Auto Books

TOYOTA

PICK-UPS/LAND CRUISER/4RUNNER
1997-00 REPAIR MANUAL

CHILTON'S

Deleted

Covers all U.S. and Canadian models of T100, Tacoma and Tundra Pick-Ups, Land Cruiser and 4Runner; 2 and 4 wheel drive

D0890280

by Bob Doughten

CHILTON Automotive Books

PUBLISHED BY **HAYNES NORTH AMERICA, Inc.**

Haynes ®

APA AUTOMOTIVE PARTS & ACCESSORIES ASSOCIATION MEMBER

Manufactured in USA

ISBN 1 56392 417 X
Library of Congress Control No. 2001092096

Haynes Publishing Group
Sparkford Nr Yeovil
Somerset BA22 7JJ England

Haynes North America, Inc
861 Lawrence Drive
Newbury Park
California 91320 USA

ABCDE
FGHIJ
KLMNO
PQRST

8-24-01

Contents

Contents

SAFETY NOTICE

Proper service and repair procedures are vital to the safe, reliable operation of all motor vehicles, as well as the personal safety of those performing repairs. This manual outlines procedures for servicing and repairing vehicles using safe, effective methods. The procedures contain many NOTES, CAUTIONS and WARNINGS which should be followed, along with standard procedures to eliminate the possibility of personal injury or improper service which could damage the vehicle or compromise its safety.

It is important to note that repair procedures and techniques, tools and parts for servicing motor vehicles, as well as the skill and experience of the individual performing the work vary widely. It is not possible to anticipate all of the conceivable ways or conditions under which vehicles may be serviced, or to provide cautions as to all possible hazards that may result. Standard and accepted safety precautions and equipment should be used when handling toxic or flammable fluids, and safety goggles or other protection should be used during cutting, grinding, chiseling, prying, or any other process that can cause material removal or projectiles.

Some procedures require the use of tools specially designed for a specific purpose. Before substituting another tool or procedure, you must be completely satisfied that neither your personal safety, nor the performance of the vehicle will be endangered.

Although information in this manual is based on industry sources and is complete as possible at the time of publication, the possibility exists that some car manufacturers made later changes which could not be included here. While striving for total accuracy, the authors or publishers cannot assume responsibility for any errors, changes or omissions that may occur in the compilation of this data.

PART NUMBERS

Part numbers listed in this reference are not recommendations by Haynes North America, Inc. for any product brand name. They are references that can be used with interchange manuals and aftermarket supplier catalogs to locate each brand supplier's discrete part number.

SPECIAL TOOLS

Special tools are recommended by the vehicle manufacturer to perform their specific job. Use has been kept to a minimum, but where absolutely necessary, they are referred to in the text by the part number of the tool manufacturer. These tools can be purchased, under the appropriate part number, from your local dealer or regional distributor, or an equivalent tool can be purchased locally from a tool supplier or parts outlet. Before substituting any tool for the one recommended, read the SAFETY NOTICE at the top of this page.

ACKNOWLEDGMENTS

We are grateful for the help and cooperation of the Toyota Motor Company for their generous assistance with technical information and certain illustrations. Technical authors who contributed to this project include Paul T. DeSanto, A.S.E., and Kevin M. G. Maher, A.S.E.

01-464

1

GENERAL INFORMATION AND MAINTENANCE

HOW TO USE THIS BOOK

Chilton's Total Car Care manual for the 1997–00 series of Toyota Trucks, including the Land Cruiser, Tacoma, T-100 Pick-Up Truck, 4Runner and Tundra, is intended to help you learn more about the inner workings of your vehicle, saving you money on its upkeep and operation.

The beginning of the book will likely be referred to the most, since that is where you will find information for maintenance and tune-up. The other sections deal with the more complex systems of your vehicle. Systems (from engine through brakes) are covered to the extent that the average do-it-yourselfer can attempt. This book will not explain such things as rebuilding a differential because the expertise required and the special tools necessary make this uneconomical. It will, however, give you detailed instructions to help you change your own brake pads and shoes, replace spark plugs, and perform many more jobs that can save you money and help avoid expensive problems.

A secondary purpose of this book is a reference for owners who want to understand their vehicle and/or their mechanics better.

Where to Begin

Before removing any bolts, read through the entire procedure. This will give you the overall view of what tools and supplies will be required. So read ahead and plan ahead. Each operation should be approached logically and all procedures thoroughly understood before attempting any work.

If repair of a component is not considered practical, we tell you how to remove the part and then how to install the new or rebuilt replacement. In this way, you at least save labor costs.

Avoiding Trouble

Many procedures in this book require you to "label and disconnect . . . " a group of lines, hoses or wires. Don't be think you can remember where everything goes—you won't. If you hook up vacuum or fuel lines incorrectly, the vehicle may run poorly, if at all. If you hook up electrical wiring incorrectly, you may instantly learn a very expensive lesson.

You don't need to know the proper name for each hose or line. A piece of masking tape on the hose and a piece on its fitting will allow you to assign your own label. As long as you remember your own code, the lines can be reconnected by matching your tags. Remember that tape will dissolve in gasoline or solvents; if a part is to be washed or cleaned, use another method of identification. A permanent felt-tipped marker or a metal scribe can be very handy for marking metal parts. Remove any tape or paper labels after assembly.

Maintenance or Repair?

Maintenance includes routine inspections, adjustments, and replacement of parts which show signs of normal wear. Maintenance compensates for wear or deterioration. Repair implies that something has broken or is not working. A need for a repair is often caused by lack of maintenance. for example: draining and refilling automatic transmission fluid is maintenance recommended at specific intervals. Failure to do this can shorten the life of the transmission/transaxle, requiring very expensive repairs. While no maintenance program can prevent items from eventually breaking or wearing out, a general rule is true: MAINTENANCE IS CHEAPER THAN REPAIR.

Two basic mechanic's rules should be mentioned here. First, whenever the left side of the vehicle or engine is referred to, it means the driver's side. Conversely, the right side of the vehicle means the passenger's side. Second, screws and bolts are removed by turning counterclockwise, and tightened by turning clockwise unless specifically noted.

Safety is always the most important rule. Constantly be aware of the dangers involved in working on an automobile and take the proper precautions. Please refer to the information in this section regarding SERVICING YOUR VEHICLE SAFELY and the SAFETY NOTICE on the acknowledgment page.

Avoiding the Most Common Mistakes

Pay attention to the instructions provided. There are 3 common mistakes in mechanical work:

1. Incorrect order of assembly, disassembly or adjustment. When taking something apart or putting it together, performing steps in the wrong order usually just costs you extra time; however, it CAN break something. Read the entire procedure before beginning. Perform everything in the order in which the instructions say you should, even if you can't see a reason for it. When you're taking apart something that is very intricate, you might want to draw a picture of how it looks when assembled in order to make sure you get everything back in its proper position. When making adjustments, perform them in the proper order. One adjustment possibly will affect another.

2. Overtorquing (or undertorquing). While it is more common for overtorquing to cause damage, undertorquing may allow a fastener to vibrate loose causing serious damage. Especially when dealing with aluminum parts, pay attention to torque specifications and utilize a torque wrench in assembly. If a torque figure is not available, remember that if you are using the right tool to perform the job, you will probably not have to strain yourself to get a fastener tight enough. The pitch of most threads is so slight that the tension you put on the wrench will be multiplied many times in actual force on what you are tightening.

There are many commercial products available for ensuring that fasteners won't come loose, even if they are not torqued just right (a very common brand is Loctite®). If you're worried about getting something together tight enough to hold, but loose enough to avoid mechanical damage during assembly, one of these products might offer substantial insurance. Before choosing a threadlocking compound, read the label on the package and make sure the product is compatible with the materials, fluids, etc. involved.

3. Crossthreading. This occurs when a part such as a bolt is screwed into a nut or casting at the wrong angle and forced. Crossthreading is more likely to occur if access is difficult. It helps to clean and lubricate fasteners, then to start threading the bolt, spark plug, etc. with your fingers. If you encounter resistance, unscrew the part and start over again at a different angle until it can be inserted and turned several times without much effort. Keep in mind that many parts have tapered threads, so that gentle turning will automatically bring the part you're threading to the proper angle. Don't put a wrench on the part until it's been tightened a couple of turns by hand. If you suddenly encounter resistance, and the part has not seated fully, don't force it. Pull it back out to make sure it's clean and threading properly.

Be sure to take your time and be patient, and always plan ahead. Allow yourself ample time to perform repairs and maintenance.

TOOLS AND EQUIPMENT

See Figures 1 thru 15

Without the proper tools and equipment it is impossible to properly service your vehicle. It would be virtually impossible to catalog every tool that you would need to perform all of the operations in this book. It would be unwise for the amateur to rush out and buy an expensive set of tools on the theory that he/she may need one or more of them at some time.

The best approach is to proceed slowly, gathering a good quality set of those tools that are used most frequently. Don't be misled by the low cost of bargain tools. It is far better to spend a little more for better quality. Forged wrenches, 6 or 12-point sockets and fine tooth ratchets are by far preferable to their less expensive counterparts. As any good mechanic can tell you, there are few worse experiences than trying to work on a vehicle with bad tools. Your monetary savings will be far outweighed by frustration and mangled knuckles.

Begin accumulating those tools that are used most frequently: those associated with routine maintenance and tune-up. In addition to the normal assortment of screwdrivers and pliers, you should have the following tools:

- Wrenches/sockets and combination open end/box end wrenches in sizes from $^1/_8$–$^3/_4$ in. or 3–19mm, as well as a $^{13}/_{16}$ in. or $^5/_8$ in. spark plug socket (depending on plug type).

➡If possible, buy various length socket drive extensions. Universal-joint and wobble extensions can be extremely useful, but be careful when using them, as they can change the amount of torque applied to the socket.

- Jackstands for support.
- Oil filter wrench.
- Spout or funnel for pouring fluids.
- Grease gun for chassis lubrication (unless your vehicle is not equipped with any grease fittings)
- Hydrometer for checking the battery (unless equipped with a sealed, maintenance-free battery).
- A container for draining oil and other fluids.
- Rags for wiping up the inevitable mess.

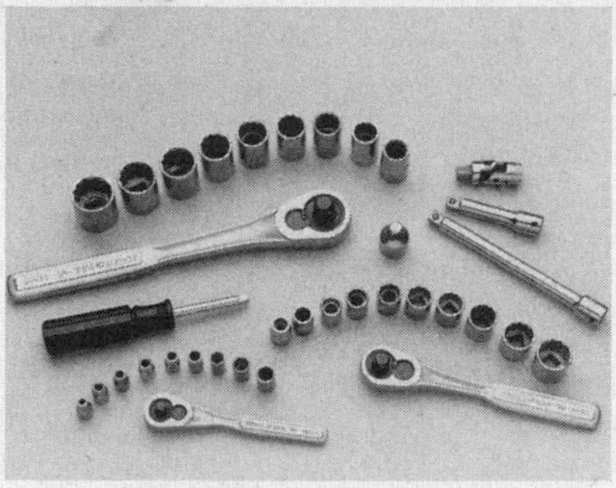

tccs1200

Fig. 1 All but the most basic procedures will require an assortment of ratchets and sockets

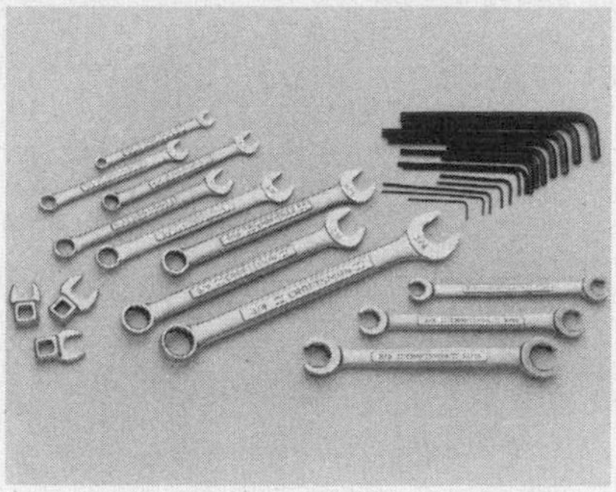

tccs1201

Fig. 2 In addition to ratchets, a good set of wrenches and hex keys will be necessary

tccs1202

Fig. 3 A hydraulic floor jack and a set of jackstands are essential for lifting and supporting the vehicle

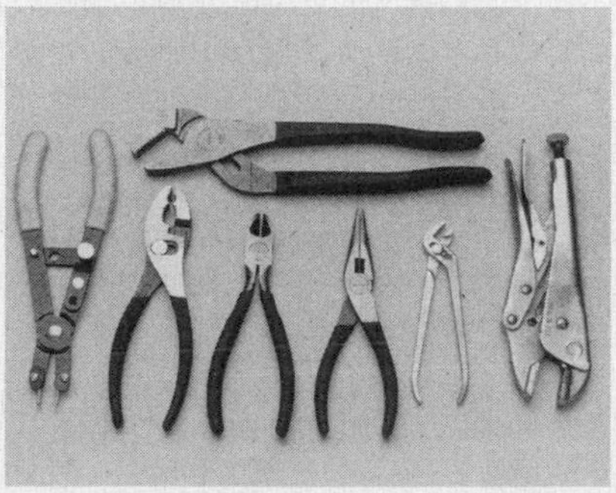

tccs1203

Fig. 4 An assortment of pliers, grippers and cutters will be handy for old rusted parts and stripped bolt heads

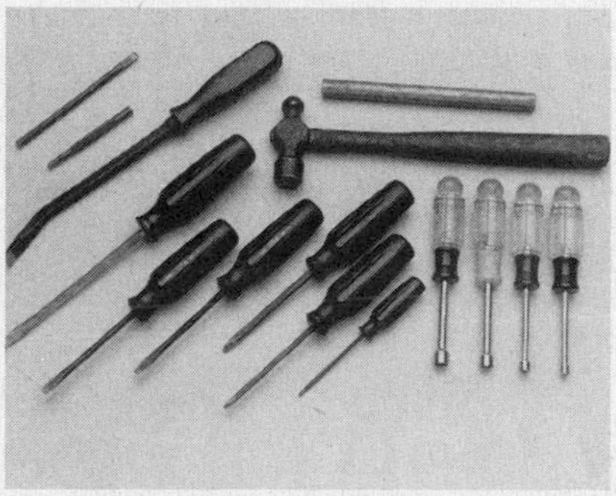

tccs1204

Fig. 5 Various drivers, chisels and prybars are great tools to have in your toolbox

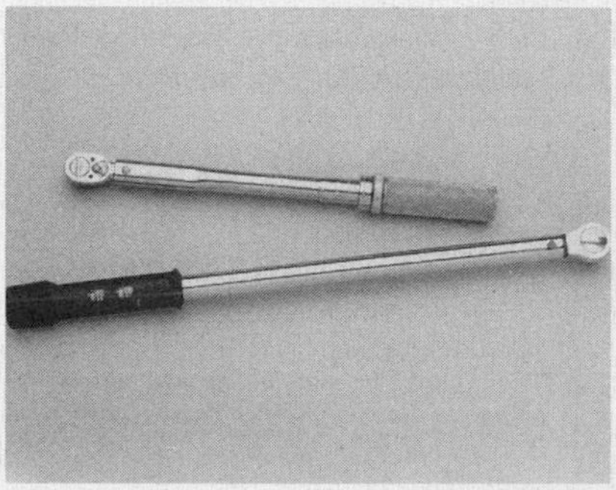

tccs1205

Fig. 6 Many repairs will require the use of a torque wrench to assure the components are properly fastened

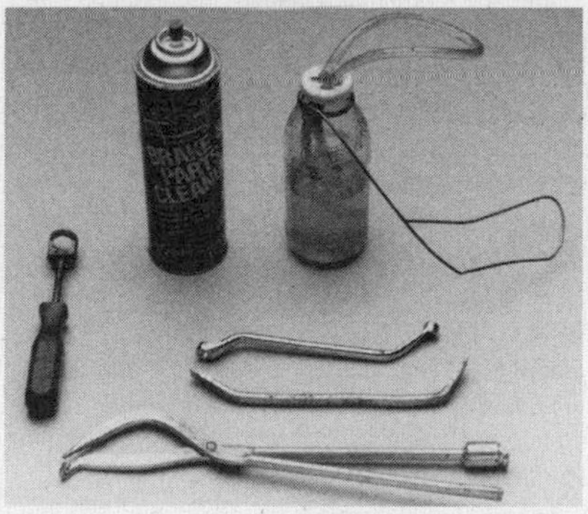

tccs1209

Fig. 7 Although not always necessary, using specialized brake tools will save time

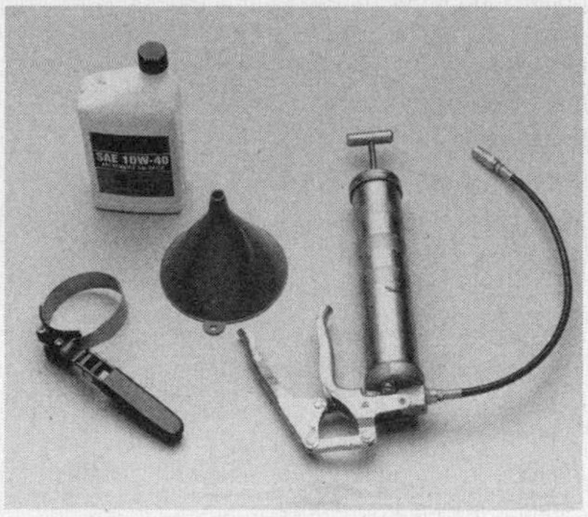

tccs1210

Fig. 8 A few inexpensive lubrication tools will make maintenance easier

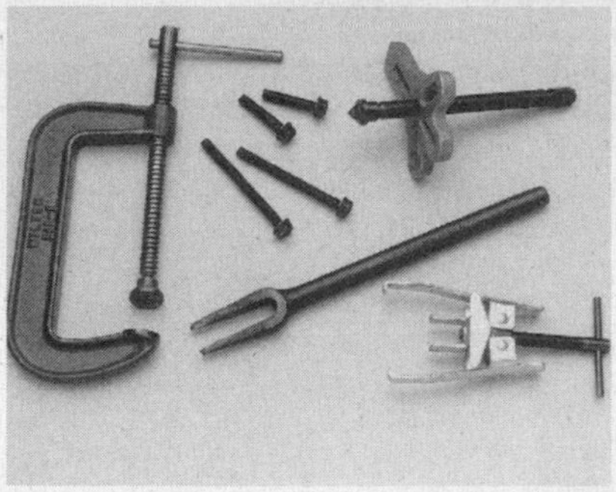

tccs1211

Fig. 9 Various pullers, clamps and separator tools are needed for many larger, more complicated repairs

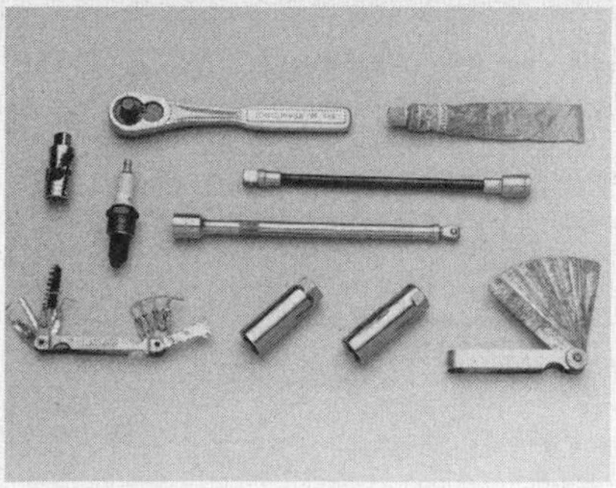

tccs1212

Fig. 10 A variety of tools and gauges should be used for spark plug gapping and installation

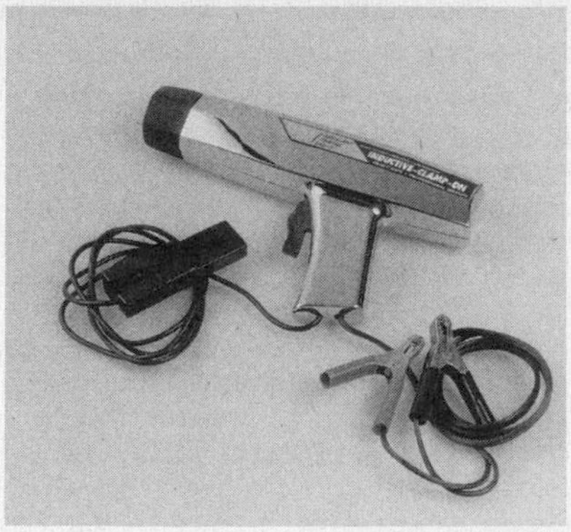

tccx1p01

Fig. 11 Inductive type timing light

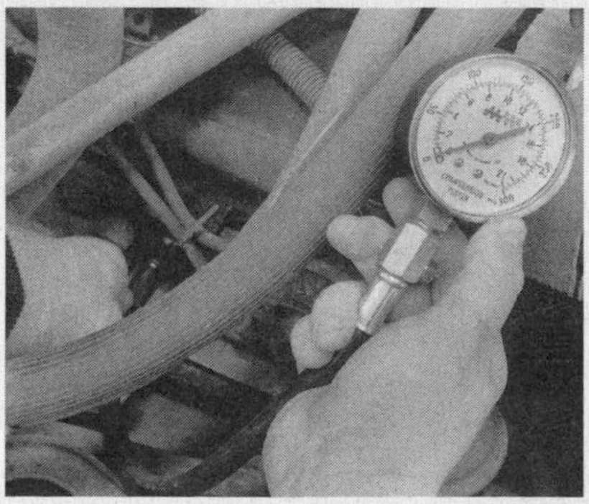

tccx1p02

Fig. 12 A screw-in type compression gauge is recommended for compression testing

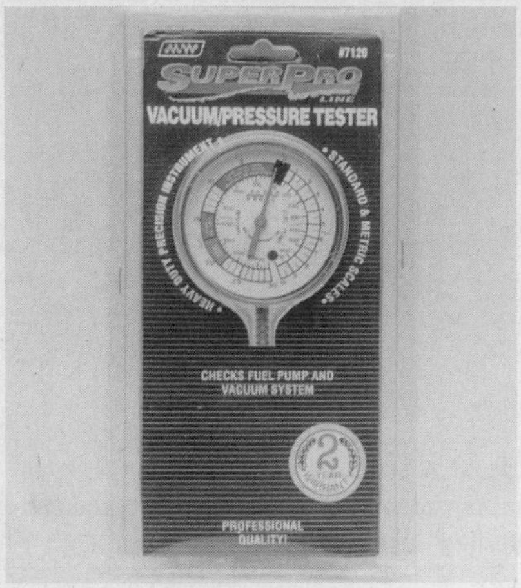

tccx1p03

Fig. 13 A vacuum/pressure tester is necessary for many testing procedures

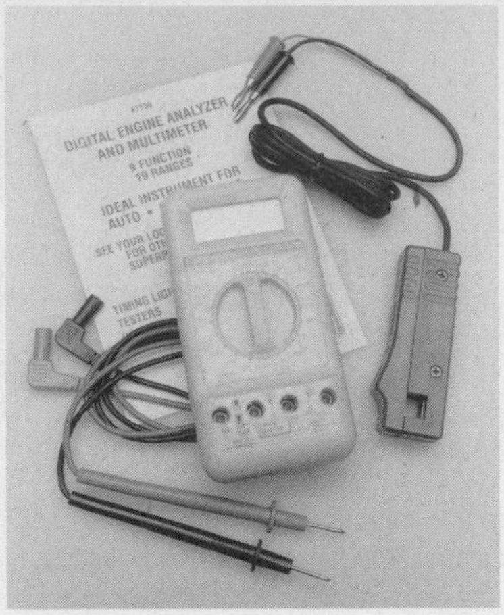

tccx1p06

Fig. 14 Most modern automotive multimeters incorporate many helpful features

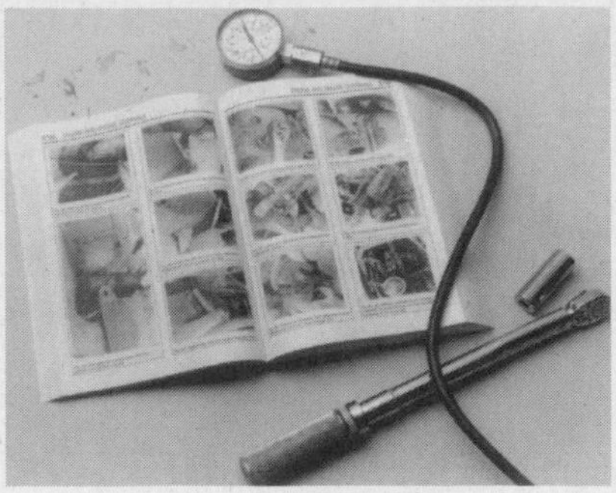

tccs1213

Fig. 15 Proper information is vital, so always have a Chilton Total Car Care manual handy

In addition to the above items there are several others that are not absolutely necessary, but handy to have around. These include an equivalent oil absorbent gravel, like cat litter, and the usual supply of lubricants, antifreeze and fluids. This is a basic list for routine maintenance, but only your personal needs and desire can accurately determine your list of tools.

After performing a few projects on the vehicle, you'll be amazed at the other tools and non-tools on your workbench. Some useful household items are: a large turkey baster or siphon, empty coffee cans and ice trays (to store parts), a ball of twine, electrical tape for wiring, small rolls of colored tape for tagging lines or hoses, markers and pens, a note pad, golf tees (for plugging vacuum lines), metal coat hangers or a roll of mechanic's wire (to hold things out of the way), dental pick or similar long, pointed probe, a strong magnet, and a small mirror (to see into recesses and under manifolds).

A more advanced set of tools, suitable for tune-up work, can be drawn up easily. While the tools are slightly more sophisticated, they need not be outrageously expensive. There are several inexpensive tach/dwell meters on the market that are every bit as good for the average mechanic as a professional model. Just be sure that it goes to a least 1200–1500 rpm on the tach scale and that it works on 4, 6 and 8-cylinder engines. The key to these purchases is to make them with an eye towards adaptability and wide range. A basic list of tune-up tools could include:

- Tach/dwell meter.
- Spark plug wrench and gapping tool.
- Feeler gauges for valve adjustment.
- Timing light.

The choice of a timing light should be made carefully. A light which works on the DC current supplied by the vehicle's battery is the best choice; it should have a xenon tube for brightness. On any vehicle with an electronic ignition system, a timing light with an inductive pickup that clamps around the No. 1 spark plug cable is preferred.

In addition to these basic tools, there are several other tools and gauges you may find useful. These include:

- Compression gauge. The screw-in type is slower to use, but eliminates the possibility of a faulty reading due to escaping pressure.
- Manifold vacuum gauge.
- 12V test light.
- A combination volt/ohmmeter
- Induction Ammeter. This is used for determining whether or not there is current in a wire. These are handy for use if a wire is broken somewhere in a wiring harness.

As a final note, you will probably find a torque wrench necessary for all but the most basic work. The beam type models are perfectly adequate, although the newer click types (breakaway) are easier to use. The click type torque wrenches tend to be more expensive. Also keep in mind that all types of torque wrenches should be periodically checked and/or recalibrated. You will have to decide for yourself which better fits your pocketbook, and purpose.

Special Tools

Normally, the use of special factory tools is avoided for repair procedures, since these are not readily available for the do-it-yourself mechanic. When it is possible to perform the job with more commonly available tools, it will be pointed out, but occasionally, a special tool was designed to perform a specific function and should be used. Before substituting another tool, you should be convinced that neither your safety nor the performance of the vehicle will be compromised.

Special tools can usually be purchased from an automotive parts store or from your dealer. In some cases special tools may be available directly from the tool manufacturer.

SERVICING YOUR VEHICLE SAFELY

➧ See Figures 16, 17, and 18

It is virtually impossible to anticipate all of the hazards involved with automotive maintenance and service, but care and common sense will prevent most accidents.

The rules of safety for mechanics range from "don't smoke around gasoline," to "use the proper tool(s) for the job." The trick to avoiding injuries is to develop safe work habits and to take every possible precaution.

Do's

- Do keep a fire extinguisher and first aid kit handy.
- Do wear safety glasses or goggles when cutting, drilling, grinding or prying, even if you have 20–20 vision. If you wear glasses for the sake of vision, wear safety goggles over your regular glasses.
- Do shield your eyes whenever you work around the battery. Batteries contain sulfuric acid. In case of contact with, flush the area with water or a mixture of water and baking soda, then seek immediate medical attention.
- Do use safety stands (jackstands) for any undervehicle service. Jacks are for raising vehicles; jackstands are for making sure the vehicle stays raised until you want it to come down.
- Do use adequate ventilation when working with any chemicals or hazardous materials. Like carbon monoxide, the asbestos dust resulting from some brake lining wear can be hazardous in sufficient quantities.
- Do disconnect the negative battery cable when working on the electrical system. The secondary ignition system contains EXTREMELY HIGH VOLTAGE. In some cases it can even exceed 50,000 volts.
- Do follow manufacturer's directions whenever working with potentially hazardous materials. Most chemicals and fluids are poisonous.
- Do properly maintain your tools. Loose hammerheads, mushroomed punches and chisels, frayed or poorly grounded electrical cords, excessively worn screwdrivers, spread wrenches (open end), cracked sockets, slipping ratchets, or faulty droplight sockets can cause accidents.

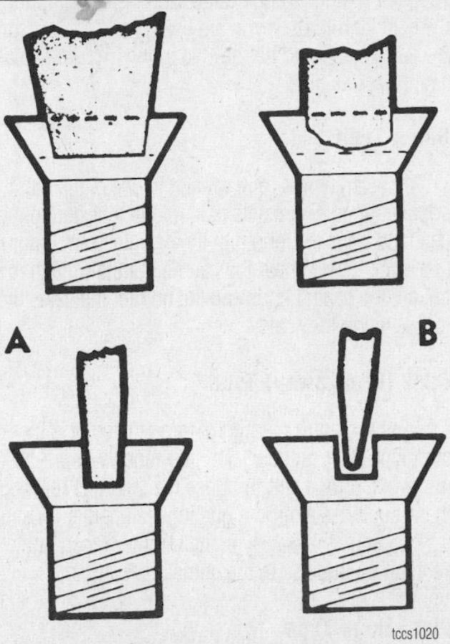

Fig. 16 Screwdrivers should be kept in good condition to prevent injury or damage which could result if the blade slips from the screw

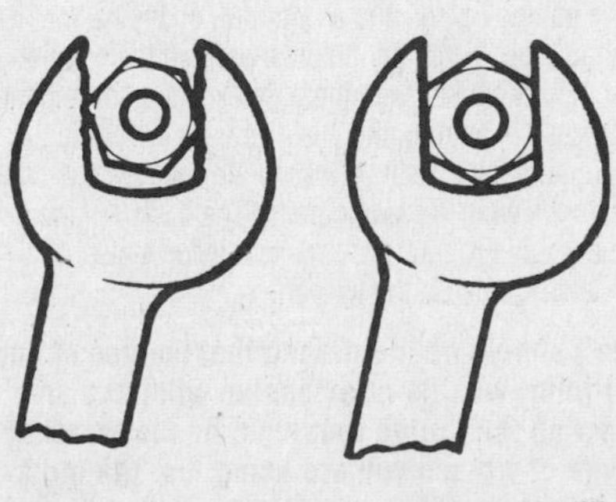

Fig. 17 Using the correct size wrench will help prevent the possibility of rounding off a nut

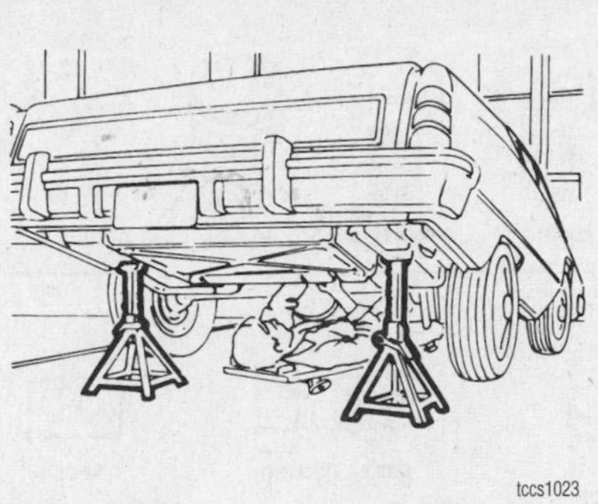

Fig. 18 NEVER work under a vehicle unless it is supported using safety stands (jackstands)

- Likewise, keep your tools clean; a greasy wrench can slip off a bolt head, ruining the bolt and often harming your knuckles in the process.
- Do use the proper size and type of tool for the job at hand. Do select a wrench or socket that fits the nut or bolt. The wrench or socket should sit straight, not cocked.
- Do, when possible, pull on a wrench handle rather than push on it, and adjust your stance to prevent a fall.
- Do be sure that adjustable wrenches are tightly closed on the nut or bolt and pulled so that the force is on the side of the fixed jaw.
- Do strike squarely with a hammer; avoid glancing blows.
- Do set the parking brake and block the drive wheels if the work requires a running engine.

Don'ts

- Don't run the engine in a garage or anywhere else without proper ventilation—EVER! Carbon monoxide is poisonous; it takes a long time to leave the human body and you can build up a deadly supply of it in your system by simply breathing in a little at a time. You may not realize you are slowly poisoning yourself. Always use power vents, windows, fans and/or open the garage door.
- Don't work around moving parts while wearing loose clothing. Short sleeves are much safer than long, loose sleeves. Hard-toed shoes with neoprene soles protect your toes and give a better grip on slippery surfaces. Watches and jewelry is not safe working around a vehicle. Long hair should be tied back under a hat or cap.
- Don't use pockets for toolboxes. A fall or bump can drive a screwdriver deep into your body. Even a rag hanging from your back pocket can wrap around a spinning shaft or fan.
- Don't smoke when working around gasoline, cleaning solvent or other flammable material.
- Don't smoke when working around the battery. When the battery is being charged, it gives off explosive hydrogen gas.
- Don't use gasoline to wash your hands; there are excellent soaps available. Gasoline contains dangerous additives which can enter the body through a cut or through your pores. Gasoline also removes all the natural oils from the skin so that bone dry hands will suck up oil and grease.
- Don't service the air conditioning system unless you are equipped with the necessary tools and training. When liquid or compressed gas refrigerant is released to atmospheric pressure it will absorb heat from whatever it contacts. This will chill or freeze anything it touches.
- Don't use screwdrivers for anything other than driving screws! A screwdriver used as an prying tool can snap when you least expect it, causing injurles. At the very least, you'll ruin a good screwdriver.
- Don't use an emergency jack (that little ratchet, scissors, or pantograph jack supplied with the vehicle) for anything other than changing a flat! These jacks are only intended for emergency use out on the road; they are NOT designed as a maintenance tool. If you are serious about maintaining your vehicle yourself, invest in a hydraulic floor jack of at least a $1^1/_2$ ton capacity, and at least two sturdy jackstands.

FASTENERS, MEASUREMENTS AND CONVERSIONS

Bolts, Nuts and Other Threaded Retainers

See Figures 19 and 20

Although there are a great variety of fasteners found in the modern car or truck, the most commonly used retainer is the threaded fastener (nuts, bolts, screws, studs, etc.). Most threaded retainers may be reused, provided that they are not damaged in use or during the repair. Some retainers (such as stretch bolts or torque prevailing nuts) are designed to deform when tightened or in use and should not be reinstalled.

Whenever possible, we will note any special retainers which should be replaced during a procedure. But you should always inspect the condition of a retainer when it is removed and replace any that show signs of damage. Check all threads for rust or corrosion which can increase the torque necessary to achieve the desired clamp load for which that fastener was originally selected. Additionally, be sure that the driver surface of the fastener has not been compromised by rounding or other damage. In some cases a driver surface may become only partially rounded, allowing the driver to catch in only one direction. In many of these occurrences, a fastener may be installed and tightened, but the driver would not be able to grip and loosen the fastener again.

If you must replace a fastener, whether due to design or damage, you must ALWAYS be sure to use the proper replacement. In all cases, a retainer of the same design, material and strength should be used. Markings on the heads of most bolts will help determine the proper strength of the fastener. The same material, thread and pitch must be selected to assure proper installation and safe operation of the vehicle afterwards.

Thread gauges are available to help measure a bolt or stud's thread. Most automotive and hardware stores keep gauges available to help you select the proper size. In a pinch, you can use another nut or bolt for a thread gauge. If the bolt you are replacing is not too badly damaged, you can select a match by finding another bolt which will thread in its place. If you find a nut which threads properly onto the damaged bolt, then use that nut to help select the replacement bolt.

** WARNING

Be aware that when you find a bolt with damaged threads, you may also find the nut or drilled hole it was threaded into has also been damaged. If this is the case, you may have to drill and tap the hole, replace the nut or otherwise repair the threads. NEVER try to force a replacement bolt to fit into the damaged threads.

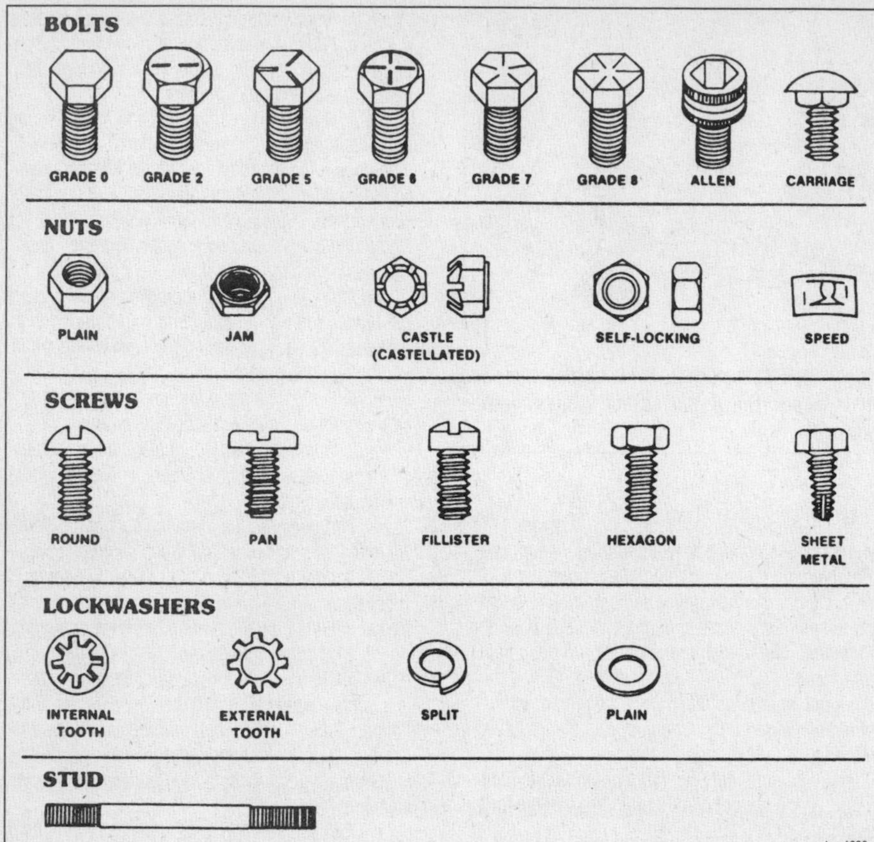

tccs1036

Fig. 19 There are many different types of threaded retainers found on vehicles

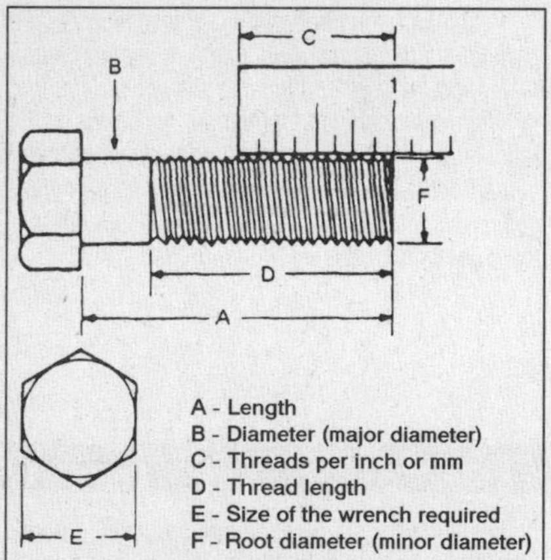

tccs1038

Fig. 20 Threaded retainer sizes are determined using these measurements

Torque

Torque is defined as the measurement of resistance to turning or rotating. It tends to twist a body about an axis of rotation. A common example of this would be tightening a threaded retainer such as a nut, bolt or screw. Measuring torque is one of the most common ways to help assure that a threaded retainer has been properly fastened.

When tightening a threaded fastener, torque is applied in three distinct areas, the head, the bearing surface and the clamp load. About 50 percent of the measured torque is used in overcoming bearing friction. This is the friction between the bearing surface of the bolt head, screw head or nut face and the base material or washer (the surface on which the fastener is rotating). Approximately 40 percent of the applied torque is used in overcoming thread friction. This leaves only about 10 percent of the applied torque to develop a useful clamp load (the force which holds a joint together). This means that friction can account for as much as 90 percent of the applied torque on a fastener.

TORQUE WRENCHES

➧ **See Figure 21**

In most applications, a torque wrench can be used to assure proper installation of a fastener. Torque wrenches come in various designs and most automotive supply stores will carry a variety to suit your needs. A torque wrench should be used any time we supply a specific torque value for a fastener. Again, the general rule of "if you are using the right tool for the job, you should not have to strain to tighten a fastener" applies here.

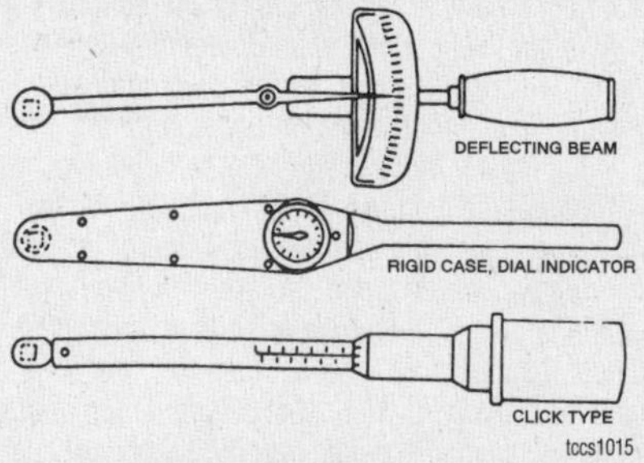

tccs1015

Fig. 21 Various styles of torque wrenches are usually available at your local automotive supply store

Beam Type

The beam type torque wrench is one of the most popular types. It consists of a pointer attached to the head that runs the length of the flexible beam (shaft) to a scale located near the handle. As the wrench is pulled, the beam bends and the pointer indicates the torque using the scale.

Click (Breakaway) Type

Another popular design of torque wrench is the click type. To use the click type wrench you pre-adjust it to a torque setting. Once the torque is reached, the wrench has a reflex signaling feature that causes a momentary breakaway of the torque wrench body, sending an impulse to the operator's hand.

Pivot Head Type

➧ **See Figure 22**

Some torque wrenches (usually of the click type) may be equipped with a pivot head which can allow it to be used in areas of limited access. BUT, it must be used properly. To hold a pivot head wrench, grasp the handle lightly, and as you pull on the handle, it should be floated on the pivot point. If the handle comes in contact with the yoke extension during the process of pulling, there is a very good chance the torque readings will be inaccurate because this could alter the wrench loading point. The design of the handle is usually such as to make it inconvenient to deliberately misuse the wrench.

➡It should be mentioned that the use of any U-joint, wobble or extension will have an effect on the torque readings, no matter what type of wrench you are using. For the most accurate readings, install the socket directly on the wrench driver. If necessary, straight extensions (which hold a socket directly under the wrench driver) will have the least effect on the torque reading. Avoid any extension that alters the length of the wrench from the handle to the head/driving point (such as a crow's foot). U-joint or wobble extensions can greatly affect the readings; avoid their use at all times.

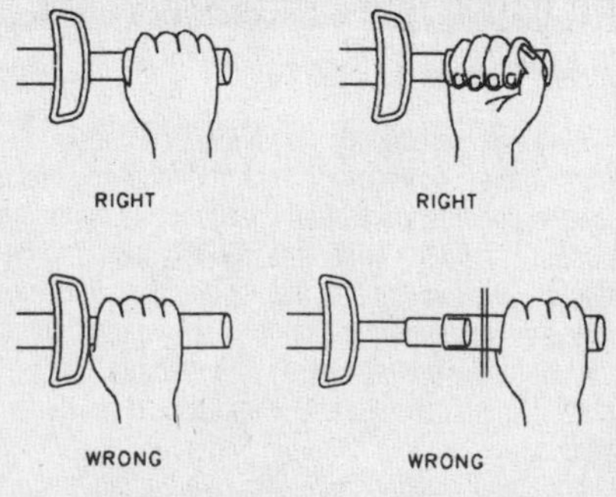

tccs1041

Fig. 22 Torque wrenches with pivoting heads must be grasped and used properly to prevent an incorrect reading

Rigid Case (Direct Reading)

A rigid case or direct reading torque wrench is equipped with a dial indicator to show torque values. One advantage of these wrenches is that they can be held at any position on the wrench without affecting accuracy. These wrenches are often preferred because they tend to be compact, easy to read and have a great degree of accuracy.

TORQUE ANGLE METERS

Because the frictional characteristics of each fastener or threaded hole will vary, clamp loads which are based strictly on torque will vary as well. In most applications, this variance is not significant enough to cause worry. But, in certain applications, a manufacturer's engineers may determine that more precise clamp loads are necessary (such is the case with many aluminum cylinder heads). In these cases, a torque angle method of installation would be specified. When installing fasteners which are torque angle tightened, a predetermined seating torque and standard torque wrench are usually used first to remove any compliance from the joint. The fastener is then tightened the specified additional portion of a turn measured in degrees. A torque angle gauge (mechanical protractor) is used for these applications.

Standard and Metric Measurements

➧ See Figure 23

Throughout this manual, specifications are given to help you determine the condition of various components on your vehicle, or to assist you in their installation. Some of the most common measurements include length (in. or cm/mm), torque (ft. lbs., inch lbs. or Nm) and pressure (psi, in. Hg, kPa or mm Hg). In most cases, we strive to provide the proper measurement as determined by the manufacturer's engineers.

Though, in some cases, that value may not be conveniently measured with what is available in your toolbox. Luckily, many of the measuring devices which are available today will have two scales so the Standard or Metric measurements may easily be taken. If any of the various measuring tools which are available to you do not contain the same scale as listed in the specifications, use the accompanying conversion factors to determine the proper value.

The conversion factor chart is used by taking the given specification and multiplying it by the necessary conversion factor. For instance, looking at the first line, if you have a measurement in inches such as "free-play should be 2 in." but your ruler reads only in millimeters, multiply 2 in. by the conversion factor of 25.4 to get the metric equivalent of 50.8mm. Likewise, if the specification was given only in a Metric measurement, for example in Newton Meters (Nm), then look at the center column first. If the measurement is 100 Nm, multiply it by the conversion factor of 0.738 to get 73.8 ft. lbs.

CONVERSION FACTORS

LENGTH–DISTANCE				
Inches (in.)	x 25.4	= Millimeters (mm)	x .0394	= Inches
Feet (ft.)	x .305	= Meters (m)	x 3.281	= Feet
Miles	x 1.609	= Kilometers (km)	x .0621	= Miles
VOLUME				
Cubic Inches (in3)	x 16.387	= Cubic Centimeters	x .061	= in3
IMP Pints (IMP pt.)	x .568	= Liters (L)	x 1.76	= IMP pt.
IMP Quarts (IMP qt.)	x 1.137	= Liters (L)	x .88	= IMP qt.
IMP Gallons (IMP gal.)	x 4.546	= Liters (L)	x .22	= IMP gal.
IMP Quarts (IMP qt.)	x 1.201	= US Quarts (US qt.)	x .833	= IMP qt.
IMP Gallons (IMP gal.)	x 1.201	= US Gallons (US gal.)	x .833	= IMP gal.
Fl. Ounces	x 29.573	= Milliliters	x .034	= Ounces
US Pints (US pt.)	x .473	= Liters (L)	x 2.113	= Pints
US Quarts (US qt.)	x .946	= Liters (L)	x 1.057	= Quarts
US Gallons (US gal.)	x 3.785	= Liters (L)	x .264	= Gallons
MASS–WEIGHT				
Ounces (oz.)	x 28.35	= Grams (g)	x .035	= Ounces
Pounds (lb.)	x .454	= Kilograms (kg)	x 2.205	= Pounds
PRESSURE				
Pounds Per Sq. In. (psi)	x 6.895	= Kilopascals (kPa)	x .145	= psi
Inches of Mercury (Hg)	x .4912	= psi	x 2.036	= Hg
Inches of Mercury (Hg)	x 3.377	= Kilopascals (kPa)	x .2961	= Hg
Inches of Water (H_2O)	x .07355	= Inches of Mercury	x 13.783	= H_2O
Inches of Water (H_2O)	x .03613	= psi	x 27.684	= H_2O
Inches of Water (H_2O)	x .248	= Kilopascals (kPa)	x 4.026	= H_2O
TORQUE				
Pounds–Force Inches (in–lb)	x .113	= Newton Meters (N·m)	x 8.85	= in–lb
Pounds–Force Feet (ft–lb)	x 1.356	= Newton Meters (N·m)	x .738	= ft–lb
VELOCITY				
Miles Per Hour (MPH)	x 1.609	= Kilometers Per Hour (KPH)	x .621	= MPH
POWER				
Horsepower (Hp)	x .745	= Kilowatts	x 1.34	= Horsepower
FUEL CONSUMPTION*				
Miles Per Gallon IMP (MPG)	x .354	= Kilometers Per Liter (Km/L)		
Kilometers Per Liter (Km/L)	x 2.352	= IMP MPG		
Miles Per Gallon US (MPG)	x .425	= Kilometers Per Liter (Km/L)		
Kilometers Per Liter (Km/L)	x 2.352	= US MPG		

*It is common to covert from miles per gallon (mpg) to liters/100 kilometers (1/100 km), where mpg (IMP) x 1/100 km = 282 and mpg (US) x 1/100 km = 235.

TEMPERATURE

Degree Fahrenheit (°F) = (°C x 1.8) + 32

Degree Celsius (°C) = (°F – 32) x .56

tccs1044

Fig. 23 Standard and metric conversion factors chart

SERIAL NUMBER IDENTIFICATION

VEHICLE IDENTIFICATION CHART

Engine Code					
Code	**Liters (cc)**	**Engine ID**	**Cyl.**	**Fuel Sys.**	**Eng. Mfg.**
VIN F	4.5 (4477)	1FZ-FE	6	EFI	TMC
VIN L	2.4 (2438)	2RZ-FE	4	EFI	TMC
VIN M	2.7 (2694)	3RZ-FE	4	EFI	TMC
VIN N	3.4 (3378)	5VZ-FE	6	EFI	TMC
VIN T	4.7 (4663)	2UZ-FE	8	EFI	TMC

Model Year	
Code	**Year**
V	1997
W	1998
X	1999
Y	2000

EFI - Electronic Fuel Injection

TMC - Toyota Motor Corporation

Engine VIN is the 8th digit of the Vehicle Indentification Number (VIN)

Model Year VIN is the 10th letter of the Vehicle Identification Number (VIN)

93161c01

Vehicle

➧ See Figure 24

The Vehicle Identification Number (VIN) plate is located on the left upper instrument panel and is visible from the outside of the vehicle at the lower left (driver's side) of the windshield. The VIN consists of 17 characters. These numbers are an important source of identification for your vehicle and its equipment. The fifth position of the VIN identifies the engine used in the vehicle. The tenth position represents the model year.

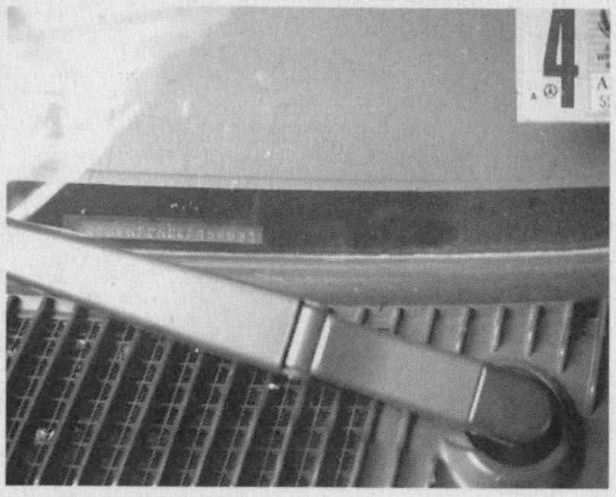

93161pe2

Fig. 24 The VIN can easily be viewed through the windshield. It is located on the driver's side of the vehicle where the dashboard meets the windshield

93161p04

Fig. 25 The engine type and or displacement may be printed on the timing cover

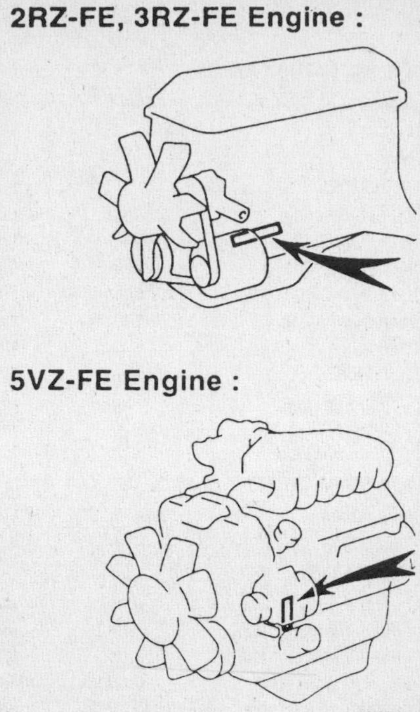

86821036

Fig. 26 Engine number location on the 2RZ-FE, 3RZ-FE and 5VZ-FE engines

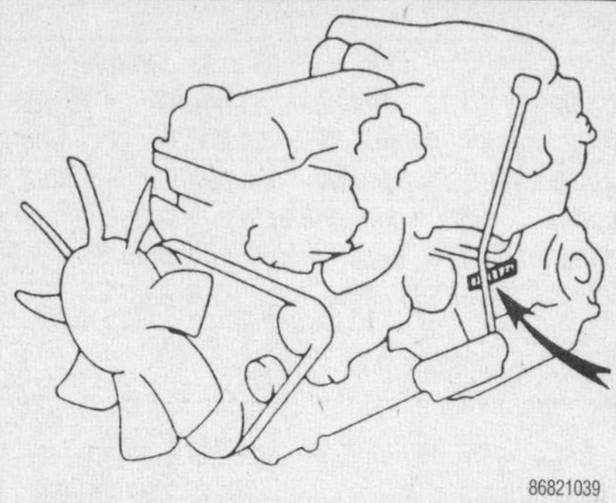

86821039

Fig. 27 Engine number location on the 1FZ-FE engine

93161G03

Fig. 28 Engine number location on the 2UZ-FE engine

Engine

See Figures 25, 26, 27, and 28

Each engine is referred to by both its family designation, such as 2RZ-FE, and its production or serial number. The serial number can be important when ordering parts. Certain changes may have been made during production of the engine; different parts will be required if the engine was assembled before or after the change date. Generally, parts stores and dealers list this data in their catalogs, so have the engine number handy when you go. Refer to the illustrations to determine the engine number location.

It is a good idea to record the engine number, perhaps jotting it inside the cover of the owner's manual or similar easy-to-find location for future reference.

Transmission

Automatic and manual transmissions are used in all of the trucks excluding the Land Cruiser. The Land Cruiser only uses an automatic transmission. The identity of the transmission is on the driver's door tag. You can also obtain the type of transmission from the model number.

TRANSMISSION APPLICATIONS

Model Year	Vehicle Model	Engine Used	AutomaticTransmissions Used	Manual Transmissions Used
1997	Tacoma	2RZ-FE	A43D	W59
	Tacoma	3RZ-FE	A340F	W59
	Tacoma	5VZ-FE	A340E, A340F	R150
	4Runner	3RZ-FE	A340E, A340F	W59
	4Runner	5VZ-FE	A340E, A340F	R150
	T100 Pickup Truck	3RZ-FE	A340E	W59
	T100 Pickup Truck	5VZ-FE	A340E, A340F	R150, R150F
	Land Cruiser	1FZ-FE	A343F	-
1998	Tacoma	2RZ-FE	A43D	W59
	Tacoma	3RZ-FE	A340F	W59
	Tacoma	5VZ-FE	A340E, A340F	R150
	4Runner	3RZ-FE	A340E, A340F	W59
	4Runner	5VZ-FE	A340E, A340F	R150
	T100 Pickup Truck	3RZ-FE	A340E	W59
	T100 Pickup Truck	5VZ-FE	A340E, A340F	R150, R150F
	Land Cruiser	1FZ-FE	A343F	-
1999	Tacoma	2RZ-FE	A43D	W59
	Tacoma	3RZ-FE	A340F	W59
	Tacoma	5VZ-FE	A340E, A340F	R150
	4Runner	3RZ-FE	A340E, A340F	W59
	4Runner	5VZ-FE	A340E, A340F	R150
	T100 Pickup Truck	3RZ-FE	A340E	W59
	T100 Pickup Truck	5VZ-FE	A340E, A340F	R150, R150F
	Land Cruiser	2UZ-FE	A343F	-
2000	Tacoma	2RZ-FE	A43D	W59
	Tacoma	3RZ-FE	A340F	W59
	Tacoma	5VZ-FE	A340E, A340F	R150
	4Runner	3RZ-FE	A340E, A340F	W59
	4Runner	5VZ-FE	A340E, A340F	R150
	Tundra	2UZ-FE	A340E, A340F	-
	Tundra	5VZ-FE	A340E, A340F	R150, R150F
	Land Cruiser	2UZ-FE	A343F	-

93161G04

GENERAL ENGINE SPECIFICATIONS

Year	Model	Engine ID/VIN	Engine Displacement Liters (cc)	No. of Cyl.	Engine Type	Fuel System Type	Net Horsepower @ rpm	Net Torque @ rpm (ft. lbs.)	Bore x Stroke (in.)	Com- pression Ratio	Oil Pressure @ rpm
1997	Land Cruiser	1FZ-FE	4.5 (4477)	6	DOHC	EFI	212@4600	275@3200	3.94 x 3.74	9.0:1	43-85@3000
	T100 Pick-Up	3RZ-FE	2.7 (2694)	4	DOHC	EFI	150@4800	177@4000	3.74 x 3.74	9.5:1	36-71@3000
	T100 Pick-Up	5VZ-FE	3.4 (3378)	6	DOHC	EFI	190@4800	220@3600	3.68 x 3.23	9.6:1	36-75@3000
	Tacoma	2RZ-FE	2.4 (2438)	4	DOHC	EFI	142@5000	160@4000	3.74 x 3.38	9.5:1	36-71@3000
	Tacoma	3RZ-FE	2.7 (2694)	4	DOHC	EFI	150@4800	177@4000	3.74 x 3.74	9.5:1	36-71@3000
	Tacoma	5VZ-FE	3.4 (3378)	6	DOHC	EFI	190@4800	220@3600	3.68 x 3.23	9.6:1	36-75@3000
	4Runner	3RZ-FE	2.7 (2694)	4	DOHC	EFI	150@4800	177@4000	3.74 x 3.74	9.5:1	36-71@3000
	4Runner	5VZ-FE	3.4 (3378)	6	DOHC	EFI	183@4800	217@3600	3.68 x 3.23	9.6:1	36-75@3000
1998	Land Cruiser	2UZ-FE	4.7 (4664)	8	DOHC	EFI	230@4800	320@3600	3.70 x 3.31	9.6:1	43-85@3000
	T100 Pick-Up	3RZ-FE	2.7 (2694)	4	DOHC	EFI	150@4800	177@4000	3.74 x 3.74	9.5:1	36-71@3000
	T100 Pick-Up	5VZ-FE	3.4 (3378)	6	DOHC	EFI	190@4800	220@3600	3.68 x 3.23	9.6:1	36-75@3000
	Tacoma	2RZ-FE	2.4 (2438)	4	DOHC	EFI	142@5000	160@4000	3.74 x 3.38	9.5:1	36-71@3000
	Tacoma	3RZ-FE	2.7 (2694)	4	DOHC	EFI	150@4800	177@4000	3.74 x 3.74	9.5:1	36-71@3000
	Tacoma	5VZ-FE	3.4 (3378)	6	DOHC	EFI	190@4800	220@3600	3.68 x 3.23	9.6:1	36-75@3000
	4Runner	3RZ-FE	2.7 (2694)	4	DOHC	EFI	150@4800	177@4000	3.74 x 3.74	9.5:1	36-71@3000
	4Runner	5VZ-FE	3.4 (3378)	6	DOHC	EFI	183@4800	217@3600	3.68 x 3.23	9.6:1	36-75@3000
1999	Land Cruiser	2UZ-FE	4.7 (4663)	8	DOHC	EFI	230@4800	320@3600	3.70 x 3.31	9.6:1	43-85@3000
	T100 Pick-Up	3RZ-FE	2.7 (2694)	4	DOHC	EFI	150@4800	177@4000	3.74 x 3.74	9.5:1	36-71@3000
	T100 Pick-Up	5VZ-FE	3.4 (3378)	6	DOHC	EFI	190@4800	220@3600	3.68 x 3.23	9.6:1	36-75@3000
	Tacoma	2RZ-FE	2.4 (2438)	4	DOHC	EFI	142@5000	160@4000	3.74 x 3.38	9.5:1	36-71@3000
	Tacoma	3RZ-FE	2.7 (2694)	4	DOHC	EFI	150@4800	177@4000	3.74 x 3.74	9.5:1	36-71@3000
	Tacoma	5VZ-FE	3.4 (3378)	6	DOHC	EFI	190@4800	220@3600	3.68 x 3.23	9.6:1	36-75@3000
	4Runner	3RZ-FE	2.7 (2694)	4	DOHC	EFI	150@4800	177@4000	3.74 x 3.74	9.5:1	36-71@3000
	4Runner	5VZ-FE	3.4 (3378)	6	DOHC	EFI	183@4800	217@3600	3.68 x 3.23	9.6:1	36-75@3000
2000	Land Cruiser	2UZ-FE	4.7 (4663)	8	DOHC	EFI	230@4800	320@3600	3.70 x 3.31	9.6:1	43-85@3000
	Tundra	5VZ-FE	3.4 (3378)	6	DOHC	EFI	190@4800	220@3600	3.68 x 3.23	9.6:1	36-75@3000
	Tundra	2UZ-FE	4.7 (4664)	8	DOHC	EFI	245@4800	315@3400	3.70 x 3.31	9.6:1	43-85@3000
	Tacoma	2RZ-FE	2.4 (2438)	4	DOHC	EFI	142@5000	160@4000	3.74 x 3.38	9.5:1	36-71@3000
	Tacoma	3RZ-FE	2.7 (2694)	4	DOHC	EFI	150@4800	177@4000	3.74 x 3.74	9.5:1	36-71@3000
	Tacoma	5VZ-FE	3.4 (3378)	6	DOHC	EFI	190@4800	220@3600	3.68 x 3.23	9.6:1	36-75@3000
	4Runner	3RZ-FE	2.7 (2694)	4	DOHC	EFI	150@4800	177@4000	3.74 x 3.74	9.5:1	36-71@3000
	4Runner	5VZ-FE	3.4 (3378)	6	DOHC	EFI	183@4800	217@3600	3.68 x 3.23	9.6:1	36-75@3000

93161c02

ROUTINE MAINTENANCE

See Figures 30 thru 35

Proper maintenance is the key to long and trouble-free vehicle life. As a conscientious owner and driver, set aside a Saturday morning, say once a month, to check or replace items which could cause major problems later. Keep your own personal log to jot down which services you performed, how much the parts cost you, the date, and the exact odometer reading at the time. Keep all receipts for such items as engine oil and filters, so that they may be referred to in case of related problems or to determine operating expenses. As a do-it-yourselfer, these receipts are the only proof you have that the required maintenance was performed. In the event of a warranty problem, these receipts will be invaluable.

The literature provided with your vehicle when it was originally delivered includes the factory recommended maintenance schedule. If you no longer have this literature, replacement copies are usually available from the dealer. A maintenance schedule is provided later in this section, in case you do not have the factory literature.

These checks and inspections can be done either by yourself, a reputable independent shop, or the Toyota dealer.

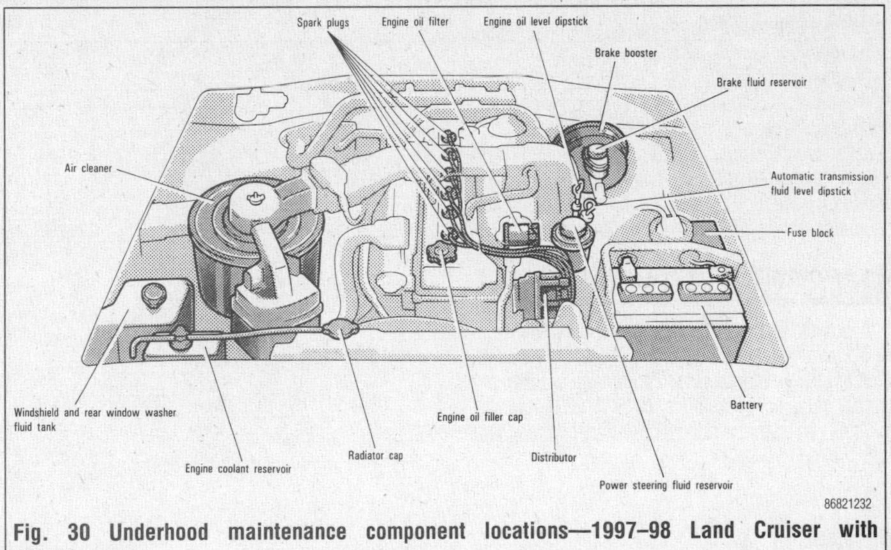

Fig. 30 Underhood maintenance component locations—1997–98 Land Cruiser with 1FZ-FE engine

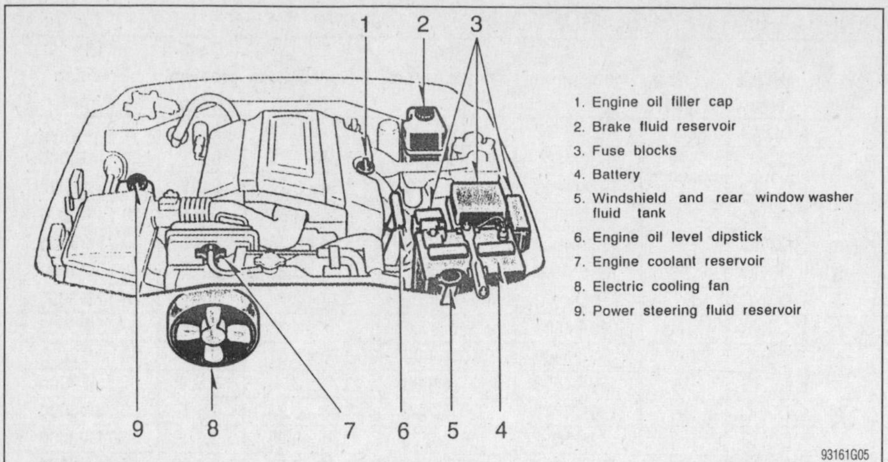

Fig. 31 Underhood maintenance component locations—1999–00 Land Cruiser with 2UZ-FE engine

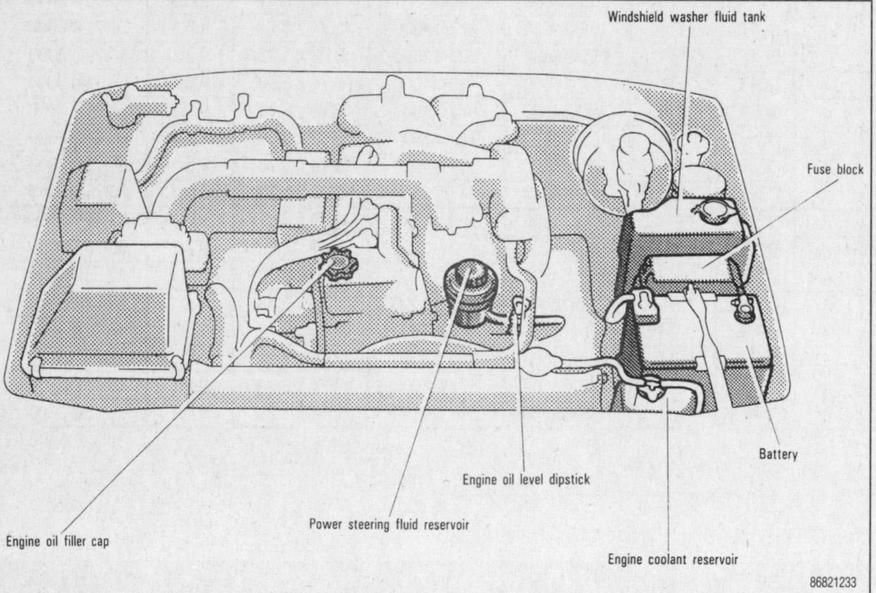

Fig. 32 Underhood maintenance component locations—1997–99 T-100 and 1997–00 4Runner with 3RZ-FE engine

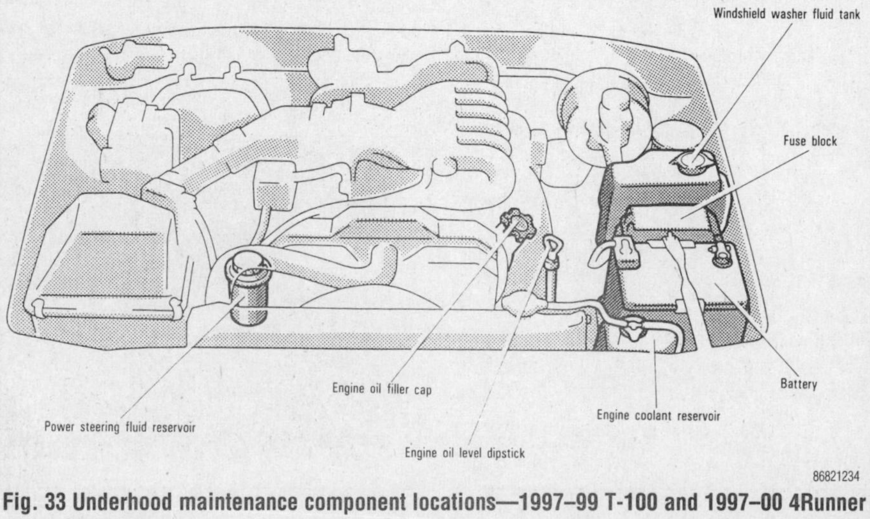

Fig. 33 Underhood maintenance component locations—1997–99 T-100 and 1997–00 4Runner with 5VZ-FE engine

Here are a few of the scheduled maintenance items that need to be checked frequently:

OUTSIDE THE VEHICLE

- Tire pressure—use a gauge to check the pressure.
- Tire surfaces and lug nuts—check the tread depth and ensure all the lug nuts are in place.
- Tire rotation—rotate every 6,200 miles (10,000 km).
- Fluid leaks—check the underneath for leaks of any kind.
- Doors and the engine hood—check the latches ensuring they are securing properly.

INSIDE THE VEHICLE

- Lights—make sure all the lights are in working order.
- Reminder indicators—ensue all the warning lights and buzzers function properly.
- Horn—test the horn to make sure it works when needed.
- Seats—be aware of any adjuster problems. A moving seat while you're driving is dangerous.
- Seat belts—are they all working properly.
- Accelerator pedal—check for smooth operation.
- Clutch pedal—check for smooth operation and free-play.
- Brake pedal—check for smooth operation and free-play.
- Brakes—in a safe location, check for any brake pull.

IN THE ENGINE COMPARTMENT

- Washer fluid—check the fluid level
- Engine coolant level—make sure the level is between the FULL and LOW marks
- Battery—if you have a maintenance battery, check the electrolyte levels
- Brake and clutch fluid levels—have the levels near the upper line of the reservoirs
- Engine oil level—with the engine OFF, check fluid level on the dipstick
- Power steering fluid—the level should be between HOT and COLD
- Exhaust system—visually check for cracks, holes and loose supports. Be aware of a sudden noise change in the exhaust

Your Toyota's on-board computer controls most driveline related functions, including many of the functions that at one time, were considered part of a standard tune-up. Fuel mixture adjustment, for example, is now controlled by the Electronic Control Module (ECM), so no adjustment is possible on these systems. So underhood tune-up has taken on a new meaning, generally being centered around engine oil and filter changes, spark plug changes and maintaining the cooling system. Owners are encouraged to set aside time to check or replace items which could cause major problems later. Keep a personal log of services performed, how much the parts cost and the exact odometer reading at the time of service work. Keep all receipts for such items as engine oil and filters, so that they may be referred to in case of related problems or to determine operating expenses. These receipts are the only proof you have that the required maintenance was performed. In the event of a warranty problem, these receipts will be valuable.

Air Cleaner Element

The air cleaner filter element should be replaced at the recommended intervals shown in the Mainte-

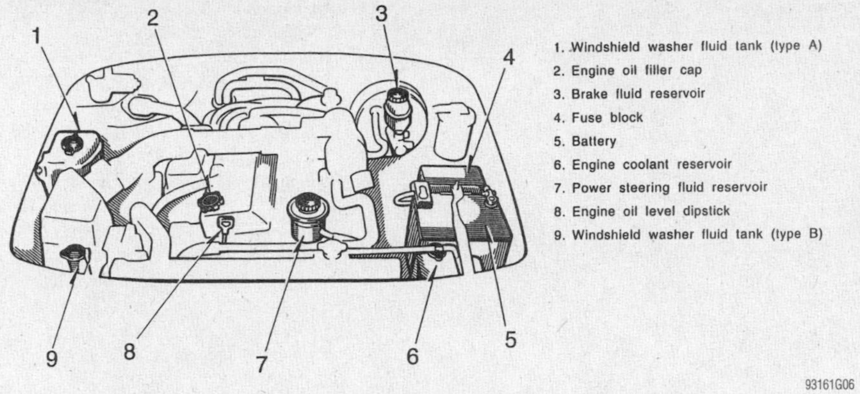

Fig. 34 Underhood maintenance component locations—1997–00 Tacoma with 2RZ-FE and 3RZ-FE engines

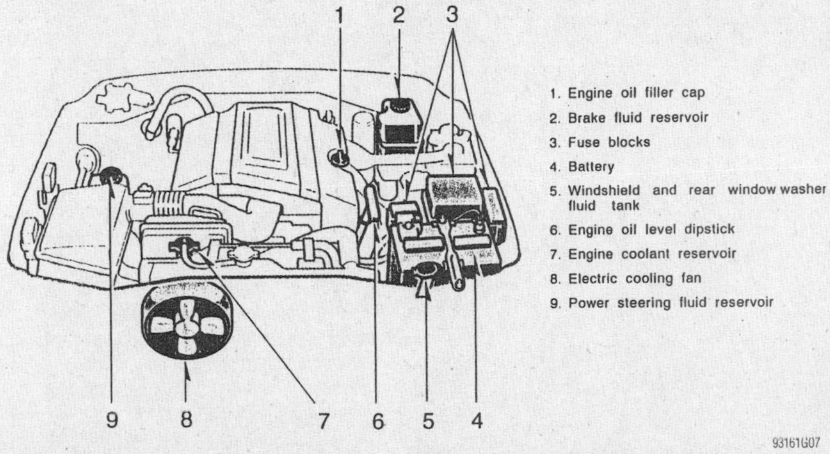

Fig. 35 Underhood maintenance component locations—1997–00 Tacoma with 5VZ-FE engine

nance Intervals chart. If your truck is operated under severely dusty conditions or severe operating conditions, more frequent changes will certainly be necessary. Inspect the element at least twice a year. Early spring and early fall are always good times for inspection. Remove the element and check for any perforations or tears in the filter. Check the cleaner housing for signs of dirt or dust that may have leaked through the filter element or in through the snorkel tube. Shine a bright light on one side of the element and look through the filter at the light. If no glow of light can be seen through the element material, replace the filter. If holes in the filter element are apparent or signs of dirt seepage through the filter are evident, replace the filter.

Maintenance of the air intake system on these engine is very important. The computerized engine management system measures the amount of air entering the engine, using a Mass Air Flow (MAF) sensor. The amount of fuel injected into the engine is based on computations with input from many engine control sensors, including the MAF sensor. Any air entering the engine that is not measured by the MAF sensor will upset the results of the computer's computations and will cause the engine to run badly. Separation or looseness of the engine oil dipstick, oil filler cap, PCV hose, or cracks or looseness in any part of the air induction system between the throttle body and cylinder head will allow suction and cause the engine to run out of tune. Make sure all air ducting and induction-related components are properly installed and sealed.

REMOVAL & INSTALLATION

➧ **See Figures 36 thru 42**

1. Disconnect all hoses, ducts and vacuum tubes which would block removal of the top of the air cleaner assembly.
2. Release the clips holding the top of the air box and lift the lid. Note that some of these clips may be in close quarters against bodywork or other components; don't pry or force the clips.
3. Remove the filter element. Clean or replace as needed. Wipe clean all surfaces of the air cleaner housing and cover. Check the condition of the mounting gasket and replace it if it appears worn or broken.

To install:

4. Reposition the filter element in the case and install the cover. The lid of the air cleaner housing must be correctly installed and fit snugly. Air leaks around the top can cause air to bypass the filter and allow dirt into the engine.

➡Filter elements may have a TOP and BOTTOM side. Look for any identifying marks and make sure the element is correctly installed.

5. Connect all hoses, duct work and vacuum lines, as required.

➡Never operate the engine without the air filter element in place.

Fig. 36 Release the clips securing the air cleaner housing lid

Fig. 37 Location of the air cleaner housing lid clips—1998 Toyota Tacoma shown

Fig. 38 Lift the air cleaner housing lid, remove the old filter and insert a new filter

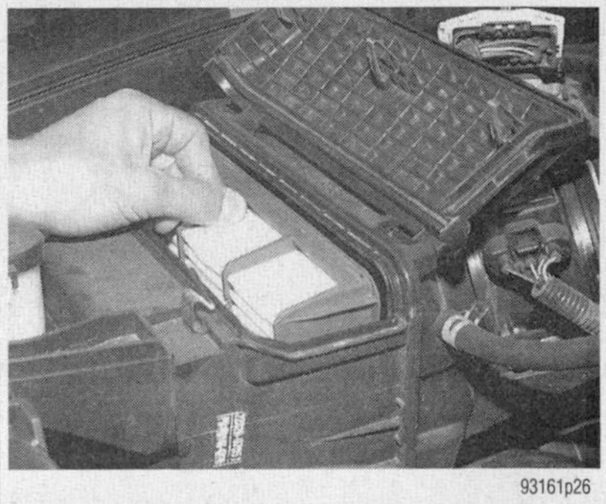

Fig. 39 Pull the air filter straight up and out of the housing

UNDERHOOD MAINTENANCE COMPONENT LOCATIONS—5VZ-FE ENGINE

1. Windshield washer solvent reservoir
2. Air cleaner assembly
3. Power steering fluid reservoir
4. PCV valve
5. Transmission oil filler dipstick
6. Spark plugs (located beneath the cover)
7. Spark plug wires
8. Accessory drive belt
9. Engine oil dipstick
10. Engine oil filler cap
11. Brake fluid reservoir
12. Battery
13. Engine fuse box
14. Coolant recovery tank
15. Radiator cap

93161pm1

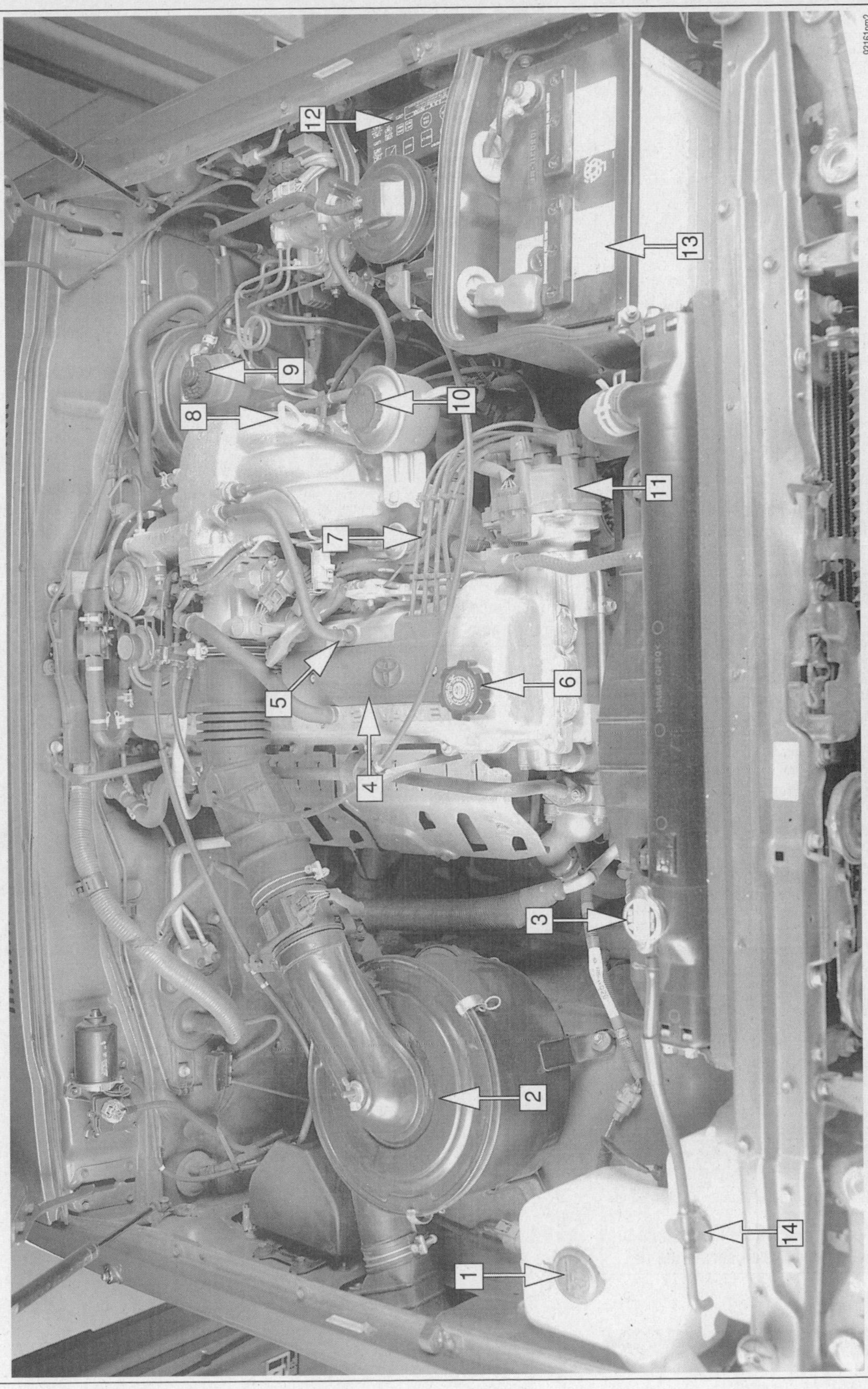

UNDERHOOD MAINTENANCE COMPONENT LOCATIONS—1FZ-FE ENGINE

1. Windshield washer solvent reservoir
2. Air cleaner assembly
3. Radiator cap
4. Spark plugs (located beneath the cover)
5. PCV valve
6. Engine oil fill cap
7. Spark plug wires
8. Engine oil dipstick
9. Brake fluid reservoir
10. Power steering fluid reservoir
11. Distributor cap
12. Engine fuse box
13. Battery
14. Coolant recovery tank

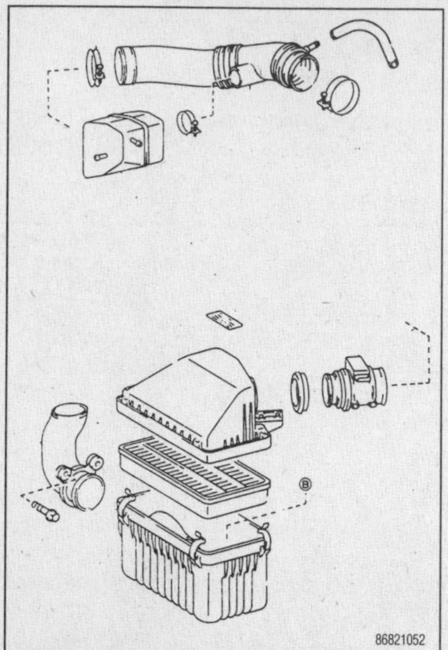

86821052

Fig. 40 Exploded view of a common air cleaner assembly found on Toyota trucks

93161p28

Fig. 41 Check the air filter for dirt and debris and replace if necessary

93161p27

Fig. 42 Slide a new filter element into the air cleaner housing, then secure the lid

Fuel Filter

REMOVAL & INSTALLATION

See Figures 43 thru 49

CAUTION

Never smoke when working around or near gasoline. Make sure that there are no active ignition sources (heaters, electric motors or fans, welders, anything with sparks or open flame.) in the area. Have a fire extinguisher within arm's reach at all times.

The fuel filter is in a metal cylinder, located either on the rear frame rail or in the engine compartment, depending on the Model Year and vehicle. You may also find it under the injection manifold on some models.

93165p03

Fig. 43 The fuel filter on this 1998 Toyota Tacoma is located under the vehicle on the rear frame rail

1. Unbolt the retaining screws and remove the protective shield from the fuel filter.
2. Place a pan under the delivery pipe to catch the dripping fuel and SLOWLY loosen the union bolt to bleed off the fuel pressure. The fuel system is under pressure. Release pressure slowly and contain spillage. Observe all "No Smoking/No Open Flame" precautions
3. Remove the union bolt and drain the remaining fuel.
4. Disconnect and plug the inlet line.
5. Unbolt and remove the fuel filter.

To install:

➡When tightening the fuel line bolts to the fuel filter, use a torque wrench. The tightening torque is very important, as under or over tightening may cause fuel leakage. Insure that there is no fuel line interference and that there is sufficient space between the fuel lines and other components.

6. Coat the flare unit, union nut and all bolt threads with light engine oil.
7. Hand-tighten the inlet line to the fuel filter.
8. Install the fuel filter and then tighten the inlet line nut to 22 ft. lbs. (29 Nm).
9. Reconnect the delivery pipe using new gaskets and then tighten the union bolt to 22 ft. lbs. (29 Nm).

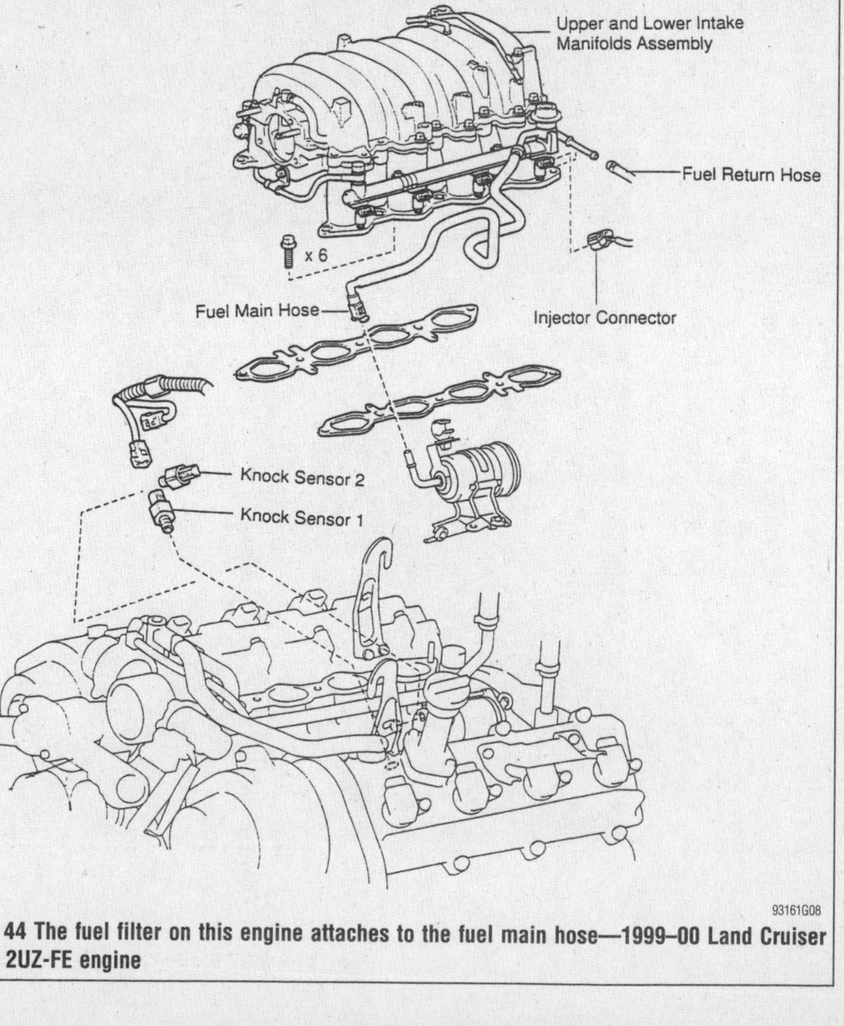

93161G08

Fig. 44 The fuel filter on this engine attaches to the fuel main hose—1999-00 Land Cruiser with 2UZ-FE engine

Fig. 45 Always use a line wrench to remove a fuel line nut

Fig. 46 The use of a three sided wrench such as this line wrench will prevent you from rounding the nut off

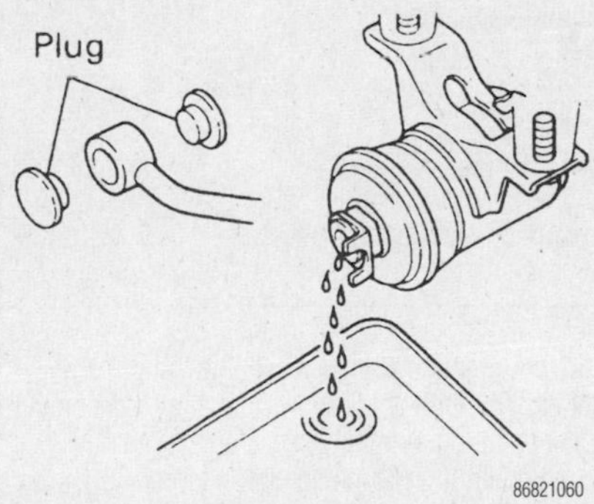

Fig. 47 Place a pan under the delivery pipe to catch the dripping fuel

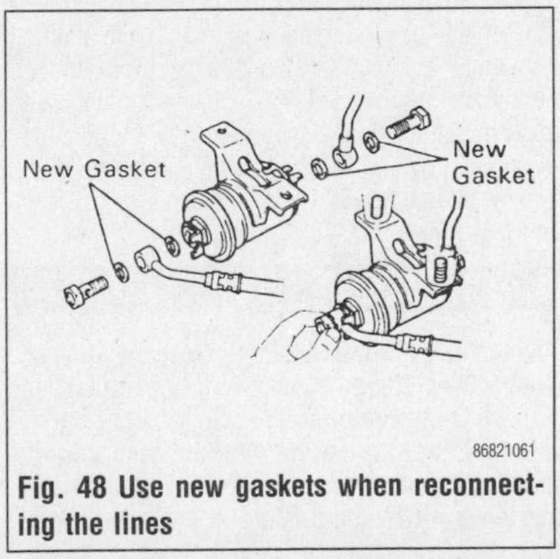

Fig. 48 Use new gaskets when reconnecting the lines

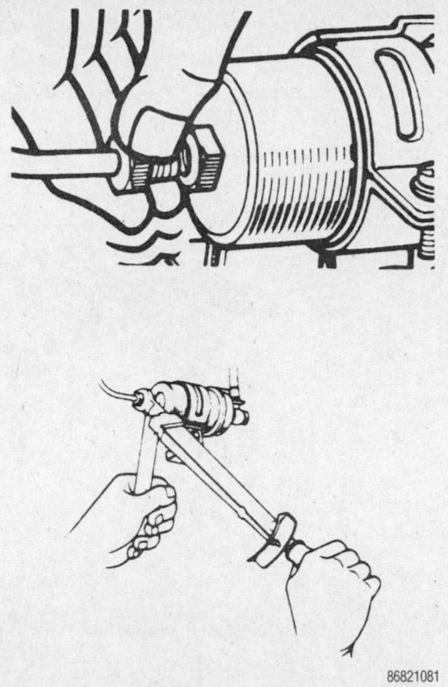

Fig. 49 Hand-tighten the fuel lines first, then final tighten with a torque wrench

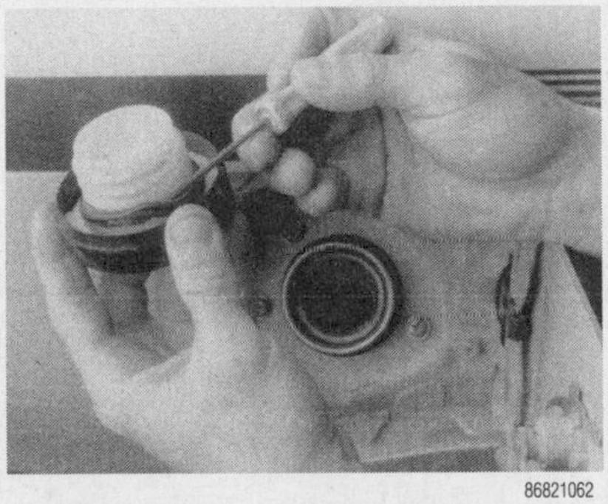

Fig. 50 A seal pick can be used to remove the fuel tank cap gasket

10. Run the engine for a short period and check for any fuel leaks.
11. Install the protective shield.

Fuel Cap Gasket

REMOVAL & INSTALLATION

See Figure 50

All vehicles require the replacement of the fuel filler cap gasket at 60,000 miles (96,558 km), to maintain the integrity of the evaporative emission control system. The gasket is important in sealing the filler neck and keeping the vapors from the tank routed through the vapor emission system. Some vehicles may have the gasket is held in with 4 small screws and a retaining plate which must be removed. Other models eliminate the screws and retainer. Gently pry the gasket off with your fingers or a tool. Install the new gasket and make certain it is not twisted or crimped.

PCV Valve

See Figure 51

The PCV valve regulates crankcase ventilation during various engine operating conditions. At high vacuum (idle speed and partial load range) it will open slightly and at low vacuum (full throttle) it will open fully. This causes vapor to be removed from the crankcase by the engine vacuum and then sucked into the combustion chamber where it is burned along with the fuel.

➡The PCV system will not function properly unless the oil filler cap and the engine oil dipstick are tightly sealed. Check the seals on the cap and dipstick. Replace components as necessary to ensure proper sealing.

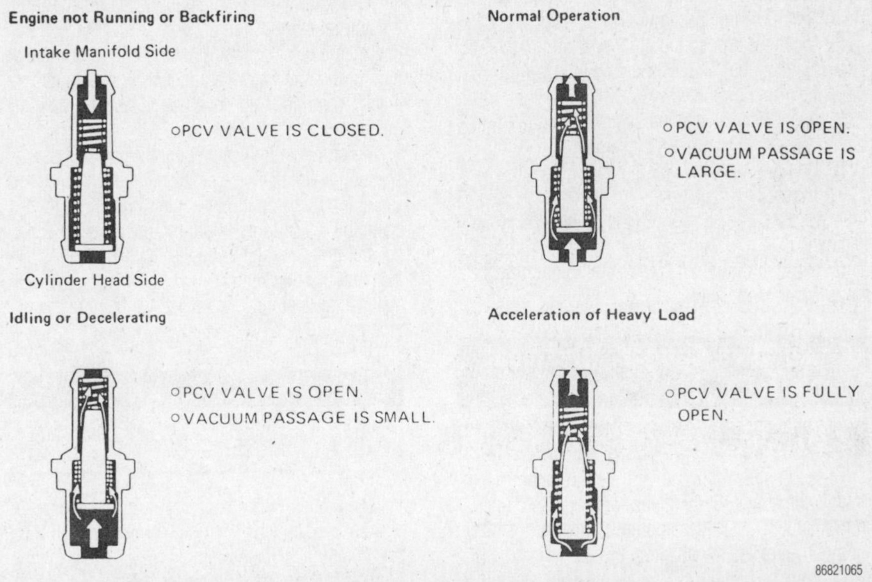

Fig. 51 The PCV valve regulates crankcase ventilation according to engine running conditions

93161pc8

Fig. 52 Locate the PCV valve in the cylinder head cover and remove it by pulling it upward

86821072

Fig. 53 Pull the PCV valve off of the vacuum hose

REMOVAL & INSTALLATION

➧ **See Figures 52 and 53**

1. Check the ventilation hoses and lines for leaks or clogging. Clean or replace as necessary.
2. Locate the PCV valve in the cylinder head cover and remove it by pulling it upward.
3. Test the valve by attaching a clean tube to the crankcase end of the valve, then blow through it. There should be free passage of air through the valve.
4. Move the tube to the other end of the valve. Blow into the tube. There should be little or no passage of air through the valve.
5. If the PCV valve failed either of the preceding two checks, it will require replacement.
6. Pull the PCV valve off the hose.

To install:

7. Slip the hose back onto the proper end of the PCV valve.
8. Press the valve into the retaining grommet in the cylinder head cover.

Evaporative Canister (Charcoal Canister)

➧ **See Figure 54**

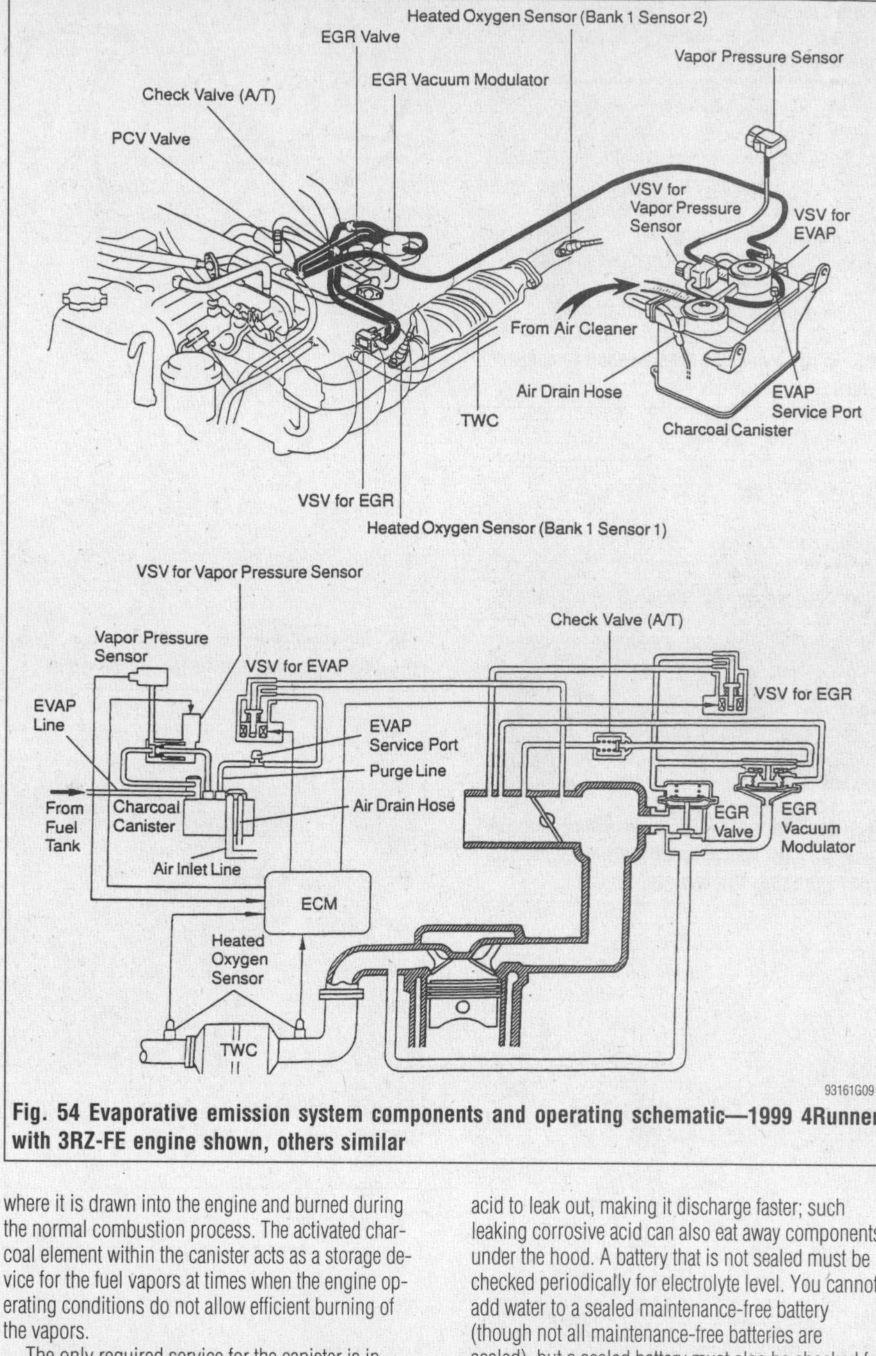

93161G09

Fig. 54 Evaporative emission system components and operating schematic—1999 4Runner with 3RZ-FE engine shown, others similar

The evaporative emissions system is designed to prevent the atmospheric release of evaporated fuel from the fuel tank. The evaporative emission canister (sometimes called the charcoal canister) directs fuel vapor from the fuel tank. A system of valves meters the vapor from the canister to the intake manifold, where it is drawn into the engine and burned during the normal combustion process. The activated charcoal element within the canister acts as a storage device for the fuel vapors at times when the engine operating conditions do not allow efficient burning of the vapors.

The only required service for the canister is inspection at the intervals specified in the Maintenance Chart. If the charcoal element is saturated or damaged, the entire canister will require replacement. Label and disconnect the canister purge hoses, loosen the retaining bracket bolt(s) and lift out the canister. Installation is simply the reverse of the removal process.

Battery

GENERAL MAINTENANCE

All batteries, regardless of type, should be carefully secured by a battery hold-down device. If this is not done, the battery terminals or casing may crack from stress applied to the battery during vehicle operation. A battery which is not secured may allow acid to leak out, making it discharge faster; such leaking corrosive acid can also eat away components under the hood. A battery that is not sealed must be checked periodically for electrolyte level. You cannot add water to a sealed maintenance-free battery (though not all maintenance-free batteries are sealed), but a sealed battery must also be checked for proper electrolyte level as indicated by the color of the built-in hydrometer "eye."

Keep the top of the battery clean, as a film of dirt can completely discharge a battery that is not used for long periods. A solution of baking soda and water may be used for cleaning, but be careful to flush this off with clear water. DO NOT let any of the solution into the filler holes. Baking soda neutralizes battery acid and will de-activate a battery cell.

✲✲ CAUTION

Always use caution when working on or near the battery. Never allow a tool to bridge the gap between the negative and positive battery terminals. Also, be careful not to allow a tool to provide a ground between the positive cable/terminal and any metal component on

the vehicle. Either of these conditions will cause a short circuit leading to sparks and possible personal injury.

Batteries in vehicles which are not operated on a regular basis can fall victim to parasitic loads (small current drains which are constantly drawing current from the battery). Normal parasitic loads may drain a battery on a vehicle that is in storage and not used for 6–8 weeks. Vehicles that have additional accessories such as a cellular phone, an alarm system or other devices that increase parasitic load may discharge a battery sooner. If the vehicle is to be stored for 6–8 weeks in a secure area and the alarm system, if present, is not necessary, the negative battery cable should be disconnected at the onset of storage to protect the battery charge.

Remember that constantly discharging and recharging will shorten battery life. Take care not to allow a battery to be needlessly discharged.

BATTERY FLUID

➧ See Figures 55, 56, and 57

⁂ CAUTION

Battery electrolyte contains sulfuric acid. If you should splash any on your skin or in your eyes, flush the affected area with plenty of clear water. If it lands in your eyes, get medical help immediately.

The fluid (sulfuric acid solution) contained in the battery cells will tell you many things about the condition of the battery. Because the cell plates must be kept submerged below the fluid level in order to operate, maintaining the fluid level is extremely important. And, because the specific gravity of the acid is an indication of electrical charge, testing the fluid can be an aid in determining if the battery must be replaced. A battery in a vehicle with a properly operating charging system should require little maintenance, but careful, periodic inspection should reveal problems before they leave you stranded.

Fluid Level

Check the battery electrolyte level at least once a month, or more often in hot weather or during periods of extended vehicle operation. On non-sealed batteries, the level can be checked either through the case on translucent batteries or by removing the cell caps on opaque-cased types. The electrolyte level in each cell should be kept filled to the split ring inside each cell, or the line marked on the outside the case.

If the level is low, add only distilled water through the opening until the level is correct. Each cell is separate from the others, so each must be checked and filled individually. Distilled water should be used, because the chemicals and minerals found in most drinking water are harmful to the battery and could significantly shorten its life.

If water is added in freezing weather, the vehicle should be driven several miles to allow the water to mix with the electrolyte. Otherwise, the battery could freeze.

Although some maintenance-free batteries have removable cell caps for access to the electrolyte, the electrolyte condition and level on all sealed maintenance-free batteries must be checked using the built-in hydrometer "eye." The exact type of eye varies between battery manufacturers, but most apply a sticker to the battery itself explaining the possible readings. When in doubt, refer to the battery manufacturer's instructions to interpret battery condition using the built-in hydrometer.

➡Although the readings from built-in hydrometers found in sealed batteries may vary, a green eye usually indicates a properly charged battery with sufficient fluid level. A dark eye is normally an indicator of a battery with sufficient fluid, but one which may be low in charge. And a light or yellow eye is usually an indication that electrolyte supply has dropped below the necessary level for battery (and hydrometer) operation. In this last case, sealed batteries with an insufficient electrolyte level must usually be discarded.

Specific Gravity

➧ See Figures 58, 59, and 60

As stated earlier, the specific gravity of a battery's electrolyte level can be used as an indication of battery charge. At least once a year, check the specific gravity of the battery. It should be between 1.20 and 1.26 on the gravity scale. Most auto supply stores carry a variety of inexpensive battery testing hydrometers. These can be used on any non-sealed battery to test the specific gravity in each cell.

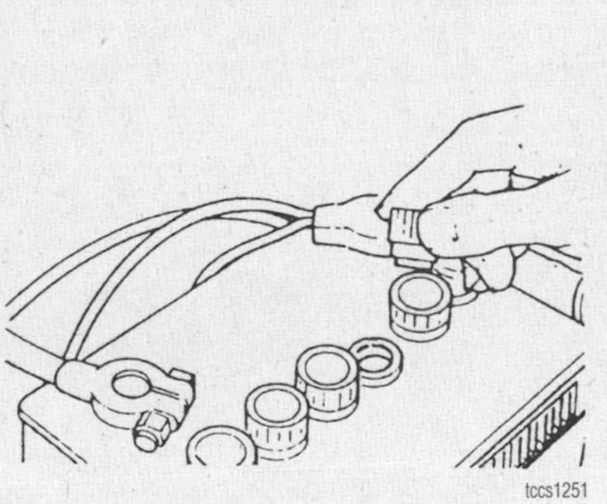

Fig. 55 On non-maintenance free batteries, the level can be checked through the case on translucent batteries; the cell caps must be removed on other models

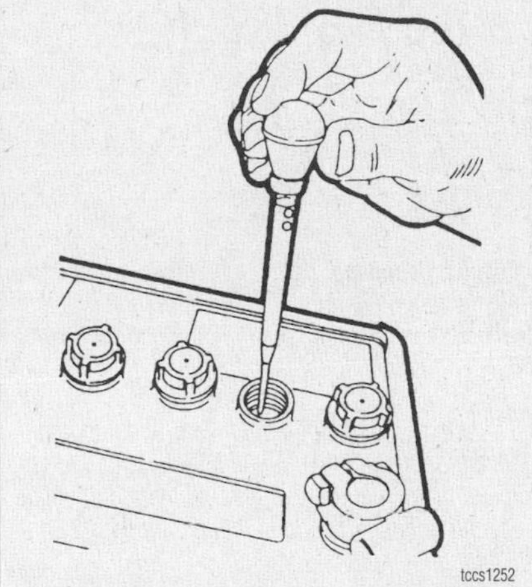

Fig. 56 Check the specific gravity of the battery's electrolyte with a hydrometer

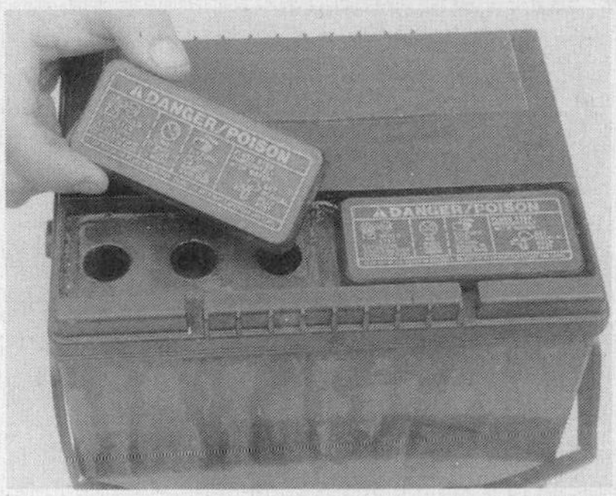

Fig. 58 On non-sealed batteries, the fluid level can be checked by removing the cell caps

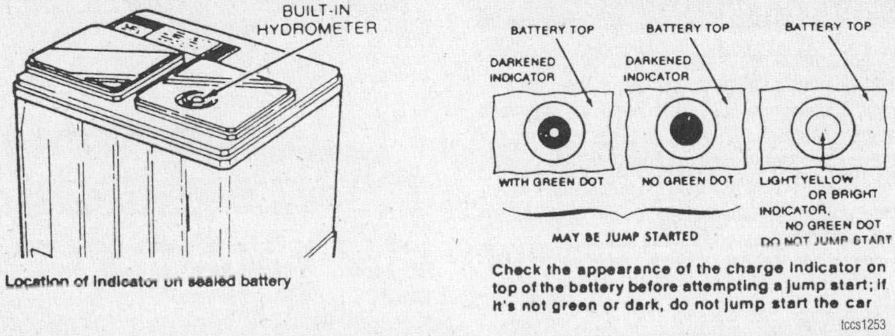

Fig. 57 A typical sealed (maintenance-free) battery with a built-in hydrometer. Note that the hydrometer eye may vary between battery manufacturers; always refer to the battery's label

Fig. 59 If the fluid level is low, add only distilled water until the level is correct

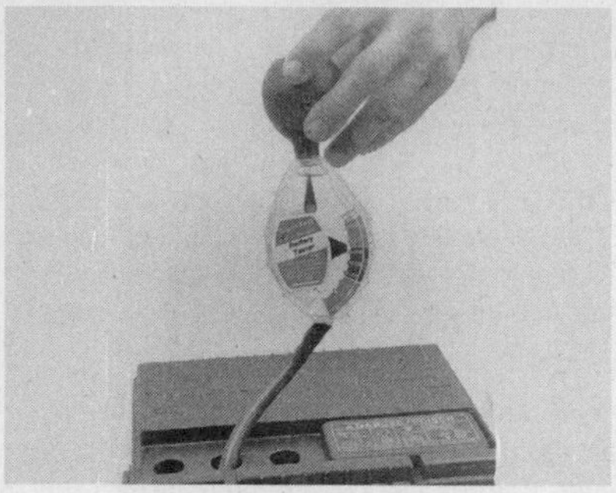

TCCA1P09

Fig. 60 Check the specific gravity of the battery's electrolyte with a hydrometer

The battery testing hydrometer has a squeeze bulb at one end and a nozzle at the other. Battery electrolyte is sucked into the hydrometer until the float is lifted from its seat. The specific gravity is then read by noting the position of the float. If gravity is low in one or more cells, the battery should be slowly charged and checked again to see if the gravity has come up. Generally, if after charging, the specific gravity between any two cells varies more than 50 points (0.50), the battery should be replaced as it can no longer produce sufficient voltage to guarantee proper operation.

On sealed batteries, the built-in hydrometer is the only way of checking specific gravity. Again, check with your battery's manufacturer for proper interpretation of its built-in hydrometer readings.

CABLES

See Figures 61 and 62

Once a year (or as necessary), the battery terminals and the cable clamps should be cleaned. Loosen the clamps and remove the cables, negative cable first. On batteries with posts on top, the use of a puller specially made for this purpose is recommended. These are inexpensive and available in most auto parts stores. Side terminal battery cables are secured with a small bolt.

Clean the cable clamps and the battery terminal with a wire brush, until all corrosion, grease, etc., is removed and the metal is shiny. It is especially important to clean the inside of the clamp (an old knife is useful here) thoroughly, since a small deposit of foreign material or oxidation there will prevent a sound electrical connection and inhibit either starting or charging. Special tools are available for cleaning these parts, one type for conventional top post batteries and another type for side terminal batteries.

Before installing the cables, loosen the battery hold-down clamp or strap, remove the battery and check the battery tray. Clear it of any debris, and check it for soundness (the battery tray can be cleaned with a baking soda and water solution). Rust should be wire brushed away, and the metal given a couple coats of anti-rust paint. Install the battery and tighten the hold-down clamp or strap securely. Do not overtighten, as this can crack the battery case.

After the clamps and terminals are clean, reinstall the cables, negative cable last; DO NOT hammer the clamps onto post batteries. Tighten the clamps securely, but do not distort them. Give the clamps and terminals a thin external coating of grease after installation, to retard corrosion.

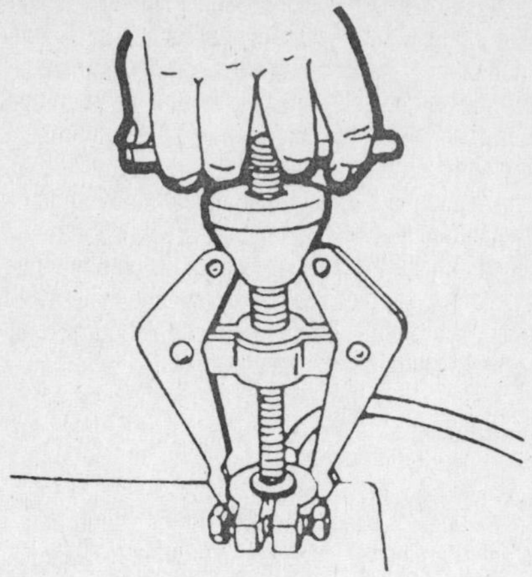

tccs1254

Fig. 61 A special tool is available to pull the clamp from the post

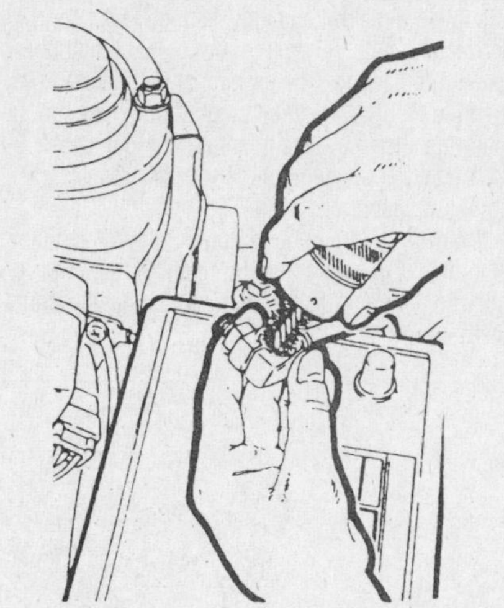

tccs1256

Fig. 62 Clean the battery terminals until the metal is shiny

Check the cables at the same time that the terminals are cleaned. If the cable insulation is cracked or broken, or if the ends are frayed, the cable should be replaced with a new cable of the same length and gauge.

CHARGING

CAUTION

The chemical reaction which takes place in all batteries generates explosive hydrogen gas. A spark can cause the battery to explode and splash acid. To avoid serious personal injury, be sure there is proper ventilation and take appropriate fire safety precautions when connecting, disconnecting, or charging a battery and when using jumper cables.

A battery should be charged at a slow rate to keep the plates inside from getting too hot. However, if some maintenance-free batteries are allowed to discharge until they are almost "dead", they may have to be charged at a high rate to bring them back to "life". Always follow the charger manufacturer's instructions on charging the battery.

REPLACEMENT

When it becomes necessary to replace the battery, select one with a rating equal to or greater than the battery originally installed. Deterioration and just plain aging of the battery cables, starter motor, and associated wires makes the battery's job harder in successive years. The slow increase in electrical resistance over time makes it prudent to install a new battery with a greater capacity than the old.

Belts

INSPECTION

See Figures 63, 64, 65, 66, and 67

Check the condition of the drive belts and check the belt tension at least every 15,000 miles (24,000 km). Inspect the belts for signs of glazing or cracking. A glazed belt will be perfectly smooth from slippage, while a good belt will have a slight texture of fabric visible. Cracks will generally start at the inner edge of the belt and run outward. Replace the belt at the first sign of cracking or if the glazing is severe.

Belt tension does not refer to play or droop. By placing your thumb midway between the two pulleys, it should be possible to depress the belt $^{1}/_{4}$–$^{1}/_{2}$ inch. (6–13mm). If any of the belts can be depressed more than this, or cannot be depressed this much, adjust the tension. While this is an inaccurate test, it provides a quick reference. Inadequate tension will always result in slippage or wear, while excessive ten-

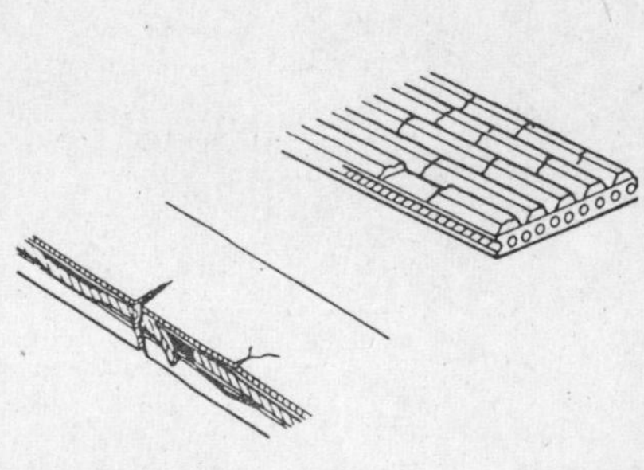

86821102

Fig. 63 There are two types of drive belts, ribbed and non-ribbed

tccs1214

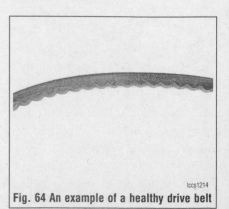

Fig. 64 An example of a healthy drive belt

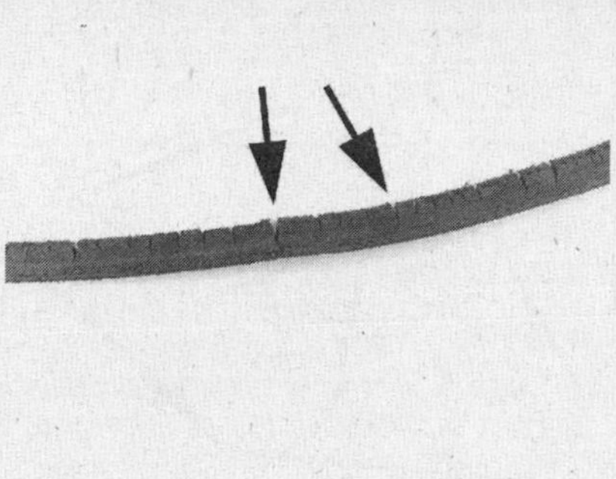

tccs1215

Fig. 65 The deep cracks in this belt will cause it to flex, causing heat that will eventually lead to failure

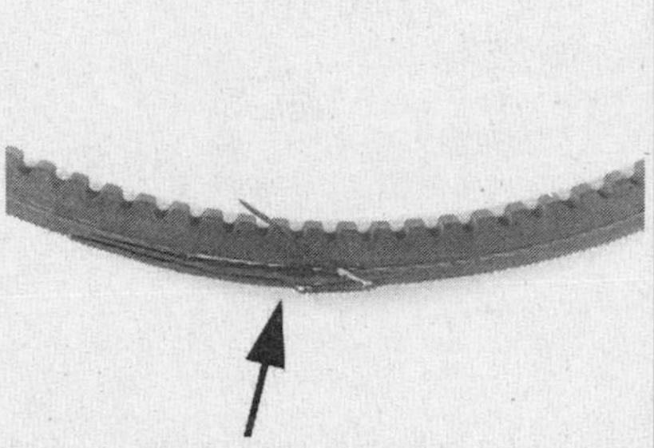

tccs1216

Fig. 66 The cover of this belt is worn exposing the critical reinforcing cords to excessive wear

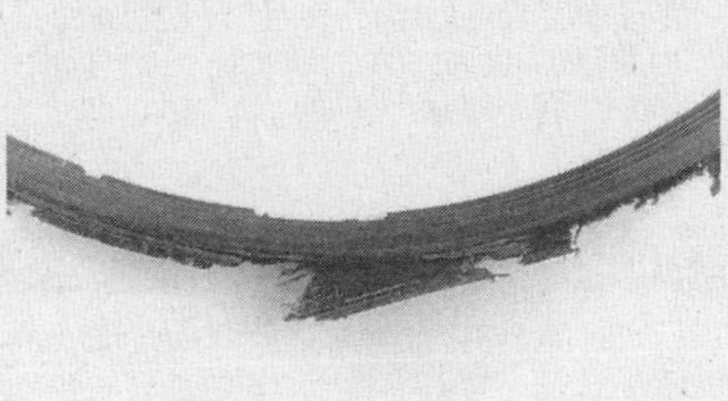

tccs1217

Fig. 67 Too wide a belt on a narrow pulley can groove the belt's side, as well as damage the cover and seat

sion will damage pulley bearings and cause belts to fray and crack. A belt should be just tight enough to perform without slipping or squealing.

It is good practice to replace all drive belts at 60,000 miles (96,000 km) regardless of their condition.

ADJUSTMENT

➧ See Figure 68

Toyota measures belt tension in pounds of force as determined by a belt tension tester. The Nippondenso and Burroughs testers are available through dealers or may be found at retail auto parts stores. The tester slips over a short section of the drive belt, and, when tightened, reads the deflection pressure on a dial. This is one of the most exact ways of setting tension and purchase of this tool or its equivalent is recommended.

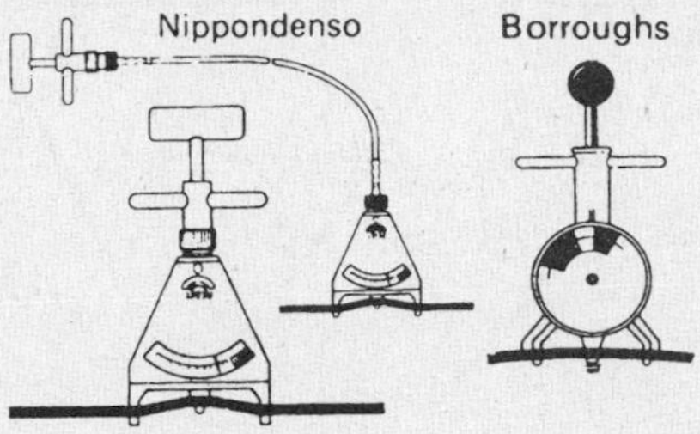

86821103

Fig. 68 The Nippondenso and Burroughs testers are available through dealers or may be found at retail auto parts stores

Following are the belt tension specifications for the engines covered by this manual. Specifications for new belts are slightly higher than for used belts. A new belt is one which has not been run under tension for more than 5 minutes. Anything else is considered a used belt.

5VZ-E Engine

- Alternator: New—160 lbs. (712 N); Used—100 lbs. (445 N)
- Power Steering: New—158 lbs. (702 N); Used—103 lbs. (458 N)
- Air Conditioning: New—160 lbs. (712 N); Used—100 lbs. (445 N)

2RZ-FE and 3RZ-FE Engines

- Alternator: New—165 lbs. (734 N); Used—115 lbs. (511 N)
- Power Steering: New—158 lbs. (702 N); Used—103 lbs. (458 N)
- Air Conditioning: New—160 lbs. (712 N); Used—100 lbs. (445 N)

1FZ-FE Engine

- Alternator: New—110 lbs. (489 N); Used—67 lbs. (298 N)
- Air Conditioning: New—125 lbs. (556 N); Used—80 lbs. (356 N)

2UZ-FE Engine

➧ See Figures 69 and 70

Belt tension adjustment is not necessary, as an automatic belt tensioner is used to maintain proper belt tension. However, you can check to be sure the tensioner is operating properly as follows.

1. Check that the tensioner moves downward when the belt is pressed down at the locations shown in the accompanying figure, with about 22 lbs. (98 N) of force.
2. Check the alignment of the belt tensioner pulley to make sure the belt will not slip off the pulley. If necessary, replace the belt tensioner.
3. Check to be sure the arrow mark on the belt tensioner falls within area "A" of the scale, as shown in the accompanying figure. If the mark falls outside of the area indicated by the "A", you must replace the belt. However, when a new belt is installed, the mark should fall within area "B".

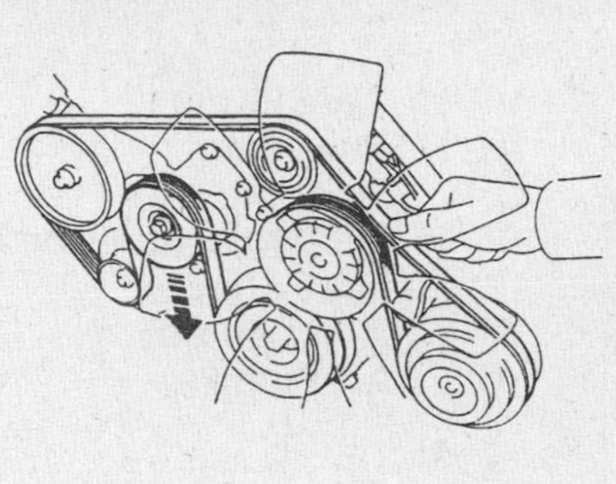

93161g41

Fig. 69 When the belt is pressed down, make sure the tensioner moves downward as shown

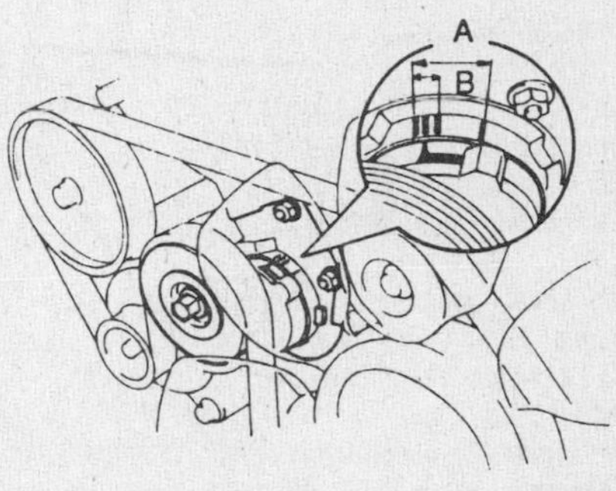

93161g42

Fig. 70 If the mark falls outside of the area indicated by the "A", you must replace the belt

REMOVAL & INSTALLATION

Except 2UZ-FE Engine

➧ See Figures 71 thru 75

When buying replacement belts, remember that the fit is critical according to the length of the belt (diameter), the width of the belt, the depth of the belt and the angle or profile of the V shape. The belt shape should exactly match the shape of the pulley; belts that are not an exact match can cause noise, slippage and premature failure.

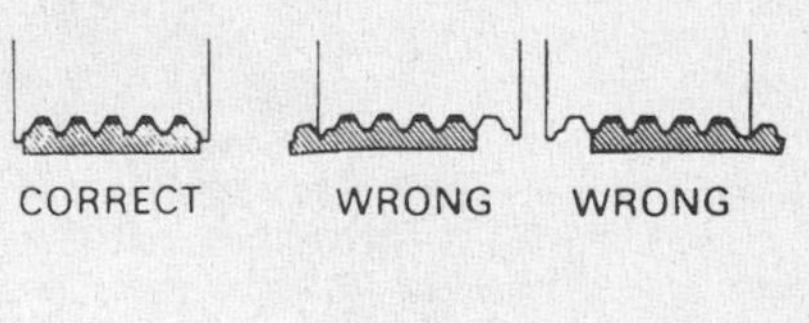

86821104

Fig. 71 When installing a new or used belt, make certain the belt is installed in the grooves correctly

VP : Vane Pump
AL : Alternator
CK : Crankshaft
CC : Cooler Compressor
IP : Idle Pulley
WP : Water Pump
AP : Air Pump

86821126

Fig. 72 Listing of pulley abbreviations

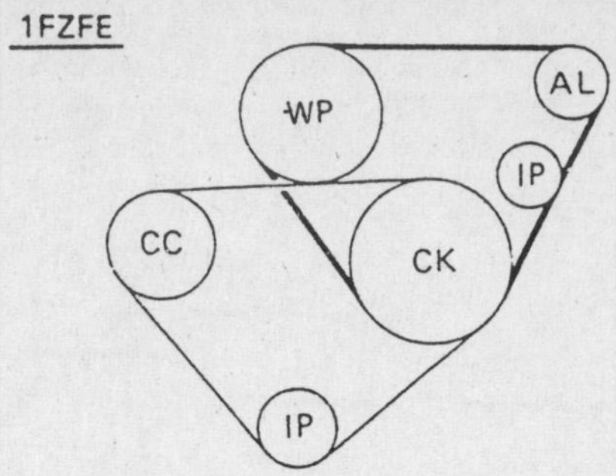

86821128

Fig. 73 Belt routings on the 1FZ-FE engine

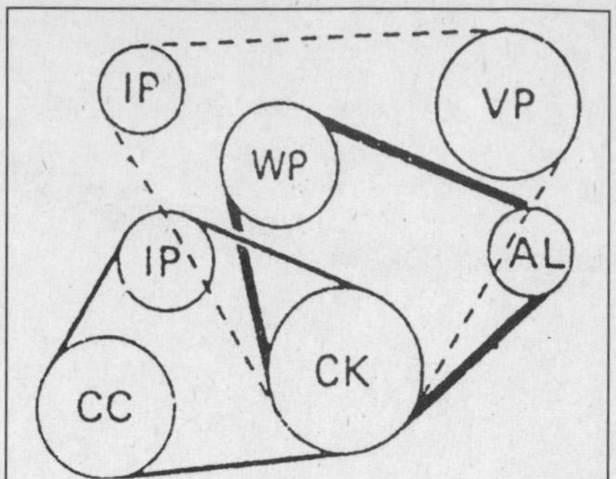

86821129

Fig. 74 Belt routings on the 3RZ-FE engine

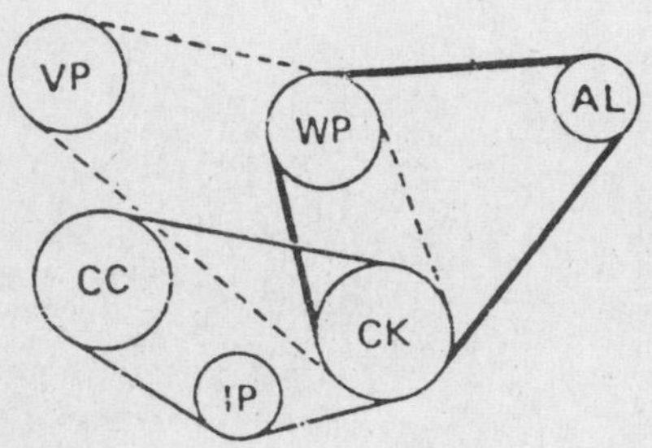

86821130

Fig. 75 Belt routings on the 5VZ-FE engine

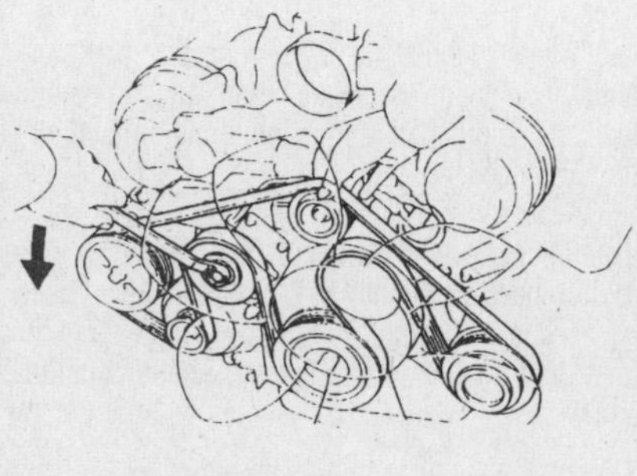

TCCS1242

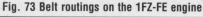

Fig. 76 On the 2UZ-FE engine, rotate the belt tensioner counterclockwise to release the belt tension

93161g43

Fig. 77 Do not bend, twist or turn the timing belt inside out. Never allow oil, water or steam to contact the belt

If a belt must be replaced, the driven unit must be loosened and moved to its extreme loosest position, generally by moving it toward the center of the motor. After removing the old belt, check the pulleys for dirt or built-up material which could affect belt contact. Carefully install the new belt, remembering that it is new and unused, so it may appear to be just a little too small to fit over the pulley flanges.

Fit the belt over the largest pulley (usually the crankshaft pulley at the bottom center of the motor) first, then work on the smaller one(s). Gentle pressure in the direction of rotation is helpful. Some belts run around a third or idler pulley, which acts as an additional pivot in the belt's path. It may be possible to loosen the idler pulley as well as the main component, making your job much easier. Depending on which belt(s) you are changing, it may be necessary to loosen or remove other interfering belts to get at the one(s) you want.

After the new belt is installed, draw tension on it by moving the driven unit away from the motor and tighten its mounting bolts. This is sometimes a three or four-handed job; you may find an assistant helpful. Make sure that all the bolts you loosened get re-tightened and that any other loosened belts also have the correct tension. A new belt can be expected to stretch a bit after installation so be prepared to re-adjust your new belt, if needed, within the first hundred miles/kilometers of use.

2UZ-FE Engine

➧ See Figure 76

To remove the serpentine belt on the 2UZ-FE engine, position a suitable sized wrench or ratchet and socket over the belt tensioner bolt, rotate the tensioner counterclockwise to release the belt tension, then remove the belt. The pulley bolt for the tensioner has a left-hand thread.

When installing the belt, make sure it fits properly in the ribbed grooves and check to be sure the belt has not slipped out of the groove on the bottom of the pulley.

Timing Belts

Of the Toyota trucks covered by this manual, only the 5VZ-FE V6 and 2UZ-FE V8 engines use timing belts. All others use timing chains.

INSPECTION

➧ See Figures 77, 78, 79, and 80

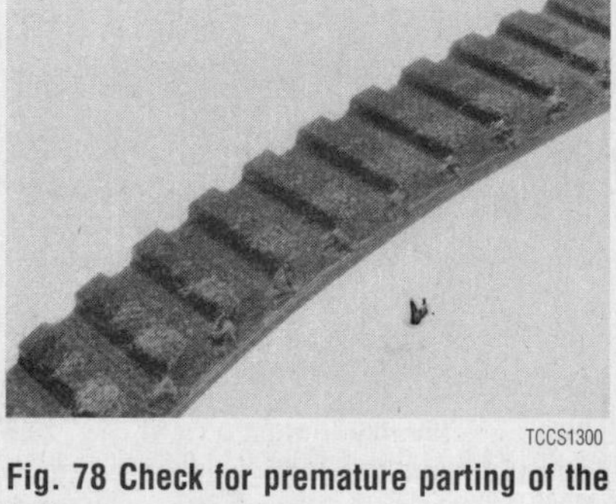

TCCS1300

Fig. 78 Check for premature parting of the belt

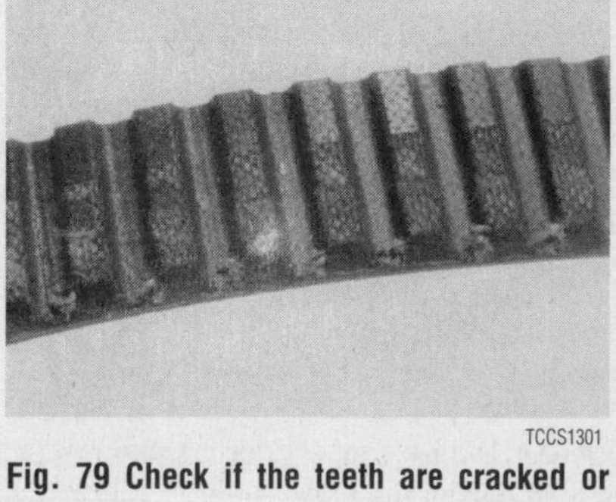

TCCS1301

Fig. 79 Check if the teeth are cracked or damaged

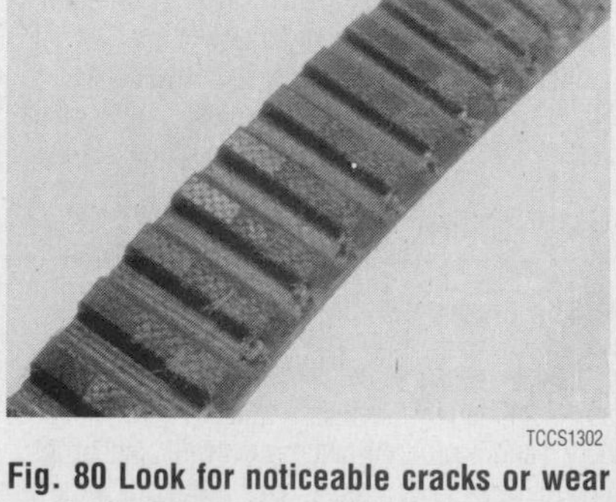

TCCS1302

Fig. 80 Look for noticeable cracks or wear on the belt face

Toyota recommends that the timing belt be replaced at 60,000 miles (96,000 km) on vehicles that are used in extensive idling or low speed driving for long distances. Police, taxi and door-to-door deliveries are commonly used in this manner. This is considered severe service and the timing belt should be replaced every 60,000 miles (96,000 km) in these cases. If your vehicle has high mileage, you may want to consider replacing the belt to prevent the possibility of having it snap. If your engine is being overhauled, inspect the belt for wear and replace if needed. In the event the belt does snap while you are driving, turn the engine **OFF** immediately. For removal and installation procedures, please refer to the following topic(s): Engine Mechanical, Timing Belt.

Hoses

➧ See Figures 81, 82, 83, and 84

Upper and lower radiator hoses along with the heater hoses should be checked for deterioration, leaks and loose hose clamps at least every 15,000 miles (24,000 km). It is also wise to check the hoses periodically in early spring and at the beginning of the fall or winter when you are performing other maintenance. A quick visual inspection could discover a weakened hose which might have left you stranded if it had remained unrepaired.

Whenever you are checking the hoses, make sure the engine and cooling system is cold. Visually inspect for cracking, rotting or collapsed hoses, replace as necessary. Run your hand along the length of the hose. If a weak or swollen spot is noted when squeezing the hose wall, the hose should be replaced.

REMOVAL & INSTALLATION

➧ See Figures 85 thru 91

tccs1219

Fig. 81 The cracks developing along this hose are a result of age and hardening

tccs1220

Fig. 82 A hose clamp that is too tight can cause older hoses to separate and tear

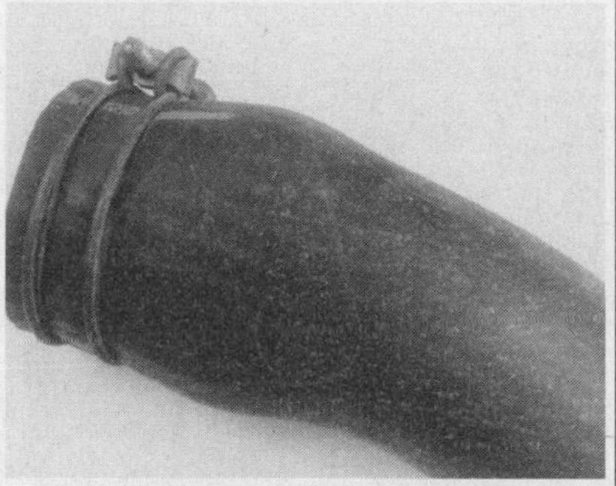

tccs1221

Fig. 83 Check for soft, spongy hoses like this one (swollen at the clamp)—this hose will eventually burst

tccs1222

Fig. 84 Debris or contaminants in the cooling system can cause a hose to weaken from the inside out

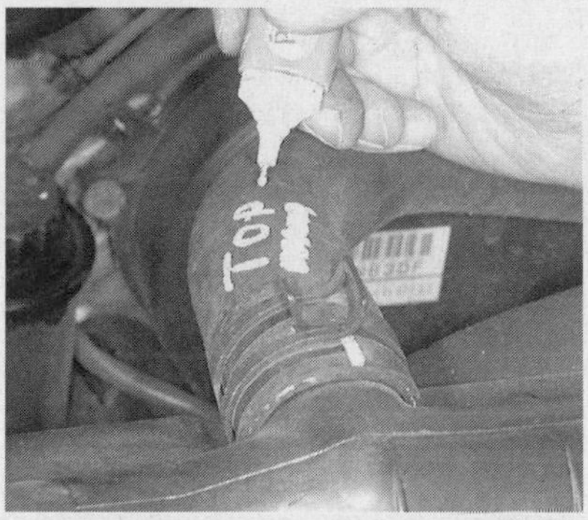

93163p33

Fig. 85 Mark the hoses so that they can be reinstalled in their original positions

93161p34

Fig. 86 When the engine is cool, remove the radiator cap

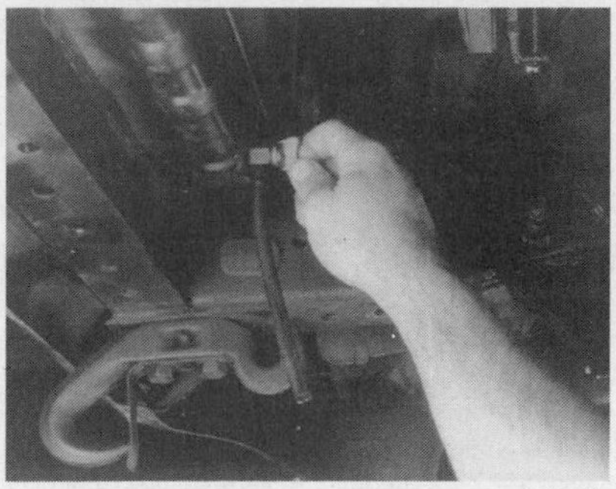

86821111

Fig. 87 Attach a short length of hose to the petcock before loosening the nut

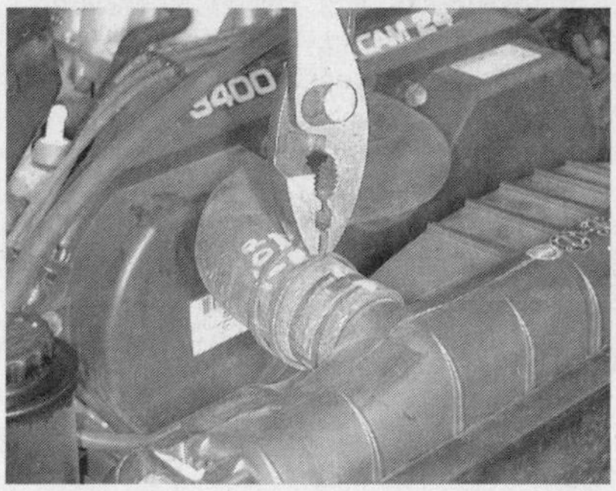

93163p34

Fig. 88 Using a pair of pliers, squeeze the tabs to loosen the upper hose

86821113

Fig. 89 As you grasp the hose clamp, slide it back

93163p35

Fig. 90 Carefully twist, then pull the hose off the neck

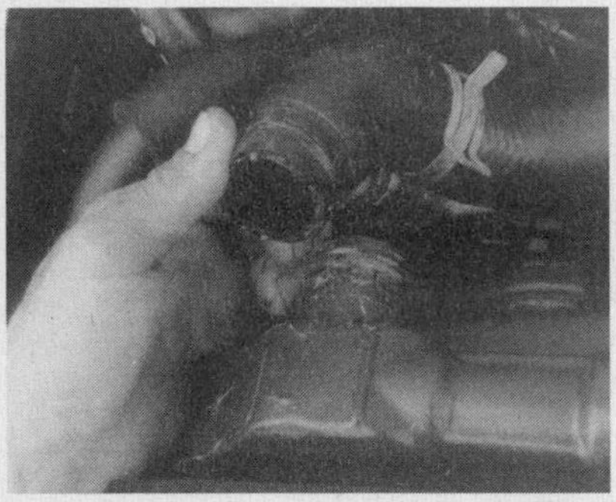

86821114

Fig. 91 When sliding the lower hose off, remember there will be a small amount of fluid still in the hose

CAUTION

Never remove the pressure cap while the engine is running or personal injury from scalding hot coolant or steam may result. If possible, wait until the engine has cooled to remove the pressure cap. If this is not possible, wrap a thick cloth around the pressure cap and turn it slowly to the stop. Step back while the pressure is released from the cooling system. When you are sure all the pressure has been released, still using the cloth, turn and remove the cap.

1. Remove the radiator pressure cap.
2. Position a clean container under the radiator and/or engine petcock or plug, then open the drain and allow the cooling system to drain to an appropriate level. For some upper hoses only a little coolant must be drained. To remove hoses positioned lower on the engine, such as a lower radiator hose, the entire cooling system must be emptied.

CAUTION

When draining coolant, keep in mind that cats and dogs are attracted by ethylene glycol antifreeze, and are quite likely to drink any that is left in an uncovered container or in puddles on the ground. This will prove fatal in sufficient quantity. Always drain coolant into a sealable container. Coolant may be reused unless it is contaminated or several years old.

3. Loosen the hose clamps at each end of the hose requiring replacement. Clamps are usually either of the spring tension type (which require pliers to squeeze the tabs and loosen) or of the screw tension type (which require screw or hex drivers to loosen). Pull the clamps back on the hose away from the connection.
4. Twist, pull and slide the hose off the fitting taking care not to damage the neck of the component from which the hose is being removed.

➡If the hose is stuck at the connection, do not try to insert a screwdriver or other sharp tool under the hose end in an effort to free it, as the connection and/or hose may become damaged. Heater core connections especially may be easily damaged by such a procedure. If the hose is to be replaced, use a single-edged razor blade to make a slice along the portion of the hose which is stuck on the connection, perpendicular to the end of the hose. Do not cut deep so as to prevent damaging the connection. The hose can then be peeled from the connection and discarded.

5. Clean both hose mounting connections. Inspect the condition of the hose clamps and replace them, if necessary.

To install:

6. Dip the ends of the new hose into clean engine coolant to lubricate and ease installation.
7. If a clamp shows signs of any damage (bent, too loose, hard to tighten, etc.), replace it. A good rule is that a new hose is always worth new clamps. Slide the clamps over the replacement hose, then slide the hose ends over the connections into position.
8. Position and secure the clamps at least $^1/_4$ inch (6.35mm) from the ends of the hose. Make sure they are located inside the raised bead of the connector.
9. Reinstall the petcock and properly refill the cooling system with the clean drained engine coolant or a suitable mixture of ethylene glycol coolant and water.
10. If available, install a pressure tester and check for leaks. If a pressure tester is not available, run the engine until normal operating temperature is reached (allowing the system to naturally pressurize), then check for leaks.

CAUTION

If you are checking for leaks with the system at normal operating temperature, BE EXTREMELY CAREFUL not to touch any moving or hot engine parts. Once temperature has been reached, shut the engine OFF, and check for leaks around the hose fittings and connections which were removed earlier.

CV-Boots

INSPECTION

➧ **See Figures 92, 93, and 94**

The Constant Velocity (CV) Joint covers, known as 'boots' should be checked for damage each time the oil is changed and any other time the vehicle is raised for service. These boots keep water, grime, dirt and other damaging matter from entering the CV-joints. Any of these could cause early CV-joint failure which can be expensive to repair. Heavy grease thrown around the inside of the front wheel(s) and on the brake caliper can be an indication of a torn boot. Thoroughly check the boots for missing clamps and tears. If the boot is damaged, have it replaced immediately.

93167p01

Fig. 92 Inspect the CV-boots for cracks or tears at every oil change

TCCS1011

Fig. 93 CV-boots must be inspected periodically for damage

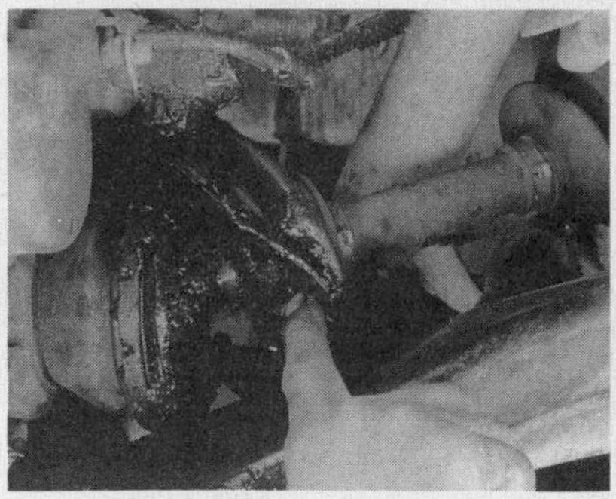

TCCS1010

Fig. 94 A torn CV-boot should be replaced immediately

Spark Plugs

➧ **See Figure 95**

A typical spark plug consists of a metal shell surrounding a ceramic insulator. A metal electrode extends downward through the center of the insulator and protrudes a small distance. Located at the end of the plug and attached to the side of the outer metal shell is the side electrode. The side electrode bends

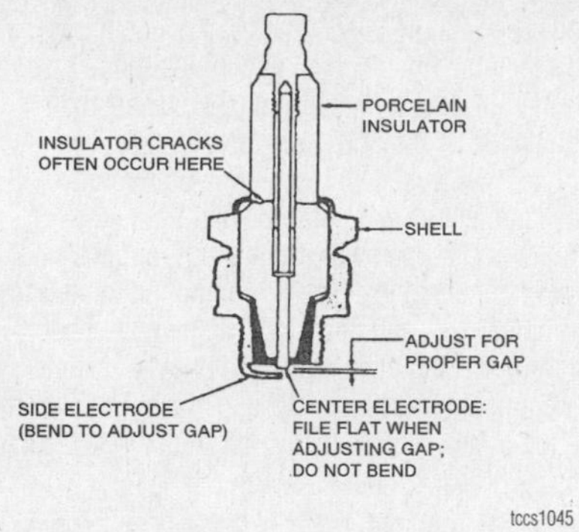

Fig. 95 Cross-section of a spark plug

in at a 90 degree angle so that its tip is just past and parallel to the tip of the center electrode. The distance between these two electrodes (measured in thousandths of an inch or hundredths of a millimeter) is called the spark plug gap.

The spark plug does not produce a spark but instead provides a gap across which the current can arc. The coil produces anywhere from 20,000 to 50,000 volts (depending on the type and application) which travels through the wires to the spark plugs. The current passes along the center electrode and jumps the gap to the side electrode, and in doing so, ignites the air/fuel mixture in the combustion chamber.

SPARK PLUG HEAT RANGE

▸ **See Figure 96**

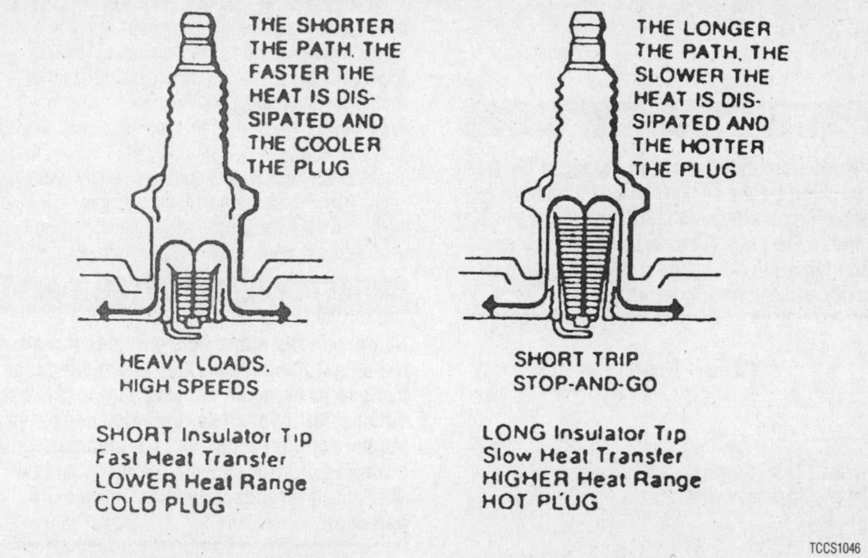

Fig. 96 Typical spark plug heat range

Spark plug heat range is the ability of the plug to dissipate heat. The longer the insulator (or the farther it extends into the engine), the hotter the plug will operate; the shorter the insulator (the closer the electrode is to the block's cooling passages) the cooler it will operate. A plug that absorbs little heat and remains too cool will quickly accumulate deposits of oil and carbon since it is not hot enough to burn them off. This leads to plug fouling and consequently to misfiring. A plug that absorbs too much heat will have no deposits but, due to the excessive heat, the electrodes will burn away quickly and might possibly lead to preignition or other ignition problems. Preignition takes place when plug tips get so hot that they glow sufficiently to ignite the air/fuel mixture before the actual spark occurs. This early ignition will usually cause a pinging during low speeds and heavy loads.

Since spark plugs are considered to be an "Emissions-Related" component, always use the spark plug recommended by the vehicle manufacturer.

REMOVAL & INSTALLATION

▸ **See Figures 97, 98, 99, and 100**

➡**Remove the spark plugs and wires one at a time to avoid confusion and incorrect wiring during installation.**

1. Disconnect the negative battery cable, and if the vehicle has been run recently, allow the engine to thoroughly cool.
2. On engines equipped with spark plugs, carefully twist the spark plug wire boot to loosen it, then pull upward and remove the boot from the plug. Be sure to pull on the boot and not on the wire, otherwise the connector located inside the boot may become separated.
3. On engines with coil-over-plug ignition, remove the ignition coil for access to the spark plug. For additional information, please refer to the following topic(s): Engine Electrical, Ignition Coil.
4. Using compressed air, blow any water or debris from the spark plug well to assure that no harmful contaminants are allowed to enter the combustion chamber when the spark plug is removed. If compressed air is not available, use a rag or a brush to clean the area.

➡**Remove the spark plugs when the engine is cold, if possible, to prevent damage to the threads. If removal of the plugs is difficult, apply a few drops of penetrating oil or silicone spray to the area around the base of the plug, and allow it a few minutes to work.**

93161pb8

Fig. 97 On the 5VZ-FE engine, you must remove the coil for access to the spark plug

93161pc2

Fig. 98 Use a $^{3}/_{8}$ in. ratchet, a locking extension, and a spark plug socket to reach the spark plugs which are deep down in the cylinder head

93161pc3

Fig. 99 Once loosened, carefully withdraw the spark plug from the cylinder head

93161pc7

Fig. 100 View of a twin electrode plug that is found in the 5VZ-FE engine

5. Using a spark plug socket that is equipped with a rubber insert to properly hold the plug, turn the spark plug counterclockwise to loosen and remove the spark plug from the bore.

WARNING

It is recommended that you not use a flexible extension on the socket. Use of a flexible extension may allow a shear force to be applied to the plug. A shear force could break the plug off in the cylinder head, leading to costly and frustrating repairs.

To install:

6. Inspect the spark plug boot for tears or damage. If a damaged boot is found, the spark plug wire must be replaced.

7. Using a wire feeler gauge, check and adjust the spark plug gap. When using a gauge, the proper size should pass between the electrodes with a slight drag. The next larger size should not be able to pass while the next smaller size should pass freely.

8. Carefully thread the plug into the bore by hand. If resistance is felt before the plug is almost completely threaded, back the plug out and begin threading again. In small to reach areas, an old spark plug wire and boot or a short length of rubber hose, placed on the spark plug, could be used as a threading tool. The boot will hold the plug while you twist the end of the wire and the wire is supple enough to twist before it would allow the plug to crossthread.

WARNING

Do not use the spark plug socket to thread the plugs. Always carefully thread the plug by hand or using an old plug wire to prevent the possibility of cross-threading and damaging the cylinder head bore. Remember, your truck has aluminum cylinder heads and the spark plug threads in the head are easily damaged.

9. Carefully tighten the spark plug. If the plug you are installing is equipped with a crush washer, seat the plug, then tighten about 1/4 turn to crush the washer. If you are installing a tapered seat plug, tighten the plug to 11–15 ft. lbs. (15–20 Nm).

10. If equipped with coil-over-plug ignition, install the ignition coil assembly(ies).

11. If equipped with spark plugs, apply a small amount of silicone dielectric compound to the end of the spark plug lead or inside the spark plug boot to prevent sticking, then install the boot to the spark plug and push until it clicks into place. The click may be felt or heard, then gently pull back on the boot to assure proper contact.

INSPECTION & GAPPING

See Figures 101, 102, 103, and 104

Check the plugs for deposits and wear. If they are not going to be replaced, clean the plugs thoroughly.

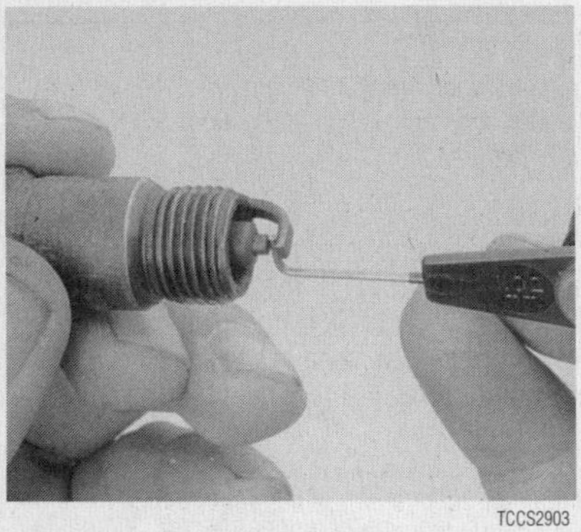

Fig. 101 Checking the spark plug gap with a wire feeler gauge

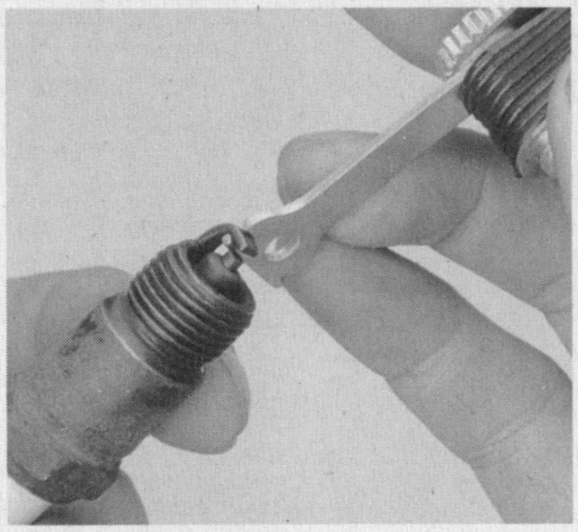

Fig. 102 Adjusting the spark plug gap

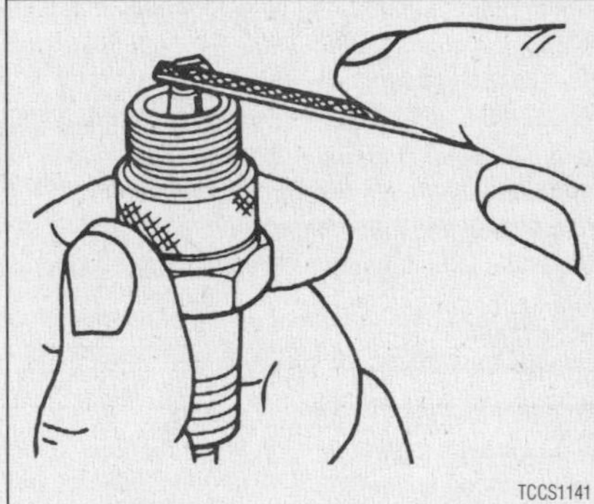

Fig. 103 If the spark plug is in good condition, the electrode may be filed flat—WARNING: Do not file platinum plugs

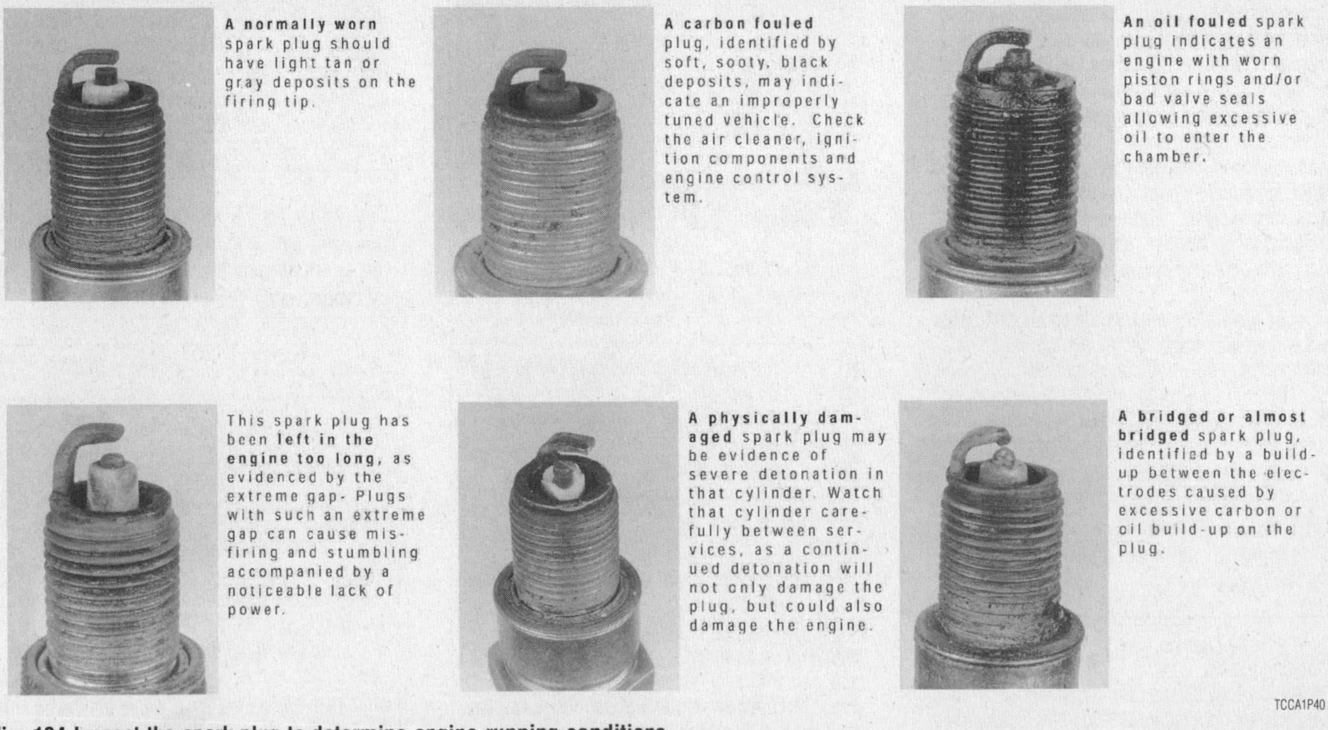

A normally worn spark plug should have light tan or gray deposits on the firing tip.
A carbon fouled plug, identified by soft, sooty, black deposits, may indicate an improperly tuned vehicle. Check the air cleaner, ignition components and engine control system.
An oil fouled spark plug indicates an engine with worn piston rings and/or bad valve seals allowing excessive oil to enter the chamber.
This spark plug has been **left in the engine too long**, as evidenced by the extreme gap- Plugs with such an extreme gap can cause misfiring and stumbling accompanied by a noticeable lack of power.
A physically damaged spark plug may be evidence of severe detonation in that cylinder. Watch that cylinder carefully between services, as a continued detonation will not only damage the plug, but could also damage the engine.
A bridged or almost bridged spark plug, identified by a build-up between the electrodes caused by excessive carbon or oil build-up on the plug.
TCCA1P40

Fig. 104 Inspect the spark plug to determine engine running conditions

Remember that any kind of deposit will decrease the efficiency of the plug. Plugs can be cleaned on a spark plug cleaning machine, which can sometimes be found in service stations, or you can do an acceptable job of cleaning with a stiff brush. If the plugs are cleaned, the electrodes must be filed flat. Use an ignition points file, not an emery board or the like, which will leave deposits. The electrodes must be filed perfectly flat with sharp edges; rounded edges reduce the spark plug voltage by as much as 50%.

Check spark plug gap before installation. The ground electrode (the L-shaped one connected to the body of the plug) must be parallel to the center electrode and the specified size wire gauge (please refer to the Tune-Up Specifications chart for details) must pass between the electrodes with a slight drag.

Always check the gap on new plugs as they are not always set correctly at the factory. Do not use a flat feeler gauge when measuring the gap on a used plug, because the reading may be inaccurate. A wire type gapping tool is the best way to check the gap. Wire gapping tools usually have a bending tool attached. Use that to adjust the side electrode until the proper distance is obtained. Absolutely never attempt to bend the center electrode. Also, be careful not to bend the side electrode too far or too often as it may weaken and break off within the engine, requiring removal of the cylinder head to retrieve it.

Spark Plug Wires

TESTING

➧ **See Figures 105, 106, and 107**

Every 36,000 miles (58,000 km) or so, the resistance of the wires should be checked with an ohmmeter. Wires with excessive resistance will cause misfiring, and may make the engine difficult to start in damp weather. Generally, the useful life of the cables is 36,000–50,000 miles (58,000–80,000 km).

To check resistance, remove the distributor cap, leaving the wires attached to the cap but removing them from the spark plugs. Look at each contact inside the cap for any sign of cracking or burning. A small amount of discoloration is normal but there should be no heavy burn marks or contact marks. Connect one lead of an ohmmeter to an electrode within the cap; connect the other lead to the corresponding spark plug terminal. Replace any wire which shows a resistance over 25,000 ohms.

Test the high tension lead from the coil by connecting the ohmmeter between the center contact in the distributor cap and either of the primary terminals of the coil. If resistance is more than 25,000 ohms, remove the cable from the coil and check the resistance of the cable alone. Anything over 15,000 ohms is cause for replacement. It should be remembered that resistance is also a function of length; the longer the cable, the greater the resistance. Thus, if the cables on your truck are longer than the factory originals, resistance will be higher, quite possibly outside these limits. Toyota recommends the 25,000 ohm limit be observed in all cases.

REMOVAL & INSTALLATION

➧ **See Figures 108 and 109**

At every tune-up, visually inspect the spark plug cables for burns, cuts, or breaks in the insulation.

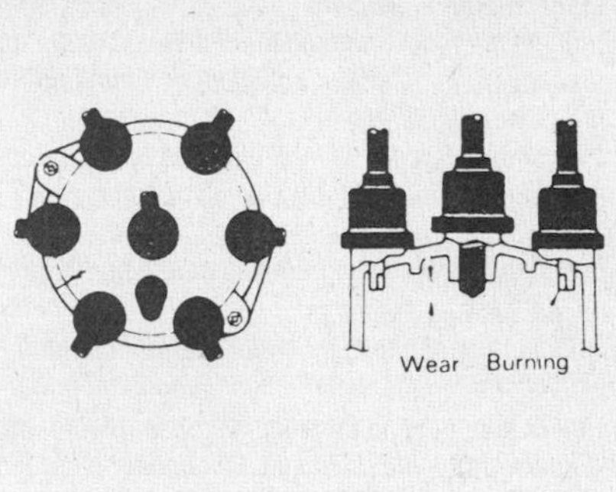

Fig. 105 Check the inside of the cap for burning, cracks or wear

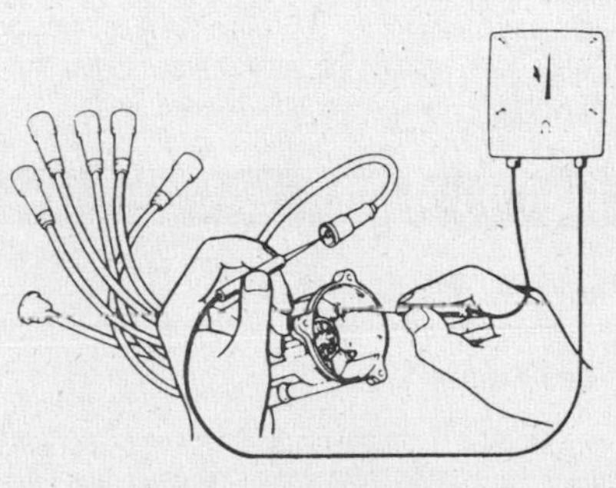

Fig. 106 Use an ohmmeter to test the high tension wires

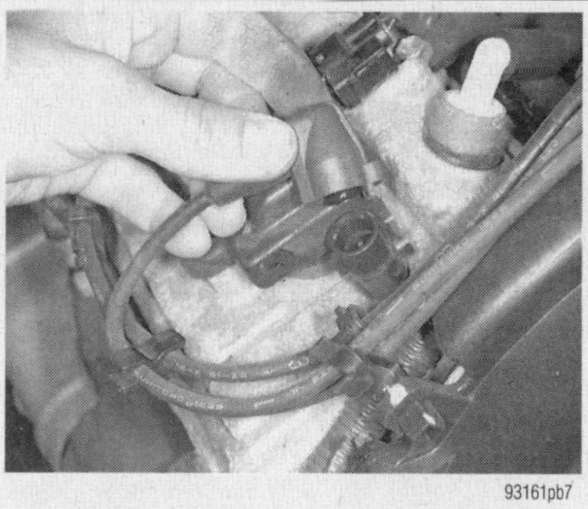

Fig. 107 Removing the spark plug wire from the ignition coil pack

Check the boots and the nipples on the distributor cap and coil. Replace any damaged wiring. Always replace spark plug wiring in sets, with a coil wire as well. Length is important; get the correct set for your vehicle.

When installing new cables, replace them one at a time to avoid mix-ups. Start by replacing the longest one first. Install the boot firmly over the spark plug. Route the wire over the same path as the original. Insert the nipple firmly into the tower on the cap or the coil.

➡The 5VZ-FE (V6) and 2UZ-FE (V8) engines do not use a distributor or spark plug wires. Individual coils (one for each spark plug) are mounted on the spark plug boots. Each coil is retained to the cylinder head cover with a small bolt. Remove the bolt and pull out the ignition coil to access the spark plug.

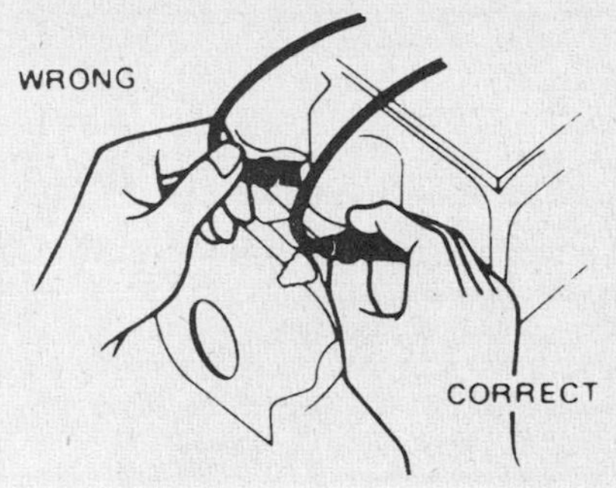

Fig. 108 Never pull on the wire; always grasp the boot of the spark plug wire

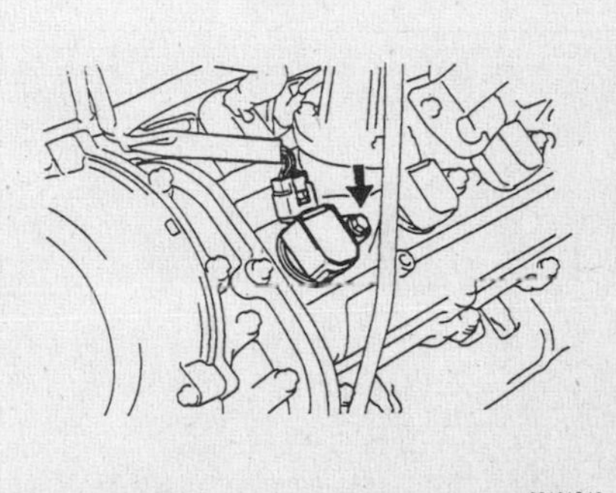

Fig. 109 The 5VZ-FE and 2UZ-FE engines use individual coils mounted on the spark plug boots. There are no spark plug wires or distributor

Distributor Cap and Rotor

The 3RZ-FE, 5VZ-FE and 2UZ-FE engines do not use a conventional distributor. The 3RZ-FE engine uses two dual-terminal coils to fire the four spark plugs. The 5VZ-FE and 2UZ-FE engines use individual coils mounted on the spark plug boots. The 1FZ-FE and 2RZ-FE engines, on the other hand, do use a distributor. The 1FZ-FE engine uses a remote-mounted coil with a long secondary cable to the distributor cap. The 2RZ-FE engine uses a solid-state coil that mounts on the distributor body. None of these engines have a provision for spark advance (timing) adjustment. All ignition timing computations and adjustments are handled by the Electronic Control Unit (ECU).

REMOVAL & INSTALLATION

➧ **See Figures 110, 111, 112, and 113**

1. Disconnect the negative battery cable.
2. Remove the distributor cap rubber boot if equipped.
3. Loosen the screws securing the cap on the distributor.
4. Usually it is helpful to tag the wires leading to the cap for easy identification on installation.
5. Lift the cap off the distributor. Pulling from the wire boot, remove the plug wires from the cap.
6. Once the cap and wires are off, lift the rotor off the shaft.

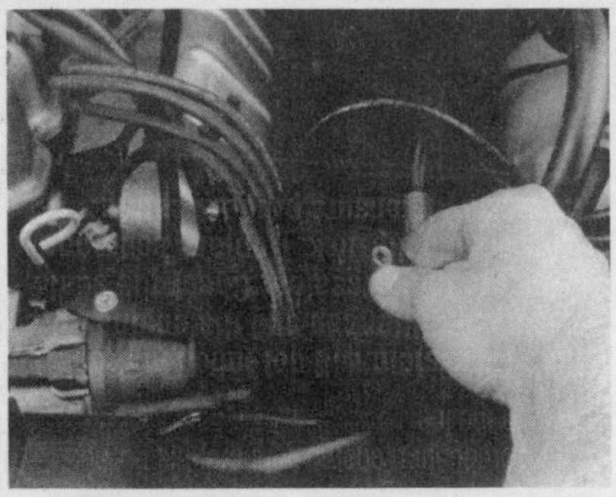

86821153

Fig. 110 Unsnap and remove the distributor boot

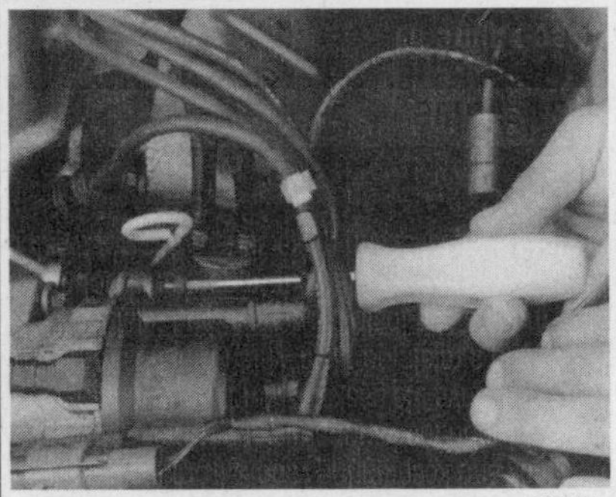

86821154

Fig. 111 Loosen the screws securing the cap

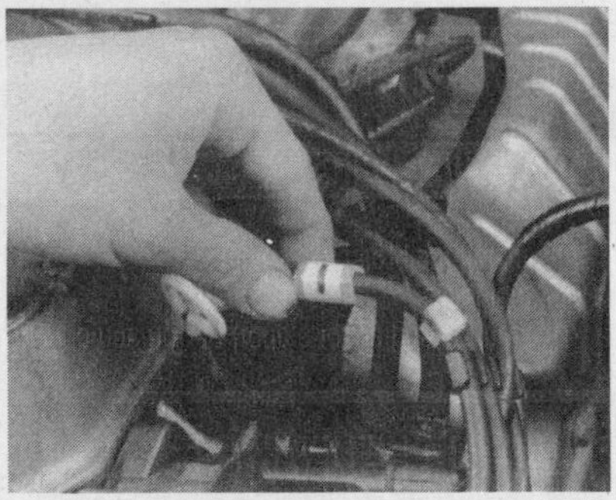

86821155

Fig. 112 It is helpful to tag the wires on the cap

86821156

Fig. 113 Pull the wires off the cap by the boot, not the wire itself

To install:

7. Install the rotor onto the distributor shaft. The rotor only goes on one way so there should be no mix-up in replacement.
8. Apply a small amount of dielectric grease on the tip of the rotor and the inside of the cap carbon ends.
9. Attach the tagged wires to their proper locations on the cap.
10. Fit the cap onto the distributor, then tighten the bolts.
11. Make sure all the wires are secure on the cap and spark plugs. Install the negative battery cable.
12. Start the vehicle and check for any misses.

INSPECTION

When inspecting a cap and rotor, look for signs of cracks, burns and wear. The inside of the cap may be burnt or have wear on the carbon ends. On the rotor look at the tip for burning and excessive wear.

Ignition Timing

GENERAL INFORMATION

➧ See Figure 114

Ignition timing is the measurement in degrees of crankshaft rotation at the instant the spark plug fires while the piston is on its compression stroke.

Ideally, the air/fuel mixture in the cylinder will be ignited by the spark plug and just beginning its rapid expansion as the piston passes Top Dead Center (TDC) of the compression stroke. If this happens, the piston will be beginning the power stroke just as the compressed air/fuel mixture starts to burn and expand. The expansion (explosion) of the air/fuel mixture will then force the piston down on the power stroke and turn the crankshaft.

It takes a fraction of a second for the spark from the plug to completely ignite the mixture in the cylinder. Because of this, the spark plug must fire before the piston reaches TDC, if the mixture is to be completely ignited as the piston passes TDC. This measurement is given in degrees of crankshaft rotation before the piston reaches top dead center (BTDC). If the ignition timing setting for your engine is 7 degrees BTDC, this means that the spark plug must fire at the time when the piston for that cylinder is 7 degrees before reaching the top of its compression stroke. However, this only holds true while your engine is at idle speed.

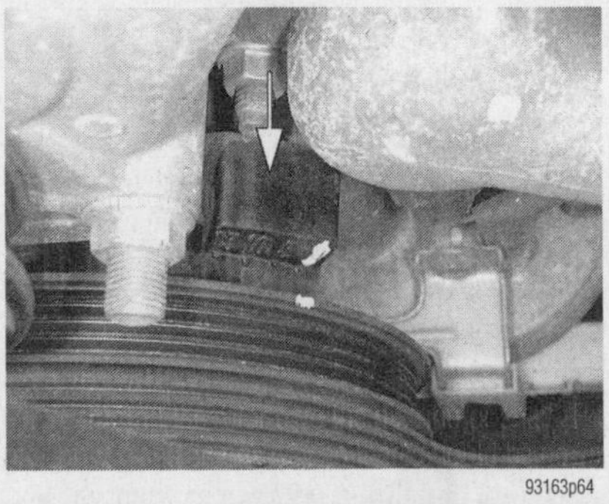

93163p64

Fig. 114 The ignition timing marks can usually be found stamped into a bracket located just above the crankshaft accessory drive pulley

As the engine accelerates from idle, the speed of the engine (rpm, or revolutions per minute) increases. The increase in rpm means that the pistons are now traveling up and down much faster. Because of this, the spark plugs will have to fire even sooner if the mixture is to be completely ignited as the piston passes TDC. To accomplish this, the truck's on-board computer (ECU) controls the timing of the spark as engine speed increases.

The ignition timing on the Toyota trucks covered by this manual is regulated completely by the Electronic Control Unit (ECU). On some engines, the timing can checked and adjusted using a timing light. On other engines, the timing cannot be adjusted.

The electronic control of the ignition timing function is known as Electronic Spark Advance (ESA) and is accomplished by Toyota's programming of the ECU. By monitoring the rpm, intake air volume, engine temperature, throttle position and other variables, the microprocessor decides the correct moment to trigger the spark for any engine operating condition from cold idle through wide open throttle. The system is simple, non-adjustable and reliable.

1FZ-FE Engine

➧ See Figures 115, 116, and 117

➡Toyota's hand-held tester or an equivalent OBD-II scan tool must be used for this procedure.

1. Warm the engine to normal operating temperature.

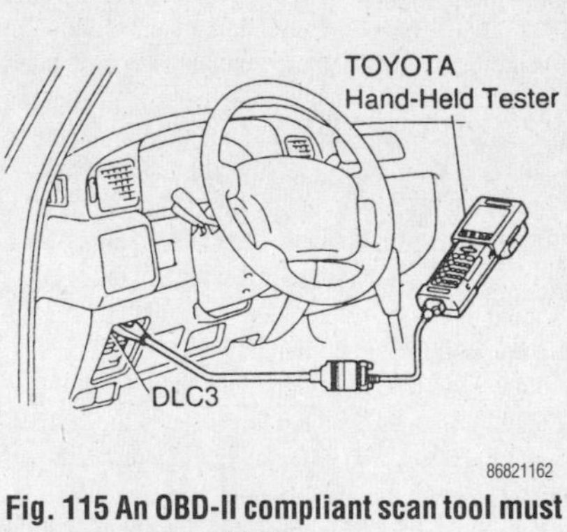

86821162

Fig. 115 An OBD-II compliant scan tool must be connected to DLC3

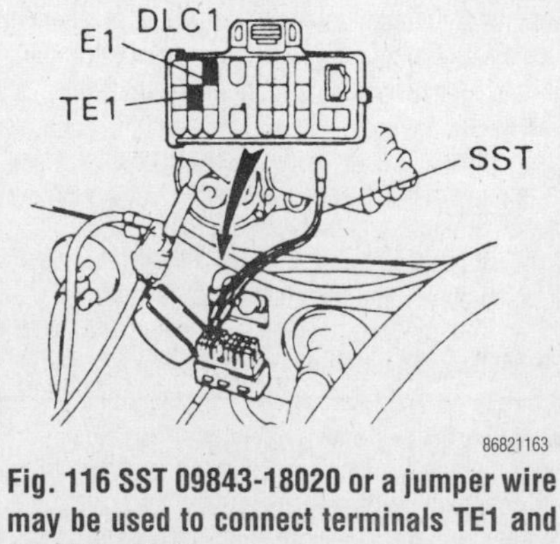

86821163

Fig. 116 SST 09843-18020 or a jumper wire may be used to connect terminals TE1 and E1 of the DLC1

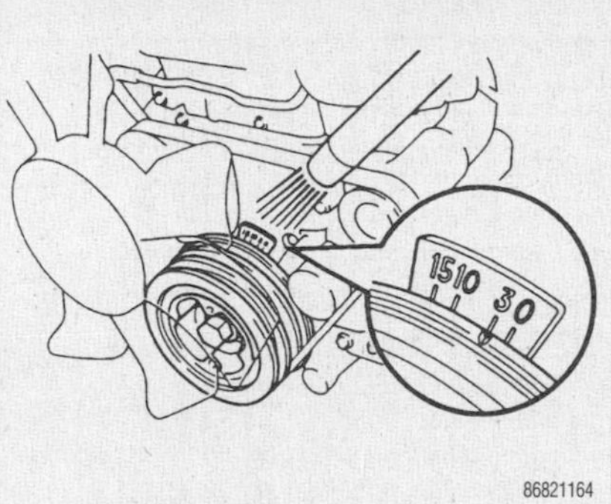

Fig. 117 The timing should be 3 degrees BTDC at idle—1FZ-FE engine

2. Connect an OBD-II compliant scan tool to the DLC3 located under the dash on the driver's side. For additional information, please refer to the following topic(s): Driveability and Emission Controls, Reading Codes.
3. Connect the timing light to the engine.
4. Race the engine to 2500 rpm for approximately 90 seconds. Check the idle speed. It should read 600–700 rpm.
5. Using SST 09843-18020 or its equivalent jumper wire, connect terminals TE1 and E1 of the DLC1 under the hood.
6. With the transmission in neutral and the A/C off, check the timing. It should read 3 degrees BTDC at idle.
7. Loosen the hold-down bolt, and adjust it by turning the distributor. Tighten the hold-down bolt to 13 ft. lbs. (18 Nm), then recheck the ignition timing again.
8. Remove the jumper wire from the DLC1.
9. Check the timing, the reading should now be 2–13 degrees BTDC at idle. The timing mark will move in this range.
10. Disconnect the timing light from the engine.
11. Disconnect the scan tool.

2RZ-FE and 3RZ-FE Engines

➧ **See Figures 118 and 119**

➡Toyota's hand-held tester or an equivalent OBD-II scan tool must be used for this procedure.

1. Warm the engine to normal operating temperature.
2. Connect an OBD-II compliant scan tool to the DLC3 located under the dash on the driver's side. For additional information, please refer to the following topic(s): Driveability and Emission Controls, Reading Codes.
3. Connect the timing light to the engine.
4. Using SST 09843-18020 or its equivalent jumper wire, connect terminals TE1 and E1 of the DLC1 under the hood.
5. After the engine speed is kept at about 1000 rpm for 5 seconds, check that it returns to idle speed.
6. Check the ignition timing, the reading should be 3–7 degrees BTDC at idle.
7. Remove the jumper wire from the DLC1.
8. Recheck the timing, the mark ranges from 7–18 degrees BTDC at idle.
9. Disconnect the scan tool.
10. Disconnect the timing light.

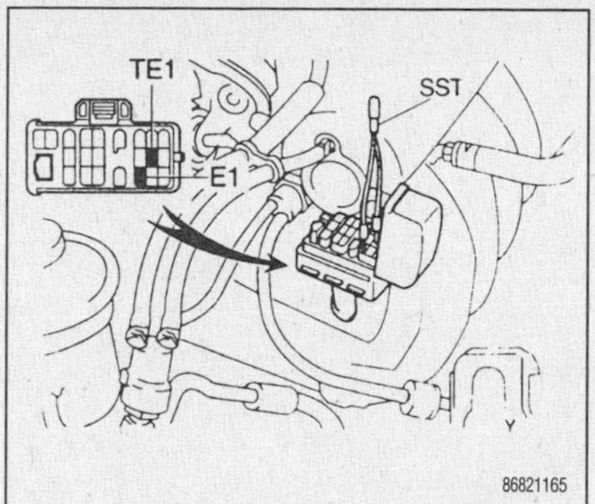

Fig. 118 Using the SST 09843-18020 or a jumper wire, connect terminals TE1 and E1 of the DLC1

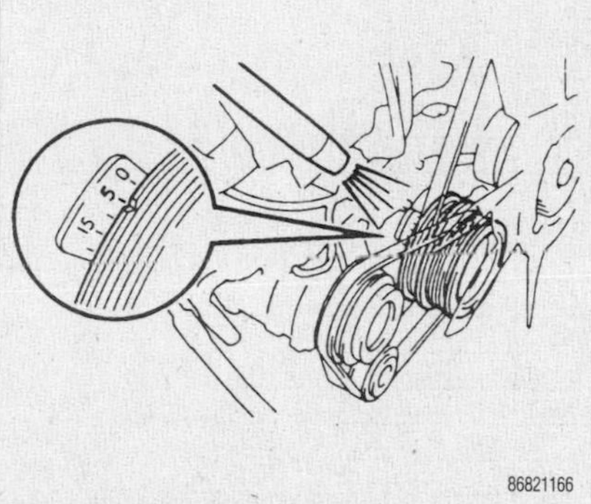

Fig. 119 The timing should be between 3–7 degrees BTDC at idle

2UZ-FE Engine

➧ **See Figures 120 and 121**

➡Toyota's hand-held tester or an equivalent OBD-II scan tool must be used for this procedure.

1. Warm the engine to normal operating temperature.
2. Connect an OBD-II compliant scan tool to the DLC3 (Diagnostic Link Connector 3) located under the instrument panel on the driver's side. For additional information, please refer to the following topic(s): Driveability and Emission Controls, Reading Codes.
3. Shift the transmission to the **N** position.
4. Connect the tester probe of a timing light to the wire of the ignition coil connector for No. 1 cylinder.
5. Race the engine speed to 2500 rpm for approximately 90 seconds. Allow the engine speed to return to idle, which should be 650–750 rpm.
6. Using SST 09843-18020 or its equivalent jumper wire, connect terminals TC and E1 of the DLC1 under the hood.
7. Using a timing light, check the ignition timing. It should be 5–15 degrees BTDC at idle.

Valve Lash

➧ **See Figures 122 and 123**

As part of every major tune-up or service interval, the valve clearance should be checked and adjusted if necessary. For all pickup trucks and 4Runners covered by this book, the specification is every 30,000

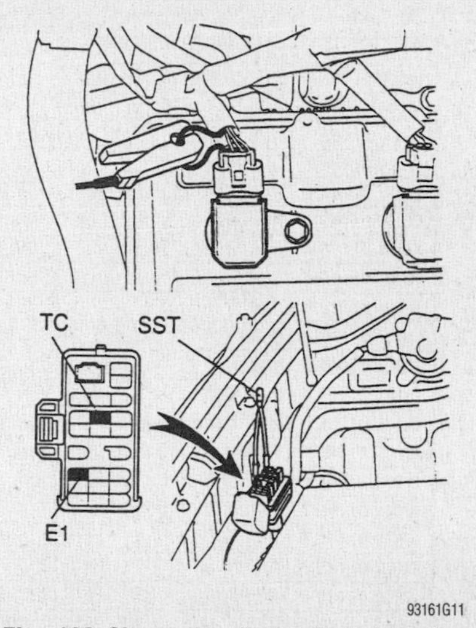

Fig. 120 Clamp the timing light inductive pickup to the wire of the ignition coil connector for No. 1 cylinder and jumper the Diagnostic Link Connector 1 terminals TC and E1—2UZ-FE engine

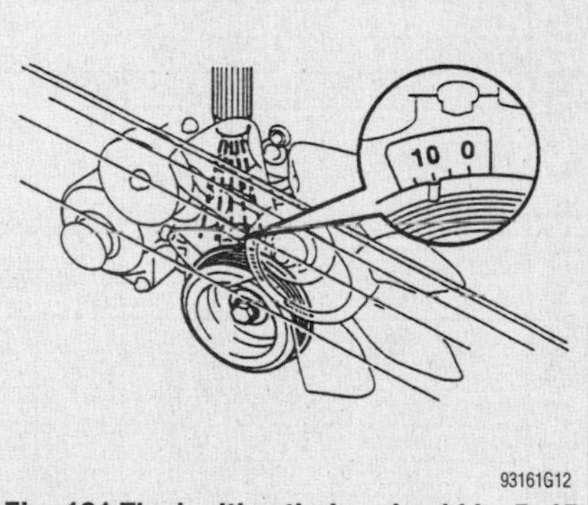

Fig. 121 The ignition timing should be 5–15 degrees BTDC at idle—2UZ-FE engine

miles (48,000 km) or 36 months. For all Land Cruisers, the requirement is 15,000 miles (24,000 km) or 18 months.

If the valve clearance is too large, part of the lift of the camshaft will be used up in removing the excessive clearance, thus the valves will not be opened far enough. This condition makes the valve train noisy as they take up the excessive clearance, and the engine will perform poorly, since a smaller amount of air/fuel mixture will be admitted to the cylinders. The exhaust valves will not open far enough to vent the cylinder completely; retained pressure (back pressure) will restrict the entry of the next air/fuel charge. If the valve clearance is too small, the intake and exhaust valves will not fully seat on the cylinder head when they close. This causes internal cylinder leakage and prevents the hot valve from transferring some heat to the head and cooling off. Therefore, the engine will run poorly (due to gases escaping from the combustion chamber), and the valves will overheat and warp (since they cannot transfer heat unless they are firmly touching the seat in the cylinder head).

One of the things to consider when adjusting valves is that on these engines, the valve adjustment is made by installing a thin wafer-like shim of the

Adjusting Shim Selection Chart (Intake)

Installed shim thickness mm (in.) / Measured clearance mm (in.)	2.000 (0.0787)	2.020 (0.0795)	2.040 (0.0803)	2.060 (0.0811)	2.080 (0.0819)	2.100 (0.0827)	2.120 (0.0835)	2.140 (0.0843)	2.160 (0.0850)	2.180 (0.0858)	2.200 (0.0866)	2.210 (0.0870)	2.220 (0.0874)	2.230 (0.0878)	2.240 (0.0882)	2.250 (0.0886)	2.260 (0.0890)	2.270 (0.0894)	2.280 (0.0898)	2.290 (0.0902)	2.300 (0.0906)	2.310 (0.0909)	2.320 (0.0913)	2.330 (0.0917)	2.340 (0.0921)	2.350 (0.0925)	2.360 (0.0929)	2.370 (0.0933)	2.380 (0.0937)	2.390 (0.0941)	2.400 (0.0945)	2.410 (0.0949)	2.420 (0.0953)	2.430 (0.0957)	2.440 (0.0961)	2.450 (0.0965)	2.460 (0.0969)	2.470 (0.0972)	2.480 (0.0976)	2.490 (0.0980)	2.500 (0.0984)	2.510 (0.0988)	2.520 (0.0992)	2.530 (0.0996)	2.540 (0.1000)	2.550 (0.1004)	2.560 (0.1008)	2.570 (0.1012)	2.580 (0.1016)	2.590 (0.1020)	2.600 (0.1024)	2.620 (0.1031)	2.640 (0.1039)	2.660 (0.1047)	2.680 (0.1055)	2.700 (0.1063)	2.720 (0.1071)	2.740 (0.1079)	2.760 (0.1087)	2.780 (0.1094)	2.800 (0.1102)
0.000-0.030 (0.0000-0.0012)							00	00	00	00	02	02	04	04	06	06	08	08	10	10	12	12	14	14	16	16	18	18	20	20	22	22	24	24	26	26	28	28	30	30	32	32	34	34	36	36	38	38	40	40	42	44	46	48	50	52	54	56	58	60	62
0.031-0.050 (0.0012-0.0020)						00	00	00	00	02	04	06	06	08	08	10	10	12	12	14	14	16	16	18	18	20	20	22	22	24	24	26	26	28	28	30	30	32	32	34	34	36	36	38	38	40	40	42	42	44	44	46	48	50	52	54	56	58	60	62	64
0.051-0.070 (0.0020-0.0028)					00	00	00	00	02	04	06	08	08	10	10	12	12	14	14	16	16	18	18	20	20	22	22	24	24	26	26	28	28	30	30	32	32	34	34	36	36	38	38	40	40	42	42	44	44	46	46	48	50	52	54	56	58	60	62	64	66
0.071-0.090 (0.0028-0.0035)				00	00	00	00	02	04	06	08	10	10	12	12	14	14	16	16	18	18	20	20	22	22	24	24	26	26	28	28	30	30	32	32	34	34	36	36	38	38	40	40	42	42	44	44	46	46	48	48	50	52	54	56	58	60	62	64	66	68
0.091-0.110 (0.0036-0.0043)			00	00	00	00	02	04	06	08	10	12	12	14	14	16	16	18	18	20	20	22	22	24	24	26	26	28	28	30	30	32	32	34	34	36	36	38	38	40	40	42	42	44	44	46	46	48	48	50	50	52	54	56	58	60	62	64	66	68	70
0.111-0.130 (0.0044-0.0051)		00	00	00	00	02	04	06	08	10	12	14	14	16	16	18	18	20	20	22	22	24	24	26	26	28	28	30	30	32	32	34	34	36	36	38	38	40	40	42	42	44	44	46	46	48	48	50	50	52	52	54	56	58	60	62	64	66	68	70	72
0.131-0.149 (0.0052-0.0059)		00	00	00	02	04	06	08	10	12	14	16	16	18	18	20	20	22	22	24	24	26	26	28	28	30	30	32	32	34	34	36	36	38	38	40	40	42	42	44	44	46	46	48	48	50	50	52	52	54	54	56	58	60	62	64	66	68	70	72	74
0.150-0.250 (0.0059-0.0098)																																																													
0.251-0.270 (0.0099-0.0106)	06	08	10	12	14	16	18	20	22	24	26	28	28	30	30	32	32	34	34	36	36	38	38	40	40	42	42	44	44	46	46	48	48	50	50	52	52	54	54	56	56	58	58	60	60	62	62	64	64	66	66	68	70	72	74	76	78	80	80	80	
0.271-0.290 (0.0107-0.0114)	08	10	12	14	16	18	20	22	24	26	28	30	30	32	32	34	34	36	36	38	38	40	40	42	42	44	44	46	46	48	48	50	50	52	52	54	54	56	56	58	58	60	60	62	62	64	64	66	66	68	68	70	72	74	76	78	80	80	80		
0.291-0.310 (0.0115-0.0122)	10	12	14	16	18	20	22	24	26	28	30	32	32	34	34	36	36	38	38	40	40	42	42	44	44	46	46	48	48	50	50	52	52	54	54	56	56	58	58	60	60	62	62	64	64	66	66	68	68	70	70	72	74	76	78	80	80	80			
0.311-0.330 (0.0122-0.0130)	12	14	16	18	20	22	24	26	28	30	32	34	34	36	36	38	38	40	40	42	42	44	44	46	46	48	48	50	50	52	52	54	54	56	56	58	58	60	60	62	62	64	64	66	66	68	68	70	70	72	72	74	76	78	80	80	80				
0.331-0.350 (0.0130-0.0138)	14	16	18	20	22	24	26	28	30	32	34	36	36	38	38	40	40	42	42	44	44	46	46	48	48	50	50	52	52	54	54	56	56	58	58	60	60	62	62	64	64	66	66	68	68	70	70	72	72	74	74	76	78	80	80	80					
0.351-0.370 (0.0138-0.0146)	16	18	20	22	24	26	28	30	32	34	36	38	38	40	40	42	42	44	44	46	46	48	48	50	50	52	52	54	54	56	56	58	58	60	60	62	62	64	64	66	66	68	68	70	70	72	72	74	74	76	76	78	80	80	80						
0.371-0.390 (0.0146-0.0154)	18	20	22	24	26	28	30	32	34	36	38	40	40	42	42	44	44	46	46	48	48	50	50	52	52	54	54	56	56	58	58	60	60	62	62	64	64	66	66	68	68	70	70	72	72	74	74	76	76	78	78	80	80	80							
0.391-0.410 (0.0154-0.0161)	20	22	24	26	28	30	32	34	36	38	40	42	42	44	44	46	46	48	48	50	50	52	52	54	54	56	56	58	58	60	60	62	62	64	64	66	66	68	68	70	70	72	72	74	74	76	76	78	78	80	80	80	80								
0.411-0.430 (0.0162-0.0169)	22	24	26	28	30	32	34	36	38	40	42	44	44	46	46	48	48	50	50	52	52	54	54	56	56	58	58	60	60	62	62	64	64	66	66	68	68	70	70	72	72	74	74	76	76	78	78	80	80	80	80	80									
0.431-0.450 (0.0170-0.0177)	24	26	28	30	32	34	36	38	40	42	44	46	46	48	48	50	50	52	52	54	54	56	56	58	58	60	60	62	62	64	64	66	66	68	68	70	70	72	72	74	74	76	76	78	78	80	80	80	80	80	80										
0.451-0.470 (0.0178-0.0185)	26	28	30	32	34	36	38	40	42	44	46	48	48	50	50	52	52	54	54	56	56	58	58	60	60	62	62	64	64	66	66	68	68	70	70	72	72	74	74	76	76	78	78	80	80	80	80	80	80	80											
0.471-0.490 (0.0185-0.0193)	28	30	32	34	36	38	40	42	44	46	48	50	50	52	52	54	54	56	56	58	58	60	60	62	62	64	64	66	66	68	68	70	70	72	72	74	74	76	76	78	78	80	80	80	80	80	80	80													
0.491-0.510 (0.0193-0.0201)	30	32	34	36	38	40	42	44	46	48	50	52	52	54	54	56	56	58	58	60	60	62	62	64	64	66	66	68	68	70	70	72	72	74	74	76	76	78	78	80	80	80	80	80	80	80															
0.511-0.530 (0.0201-0.0209)	32	34	36	38	40	42	44	46	48	50	52	54	54	56	56	58	58	60	60	62	62	64	64	66	66	68	68	70	70	72	72	74	74	76	76	78	78	80	80	80	80	80	80	80																	
0.531-0.550 (0.0209-0.0217)	34	36	38	40	42	44	46	48	50	52	54	56	56	58	58	60	60	62	62	64	64	66	66	68	68	70	70	72	72	74	74	76	76	78	78	80	80	80	80	80	80	80																			
0.551-0.570 (0.0217-0.0224)	36	38	40	42	44	46	48	50	52	54	56	58	58	60	60	62	62	64	64	66	66	68	68	70	70	72	72	74	74	76	76	78	78	80	80	80	80	80	80	80																					
0.571-0.590 (0.0225-0.0232)	38	40	42	44	46	48	50	52	54	56	58	60	60	62	62	64	64	66	66	68	68	70	70	72	72	74	74	76	76	78	78	80	80	80	80	80	80	80																							
0.591-0.610 (0.0233-0.0240)	40	42	44	46	48	50	52	54	56	58	60	62	62	64	64	66	66	68	68	70	70	72	72	74	74	76	76	78	78	80	80	80	80	80	80	80																									
0.611-0.630 (0.0241-0.0248)	42	44	46	48	50	52	54	56	58	60	62	64	64	66	66	68	68	70	70	72	72	74	74	76	76	78	78	80	80	80	80	80	80	80																											
0.631-0.650 (0.0248-0.0256)	44	46	48	50	52	54	56	58	60	62	64	66	66	68	68	70	70	72	72	74	74	76	76	78	78	80	80	80	80	80	80	80																													
0.651-0.670 (0.0256-0.0264)	46	48	50	52	54	56	58	60	62	64	66	68	68	70	70	72	72	74	74	76	76	78	78	80	80	80	80	80	80	80																															
0.671-0.690 (0.0264-0.0272)	48	50	52	54	56	58	60	62	64	66	68	70	70	72	72	74	74	76	76	78	78	80	80	80	80	80	80	80																																	
0.691-0.710 (0.0272-0.0280)	50	52	54	56	58	60	62	64	66	68	70	72	72	74	74	76	76	78	78	80	80	80	80	80	80	80																																			
0.711-0.730 (0.0280-0.0287)	52	54	56	58	60	62	64	66	68	70	72	74	74	76	76	78	78	80	80	80	80	80	80	80																																					
0.731-0.750 (0.0288-0.0295)	54	56	58	60	62	64	66	68	70	72	74	76	76	78	78	80	80	80	80	80	80	80																																							
0.751-0.770 (0.0296-0.0303)	56	58	60	62	64	66	68	70	72	74	76	78	78	80	80	80	80	80	80	80																																									
0.771-0.790 (0.0304-0.0311)	58	60	62	64	66	68	70	72	74	76	78	80	80	80	80	80	80	80																																											
0.791-0.810 (0.0311-0.0319)	60	62	64	66	68	70	72	74	76	78	80	80	80	80	80	80																																													
0.811-0.830 (0.0319-0.0327)	62	64	66	68	70	72	74	76	78	80	80	80	80	80																																															
0.831-0.850 (0.0327-0.0335)	64	66	68	70	72	74	76	78	80	80	80	80																																																	
0.851-0.870 (0.0335-0.0343)	66	68	70	72	74	76	78	80	80	80																																																			
0.871-0.890 (0.0343-0.0350)	68	70	72	74	76	78	80	80	80																																																				
0.891-0.910 (0.0351-0.0358)	70	72	74	76	78	80	80	80																																																					
0.911-0.930 (0.0359-0.0366)	72	74	76	78	80	80	80																																																						
0.931-0.950 (0.0367-0.0374)	74	76	78	80	80	80																																																							
0.951-0.970 (0.0374-0.0382)	76	78	80	80	80																																																								
0.971-0.990 (0.0382-0.0390)	78	80	80	80																																																									
0.991-1.010 (0.0390-0.0398)	80	80	80																																																										
1.011-1.030 (0.0398-0.0406)	80	80																																																											
1.031-1.050 (0.0406-0.0413)	80																																																												

Intake valve clearance (Cold):
0.15 – 0.25 mm (0.006 – 0.010 in.)

EXAMPLE:
The 2.300 mm (0.0906 in.) shim is installed, and the measured clearance is 0.440 mm (0.0173 in.). Replace the 2.300 mm (0.0906 in.) shim with a No. 54 shim.

New shim thickness mm (in.)

Shim No.	Thickness	Shim No.	Thickness	Shim No.	Thickness
00	2.000 (0.0787)	28	2.280 (0.0898)	56	2.560 (0.1008)
02	2.020 (0.0795)	30	2.300 (0.0906)	58	2.580 (0.1016)
04	2.040 (0.0803)	32	2.320 (0.0913)	60	2.600 (0.1024)
06	2.060 (0.0811)	34	2.340 (0.0921)	62	2.620 (0.1031)
08	2.080 (0.0819)	36	2.360 (0.0929)	64	2.640 (0.1039)
10	2.100 (0.0827)	38	2.380 (0.0937)	66	2.660 (0.1047)
12	2.120 (0.0835)	40	2.400 (0.0945)	68	2.680 (0.1055)
14	2.140 (0.0843)	42	2.420 (0.0953)	70	2.700 (0.1063)
16	2.160 (0.0850)	44	2.440 (0.0961)	72	2.720 (0.1071)
18	2.180 (0.0858)	46	2.460 (0.0969)	74	2.740 (0.1079)
20	2.200 (0.0866)	48	2.480 (0.0976)	76	2.760 (0.1087)
22	2.220 (0.0874)	50	2.500 (0.0984)	78	2.780 (0.1094)
24	2.240 (0.0882)	52	2.520 (0.0992)	80	2.800 (0.1102)
26	2.260 (0.0890)	54	2.540 (0.1000)		

93161G13

Fig. 122 Adjusting shim chart for the intake valves

Adjusting Shim Selection Chart (Exhaust)

Measured clearance mm (in.) \ Installed shim thickness mm (in.)	2.000 (0.0787)	2.020 (0.0795)	2.040 (0.0803)	2.060 (0.0811)	2.080 (0.0819)	2.100 (0.0827)	2.120 (0.0835)	2.140 (0.0843)	2.160 (0.0850)	2.180 (0.0858)	2.200 (0.0866)	2.210 (0.0870)	2.220 (0.0874)	2.230 (0.0878)	2.240 (0.0882)	2.250 (0.0886)	2.260 (0.0890)	2.270 (0.0894)	2.280 (0.0898)	2.290 (0.0902)	2.300 (0.0906)	2.310 (0.0909)	2.320 (0.0913)	2.330 (0.0917)	2.340 (0.0921)	2.350 (0.0925)	2.360 (0.0929)	2.370 (0.0933)	2.380 (0.0937)	2.390 (0.0941)	2.400 (0.0945)	2.410 (0.0949)	2.420 (0.0953)	2.430 (0.0957)	2.440 (0.0961)	2.450 (0.0965)	2.460 (0.0969)	2.470 (0.0972)	2.480 (0.0976)	2.490 (0.0980)	2.500 (0.0984)	2.510 (0.0988)	2.520 (0.0992)	2.530 (0.0996)	2.540 (0.1000)	2.550 (0.1004)	2.560 (0.1008)	2.570 (0.1012)	2.580 (0.1016)	2.590 (0.1020)	2.600 (0.1024)	2.620 (0.1031)	2.640 (0.1039)	2.660 (0.1047)	2.680 (0.1055)	2.700 (0.1063)	2.720 (0.1071)	2.740 (0.1079)	2.760 (0.1087)	2.780 (0.1094)	2.800 (0.1102)
0.000-0.030 (0.0000-0.0012)												00	00	00	00	00	00	00	00	00	02	02	04	04	06	06	08	08	10	10	12	12	14	14	16	16	18	18	20	20	22	22	24	24	26	26	28	28	30	30	32	34	36	38	40	42	44	46	48	50	52
0.031-0.050 (0.0012-0.0020)											00	00	00	00	00	00	00	02	02	04	04	06	06	08	08	10	10	12	12	14	14	16	16	18	18	20	20	22	22	24	24	26	26	28	28	30	30	32	32	34	34	36	38	40	42	44	46	48	50	52	54
0.051-0.070 (0.0020-0.0028)										00	00	00	00	00	00	02	02	04	04	06	06	08	08	10	10	12	12	14	14	16	16	18	18	20	20	22	22	24	24	26	26	28	28	30	30	32	32	34	34	36	36	38	40	42	44	46	48	50	52	54	56
0.071-0.090 (0.0028-0.0035)									00	00	00	00	00	02	02	04	04	06	06	08	08	10	10	12	12	14	14	16	16	18	18	20	20	22	22	24	24	26	26	28	28	30	30	32	32	34	34	36	36	38	38	40	42	44	46	48	50	52	54	56	58
0.091-0.110 (0.0036-0.0043)								00	00	00	00	02	02	04	04	06	06	08	08	10	10	12	12	14	14	16	16	18	18	20	20	22	22	24	24	26	26	28	28	30	30	32	32	34	34	36	36	38	38	40	40	42	44	46	48	50	52	54	56	58	60
0.111-0.130 (0.0044-0.0051)							00	00	00	00	02	04	04	06	06	08	08	10	10	12	12	14	14	16	16	18	18	20	20	22	22	24	24	26	26	28	28	30	30	32	32	34	34	36	36	38	38	40	40	42	42	44	46	48	50	52	54	56	58	60	62
0.131-0.150 (0.0052-0.0059)						00	00	00	00	02	04	06	06	08	08	10	10	12	12	14	14	16	16	18	18	20	20	22	22	24	24	26	26	28	28	30	30	32	32	34	34	36	36	38	38	40	40	42	42	44	44	46	48	50	52	54	56	58	60	62	64
0.151-0.170 (0.0059-0.0067)					00	00	00	00	02	04	06	08	08	10	10	12	12	14	14	16	16	18	18	20	20	22	22	24	24	26	26	28	28	30	30	32	32	34	34	36	36	38	38	40	40	42	42	44	44	46	46	48	50	52	54	56	58	60	62	64	66
0.171-0.190 (0.0067-0.0075)				00	00	00	00	02	04	06	08	10	10	12	12	14	14	16	16	18	18	20	20	22	22	24	24	26	26	28	28	30	30	32	32	34	34	36	36	38	38	40	40	42	42	44	44	46	46	48	48	50	52	54	56	58	60	62	64	66	68
0.191-0.210 (0.0075-0.0083)			00	00	00	00	02	04	06	08	10	12	12	14	14	16	16	18	18	20	20	22	22	24	24	26	26	28	28	30	30	32	32	34	34	36	36	38	38	40	40	42	42	44	44	46	46	48	48	50	50	52	54	56	58	60	62	64	66	68	70
0.211-0.230 (0.0083-0.0091)		00	00	00	00	02	04	06	08	10	12	14	14	16	16	18	18	20	20	22	22	24	24	26	26	28	28	30	30	32	32	34	34	36	36	38	38	40	40	42	42	44	44	46	46	48	48	50	50	52	52	54	56	58	60	62	64	66	68	70	72
0.231-0.249 (0.0091-0.0098)		00	00	00	02	04	06	08	10	12	14	16	16	18	18	20	20	22	22	24	24	26	26	28	28	30	30	32	32	34	34	36	36	38	38	40	40	42	42	44	44	46	46	48	48	50	50	52	52	54	54	56	58	60	62	64	66	68	70	72	74
0.250-0.350 (0.0098-0.0138)|																																																													
0.351-0.370 (0.0138-0.0146)	06	08	10	12	14	16	18	20	22	24	26	28	28	30	30	32	32	34	34	36	36	38	38	40	40	42	42	44	44	46	46	48	48	50	50	52	52	54	54	56	56	58	58	60	60	62	62	64	64	66	66	68	70	72	74	76	78	80	80	80	
0.371-0.390 (0.0146-0.0154)	08	10	12	14	16	18	20	22	24	26	28	30	30	32	32	34	34	36	36	38	38	40	40	42	42	44	44	46	46	48	48	50	50	52	52	54	54	56	56	58	58	60	60	62	62	64	64	66	66	68	68	70	72	74	76	78	80	80	80		
0.391-0.410 (0.0154-0.0161)	10	12	14	16	18	20	22	24	26	28	30	32	32	34	34	36	36	38	38	40	40	42	42	44	44	46	46	48	48	50	50	52	52	54	54	56	56	58	58	60	60	62	62	64	64	66	66	68	68	70	70	72	74	76	78	80	80	80			
0.411-0.430 (0.0162-0.0169)	12	14	16	18	20	22	24	26	28	30	32	34	34	36	36	38	38	40	40	42	42	44	44	46	46	48	48	50	50	52	52	54	54	56	56	58	58	60	60	62	62	64	64	66	66	68	68	70	70	72	72	74	76	78	80	80	80				
0.431-0.450 (0.0170-0.0177)	14	16	18	20	22	24	26	28	30	32	34	36	36	38	38	40	40	42	42	44	44	46	46	48	48	50	50	52	52	54	54	56	56	58	58	60	60	62	62	64	64	66	66	68	68	70	70	72	72	74	74	76	78	80	80	80					
0.451-0.470 (0.0178-0.0185)	16	18	20	22	24	26	28	30	32	34	36	38	38	40	40	42	42	44	44	46	46	48	48	50	50	52	52	54	54	56	56	58	58	60	60	62	62	64	64	66	66	68	68	70	70	72	72	74	74	76	76	78	80	80	80						
0.471-0.490 (0.0185-0.0193)	18	20	22	24	26	28	30	32	34	36	38	40	40	42	42	44	44	46	46	48	48	50	50	52	52	54	54	56	56	58	58	60	60	62	62	64	64	66	66	68	68	70	70	72	72	74	74	76	76	78	78	80	80	80							
0.491-0.510 (0.0193-0.0201)	20	22	24	26	28	30	32	34	36	38	40	42	42	44	44	46	46	48	48	50	50	52	52	54	54	56	56	58	58	60	60	62	62	64	64	66	66	68	68	70	70	72	72	74	74	76	76	78	78	80	80	80	80								
0.511-0.530 (0.0201-0.0209)	22	24	26	28	30	32	34	36	38	40	42	44	44	46	46	48	48	50	50	52	52	54	54	56	56	58	58	60	60	62	62	64	64	66	66	68	68	70	70	72	72	74	74	76	76	78	78	80	80	80	80	80									
0.531-0.550 (0.0209-0.0217)	24	26	28	30	32	34	36	38	40	42	44	46	46	48	48	50	50	52	52	54	54	56	56	58	58	60	60	62	62	64	64	66	66	68	68	70	70	72	72	74	74	76	76	78	78	80	80	80	80	80	80										
0.551-0.570 (0.0217-0.0224)	26	28	30	32	34	36	38	40	42	44	46	48	48	50	50	52	52	54	54	56	56	58	58	60	60	62	62	64	64	66	66	68	68	70	70	72	72	74	74	76	76	78	78	80	80	80	80	80	80	80											
0.571-0.590 (0.0225-0.0232)	28	30	32	34	36	38	40	42	44	46	48	50	50	52	52	54	54	56	56	58	58	60	60	62	62	64	64	66	66	68	68	70	70	72	72	74	74	76	76	78	78	80	80	80	80	80	80	80													
0.591-0.610 (0.0233-0.0240)	30	32	34	36	38	40	42	44	46	48	50	52	52	54	54	56	56	58	58	60	60	62	62	64	64	66	66	68	68	70	70	72	72	74	74	76	76	78	78	80	80	80	80	80	80	80															
0.611-0.630 (0.0241-0.0248)	32	34	36	38	40	42	44	46	48	50	52	54	54	56	56	58	58	60	60	62	62	64	64	66	66	68	68	70	70	72	72	74	74	76	76	78	78	80	80	80	80	80	80	80																	
0.631-0.650 (0.0248-0.0256)	34	36	38	40	42	44	46	48	50	52	54	56	56	58	58	60	60	62	62	64	64	66	66	68	68	70	70	72	72	74	74	76	76	78	78	80	80	80	80	80	80	80																			
0.651-0.670 (0.0256-0.0264)	36	38	40	42	44	46	48	50	52	54	56	58	58	60	60	62	62	64	64	66	66	68	68	70	70	72	72	74	74	76	76	78	78	80	80	80	80	80	80	80																					
0.671-0.690 (0.0264-0.0272)	38	40	42	44	46	48	50	52	54	56	58	60	60	62	62	64	64	66	66	68	68	70	70	72	72	74	74	76	76	78	78	80	80	80	80	80	80	80																							
0.691-0.710 (0.0272-0.0280)	40	42	44	46	48	50	52	54	56	58	60	62	62	64	64	66	66	68	68	70	70	72	72	74	74	76	76	78	78	80	80	80	80	80	80	80																									
0.711-0.730 (0.0280-0.0287)	42	44	46	48	50	52	54	56	58	60	62	64	64	66	66	68	68	70	70	72	72	74	74	76	76	78	78	80	80	80	80	80	80	80																											
0.731-0.750 (0.0288-0.0295)	44	46	48	50	52	54	56	58	60	62	64	66	66	68	68	70	70	72	72	74	74	76	76	78	78	80	80	80	80	80	80	80																													
0.751-0.770 (0.0296-0.0303)	46	48	50	52	54	56	58	60	62	64	66	68	68	70	70	72	72	74	74	76	76	78	78	80	80	80	80	80	80	80																															
0.771-0.790 (0.0304-0.0311)	48	50	52	54	56	58	60	62	64	66	68	70	70	72	72	74	74	76	76	78	78	80	80	80	80	80	80	80																																	
0.791-0.810 (0.0311-0.0319)	50	52	54	56	58	60	62	64	66	68	70	72	72	74	74	76	76	78	78	80	80	80	80	80	80	80																																			
0.811-0.830 (0.0319-0.0327)	52	54	56	58	60	62	64	66	68	70	72	74	74	76	76	78	78	80	80	80	80	80	80	80																																					
0.831-0.850 (0.0327-0.0335)	54	56	58	60	62	64	66	68	70	72	74	76	76	78	78	80	80	80	80	80	80	80																																							
0.851-0.870 (0.0335-0.0343)	56	58	60	62	64	66	68	70	72	74	76	78	78	80	80	80	80	80	80	80																																									
0.871-0.890 (0.0343-0.0350)	58	60	62	64	66	68	70	72	74	76	78	80	80	80	80	80	80	80																																											
0.891-0.910 (0.0351-0.0358)	60	62	64	66	68	70	72	74	76	78	80	80	80	80	80	80																																													
0.911-0.930 (0.0359-0.0366)	62	64	66	68	70	72	74	76	78	80	80	80	80	80																																															
0.931-0.950 (0.0367-0.0374)	64	66	68	70	72	74	76	78	80	80	80	80																																																	
0.951-0.970 (0.0374-0.0382)	66	68	70	72	74	76	78	80	80	80																																																			
0.971-0.990 (0.0382-0.0390)	68	70	72	74	76	78	80	80	80																																																					
0.991-1.010 (0.0390-0.0398)	70	72	74	76	78	80	80	80																																																						
1.011-1.030 (0.0398-0.0406)	72	74	76	78	80	80	80																																																							
1.031-1.050 (0.0406-0.0413)	74	76	78	80	80	80																																																								
1.051-1.070 (0.0414-0.0421)	76	78	80	80	80																																																									
1.071-1.090 (0.0422-0.0429)	78	80	80	80																																																										
1.091-1.110 (0.0430-0.0437)	80	80	80																																																											
1.111-1.130 (0.0437-0.0445)	80	80																																																												
1.131-1.150 (0.0445-0.0453)|80|																																																												

Exhaust valve clearance (Cold):
0.25 – 0.35 mm (0.010 – 0.014 in.)

EXAMPLE:
The 2.300 mm (0.0906 in.) shim is installed, and the measured clearance is 0.440 mm (0.0173 in.). Replace the 2.300 mm (0.0906 in.) shim with a No. 44 shim.

New shim thickness — mm (in.)

Shim No.	Thickness	Shim No.	Thickness	Shim No.	Thickness
00	2.000 (0.0787)	28	2.280 (0.0898)	56	2.560 (0.1008)
02	2.020 (0.0795)	30	2.300 (0.0906)	58	2.580 (0.1016)
04	2.040 (0.0803)	32	2.320 (0.0913)	60	2.600 (0.1024)
06	2.060 (0.0811)	34	2.340 (0.0921)	62	2.620 (0.1031)
08	2.080 (0.0819)	36	2.360 (0.0929)	64	2.640 (0.1039)
10	2.100 (0.0827)	38	2.380 (0.0937)	66	2.660 (0.1047)
12	2.120 (0.0835)	40	2.400 (0.0945)	68	2.680 (0.1055)
14	2.140 (0.0843)	42	2.420 (0.0953)	70	2.700 (0.1063)
16	2.160 (0.0850)	44	2.440 (0.0961)	72	2.720 (0.1071)
18	2.180 (0.0858)	46	2.460 (0.0969)	74	2.740 (0.1079)
20	2.200 (0.0866)	48	2.480 (0.0976)	76	2.760 (0.1087)
22	2.220 (0.0874)	50	2.500 (0.0984)	78	2.780 (0.1094)
24	2.240 (0.0882)	52	2.520 (0.0992)	80	2.800 (0.1102)
26	2.260 (0.0890)	54	2.540 (0.1000)		

93161G14

Fig.123 Adjusting shim chart for the exhaust valves

correct thickness to take up the valve lash. Each valve will require a slightly different thickness, due to manufacturing and operating tolerances in the valve train. Toyota uses numerous shims in increments of less than 0.001 inch. Only a Toyota dealer is likely to have the correct shims in an assortment covering the wide range of sizes required for accurate valve lash adjustment. In some cases, it is possible to swap shims from one cam follower to another, but it would be unusual for this to work on all of the cam followers. Valve adjustment requires an assortment of valve shims, very careful work and proficient ability with a micrometer. The valve adjustment procedure is given here, however, do not attempt this procedure without the proper tools and knowledge of the job.

➡While all valve adjustments must be as accurate as possible, it is better to have the valve adjustment slightly loose than slightly tight, as burnt valves may result from overly tight adjustments.

ADJUSTMENT

2RZ-FE and 3RZ-FE Engines

See Figures 124 thru 129

Toyota's Special Service Tools (SST) for valve adjustment, or their equivalent, are required for this procedure. The valve adjusting shims are set inside bucket-like cam followers. Part of the Toyota SST Valve Adjust Tool Set is a pliers-like tool to press down on the cam follower (also called a valve lifter) for enough clearance to withdraw the shim, and a lever-like tool that fits between the camshaft and the valve lifter flange to hold that clearance for shim extraction and insertion. In addition, a magnet to remove the adjustment shim from the cam follower and an accurate micrometer is required to properly measure the valve shim thickness. If all of these items are not available, valve adjustment is not recommended.

➡Only adjust the valve clearance when the engine is cold.

1. Disconnect the negative battery cable.
2. Remove the cylinder head (valve) cover.
3. Turn the crankshaft pulley clockwise and align its groove with the timing mark 0of the timing chain cover. If all of the spark plugs are removed, it will be easier to turn the engine by hand.
4. Check that the timing marks (1 and 2 dots) on the camshaft drive and driven gears are in a straight line on the cylinder head surface. If not, turn the crankshaft 1 complete revolution (360 degrees). This should be Top Dead Center (TDC) for cylinder No. 1.
5. Using an accurate feeler gauge, measure the clearance between the valve lifter and the camshaft. Record the measurements on the intake valves on cylinder No. 1 and 2. Measure the exhaust valves at cylinder No. 1 and 3.
   a. The intake valve clearance cold should be 0.006–0.010 in. (0.15–0.25mm).
   b. The exhaust valve clearance cold should be 0.010–0.014 in. (0.25–0.35mm).
6. Turn the crankshaft pulley exactly 1 complete revolution (360 degrees) and align the pulley groove with the timing mark **0** on the timing chain cover. This should now be Top Dead Center for cylinder No. 4.
7. Measure the clearance between the valve lifter and the camshaft. Record the measurements on

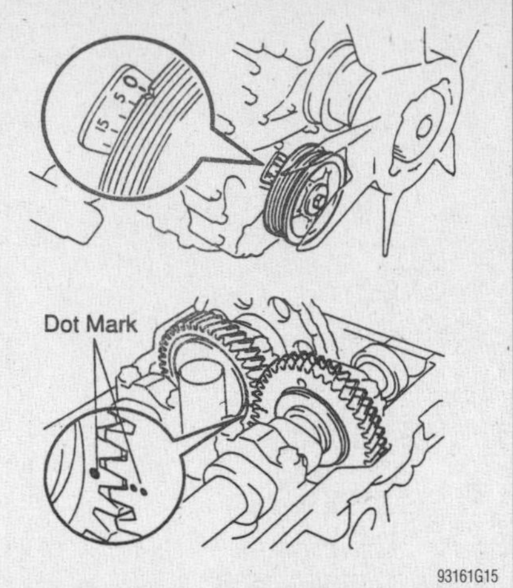

Fig. 124 Align the timing marks at the crankshaft pulley. Verify that the marks (1 and 2 dots) on the camshaft drive and driven gears are in a straight line—2RZ-FE and 3RZ-FE Engines

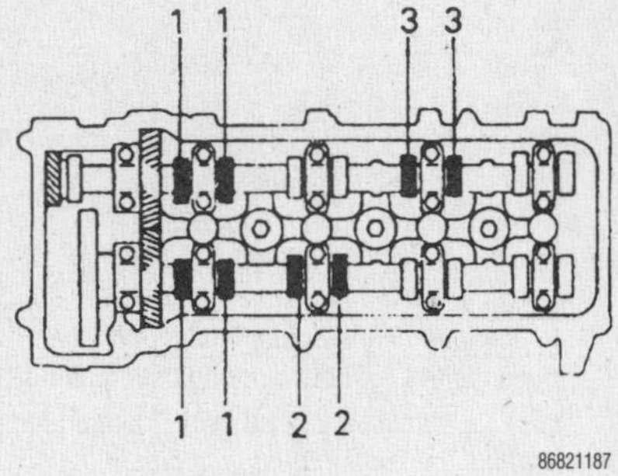

Fig. 125 Intake valves No. 1 and 2 and exhaust valves No. 1 and 3—2RZ-FE and 3RZ-FE Engines

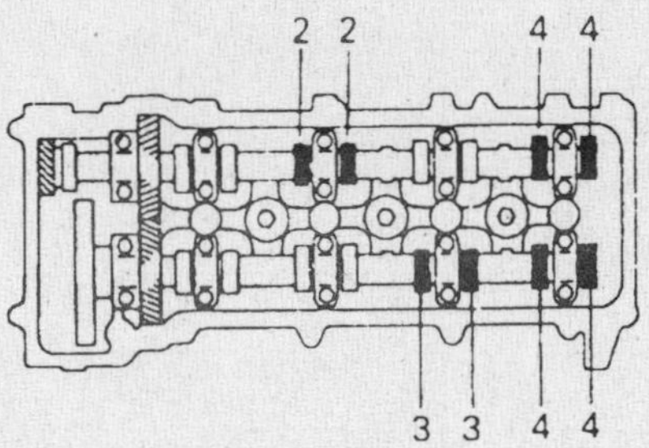

Fig. 126 Intake valves No. 3 and 4 and exhaust valves No. 2 and 4—2RZ-FE and 3RZ-FE Engines

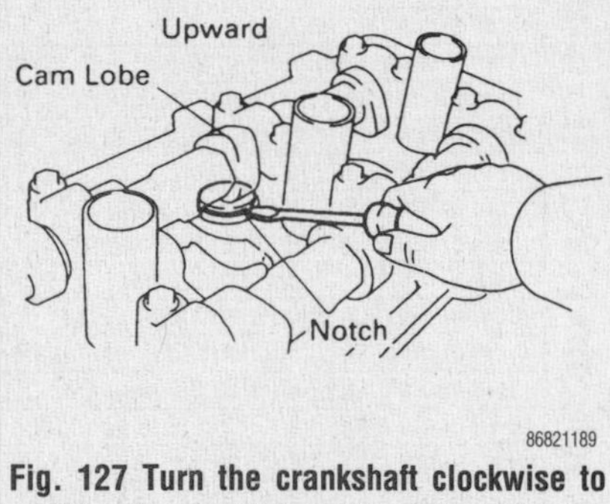

Fig. 127 Turn the crankshaft clockwise to position the cam lobe of the valve to be adjusted, upward. Rotate the notch in the valve lifter to face the spark plug side—2RZ-FE and 3RZ-FE Engines

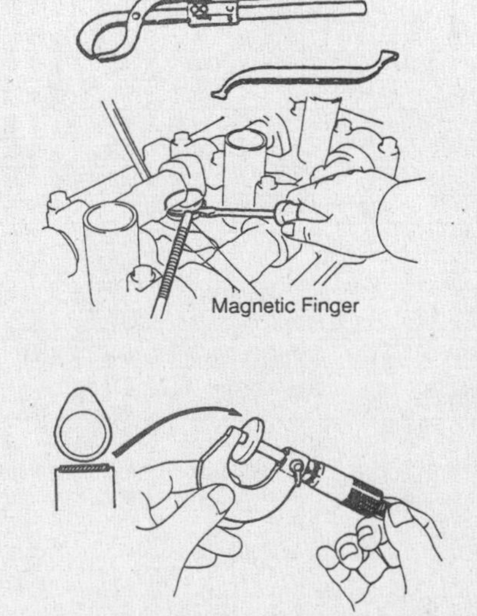

Fig. 128 These special tools are required for valve adjustment

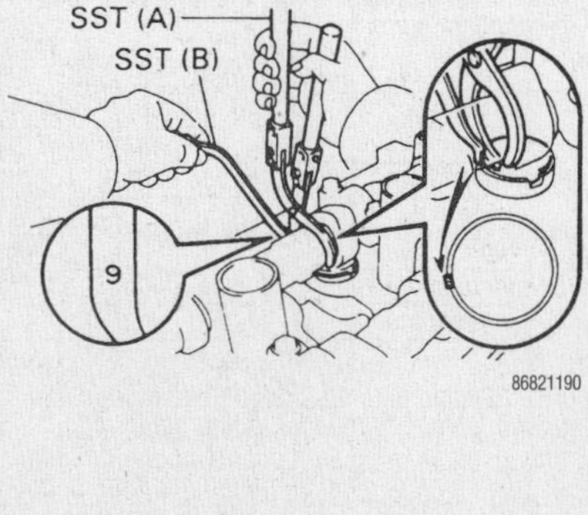

Fig. 129 Apply the SST (B) at a slight angle on the side marked with a '9', at the position shown in the illustration—2RZ-FE and 3RZ-FE Engines

the intake valves for cylinder No. 3 and 4. Measure the exhaust valves at the cylinder No. 2 and 4.

a. The intake valve clearance cold should be 0.006–0.010 in. (0.15–0.25mm).

b. The exhaust valve clearance cold is 0.010–0.014 in. (0.25–0.35mm).

8. To adjust the intake valve clearance:

a. Turn the crankshaft to position the cam lobe of the valve to be adjusted, facing upward.

b. Look closely for a notch in the valve lifter. Position the notch of the valve lifter toward the spark plug side.

c. Using the pliers-like Toyota SST tool, press down on the valve lifter and place the lever-like part of the SST valve adjusting tool set between the camshaft and valve lifter flange. The tip on the lever should fit into the notch in the valve lifter. With the valve lifter retained in this way, remove the pliers-like tool.

d. Using a small flat-bladed tool and a magnet, remove the adjusting shim.

e. Using an accurate micrometer, measure the thickness of the removed shim.

f. Calculate the thickness of a new shim so that the valve clearance comes within the specified value. Determine the replacement adjusting shim size by either using the chart or the following formula:

- Intake—N=T+(A-0.008 in./0.20mm)
- Exhaust—N=T+(A-0.012 in./0.30mm)
- T=Thickness of removed shim
- A=Measured valve clearance
- N=Thickness of new shim

g. Select a new shim with a thickness as close as possible to the calculated value.

9. Place a new adjusting shim on the valve lifter. Using the pliers-like Special Service Tool, press down on the valve lifter and remove the lever-like tool.

10. With feeler gauges, recheck the valve clearance.

11. The same procedures and tools are used for both intake and exhaust valve lifter adjustment.

12. When satisfied that all lifter clearances are correct, reinstall the cylinder head (valve) cover.

13. Connect the spark plug wires and any wiring removed or displaced for cylinder head cover removal.

14. Connect the remaining components such as PCV hoses and intake air connector.

15. Check engine oil level and connect the negative battery cable.

5VZ-FE Engine

➧ **See Figures 130 thru 135**

➡Adjust the valves when the engine is cold.

Toyota's Special Service Tools (SST) for valve adjustment, or their equivalent, are required for this procedure. The valve adjusting shims are set inside bucket-like cam followers. Part of the Toyota SST Valve Adjust Tool Set is a pliers-like tool to press down on the cam follower (also called a valve lifter) for enough clearance to withdraw the shim, and a lever-like tool that fits between the camshaft and the valve lifter flange to hold that clearance for shim extraction and insertion. In addition, a magnet to remove the adjustment shim from the cam follower and an accurate micrometer is required to properly measure the valve shim thickness. If all of these items are

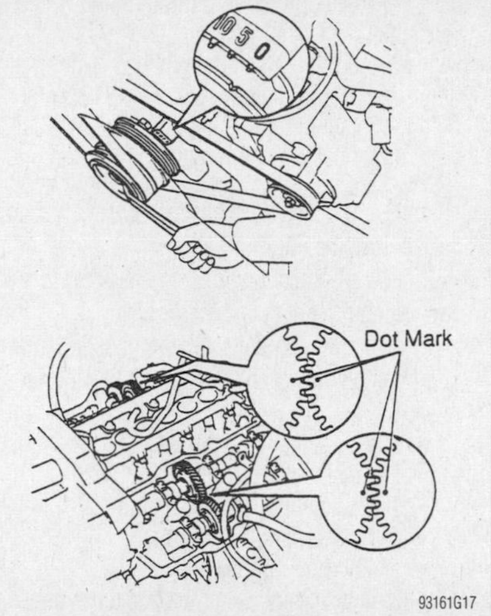

Fig. 130 Align the timing marks at the crankshaft pulley. Verify that the dot marks on the camshaft drive and driven gears are in a straight line—5VZ-FE Engine

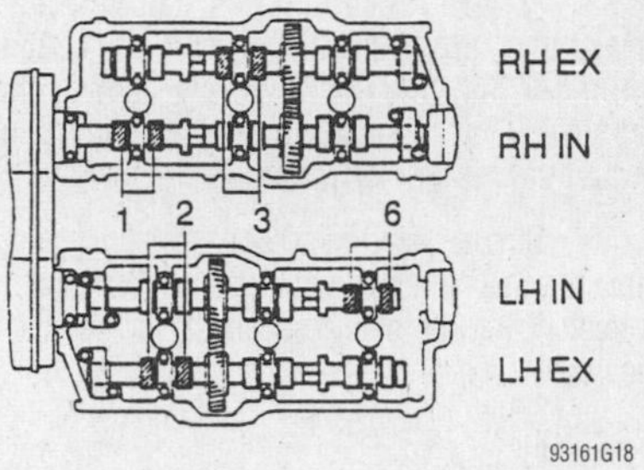

Fig. 131 Adjust these valves in the first step—5VZ-FE Engine

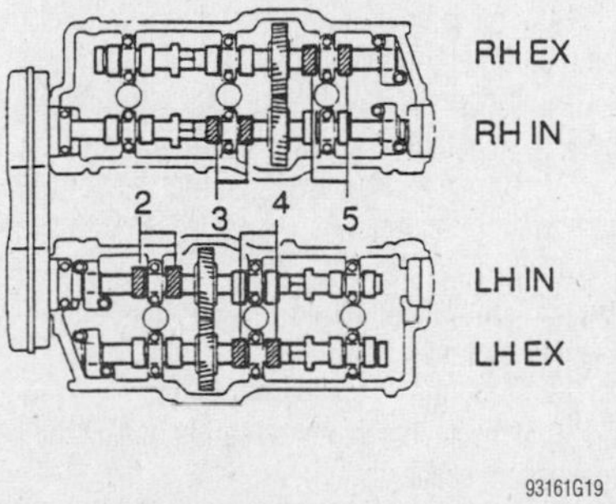

Fig. 132 Adjust these valves in the second step—5VZ-FE Engine

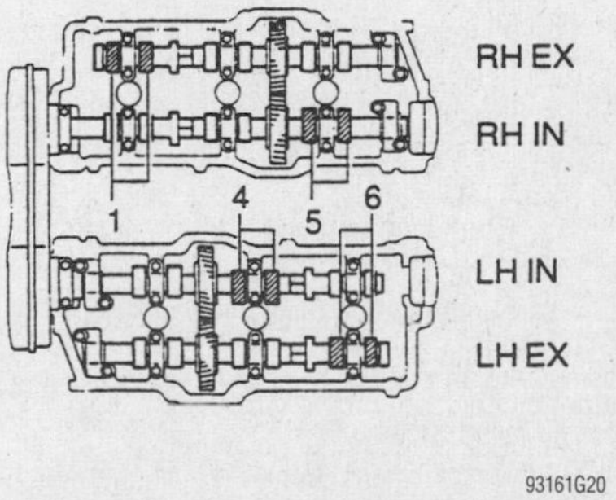

Fig. 133 Adjust these valves in the third step—5VZ-FE Engine

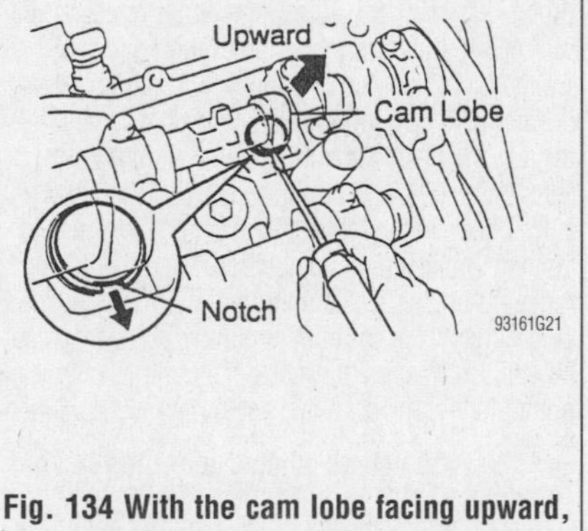

Fig. 134 With the cam lobe facing upward, turn the lifter so the notches are perpendicular to the camshaft—5VZ-FE Engine

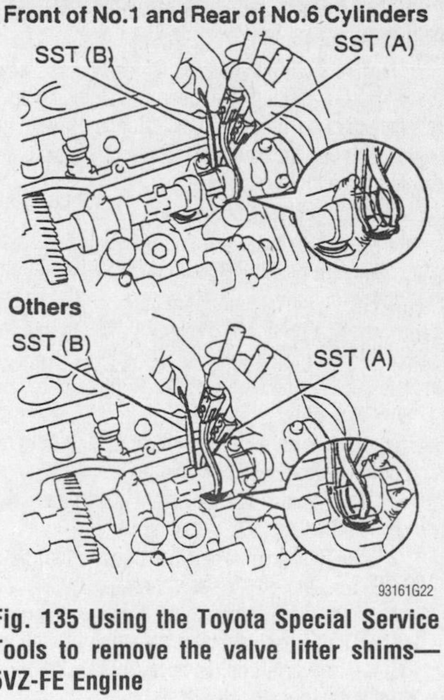

Fig. 135 Using the Toyota Special Service Tools to remove the valve lifter shims—5VZ-FE Engine

not available, valve adjustment is not recommended.

1. Disconnect the negative battery cable.
2. Drain the engine coolant.
3. Remove the intake air connector.
4. Remove the cylinder head (valve) covers.
5. Turn the crankshaft pulley clockwise and align its groove with the timing mark **0** on the timing belt cover. If all of the spark plugs are removed, it will be easier to turn the engine by hand.
6. Check that the timing marks (1 dot) on the camshaft drive and driven gears are in a straight line

on the cylinder head surface. If not, turn the crankshaft 1 complete revolution (360 degrees). This should be Top Dead Center for cylinder No. 1.

➡The cylinder layout for this V6 engine is: Right Cylinder Bank—1-3-5; Left Cylinder Bank—2-4-6. All cylinders are numbered starting at the front (timing belt end). Remember that this is a four-valve per cylinder engine. That means two intake and two exhaust valves per cylinder.

7. Step 1: Using an accurate feeler gauge, measure the clearance between the valve lifters and the camshaft. Record the measurements for the following valves:
   a. Both Intake Valves on cylinder No. 1—Right Hand Side
   b. Both Exhaust Valves on cylinder No. 2—Left Hand Side.
   c. Both Exhaust Valves on cylinder No. 3—Right Hand Side.
   d. Both Intake Valves on cylinder No. 6—Left Hand Side.
   e. The intake valve clearance cold should be 0.006–0.009 in. (0.13–0.23mm).
   f. The exhaust valve clearance cold should be 0.011–0.014 in. (0.27–0.37mm).
8. Step 2: Turn the crankshaft clockwise $^2/_3$ of a revolution (240 degrees). Using an accurate feeler gauge, measure the clearance between the valve lifters and the camshaft. Record the measurements for the following valves:
   a. Both Intake Valves on cylinder No. 2—Left Hand Side.
   b. Both Intake Valves on cylinder No. 3—Right Hand Side.
   c. Both Exhaust Valves on cylinder No. 4—Left Hand Side.
   d. Both Exhaust Valves on cylinder No. 5—Right Hand Side.
   e. The intake valve clearance cold should be 0.006–0.009 in. (0.13–0.23mm).
   f. The exhaust valve clearance cold should be 0.011–0.014 in. (0.27–0.37mm).
9. Step 3: Turn the crankshaft clockwise a further $^2/_3$ of a revolution (240 degrees). Using an accurate feeler gauge, measure the clearance between the valve lifters and the camshaft. Record the measurements for the following valves:
   a. Both Exhaust Valves on cylinder No. 1—Right Hand Side.
   b. Both Intake Valves on cylinder No. 4—Left Hand Side.
   c. Both Intake Valves on cylinder No. 5—Right Hand Side.
   d. Both Exhaust Valves on cylinder No. 6—Left Hand Side.
   e. The intake valve clearance cold should be 0.006–0.009 in. (0.13–0.23mm).
   f. The exhaust valve clearance cold should be 0.011–0.014 in. (0.27–0.37mm).
10. To adjust the intake valve clearance:
   a. Turn the crankshaft to position the cam lobe of the valve to be adjusted, facing upward.
   b. Look closely for a notch in the valve lifter. Position the notch of the valve lifter so it is perpendicular to the camshaft.
   c. Using the pliers-like Toyota SST tool, press down on the valve lifter and place the lever-like part of the SST valve adjusting tool set between the camshaft and valve lifter flange. The tip on the lever should fit into the notch in the valve lifter. Use care. If the tip of the tool is inserted too deeply, it will get pinched by the shim. To prevent it from being stuck, insert it gently from the intake side, at a slight angle. With the valve lifter retained in this way, remove the pliers-like tool.
   d. Using a small flat-bladed tool and a magnet, remove the adjusting shim.
   e. Using an accurate micrometer, measure the thickness of the removed shim.
   f. Determine the replacement adjusting shim size by either using charts or the following formula:
   - Intake—N=T+(A-0.007 in./0.18mm)
   - Exhaust—N=T+(A-0.013 in./0.32mm)
   - T=Thickness of removed shim
   - A=Measured valve clearance
   - N=Thickness of new shim
11. Select a new shim with the thickness as close as possible to the calculated value.
12. Place the new adjusting shim on the valve lifter, with the imprinted numbers facing down. Using the pliers-like Special Service Tool, press down on the valve lifter and remove the lever-like tool.
13. With feeler gauges, recheck the valve clearance.
14. The same procedures and tools are used for both intake and exhaust valve lifter adjustment.
15. When satisfied that all lifter clearances are correct, reinstall the cylinder head covers.
16. Connect the spark plug wires and any wiring removed or displaced for cylinder head cover removal.
17. Connect the remaining components such as the intake air connector.
18. Refill the engine with coolant.
19. Check engine oil level and connect the negative battery cable.

1FZ-FE Engine

➧ See Figures 136, 137, 138, 139, and 140

Toyota's Special Service Tools (SST) for valve adjustment, or their equivalent, are required for this procedure. The valve adjusting shims are set inside bucket-like cam followers. Part of the Toyota SST Valve Adjust Tool Set is a pliers-like tool to press down on the cam follower (also called a valve lifter) for enough clearance to withdraw the shim, and a lever-like tool that fits between the camshaft and the valve lifter flange to hold that clearance for shim extraction and insertion. In addition, a magnet to remove the adjustment shim from the cam follower and an accurate micrometer is required to properly measure the valve shim thickness. If all of these items are not available, valve adjustment is not recommended.

➡Adjust the valves when the engine is cold.

1. Disconnect the negative battery cable.
2. Drain the engine coolant.
3. Remove the throttle body. For additional information, please refer to the following topic(s): Fuel System, Throttle Body.
4. Disconnect the engine wires and heater valve from their locations on the cowl panel.
5. Remove the spark plug cables.
6. Remove the cylinder head (valve) covers.
7. Turn the crankshaft pulley clockwise and align its groove with the timing mark 0of the timing belt cover. If all of the spark plugs are removed, it will be easier to turn the engine by hand.

Fig. 136 Disconnect the engine wires and heater valve from the cowl panel and remove the cylinder head cover—1FZ-FE Engine

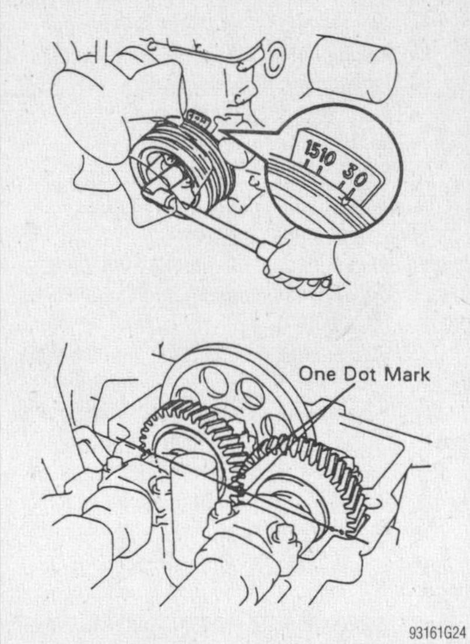

Fig. 137 Align the timing marks at the crankshaft pulley. Verify that the timing marks (one and two dots) on the camshaft drive and driven gears are in a straight line—1FZ-FE Engine

8. Turn the crankshaft pulley clockwise and align its groove with the timing mark **0** on the timing chain cover. If all of the spark plugs are removed, it will be easier to turn the engine by hand.
9. Check that the timing marks (1 and 2 dots) on the camshaft drive and driven gears are in a straight line on the cylinder head surface. If not, turn the crankshaft 1 complete revolution (360 degrees). This should be Top Dead Center for cylinder No. 1.

➡The cylinder layout for this Inline Six Cylinder is: 1-2-3-4-5-6. Cylinders are numbered starting at the front (timing chain end). Remember that this is a four-valve per cylinder engine. That means two intake and two exhaust valves per cylinder.

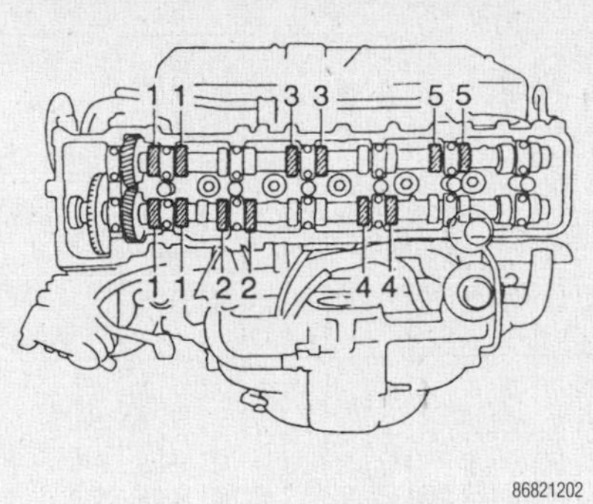

Fig. 138 Check these valves first—1FZ-FE Engine

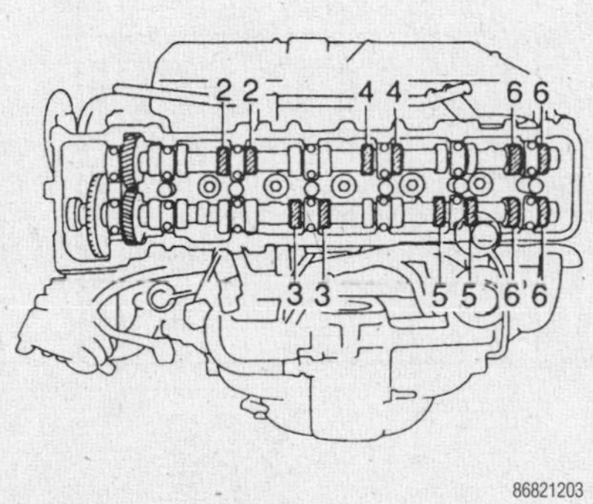

Fig. 139 Check these valves second—1FZ-FE Engine

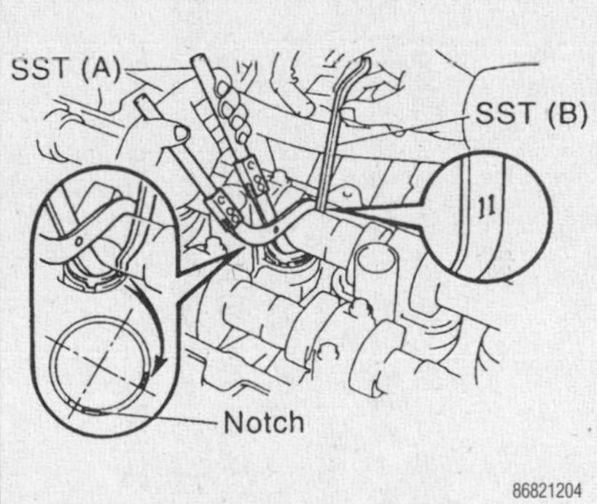

Fig. 140 Using Toyota's Special Service Tools to remove the valve adjusting shims—1FZ-FE Engine

10. Step 1: Using an accurate feeler gauge, measure the clearance between the valve lifters and the camshaft. Record the measurements for the following valves:
   a. Both Intake and Both Exhaust Valves on cylinder No. 1
   b. Both Intake Valves on cylinder No. 2
   c. Both Exhaust Valves on cylinder No. 3
   d. Both Intake Valves on cylinder No. 4
   e. Both Exhaust Valves on cylinder No. 5
   f. The intake valve clearance cold should be 0.006–0.010 in. (0.15–0.25mm).
   g. The exhaust valve clearance cold should be 0.010–0.014 in. (0.25–0.35mm).
11. Now turn the crankshaft pulley clockwise 1 complete revolution (360 degrees) and align its groove with the timing mark **0** on the timing chain cover. This should be Top Dead Center for cylinder No. 6.
12. Step 2: Using an accurate feeler gauge, measure the clearance between the valve lifters and the camshaft. Record the measurements for the following valves:
   a. Both Exhaust Valves on cylinder No. 2
   b. Both Intake Valves on cylinder No. 3
   c. Both Exhaust Valves on cylinder No. 4
   d. Both Intake Valves on cylinder No. 5
   e. Both Intake and Both Exhaust Valves on cylinder No. 6
   f. The intake valve clearance cold should be 0.006–0.010 in. (0.15–0.25mm).
   g. The exhaust valve clearance cold should be 0.010–0.014 in. (0.25–0.35mm).

➡The following procedure applies to all valves EXCEPT the rear valves for No. 6 cylinder.

13. To adjust the valve clearance:
   a. Turn the crankshaft to position the cam lobe of the valve to be adjusted, facing upward.
   b. Look closely for a notch in the valve lifter. Position the notch of the valve lifter toward the spark plug side.
   c. Using the pliers-like Toyota SST tool, press down on the valve lifter and place the lever-like part of the SST valve adjusting tool set between the camshaft and valve lifter flange. The tip on the lever should fit into the notch in the valve lifter. Use care. If the tip of the tool is inserted too deeply, it will get pinched by the shim. To prevent it from being stuck, insert it shallowly from the outside of the cylinder head, at a slight angle. With the valve lifter retained in this way, remove the pliers-like tool.
   d. Using a small flat-bladed tool and a magnet, remove the adjusting shim.
   e. Using an accurate micrometer, measure the thickness of the removed shim.
14. Determine the replacement adjusting shim size by either using charts or the following formula:
   - Intake—N=T+(A-0.008 in./0.20mm)
   - Exhaust—N=T+(A-0.012 in./0.30mm)
   - T=Thickness of removed shim
   - A=Measured valve clearance
   - N=Thickness of new shim
15. Select a new shim with the thickness as close as possible to the calculated value.
16. Place the new adjusting shim on the valve lifter, with the imprinted numbers facing down. Using the pliers-like Special Service Tool, press down on the valve lifter and remove the lever-like tool.
17. With feeler gauges, recheck the valve clearance.
18. The same procedures and tools are used for both intake and exhaust valve lifter adjustment.

➡The following procedure applies to ONLY THE REAR VALVES for No. 6 cylinder.

19. To adjust the rear valves on No. 6 cylinder:
   a. Remove the distributor.
   b. Remove the camshafts; refer to the following topics: Engine Mechanical, Camshafts.
   c. Remove the valve adjusting shim and measure using the formula given above. Select the proper replacement valve shim.
   d. Install the new shim. Make sure it is seated properly.
   e. Install the camshafts.
   f. Recheck the valve clearance.
   g. Install the distributor.
20. When satisfied that all lifter clearances are correct, reinstall the cylinder head cover.
21. Connect the spark plug wires and any wiring removed or displaced for cylinder head cover removal.
22. Connect the remaining components such as the throttle body.
23. Refill the engine with coolant.
24. Check engine oil level and connect the negative battery cable.
25. Run the engine to check for leaks and, if the distributor was removed, to adjust the ignition timing.

2UZ-FE Engine

➧ See Figures 141, 142, 143, and 144

➡The procedure should be done while the engine is cold.

1. Drain the engine coolant.
2. Remove the battery clamp cover.

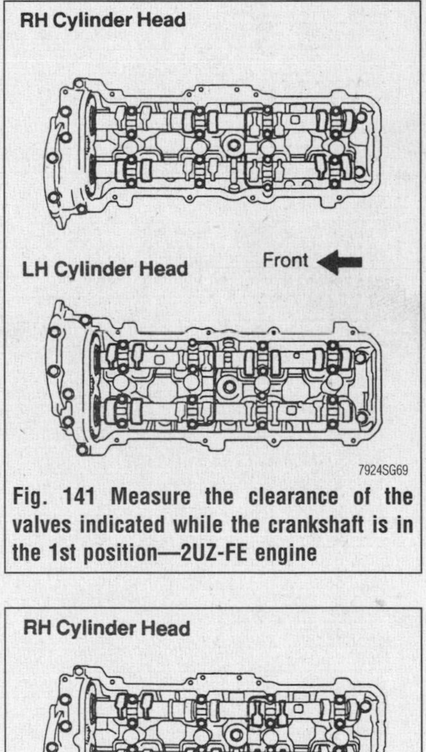

Fig. 141 Measure the clearance of the valves indicated while the crankshaft is in the 1st position—2UZ-FE engine

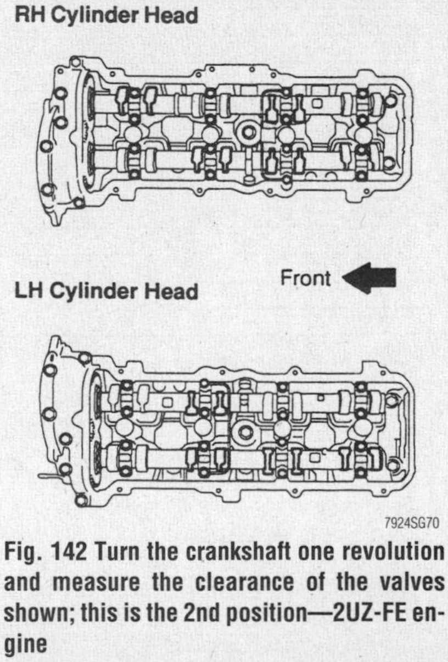

Fig. 142 Turn the crankshaft one revolution and measure the clearance of the valves shown; this is the 2nd position—2UZ-FE engine

Measured clearance mm (in.) \ Installed shim thickness mm (in.)	2.000 (0.0787)	2.020 (0.0795)	2.040 (0.0803)	2.060 (0.0811)	2.080 (0.0819)	2.100 (0.0827)	2.120 (0.0835)	2.140 (0.0843)	2.160 (0.0850)	2.180 (0.0858)	2.200 (0.0866)	2.210 (0.0870)	2.220 (0.0874)	2.230 (0.0878)	2.240 (0.0882)	2.250 (0.0886)	2.260 (0.0890)	2.270 (0.0894)	2.280 (0.0898)	2.290 (0.0902)	2.300 (0.0906)
0.000-0.030 (0.0000-0.0012)							00	00	00	00	02	02	04	04	06	06	08	08	10	10	12
0.031-0.050 (0.0012-0.0020)						00	00	00	00	02	04	06	06	08	08	10	10	12	12	14	14
0.051-0.070 (0.0020-0.0028)					00	00	00	00	02	04	06	08	08	10	10	12	12	14	14	16	16
0.071-0.090 (0.0028-0.0035)				00	00	00	00	02	04	06	08	10	10	12	12	14	14	16	16	18	18
0.091-0.110 (0.0036-0.0043)			00	00	00	00	02	04	06	08	10	12	12	14	14	16	16	18	18	20	20
0.111-0.130 (0.0044-0.0051)		00	00	00	00	02	04	06	08	10	12	14	14	16	16	18	18	20	20	22	22
0.131-0.149 (0.0052-0.0059)		00	00	00	02	04	06	08	10	12	14	16	16	18	18	20	20	22	22	24	24
0.150-0.250 (0.0059-0.0098)																					
0.251-0.270 (0.0099-0.0106)	06	08	10	12	14	16	18	20	22	24	26	28	28	30	30	32	32	34	34	36	36
0.271-0.290 (0.0107-0.0114)	08	10	12	14	16	18	20	22	24	26	28	30	30	32	32	34	34	36	36	38	38
0.291-0.310 (0.0115-0.0122)	10	12	14	16	18	20	22	24	26	28	30	32	32	34	34	36	36	38	38	40	40
0.311-0.330 (0.0122-0.0130)	12	14	16	18	20	22	24	26	28	30	32	34	34	36	36	38	38	40	40	42	42
0.331-0.350 (0.0130-0.0138)	14	16	18	20	22	24	26	28	30	32	34	36	36	38	38	40	40	42	42	44	44
0.351-0.370 (0.0138-0.0146)	16	18	20	22	24	26	28	30	32	34	36	38	38	40	40	42	42	44	44	46	46
0.371-0.390 (0.0146-0.0154)	18	20	22	24	26	28	30	32	34	36	38	40	40	42	42	44	44	46	46	48	48
0.391-0.410 (0.0154-0.0161)	20	22	24	26	28	30	32	34	36	38	40	42	42	44	44	46	46	48	48	50	50
0.411-0.430 (0.0162-0.0169)	22	24	26	28	30	32	34	36	38	40	42	44	44	46	46	48	48	50	50	52	52
0.431-0.450 (0.0170-0.0177)	24	26	28	30	32	34	36	38	40	42	44	46	46	48	48	50	50	52	52	54	54
0.451-0.470 (0.0178-0.0185)	26	28	30	32	34	36	38	40	42	44	46	48	48	50	50	52	52	54	54	56	56
0.471-0.490 (0.0185-0.0193)	28	30	32	34	36	38	40	42	44	46	48	50	50	52	52	54	54	56	56	58	58
0.491-0.510 (0.0193-0.0201)	30	32	34	36	38	40	42	44	46	48	50	52	52	54	54	56	56	58	58	60	60
0.511-0.530 (0.0201-0.0209)	32	34	36	38	40	42	44	46	48	50	52	54	54	56	56	58	58	60	60	62	62
0.531-0.550 (0.0209-0.0217)	34	36	38	40	42	44	46	48	50	52	54	56	56	58	58	60	60	62	62	64	64
0.551-0.570 (0.0217-0.0224)	36	38	40	42	44	46	48	50	52	54	56	58	58	60	60	62	62	64	64	66	66
0.571-0.590 (0.0225-0.0232)	38	40	42	44	46	48	50	52	54	56	58	60	60	62	62	64	64	66	66	68	68
0.591-0.610 (0.0233-0.0240)	40	42	44	46	48	50	52	54	56	58	60	62	62	64	64	66	66	68	68	70	70
0.611-0.630 (0.0241-0.0248)	42	44	46	48	50	52	54	56	58	60	62	64	64	66	66	68	68	70	70	72	72
0.631-0.650 (0.0248-0.0256)	44	46	48	50	52	54	56	58	60	62	64	66	66	68	68	70	70	72	72	74	74
0.651-0.670 (0.0256-0.0264)	46	48	50	52	54	56	58	60	62	64	66	68	68	70	70	72	72	74	74	76	76
0.671-0.690 (0.0264-0.0272)	48	50	52	54	56	58	60	62	64	66	68	70	70	72	72	74	74	76	76	78	78
0.691-0.710 (0.0272-0.0280)	50	52	54	56	58	60	62	64	66	68	70	72	72	74	74	76	76	78	78	80	80
0.711-0.730 (0.0280-0.0287)	52	54	56	58	60	62	64	66	68	70	72	74	74	76	76	78	78	80	80	80	80
0.731-0.750 (0.0288-0.0295)	54	56	58	60	62	64	66	68	70	72	74	76	76	78	78	80	80	80	80	80	80
0.751-0.770 (0.0296-0.0303)	56	58	60	62	64	66	68	70	72	74	76	78	78	80	80	80	80	80	80	80	
0.771-0.790 (0.0304-0.0311)	58	60	62	64	66	68	70	72	74	76	78	80	80	80	80	80	80	80			
0.791-0.810 (0.0311-0.0319)	60	62	64	66	68	70	72	74	76	78	80	80	80	80	80	80					
0.811-0.830 (0.0319-0.0327)	62	64	66	68	70	72	74	76	78	80	80	80	80	80							
0.831-0.850 (0.0327-0.0335)	64	66	68	70	72	74	76	78	80	80	80	80									
0.851-0.870 (0.0335-0.0343)	66	68	70	72	74	76	78	80	80	80											
0.871-0.890 (0.0343-0.0350)	68	70	72	74	76	78	80	80	80												
0.891-0.910 (0.0351-0.0358)	70	72	74	76	78	80	80	80													
0.911-0.930 (0.0359-0.0366)	72	74	76	78	80	80	80														
0.931-0.950 (0.0367-0.0374)	74	76	78	80	80	80															
0.951-0.970 (0.0374-0.0382)	76	78	80	80	80																
0.971-0.990 (0.0382-0.0390)	78	80	80	80																	
0.991-1.010 (0.0390-0.0398)	80	80	80																		
1.011-1.030 (0.0398-0.0406)	80	80																			
1.031-1.050 (0.0406-0.0413)	80																				

Measured clearance mm (in.) \ Installed shim thickness mm (in.)	2.310 (0.0909)	2.320 (0.0913)	2.330 (0.0917)	2.340 (0.0921)	2.350 (0.0925)	2.360 (0.0929)	2.370 (0.0933)	2.380 (0.0937)	2.390 (0.0941)	2.400 (0.0945)	2.410 (0.0949)	2.420 (0.0953)	2.430 (0.0957)	2.440 (0.0961)	2.450 (0.0965)	2.460 (0.0969)	2.470 (0.0972)	2.480 (0.0976)	2.490 (0.0980)	2.500 (0.0984)
0.000-0.030 (0.0000-0.0012)	12	14	14	16	16	18	18	20	20	22	22	24	24	26	26	28	28	30	30	32
0.031-0.050 (0.0012-0.0020)	16	16	18	18	20	20	22	22	24	24	26	26	28	28	30	30	32	32	34	34
0.051-0.070 (0.0020-0.0028)	18	18	20	20	22	22	24	24	26	26	28	28	30	30	32	32	34	34	36	36
0.071-0.090 (0.0028-0.0035)	20	20	22	22	24	24	26	26	28	28	30	30	32	32	34	34	36	36	38	38
0.091-0.110 (0.0036-0.0043)	22	22	24	24	26	26	28	28	30	30	32	32	34	34	36	36	38	38	40	40
0.111-0.130 (0.0044-0.0051)	24	24	26	26	28	28	30	30	32	32	34	34	36	36	38	38	40	40	42	42
0.131-0.149 (0.0052-0.0059)	26	26	28	28	30	30	32	32	34	34	36	36	38	38	40	40	42	42	44	44
0.150-0.250 (0.0059-0.0098)																				
0.251-0.270 (0.0099-0.0106)	38	38	40	40	42	42	44	44	46	46	48	48	50	50	52	52	54	54	56	56
0.271-0.290 (0.0107-0.0114)	40	40	42	42	44	44	46	46	48	48	50	50	52	52	54	54	56	56	58	58
0.291-0.310 (0.0115-0.0122)	42	42	44	44	46	46	48	48	50	50	52	52	54	54	56	56	58	58	60	60
0.311-0.330 (0.0122-0.0130)	44	44	46	46	48	48	50	50	52	52	54	54	56	56	58	58	60	60	62	62
0.331-0.350 (0.0130-0.0138)	46	46	48	48	50	50	52	52	54	54	56	56	58	58	60	60	62	62	64	64
0.351-0.370 (0.0138-0.0146)	48	48	50	50	52	52	54	54	56	56	58	58	60	60	62	62	64	64	66	66
0.371-0.390 (0.0146-0.0154)	50	50	52	52	54	54	56	56	58	58	60	60	62	62	64	64	66	66	68	68
0.391-0.410 (0.0154-0.0161)	52	52	54	54	56	56	58	58	60	60	62	62	64	64	66	66	68	68	70	70
0.411-0.430 (0.0162-0.0169)	54	54	56	56	58	58	60	60	62	62	64	64	66	66	68	68	70	70	72	72
0.431-0.450 (0.0170-0.0177)	56	56	58	58	60	60	62	62	64	64	66	66	68	68	70	70	72	72	74	74
0.451-0.470 (0.0178-0.0185)	58	58	60	60	62	62	64	64	66	66	68	68	70	70	72	72	74	74	76	76
0.471-0.490 (0.0185-0.0193)	60	60	62	62	64	64	66	66	68	68	70	70	72	72	74	74	76	76	78	78
0.491-0.510 (0.0193-0.0201)	62	62	64	64	66	66	68	68	70	70	72	72	74	74	76	76	78	78	80	80
0.511-0.530 (0.0201-0.0209)	64	64	66	66	68	68	70	70	72	72	74	74	76	76	78	78	80	80	80	80
0.531-0.550 (0.0209-0.0217)	66	66	68	68	70	70	72	72	74	74	76	76	78	78	80	80	80	80	80	80
0.551-0.570 (0.0217-0.0224)	68	68	70	70	72	72	74	74	76	76	78	78	80	80	80	80	80	80	80	
0.571-0.590 (0.0225-0.0232)	70	70	72	72	74	74	76	76	78	78	80	80	80	80	80	80	80			
0.591-0.610 (0.0233-0.0240)	72	72	74	74	76	76	78	78	80	80	80	80	80	80	80					
0.611-0.630 (0.0241-0.0248)	74	74	76	76	78	78	80	80	80	80	80	80	80							
0.631-0.650 (0.0248-0.0256)	76	76	78	78	80	80	80	80	80	80	80									
0.651-0.670 (0.0256-0.0264)	78	78	80	80	80	80	80	80	80											
0.671-0.690 (0.0264-0.0272)	80	80	80	80	80	80	80													
0.691-0.710 (0.0272-0.0280)	80	80	80	80	80															
0.711-0.730 (0.0280-0.0287)	80	80	80																	
0.731-0.750 (0.0288-0.0295)	80																			
0.751-0.770 (0.0296-0.0303)																				
0.771-0.790 (0.0304-0.0311)																				
0.791-0.810 (0.0311-0.0319)																				
0.811-0.830 (0.0319-0.0327)																				
0.831-0.850 (0.0327-0.0335)																				
0.851-0.870 (0.0335-0.0343)																				
0.871-0.890 (0.0343-0.0350)																				
0.891-0.910 (0.0351-0.0358)																				
0.911-0.930 (0.0359-0.0366)																				
0.931-0.950 (0.0367-0.0374)																				
0.951-0.970 (0.0374-0.0382)																				
0.971-0.990 (0.0382-0.0390)																				
0.991-1.010 (0.0390-0.0398)																				
1.011-1.030 (0.0398-0.0406)																				
1.031-1.050 (0.0406-0.0413)																				

Measured clearance mm (in.) \ Installed shim thickness mm (in.)	2.510 (0.0988)	2.520 (0.0992)	2.530 (0.0996)	2.540 (0.1000)	2.550 (0.1004)	2.560 (0.1008)	2.570 (0.1012)	2.580 (0.1016)	2.590 (0.1020)	2.600 (0.1024)	2.620 (0.1031)	2.640 (0.1039)	2.660 (0.1047)	2.680 (0.1055)	2.700 (0.1063)	2.720 (0.1071)	2.740 (0.1079)	2.760 (0.1087)	2.780 (0.1094)	2.800 (0.1102)
0.000-0.030 (0.0000-0.0012)	32	34	34	36	36	38	38	40	40	42	44	46	48	50	52	54	56	58	60	62
0.031-0.050 (0.0012-0.0020)	36	36	38	38	40	40	42	42	44	44	46	48	50	52	54	56	58	60	62	64
0.051-0.070 (0.0020-0.0028)	38	38	40	40	42	42	44	44	46	46	48	50	52	54	56	58	60	62	64	66
0.071-0.090 (0.0028-0.0035)	40	40	42	42	44	44	46	46	48	48	50	52	54	56	58	60	62	64	66	68
0.091-0.110 (0.0036-0.0043)	42	42	44	44	46	46	48	48	50	50	52	54	56	58	60	62	64	66	68	70
0.111-0.130 (0.0044-0.0051)	44	44	46	46	48	48	50	50	52	52	54	56	58	60	62	64	66	68	70	72
0.131-0.149 (0.0052-0.0059)	46	46	48	48	50	50	52	52	54	54	56	58	60	62	64	66	68	70	72	74
0.150-0.250 (0.0059-0.0098)																				
0.251-0.270 (0.0099-0.0106)	58	58	60	60	62	62	64	64	66	66	68	70	72	74	76	78	80	80	80	
0.271-0.290 (0.0107-0.0114)	60	60	62	62	64	64	66	66	68	68	70	72	74	76	78	80	80	80		
0.291-0.310 (0.0115-0.0122)	62	62	64	64	66	66	68	68	70	70	72	74	76	78	80	80	80			
0.311-0.330 (0.0122-0.0130)	64	64	66	66	68	68	70	70	72	72	74	76	78	80	80	80				
0.331-0.350 (0.0130-0.0138)	66	66	68	68	70	70	72	72	74	74	76	78	80	80	80					
0.351-0.370 (0.0138-0.0146)	68	68	70	70	72	72	74	74	76	76	78	80	80	80						
0.371-0.390 (0.0146-0.0154)	70	70	72	72	74	74	76	76	78	78	80	80	80							
0.391-0.410 (0.0154-0.0161)	72	72	74	74	76	76	78	78	80	80	80	80								
0.411-0.430 (0.0162-0.0169)	74	74	76	76	78	78	80	80	80	80	80									
0.431-0.450 (0.0170-0.0177)	76	76	78	78	80	80	80	80	80	80										
0.451-0.470 (0.0178-0.0185)	78	78	80	80	80	80	80	80	80											
0.471-0.490 (0.0185-0.0193)	80	80	80	80	80	80	80													
0.491-0.510 (0.0193-0.0201)	80	80	80	80	80															
0.511-0.530 (0.0201-0.0209)	80	80	80																	
0.531-0.550 (0.0209-0.0217)	80																			
0.551-0.570 (0.0217-0.0224)																				
0.571-0.590 (0.0225-0.0232)																				
0.591-0.610 (0.0233-0.0240)																				
0.611-0.630 (0.0241-0.0248)																				
0.631-0.650 (0.0248-0.0256)																				
0.651-0.670 (0.0256-0.0264)																				
0.671-0.690 (0.0264-0.0272)																				
0.691-0.710 (0.0272-0.0280)																				
0.711-0.730 (0.0280-0.0287)																				
0.731-0.750 (0.0288-0.0295)																				
0.751-0.770 (0.0296-0.0303)																				
0.771-0.790 (0.0304-0.0311)																				
0.791-0.810 (0.0311-0.0319)																				
0.811-0.830 (0.0319-0.0327)																				
0.831-0.850 (0.0327-0.0335)																				
0.851-0.870 (0.0335-0.0343)																				
0.871-0.890 (0.0343-0.0350)																				
0.891-0.910 (0.0351-0.0358)																				
0.911-0.930 (0.0359-0.0366)																				
0.931-0.950 (0.0367-0.0374)																				
0.951-0.970 (0.0374-0.0382)																				
0.971-0.990 (0.0382-0.0390)																				
0.991-1.010 (0.0390-0.0398)																				
1.011-1.030 (0.0398-0.0406)																				
1.031-1.050 (0.0406-0.0413)																				

Intake valve clearance (Cold):
0.15 – 0.25 mm (0.006 – 0.010 in.)

EXAMPLE:
The 2.300 mm (0.0906 in.) shim is installed, and the measured clearance is 0.440 mm (0.0173 in.). Replace the 2.300 mm (0.0906 in.) shim with a No. 54 shim.

New shim thickness — mm (in.)

Shim No.	Thickness	Shim No.	Thickness	Shim No.	Thickness
00	2.000 (0.0787)	28	2.280 (0.0898)	56	2.560 (0.1008)
02	2.020 (0.0795)	30	2.300 (0.0906)	58	2.580 (0.1016)
04	2.040 (0.0803)	32	2.320 (0.0913)	60	2.600 (0.1024)
06	2.060 (0.0811)	34	2.340 (0.0921)	62	2.620 (0.1031)
08	2.080 (0.0819)	36	2.360 (0.0929)	64	2.640 (0.1039)
10	2.100 (0.0827)	38	2.380 (0.0937)	66	2.660 (0.1047)
12	2.120 (0.0835)	40	2.400 (0.0945)	68	2.680 (0.1055)
14	2.140 (0.0843)	42	2.420 (0.0953)	70	2.700 (0.1063)
16	2.160 (0.0850)	44	2.440 (0.0961)	72	2.720 (0.1071)
18	2.180 (0.0858)	46	2.460 (0.0969)	74	2.740 (0.1079)
20	2.200 (0.0866)	48	2.480 (0.0976)	76	2.760 (0.1087)
22	2.220 (0.0874)	50	2.500 (0.0984)	78	2.780 (0.1094)
24	2.240 (0.0882)	52	2.520 (0.0992)	80	2.800 (0.1102)
26	2.260 (0.0890)	54	2.540 (0.1000)		

7924SG71

Fig. 143 Intake valve clearance shim selection chart—2UZ-FE engine

Installed shim thickness mm (in.) / Measured clearance mm (in.) — installed shim thickness 2.000–2.400 mm:

Measured clearance mm (in.)	2.000 (0.0787)	2.020 (0.0795)	2.040 (0.0803)	2.060 (0.0811)	2.080 (0.0819)	2.100 (0.0827)	2.120 (0.0835)	2.140 (0.0843)	2.160 (0.0850)	2.180 (0.0858)	2.200 (0.0866)	2.210 (0.0870)	2.220 (0.0874)	2.230 (0.0878)	2.240 (0.0882)	2.250 (0.0886)	2.260 (0.0890)	2.270 (0.0894)	2.280 (0.0898)	2.290 (0.0902)	2.300 (0.0906)	2.310 (0.0909)	2.320 (0.0913)	2.330 (0.0917)	2.340 (0.0921)	2.350 (0.0925)	2.360 (0.0929)	2.370 (0.0933)	2.380 (0.0937)	2.390 (0.0941)	2.400 (0.0945)
0.000-0.030 (0.0000-0.0012)												00	00	00	00	00	00	00	00	00	02	02	04	04	06	06	08	08	10	10	12
0.031-0.050 (0.0012-0.0020)											00	00	00	00	00	00	00	02	02	04	04	06	06	08	08	10	10	12	12	14	14
0.051-0.070 (0.0020-0.0028)										00	00	00	00	00	00	02	02	04	04	06	06	08	08	10	10	12	12	14	14	16	16
0.071-0.090 (0.0028-0.0035)									00	00	00	00	00	02	02	04	04	06	06	08	08	10	10	12	12	14	14	16	16	18	18
0.091-0.110 (0.0036-0.0043)								00	00	00	00	02	02	04	04	06	06	08	08	10	10	12	12	14	14	16	16	18	18	20	20
0.111-0.130 (0.0044-0.0051)							00	00	00	00	02	04	04	06	06	08	08	10	10	12	12	14	14	16	16	18	18	20	20	22	22
0.131-0.150 (0.0052-0.0059)						00	00	00	00	02	04	06	06	08	08	10	10	12	12	14	14	16	16	18	18	20	20	22	22	24	24
0.151-0.170 (0.0059-0.0067)					00	00	00	00	02	04	06	08	08	10	10	12	12	14	14	16	16	18	18	20	20	22	22	24	24	26	26
0.171-0.190 (0.0067-0.0075)				00	00	00	00	02	04	06	08	10	10	12	12	14	14	16	16	18	18	20	20	22	22	24	24	26	26	28	28
0.191-0.210 (0.0075-0.0083)			00	00	00	00	02	04	06	08	10	12	12	14	14	16	16	18	18	20	20	22	22	24	24	26	26	28	28	30	30
0.211-0.230 (0.0083-0.0091)		00	00	00	00	02	04	06	08	10	12	14	14	16	16	18	18	20	20	22	22	24	24	26	26	28	28	30	30	32	32
0.231-0.249 (0.0091-0.0098)		00	00	00	02	04	06	08	10	12	14	16	16	18	18	20	20	22	22	24	24	26	26	28	28	30	30	32	32	34	34
0.250-0.350 (0.0098-0.0138)																															
0.351-0.370 (0.0138-0.0146)	06	08	10	12	14	16	18	20	22	24	26	28	28	30	30	32	32	34	34	36	36	38	38	40	40	42	42	44	44	46	46
0.371-0.390 (0.0146-0.0154)	08	10	12	14	16	18	20	22	24	26	28	30	30	32	32	34	34	36	36	38	38	40	40	42	42	44	44	46	46	48	48
0.391-0.410 (0.0154-0.0161)	10	12	14	16	18	20	22	24	26	28	30	32	32	34	34	36	36	38	38	40	40	42	42	44	44	46	46	48	48	50	50
0.411-0.430 (0.0162-0.0169)	12	14	16	18	20	22	24	26	28	30	32	34	34	36	36	38	38	40	40	42	42	44	44	46	46	48	48	50	50	52	52
0.431-0.450 (0.0170-0.0177)	14	16	18	20	22	24	26	28	30	32	34	36	36	38	38	40	40	42	42	44	44	46	46	48	48	50	50	52	52	54	54
0.451-0.470 (0.0178-0.0185)	16	18	20	22	24	26	28	30	32	34	36	38	38	40	40	42	42	44	44	46	46	48	48	50	50	52	52	54	54	56	56
0.471-0.490 (0.0185-0.0193)	18	20	22	24	26	28	30	32	34	36	38	40	40	42	42	44	44	46	46	48	48	50	50	52	52	54	54	56	56	58	58
0.491-0.510 (0.0193-0.0201)	20	22	24	26	28	30	32	34	36	38	40	42	42	44	44	46	46	48	48	50	50	52	52	54	54	56	56	58	58	60	60
0.511-0.530 (0.0201-0.0209)	22	24	26	28	30	32	34	36	38	40	42	44	44	46	46	48	48	50	50	52	52	54	54	56	56	58	58	60	60	62	62
0.531-0.550 (0.0209-0.0217)	24	26	28	30	32	34	36	38	40	42	44	46	46	48	48	50	50	52	52	54	54	56	56	58	58	60	60	62	62	64	64
0.551-0.570 (0.0217-0.0224)	26	28	30	32	34	36	38	40	42	44	46	48	48	50	50	52	52	54	54	56	56	58	58	60	60	62	62	64	64	66	66
0.571-0.590 (0.0225-0.0232)	28	30	32	34	36	38	40	42	44	46	48	50	50	52	52	54	54	56	56	58	58	60	60	62	62	64	64	66	66	68	68
0.591-0.610 (0.0233-0.0240)	30	32	34	36	38	40	42	44	46	48	50	52	52	54	54	56	56	58	58	60	60	62	62	64	64	66	66	68	68	70	70
0.611-0.630 (0.0241-0.0248)	32	34	36	38	40	42	44	46	48	50	52	54	54	56	56	58	58	60	60	62	62	64	64	66	66	68	68	70	70	72	72
0.631-0.650 (0.0248-0.0256)	34	36	38	40	42	44	46	48	50	52	54	56	56	58	58	60	60	62	62	64	64	66	66	68	68	70	70	72	72	74	74
0.651-0.670 (0.0256-0.0264)	36	38	40	42	44	46	48	50	52	54	56	58	58	60	60	62	62	64	64	66	66	68	68	70	70	72	72	74	74	76	76
0.671-0.690 (0.0264-0.0272)	38	40	42	44	46	48	50	52	54	56	58	60	60	62	62	64	64	66	66	68	68	70	70	72	72	74	74	76	76	78	78
0.691-0.710 (0.0272-0.0280)	40	42	44	46	48	50	52	54	56	58	60	62	62	64	64	66	66	68	68	70	70	72	72	74	74	76	76	78	78	80	80
0.711-0.730 (0.0280-0.0287)	42	44	46	48	50	52	54	56	58	60	62	64	64	66	66	68	68	70	70	72	72	74	74	76	76	78	78	80	80	80	80
0.731-0.750 (0.0288-0.0295)	44	46	48	50	52	54	56	58	60	62	64	66	66	68	68	70	70	72	72	74	74	76	76	78	78	80	80	80	80	80	80
0.751-0.770 (0.0296-0.0303)	46	48	50	52	54	56	58	60	62	64	66	68	68	70	70	72	72	74	74	76	76	78	78	80	80	80	80	80	80	80	
0.771-0.790 (0.0304-0.0311)	48	50	52	54	56	58	60	62	64	66	68	70	70	72	72	74	74	76	76	78	78	80	80	80	80	80	80	80			
0.791-0.810 (0.0311-0.0319)	50	52	54	56	58	60	62	64	66	68	70	72	72	74	74	76	76	78	78	80	80	80	80	80	80	80					
0.811-0.830 (0.0319-0.0327)	52	54	56	58	60	62	64	66	68	70	72	74	74	76	76	78	78	80	80	80	80	80	80	80							
0.831-0.850 (0.0327-0.0335)	54	56	58	60	62	64	66	68	70	72	74	76	76	78	78	80	80	80	80	80	80	80									
0.851-0.870 (0.0335-0.0343)	56	58	60	62	64	66	68	70	72	74	76	78	78	80	80	80	80	80	80	80											
0.871-0.890 (0.0343-0.0350)	58	60	62	64	66	68	70	72	74	76	78	80	80	80	80	80	80	80													
0.891-0.910 (0.0351-0.0358)	60	62	64	66	68	70	72	74	76	78	80	80	80	80	80	80															
0.911-0.930 (0.0359-0.0366)	62	64	66	68	70	72	74	76	78	80	80	80	80	80																	
0.931-0.950 (0.0367-0.0374)	64	66	68	70	72	74	76	78	80	80	80	80																			
0.951-0.970 (0.0374-0.0382)	66	68	70	72	74	76	78	80	80	80																					
0.971-0.990 (0.0382-0.0390)	68	70	72	74	76	78	80	80	80																						
0.991-1.010 (0.0390-0.0398)	70	72	74	76	78	80	80	80																							
1.011-1.030 (0.0398-0.0406)	72	74	76	78	80	80	80																								
1.031-1.050 (0.0406-0.0413)	74	76	78	80	80	80																									
1.051-1.070 (0.0414-0.0421)	76	78	80	80	80																										
1.071-1.090 (0.0422-0.0429)	78	80	80	80																											
1.091-1.110 (0.0430-0.0437)	80	80	80																												
1.111-1.130 (0.0437-0.0445)	80	80																													
1.131-1.150 (0.0445-0.0453)	80																														

Installed shim thickness 2.410–2.800 mm:

Measured clearance mm (in.)	2.410 (0.0949)	2.420 (0.0953)	2.430 (0.0957)	2.440 (0.0961)	2.450 (0.0965)	2.460 (0.0969)	2.470 (0.0972)	2.480 (0.0976)	2.490 (0.0980)	2.500 (0.0984)	2.510 (0.0988)	2.520 (0.0992)	2.530 (0.0996)	2.540 (0.1000)	2.550 (0.1004)	2.560 (0.1008)	2.570 (0.1012)	2.580 (0.1016)	2.590 (0.1020)	2.600 (0.1024)	2.620 (0.1031)	2.640 (0.1039)	2.660 (0.1047)	2.680 (0.1055)	2.700 (0.1063)	2.720 (0.1071)	2.740 (0.1079)	2.760 (0.1087)	2.780 (0.1094)	2.800 (0.1102)
0.000-0.030 (0.0000-0.0012)	12	14	14	16	16	18	18	20	20	22	22	24	24	26	26	28	28	30	30	32	34	36	38	40	42	44	46	48	50	52
0.031-0.050 (0.0012-0.0020)	16	16	18	18	20	20	22	22	24	24	26	26	28	28	30	30	32	32	34	34	36	38	40	42	44	46	48	50	52	54
0.051-0.070 (0.0020-0.0028)	18	18	20	20	22	22	24	24	26	26	28	28	30	30	32	32	34	34	36	36	38	40	42	44	46	48	50	52	54	56
0.071-0.090 (0.0028-0.0035)	20	20	22	22	24	24	26	26	28	28	30	30	32	32	34	34	36	36	38	38	40	42	44	46	48	50	52	54	56	58
0.091-0.110 (0.0036-0.0043)	22	22	24	24	26	26	28	28	30	30	32	32	34	34	36	36	38	38	40	40	42	44	46	48	50	52	54	56	58	60
0.111-0.130 (0.0044-0.0051)	24	24	26	26	28	28	30	30	32	32	34	34	36	36	38	38	40	40	42	42	44	46	48	50	52	54	56	58	60	62
0.131-0.150 (0.0052-0.0059)	26	26	28	28	30	30	32	32	34	34	36	36	38	38	40	40	42	42	44	44	46	48	50	52	54	56	58	60	62	64
0.151-0.170 (0.0059-0.0067)	28	28	30	30	32	32	34	34	36	36	38	38	40	40	42	42	44	44	46	46	48	50	52	54	56	58	60	62	64	66
0.171-0.190 (0.0067-0.0075)	30	30	32	32	34	34	36	36	38	38	40	40	42	42	44	44	46	46	48	48	50	52	54	56	58	60	62	64	66	68
0.191-0.210 (0.0075-0.0083)	32	32	34	34	36	36	38	38	40	40	42	42	44	44	46	46	48	48	50	50	52	54	56	58	60	62	64	66	68	70
0.211-0.230 (0.0083-0.0091)	34	34	36	36	38	38	40	40	42	42	44	44	46	46	48	48	50	50	52	52	54	56	58	60	62	64	66	68	70	72
0.231-0.249 (0.0091-0.0098)	36	36	38	38	40	40	42	42	44	44	46	46	48	48	50	50	52	52	54	54	56	58	60	62	64	66	68	70	72	74
0.250-0.350 (0.0098-0.0138)																														
0.351-0.370 (0.0138-0.0146)	48	48	50	50	52	52	54	54	56	56	58	58	60	60	62	62	64	64	66	66	68	70	72	74	76	78	80	80	80	
0.371-0.390 (0.0146-0.0154)	50	50	52	52	54	54	56	56	58	58	60	60	62	62	64	64	66	66	68	68	70	72	74	76	78	80	80	80		
0.391-0.410 (0.0154-0.0161)	52	52	54	54	56	56	58	58	60	60	62	62	64	64	66	66	68	68	70	70	72	74	76	78	80	80	80			
0.411-0.430 (0.0162-0.0169)	54	54	56	56	58	58	60	60	62	62	64	64	66	66	68	68	70	70	72	72	74	76	78	80	80	80				
0.431-0.450 (0.0170-0.0177)	56	56	58	58	60	60	62	62	64	64	66	66	68	68	70	70	72	72	74	74	76	78	80	80	80					
0.451-0.470 (0.0178-0.0185)	58	58	60	60	62	62	64	64	66	66	68	68	70	70	72	72	74	74	76	76	78	80	80	80						
0.471-0.490 (0.0185-0.0193)	60	60	62	62	64	64	66	66	68	68	70	70	72	72	74	74	76	76	78	78	80	80	80							
0.491-0.510 (0.0193-0.0201)	62	62	64	64	66	66	68	68	70	70	72	72	74	74	76	76	78	78	80	80	80	80								
0.511-0.530 (0.0201-0.0209)	64	64	66	66	68	68	70	70	72	72	74	74	76	76	78	78	80	80	80	80	80									
0.531-0.550 (0.0209-0.0217)	66	66	68	68	70	70	72	72	74	74	76	76	78	78	80	80	80	80	80	80										
0.551-0.570 (0.0217-0.0224)	68	68	70	70	72	72	74	74	76	76	78	78	80	80	80	80	80	80	80											
0.571-0.590 (0.0225-0.0232)	70	70	72	72	74	74	76	76	78	78	80	80	80	80	80	80	80													
0.591-0.610 (0.0233-0.0240)	72	72	74	74	76	76	78	78	80	80	80	80	80	80	80															
0.611-0.630 (0.0241-0.0248)	74	74	76	76	78	78	80	80	80	80	80	80	80																	
0.631-0.650 (0.0248-0.0256)	76	76	78	78	80	80	80	80	80	80	80																			
0.651-0.670 (0.0256-0.0264)	78	78	80	80	80	80	80	80	80																					
0.671-0.690 (0.0264-0.0272)	80	80	80	80	80	80	80																							
0.691-0.710 (0.0272-0.0280)	80	80	80	80	80																									
0.711-0.730 (0.0280-0.0287)	80	80	80																											
0.731-0.750 (0.0288-0.0295)	80																													

New shim thickness mm (in.)

Shim No.	Thickness	Shim No.	Thickness	Shim No.	Thickness
00	2.000 (0.0787)	28	2.280 (0.0898)	56	2.560 (0.1008)
02	2.020 (0.0795)	30	2.300 (0.0906)	58	2.580 (0.1016)
04	2.040 (0.0803)	32	2.320 (0.0913)	60	2.600 (0.1024)
06	2.060 (0.0811)	34	2.340 (0.0921)	62	2.620 (0.1031)
08	2.080 (0.0819)	36	2.360 (0.0929)	64	2.640 (0.1039)
10	2.100 (0.0827)	38	2.380 (0.0937)	66	2.660 (0.1047)
12	2.120 (0.0835)	40	2.400 (0.0945)	68	2.680 (0.1055)
14	2.140 (0.0843)	42	2.420 (0.0953)	70	2.700 (0.1063)
16	2.160 (0.0850)	44	2.440 (0.0961)	72	2.720 (0.1071)
18	2.180 (0.0858)	46	2.460 (0.0969)	74	2.740 (0.1079)
20	2.200 (0.0866)	48	2.480 (0.0976)	76	2.760 (0.1087)
22	2.220 (0.0874)	50	2.500 (0.0984)	78	2.780 (0.1094)
24	2.240 (0.0882)	52	2.520 (0.0992)	80	2.800 (0.1102)
26	2.260 (0.0890)	54	2.540 (0.1000)		

Exhaust valve clearance (Cold):
0.25 – 0.35 mm (0.010 – 0.014 in.)

EXAMPLE:
The 2.300 mm (0.0906 in.) shim is installed, and the measured clearance is 0.440 mm (0.0173 in.). Replace the 2.300 mm (0.0906 in.) shim with a No. 44 shim.

7924SG72

Fig. 144 Exhaust valve clearance shim selection chart—2UZ-FE engine

ENGINE TUNE-UP SPECIFICATIONS

Year	Engine ID/VIN	Engine Displacement Liters (cc)	Spark Plug Gap (in.)	Ignition Timing (deg.) MT	Ignition Timing (deg.) AT	Fuel Pump (psi)	Idle Speed (rpm) MT	Idle Speed (rpm) AT	Valve Clearance In.	Valve Clearance Ex.
1997	1FZ-FE	4.5 (4477)	0.043	-	5-15B ②	28-34 ①	-	650-750	0.006-0.010	0.010-0.014
	3RZ-FE	2.7 (2694)	0.031	3-7B ②	3-7B ②	31-37 ①	650-750	650-750	0.006-0.010	0.010-0.014
	5VZ-FE	3.4 (3378)	0.043	8-12B ②	8-12B ②	33-38 ①	650-750	650-750	0.006-0.009	0.011-0.014
	2RZ-FE	2.4 (2438)	0.031	3-7B ②	3-7B ②	31-37 ①	650-750	650-750	0.006-0.010	0.010-0.014
1998	2UZ-FE	4.7 (4663)	0.043	-	5-15B ②	38-44 ①	-	650-750	0.006-0.010	0.010-0.014
	3RZ-FE	2.7 (2694)	0.031	3-7B ②	3-7B ②	31-37 ①	650-750	650-750	0.006-0.010	0.010-0.014
	5VZ-FE	3.4 (3378)	0.043	8-12B ②	8-12B ②	33-38 ①	650-750	650-750	0.006-0.009	0.011-0.014
	2RZ-FE	2.4 (2438)	0.031	3-7B ②	3-7B ②	31-37 ①	650-750	650-750	0.006-0.010	0.010-0.014
1999	2UZ-FE	4.7 (4663)	0.043	-	5-15B ②	38-44 ①	650-750	650-750	0.006-0.010	0.010-0.014
	3RZ-FE	2.7 (2694)	0.031	3-7B ②	3-7B ②	31-37 ①	650-750	650-750	0.006-0.010	0.010-0.014
	5VZ-FE	3.4 (3378)	0.043	3-19B ②	3-19B ②	33-38 ①	650-750	650-750	0.006-0.009	0.011-0.014
	2RZ-FE	2.4 (2438)	0.031	3-7B ②	3-7B ②	31-37 ①	650-750	650-750	0.006-0.010	0.010-0.014
2000	2UZ-FE	4.7 (4663)	0.043	-	5-15B ②	38-44 ①	650-750	650-750	0.006-0.010	0.010-0.014
	3RZ-FE	2.7 (2694)	0.031	3-7B ②	3-7B ②	31-37 ①	650-750	650-750	0.006-0.010	0.010-0.014
	5VZ-FE	3.4 (3378)	0.043	3-19B ②	3-19B ②	33-38 ①	650-750	650-750	0.006-0.009	0.011-0.014
	2RZ-FE	2.4 (2438)	0.031	3-7B ②	3-7B ②	31-37 ①	650-750	650-750	0.006-0.010	0.010-0.014

NOTE: The Vehicle Emission Control Information label reflects specification changes during production and must be used if they differ from this chart.

B - Before Top Dead Center

① At idle, pressure regulator vacuum hose and fuel lines all connected

② Timing with TW1 and E1 Connected

93161c03

3. Remove the V-bank cover.
4. Remove the air cleaner and duct assembly.
5. Remove the No. 3 timing belt covers.
6. Remove the ignition coils.
7. Remove the cylinder head covers.
8. Turn the crankshaft so the No. 1 piston is at TDC on compression (1st position). Be sure the camshaft timing marks align with the marks on the rear covers.
9. Measure the clearance with a feeler gauge of the valves indicated and record the measurement of any valve out of specification.
   - Intake—0.006–0.010 inch (0.15–0.25mm)
   - Exhaust—0.010–0.014 inch (0.25–0.35mm)
10. Turn the crankshaft one revolution and measure the clearance of the valves indicated (2nd position). Record the measurement of any valves out of specification.

➡The camshafts must be removed to allow access to the adjusting shims.

11. Remove the timing belt and camshafts.
12. Remove the valve lifter and adjusting shim.
13. Using a micrometer, measure the thickness of the removed shim. Calculate the thickness of a new shim so that the valve clearance comes within the specified value.
14. Determine the size of the replacement shim by using the following formula, or the adjusting shim charts.
   - T = Thickness of the removed shim
   - A = Measured valve clearance
   - N = Thickness of the new shim
   a. Intake: N = T + (A - 0.008 in. (0.20mm))
   b. Exhaust: N = T + (A - 0.012 in. (0.30mm))
15. Install the lifter with the new shim.
16. Install the camshafts and timing belt.
17. Recheck the valve clearance.
18. Install the cylinder head covers.
19. Install the ignition coils and the No. 3 timing belt covers.
20. Install the air cleaner and duct assembly.
21. Refill the cooling system.
22. Start the engine and check for leaks.
23. Install the V-bank cover.
24. Recheck the coolant level.
25. Install the battery clamp cover.

Idle Speed and Mixture Adjustments

MIXTURE ADJUSTMENT

On fuel injected engines, fuel mixture is handled by the computer, based on signals from the oxygen sensor in the exhaust system and many other engine sensors. By having a 'picture' of the engine operating conditions at any given moment, the computer determines the exact amount of fuel to maintain proper combustion and signals the injectors accordingly. Any investigation of the air/fuel mixture on a fuel injected engine requires the use of an HC/CO emissions tester, which is well out of the reach of the home mechanic.

IDLE SPEED ADJUSTMENT

The idle speed on fuel injected engines is electronically controlled by the Engine Control Module (ECM) computer. The Idle Speed Control (ISC) system electrically oversees the proper idle speed for all operating conditions. There are no adjustments possible with this system. Any roughness or uneven idle is almost always due to other causes such as a clogged injector, air leak or loose, corroded terminals in the wiring harness, etc.

Air Conditioning System

SYSTEM SERVICE & REPAIR

➡It is recommended that the A/C system be serviced by an EPA Section 609 certified automotive technician utilizing a refrigerant recovery/recycling machine.

The do-it-yourselfer should not service his/her own vehicle's A/C system for many reasons, including legal concerns, personal injury, environmental damage and cost.

According to the U.S. Clean Air Act, it is a federal crime to service or repair (involving the refrigerant) a Motor Vehicle Air Conditioning (MVAC) system for money without being EPA certified. It is also illegal to vent R-134a refrigerant into the atmosphere. State and/or local laws may be more strict than the federal regulations, so be sure to check with your state and/or local authorities for further information.

➡Federal law dictates that a fine of up to $25,000 may be levied on people convicted of venting refrigerant into the atmosphere.

When servicing an A/C system you run the risk of handling or coming in contact with refrigerant, which may result in skin or eye irritation or frostbite. Although low in toxicity (due to chemical stability), inhalation of concentrated refrigerant fumes is dangerous and can result in death; cases of fatal cardiac arrhythmia have been reported in people accidentally subjected to high levels of refrigerant. Some early symptoms include loss of concentration and drowsiness.

Also, some refrigerants can decompose at high temperatures (near gas heaters or open flame), which may result in hydrofluoric acid, hydrochloric acid and phosgene (a fatal nerve gas).

It is usually more economically feasible to have a certified MVAC automotive technician perform A/C system service on your vehicle.

PREVENTIVE MAINTENANCE

Although the A/C system should not be serviced by the do-it-yourselfer, preventive maintenance should be practiced to help maintain the efficiency of the vehicle's A/C system. Be sure to perform the following:

- The easiest and most important preventive maintenance for your A/C system is to be sure that it is used on a regular basis. Running the system for five minutes each month (no matter what the season) will help ensure that the seals and all internal components remain lubricated.

➡Some vehicles automatically operate the A/C system compressor whenever the windshield defroster is activated. Therefore, the A/C system would not need to be operated each month if the defroster was used.

- In order to prevent heater core freeze-up during A/C operation, it is necessary to maintain proper antifreeze protection. Be sure to properly maintain the engine cooling system.
- Any obstruction of or damage to the condenser configuration will restrict air flow which is essential to its efficient operation. Keep this unit clean and in proper physical shape.

➡Bug screens which are mounted in front of the condenser (unless they are original equipment) are regarded as obstructions.

- The condensation drain tube expels any water which accumulates on the bottom of the evaporator housing into the engine compartment. If this tube is obstructed, the air conditioning performance can be restricted and condensation buildup can spill over onto the vehicle's floor.

SYSTEM INSPECTION

Although the A/C system should not be serviced by the do-it-yourselfer, system inspections should be performed to help maintain the efficiency of the vehicle's A/C system. Be sure to perform the following:

The easiest and often most important check for the air conditioning system consists of a visual inspection of the system components. Visually inspect the system for refrigerant leaks, damaged compressor clutch, abnormal compressor drive belt tension and/or condition, plugged evaporator drain tube, blocked condenser fins, disconnected or broken wires, blown fuses, corroded connections and poor insulation.

A refrigerant leak will usually appear as an oily residue at the leakage point in the system. The oily residue soon picks up dust or dirt particles from the surrounding air and appears greasy. Through time, this will build up and appear to be a heavy dirt impregnated grease.

For a thorough visual and operational inspection, check the following:

- Check the surface of the radiator and condenser for dirt, leaves or other material which might block air flow.
- Check for kinks in hoses and lines. Check the system for leaks.
- Make sure the drive belt is properly tensioned. During operation, make sure the belt is free of noise or slippage.
- Make sure the blower motor operates at all appropriate positions, then check for distribution of the air from all outlets.

➡Remember that in high humidity, air discharged from the vents may not feel as cold as expected, even if the system is working properly. This is because moisture in humid air retains heat more effectively than dry air, thereby making humid air more difficult to cool.

Windshield Wipers

ELEMENT (REFILL) CARE & REPLACEMENT

➧ See Figures 145, 146, and 147

For maximum effectiveness and longest element life, the windshield and wiper blades should be kept clean. Dirt, tree sap, road tar and so on will cause streaking, smearing and blade deterioration if left on the glass. It is advisable to wash the windshield carefully with a commercial glass cleaner at least once a month. Wipe off the rubber blades with the wet rag afterwards. Do not attempt to move wipers across the windshield by hand; damage to the motor and drive mechanism will result.

To inspect and/or replace the wiper blade elements, place the wiper switch in the **LOW** speed position and the ignition switch in the **ACC** position. When the wiper blades are approximately vertical on the windshield, turn the ignition switch to **OFF**.

Examine the wiper blade elements. If they are found to be cracked, broken or torn, they should be replaced immediately. Replacement intervals will vary with usage, although ozone deterioration usually limits element life to about one year. If the wiper pattern is smeared or streaked, or if the blade chatters across the glass, the elements should be replaced. It is easiest and most sensible to replace the elements in pairs.

If your vehicle is equipped with aftermarket blades, there are several different types of refills and your vehicle might have any kind. Aftermarket blades and arms rarely use the exact same type blade or refill as the original equipment.

Regardless of the type of refill used, be sure to follow the part manufacturer's instructions closely. Make sure that all of the frame jaws are engaged as the refill is pushed into place and locked. If the metal blade holder and frame are allowed to touch the glass during wiper operation, the glass will be scratched.

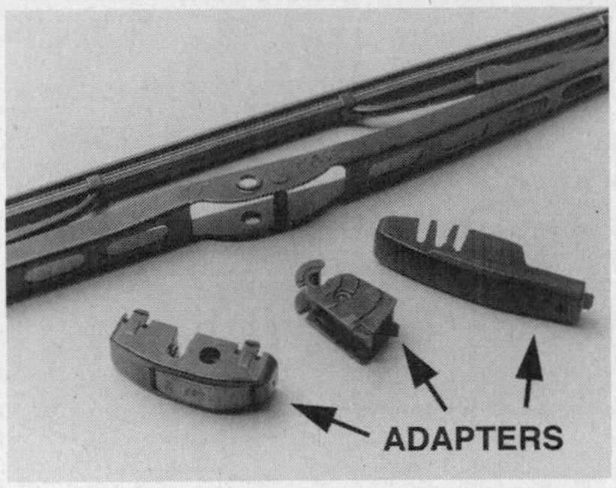

tccs1223

Fig. 145 Most aftermarket blades are available with multiple adapters to fit different vehicles

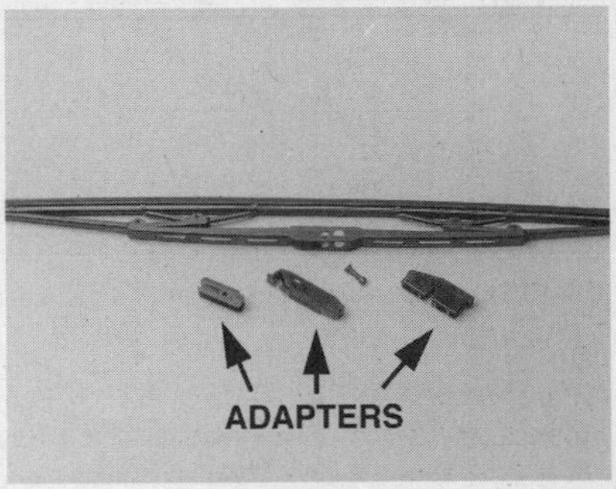

tccs1224

Fig. 146 Choose a blade which will fit your vehicle, and that will be readily available next time you need blades

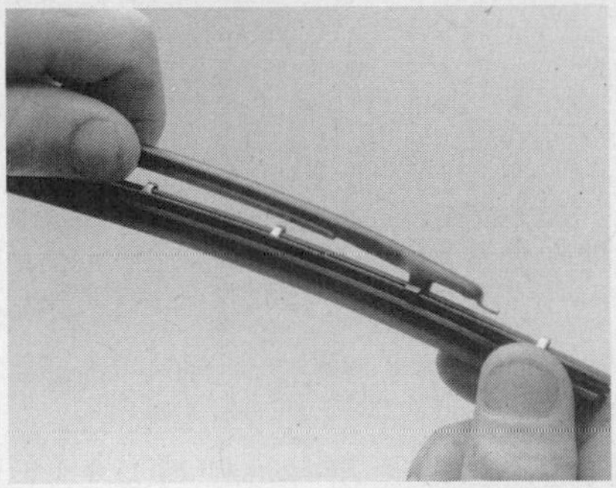

tccs1231

Fig. 147 When installed, be certain the blade is fully inserted into the backing

Tires and Wheels

Common sense and good driving habits will afford maximum tire life. Make sure that you don't overload the vehicle or run with incorrect pressure in the tires. Either of these will increase tread wear. Fast starts, sudden stops and sharp cornering are hard on tires and will shorten their useful life span.

➡For optimum tire life, keep the tires properly inflated, rotate them often and have the wheel alignment checked periodically.

Inspect your tires frequently. Be especially careful to watch for bubbles in the tread or sidewall, deep cuts or underinflation. Replace any tires with bubbles in the sidewall. If cuts are so deep that they penetrate to the cords, discard the tire. Any cut in the sidewall of a radial tire renders it unsafe. Also look for uneven tread wear patterns that may indicate the front end is out of alignment or that the tires are out of balance.

TIRE ROTATION

➧ See Figure 148

Tires must be rotated periodically to equalize wear patterns that vary with a tire's position on the vehicle. Tires will also wear in an uneven way as the front steering/suspension system wears to the point where the alignment should be reset.

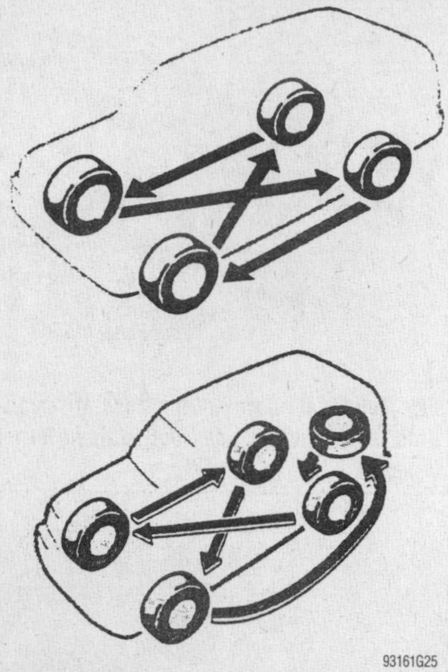

Fig. 148 Toyota's recommended four wheel (top) and five wheel (bottom) tire rotation pattern

Rotating the tires will ensure maximum life for the tires as a set, so you will not have to discard a tire early due to wear on only part of the tread. Regular rotation is required to equalize wear.

When rotating "unidirectional tires," make sure that they always roll in the same direction. This means that a tire used on the left side of the vehicle must not be switched to the right side and vice-versa. Such tires should only be rotated front-to-rear or rear-to-front, while always remaining on the same side of the vehicle. These tires are marked on the sidewall as to the direction of rotation; observe the marks when reinstalling the tire(s).

Some styled or "mag" wheels may have different offsets front to rear. In these cases, the rear wheels must not be used up front and vice-versa. Furthermore, if these wheels are equipped with unidirectional tires, they cannot be rotated unless the tire is remounted for the proper direction of rotation.

➡The compact or space-saver spare is strictly for emergency use. It must never be included in the tire rotation or placed on the vehicle for everyday use.

TIRE DESIGN

See Figure 149

For maximum satisfaction, tires should be used in sets of four. Mixing of different brands or types (radial, bias-belted, fiberglass belted) should be avoided. In most cases, the vehicle manufacturer has designated a type of tire on which the vehicle will perform best. Your first choice when replacing tires should be to use the same type of tire that the manufacturer recommends.

When radial tires are used, tire sizes and wheel diameters should be selected to maintain ground clearance and tire load capacity equivalent to the original specified tire. Radial tires should always be used in sets of four.

CAUTION

Radial tires should never be used on only the front axle.

When selecting tires, pay attention to the original size as marked on the tire. Most tires are described using an industry size code sometimes referred to as P-Metric. This allows the exact identification of the tire specifications, regardless of the manufacturer. If selecting a different tire size or brand, remember to check the installed tire for any sign of interference with the body or suspension while the vehicle is stopping, turning sharply or heavily loaded.

Snow Tires

Good radial tires can produce a big advantage in slippery weather, but in snow, a street radial tire does not have sufficient tread to provide traction and control. The small grooves of a street tire quickly pack with snow and the tire behaves like a billiard ball on a marble floor. The more open, chunky tread of a snow tire will self-clean as the tire turns, providing much better grip on snowy surfaces.

To satisfy municipalities requiring snow tires during weather emergencies, most snow tires carry either an M + S designation after the tire size stamped on the sidewall, or the designation "all-season." In general, no change in tire size is necessary when buying snow tires.

Most manufacturers strongly recommend the use of 4 snow tires on their vehicles for reasons of stability. If snow tires are fitted only to the drive wheels, the opposite end of the vehicle may become very unstable when braking or turning on slippery surfaces. This instability can lead to unpleasant endings if the driver can't counteract the slide in time.

Note that snow tires, whether 2 or 4, will affect vehicle handling in all non-snow situations. The stiffer, heavier snow tires will noticeably change the turning and braking characteristics of the vehicle. Once the snow tires are installed, you must re-learn the behavior of the vehicle and drive accordingly.

➡Consider buying extra wheels on which to mount the snow tires. Once done, the "snow wheels" can be installed and removed as needed. This eliminates the potential damage to tires or wheels from seasonal removal and installation. Even if your vehicle has styled wheels, see if inexpensive steel wheels are available. Although the look of the vehicle will change, the expensive wheels will be protected from salt, curb hits and pothole damage.

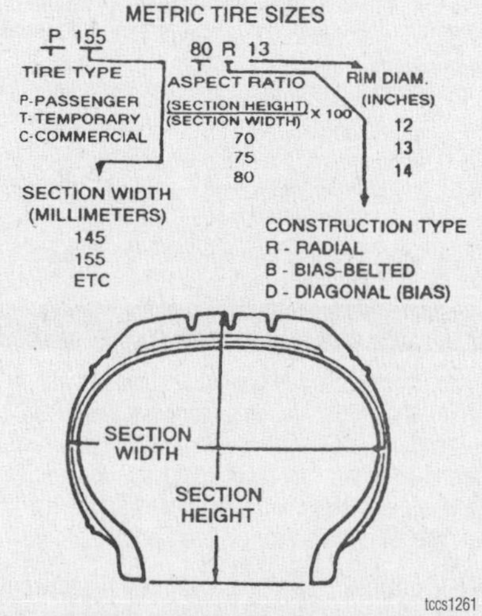

Fig. 149 P-Metric tire coding

TIRE STORAGE

If they are mounted on wheels, store the tires at proper inflation pressure. All tires should be kept in a cool, dry place. If they are stored in the garage or basement, do not let them stand on a concrete floor; set them on strips of wood, a mat or a large stack of newspaper. Keeping them away from direct moisture is of paramount importance. Tires should not be stored upright, but in a flat position.

INFLATION & INSPECTION

See Figures 150 thru 155

The importance of proper tire inflation cannot be overemphasized. A tire employs air as part of its structure. It is designed around the supporting strength of the air at a specified pressure. For this reason, improper inflation drastically reduces the tire's ability to perform as intended. A tire will lose some air in day-to-day use; having to add a few pounds of air periodically is not necessarily a sign of a leaking tire.

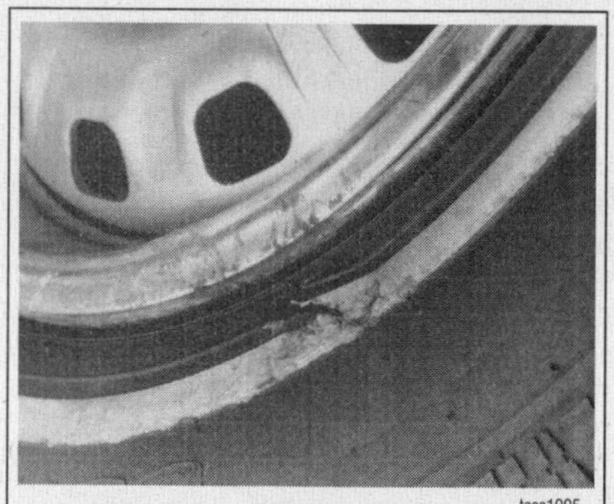

Fig. 150 Tires with deep cuts, or cuts which bulge, should be replaced immediately

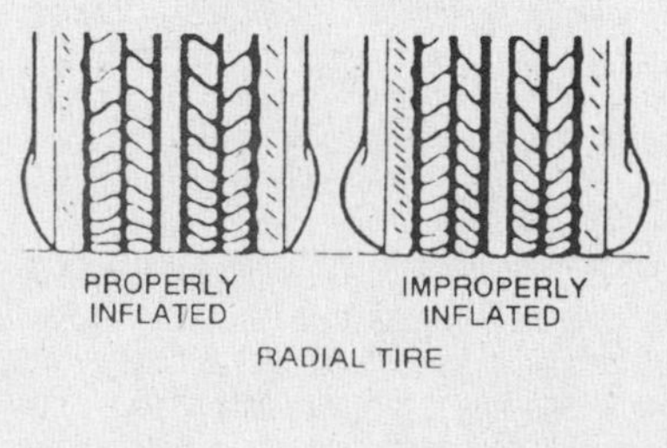

Fig. 151 Radial tires have a characteristic sidewall bulge; don't try to measure pressure by looking at the tire. Use a quality air pressure gauge

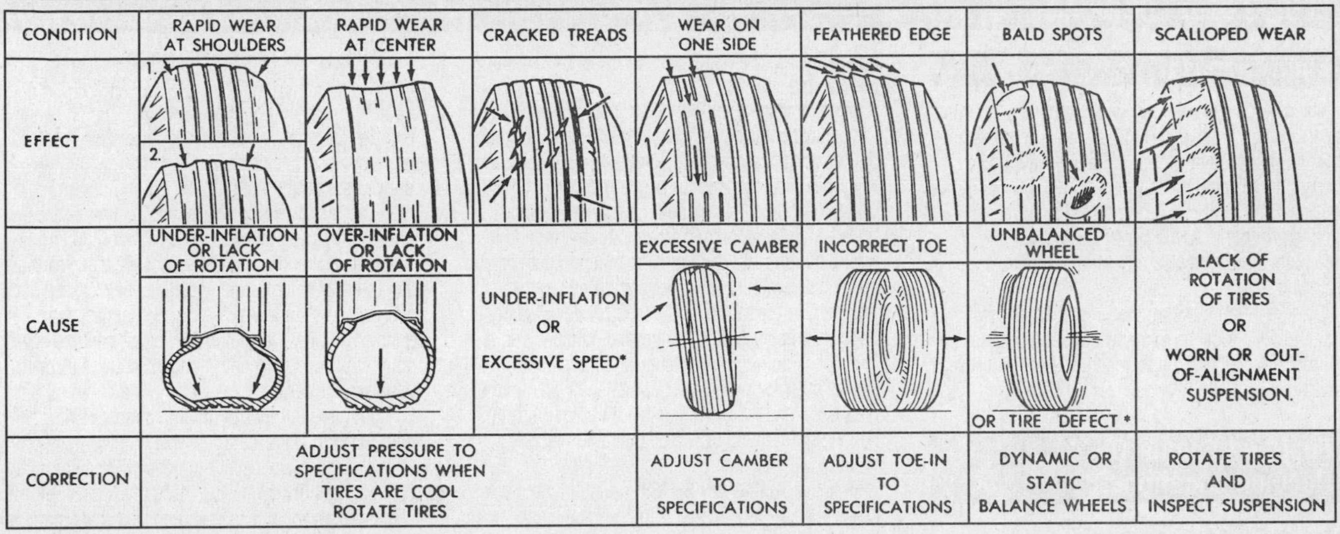

CONDITION
RAPID WEAR AT SHOULDERS
RAPID WEAR AT CENTER
CRACKED TREADS
WEAR ON ONE SIDE
FEATHERED EDGE
BALD SPOTS
SCALLOPED WEAR
EFFECT
1.
2.
CAUSE
UNDER-INFLATION OR LACK OF ROTATION
OVER-INFLATION OR LACK OF ROTATION
UNDER-INFLATION OR EXCESSIVE SPEED*
EXCESSIVE CAMBER
INCORRECT TOE
UNBALANCED WHEEL
OR TIRE DEFECT *
LACK OF ROTATION OF TIRES OR WORN OR OUT-OF-ALIGNMENT SUSPENSION.
CORRECTION
ADJUST PRESSURE TO SPECIFICATIONS WHEN TIRES ARE COOL ROTATE TIRES
ADJUST CAMBER TO SPECIFICATIONS
ADJUST TOE-IN TO SPECIFICATIONS
DYNAMIC OR STATIC BALANCE WHEELS
ROTATE TIRES AND INSPECT SUSPENSION

*HAVE TIRE INSPECTED FOR FURTHER USE.

tccs1267

Fig. 152 Common tire wear patterns and causes

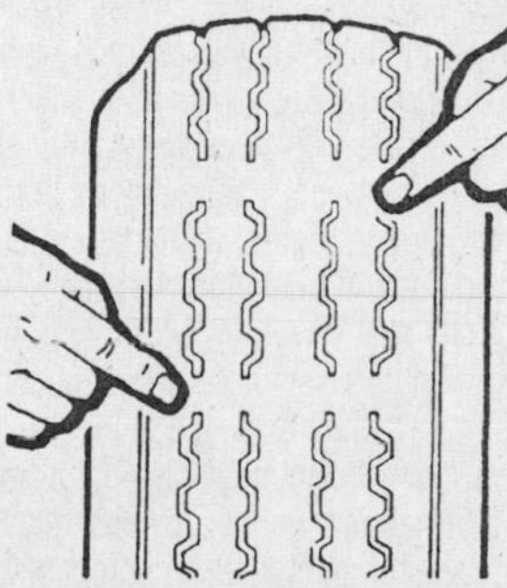

tccs1265

Fig. 153 Tread wear indicators will appear when the tire is worn

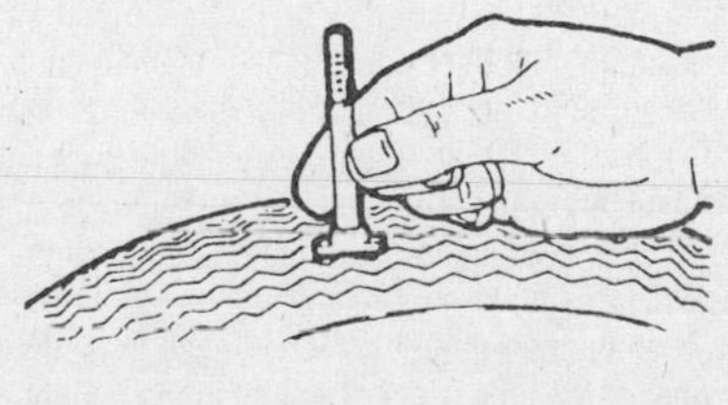

tccs1264

Fig. 154 Accurate tread depth indicators are inexpensive and handy

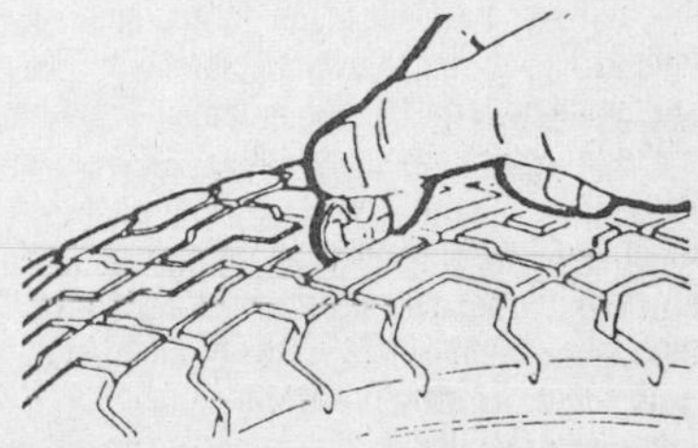

tccs1266

Fig. 155 A penny works well for a quick check of tread depth

Two items should be a permanent fixture in every glove compartment: an accurate tire pressure gauge and a tread depth gauge. Check the tire pressure (including the spare) regularly with a pocket type gauge. Too often, the gauge on the end of the air hose at your corner garage is not accurate because it suffers too much abuse. Always check tire pressure when the tires are cold, as pressure increases with temperature. If you must move the vehicle to check the tire inflation, do not drive more than a mile before checking. A cold tire is generally one that has not been driven for more than three hours.

A plate or sticker is normally provided somewhere in the vehicle (door post, hood, tailgate or trunk lid) which shows the proper pressure for the tires. Never counteract excessive pressure build-up by bleeding off air pressure (letting some air out). This will cause the tire to run hotter and wear quicker.

CAUTION

Never exceed the maximum tire pressure embossed on the tire! This is the pressure to be used when the tire is at maximum loading, but it is rarely the correct pressure for everyday driving. Consult the owner's manual or the tire pressure sticker for the correct tire pressure.

Once you've maintained the correct tire pressures for several weeks, you'll be familiar with the vehicle's braking and handling personality. Slight adjustments in tire pressures can fine-tune these characteristics, but never change the cold pressure specification by more than 2 psi. A slightly softer tire pressure will give a softer ride but also yield lower fuel mileage. A slightly harder tire will give crisper dry road handling but can cause skidding on wet surfaces. Unless you're fully attuned to the vehicle, stick to the recommended inflation pressures.

All automotive tires have built-in tread wear indicator bars that show up as $^1/_2$ in. (13mm) wide smooth bands across the tire when $^1/_{16}$ in. (1.5mm) of tread remains. The appearance of tread wear indicators means that the tires should be replaced. In fact, many states have laws prohibiting the use of tires with less than this amount of tread.

You can check your own tread depth with an inexpensive gauge or by using a Lincoln head penny. Slip the Lincoln penny (with Lincoln's head upside-down) into several tread grooves. If you can see the top of Lincoln's head in 2 adjacent grooves, the tire has less than $^1/_{16}$ in. (1.5mm) tread left and should be replaced. You can measure snow tires in the same manner by using the "tails" side of the Lincoln penny. If you can see the top of the Lincoln memorial, it's time to replace the snow tire(s).

FLUIDS AND LUBRICANTS

Fluid Disposal

Used fluids such as engine oil, transmission fluid, antifreeze and brake fluid are hazardous wastes and must be disposed of properly. Before draining any fluids, consult with your local authorities; in many areas, waste oil, etc. is being accepted as a part of recycling programs. A number of service stations and auto parts stores are also accepting waste fluids for recycling.

Be sure of the recycling center's policies before draining any fluids, as many will not accept different fluids that have been mixed together, such as oil and antifreeze.

Fuel and Engine Oil Recommendations

GENERAL INFORMATION

Engine Oil

➧ **See Figures 156 and 157**

The SAE (Society of Automotive Engineers) grade number indicates the viscosity of the engine oil; its resistance to flow at a given temperature. The lower the SAE grade number, the lighter the oil. For example, the mono-grade oils begin with SAE 5 weight, which is a thin, light oil, and continue in viscosity up to SAE 80 or 90 weight, which are heavy gear lubricants. These oils are also known as 'straight weight', meaning they are of a single viscosity, and do not vary with engine temperature.

Multi-viscosity oils offer the important advantage of being adaptable to temperature extremes. These oils have designations such as 10W–40, 20W–50, etc. The '10W–40' means that in winter (the 'W' in the designation) the oil acts like a thin 10 weight oil, allowing the engine to spin easily when cold and offering rapid lubrication. Once the engine has warmed up, however, the oil acts like a straight 40 weight, maintaining good lubrication and protection for the engine's internal components. A 20W–50 oil would therefore be slightly heavier than and not as ideal in cold weather as the 10W–40, but would offer better protection at higher rpm and temperatures because when warm it acts like a 50 weight oil. Whichever oil viscosity you choose when changing the oil, make sure you are anticipating the temperatures your engine will be operating in until the oil is changed again. Refer to the oil viscosity chart for oil recommendations according to temperature.

The API (American Petroleum Institute) designation indicates the classification of engine oil used under certain given operating conditions. Only oils designated for use 'Service SJ' or greater should be used. Oils of the SJ type perform a variety of functions inside the engine in addition to the basic function as a lubricant. Through a balanced system of metallic detergents and polymeric dispersants, the oil prevents the formation of high and low temperature deposits and also keeps sludge and particles of dirt in suspension. Acids, particularly sulfuric acid, as well as other by-products of combustion, are neutralized. Both the SAE grade number and the API designation can be found on the oil bottle. For recommended oil viscosities, refer to the chart.

Toyota specifies API SH (SJ starting in 1999 vehicles) "Energy-Conserving II" multi-grade engine oil be used in their engines. Toyota says that SAE 5W–30 is the best choice for good fuel economy and good starting in cold weather. SAE 10W–30 can also be used by Toyota says that extremely low temperatures, the engine may become difficult to start, so SAE 5W-30 engine oil is recommended. If you have any questions about engine oil, please consult your Owner's Manual for the latest recommendations specific to your vehicle.

Remember that Over Head Camshaft (OHC) engines as used in these vehicles have a lot of moving parts. The camshaft lifters and camshaft bearings need lubrication as soon as the engine begins to turn. In cold weather, an oil with too heavy a weight (thicker viscosity) takes a long time to get to the more remote parts of the engine. An engine can be badly damaged in the time it takes thick oil to reach all of the locations in an engine, especially those the greatest distance from the oil pump. Use the oil recommended in your Owner's Manual.

SYNTHETIC OIL

There are many excellent synthetic oils currently available that can provide better gas mileage, longer service life, and in some cases better engine protection. These benefits do not come without a few hitches, however; the main one being the price of synthetic oils, which is three or four times the price per quart of conventional oil.

Synthetic oil is not for every truck and every type of driving, so you should consider your engine's condition and your type of driving. Also, check your truck's warranty conditions regarding the use of synthetic oils.

Both brand new engines and older, high mileage engines are often the wrong candidates for synthetic oil. A synthetic oil can be so slippery that they can prevent the proper break-in of new engines; most manufacturers recommend that you wait until the engine is properly broken in 3000 miles (4830 km) before using synthetic oil. Older engines with wear have a different problem with synthetics: they leak more oil as they age. Slippery synthetic oils get past worn parts easily. If your truck is leaking oil past old seals you'll most probably have a much greater leak problem with synthetics.

Consider your type of driving. If most of your accumulated mileage is high speed, highway type driving, the more expensive synthetic oils may be a benefit. Extended highway driving gives the engine a chance to warm up, accumulating less acids in the oil and putting less stress on the engine over the long run. Trucks with synthetic oils may show increased fuel economy in highway driving, due to less internal friction.

If synthetic oil is used, it should still be replaced at regular intervals as stated in the maintenance schedule. While the oil itself will last much longer than regular oil, pollutants such as soot, water and unburned fuel still accumulate within the oil. These are the damaging elements within a motor and must be drained regularly to prevent damage.

Trucks used under harder circumstances, such as stop-and-go, city type driving, short trips, or extended idling, should be serviced more frequently. For the engines in these trucks, the much greater cost of synthetic or fuel-efficient oils may not be worth the investment. Internal wear increases much quicker on these trucks, causing greater oil consumption and leakage.

Fuel

Your Toyota truck is designed to use unleaded gasoline only. Do not use leaded gasoline. Use of any leaded gasoline will cause the three-way catalytic converter to lose its effectiveness and the emission control system to function improperly. This can lead to expensive repairs.

It is important to use fuel of the proper octane rating in your truck. Octane rating is based on the quantity of anti-knock compounds added to the fuel and it determines the speed at which the gas will burn. The lower the octane rating, the faster it burns. The higher

tccs1235

Fig. 156 Look for the API oil identification label when choosing your engine oil

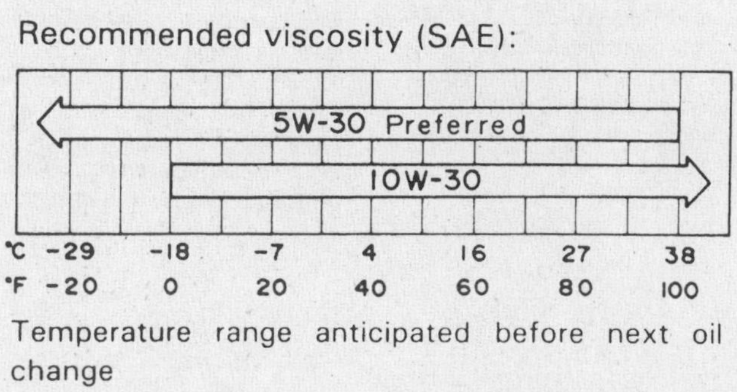

86821236

Fig. 157 Engine oil viscosity chart

the octane, the slower the fuel will burn and a greater percentage of compounds in the fuel prevent spark ping (knock), detonation and pre-ignition (dieseling).

As the temperature of the engine increases, the air/fuel mixture exhibits a tendency to ignite before the spark plug is fired. If fuel of an octane rating too low for the engine is used, this will allow combustion to occur before the piston has completed its compression stroke, thereby creating a very high pressure very rapidly.

Toyota's octane recommendations depends on the vehicle model and even. Some vehicles can use gasoline with an Octane Rating of 87. Others require an Octane Rating of 91 or higher. Consult your Owner's manual. Use of unleaded fuel with an octane number lower than recommended will cause persistent heavy knocking. If severe, this will lead to engine damage.

Toyota says that heavy knocking, even when using the recommended fuel, or a steady knocking while holding a steady speed, should be investigated as there may be a problem with the engine. However, now and then, you may notice a light knocking for a short time while accelerating or driving up hills. This should be no cause for concern.

Toyota recommends the use of gasoline that contains detergent additives to avoid build-up of engine deposits. If you use gasohol in your Toyota, be sure that it is unleaded, has an octane rating no lower than 87 and does not contain more than 10 percent ethanol. Toyota does not recommend gasoline containing methanol. If you must use gasoline containing methanol, it must contain less than 5 percent methanol with cosolvents and corrosion inhibitors for methanol.

Engine

OIL LEVEL CHECK

➧ See Figures 158 thru 163

⁂ CAUTION

Prolonged and repeated skin contact with used engine oil, with no effort to remove the oil, may cause skin cancer. Always follow these simple precautions when handling used motor oil:

- Avoid prolonged skin contact with used motor oil.
- Remove oil from skin by washing thoroughly with soap and water or waterless hand cleaner. Do not use gasoline, thinners or other solvents.
- Avoid prolonged skin contact with oil-soaked clothing.

Every time you stop for fuel, check the engine oil as follows:

1. Park the truck on level ground.
2. When checking the oil level it is best for the engine to be at operating temperature, although checking the oil immediately after a stopping will lead to a false reading. Wait a few minutes after turning off the engine to allow the oil to drain back into the oil pan (crankcase).
3. Open the hood and locate the dipstick. Pull the dipstick from its tube, wipe it clean and reinsert it.
4. Pull the dipstick out again and, holding it horizontally, read the oil level. The oil should be between the **F** and **L** marks on the dipstick. If the oil is below the **L** mark, add oil of the proper viscosity through the capped opening on the top of the cylinder head cover.
5. Reinsert the dipstick and check the oil level again after adding any oil. Be careful not to overfill the crankcase. Approximately one quart of oil will raise the level from the **L** to the **F**. Excess oil will generally be consumed at an accelerated rate as well as hampering engine operation.

OIL AND FILTER CHANGE

➧ See Figures 164 thru 177

The oil and filter should be changed every 7,500 miles (12,000 km). The mileage figures given are the Toyota recommended intervals assuming normal driving and conditions. Normal driving requires that the vehicle be driven far enough to warm up the oil; usually this is about 10 miles (16 km) or so. If your everyday use is shorter than this (one way), your use qualifies as severe duty.

Severe duty includes dusty, polluted or off-road conditions, as well as stop-and-go short haul uses. Regularly towing a trailer also puts the truck in this category, as does constant operation with a near capacity load. Change the oil and filter at $^1/_2$ the normal interval. Half of 7,500 equals 3,250 miles (5,229 km); round it down to the easily remembered 3,000 mile (5,000 km) interval. For some owners, that may be once a month; for others, it may be six months.

⁂ CAUTION

Prolonged and repeated skin contact with used engine oil, with no effort to remove the oil, may cause skin cancer. Always follow these simple precautions when handling used motor oil:

93161p17

Fig. 158 Pull the engine oil dipstick from its tube

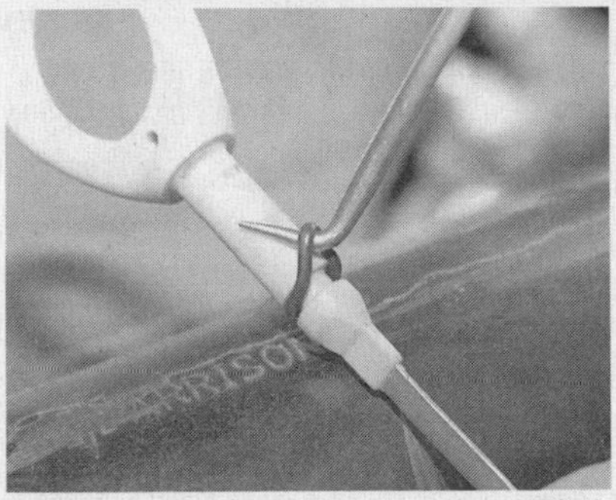
93161p18

Fig. 159 Periodically check the dipstick's O-ring for cracks or tears

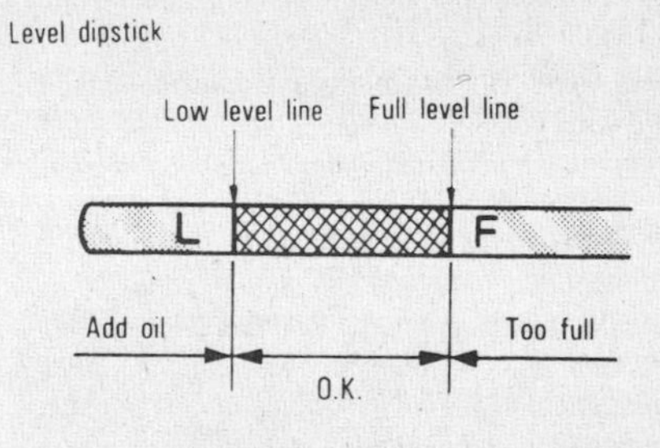

86821235

Fig. 160 Read the dipstick carefully, add oil when the level is below the L mark; do not overfill

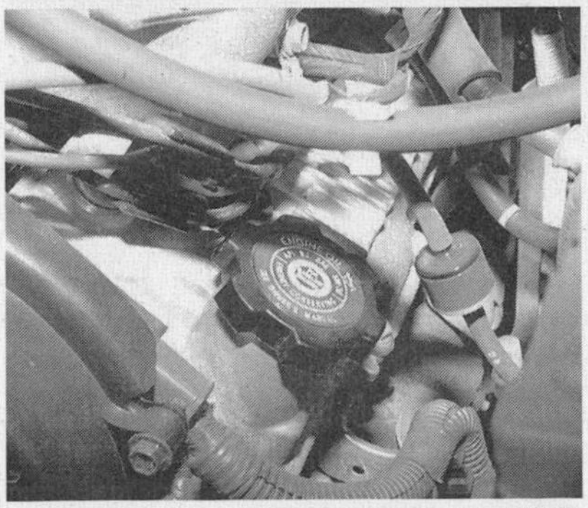
93161p15

Fig. 161 Location of the oil filler cap

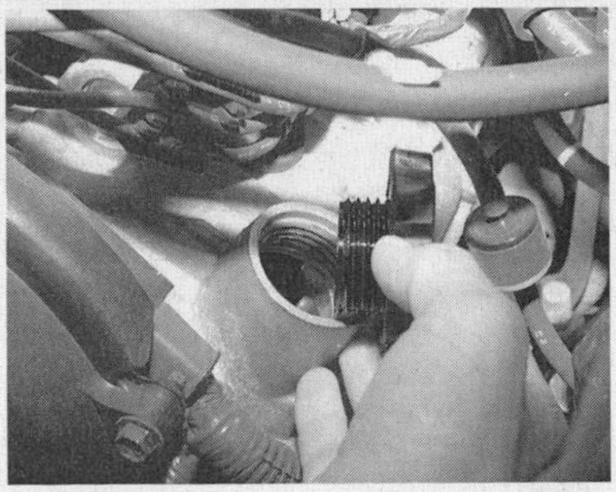
93161p16

Fig. 162 If engine oil level is low, remove the oil fill cap . . .

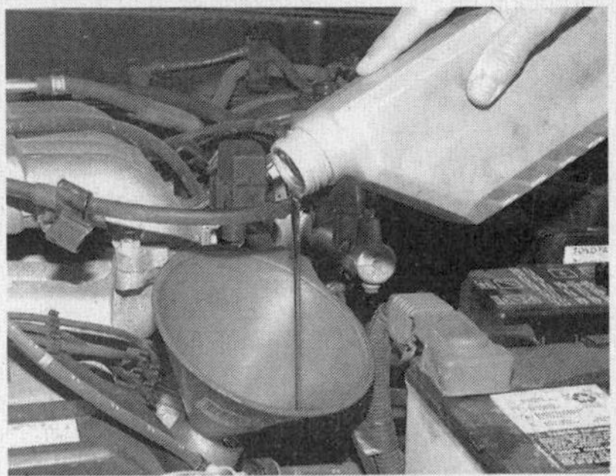
93161p59

Fig. 163 . . then add oil, using a funnel to prevent spills

Fig. 164 In order to change the oil and filter, you may have to remove the skid plate from the truck

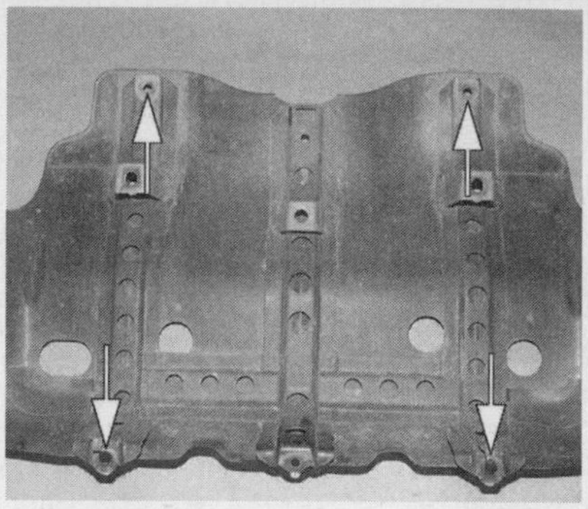

Fig. 165 View of the inside of the skid plate and its mounting points

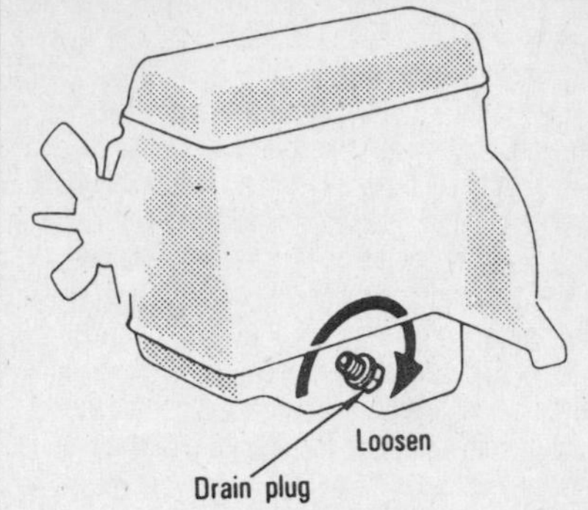

Fig. 166 Oil drain plug location—1FZ-FE Engine

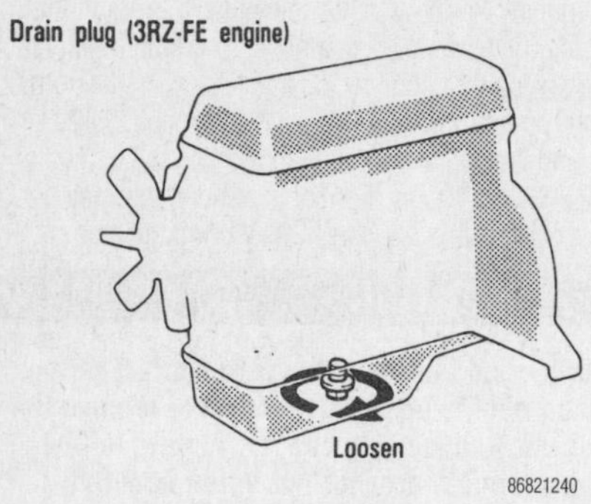

Fig. 167 Oil drain plug location—3RZ-FE Engine

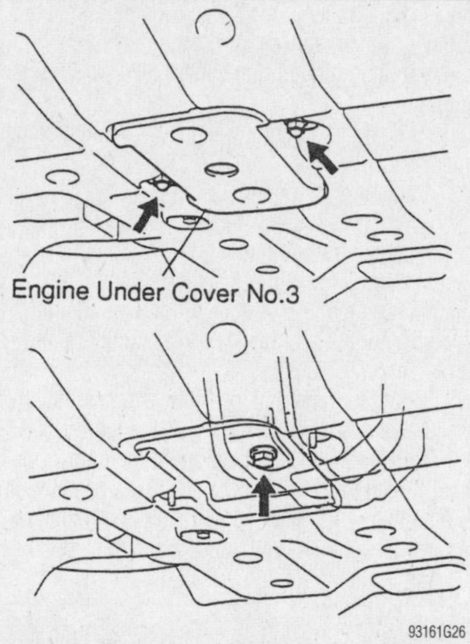

Fig. 168 The oil drain plug on this V8 powered Land Cruiser is behind Engine Under Cover No. 3—2UZ-FE Engine

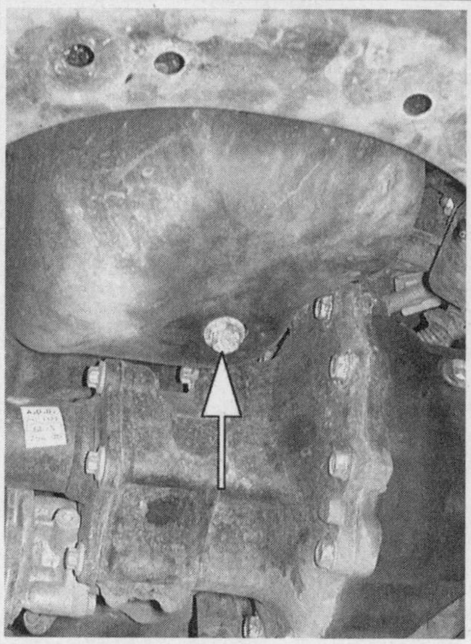

Fig. 169 Location of the engine oil drain plug on the 5VZ-FE engine

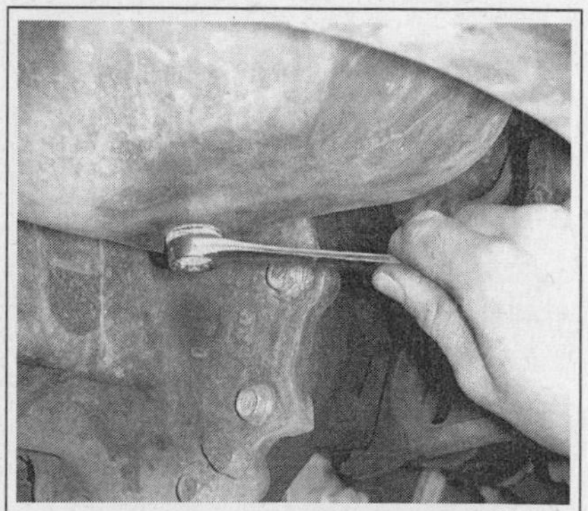

Fig. 170 Use a closed end wrench to loosen the engine oil drain plug

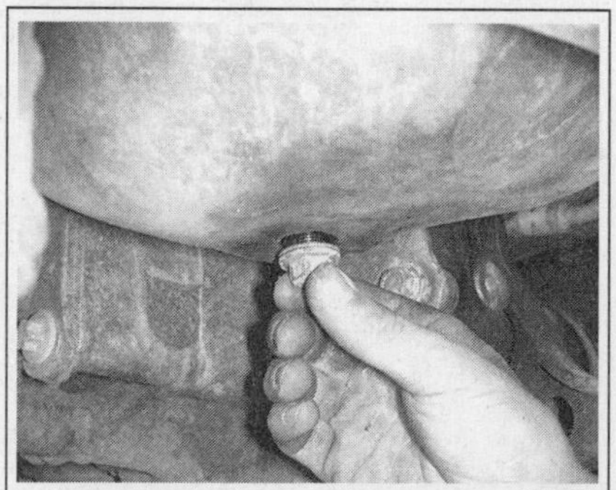

Fig. 171 Keeping an upward pressure on the drain plug while unscrewing it will prevent oil leakage until you're ready for it

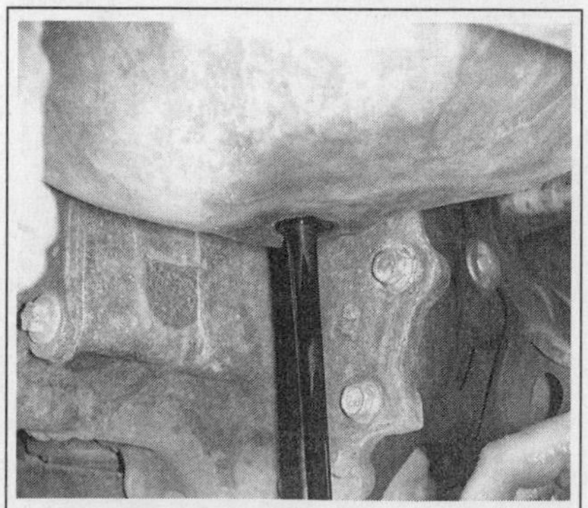

Fig. 172 Quickly withdraw the plug and allow all of the oil to drain out

- Avoid prolonged skin contact with used motor oil.
- Remove oil from skin by washing thoroughly with soap and water or waterless hand cleaner. Do not use gasoline, thinners or other solvents.
- Avoid prolonged skin contact with oil-soaked clothing.

The oil drain plug is located on the bottom, rear of the oil pan (bottom of the engine, underneath the truck). The oil filter is located on the side of the engine. One some vehicles, the oil drain plug and the filter may be located behind access panels in the engine under covers.

Always drain the oil after the engine has been running long enough to bring it to normal operating temperature. Hot oil will flow easier and more contaminants will be removed along with the oil than if it were drained cold. To change the oil and filter:

1. Run the engine until it reaches normal operating temperature. Shut down the engine.
2. Raise and safely support the front of the truck on safety stands.
3. Slide a drain pan of at least 8 quarts capacity under the oil pan.
4. Loosen the drain plug with a wrench. Turn the plug out by hand. By keeping an inward pressure on the plug as you unscrew it, oil won't escape past

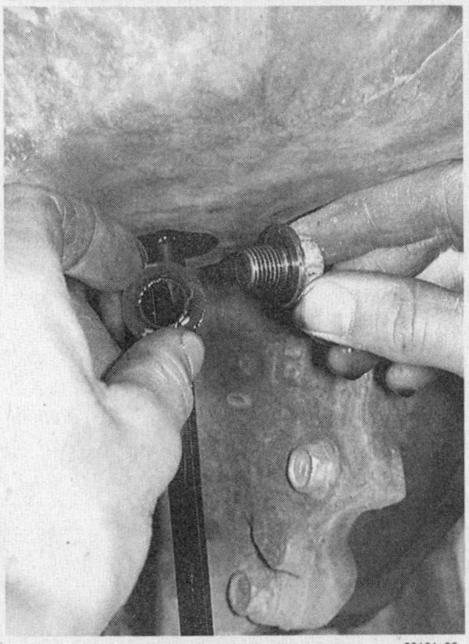
93161p96

Fig. 173 Engine oil drain plug and sealing O-ring

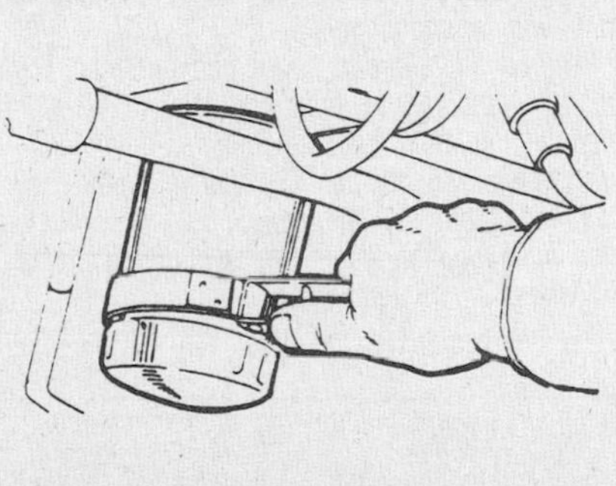
86821248

Fig. 175 A strap-type wrench can be used if space permits. Other applications may require a cap-type wrench that grabs the end of the filter

TCCS1901

Fig. 177 Before installing a new oil filter, coat the rubber gasket with clean oil

the threads and you can remove it without being burned by hot oil.

5. Allow the oil to drain completely and then install the drain plug. Don't overtighten the plug, or you'll be buying a new pan or a replacement plug for stripped threads.

6. Using a filter wrench, remove the oil filter. Keep in mind that it's holding about one quart of

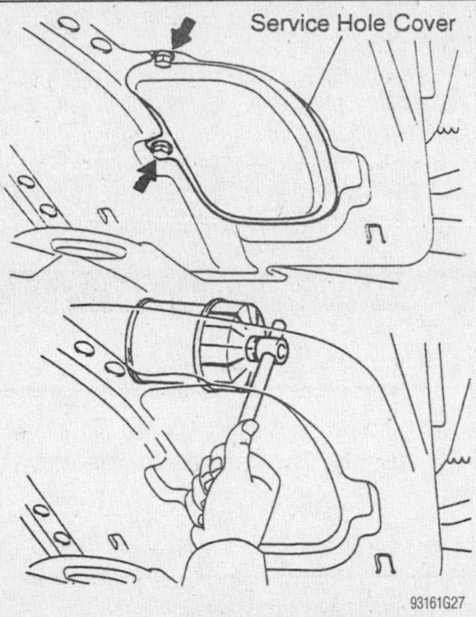

93161G27

Fig. 174 The oil filter on this V8 powered Land Cruiser is behind a removable Service Hole Cover and is serviced using a cap-type oil filter tool—2UZ-FE Engine

86821247

Fig. 176 With a lint free rag, clean the surface of the filter contact

dirty, hot oil. Make certain the old gasket comes off with the filter and is not stuck to the block.

7. Empty the old filter into the drain pan and dispose of the filter.

8. Using a clean rag, wipe off the filter adapter on the engine block. Be sure that the rag doesn't leave any lint which could clog an oil passage.

9. Coat the rubber gasket on the filter with fresh oil. The reason for this is that the rubber will react with the oil and swell a small amount, making a good, tight seal without having to tighten the filter excessively. Spin it onto the engine by hand; when the gasket touches the adapter surface give it another $^1/_2$–$^3/_4$ turn. No more, or you'll crush the gasket and it will leak.

10. Refill the engine with the correct amount of fresh oil. See the "Capacities" chart.

11. Check the oil level on the dipstick. It is normal for the level to be a bit above the full mark. Start the engine and allow it to idle for a few minutes.

WARNING

Do not run the engine above idle speed until it has built up oil pressure, indicated when the oil light goes out.

12. Shut **OFF** the engine, allow the oil to drain for a minute, and check the oil level. Check around the filter and drain plug for any leaks, and correct as necessary.

Manual Transmission

FLUID RECOMMENDATIONS

All vehicles use a multipurpose gear oil in the manual transmission. The recommended types are: API GL–4 or GL–5 with the viscosity SAE 75W–90 or 80W–90.

LEVEL CHECK

See Figures 178, 179, and 180

The oil in the manual transmission should be checked at least every 7500 miles (12,000 km) and

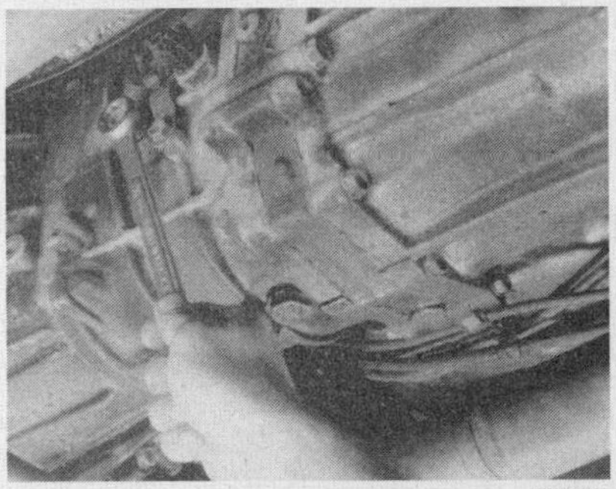
86821250

Fig. 178 Use a wrench to remove the filler plug from the side of the case

86821251

Fig. 179 A gear oil pump with a nozzle is the easiest way to add gear oil to a manual transmission

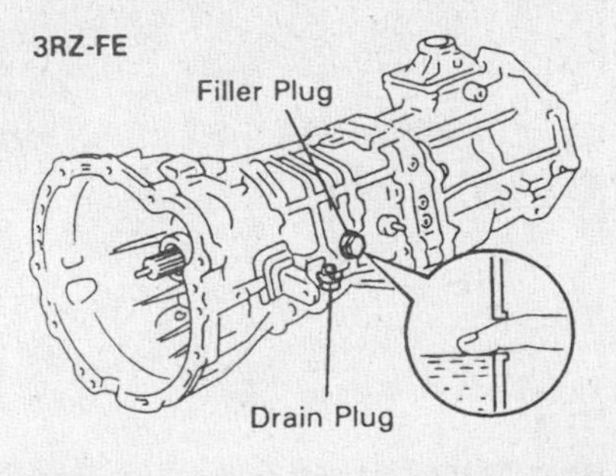

86821256

Fig. 180 Typical manual transmission fill plug and drain plug locations

replaced every 25,000–30,000 miles (40,000–48,000 km). Even more frequently if driven in deep water.

1. With the truck parked on a level surface, remove the filler plug (usually 17mm) from the side of the transmission housing. A gasket will also have to be removed and replaced.
2. If the lubricant begins to trickle out of the hole, there is enough. Otherwise, carefully insert your finger (watch out for sharp threads) and check to see if the oil is up to the edge of the hole.
3. If not, add oil through the hole until the level is at the edge of the hole. Most gear lubricants come in a plastic squeeze bottle with a nozzle, making additions somewhat easier, though not always simple.
4. Install the filler plug with a new gasket. Run the engine and check for leaks.

DRAIN AND REFILL

See Figures 181, 182, and 183

The oil in the manual transmission should be changed at least every 30,000 miles (48,000 km).

1. The transmission oil should be warmed to normal operating temperature before it is drained.
2. Raise and safely support the truck on safety stands so that you can safely work underneath. You will probably not have enough room to work if the truck is not raised.
3. The drain plug is located on the bottom of the transmission. It is usually on the passenger side on four speeds, and on the bottom center of five speeds. Place a pan under the drain plug, then remove it. Keep a slight upward pressure on the plug while unscrewing it, this will keep the oil from pouring out until the plug is removed.

**** CAUTION**

The oil may be hot if the vehicle had been recently run a long distance. Be careful when you remove the plug to avoid spilling hot oil on your skin.

4. Allow the oil to drain completely.
5. Clean off the plug then install it, tightening it until just snug.
6. Remove the filler plug from the side of the transmission case. It is usually on the driver's side of four speeds, and on the passenger side on five speeds. There will be a gasket underneath this plug. Replace it every time the bolt is removed.
7. Fill the transmission with gear oil through the filler plug hole.
8. The oil level should come right up to the edge of the hole. You can stick your finger in to verify this. Watch out for sharp threads.
9. Install the filler plug and gasket, lower the truck, then check for leaks. Dispose of the old oil in the proper manner.

Automatic Transmission

FLUID RECOMMENDATIONS

All automatic transmissions covered in this manual use DEXRON®II or III automatic transmission fluid.

LEVEL CHECK

See Figures 184 and 185

Check the automatic transmission fluid level at least every 15,000 miles (24,000 km) or more if possible. The dipstick is usually located in the rear of the engine compartment. The fluid level should be checked only when the transmission is hot (normal operating temperature) and with the engine running. The transmission is considered hot after about 20 miles (32 km) of highway driving.

1. Park the truck on a level surface with the engine idling. Shift the transmission into Neutral or Park and set the parking brake.
2. Remove the dipstick, wipe it clean and reinsert if firmly. Be sure that it has been pushed all the way in. Remove the dipstick and check the fluid level while holding it horizontally. With the engine running, the fluid level should be between the second and third notches on the dipstick.
3. If the fluid level is below the second notch, add fluid with the aid of a funnel.
4. Check the level often as you are filling the transmission. Be extremely careful not to overfill it. Overfilling will cause slippage, seal damage and overheating. Approximately one pint of ATF will raise the level from one notch to the other.

The fluid on the dipstick should always be a bright red color. It if is discolored (brown or black), or smells burnt, serious transmission troubles, probably due to overheating, should be suspected. The transmission should be inspected by a qualified service technician to locate the cause of the burnt fluid.

DRAIN AND REFILL

See Figures 186, 187, and 188

The automatic transmission fluid should be changed at least every 25,000–30,000 miles (40,000–48,000 km). If the truck is normally used in severe service, such as stop-and-go driving, trailer towing or the like, the interval should be halved. The fluid should be hot before it is drained; a 20 minute drive will accomplish this.

Unlike many other automatic transmissions, Toyota automatic transmissions are equipped with a drain plug in the pan, so that fluid may be drained without removing the pan. The filter within the pan is not replaceable as a maintenance item; removing the pan is not required or recommended during normal transmission maintenance.

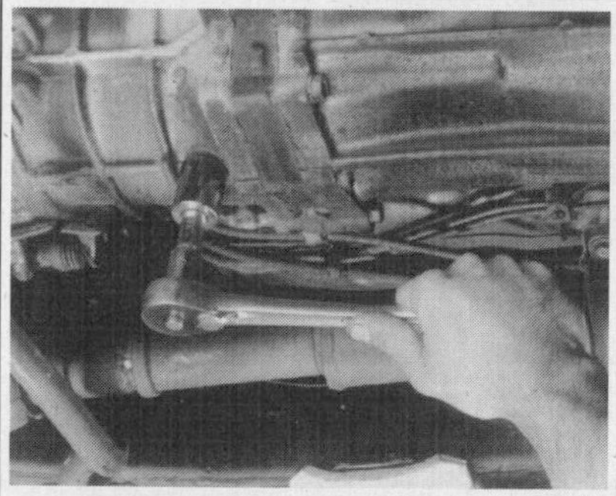

86821252

Fig. 181 Use a short extension to aid in removing the drain plug

86821253

Fig. 182 Quickly withdraw the plug and allow the oil to drain into a suitable container

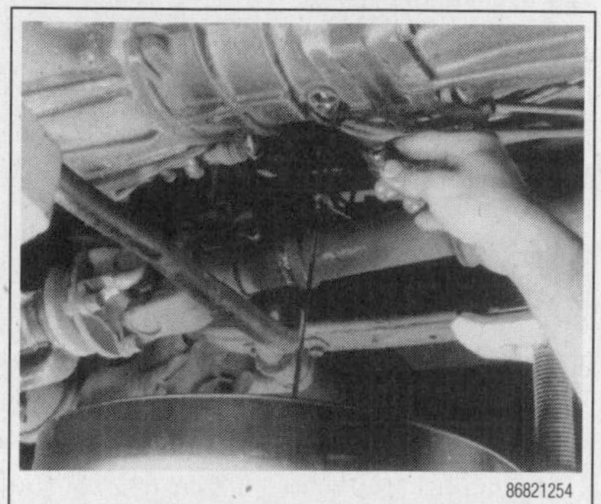

86821254

Fig. 183 Allow enough time for the fluid to drain completely before reinstalling the plug

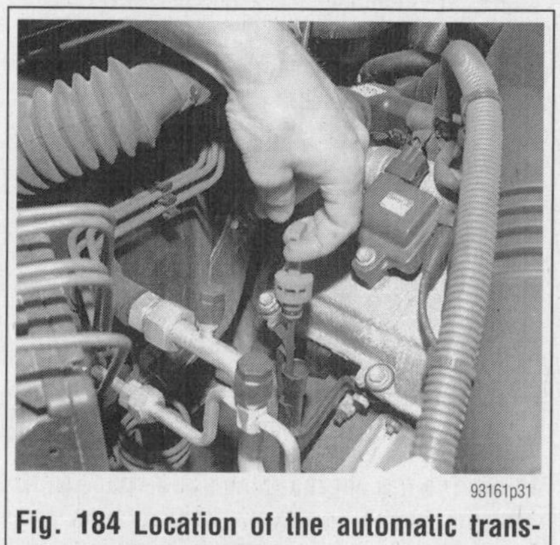

93161p31

Fig. 184 Location of the automatic transmission fluid dipstick

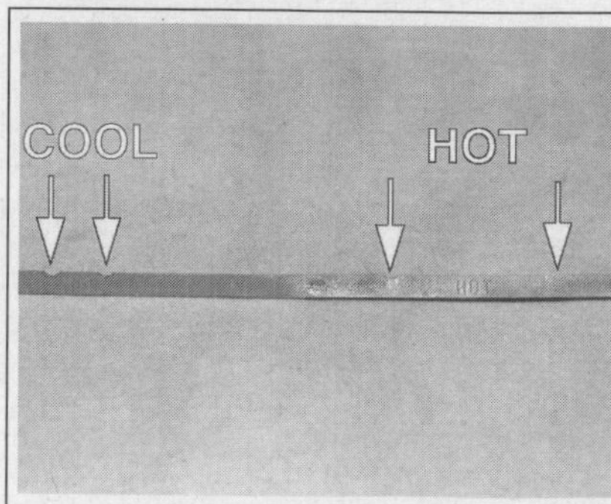

93161p22

Fig. 185 When checking the fluid level on the automatic transmission dipstick, be sure to read the dipstick carefully

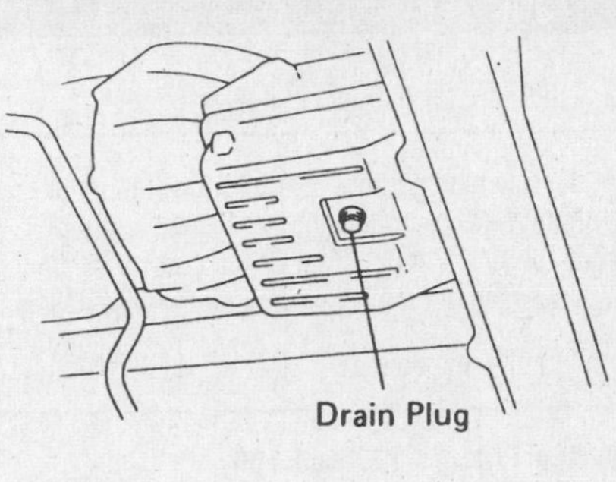

Fig. 186 All Toyota automatic transmissions have a drain plug to ease the removal of fluid

Fig. 187 Remove the drain plug with an appropriate wrench

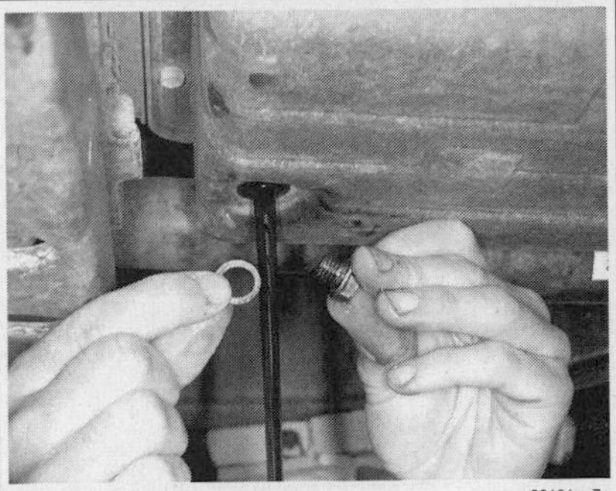

Fig. 188 When installing the automatic transmission pan drain plug, always use a new sealing washer

1. With the truck safely supported on safety stands, position a large catch pan below the drain plug.
2. Remove the plug and gasket slowly, and be prepared for a rush of HOTfluid. Allow enough time for the fluid to drain completely.
3. Install the drain plug with a new gasket if used, and tighten just snug. Add transmission fluid through the dipstick tube under the hood.
4. Reinsert the dipstick after filling, then start the engine and allow it to idle. DO NOT race the engine.
5. After the engine has idled for a few minutes, shift the transmission slowly through the gears, then return it to Park. With the engine still idling, check the fluid level on the dipstick. If necessary, add more fluid to raise the level.

Fig. 189 Use a ratchet to remove the bolts from the automatic transmission pan

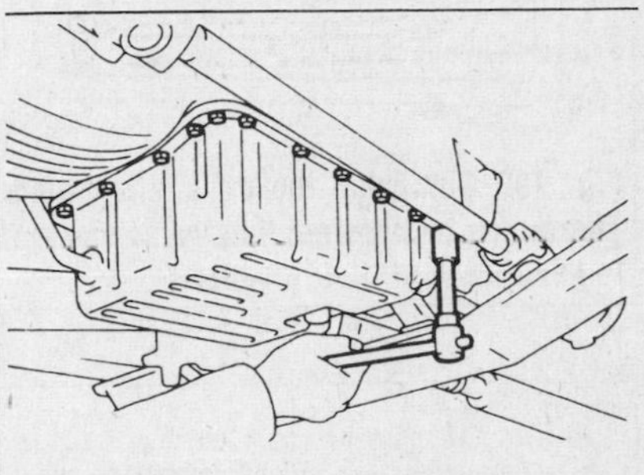

Fig. 190 Most of the pan bolts should be accessible; you may need to remove another part to obtain access for some

PAN AND FILTER SERVICE

➧ **See Figures 187 thru 196**

➡The automatic transmission fluid can be drained without removing the pan. The filter within the pan is not replaceable as a maintenance item. Removing the pan is not required or recommended during normal transmission maintenance.

1. Raise and safely support the vehicle using safety stands.
2. Place a container under the transmission drain plug and drain the transmission fluid. Install the drain plug with a new sealing and tighten securely.
3. Remove the pan securing bolts and remove the pan and gasket. The transmission pans are installed with Formed In Place Gasket (FIPG) sealer which means that even after the bolts are removed, the pan will likely still be stuck in place, held fast by the sealer. Toyota has a Special Service Tool (SST) that uses a thin, sharp blade in a holder designed to be tapped with a hammer, to slice through the sealer so the parts can be separated. Use care if using substitute tools. The oil pan flange and the sealing surface of the aluminum transmission case are easily damaged. Do NOT use a screwdriver (you'll deform the pan lip) and do NOT drive the tool straight into the seam; if it goes too far, internal damage will result. Work on an angle to the pan and tap the tool just deeply enough to cut the sealer.
4. Before cleaning the transmission oil pan, examine the contents carefully. Some minor amounts of debris will be found from normal operation. Magnets

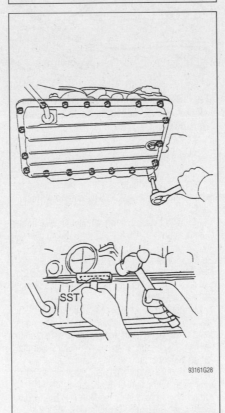

Fig. 191 Using Toyota's Special Service Tool (SST) to cut through the sealer holding the pan to the case

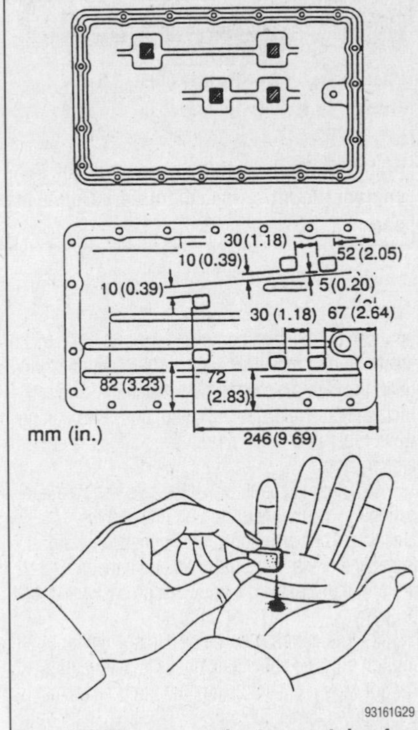

Fig. 192 The pan at the top contains four magnets, the pan in the middle has six magnets to trap steel particle debris. They require surprisingly precise placement to avoid interference with valve body components

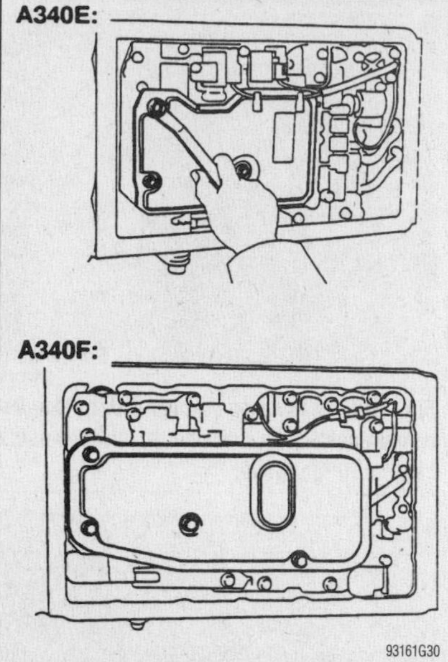

Fig. 193 Removing the oil strainer bolts. There may be different lengths so use care to keep track of their locations

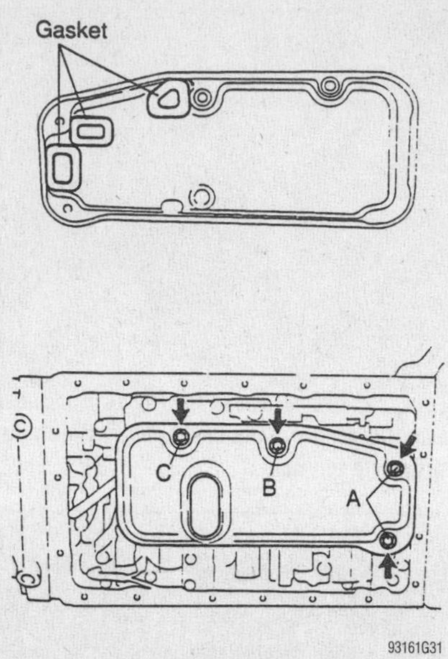

Fig. 194 This filter screen uses three gaskets that must be carefully positioned and three different length bolts

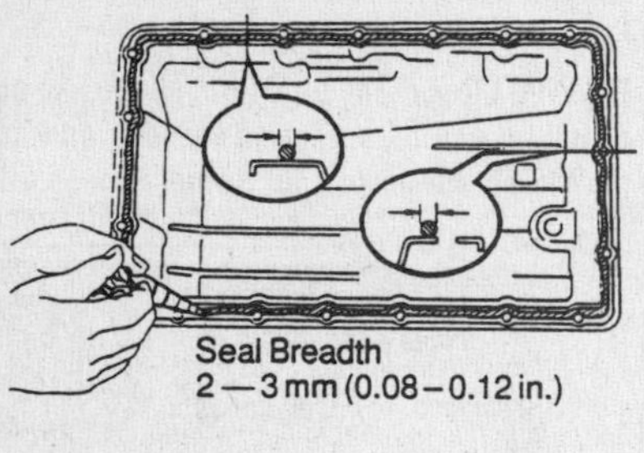

Fig. 195 Apply a thin, even bead of FIPG sealant (about $^1/_8$ inch diameter) around the pan

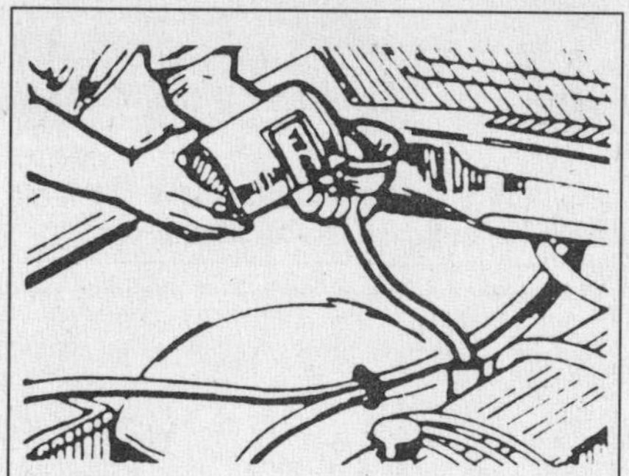

Fig. 196 A funnel with a long, flexible neck allows you to add fluid to the automatic transmission

are used to trap steel particles. Excessive amounts of steel particles may indicate a problem with bearing, gear or clutch plate wear. Non-metallic debris could include brass particles indicating possible bushing wear. Fiber particles are from the friction plates in the clutch packs.

5. Clean all parts well. Use care to note the locations of the magnets before removing them for cleaning. The valve body and the metal oil transfer tubes and close to the magnets and if the magnets are out of place, the oil pan won't go back into place properly.

6. The pan may be washed in solvent for cleaning but must be absolutely dry when it is reinstalled. Do not wipe it out with a rag; the lint from the rag can damage the transmission.

7. Remove all traces of the old sealer from the pan and from the transmission..

8. Inspect, clean or replace the transmission filter or strainer at this time, if necessary. If the filter is removed, additional fluid will drain out. Note that some of the oil strainer bolts will be of different lengths and care should be taken to mark their locations so they can be installed in their original locations.

9. With the replacement strainer in place tighten to bolts to just 84 inch lbs. (10 Nm). Do not overtighten.

10. Make sure the oil pan is clean, the magnets have been returned to their proper locations and the sealing flanges of both the pan and the transmission are clean and free of oil.

11. Apply a thin, even bead of FIPG sealant (about $^1/_8$-inch diameter) around the pan, staying inboard of the screw holes and roughly centered on the pan flange. Use care not to use too much sealer that will get squeezed out into the transmission.

12. Install the pan, tightening the securing bolts to the proper torque in a crisscrossing pattern. Torque the pan bolts to 65 inch lbs. (7.4 Nm). Do not overtighten. The pan bolts with break and/or the threaded holes in the transmission case may strip.

13. Carefully lower the vehicle, then fill the transmission to the correct level with DEXRON®II or III.

Transfer Case

FLUID RECOMMENDATIONS

1. Use multipurpose gear oil API GL–4 or GL–5 SAE 75W–90 gear oil in the transfer case. Check your Owner's Manual under Specifications for any late changes that may apply to your specific vehicle.

LEVEL CHECK

See Figures 197 and 198

The oil in the transfer case should be checked at least every 7,500 miles (12,000 km) and replaced every 25,000–30,000 miles (40,000–48,000 km), even more frequently if driven in deep water.

1. With the truck parked on a level surface, remove the filler plug from the side of the transfer housing.

2. If the lubricant begins to trickle out of the hole, there is enough. Otherwise, carefully insert a finger and check to see if the oil is up to the edge of the hole.

3. If not, add oil through the hole until the level is at the edge of the hole. Most gear lubricants come in a plastic squeeze bottle with a nozzle; making additions simple.

4. Install the filler plug and gasket, then run the engine and check for leaks.

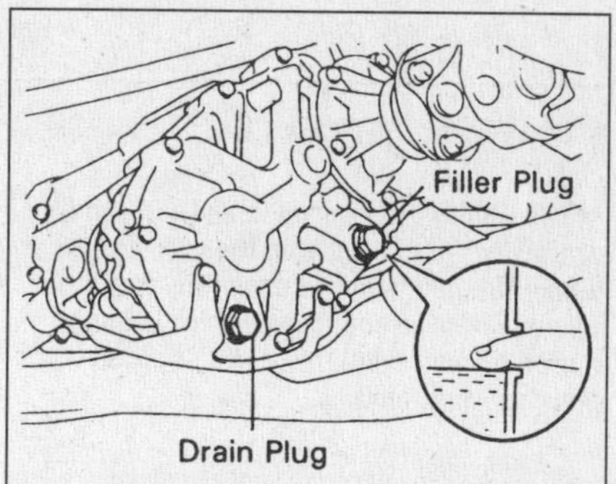

Fig. 197 When checking the transfer case fluid level, watch the threads in the filler plug opening, they can be sharp

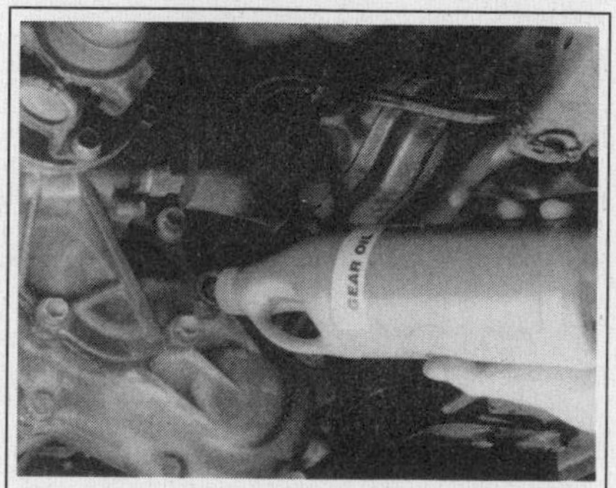

Fig. 198 The gear oil usually comes in a long container with a built-in spout

DRAIN AND REFILL

➧ **See Figures 199, 200, 201, and 202**

1. The transfer case oil should be hot before it is drained. If the engine is at normal operating temperature, the oil should be hot enough.
2. Raise and safely support the truck using safety stands.
3. The drain plug is usually located on the bottom of the transfer case. Place a pan under the drain plug and remove it.
4. Allow the oil to drain completely. Clean off the plug and install it, tightening it until it is just snug.
5. Remove the filler plug from the side of the case.
6. Fill the transfer case with the correct oil through the filler plug hole as detailed previously. Refer to the Capacities chart for the amount of oil needed to refill your transfer case.
7. The oil level should come right up to the edge of the hole.
8. Install the filler plug with a new gasket, lower the truck, and check for leaks. Dispose of the old oil in the proper manner.

Drive Axles

FLUID RECOMMENDATIONS

Use Hypoid gear oil API GL–5. Above 0°F (–18°C) use SAE 90W. Below 0°F (–18°C) use SAE 80W or 80W–90.

LEVEL CHECK

Front

➧ **See Figures 203, 204, and 205**

The oil in the front differential should be checked at least every 7,500 miles (12,000 km).

1. With the truck parked on a level surface, remove the filler plug from the back of the differential.

➡**The plug on the bottom is the drain plug.**

2. If the oil begins to trickle out of the hole, there is enough. Otherwise, carefully insert your finger into the hole and check to see if the oil is up to the bottom edge of the filler hole.
3. If not, add oil through the hole until the level is at the edge of the hole. Most gear oils come in a plastic squeeze bottle with a nozzle, making oil addition easier.
4. Install the filler plug and drive the truck for a short distance. Stop the truck and check for leaks.

Rear

➧ **See Figures 206, 207, 208, 209, and 210**

The oil in the rear differential should be checked at least every 7,500 miles (12,000 km).

1. With the truck parked on a level surface, remove the filler plug from the back of the differential.

➡**The plug on the bottom is the drain plug.**

2. If the oil begins to trickle out of the hole, there is enough. Otherwise, carefully insert your finger (watch out for sharp threads) into the hole and check to see if the oil is up to the bottom edge of the filler hole.

93161p99

Fig. 199 Using a ratchet to remove the transfer case drain plug

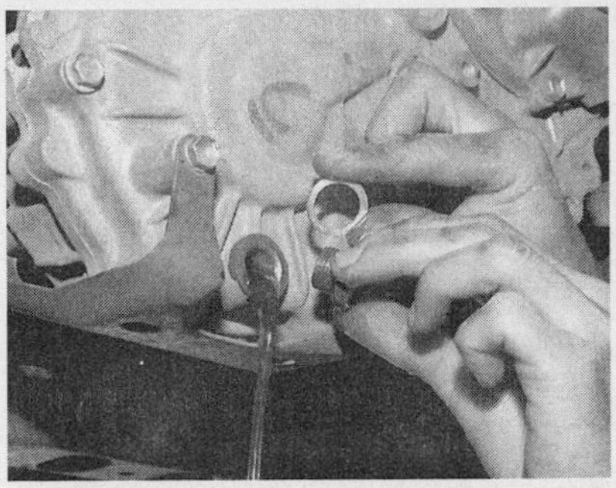

93161p97

Fig. 200 When removing the filler plug, remember there is a gasket, usually metal

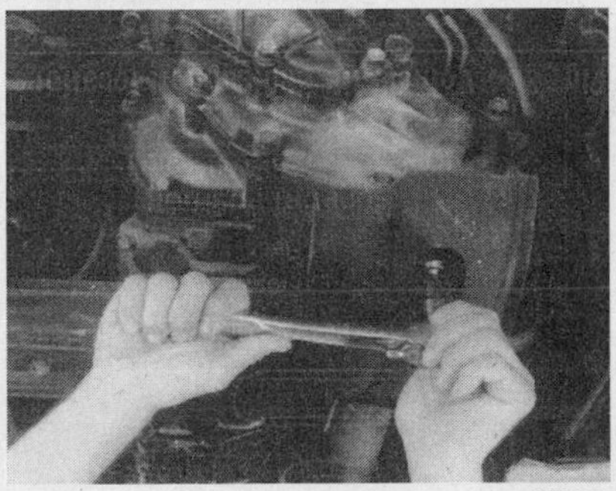

86821265

Fig. 201 This truck has a bracket/shield where you access the plug. You may need to use an extension

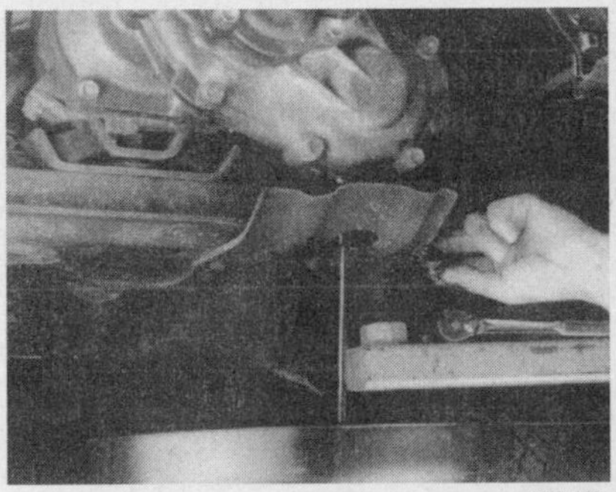

86821266

Fig. 202 There will be just enough room to remove the plug with your hands. Be careful of the hot oil

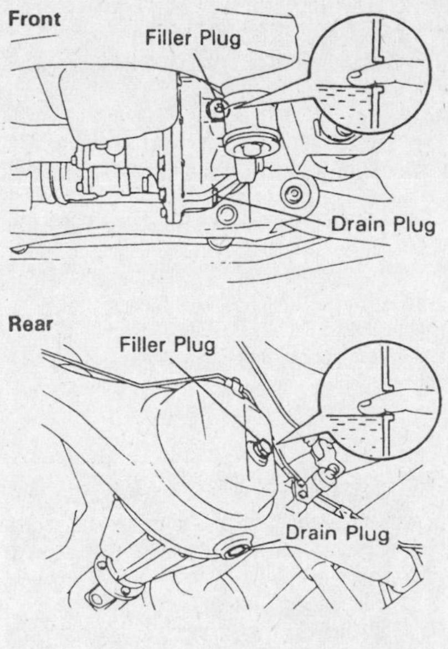

86821275

Fig. 203 The front and rear filler plugs on most of the trucks covered by this manual are located in these areas shown

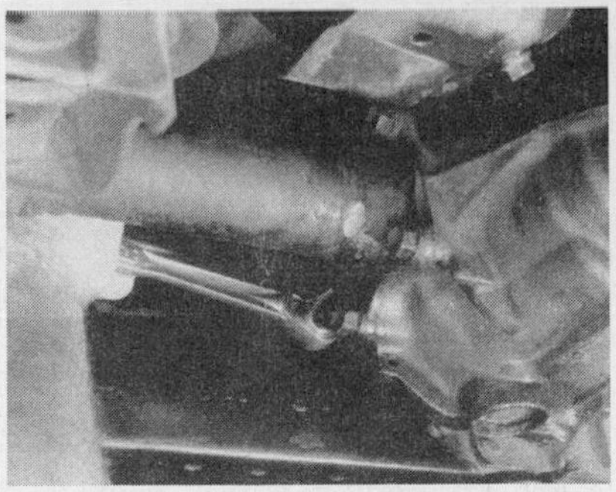

86821267

Fig. 204 Locate the filler plug . . .

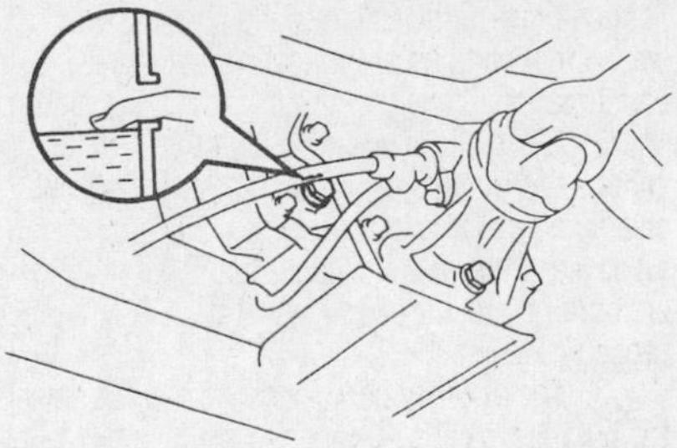

86821269

Fig. 205 . . . then check the fluid level with your finger

3. If not, add oil through the hole until the level is at the edge of the hole. Most gear oils come in a plastic squeeze bottle with a nozzle, making oil addition easier.
4. Install the filler plug and drive the truck for a short distance. Stop the truck and check for leaks.

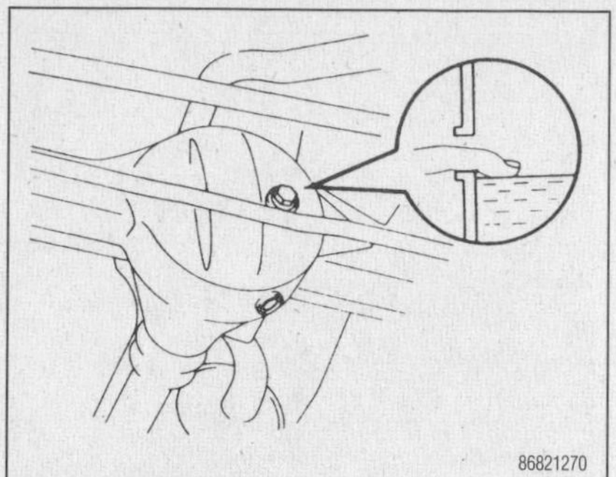

86821270

Fig. 206 Check the gear oil level. The oil should be level with the threads in the plug opening

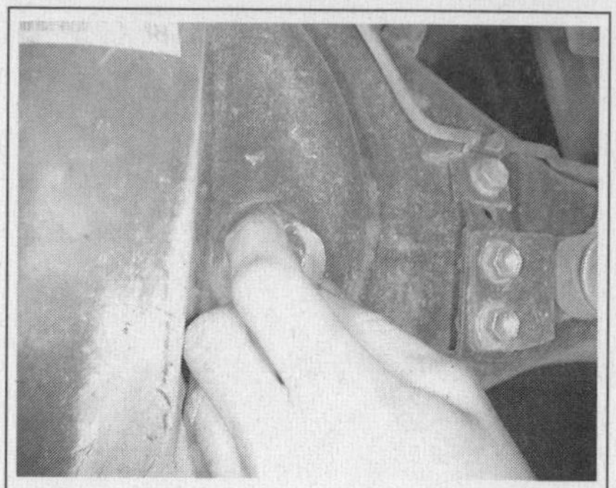

93161p85

Fig. 207 Once loose, unscrew the filler plug by hand . . .

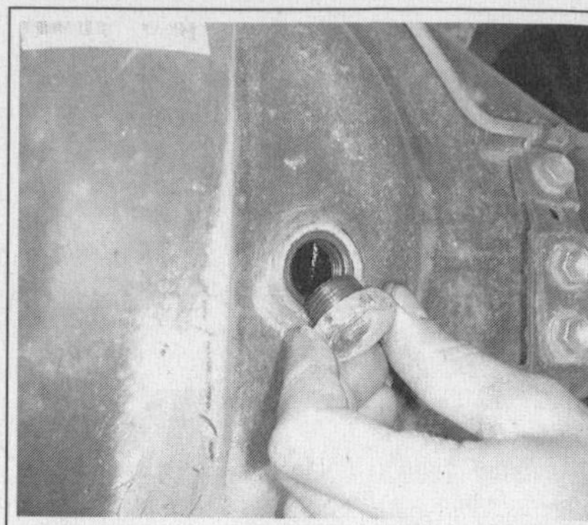

93161p86

Fig. 208 . . . then remove the filler plug

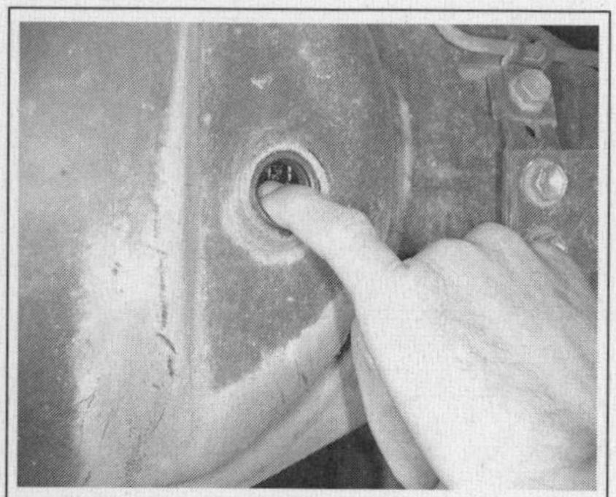

93161p87

Fig. 209 Using your finger, carefully check the oil level

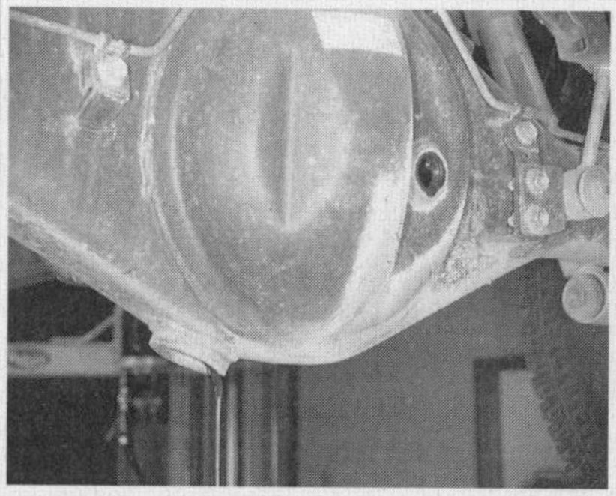

93161p88

Fig. 210 The oil level should be level with the bottom threads

DRAIN AND REFILL

Front

➧ See Figures 211, 212, and 213

The gear oil in the front axle should be changed at least every 25,000–30,000 miles (40,000–48,000 km), or immediately if driven in deep water.

1. Park the vehicle on a level surface. Set the parking brake.
2. Clean the area around the drain plug.
3. Remove the filler (upper) plug. Place a container which is large enough to catch all of the differential oil under the drain plug.
4. Remove the drain (lower) plug and gasket, if so equipped. Allow all of the oil to drain into the container.
5. Install the drain plug. Tighten it so that it will not leak, but do not overtighten.
6. Refill with the proper grade and viscosity of axle lubricant. Be sure that the level reaches the bottom of the filler plug. DO NOT overfill.
7. Install the filler plug and check for leakage.

Rear

➧ See Figures 214, 215, 216, 217, and 218

The gear oil in the rear axle should be changed at least every 25,000–30,000 miles (40,000–48,000 km), or immediately if driven in deep water.

1. Park the vehicle on a level surface. Set the parking brake.
2. Clean the area around the drain plug.
3. Remove the filler (upper) plug. Place a container which is large enough to catch all of the differential oil under the drain plug.
4. Remove the drain (lower) plug and gasket, if so equipped. Allow all of the oil to drain into the container.
5. Install the drain plug. Tighten it so that it will not leak, but do not overtighten.
6. Refill with the proper grade and viscosity of axle lubricant. Be sure that the level reaches the bottom of the filler plug. DO NOT overfill.
7. Install the filler plug and check for leakage.

Cooling System

FLUID RECOMMENDATIONS

When additional coolant is required to maintain the proper level, always add a 50/50 mixture of ethylene-glycol antifreeze/coolant and water. Toyota specifies the use of ethylene-glycol antifreeze to not only provide freezing protection but to also prevent corrosion. The use of supplementary inhibitors or additives is neither required nor recommended.

➡Do not use alcohol type antifreeze or plain water alone.

LEVEL CHECK

➧ See Figures 219, 220, and 221

All vehicles use a coolant reservoir tank (expansion tank) connected to the radiator by a small hose. Look through the plastic tank; the fluid level should be between FULL and LOW lines. Note that the FULL

86821271

Fig. 211 Drain the axle's gear oil into a suitable container

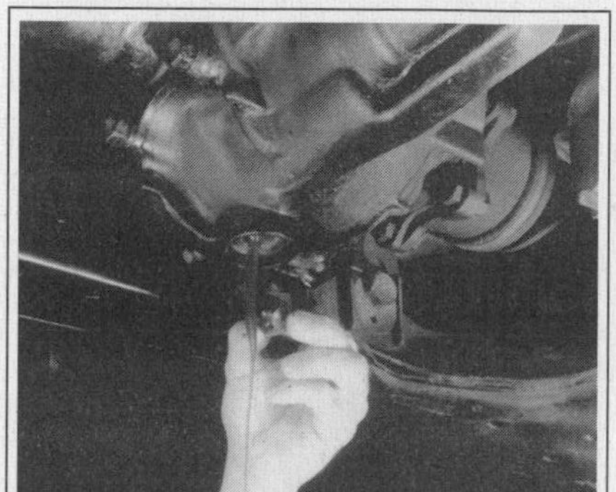

86821272

Fig. 212 Remove the drain (lower) plug and gasket, if so equipped

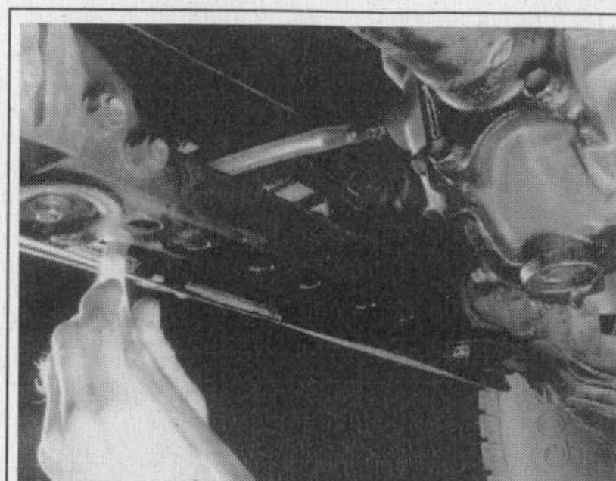

86821268

Fig. 213 Slide the pump's tube (shown) into the filler hole, or use bottled fluid with a built-in funnel

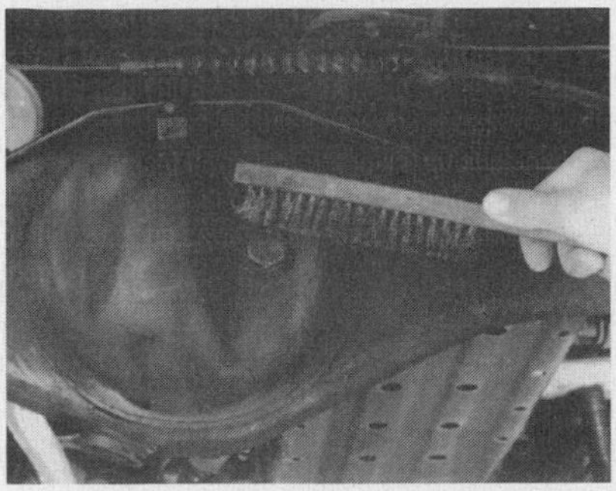

86821277

Fig. 214 Clean the area around the drain plug—rear axle shown

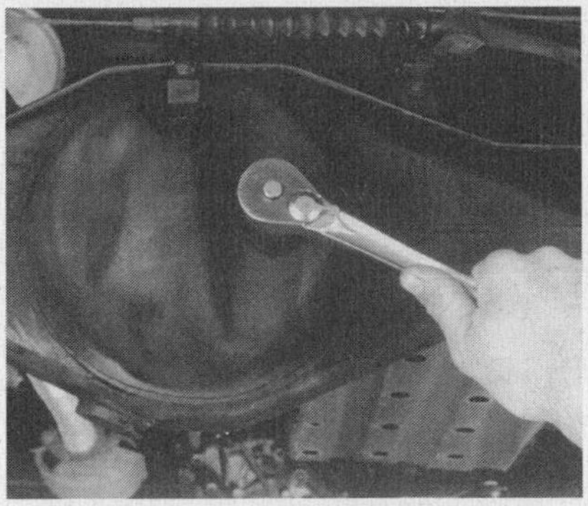

86821278

Fig. 215 Unscrew the filler plug

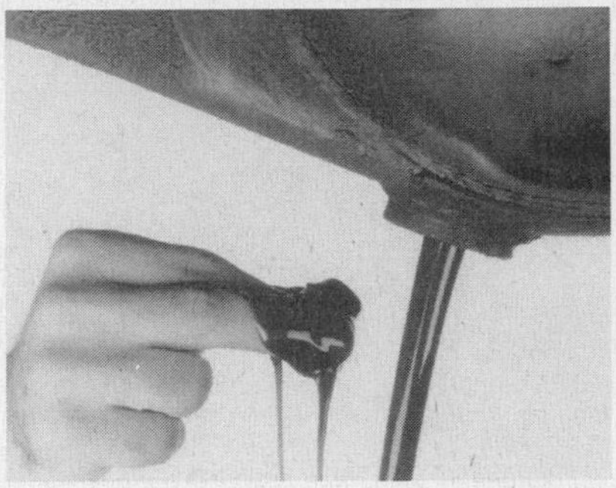

86821279

Fig. 216 Drain the oil into a suitable container

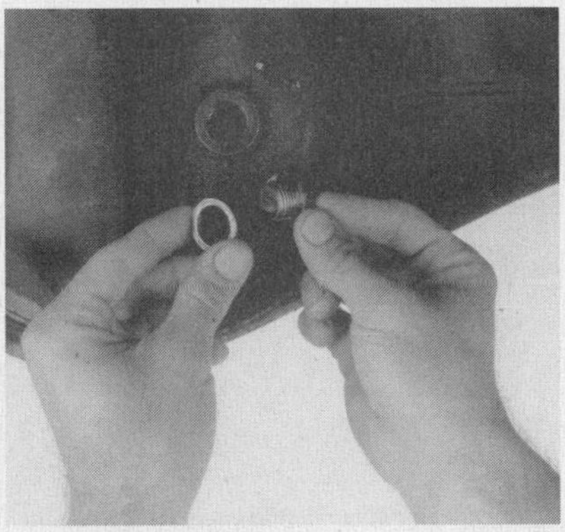

86821280

Fig. 217 Install the filler (shown) and drain plugs along with the gaskets, securely

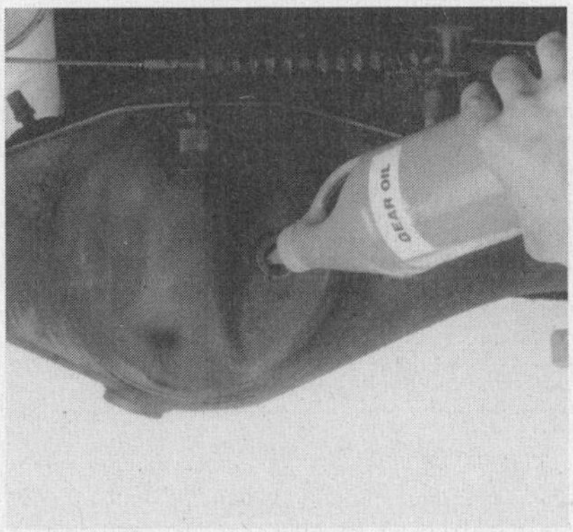

86821281

Fig. 218 Refill the axle with the proper gear oil

93161p35

Fig. 219 The engine coolant reservoir can be used for checking fluid level and adding coolant. Simply remove the cap from the coolant recovery tank reservoir . . .

93161p55

Fig. 220 . . . then, if the coolant is low, add an equal amount of ethylene-glycol based antifreeze and distilled water to the recovery system

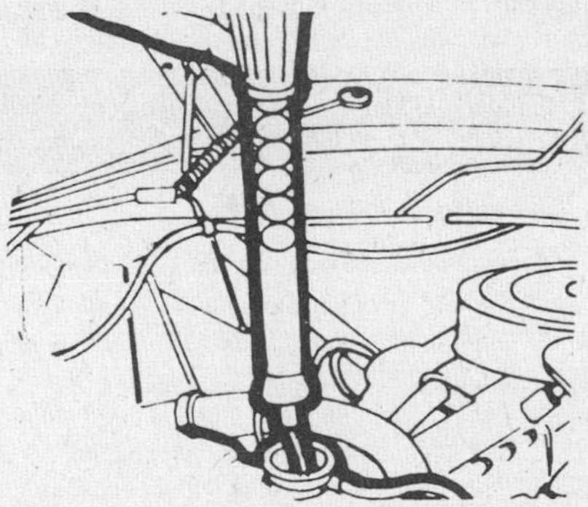

86821290

Fig. 221 A coolant hydrometer will show you the boiling and freezing points of the coolant present

line is below the very top of the tank, allowing room for expansion. If the level in the tank is low, remove the cap of the tank and add coolant to the FULL line.

⁂ CAUTION

Never remove the radiator cap to check fluid level; there is a high risk of scalding from escaping hot fluid.

If the coolant level is low, add an equal amount of ethylene-glycol based antifreeze. Avoid using water that is known to have a high alkaline content or is very hard, except in emergency situations. Drain and flush the cooling system as soon as possible after using such water.

The radiator hoses and clamps and the radiator cap should be checked at the same time as the coolant level. Hoses which are brittle, cracked, or swollen should be replaced. Clamps should be checked for tightness (screwdriver tight only.) Do not allow the clamp to cut into the hose or crush the fitting. The radiator cap gasket should be checked for any obvious tears, cracks or swelling, or any signs of incorrect seating in the radiator neck.

A 50/50 mix of coolant concentrate and water will usually provide protection to −35°F. (−37°C). Freeze protection may be checked by using a cooling system hydrometer. Inexpensive hydrometers may be obtained from a local auto supply store. Follow the directions packaged with the coolant hydrometer when checking protection.

DRAIN AND REFILL

➧ See Figures 222, 223, 224, and 225

⁂ CAUTION

When draining coolant, keep in mind that cats and dogs are attracted by ethylene glycol-antifreeze, and are quite likely to drink any that is left in an uncovered container or in puddles on the ground. This will prove fatal in sufficient quantity. Always drain coolant into a sealable container. Coolant may be reused unless it is contaminated or several years old.

Completely draining and refilling the cooling system every two years will remove accumulated rust, scale and other deposits.

1. Make certain the engine is COLD. Generally, this means at least 3 hours from last operation, longer in hot weather. Overnight cold is best.
2. Remove the radiator cap. Drain the existing antifreeze and coolant. Open the radiator and engine drain petcocks, or disconnect the bottom radiator hose at the radiator outlet. Set the heater temperature controls to the full HOT position.

➡Before opening the radiator petcock, spray it with some penetrating lubricant.

3. Close the petcocks or reconnect the lower hose and fill the system with the correct mixture of antifreeze and water in the correct amount. It will take a bit of time for the level to stabilize within the radiator.

86821110

Fig. 222 When the engine is cool, remove the radiator cap

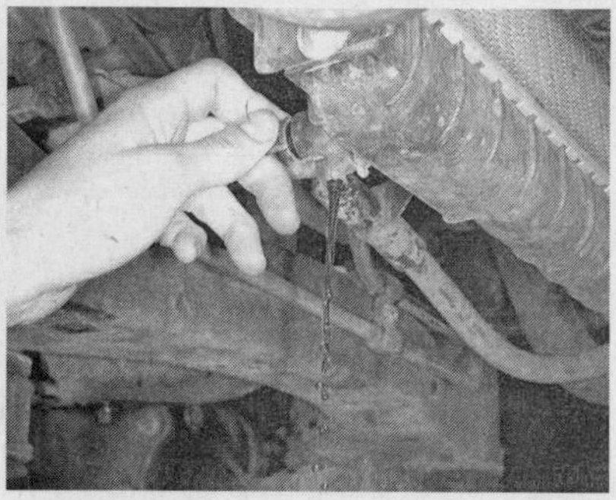

93161pb2

Fig. 223 Unscrew the petcock and let the coolant drain

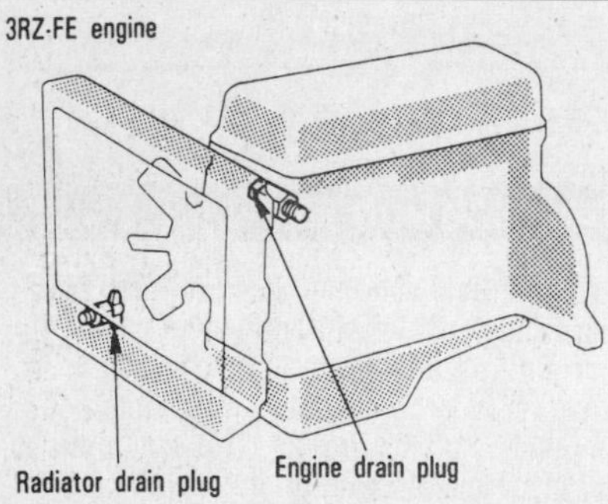

86821286

Fig. 224 Radiator and engine coolant plugs—3RZ-FE engine shown, others similar

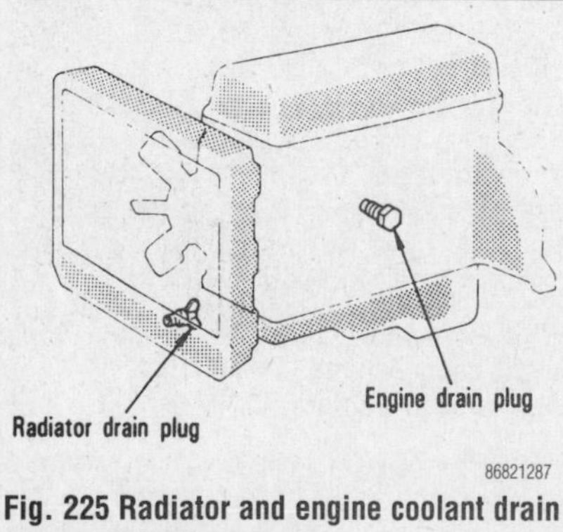

86821287

Fig. 225 Radiator and engine coolant drain plugs—1FZ-FE engine

4. Double check the petcocks for closure.
5. Install the radiator cap.
6. Flush the reservoir with water, empty it, then install fresh coolant mixture to the FULL line.
7. Start the engine, allowing it to idle. As it warms up, keep a close watch on the petcocks and/or hose fittings used to drain the system. If any leakage is seen, shut the engine **OFF** and fix the leak.
8. After the engine has warmed up, shut the engine **OFF**. Check the level in the reservoir tank and adjust the fluid level as needed.

➡Fresh antifreeze has a detergent quality. Fluid in the reservoir may appear muddy or discolored due to the cleaning action of the new coolant. If the system has been neglected for a period of time, it may be necessary to redrain the system to eliminate this sludge.

FLUSHING AND CLEANING THE SYSTEM

Several aftermarket radiator flushing and cleaning kits can be purchased at your local auto parts store. It is recommended that the radiator be cleaned and flushed of sludge and any rust build-up once a year. Manufacturers directions for proper use, and safety precautions, come in each kit.

CLEAN RADIATOR OF DEBRIS

Periodically clean any debris such as leaves, paper, insects, etc., from the radiator fins. Pick the large pieces off by hand. The smaller pieces can be washed away with water pressure from a hose.

Carefully straighten any bent radiator fins with a pair of needle nose pliers. Be careful, the fins are very soft. Don't wiggle the fins back and forth too much. Straighten them once and try not to move them again.

Master Cylinder (Brake and Clutch)

➧ See Figures 226 and 227

All models have the brake master cylinder reservoir on the left side of the firewall under the hood. Trucks and 4Runners with manual transmissions use a hydraulic (fluid actuated) clutch. The clutch fluid reservoir is located in the same area as brake reservoir. The clutch master cylinder uses the same fluid as the brakes, and should be checked at the same time as the brake master cylinder.

FLUID RECOMMENDATIONS

Use only Heavy Duty Brake fluid meeting DOT 3 or SAE J1703 specifications.

LEVEL CHECK

➧ See Figures 228 thru 233

The fluid in the brake and/or clutch master cylinders should be checked every 6 months or 6,000 miles (9,600 km). Check the fluid level at the side of the reservoir. If fluid is required, thoroughly wipe the top of the reservoir and the sides of the plastic housing with a rag before opening. The fluid must be kept free from dirt and grit. Fill the reservoir to the MAX line in the reservoir. Never overfill the reservoir. Install the reservoir cap, making sure the gasket is properly seated in the cap.

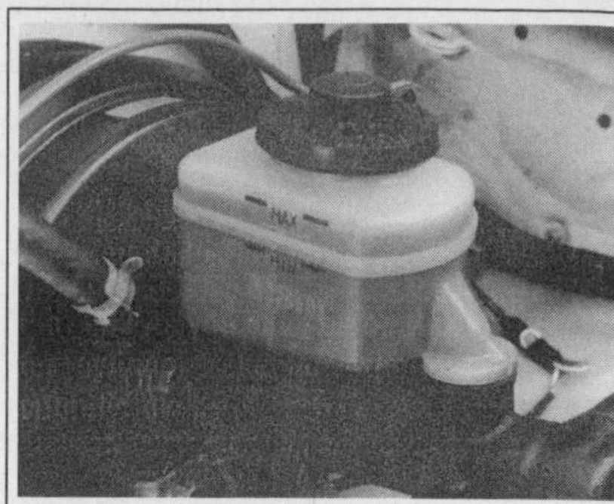

86821291

Fig. 226 The brake master cylinder is attached to the booster

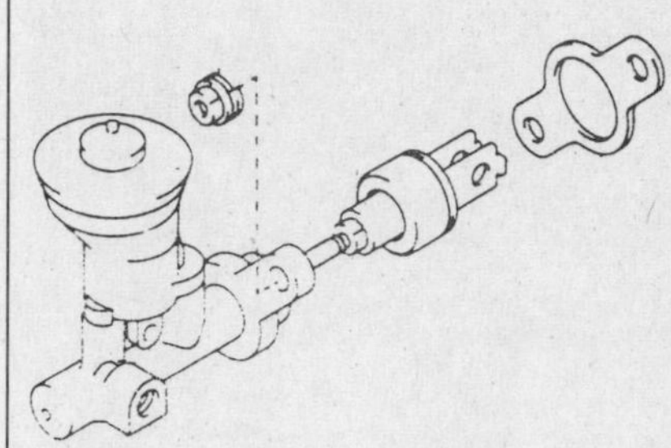

86821293

Fig. 227 The clutch master cylinder is located next to the brake master cylinder

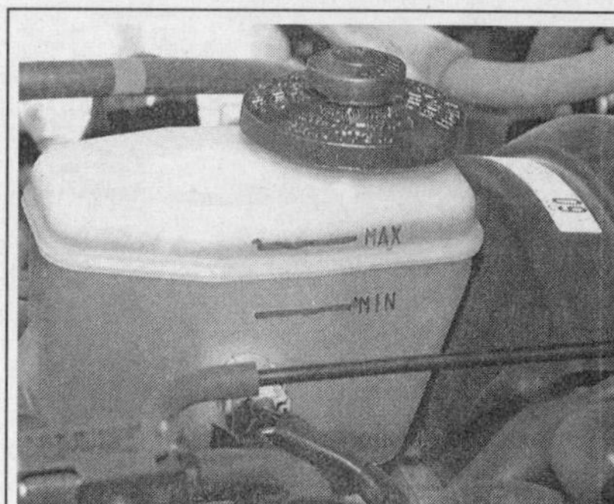

93161p39

Fig. 228 The brake fluid level must be between the MIN and MAX lines on the side of the reservoir

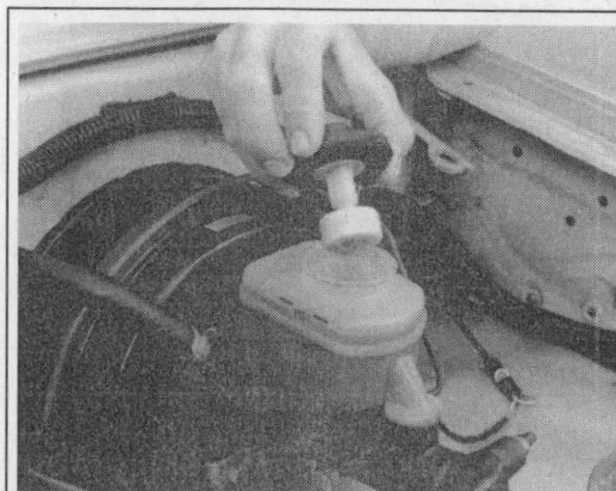

86821295

Fig. 229 As you can see on this brake master cylinder reservoir, the fluid level is slightly low

86821296

Fig. 230 Use a clean funnel and take care to keep brake fluid off painted surfaces

93161p57

Fig. 231 Adding brake fluid to the brake master cylinder reservoir

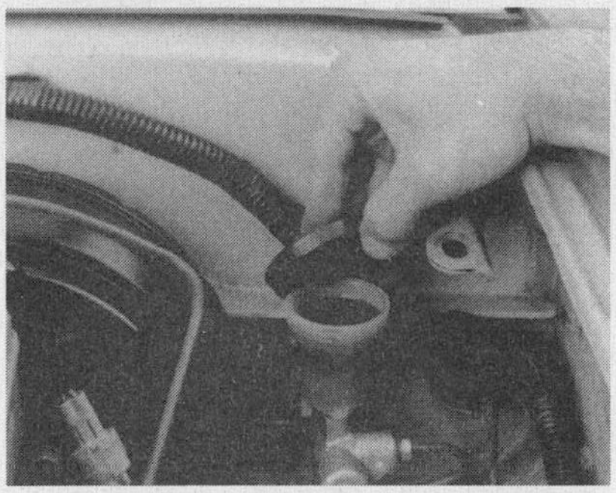

86821292

Fig. 232 Check the fluid level on the side of the clutch master cylinder reservoir. If necessary, lift the cap . . .

86821294

Fig. 233 . . . then fill to the appropriate line with DOT 3 fluid

⁂ WARNING

Brake fluid damages painted surfaces. If any fluid is spilled, immediately clean it off with plenty of clean water. It also absorbs moisture from the air; never leave a container of fluid or the master cylinder or the clutch cylinder uncovered any longer than necessary.

It is normal for the fluid level to fall as the disc brake pads wear. However, if the master cylinder requires filling frequently, you should check the system for leaks in the hoses, master cylinder, or wheel cylinders.

Power Steering Pump

FLUID RECOMMENDATIONS

Use only DEXRON®II or III Automatic Transmission Fluid (ATF) in the power steering system.

FLUID LEVEL CHECK

See Figures 234, 235, 236, and 237

Check the power steering fluid level every 6 months or 6,000 miles (9,600 km).

1. Park the vehicle on a level surface. Run the engine until normal operating temperature is reached.
2. Turn the steering all the way to the left and then all the way to the right several times. Center the steering wheel and shut off the engine.
3. Open the hood.
4. Remove the filler cap on the power steering fluid reservoir and wipe the dipstick clean.
5. Reinsert the dipstick and tighten the cap. Remove the dipstick and note the fluid level indicated on the dipstick.
6. The level should be at any point below the Full mark, but not below the ADD mark (in the HOT or COLD ranges).
7. Add fluid as necessary. Do not overfill.

Chassis Greasing

See Figures 238, 239, and 240

Complete chassis greasing should include an inspection of all rubber suspension bushings, as well as proper greasing of the front suspension upper and lower ball joints, control arm bushings and especially the driveshaft universal joints. To provide correct operation, the chassis should be greased with every oil and filter change or 7,500 miles (12,070 km). Use a standard, good quality lithium base chassis grease (NLGI No. 2).

To lubricate the chassis of your Toyota truck, use a cartridge-type grease gun and good quality lithium grease. Clean the grease fitting first, to avoid pushing dirt into the joint. Push the nozzle of the grease gun onto the fitting and while applying pressure, force the new grease into the fitting. Force sufficient grease into the fitting to cause some old grease to be expelled (called purging the joint) and until you see fresh grease begin to run out of the joint. Wipe off expelled grease; keep the fittings and joints free of excess grease. Take care to keep chassis grease off rubber components such as tires and flexible brake lines.

86821297

Fig. 234 Remove the filler cap on the power steering fluid reservoir and wipe the dipstick clean

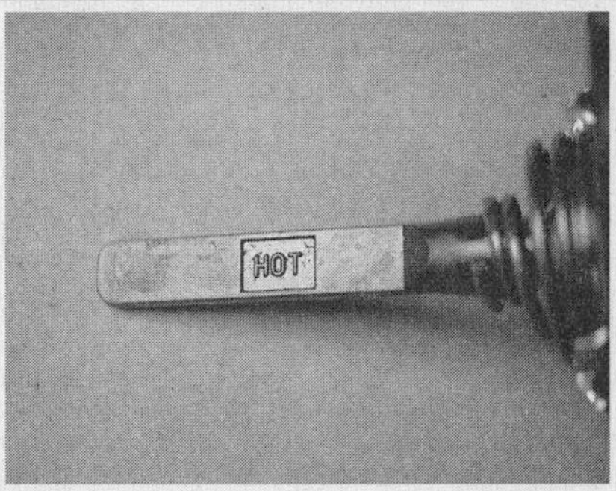

93161p13

Fig. 235 The power steering fluid dipstick has a full when hot mark on one side . . .

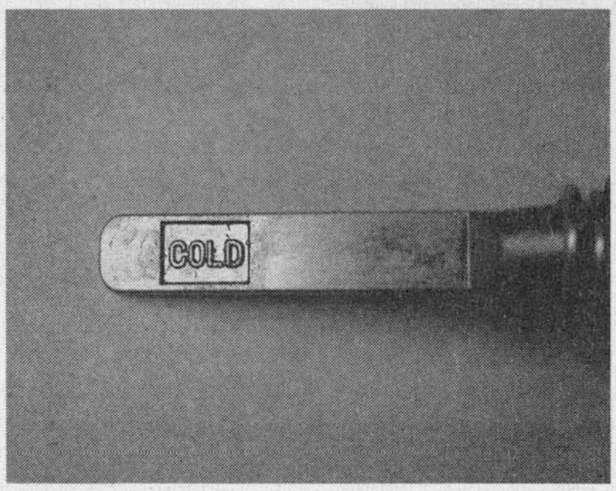

93161p14

Fig. 236 . . . and a full cold mark on the other side

93161p56

Fig. 237 If necessary, add the proper type and amount of fluid to the power steering pump

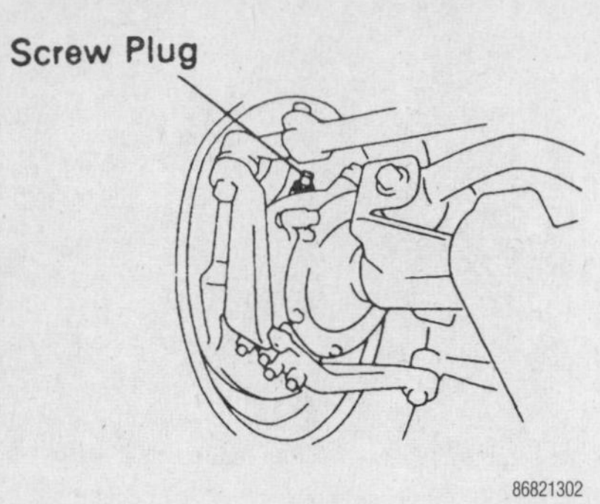

Fig. 238 On the steering knuckles, there is a screw plug to be removed and lubricated

Not all areas can be greased. Some steering and suspension components are lubricated at the factory and use permanently sealed joints; no lubrication is necessary.

Four wheel drive vehicles have several lubrication points within the driveshaft and driveline. Some of these fittings are tucked into hard to see places; make certain each one is accounted for.

PARKING BRAKE LINKAGE

At yearly intervals or whenever binding is noticeable in the parking brake linkage, lubricate the cable guides, levers and linkage with a suitable chassis grease.

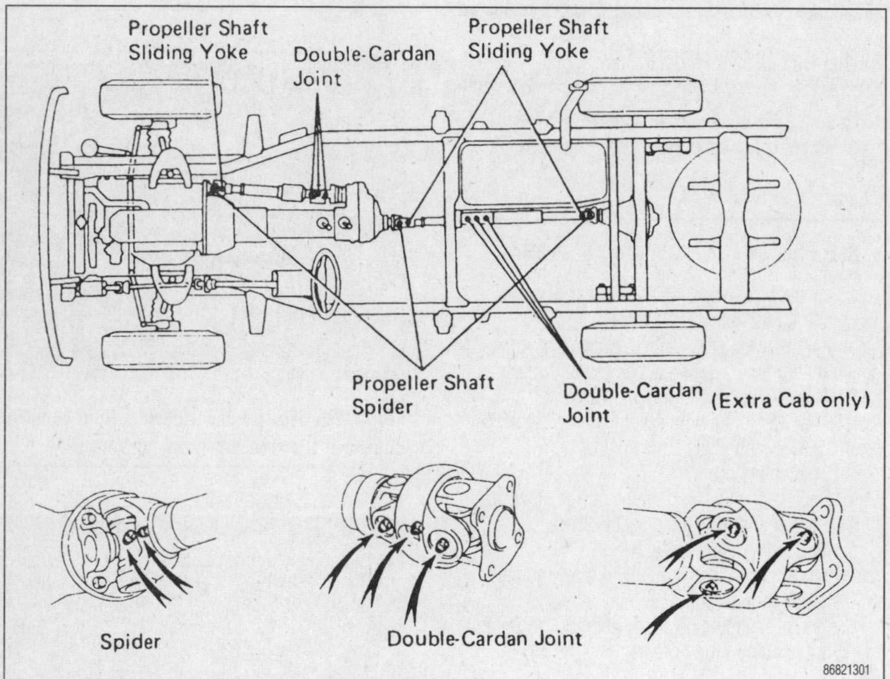

Fig. 239 Typical Toyota truck chassis grease points

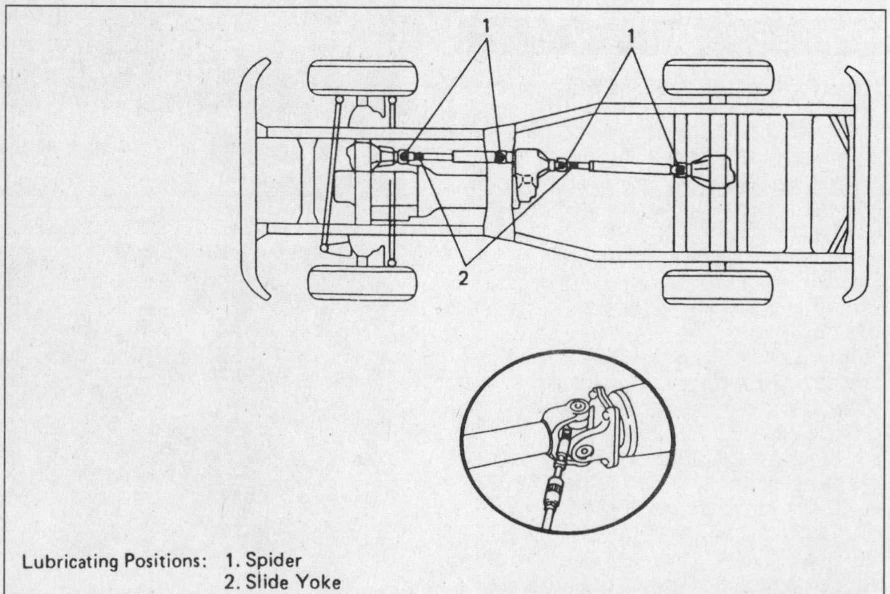

Fig. 240 Grease points on the Land Cruiser. Pay particular attention to the driveshaft universal joints

Body Lubrication and Maintenance

Door handles, hinges, and locks should be lubricated at least once a year. Use a light lithium grease for hinges and handles. Use spray graphite for door locks. Do not inject oil into door locks; it attracts and holds dirt and grit, causing binding and stiff operation, particularly in cold weather.

Additionally, a small amount of grease should be applied to the hood and trunk latches and hinges periodically. Other moving components such as seat back pivots or cargo compartments should be attended to on as-needed basis.

➡When performing lubrication of any item in the passenger area (doors, locks, etc.) apply lubricant sparingly and thoroughly wipe up the excess to prevent lubricant getting onto upholstery and/or clothing.

EXTERIOR CARE

Keep the exterior of the vehicle clean. Dirt can cause small scratches in the paint and the chemicals in road dirt and air pollution can cause paint damage. Frequent washing is recommended; this is particularly important for vehicles used in snowy areas, near salt water or any vehicle used off the road.

Wash the vehicle in the shade when the body is not hot to the touch. Wash with mild car-wash soap and rinse thoroughly before the soap dries on the paint. It may be necessary to wash and rinse the vehicle in sections to prevent the soap from streaking the paint. Never use gasoline or strong solvents to clean painted surfaces.

Use a chamois or soft, lint-free rag to dry the exterior. Wring the drying rag out frequently and keep it away from areas in which it may pick up dirt or grit. If the rag or chamois is dropped on the ground, rinse it thoroughly before continuing; it may carry grit which will scratch the finish.

After the paint is completely dry, the bodywork may be waxed with any of the commercial car polishes or waxes. Read the can carefully before purchase; use good judgment in deciding the condition of the finish. A wax for older finishes will have more abrasive to remove oxidized paint. A 'new car' wax will have much less abrasive. Toyota has some suggestions on washing and waxing your Toyota truck in the Owner's Manual.

Wheel Bearings

➡Front wheel bearings on 4WD vehicles are covered in Section 7. Do not attempt to disassemble the bearings and hubs on these vehicles without referring to the appropriate procedures.

Only the front wheel bearings require periodic service. The lubricant to use is high temperature disc brake-rated wheel bearing grease meeting NLGI No. 2 specifications. This service is recommended at 30,000 miles or every 36 months or whenever the truck has been driven in water up to the hub.

Wheel Bearing Service Precautions

Before servicing wheel bearings, observe the following:

- Remove all outside dirt from the housing before exposing the bearing.

- Treat a used bearing as carefully as a new one.
- Work with clean tools in clean surroundings.
- Use clean, dry canvas gloves, or at least clean, dry hands.
- Clean solvents and flushing fluids are a must.
- Use clean paper when laying out the bearings to dry.
- Protect disassembled bearings from rust and dirt. Cover them up.
- Use clean cloths to wipe bearings.
- Keep the bearings in oil-proof paper when they are to be stored or are not in use.
- Clean the inside of the housing before replacing the bearings.
- Do not spin dry bearings with compressed air. They will be damaged.

REMOVAL, PACKING, AND INSTALLATION

2 Wheel Drive (2WD) Vehicles

See Figures 241, 242, 243, 244, and 245

1. Loosen the wheel lugnuts.
2. Raise and safely support the vehicle on safety stands.
3. Remove the wheels.
4. Remove the brake caliper from its mount. Use stiff wire to suspend it out of the way; do not loosen the brake hose at the caliper. Remove the brake pads.
5. Remove the grease cap. Remove the cotter pin and locknut. Use a socket of the correct size to loosen and remove the axle nut.
6. Remove the hub and brake disc together with the outer bearing and thrust washer. Use your thumbs to keep the pieces inside the hub as the unit is removed. Be careful not to drop the outer bearing.
7. Use a small prying tool to remove the inner bearing seal. Once the seal is out, remove the bearing from the hub.
8. Place both bearings and all the nuts, caps, etc., into a wide container of cleaning solvent. Cleanliness is essential to wheel bearing maintenance. Use a soft bristle brush to clean every bit of grease from every component. Place each cleaned component on a clean, lint-free cloth and allow them to air dry.
9. Inspect the bearings for pitting, flat spots, rust, and rough areas. Check the races (inner surfaces of the hub) for the same conditions. If any damage is seen, the components must be replaced. As a general rule, if either a bearing or race is damaged, the matching part that contacts it should also be replaced. Replacement bearings, seals and other required parts can be bought at an auto parts store. The old parts that are to be replaced should be taken along to be compared with the replacement part to insure a perfect match.

To pack:

10. Pack the wheel bearings with grease. There are special devices made for the specific purpose of greasing bearings, but if one is not available, pack the wheel bearings by hand. Put a large dab of grease in the palm of your hand and push the bearing through it with a sliding motion. The grease must be forced through the side of the bearing and in between each roller. Continue until the grease begins to ooze out the other side and through the gaps between the rollers; the bearing must be completely packed with grease.
11. Coat the inside of the hub and cap with grease, but do not pack it solid. Remember that the spindle (axle) has to pass through the center.

To install:

12. Clean the spindle thoroughly and inspect it for any sign of damage. Coat it with a very light layer of bearing grease.
13. Install the inner bearing into the race. Use a seal driver of the correct diameter to install a NEW grease seal over the bearing. Reusing the old seal may cost more money than it saves; if the grease leaks out and the bearing fails, the wheel may seize while in motion.

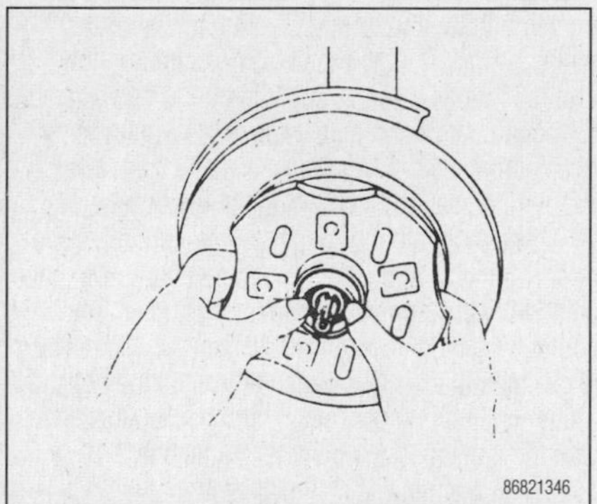

Fig. 241 Use your thumbs to keep the parts inside the hub as the unit is removed

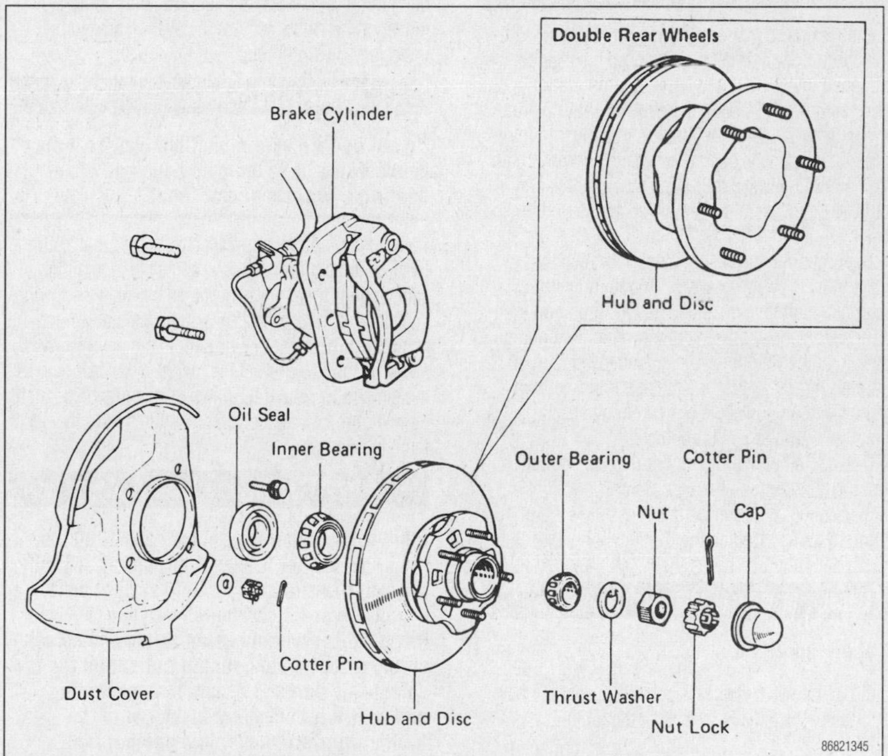

Fig. 242 Exploded view of the 2WD front wheel bearing components

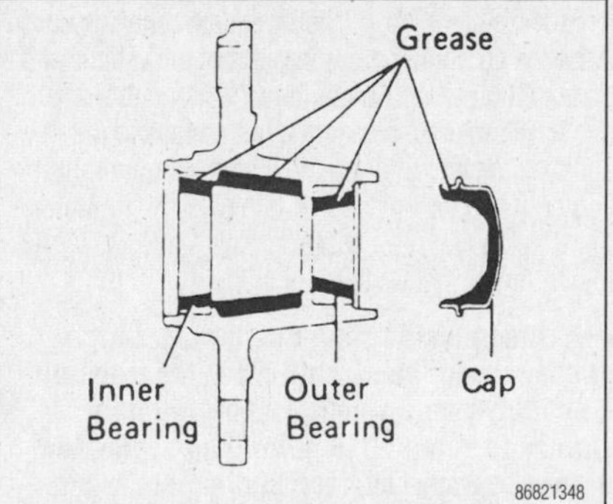

Fig. 243 These areas should be cleaned and regreased during front wheel bearing maintenance

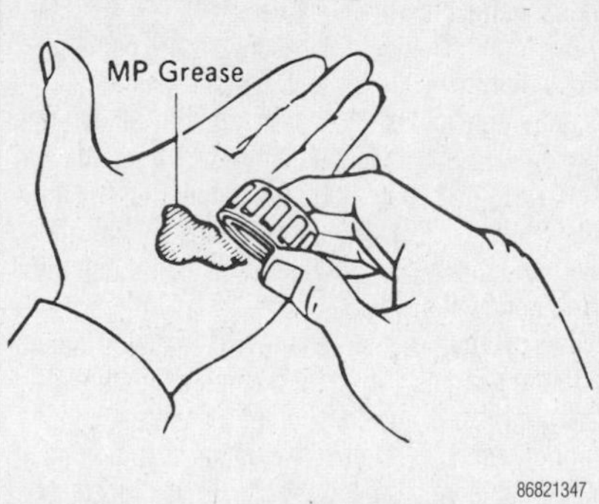

Fig. 244 Put a large dab of grease into the palm of your hand, then move the bearing in a sliding motion through the grease

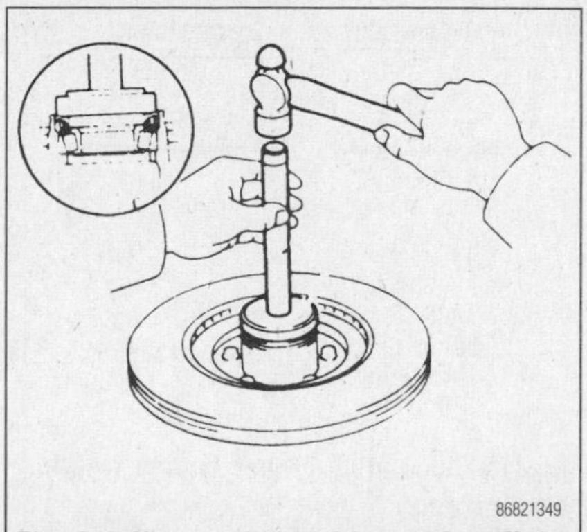

Fig. 245 Use a suitable driver to install the grease seal

14. Place the hub and disc onto the spindle. Install the outer bearing and the flat thrust washer.

15. Install the locknut and use a torque wrench to adjust the nut to 25 ft. lbs. (34 Nm).

16. Turn the hub in each direction several times to seat and snug the bearing. Loosen the locknut until it can be turned by hand without the wrench. Don't loosen it any more than necessary to be finger-loose. (Loosening the nut takes the pre-tension off the bearing.)

17. Install the locknut, cotter pin and grease cap. Make certain the cap is not crooked or loose.

18. Install the brake pads and caliper.

19. Install the wheel and lugnuts (hand-tight). Lower the vehicle to the ground and tighten the lugnuts.

TRAILER TOWING

General Recommendations

Your vehicle was primarily designed to carry passengers and cargo. It is important to remember that towing a trailer will place additional loads on your vehicle's engine, drive train, steering, braking and other systems. However, if you find decide to tow a trailer, using the proper equipment is a must.

Local laws may require specific equipment such as trailer brakes or fender mounted mirrors. Check your local laws.

Trailer Weight

The maximum gross trailer weight (trailer weight plus cargo weight) must never exceed the weights published in your Owner's Manual. This weight varies across the Toyota truck product line. It varies from vehicle to vehicle and is also dependent on the engine size and whether the vehicle is equipped with 2WD or 4WD. Always follow the recommendation in your Owner's Manual or consult an authorized Toyota dealer.

The gross vehicle weight must not exceed the Gross Vehicle Weight Rating (GVWR) indicated on the truck's Certification Label, usually found on the driver's side door post. The gross vehicle weight is the sum of the weights of the unloaded vehicle, driver, passengers, luggage, hitch and trailer tongue loads. It also includes the weight of any special equipment installed on the vehicle.

The load on either the front or rear axle resulting from the distribution of the gross vehicle weight on both axles must not exceed the Gross Axle Weight Rating (GAWR) listed on the Certification Label.

Hitch (Tongue) Weight

➧ **See Figure 246**

Figure the hitch weight to select a proper hitch. Hitch weight is usually 9–11% of the trailer gross weight and should be measured with the trailer loaded. Never load the trailer with more weight in the back than in the front. About 60% of the trailer load should be in the front half of the trailer and the remaining 40% in the rear.

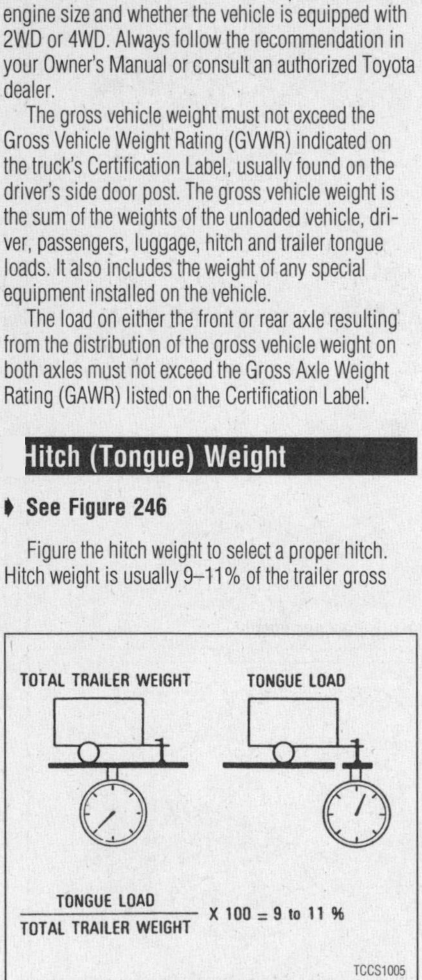

Fig. 246 Calculating proper tongue weight for your trailer

Use only a weight carrying hitch designed for the total trailer weight. Toyota does not recommend using a weight distribution (load equalizing) hitch. The hitch must be bolted securely to the vehicle frame and installed according to the hitch manufacturer's instructions.

Toyota recommends removing the hitch when not towing to prevent injury and/or damage due to the hitch in the event of a rear end collision. After removal of the hitch, seal the installation area to prevent entry of dirt or mud.

WARNING

Do not use an axle-mounting hitch as it may cause damage to the axle housing, wheel bearings, wheels and/or tires.

Toyota recommends trailers with brakes that conform to all applicable federal and state regulations. A safety chain must always be used between the towing vehicle and the trailer. Leave sufficient slack in the chain for turns. The chains should cross under the trailer tongue to prevent the tongue from dropping to the ground in case it becomes damaged or separated. Follow correct safety chain procedures from the hitch manufacturer.

WARNING

If the total trailer weight exceeds 1000 lbs. (453 kg), trailer brakes are required. NEVER tap into the truck's hydraulic system as it would lower its braking effectiveness. Never tow a trailer without using safety chains securely attached to both the trailer and the tow vehicle. If damage occurs to the coupling unit or hitch ball, there is danger of the trailer wandering over into another lane.

Check the gross weight rating of your trailer. Tongue weight is usually figured as 10% of gross trailer weight. Therefore, a trailer with a maximum gross weight of 2000 lbs. will have a maximum tongue weight of 200 lbs. Class I trailers fall into this category. Class II trailers are those with a gross weight rating of 2000–3000 lbs., while Class III trailers fall into the 3500–6000 lbs. category. Class IV trailers are those over 6000 lbs. and are for use with fifth wheel trucks, only.

When you've determined the hitch that you'll need, follow the manufacturer's installation instructions, exactly, especially when it comes to fastener torque. The hitch will subjected to a lot of stress and good hitches come with hardened bolts. Never substitute an inferior bolt for a hardened bolt.

Cooling

ENGINE

One of the most common, if not THE most common, problems associated with trailer towing is engine overheating. The vehicle's cooling system should be regularly serviced so it will operate at peak efficiency.

Aftermarket engine oil coolers are helpful for prolonging engine oil life and reducing overall engine temperatures. Both of these factors increase engine life. While not absolutely necessary in towing Class I and some Class II trailers, they are recommended for heavier Class II and all Class III towing. Engine oil cooler systems consists of an adapter, screwed on in place of the oil filter, a remote filter mounting and a multi-tube, finned heat exchanger, which is mounted in front of the radiator or air conditioning condenser. It would be wise to consult with your Toyota dealer before making any modifications to your truck's cooling or engine oil systems.

TRANSMISSION

An automatic transmission is usually recommended for trailer towing. Modern automatics have proven reliable and, of course, easy to operate, in trailer towing. The increased load of a trailer, however, causes an increase in the temperature of the automatic transmission fluid. Heat is the worst enemy of an automatic transmission. As the temperature of the fluid increases, the life of the fluid decreases.

Although automatic transmissions normally have remote coolers, many trailer towing vehicles will have an additional automatic transmission cooler. The cooler, which consists of a multi-tube, finned heat exchanger, is usually installed in front of the radiator or air conditioning condenser, and hooked in-line with the transmission cooler tank inlet line. Follow the cooler manufacturer's installation instructions and consult with your Toyota dealer before making any modifications to your truck's transmission fluid systems.

Select a cooler of at least adequate capacity, based upon the combined gross weights of the vehicle and trailer. Cooler manufacturers recommend that you use an aftermarket cooler in addition to, and not instead of, the factory-installed automatic transmission cooler. If you do want to use it in place of the factory-installed cooler, get a cooler at least two sizes larger than normally necessary.

➡A transmission cooler can, sometimes, cause slow or harsh shifting in the transmission during cold weather, until the fluid has a chance to come up to normal operating temperature. Some coolers can be purchased with or retrofitted with a temperature bypass valve which will allow fluid flow through the cooler only when the fluid has reached above a certain operating temperature.

TOWING THE VEHICLE

➧ See Figure 247

✻✻ WARNING

Push-starting your Toyota truck is not recommended. All trucks are equipped with a catalytic converter. Raw gas collecting in the converter may cause damage. Additionally, computer controlled fuel injection system components may be damaged. Jump starting from a known good battery is the only recommended method of starting a disabled vehicle.

If a Toyota truck needs to be towed, the best way is to use a flatbed or rollback tow vehicle which can carry the vehicle with all 4 wheels off the ground.

Trucks and 4Runners with manual transmissions may also be towed with either end elevated. To tow with rear wheels on the ground, release the parking bake and put the transmission in NEUTRAL. The transfer case (if 4WD) must be in H2. The H4 button must be off. With automatic transmissions, the rear drive shaft must be disconnected at the differential if towing will exceed 30 mph (48 kph) or a total of 50 miles (80 km). Failure to disconnect the driveshaft will damage the transmission.

Towing trucks and 4Runners with the front wheels on the ground requires the ignition key to be in the **ACC** position to release the steering lock. On 4WD units, put the transmission in NEUTRAL and the transfer case selector in H2. Disengage the free-wheeling hubs if so equipped. To tow with the front wheels on the ground, the steering wheel must be held in place with special equipment commonly carried on tow trucks. The anti-theft lock is not strong enough to hold the front wheels straight during towing.

Land Cruisers may be towed in similar manners but in all cases the center differential switch must be OFF and the center differential set in the FREE position.

All vehicles are equipped with tow hooks front and rear which may be used for flat towing with a rope or chain. A driver must be in the vehicle to steer it and operate the brakes. Towing in this manner must only be done for a short distance at low speeds. The entire drive line, wheels, axles, etc., must be in serviceable condition. The transmission must be in NEUTRAL and, on 4WD models, the transfer case in H2. On Land Cruisers, switch the center differential lock OFF.

Consult your Owner's Manual for additional towing cautions that may apply specifically to your model truck.

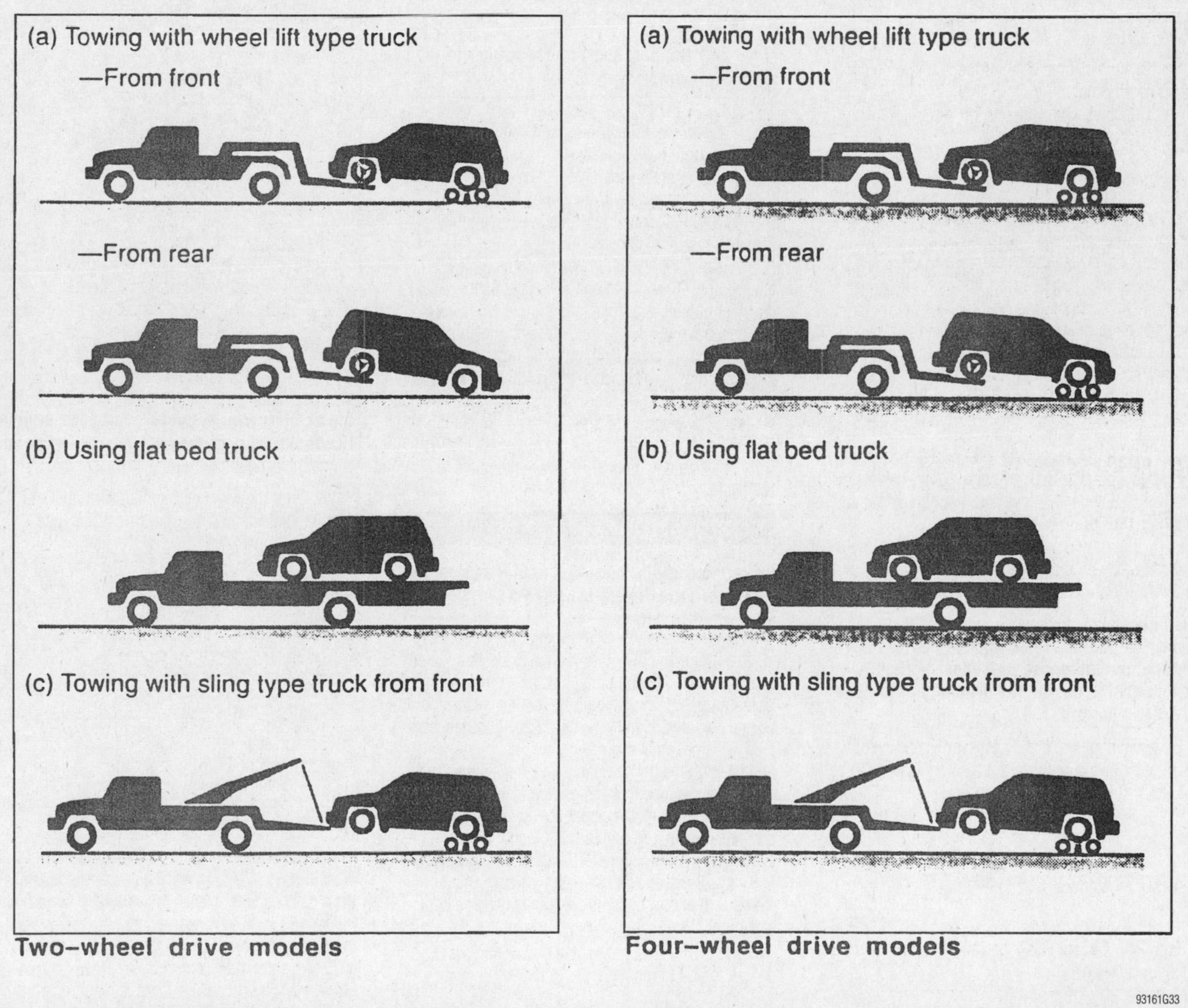

Fig. 247 Suggested ways of towing a Toyota truck—4Runner shown, others similar

JUMP STARTING A DEAD BATTERY

➧ **See Figures 248 and 249**

Whenever a vehicle is jump started, precautions must be followed in order to prevent the possibility of personal injury. Remember that batteries contain a small amount of explosive hydrogen gas which is a by-product of battery charging. Sparks should always be avoided when working around batteries, especially when attaching jumper cables. To minimize the possibility of accidental sparks, follow the procedure carefully.

✲✲ WARNING

NEVER hook the batteries up in a series circuit or the entire electrical system can be damaged.

JUMP STARTING PRECAUTIONS

- Be sure that both batteries are of the same voltage. Vehicles covered by this manual and most vehicles on the road today use a 12 volt charging system.
- Be sure that both batteries are of the same polarity (have the same terminal, in most cases NEGATIVE grounded).
- Be sure that the vehicles are not touching or a short could occur.
- On serviceable batteries, be sure the vent cap holes are not obstructed.
- Do not smoke or allow sparks anywhere near the batteries.
- In cold weather, make sure the battery electrolyte is not frozen. This can occur more readily in a battery that has been in a state of discharge.
- Do not allow electrolyte to contact your skin or clothing.

JUMP STARTING PROCEDURE

1. Make sure that the voltages of the 2 batteries are the same. Most batteries and charging systems are of the 12 volt variety.
2. Pull the jumping vehicle (with the good battery) into a position so the jumper cables can reach the dead battery and that vehicle's engine. Make sure that the vehicles do NOT touch.
3. Place the transmissions of both vehicles in Neutral or Park, Os applicable, then firmly set their parking brakes.

➡If necessary for safety reasons, the hazard lights on both vehicles may be operated throughout the entire procedure without significantly increasing the difficulty of jumping the dead battery.

4. Turn all lights and accessories off on both vehicles. Make sure the ignition switches on both vehicles are turned to the **OFF** position.
5. Use a cloth to cover the battery cell caps, if equipped, but do not cover the terminals.
6. Make sure the terminals on both batteries are clean and free of corrosion or proper electrical connection will be impeded. If necessary, clean the battery terminals before proceeding.

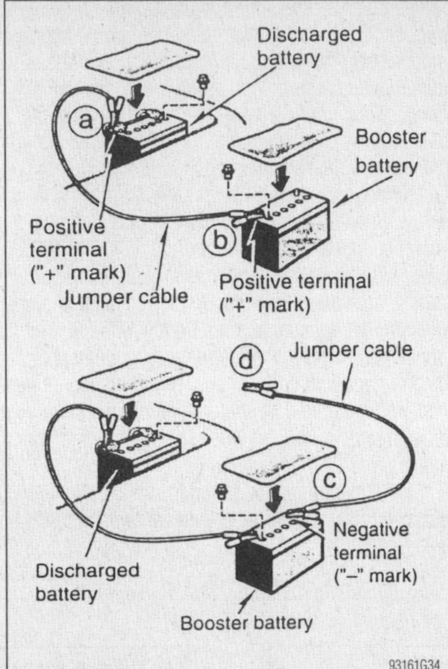

Fig. 248 Connect the jumper cables in the following order: a, b, c, d

7. Identify the positive (+) and negative (–) terminals on both battery posts.
8. Connect the first jumper cable to the positive (+) terminal of the dead battery, then connect the other end of that cable to the positive (+) terminal of the booster (good) battery.
9. Connect one end of the other jumper cable to the negative (–) terminal on the booster battery and the other cable clamp to a good ground, away from the dead battery. Toyota seems to favor the engine removal hooks or possibly the bracket retaining the throttle cables. Try to pick a ground on the engine that is positioned away from the battery in order to minimize the possibility of the 2 clamps touching should one loosen during the procedure. DO NOT connect this clamp to the negative (–) terminal of the bad battery.

✲✲ CAUTION

Be very careful to keep the jumper cables away from moving parts (cooling fan, belts, etc.) on both engines.

10. Check to make sure that the cables are routed away from any moving parts, then start the donor vehicle's engine. Run the engine at moderate speed for several minutes to allow the dead battery a chance to receive some initial charge.
11. With the donor vehicle's engine still running slightly above idle, try to start the vehicle with the dead battery. Crank the engine for no more than 10 seconds at a time and let the starter cool for at least 20 seconds between tries. If the vehicle does not start in 3 tries, it is likely that something else is also wrong or that the battery needs additional time to charge.

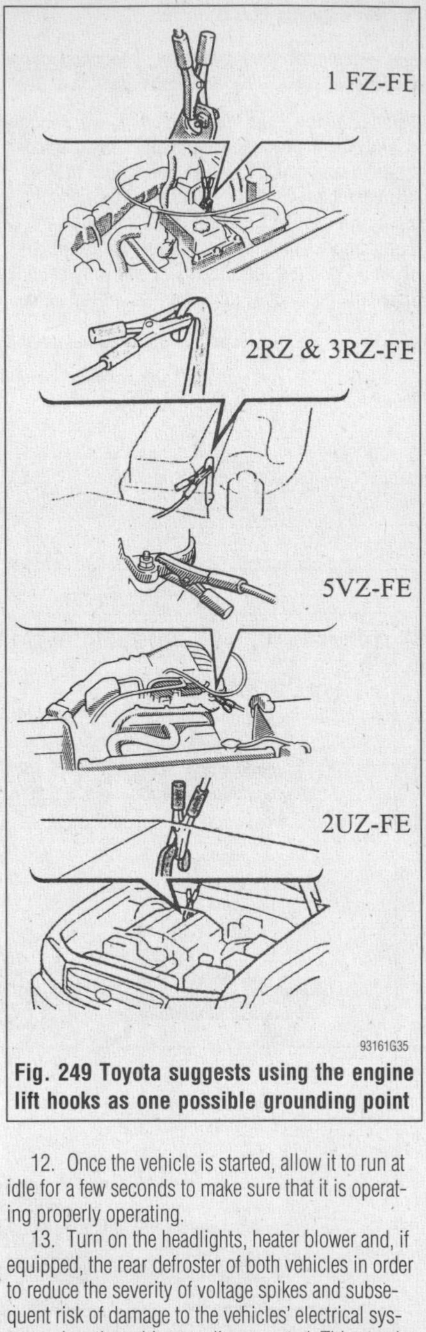

Fig. 249 Toyota suggests using the engine lift hooks as one possible grounding point

12. Once the vehicle is started, allow it to run at idle for a few seconds to make sure that it is operating properly operating.
13. Turn on the headlights, heater blower and, if equipped, the rear defroster of both vehicles in order to reduce the severity of voltage spikes and subsequent risk of damage to the vehicles' electrical systems when the cables are disconnected. This step is especially important to late model vehicles equipped with computer control modules.
14. Carefully disconnect the cables in the reverse order of connection. Start with the negative cable that is attached to the engine ground, then the negative cable on the donor battery. Disconnect the positive cable from the donor battery and finally, disconnect the positive cable from the formerly dead battery. Be careful when disconnecting the cables from the positive terminals not to allow the alligator clips to touch any metal on either vehicle or a short and sparks will occur.

JACKING

See Figures 250 thru 268

Your vehicle was supplied with a jack for emergency road repairs. This jack is adequate for the job it was designed to do—for changing a flat tire in an emergency where you are not required to go beneath the vehicle. If it is used in an emergency situation, carefully follow the instructions provided either with the jack or in your Owner's Manual. The Toyota truck Owner's Manual have good coverage of how to use their jack in an emergency. Do not attempt to use the jack in any places other than specified by the vehicle manufacturer. Always block the diagonally opposite wheel when using a jack.

A more convenient way of jacking is the use of a garage or floor jack. Never place the jack under the radiator, engine or transmission components. Severe and expensive damage will result when the jack is raised. Additionally, never jack under the floorpan or bodywork; the metal will deform.

Whenever you plan to work under the vehicle, you must support it on safety stands or ramps. Never use cinder blocks or stacks of wood to support the vehicle, even if you're only going to be under it for a few minutes. Never crawl under the vehicle when it is supported only by the tire-changing jack or other floor jack.

Small hydraulic, screw, or scissors jacks are satisfactory for raising the vehicle. Drive-on trestles or ramps are also a handy and safe way to both raise and support the vehicle. Be careful though, some ramps may be too steep to drive your vehicle onto without scraping the front bottom panels. Never support the vehicle on any suspension member (unless specifically instructed to do so by a repair manual) or underbody panel.

The following safety points cannot be overemphasized:

- Always block the opposite wheel or wheels to keep the vehicle from rolling off the jack.
- When raising the front of the vehicle, firmly apply the parking brake.
- Always use safety stands to support the vehicle when you are working underneath. Place the stands beneath the scissors jacking brackets. Before climbing underneath, rock the vehicle a bit to make sure it is firmly supported.

93161p78

Fig. 250 If necessary, remove the center cap

93161p75

Fig. 251 A wheel lock key is the only way to remove the wheel locks from the wheels. Make sure to keep it in the vehicle at all times

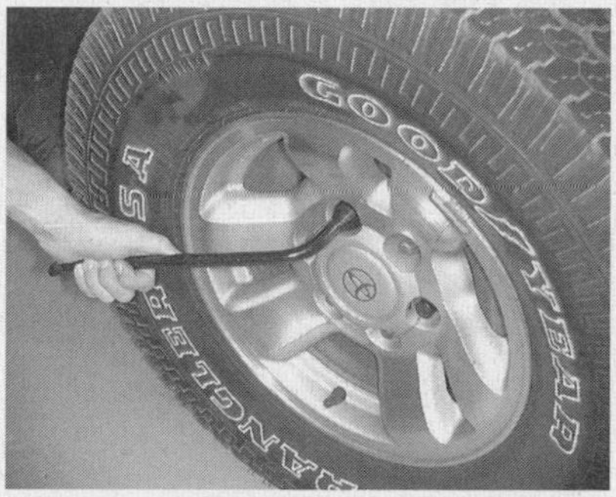

93161p74

Fig. 252 Removing the lug nuts with the supplied lug wrench

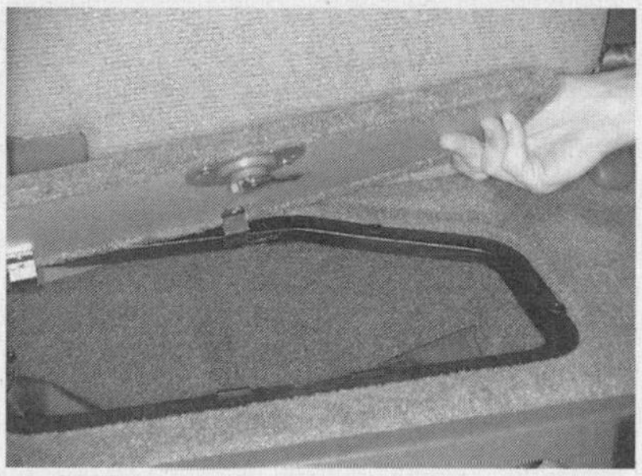

93161p61

Fig. 253 Detach the storage compartment cover to access the jack—1998 Tacoma shown

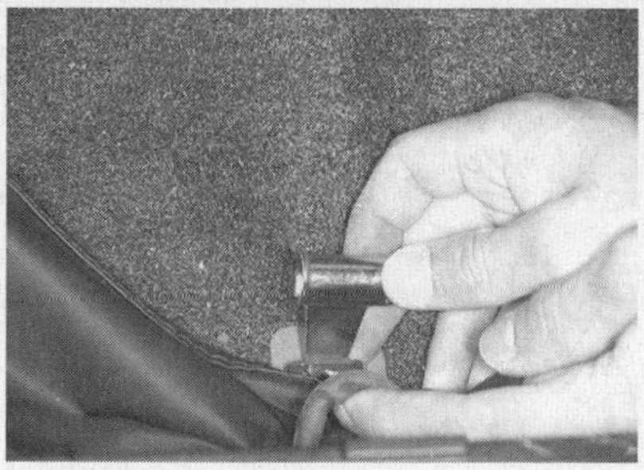

93161p62

Fig. 254 Remove the rubber band that secures the lug wrench to the inner compartment

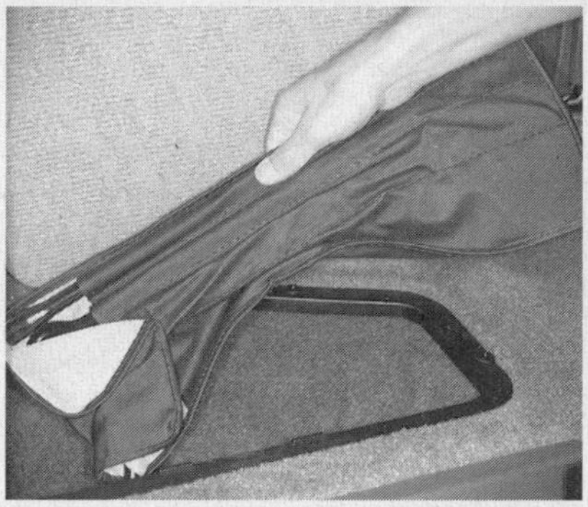

93161p63

Fig. 255 Removing the tool kit from the storage compartment

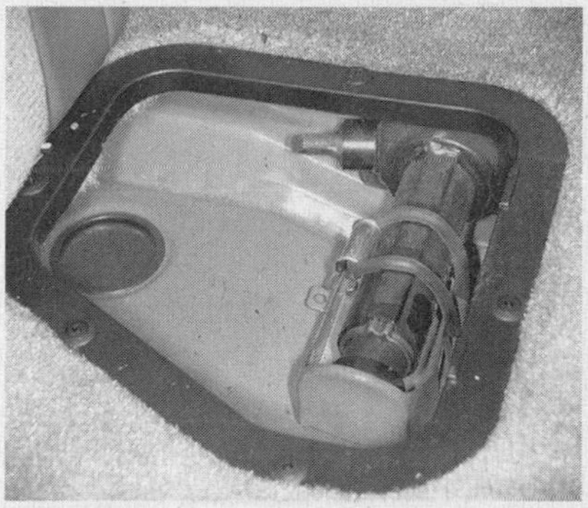

93161p65

Fig. 256 Location of the jack

93161p71

Fig. 257 Front jacking point—1998 Tacoma shown

93161p66

Fig. 258 Using the supplied jack to lift the rear axle—1998 Tacoma shown

93161p69

Fig. 259 Put the jack handle, the extension, and the handle end together and insert the assembly into the hole just above the trailer hitch ball as shown

93161p70

Fig. 260 Insert the end of the jack handle into the lowering screw

93161p68

Fig. 261 Lowering the spare tire from the vehicle

93161pf2

Fig. 262 Always tighten the lug nuts to the proper torque

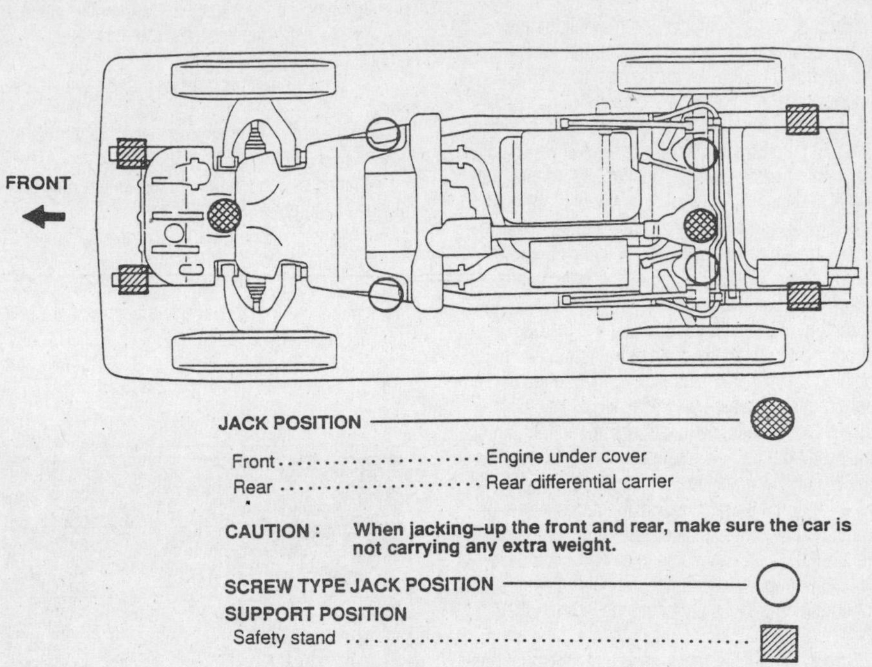

93161G36

Fig. 263 Vehicle lift and support locations—Land Cruiser shown

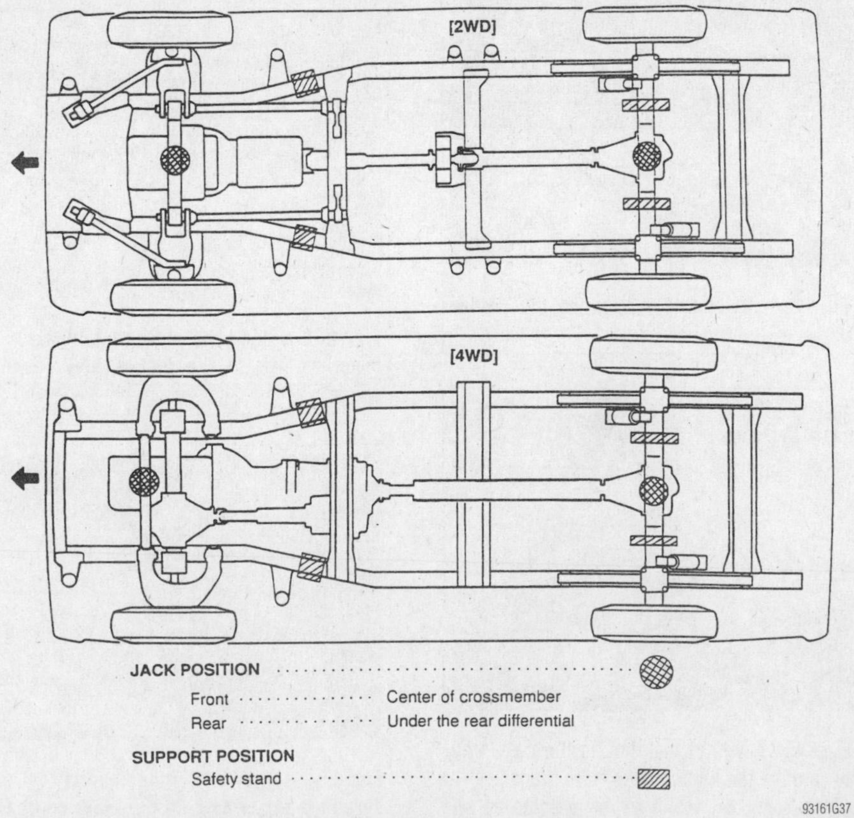

93161G37

Fig. 264 Vehicle lift and support locations—T100 Pick-Up Trucks shown

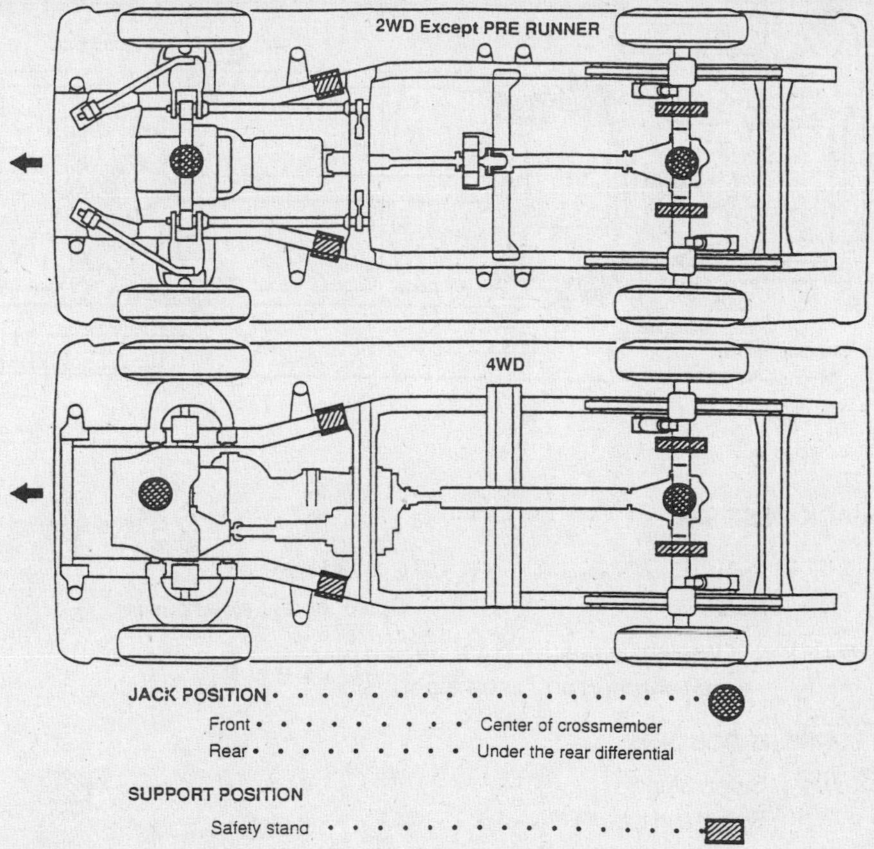

Fig. 265 Vehicle lift and support locations—Tacoma shown

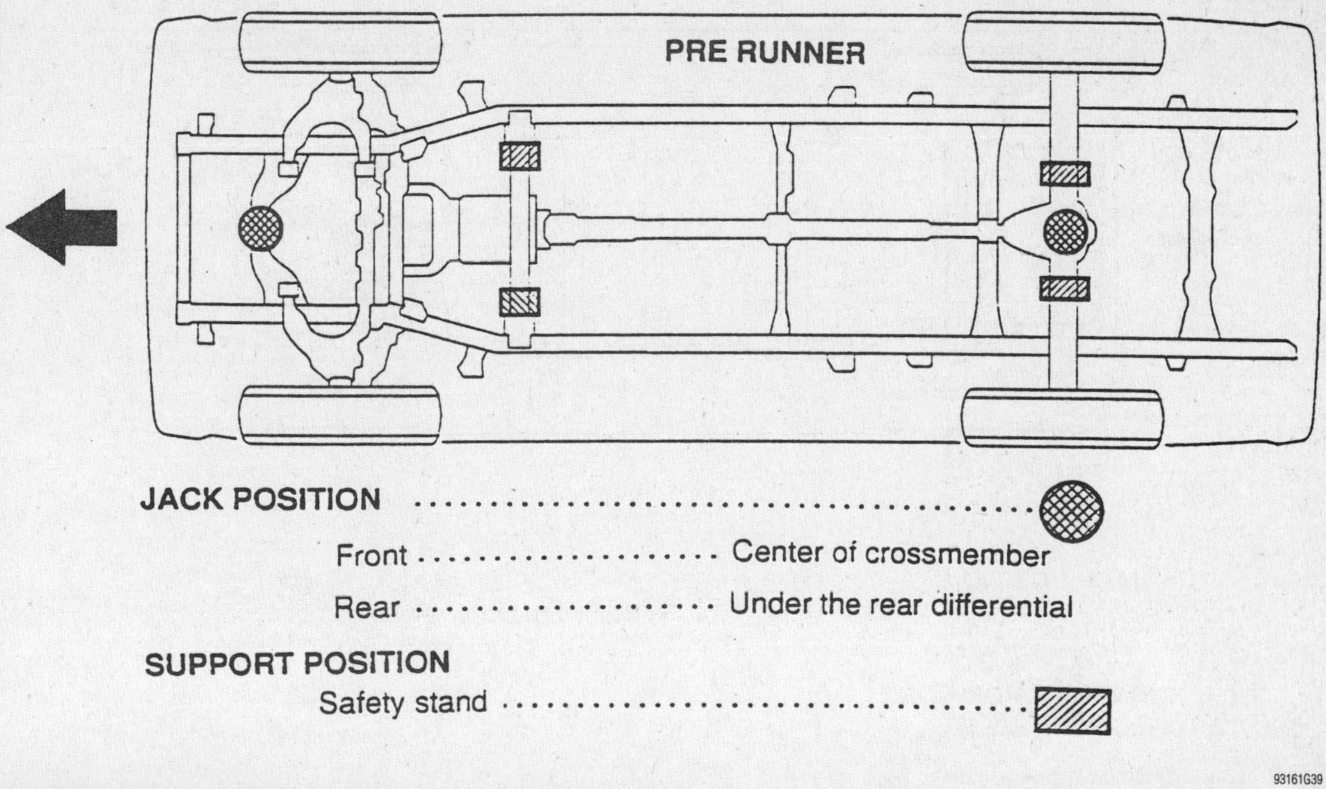

Fig. 266 Vehicle lift and support locations—Tacoma Pre Runner shown

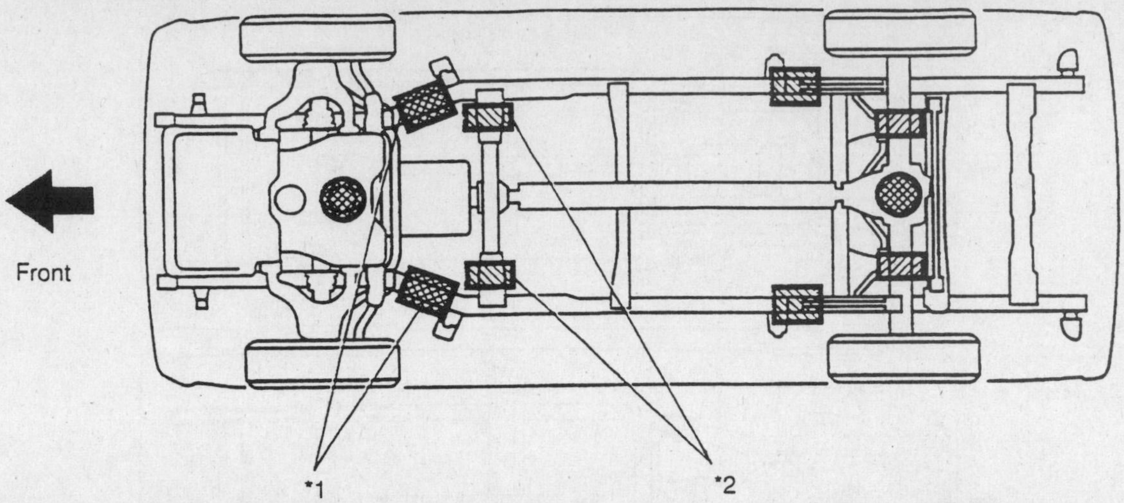

JACK POSITION . . . .

Front . . . . Center of crossmember
Rear . . . . Center of rear axle housing

CAUTION: When jacking–up the front and rear make sure the car is not carrying any extra eight.

SUPPORT POSITION

Safety stand . . . .
Swing arm type lift . . . .

*1: Support position when equipping without side step.
*2: Support position when equipping with side step.

93161G40

Fig. 267 Vehicle lift and support locations—4Runner shown

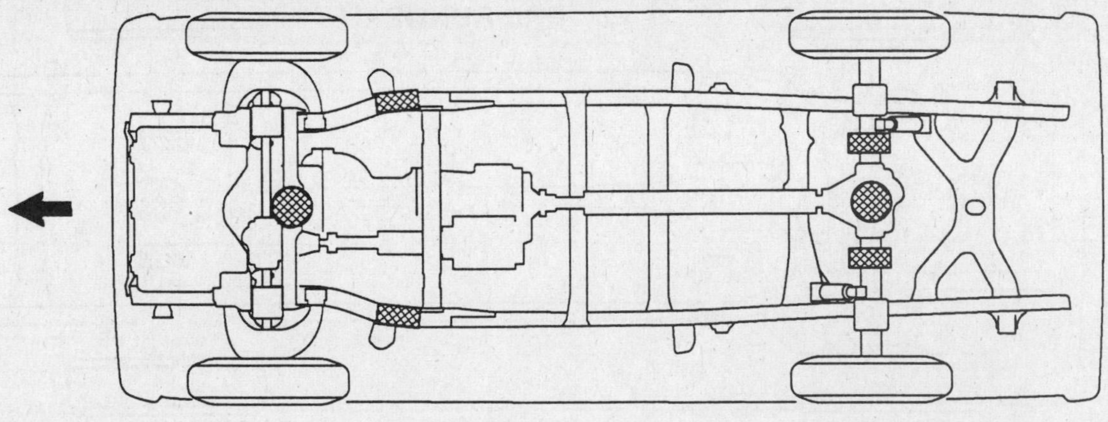

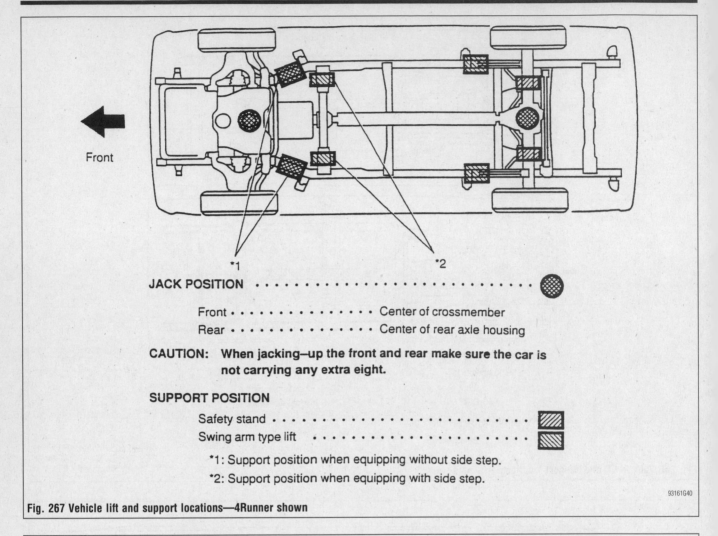

JACK POSITION • • • • • • • • • • • • • • • • • •
Front • • • • • • • • • • Center of crossmember
Rear • • • • • • • • • • Center of rear axle housing

SUPPORT POSITION
Safety stand • • • • • • • • • • • • • • • • •

93161g44

Fig. 268 Vehicle lift and support locations—Tundra shown

MANUFACTURER RECOMMENDED NORMAL MAINTENANCE INTERVALS

		VEHICLE MAINTENANCE INTERVAL (x1000)																		
	Miles	5	10	15	20	25	30	35	40	45	50	55	60	65	70	75	80	85	90	95
	km	8	16	24	32	40	48	56	64	72	80	88	96	104	112	121	128	136	144	153
TO BE SERVICED	**TYPE OF SERVICE**																			
Automatic transmission and differential fluid	S/I			✓			✓			✓			✓			✓			✓	
Ball joints and boots	S/I			✓			✓			✓			✓			✓			✓	
Brake linings, discs/drums, lines & hoses	S/I			✓			✓			✓			✓			✓			✓	
Charcoal canister	S/I												✓							
Drive belts	S/I						✓						✓						✓	
Driveshaft bushing (4WD)	L						✓						✓						✓	
Engine coolant	R						✓						✓						✓	
Engine oil & filter	R	✓	✓	✓	✓	✓	✓	✓	✓	✓	✓	✓	✓	✓	✓	✓	✓	✓	✓	✓
Exhaust pipes & mounts	S/I			✓			✓			✓			✓			✓			✓	
Fuel lines & connections, fuel tank vapor vent system hoses, fuel tank band	S/I						✓						✓						✓	
Fuel tank cap gasket	S/I						✓						✓						✓	
Halfshaft boots & flange bolts	S/I			✓			✓			✓			✓			✓			✓	
Limited slip differential fluid	R						✓						✓						✓	
Manual transmission and differential fluid	S/I						✓						✓						✓	
Non-platinum spark plugs	R						✓						✓						✓	
Platinum spark plugs	R												✓							
Propeller shaft (4WD models)	L			✓			✓			✓			✓			✓			✓	
Propeller shaft bolts	S/I			✓			✓			✓			✓			✓			✓	
Rack and pinion assembly	S/I			✓			✓			✓			✓			✓			✓	
Rear wheel bearing	L						✓						✓						✓	
Steering Knuckle	L			✓			✓			✓			✓			✓			✓	
Steering linkage	S/I			✓			✓			✓			✓			✓			✓	
Transfer case and differential fluid	S/I			✓			✓			✓			✓			✓			✓	
Valves	S/I												✓							

R - Replace S/I - Service or Inspect L - Lubricate

93161c05

MANUFACTURER RECOMMENDED SEVERE MAINTENANCE INTERVALS

		VEHICLE MAINTENANCE INTERVAL (x1000)																		
	Miles	5	10	15	20	25	30	35	40	45	50	55	60	65	70	75	80	85	90	95
	km	8	16	24	32	40	48	56	64	72	80	88	96	104	112	121	128	136	144	153
TO BE SERVICED	**TYPE OF SERVICE**																			
Automatic transmission and differential fluid	S/I			✓			✓			✓			✓			✓			✓	
Ball joints and boots	S/I	✓	✓	✓	✓	✓	✓	✓	✓	✓	✓	✓	✓	✓	✓	✓	✓	✓	✓	✓
Brake linings, discs/drums, lines & hoses	S/I	✓	✓	✓	✓	✓	✓	✓	✓	✓	✓	✓	✓	✓	✓	✓	✓	✓	✓	✓
Charcoal canister	S/I												✓							
Drive belts	S/I						✓						✓						✓	
Driveshaft bushing (4WD)	L						✓						✓						✓	
Engine coolant	R						✓						✓						✓	
Engine oil & filter	R	✓	✓	✓	✓	✓	✓	✓	✓	✓	✓	✓	✓	✓	✓	✓	✓	✓	✓	✓
Exhaust pipes & mounts	S/I			✓			✓			✓			✓			✓			✓	
Fuel lines & connections, fuel tank vapor vent system hoses, fuel tank band	S/I						✓						✓						✓	
Fuel tank cap gasket	S/I						✓						✓						✓	
Halfshaft boots & flange bolts	S/I	✓	✓	✓	✓	✓	✓	✓	✓	✓	✓	✓	✓	✓	✓	✓	✓	✓	✓	✓
Limited slip differential fluid	R						✓						✓						✓	
Manual transmission and differential fluid	S/I						✓						✓						✓	
Non-platinum spark plugs	R						✓						✓						✓	

93161c06

MANUFACTURER RECOMMENDED SEVERE MAINTENANCE INTERVALS

		VEHICLE MAINTENANCE INTERVAL (x1000)																		
	Miles	5	10	15	20	25	30	35	40	45	50	55	60	65	70	75	80	85	90	95
	km	8	16	24	32	40	48	56	64	72	80	88	96	104	112	121	128	136	144	153
TO BE SERVICED	TYPE OF SERVICE																			
Platinum spark plugs	R												✓							
Propeller shaft (4WD models)	L			✓			✓			✓			✓			✓			✓	
Propeller shaft bolts	S/I			✓			✓			✓			✓			✓			✓	
Rack and pinion assembly	S/I			✓			✓			✓			✓			✓			✓	
Rear wheel bearing	L						✓						✓						✓	
Steering knuckle	L			✓			✓			✓			✓			✓			✓	
Steering linkage	S/I	✓	✓	✓	✓	✓	✓	✓	✓	✓	✓	✓	✓	✓	✓	✓	✓	✓	✓	✓
Timing belt	R												✓							
Transfer case and differential fluid	S/I			✓			✓			✓			✓			✓			✓	
Valves	S/I												✓							

R - Replace S/I - Service or Inspect L - Lubricate

FREQUENT OPERATION MAINTENANCE (SEVERE SERVICE)

If a vehicle is operated under any of the following conditions it is considered severe service:

- Towing a trailer or using a camper or car-top carrier.

- Repeated short trips of less than 5 miles in temperatures below freezing.

- Excessive idling or low-speed driving for long distances as in heavy commercial use, such as delivery, taxi or police cars.

- Operating on rough, muddy or salt-covered roads.

- Operating on unpaved or dusty roads.

93161c07

CAPACITIES

Year	Model	Engine Displacement Liters (cc)	Engine Identification	Engine Oil with Filter (qts.)	Transmission (pts.) M/T	Transmission (pts.) A/T	Transmission (pts.) 4WD	Drive Axle (pts.)	Fuel Tank (gal.)	Cooling System (qts.)
1997	Land Cruiser	4.5 (4477)	1FZ-FE	7.2	-	②	③	④ ⑤	25.4	14.5
	T100 Pick-Up	2.7 (2694)	3RZ-FE	5.8	①	②	③	④ ⑤	24.0	8.1
	T100 Pick-Up	3.4 (3378)	5VZ-FE	5.5	①	②	③	④ ⑤	24.0	10.6
	Tacoma	2.4 (2438)	2RZ-FE	5.1	①	②	③	④ ⑤	18.0	8.5
	Tacoma	2.7 (2694)	3RZ-FE	5.0	①	②	③	④ ⑤	18.0	8.8
	Tacoma	3.4 (3378)	5VZ-FE	5.4	①	②	③	④ ⑤	18.0	10.3
	4Runner	2.7 (2694)	3RZ-FE	5.0	①	②	③	④ ⑤	18.5	10.6
	4Runner	3.4 (3378)	5VZ-FE	5.2	①	②	③	④ ⑤	18.5	9.4
1998	Land Cruiser	4.7 (4663)	2UZ-FE	7.2	-	②	③	④ ⑤	25.4	15.6 ⑥
	T100 Pick-Up	2.7 (2694)	3RZ-FE	5.8	①	②	③	④ ⑤	24.0	8.1
	T100 Pick-Up	3.4 (3378)	5VZ-FE	5.5	①	②	③	④ ⑤	24.0	10.6
	Tacoma	2.4 (2438)	2RZ-FE	5.1	①	②	③	④ ⑤	18.0	8.5
	Tacoma	2.7 (2694)	3RZ-FE	5.0	①	②	③	④ ⑤	18.0	8.8
	Tacoma	3.4 (3378)	5VZ-FE	5.4	①	②	③	④ ⑤	18.0	10.3
	4Runner	2.7 (2694)	3RZ-FE	5.0	①	②	③	④ ⑤	18.5	10.6
	4Runner	3.4 (3378)	5VZ-FE	5.2	①	②	③	④ ⑤	18.5	9.4
1999	Land Cruiser	4.7 (4664)	2UZ-FE	7.2	-	②	③	④ ⑤	25.4	15.6 ⑥
	T100 Pick-Up	2.7 (2694)	3RZ-FE	5.8	①	②	③	④ ⑤	24.0	8.1
	T100 Pick-Up	3.4 (3378)	5VZ-FE	5.5	①	②	③	④ ⑤	24.0	10.6
	Tacoma	2.4 (2438)	2RZ-FE	5.1	①	②	③	④ ⑤	18.0	8.5
	Tacoma	2.7 (2694)	3RZ-FE	5.0	①	②	③	④ ⑤	18.0	8.8
	Tacoma	3.4 (3378)	5VZ-FE	5.4	①	②	③	④ ⑤	18.0	10.3
	4Runner	2.7 (2694)	3RZ-FE	5.0	①	②	③	④ ⑤	18.5	10.6
	4Runner	3.4 (3378)	5VZ-FE	5.2	①	②	③	④ ⑤	18.5	9.4
2000	Land Cruiser	4.7 (4664)	2UZ-FE	7.2	-	②	③	④ ⑤	25.4	15.6 ⑥
	Tundra	3.4 (3378)	5VZ-FE	5.2	①	②	③	④ ⑤	26.4	10.6
	Tundra	4.7 (4664)	2UZ-FE	6.0	①	②	③	④ ⑤	26.4	12.3
	Tacoma	2.4 (2438)	2RZ-FE	5.1	①	②	③	④ ⑤	18.0	8.5
	Tacoma	2.7 (2694)	3RZ-FE	5.0	①	②	③	④ ⑤	18.0	8.8
	Tacoma	3.4 (3378)	5VZ-FE	5.4	①	②	③	④ ⑤	18.0	10.3
	4Runner	2.7 (2694)	3RZ-FE	5.0	①	②	③	④ ⑤	18.5	10.6
	4Runner	3.4 (3378)	5VZ-FE	5.2	①	②	③	④ ⑤	18.5	9.4

NOTE: All capacities are approximate. Add fluid gradually and ensure a proper fluid level is obtained. Capacities given are service, not overhaul capacities

M/T = Manual Transmission - Use SAE 75W-90 GL4 or GL5 Gear Oil

A/T = Automatic Transmission - Use DEXRON II or DEXRON III Automatic Transmission Fluid

4WD = Transfer Case - Use SAE 75W-90 GL4 or GL5 Gear Oil

Front Drive Axle - Use SAE 90 GL5 Hypoid Gear Oil

Front Drive Axle With Automatic Disconnecting Differential (A.D.D.) - Use SAE 75W-90 GL5 Hypoid Gear Oil

Rear Drive Axle - Use SAE 90 GL5 Hypoid Gear Oil

① Manual Transmission (2WD) - 5.4 pts.
Manual Transmission (4WD) - 4.6 pts.

② Automatic Transmission A43D - 5.0 pts.
Automatic Transmission A340E - 3.4 pts.
Automatic Transmission A340F - 4.3 pts.

③ Transfer Case VF2A - 2.2 pts.
Transfer Case VF3AM - 2.6 pts.

④ Front Drive Axle, without Automatic Disconnecting Differential (A.D.D.) - 2.3pts
Front Drive Axle, with Automatic Disconnecting Differential (A.D.D.) - 2.4pts

⑤ Rear Drive Axle, 2WD - 5.8 pts
Rear Drive Axle, 4WD without Differential lock - 5.2 pts
Rear Drive Axle, 4WD with Differential lock - 5.8 pts

⑥ Without Rear Heater, 16.2 With Rear Heater

93161c04

2

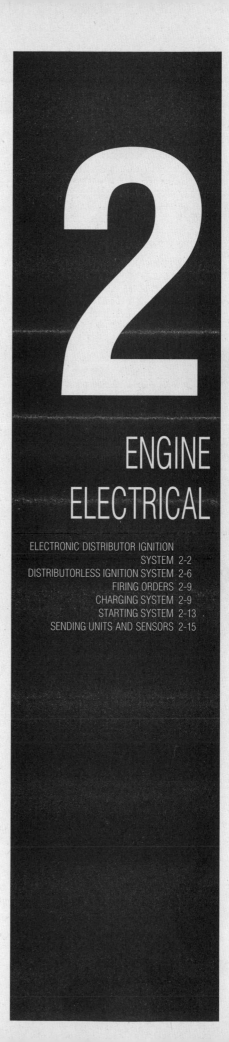

ENGINE ELECTRICAL

ELECTRONIC DISTRIBUTOR IGNITION SYSTEM

General Information

In order to extract the best performance and economy from your engine it is essential that it be properly tuned at regular intervals. Although computerized engine controls and more durable components have reduced ignition maintenance, a regular tune-up will keep your Toyota's engine running smoothly and will prevent the annoying minor breakdowns and poor performance associated with an untuned engine.

➡The 1FZ-FE engine and early 2RZ-FE engines are the only engines covered by this manual that are equipped with distributor ignition systems. All other engines have distributorless ignition systems, and are covered later in this section.

Electronic ignition systems offer many advantages over the conventional breaker points ignition system. By eliminating the points, maintenance requirements are greatly reduced. An electronic ignition system is capable of producing much higher voltage which in turn aids in starting, reduces spark plug fouling and provides better emission control.

The system Toyota uses consists of a distributor with a signal generator, an ignition coil and an electronic igniter. The signal generator is used to activate the electronic components of the igniter. It is located in the distributor and consists of three main components; the signal rotor, the pick-up coil and the permanent magnet. The signal rotor (not to be confused with the distributor rotor) revolves with the distributor shaft, while the pick-up coil and the permanent magnet are stationary. As the signal rotor spins, the teeth on it pass a projection leading from the pick-up coil. When this happens, voltage is allowed to flow through the system, firing the spark plugs. There is no physical contact and no electrical arcing, hence no need to replace burnt or worn parts.

Service consists of inspection of the distributor cap, rotor and the ignition wires, replacing them as necessary. In addition, the air gap between the signal rotor and the projection on the pick-up coil should be checked periodically. The resistances of the coil and pick-up circuits should be measured periodically.

Diagnosis and Testing

PRECAUTIONS

- Do not allow the ignition switch to be **ON** for more than ten minutes if the engine will not start.
- When a tachometer is connected to the system, always connect the tachometer positive lead to the ignition coil negative terminal. Some tachometers are not compatible with this system; it is recommended that you consult with the manufacturer.
- NEVER allow the ignition coil terminals to touch ground as it could result in damage to the igniter and/or the ignition coil itself.
- Do not disconnect the battery when the engine is running.
- Make sure that the igniter is always properly grounded to the body.

SPARK TEST

➧ See Figure 1

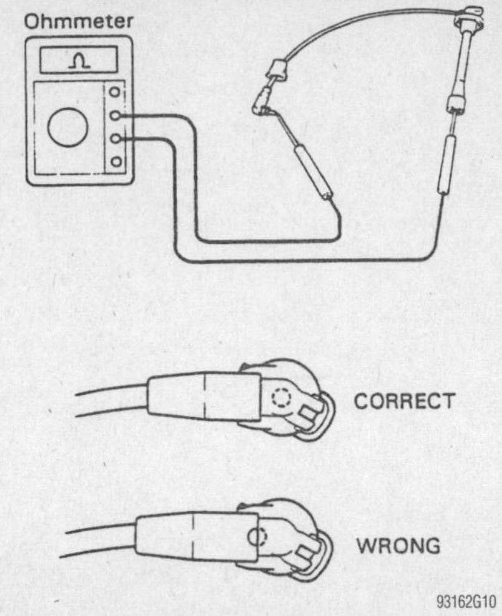

Fig. 1 Test the spark plug cables with an ohmmeter and make sure the terminals are properly secured

The spark test is used to see if the ignition system is delivering electricity through the coil wire to the distributor. Use this test as a preliminary test if the engine cranks but won't start. It's a simple test, but can give a nasty shock if not performed correctly.

Spark plug cables should be treated carefully and always routed in the factory locations and secured with the factory clips. The high voltages these systems can produce can cause improperly routed cables to induce crossfire voltages into other cables, resulting in misfire and possible engine damage. Makes sure the spark plug cables are in good condition and properly positioned.

Spark plug cables can be removed and tested with an ohmmeter. All systems using spark plug cables carry a specification of 25 kohms per cable.

1FZ-FE and 2RZ-FE Engines

➧ See Figure 2

1. Disconnect the end of the coil wire at the distributor.
2. Use a well-insulated tool (such as ignition wire pliers) to hold the exposed end of the wire about 1/2 inch (13mm) from the metal of the engine block.

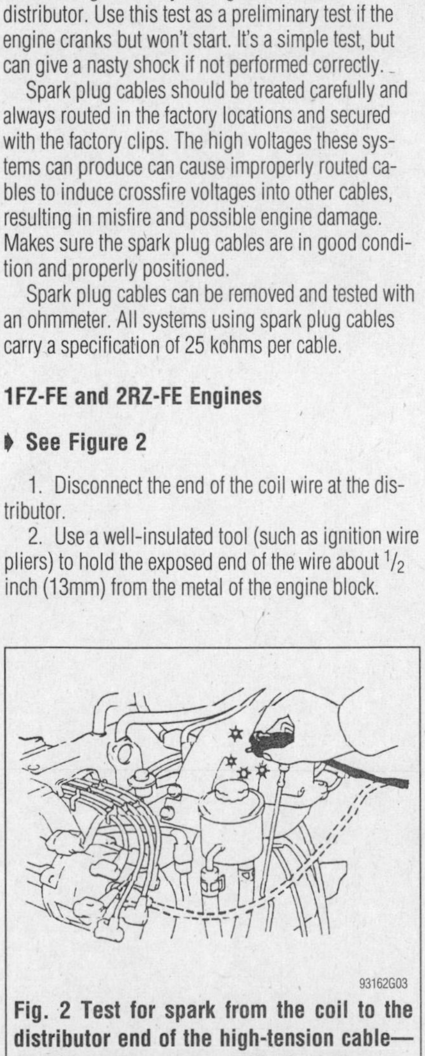

Fig. 2 Test for spark from the coil to the distributor end of the high-tension cable—1FZ-FE engine shown, 2RZ-FE similar

⁂ CAUTION

Do not attempt to hold the wire with your bare hand. Use as much insulation as possible between the wire and the tool holding it. Do not stand on wet concrete while testing. Do not lean on the bodywork of the car while testing. The electrical charge will pass through the easiest path to ground, make certain it's not you. Make sure the metal ground point nearest the cable end is safe; don't choose components that might contain fluids or electronic components.

3. Have an assistant crank the engine by turning the ignition switch to the **START** position, but only for 1 or 2 seconds. Keep clear of moving parts under the hood, and keep clothing and hair well out of the way. If the cable end is the correct distance from solid metal, and if the ignition system is in good condition, a distinct, blue-white spark should jump to the metal as the engine cranks.
4. The engine should only be cranked in 1–2 seconds bursts. Longer cranking will cause the fuel injectors to deliver additional fuel into the cylinders, flooding the engine or at least fouling the spark plugs.
5. If no spark is present, turn the ignition switch **OFF** and proceed to check the resistance of the of the coil wire, the voltage supply to the coil (12 volts with the ignition **ON**), the coil resistance, the resistance of the pickup coil and the air gap within the distributor.

Adjustments

AIR GAP

1FZ-FE and 2RZ-FE Engine

➧ See Figures 3 and 4

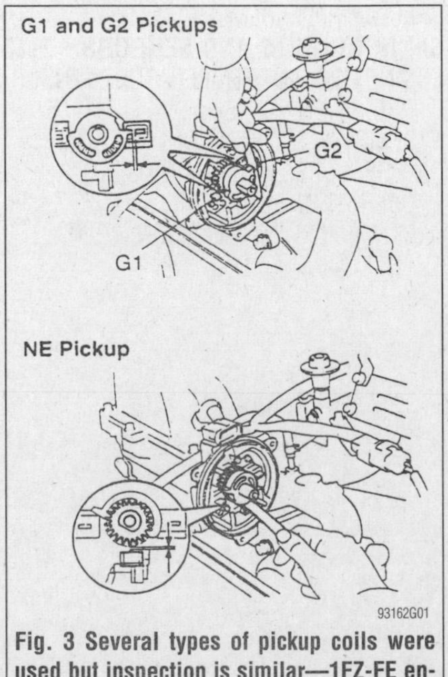

Fig. 3 Several types of pickup coils were used but inspection is similar—1FZ-FE engine

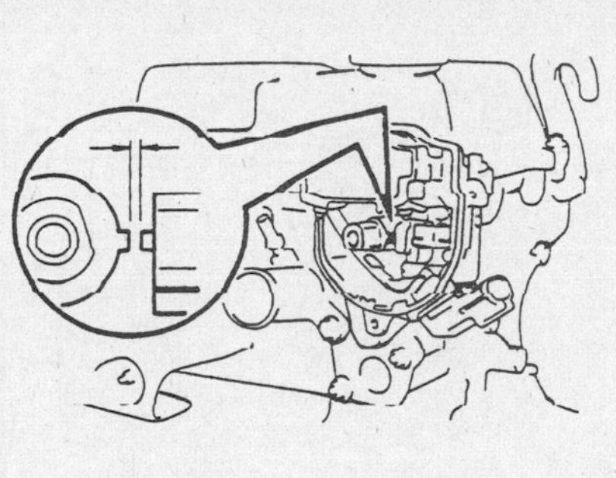

93162G02

Fig. 4 A non-magnetic feeler gauge is used to check pickup coil air gap—2RZ-FE engine

➡The air gap is NOT adjustable. If the gap is not within specifications, the distributor must be replaced.

1. Remove the distributor cap. Inspect the cap for cracks, carbon tracks or a worn center contact. Replace it if necessary, transferring the wires one at a time from the old cap to the new one.
2. Pull the ignition rotor (not the signal rotor) straight up and remove it. Replace it if the contact is worn, burned or pitted. Do not file the contacts.
3. Turn the crankshaft (you may use a socket wrench on the front pulley bolt to do this) until the projection on the pickup coil is directly opposite the signal rotor tooth.
4. Use only a non-ferrous, non-magnetic (paper, brass, or plastic) feeler gauge set.
5. Select a non-ferrous feeler blade of 0.020 in. (0.30mm) thickness, and insert it into the pick-up air gap. The gauge should just touch either side of the gap. The permissible range is 0.008–0.016 in. (0.20–0.40mm).

Ignition Coil

TESTING

➡All of the coil testing procedures have Cold and Hot specifications. This is the temperature of the coils themselves. Cold is from 14–122°F (-10–50°C) and Hot is from 122–212°F (50–100°C).

1FZ-FE and 2RZ-FE Engines

➧ See Figures 5 and 6

The 1FZ-FE and early 2RZ-FE engines use a conventional electronic ignition distributor.

1. With the ignition switch **OFF**, carefully remove the high-tension cable (coil-to-distributor wire) from the coil.
2. Carefully unplug the smaller electrical connector from the coil.
3. Using an ohmmeter, measure the primary coil resistance between the positive (+) and negative (–) terminals. The readings should be:
   a. Cold: 0.36–0.55 ohms
   b. Hot: 0.45–0.65 ohms
4. Using an ohmmeter, measure the secondary coil resistance between the positive (+) and high-tension terminals. The readings should be:
   a. Cold: 9.0–15.4 kohms
   b. Hot: 11.4–18.1 kohms
5. If the resistance is not as specified, replace the ignition coil.

REMOVAL & INSTALLATION

External Mount

➧ See Figures 7, 8, 9, 10, and 11

1. Disconnect the negative battery cable.
2. If equipped, remove the ignition coil cover.
3. Remove the coil wire lead.
4. Tag and disconnect all electrical leads from the coil. If applicable, remove the igniter.
5. Remove the two mounting bolts and lift off the ignition coil.

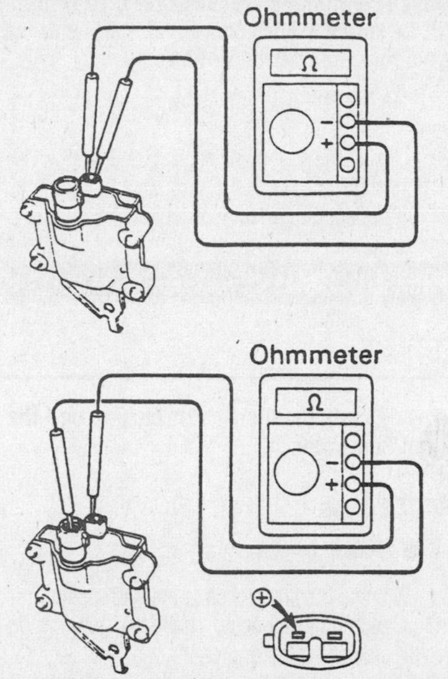

93162G04

Fig. 5 Checking the coil's primary circuit resistance (top) and secondary resistance (bottom)—1FZ-FE engine

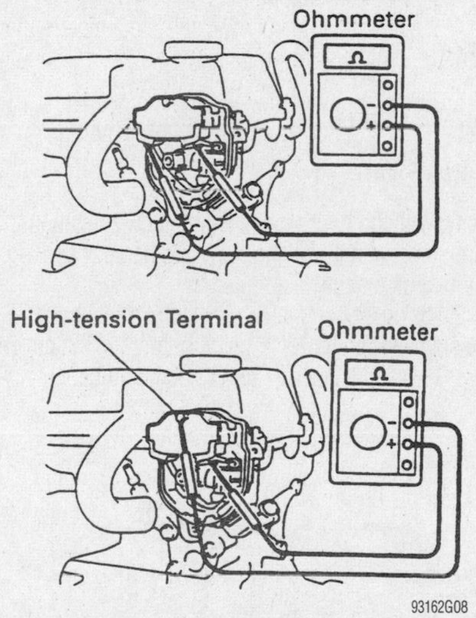

93162G08

Fig. 6 Checking the coil's primary circuit resistance (top) and secondary resistance (bottom)—2RZ-FE engine

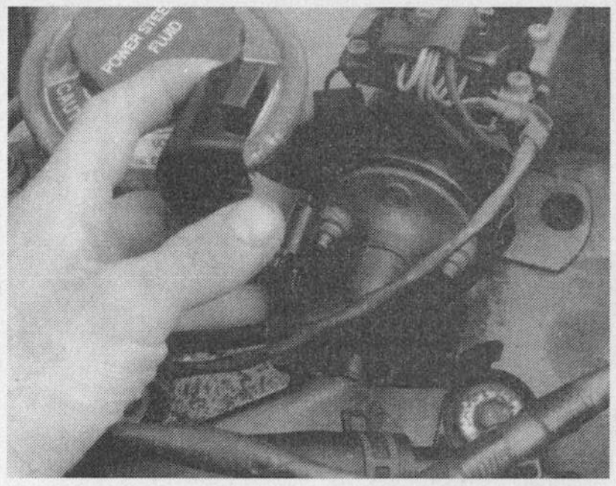

86822004

Fig. 7 Remove the cover from the ignition coil

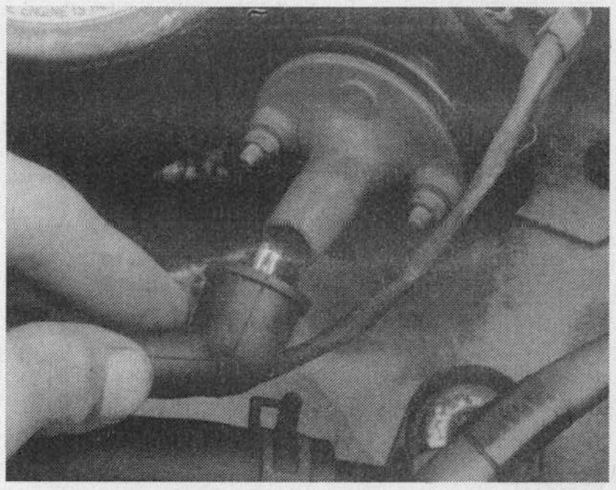

86822005

Fig. 8 Detach the coil wire from the unit

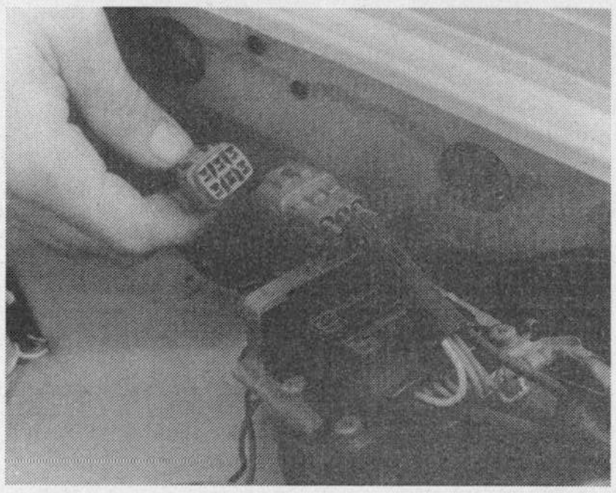

86822006

Fig. 9 Unplug the connector and remove the igniter

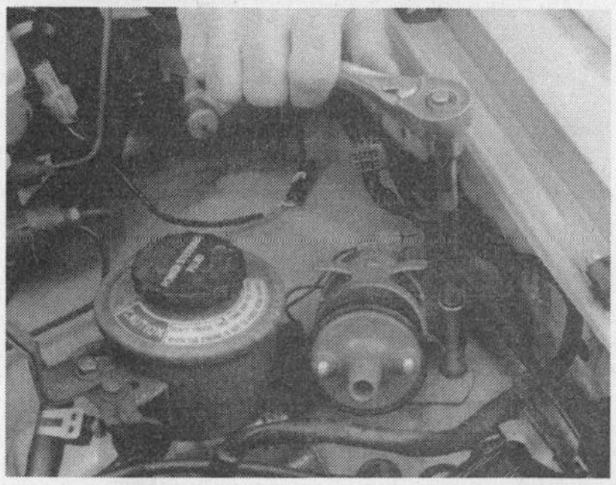

86822007

Fig. 10 Loosen and remove the mounting bolts securing the coil

Fig. 11 Once all leads and bolts are removed, lift the ignition coil from the fenderwell

To install:

6. Install the coil in position and tighten the mounting bolts.
7. Connect all wires and install the igniter.
8. Connect the negative battery cable.

Internally Mounted

➧ **See Figure 12**

1. Disconnect the negative battery cable.
2. Remove the distributor cap and rotor.
3. Remove the ignition coil dust cover and dust proof packing.
4. Unfasten the two nuts and disconnect the three ignition coil terminals.
5. Remove the ignition coil retaining screws and the coil from the distributor.

To install:

6. Before installing, remove any old sealing material from the ignition coil. Apply sealer (Formed In Place Gasket, or FIPG or equivalent) to the coil mounting surface.
7. Install the ignition coil to the distributor with the four screws.

➡When connecting the wires for the ignition coil, be sure the wires do not contact with the signal rotor or distributor housing.

8. Connect the ignition coil wires and install the two nuts.
9. Install the dust proof packing and dust cover.
10. Install the rotor and distributor cap.
11. Connect the negative battery cable.

Pick-Up Coils

TESTING

➡Toyota calls the distributor pick-up coil the Signal Generator.

1FZ-FE Engine

➧ **See Figure 13**

1. With the ignition switch in the **OFF** position, carefully detach the connector in the harness coming from the side of the distributor.
2. Using an ohmmeter, check the resistance of the signal generator (pick-up coil).
3. Measure between at terminals G1 and G(–), G2 and G(–) and NE and G(–). In all cases, the readings should be:
   a. Cold: 185–275 kohms
   b. Hot: 240–325 kohms
4. If the resistance is not as specified, replace the distributor housing assembly.

2RZ-FE Engine

➧ **See Figure 14**

1. With the ignition switch in the **OFF** position, carefully detach the connector in the harness coming from the side of the distributor.
2. Using an ohmmeter, check the resistance of the signal generator (pick-up coil). Measure at terminals G (–) and G (+). The readings should be:

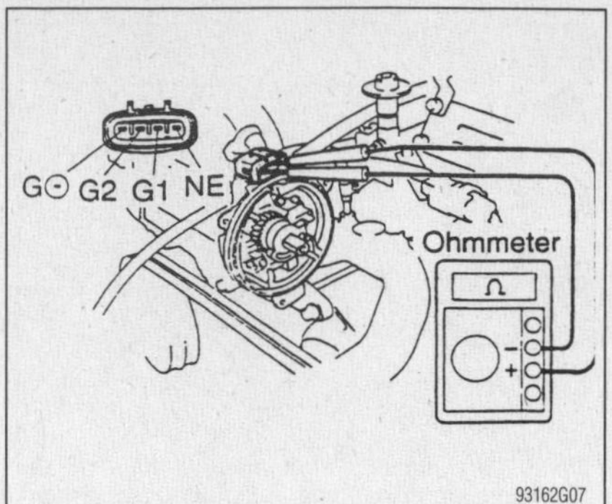

Fig. 13 Checking the distributor pickup coil and terminal identification—1FZ-FE engine

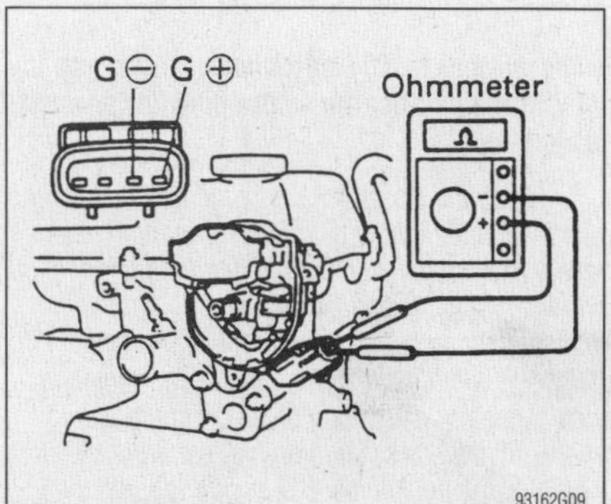

Fig. 14 Checking the distributor pickup coil and terminal identification—1997 2RZ-FE engine

   a. Cold: 185–275 kohms
   b. Hot: 240–325 kohms
3. If the resistance is not as specified, replace the distributor housing assembly.

Igniter

REMOVAL & INSTALLATION

➧ **See Figures 15, 16, 17, and 18**

Igniters are mounted in one of two places on your Toyota truck. On the remotely mounted coils, the igniter is secured to the coil. On the integral coil vehicles (where the coil is in the distributor) the igniter is secured to the fenderwell.

1. Disconnect the negative battery cable.

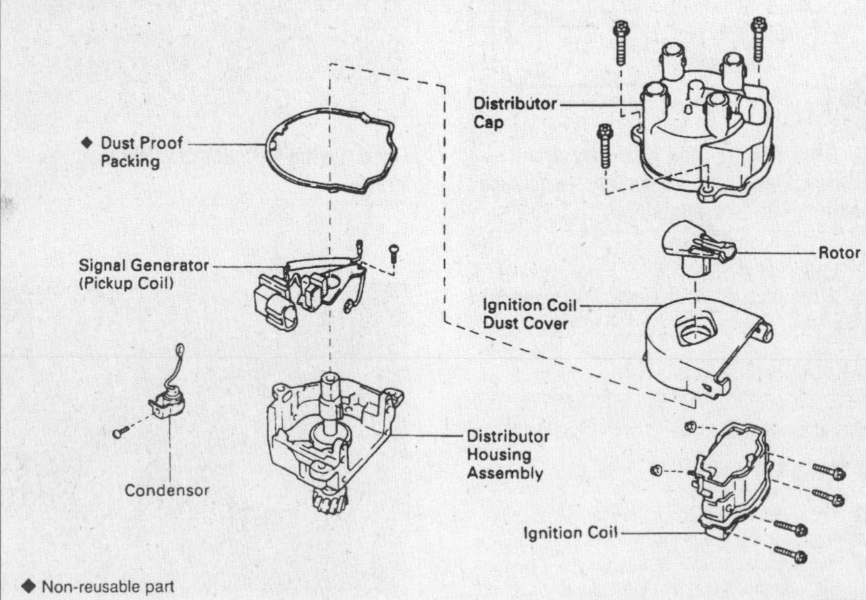

Fig. 12 Exploded view of the internally mounted ignition coil distributor—1997 2RZ-FE engine shown

Fig. 15 The igniter can be found mounted on the remote ignition coil

86822010

Fig. 16 Unplug the connector and remove the retaining screws

86822011

Fig. 17 If mounted to the coil, detach the wire

86822013

Fig. 18 Check that all the connections are separated, then lift the unit from the vehicle

2. Separate the wiring harness connections.
3. Unbolt the igniter.
4. If mounted to the coil, loosen the nut holding the wire lead.
5. Tag and disconnect the wire lead.
6. Lift the igniter off its mount.

To install:

7. Mount the igniter to the bracket.
8. Attach the wire lead to the coil if used.
9. Connect the harness.
10. Connect the negative battery cable.

Distributor

REMOVAL

➧ **See Figures 19 thru 25**

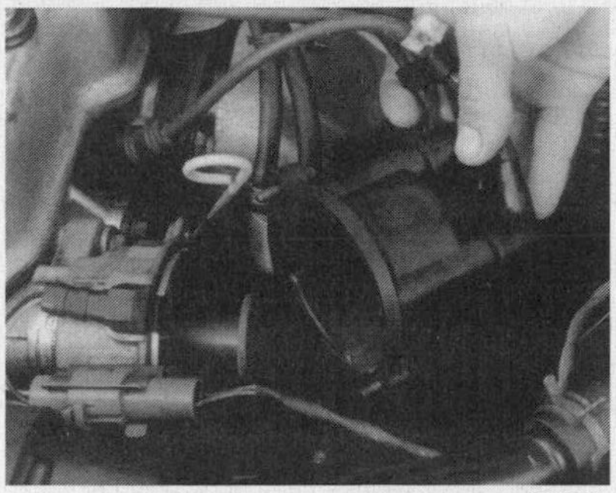

86822020

Fig. 19 Remove the distributor cap with the wires attached

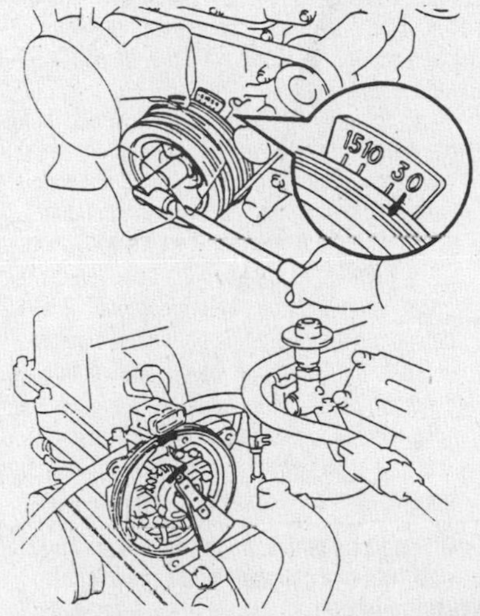

93162G11

Fig. 20 On this 1997 Land Cruiser, the distributor body has a notch which should align with the tip of the rotor when No. 1 cylinder is at TDC, compression stroke (firing position)

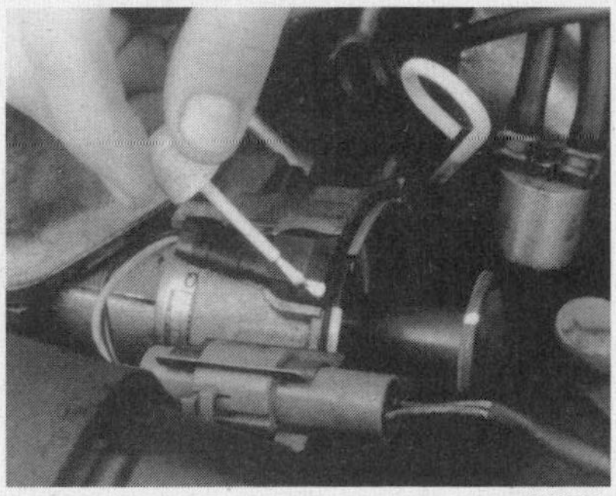

86822022

Fig. 21 If the crankshaft timing mark and notch on the distributor body are not aligned, at least mark the position of the rotor . . .

1. Unfasten the retaining clips or remove the retaining screws and lift the distributor cap straight off. It will be easier to install the distributor if the wiring is left connected to the cap. If the wires must be removed from the cap, mark their positions to aid in installation.

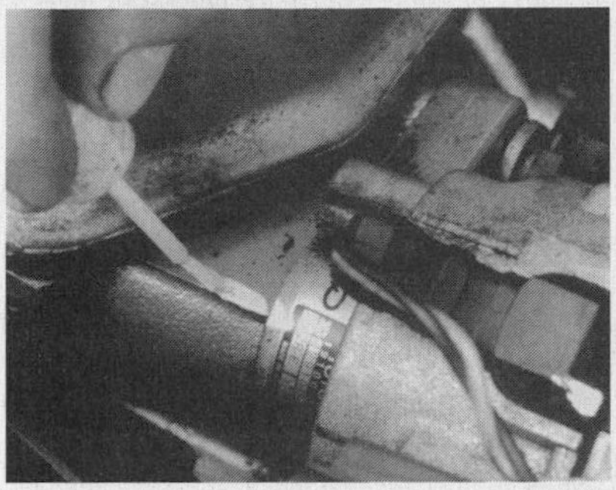

86822023

Fig. 22 . . . and the distributor base

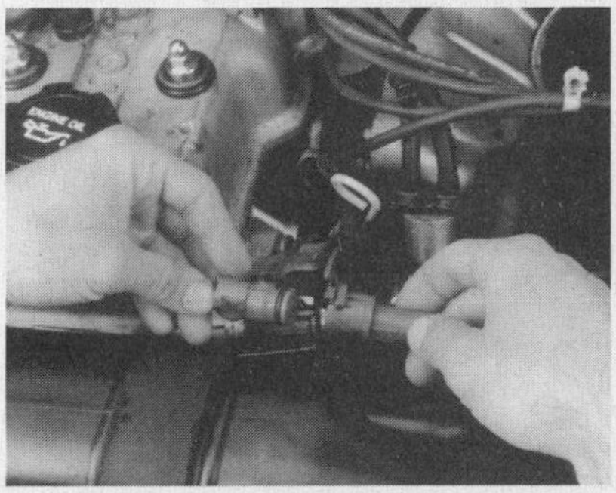

86822024

Fig. 23 Detach the electrical connections

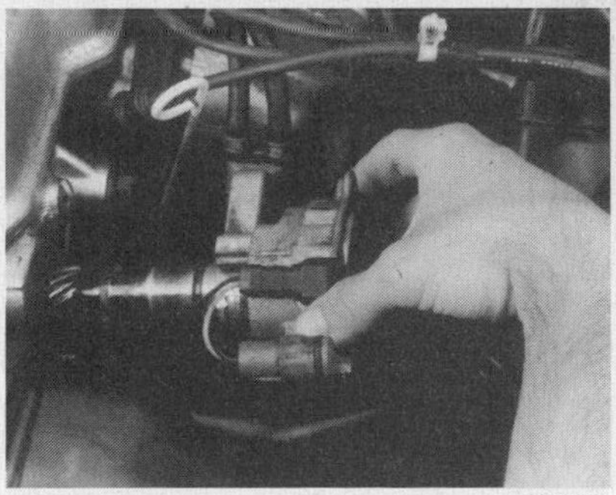

86822025

Fig. 24 After the pinch-bolt is removed, carefully pull the distributor out of the engine

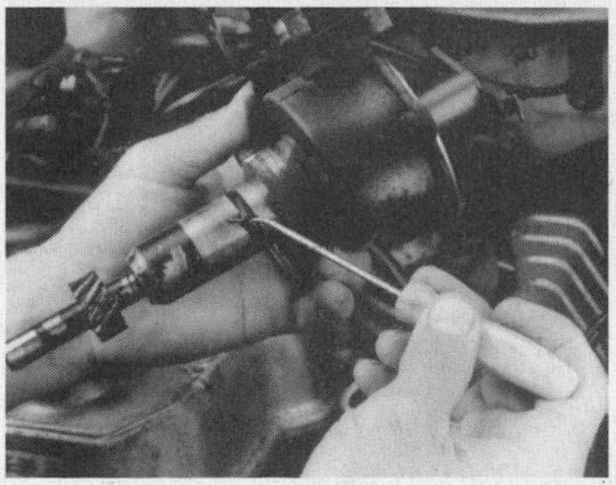

86822026

Fig. 25 Discard the O-ring. A new one should be used during installation

➡While it is possible to remove and install the distributor without setting up No. 1 to TDC by marking the rotor's position in relation to the distributor body, it is good practice to always set the engine with cylinder No. 1 at TDC of the compression stroke. This is the best point of reference.

2. Remove the dust cover and mark the position of the rotor relative to the distributor body; then mark the position of the body relative to the cylinder head.
3. Tag and disconnect the electrical wires and vacuum lines.
4. Remove the pinch-bolt and lift the distributor straight out, away from the engine. The rotor and body are marked so that they can be returned to the position from which they were removed. Do not turn or disturb the engine (unless absolutely necessary, such as for engine rebuilding), after the distributor has been removed. The relationship between the position of the distributor and the position of the engine is critical if the spark is to be sent to the proper place at the proper time.
5. Remove the distributor O-ring, discard and install a new one. Apply a light coat of engine oil on the O-ring.

INSTALLATION

Timing Not Disturbed

1. If the crankshaft timing mark and notch on the distributor body were not aligned at removal but alignment marks were made on the rotor, distributor body and cylinder head before removal, align these matchmarks on the distributor with the rotor. Position the distributor to align with the mark made on the block. Insert the distributor in the block, taking care not to damage the drive gear at the bottom or to knock all the marks out of alignment.
2. Tighten the pinch-bolt to 14 ft. lbs. (19 Nm).
3. Install the distributor cap and wires. Check the ignition timing.
4. Check the idle speed.

Timing Disturbed

➧ See Figure 26

If the engine has been cranked, dismantled, or the timing otherwise lost, proceed as follows:

1. Determine Top Dead Center (TDC) of the No. 1 cylinder's compression stroke by removing the spark plug from the No. 1 cylinder and placing your finger over the spark plug hole. Turn the engine (with a wrench on the crank pulley bolt) until the timing marks align at 0 degrees. A definite compression can be felt pressing against your finger. Doing this is most important, because the timing marks also align during the exhaust stroke, but no compression will be felt. If the distributor is installed incorrectly (180 degrees out of time), the engine may be damaged, if it starts at all.
   a. To verify that the timing is correct, remove the cylinder head cover. With a wrench on the crankshaft balancer center bolt turn the crankshaft pulley clockwise until the notch on the pulley aligns with the **0** mark on the timing chain cover.
   b. Look at the backs of the camshaft drive gears. Verify that the timing marks with 1 and 2 dots are in a straight line on the head surface. If not, turn the crankshaft exactly one full turn (360 degrees).
   c. Locate the notch marks on the distributor end next to the drive gear. Align groove on the housing with the protrusion on the drive gear.

➡On engines which have the spark plugs buried into the cylinder head, use a compression gauge.

2. Install the rotor. Position the rotor so it is at the No. 1 cylinder firing position.

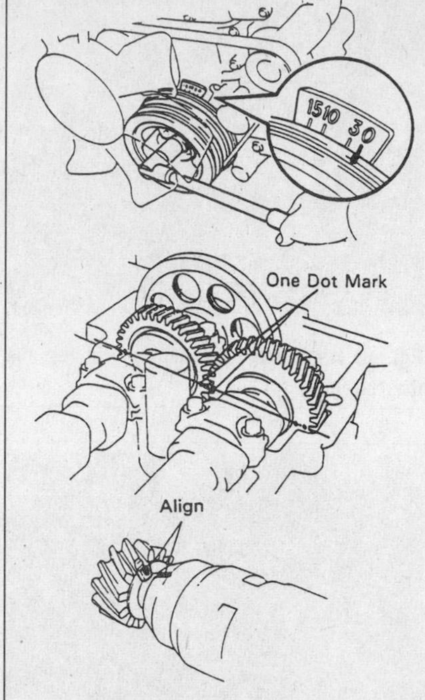

Fig. 26 All of these marks must be in alignment before installing the distributor—1FZ-FE engine shown, 2RZ-FE similar

3. Install a replacement O-ring on the distributor body and lightly oil. Slowly insert the distributor into the cylinder block aligning the center of the flange with the bolt hole in the cylinder head.
4. Tighten the pinch-bolt to 14 ft. lbs. (19 Nm).
5. Install the distributor cap and wires. Check the ignition timing.
6. Check the idle speed.

DISTRIBUTORLESS IGNITION SYSTEM

General Information

In Model Year 1998, the 2RZ-FE engine transitioned from distributor ignition to a distributorless system. The 2RZ-FE and 3RZ-FE engines have no distributor, but are equipped with two dual-terminal coils. When signaled by the on-board computer, the coils fire in sequence and distribute the spark through conventional spark plug cables.

The 5VZ-FE engines are equipped with what is called the Toyota Direct Ignition (TDI). This system improves the timing accuracy and enhances the overall reliability of the ignition system. The TDI uses a two-cylinder simultaneous (waste spark) ignition system which fires two cylinders at the same time with one coil. In a waste spark system, one spark plug is attached to each end of the secondary coil winding. This circuit arrangement causes one of the plugs in each cylinder pair to fire in a forward direction, and the other to fire in a reverse direction. The cylinder on the compression stroke is defined as the 'event' cylinder, while the cylinder in the exhaust stroke is called the 'waste' cylinder. The coils are positioned over one bank of the plugs. This arrangement has eliminated half of the normal required plug wires.

The 2UZ-FE engine use an arrangement where each spark plug has its own coil. There are no spark plug wires.

Diagnosis and Testing

SPARK TEST

3RZ-FE, 5VZ-FE and 2UZ-FE Engines

➧ See Figure 27

1. Remove the ignition coils (with igniter) from the spark plugs. On the 3RZ-FE engine, disconnect the spark plug wires from the spark plugs.
2. Remove the spark plugs.
3. Install the spark plugs to each ignition coil (or spark plug cables if 3RZ-FE) and attach the ignition coil electrical connector.
4. Detach the electrical connection from each fuel injector.
5. Ground the spark plug.
6. Crank the engine and check for spark while the engine is being cranked.

➡To prevent overloading the engine with gasoline, crank the engine no more than 5–10 seconds at a time.

7. If no spark is present, check the power supply to the coil.
   a. Turn the ignition switch to the **ON** position.
   b. Check that there is battery voltage at the ignition coil positive (+) terminal.
   c. If okay, check the Camshaft Position (CMP) sensor and Crankshaft Position (CKP) sensor. For additional information, please refer to the following topic(s): Driveability and Emission Controls, Camshaft and Crankshaft Position Sensors.

⁂ CAUTION

Do not attempt to hold the wire with your bare hand. Use as much insulation as possible between the wire and the tool holding it. Do not stand on wet concrete while testing. Do not lean on the bodywork of the car while testing. The electrical charge will pass through the easiest path to ground, make

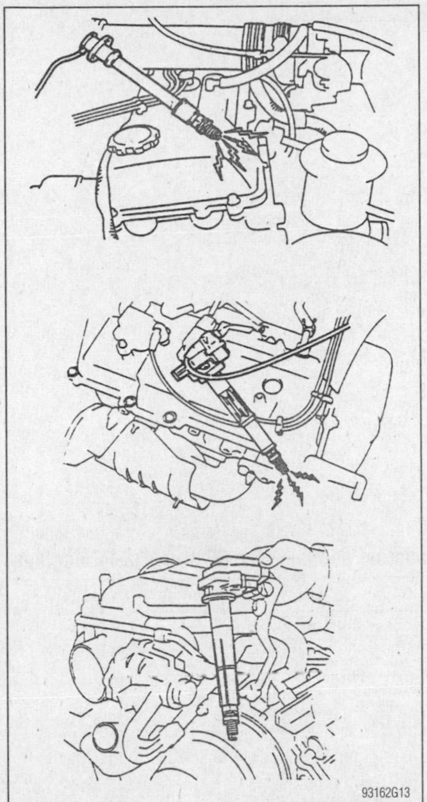

93162G13

Fig. 27 Testing for spark—Top: 2RZ-FE & 3RZ-FE engines; Middle: 5VZ-FE engine; Bottom: 2UZ-FE engine

certain its not you. Make sure the metal ground point nearest the cable end is safe; don't choose components that might contain fluids or electronic components.

8. Check to see if a bright blue spark occurs when the engine is being cranked.

➡To prevent any gasoline from being injected during this test, crank the engine no more than 1–2 seconds at one time.

9. If the spark does not occur, perform the following:

a. Check the connection to the ignition coil and igniter. If this is OK then proceed.

b. Inspect the resistance of the wires where used. It should be 25kohms. Replace the wires if not to specifications. If the wires are good proceed.

c. Check the power supply to the coil and the igniter. Turn the ignition **ON**. Check that there is battery voltage at the ignition coil positive terminal. If not, check the wiring between the ignition switch to the coil and igniter assemblies. If this is OK, proceed.

d. Check the resistance of the ignition coils, if not within specifications, replace the coil. If this is not correct replace the coil. If it is good, continue.

➡For additional information on sensor testing, please refer to the following topic(s): Driveability and Emission Controls.

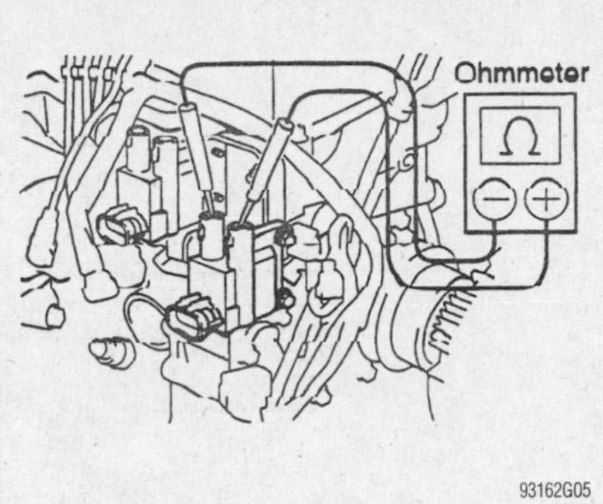

93162G05

Fig. 28 On this coil, only the secondary resistance is checked—2RZ-FE and 3RZ-FE engines

e. Check the resistance of the Camshaft Position (CMP) sensor. If this is not correct, replace the sensor. If this is correct, proceed.

f. Check the resistance of the Crankshaft Position (CKP) sensor. If this is not correct, replace the sensor. If this is correct, proceed.

g. If the spark is still not present, check the wiring between the ECM, distributor and igniter. If the wiring is OK, replace the igniter.

Ignition Coil Pack

TESTING

2RZ-FE and 3RZ-FE Engines

➧ See Figure 28

The late 2RZ-FE and all 3RZ-FE engines have an electronic ignition system using no distributor but it does use two coils, each with dual-output terminals, and spark plug cables from the coils to the spark plugs.

1. Disconnect the high-tension (spark plug wires) cables from the ignition coils.
2. Detach the ignition coil electrical connectors.
3. Using an ohmmeter, measure the secondary coil resistance between the positive (+) and high-tension terminals. The readings should be:
   a. Cold: 9.7–16.7 kohms
   b. Hot: 12.4–19.6 kohms
4. If the resistance is not as specified, replace the ignition coil.

5VZ-FE Engine

➧ See Figures 29 and 30

The 5VZ-FE engine has an electronic distributorless ignition system, with six separate coils, each with their own spark plug wire.

1. If there is no spark at the spark plugs, check for power to the ignition coil, as follows:
   a. Turn the ignition switch to the **ON** position.
   b. Check that there is battery voltage at the ignition coil positive (+) terminal.
2. If there is battery voltage at the ignition coil positive (+) terminal, but no spark at the plugs, the coils should be checked.
3. Disconnect the high-tension (spark plug wires) cables and the smaller ignition harness connectors from the ignition coils.

93161pb9

Fig. 29 View of the ignition coil assembly used on the 5VZ-FE engine

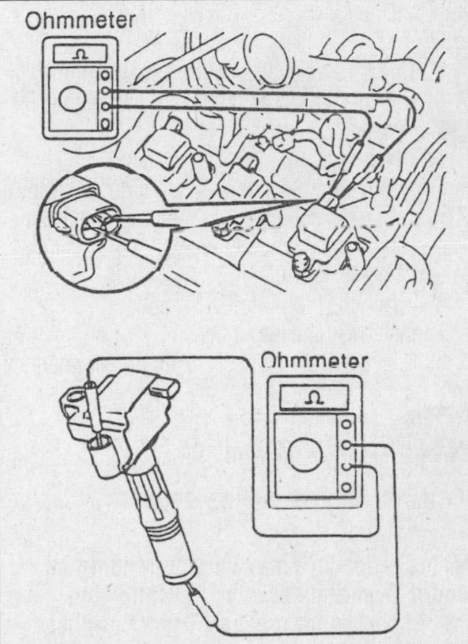

93162G06

Fig. 30 Checking the coil's primary circuit resistance (top) and secondary resistance (bottom)—5VZ-FE engine

4. Using an ohmmeter, measure the primary coil resistance between the positive (+) and negative (–) terminals. The reading should be:
   a. Cold: 0.67–1.05 ohms
   b. Hot: 0.85–1.23 ohms
5. Using an ohmmeter, measure the secondary coil resistance between the positive (+) and high-tension terminals. The readings should be:
   a. Cold: 9.3–16.0 kohms
   b. Hot: 11.7–18.8 kohms
6. If the resistance is not as specified, replace the ignition coil.

2UZ-FE Engine

The 2UZ-FE engine has an electronic distributorless ignition system, with eight separate coils and no spark plug wires. Each spark plug has its own coil on top of the connector.

1. If there is no spark at the spark plugs, check for power to the ignition coil, as follows:
   a. Turn the ignition switch to the **ON** position.
   b. Check that there is battery voltage at the ignition coil positive (+) terminal.
2. If there is battery voltage at the ignition coil positive (+) terminal, but no spark at the plugs, the

Camshaft Position (CMP) sensor and Crankshaft Position (CKP) sensor should be checked. For additional information, please refer to the following topic(s): Driveability and Emission Controls.

REMOVAL & INSTALLATION

2RZ-FE and 3RZ-FE Engines

See Figure 31

This procedure may vary depending on Model Year and chassis. The following should suffice for most all Toyota applications using these engines.

1. Remove the air cleaner hose.
2. Tag for identification, then disconnect the high-tension (spark plug) cables from the ignition coils.
3. Unplug the connectors from the ignition coils.
4. Remove the 4 mounting bolts and remove the coils from their bracket.

To install:

5. Install the coils in the reverse order of removal. Make certain the correct coil is replaced in the same place where it was removed. Tighten the mounting bolts to 84 inch lbs. (10 Nm).
6. Attach the plug wires to the coils.
7. Install the air cleaner hose.
8. Start the engine and check for proper operation.

5VZ-FE and 2UZ-FE Engines

See Figures 32 and 33

This procedure may vary depending on Model Year and chassis. The following should suffice for most all Toyota applications using these engines.

1. Remove the air cleaner hose.
2. If equipped, tag for identification, then disconnect the high-tension (spark plug) cables from the ignition coils.
3. Unplug the connectors from the ignition coils.
4. On these engines, the coils mount to the left side cylinder head. Remove the 3 mounting bolts and remove the coils from the cylinder head

To install:

5. Install the coils in the reverse order of removal. Make certain the correct coil is replaced in the same place where it was removed. Tighten the mounting bolts to 69 inch lbs. (7.8 Nm).
6. Attach the plug wires to the coils, if applicable.
7. Install the air cleaner hose.
8. Start the engine and check for proper operation.

Crankshaft Position Sensor

For additional information, please refer to the following topic(s): Electronic Engine Controls, Crankshaft Position Sensor

Camshaft Position Sensor

For additional information, please refer to the following topic(s): Electronic Engine Controls, Camshaft Position Sensor

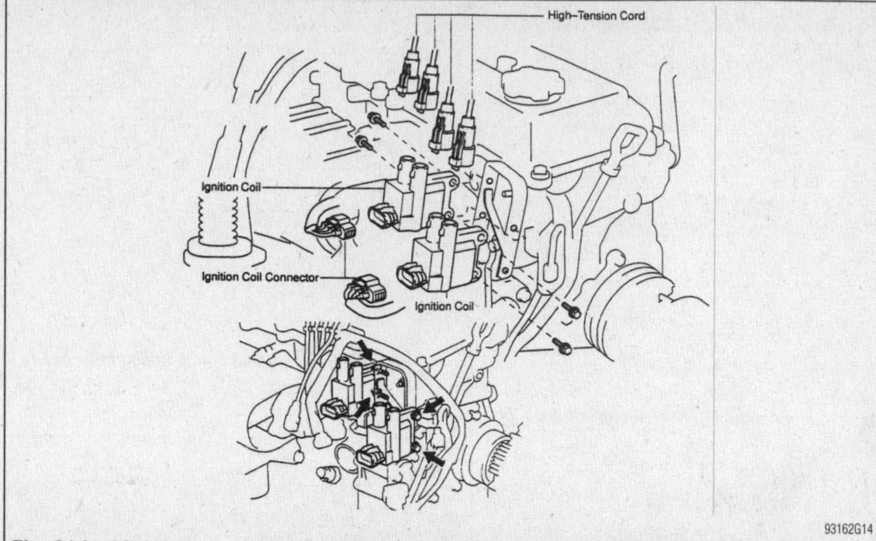

Fig. 31 Ignition coils, related components and mounting points—2RZ-FE and 3RZ-FE engines

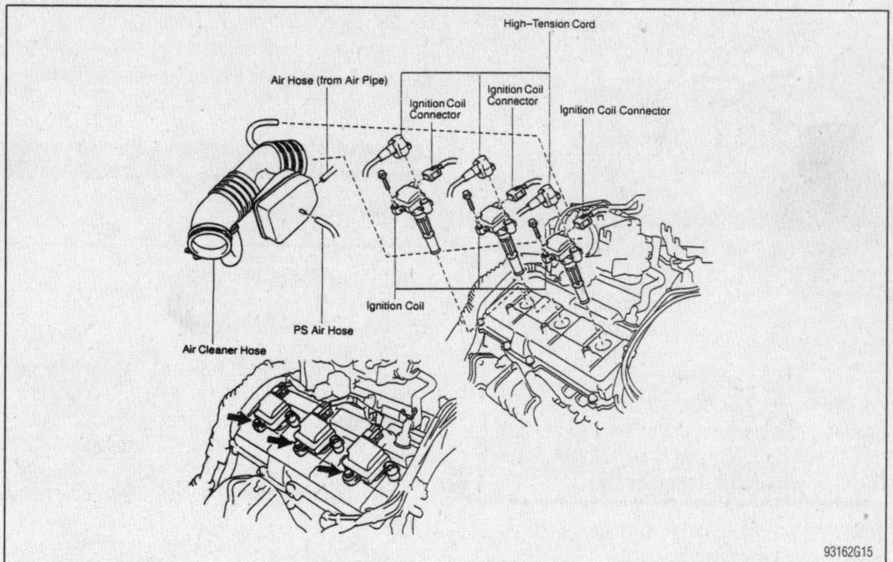

Fig. 32 Exploded view of the ignition coils, related components and mounting points—5VZ-FE engine

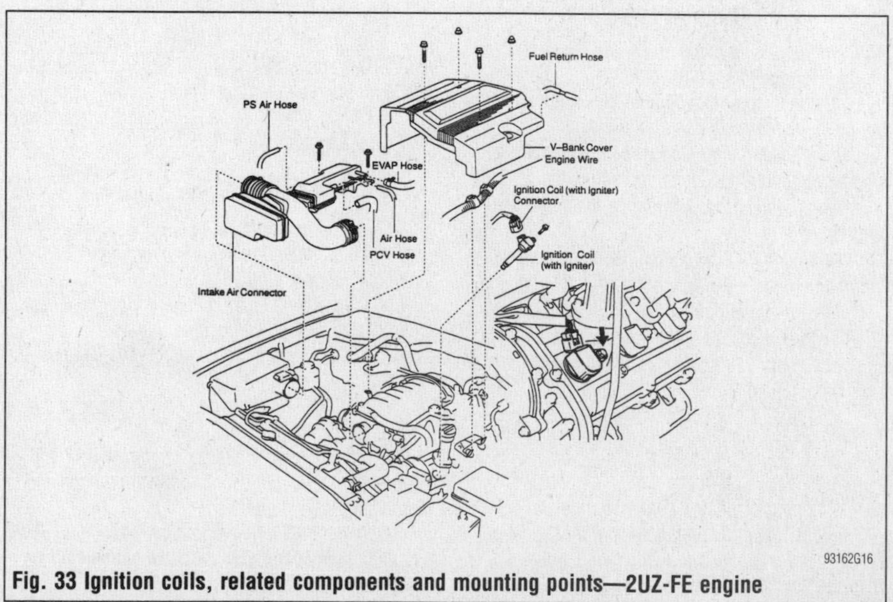

Fig. 33 Ignition coils, related components and mounting points—2UZ-FE engine

FIRING ORDERS

➧ See Figures 34, 35, 36, 37, and 38

The firing order is the order in which spark is sent to each cylinder. The spark must arrive at the correct time in the combustion cycle or damage may result. For this reason, connecting the correct plug to the correct distributor or coil terminal is critical. To avoid confusion, always replace the spark plug wires one at a time.

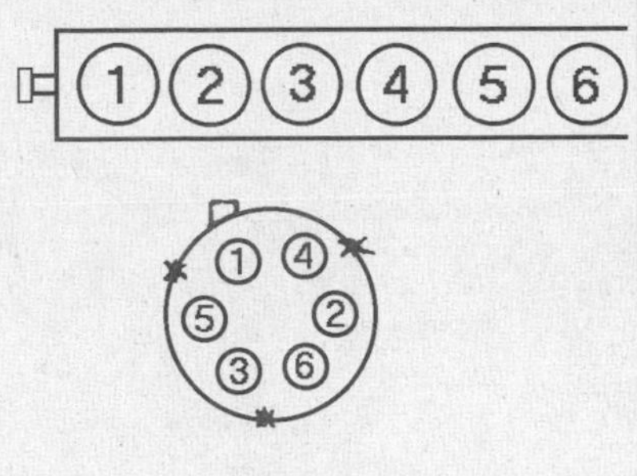

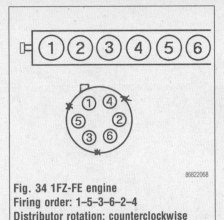

Fig. 34 1FZ-FE engine
Firing order: 1–5–3–6–2–4
Distributor rotation: counterclockwise

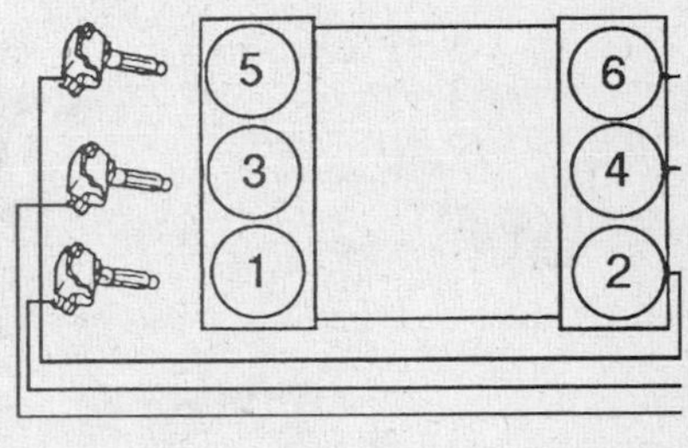

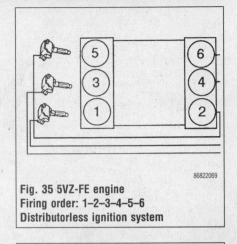

Fig. 35 5VZ-FE engine
Firing order: 1–2–3–4–5–6
Distributorless ignition system

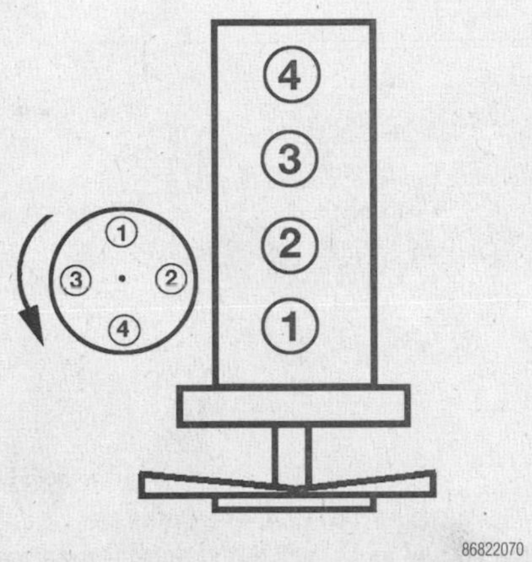

Fig. 36 2RZ-FE and 3RZ-FE engines
Firing order: 1–3–4–2
Distributor rotation: clockwise

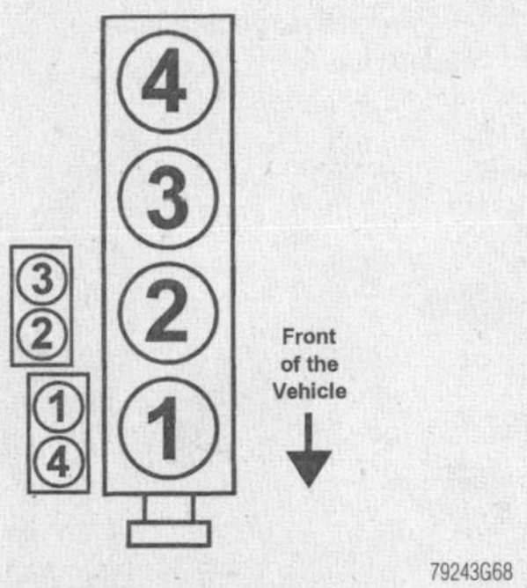

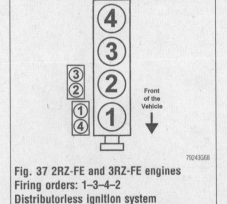

Fig. 37 2RZ-FE and 3RZ-FE engines
Firing orders: 1–3–4–2
Distributorless ignitlon system

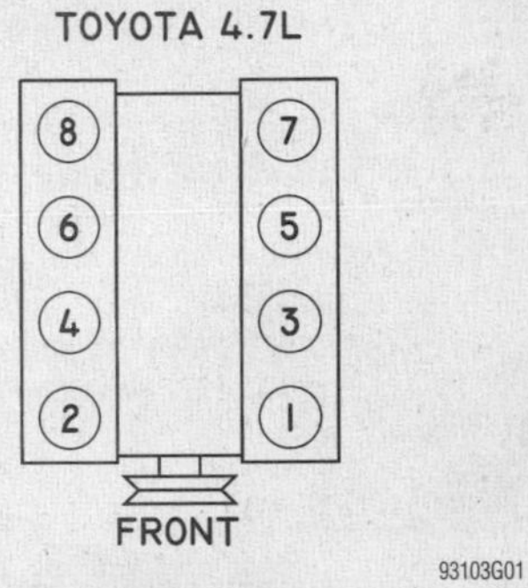

Fig. 38 2UZ-FE engine
Firing order: 1–8–4–3–6–5–7–2
Distributorless ignition system

CHARGING SYSTEM

Alternator Precautions

➧ See Figures 39 and 40

To prevent damage to the alternator and regulator, the following precautionary measures must be taken when working with the electrical system.

- Never reverse the battery connections. Always check the battery polarity visually. This is to be done before any connections are made to ensure that all of the connections correspond to the battery ground polarity of the truck.
- Booster batteries must be connected properly. Make sure the positive cable of the booster battery is connected to the positive terminal of the battery which is getting the boost.
- Disconnect the battery cables before using a fast charger; the charger has a tendency to force current through the diodes in the opposite direction. This causes damage.
- Never use a fast charger as a booster for starting the truck.
- Never disconnect the voltage regulator while the engine is running.
- Do not ground the alternator output terminal.
- Do not operate the alternator on an open circuit with the field energized.
- Do not attempt to polarize the alternator.

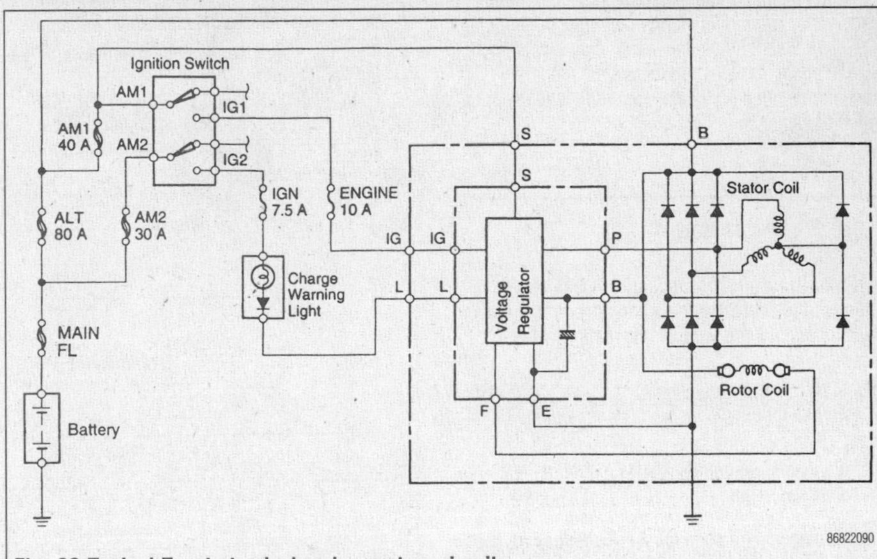

Fig. 39 Typical Toyota truck charging system circuit

- Disconnect the battery cables and remove the alternator before using an electric arc welder on the truck.
- Protect the alternator from excessive moisture. If the engine is to be steam cleaned, cover or remove the alternator.

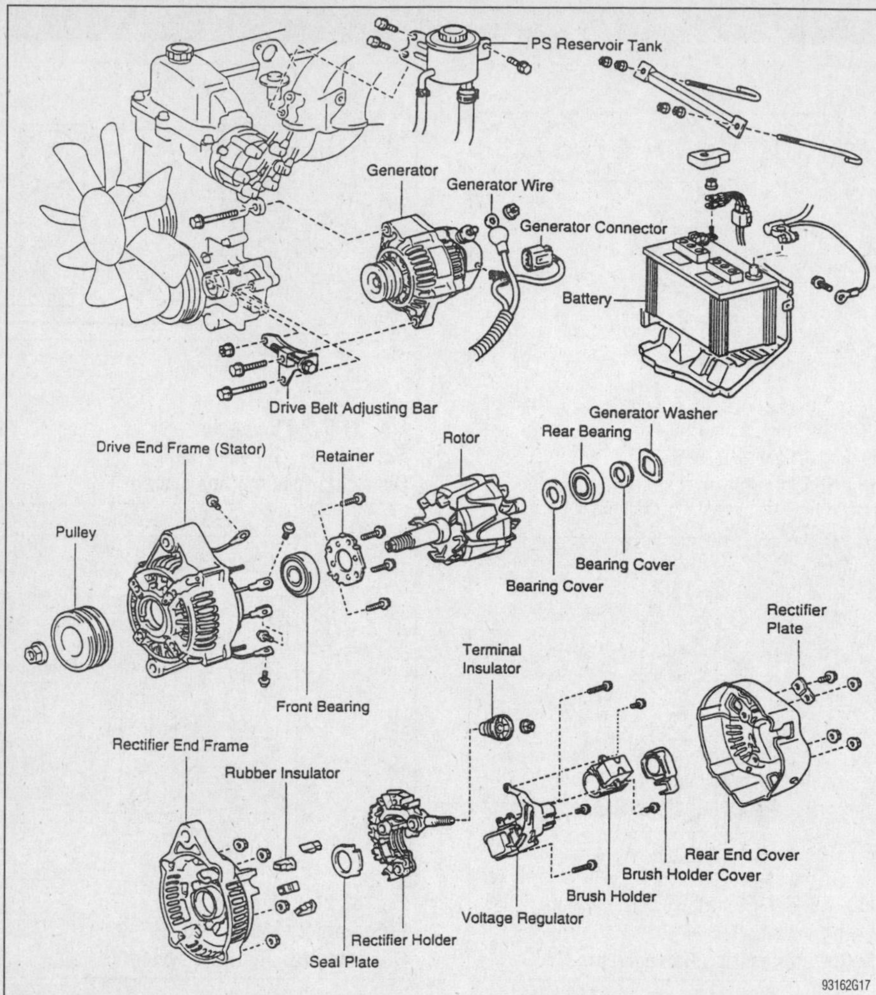

Fig. 40 Exploded view of a typical Toyota truck alternator and related components

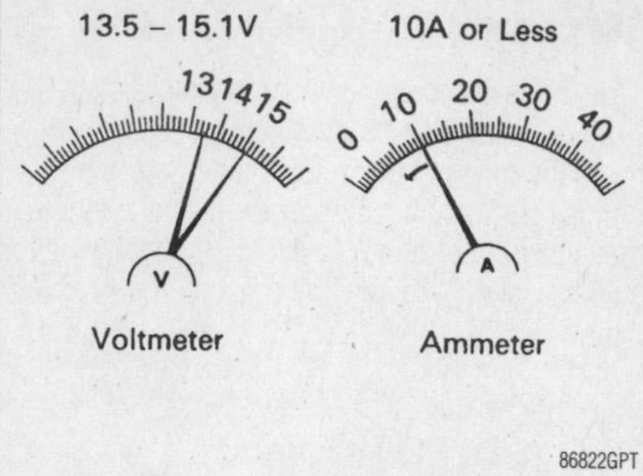

Fig. 42 With the engine running from idle to 2000 rpm, the readings should be as shown

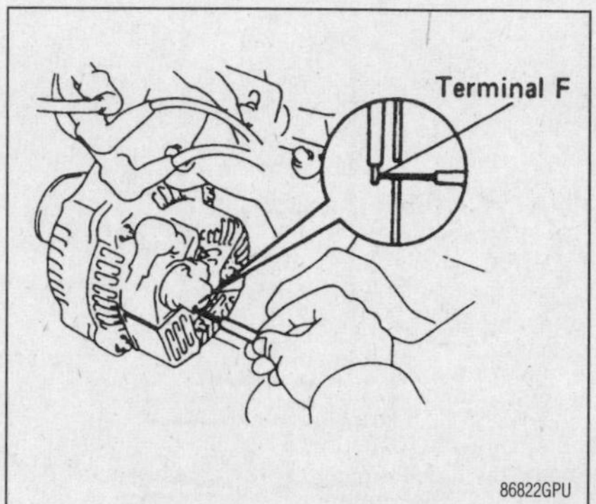

Fig. 43 With terminal (F) grounded, start the engine and check the voltmeter reading of terminal (B)

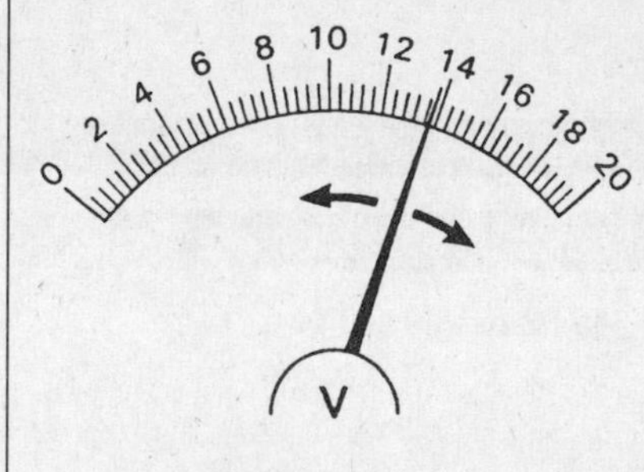

Fig. 44 Note whether the reading is above or below the standard voltage

Alternator

All current trucks use a nominal 12 volt alternator. (Exact output should be slightly higher, generally 13.5–14.4 volts). Amperage ratings may vary according to the year, model and accessories. All have a transistorized, non-adjustable regulator, integrated with the alternator.

TESTING

➧ See Figures 41 thru 46

➡If a battery/alternator tester is available, connect the tester to the charging circuit recommended by the manufacturer's instructions.

If a tester is not available, connect a voltmeter and an ammeter to the charging circuit by doing the following:

1. Disconnect the wire from terminal (B) of the alternator and attach to the negative (–) lead of the ammeter.
2. Connect the positive (+) lead of the ammeter to terminal (B) of the alternator.
3. Connect the positive (+) lead of the voltmeter to terminal (B) of the alternator.
4. Ground the negative (–) lead of the voltmeter.
5. With the engine running from idle to 2000 rpm, check the reading on the ammeter and voltmeter. The standard amperage should be 10 A or less; standard voltage cold is 13.9–15.1 volts, and 13.5–14.3 volts hot. If the reading is greater than standard voltage, replace the regulator.
6. If the reading is less than the standard voltage, check the regulator and alternator:
7. With terminal (F) grounded, start the engine and check the voltmeter reading of terminal (B).
8. If the voltmeter reading is more than the standard voltage, replace the regulator.
9. If the voltmeter reading is less than standard voltage, the alternator may be faulty.

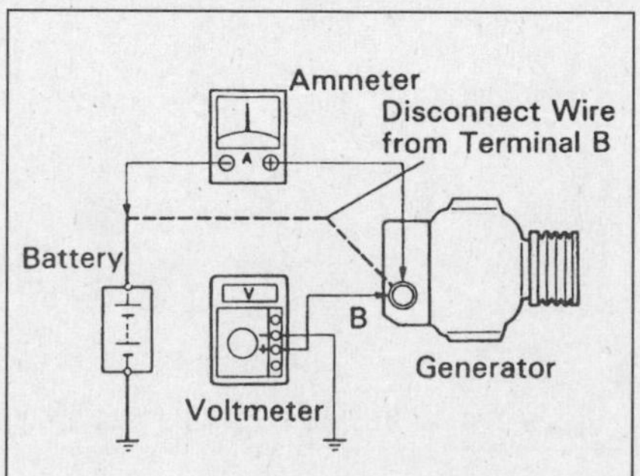

Fig. 41 Attach the ammeter and voltmeter as shown to test the charging system

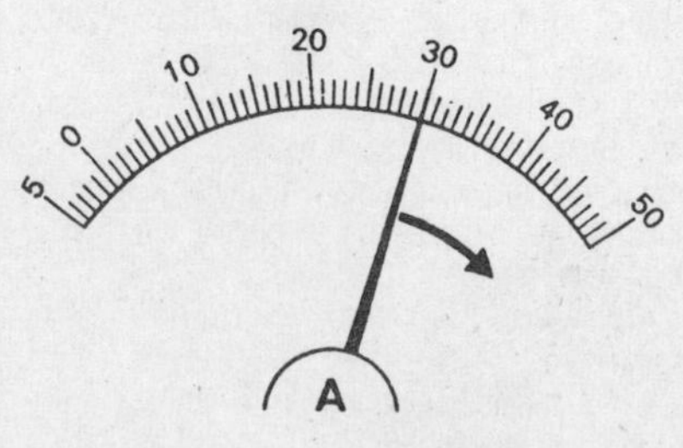

Fig. 45 The ammeter reading should be above 30 A

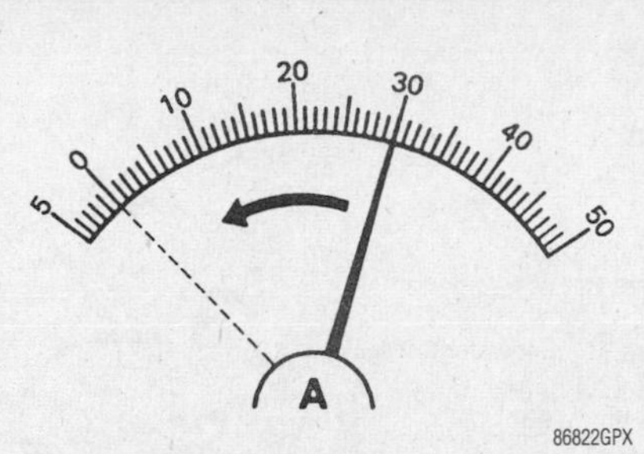

Fig. 46 If the ammeter reading is below 30 A, replace the alternator

10. With the engine running at 2000 rpm turn on the high beam headlights and place the heater switch on high.
11. Check the reading on the ammeter. It should be 30 A or more.
12. If the ammeter reading is less than the standard amperage, replace the alternator.

➡If the battery is fully charged, the indication will sometimes be slightly less than the standard amperage.

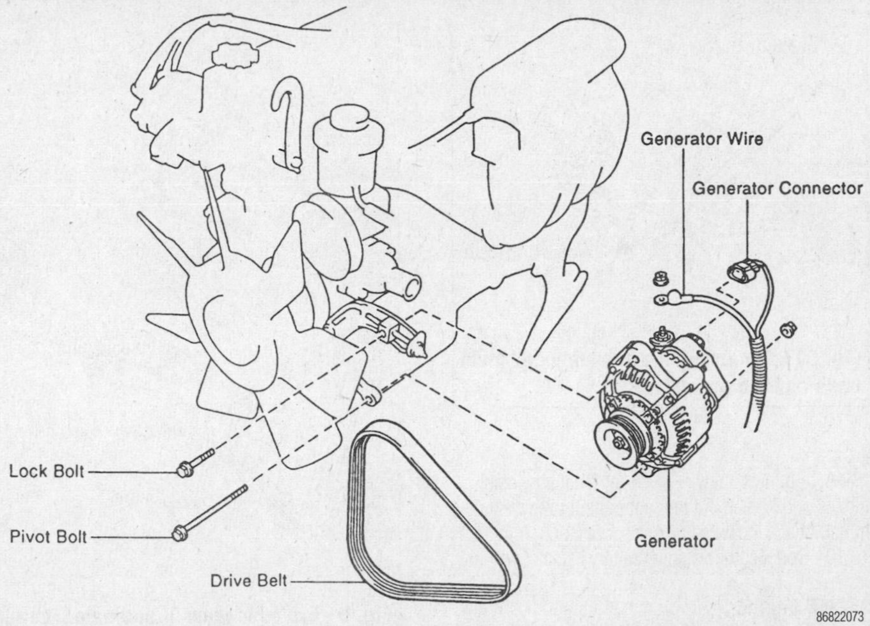

Fig. 47 Exploded view of the alternator and drive belt—2RZ-FE and 3RZ-FE engines

REMOVAL & INSTALLATION

➡On some models, the alternator is mounted very low on the engine. On these models, it may be necessary to remove the gravel shield and work from beneath the truck in order to gain access to the alternator. Replacing the alternator while the engine is cold is recommended. A hot engine can result in personal injury.

2RZ-FE and 3RZ-FE Engines

➧ See Figures 47 and 48

1. Disconnect the negative battery cable.
2. Disconnect the wiring at the back of the alternator. Lift the rubber boot, remove the nut from the external terminal and the wire.
3. Loosen the alternator lockbolt, pivot bolt, nut and adjusting bolt.
4. Push the alternator towards the engine and remove the belt.
5. Remove the wiring harness with the clip.
6. Remove the alternator lockbolt, pivot bolt, nut.
7. Remove the alternator.

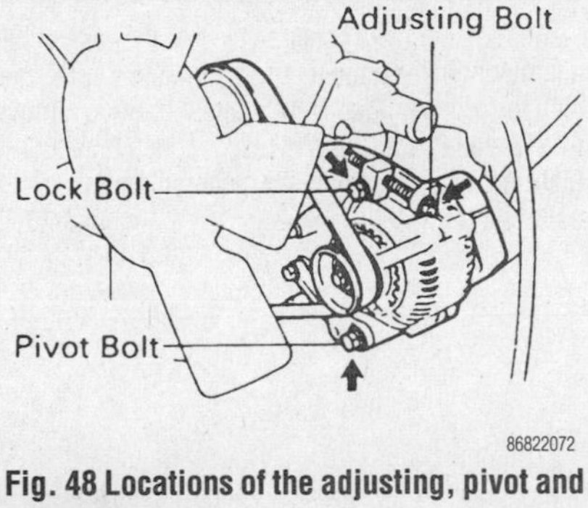

Fig. 48 Locations of the adjusting, pivot and lockbolts

To install:

8. Place the alternator into position and loosely install the pivot and adjusting bolts.
9. Install the drive belt; adjust it to the proper tension. Tighten the lockbolt to 21 ft. lbs. (29 Nm) and the pivot bolt to 43 ft. lbs. (59 Nm).
10. Connect the wire harness with clip.
11. Connect the wire to the terminal. Install the nut and tighten to 7 ft. lbs. (10 Nm). Fit the rubber boot over the terminal. Attach the wire harness connector.
12. Connect the negative battery cable.

5VZ-FE Engine

➧ See Figures 49 and 50

1. Disconnect the negative battery cable.
2. Disconnect the wiring at the back of the alternator. Lift the rubber boot, remove the nut from the external terminal and the wire.
3. Loosen the alternator locknut, pivot bolt, nut and adjusting bolt.
4. Push the alternator towards the engine and remove the belt.
5. Remove the alternator lockbolt, pivot bolt, nut.
6. Remove the alternator.

To install:

7. Place the alternator into position and loosely install the pivot and adjusting bolts.
8. Install the drive belt; adjust it to the proper tension. Tighten the locknut 25 ft. lbs. (33 Nm) and the pivot bolt 38 ft. lbs. (51 Nm).

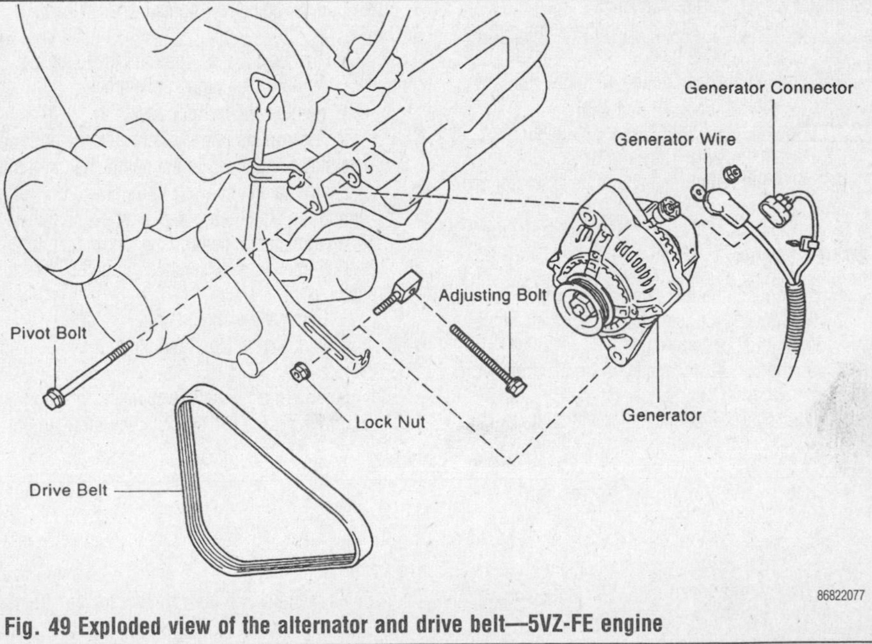

Fig. 49 Exploded view of the alternator and drive belt—5VZ-FE engine

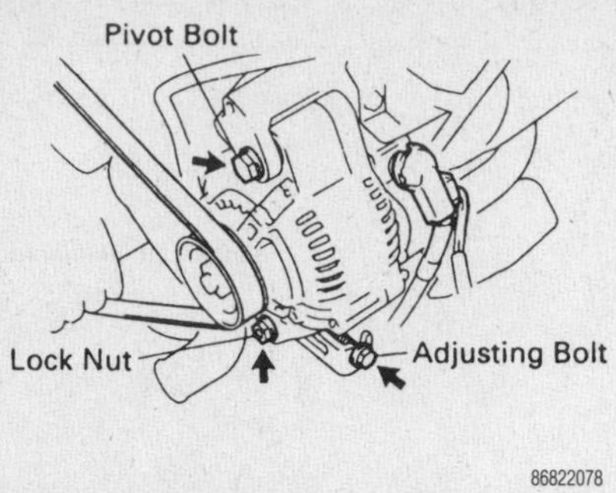

Fig. 50 Locations of the adjusting and pivot bolts and the locknut

9. Connect the wire to the terminal and install the nut and tighten. Fit the rubber boot over the terminal. Attach the wire harness connector.
10. Connect the negative battery cable.

1FZ-FE Engine

➧ **See Figures 51, 52, and 53**

1. Disconnect the negative battery terminal.
2. Remove the battery and tray.
3. Disconnect the power steering reservoir tank.
4. Loosen the lock, pivot and adjusting bolts.
5. Remove the 2 drive belts.
6. Disconnect the wiring at the back of the alternator. Lift the rubber boot, remove the nut from the external terminal and the wire.
7. Remove the wire clamp from the alternator.
8. Remove the lockbolt, nut and drive belt adjusting bar.
9. Hold the alternator; remove the pivot bolt then the alternator.

To install:

10. Mount the alternator on the bracket with the pivot bolt. Do not tighten the bolt yet.
11. Install the drive belt adjusting bar with the bolt and nut. Tighten the bolt to 15 ft. lbs. (21 Nm).
12. Temporarily install the lockbolt. Connect the alternator wiring, nut and rubber cap.
13. Connect the wire clamp to the alternator.
14. Install the drive belts.
15. Tighten the pivot bolt to 43 ft. lbs. (59 Nm) and the lockbolt to 15 ft. lbs. (21 Nm).
16. Connect the power steering reservoir tank.
17. Install the battery tray and battery.
18. Start the vehicle and check the alternator operation.

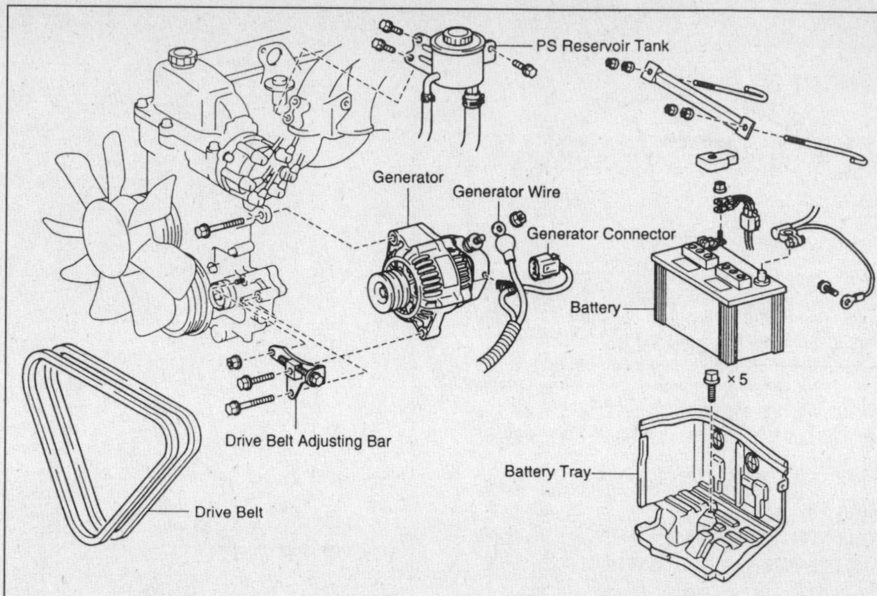

Fig. 51 Exploded view of alternator, battery, belt and related components—1FZ-FE engine

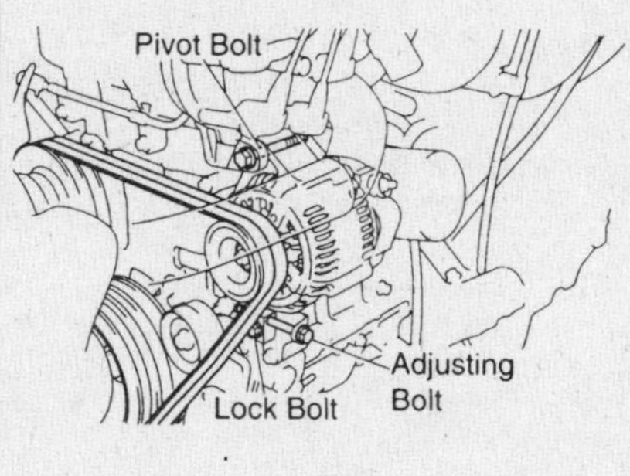

Fig. 52 Lock, pivot and adjusting bolt locations

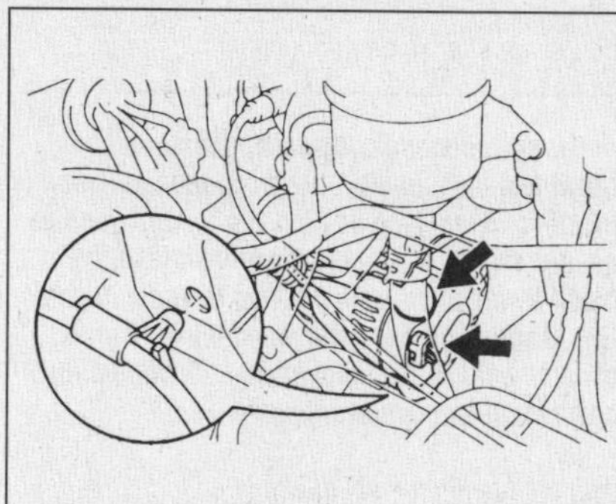

Fig. 53 The wiring clamp is mounted into the alternator as shown

2UZ-FE Engine

1. Disconnect the negative battery cable.
2. On the Land Cruiser, drain the coolant since the radiator must be removed.
3. On the Tundra and the Land Cruiser, remove the alternator drive belt. Loosen the belt tension by turning the tensioner counterclockwise. Note that the pulley bolt for the belt tensioner has a left-hand thread.
4. On the Land Cruiser, perform the following:
   a. Remove the engine under cover.
   b. Remove the radiator assembly.
   c. Remove the power steering pump pulley. Note that it is splined to the pump shaft and may take some careful coaxing for removal. Do not hammer on either the pump shaft or the pulley.
5. On the Tundra, perform the following:
   a. Remove the power steering pump from the engine.
   b. Remove the engine under cover.
   c. Remove the No. 2 fan shroud, by removing the clips.
6. Remove the alternator electrical connector. There will likely be a clip securing the wiring to the alternator body. Gently work this clip free. Unbolt the alternator.

To install:

7. Installation is the reverse of removal. Verify that all electrical connections are tight. On Land Cruiser, if the pump pulley has been removed, install with a new pulley nut and torque to 32 ft. lbs. (43 Nm).

Regulator

All regulators are contained inside the case of the alternator. The voltage regulator is usually combined with the brush holder. Once the rear cover is removed from the alternator, brush holder/voltage regulator replacement is generally just a matter of removing some screws.

STARTING SYSTEM

▸ See Figure 54

Starter

TESTING

⁂ WARNING

These tests must be performed within a 3 to 5 seconds to avoid burning out the coil.

Pull-In

▸ **See Figure 55**

1. Disconnect the field coil lead wire from terminal C.
2. Connect the battery to the magnetic switch shown in the diagram.
3. Check that the clutch pinion gear moves in the outward motion.

Hold-In

▸ **See Figure 56**

With the battery connected as in the picture and with the clutch pinion gear out, disconnect the negative (–) lead from terminal C. Check that the pinion gear stays in the outward position.

Inspect Clutch Pinion Gear Return

▸ **See Figure 57**

Disconnect the negative lead from the magnetic switch body. Check that the pinion gear returns to the inward position.

No-Load

▸ **See Figure 58**

1. Connect the battery ammeter to the starter as shown in the illustration.
2. Check the rotation of the starter, it must be smooth and steady with the pinion gear moving outwards. Compare the ammeter reading to the starter specifications chart.

REMOVAL & INSTALLATION

➡On all engines except the 2UZ-FE, the starter is external, mounted in a conventional manner, alongside the engine block. One the 2UZ-FE, however, the starter is mounted in the 'V' of the engine, between the cylinder head banks. The entire intake manifold assembly must be removed to access the starter motor and solenoid (Toyota calls the solenoid a magnetic switch).

Except 2UZ-FE Engine

▸ **See Figures 59, 60, and 61**

1. Disconnect the negative battery cable.
2. Remove the nut and disconnect the battery cable from the magnetic switch on the starter motor.

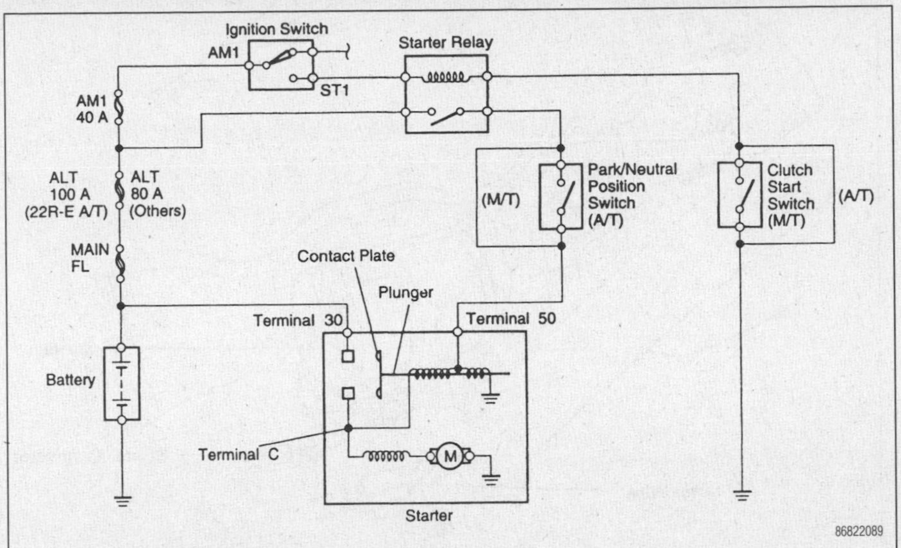

Fig. 54 Typical Toyota truck starting system circuit

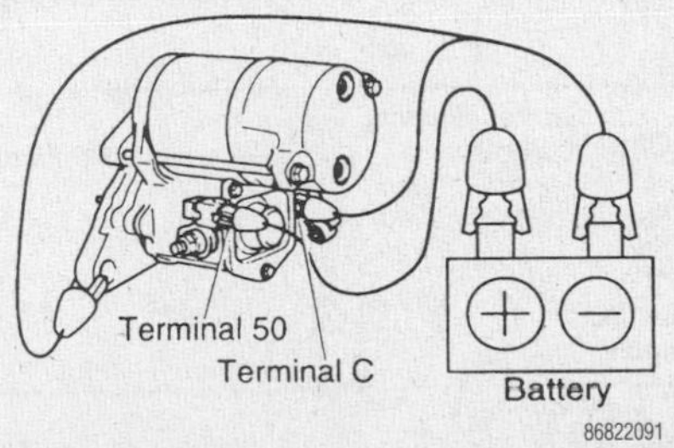

Fig. 55 Connect the battery to the magnetic switch as shown here

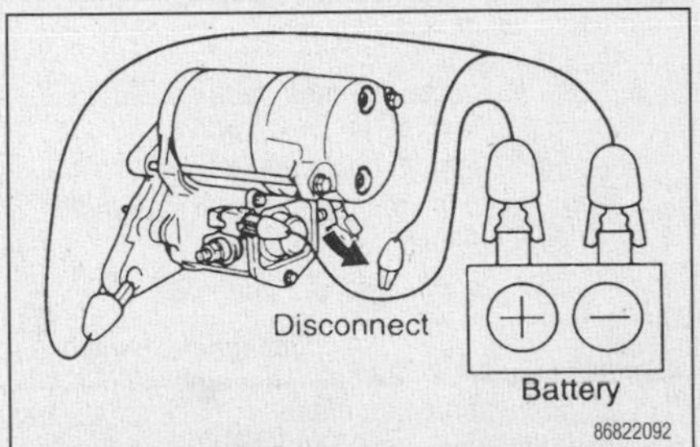

Fig. 56 Connect the battery as shown here to test the hold-in windings

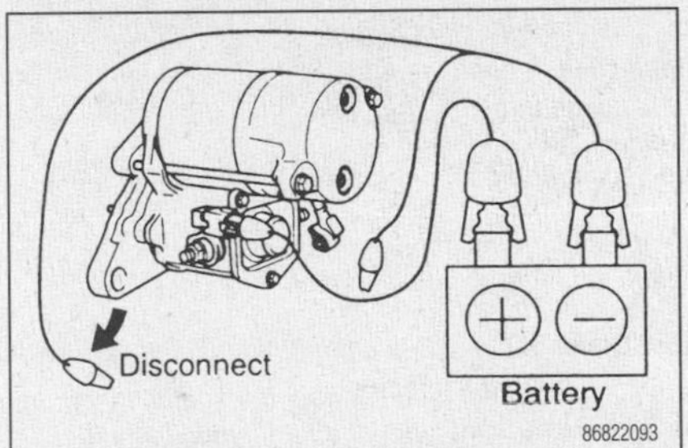

Fig. 57 Disconnect the negative lead from the starter as shown here

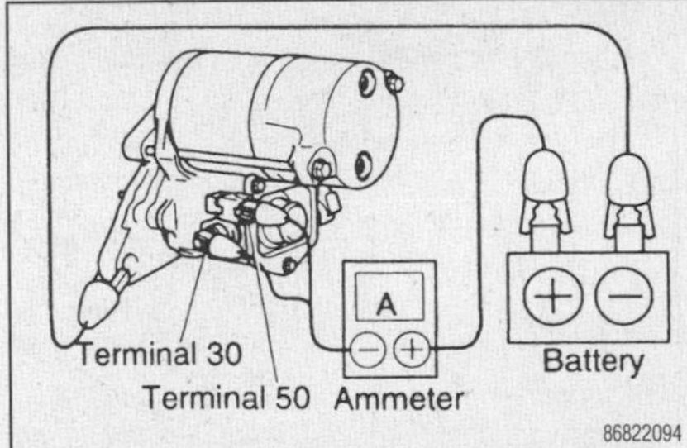

Fig. 58 Make the connections to the battery, ammeter and starter as shown here

Fig. 59 Unfasten the starter mounting bolts . . .

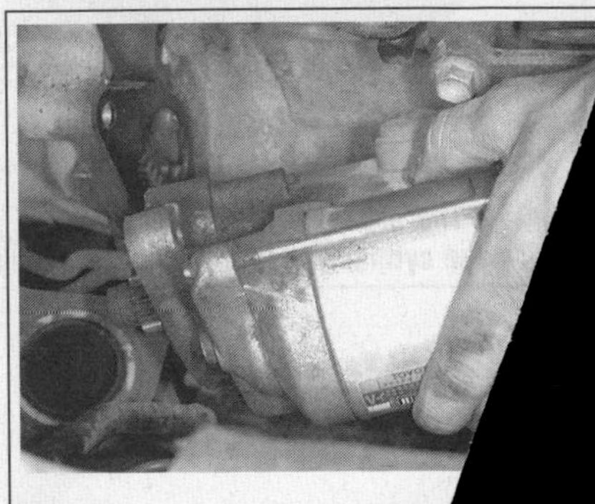

Fig. 60 . . . then pull the starte front of the vehicle to remove i ponents removed for clarity)

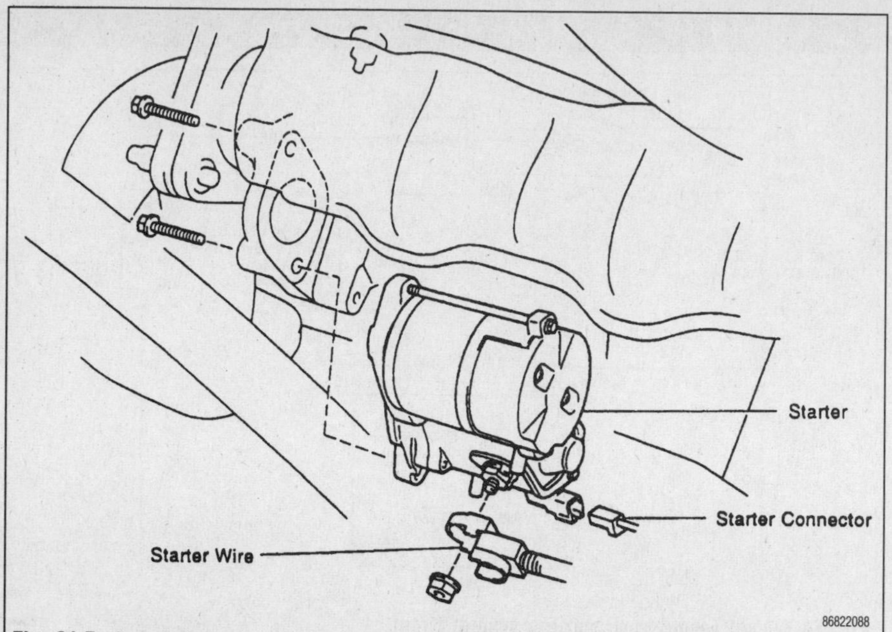

Fig. 61 Exploded view of a common starter mounting found on Toyota trucks

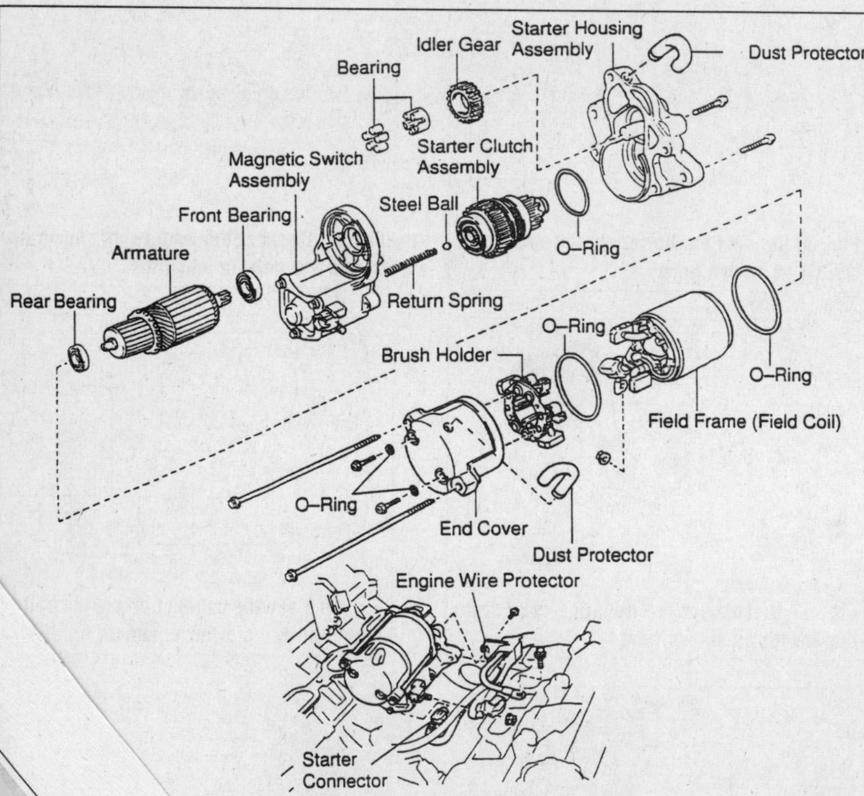

...motor on this 2UZ-FE engine is installed under the intake manifold be-...ds, making it a lengthy procedure to perform

3. Detach the remaining electrical connections at the starter.

4. Remove the nuts and/or bolts securing the starter to the bell housing, then pull the starter toward the front of the vehicle to remove.

To install:

5. Insert the starter into the bell housing being sure that the starter drive teeth are engaged with the flywheel teeth, not jammed against the flywheel.

6. Tighten the attaching hardware to 29 ft. lbs. (39 Nm) and replace all electrical connections.

7. Connect the positive battery cable (starter wire) to the starter.

8. Connect the negative battery cable.

2UZ-FE Engine

See Figure 62

1. Disconnect the negative battery cable.
2. Remove the cosmetic/acoustic engine cover.
3. Disconnect the accelerator cable and intake air connector.
4. Remove the intake manifold assembly. For additional information, please refer to the following topic(s): Engine Mechanical, Intake Manifold.
5. Remove the two bolts holding the starter motor to the engine block and lift the starter away from the block.
6. Detach the electrical connectors from the starter and remove the starter from the vehicle.

To install:

7. Installation is the reverse of the removal procedure. Make sure all electrical connections are tight and that the harness is secure.
8. Install the starter and torque the two bolts to 29 ft. lbs. (39 Nm).
9. Install the intake manifold.
10. Connect the negative battery cable.

RELAY REPLACEMENT

See Figures 63 and 64

The starter relays on most Toyota trucks are located either in the relay block in the engine compartment or on the driver's side junction block. The cover for the relay compartments should be marked, 'starter' (or something similar) or the relay will have a part number with a suffix of 28300-XXXXX. Simply locate the relay, pull it out, and install a new one if needed.

93163p15
...toward the
...(other com-

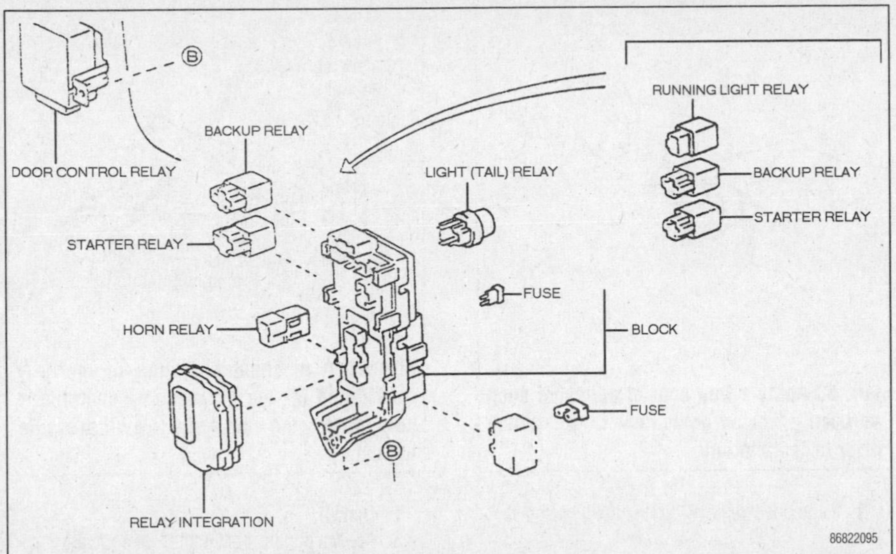

Fig. 63 The relay may be located in the driver's side junction block or in the engine compartment relay block

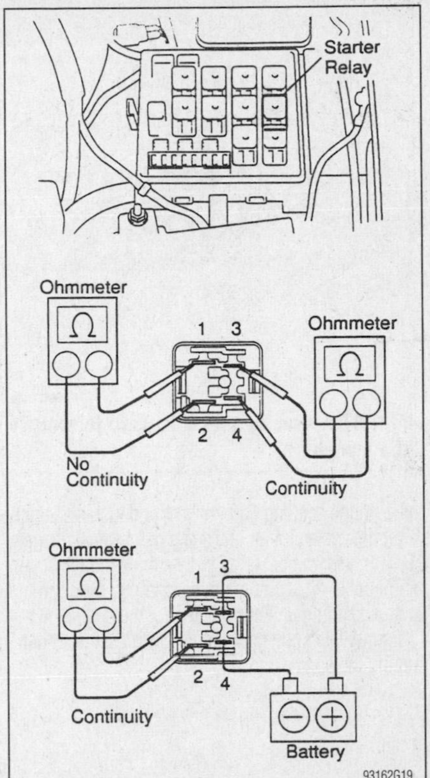

Fig. 64 This relay is marked ST and can be tested for continuity with an ohmmeter—1998 2UZ-FE engine shown, others similar

SENDING UNITS AND SENSORS

Engine Coolant Temperature Sensor

OPERATION

▶ **See Figure 65**

The engine coolant temperature sensor is usually located on the thermostat housing. This sensor controls the readings of the coolant temperature gauge in your vehicle when the ignition switch is **ON**.

There is a needle that shows the temperature area of the engine. If the needle points in the red zone or higher (this is overheating), you should pull to the side of the road, turn your engine OFF immediately and allow it to cool.

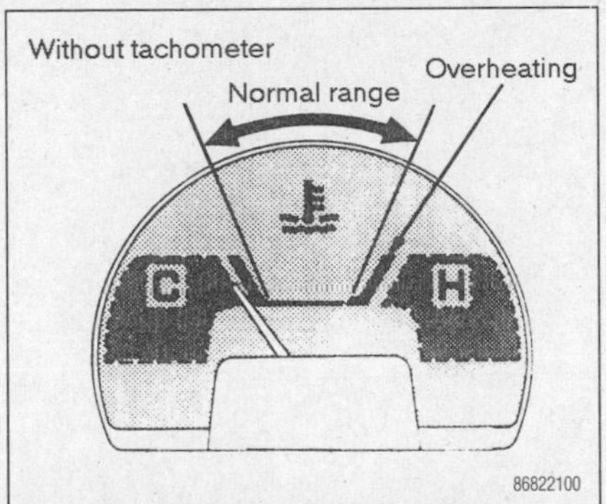

Fig. 65 A common engine coolant temperature gauge found on Toyota trucks

REMOVAL & INSTALLATION

1. Drain the coolant from the vehicle.
2. Disconnect the engine wiring protector from the brackets.
3. Disconnect the sensor wire.
4. Using a 19mm deep socket, remove the sensor and gasket.

To install:

5. Apply a thin coat of Loctite® or equivalent to the switch. By hand, carefully thread the switch into the engine. If resistance is felt at all, remove the switch and inspect the threads for any damage. Continue to install the switch. Once installed, tighten to 14 ft. lbs. (20 Nm).
6. Connect the sensor wiring.
7. Install the engine wire protector to the brackets.
8. Refill the coolant. Start the engine and check for leaks.

Oil Pressure Light/Gauge Sender

OPERATION

▶ **See Figure 66**

The oil pressure sender/switch controls the gauge in the instrument cluster of your vehicle while the engine is **ON**. The gauge will fluctuate during engine operation. If the pressure should stay below the normal range, you should pull to the side of the road and turn your engine **OFF** immediately. Check your oil level of the vehicle on level ground, if it is low, fill to the proper level. Start the engine and recheck after a few minutes. Oil pressure may not build up when the level is too low.

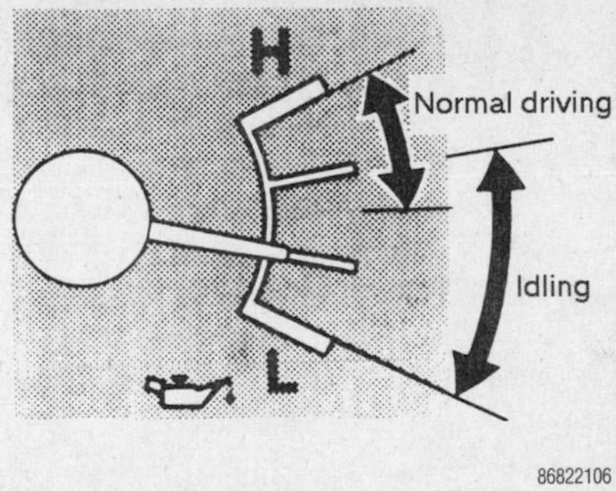

Fig. 66 A common oil pressure gauge found on Toyota trucks

REMOVAL & INSTALLATION

See Figures 67, 68, and 69

When troubleshooting a suspected oil pressure problem, it is possible to remove the electric oil pres-

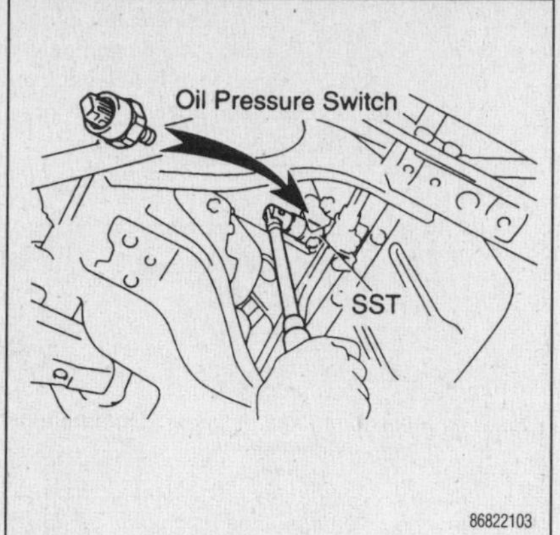

Fig. 67 A special socket is used to remove the switch

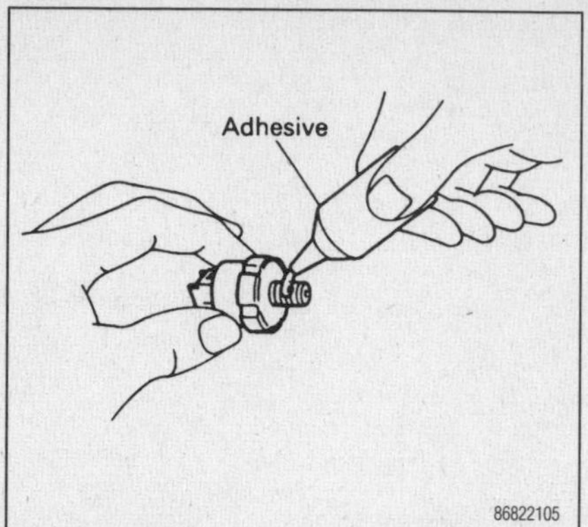

Fig. 68 Apply a thin coat of adhesive such as Loctite® or an equivalent to the switch prior to installation

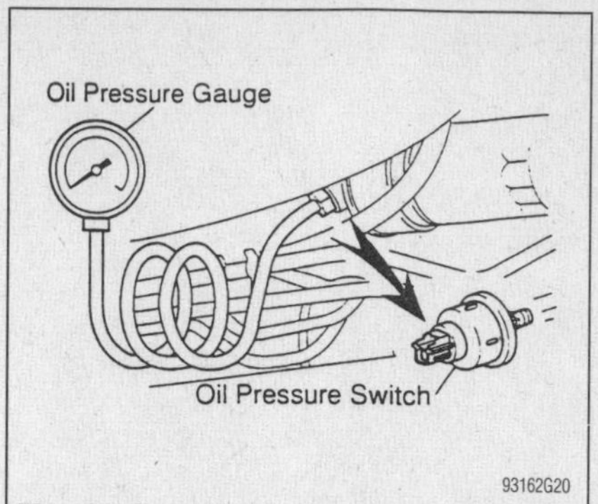

Fig. 69 A mechanical gauge temporarily substituted for the oil pressure switch can help identify the cause of a low oil pressure indication

sure gauge sending unit (switch) and install a length of appropriate size oil line and a mechanical gauge. This is often the best way to determine if the instrument panel oil pressure gauge is faulty, the electric gauge sending unit has failed, or if the engine oil pump really is putting out only low pressure, endangering the engine.

1. If equipped, remove the lower engine splash shield.
2. Due to the shape of the switch body it may be necessary to use a specially-shaped socket. Toyota recommends their Special Service Tool (SST) 09816-33010 or an equivalent oil pressure switch socket. Using an appropriate socket extension, as required, remove the switch.

To install:

3. Apply a thin coat of Loctite® or equivalent to the switch. By hand, carefully thread the switch into the engine. If resistance is felt at all, remove the switch and inspect the threads for any damage. Continue to install the switch. Once installed tighten to 11 ft. lbs. (15 Nm).
4. If removed, install the engine splash shield.
5. Start the engine and inspect for leaks.

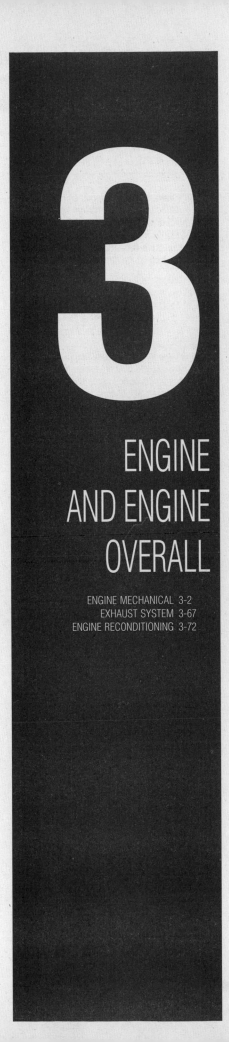

3 ENGINE AND ENGINE OVERALL

ENGINE MECHANICAL

Engine

REMOVAL & INSTALLATION

➡If your vehicle is equipped with air conditioning, refer to the information regarding the implications of servicing your A/C system yourself. Only an MVAC-trained, EPA-certified, automotive technician should service the A/C system or its components.

In the process of removing the engine, you will come across a number of steps which call for the removal of a separate component or system, such as "disconnect the exhaust system" or "remove the radiator." In most instances, a detailed removal procedure can be found elsewhere.

It is virtually impossible to list each individual wire and hose which must be disconnected, simply because so many different model and engine combinations have been manufactured. Careful observation and common sense are the best possible additions to any repair procedure. Be absolutely sure to tag and wire or hose before it is disconnected, so that you can be assured of proper reconnection during installation.

5VZ-FE Engine

2WD MODELS

➧ **See Figures 1, 2, 3, 4, and 5**

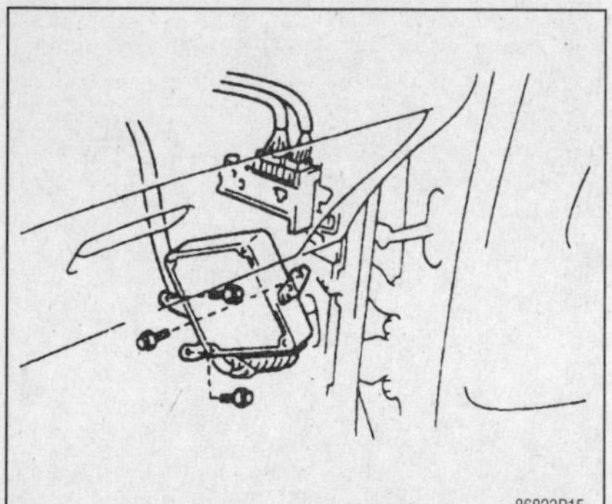

Fig. 1 The Electronic Control Unit (ECU) can be found behind the passenger's side kick panel

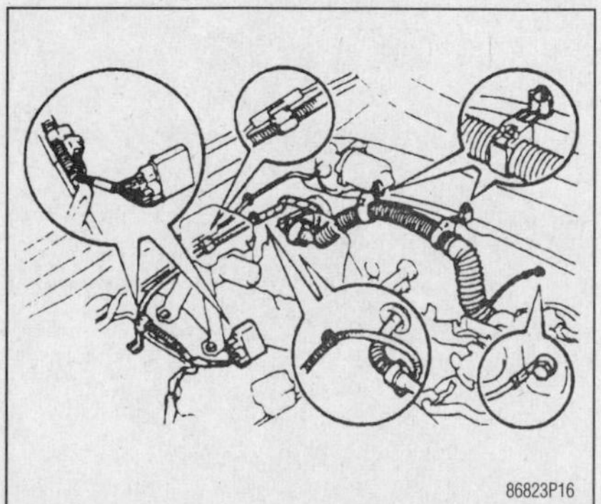

Fig. 2 Remove the clamps securing the engine wiring harness at the points shown

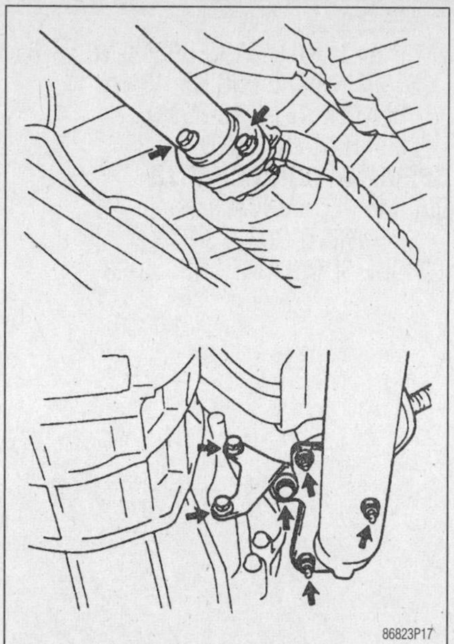

Fig. 3 Remove the bolts securing the front exhaust pipe to the manifold, support bracket and catalytic converter

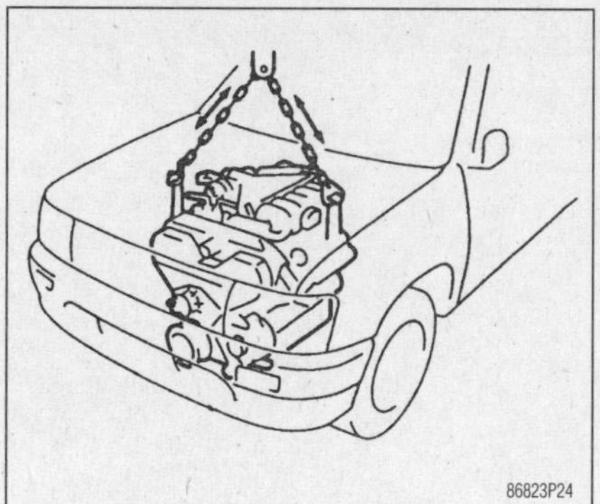

Fig. 4 Attach the engine hoist chain to the engine hangers

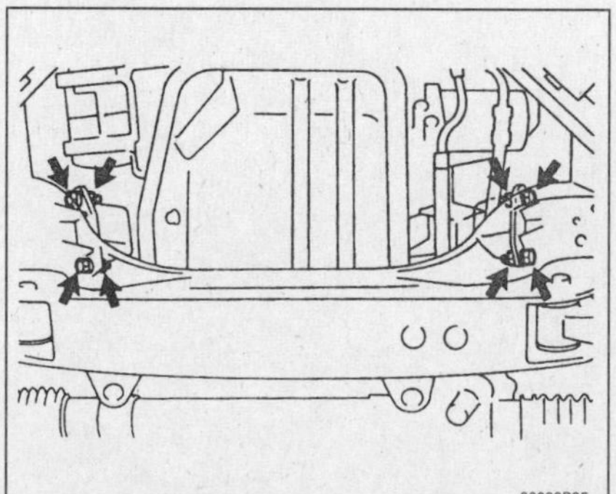

Fig. 5 Remove these four bolts and nuts that secure the engine mounting insulators to the frame

1. Remove the hood.
2. Relieve the fuel pressure. For additional information, please refer the following topic(s): Fuel System, Relieving Fuel System Pressure.
3. Disable the air bag system. For additional information, please refer to the following topic(s): Chassis Electrical, SRS system.
4. Disconnect the battery and remove it from the vehicle.
5. Raise and safely support the vehicle.
6. Remove the engine undercovers.
7. Drain the engine coolant.
8. Drain the engine oil.
9. Remove the radiator.
10. Remove the power steering drive belt, as follows:
    a. Stretch the belt and loosen the fan pulley mounting bolts.
    b. Loosen the lock, pivot and adjusting bolts. Remove the drive belt from the engine.
11. If equipped with A/C, remove the A/C drive belt by loosening the idle pulley nut and adjusting bolt.
12. Loosen the lock, pivot and adjusting bolts, then remove the alternator belt.
13. Remove the fan with the fluid coupling and the fan pulleys.
14. Disconnect the power steering pump from the engine and set aside. Do not disconnect the lines from the pump.
15. If equipped with A/C, disconnect the compressor from the engine and set aside. Do not disconnect the lines from the compressor.
16. Remove the air cleaner lid, Mass Air Flow (MAF) meter and resonator.
17. Remove the air cleaner case and filter assembly.
18. Disconnect the following cables:
    - Detent cable, if equipped with cruise control
    - Accelerator cable
    - Throttle cable, if automatic
19. Disconnect the heater hoses.
20. Disconnect the following hoses:
    - Brake booster vacuum hose
    - Evaporative emissions (EVAP) hose
    - Fuel return and inlet hoses
21. Disconnect the starter wire and connectors as follows:
    a. Remove the bolt retaining the ground strap.
    b. Disconnect the positive battery cable.
    c. Disconnect the starter wires and connectors.
22. Disconnect the alternator harness.
23. Remove the engine harness as follows:
    a. Remove the four screws to the right front door scuff plate.
    b. Remove clip retaining the cowl panel side trim.
    c. Disconnect the Electronic Control Unit (ECU) wiring.
    d. Detach the two connectors from the cowl wire.
    e. Disconnect the igniter.
    f. Detach the ground strap.
    g. Disconnect the six engine wire clamps.
    h. Pull the engine wire from the compartment.
24. If equipped with a manual transmission, remove the shift lever as follows:
    a. Remove the shift lever knob.
    b. Remove the four screws and the shift lever boot.
    c. Remove the six bolts to retrieve the shift lever assembly and gasket.

25. Remove the stabilizer bar.
26. Remove the driveshaft from the transmission.
27. Disconnect the speedometer cable.
28. Remove the front exhaust pipe as follows:
  a. Disconnect the heated oxygen sensor.
  b. Remove the two bolts and retainer holding the front pipe to the catalytic converter.
  c. Remove the three bolts and the support bracket.
  d. Loosen and remove the three nuts holding the front pipe and gaskets.
29. If equipped with a manual transmission, remove the slave cylinder.
30. On automatic transmissions, remove the cross-shaft.
31. Place a jack under the transmission.
32. Remove the eight bolts retaining the transmission rear mounting bracket.
33. If equipped with A/C, remove the bolt and disconnect the wire.
34. Attach the engine hoist chain to the two engine hangers.
35. Remove the four bolts and nuts holding the front mounting insulators to the frame.
36. Lift the engine and transmission out of the vehicle.

To install:

37. Install the engine assembly to the vehicle. Attach the engine mounts to the body mountings, then install bolts and nuts. Do not tighten them.
38. Remove the engine hoist from the engine hangers.
39. The remainder of installation is the reverse of the removal procedure. Make sure to note the following steps and tightening specifications:
  - Transmission-to-frame bolts: 43 ft. lbs. (58 Nm)
  - Mounting bracket insulator bolts: 13 ft. lbs. (18 Nm)
  - Engine mounting nuts and bolts: 28 ft. lbs. (38 Nm)
  - Front exhaust pipe-to-engine nuts: 36 ft. lbs. (44 Nm).
  - Support bracket bolts: 33 ft. lbs. (44 Nm)
  - Exhaust pipe-to-catalytic converter bolts: 35 ft. lbs. (48 Nm)
40. Fill the engine with oil.
41. Fill the cooling system.
42. Start the engine and check for leaks.
43. Top off any fluid levels.

4WD MODELS

➧ **See Figure 1, 5, and 6**

1. Disable the air bag system. For additional information, please refer to the following topic(s): Chassis Electrical, SRS system.
2. Remove the transmission from the vehicle.
3. Remove the hood.
4. Disconnect the battery and remove it from the vehicle.
5. Raise and support the vehicle safely.
6. Remove the engine splash shields.
7. Drain the engine coolant.
8. Drain the engine oil.
9. Remove the radiator.
10. Remove the power steering drive belt, as follows:
  a. Loosen the fan pulley mounting bolts.
  b. Loosen the lock, pivot and adjusting bolts. Remove the drive belt.
11. On A/C vehicles, loosen the idle pulley nut and adjusting bolt to remove the A/C drive belt.
12. Loosen the lock, pivot and adjusting bolts. Remove the drive belt.
13. Remove the fan, fluid coupling and pulleys.
14. Disconnect the power steering pump from the engine and set aside. Do not disconnect the lines from the pump.
15. On A/C vehicles, disconnect the compressor from the engine and set aside. Do not disconnect the lines from the compressor.
16. Remove the air cleaner lid, Mass Air Flow (MAF) meter and resonator.
17. Remove the air cleaner assembly.
18. Disconnect the following cables:
  - Cruise control actuator and bracket
  - Accelerator cable
  - On automatics, remove the throttle cable
19. Disconnect the heater hoses.
20. Disconnect the following hoses:
  - Brake booster vacuum hose
  - Evaporative emissions (EVAP) hose
  - Fuel return and inlet hoses
21. Disconnect the starter wire, as follows:
  a. Remove the ground strap.
  b. Remove the nuts and disconnect the positive battery cable.
  c. Disconnect the three starter wire clamps.
22. Disconnect the alternator harness.
23. Detach the engine harness:
  a. Remove the right front door scuff plate.
  b. Remove the cowl panel side trim.
  c. Disconnect the Electronic Control Unit (ECU).
  d. Disconnect the wires leading to the cowl.
  e. Remove the wiring to the igniter.
  f. Disconnect the ground strap.
  g. Remove the wire clamps.
  h. Pull out the engine wire from the cabin.
24. On A/C vehicles, remove the bolt and disconnect the compressor wire clamp.
25. Attach the engine hoist chain to the two engine hangers.
26. Remove the bolts and nuts holding the engine front mounting insulators to the frame.
27. Lift the engine out of the vehicle.

To install:

28. Install the engine assembly in the vehicle. Attach the engine mounts to the body mountings. Install the bolts and nuts but do not tighten them.
29. Remove the engine hoist chain from engine hangers.

93163pl9

Fig. 6 Always use an engine hoist of the correct capacity when removing an engine. Never overload the hoist for bodily injury may occur

30. The remainder of installation is the reverse of the removal procedure. Tighten the engine mounting nuts and bolts to 28 ft. lbs. (38 Nm).
31. Fill the engine with oil.
32. Fill the cooling system.
33. Install the hood.
34. Attach the engine splash shield.
35. Install the transmission in the vehicle.
36. Start the engine and check for leaks.
37. Top off any fluid levels.

2RZ-FE and 3RZ-FE Engines

➧ **See Figures 7 thru 13**

1. Turn the ignition **OFF.** Disable the air bag system using the procedures in Section 6.
2. If not already done, disconnect the battery cables, negative first.

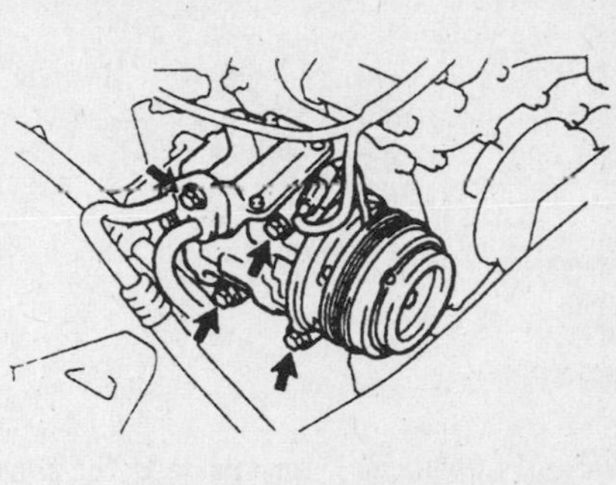

86823P32

Fig. 7 Remove the bolts securing the A/C compressor, then position it aside

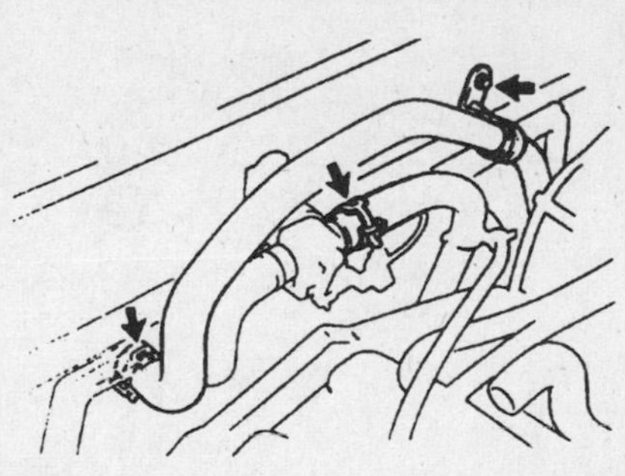

86823P35

Fig. 8 Remove the clamps shown securing the heater hoses

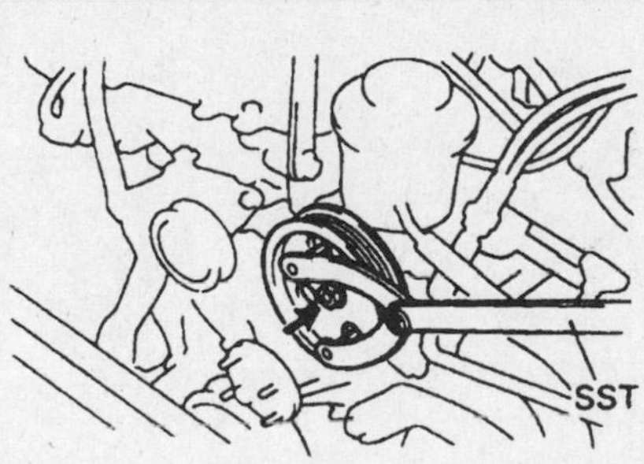

86823P33

Fig. 9 A spanner wrench can be used to hold the pulley while removing the bolt

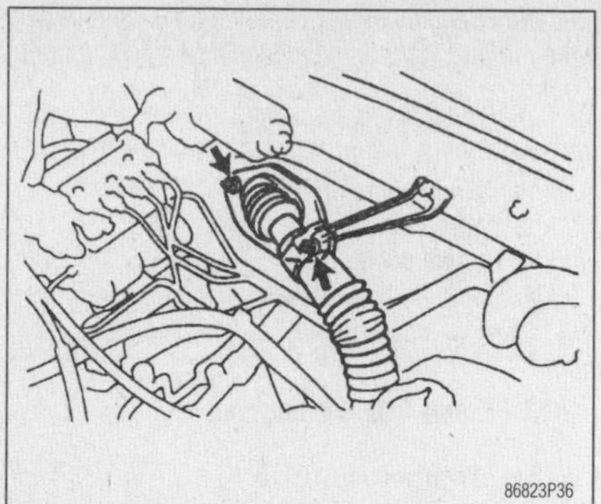

Fig. 10 Remove the bolts securing the engine wiring clamps

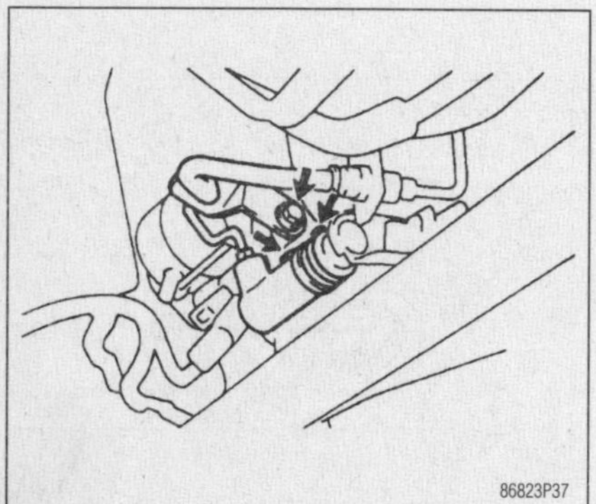

Fig. 11 On manual transmissions, the slave cylinder must be removed

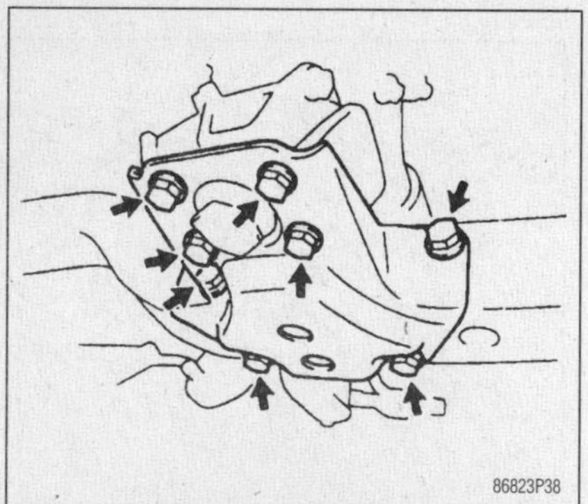

Fig. 12 Remove the bolts retaining the rear engine mounting bracket

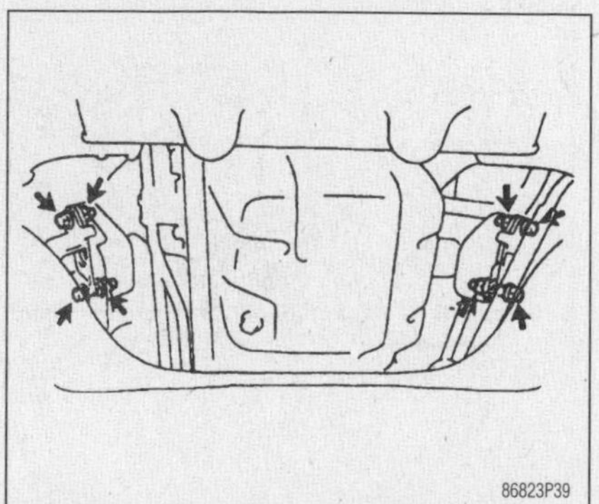

Fig. 13 The left and right engine mount retainers must be removed

3. Matchmark the hood hinges, then remove the hood.

4. Relieve the fuel system pressure. For additional information, please refer to the following topic(s): Fuel System, Relieving the Fuel System Pressure.

5. Remove the engine splash shield.

6. Drain the engine oil, transmission fluid and cooling system.

7. To remove the radiator:

a. Remove the parking lights from the grille.

b. Remove the two fillers.

c. Remove the grille from the vehicle.

d. On some California models you may need to remove the bolts retaining the air pipe.

e. Disconnect the upper radiator hose and the reservoir hose.

f. Remove the No. 2 fan shroud if equipped.

g. On automatics, disconnect the oil cooler hoses.

h. Remove the lower radiator hose.

i. Remove the four bolts retaining the radiator, and pull the radiator from the vehicle.

8. If equipped with power steering, loosen the lock bolt and adjusting bolt to the idler pulley, then remove the drive belt.

9. On A/C vehicles, loosen the idler pulley nut and adjusting bolt. Remove the drive belt.

10. Remove the alternator drive belt, fan, fan clutch, water pump pulley, and fan shroud as follows:

a. Loosen the water pump pulley mounting bolts.

b. Loosen the lock, pivot and adjusting bolts for the alternator and remove the alternator drive belt.

c. Remove the water pump pulley mount nuts.

d. Remove the fan (with clutch) and the water pump pulley.

11. On manual transmissions, disconnect the accelerator cable from the throttle body.

12. On automatics, disconnect the accelerator and throttle cables from the throttle body.

13. For vehicles with cruise control, remove the actuator cover and disconnect the cable.

14. Remove the air cleaner top, Mass Air Flow (MAF) meter and resonator. Remove the air cleaner assembly.

15. Remove the intake air connector.

16. On vehicles with A/C, disconnect the compressor and bracket:

a. Disconnect the A/C compressor wiring.

b. Remove the mounting bolts and mounting bracket. Do not disconnect the A/C pressure lines from the compressor. Suspend the compressor away from the engine.

c. Remove the compressor bracket.

17. Detach the alternator wiring.

18. Remove the heater hoses at the cowl.

19. Disconnect the following hoses:

- Brake booster vacuum hose
- Evaporative emissions (EVAP) hose
- On vehicles with power steering, disconnect the two hoses
- Fuel return and inlet hoses

20. Remove the power steering pump:

a. Using special service tool 09960–10010 or an equivalent spanner wrench, remove the nut and power steering pulley.

b. Remove the two bolts and disconnect the power steering pump.

21. Disconnect the following engine wiring:

a. Remove the igniter connection

b. Disconnect the ground strap from the cowl top panel.

c. Disconnect the two engine wire clamps.

d. Remove the nuts holding the engine wire retainer to the cowl panel and pull out the engine wire from the vehicles cabin.

22. Disconnect the front exhaust pipe from the exhaust manifold and catalytic converter as follows:

a. Disconnect the two heated oxygen sensors connectors.

b. Remove the two bolts and retainer holding the front exhaust pipe to the catalytic converter.

c. Loosen the clamp bolt and disconnect the clamp from the support bracket.

d. Remove the two bolts to release the support bracket.

e. Disconnect the three nuts, front exhaust pipe and gaskets from the exhaust manifold.

23. On manual transmissions, remove the shift lever assembly as follows:

a. Remove the shift lever knob.

b. Remove the shift lever boot.

c. Loosen the retaining bolts for the shift lever assembly and baffle, then remove.

24. Remove the driveshaft from the vehicle.

25. Disconnect the speedometer cable from the transmission.

26. On manual transmissions, remove the slave cylinder.

27. On automatics, remove the cross-shaft.

28. Disconnect the wires at the starter.

29. Position a jack and wooden block under the transmission, then remove the rear engine mounting bracket.

30. Attach a suitable engine hoist to the engine hangers.

31. Remove the nuts and bolts from the engine mounts.

➡Make sure the engine/transmission assembly is clear of all the wiring and hoses.

32. Carefully lift the engine/transmission out of the vehicle.

To install:

33. Attach the engine hoist to the engine hangers. Carefully lower the engine/transmission into the vehicle. Keep the engine level, while aligning the engine mounts.

34. Install the engine mount fasteners, but do not fully tighten them.

35. Position a jack and wooden block under the transmission, then install the rear engine mounting bracket. Tighten the bolts to the frame to 19 ft. lbs. (58 Nm) and the bolts to the mount to 13 ft. lbs. (18 Nm).

36. Remove the jack and engine hoist. Tighten the engine mounts to 28 ft. lbs. (38 Nm).

37. The remainder of installation is the reverse of the removal procedure, making sure to note the following tightening specifications and steps:

- Front exhaust pipe-to-manifold nuts: 46 ft. lbs. (62 Nm)
- Support bracket bolts: 29 ft. lbs. (39 Nm)
- Front pipe-to-catalytic converter bolts: 29 ft. lbs. (39 Nm)
- Power steering pump-to-bracket bolts: 43 ft. lbs. (58 Nm)
- With special service tool 09960–10010 or an equivalent spanner wrench, install the power steering pulley, tighten the nut to 32 ft. lbs. (43 Nm).

38. Fill the engine oil, coolant and transmission oil.
39. Connect the negative battery cable, then the positive cable.
40. Start the engine and check for leaks.
41. Check the ignition timing.
42. Install the engine splash shield.
43. Install the hood.
44. Road test the vehicle and recheck the fluids.

1FZ-FE Engine

➧ See Figures 14 thru 24

1. Disable the air bag system. For additional information, please refer to the following topic(s): Chassis Electrical, SRS system.
2. Release the fuel pressure. For additional information, please refer to the following topic(s): Fuel System, Relieving Fuel System Pressure.
3. Disconnect the battery cables, negative first. Remove the battery and tray assembly.
4. Raise and safely support the vehicle.
5. Drain the engine coolant, transmission fluid and engine oil.
6. Scribe the hood hinges and remove the hood.
7. Remove the radiator grille and radiator.
8. Disconnect the oil cooler hose from the oil cooler pipe.
9. Remove the air cleaner hose, cap and case assembly.
10. Disconnect the cruise control actuator cable from the throttle body.
11. Disconnect the accelerator actuator cable from the throttle body.
12. Disconnect the heater hoses.
13. Disconnect the ground wire and heater control valve from the cowl panel.
14. Remove the brake booster vacuum hose.
15. Disconnect the evaporative emissions (EVAP) hoses and fuel hoses.

✱✱ CAUTION

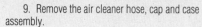

Fuel injected engines remain under constant pressure after the ignition has been turned OFF. Properly relieve the pressure before disconnecting any fuel lines. Failure to do so may result in personal injury. Please see the fuel pressure relief procedure in the Fuel System section.

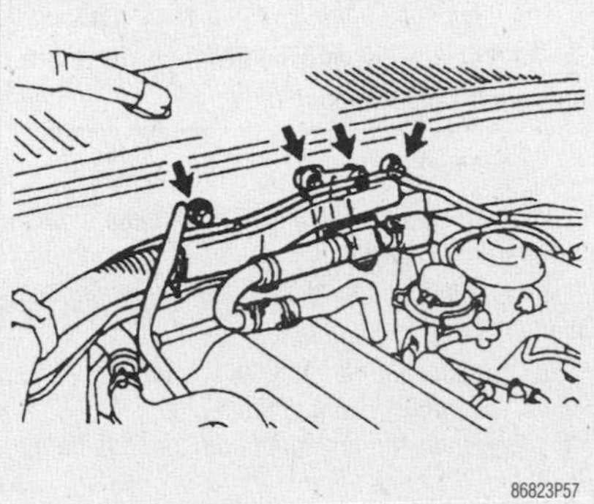

Fig. 14 Remove the bolts securing the engine ground wire and heater control valve

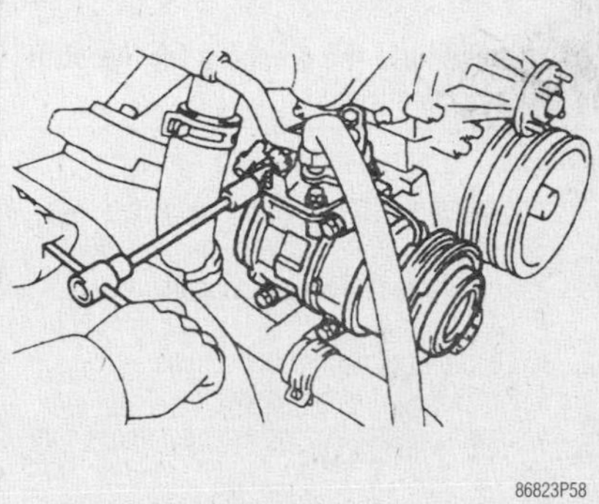

Fig. 15 Remove the bolts securing the compressor, then position it aside

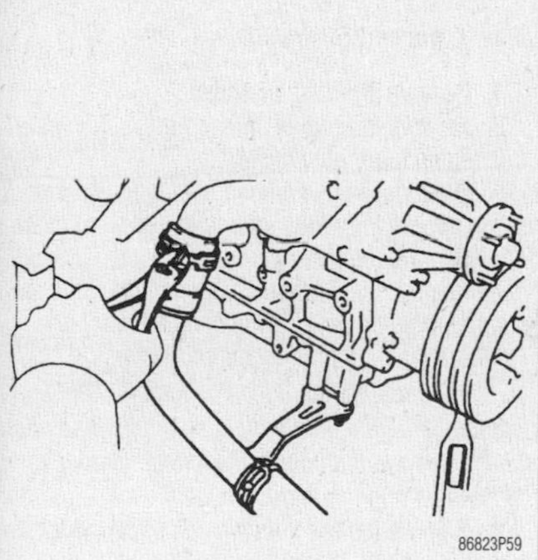

Fig. 16 Disconnect the No. 2 radiator hose from the water inlet

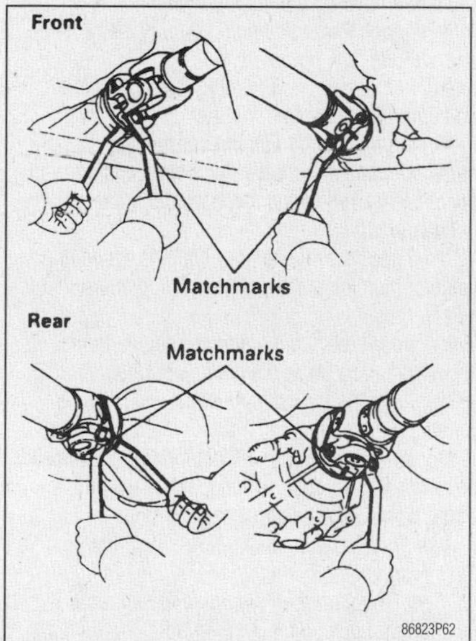

Fig. 17 Always matchmark the driveshaft flanges prior to removal

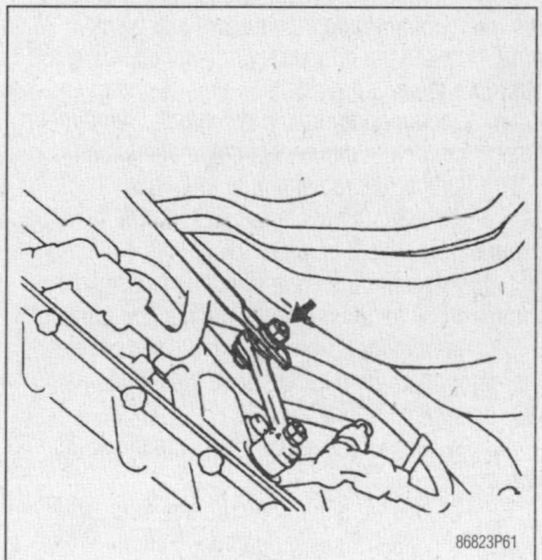

Fig. 18 Remove this nut to release the control rod

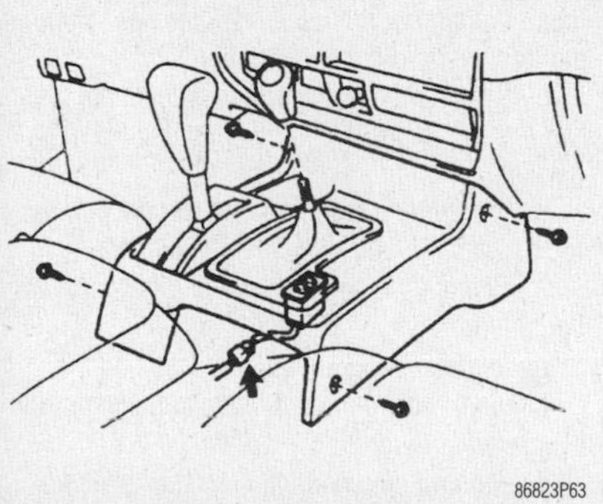

Fig. 19 Remove the screws securing the shifter console, then detach the wiring

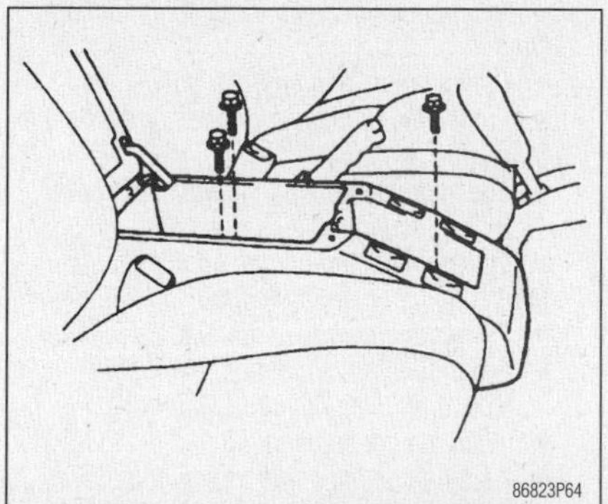

Fig. 20 The center console should also be removed

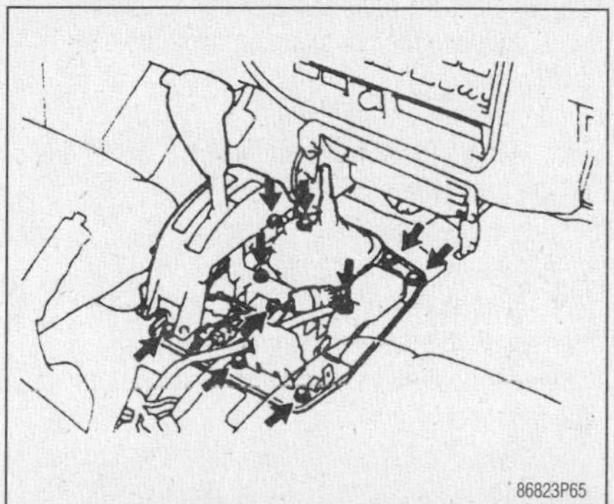

Fig. 21 Bolt locations for removing the shift lever assembly

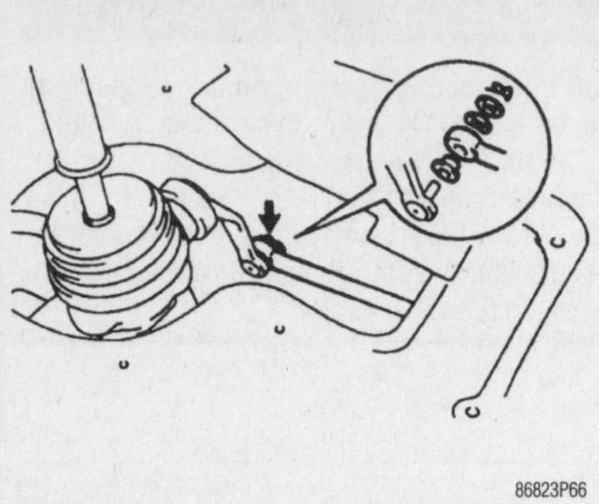

Fig. 22 Assemble the washers for the shift rod linkage as shown

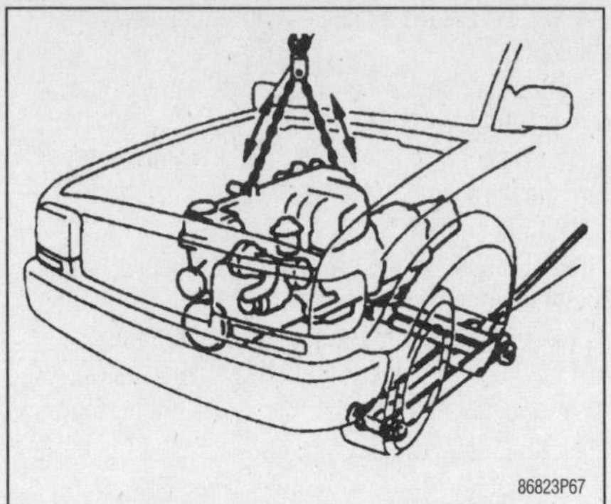

Fig. 23 Secure the engine hoist chain to the engine as shown

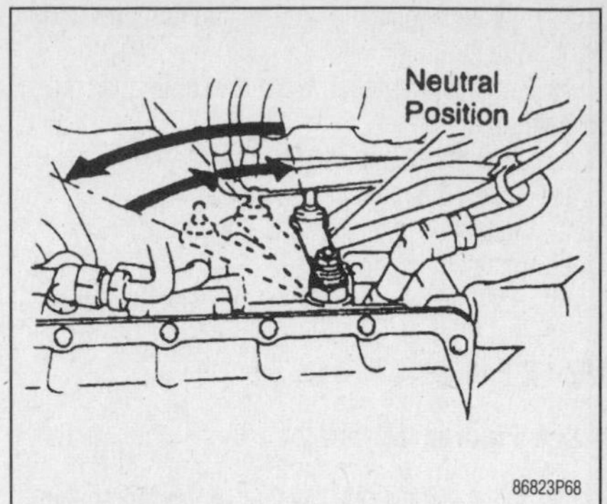

Fig. 24 The shift lever must be placed in the neutral position

16. Disconnect the following wires and connectors:
  - The two heated oxygen sensors
  - DCL1 clamp
  - Oil pressure gauge connections
  - Alternator wire and connector
  - Intake manifold from the fender apron connection
  - High tension cord leading to the ignition coil
  - Ground strap from the No. 1 engine hanger
  - Ground strap from the air intake chamber
  - Ground cable from the cylinder block
17. Loosen the idler pulley nut and adjusting nut to remove the A/C drive belt.
18. Disconnect the A/C compressor, then remove the bracket. Do not disconnect the refrigerant lines.
19. Remove the radiator pipe as follows:
  a. Remove the two nuts retaining the radiator pipe to the No. 1 oil pan.
  b. Disconnect the No. 2 radiator hose from the water inlet, then remove the radiator pipe.
20. Remove the union bolt and the two gaskets, then disconnect the pressure hose from the power steering reservoir pump.
21. Disconnect the return hose from the power steering reservoir tank.
22. Remove the glove compartment door.
23. Remove the speaker panel.
24. Disconnect the A/C amplifier.
25. Disconnect the wires leading to the Electronic Control Unit (ECU) and cowl wire.
26. Pull the engine wire out from the cabin of the vehicle.
27. Remove the stabilizer bar.
28. Matchmark the flanges of the front and rear driveshafts, then remove the shafts.
29. Remove the transfer shift lever, as follows:
  a. Remove the nut retaining the transmission control rod.
  b. Remove the shift knob.
  c. Lift up the console slightly in order to disconnect the wire.
  d. Remove the shifter console.
  e. Remove the center console box.
  f. Disconnect the wires, then remove the transfer shift lever boot and lever assembly.
  g. Pull out the retaining pin, then disconnect the shift rod.
  h. Remove the hose clamp, then the transfer shift lever.
30. Remove the front exhaust pipe, as follows:
  a. Disconnect the heated oxygen sensor.
  b. Remove the nuts and bolts holding the exhaust to the catalyst.
  c. Loosen the clamp then disconnect the from the No. 1 support bracket.
  d. Remove the No. 1 support bracket.
  e. Remove the front exhaust pipe.
31. Detach the ground strap from the heat insulator.
32. Place a jack under the transmission. Put a wooden block between the jack and the transmission oil pan to prevent damages to the pan.
33. Remove the frame crossmember.
34. Attach the engine hoist chain to the two engine hangers.
35. Remove the nuts holding the engine front mounting insulators to the frame.
36. Lift the engine with the transmission out of the vehicle slowly and carefully. Make certain the engine is clear of all wiring and hoses.

To install:

37. Attach the engine hoist chain to the engine hangers, then lower the engine and transmission into the vehicle.
38. Install the nuts holding the engine front mounting insulators to the frame crossmember.
39. Keep the engine level with a jack, then remove the chain hoist.
40. The remainder of installation is the reverse of the removal procedure, making sure to note the following tightening specifications and steps.
  - Front crossmember bolts: 45 ft. lbs. (61 Nm)
  - Crossmember-to-engine rear mounting insulator nuts: 54 ft. lbs. (74 Nm)
  - Engine front mounting insulators-to-frame nuts: 54 ft. lbs. (74 Nm)
  - Front exhaust pipe nuts: 46 ft. lbs. (63 Nm)
  - No. 1 support bracket bolts: 17 ft. lbs. (24 Nm)
  - Clamp bolts: 14 ft. lbs. (19 Nm)
  - Front exhaust pipe-to-rear catalyst bolts: 34 ft. lbs. (46 Nm)
  - Transfer shift lever and hose clamp bolts: 13 ft. lbs. (18 Nm)
  - Transfer shift lever bolts: 48 inch lbs. (5 Nm)
  - Transmission control rod: 9 ft. lbs. (13 Nm)
  - Front driveshaft: 54 ft. lbs. (74 Nm)
  - Rear driveshaft: 65 ft. lbs. (88 Nm)
  - Stabilizer bar brackets: 13 ft. lbs. (18 Nm)
  - Stabilizer bar-to-axle housing bolts: 19 ft. lbs. (25 Nm)
  - Power steering pressure hose union bolt: 42 ft. lbs. (56 Nm)
  - A/C bracket bolts: 27 ft. lbs. (37 Nm)
  - A/C compressor bolts: 18 ft. lbs. (25 Nm)
41. Fill the engine with oil and the transmission with proper amount and type of fluid.
42. Fill the cooling system with coolant.
43. Start the engine and check for leaks.
44. Check the automatic transmission fluid level.
45. Check the timing.
46. Install the hood and test drive the vehicle.
47. Top off any fluid levels.

2UZ-FE Engine

➧ **See Figures 25 thru 30**

1. Remove the hood assembly.
2. Remove the engine undercovers.
3. Drain the engine coolant.
4. Drain the engine oil.
5. Remove the acoustic/cosmetic engine cover.
6. Remove the battery.
7. Remove the air cleaner assembly with the air cleaner hose using the following procedure:
  a. Detach the MAF meter connector.
  b. Disconnect the hose and remove the clamp.
  c. Remove the three bolts and air cleaner assembly with the air cleaner hose.
8. Remove the coolant reservoir using the following procedure:
  a. Disconnect the clamp on the wire from the reservoir.
  b. Disconnect the reservoir hose from the radiator.
  c. Remove the two bolts, reservoir and grommet.
9. Remove the radiator and fan shroud using the following procedure:
  a. Disconnect the upper radiator hose from the front water bypass connection.
  b. Remove the two nuts and disconnect the two clamps on the A/C discharge tube from the bracket.
  c. Remove the two bolts and disconnect the two brackets on the wire from the radiator.
  d. Remove the three bolts and disconnect the fan shroud from the radiator.
  e. Remove the lower radiator hose.
  f. Disconnect the two automatic transmission oil cooler hoses from the radiator.
  g. Remove the two bolts, two nuts and two support collars and lift out the radiator.
  h. Remove the fan shroud.

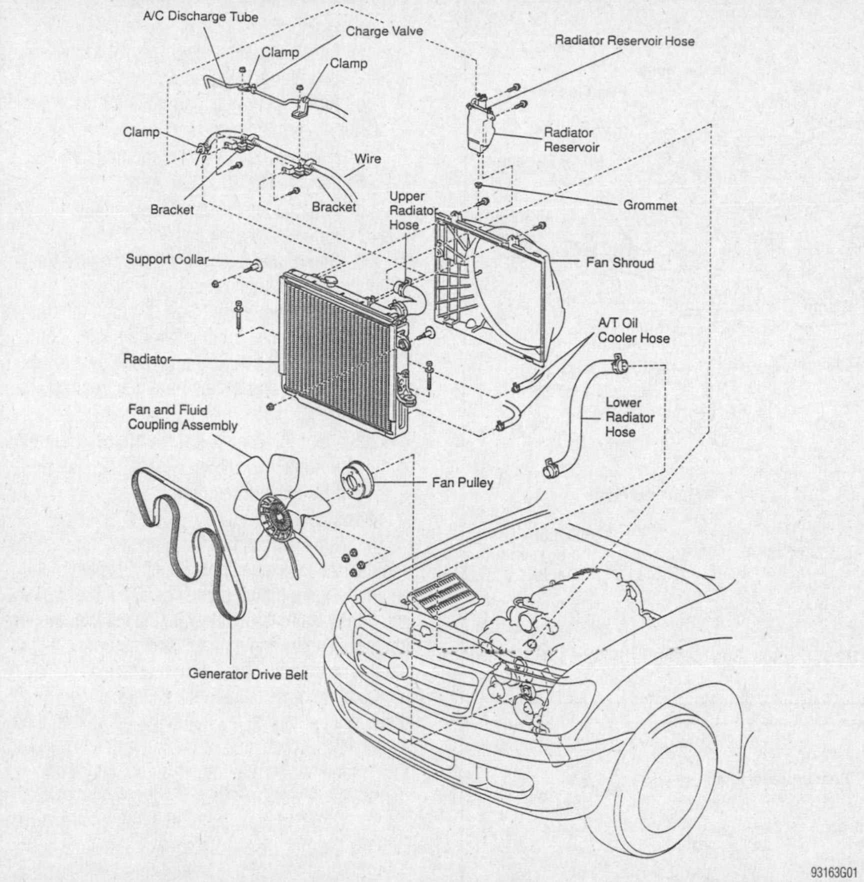

Fig. 25 Some of the underhood components that must be removed for engine removal—1999 Land Cruiser with 2UZ-FE engine shown

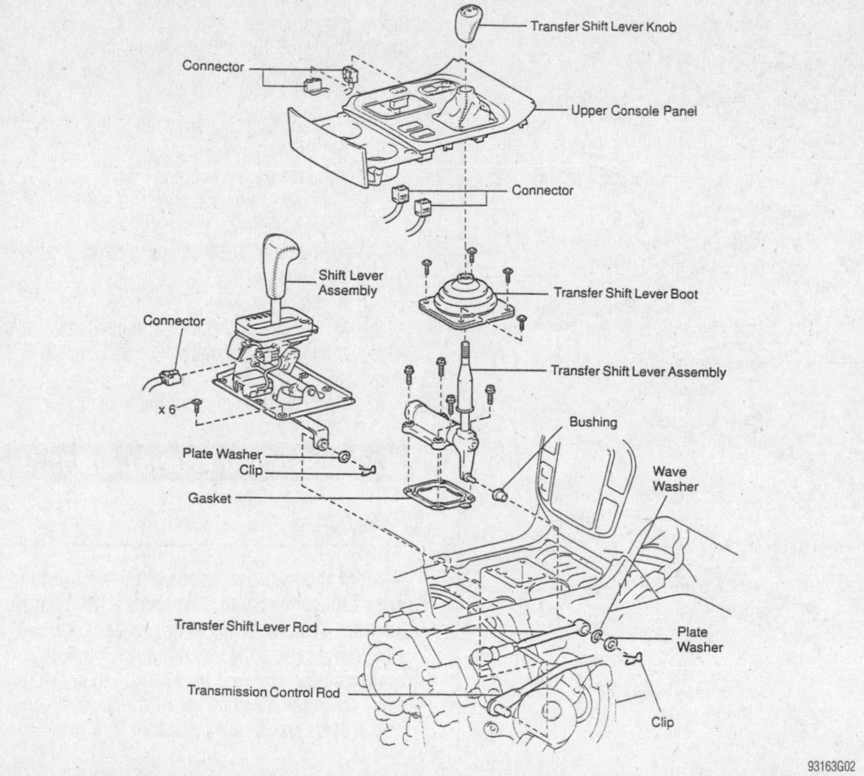

Fig. 26 Disconnect the transmission and transfer case shifters—1999 Land Cruiser with 2UZ-FE engine shown

10. Remove the alternator drive belt, fan, fluid coupling (fan clutch) and fan pulley using the following procedure:
    a. Loosen the four nuts holding the fluid coupling to the fan bracket.
    b. Remove the alternator drive belt.
    c. Remove the four nuts, the fan and fluid coupling assembly and the fan pulley.
11. Disconnect the engine wiring harness from the Electronic Control Module (ECM) which is inside the passenger compartment behind the glove box. Use the following procedure:
    a. Remove the glove compartment door.
    b. Remove the panel found behind the glove compartment.
    c. Detach the three harness connectors from the ECM.
    d. Remove the three screws and disconnect the ECM from the body bracket.
    e. Disconnect the three wire harness connectors.
12. Disconnect the following hoses, wires, connectors, clamps, grommet and cables:
    - Accelerator cable
    - Two power steering vacuum hoses from the clamp on the No. 3 right side timing belt cover.
    - Alternator wiring.
    - Loosen the hose clamp for the power steering vacuum line and remove the vacuum line from the upper intake manifold.
    - Two heater hoses
    - Engine harness clamp and the grommet from the bracket on the cowl panel.
    - Ground strap
    - Fuel feed and return hoses
    - Hose from the EVAP charcoal canister
    - Engine wiring harness from the clamp on the right fender apron.
    - Clamp on the battery negative cable from the relay box and remove the cable from the right fender apron.
    - Battery positive cable
13. Remove the transmission shift lever assembly and transfer case shift lever assembly using the following procedure:
    a. Remove the transfer case shift lever knob.
    b. Remove the upper console panel.
    c. Remove the shift lever assembly. First, remove the retaining clip, then disconnect the transmission control rod from the shift lever assembly. Remove the shift lever assembly. Remove the four bolts from the transfer case shift lever boot, then remove the retainer clip and washers and disconnect the transfer case rod from the shift lever. Remove the bushing, four bolts, shift lever and gasket.
14. Remove the front exhaust pipes.
15. Remove the driveshafts. For additional information, please refer to the following topic(s): Drivetrain, Driveshafts.
16. Disconnect the Air Conditioning (A/C) compressor using the following procedure:
    a. Detach the A/C electrical connector.
    b. Remove the three bolts and disconnect the A/C compressor from the engine. Securely wire the compressor out of the way. Do not disconnect the refrigerant lines.
    c. Remove the three bolts and disconnect the power steering pump from the engine. Securely wire the pump out of the way.

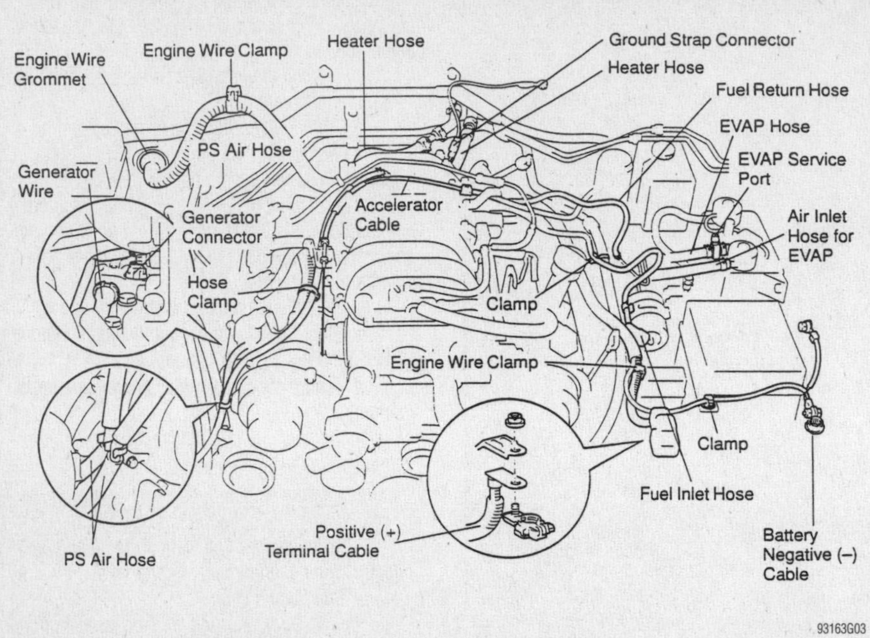

Fig. 27 Tag for identification, then detach these wires, hoses and connections—1999 Land Cruiser with 2UZ-FE engine shown

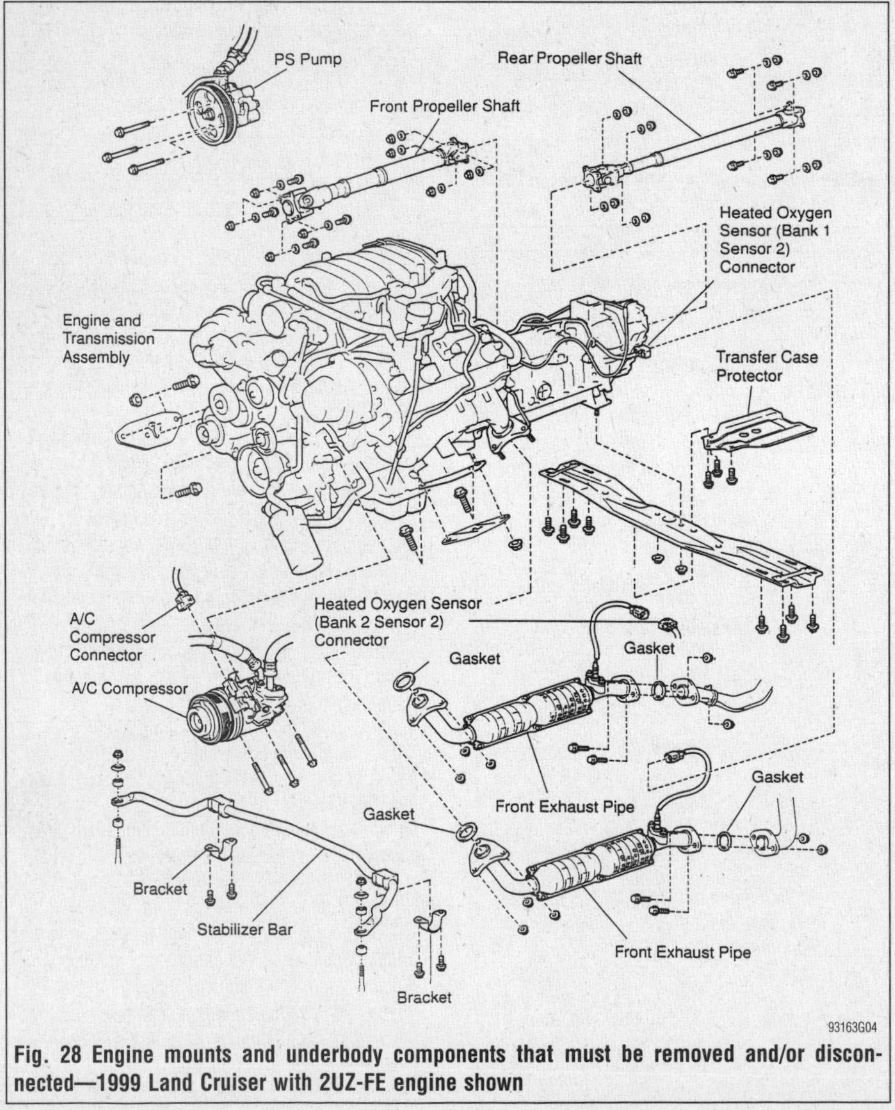

Fig. 28 Engine mounts and underbody components that must be removed and/or disconnected—1999 Land Cruiser with 2UZ-FE engine shown

17. Remove the engine assembly using the following procedure:
   a. Attach a suitable engine hoist to the engine hangers (lifting hooks).
   b. Remove the nuts and bolts from the engine mounts-to-frame brackets.
   c. Remove the bolts from the transfer case protector.
   d. Remove the crossmember nuts and bolts and remove the crossmember.
   e. Slowly and carefully lift the engine and transmission as an assembly. The rear of the transmission will have to go down as the front of the engine comes up to clear the engine compartment. Work carefully and make sure all wiring, hoses and cables have been disconnected, as required.
   f. Place the engine and transmission on a suitable work stand. Separate the transmission from the engine, if required.

To install:

18. With the transmission properly bolted to the engine, use a suitable engine hoist attached to the engine hangers (lifting hooks) to install the engine and transmission assembly into the vehicle. Slowly lower the engine and transmission assembly aligning the engine mounts with the frame brackets. It may be necessary to place a floor jack under the rear of transmission, raising the transmission to keep the engine level. When satisfied with the fit and alignment of the engine and transmission, install the transmission crossmember. Tighten the bolts to 37 ft. lbs. (50 Nm) and the nuts to 55 ft. lbs. (74 Nm). Install the transfer case protector with the three bolts.
19. Install the engine mount-to-frame fasteners and tighten to 22 ft. lbs. (30 Nm). With the engine mounts and transmission crossmember securely fastened, remove the engine hoist.
20. The remainder of installation is the reverse of the removal procedure, making sure to note the following steps and tightening specifications.
   - Power steering pump bolts: 13 ft. lbs. (17 Nm)
   - A/C compressor bolts: 36 ft. lbs. (49 Nm)
21. Refill the engine oil.
22. Refill the engine coolant.
23. Start the engine and check for leaks
24. When satisfied with the engine installation, install the engine acoustic/cosmetic cover and the engine undercovers.
25. Install the hood.
26. Road test and check for abnormal noise, slippage, vibration, correct shift points and smooth operation.
27. Recheck the engine oil and coolant levels.

Cylinder Head (Valve) Cover

REMOVAL & INSTALLATION

➡All of the engines covered by the manual are of the Over Head Camshaft (OHC) configuration. The covering over the camshafts is variously called the valve cover, cam cover, rocker cover and cylinder head cover. In general, cylinder head cover is most accurate and will be used most often in this manual.

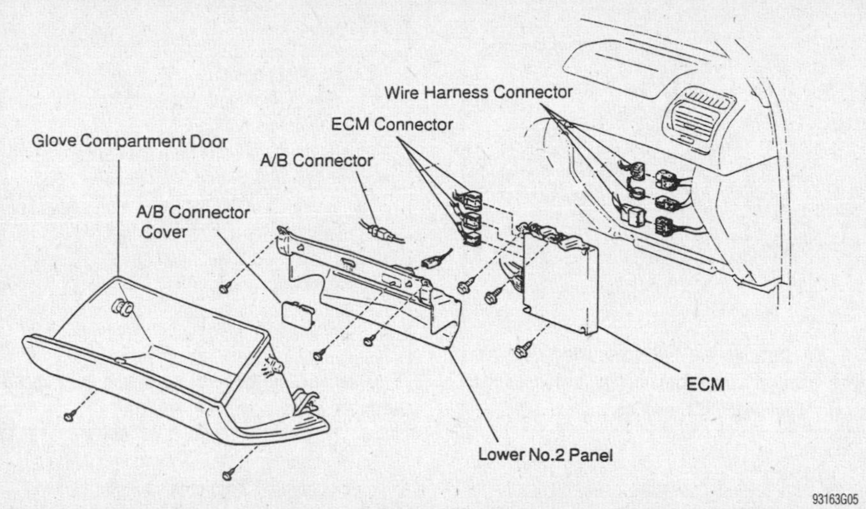

Fig. 29 The engine wiring harness ends at the ECM, which is mounted behind the glove box—1999 Land Cruiser with 2UZ-FE engine shown

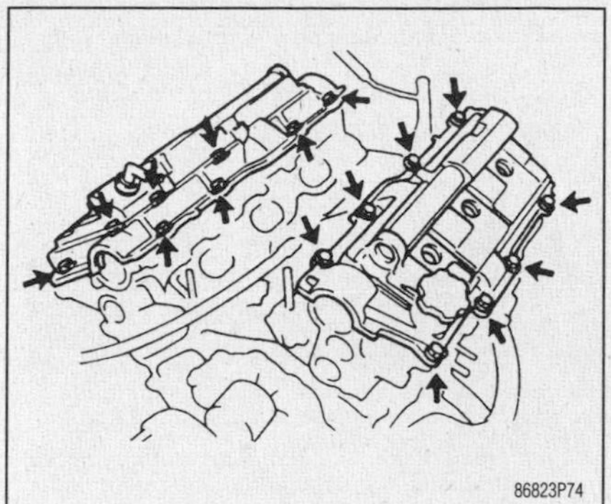

Fig. 32 The cylinder head covers are secured to the heads by the bolts shown on 5VZ-FE engines

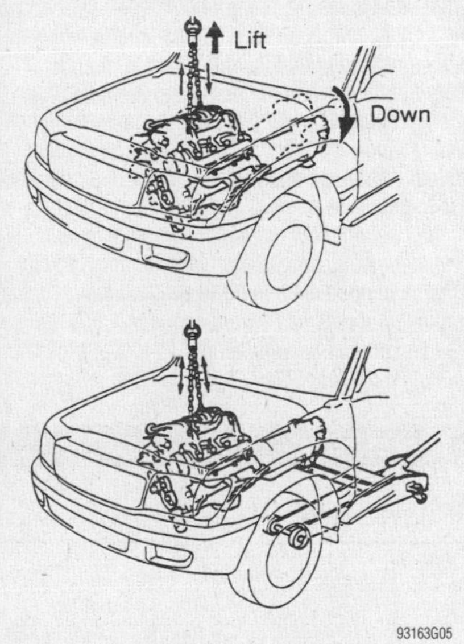

Fig. 30 Tilt the transmission down when removing the engine (Top) and raise the transmission with a floor jack when installing (Bottom)—1999 Land Cruiser with 2UZ-FE engine shown

2RZ-FE and 3RZ-FE Engines

➧ See Figure 31

1. On manual transmissions, disconnect the accelerator cable from the throttle body.
2. On automatics, disconnect the accelerator and throttle cables from the throttle body.
3. On cruise control, remove the actuator cover, then disconnect the cruise control cable from the actuator.
4. Disconnect the 3 wire clamps for the engine harness.
5. Detach the Mass Air Flow (MAF) meter and Intake Air Temperature (IAT) sensor connections.
6. On the 3RZ-FE engine, disconnect the air hose from the air cleaner cap, then loosen the air cleaner hose clamp.
7. Loosen the 4 clips, and remove the air cleaner cover, Mass Air Flow (MAF) meter and resonator sensor.
8. Remove the air intake sensor by disconnecting the air hose for the Idle Air Control (IAC) valve.
   a. Remove the vacuum sensing hose and wire clamp for the engine wire.
   b. Loosen the hose clamp, and remove the bolts retaining the air intake connector.
9. Remove the PCV hoses.
10. Tag and disconnect the spark plug wires.
11. Disconnect the following wires:
    - A/C connector if equipped
    - Oil pressure sensor wire
    - Engine coolant temperature sensor
    - Distributor wire
    - 4 engine wire clamps and engine wire
12. Remove the cylinder head cover bolts, seal washers, cover and gasket.
13. Installation is the reverse of the removal procedure. Make sure to clean the mating areas well and use new seal washers.
14. Start the engine and check for leaks. Check and add fluids as required.

5VZ-FE Engine

➧ See Figures 32, 33, 34, 35, and 36

1. Disconnect the accelerator and throttle cables from the throttle linkage.

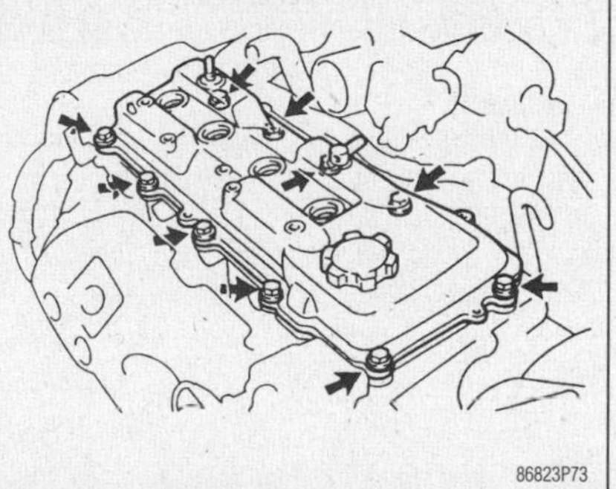

Fig. 31 On 2RZ-FE and 3RZ-FE engines, the cylinder head cover is secured by 10 bolts

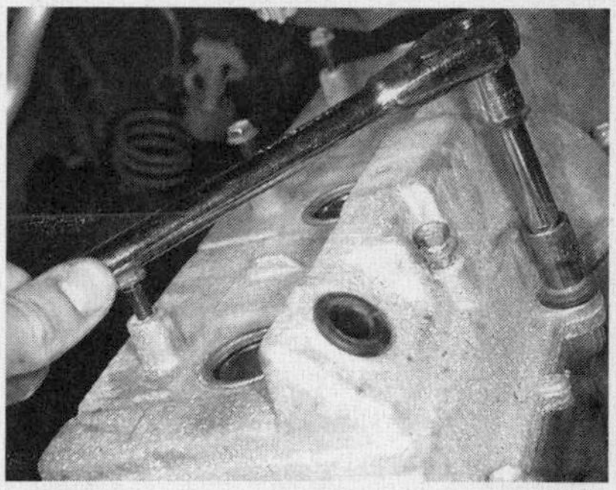

Fig. 33 Use a ratchet, an extension, and a socket to remove the cylinder head cover bolts

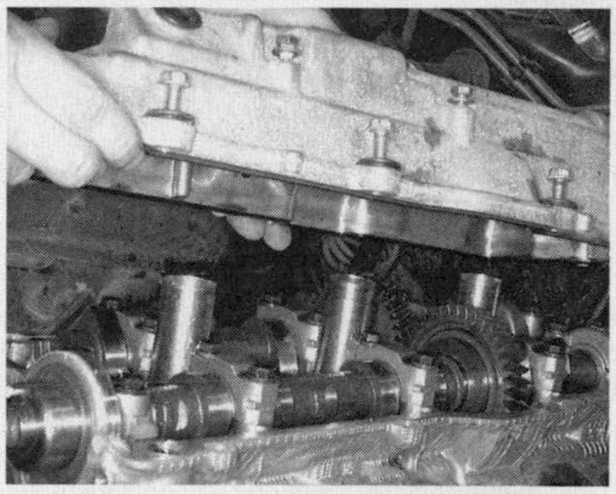

Fig. 34 Lift off the cylinder head cover

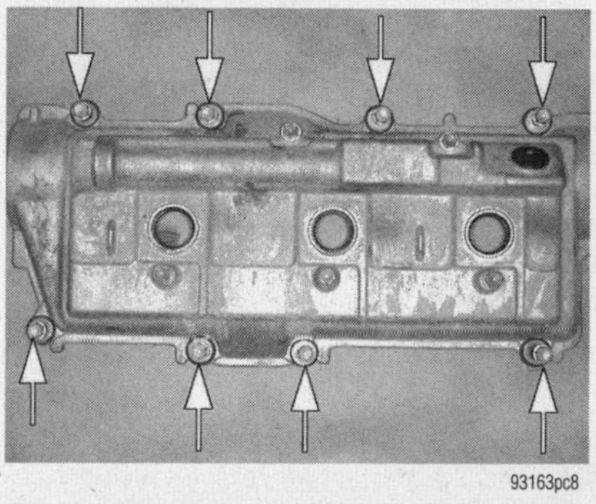

Fig. 35 Cylinder head cover bolt locations

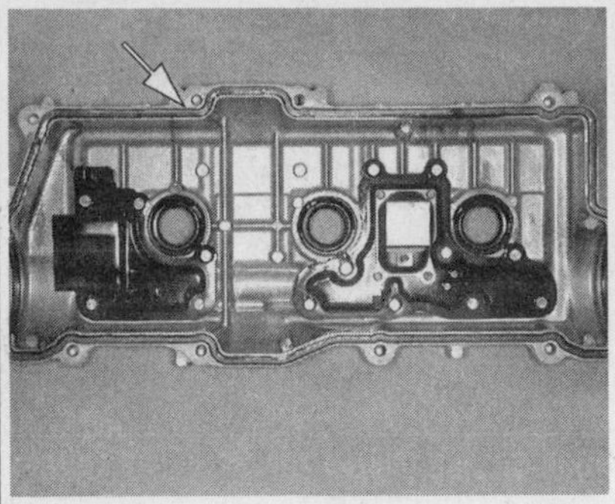

93163pc9

Fig. 36 Remove the gasket from the groove in the cylinder head cover

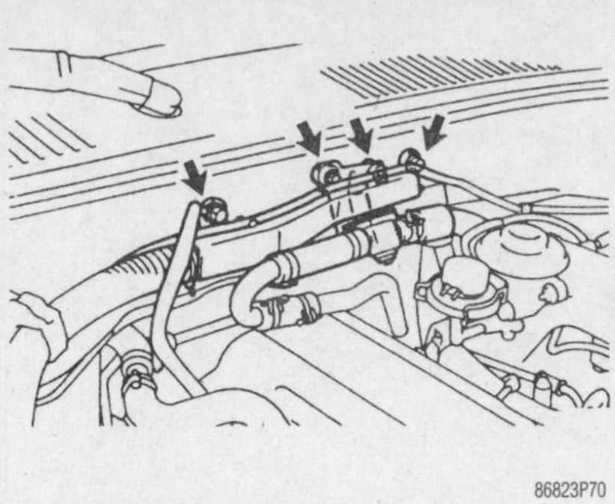

86823P70

Fig. 37 Remove the bolts securing the harness ground strap and heater valve to the cowl panel—1FZ-FE engine

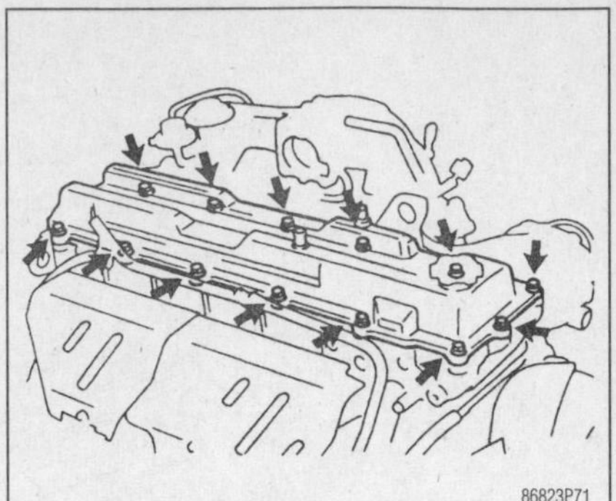

86823P71

Fig. 38 The cylinder head cover is secured with 13 bolts—1FZ-FE engine

2. Remove the air cleaner cover, air flow meter, and air duct assembly. It will be necessary to disconnect the wiring to the meter and unbolt the assembly, prior to removal.
3. Loosen and remove the cylinder head cover bolts.
4. Remove the cylinder head covers, work on one at a time to avoid confusion.

To install:

5. Clean the mating areas on the cover and cylinder head.
6. Install the gasket to the head and seal washers. Attach the cover with the mounting bolts. Tighten until snug.
7. Install the air flow meter, air duct, and the air cleaner cover.
8. Connect the accelerator and throttle cables to the throttle linkage.
9. Start the engine and check for leaks. Check and add fluids as required.

1FZ-FE Engine

See Figures 37 and 38

1. Drain the cooling system.
2. Remove the throttle body.
3. Disconnect the engine wiring harness and heater control valve from the cowl panel. A ground strap holds the harness in place.
4. Tag and disconnect the spark plug wires.
5. Remove the cylinder head cover bolts, gasket and the cover.

To install:

6. Clean the cylinder head cover and mating areas on the engine.
7. Install a new gasket into the groove of the cover.
8. Install and tighten the 13 bolts evenly.
9. Attach the spark plug wires to their proper locations.
10. Bolt the engine harness to the cowl. Attach the heater control valve.
11. Install the throttle body with a new gasket.
12. Fill the cooling system.
13. Start the engine and check for leaks. Check and add fluids as required.

2UZ-FE Engine

See Figure 39

1. Disconnect the negative battery cable.
2. Remove the four bolts retaining the ignition coils to the cylinder head cover and the spark plugs. Tag for identification, then remove the coil assemblies.
3. On the left side (drivers side):
   a. The engine oil dipstick may interfere with cylinder head cover removal, so pull the dipstick out and set it aside.
   b. Reposition the fuel lines and EVAP hoses as necessary. It shouldn't be necessary to disconnect them, just unclip from their retainers and reposition.
   c. Disconnect the breather hose.
4. On the right side (passengers side):
5. Disconnect the L-Shaped PCV breather hose.
6. Unclip the power steering vacuum switch hose that runs to the intake manifold plenum and reposition.
7. Remove the nine cylinder head cover bolts and carefully remove the cylinder head cover. Use care. The cover is aluminum. Light alloy parts can be easily damaged.

To install:

8. Clean all parts well. In addition to the cylinder head cover gaskets, Toyota uses small amounts of FIPG sealer in two spots at the camshaft drive end of the cylinder head next to the timing belt covers. Note the position of this sealer before cleaning it off since new sealer must be installed in the same locations. All of this old sealer must be removed. Use care not to gouge the aluminum sealing surfaces on either the head or the cylinder head cover. Note the semi-circular sealing plugs that are in the cylinder head on the end opposite the camshaft drive. These seals must be in good condition and properly installed or there will be a massive oil leak on startup.
9. Installation is the reverse of the removal procedure. Apply fresh FIPG material (sealer, Toyota #08826-00080, or equivalent) at the places indicated. Verify that the semi-circular plugs are in place.
10. Install a new gasket to the cylinder head cover. The bolts also have seals under them and they must be in good condition and properly installed. Install the cylinder head cover and the bolts.
11. Torque the cylinder head cover bolts evenly in several passes to 53 inch lbs. (6 Nm).

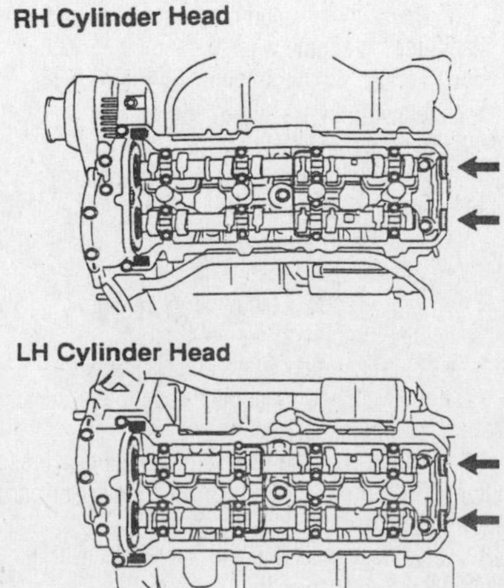

93163G07

Fig. 39 Make sure the semi-circular seal plugs are in place (arrows) and that FIPG sealer is applied at the places indicated—2UZ-FE engine

Thermostat

REMOVAL & INSTALLATION

See Figures 40 thru 47

On all Toyota engines covered by this manual, the thermostat is located under the upper radiator hose water inlet connection.

1. Drain the cooling system into a suitable container.
2. The water inlet connection is usually retained by studs with nuts. Remove the nuts, then carefully work loose the water inlet with the hose attached. If there is not enough room to pull both housing and hose out, you may want to disconnect the hose first. Make certain to remove the gasket (usually an O-ring seal which should be replaced) with the water inlet.

To install:

3. Clean all parts well. A small wire brush may be helpful to clean the threads on the studs. The water inlet is light alloy and easily damaged. At assembly, you want the nuts to tighten down evenly to avoid distorting and cracking the water inlet. Thread the nuts up and down the cleaned studs a few times to make sure the threads are clean. Apply a small amount of oil on the threads of the studs.
4. When installing a new thermostat always use a new seal. Be sure that the thermostat is positioned with the spring down or into the housing. Some thermostats use a jiggle valve (looks like a small rivet in

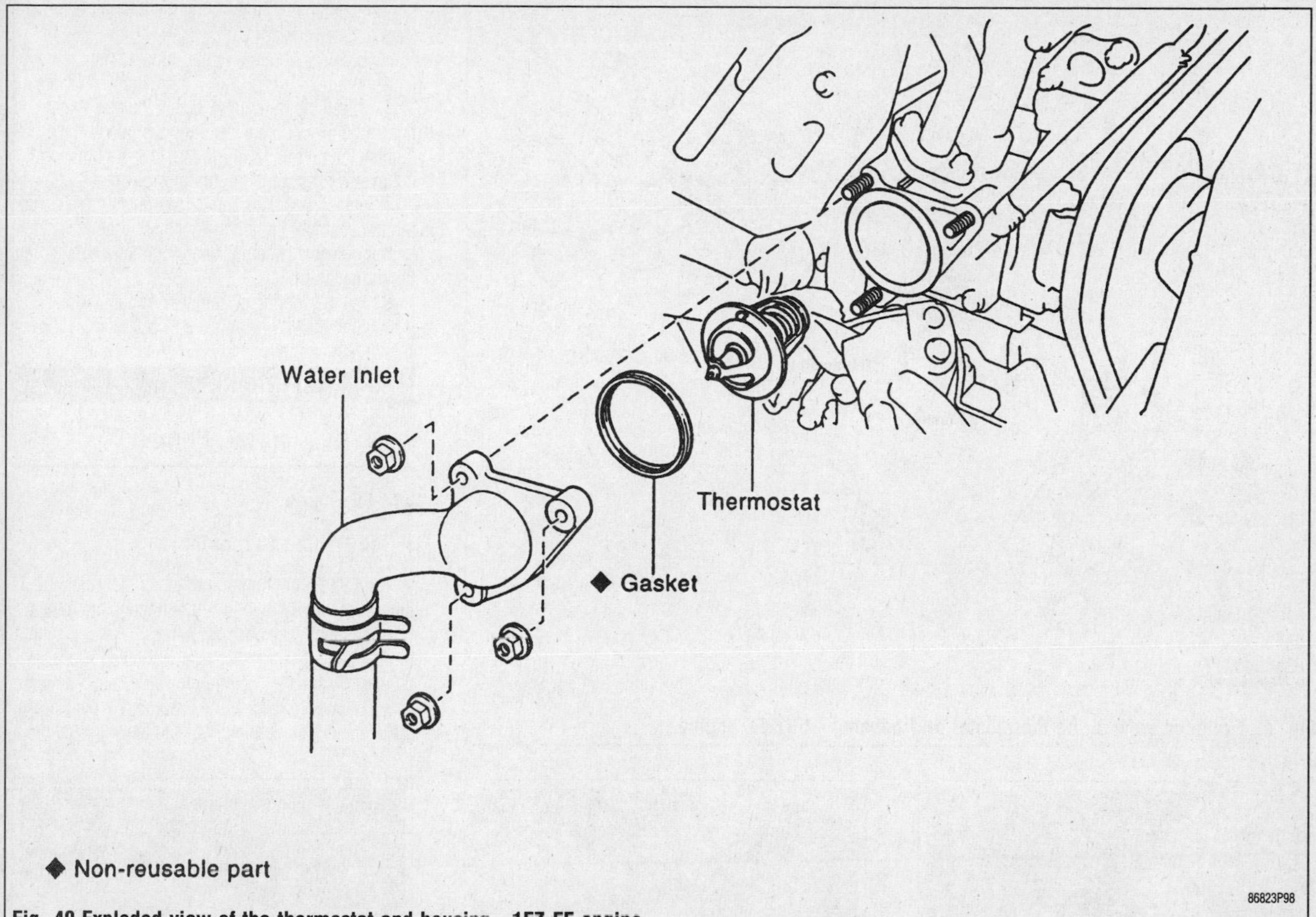

Fig. 40 Exploded view of the thermostat and housing—1FZ-FE engine

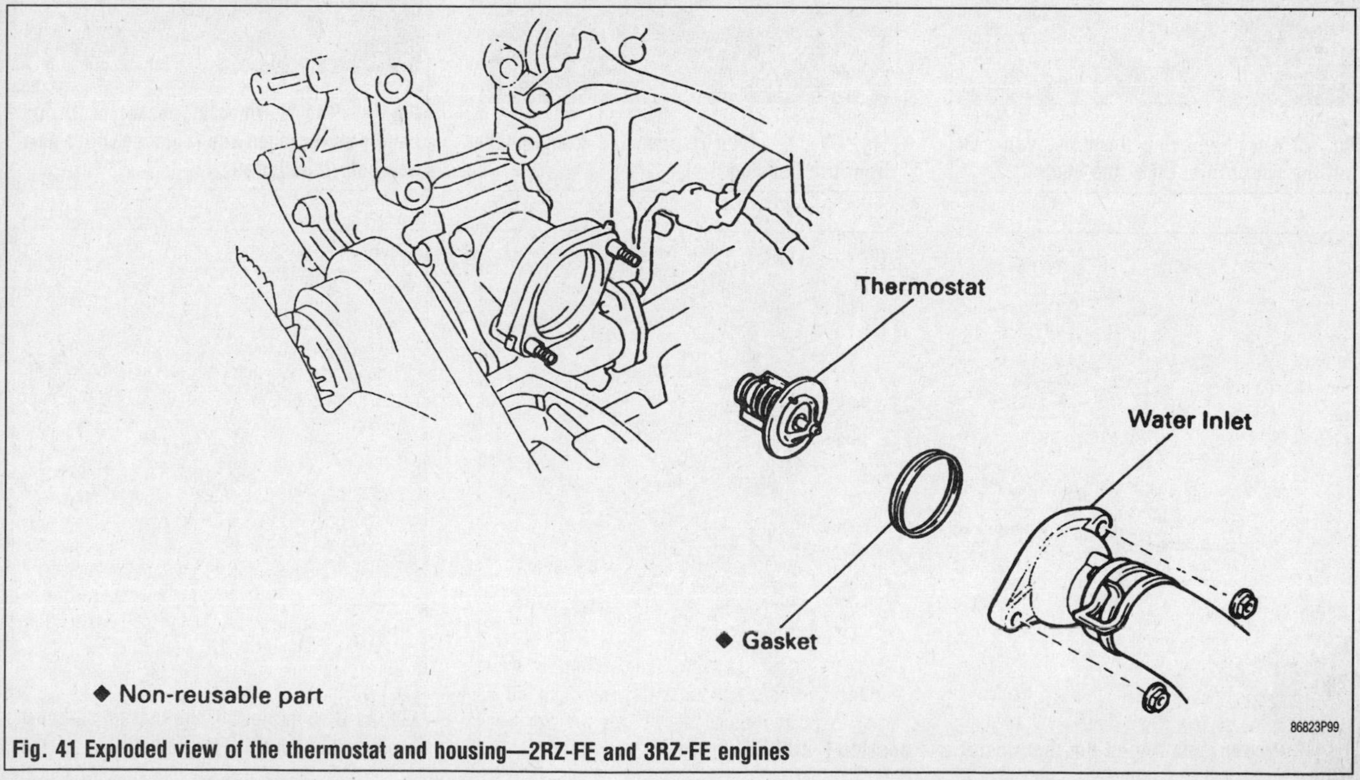

Fig. 41 Exploded view of the thermostat and housing—2RZ-FE and 3RZ-FE engines

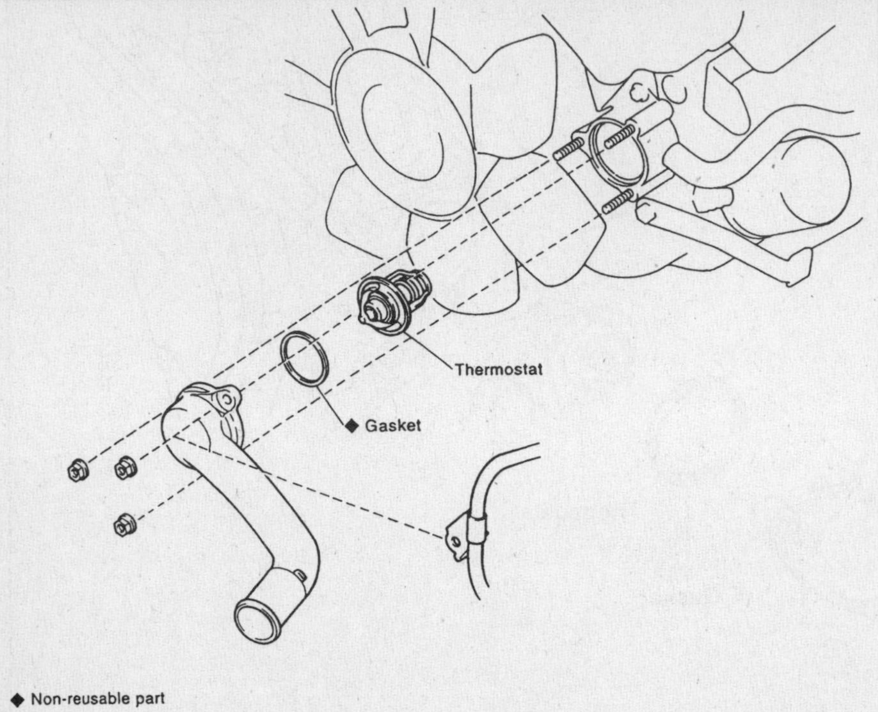

Fig. 42 Exploded view of the thermostat and housing—5VZ-FE engine

the edge of the thermostat) that must be at the top or 12 o'clock position.

5. Lubricate the new replacement O-ring seal with anti-freeze.

6. Install the water inlet. Install the nuts finger-tight making sure the water inlet is properly seated. Tighten the nuts to 10–14 ft. lbs. (13–19 Nm). Do not over-tighten, or the water inlet may crack.

7. Install the hoses and wire connectors removed for access. Make certain the coolant hoses are not kinked or twisted after installation. Do not overtighten the hose clamps.

8. Fill the cooling system with coolant.

9. Start the engine and check for leaks.

Intake Manifold

REMOVAL & INSTALLATION

5VZ-FE Engine

▸ See Figures 48 thru 60

The 5VZ-FE engine uses what could be called a three-piece intake manifold. The upper part (Toyota calls it an air intake chamber assembly) mounts the throttle body. The middle part is called an intake air connector assembly, jointing the air intake chamber with the lower manifold. The lower part is considered the actual intake manifold, bolts to the engine and

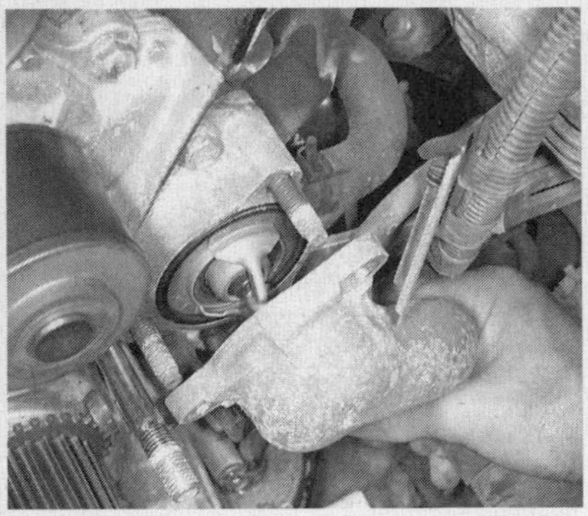

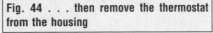

Fig. 43 After removing the nuts, you can pull the water inlet off of the studs . . .

Fig. 44 . . . then remove the thermostat from the housing

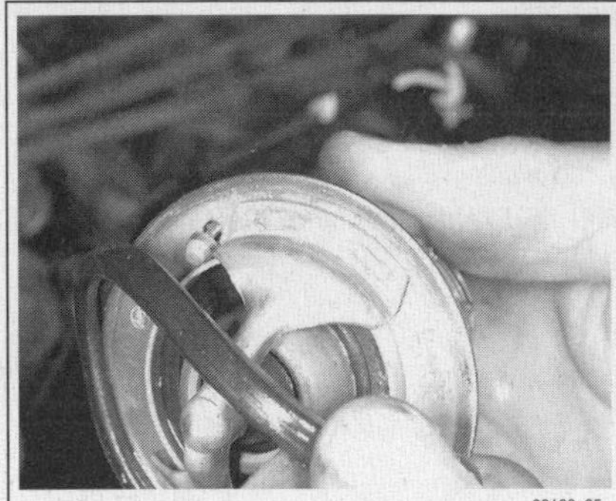

Fig. 45 The thermostat gasket or O-ring should be removed and replaced with a new one before installation

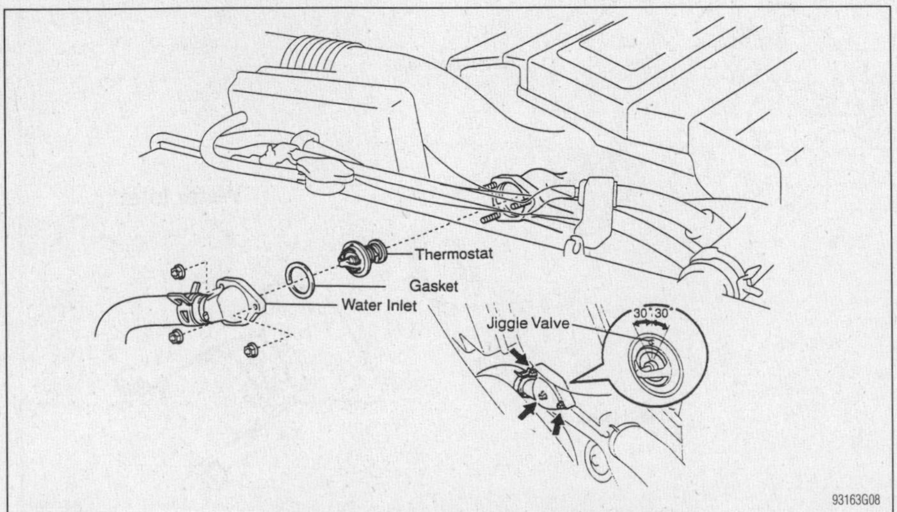

Fig. 46 Proper mounting of the thermostat and housing—2UZ-FE engine

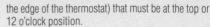

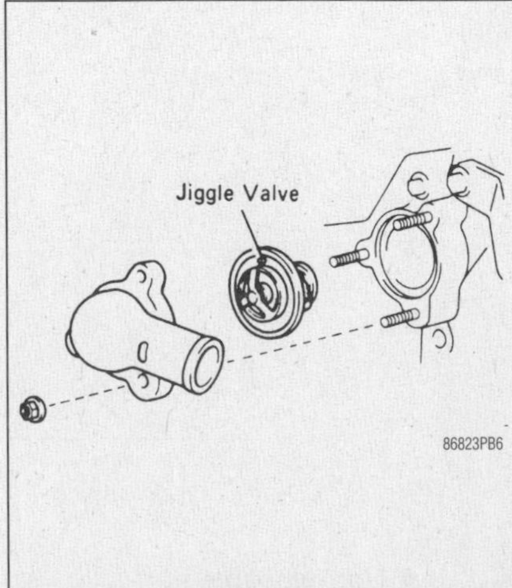

Fig. 47 If so equipped, the thermostat must be installed with the jiggle valve at the top

93163p09

Fig. 48 Use a ratchet to remove the upper intake manifold bolts

93163p10

Fig. 49 Once all the fasteners have been removed, lift off the upper intake manifold

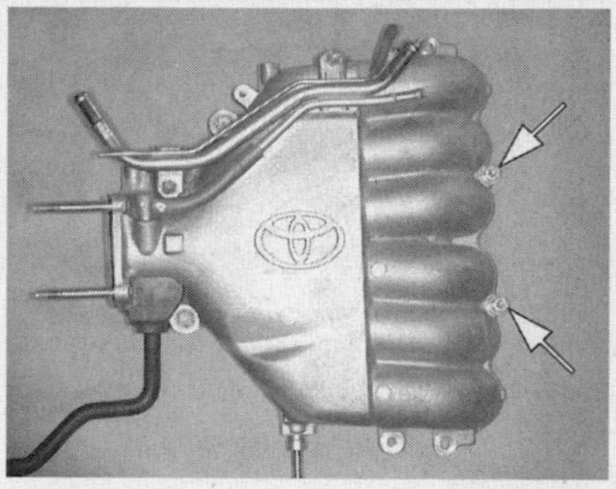

93163p11

Fig. 50 View of the upper intake manifold and its bolt locations

93163p12

Fig. 51 Remove the upper intake manifold gasket from the lower intake runners

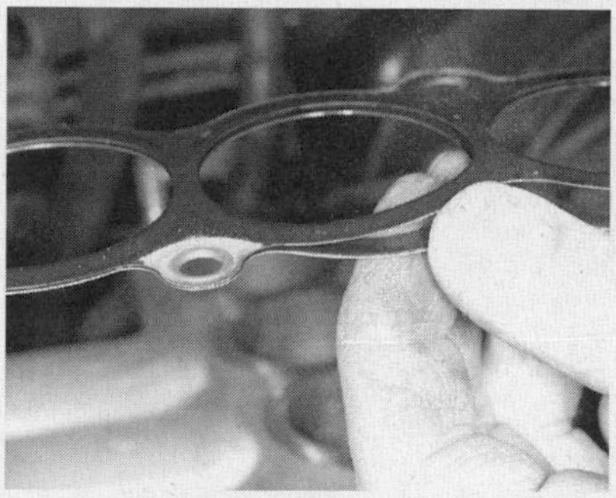

93163p13

Fig. 52 The upper intake manifold gasket may be made from several steel shims riveted together

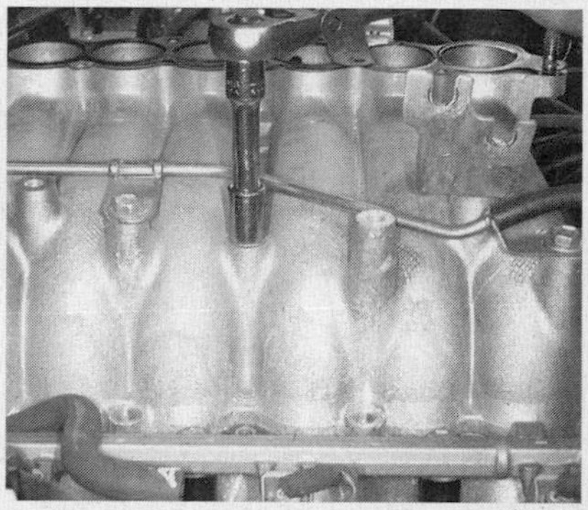

93163p21

Fig. 53 Remove the middle-to-lower intake manifold bolts

93163p19

Fig. 54 Once all fasteners have been removed from the middle intake manifold, lift it off the lower intake manifold

93163p15

Fig. 55 Inspecting the intake manifold gasket for cracks or deterioration

93163p16

Fig. 56 Stuff shop towels into the intake runners to prevent dirt and debris from entering the engine

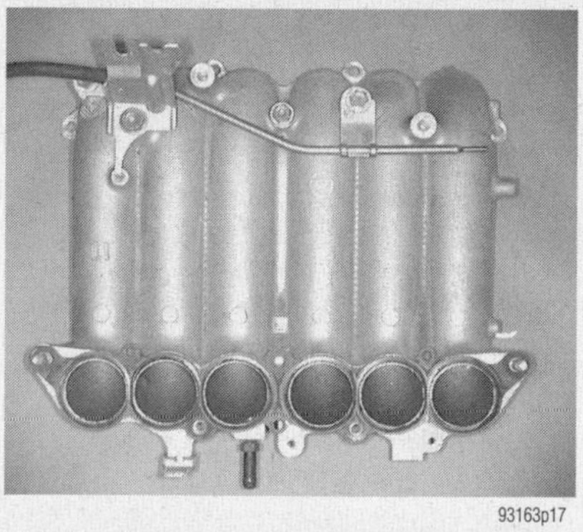

93163p17

Fig. 57 View of the middle intake runners

93163pb1

Fig. 58 View of the lower intake manifold after it has been removed from the vehicle

mounts the fuel injectors. Toyota uses aluminum for many engine parts. Use care when working with light alloy parts as they are easily damaged.

***** CAUTION**

The Fuel injection system remains under pressure after the engine has been turned OFF. Properly relieve the fuel pressure before disconnecting any fuel lines. Failure to do so may result in fire or personal injury.

1. Relieve the fuel system pressure. For additional information, please refer to the following topic(s): Fuel System, Relieving Fuel System Pressure.
2. Disconnect the negative battery cable.

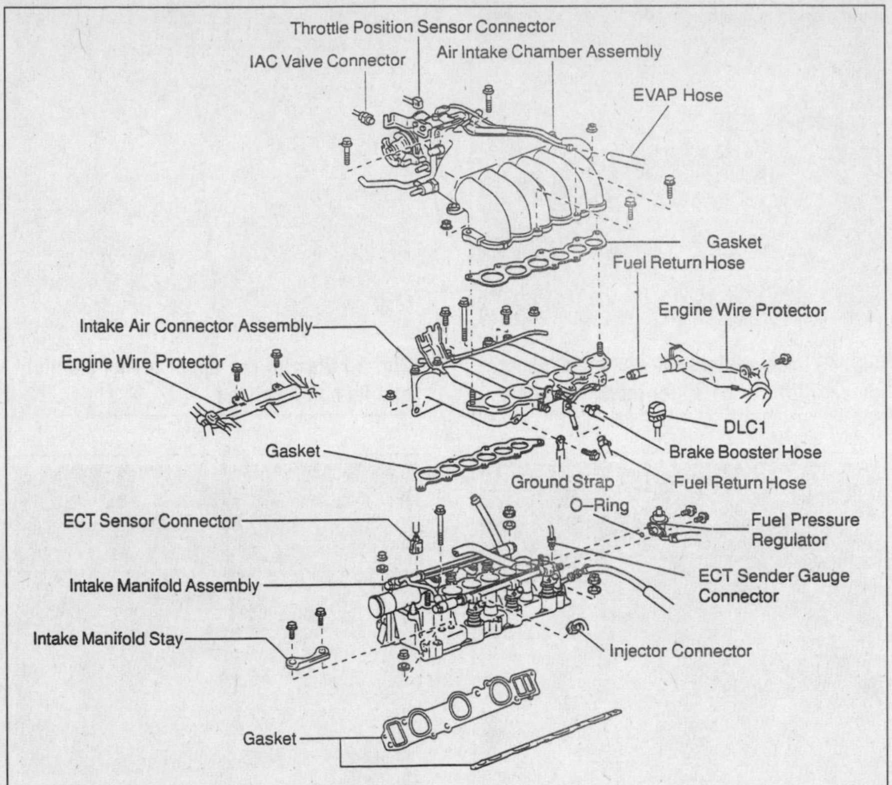

Fig. 59 Exploded view of the upper and lower intake manifolds—1999 Tacoma with 5VZ-FE engine

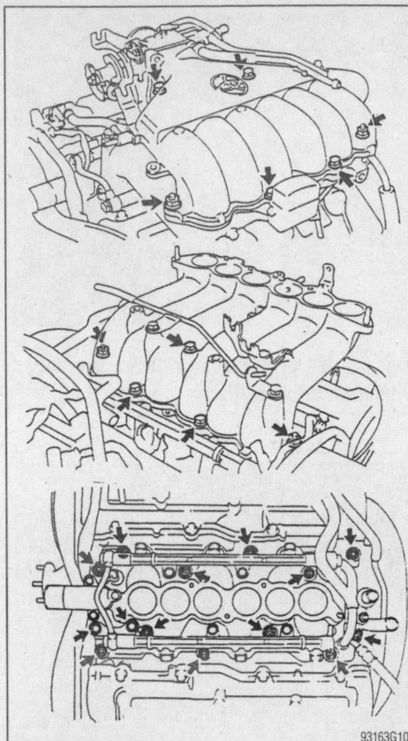

Fig. 60 Mounting bolt locations on the upper, middle and lower portions of the intake manifolds—1999 Tacoma with 5VZ-FE engine

3. Drain the engine coolant.
4. Remove the air cleaner hose.
5. Disconnect the following cables:
   - On cruise control vehicles, the actuator cable with bracket
   - Accelerator cable
   - On automatics, the throttle cable
6. Tag for identification, then disconnect the brake booster hose, the EVAP hose, and if 4WD equipped with Automatic Disconnecting Differential (ADD), disconnect the ADD vacuum hose.
7. Disconnect the fuel return and fuel feed hoses.
8. Remove the upper intake manifold (air chamber) brace (Toyota calls it a stay). Remove the two bolts holding the throttle cable clamp, then remove the two bolts holding the brace.
9. Remove the No. 2 timing belt cover. This is the cover that goes over the cam belt sprockets. It will be necessary to disconnect the four spark plug cable clamps that run across the top of the cover. Then remove the six retaining bolts and carefully separate the cover from the engine. Look for the wire from the Camshaft Position Sensor and detach the connector, if required.
10. At the upper intake manifold (air intake chamber), disconnect the following:
    - Throttle Position (TP) sensor connector
    - Idle Air Control (IAC) connector
    - Two PCV hoses
    - Two water bypass hoses
11. Remove the nuts and bolts holding the upper intake manifold (air intake chamber) assembly. Discard the gasket.
12. Remove the middle part of the intake manifold assembly (air connector) by unbolting the engine ground wire, disconnecting the fuel return hose, if not done so already, and the vacuum line to the fuel pressure regulator. Detach the Diagnostic Connector (DLC1) from the bracket. Remove the nuts and bolts and separate the middle part of the intake manifold. Discard the gasket.
13. Locate the engine wiring harness protector. Detach the six fuel injector connectors, the Engine Coolant Temperature (ECT) sensor connector(s) and unbolt the wiring harness protector assembly from the cylinder head.
14. Disconnect the fuel pressure regulator.
15. Remove the nuts and bolts from the lower part of the intake manifold and carefully work the manifold free of the cylinder heads. Discard the gasket.

To install:

16. Clean all parts well. Pay particular attention to the gasket sealing surfaces. Use care not to damage the light alloy parts.
17. Installation is the reverse of the removal process. Always use new gaskets. Carefully place the lower part of the intake manifold to the cylinder heads. Make sure all flat washers, nuts and bolts are installed. Tighten to 160 inch lbs. (18 Nm), working from the center fasteners, outward.
18. Install the engine wiring harness protector and attach all removed connectors.
19. Using a new gasket, install the middle part of the intake manifold (air connector). Install the nuts and bolts and tighten to 160 inch lbs. (18 Nm), working from the center fasteners, outward.
20. Place the Diagnostic Connector (DLC1) back on its bracket. Connect the engine ground wire and all the vacuum hoses detached at removal, using the identification tags made earlier.
21. Using a new gasket, install the upper part of the intake manifold (air chamber). Install the nuts and bolts and tighten to 160 inch lbs. (18 Nm), working from the center fasteners, outward.
22. Connect all remaining wires, hoses and cables, as required.
23. Install the timing belt cover and air cleaner hose.
24. Refill the engine with fresh coolant. Test run the engine and check for coolant and vacuum leaks.

1FZ-FE Engine

See Figure 61

The 1FZ-FE engine uses what could be called a two-piece intake manifold. The upper part (Toyota calls it an air intake chamber assembly) mounts the throttle body. The lower part is considered the actual intake manifold, bolts to the cylinder head and mounts the fuel injectors. Toyota uses aluminum for many engine parts. Use care when working with light alloy parts as they are easily damaged.

CAUTION

Fuel injected engine systems remain under pressure after the engine has been turned OFF. Properly relieve the fuel pressure before disconnecting any fuel lines. Failure to do so may result in fire or personal injury.

1. Relieve the fuel pressure. For additional information, please refer to the following topic(s): Fuel System, Relieving Fuel System Pressure.
2. Drain the engine coolant.
3. Remove the battery and the battery tray.

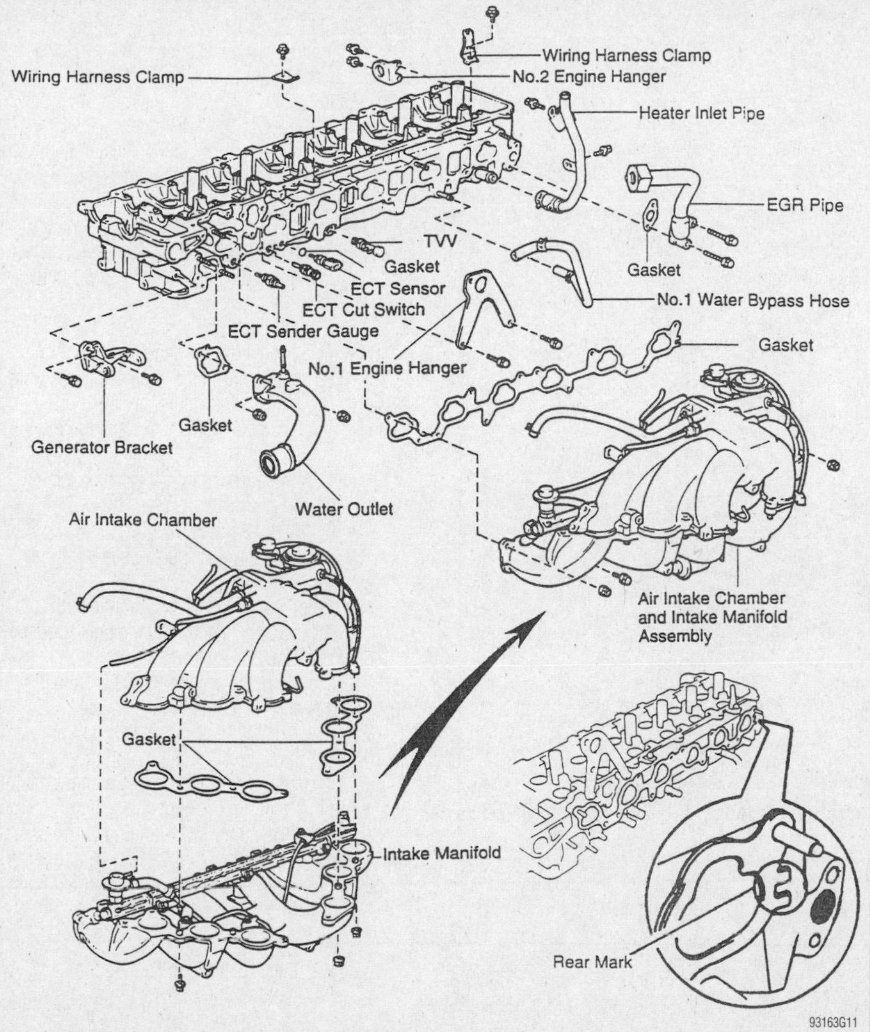

Fig. 61 Upper and lower intake manifolds and related components—Land Cruiser with 1FZ-FE engine

4. Remove the air cleaner hose and cap.
5. Disconnect the following cables:
   - On cruise control vehicles, the actuator cable from the throttle body
   - Accelerator cable
   - Throttle cable (auto transmission)
6. Disconnect the engine ground straps from the engine hanger and from the upper half of the intake manifold.
7. Detach the connection on the intake manifold from the left fender apron.
8. Disconnect the brake booster and EVAP hoses.
9. Separate the fuel inlet and return lines from the fuel rail.
10. Disconnect the heater hoses and the radiator inlet and bypass hoses.
11. If necessary for clearance, remove the alternator and its bracket.
12. For more working room, remove the dipsticks for the engine oil and automatic transmission. Remove the mounting bolts and pull the dipstick tubes straight out. The O-rings should be replaced at assembly.
13. Remove the intake manifold brace (Toyota calls it a stay).
14. If necessary for clearance, remove the two nuts and take off the water outlet pipe. The gasket must be replaced at assembly.
15. Locate and disconnect the EGR pipe from the cylinder head and intake manifold.
16. Remove the retaining nuts and bolts and remove upper and lower intake manifold as an assembly. Use care and make sure all vacuum connections are tagged for identification and disconnected, including the Thermal Vacuum Valve (TVV) hoses. Discard the gaskets.

To install:

17. Installation is the reverse of the removal process, making sure to note the following steps.
    a. If separated, install the air intake chamber (upper) and intake manifold (lower) assembly:
    b. Inspect the new manifold-to-head gasket. There should be a notch in the gasket that indicates that end should be placed to the rear. Install the new gasket so that the rear mark is toward the rear of the cylinder head, near the EGR pipe opening in the head.
    c. Tighten the intake manifold nuts and bolts evenly to 15 ft. lbs. (20 Nm), working from the center, outward.
18. Refill the engine with fresh coolant. Test run the engine and check for coolant and vacuum leaks.

2RZ-FE and 3RZ-FE Engines

See Figure 62

The 2RZ-FE and 3RZ-FE engines use what could be called a two-piece intake manifold. The upper part (Toyota calls it an air intake chamber assembly) mounts the throttle body. The lower part is considered the actual intake manifold and bolts to the cylinder head. Toyota uses aluminum for many engine parts. Use care when working with light alloy parts as they are easily damaged.

CAUTION

Fuel injected engine systems remain under pressure after the engine has been turned OFF. Properly relieve the fuel pressure before disconnecting any fuel lines. Failure to do so may result in fire or personal injury.

1. Relieve the fuel pressure. For additional information, please refer to the following topic(s): Fuel System, Relieving Fuel System Pressure.
2. Drain the coolant.
3. Disconnect the accelerator cable, the automatic transmission throttle valve cable (if equipped) and the cruise control cable (if equipped) from the throttle body.
4. Remove the air cleaner lid, detach the Mass Air Flow (MAF) meter electrical connector and the intake air connector pipe.
5. Disconnect the EGR pipe at the upper intake manifold.
6. Remove the intake manifold brace (Toyota calls it a stay).
7. Tag for identification and remove the following:
   - EVAP hose from the throttle body
   - Brake booster vacuum hose
   - Water bypass hose from the water bypass pipe
   - Water bypass hose from the cylinder head rear cover
8. Locate and remove the nuts and bolts that hold the upper intake manifold to the lower intake manifold. Discard the gasket.
9. Locate and remove the nuts and bolts that hold the lower intake manifold to the cylinder head. Please note that if are clearance problems with the fuel rail and injectors and they need to be removed, use the following procedure:
   a. Tag for identification the fuel injector connectors and detach the connectors.
   b. Remove the fuel inlet and return lines.
   c. Remove the two bolts that retain the fuel rail. Carefully lift the fuel rail upwards with the injectors. Use caution. The fuel injectors will tend to drop out of the fuel rail.

To install:

10. Clean all parts well. Check the sealing surfaces of the intake manifold parts. Using a precision straightedge and feeler gauge, check all of the sealing surfaces for warping. Maximum distortion allowed is 0.0078 inch (0.20mm). If the distortion is greater than this, the manifolds may not seal properly. The parts should be replaced.
11. Using a new gaskets install the lower half intake manifold to the cylinder head. Torque the nuts and bolts to 22 ft. lbs. (29 Nm).

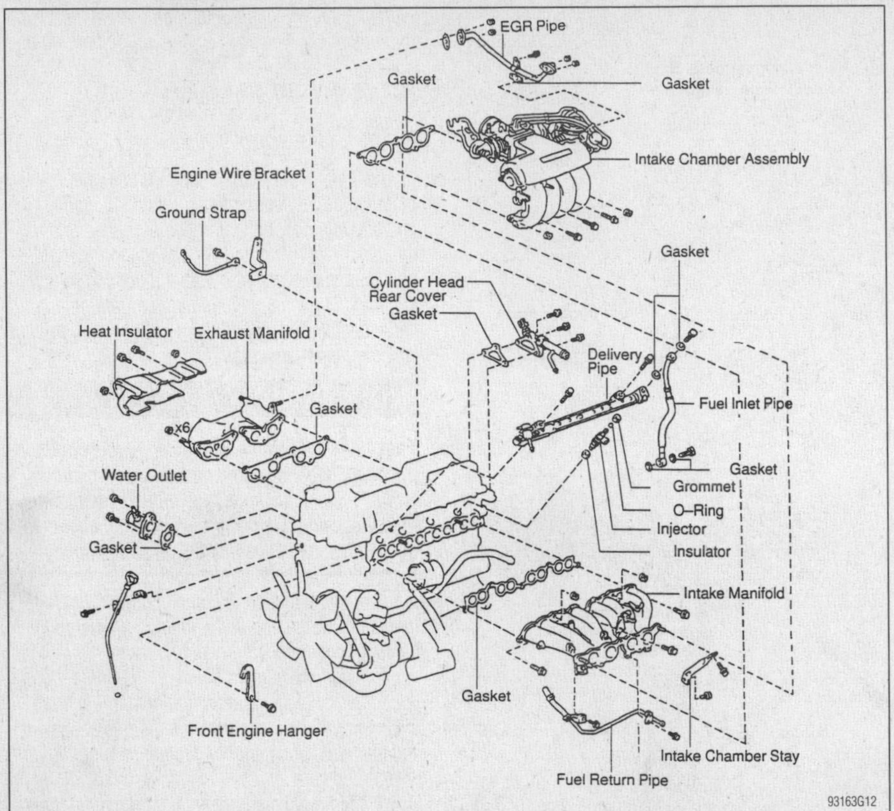

Fig. 62 Upper and lower intake manifolds and related components—2RZ-FE and 3RZ-FE engines

12. If removed, install the fuel injectors and the fuel rail. Connect the fuel lines using new seals.
13. Using a new gasket, Install the upper half of the intake manifold. Torque the nuts and bolts to 15 ft. lbs. (20 Nm).
14. The remainder of installation is the reverse of the removal procedure.
15. Refill with coolant. Test run the engine and check for coolant and vacuum leaks.

2UZ-FE Engine

See Figure 63

The 2UZ-FE engine uses a two-piece intake manifold. The upper part mounts the throttle body. The lower intake manifold bolts to the cylinder heads and hold the fuel rails and injectors. Toyota uses aluminum for many engine parts. Use care when working with light alloy parts as they are easily damaged. Note that on this engine, the starter motor is mounted to the lower intake manifold, facing to the rear, engaging the flywheel at the top.

✲✲ CAUTION

Fuel injected engine systems remain under pressure after the engine has been turned OFF. Properly relieve the fuel pressure before disconnecting any fuel lines. Failure to do so may result in fire or personal injury.

1. Relieve the fuel pressure. For additional information, please refer to the following topic(s): Fuel System, Relieving Fuel System Pressure.
2. Drain the coolant.
3. Disconnect the accelerator cable, the automatic transmission throttle valve cable (if equipped) and the cruise control cable (if equipped) from the throttle body.
4. Disconnect the fuel lines.
5. Detach the following connectors from the intake manifolds:
   - Throttle Position (TP) sensor
   - Accelerator pedal position sensor connector
   - Throttle control motor connector
   - EVAP control connector
   - Eight fuel injector connectors (tag first)
   - Engine Coolant Temperature (ECT) sensor and water temperature sender gauge connections
   - Eight ignition coil connectors (tag first)
   - Two heated oxygen sensor connectors
6. Tag for identification and detach the following hoses from the intake manifolds.
   - Vacuum hose from the fuel pressure regulator
   - PCV hose from the PCV valve on the left side head
   - Three EVAP hoses
   - Power steering vacuum hoses from the intake manifold
   - If not equipped with a hydraulic brake booster system, disconnect the brake booster vacuum tube
7. Disconnect the accelerator cable from the throttle body and remove the wire clamps.
8. Disconnect the water bypass hose from the front water bypass joint.
9. Disconnect the engine wiring harness retainers where it attaches to the right side fuel rail.
10. Remove the three bolts holding the engine wiring harness protector from the rear water bypass joint, on both cylinder heads.

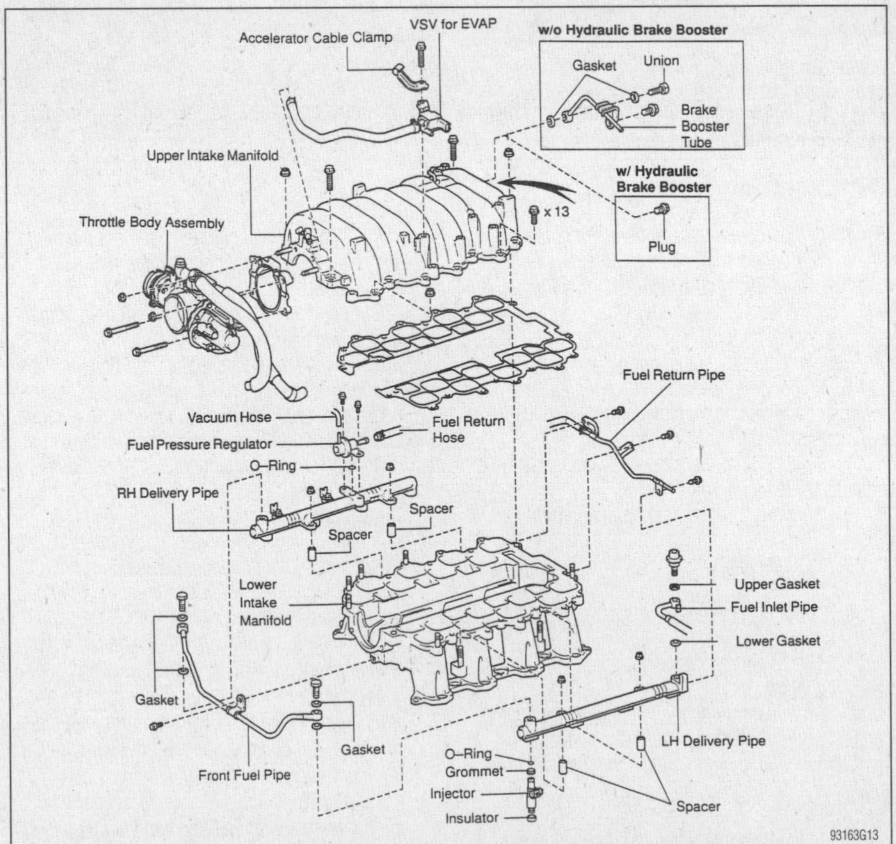

Fig. 63 Upper and lower intake manifolds and related components—2UZ-FE engine

11. Remove the ground cables from both cylinder heads.
12. Remove the Diagnostic Connector (DLC1) from the throttle body cover bracket and remove the bracket from the intake manifold.
13. Remove the two nuts and the accelerator cable bracket from the intake manifold.
14. Remove the nuts and bolts and carefully lift off the upper and lower intake manifolds and the fuel rails as an assembly.
15. If required, remove the nuts and bolts and separate the upper and lower intake manifolds.

To install:

16. Clean all parts well. Check the sealing surfaces of the intake manifold parts. Using a precision straightedge and feeler gauge, check all of the sealing surfaces for warping. Maximum distortion allowed is 0.0059 inch (0.15mm). If the distortion is greater than this, the manifolds may not seal properly. The parts should be replaced.
17. Inspect the new gaskets. Factory-type gaskets should have a white painted mark to indicate facing upward. Use care to align the port hole of the gasket and cylinder head. Using two new gaskets on the cylinder heads, carefully lower the intake manifold assembly into place on the cylinder heads. Torque the nuts and bolts to 160 inch ft. lbs. (18 Nm).
18. Install the remaining components in the reverse of the removal procedure.
19. Refill with coolant. Test run the engine and check for coolant and vacuum leaks.

Exhaust Manifolds

REMOVAL & INSTALLATION

***** CAUTION**

When working on or around an exhaust manifold, make certain all surfaces are cool to the touch before beginning to work.

5VZ-FE Engine

LEFT SIDE

See Figures 64, 65, and 66

1. Disconnect the exhaust crossover pipe from the exhaust manifold.
2. Remove the EGR pipe from the manifold.
3. Remove the heat insulator from the manifold.
4. Unfasten the retainers, then remove the manifold.

To install:

5. Install the exhaust manifold to the engine with a new gasket. Tighten the nuts to 30 ft. lbs. (40 Nm).
6. Install the heat insulator, tighten the nuts down to 71 inch lbs. (8 Nm).
7. Connect the EGR pipe to the manifold. Tighten the nuts to 14 ft. lbs. (18 Nm). Tighten the clamp nuts to 71 inch lbs. (8 Nm).
8. Attach the crossover pipe to the exhaust manifold, tighten the nuts to 33 ft. lbs. (45 Nm).

RIGHT SIDE

See Figures 64, 65, and 66

1. Disconnect the exhaust crossover pipe from the exhaust manifold.

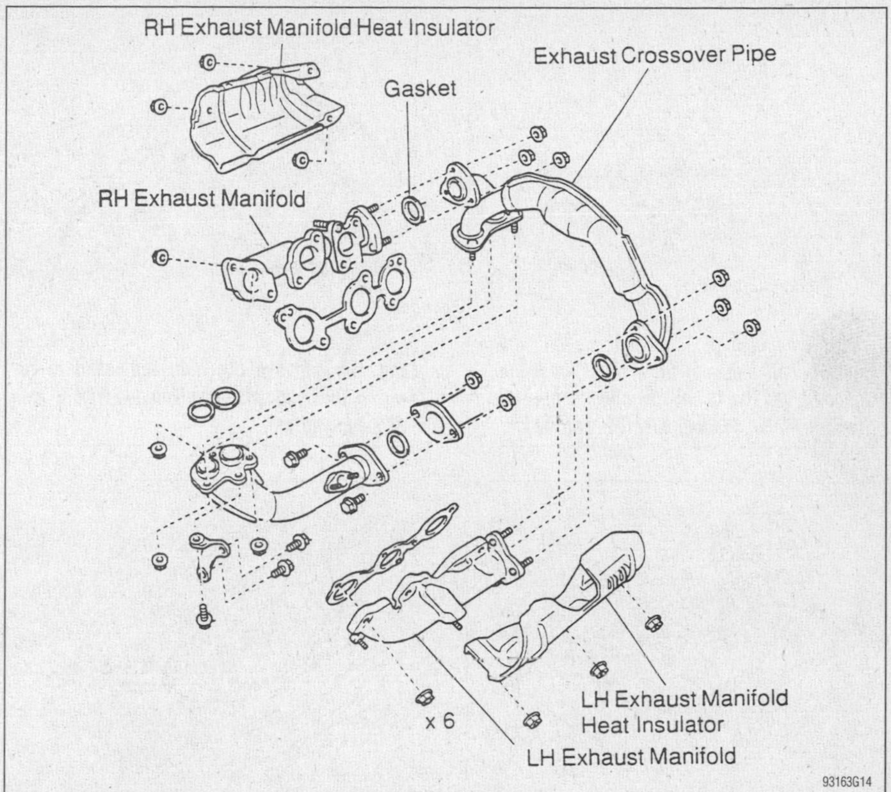

Fig. 64 Exhaust manifold arrangement—5VZ-FE engine

Fig. 65 Removing the bolts securing the crossover pipe to the manifolds—5VZ-FE engine

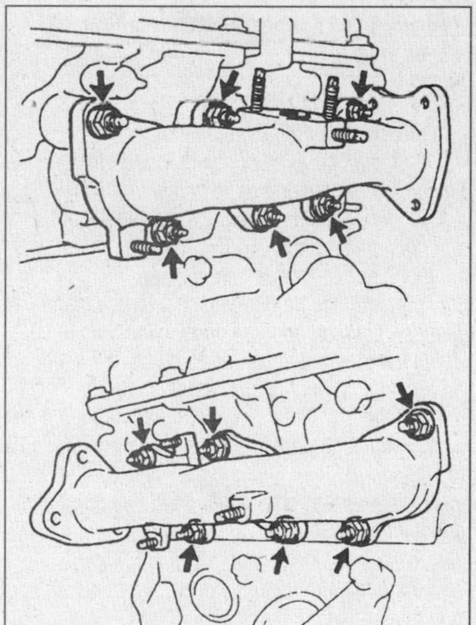

Fig. 66 Exhaust manifold retaining nut locations—5VZ-FE engine

2. Remove the exhaust manifold heat insulator.
3. Unfasten the six nuts securing the manifold, then remove the manifold from the engine.

To install:

4. Install the exhaust manifold with the new gasket, tighten the six nuts to 30 ft. lbs. (40 Nm).
5. Attach the heat insulator, tighten the nuts to 71 inch lbs. (8 Nm).
6. Connect the crossover pipe with a new gasket, to the exhaust manifold. Tighten the nuts to 33 ft. lbs. (45 Nm).

2RZ-FE and 3RZ-FE Engines

See Figures 67 and 68

1. Raise and safely support the vehicle.
2. Disconnect the front exhaust pipe from the manifold and mounting bracket.
3. Lower the vehicle.
4. Remove the heat insulator.
5. Remove the exhaust manifold and gasket.

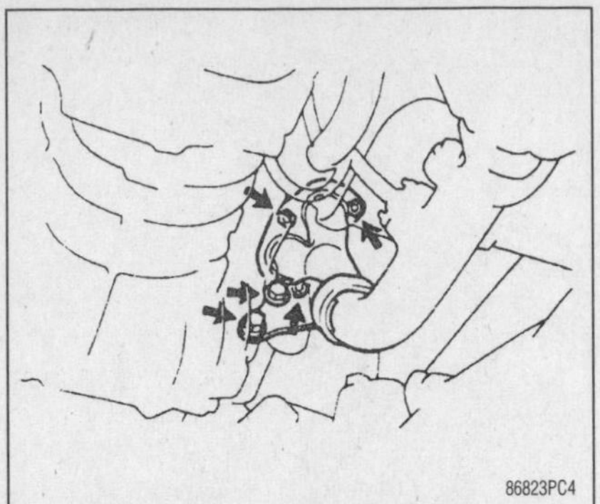

Fig. 67 The exhaust pipe must be disconnected from the manifold and its mounting bracket—2RZ-FE and 3RZ-FE engines

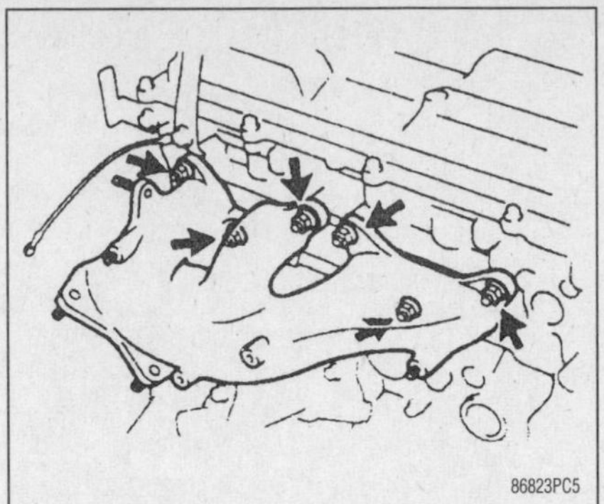

Fig. 68 Remove the nuts indicated to remove the exhaust manifold—2RZ-FE and 3RZ-FE engines

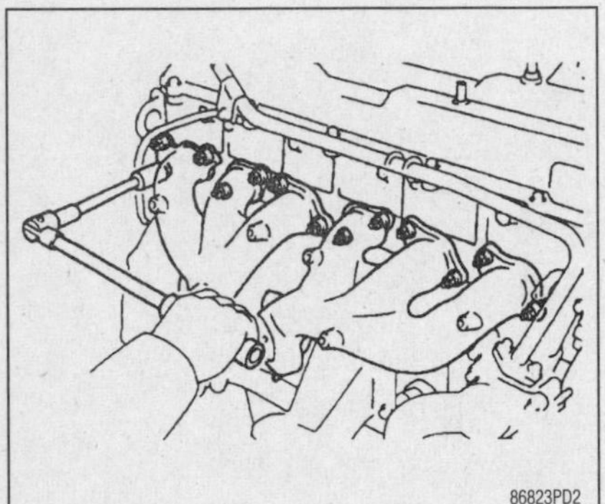

Fig. 69 An extension can be useful for reaching the manifold retaining nuts—1FZ-FE engine

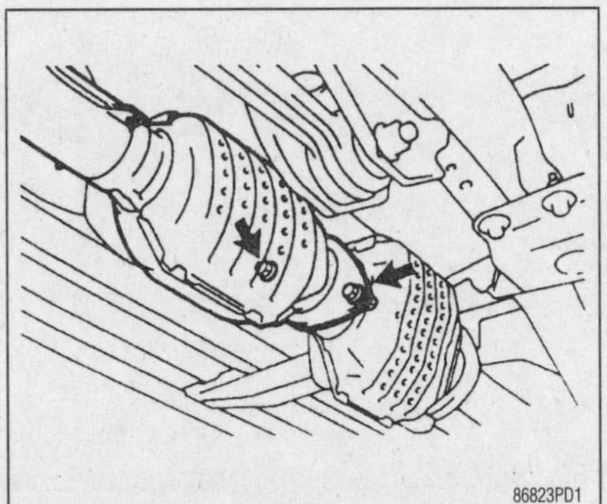

Fig. 70 Be sure to use new gaskets when attaching the front header pipe to the catalyst—1FZ-FE engine

To install:

6. Install the exhaust manifold and gasket to the engine, tighten the nuts to 36 ft. lbs. (49 Nm).
7. Attach the heat insulator, tighten the bolts and nuts to 48 inch lbs. (5 Nm).
8. Raise and support the vehicle.
9. Install the front exhaust pipe to the manifold with new gaskets. Apply a gasket to the front pipe, install the nuts and tighten to 46 ft. lbs. (62 Nm).
10. Attach the support bracket, tighten to 29 ft. lbs. (39 Nm).
11. Attach the clamp and tighten to 14 ft. lbs. (19 Nm).
12. Lower the vehicle, then start the engine and check for exhaust leaks.

1FZ-FE Engine

➧ See Figures 69 and 70

1. Disconnect the negative battery cable.
2. Raise and safely support the vehicle.
3. Working from underneath the vehicle, disconnect the oxygen sensor wire.
4. Remove the nuts and bolts holding the front header pipe to the catalytic converter.
5. Loosen the pipe clamp.
6. Remove the pipe bracket.
7. Unbolt the front header pipe and remove the gasket.
8. Lower the vehicle, remove the exhaust manifold heat shield insulators.
9. Remove the nuts from the exhaust manifolds, then the gaskets.

To install:

10. Install the exhaust manifolds to the engine with new gaskets. Uniformly tighten the nuts in several passes. Tighten the nuts to 29 ft. lbs. (39 Nm).
11. Install the exhaust manifold heat insulators, tighten down to 14 ft. lbs. (19 Nm).
12. Attach the header pipe to the exhaust manifold using new gaskets, tighten the nuts to 46 ft. lbs. (63 Nm).
13. Install the support bracket, then tighten to 17 ft. lbs. (24 Nm).
14. Attach the clamp, tighten to 14 ft. lbs. (19 Nm).
15. Connect the header pipe to the catalyst using a new gasket to prevent leaks. Tighten to 34 ft. lbs. (46 Nm).
16. Attach the oxygen sensor wire.
17. Connect the negative battery cable, then start the engine and check for exhaust leaks.

2UZ-FE Engine

➧ See Figure 71

➡The gaskets between the manifold and head and between the manifold and front exhaust pipe are not reusable. Toyota also specifies that the nuts be replaced with new service parts.

1. Disconnect the negative battery cable.
2. Apply penetrating oil to the nuts and bolts, as required.
3. Remove the nuts from the front pipe that connects the manifold to the three-way catalytic converter
4. Detach the oxygen sensor electrical connector.
5. Remove the small bolts that hold the heat insulator to the manifold.
6. Remove the eight nuts and separate the manifold from the cylinder head. Discard the gasket.

To install:

7. Installation is the reverse of the removal process. Examine the replacement exhaust manifold-to-head gasket. Original equipment Toyota gaskets should have white paint marks on them. The white painted marks should face the manifold side. Use care to install the gasket in the correct direction.
8. Using a new gasket, install the manifold using care to align the studs with the front pipe. A new gasket between the manifold outlet and the front pipe is also required. Use new service replacement nuts. Uniformly tighten the nuts to 32 ft. lbs. (44 Nm).
9. Install the heat insulator and tighten the four bolts to just 66 inch lbs. (7.5 Nm).

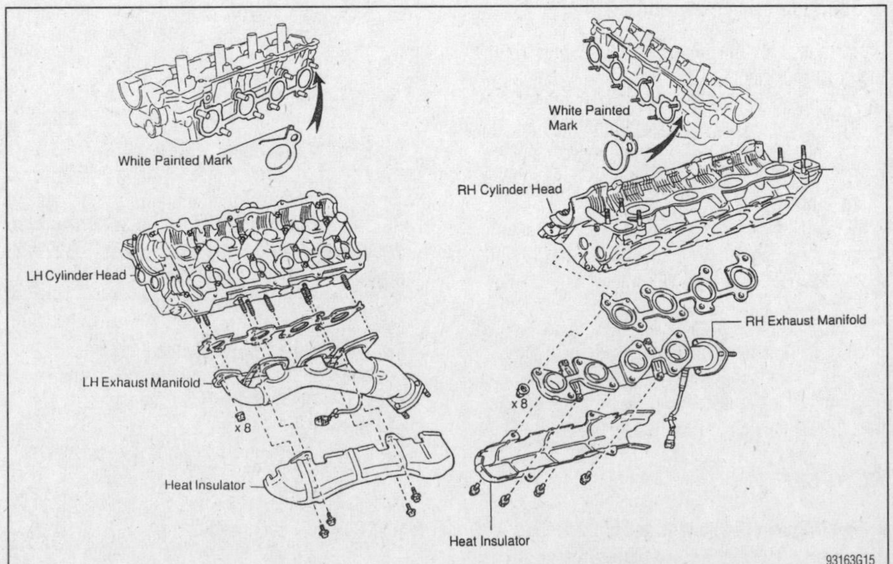

Fig. 71 Exhaust manifold arrangement and gasket markings—2UZ-FE engine

10. Tighten the manifold-to-front pipe nuts to 46 ft. lbs. (62 Nm).
11. Connect the negative battery cable, start the engine and verify no exhaust leaks.

Radiator

REMOVAL & INSTALLATION

2RZ-FE and 3RZ-FE Engines

See Figures 72, 73, and 74

1. Drain the engine cooling system. Have a large enough suitable container to collect the fluid.
2. Remove the grille, filler and clearance lamps.
3. On the 3RZ-FE California models, disconnect the air pipe.

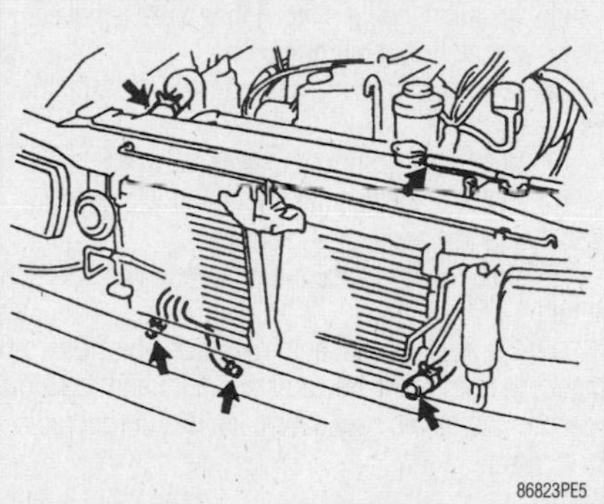

Fig. 72 Disconnect the hoses at the points shown

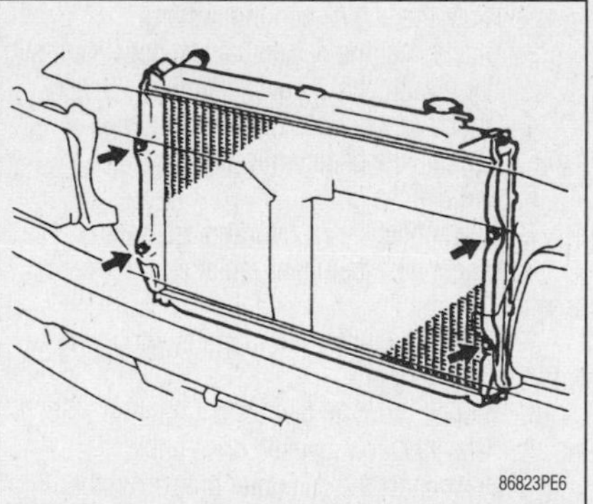

Fig. 73 The radiator is usually secured by four bolts

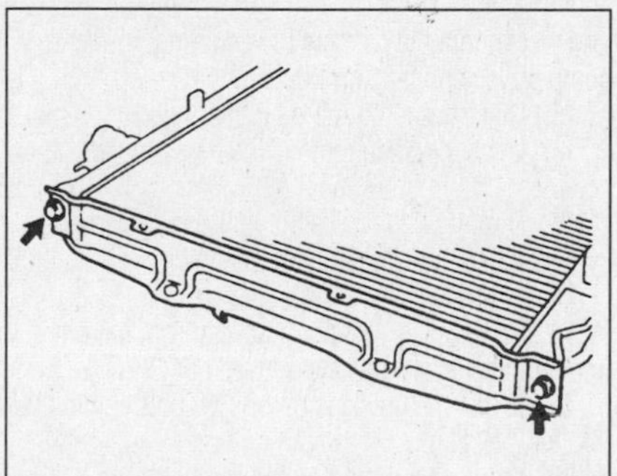

Fig. 74 If the radiator is being replaced, the support brackets should be transferred to the new radiator

4. Disconnect the upper radiator hose.
5. Unsecure the radiator reservoir hose.
6. On some T100 models you will need to remove the power steering belt. With A/C vehicles, loosen the idler pulley nut and adjusting bolt, then remove the belt. Remove the alternator belt, fan with coupling, water pump pulley and fan shroud.
7. Remove the lower radiator hose, remember there will still be some fluid left in the lower hose. Have a catch pan available.
8. Remove the fan shroud.
9. On A/T vehicles, disconnect the oil cooler hoses. Plug the openings so oil does not drip out.
10. Remove the 4 mounting bolts for the radiator. When lifting the radiator from the vehicle, you will have some fluid still in the tank. Watch for spillage.

To install:

11. After the radiator has been removed there may be supports on the old unit. Remove them and install on the new radiator.
12. If replacing with a used radiator or your old one, install a new O-ring onto the petcock.
13. With the supports on the new unit, install into the vehicle. Insert the tabs of the support through the radiator service holes. Tighten the radiator down to 9 ft. lbs. (12 Nm).
14. Connect the outlet hose.
15. If removed on the T100; install the water pump pulley, fan shroud, fan with coupling and drive belt vehicles with A/C, install the compressor belt then adjust. Install the power steering belt and adjust.
16. Connect the radiator reservoir hose.
17. With new hose clamps, connect the upper radiator hose.
18. Attach the radiator grille with the clips and screws. Install both clearance lamp assemblies.
19. Fill the engine with a water coolant mixture. Start the engine, check for leaks, and add as required.
20. Check the A/T fluid level, and add, if required.

5VZ-FE Engine

See Figures 75 thru 85

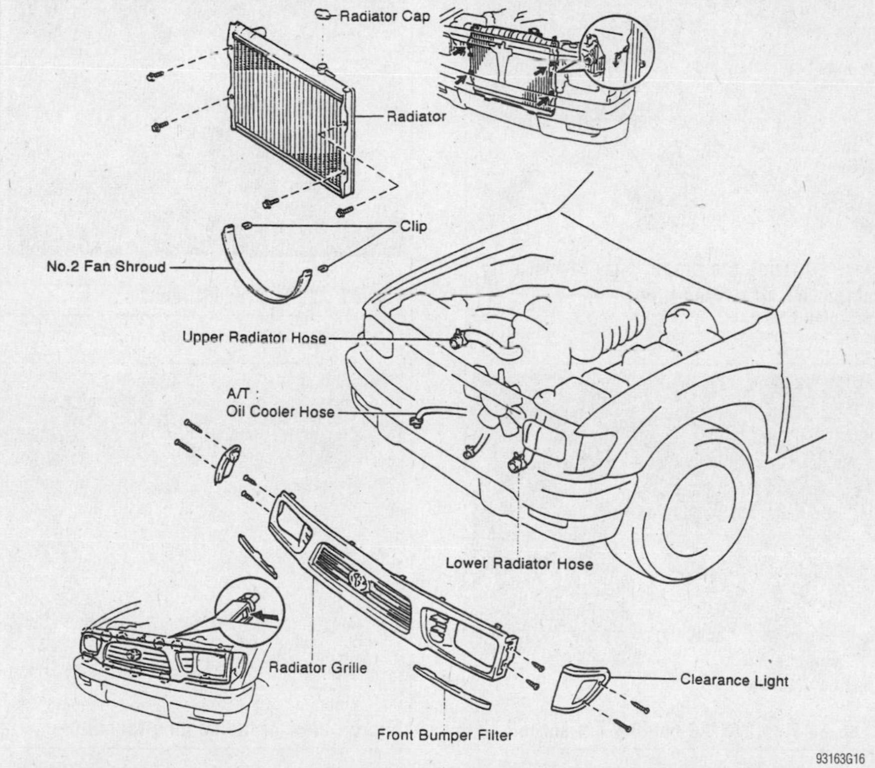

Fig. 75 Radiator and related components—1999 Tacoma with 5VZ-FE engine shown

Fig. 76 Remove the upper radiator hose

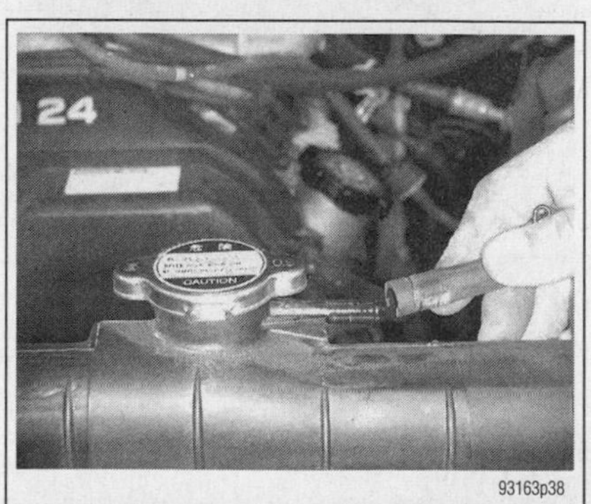

Fig. 77 Detach the overflow hose from the filler neck of the radiator

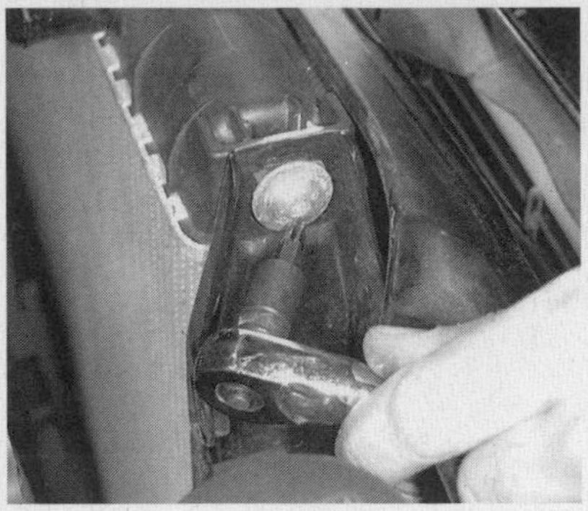

93163p39

Fig. 78 Remove all mounting fasteners from the radiator

93163p40

Fig. 79 Squeeze the lower radiator hose clamp, slide it back a few inches, then twist and remove the lower hose

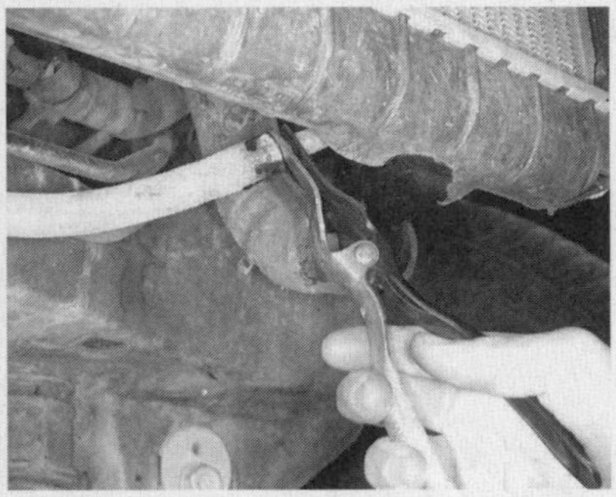

93163p41

Fig. 80 Using the proper type of tool only, clamp off all related lines . . .

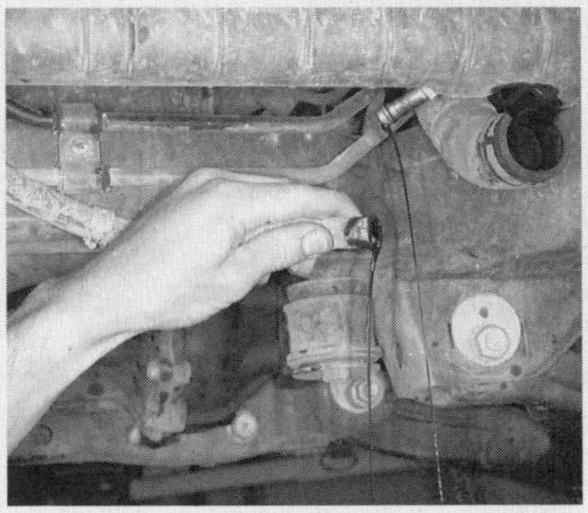

93163p42

Fig. 81 . . . to prevent leaks

93163p48

Fig. 82 Remove the cooling fan shroud

93163p50

Fig. 83 View of the cooling fan shroud

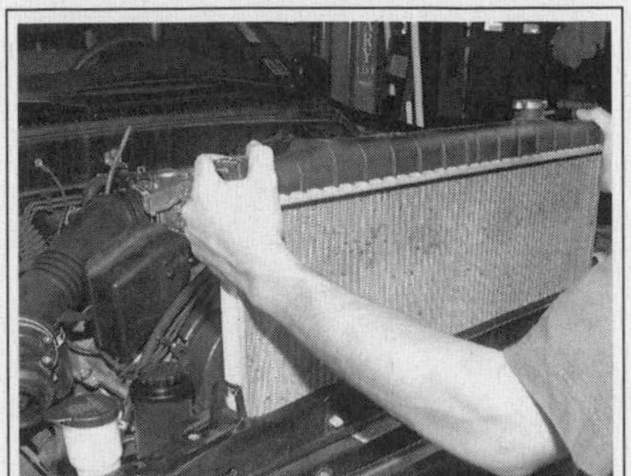

93163p45

Fig. 84 Remove the radiator by carefully pulling it straight up and out of the vehicle

93163p47

Fig. 85 After removing the radiator from the vehicle, place it in a safe place so it doesn't get damaged

1. Drain the engine cooling system, discard the O-ring.
2. Remove the front bumper filler.
3. Take off the clearance lamps.
4. Remove the grille assembly. The grille is held in place by a combination of screws and clips.
5. Disconnect the upper and lower radiator hoses and disconnect the hose to the overflow reservoir.
6. Unbolt the fan shroud.
7. On A/T vehicles, disconnect and plug the oil cooler lines.
8. Unbolt the radiator and lift out of the vehicle.

To install:

9. If replacing with a used radiator or your old one, install a new O-ring onto the petcock.
10. Install the radiator and tighten the mounting bolts to 9 ft. lbs. (12 Nm). Make certain all the rubber mounts and bushings are present and correctly placed.
11. Install oil cooler lines if they were removed.
12. Install the fan shrouds.
13. With new hose clamps, connect the radiator hoses.
14. Attach the grille and clearance lamps.
15. Fill the radiator with a water coolant mixture, start the engine and check for leaks.
16. Add coolant to the overflow reservoir, as required.
17. On vehicles with automatic transmissions, check the level of the transmission fluid and adjust as needed. Some fluid may have been lost during radiator removal.

1FZ-FE Engine

➧ See Figures 86 thru 91

1. Drain the engine cooling system.
2. Disconnect the battery cables, negative first.
3. Remove the hold-down clamp and battery.
4. Unbolt and remove the ground strap.
5. Remove the battery tray.
6. Remove the grille.
7. Disconnect the radiator bypass hose.
8. Disconnect the upper radiator and reservoir hoses.
9. Loosen the water pump pulley mounting nuts.
10. Loosen the lock, pivot and adjusting bolts of the alternator, then remove the drive belts.
11. Disconnect the oil cooler hose from the clamp on the fan shroud.
12. Unbolt and remove the fan shroud.
13. Remove the water pump pulley mounting nuts.
14. Pull out the fan with the coupling, water pump pulley and fan shroud.
15. Disconnect the A/T oil cooler hoses.
16. Unclamp, then remove the lower radiator hose.
17. Unbolt and remove the radiator, remember there will be some fluid still in the unit.

To install:

18. Remove the radiator brackets from the old unit if replacing with a new or used one.
19. Install the brackets to the new unit, tighten to 9 ft. lbs. (12 Nm).
20. Use a new O-ring on the petcock.
21. Install the radiator, tighten the mounting nuts to 9 ft. lbs. (12 Nm) and bolts to 13 ft. lbs. (18 Nm).
22. Connect the A/T oil cooler hoses.
23. Attach the lower radiator hose.

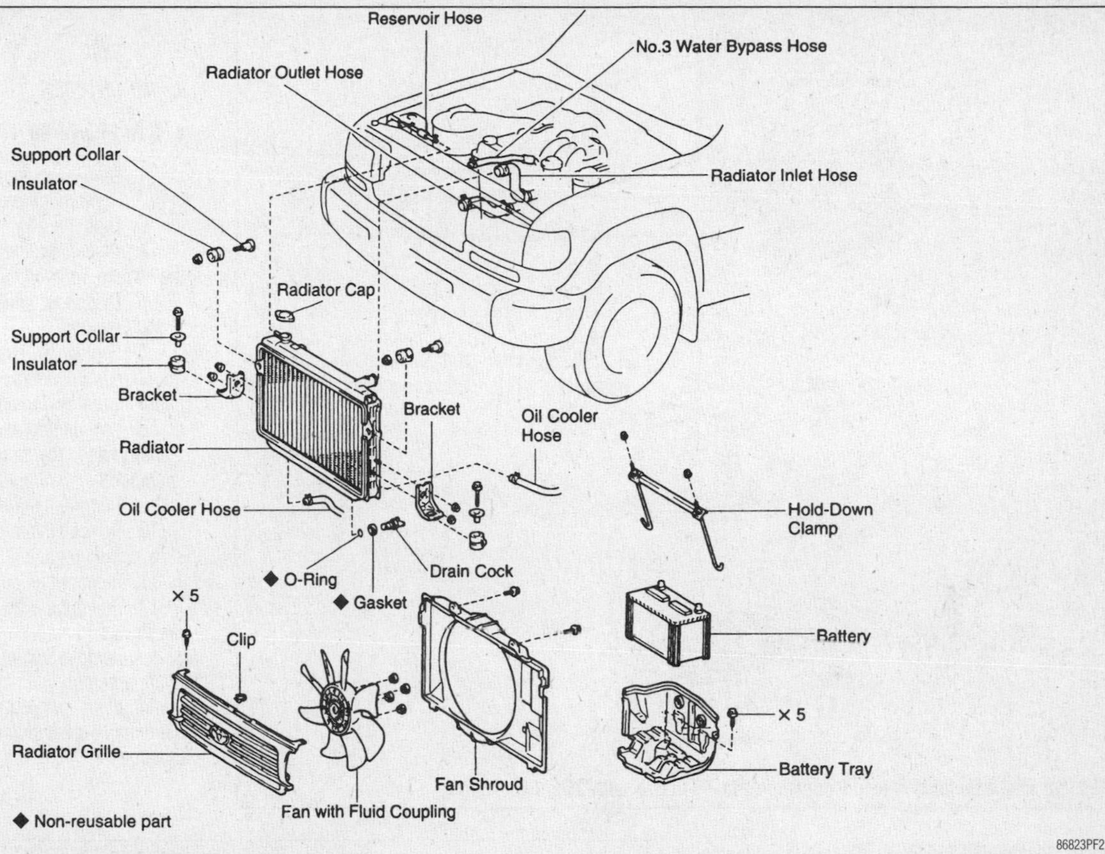

Fig. 86 Exploded view of the radiator mounting on 1FZ-FE engines

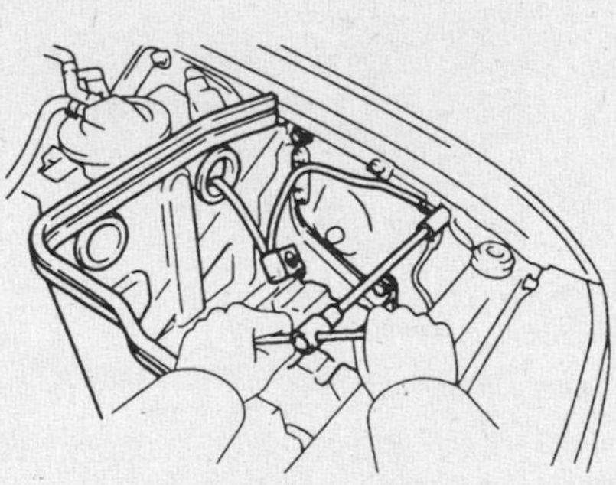

Fig. 87 The battery tray must be removed from the vehicle

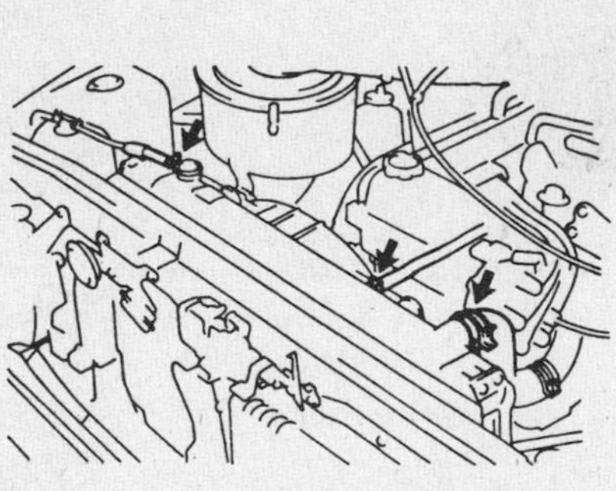

Fig. 88 Disconnect the indicated hoses from the radiator

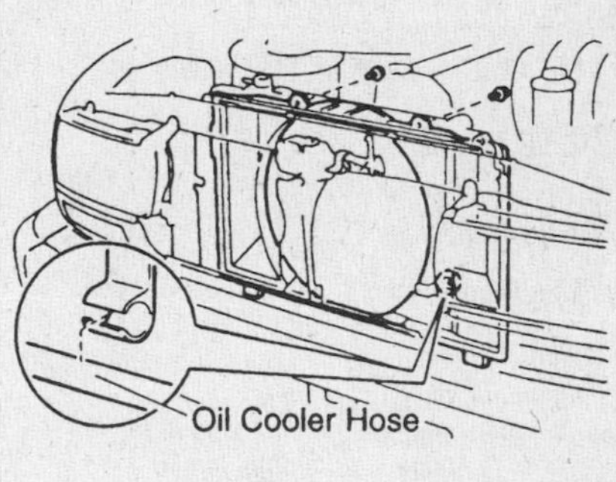

Fig. 89 Be sure to release the oil cooler hose from the clamp before removing the fan shroud

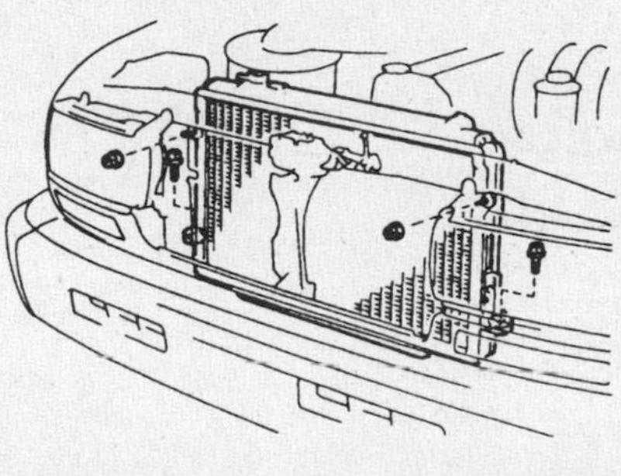

Fig. 90 Remove the fasteners securing the radiator, then remove the radiator from the vehicle

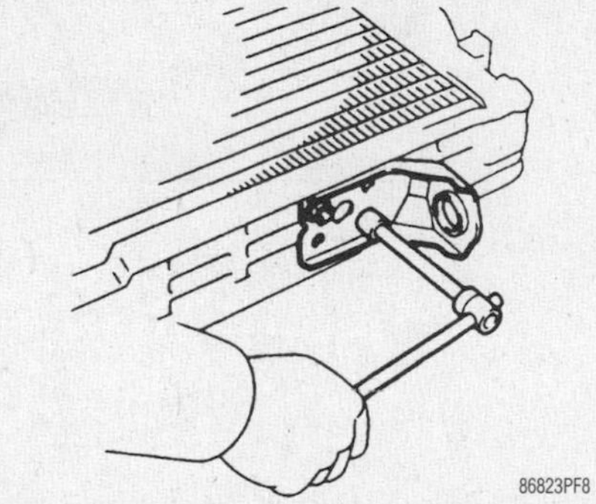

Fig. 91 If replacing the radiator, transfer the brackets to the new unit

24. Place the fan, coupling, water pump pulley and shroud in position on the engine. Temporarily install the pulley mounting nuts.
25. Install the shroud and tighten to 43 inch lbs. (5 Nm).
26. Attach the oil cooler hose to the clamp on the fan shroud.
27. Install the drive belts with the adjusting and pivot bolts.
28. Stretch the belts tight, then tighten the pulley mounting nuts.
29. Adjust the drive belts.
30. Attach the reservoir, upper radiator and bypass hoses.
31. Install the grille.
32. Install the battery tray, connect the ground strap. Install the battery with the hold-down clamp and nuts.

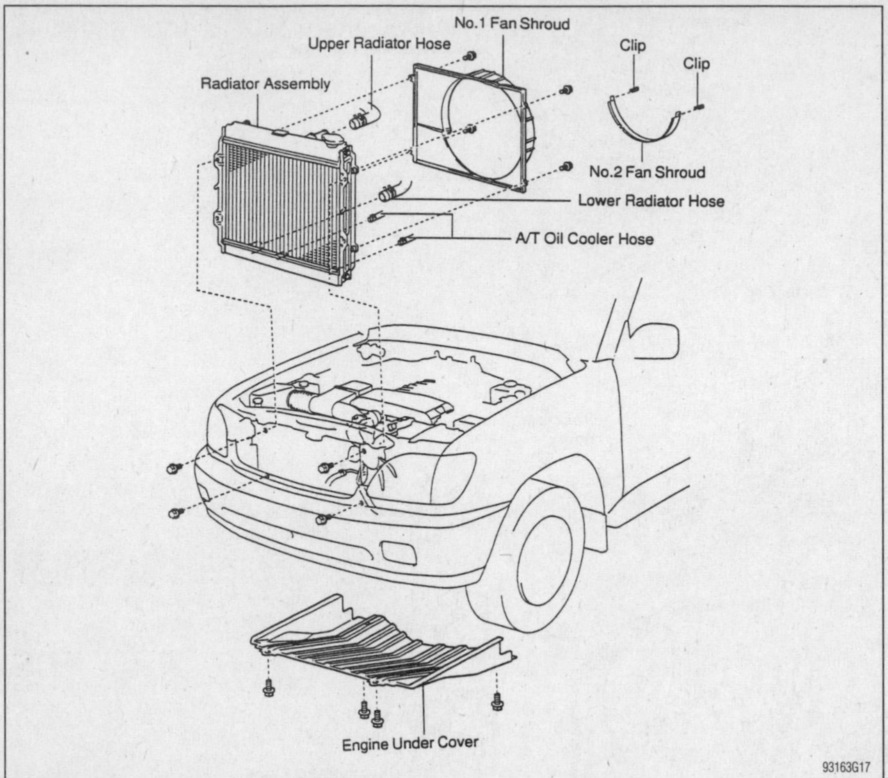

Fig. 92 Radiator and related components—Tundra with 2UZ-FE engine

33. Connect the battery cables.
34. Fill the engine with the correct amount of water and coolant mixture.
35. Start the engine, check for leaks and add coolant, if required.
36. Check and add A/T fluid, if required.

2UZ-FE Engine

TUNDRA

➧ See Figure 92

Use care handling this radiator. It is constructed of aluminum with plastic tanks.

1. Disconnect the negative battery cable.
2. Remove the engine undercover.
3. Drain the engine coolant.
4. Disconnect the upper and lower radiator hoses and the hose to the overflow reservoir.
5. Disconnect the automatic transmission cooler lines, if equipped.
6. Unclip and remove the No. 2 (small) fan shroud.
7. Remove the four bolts and remove the radiator assembly. It may be necessary to remove the four bolts and remove the No. 1 (large) fan shroud.

To install:

8. If removed, install the No. 1 (large) fan shroud.
9. Install the radiator, guiding the bracket hooks to the radiator support holes. Install the four bolts and torque to 108 inch lbs. (12 Nm).
10. Install the No. 2 (small) fan shroud.
11. Connect the automatic transmission cooler hoses to the radiator.
12. Connect the upper and lower radiator hoses and the hose to the coolant overflow reservoir.
13. Fill the radiator with coolant, start the engine and check for leaks.
14. Recheck the engine coolant level.
15. Install the engine undercover.

LAND CRUISER

➧ See Figure 93

1. Disconnect the negative battery cable.
2. Remove the engine undercover.
3. Drain the engine coolant.
4. Disconnect the upper and lower radiators and the hose to the overflow reservoir tank.
5. Disconnect the automatic transmission cooler lines.
6. Remove the overflow reservoir tank.
7. Disconnect the automatic transmission cooler lines from the clamp on the fan shroud.
8. Loosen the fan pulley mounting nuts holding the fan clutch (Toyota calls it a fluid coupling) to the fan bracket.
9. Remove the alternator drive belt.
10. Remove the three bolts holding the fan shroud to the radiator.
11. Remove the four fan pulley mounting nuts.
12. Pull out the fan with the clutch, fan pulley and fan shroud.
13. Remove the nuts and bolts and lift out the radiator assembly.
14. If changing out the radiator to a new replacement, transfer the radiator side supports to the new radiator.

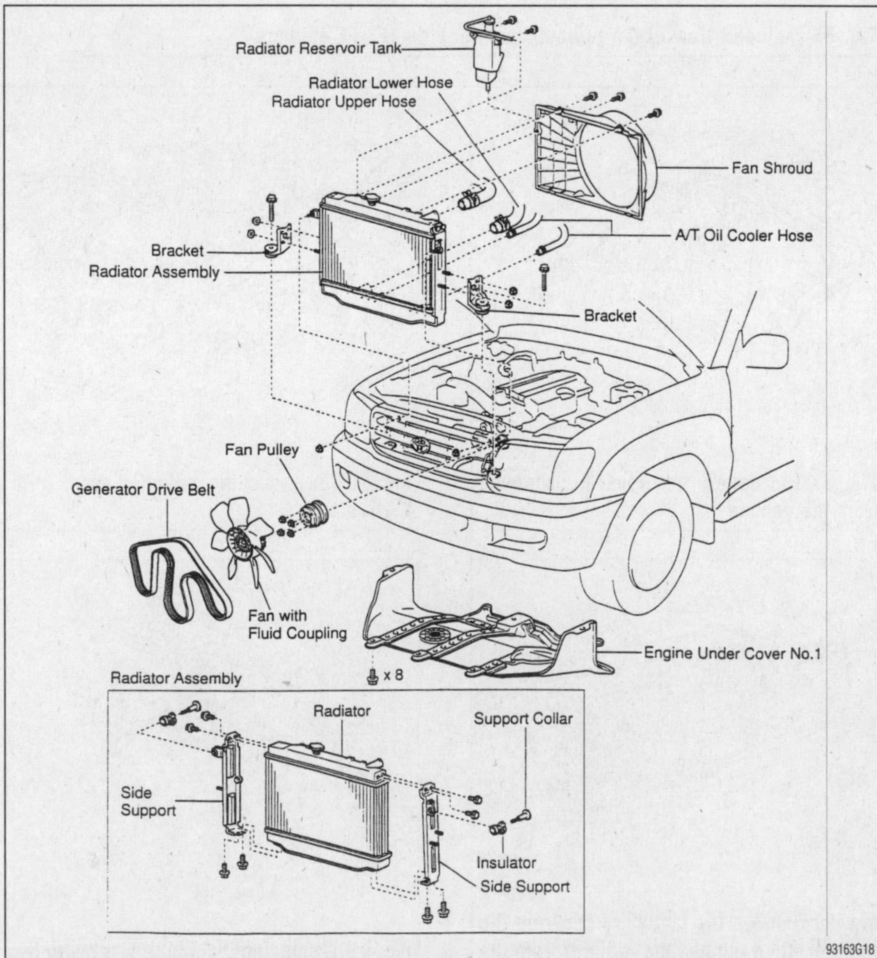

Fig. 93 Radiator and related components—1999 Land Cruiser with 2UZ-FE engine

To install:

15. Install the radiator in the truck. Tighten the nuts to 15 ft. lbs. (20 Nm) and the bolts to 13 ft. lbs. (18 Nm).
16. Place the fan using the following sequence:
    a. Place the fan with the clutch, fan pulley and shroud in position.
    b. Temporarily install the fan pulley mounting nuts.
    c. Install the fan shroud with the 3 bolts
    d. Connect the automatic transmission cooler lines to the clamp on the fan shroud.
    e. Install the alternator drive belt.
    f. Tighten the fan pulley mounting nuts.
17. Install the coolant overflow reservoir tank.
18. Connect the automatic transmission cooler lines, the upper and lower radiator hoses and the hose to the overflow reservoir.
19. Fill the radiator with coolant.
20. Start the engine and check for engine coolant leaks.
21. Recheck the coolant level.
22. Install the engine undercover.

Engine Cooling Fan

REMOVAL & INSTALLATION

▶ See Figures 94, 95, and 96

1. Disconnect the negative battery cable.
2. Remove the alternator, A/C and power steering (if applicable) belts.
3. Loosen the bolts holding the water pump pulley (not the pump).
4. Remove the nuts, then remove the fan clutch (fluid coupling), fan and pulley.

To install:

5. Install the pulley, clutch and fan; loosely fit the nuts in place.
6. Install the drive belt to the water pump pulley. Tighten the nuts to 16 ft. lbs. (22 Nm).
7. Install the belts to the other pulleys and adjust.
8. Connect the negative battery cable.

Water Pump

REMOVAL & INSTALLATION

5VZ-FE Engines

▶ See Figures 97 thru 104

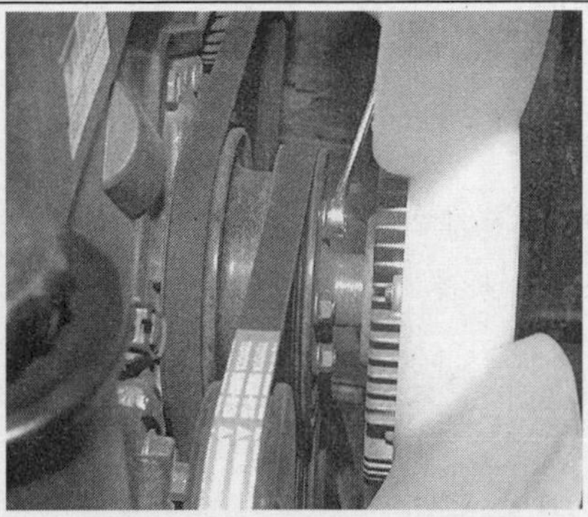

93163p51

Fig. 94 Remove the nuts that hold the fan to the drive pulley

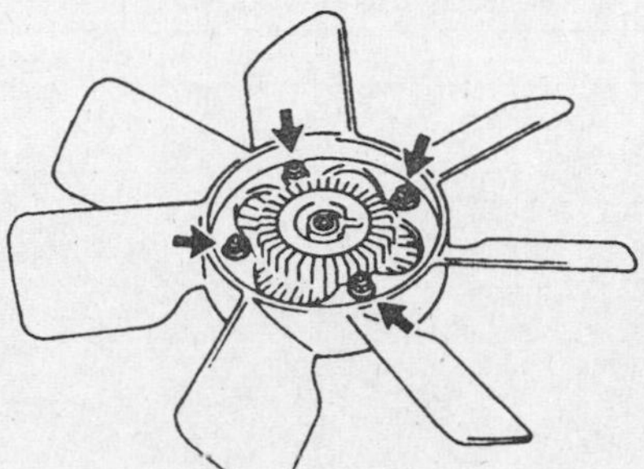

86823PI5

Fig. 95 There are four nuts retaining the fan blade to the fluid coupling. Tighten to 47 inch lbs. (5.4 Nm)

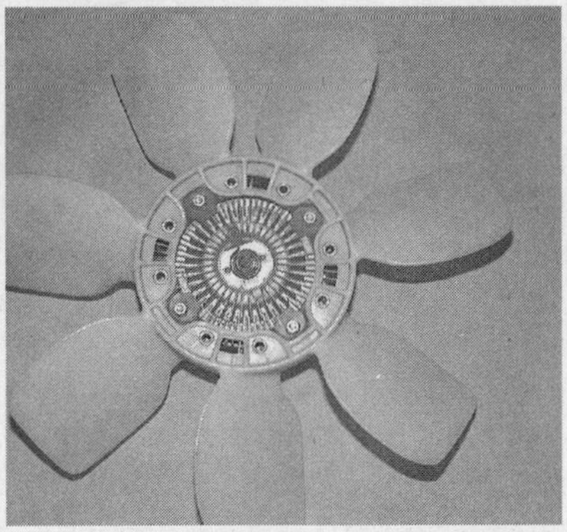

93163p52

Fig. 96 Front view of the cooling fan blades

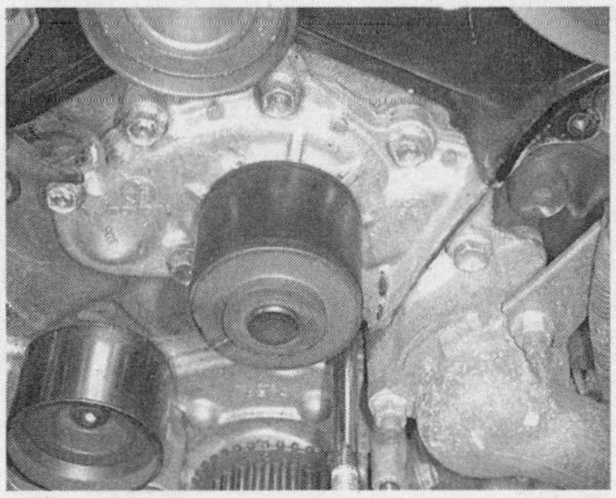

93163p92

Fig. 97 The water pump is located on the front of the engine block, behind the timing cover

93163p97

Fig. 98 Once the retainers are removed, pull the pump away from the block

93163p98

Fig. 99 Scrape any remaining gasket material from the block before installing the new pump

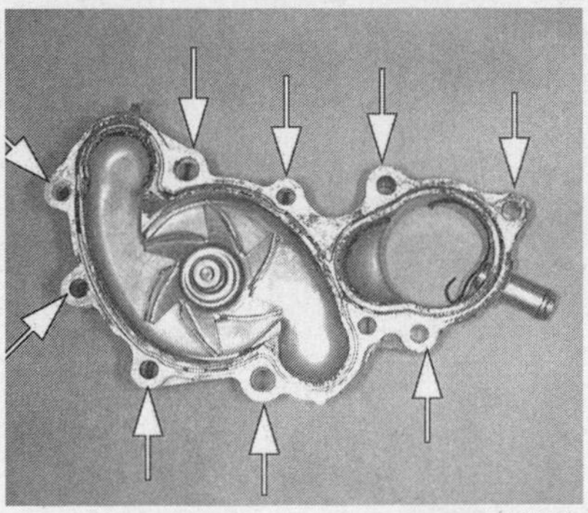

93163p88

Fig. 100 Water pump mounting bolt locations

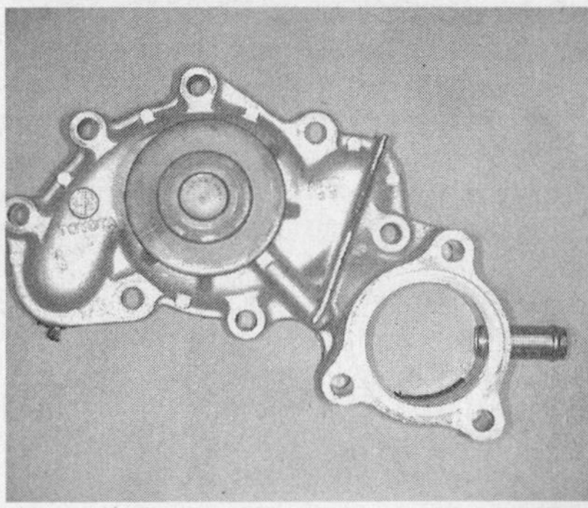

93163p99

Fig. 101 Front view of the water pump and thermostat housing

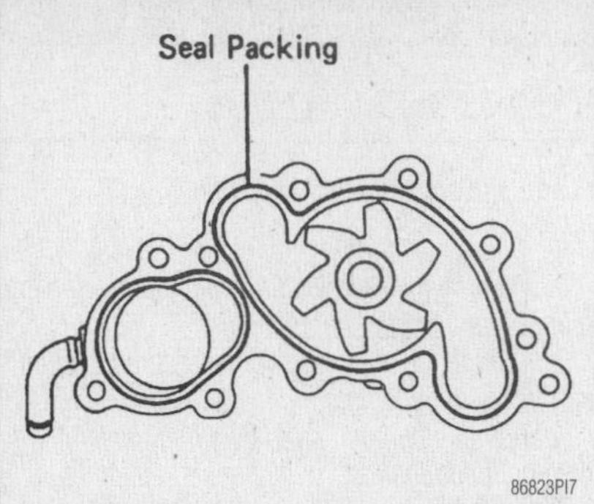

Fig. 102 Apply sealant to the areas shown

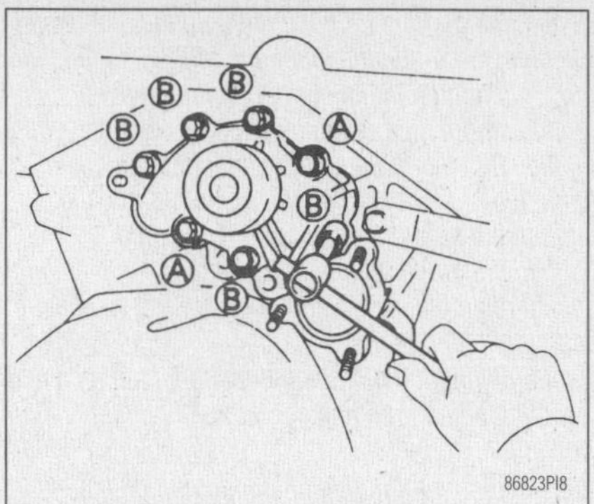

Fig. 103 A and B bolt locations

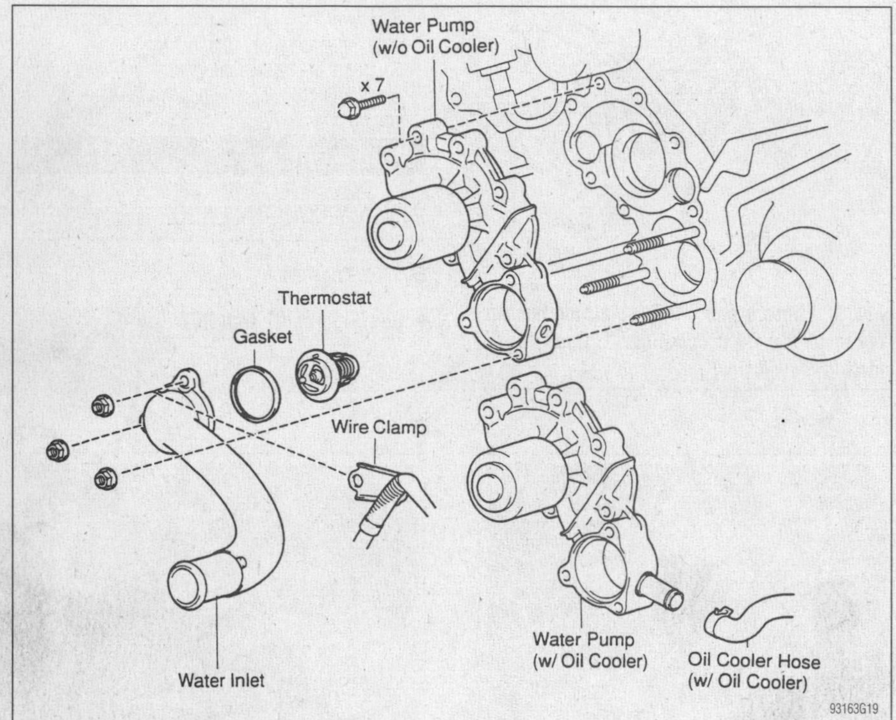

Fig. 104 Exploded view of the water pump arrangement—5VZ-FE engine

WARNING

This procedure requires the removal of the timing belt. This is an extensive procedure requiring precision work, particularly at assembly. For more information, refer to Timing Belt Removal and Installation. Do not attempt to remove the belt without consulting the procedure; extreme engine damage may occur.

1. Drain the cooling system.
2. Remove the timing belt. For additional information, please refer to the following topic(s): Timing Belt Removal and Installation.
3. Remove the idler pulley.
4. Remove the thermostat.
5. Disconnect the oil cooler hose from the pump.
6. Remove the seven bolts and the tension spring bracket and then remove the water pump.

To install:

7. Clean all parts well. It is good practice to carefully clean all threaded openings, especially those exposed to coolant to remove rust and scale so at assembly, an accurate torque reading is obtained. This is important since gasketless applications like this depend on even clamp loads from the fasteners to avoid distortion and leaks. Remove any old sealer (Toyota calls it packing) from the pump and mounting area of the engine. Keep oil off the mating areas.
8. Apply Formed In Place Gasket (FIPG) sealer to the pump-to-block mating surface and then tighten the bolts marked **A** in the illustration to 13 ft. lbs. (18 Nm). Tighten those marked **B** to 14 ft. lbs. (20 Nm).

➡The parts must be installed within 5 minutes of application of the sealant. Otherwise you must remove and reapply the sealer.

9. Install the remaining components in the reverse of the removal procedure.
10. Refill the cooling system and check for leaks.

2RZ-FE and 3RZ-FE Engines

1. Disconnect the negative battery cable.
2. Drain the cooling system.
3. If equipped with an air conditioning compressor or power steering pump drive belts, it may be necessary to loosen the adjusting bolt, remove the drive belt(s) and move the component(s) out of the way.
4. Remove the fluid coupling with the fan and water pump pulley.
5. Remove the water pump.

To install:

6. Clean the gasket mounting surfaces.
7. Install the replacement water pump using a new gasket.
8. Install the water pump pulley and fluid coupling with the fan.
9. Install the removed engine drive belts.
10. Fill the cooling system.
11. Connect the negative battery cable. Start the engine and check for leaks.
12. Bleed the cooling system.

1FZ-FE Engine

➧ See Figures 105 and 106

1. Disconnect the negative battery cable.
2. Drain the engine coolant.
3. Disconnect the water bypass and radiator inlet hoses.
4. Remove the drive belts, fan assembly, and the fan shroud.
5. Disconnect the oil cooler hose from the clamp on the fan shroud. Remove the bolts holding the fan shroud to the radiator.
6. Remove the 4 bolts, 2 nuts, water pump, and the gasket.

To install:

7. Install the water pump using a new gasket. Tighten the fasteners to 15 ft. lbs. (21 Nm).
8. Install the water pump pulley, fan shroud, and the drive belts as follows:
   a. Place the fan with the fluid coupling, water pump pulley, and the fan shroud in position.
   b. Temporarily install the fan pulley mounting nuts.
   c. Install the fan shroud and tighten the bolts to 43 inch lbs. (5 Nm).
   d. Connect the oil cooler hose to the clamp on the fan shroud.
9. Connect the water bypass and radiator hoses. Fill the cooling system.
10. Connect the negative battery cable.
11. Start the engine, check for leaks. Add fluids as required.

2UZ-FE Engine

➧ See Figure 107

WARNING

This procedure requires the removal of the timing belt. This is an extensive procedure requiring precision work, particularly at assembly. Refer to Timing Belt—Removal and Installation. Do not attempt to remove the belt without consulting the procedure; extreme engine damage may occur.

1. Disconnect the negative battery cable.
2. Drain the engine coolant.
3. Remove the camshaft timing belt. For additional information, please refer to the following topic(s): Timing Belt Removal and Installation.
4. Remove the No. 2 idler pulley.

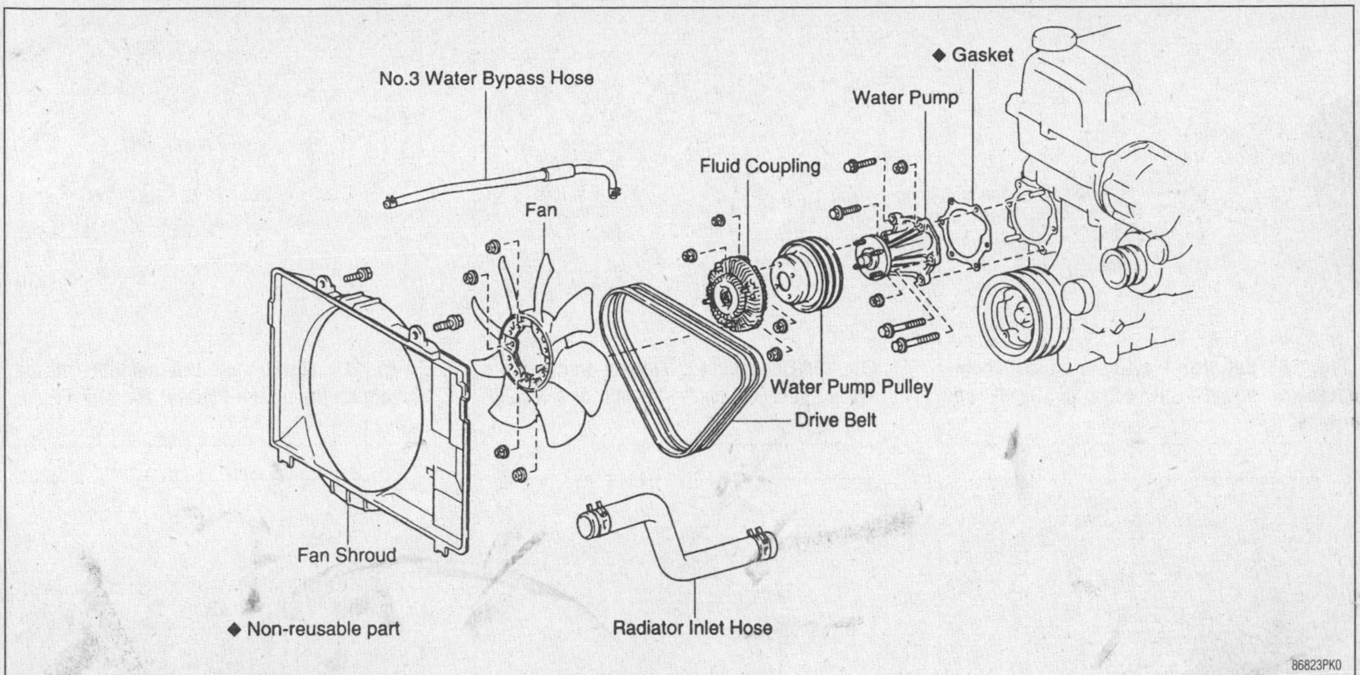

Fig. 105 Exploded view of the water pump mounting on the 1FZ-FE engine

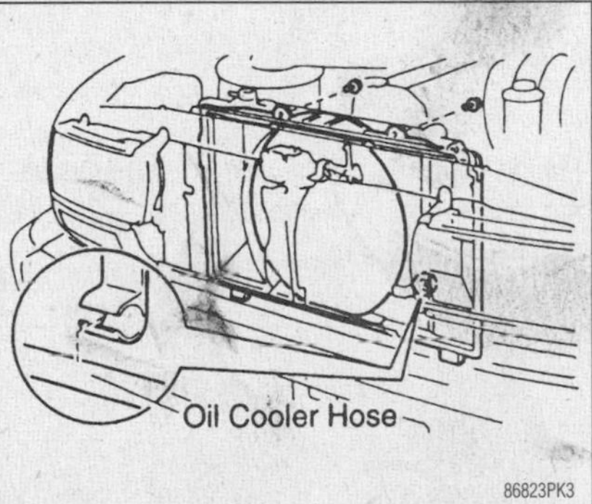

Fig. 106 Detach the oil cooler hose from the clamp on the fan shroud

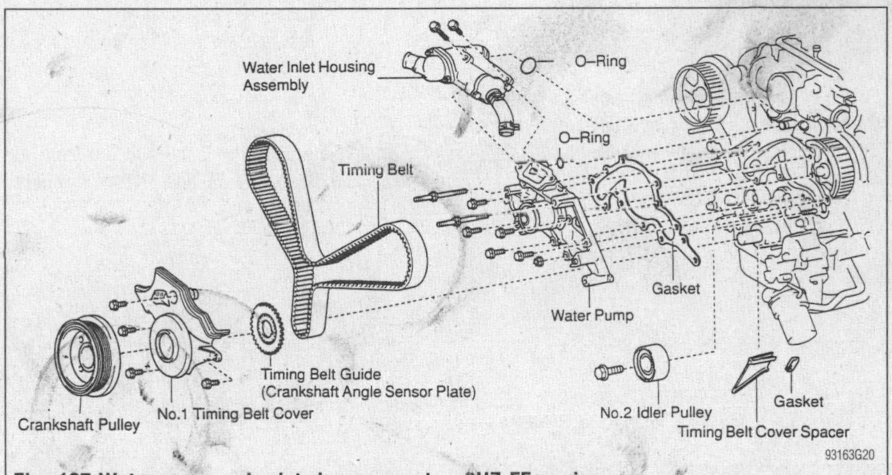

Fig. 107 Water pump and related components—2UZ-FE engine

5. Remove the water inlet and thermostat.
6. Remove the five bolts, two stud bolts and nut and separate the water pump from the engine block. Discard the gasket.

To install:

7. Installation is the reverse of the removal procedure. Clean all parts well. It is good practice to carefully clean all threaded openings, especially those exposed to coolant to remove rust and scale so at assembly, an accurate torque reading is obtained. Remove any old gasket material from the pump and mounting area of the engine using a razor blade and/or gasket scraper. Use care not to gouge aluminum parts.
8. Inspect the pump. Check the air hole (vent) and water holes for coolant leakage. If coolant has been leaking on the timing belt, replace the timing belt. Turn the pump pulley and check that the water pump bearing moves smoothly and quietly. If not, replace the water pump. Check the fan coupling (sometime called the fan clutch). It contains silicone oil. If it is leaking, it must be replaced.
9. Install a new O-ring to the water bypass pipe end. Lubricate with soapy water and connect the water pump to the water bypass pipe end. Using a new gasket, install the water pump. Uniformly tighten the bolts, stud bolts and nut, in several passes. Final torque should be:
   a. Bolts—180 inch lbs. (21 Nm)
   b. Std bolts and nut—156 inch lbs. (18 Nm)
10. Install the water inlet and inlet housing assembly. Use FIPG material. Make sure all old sealer is cleaned off. Apply a $^1/_8$-bead of sealer and install immediately. Tighten the bolts to 156 inch lbs. (18 Nm). Connect the water bypass hose.
11. Install the No. 2 idler pulley.
12. Install the timing belt.
13. Fill the engine with coolant, start the engine and check for leaks. When cool, recheck engine coolant level.

Cylinder Head

REMOVAL & INSTALLATION

2RZ-FE and 3RZ-FE Engines

➧ See Figures 108 thru 116

1. Disconnect the negative battery cable.
2. Drain the engine coolant.
3. Remove the air cleaner cap, Mass Air Flow (MAF) meter, and the resonator.
4. If equipped with a manual transmission, disconnect the accelerator cable from the throttle body.
5. If equipped with a automatic transmission, disconnect the accelerator and throttle cables from the throttle body.
6. Remove the intake air connector, as follows:
   - Air hose for the IAC
   - Vacuum sensing hose
   - Wire clamp for the engine

Fig. 108 Set No. 1 cylinder to TDC compression stroke—2RZ-FE and 3RZ-FE engines

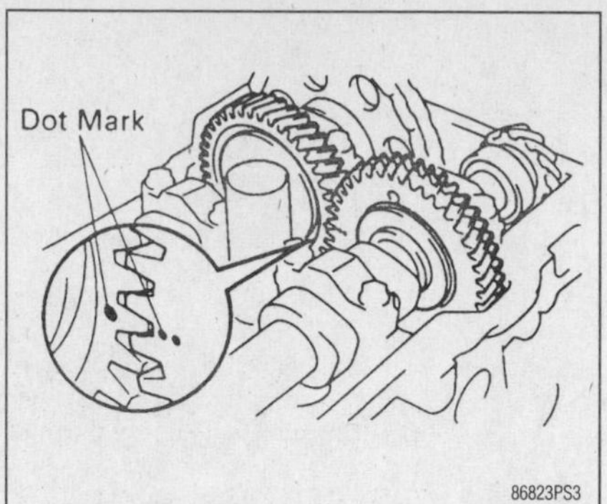

Fig. 109 Check that the marks on the gears are properly aligned—2RZ-FE and 3RZ-FE engines

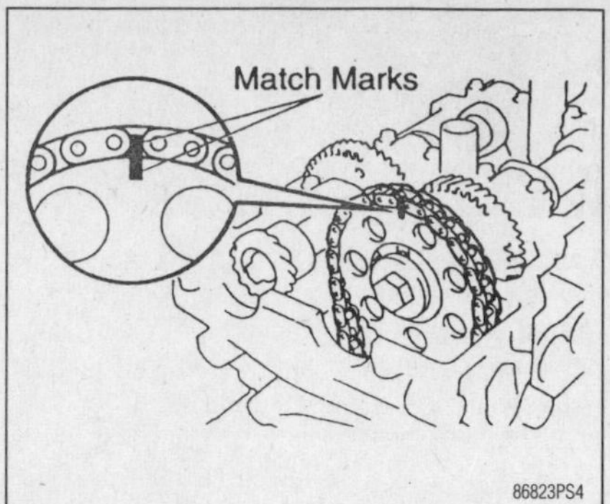

Fig. 110 Matchmark the position of the chain on the gear—2RZ-FE and 3RZ-FE engines

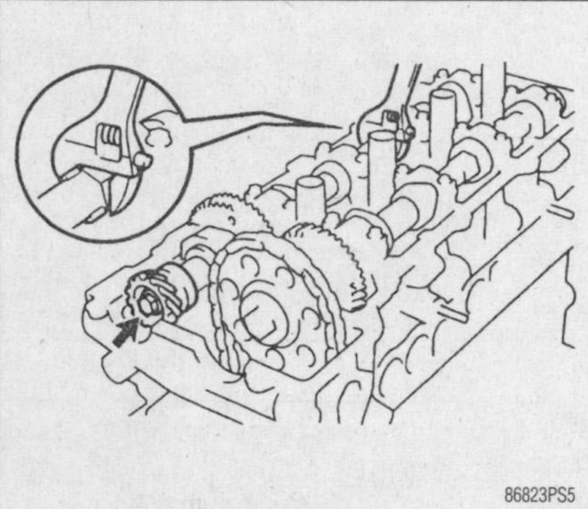

Fig. 111 Hold the hexagon head portion of the camshaft with a wrench and remove the bolt securing the gear—2RZ-FE and 3RZ-FE engines

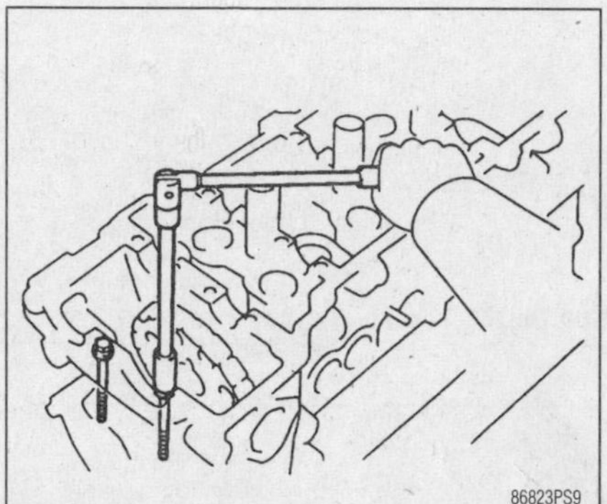

Fig. 112 Remove the 2 bolts at the front of the head first—2RZ-FE and 3RZ-FE engines

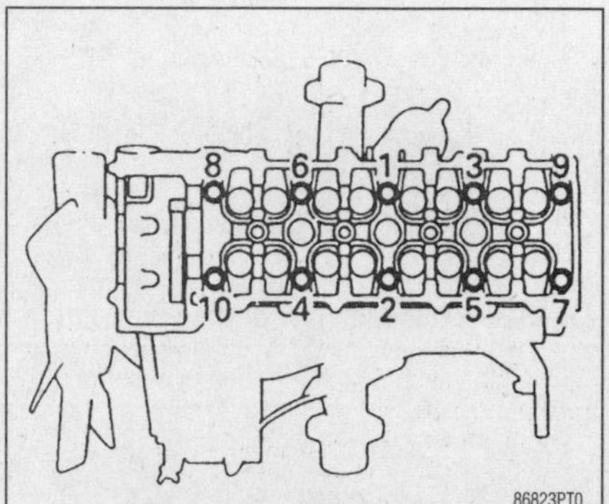

Fig. 113 Remove the cylinder head bolts using this order, in several passes—2RZ-FE and 3RZ-FE engines

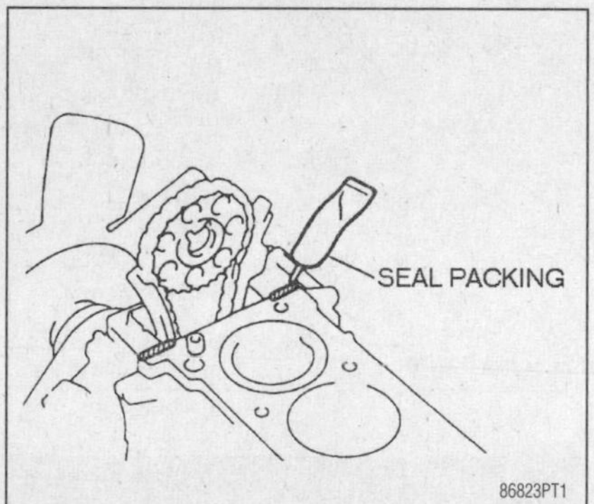

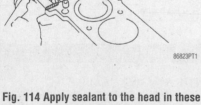

Fig. 114 Apply sealant to the head in these areas—2RZ-FE and 3RZ-FE engines

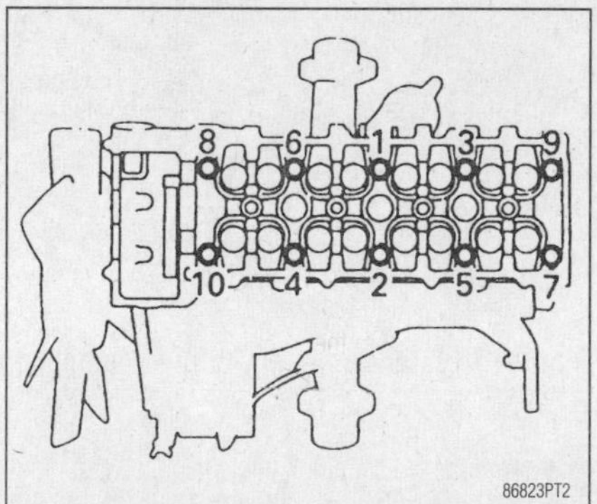

Fig. 115 New head bolts are strongly recommended. Tighten the head bolts down uniformly using this sequence in several passes—2RZ-FE and 3RZ-FE engines

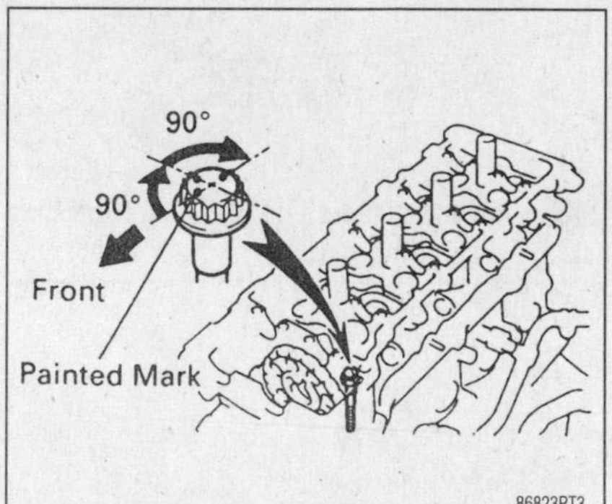

Fig. 116 Mark the front of the bolt with paint and retighten bolts 90 degrees in the proper sequence—2RZ-FE and 3RZ-FE Engines

7. Remove the oil dipstick guide.
8. If equipped with A/C, remove the air conditioning idle-up valve.
9. Remove the power steering drive belt.
10. Remove the idler pulley by removing the three bolts.
11. Remove the power steering drive belt, pump and bracket.
12. Remove the PCV hoses.
13. Remove the distributor connector, hold-down bolts, and the distributor.
14. Remove the water housing as follows:
   a. Disconnect the radiator inlet hose.
   b. Detach the ECT sender gauge connector.
   c. Remove the two bolts, water housing, and the gasket.
15. Remove the throttle body.
16. Tag for identification then disconnect the following harnesses:
   - A/C compressor wiring, if equipped
   - Oil pressure sensor
   - ECT sensor
   - EGR gas temperature sensor
   - EGR Vacuum Switching Valve (VSV)
17. Disconnect the engine wire as follows:
   a. Remove the two bolts and disconnect the engine wire from the intake chamber.
   b. Disconnect the five engine wire clamps and engine wire.
   c. Detach the connectors from the following:
      - Knock sensor
      - Crankshaft position sensor
      - Fuel pressure control VSV
   d. Disconnect the DLC1 from the bracket.
   e. Disconnect the two engine wire clamps.
   f. Remove the bolt, then disconnect the engine wire from the engine.
18. Disconnect the fuel injectors.
19. Remove the cylinder head rear cover by disconnecting the heater bypass hose, then remove the three bolts.

20. Remove the EGR valve and vacuum modulator.

21. Remove the intake chamber stay by removing the two bolts.

CAUTION

Fuel injection systems remain under pressure after the engine has been turned OFF. Properly relieve fuel pressure before disconnecting any fuel lines. Failure to do so may result in fire or personal injury.

22. Unbolt the fuel return pipe and separate from the hoses.

23. Remove the intake chamber as follows:
   a. Disconnect the vacuum hose from the gas filter.
   b. Disconnect the brake booster vacuum hose from the intake chamber.
   c. Remove the three bolts, two nuts, air intake chamber, and the gasket.

24. Remove the fuel inlet tube by removing the union bolts.

25. Remove the delivery pipe (also called the fuel rail) and injectors.

➡Be careful not to drop the injectors when removing the delivery pipe.

26. Remove the intake manifold by removing the three bolts and two nuts.

27. Disconnect the front exhaust pipe from the exhaust manifold.

28. Remove the heat insulator by loosening the two bolts and two nuts.

29. Remove the exhaust manifold and gasket.

30. Remove the engine hangers.

31. Remove the valve cover and gasket.

32. Remove the spark plug wires and plugs from the engine.

33. Set No. 1 cylinder to TDC compression stroke. The groove on the crankshaft pulley should align with the **0** mark on the timing chain cover and the timing marks (one and two dots) of the camshaft gears should form a straight line in respect to the cylinder head surface. If not, turn the crankshaft 1 revolution (360 degrees).

34. Remove the chain tensioner and gasket by removing the two nuts.

35. Remove the camshaft timing gear.

➡Since the thrust clearance of the camshaft is small, the camshaft must be kept level while it is being removed. If the camshaft is not kept level, the portion of the cylinder head receiving the shaft thrust may crack or be damaged, causing the camshaft to seize or break.

36. Remove the exhaust camshaft.

WARNING

When removing the camshaft, make sure that the torsional spring force of the sub-gear has been eliminated by the above operation.

37. Remove the intake camshaft.

➡Do not pry on or attempt to force the camshaft with a tool or other object.

38. Remove the 2 bolts in the front of the head before the other head bolts are removed. Uniformly loosen and remove the remaining head bolts, in several passes, in the sequence shown.

39. Lift the cylinder head from the block and place the head on wooden blocks on a bench.

To install:

40. Clean all parts well. Cylinder head rebuilding is best left to professionals. The head should be cleaned and inspected before installation. More information is available in the Engine Reconditioning section.

➡The head bolts used in this engine are designed to stretch and deform slightly. They should be carefully inspected. New service replacement head bolts are strongly recommended.

41. Before installing, thoroughly clean the gasket mating surfaces and check for warpage.

42. Apply sealant (08826–00080 or equivalent) to the 2 locations, as shown. Place a new head gasket on the block and install the cylinder head.

43. Lightly coat the cylinder head bolts with engine oil. Install the bolts and tighten in several passes in the sequence shown:
   a. Tighten all bolts to 29 ft. lbs. (39 Nm).
   b. Mark the front of the bolt with paint and retighten bolts 90 degrees in the proper sequence.
   c. Retighten an additional 90 degrees. Check that the painted mark is now facing rearward.

44. Install and tighten the 2 front mounting bolts to 15 ft. lbs. (20 Nm).

45. Install the intake camshaft.

46. Install the exhaust camshaft.

47. Set No. 1 cylinder to TDC compression stroke: the crankshaft pulley groove will align with the **0** mark on timing cover and camshafts timing marks with one dot and two dots will be in a straight line on the cylinder head surface.

48. Install the timing gear. Place the gear over the straight pin of the intake camshaft.
   a. Hold the intake camshaft with a wrench. Install and tighten the bolt to 54 ft. lbs. (74 Nm).
   b. Hold the exhaust camshaft and install the bolt and distributor gear. Tighten the bolt to 34 ft. lbs. (46 Nm).

49. Install the chain tensioner, using a new gasket (mark toward the front) as follows:
   a. Release the ratchet pawl, fully push in the plunger and apply the hook to the pin so that the plunger cannot spring out.
   b. Turn the crankshaft pulley clockwise to provide some slack for the chain on the tensioner side.
   c. Push the tensioner by hand until it touches the head installation surface, then install the 2 nuts. Tighten the nuts to 13 ft. lbs. (18 Nm). Check that the hook of the tensioner is not released.
   d. Turn the crankshaft to the left so that the hook of the chain tensioner is released from the pin of the plunger, allowing the plunger to spring out and the slipper to be pushed into the chain.

50. Check and adjust the valve clearance. Intake valve clearance is 0.006–0.010 inch (0.15–0.25mm) and exhaust valve clearance is 0.010–0.014 inch (0.25–0.35mm).

51. Recheck the engine for proper valve timing. Check and adjust the valve clearance.

52. Install the spark plugs and the semi-circular plug.

53. Recheck the engine for proper valve timing. Install the valve cover and engine hangers. Tighten the engine hanger bolts to 30 ft. lbs. (42 Nm).

54. Install the exhaust manifold and gasket to the engine and install the six nuts. Tighten the nuts to 36 ft. lbs. (49 Nm).

55. Install the heat insulator with the two bolts and two nuts. Tighten the bolts and nuts to 48 inch lbs. (6 Nm).

56. Install the front exhaust pipe to the exhaust manifold.

57. Install the intake manifold using a new gasket. Tighten the bolts and nuts to 22 ft. lbs. (29 Nm).

58. Install the injectors and delivery pipe. Tighten the bolts holding the delivery pipe to 15 ft. lbs. (21 Nm).

59. Install the fuel tube with four new gaskets. Tighten the union bolts to 22 ft. lbs. (29 Nm).

60. Install the air intake chamber as follows:
   a. Install a new gasket and the air intake chamber with the three bolts and two nuts. Tighten the bolts and nuts to 15 ft. lbs. (20 Nm).
   b. Connect the vacuum hose to the gas filter.
   c. Connect the brake booster vacuum hose to the intake chamber.

61. Install the fuel return pipe by installing the two bolts and hoses.

62. Install the intake chamber stay by installing the two bolts. Tighten the bolts to 14 ft. lbs. (19 Nm).

63. Install the EGR valve and vacuum modulator.

64. Install the cylinder head rear cover with a new gasket. Tighten the three bolts to 10 ft. lbs. (14 Nm).

65. Connect the heater water bypass pipe.

66. Connect the injector wiring.

67. Connect the engine wire to the engine as follows:
   a. Secure the engine wire to the intake manifold.
   b. Connect the two engine wire clamps.
   c. Attach the DLC1 to the bracket.
   d. Attach all electrical connections, as tagged during removal.

68. Install the throttle body.

69. Install the water outlet with a new gasket. Install the two bolts and tighten the bolts to 14 ft. lbs. (20 Nm). Connect the ECT sender gauge connector and radiator inlet hose.

70. Install the distributor.

71. Install the 2 PCV hoses.

72. Install the power steering pump bracket by installing the four bolts, tighten to 14 ft. lbs. (20 Nm).

73. Install the power steering pump to the bracket.

74. Install the idler pulley with the three bolts, tighten to 14 ft. lbs. (20 Nm).

75. With A/C, install the A/C idle up valve.

76. Install the air intake connector by installing the two bolts, hose clamp, and two air hoses.

77. If equipped with a manual transaxle, connect the accelerator cable to the throttle body.

78. If equipped with a automatic transaxle, connect the throttle and accelerator cables to the throttle body.

79. Install the MAF meter, resonator, and the air cleaner cap.

80. Refill the cooling system. Since coolant can contaminate the oil system when a cylinder head is removed, it is important to drain and refill the engine oil.

81. Connect the negative battery cable. Start the engine and check for leaks.

82. Road test the vehicle for proper operation.

83. Recheck all fluid levels and add as required.

5VZ-FE Engine

➧ See Figures 117, 118, 119, 120, and 121

1. Disconnect the negative battery cable.

93163pe5

Fig. 117 Use a breaker bar and deep socket to remove the cylinder head bolts

2. Relieve the fuel system pressure using the procedures found in Section 4.
3. Remove the engine undercover.
4. Drain the cooling system.

93163pe9

Fig. 118 Removing the cylinder head from the block

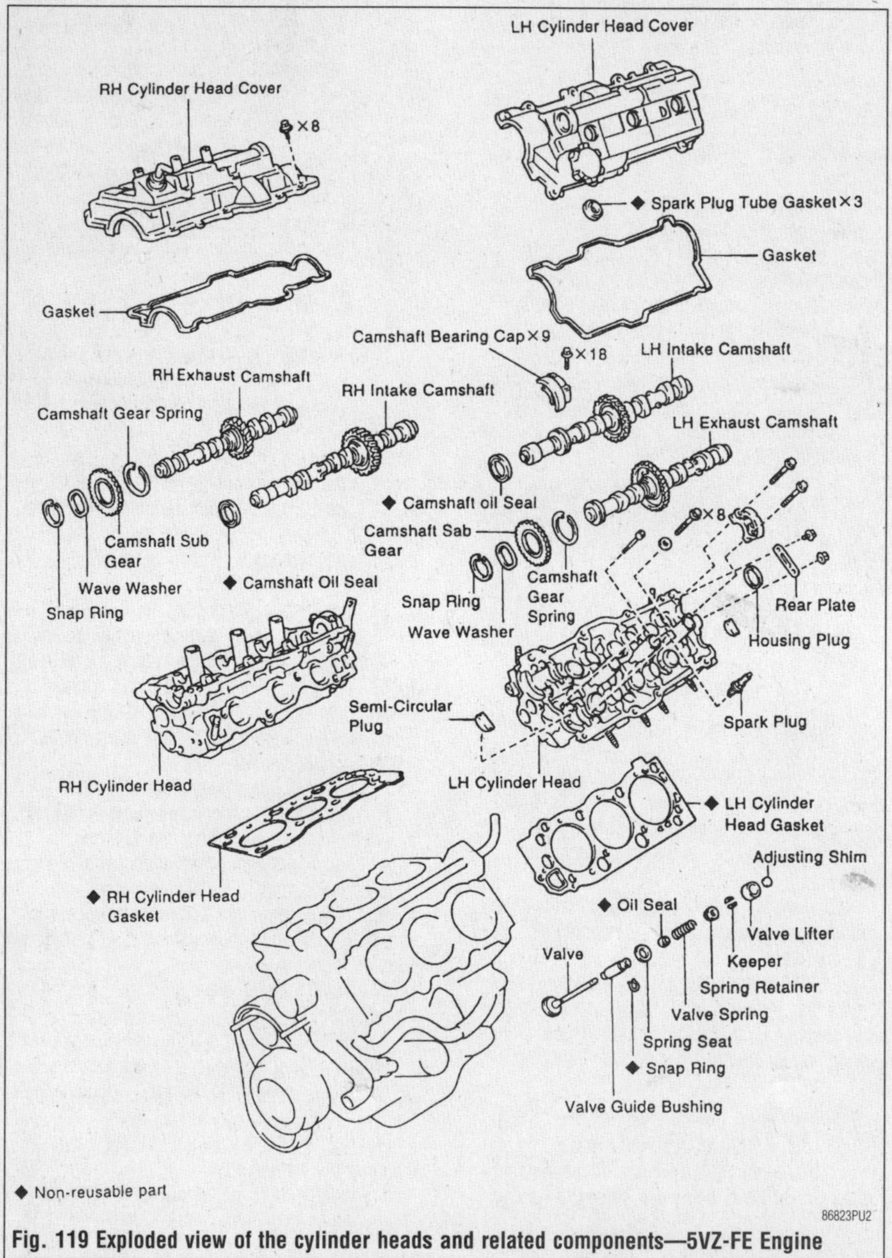

86823PU2

Fig. 119 Exploded view of the cylinder heads and related components—5VZ-FE Engine

5. Remove the front exhaust pipe.
6. Disconnect the air cleaner cap, Mass Air Flow (MAF) meter and the resonator.
7. Disconnect the following cables:
   - Actuator cable with the bracket, if equipped with cruise control
   - Accelerator cable
   - Throttle cable if equipped with an automatic transmission
8. Disconnect the heater hose.
9. Disconnect the upper radiator hose from the engine.
10. Remove the power steering drive belt.
11. Remove the A/C drive belt by loosening the idle pulley nut and adjusting bolt.
12. Loosen the lock bolt, pivot bolt and adjusting bolt and the alternator drive belt.
13. Remove the fan shroud by removing the two clips.
14. Remove the fan with the fluid coupling and fan pulleys.
15. Disconnect the power steering pump from the engine and set aside. Do not disconnect the lines from the pump.
16. If equipped with A/C, remove the compressor from the engine and set aside. Do not disconnect the lines from the compressor.
17. If equipped with A/C, remove the A/C bracket.
18. Remove the spark plug wires with the ignition coils.
19. Remove the spark plugs.
20. Remove the timing belt cover.
21. Remove the fan bracket.
22. Set the No. 1 cylinder at TDC of the compression stroke.
    a. Turn the crankshaft pulley and align its groove with the timing mark **O** of the No. 1 timing belt cover.
    b. Check that the timing marks of the camshaft timing pulleys and the No. 3 timing belt cover are aligned. If not, turn the crankshaft pulley one revolution (360 degrees).

➡If reusing the timing belt, make sure that you can still read the installation marks. If not, place new installation marks on the timing belt to match the timing marks of the camshaft timing pulleys.

23. Remove the timing belt tensioner by alternately loosening the two bolts.
24. Remove the camshaft timing pulleys. Using SST 09960–10010 or equivalent to hold the pulley to keep it from turning, remove the pulley bolt, the timing pulley and the straight pin. Remove the two timing pulleys with the timing belt.
25. Remove the bolt and the idler pulley.
26. Remove the alternator from the engine.
27. Remove the nuts and remove the EGR pipe and two gaskets.
28. Remove the oil filler tube and throttle cable clamp by removing the bolt and two nuts.
29. Remove the intake chamber stay by removing the two bolts.
30. Remove the following connectors:
    - Vacuum Switching Valve (VSV) for the fuel pressure control
    - Throttle Position (TP) sensor
    - IAC valve
    - Disconnect the EGR gas temperature wire
    - Disconnect the VSV wire for the EGR valve
31. Disconnect the following hoses:
    - PCV hoses

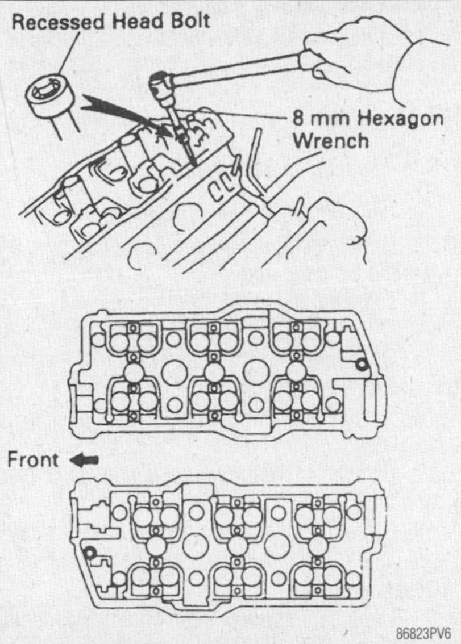

Fig. 120 The recessed bolts must be removed first—5VZ-FE engine

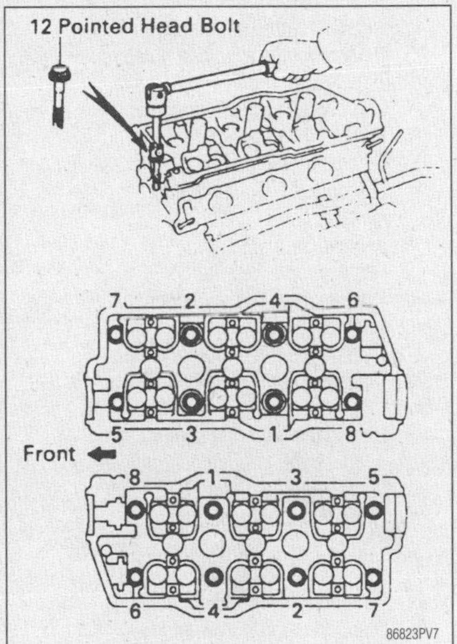

Fig. 121 Cylinder head bolt tightening sequence—5VZ-FE engine

- Water bypass
- Air assist hose from the intake air wire
- Two vacuum sensing hoses from the VSV
- EVAP
- Air hose from the power steering
- If equipped with A/C, disconnect the air hose from the A/C idle up valve.

32. Remove the four bolts, two nuts and remove the air intake chamber assembly from the engine.
33. Remove the intake air connector as follows:
    a. Disconnect the engine wire from the intake air connector by removing the bolt.
    b. Disconnect the two fuel return hoses.
    c. Disconnect the brake booster vacuum hose from the intake air connector.
    d. Remove the bolt and disconnect the ground strap from the intake air harness.
    e. Disconnect the DLC1 from the bracket of the intake air harness.
    f. If equipped with A/C, disconnect idle up valve.
    g. Remove the intake air connector from the engine by removing the three bolts and two nuts.
34. Disconnect the engine wire from the intake manifold as follows:
    a. Tag for identification, then disconnect the wiring from the following:
       - Oil pressure sensor
       - Crankshaft position sensor
       - Six injectors
       - ECT sender gauge
       - ECT sensor
       - Knock sensor
       - Camshaft position sensor
    b. Disconnect the three engine wire clamps.
    c. Remove the three bolts, then disconnect the engine wire from the cylinder head.
35. Remove the camshaft position sensor.
36. Remove the (rear) timing belt cover by removing the six bolts.
37. Remove the fuel pressure regulator.
38. Remove the intake manifold assembly.
39. Remove the power steering pump bracket.
40. Remove the oil dipstick and guide.
41. Remove the exhaust crossover pipe and gaskets by removing the six nuts.
42. Remove the left hand exhaust manifold by unbolting the heat insulator and nuts for the exhaust manifold.
43. Remove the right hand exhaust manifold by unbolting the heat insulator and six nuts for the exhaust manifold.
44. Remove the eight bolts, seal washers, valve cover and gasket. Remove both valve covers.
45. Remove the semi-circular plugs.
46. Remove the right side exhaust camshaft.

✲✲ WARNING

Do not pry on or attempt to force the camshaft with a tool or other object.

47. Remove the right side intake camshaft.
48. Remove the left side exhaust camshaft.
49. Remove the left side intake camshaft.
50. Remove the valve lifters and shims from the cylinder head. Arrange the valve lifters and shims in correct order.
51. Using a 8mm hexagon wrench, remove the cylinder head (recessed head) bolt on each cylinder head, then repeat for the other side.
52. Uniformly loosen and remove the eight cylinder head (12 pointed head) bolts on each cylinder head. Loosen the bolts in several passes using the reverse of the tightening sequence.
53. Remove the 16 cylinder head bolts and flat washers.
54. Lift the cylinder head from the dowels on the cylinder block.

To install:

55. Clean all parts well. Cylinder head rebuilding is best left to professionals. The head should be cleaned and inspected before installation. More information is available in the Engine Reconditioning section.

➡The head bolts used in this engine are designed to stretch and deform slightly. They should be carefully inspected. New service replacement head bolts are strongly recommended.

56. Place two new cylinder head gaskets in position on the cylinder block.
57. Place the two cylinder heads on the dowels of the cylinder block.
58. Apply a light coat of engine oil on the threads and under the heads of the cylinder head bolts.
59. Install and uniformly tighten the cylinder head bolts on each cylinder as follows:
    a. In several passes and in the sequence shown, tighten the cylinder bolts to 25 ft. lbs. (34 Nm).
    b. Mark the front of the cylinder head bolt with paint.
    c. Retighten the cylinder head bolts by 90 degrees in order.
    d. Check that the painted mark is now at a 90 degrees angle to the front.
60. Apply a light coat of engine oil on the threads and under the heads of the recessed cylinder head bolts. Using a 8mm hexagon wrench, install the cylinder head bolt on each cylinder head, then repeat for the other side. Tighten the bolts to 13 ft. lbs. (18 Nm).
61. Install the valve lifters and shims. Check that the valve lifter rotates smoothly by hand.
62. Install the right intake camshaft.
63. Install the right exhaust camshaft.
64. Install the left intake camshaft.
65. Install the left exhaust camshaft.
66. Check and adjust the valve clearance.
67. Install the semi circular plugs.
68. Install the cylinder head covers. Uniformly tighten the bolts in several passes to 53 inch lbs. (6 Nm).
69. Attach the exhaust manifolds with new gaskets, tighten the nuts to 30 ft. lbs. (40 Nm).
70. Install the exhaust manifold heat insulators with the nuts, tighten to 71 inch lbs. (8 Nm).
71. Install the exhaust crossover pipe and tighten the nuts to 33 ft. lbs. (45 Nm).
72. Install the alternator bracket and tighten to 14 ft. lbs. (18 Nm).
73. Install the oil dipstick and guide using a new O-ring.
74. Install the power steering bracket and tighten to 14 ft. lbs. (18 Nm).
75. Install two new gaskets and the intake manifold assembly. Install the four flat washers, eight bolts and four nuts. Tighten the bolts and nuts to 13 ft. lbs. (18 Nm).
76. Install the intake manifold stay with the two bolts. Tighten the bolts to 14 ft. lbs. (18 Nm).
77. Connect the fuel inlet hose.
78. Install the fuel pressure regulator.
79. Install the timing belt cover with the six bolts. Tighten the bolts to 80 inch lbs. (9 Nm).
80. Install the camshaft position sensor, tighten to 71 inch lbs. (8 Nm).
81. Connect the engine wire to the intake manifold as follows:
    a. Install the engine wire to the cylinder head by installing the three bolts.
    b. Connect the three engine wire clamps.
    c. Attach the electrical connectors that were detached, as tagged during removal.
82. Install the intake air connector as follows:
    a. Install the intake manifold to the engine by installing the three bolts and two nuts. Tighten the bolts and nuts to 14 ft. lbs. (19 Nm).
    b. Attach the DLC1 to the bracket on the intake manifold.

c. Attach the ground strap to the intake manifold by installing the bolt.
d. Connect the brake booster vacuum hose to the intake air connector.
e. Connect the two fuel return hoses.
f. Connect the engine wire to the intake manifold by installing the bolt.
g. If equipped with A/C, attach the idle up valve connector.
83. Install the air intake chamber assembly to the engine by installing the four bolts and two nuts. Tighten the bolts and nuts to 14 ft. lbs. (19 Nm).
84. Connect all hoses disconnected during removal.
85. Attach the following connectors:
- VSV for the fuel pressure control
- Throttle position sensor
- Idle Air Control (IAC) Valve
- Connect the EGR gas temperature sensor
- Connect the VSV wire for the EGR valve

86. Install the intake chamber stay. Tighten to 30 ft. lbs. (40 Nm)
87. Install a new O-ring to the oil filler tube. Push in the oil filler tube end into the tube hole in the oil pan. Install the oil filler tube and throttle cable clamp and install the bolt and two nuts.
88. Install two new gaskets and the EGR pipe with the nuts. Tighten the clamp nuts to 71 inch lbs. (8 Nm) and the EGR pipe nuts to 14 ft. lbs. (19 Nm).
89. Install the alternator but do not tighten the bolts and nuts at this time.
90. Install the timing belt idler with the bolt, tighten to 30 ft. lbs. (40 Nm). Check that the pulley bracket moves smoothly.
91. Install the left camshaft timing pulley as follows:
a. Install the knock pin to the camshaft.
b. Align the knock pin hole of the camshaft with the knock pin groove of the timing pulley.
c. Slide the timing pulley on the camshaft with the flange side facing outward. Tighten the pulley bolt to 81 ft. lbs. (110 Nm).
92. Set the No. 1 cylinder to TDC of the compression stroke:
a. Turn the crankshaft pulley, and align its groove with the timing mark **0** of the timing belt cover.
b. Turn the camshaft, align the knock pin hole of the camshaft with the timing mark of the timing belt cover.
c. Turn the camshaft timing pulley, align the timing marks of the camshaft timing pulley and the timing belt cover.
93. Connect the timing belt to the left camshaft timing pulley. Check that the installation mark on the timing belt is aligned with the end of the timing belt cover.
a. Using SST 09960–01000 or equivalent, slightly turn the left camshaft timing pulley clockwise. Align the installation mark on the timing belt with the timing mark of the camshaft timing pulley, and hang the timing belt on the left camshaft timing pulley.
b. Align the timing marks of the left camshaft pulley and the timing belt cover.
c. Check that the timing belt has tension between the crankshaft timing pulley and the left camshaft timing pulley.
94. Install the right camshaft timing pulley and the timing belt as follows:
a. Align the installation mark on the timing belt with the timing mark of the right camshaft timing pulley, and hang the timing belt on the right camshaft timing pulley with the flange side facing inward.
b. Slide the right camshaft timing pulley on the camshaft. Align the timing marks on the right camshaft timing pulley and the timing belt cover.
c. Align the knock pin hole of the camshaft with the knock pin groove of the pulley and install the knock pin. Install the bolt and tighten to 81 ft. lbs. (110 Nm).
95. Set the timing belt tensioner as follows:
a. Using a press, slowly press in the pushrod.
b. Align the holes of the pushrod and housing, pass a 1.5mm hexagon wrench through the holes to keep the setting position of the pushrod.
c. Release the press and install the dust boot to the tensioner.
96. Install the timing belt tensioner and alternately tighten the bolts to 20 ft. lbs. (28 Nm). Using pliers, remove the 1.5mm hexagon wrench from the belt tensioner.
97. Slowly turn the crankshaft pulley two revolutions from the TDC to TDC. Always turn the crankshaft pulley clockwise. Check that each pulley aligns with the timing marks. If the timing marks do not align, remove the timing belt and reinstall it.
98. Install the fan bracket with the bolt and nut.
99. Install the power steering adjusting strut with the nut.
100. Install the timing belt cover, tighten the bolts to 80 inch lbs. (9 Nm).
101. Connect the three clamps for the spark plug wires to the timing belt cover.
102. Connect the camshaft position sensor connector to the timing belt cover.
103. Install the spark plugs.
104. Install the spark plug wires with the ignition coils.
105. If equipped, install the A/C compressor bracket.
106. If equipped, install the A/C compressor.
107. Install the fan with the fluid coupling and fan pulleys, tighten the nuts to 48 inch lbs. (5 Nm).
108. Install the fan shroud.
109. Install the alternator drive belt.
110. Install the cooling fan, then tighten the nuts to 4 ft. lbs. (5 Nm).
111. If equipped, install and adjust the A/C drive belt.
112. Install the power steering pump, pump pulley and the drive belt.
113. Connect the upper radiator hose.
114. Connect the heater hose.
115. Connect the following cables:
- On cruise control, attach the actuator cable with bracket
- Accelerator cable
- With A/T, the throttle cable

116. Install the MAF meter, resonator and air cleaner cap.
117. Install the front exhaust pipe.
118. Fill the radiator with engine coolant.
119. Because coolant can contaminate the oil system when cylinder heads are removed, it is important to drain the oil and refill with fresh oil. A filter change is recommended.
120. Connect the negative battery cable.
121. Start the engine and check for leaks.
122. Check the ignition timing.
123. Install the engine undercover.
124. Road test the vehicle.
125. Recheck all fluid levels and add as required.

1FZ-FE Engine

➧ See Figures 122 thru 128

1. Relieve the fuel system pressure.
2. Disconnect the battery cables and remove the battery and the battery tray.
3. Drain the engine coolant.
4. Remove the air cleaner hose and cap.
5. Disconnect the cruise control actuator cable from the throttle body.
6. Disconnect the accelerator cable from the throttle body.
7. Disconnect the throttle cable from the throttle body.
8. Disconnect the engine ground strap from the engine hanger and the ground strap from the air intake chamber.
9. Unplug the connector on the intake manifold from the left fender apron.
10. Disconnect the brake booster vacuum hose.
11. Disconnect the EVAP hose and disconnect the fuel return hose.
12. Disconnect the heater hoses.
13. Disconnect the engine wire and heater valve from the cowl panel.
14. Remove the cylinder head covers
15. Remove the distributor.
16. Disconnect the power steering reservoir tank.
17. Disconnect the radiator inlet hose and the water bypass hose.
18. Remove the alternator.
19. Remove the throttle body.
20. Remove the oil dipsticks and guides for the engine and transmission.
21. Remove the intake manifold stay.
22. Disconnect the fuel inlet hose from the fuel filter.
23. Unplug the following connectors:
a. ECT sender gauge connector, the ECT cut switch connector, and the ECT sensor connector
b. Knock sensor connector
c. Crankshaft position sensor connector
24. Remove the bolt and disconnect the engine wire harness from the cylinder block.
25. Disconnect the following:
a. Oil level sensor connector
b. Two connectors from the transmission
c. Starter connector
d. Two heated oxygen sensor connectors
e. Park/Neutral Position (PNP) switch connector
26. Remove the two bolts and disconnect the engine wire from the intake manifold and the cylinder block
27. Disconnect the PCV hose from the PCV valve
28. Remove the bolt holding the engine wire to the intake manifold
29. Unplug the connector for the emission control valve set assembly and the three injector connectors
30. Disconnect the engine wire harness clamp
31. Disconnect the EGR gas temperature sensor connector
32. Disconnect the clamp of the No. 6 injector wire from the bracket
33. Disconnect the engine wire harness from the cylinder head and the intake manifold

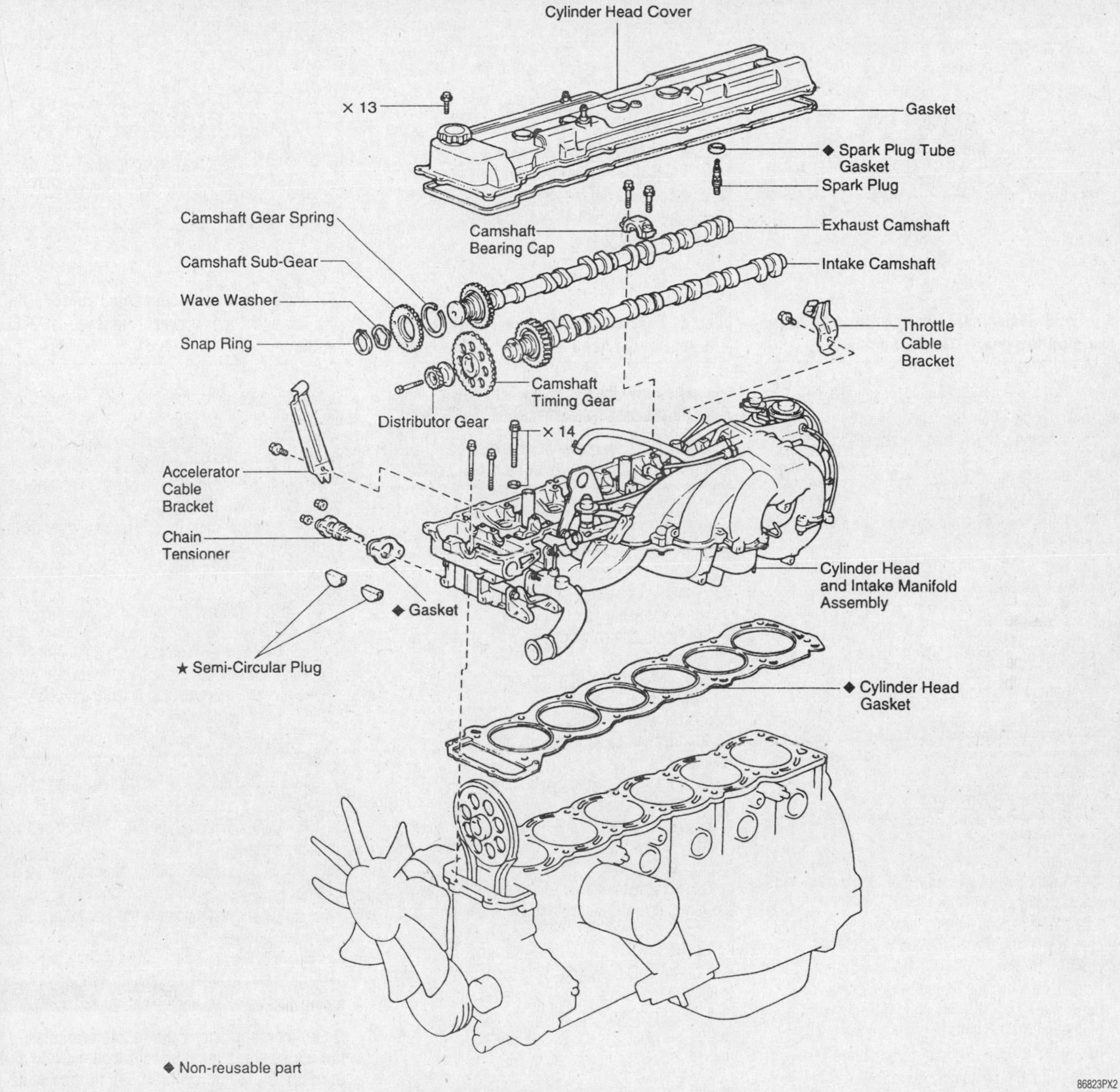

Fig. 122 Exploded view of the cylinder head components—1FZ-FE engine

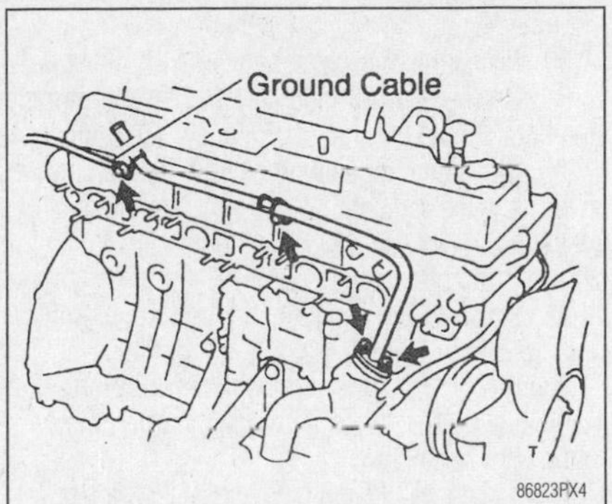

Fig. 123 The ground cable is secured to the front of the heater pipe—1FZ-FE engine

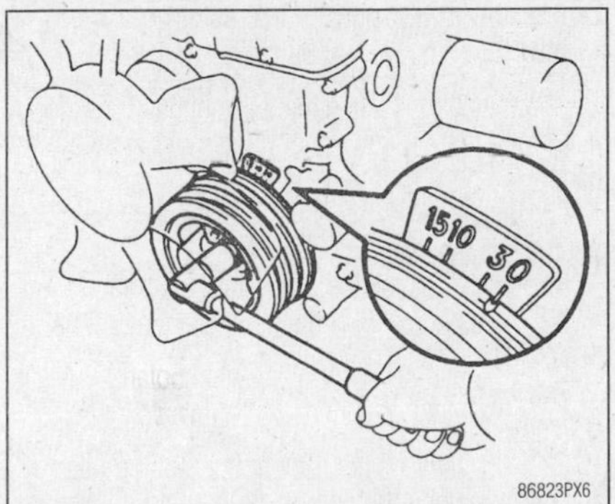

Fig. 124 Turn the crankshaft pulley and align its groove with the 0 mark on the timing chain cover—1FZ-FE engine

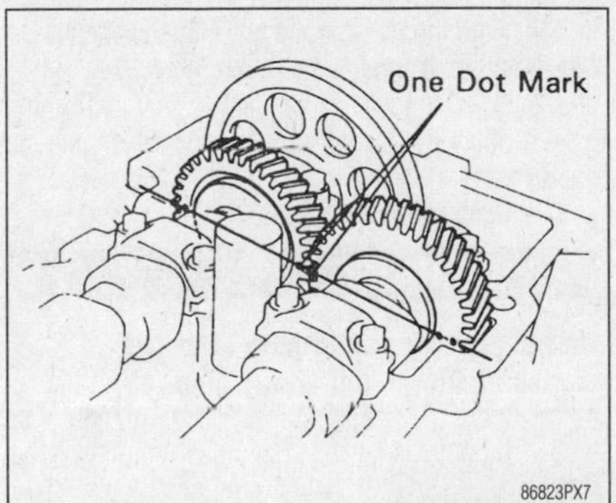

Fig. 125 Check that the marks on the camshaft pulley are aligned—1FZ-FE engine

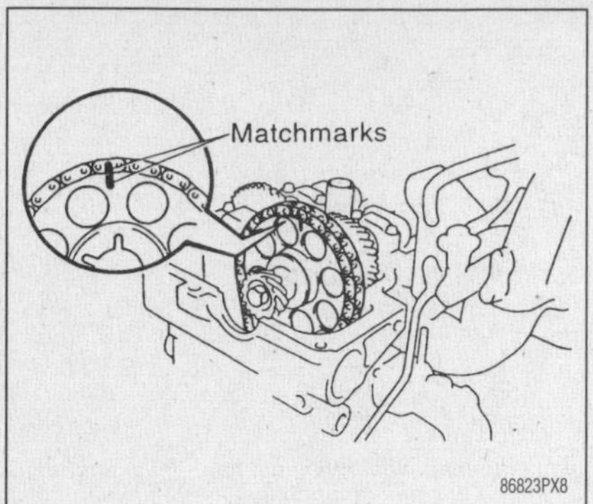

Fig. 126 Matchmark the position of the chain on the gear—1FZ-FE engine

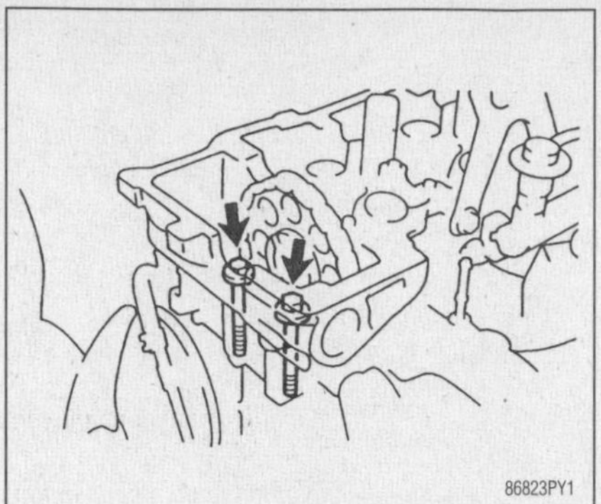

Fig. 127 Remove these two bolts prior to the rest of the head bolts—1FZ-FE engine

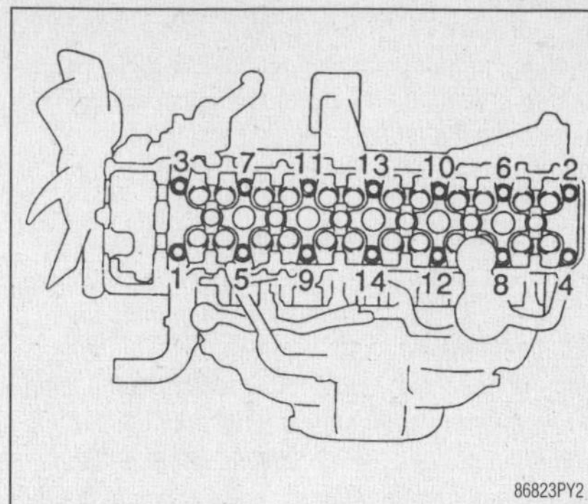

Fig. 128 Uniformly loosen and remove the 14 head bolts in several passes—1FZ-FE engine

34. Remove the three bolts and disconnect the water bypass pipe from the cylinder head.
35. Disconnect the heated oxygen sensor connector.
36. Remove the nuts and bolts holding the front exhaust pipe to the rear TWC.
37. Disconnect the front exhaust pipe and remove the gasket.
38. Remove the clamp from the support bracket and remove the bracket.
39. Remove the front exhaust pipe and the gaskets.
40. Remove the exhaust manifolds.
41. Remove the heat insulators.
42. Remove the ground cable, heater pipe and gasket.
43. Remove the water bypass outlet and the pipe. Remove the three O-rings from the water bypass outlet and the pipe.
44. Remove the valve cover.
45. Remove the semi–circular plug from the cylinder head.
46. Remove the spark plugs.
47. Set the No. 1 cylinder to TDC of the compression stroke as follows:
    a. Turn the crankshaft pulley and align its groove with the **0** mark on the timing chain cover.
    b. Check that the timing marks (one and two dots) of the camshaft drive and driven gears are in straight line on the cylinder head surface. If not, turn the crankshaft one revolution (360 degrees) and align the marks as above.
48. Remove the chain tensioner.
49. Place matchmarks on the camshaft timing gear and the timing chain.
50. Hold the intake camshaft with a wrench and remove the bolt and the distributor gear.
51. Remove the camshaft timing gear and chain from the intake camshaft and leave on the slipper and the damper.
52. Remove the camshafts.

⁂ WARNING

Do not pry on or attempt to force the camshaft with a tool or any other object.

53. Remove the two bolts in the front of the head first.
54. Loosen and remove the 14 cylinder head bolts in sequence using several passes.

⁂ WARNING

Cylinder head warpage or cracking could result from removing bolts in incorrect order.

55. Lift the cylinder head from the dowels on the cylinder block and place the cylinder head on wooden blocks on the bench. If the cylinder head is difficult to lift off, pry between the cylinder head and the cylinder block with a flat prying tool.
56. Remove the alternator bracket.
57. Remove the two nuts, the water outlet, and the gasket.
58. Loosen the union nut and remove the EGR pipe and gasket.
59. Remove the heater inlet pipe and hose.
60. Remove the air intake chamber and the intake manifold assembly.
61. Remove the water bypass hose.
62. Remove the engine hanger brackets.
63. Remove the two engine wire clamp brackets.
64. Remove the accelerator cable bracket and the throttle cable bracket.
65. Remove the valve lifters and shims. Arrange the valve lifters and shims in correct order for reinstallation.

To install:

66. Clean all parts well. Cylinder head rebuilding is best left to professionals. The head should be cleaned and inspected before installation. More information is available in the Engine Reconditioning section.

➡The head bolts used in this engine are designed to stretch and deform slightly. They should be carefully inspected. New service replacement head bolts are strongly recommended.

67. Install the valve lifters and shims. Check to make sure that the valve lifter rotates smoothly by hand.
68. Install the accelerator cable bracket and the throttle cable bracket.
69. Install the engine wire clamp brackets.
70. Install the engine hangers. Tighten to 30 ft. lbs. (41 Nm).
71. Install the air intake chamber and intake manifold assembly.
72. Install the heater hose to the cylinder head, and connect the pipe to the intake manifold. Tighten the bolts to 15 ft. lbs. (21 Nm).
73. Temporarily install the union nut to the EGR valve. Install the EGR pipe to the cylinder head. Tighten the bolts to 15 ft. lbs. (21 Nm). Tighten the union nut to 58 ft. lbs. (78 Nm).
74. Install a new gasket and the water outlet. Tighten the nuts to 15 ft. lbs. (21 Nm).
75. Install the alternator bracket and tighten the bolts to 32 ft. lbs. (43 Nm).
76. Apply sealant on the end of the engine block by the timing belt.
77. Install a new cylinder head gasket on the cylinder block.
78. Install the cylinder head.
79. Install the cylinder head bolts as follows:
    a. The cylinder head bolts are tightened in three progressive steps. Apply a light coat of engine oil on the threads and under the heads of the cylinder head bolts.
    b. Install the 14 cylinder head bolts and tighten progressively in sequence to 29 ft. lbs. (39 Nm). Use the reverse of the loosening sequence.
    c. Mark the front of the cylinder head bolt head with paint.
    d. Retighten the cylinder head bolts by 90 degrees in numerical order.
    e. Retighten the cylinder head bolts an additional 90 degrees so that the painted mark is now facing to the rear.

⁂ WARNING

Do not combine steps D and E in one pass; the above steps must be followed exactly and in order to prevent cylinder head damage or pre-mature gasket failure.

    f. Install and tighten the two bolts at the front of the head to 15 ft. lbs. (21 Nm).
80. Install the camshafts.
81. Set the No. 1 cylinder to TDC of the compression stroke. Turn the crankshaft pulley, and align its groove with the timing mark **0** of the timing chain cover. Turn the camshaft so that the timing marks with one and two dots will be in straight line on the cylinder head surface.
82. Install the camshaft timing gear as follows:
    a. Check that the matchmarks on the camshaft timing gear and the timing chain are aligned. Place the gear over the straight pin of the intake camshaft.
    b. Align the straight pin of the distributor gear with the straight pin groove of the intake camshaft gear.

c. Hold the intake camshaft with a wrench, install and tighten the bolt to 54 ft. lbs. (74 Nm).

83. Install the chain tensioner. Push the tensioner by hand until it touches the head installation surface, then install and tighten the two nuts to 15 ft. lbs. (21 Nm).

84. Turn the crankshaft pulley, and align its groove with the timing mark **0** of the timing chain cover. Always turn the crankshaft clockwise. Check that the timing marks (one and two dots) of the camshaft drive and driven gears are in straight line on the cylinder head surface. If not, turn the crankshaft one revolution (360 degrees) and align the marks.

85. Check valve clearance and adjust if necessary.

86. Install the spark plugs.

87. Install the semi-circular plug to the cylinder head.

88. Make sure that the No. 1 cylinder is in TDC of the compression stroke.

89. Install the valve cover.

90. Install the water bypass outlet and the pipe as flows:

a. Install a new O-ring to the water bypass outlet. Install new O-rings to the water bypass pipe.

b. Assemble the water bypass outlet and the pipe and install with the two bolts tightened to 15 ft. lbs. (21 Nm).

91. Install the heater pipe and the ground cable. Tighten the heater pipe bolt to 14 ft. lbs. (20 Nm) and the nut to 15 ft. lbs. (21 Nm).

92. Install the exhaust manifolds. Tighten the nuts to 29 ft. lbs. (39 Nm).

93. Install the insulator and heat insulator and tighten the bolts to 14 ft. lbs. (20 Nm).

94. Install the front exhaust pipe. Tighten the nuts to 46 ft. lbs. (63 Nm).

95. Install the support bracket and tighten to 17 ft. lbs. (24 Nm).

96. Connect the clamp and tighten the clamp bolt to 14 ft. lbs. (20 Nm).

97. Connect the front exhaust pipe to the rear catalytic converter and tighten the bolts to 34 ft. lbs. (46 Nm).

98. Connect the water bypass pipe to the cylinder head and tighten the bolts to 14 ft. lbs. (20 Nm).

99. Connect the following:

a. Connect the engine wire harness to the cylinder head and the intake manifold

b. Connect the clamp of the No. 6 injector wire to the bracket

c. Connect the EGR gas temperature sensor connector

d. Connect the engine wire harness clamp

e. Attach the connector for the emission control valve set assembly and the three injector connectors

f. Install the bolt holding the engine wire to the intake manifold

g. Connect the PCV hose from the PCV valve

h. Install the two bolts and connect the engine wire to the intake manifold and the cylinder block

i. Connect the Park/Neutral Position (PNP) switch connector

j. Connect the two heated oxygen sensor connectors

k. Starter connector

l. Two connectors to the transmission

m. Oil level sensor connector

100. Install the bolt and connect the engine wire harness from the cylinder block.

101. Engage the following connectors:

a. ECT sender gauge connector, the ECT cut switch connector, and the ECT sensor connector

b. Knock sensor connector

c. Crankshaft position sensor connector

102. Connect the fuel inlet hose to the fuel filter with the union bolt. Tighten to 22 ft. lbs. (29 Nm).

103. Install the intake manifold stay and tighten the bolts to 26 ft. lbs. (36 Nm).

104. Install the oil dipsticks and the guides for the engine and the transmission. Tighten the oil dipstick guide bolts to 14 ft. lbs. (20 Nm).

105. Install the throttle body.

106. Install the alternator and the drive belts.

107. Connect the water bypass hose.

108. Connect the radiator inlet hose.

109. Connect the power steering reservoir tank and tighten the bolts to 14 ft. lbs. (20 Nm).

110. Install the distributor.

111. Install the cylinder head covers.

112. Connect the heater valve and the engine wire harness to the cowl panel.

113. Connect the heater hoses.

114. Connect the fuel return hose, the EVAP hose, and the brake booster vacuum hose.

115. Attach the connector on the intake manifold to the left fender apron.

116. Connect the ground strap to the engine hanger and the air intake chamber.

117. Attach the throttle cable to the throttle body. Adjust the throttle cable.

118. Connect the accelerator cable to the throttle body.

119. Connect the cruise control actuator cable to the throttle body.

120. Install the air cleaner hose and cap.

121. Install the battery tray, the battery, and connect the cables.

122. Refill the engine coolant.

123. Because coolant can contaminate the oil system when a cylinder head is removed, drain and refill the engine oil. A filter change is recommended.

124. Start the engine and check for leaks.

125. Make necessary engine adjustments.

126. Road test the vehicle and recheck the engine coolant level.

2UZ-FE Engine

➧ **See Figures 129 thru 142**

This is a lengthy and complicated procedure requiring careful and precise work.

1. Disconnect the negative battery cable.
2. Drain the engine coolant.
3. Remove the throttle body cover.
4. Disconnect the timing belt from the camshaft pulleys. For additional information, please refer to the following topic(s): Timing Belt Removal and Installation. Use care when working around the timing belt. Do not allow anything to drop inside the timing belt cover. Do not allow the timing belt to come into contact with oil, water or dust.
5. Remove the camshaft timing pulleys. Please see the timing belt procedure in this section.
6. Remove the camshaft position sensor by removing the bolt and stud bolt and then removing the sensor.
7. Disconnect the power steering pump from the engine by disconnecting the lines from the steering gear assembly.
8. Disconnect the front exhaust pipe.
9. Remove the automatic transmission dipstick and tube.
10. Remove the ignition coils.
11. Remove the three bolts and the stud bolt and remove the left side and right side timing belt rear plates.
12. Disconnect the fuel lines.
13. Tag and detach the following electrical connectors:
    - Throttle Position (TP) sensor
    - Accelerator pedal position sensor connector
    - Throttle control motor connector
    - VSV connector for the EVAP system
    - Eight fuel injector connectors
    - Engine Coolant Temperature (ECT) sensor
    - Water sender gauge connector
    - Eight ignition coil connectors
    - Two heated oxygen sensor connectors
14. Tag for identification and disconnect the following hoses:
    - Vacuum hose from the fuel pressure regulator
    - PCV hose from the PCV valve on the left side cylinder head
    - EVAP hose from the charcoal canister from the VSV for the EVAP system
    - EVAP hose from the charcoal canister from the EVAP pipe on the intake manifold
    - Power steering vacuum switch lines from the intake manifold
    - Brake booster vacuum line
15. Remove the upper and lower intake manifolds.
16. If necessary, remove the water inlet and inlet housing assembly.
17. Remove the 18 bolts and seal washers from the cylinder head covers and remove the covers and gaskets. If necessary, remove semi-circular plugs and camshaft housing plugs.

✲✲ WARNING

Since the thrust clearance of the camshaft is small, the camshaft must be kept level while it is being removed. If the camshaft is not kept level, the portion of the head receiving the shaft thrust may crack or be damaged, causing the camshaft to seize or break. To avoid this, the following steps should be carried out.

18. Remove the camshafts using the following procedure.

a. Check the crankshaft pulley position. Check that the timing mark of the crankshaft pulley is aligned with the centers of the crankshaft pulley bolt and the idler pulley.

✲✲ WARNING

Having the crankshaft pulley at the wrong angle can cause the piston head and valve head to come into contact with each other when you remove the camshaft, causing damage. Always set the crankshaft pulley at the correct angle.

b. Remove the right side camshafts. Bring the service bolt hole of the sub-gear upward by turning the hexagon wrench portion of the exhaust camshaft with a wrench. Secure the sub-gear to the main gear with a bolt 6mm in diameter x 1.0mm thread pitch x 16–20mm long.

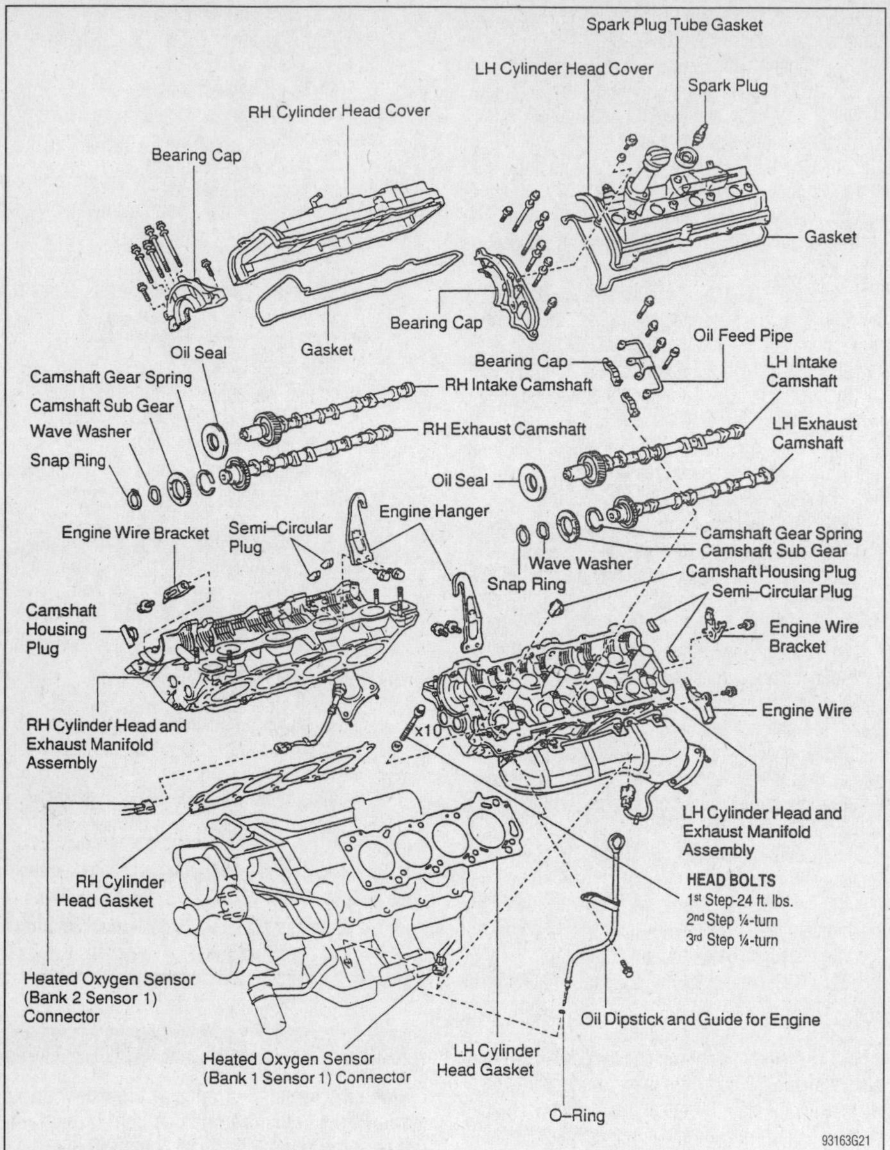

93163G21

Fig. 129 Cylinder heads, camshafts and related components—2UZ-FE engine

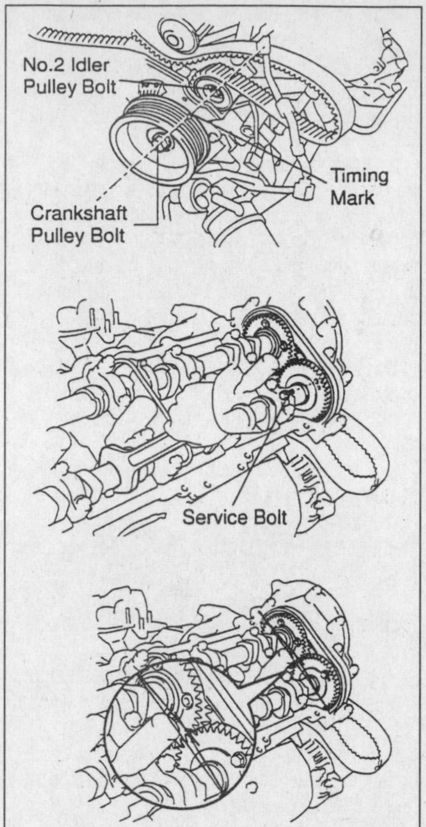

93163G22

Fig. 130 Set up the engine and align the timing marks before right side camshaft removal. Note the 6mm bolt used to lock together the two-piece cam gear—2UZ-FE engine

⁂ WARNING

When removing the camshafts, make sure that the torsion spring force of the sub-gear has been eliminated by the above operation.

c. Set the timing mark (one dot mark) of the camshaft main gear at an angle approximately 10 degrees above horizontal by turning the hexagon wrench portion of the exhaust camshaft with a wrench.

d. Uniformly loosen and remove the 22 bearing cap bolts in several passes, in the sequence illustrated.

e. Remove the oil feed pipe, the bearing caps and the camshafts.

f. Remove the left side camshafts. Bring the service bolt hole of the sub-gear upward by turning the hexagon wrench portion of the exhaust camshaft with a wrench. Secure the sub-gear to the main gear with a bolt 6mm in diameter x 1.0mm thread pitch x 16–20mm long.

⁂ WARNING

When removing the camshafts, make sure that the torsion spring force of the sub-gear has been eliminated by the above operation.

g. Align timing marks (two dot marks) of the camshaft drive gear by turning the hexagon wrench portion of the exhaust camshaft with a wrench.

h. Uniformly loosen and remove the 22 bearing cap bolts in several passes, in the sequence illustrated. Note that there are five different length bearing cap bolts that, at assembly, MUST be returned to their proper locations. Mark these bolts or place in holes punched through cardboard to make sure they will be in the proper location and sequence. Take the time to accurately measure each bolt and mark its length on the cardboard. The reason for this is that at assembly, certain lengths of bolts are handled differently, and they are identified by length.

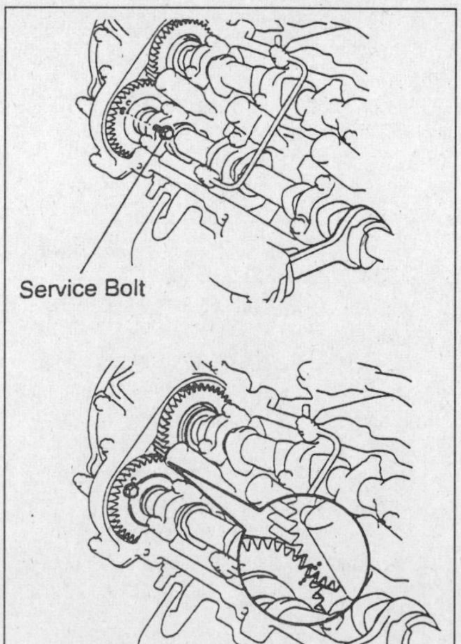

93163G23

Fig. 131 Set up the engine and align the timing marks before left side camshaft removal. Note the 6mm bolt used to lock together the two-piece cam gear—2UZ-FE engine

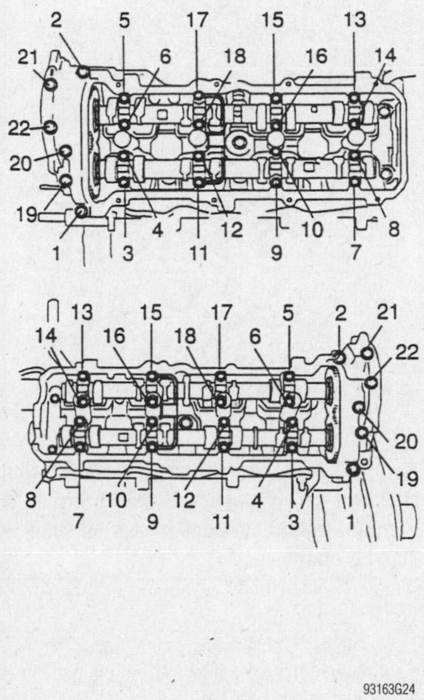

Fig. 132 Use this sequence to loosen the camshaft bearing cap bolts. Top—Left Side Bank; Bottom—Right Side Bank—2UZ-FE engine

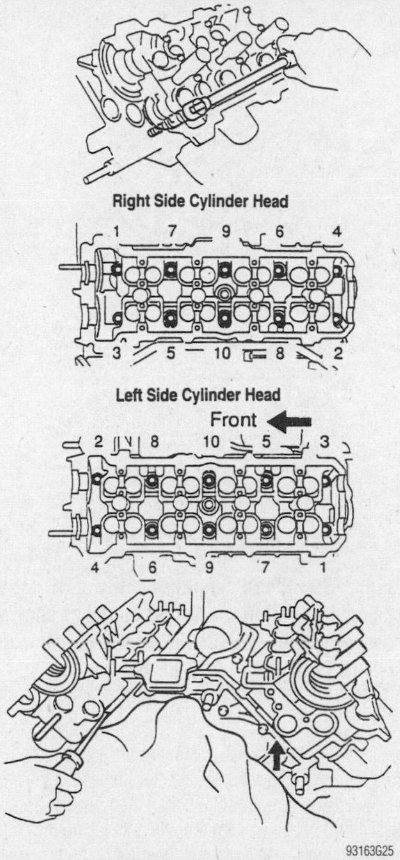

Fig. 133 Use this sequence to loosen the cylinder head bolts. If necessary, carefully pry where indicated—2UZ-FE engine

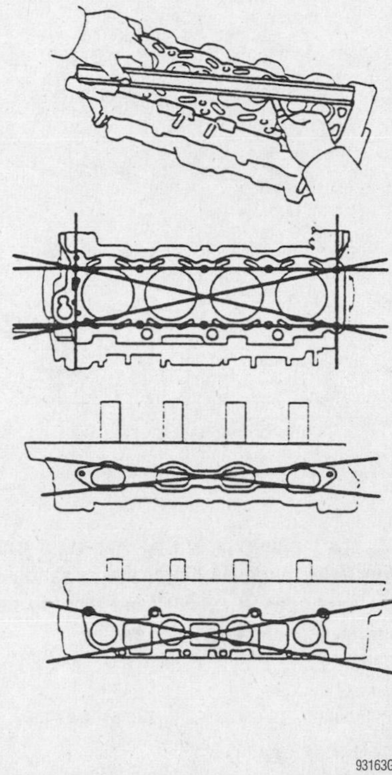

Fig. 134 Use a precision straightedge and feeler gauges to check for cylinder head distortion in the directions indicated. Maximum warpage allowed is only 0.0039 inch (0.10mm)—2UZ-FE engine

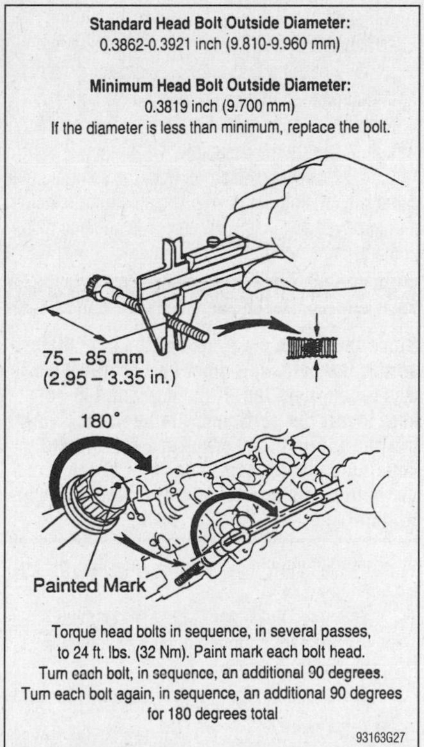

Fig. 135 Inspect and measure the outside diameter of the head bolts. New head bolts are recommended—2UZ-FE engine

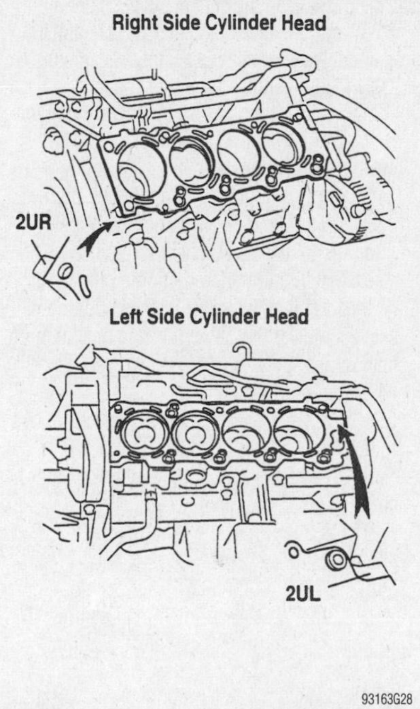

Fig. 136 Inspect the head gaskets and find the marks indicating left side or right side—2UZ-FE engine

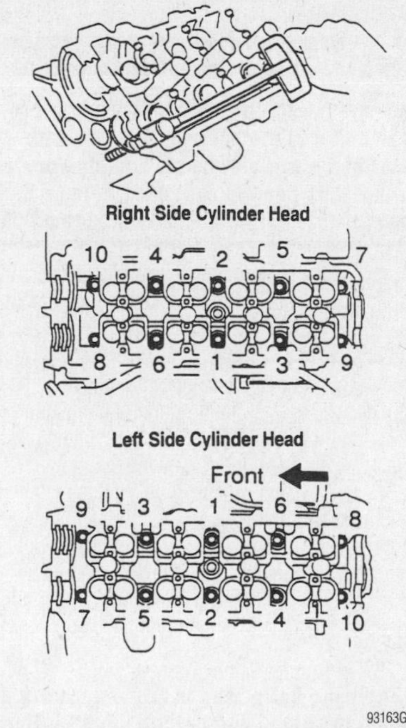

Fig. 137 Use this sequence to tighten the cylinder head bolts—2UZ-FE engine

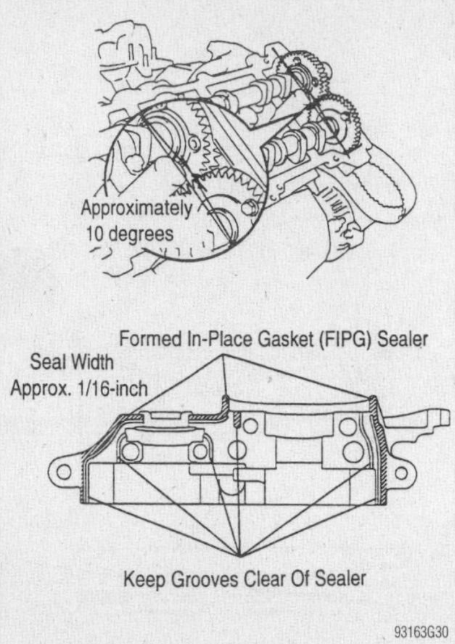

Fig. 138 When installing the right side camshafts, align the timing marks as shown and apply sealer to the front bearing cap where indicated—2UZ-FE engine

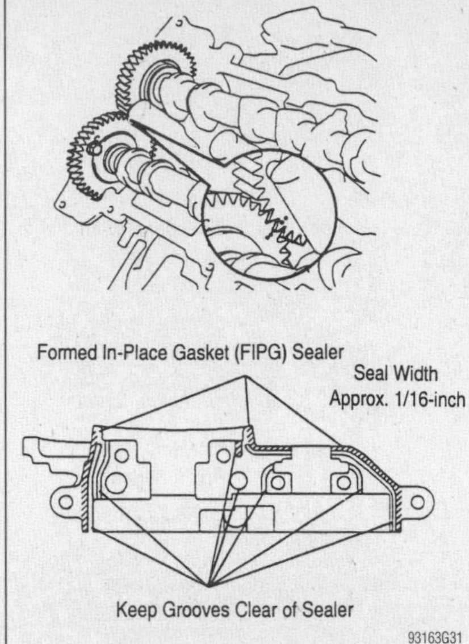

Fig. 139 When installing the left side camshafts, align the timing marks as shown and apply sealer to the front bearing cap where indicated—2UZ-FE engine

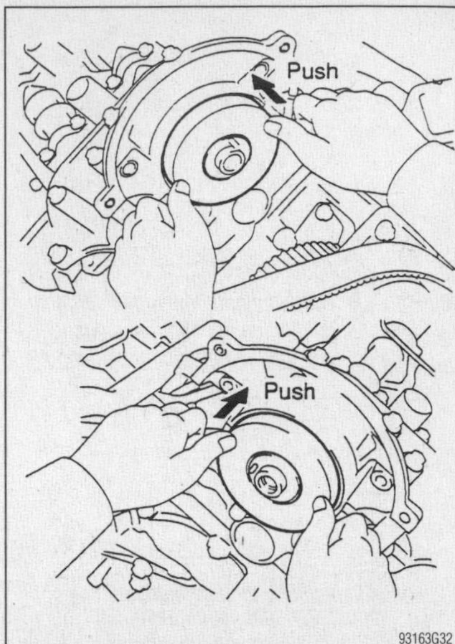

Fig. 140 After the camshaft front bearing caps are set in place, but before the bolts are final-tightened, push in new oil seals—2UZ-FE engine

i. Remove the oil feed pipe, the bearing caps and the camshafts.

➡Use care to keep the bearing caps in order, in the exact same sequence and direction as originally installed on the engine.

19. Uniformly loosen the ten cylinder head bolts on one side of each cylinder head in several passes, in the sequence illustrated, then do the other side. Remove the twenty head bolts and the flat washers under then. Use care. Cylinder head warping or cracking could result from removing the bolts in an incorrect order.

⁂ WARNING

Use care not to drop the flat washer for a head bolt into the open portion (oil drainback) of the cylinder head. Anything dropped through this opening will pass through the head and cylinder block and into the oil pan.

20. Lift the cylinder heads (with the exhaust manifolds attached) from the locating dowels in the cylinder block, and place the heads on protective soft wood block on a workbench. If the cylinder head is reluctant to come off, it may be carefully pried off but use great care not the damage the sealing surfaces of the head or the block. Do not tilt the cylinder head at removal or the valve lifters may fall out.

21. Remove the exhaust manifolds, as required.

To install:

22. Clean all parts well. Cylinder head rebuilding is best left to professionals. The head should be cleaned and inspected before installation. More information is available in the Engine Reconditioning section.

➡The head bolts used in this engine are designed to stretch and deform slightly. They should be carefully inspected. New service replacement head bolts are strongly recommended.

23. Toyota suggests installing the exhaust manifold(s) to the cylinder head before the head is installed. Use new gaskets. Factory replacement gaskets should have white painted marks facing the manifold side. Use eight new manifold nuts per manifold and tighten uniformly, in several passes, to 32 ft. lbs. (44 Nm).

24. Place new cylinder head gaskets on the block. On the rear side of the cylinder head gasket are marks to distinguish the left side and right side banks. There is a **2UR** mark on the right side bank and a **2UL** mark on the left side bank. Use care to install the gaskets on the correct sides.

25. Install the cylinder heads and prepare the head bolts. New service replacement head bolts are strongly recommended. Care must be taken when tightening the head bolts. Use the following guide:

a. The cylinder head bolts are tightened in two progressive steps.

b. Apply a light coat of engine oil on the threads and under the heads of the bolts.

c. Install the flat washers to the head bolts

d. Install and uniformly tighten the ten cylinder head bolts (per bank) in several passes in the sequence illustrated. Perform this operation on both banks. On this first pass, tighten the bolts to 24 ft. lbs. (32 Nm).

e. Mark the front of the cylinder head bolts with a small amount of paint.

f. On a second pass, tighten the cylinder head bolts, in sequence, another 90 degrees ($^1/_4$ turn).

g. On a third pass, again tighten the cylinder head bolts, in sequence, another 90 degrees ($^1/_4$ turn).

h. Check that the painted mark is now 180 degrees $^1/_2$-turn from its original position.

26. Install the spark plugs.

27. If disassembled, assemble the exhaust camshafts and sprockets using the following procedure:

a. Install the camshaft gear spring, camshaft sub-gear and wave washer. Attach the pins on the gears to the gear spring ends.

b. Install the snapring.

c. Mount the hexagon wrench head portion of the camshaft in a vise. Use care not to damage the camshaft.

d. Using Toyotas Special Service tool or a suitable pin-type spanner, align the holes of the camshaft main gear and sub-gear by turning the camshaft sub-gear counterclockwise, and temporarily install a bolt 6mm in diameter x 1.0mm thread pitch x 16–20mm long. Make sure the teeth of the gears are aligned, then tighten the bolt to secure the assembly.

28. Remove any old sealer from the semi-circular camshaft housing plugs. Apply fresh sealer to the plug grooves and install the camshaft housing plugs to the cylinder heads.

⁂ WARNING

Since the thrust clearance of the camshaft is small, the camshaft must be kept level while it is being installed. If the camshaft is not kept level, the portion of the head receiving the shaft thrust may crack or be damaged, causing the camshaft to seize or break. To avoid this, the following steps should be carried out.

29. Install the right side camshafts using the following procedure.

a. Apply engine assembly lube or multipurpose grease to the thrust portion of the intake and exhaust camshafts.

b. Lay the intake and exhaust camshafts carefully in position.

c. Set the timing mark (one dot mark) of the camshaft main gear at an angle approximately 10 degrees above horizontal by turning the hexagon

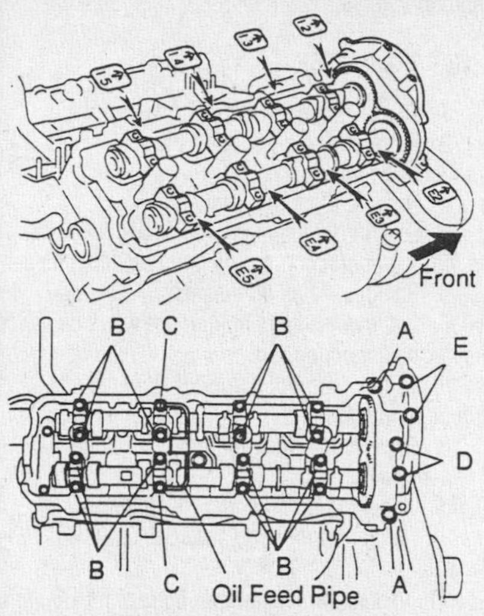

A Bolt is 0.98 inch (25 mm) long
B Bolt is 1.50 inch (38 mm) long
C Bolt is 2.05 inch (52 mm) long
D Bolt is 2.83 inch (72 mm) long
E Bolt is 3.70 inch (94 mm) long

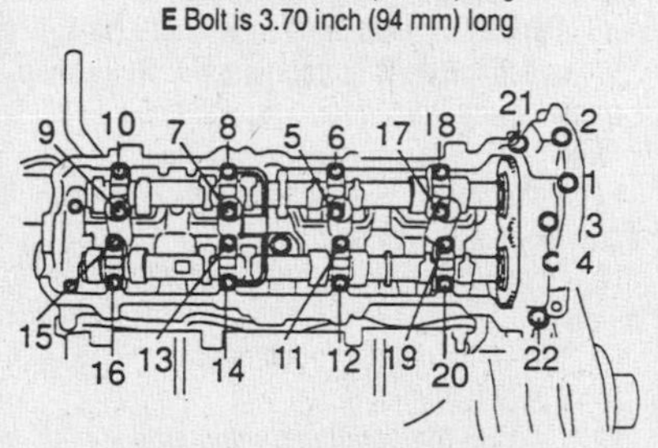

Do not apply oil under the heads of bolts **A, B** and **C**

Apply a light coat of engine oil on the threads and under the heads of bolts **D** and **E**.

A Bolts are tightened to 69 inch lbs. (7.5 Nm).
All other bolts are tightened to 144 inch lbs. (16 Nm).

93163G33

Fig. 141 Make sure the camshaft bearing caps are properly identified and correctly installed. Verify the proper length bolt is installed in the correct location, then tighten in the sequence shown—Right side bank shown

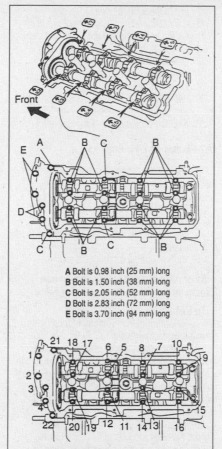

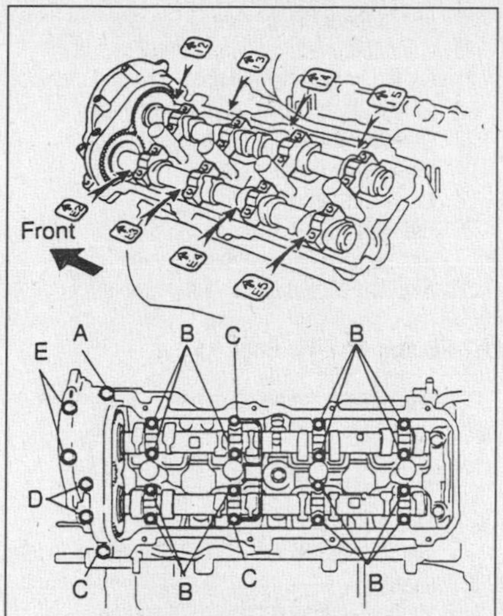

A Bolt is 0.98 inch (25 mm) long
B Bolt is 1.50 inch (38 mm) long
C Bolt is 2.05 inch (52 mm) long
D Bolt is 2.83 inch (72 mm) long
E Bolt is 3.70 inch (94 mm) long

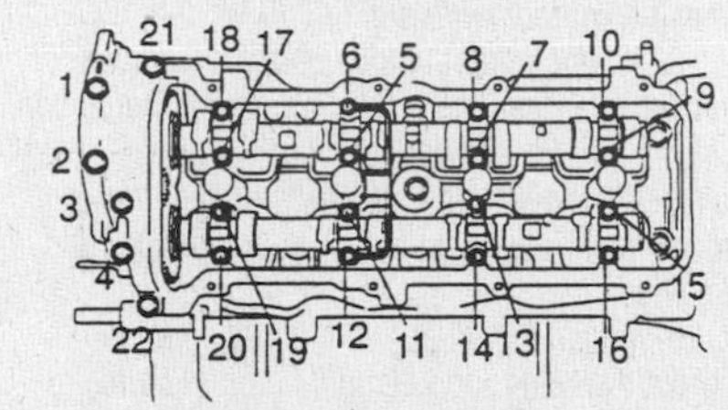

Do not apply oil under the heads of bolts **A, B** and **C**

Apply a light coat of engine oil on the threads and under the heads of bolts **D** and **E**.

A Bolts are tightened to 69 inch lbs. (7.5 Nm).
All other bolts are tightened to 144 inch lbs. (16 Nm).

93163G34

Fig. 142 Make sure the camshaft bearing caps are properly identified and correctly installed. Verify the proper length bolt is installed in the correct location, then tighten in the sequence shown—Left side bank shown

wrench portion of the exhaust camshaft with a wrench.

d. Remove any old sealer from the front bearing cap. Apply a bead of fresh sealer approximately $^{1}/_{16}$ inch in diameter, to the areas indicated in the illustration. Use care to keep sealer out of the front bearing cap grooves. Assemble the front bearing cap before the sealer has a chance to skin-over (start to cure). Note that installing the front bearing cap will determine the thrust clearance of the camshaft.

e. Install the other bearing caps in the sequence illustrated with the arrow mark facing forward. Align the arrow marks at the front and rear of the cylinder head with the mark on the bearing cap.

f. Install a new camshaft oil seal.

g. Apply a light coat of engine oil on the threads of only two sizes (the two longest) of camshaft bearing cap bolts. These bolts are:

- The 2.83 inch (72mm) bolts (called bolt D).
- The 3.70 inch (94mm) bolts (called bolt E).

h. Do not apply engine oil under the heads of the remaining camshaft bearing cap bolts. These bolts are:

- The 0.98 inch (25mm) bolts (called bolt A).
- The 1.50 inch (38mm) bolts (called bolt B).
- The 2.05 inch (52mm) bolts (called bolt C).

30. Uniformly tighten the 22 bearing cap bolts in several passes, in the sequence illustrated.

a. Torque the shortest bolts (bolt A) to 69 inch lbs. (7.5 Nm).

b. Torque all other bolts to 144 inch lbs. (16 Nm).

c. Bring the service bolt hole of the sub-gear upward by turning the hexagon wrench portion of the exhaust camshaft with a wrench. Remove the bolt. This allows the torsion spring and sub-gear to remove gear backlash.

31. Install the left side camshafts using the same procedure.

32. Turn the camshaft(s) and position so the lobes are upward, and check and adjust the valve clearance, noting the following:

a. Turn the crankshaft pulley and align its groove with the timing mark **0** on the No. 1 timing belt cover.

b. Install the timing belt rear plates.

c. Check that the timing marks of the camshaft timing pulleys and the timing belt rear plates are aligned. If not, turn the crankshaft exactly one revolution (360 degrees) and align the marks.

d. Using a feeler gauge, measure the distance between the valve lifter and camshaft. Clearance should be 0.006–0.010 inch (0.15–0.25mm) on the intake camshaft and 0.010–0.014 inch (0.25–0.35mm) on the exhaust camshaft.

33. Clean all old sealer from the four semi-circular camshaft plugs. Apply a fresh bead of sealer to the center groove of the plugs and install the plugs to the cylinder head.

34. Clean all old sealer from the cylinder head covers. Apply fresh sealer at the joint where the camshaft front bearing cap meets the cylinder head cover sealing surface. Use new cylinder head cover gaskets. Make sure the seal washers under the bolt heads are in good condition. Install the cylinder head covers. Uniformly tighten the bolts in several passes with final torque to 53 inch lbs. (6 Nm).

35. Install the engine lift hangers, if removed and the oil dipstick and guide tube.

36. Install the rear and front water bypass assemblies using new gaskets. Tighten the nuts evenly and alternately to 156 inch lbs. (18 Nm). Attach the ECT sensor and water sender gauge connectors.

37. Install the water inlet housing assembly.

38. Install the upper and lower intake manifolds using the procedures found in this section. Use care to make sure the lower intake manifold gaskets are properly installed. Factory replacement gaskets should have white paint marks which should be facing upward. Align the port holes of the gasket and the cylinder head.

39. Using the identification tags made at disassembly, connect the following hoses to the intake manifold:

- The vacuum hose from the fuel pressure regulator.
- The PCV hose from the PCV valve on the left side cylinder head.
- The EVAP hose from the charcoal canister from the VSV for the EVAP system.
- The EVAP hose from the charcoal canister from the EVAP pipe on the intake manifold.
- The power steering vacuum switch lines from the intake manifold.
- The brake booster vacuum line.

40. Using the identification tags made at disassembly, attach the electrical connectors unplugged during removal.

41. Connect the fuel lines.

42. If not done so earlier, install the timing belt rear plates and tighten the bolts to 66 inch lbs. (7.5 Nm).

43. Install the throttle body.

44. Install the ignition coils to their proper spark plug.

45. Install the automatic transmission fluid dipstick and fill tube.

46. Connect the front exhaust pipe.

47. install the power steering pump.

48. Install the camshaft position sensor.

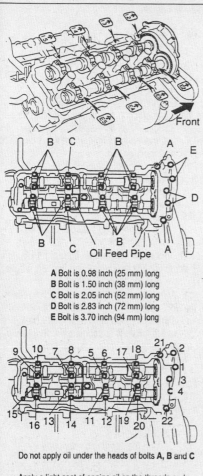

49. Install the camshaft timing pulleys and the timing belt, using the procedure found in this section.
50. Because the engine oil can become contaminated with coolant when a cylinder head is removed, change the oil and install a new filter.
51. Refill the engine with coolant.
52. Start the engine and check for leaks and abnormal noises.

Oil Pan

REMOVAL & INSTALLATION

5VZ-FE Engine

➧ See Figures 143 thru 151

1. Disconnect the negative battery cable.
2. Raise and safely support the vehicle.
3. Remove the crankshaft timing pulley.
4. Drain the engine oil.
5. If equipped with 4WD, remove the front differential.
6. On A/T remove the oil cooler tube and clamp.
7. Remove the stiffener plate.
8. Unbolt the flywheel housing dust cover.
9. Disconnect the starter wire clamp.
10. Remove the crankshaft position sensor.
11. Unbolt and lower the oil pan.
12. Using SST 0c2–00100 or equivalent and a brass bar, separate the oil pan from the cylinder block.

To install:

13. Use a razor blade or equivalent to scrape the cylinder block and oil pan mating surfaces of any old sealing material. All traces of the old gasket and sealer must be removed.
14. Clean the pan thoroughly, using solvent if necessary. If the pan has a magnet in it, examine it closely. Excess metal is a sign of engine wear. A few slivers are normal. Use good judgment in relating the amount of debris to the amount of time the pan has been in place.
15. Install the crankshaft position sensor.
16. Install the oil pan baffle plate.
17. Apply Formed In-Place Gasket (FIPG) sealer to the oil pan and install the pan to the cylinder block. Tighten the nuts and bolts to 66 inch lbs. (8 Nm). If parts are not assembled within 5 minutes of applying time, the sealer starts to skin over and cure, the effectiveness of the sealer is lost, and must be removed and reapplied.
18. Attach the flywheel housing under and cover dust.
19. Install the stiffener plate.
20. Connect the starter wire clamp.
21. On A/T install the oil cooler tube and clamp.
22. Reinstall the crankshaft timing pulley.
23. On the 4WD, install the front differential.
24. Install the engine undercover.
25. Lower the vehicle.
26. Fill with engine oil.
27. Connect the negative battery cable.
28. Start the engine and check for leaks.

2RZ-FE and 3RZ-FE Engines

1. Disconnect the negative battery cable from the battery.
2. Raise and support the vehicle safely.
3. Remove the engine undercover.
4. Drain the engine oil.
5. Remove the 16 mounting bolts and two nuts to the oil pan.
6. Remove the oil pan from the engine.

➡Be careful not to damage the oil pan flanges of the oil pan and cylinder block.

To install:

7. Before installing the oil pans, thoroughly clean the contact surfaces.
8. Apply sealant 08826-00080 or equivalent Formed In-Place Gasket (FIPG) sealer to the oil pan. Parts should be assembled within 5 minutes of application. Otherwise the sealer starts to skin over, looses its effectiveness and must be removed and reapplied.
9. Install the oil pan and mounting bolts. Tighten the bolts and nuts to 9 ft. lbs. (13 Nm).
10. Install the engine undercover. Lower the vehicle.
11. Fill the engine with oil. Connect the negative battery cable, start the engine and check for leaks.

1FZ-FE Engine

➧ See Figure 152

1. Disconnect the negative battery cable.
2. Raise and safely support the vehicle.
3. Drain the engine oil.
4. Remove the engine undercover.
5. Disconnect the oil cooler pipe bracket from the No. 1 (upper half of the oil pan assembly) oil pan.
6. Remove the oil level sensor.
7. Remove the bolts holding the No. 1 oil pan to the transmission housing.
8. Remove the No. 2 (lower half of the oil pan assembly) oil pan.
9. Remove the No. 1 oil pan.

To install:

10. Install the No. 1 oil pan, as follows:
    a. Apply Formed In-Place Gasket (FIPG) sealer to the No. 1 oil pan.
    b. Install the oil pan and tighten the 14mm bolts to 32 ft. lbs. (44 Nm) and the 12mm bolts to 14 ft. lbs. (20 Nm).
11. Apply Formed In-Place Gasket (FIPG) sealer to the No. 2 oil pan and tighten the bolt to 72 inch lbs. (8 Nm) and the nuts to 84 inch lbs. (9 Nm).
12. Install the bolts holding the No. 1 oil pan to the transmission housing and tighten to 53 ft. lbs. (72 Nm).
13. Install the oil level sensor and tighten the bolts to 60 inch lbs. (5 Nm).
14. Connect the oil cooler pipe bracket to the No. 1 oil pan.
15. Install the engine undercover.
16. Fill with engine oil.
17. Connect the negative battery cable.
18. Start the engine and check for leaks.

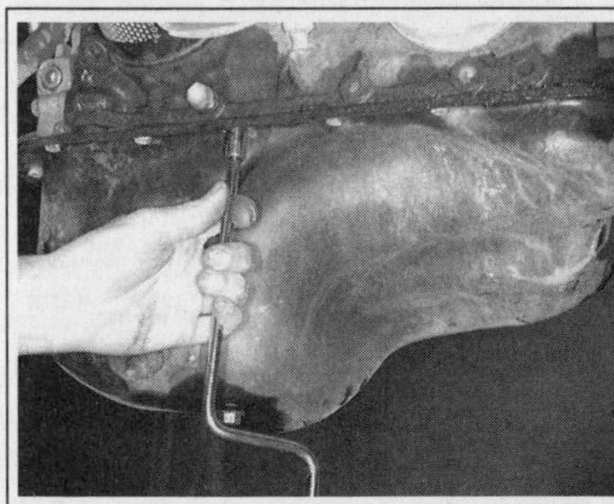

93163ph6

Fig. 143 Removing the oil pan bolts

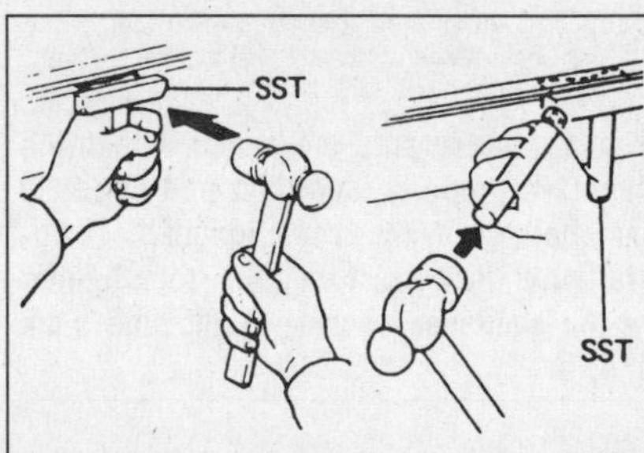

86823PBJ

Fig. 144 A special tool is available to cut through the Formed In-Place Gasket (FIPG) sealant used on the oil pan

93163pm6

Fig. 145 Carefully lower the oil pan

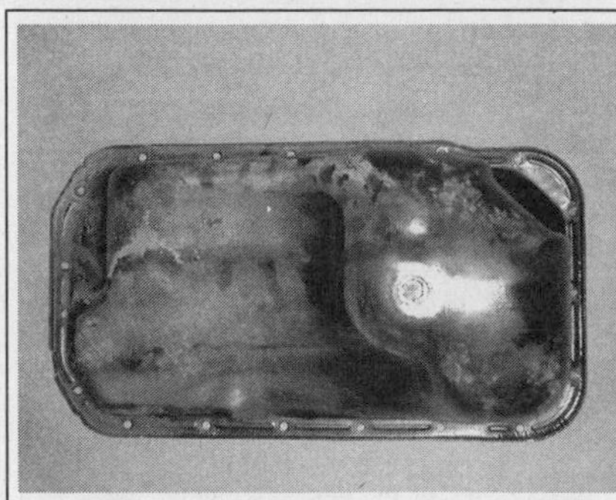

93163pi4

Fig. 146 View of the oil pan and mounting bolt hole locations

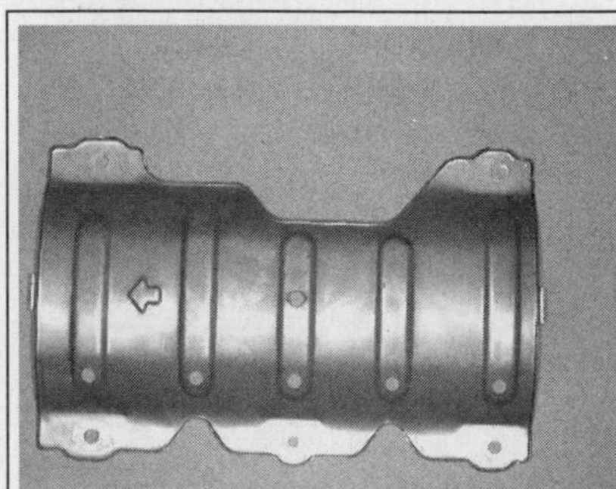

93163pm5

Fig. 147 Oil pan baffle plate

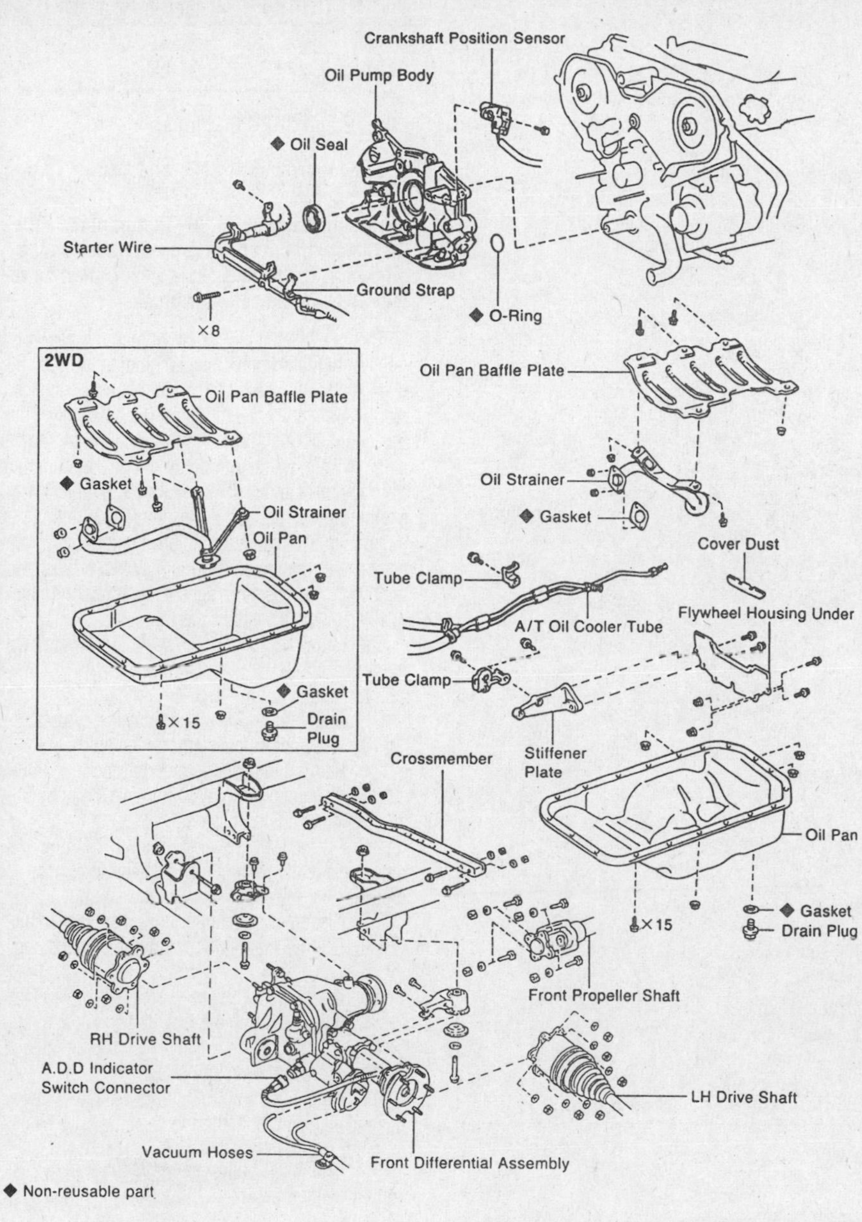

Fig. 148 Exploded view of the oil pan and related components on the 5VZ-FE engine

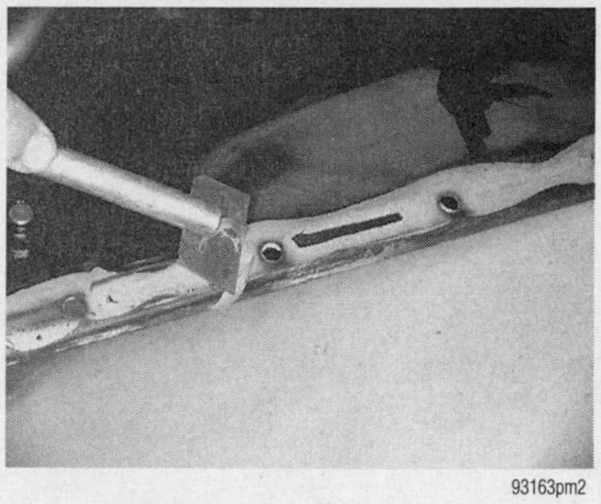

Fig. 149 Make sure to clean all old gasket material from the oil pan

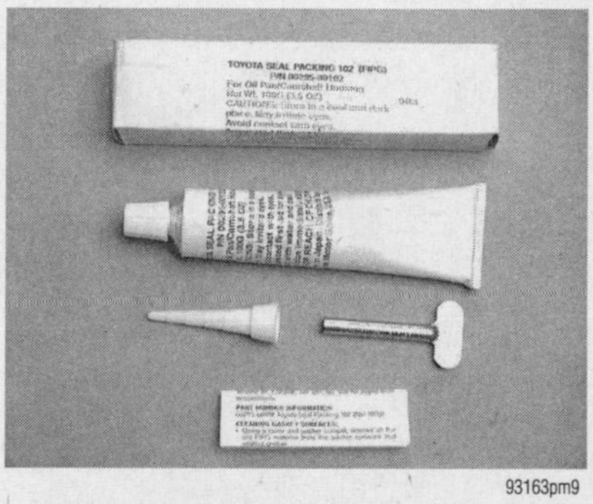

Fig. 150 Toyota's factory Formed In-Place Gasket (FIPG) sealer

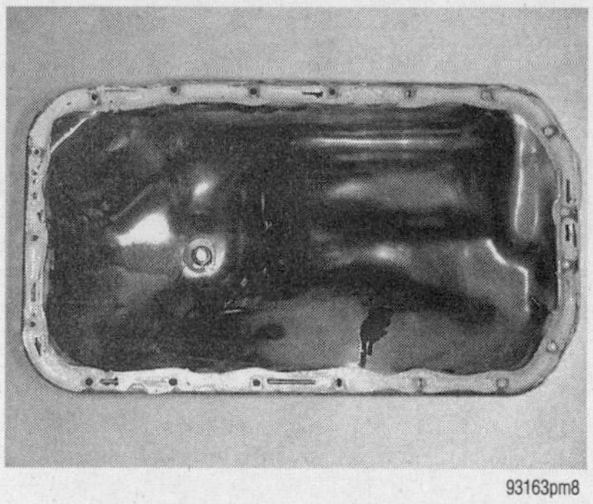

Fig. 151 Formed In-Place Gasket (FIPG) sealer applied to the oil pan

2UZ-FE Engine

➧ **See Figures 153, 154, and 155**

Like some of the other Toyota truck engines, the 2UZ-FE engine uses a two-piece oil pan, separated by a baffle plate. Toyota calls the upper part of the oil pan the No. 1 oil pan, while the lower section is called the No.2 oil pan. Please note that the oil pump is not inside the oil pan. The oil pump body bolts to the front of the engine, driven off the front of the crankshaft. For oil pump removal and installation, please see the procedure further in this section.

Oil pan removal and installation is a major job since Toyota recommends that the engine be removed from the vehicle for oil pump and oil pan service. Toyota specifies that when the oil pump is services, the oil pan and strainer should be removed and cleaned. Oil pan installation takes some care since the pan must be positioned very precisely. This is best one with the engine out of the vehicle and mounted on an appropriate engine stand. Use care and keep all parts as clean as possible.

The following procedure is based on Toyotas oil pump and oil pan service procedures which include removing the engine from the vehicle.

1. Remove the engine from the vehicle.
2. Mount the engine to a suitable engine stand.
3. Remove the oil dipstick.
4. Remove the lower half of the oil pan (Toyota calls it the No. 2 oil pan). There should be 24 bolts and two nuts. The lower oil pan is sealed with a Formed-In-Place Gasket (FIPG) sealer and it may be difficult to break the seal. Toyota recommends their special tool which is a blade mounted in a holder that can be tapped with a hammer. The blade is positioned at the seal joint and tapped with a hammer around the oil pan flange, cutting the seal. Use care not to damage the oil pan sealing flanges, especially if using substitute tools.
5. Between the lower oil pan and the upper oil pan (Toyota calls it the No. 1 oil pan), there is a baffle plate. Remove the seven bolts and two nuts and separate the baffle plate from the upper oil pan.

➡The upper oil pan uses four different length bolts. Take care to correctly identify each bolt, its length and location. It is good practice to punch holes in a piece of corrugated cardboard to closely resemble the bolt pattern of the upper oil pan. Insert the bolts in the cardboard in their corresponding locations as they are removed. A few minutes spent at removal will save much time at installation.

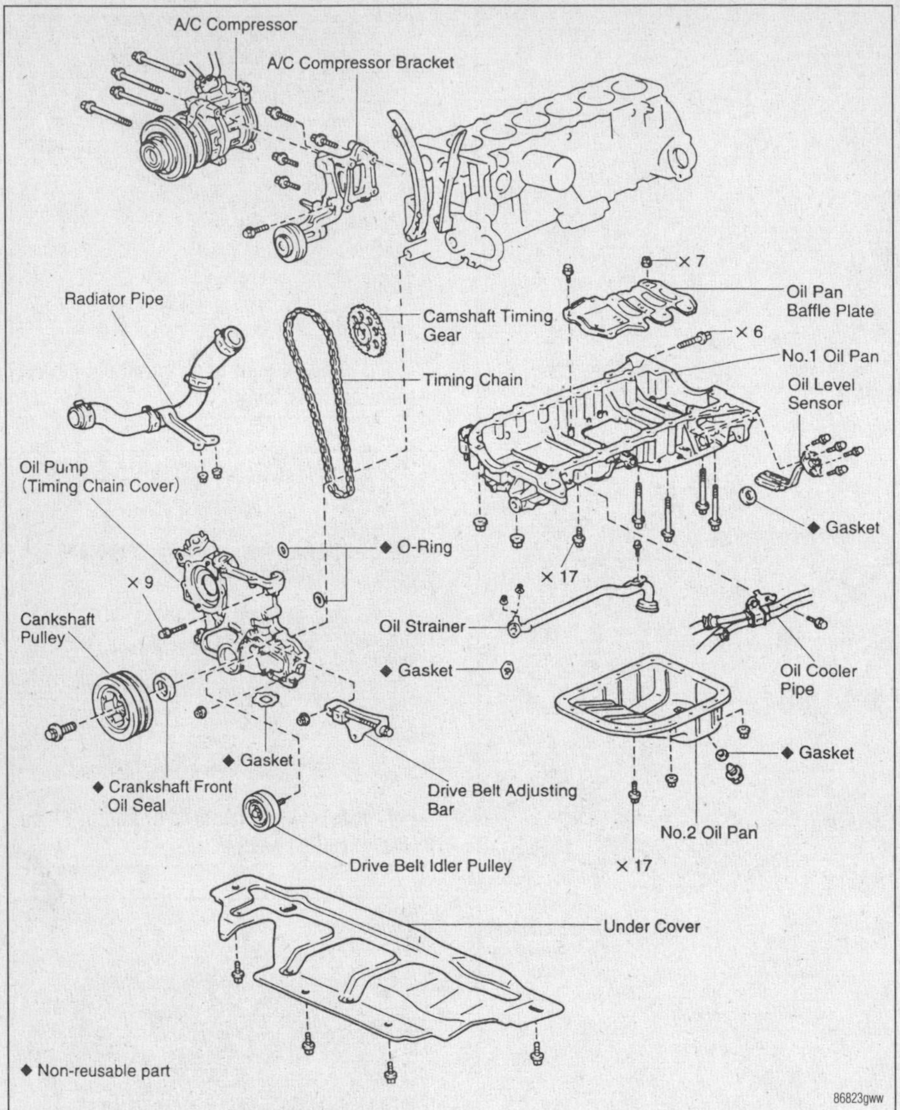

Fig. 152 Exploded view of the oil pan and related components on the 1FZ-FE engine

6. Remove the 18 bolts and two nuts from the upper pan. There are several points around the pan and engine block where it is approved to pry the upper pan from the block. Use care not to damage the sealing surface of the engine block or the upper oil pan.

To install:

7. Clean all parts well. If necessary, remove the two bolts and two nuts and remove the oil strainer and gasket. Clean the strainer well. Install the strainer with a new gasket and torque the fasteners to 66 inch lbs. (7.5 Nm).

8. Make sure all old FIPG sealer is removed. The pan sealing flanges and the engine block sealing surfaces must be clean of all oil and grease or the new FIPG sealer wont work. Apply a $^1/_8$ inch (3mm) bead of FIPG sealer to the upper oil pan flange. Most sealers start to skin over in about five minutes so assemble the oil pan to the block without hesitation. Install the bolts just a few turns, making sure all bolt holes line up. Make sure the clearance between the rear ends of the upper oil pan and the engine block is 0.008 inch (0.2mm) or less. If the clearance is more than this, the upper oil pan will be stretched. Uniformly torque the bolts and nuts in several passes as follows:

a. Tighten all bolts with a 10mm head to 66 inch lbs. (7.5 Nm).

b. Tighten all bolts with a 12mm head to 21 ft. lbs. (28 Nm).

9. Install the oil pan baffle plate and tighten the nuts and bolts to 66 inch lbs. (7.5 Nm).

10. Install the lower oil pan. It should be clean of any old sealer and any oil or grease. Apply a $^1/_8$ inch (3mm) bead of FIPG sealer to the lower oil pan flange and install the oil pan to the upper oil pan without hesitation, before the sealer starts to cure. Install the bolts just a few turns, making sure all bolt holes line up. When satisfied with the lower oil pans position, uniformly tighten the nuts and bolts, in several passes, ending with a torque of 66 inch lbs. (7.5 Nm).

11. Install the engine into the vehicle using the procedures found in this section.

Oil Pump

REMOVAL & INSTALLATION

2RZ-FE and 3RZ-FE Engines

➧ See Figures 156, 157, and 158

➡The oil pump assembly is mounted in the timing chain cover. To properly service the oil pump, the timing chain cover must be removed from the cylinder block.

This is a difficult and lengthy procedure requiring removal of many components including the front differential assembly and the cylinder head, which also requires removal of the timing chain assembly. This procedure can also be performed with the engine out of the vehicle, which may be an option, depending on the equipment and facilities available. If other heavy engine work is required (for example, a failed oil pump may have caused crankshaft and bearing damage or other engine damage) it may just be easier to remove the engine as an assembly and perform the work on a suitable engine stand.

The following procedure is based on Toyota's in-frame procedure.

1. Disconnect the negative battery cable.
2. Drain the engine oil and cooling system.
3. Raise and safely support the vehicle.
4. Remove the engine undercover.
5. If equipped with 4WD, remove the front differential and halfshaft assembly.
6. For the California vehicles with 3RZ-FE engine, remove the two bolts and disconnect the air pipe.
7. Disconnect the upper hose from the radiator.
8. Remove the oil dipstick guide by removing the bolt.
9. If equipped with power steering, remove the drive belt by loosening the lock bolt and adjusting bolt.
10. Remove the fan shrouds.
11. If equipped with A/C, loosen the idler pulley nut and adjusting bolt, then remove the drive belt from the engine.
12. Remove the alternator drive belt, fan (with fan clutch), water pump pulley, and the fan shroud as follows:

a. Loosen the water pump pulley mounting nuts.

b. Loosen the lock, pivot and adjusting bolts for the alternator and remove the alternator drive belt from the engine.

c. Remove the four water pump pulley mounting nuts.

d. Remove the fan (with fan clutch) and the water pump pulley.

13. Remove the cylinder head from the engine.
14. If equipped with A/C, disconnect the compressor and bracket as follows:

a. Remove the four mounting bolts and disconnect the compressor from the bracket. Do not disconnect the A/C pressure lines from the compressor. Suspend the compressor away from the engine.

b. Remove the A/C compressor bracket by removing the four bolts.

15. Remove the alternator, adjusting bar and bracket as follows:

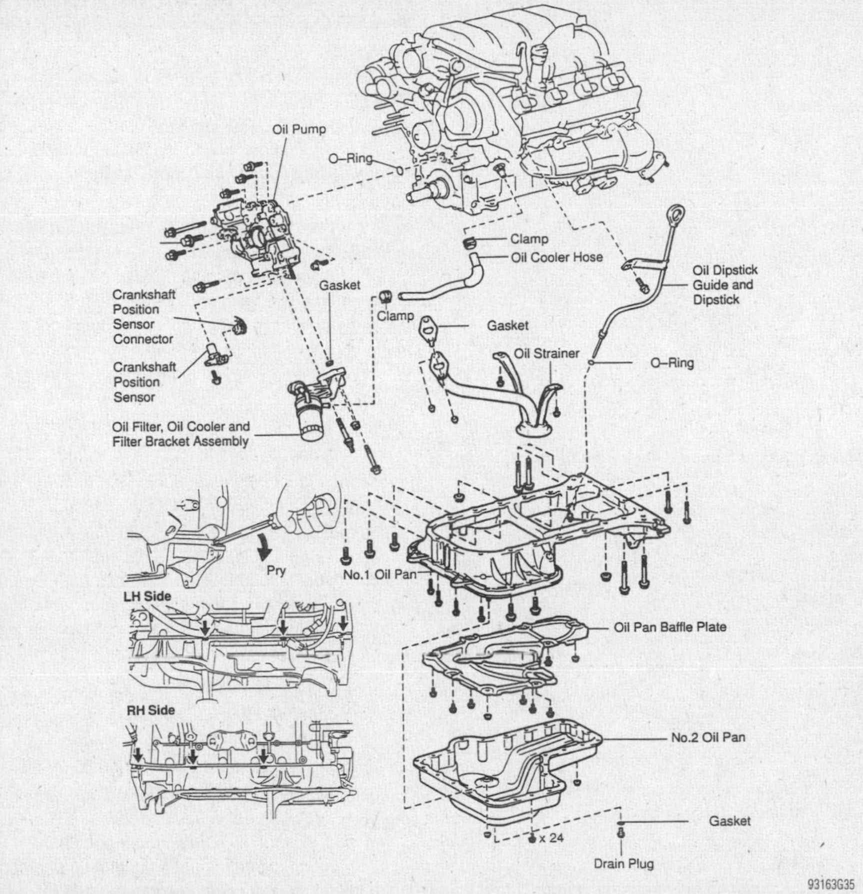

Fig. 153 Numerous engine components must be removed to service this two-piece oil pan—2UZ-FE Engine

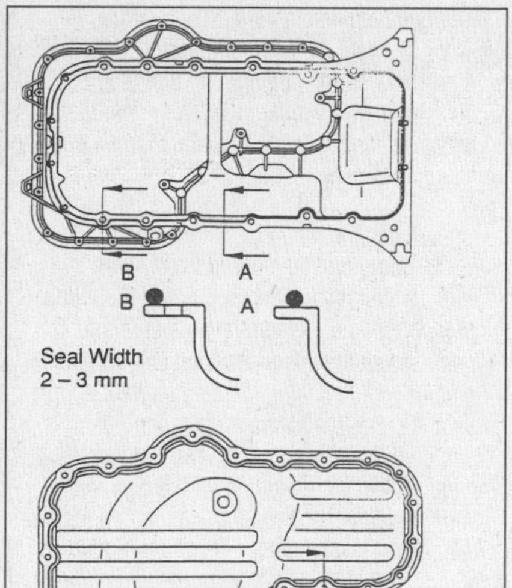

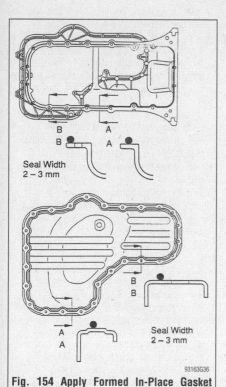

Fig. 154 Apply Formed In-Place Gasket (FIPG) sealer in places indicated—2UZ-FE Engine

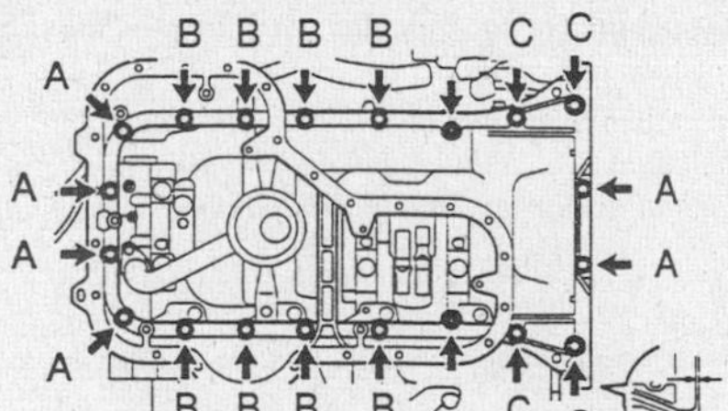

A Bolt is 0.79 inch (20 mm) long with a 10 mm head
B Bolt is 0.98 inch (25 mm) long with a 12 mm head
C Bolt is 2.36 inch (60 mm) long with a 12 mm head
D Bolt is 1.38 inch (35 mm) long with a 10 mm head

Make sure the clearance between the rear ends of the No. 1 oil pan and cylinder block is 0.008 inch (0.2mm) or less. If the clearance is more than this, the upper oil pan will be stretched. Tighten the bolts evenly, in several passes.

Tighten all bolts with a 10 mm head to 66 inch lbs. (7.5 Nm)
Tighten all bolts with a 12 mm head to 21 ft. lbs. (28 Nm)

93163G37

Fig. 155 Upper oil pan bolt installation takes care and careful work with a torque wrench—2UZ-FE Engine

a. Loosen the lock bolt, pivot bolt, nut and adjusting bolt at the alternator.

b. After loosening the adjusting bolt, remove the alternator drive belt from the engine.

c. Disconnect the alternator wiring.

d. Remove the nut, then disconnect the alternator wire.

e. Disconnect the wire harness with the clip.

f. Remove the lock bolt, pivot bolt, nut, and the alternator from the engine.

g. Unbolt and remove the adjusting bar.

h. Unbolt and remove the bracket.

16. Unbolt and remove the crankshaft position sensor.

17. If equipped with 2WD, remove the stiffener plates by removing the eight bolts.

18. Remove the flywheel housing undercover and dust seal.

19. Remove the oil pan by removing the 16 mounting bolts and 2 nuts.

➡Be careful not to damage the flanges of the oil pan and cylinder block.

20. Remove the two bolts, two nuts, oil strainer, and gasket.

21. Remove the crankshaft pulley.

a. If equipped with A/C, remove the No. 2 and No. 3 crankshaft pulleys by removing the four bolts.

b. Using SST 09213–54015 and 09330–00021 or equivalents, remove the crankshaft pulley bolts.

c. Remove the crankshaft pulley.

22. Remove the timing chain cover as follows:

a. Remove the two water bypass pipe mounting nuts.

b. Remove the two timing chain cover mounting bolts.

c. Remove the nine mounting bolts and two mounting nuts from the timing chain cover.

d. Using a rubber hammer, loosen the chain cover, timing chain cover and three gaskets.

23. Disassemble the oil pump from the front cover, pump cover, drive rotor, driven rotor and O-ring.

24. Remove the relief valve as follows:

a. Using snapring pliers, remove the snapring for the relief valve.

b. Remove the retainer, spring(s) and relief valve from the front cover.

To install:

25. Install the relief valve as follows:

a. Install the relief valve, spring(s) and retainer to the valve cover.

b. Using snapring pliers, install the snapring to hold the relief valve.

➡Pack petroleum jelly between the oil pump gears. This will prime the pump during initial startup. DO NOT use chassis grease as it will plug up the system. Ordinary petroleum jelly will seal the gear cavity long enough so the pump will prime and start drawing oil as soon as the crankshaft begins to turn, then dissolve as the engine warms.

26. Install the drive and driven rotors as follows:

a. Place the drive and driven rotors into the pump body.

b. Place a new O-ring to the pump body.

c. Install the pump cover with the nine screws.

27. Install the timing chain cover.

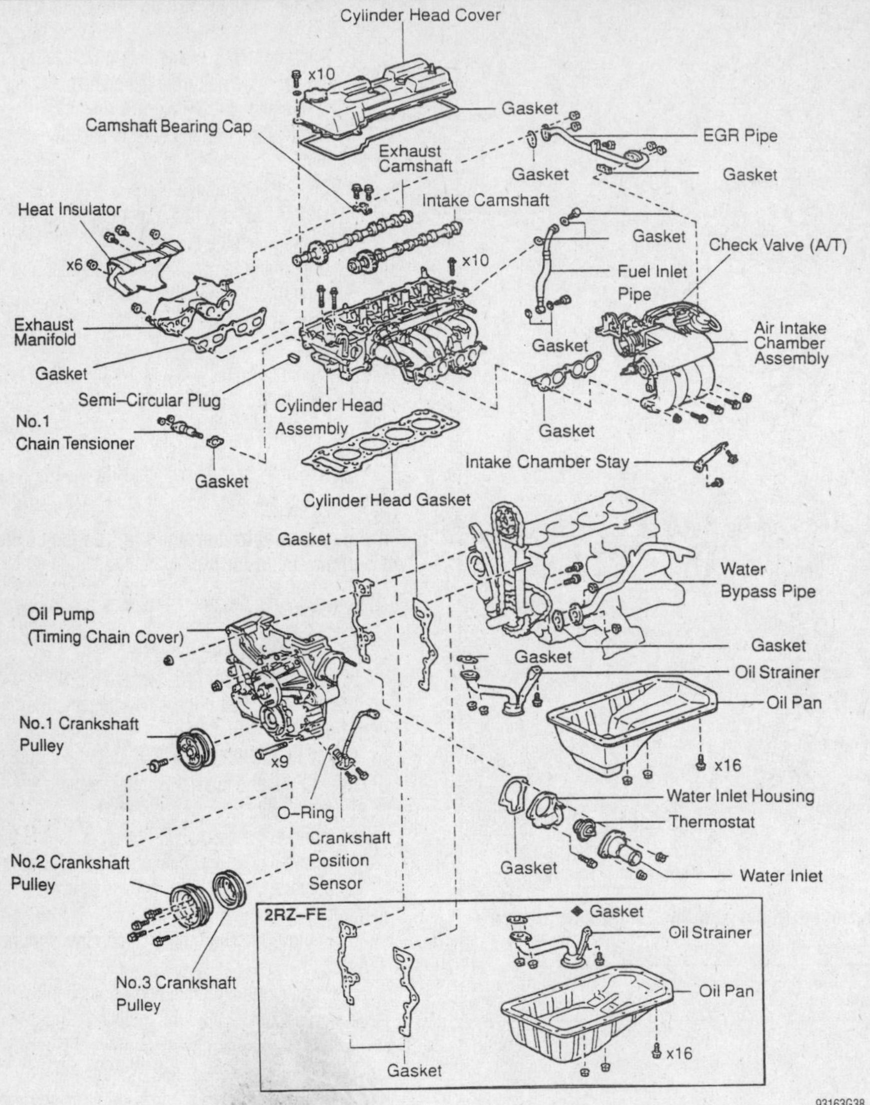

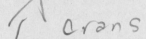

Fig. 156 Numerous engine components must be removed to service the oil pump—2RZ-FE and 3RZ-FE engines

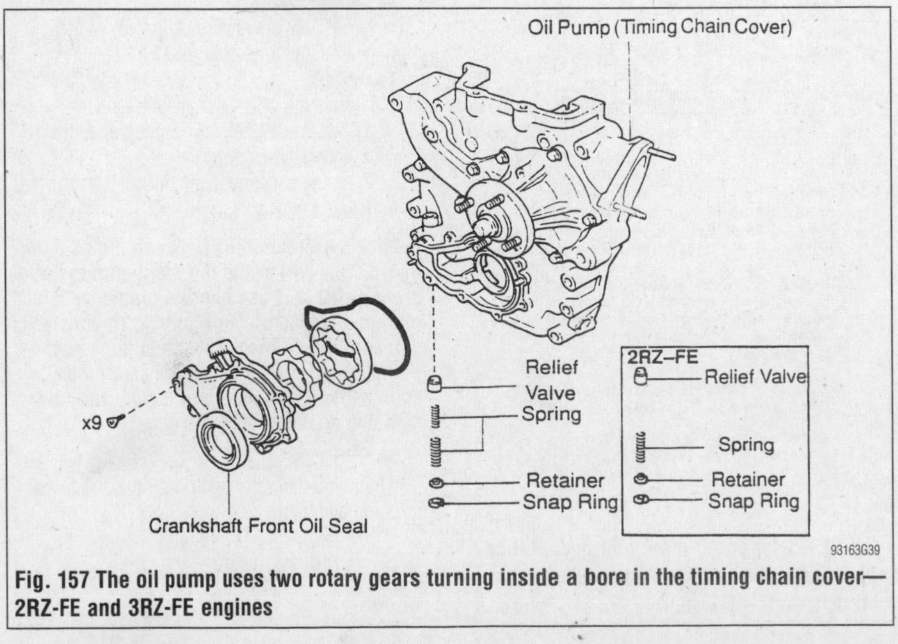

Fig. 157 The oil pump uses two rotary gears turning inside a bore in the timing chain cover—2RZ-FE and 3RZ-FE engines

28. Install the 2 rear timing chain cover mounting bolts and water bypass pipe mounting nuts. Tighten to 13 ft. lbs. (18 Nm).
29. Align the pulley set key with the key groove of the pulley and slide on the pulley. Install and tighten the pulley bolt to 193 ft. lbs. (260 Nm).
30. If equipped with A/C, install the crankshaft pulleys with the four bolts. Tighten the bolts to 18 ft. lbs. (25 Nm).
31. Install the oil strainer, then tighten the fasteners to 13 ft. lbs. (18 Nm).
32. Clean the oil pan and cylinder block mating surfaces. Apply Formed In-Place Gasket (FIPG) sealer to the oil pan. Install the oil pan and tighten the fasteners to 9 ft. lbs. (13 Nm).
33. Install the flywheel housing undercover and dust seal.
34. If equipped with 2WD, install the stiffener plates. Tighten the eight bolts to 27 ft. lbs. (37 Nm).
35. Using a new O-ring, install the crankshaft position sensor, tighten to 74 inch lbs. (9 Nm).
36. Install the alternator to the engine as follows:
    a. Attach the alternator to the engine, then install the nut, pivot bolt, and the lock bolt. Do not tighten the bolts or nut at this time.
    b. Connect the wire harness with the clip to the alternator.
    c. Install the alternator wire with the nut.
    d. Connect the alternator harness.
    e. Install the drive belt to the engine.
    f. Tighten the drive belt with the adjusting bolt. Belt tension should be as follows:
        - New belt: 155–175 lbs. (689–778 N)
        - Old belt: 75–125 lbs. (334–556 N)
    g. Once the belt is tight, tighten the pivot bolt to 43 ft. lbs. (59 Nm); lock bolt to 21 ft. lbs. (29 Nm).
37. If equipped with A/C, install the compressor as follows:
    a. Install the A/C compressor bracket with the four bolts, tighten to 32 ft. lbs. (44 Nm).
    b. Connect the A/C compressor to the bracket with the four bolts, tighten to 18 ft. lbs. (25 Nm).
38. Install the cylinder head.
39. Install the water pump pulley, fan shroud, fan (with fan clutch), and the alternator drive belt as follows:
    a. Place the fan (with the fan clutch), water pump pulley and fan shroud in position.
    b. Install the water pump pulley mounting nuts, but do not tighten the nuts at this time.
    c. Install the alternator drive belt to the engine.
    d. Stretch the alternator belt tight, then tighten the fan nuts to 16 ft. lbs. (21 Nm).
    e. Adjust the drive belt for the alternator.
40. Install the fan shrouds.
41. Install and adjust the power steering drive belt.
42. Install the oil dipstick guide with the bolt.
43. Connect the upper hose to the radiator.
44. If removed, attach the air pipe.
45. If equipped with 4WD, install the front differential and halfshaft assembly.
46. Install the engine undercover.
47. Lower the vehicle.
48. Fill the cooling system and engine oil.
49. Connect the negative battery cable.
50. Start the engine and check for leaks.
51. Recheck and top off all fluid levels.
52. Adjust ignition timing. Road test the vehicle for proper operation.

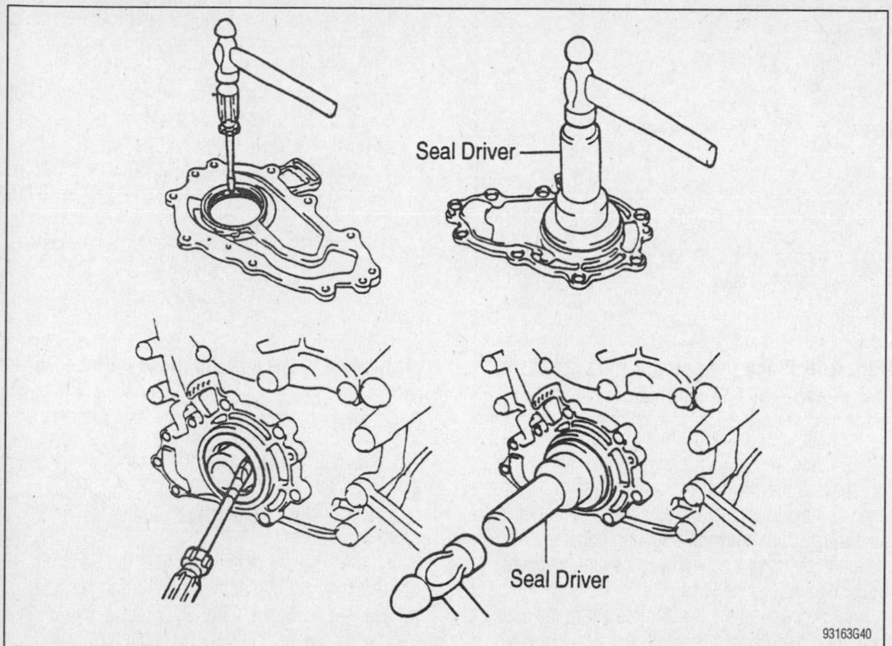

Fig. 158 Top: Removing and installing the crankshaft front oil seal with the pump cover off the engine; Bottom: Removing and installing the crankshaft front oil seal with the pump cover still on the engine—2RZ-FE and 3RZ-FE Engines

5VZ-FE Engine

See Figures 159 thru 167

1. Disconnect the negative battery cable.
2. Raise and safely support the vehicle.
3. Remove the crankshaft timing pulley.
4. Drain the engine oil.
5. If equipped with 4WD, remove the front differential.
6. On A/T remove the oil cooler tube and clamp.
7. Remove the stiffener plate.
8. Unbolt the flywheel housing dust cover.
9. Disconnect the starter wire clamp.
10. Remove the crankshaft position sensor.
11. Unbolt and lower the oil pan.
12. Remove the oil strainer and gasket.
13. Unbolt the oil pan baffle plate.
14. Remove the 8 bolts, ground strap and oil pump from the engine. Using a plastic head hammer, carefully tap the pump body. Remove the O-ring from the block.

To install:

15. Use a razor blade or equivalent to scrape the cylinder block and oil pan mating surfaces of any old sealing material. All traces of the old gasket and sealer must be removed.
16. Clean the pan thoroughly, using solvent if necessary. If the pan has a magnet in it, examine the shavings closely; excess metal is a sign of engine wear. A few slivers are normal. Use good judgment in relating the amount of debris to the amount of time the pan has been in place.
17. Apply multi-purpose grease to the oil seal lip. Using a special service tool 09306–37010 or equivalent, along with a hammer, tap in the oil seal until its surface is flush with the pump body edge.

➡Pack petroleum jelly between the oil pump gears. This will prime the pump during initial startup. DO NOT use chassis grease as it will plug up the system. Ordinary petroleum jelly will seal the gear cavity long enough so the pump will prime and start drawing oil as soon as the crankshaft begins to turn, then dissolve as the engine warms.

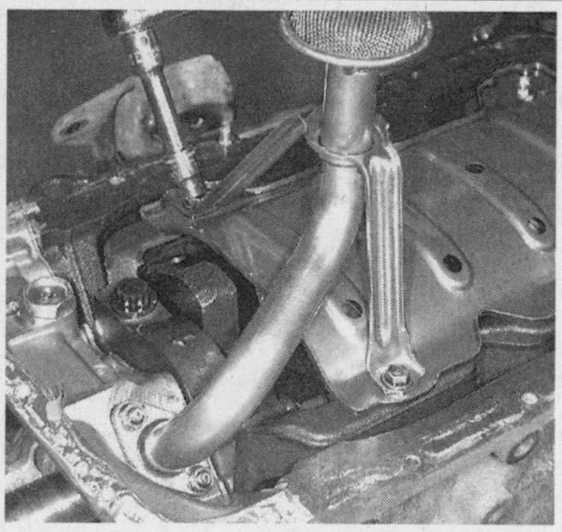

Fig. 159 Remove the oil pump screen bolts

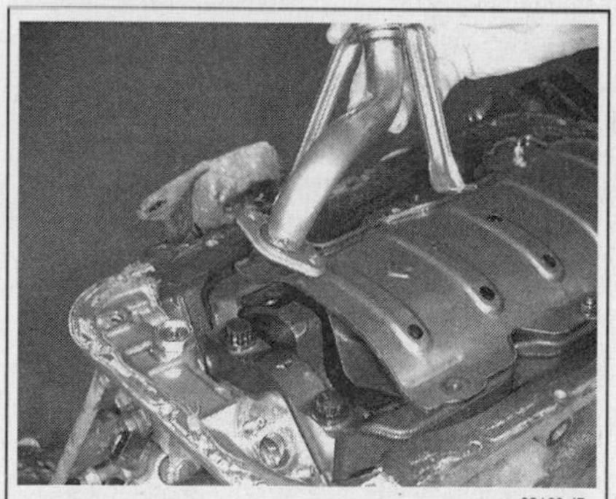

Fig. 160 After you have removed all of the fasteners, remove the oil pump screen and pick up tube

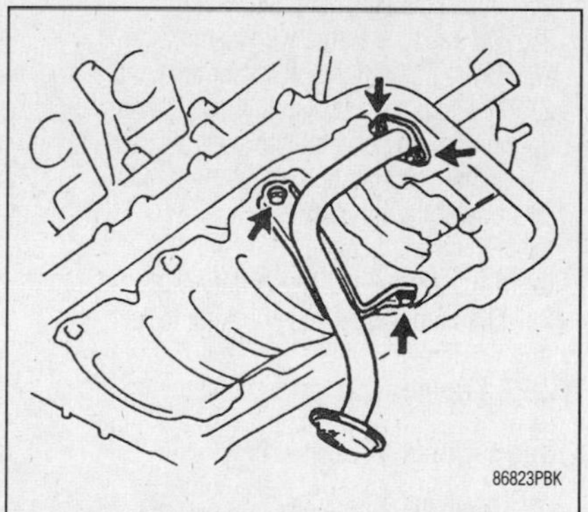

Fig. 161 Remove the bolts securing the oil strainer—5VZ-FE engine

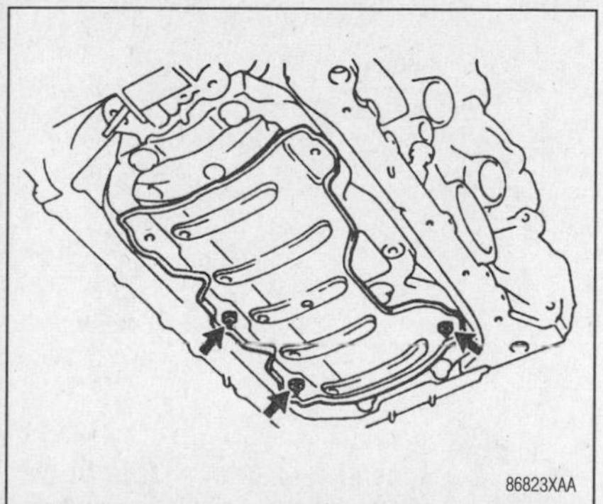

Fig. 162 Remove the three bolts retaining the oil pan baffle—5VZ-FE engine

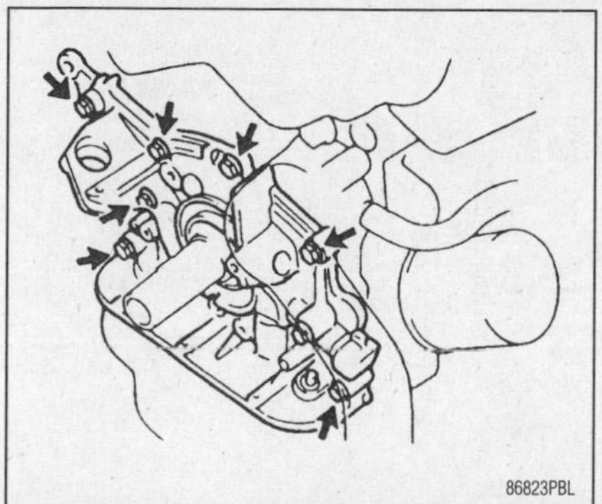

Fig. 163 Remove the bolts securing the oil pump body to the engine—5VZ-FE engine

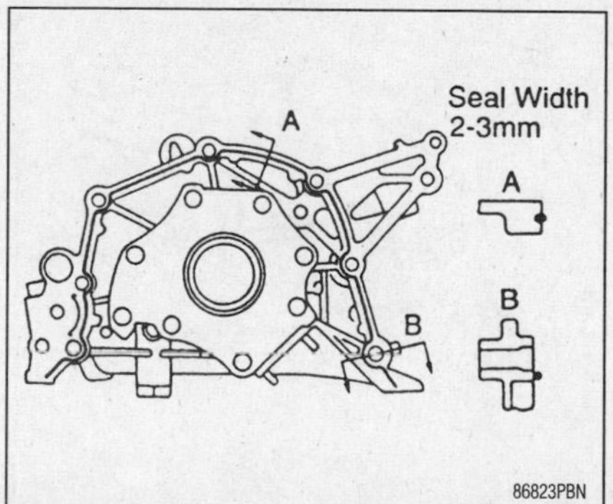

Fig. 164 Place a bead of sealant as shown—5VZ-FE engine

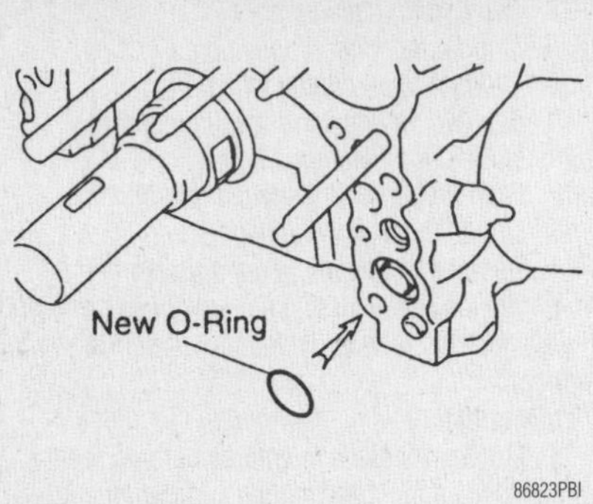

Fig. 165 Place the new O-ring into the groove of the block—5VZ-FE engine

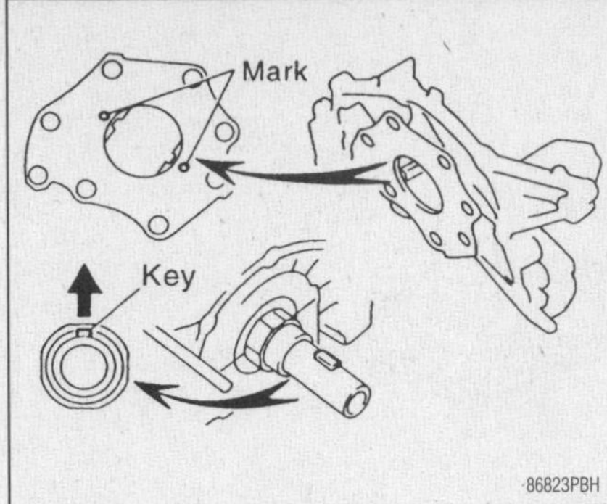

Fig. 166 Place the pump on the crankshaft as shown—5VZ-FE engine

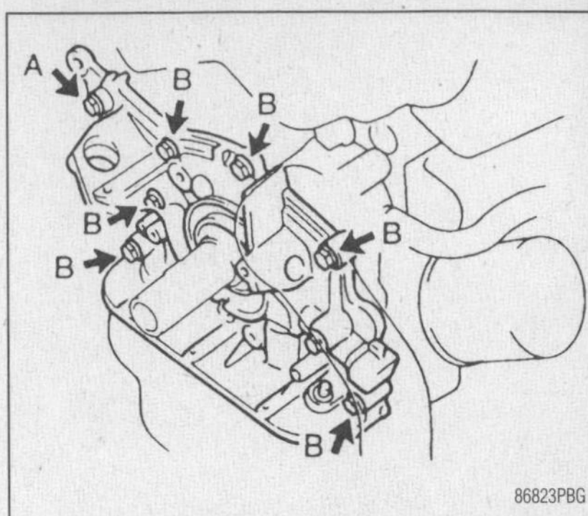

Fig. 167 A and B bolt locations—5VZ-FE engine

18. Remove any old sealant from the surface of the pump, apply new sealant to the oil pump, place the new O-ring into the groove of the block. Place the pump on the crankshaft with the spline teeth of the drive rotor engaged with the large teeth of the crankshaft.
19. Tighten fasteners A to 15 ft. lbs. (20 Nm) and B to 31 ft. lbs. (42 Nm).
20. Install the crankshaft position sensor.
21. Install the oil pan baffle plate.
22. Apply Formed In-Place Gasket (FIPG) sealer to the oil pan and install the pan to the cylinder block. Tighten the nuts and bolts to 66 inch lbs. (8 Nm). If parts are not assembled within 5 minutes of applying time, the sealer starts to skin over, the effectiveness of the sealer is lost and the sealer must be removed and reapplied.
23. Attach the flywheel housing under and cover dust.
24. Install the stiffener plate.
25. Connect the starter wire clamp.
26. On A/T install the oil cooler tube and clamp.
27. Reinstall the crankshaft timing pulley.
28. On the 4WD, install the front differential.
29. Install the engine undercover.
30. Lower the vehicle.
31. Fill with engine oil.
32. Connect the negative battery cable.
33. Start the engine and check for leaks.

1FZ-FE Engine

➧ See Figures 168 thru 175

1. Drain the engine oil.
2. Remove the engine undercover.
3. Drain the engine coolant.
4. Remove the radiator.
5. Disconnect the A/C compressor and bracket. Loosen the pulley nut and adjusting bolt, then remove the belt. Put the compressor aside but do not disconnect any of the lines.
6. Disconnect the radiator hose from the inlet, then unbolt and remove the radiator pipe.
7. Remove the water pump.
8. Remove the cylinder head using the procedures found in this section.
9. Disconnect the oil cooler bracket from the No. 1 oil pan.
10. Remove the oil level sensor and gasket.
11. Unbolt the No. 1 oil pan (upper pan) from the transmission housing.
12. Remove the No. 2 oil pan (lower pan), this is the pan with 17 mounting bolts. Insert a blade or SST 0c2–00100, between the No. 1 and No. 2 oil pans, remove the sealer and lower the No. 2 pan.
13. Remove the 21 bolts retaining the No. 1 oil pan. Pry portions A between the block and the No. 1 pan.
14. Remove the oil pan baffle plate.
15. Remove the oil strainer.
16. Unbolt the crankshaft pulley, then remove the drive belt idler pulley.
17. Unbolt the oil pump (timing chain cover), timing chain and camshaft gear.

To install:

18. Turn the crankshaft until the set key on the crankshaft faces downwards.
19. Install the timing chain and camshaft gear.
20. Attach the oil pump (timing chain cover).
21. Install the drive belt idler pulley then the crankshaft pulley.
22. Install the oil strainer to the block with a new gasket, tighten to 14 ft. lbs. (20 Nm).
23. Install the oil baffle plate, tighten to 78 inch lbs. (9 Nm).
24. Remove any old sealant from the No. 1 oil pan. Clean all the components with a non-residue solvent. Apply sealant to the No. 1 pan as shown. Install the pan within 5 minutes of application.
25. Install a new gasket into position. Pour approximately a few ounces of engine oil into the oil pump hole to help prime the pump. Install the No. 1 pan, tighten the 14mm heads to 31 ft. lbs. (44 Nm) and the 12mm heads to 14 ft. lbs. (20 Nm).
26. Apply sealant to the No. 2 pan, assemble within 5 minutes before the sealant starts to cure. Tighten the bolts to 69 inch lbs. (8 Nm) and the nuts to 78 inch lbs. (9 Nm).
27. Attach the bolts retaining the No. 1 pan to the transmission housing, tighten to 53 ft. lbs. (73 Nm).
28. Install the oil level sensor, tighten to 48 inch lbs. (5 Nm).
29. Connect the oil cooler pipe bracket to the No. 1 pan.
30. Install the cylinder head using a new gasket.
31. Install the water pump with new gaskets on the engine.
32. Connect the radiator hose to the inlet, tighten to 15 ft. lbs. (21 Nm).
33. Install the A/C compressor and bracket, tighten the bracket to 27 ft. lbs. (37 Nm) and the compressor to 18 ft. lbs. (25 Nm).
34. Install the radiator.
35. Attach the engine undercover.
36. Lower the vehicle, fill the engine with oil and coolant.
37. Start the engine and check for leaks. Add any fluid as necessary.

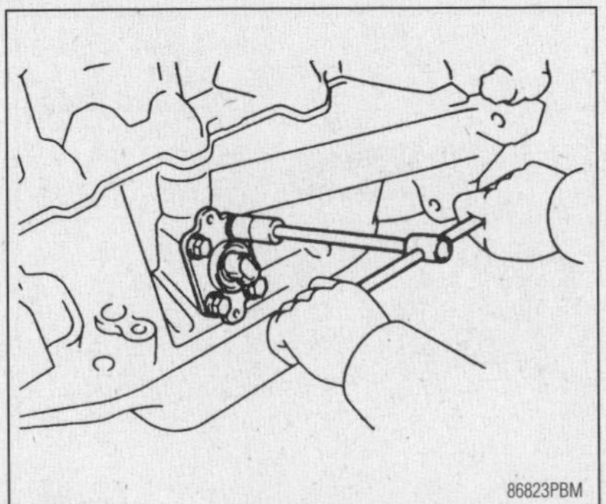

Fig. 168 Remove the oil level sensor and gasket—1FZ-FE engine

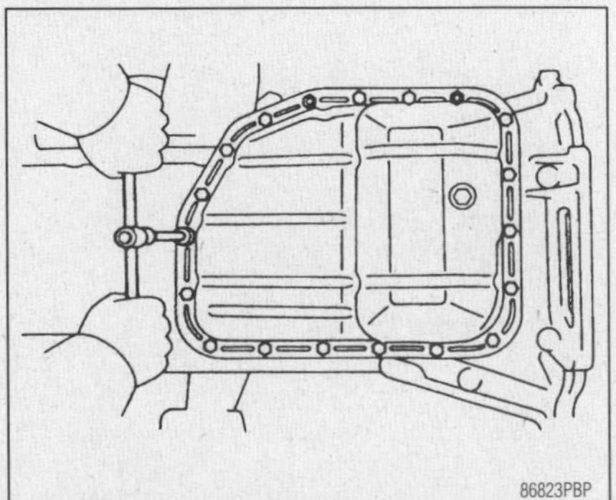

Fig. 169 Remove the bolts securing the No. 2 oil pan—1FZ-FE engine

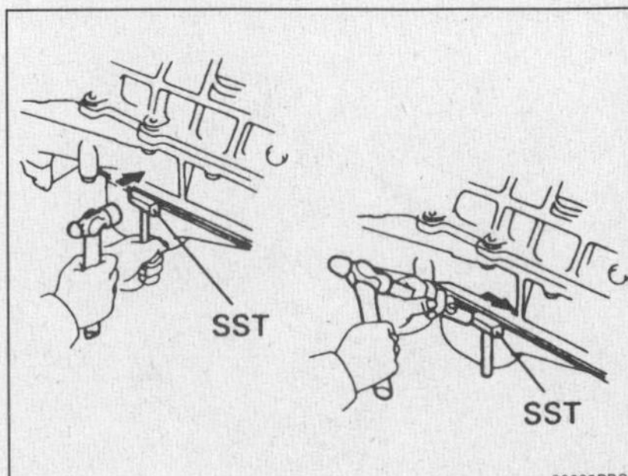

Fig. 170 A special tool is available to cut through the sealant of the oil pan—1FZ-FE engine

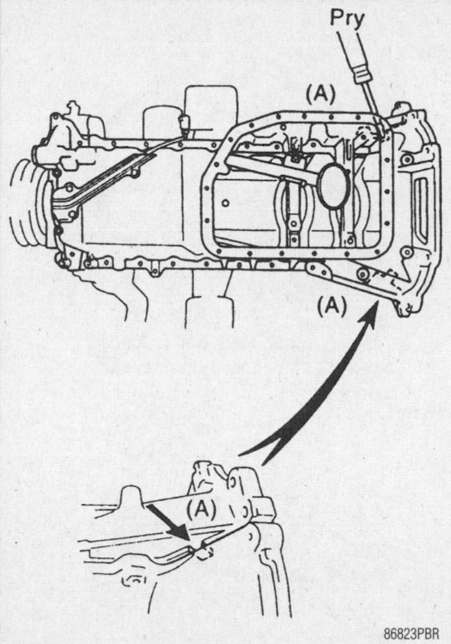

Fig. 171 Use a prybar to pry portions A between the block and the No. 1 pan—1FZ-FE engine

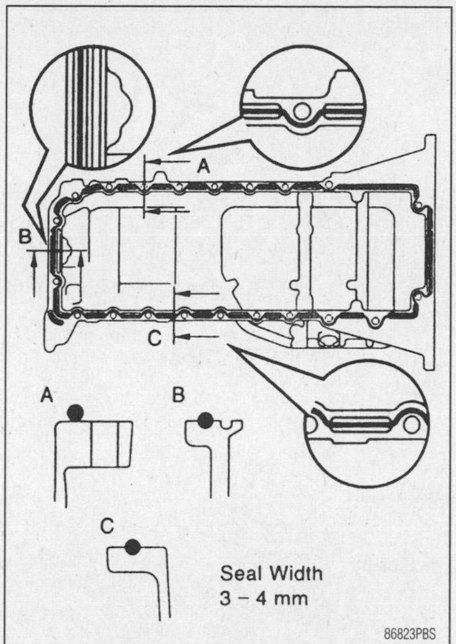

Fig. 172 Apply sealant to the areas shown—1FZ-FE engine

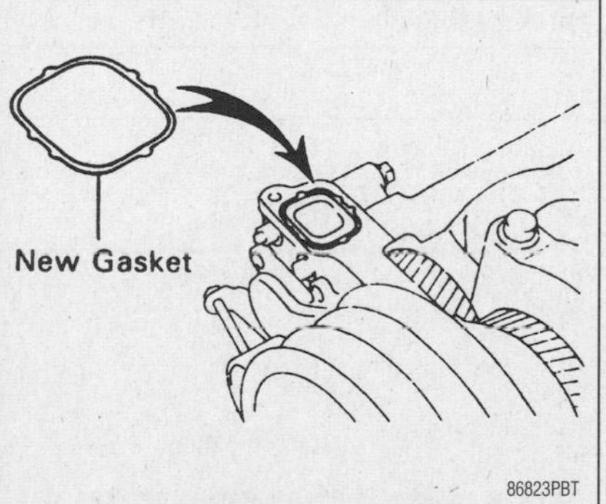

Fig. 173 Install the new gasket to the engine—1FZ-FE engine

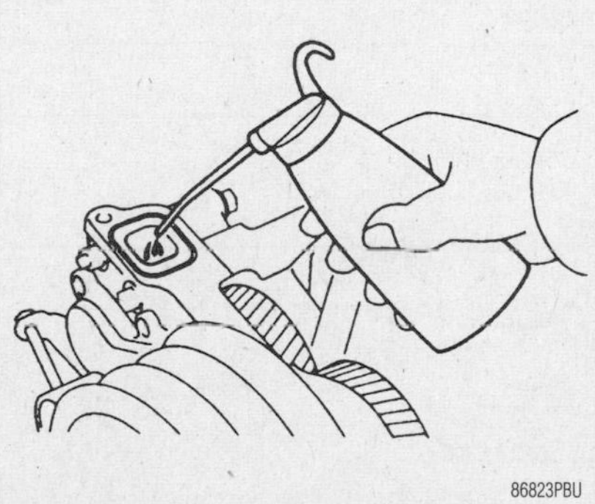

Fig. 174 Add a few ounces of engine oil to prime the pump—1FZ-FE engine

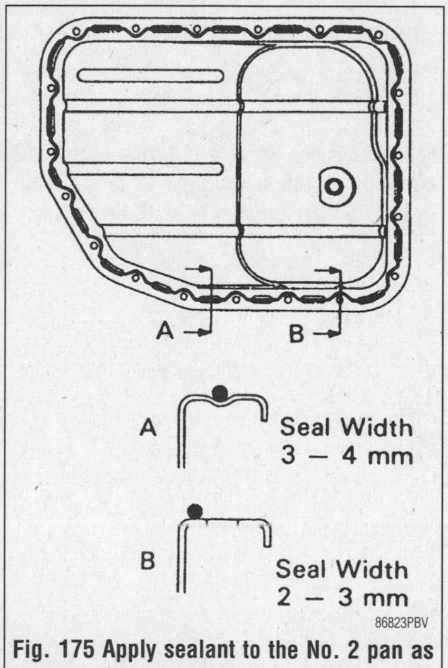

Fig. 175 Apply sealant to the No. 2 pan as shown—1FZ-FE engine

2UZ-FE Engine

➧ See Figures 176, 177, 178, and 179

Toyota specifies that the engine must be removed from the vehicle to service the oil pump. The oil pan and strainer should also be removed and cleaned at the same time.

1. Remove the engine from the vehicle.
2. Mount the engine to a suitable engine stand.
3. Remove the timing belt.
4. Remove both timing belt idler pulleys.
5. Remove the crankshaft timing belt pulley.
6. Remove the crankshaft position sensor.
7. Remove the bolt holding the oil dipstick to the left side cylinder head and pull out the dipstick tube from the oil pan.
8. Remove the oil filer, oil cooler and filter bracket assembly noting the following:
   a. Detach the oil pressure switch connector.
   b. Disconnect the oil cooler hose from the oil cooler.
   c. Remove the bolts and nut, then separate the oil filter, oil cooler and filter bracket assembly from the front of the engine block.
9. Remove the upper and lower oil pans using the procedures found in this section.
10. There are five different sizes of oil pump bolts. Take care to correctly identify each bolt, its length and location. It is good practice to punch holes in a piece of corrugated cardboard to closely resemble the bolt pattern of the oil pump. Insert the bolts in the cardboard in their corresponding locations as they are removed. A few minutes spent at removal will save much time at installation. Remove the eight bolts from oil pump and separate the pump from the engine block. Use care not to damage the sealing surfaces of the block or the pump. Discard the gasket.

To install:

11. Clean all parts well. It is recommended that the oil strainer be removed and cleaned. Install the strainer with a new gasket and torque the fasteners to 66 inch lbs. (7.5 Nm).
12. The oil pump houses the front crankshaft seal. There are two methods of seal replacement.
    a. If the pump has been removed from the engine, simply pry out the old seal. Install a replacement using a seal driver or other suitable tool and tap in the new seal until surface is flush with the oil pump body edge.
    b. If the oil pump is still on the engine, use a sharp knife to cut the oil seal lip. Insert a suitable prytool and pry out the seal. Use great care not to damage the crankshaft surface. Put tape over the removal tool to protect the crankshaft. Apply grease to the seal lip. Using a seal driver or other suitable tool and tap in the new seal until surface is flush with the oil pump body edge.
13. If the pump was disassembled, install the drive and driver rotors into the pump body with the identification marks on the rotors facing the cover side (not the pump body side). Install the cover and tighten the ten screws to 84 inch lbs. (10 Nm).
14. The relief valve, if removed, should be cleaned. Coat the valve with engine oil and check that it falls smoothly into its bore by its own weight. If not, the valve and/or the pump body may have to be replaced. Install the relief valve, spring and retainer into the oil pump body bore. Use snapring pliers to install the retaining ring.
15. There is a small O-ring in the engine block above the crankshaft that must be replaced with a new O-ring. The spline teeth of the oil pump drive gear must align with the large teeth on the crankshaft. Position the pump drive gear as required so the pump will slide onto the crankshaft at assembly.
16. Make sure all old FIPG sealer is removed. The pump sealing flanges and the engine block sealing surfaces must be clean of all oil and grease or the new FIPG sealer wont work. Apply a $^1/_8$ inch (3mm) bead of FIPG sealer to the oil pump sealing surface. Most sealers start to skin over in about five minutes so assemble the oil pump to the block without hesitation. Install the bolts just a few turns, making sure all bolt holes line up. Uniformly torque the bolts in several passes as follows:
    a. Tighten all bolts with a 14mm head to 22 ft. lbs. (30 Nm).
    b. Tighten all other bolts 11 ft. lbs. (15 Nm).
17. Install the oil pan components using the procedures found in this section.
18. Install the oil filter, oil cooler and filter bracket assembly. Torque the nuts and bolts to 13 ft. lbs. (18 Nm). Connect the oil cooler hose and attach the oil pressure switch connector.

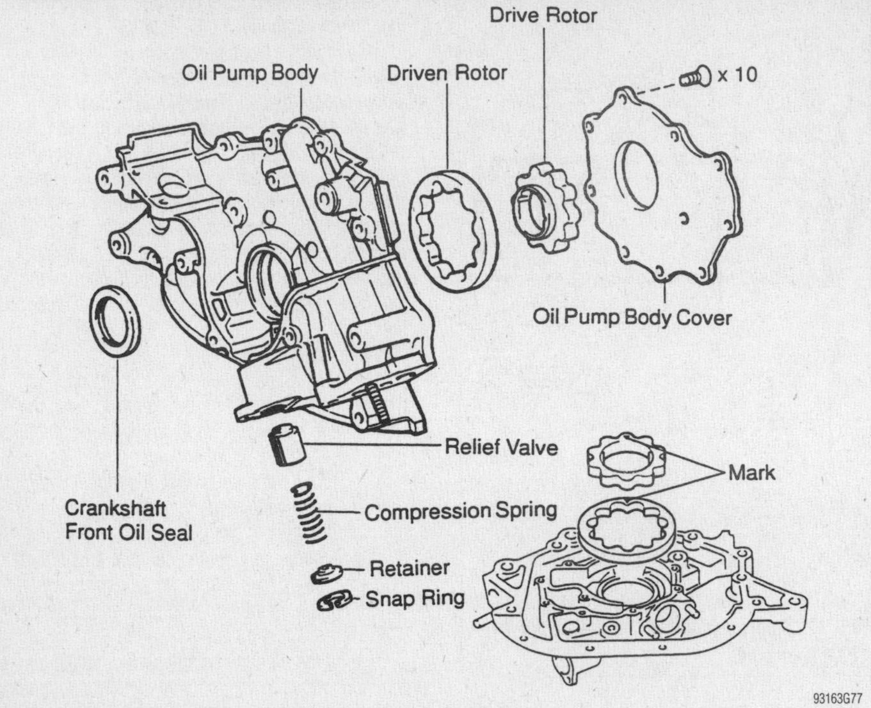

Fig. 176 Exploded view of the oil pump—2UZ-FE engine

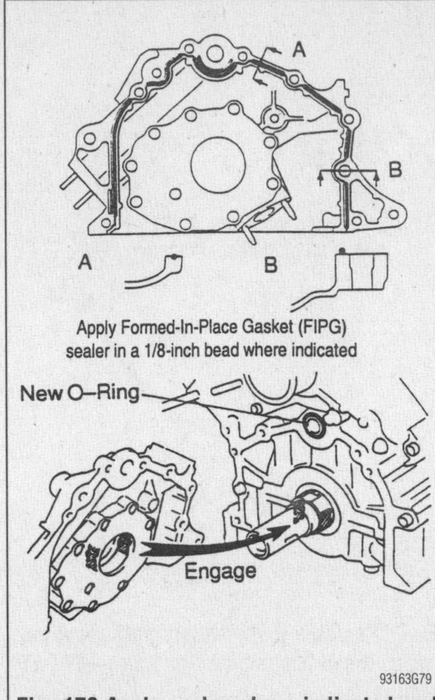

Fig. 178 Apply sealer where indicated and position the driven gear to engage the crankshaft teeth—2UZ-FE engine

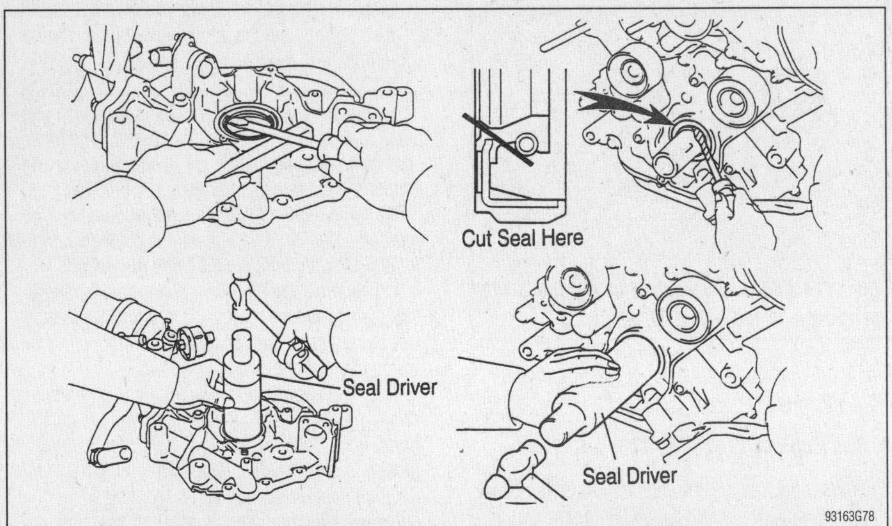

Fig. 177 Crankshaft front oil seal service. Left: Pump removed; Right: Pump in place—2UZ-FE engine

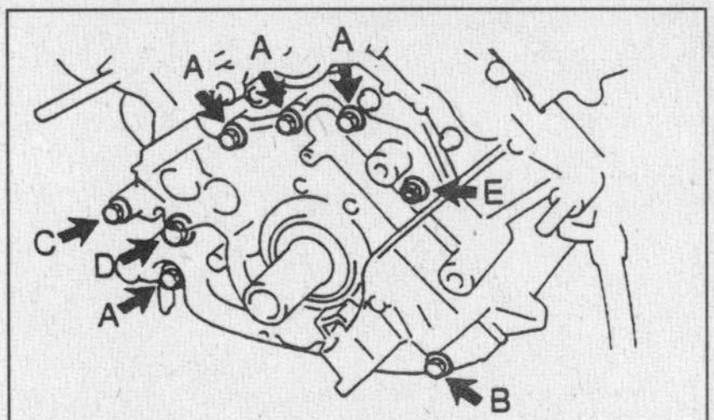

A Bolt is 1.38 inch (35 mm) long with a 12 mm head
B Bolt is 1.97 inch (50 mm) long with a 12 mm head
C Bolt is 4.17 inch (106 mm) long with a 12 mm head
D Bolt is 1.57 inch (40 mm) long with a 14 mm head
E Bolt is 1.18 inch (30 mm) long with a 6 mm hex head

Tighten the bolts evenly, in several passes

Tighten all bolts with a 14 mm head to 22 ft. lbs. (30.5 Nm)
Tighten all other bolts to 11 ft. lbs. (15.5 Nm)

93163G80

Fig. 179 There are five different length oil pump bolts. Use care to get all of the bolts in their proper locations—2UZ-FE engine

19. Using a new O-ring, install the oil dipstick tube.
20. Install both timing belt idler pulleys.
21. Install the timing belt.
22. Install the engine in the vehicle. Refill with oil and coolant. Start the engine and verify correct oil pressure.

Timing Belt Cover and Seal

REMOVAL & INSTALLATION

Refer to the timing belt procedure in this section to remove the timing belt cover.

Timing Chain Cover and Seal

REMOVAL & INSTALLATION

1FZ-FE Engine

See Figures 180 and 181

This is a lengthy procedure requiring careful work. Make sure all timing marks are properly aligned before start-up.

1. Disconnect the negative battery cable.
2. Raise and safely support the vehicle.
3. Drain the engine oil and the engine coolant.
4. Remove the engine undercover.
5. Remove the radiator.
6. Disconnect and remove the A/C compressor and the bracket.
7. Remove the radiator pipe by disconnecting the radiator hose from the water inlet.
8. Remove the water pump and the gasket.
9. Remove the cylinder head using the procedure found in this section.
10. Disconnect the oil cooler pipe bracket from the No. 1 (upper half of the two-piece assembly) oil pan.
11. Remove the oil level sensor.
12. Remove the bolts holding the No. 1 (upper half) oil pan to the transmission housing.

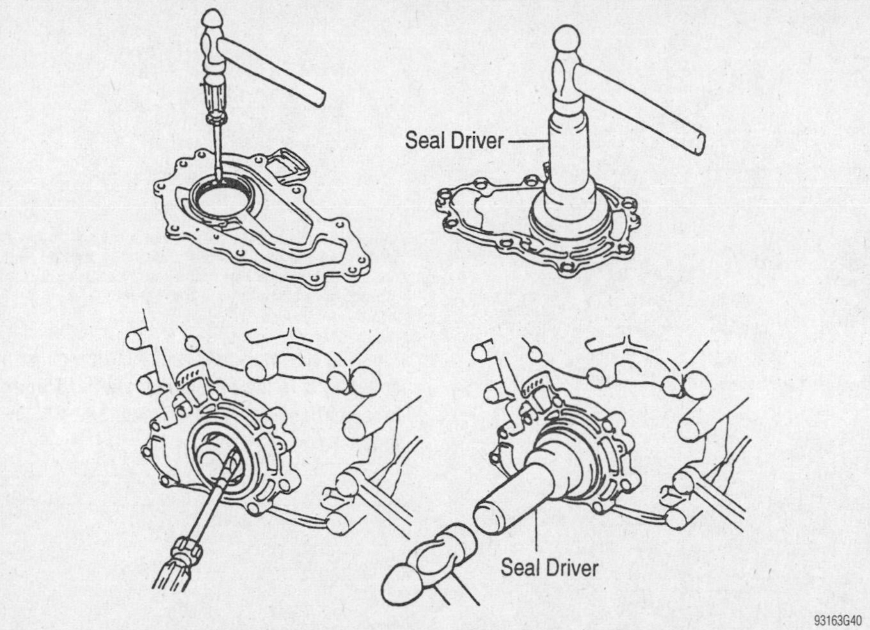

Fig. 180 A seal driver is highly recommended when installing a new seal into the cover

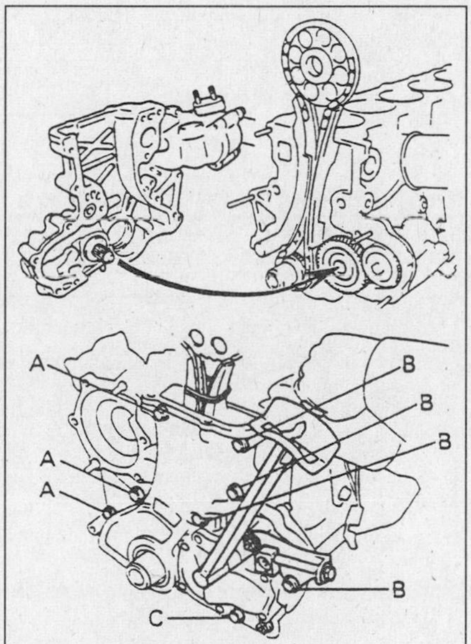

A Bolt is 1.18 inch (30 mm) long
B Bolt is 1.97 inch (50 mm) long
C Bolt is 2.38 inch (60 mm) long

93163G42

Fig. 181 Engage the gear of the oil pump rotor with the gear of the oil pump drive gear and install the front cover and oil pump assembly—1FZ-FE engine

13. Remove the No. 2 (lower half of the assembly) and No. 1 oil pans.
14. Using SST 09213–58012 and 09330–00021, or equivalent, remove the pulley bolt. Remove the crankshaft pulley.
15. Check the thrust clearance of the oil pump driveshaft gear.
  a. Using a dial indicator with a lever type attachment, measure the thrust clearance.
  b. Maximum thrust clearance is 0.0118 in. (0.30mm).
  c. If the thrust clearance is greater than maximum, replace the oil pump driveshaft gear and/or timing chain cover.
16. Remove the drive belt idler pulley.
17. Remove the bolts securing the timing chain cover, then remove the cover. Be sure to note the locations of the different sized bolts.

To install:

18. Clean the gasket mating areas well.
19. Apply Formed In-Place Gasket (FIPG) sealer to the timing chain cover and install the cover assembly.
20. Engage the gear of the oil pump drive rotor with the gear of the oil pump drive gear, and install the oil pump and cover assembly.
21. Three different length bolts are used on the front cover. Make sure they're in the correct locations. Tighten the bolts to 15 ft. lbs. (21 Nm).
22. Remove the cord from the chain.
23. Install the drive belt idler pulley and tighten the bolt to 32 ft. lbs. (43 Nm).
24. Install the crankshaft pulley as follows:
  a. Align the pulley set key with the key groove of the pulley and slide on the pulley.
  b. Install the pulley bolt and tighten to 304 ft. lbs. (412 Nm).
25. Install the No. 1 and the No. 2 oil pans.
26. Install the bolts holding the No. 1 oil pan to the transmission housing. Tighten to 53 ft. lbs. (72 Nm).
27. Install the oil level sensor with a new gasket and tighten the bolts to 48 inch lbs. (5 Nm).
28. Connect the oil cooler pipe bracket to the No. 1 oil pan.
29. Install the cylinder head using the procedures found in this section.
30. Install the water pump and tighten the bolts to 15 ft. lbs. (21 Nm).
31. Attach the No. 2 radiator hose to the water inlet. Install the nuts holding the radiator pipe to the No. 1 oil pan, then tighten to 15 ft. lbs. (21 Nm).
32. Install the A/C compressor bracket, tighten the bolts to 27 ft. lbs. (37 Nm).
33. Install the A/C compressor, tighten the bolts to 18 ft. lbs. (25 Nm). Install and adjust the drive belt.
34. Install the radiator.
35. Refill the engine oil and the engine coolant.
36. Connect the negative battery cable.
37. Start the engine, check for leaks, and check the ignition timing.
38. Install the engine undercover.
39. Add any fluids as required.

2RZ-FE and 3RZ-FE Engines

See Figures 182 and 183

This is a difficult and lengthy procedure requiring removal of many components including the front differential assembly and the cylinder head. This procedure can also be performed with the engine out of the vehicle, which may be an option, depending on the equipment and facilities available. If other heavy engine work is required (for example, a failed timing chain may have caused valve/piston damage) it may just be easier to remove the engine as an assembly and perform the work on a suitable engine stand.

The following procedure is based on Toyotas in-frame procedure.

1. Disconnect the negative battery cable.
2. Raise and safely support the vehicle.
3. Drain the engine coolant and the engine oil.
4. Remove the cylinder head.
5. Remove the radiator.
6. On 4WD vehicles, remove the front differential.
7. Remove the oil pan.
8. If equipped with power steering, remove the power steering belt.
9. If equipped with A/C, remove the A/C belt, compressor, and the bracket.
10. Remove the fluid coupling with the fan and the water pump pulley, as follows:
  a. Loosen the water pump pulley bolts. Loosen the belt adjusting bolt and the pivot bolt of the alternator and remove the drive belt.
  b. Remove the set nuts, the fluid coupling with the fan, and the water pump pulley.
11. Remove the crankshaft pulley.
12. Remove the water bypass pipe.
13. Remove the fan belt adjusting bar. With power steering, remove the lower power steering bracket.
14. Disconnect the heater water outlet pipe.
15. Remove the chain cover assembly.

To install:

16. Remove the old cover gaskets and install new gaskets.
17. Slide the timing chain cover assembly over the dowels and the pump spline. Tighten the 8mm bolts to 9 ft. lbs. (13 Nm) and the 10mm bolts to 29 ft. lbs. (13 Nm).
18. Install the fan belt adjusting bar to the chain cover and the cylinder head. Tighten to 9 ft. lbs. (13 Nm).
19. Install the heater water outlet pipe.
20. Install the water bypass pipe.
21. Install the crankshaft pulley and tighten the bolt to 116 ft. lbs. (157 Nm).
22. Install the water pump pulley and the fluid coupling with the fan. Place the belt onto each pulley. While pulling the belt tight, tighten the four nuts.
23. Adjust the drive belt tension.
24. If removed, install the A/C compressor bracket, the compressor and the belt.

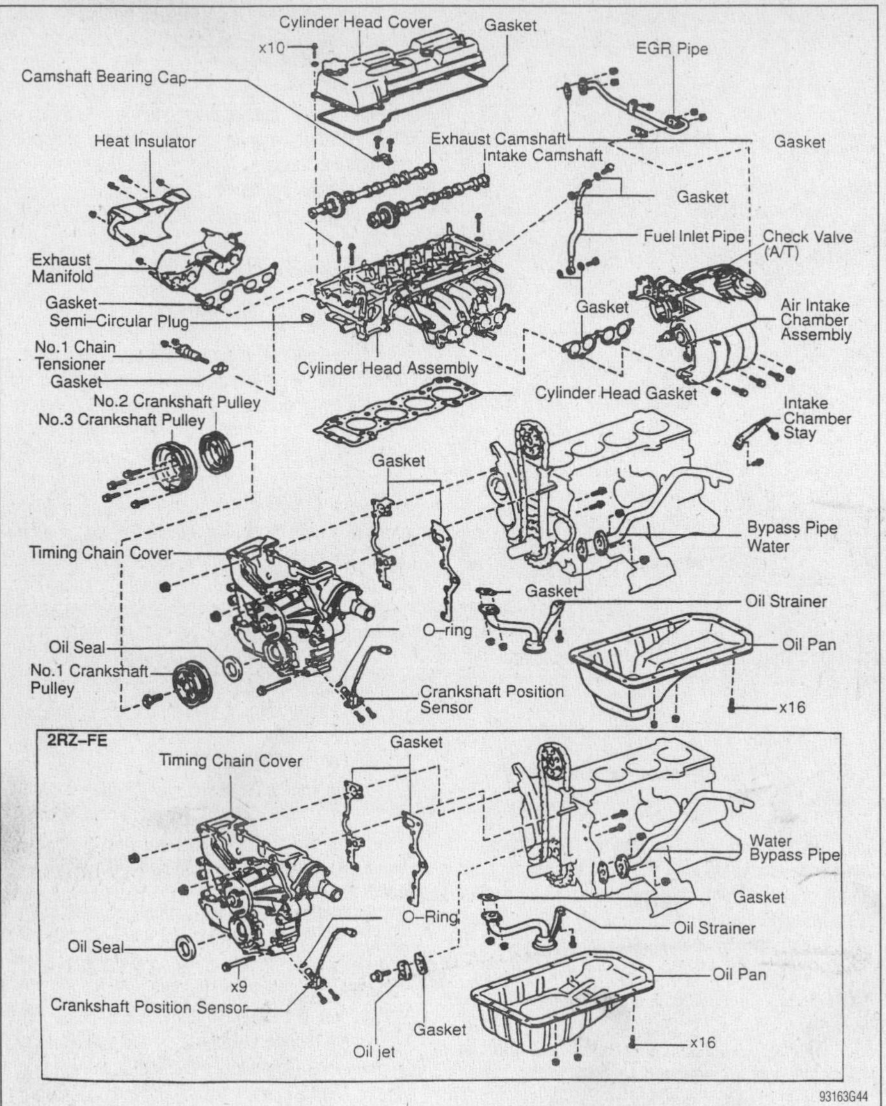

Fig. 182 Numerous components must be removed to service the timing chain cover—2RZ-FE and 3RZ-FE engines

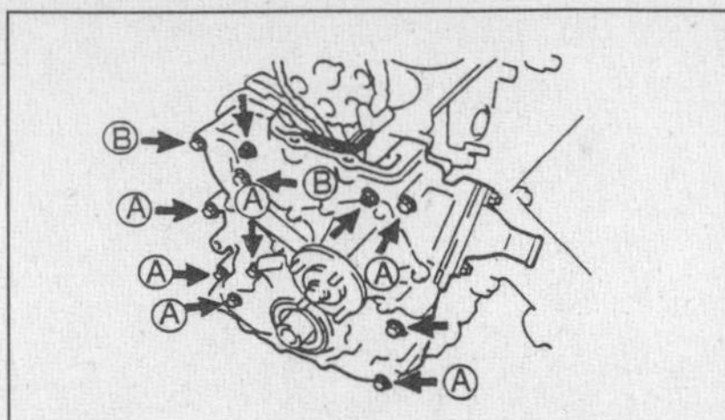

A Bolt has a 12 mm head and is tightened to 14 ft. lbs. (20 Nm)
B Bolt has a 12 mm head and is tightened to 18 ft. lbs. (24.5 Nm)
Bolts with a 14 mm head are tightened to 32 ft. lbs. (44 Nm)
The two nuts are tightened to 14 ft. lbs. (20 Nm)
93163G48

Fig. 183 Use care to install the timing chain cover bolts in their proper locations. Torque to specification—2RZ-FE and 3RZ-FE Engines

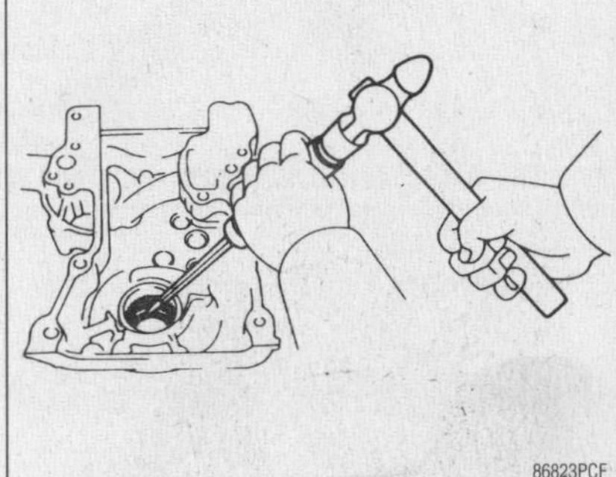

Fig. 184 Remove the seal with a flat-blade tool and hammer

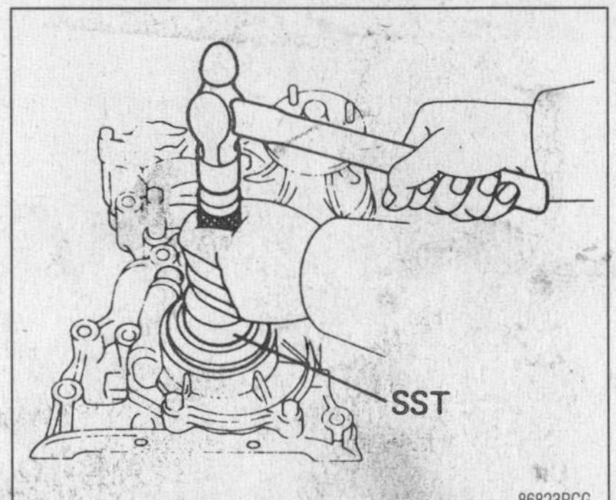

Fig. 185 Install the seal using a proper sized driver

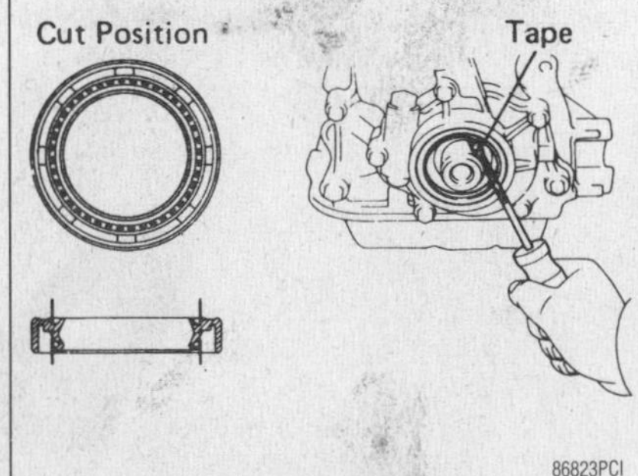

Fig. 186 Carefully cut off the oil seal lip, then pry the seal from the cover

25. If removed, install the power steering belt.
26. Apply Formed In-Place Gasket (FIPG) sealer to the joint part of the cylinder block, the chain cover, the cylinder block, the rear oil seal retainer and the oil pan. Install the oil pan over the studs on the block and tighten the nuts and bolts to 9 ft. lbs. (13 Nm).
27. Install the radiator.
28. Install the cylinder head.
29. If removed, install the front differential.
30. Fill with engine coolant and engine oil.
31. Connect the negative battery cable.
32. Start the engine and check the ignition timing.

SEAL REPLACEMENT

Cover Removed

➧ See Figures 184 and 185

1. Unbolt the timing chain cover assembly. Be careful to loosen only the correct bolts.
2. Pry out the seal from the cover with a flat-bladed tool.
3. It is a good idea to remove the oil pump from the timing cover and replace the O-ring.

To install:

4. Clean and inspect the timing cover area. Install new gaskets around the dowel areas and pump spline.
5. Apply multi-purpose grease to the new oil seal lip.
6. Tap the seal into place with SST 09223-50010/60010 or equivalent, and a hammer. Do this until the seal surface is flush with the cover edge.
7. Install the cover, tighten the bolts as specified for your engine.
8. If the oil pump was removed, install a new O-ring behind the pump prior to installation.

Cover Installed

➧ See Figures 186 and 187

1. Unbolt and remove the oil pump.
2. Using a knife, carefully cut off the oil seal lip. With a flat-bladed tool, (preferably with tape around it) pry the seal from the cover.

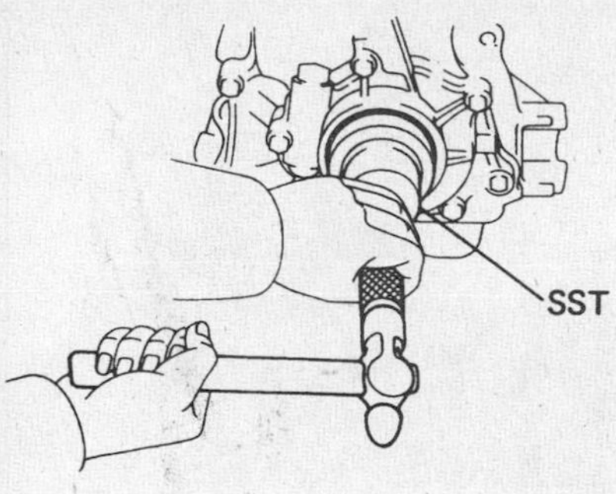

86823PCJ

Fig. 187 Drive the seal flush against the cover edge

To install:

3. Apply multi-purpose grease to the new oil seal lip.
4. Tap the seal into place with SST 09223–50010/60011 or equivalent seal driver, and a hammer. Do this until the seal surface is flush with the cover edge.
5. Install the oil pump with a new O-ring.

Timing Belt

REMOVAL & INSTALLATION

If you operate your vehicle under conditions of extensive idling and or low speed driving for long periods of time; such as a taxi, police or delivery service, replace the belt every 60,000 miles (96,000 km).

Valve timing in any engine is important but in a Dual Over Head Camshaft (DOHC) engine like this it is critical. Improperly performed, cam timing belt replacement can ruin the engine. Work carefully and verify that all timing marks properly align before attempting to start the engine.

5VZ-FE Engine

See Figures 188 thru 203

1. Disconnect the negative battery cable.
2. Remove the engine undercover.
3. Drain the engine coolant.

93163p58

Fig. 188 Remove the upper timing belt cover

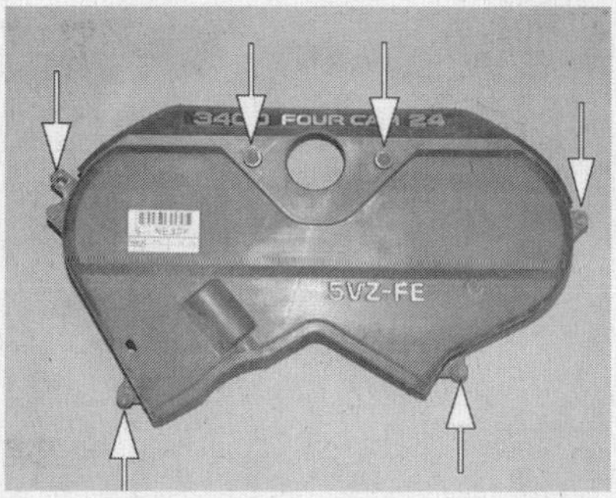

93163p59

Fig. 189 Upper timing belt cover bolt locations

93163p60

Fig. 190 Once the cover is removed, the timing belt and camshafts are in plain view

93163p63

Fig. 191 Mark the installed position of the belt . . .

93163p65

Fig. 192 . . . and direction of rotation

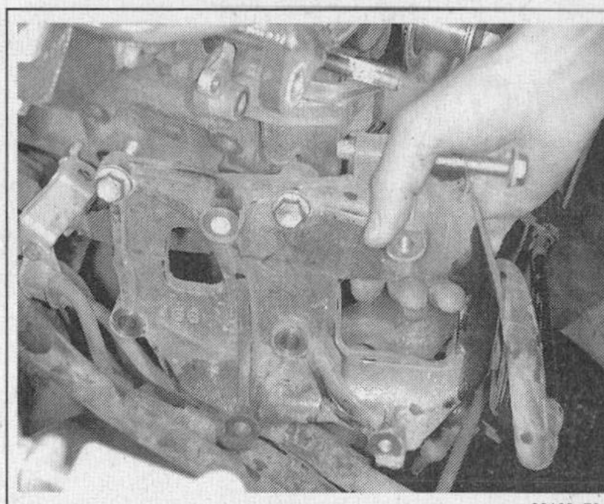

93163p79

Fig. 193 You may have to remove the A/C bracket . . .

93163p81

Fig. 194 . . . to gain access to the rear timing belt tensioner bolt

93163p80

Fig. 195 View of the A/C bracket and bolts

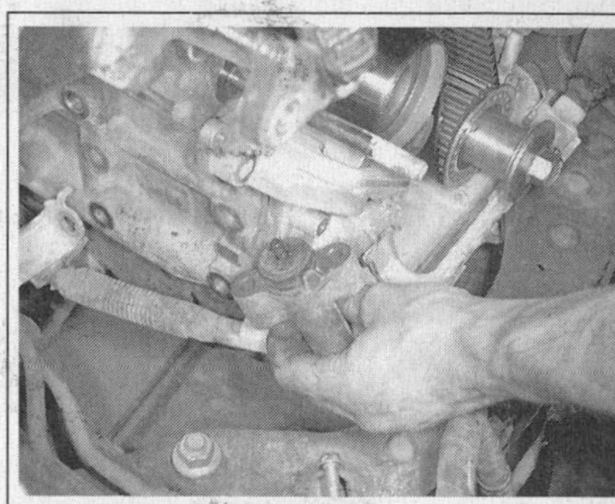

93163p83

Fig. 196 Carefully remove the timing belt tensioner

93163p84

Fig. 197 View of the crankshaft pulley and bolt

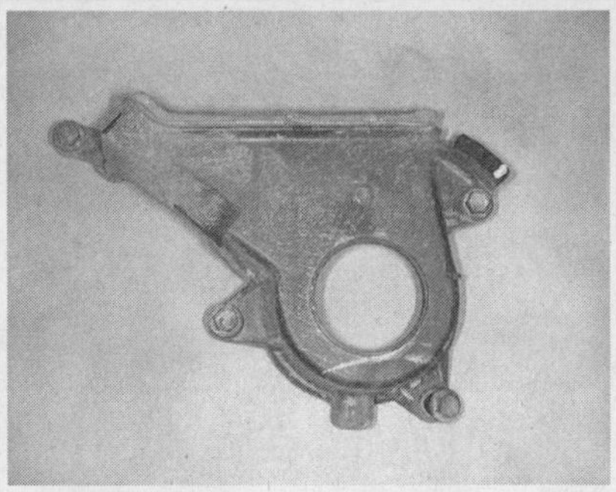

93163p86

Fig. 198 Lower timing cover, once removed from the vehicle

93163p90

Fig. 199 Carefully remove the timing belt by unrouting it from the pulleys

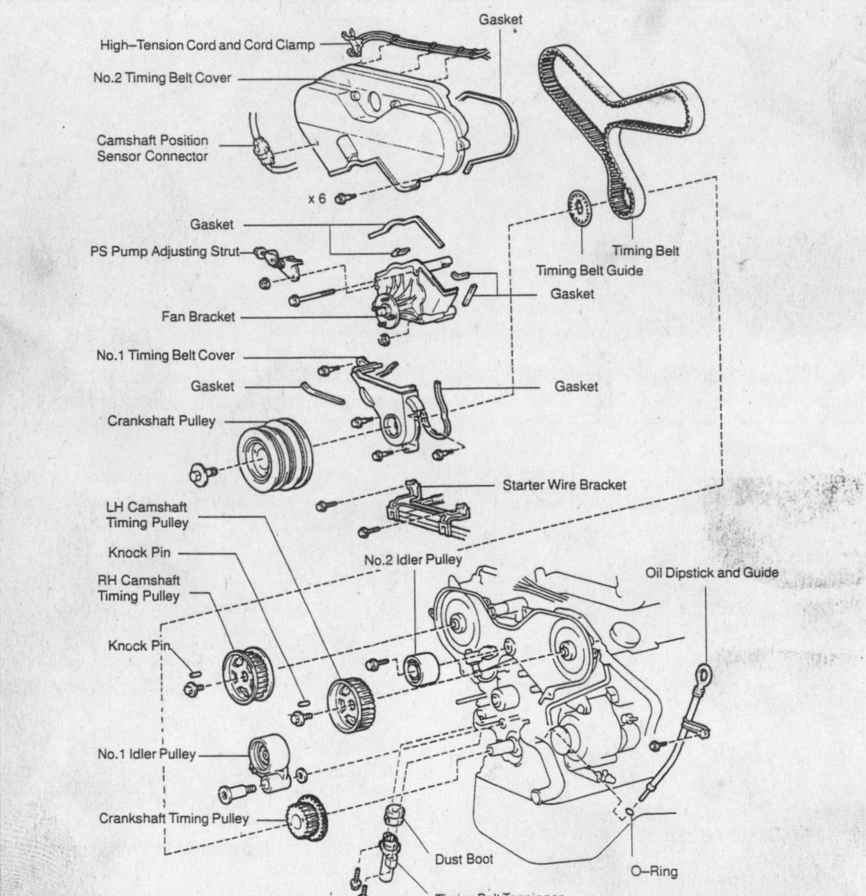

93163G49

Fig. 200 Exploded view of the timing belt and related components—5VZ-FE engine

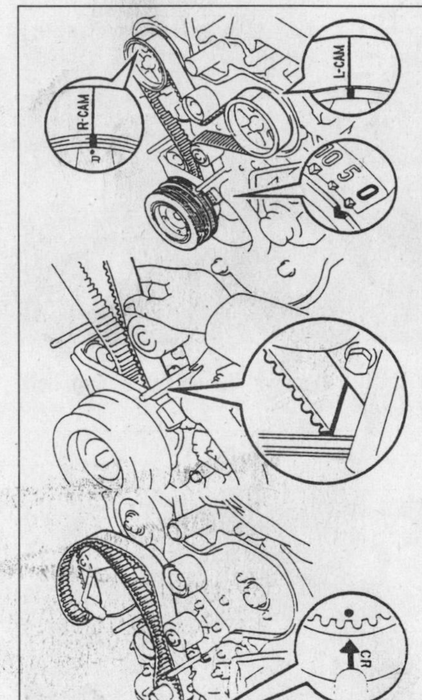

93163G50

Fig. 201 For proper installation and to avoid engine damage, all timing marks must align—5VZ-FE engine

4. Disconnect the upper radiator hose from the engine and radiator.

5. Remove the power steering pump from the engine.

6. Without disconnecting the refrigerant lines, remove the A/C compressor from the engine. Carefully secure out of the way with wire.

7. Loosen the fan with the fluid coupling (also called a fan clutch) and fan pulleys.

8. Remove the alternator belt.

9. Remove the No. 2 fan shroud. This is the small, semicircular piece below the fan.

10. Remove the fan along with the fluid coupling and fan pulleys.

11. If equipped with air conditioning, remove the five bolts and take off the compressor bracket.

12. Remove the No. 2 timing belt cover using the following procedure:

a. Disconnect the camshaft position sensor connector from the No. 2 timing belt cover.

b. Disconnect the high-tension spark plug cable clamps from the timing belt cover.

c. Remove the six bolts and take off the timing belt cover.

13. Remove the fan bracket as follows:

a. Remove the power steering pump adjusting strut by removing the nut.

b. Remove the fan bracket by removing the bolt and nut.

14. Set the No. 1 cylinder to TDC of the compression stroke as follows:

a. Turn the crankshaft pulley and align its groove with the timing mark **0** of the No. 1 timing belt cover.

b. Check that the timing marks of the camshaft timing pulleys and the No. 3 timing belt cover are aligned. If not, turn the crankshaft pulley one revolution (360 degrees).

➡If reusing the timing belt, make sure that you can still read the installation marks. If not, place new installation matchmarks on the timing belt to match the timing marks of the camshaft timing pulleys.

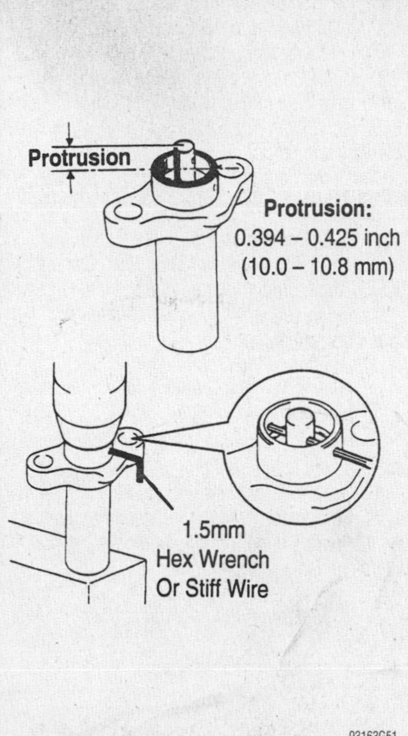

Fig. 202 Measure the tensioner's pushrod. If it's OK, compress it in a shop press and secure with a pin—5VZ-FE Engine

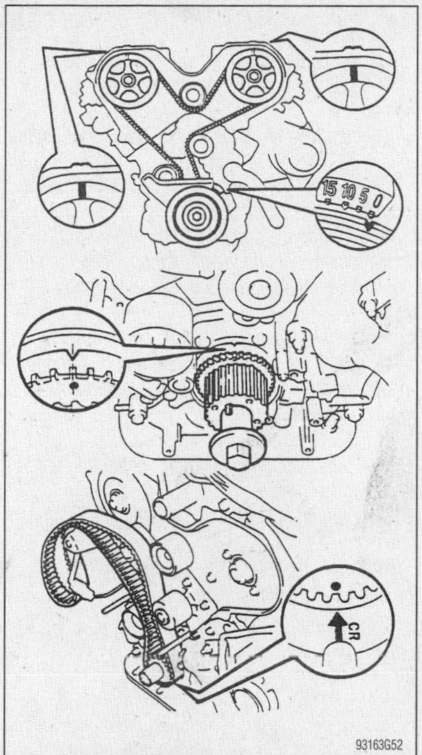

Fig. 203 As a final check, verify that all of these timing marks are properly aligned—5VZ-FE Engine

15. Remove the timing belt tensioner by alternately loosening the two bolts. Remove the bolts, the tensioner and dust boot.

16. Remove the timing belt from the camshaft timing belt pulleys (also called sprockets).

17. If the timing belt pulleys must be removed, continue with this procedure. Ordinarily, the timing belt pulleys do not need to be removed just to replace the timing belt.

18. Using SST 09960–10010 or and equivalent pin spanner-type tool to hold the pulley in place, remove the pulley bolt, the camshaft timing pulley and the small pin (Toyota calls it a knock pin) that locates the pulley to the camshaft. Remove both camshaft timing pulleys in this manner.

19. To remove the timing belt lower cover (Toyota calls it the No. 1 timing belt cover), first the crankshaft pulley must be removed. Use the following procedure:

a. Using SST 09213–54015 and 09330–00021, or equivalent holding tool to keep the crankshaft from turning, loosen the pulley center bolt.

b. Remove the holding tool, the pulley bolt, and the pulley.

20. Remove the starter wire bracket and the No. 1 timing belt cover.

21. Remove the timing belt guide and remove the timing belt from the engine.

22. Remove the bolt and the No. 2 idler pulley.

23. Remove the pivot bolt, the No. 1 idler pulley, and the flat washer.

24. Remove the crankshaft timing belt pulley. It should pull off. If not, use the a gear puller to coax the pulley from the front of the crankshaft.

To install:

25. Clean all parts well. Do not bend or turn the timing belt inside out. Check the belt for cracks or deterioration. Take care to keep solvents, oil, water and anti-freeze off the timing belt. If contaminated, the belt must be replaced.

26. Inspect the idler pulleys. Check around the seals for oil leakage. Check that the pulley turns smoothly. Replace the idler pulley if necessary.

27. Inspect the timing belt tensioner. Check the seal for signs of leakage. Hold the tensioner securely and and push the pushrod strongly to check that it doesn't move. If the pushrod moves, replace the tensioner. Never hold the tensioner pushrod facing downward. Measure the protrusion of the pushrod from the housing end. It should stick out 0.394–0.425 inch (10.0–10.8mm). If not as specified, replace the tensioner.

28. Install the crankshaft timing belt pulley. Align the key in the crankshaft groove with the key groove of the timing pulley. Slide the timing pulley onto the crankshaft with the flange side inward. The toothed flange is for the crankshaft position sensor and must be positioned properly to line up with the sensor. Use care not to bend or damage this toothed flange.

29. Install the flat washer and the No. 1 idler pulley with the pivot bolt and tighten to 26 ft. lbs. (35 Nm). Check that the pulley bracket moves smoothly.

30. Install the No. 2 timing belt idler with the bolt. Tighten the bolt to 30 ft. lbs. (40 Nm). Check that the pulley bracket moves smoothly.

31. Temporarily install the timing belt, as follows:

a. Using the crankshaft pulley bolt, turn the crankshaft and align the timing marks on the crankshaft timing pulley and the oil pump body.

b. Align the installation mark on the timing belt with the dot mark of the crankshaft timing pulley.

c. Install the timing belt on the crankshaft timing pulley, No. 1 idler, and the water pump pulleys.

32. Install the timing belt guide with the cup side facing outward.

33. Install the No. 1 timing belt cover and starter wire bracket. Tighten the timing belt cover bolts to 80 inch lbs. (9 Nm).

34. Install the crankshaft pulley as follows:

a. Align the pulley key with the key groove of the crankshaft pulley.

b. Install the pulley bolt and tighten it to 215 ft. lbs. (295 Nm). A holding tool will be required to keep the pulley from turning.

➡The left side camshaft pulley is to be installed next. Do not install the right side pulley yet since the camshafts must be timed. Follow the procedure closely.

35. Install the left camshaft timing pulley as follows:

a. Slide the timing pulley onto the end of the camshaft with the flange side facing outward.

b. Align the hole in the camshaft with the retaining pin groove of the timing belt pulley.

c. Install the retaining pin to the camshaft.

d. Tighten the pulley bolt to 81 ft. lbs. (110 Nm).

36. Set the No. 1 cylinder to TDC of the compression stroke as follows:

a. Turn the crankshaft pulley, and align its groove with the timing mark **0** of the No. 1 timing belt cover.

b. Turn the right side camshaft and align the retaining pin hole of the camshaft with the timing mark of the No. 3 timing belt cover.

c. Turn the left side camshaft timing pulley and align the timing marks of the camshaft timing pulley and the No. 3 timing belt cover.

37. Install the timing belt to the left camshaft timing pulley. Check that the installation mark on the timing belt is aligned with the end of the No. 1 timing belt cover as follows:

a. Using SST 09960–01000 or equivalent pin spanner tool, slightly turn the left camshaft timing pulley clockwise. Align the installation mark on the timing belt with the timing mark of the camshaft timing pulley, and hang the timing belt on the left camshaft timing pulley.

b. Align the timing marks of the left camshaft pulley and the No. 3 timing belt cover.

c. Check that the timing belt has tension between the crankshaft timing pulley and the left camshaft timing pulley.

38. Install the right camshaft timing pulley and the timing belt as follows:

a. Align the installation mark on the timing belt with the timing mark of the right camshaft timing pulley, and hang the timing belt on the right camshaft timing pulley with the flange side facing inward.

b. Slide the right camshaft timing pulley on the camshaft. Align the timing marks on the right camshaft timing pulley and the No. 3 timing belt cover.

c. Align the retaining pin hole in the end of the camshaft with the pin groove of the pulley and install the retaining pin. Install the bolt and tighten to 81 ft. lbs. (110 Nm).

39. Set the timing belt tensioner as follows:

a. Using a shop press, slowly press in the pushrod. A considerable amount of force may be required, as much as 220–2,200 lbs. (981–9,807 N) of force.

b. Align the holes of the pushrod and housing, pass a 1.5mm hexagon wrench or similar strong retaining pin through the holes to keep the setting position of the pushrod.

c. Release the press and install the dust boot to the tensioner.

40. Install the timing belt tensioner and alternately tighten the bolts to 20 ft. lbs. (28 Nm). Using pliers, remove the 1.5mm hexagon wrench or other retaining pin used to contain the tensioner, from the belt tensioner.

41. Check the valve timing as follows:

a. Slowly turn the crankshaft pulley two revolutions from the TDC to TDC. Always turn the crankshaft pulley clockwise.

b. Check that each pulley aligns with the timing marks. If the timing marks do not align, the job must be done over. Remove the timing belt and reinstall it.

42. Install the fan bracket with the bolt and nut.

43. Install the power steering adjusting strut with the nut.

44. Install the No. 2 timing belt cover. Tighten the bolts to 80 inch lbs. (9 Nm).

45. Connect the clamps for the spark plug wires to the No. 2 timing belt cover.

46. Connect the camshaft position sensor connector to the No. 2 timing belt cover.

47. If equipped, install the A/C compressor bracket.

48. If equipped, install the A/C compressor.

49. Install the fan with the fluid coupling and fan pulleys. Tighten the nuts to 48 inch lbs. (6 Nm).

50. Install the fan shroud.

51. Install the alternator drive belt.

52. Install the cooling fan and tighten the nuts to 48 inch lbs. (6 Nm).

53. If equipped, install and adjust the A/C drive belt.

54. Install the power steering pump, pump pulley, and the drive belt.

55. Connect the upper radiator hose.

56. Install the engine undercover.

57. Fill the cooling system with coolant.

58. Connect the negative battery cable.

59. Start the engine and check for leaks.

2UZ-FE Engine

➧ See Figures 204, 205, 206, 207, and 208

The 2UZ-FE engine is a V8 introduced during Model Year 1998. It is a Dual Over Head Camshaft (DOHC) engine and great care must be used if servicing the timing belt. If the camshaft-to-crankshaft timing is incorrect, engine damage will result.

1. Disconnect the negative battery cable.
2. Remove the engine undercover.
3. Drain the engine coolant.
4. Remove the radiator assembly using the procedures found in this section.
5. Remove the throttle body cover.
6. Remove the intake air connector assembly.
7. Remove the drive belt, fluid coupling (fan clutch) and fan pulley.

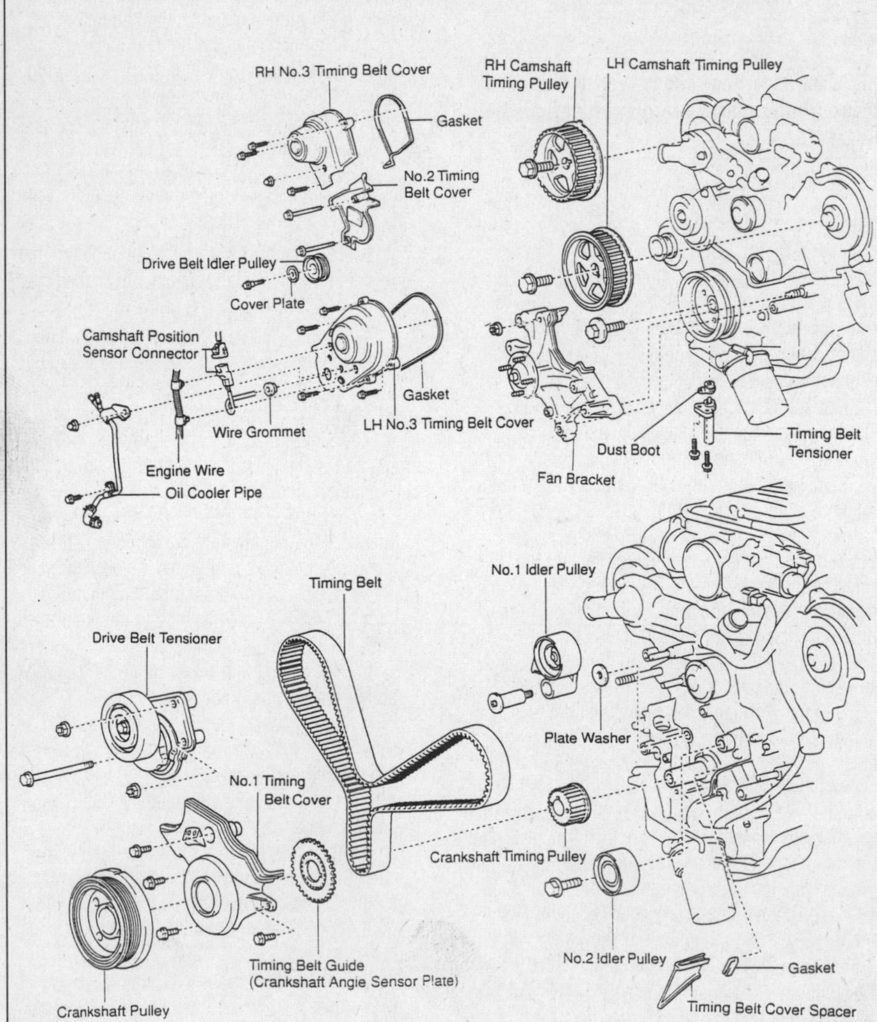

Fig. 204 Camshaft timing belt and related components—2UZ-FE engine

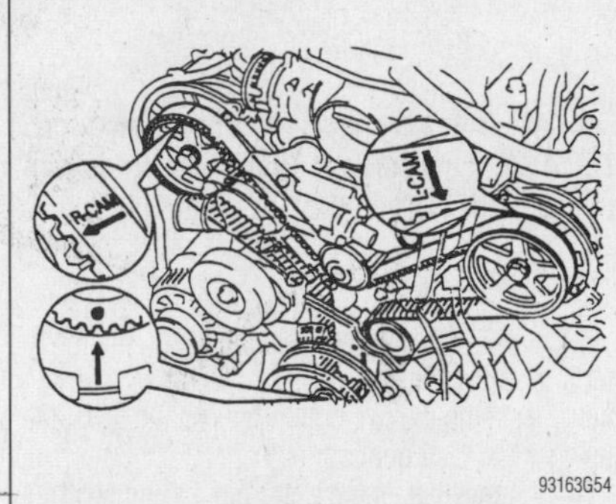

Fig. 205 If reusing the timing belt, check that these installation marks are on the timing belt—2UZ-FE engine

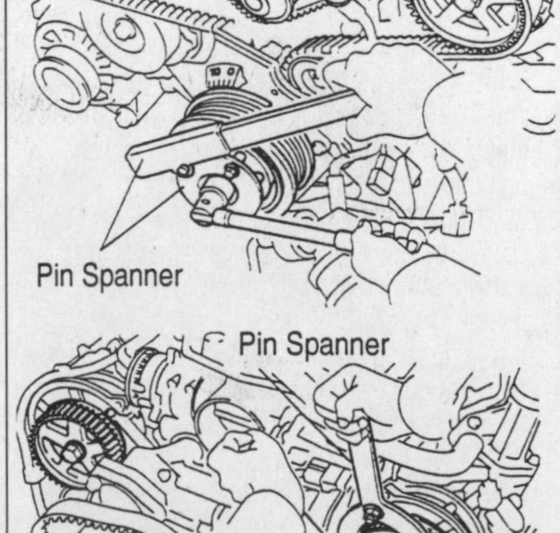

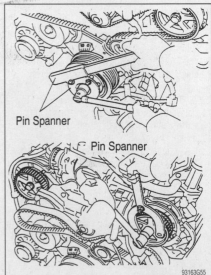

Fig. 206 A holding tool will be required when loosening the crankshaft and camshaft pulley bolts. A pin-type spanner is an adjustable tool adaptable to different sizes—2UZ-FE engine

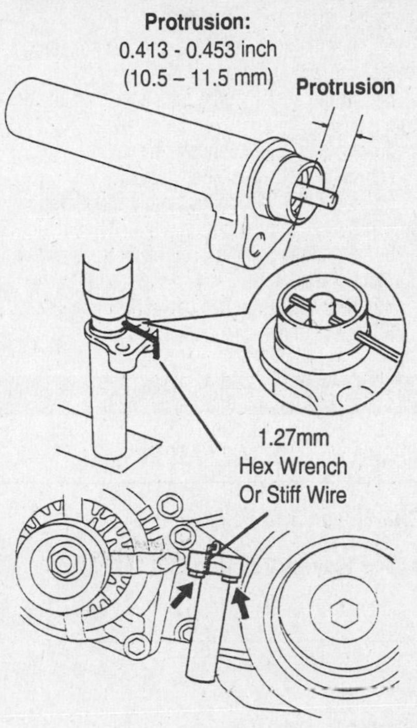

93163G56

Fig. 207 Measure the tensioner's pushrod. If it's OK, compress the tensioner in a shop press and secure with a pin—2UZ-FE engine

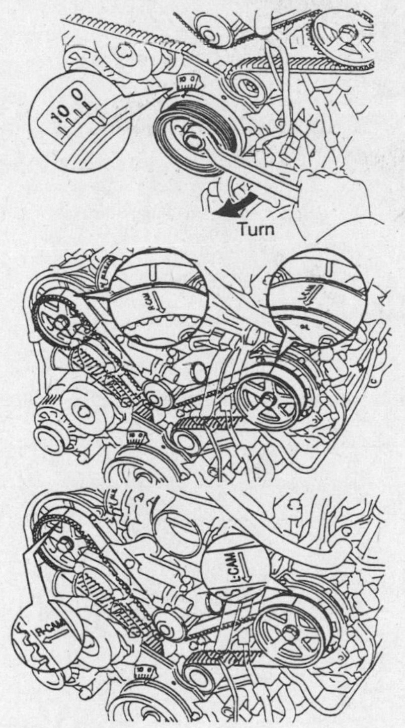

93163G57

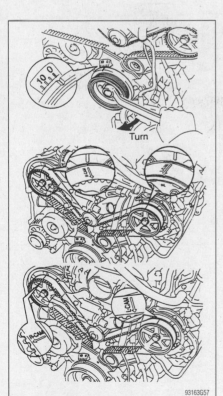

Fig. 208 With the timing belt installed, turn the crankshaft exactly two complete turns and check the timing marks again. They must be properly aligned or the engine will be damaged

8. Without disconnecting the power steering lines, unbolt the power steering pump and wire it out of the way.
9. Remove the drive belt idler pulley by removing the bolt, cover plate, then the pulley.
10. Remove the right side timing belt cover (Toyota calls it the RH No. 3 Timing Belt Cover).
11. Remove the left side timing belt cover (Toyota calls it the LH No. 3 Timing Belt Cover). Use care when detaching the camshaft position sensor wire.
12. Remove the timing belt cover that is next to the drive belt pulley position (Toyota call it the No. 2 Timing Belt Cover).
13. Without disconnecting the refrigerant lines, unbolt the air conditioning compressor and wire it out of the way.
14. Unbolt the fan bracket. Use care. The bolts are different lengths with different head sizes. Identify and mark the bolts are they are removed so they can be installed in the same locations.
15. If reusing the timing belt, look for installation marks on the timing belt. Check that there are three installation marks on the timing belt by turning the crankshaft pulley clockwise. Look for marks at the crankshaft and camshaft pulleys. If the installation marks have disappeared, place a new mark on the timing belt before removing each part.
16. Loosen (but do not remove) the crankshaft pulley bolt. A holding tool may be needed to keep the crankshaft from turning as the bolt is broken loose.
17. Set the engine up so No. 1 cylinder is at Top Dead Center (TDC) of the compression stroke, using the following as a guide:
    a. Turn the crankshaft pulley and align its groove with the timing mark **0** of the No.1 timing belt cover.
    b. Check that the timing marks of the camshaft timing pulleys and timing belt rear plates are aligned. If not, then the No. 1 cylinder is not on the compression stroke. Turn the crankshaft clockwise exactly one revolution until the crankshaft pulley groove is aligned with the timing mark **0** of the No.1 timing belt cover.
    c. Now remove the crankshaft pulley bolt, using care not to allow the pulley to turn off TDC.

**** WARNING**

Do not turn the crankshaft pulley.

18. Remove the timing belt tensioner, as follows:
    a. If reusing the timing belt, look for the installation marks. If the installation marks have disappeared, before removing the belt, paint two new installation marks on the timing belt to match the timing marks of the camshaft pulleys.
    b. When replacing the timing belt tensioner only, to avoid incorrect meshing of the timing pulley and timing belt, secure one of them with a string or wire, to keep the belt tight on the pulley. Place matchmarks on the timing belt and right side camshaft pulley.
    c. Alternately loosen the two bolts and remove them, then separate the belt tensioner and dust boot.
19. Disconnect the timing belt from the camshaft pulleys, noting the following:
    a. Using a spin spanner or equivalent tool that fits on the camshaft pulleys, loosen the tension spring between the left side and right side camshaft timing pulleys by slightly turning the left side camshaft pulley clockwise.
    b. Remove timing belt from the camshaft pulleys .
20. To remove the camshaft pulleys, use a pin spanner or equivalent tool to hold the camshaft pulleys and keep them from turning, loosen the pulley center bolts and remove the pulleys. Use care not to turn the pulleys.
21. Remove the alternator.
22. Remove the drive belt tensioner.
23. To remove the crankshaft pulley, the center bolt should have already been removed in a previous step. Use a suitable harmonic balancer-type puller draw the pulley from the nose of the crankshaft. Use care not to turn the crankshaft pulley from TDC.
24. Remove the lower timing belt cover (Toyota called it the No. 1 Timing Belt Cover).
25. Remove the timing belt guide and cover spacer.
26. Remove the timing belt from the engine. If reusing the timing belt, and the installation mark has disappeared from it, paint a new installation mark on the timing belt to match the dot mark of the crankshaft timing pulley.
27. If necessary, remove the idler pulleys and check them for smooth turning.
28. If it is necessary to remove the crankshaft timing belt pulley, use a suitable gear puller to draw the pulley from the nose of the crankshaft. Use care not to turn the crankshaft pulley from TDC.

To install:

29. Inspect the timing belt. Do not bend, twist or turn the timing belt inside out. Do not allow the timing belt to come into contact with oil, water, antifreeze or solvents. If the belt teeth are cracked or damaged, check that one of the camshafts is locked. If there is noticeable wear or cracks on the belt face, check for nicks on the side of the idler pulley and water pump. If there is wear or damage on even one side of the belt, check the belt guide and the alignment of each pulley. If there is noticeable wear on the belt teeth, check the timing cover for damage and for foreign material on the pulley teeth. If necessary, replace the timing belt. Do not use the timing belt tension when installing or removing the mount bolt of the camshaft timing pulleys.
30. Check the idler pulleys. Check seal for leaking lubricant. If necessary, replace the idler pulley. Check the belt tensioner for leaks. Push in on the tensioner pushrod. Check that it doesn't move. If it does move, replace the tensioner. Measure the protrusion (the amount the pushrod sticks out of the tensioner. It should be 0.413–0.453 inch (10.5–11.5mm).
31. Inspect the water pump for leaks. See that the shaft turns smoothly, without play.
32. If removed, install the crankshaft timing belt pulley. Align the pulley key with the groove and install the pulley. It may be necessary to gently tap the pulley in place with a suitably sided socket or short length of pipe.
33. Install the idler pulleys. Use a small amount of thread-locking compound, Loctite®242, or equivalent, on the bolt threads. Tighten the bolts to 25 ft. lbs. (35 Nm). Verify that the idler pulleys turn smoothly.
34. Temporarily install the timing belt. Remove any oil or water on the crankshaft pulley, oil pump pulley, water pump pulley, both idler pulleys and keep them clean. Wipe them clean with a clean shop cloth. Do not use solvents. Align the installation mark on the timing belt with the timing mark on the crankshaft timing pulley. Install the belt on the crankshaft timing pulley and over the idler pulleys.

35. Install the timing belt cover spacer. Make sure the gasket (seal) is in position.
36. Install the timing belt guide, facing the cup side outward.
37. Install the timing belt cover and its four bolts.
38. Install the crankshaft pulley. Align the key with the slot and install the pulley. It may be necessary to gently tap the pulley in place with a suitably sided socket or short length of pipe.
39. Install the drive belt tensioner (this is not the timing belt tensioner). The bolt should be 4.18 inches (106mm) in length. Tighten the bolt and nuts to 144 inch lbs. (16 Nm).
40. Install the alternator.
41. Check the crankshaft pulley position. Check that the timing mark of the crankshaft pulley is aligned with the timing mark **0** on the lower timing belt cover.
42. Install the right and left camshaft timing pulleys. Align the dowel pin on the camshafts with the groove in the pulleys and slide on the pulleys. Use a pin spanner or other suitable tool to keep the pulleys from turning and torque the center bolts to 80 ft. lbs. (108 Nm). Wipe the pulleys clean of any oil or water. Use a clean shop cloth. Do not use solvent.
43. Install the timing belt to the camshaft pulleys using the following as a guide:
   a. Turn the left side pulley to align the installation mark on the timing belt with the timing mark on the camshaft pulley. Hang the belt on the pulley.
   b. Turn the left side pulley counterclockwise until there is tension between the crankshaft timing pulley and the left side camshaft timing pulley.
   c. Turn the right side pulley to align the installation mark on the timing belt with the timing mark on the camshaft pulley. Hang the belt on the pulley.
44. Using a shop press, compression the tensioner pushrod. It may take anywhere from 220–2200 pounds of pressure. Align the holes of the pushrod and housing and insert a 0.50 inch (1.27mm) hex wrench or other suitable stiff pin to secure the setting position of the pushrod. Release the press and install the dust boot. Install the belt tensioner and alternately tighten the bolts to 19 ft. lbs. (26 Nm). With the tensioner securely bolted in place, use pliers to pull the restraining pin from the belt tensioner.
45. Check the valve timing. Temporarily install the crankshaft pulley bolt. Slowly turn the crankshaft pulley 2 complete revolutions from TDC to TDC. Always turn the pulley clockwise. Verify that each pulley aligns with the timing marks. If the timing marks do not align, stop. Remove he timing belt and reinstall it. It can be see how important is was to make installation marks on the belt before removal, as described earlier.
46. When satisfied that all timing marks are correctly aligned, tighten the crankshaft pulley bolt to 180 ft. lbs. (245 Nm). A holding tool may be required to keep the pulley from turning as it is tightened.
47. Install the fan bracket. Use care to get the bolts installed in the correct location. Some bolts are 4.17 inch (106mm) long and have a 12mm head. Other bolts are 4.49 inch (114mm) long and have a 14mm head. Torque the bolts as follows:
   a. Bolts with a 12mm head are tightened to 12 ft. lbs. (16 Nm).
   b. Bolts with a 14mm head are tightened to 24 ft. lbs. (32 Nm).
48. If equipped with air conditioning, install the compressor.
49. Install No. 2 timing belt cover and tighten the two bolts to 12 ft. lbs. (16 Nm).
50. Install the right side timing belt cover, matching it with the fan bracket Tighten the bolts and nut to 66 inch lbs. (7.5 Nm).
51. Install the left side timing belt cover observing the following:
   a. Install the oil cooler pipe with the nut and bolt.
   b. Run the camshaft position sensor wire through the timing belt cover hole.
   c. Install the belt cover, matching it with the fan bracket.
   d. Tighten the bolts and nut to 66 inch lbs. (7.5 Nm).
   e. Install the sensor wire grommet to the cover and attach the sensor connector and secure to its bracket.
   f. Secure the remaining wire clamps for the engine harness, as required.
52. Install the drive belt idler pulley and torque the bolt to 30 ft. lbs. (39 Nm).
53. Install the power steering pump and torque the bolts to 156 inch lbs. (17 Nm).
54. Install the fan pulley, fan, fan clutch and drive belt.
55. Install the air connector assembly.
56. Install the throttle body cover.
57. Install the radiator assembly and fill with coolant.
58. Start the engine and check for leaks and abnormal noises.
59. Recheck the engine coolant.
60. Install the engine undercover.

Timing Chain

REMOVAL & INSTALLATION

2RZ-FE and 3RZ-FE Engines

➧ See Figures 209 thru 220

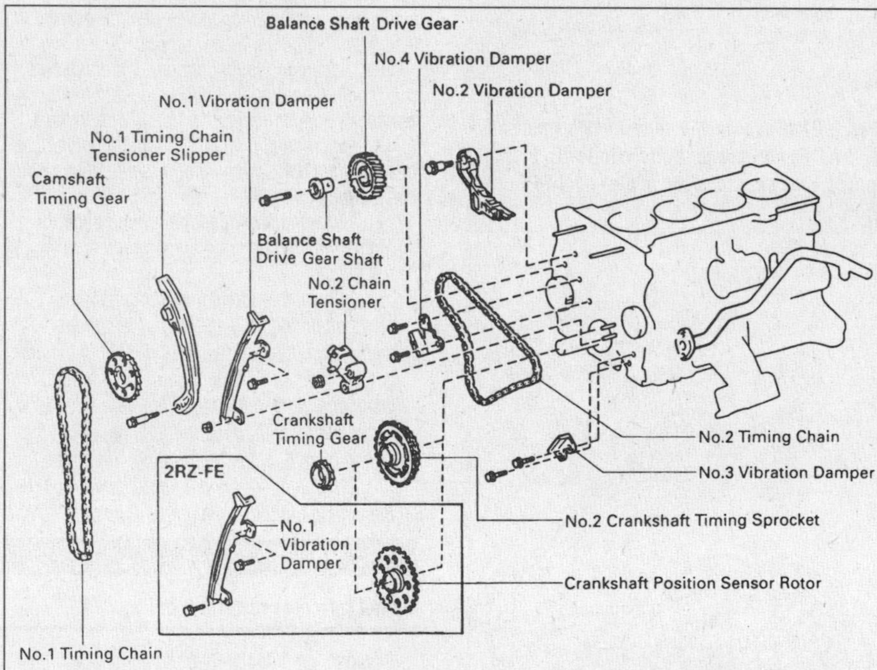

Fig. 209 Exploded view of the engine timing chains and related components—2RZ-FE and 3RZ-FE engines

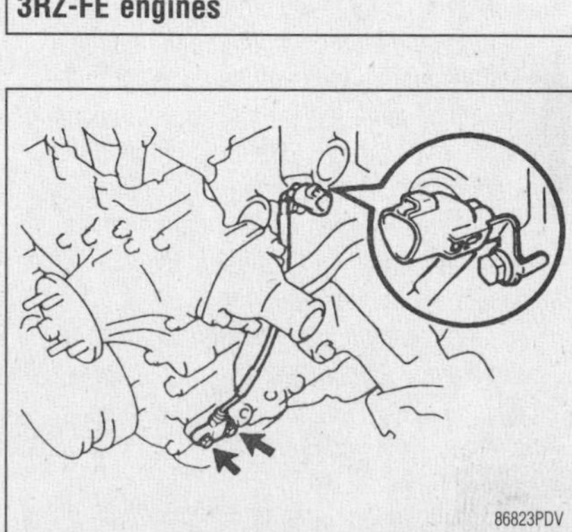

Fig. 210 The crankshaft position sensor is located below the water pump—2RZ-FE and 3RZ-FE engines

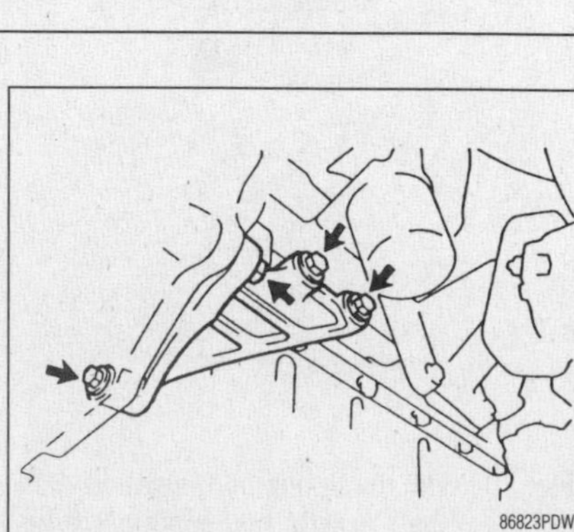

Fig. 211 Remove the bolts securing the stiffener plates

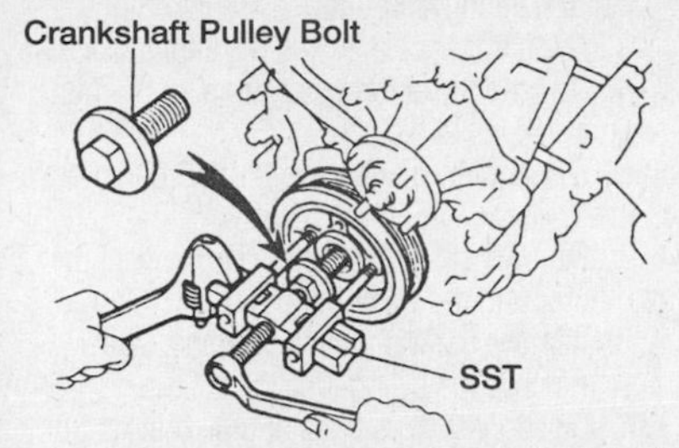

Fig. 212 The crankshaft pulley is removed with a puller. Note the crankshaft center bolt is partly installed to protect the threads in the crankshaft—2RZ-FE and 3RZ-FE engines

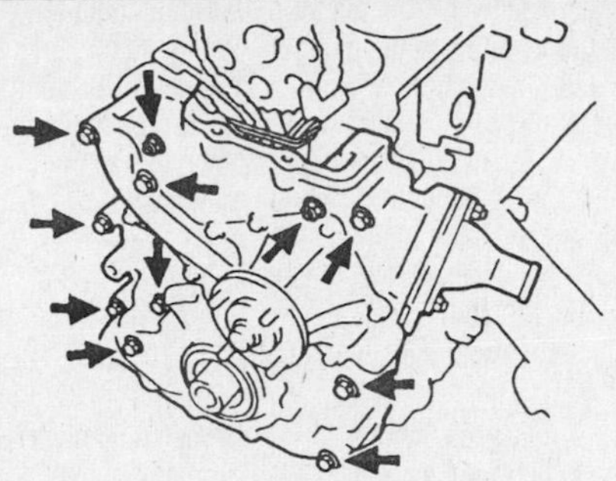

Fig. 213 Remove the bolts securing the front cover (arrows)—2RZ-FE and 3RZ-FE engines

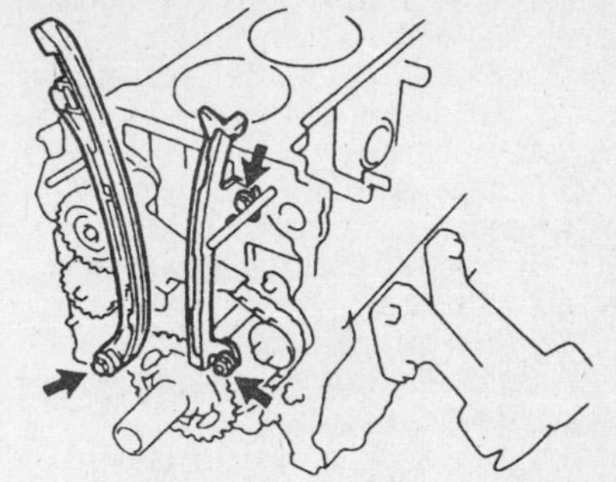

Fig. 214 Remove the bolts securing the chain dampers—2RZ-FE and 3RZ-FE engines

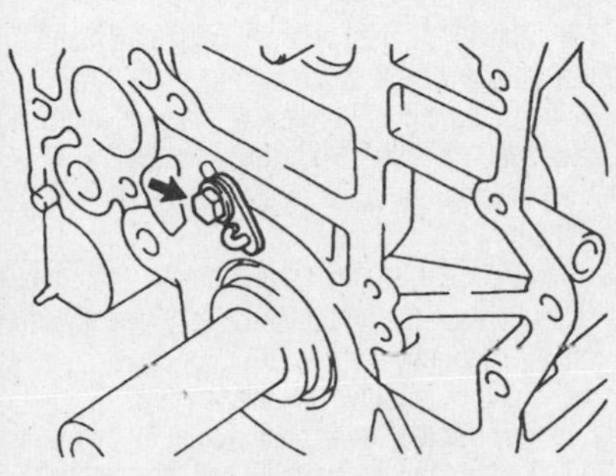

Fig. 215 The oil jet is secured by a single bolt—2RZ-FE and 3RZ-FE engines

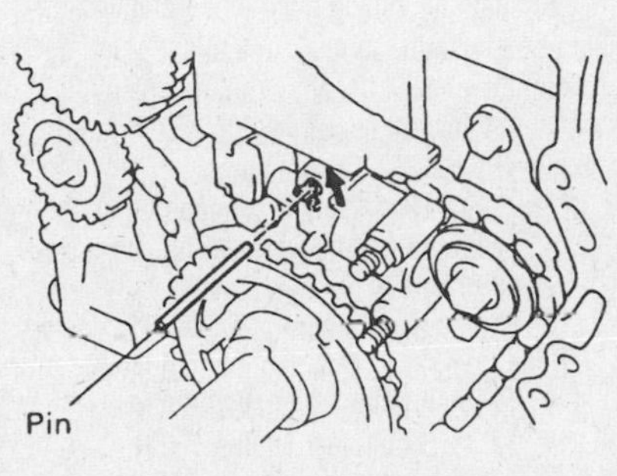

Fig. 216 Lock the plunger with an appropriate pin—2RZ-FE and 3RZ-FE engines

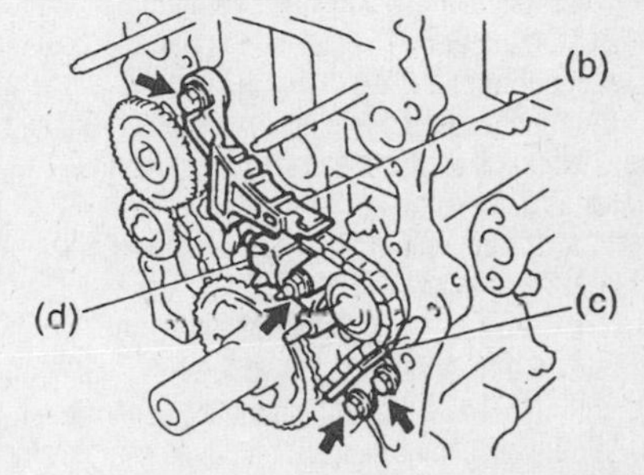

Fig. 217 Fastener locations for the tensioner and damper—2RZ-FE and 3RZ-FE engines

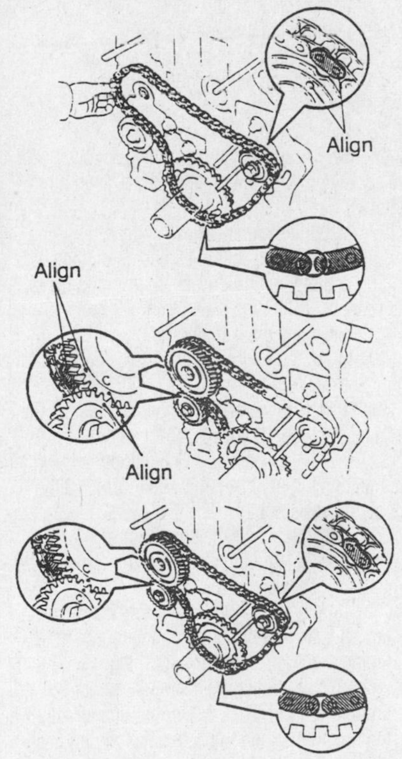

Fig. 218 With No.1 cylinder at TDC of the compression stroke and the weights of the balance shafts at the bottom, install the balance shaft chain and sprockets using care to align all of the timing marks—2RZ-FE and 3RZ-FE engines

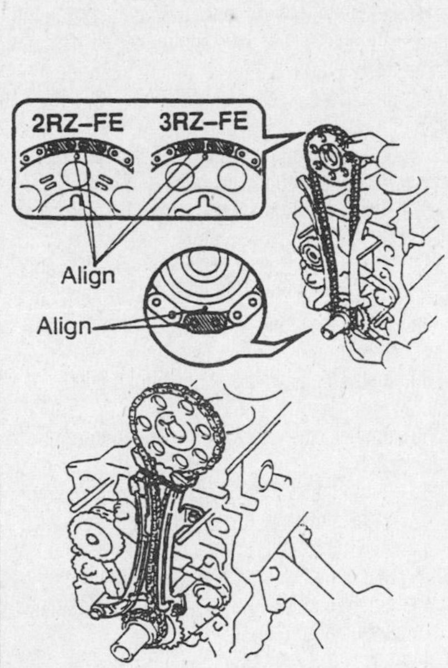

Fig. 219 Align the camshaft gear timing mark between the marked links on the timing chain, then align the timing mark on the crankshaft gear with its marked link on the chain. Wire the chain together under the gear to keep it from coming off when the head is installed—2RZ-FE and 3RZ-FE engines

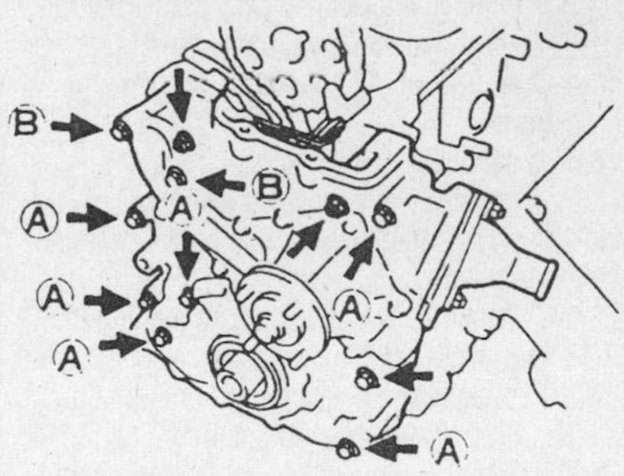

Fig. 220 Timing cover fastener identification—2RZ-FE and 3RZ-FE engines

1. Disconnect the negative battery cable.
2. Raise and safely support the vehicle.
3. Remove the engine undercover.
4. Drain the engine coolant and the engine oil.
5. On 4WD vehicles, remove the front differential.
6. Remove the alternator belt, fan with coupling and the water pump pulley.
   a. Loosen the water pump pulley bolts. Loosen the belt adjusting bolt and the pivot bolt of the alternator and remove the drive belt.
   b. Remove the set nuts, the fluid coupling with the fan, and the water pump pulley.
7. Remove the cylinder head.
8. If equipped with A/C, remove the A/C belt, compressor, and the bracket.
9. Remove the alternator adjusting bar and bracket.

10. Unbolt and remove the crankshaft position sensor and O-ring.
11. On 2WD vehicles, remove the stiffener plates.
12. Unbolt the flywheel housing undercover and dust seal.
13. Remove the oil pan.
14. Unsecure the oil strainer and gasket.
15. Remove the crankshaft pulley, a pulley bolt remover will be needed.
16. Remove the water bypass pipe.
17. Remove the chain cover assembly. Remove the bolts shown by the arrows.
18. Remove the No. 1 timing chain and camshaft gear.
19. Remove the crankshaft timing gear.
20. Remove the No. 1 timing chain tensioner slipper and No. 1 vibration damper. On the 2RZ-FE, remove the two bolts and the damper. On the 3RZ-FE, remove the bolt, nut and No. 1 damper.
21. On the 2RZ-FE remove the crankshaft position sensor rotor and the timing chain oil jet.
22. On the 3RZ-FE engine, remove the No. 2 and No. 3 vibration dampers and the No. 2 chain tensioner as follows:
   a. Install a pin to the No. 2 tensioner and lock the plunger.
   b. Remove the bolt and the No. 2 damper.
   c. Remove the 2 bolts and the No. 3 damper.
   d. Unsecure the nut and the No. 2 tensioner.
23. Remove the balance shaft driven gear, shaft, No. 2 timing chain and the No. 2 crankshaft sprocket, as follows:
   a. Unbolt the balance shaft driven gear.
   b. Remove the balance shaft gear with the shaft.
   c. Remove the No. 2 timing chain with the No. 2 crankshaft timing sprocket.
24. Remove the No. 4 vibration damper.

To install:

25. Install the No. 4 vibration dampener.
26. Install the No. 2 timing chain, No. 2 crankshaft timing sprocket, balance shaft drive gear and shaft as follows:
   a. Install the No. 2 chain by matching the marked links with the timing marks on the crankshaft sprocket and balance shaft timing sprocket.
   b. Fit the other marked link of the No. 2 chain onto the sprocket behind the large timing mark of the balance shaft gear.
   c. Insert the balance shaft gear shaft through the balance shaft drive gear so that it fits into the thrust plate hole. Align the small timing mark of the balance shaft drive gear with the timing mark of the balance shaft timing gear.
   d. Install the bolt to the balance shaft gear and tighten to 18 ft. lbs. (25 Nm).
   e. Check each timing mark is matched with the corresponding mark link.
27. Install the No. 2, No. 3 vibration dampers and the No. 2 chain tensioner, as follows:

➡Assemble the chain tensioner with the pin installed, then remove the pin after assembly.

   a. Install the No. 2 chain tensioner with the nut, tighten to 13 ft. lbs. (18 Nm).
   b. Install the No. 3 damper with the bolts, tighten to 13 ft. lbs. (18 Nm).
   c. Install the No. 2 damper, tighten to 20 ft. lbs. (27 Nm).
   d. Remove the pin from the No. 2 chain tensioner and free the plunger.
28. On the 2RZ-FE engines, install the oil jet and crankshaft position sensor rotor. Make sure the front mark of the cavity of the rotor is facing forward.
29. Install the No. 1 timing chain tensioner slipper and the No. 1 vibration damper.
   a. Install the No. 1 damper, tighten to 22 ft. lbs. (29 Nm).
   b. Install the slipper, tighten to 20 ft. lbs. (27 Nm).
   c. Check that the slipper moves smoothly.
30. Install the crankshaft timing gear.
31. Install the No. 1 timing chain and camshaft timing gear.
   a. Align the timing mark between the marked link of the No. 1 timing chain, and install the No. 1 timing chain to the gear.
   b. Align the timing mark of the crankshaft timing gear with the mark of the No. 1 timing chain, then install the No. 1 timing chain.
   c. Tie the No. 1 chain with a wire or cord, make sure it does not come loose.
32. Install the timing chain cover assembly.
   a. Remove the old cover gaskets and install new gaskets.
   b. Slide the cover assembly over the dowels and the pump spline. Tighten the following:
   - 12mm **A** bolts—14 ft. lbs. (20 Nm)
   - 12mm **B** bolts—18 ft. lbs. (25 Nm)
   - 14mm bolts—32 ft. lbs. (44 Nm)
   - 14mm nut—14 ft. lbs. (20 Nm)

   c. Attach the water bypass pipe.
   d. Remove the cord or wire from the chain.
33. Install the crankshaft pulley, tighten the bolt to 193 ft. lbs. (260 Nm). On A/C vehicles, install the crankshaft pulleys with bolts and tighten to 18 ft. lbs. (25 Nm).
34. Install the oil strainer, tighten to 13 ft. lbs. (18 Nm).
35. Attach the oil pan with fresh sealant, tighten the mounting bolts to 108 inch lbs. (13 Nm).
36. Attach the flywheel housing undercover and dust seal.
37. Attach the stiffener plates on the 2WD vehicles, tighten to 27 ft. lbs. (37 Nm).
38. Install the crankshaft position sensor with a new O-ring.
39. Install the alternator, adjusting bar and bracket.
40. For vehicles with A/C, install the compressor and bracket.
41. Install the cylinder head.
42. Install the water pump pulley and the fluid coupling with the fan. Place the belt onto each pulley. While pulling the belt tight, tighten the four nuts.
43. On 4WD vehicles, install the front differential and driveshaft assemblies.
44. Lower the vehicle.
45. Adjust the drive belt tension.
46. Fill with engine coolant and engine oil.
47. Install the engine undercover.
48. Connect the negative battery cable.
49. Start the engine and check the ignition timing.
50. Recheck fluid levels and top off.

1FZ-FE Engine

➧ See Figures 221, 222, and 223

1. Disconnect the negative battery cable.
2. Raise and safely support the vehicle.
3. Drain the engine oil and the engine coolant.
4. Remove the engine undercover.
5. Remove the radiator.
6. Disconnect and remove the A/C compressor and the bracket.
7. Remove the radiator pipe. Disconnect the radiator hose from the water inlet.
8. Remove the water pump and the gasket.
9. Remove the cylinder head.
10. Disconnect the oil cooler pipe bracket from the No. 1 oil pan.
11. Remove the oil level sensor.
12. Remove the bolts holding the No. 1 oil pan to the transmission housing.
13. Remove the No. 2 and No. 1 oil pans.
14. Using SST 09213–58012 and 09330–00021, or equivalent, remove the pulley bolt. Remove the crankshaft pulley.
15. Check the thrust clearance of the oil pump driveshaft gear as follows:
   a. Using a dial indicator with a lever type attachment, measure the thrust clearance.
   b. Maximum thrust clearance is 0.0118 in. (0.30mm).
   c. If the thrust clearance is greater than maximum, replace the oil pump driveshaft gear and/or timing chain cover.
16. Remove the drive belt idler pulley.
17. Remove the timing chain cover.
18. Remove the timing chain and the camshaft timing gear.
19. Pull out the crankshaft timing gear.
20. Remove the chain tensioner slipper and the vibration damper.
21. Remove the oil jet.
22. Remove the crankshaft rotor.
23. Remove the oil pump driveshaft gear.
24. Remove the pump driveshaft gear.

To install:

25. Clean the mating areas well.
26. Set the crankshaft. Turn the crankshaft until the set key on the crankshaft is facing downward (6 o'clock).
27. Install the pump driveshaft gear.
28. Apply a light coat of engine oil on the shaft portion of the oil pump driveshaft gear, and install the gear.
29. Install the crankshaft rotor.
30. Install the oil jet and tighten the bolt to 14 ft. lbs. (20 Nm).
31. Install the vibration damper and tighten the bolts to 14 ft. lbs. (20 Nm).
32. Install the chain tensioner slipper and tighten the bolt to 51 ft. lbs. (69 Nm). Make sure that the slipper moves smoothly.
33. Install the crankshaft timing gear.
34. Install the timing chain and the camshaft timing gear as follows:
   a. Install the timing chain on the camshaft timing gear with the bright link aligned with the timing mark on the camshaft timing gear.
   b. Install the timing chain on the crankshaft timing gear with the other bright link aligned with the timing mark on the crankshaft timing gear.
   c. Tie the timing chain with a cord to make sure that it doesn't come loose.
35. Install the timing chain cover.
36. Remove the cord from the chain.
37. Install the drive belt idler pulley and tighten the bolt to 32 ft. lbs. (43 Nm).

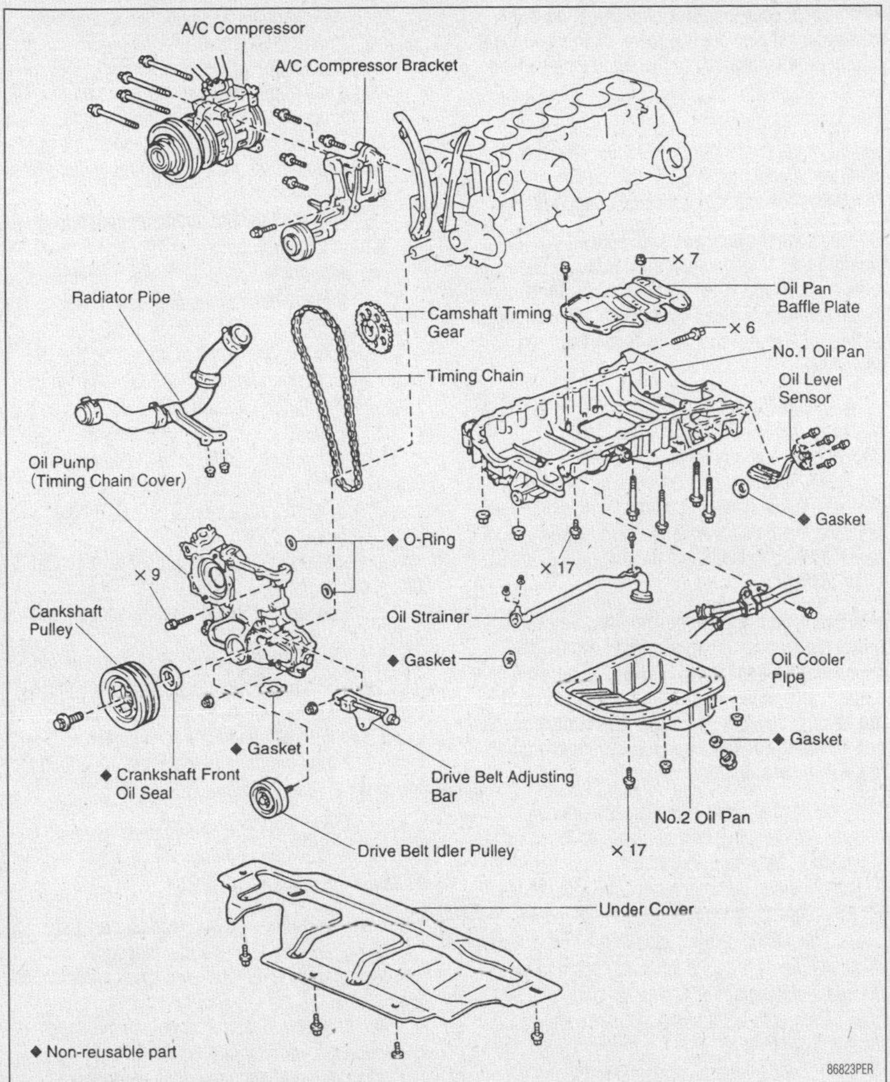

Fig. 221 Exploded view of the timing chain assembly—1FZ-FE engine

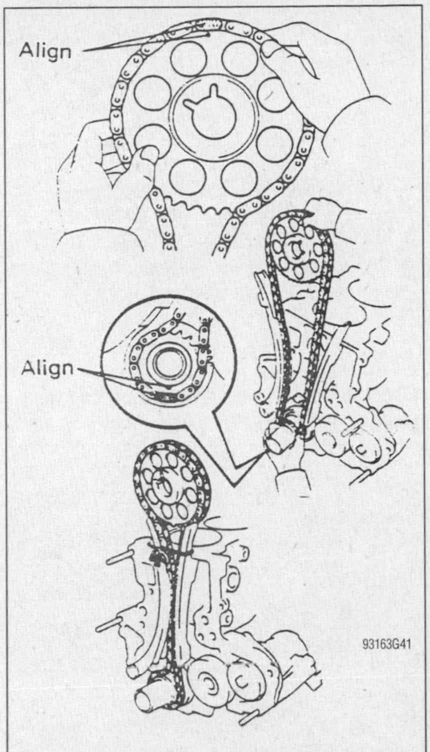

Fig. 222 Install the cam gear with the bright link aligned with the timing mark. Align the other bright link with the mark on the crankshaft gear. Tie the timing chain as shown to secure the assembly—1FZ-FE engine

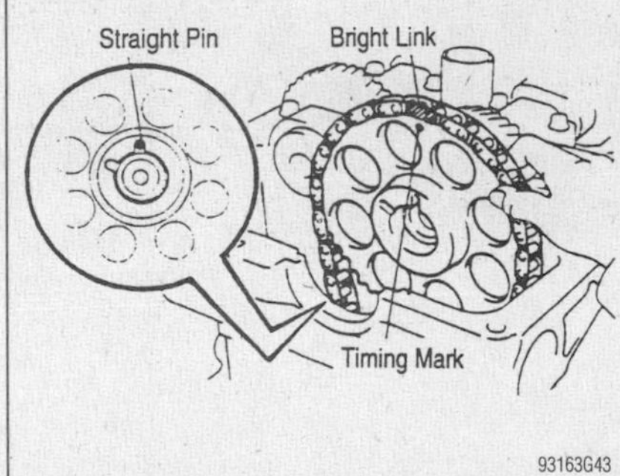

Fig. 223 With the head installed, align the bright link of the chain with the camshaft gear timing mark, then install onto the camshaft—1FZ-FE engine

38. Install the crankshaft pulley. Align the pulley set key with the key groove of the pulley and slide on the pulley. Install the pulley bolt and tighten to 304 ft. lbs. (412 Nm).
39. Install the No. 1 and the No. 2 oil pans.
40. Install the bolts holding the No. 1 oil pan to the transmission housing. Tighten the bolts to 53 ft. lbs. (72 Nm).
41. Install the oil level sensor with a new gasket and tighten the bolts to 48 inch lbs. (5 Nm).
42. Connect the oil cooler pipe bracket to the No. 1 oil pan.
43. Install the cylinder head.
44. Install the water pump and tighten the bolts to 15 ft. lbs. (21 Nm).
45. Connect the No. 2 radiator hose to the water inlet. Install the nuts holding the radiator pipe to the No. 1 oil pan and tighten to 15 ft. lbs. (21 Nm).
46. Install the A/C compressor bracket and tighten the bolts to 27 ft. lbs. (37 Nm).
47. Install the A/C compressor and tighten the bolts to 18 ft. lbs. (25 Nm). Install and adjust the drive belt.
48. Install the radiator.
49. Refill the engine oil and the engine coolant.
50. Connect the negative battery cable.
51. Start the engine, check for leaks, and check the ignition timing.
52. Install the engine undercover.

Camshaft and Bearings

➡These engines are not equipped with replaceable camshaft bearings.

REMOVAL & INSTALLATION

2RZ-FE and 3RZ-FE Engines

◗ See Figures 224, 225, 226, 227, and 228

1. Remove the timing chain from the engine using the procedures found in this section.
2. Remove the exhaust camshaft by bringing the service bolt hole of the driven sub-gear upwards. Turn the hexagon wrench head portion of the exhaust camshaft with a wrench.
3. Secure the exhaust camshaft sub-gear to the main gear with a service bolt. The thread diameter should be 6mm x 1.0mm thread 16–20mm long.

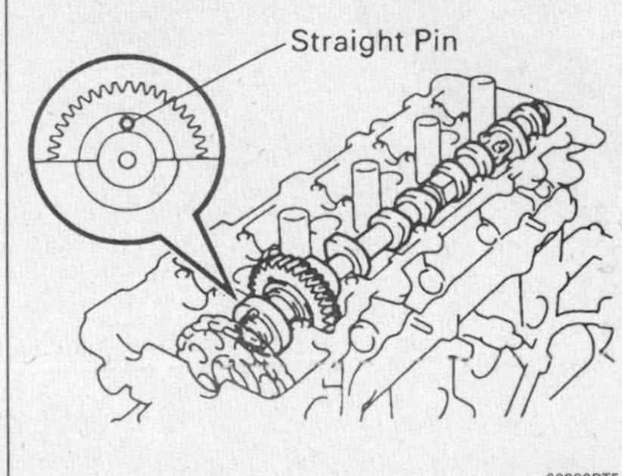

Fig. 224 Install the camshaft with the pin facing upwards—2RZ-FE and 3RZ-FE engines

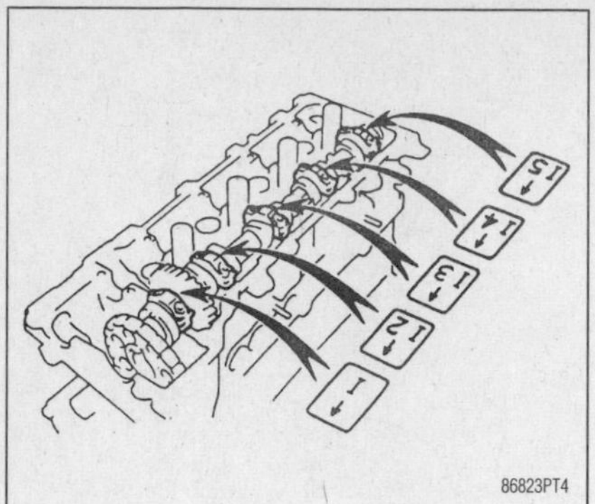

86823PT4

Fig. 225 Intake camshaft bearing cap locations—2RZ-FE and 3RZ-FE engines

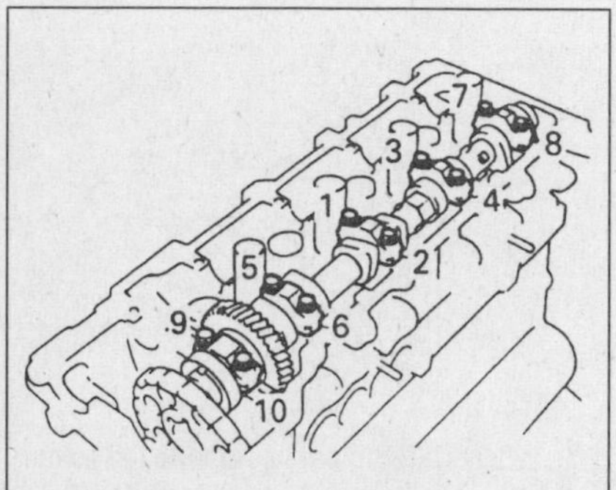

86823PT6

Fig. 226 Tighten the intake bearing caps following this order—2RZ-FE and 3RZ-FE engines

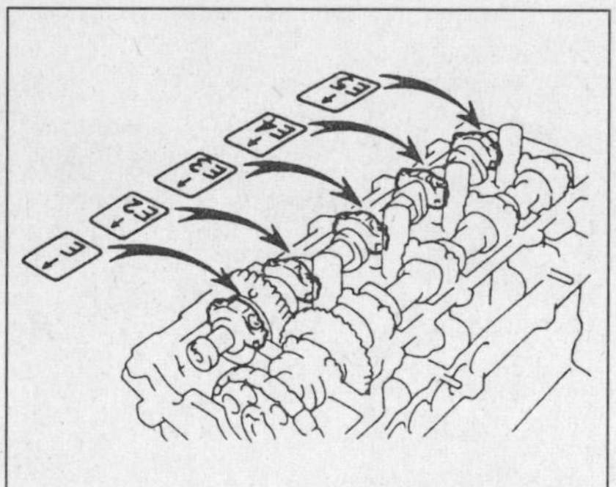

86823PT7

Fig. 227 Position the exhaust camshaft bearing caps as shown—2RZ-FE and 3RZ-FE engines

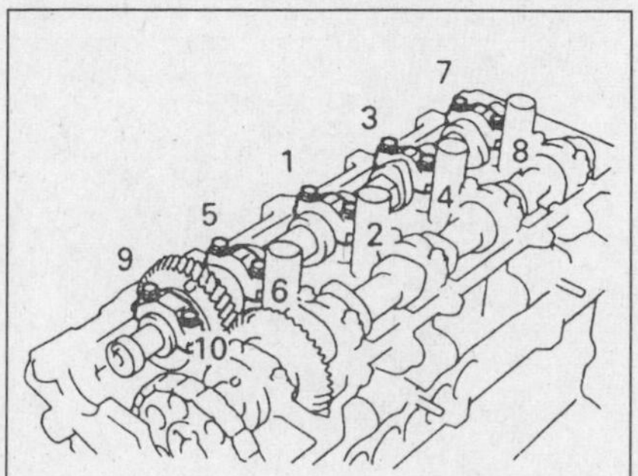

86823PT8

Fig. 228 Tighten the exhaust bearing cap bolts in this order—2RZ-FE and 3RZ-FE engines

➡When you remove the camshaft, be sure that the torsional spring force of the sub-gear has been eliminated by the above operation.

4. Uniformly loosen and remove the exhaust bearing cap bolts (10 of them), in several passes. Use the reverse order of the tightening sequence. Remove the bearing caps and lift out the exhaust side camshaft. Do the same for the intake camshafts.

➡If the camshaft is not being lifted out straight and level, reinstall the No. 3 cap with the 2 bolts. Alternately loosen then remove the bearing cap bolts with the camshaft pulled up. Do not pry on or force the camshaft.

5. Inspect the camshafts for runout. Inspect the cam lobes and journals. The bearings are part of the cylinder head and bearing caps and should be inspected for flaking or scoring. If the bearings are damaged, the caps and the cylinder head will have to be replaced as a set. The camshaft journal oil and thrust clearances should be checked.

To install:

➡When installing the camshafts; since the thrust clearance of the shafts is small, the cam must be kept level while it is being installed. If it is not kept level, the portion of the head receiving the shaft thrust may crack or be damaged. This can cause the camshaft to seize or break.

6. Install the intake camshaft as follows:
   a. Apply multi-purpose grease to the thrust portion of the intake camshaft.
   b. Position the intake camshaft with the pin facing upward.
   c. Install the bearing caps in their proper locations. Apply a light coat of engine oil to the threads and install the cap bolts. Uniformly tighten the cap bolts in the sequence shown to 12 ft. lbs. (16 Nm).
7. Install the exhaust camshaft as follows:
   a. Apply engine oil to the thrust portion of the intake camshaft.
   b. Engage the exhaust camshaft gear to the intake camshaft gear by matching the timing marks (one and two dots) on each other.
   c. Roll down the exhaust camshaft onto the bearing journals while engaging the gears with each other. Install the bearing caps in their proper locations.
   d. Apply a light coat of engine oil to the threads and install the cap bolts. Uniformly tighten the cap bolts in the sequence shown to 12 ft. lbs. (16 Nm).
   e. Remove the service bolt from the driven sub-gear. Check that the intake and exhaust camshafts turn smoothly.
8. Set No. 1 cylinder to TDC compression stroke. The crankshaft pulley groove aligns with the **0** mark on timing cover and camshaft timing marks with one dot and two dots will be in a straight line on the cylinder head surface.
9. Install the timing gear. Place the gear over the straight pin of the intake camshaft.
   a. Hold the intake camshaft with a wrench. Install and tighten the bolt to 54 ft. lbs. (74 Nm).
   b. Hold the exhaust camshaft and install the bolt and distributor gear. Tighten the bolt to 34 ft. lbs. (46 Nm).
10. Install the chain tensioner, using a new gasket (mark toward the front) as follows:
   a. Release the ratchet pawl, fully push in the plunger and apply the hook to the pin so that the plunger cannot spring out.
   b. Turn the crankshaft pulley clockwise to provide some slack for the chain on the tensioner side.
   c. Push the tensioner by hand until it touches the head installation surface, then install the 2 nuts. Tighten the nuts to 13 ft. lbs. (18 Nm). Check that the hook of the tensioner is not released.
   d. Turn the crankshaft to the left so that the hook of the chain tensioner is released from the pin of the plunger, allowing the plunger to spring out and the slipper to be pushed into the chain.
11. Check and adjust the valve clearance. Intake valve clearance is 0.006–0.010 inch (0.15–0.25mm) and exhaust valve clearance is 0.010–0.014 inch (0.25–0.35mm).
12. Recheck the engine for proper valve timing. Check and adjust the valve clearance.
13. Install the spark plugs and the semi-circular plug.
14. Recheck the engine for proper valve timing. Install the valve cover and engine hangers. Tighten the engine hanger bolts to 30 ft. lbs. (42 Nm).
15. Reinstall all other parts from the timing chain removal. Fill any fluids, start the engine, add fluid as required.

5VZ-FE Engine

➧ See Figures 229 thru 251

1. Remove both cylinder head covers.
2. Remove the semi-circular plugs.
3. Remove the right exhaust camshaft as follows:
   a. Bring the service bolt hole of the driven sub-gear upward by turning the hexagon head portion of the exhaust camshaft with a wrench.
   b. Align the timing mark (2 dot marks) of the camshaft drive and driven gears by turning the camshaft with a wrench.
   c. Secure the exhaust camshaft sub-gear to the driven gear with a service bolt 6mm in diameter by 1.0mm pitch thread, 16–20mm long.

➡When removing the camshaft, make sure that the torsional spring force of the sub-gear has been eliminated by the above operation.

   d. Uniformly loosen and remove the bearing cap bolts in several passes, in the sequence shown.
   e. Remove the bearing caps and camshaft. Make a note of the bearing cap positions for proper installation.

WARNING

Do not pry on or attempt to force the camshaft with a tool or other object.

4. Remove the right hand intake camshaft as follows:
   a. Uniformly loosen and remove the bearing cap bolts in several passes, in the sequence shown.

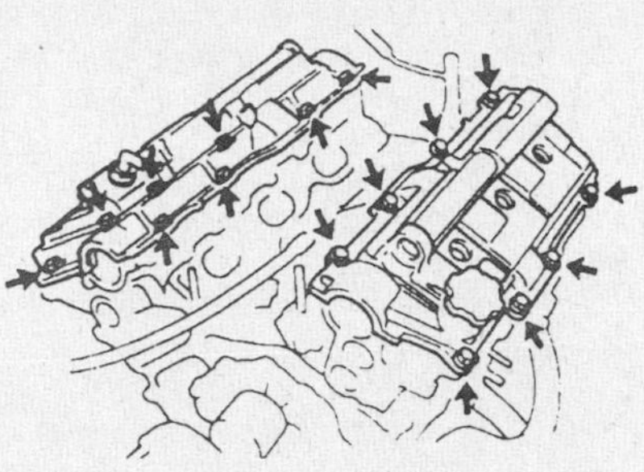

86823PU7

Fig. 229 Remove the cylinder head covers from the engine—5VZ-FE engine

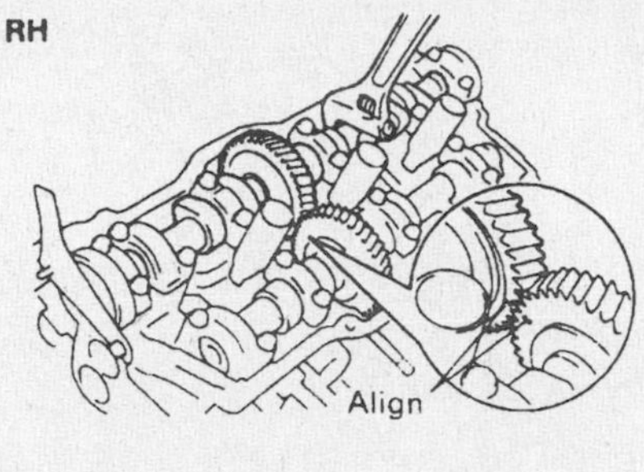

86823PU8

Fig. 230 Align the gears by turning the camshaft with a wrench on the flats provided—not the lobes—5VZ-FE engine

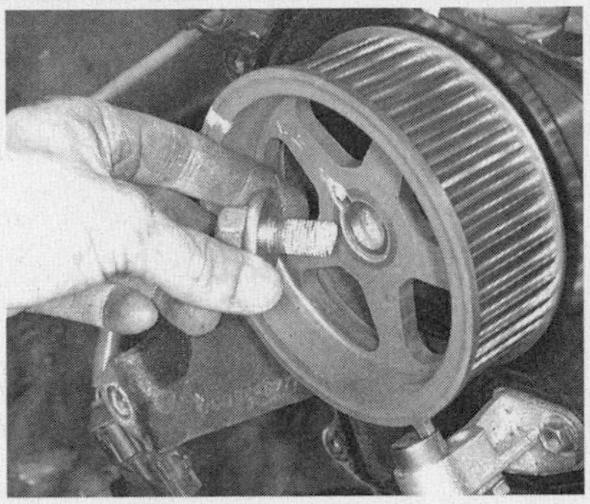

93163pa2

Fig. 231 Removing the bolt from the camshaft pulley

93163pa3

Fig. 232 Carefully detach the camshaft pulley

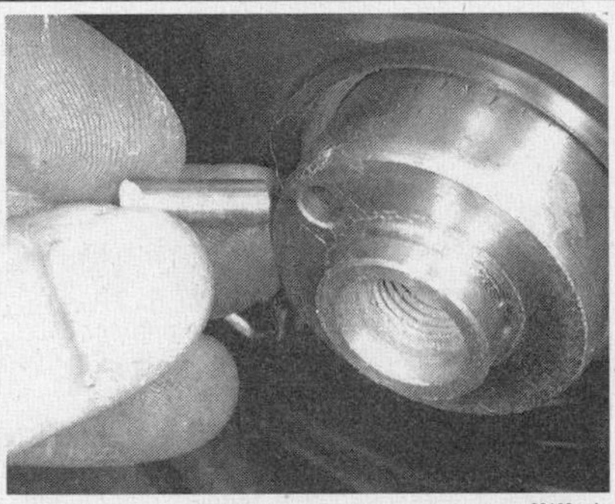

93163pa4

Fig. 233 Be careful not to lose the dowel pin

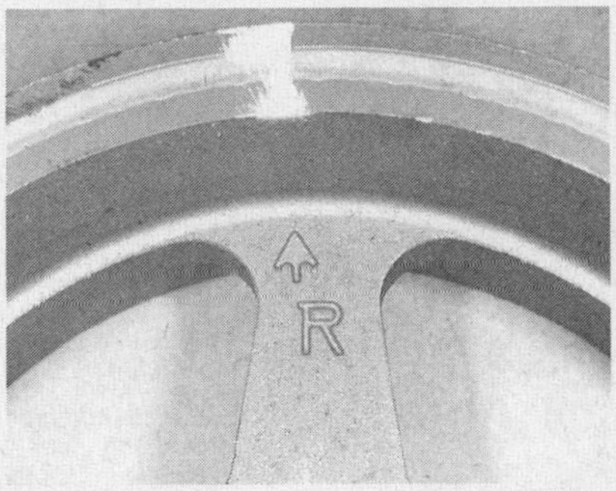

93163pa6

Fig. 234 The camshaft pulleys are marked right and left

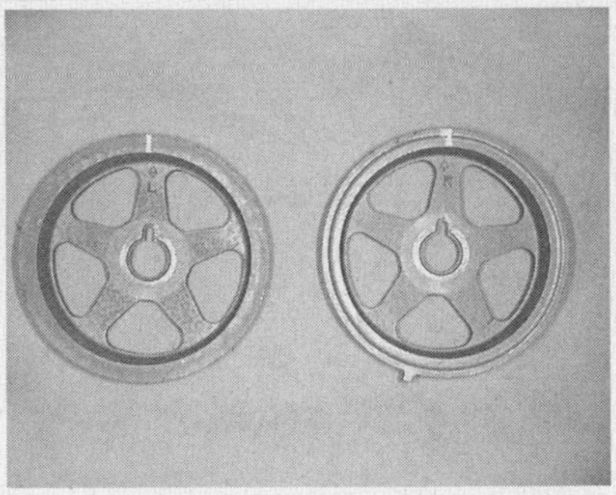

93163pa7

Fig. 235 Left and right camshaft pulleys—5VZ-FE engine

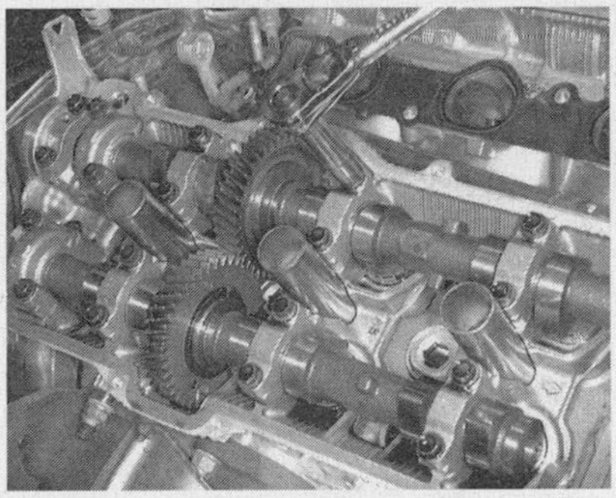

93163pd2

Fig. 236 Unfasten the camshaft's bearing cap retaining bolts . . .

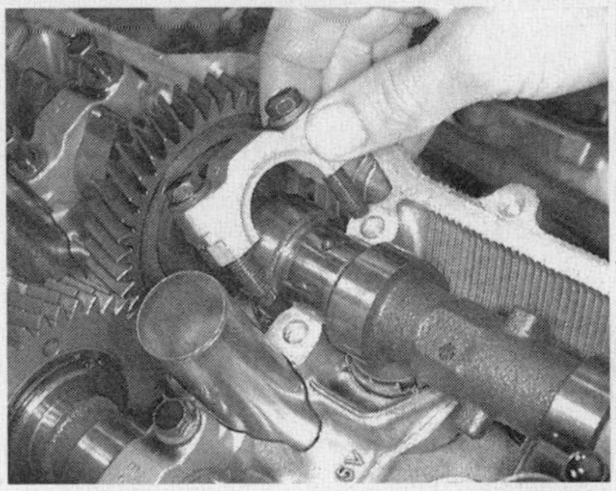

93163pd3

Fig. 237 . . . then remove the camshaft bearing cap

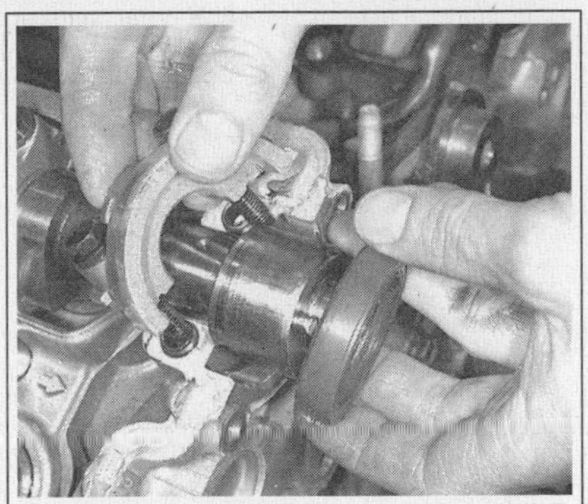

93163pd5

Fig. 238 Lift the rear bearing cap and pull out the camshaft seal

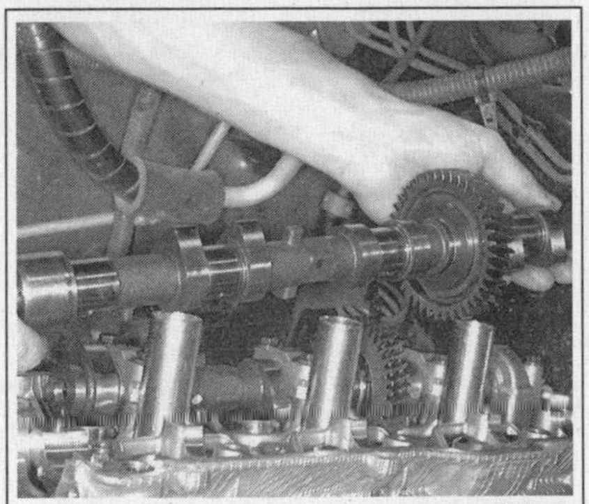

93163pd7

Fig. 239 Carefully remove the camshaft from the cylinder head

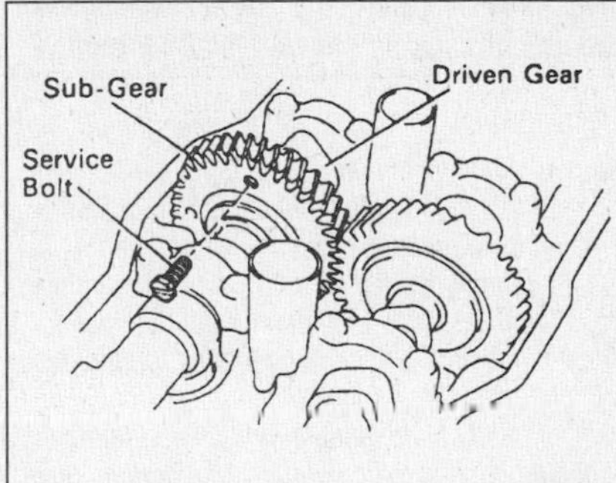

86823PU9

Fig. 240 Use an appropriate size bolt to release the spring force of the sub-gear—5VZ-FE engine

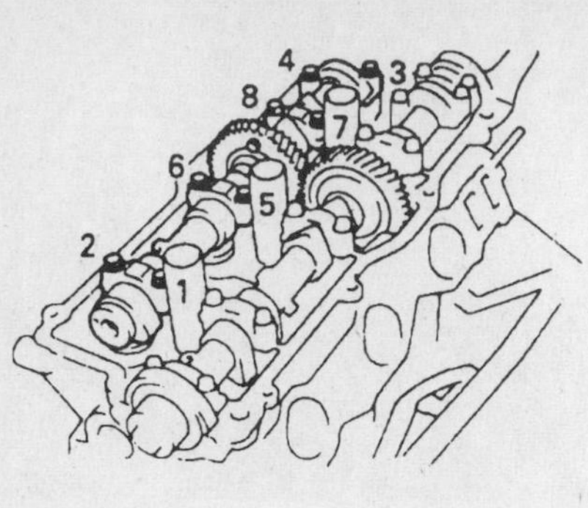

Fig. 241 Right hand exhaust camshaft bearing cap loosening sequence—5VZ-FE engine

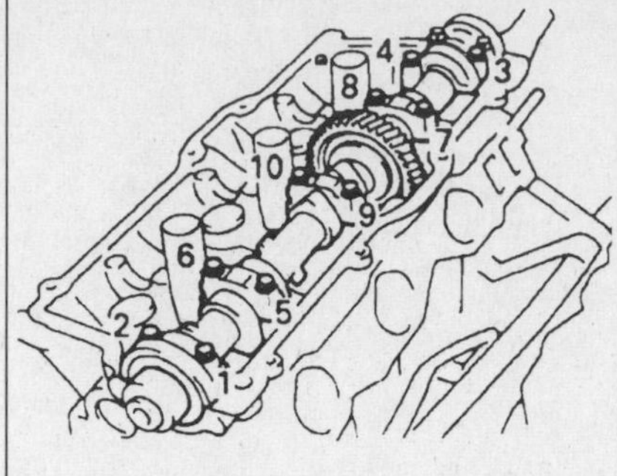

Fig. 242 Loosen the right hand intake camshaft caps as shown—5VZ-FE engine

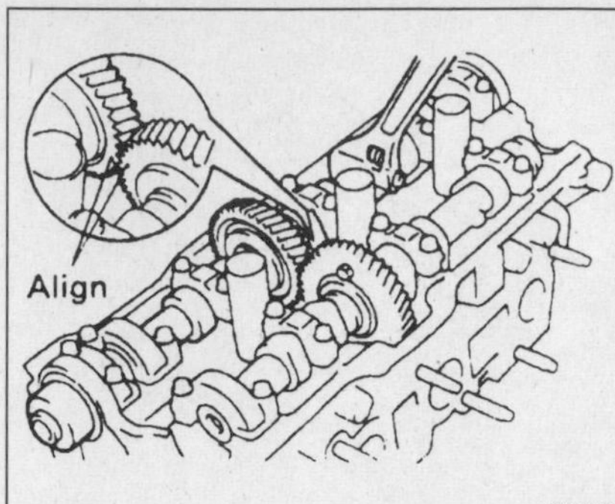

Fig. 243 When aligning the gears, turn the camshaft with the flats provided. Do not place a wrench on the lobes—5VZ-FE engine

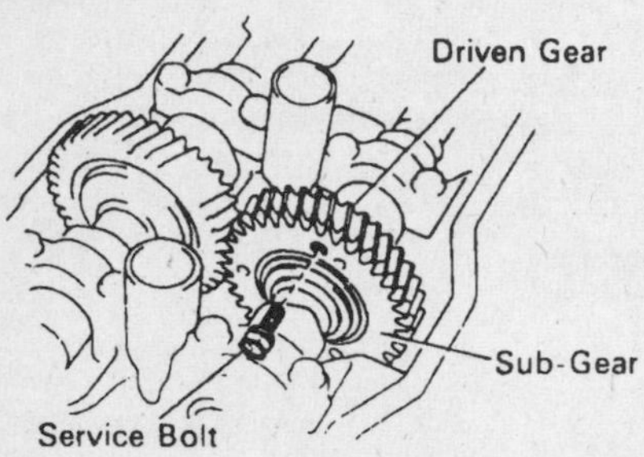

Fig. 244 The spring force of the sub-gear can be overcome by using a 6mm restraining bolt—5VZ-FE engine

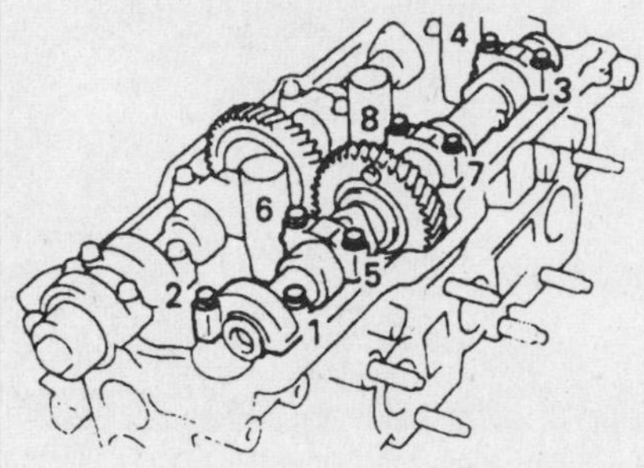

Fig. 245 Left hand exhaust camshaft bearing cap loosening sequence—5VZ-FE engine

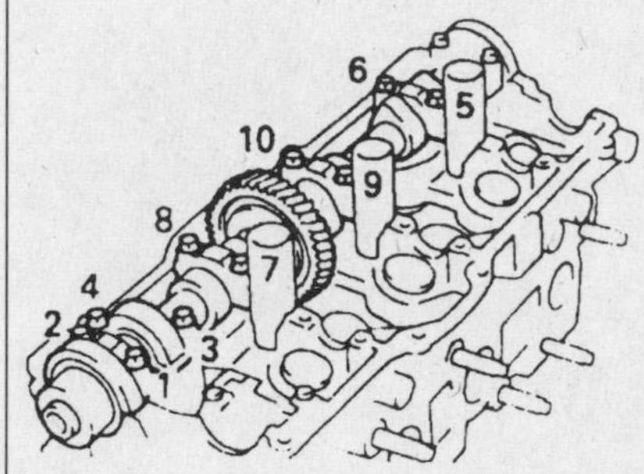

Fig. 246 The left hand intake camshaft caps must be loosened as shown—5VZ-FE engine

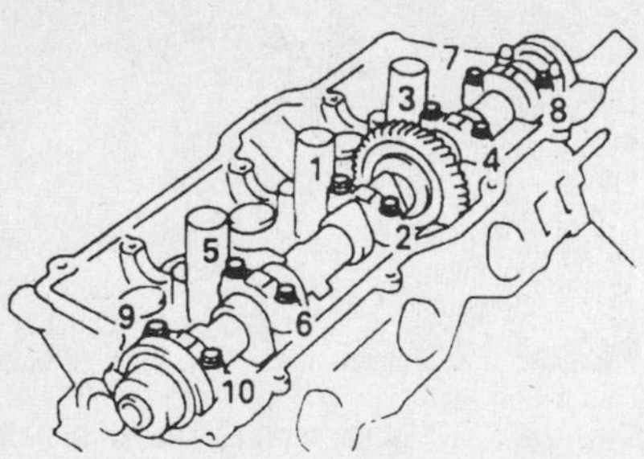

Fig. 247 Tighten the right side intake camshaft caps as shown—5VZ-FE engine

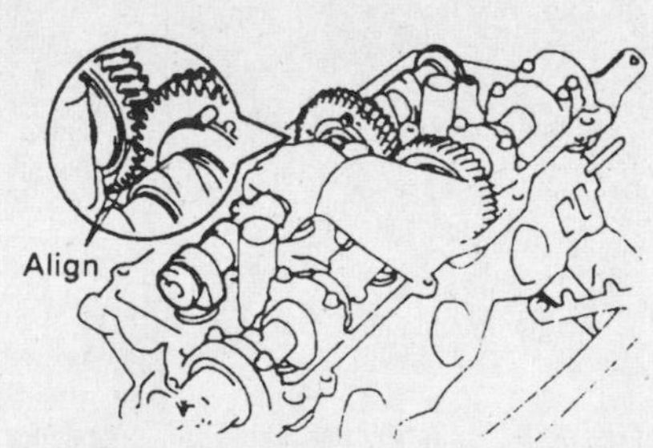

Fig. 248 When installing the exhaust camshaft, make sure the timing marks align—5VZ-FE engine

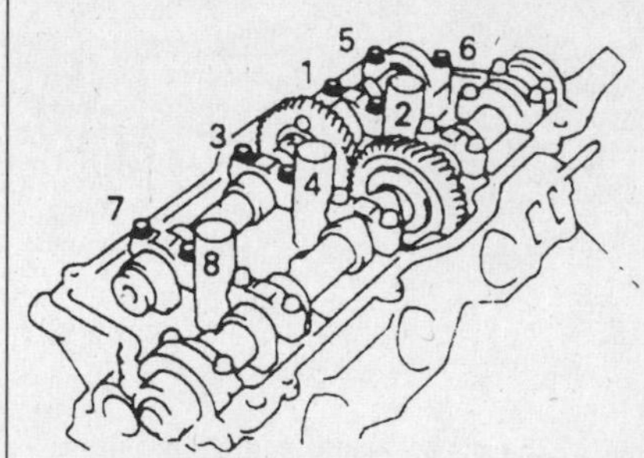

Fig. 249 Use this sequence to tighten the right hand exhaust camshaft bearing cap bolts—5VZ-FE engine

b. Remove the bearing caps, oil seal and camshaft. Make a note of the bearing cap positions for proper installation.

5. Remove the left exhaust camshaft as follows:

a. Align the timing mark (1 dot mark) of the camshaft drive and driven gears by turning the camshaft with a wrench.

b. Secure the exhaust camshaft sub-gear to the driven gear with a service bolt 6mm in diameter by 1.0mm pitch thread, 16–20mm long.

➡When removing the camshaft, make sure that the torsional spring force of the sub-gear has been eliminated by the above operation.

c. Uniformly loosen and remove the bearing cap bolts in several passes, in the sequence shown.

d. Remove the bearing caps and camshaft. Make a note of the bearing cap positions for proper installation.

✲✲ WARNING

Do not pry on or attempt to force the camshaft out.

6. Remove the left hand intake camshaft as follows:

a. Uniformly loosen and remove the bearing cap bolts in several passes, in the sequence shown.

b. Remove the bearing caps, oil seal and camshaft. Make a note of the bearing cap positions for proper installation.

To install:

7. Install the right intake camshaft as follows:

a. Apply engine oil to the thrust portion of the intake camshaft.

b. Position the intake camshaft at a 90 degree angle of the timing mark (2 dot marks) on the cylinder head.

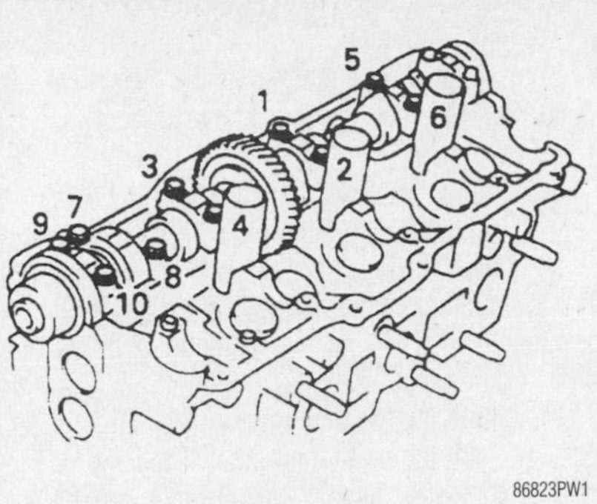

86823PW1

Fig. 250 Tightening sequence for the left hand intake camshaft cap bolts—5VZ-FE engine

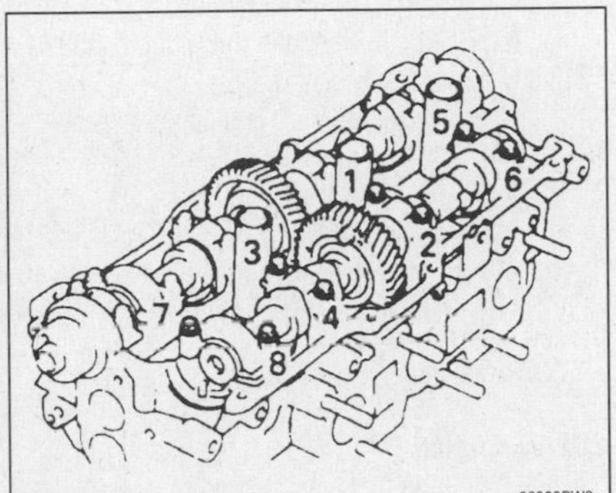

86823PW2

Fig. 251 Tighten the left side exhaust camshaft cap bolts in this sequence—5VZ-FE engine

c. Install the bearing caps in their proper locations. Apply a light coat of engine oil to the threads and under the heads of the bearing cap bolts. Install the cap bolts.

d. Uniformly tighten the cap bolts in the sequence shown to 12 ft. lbs. (16 Nm).

8. Install the right exhaust camshaft as follows:

a. Apply engine oil to the thrust portion of the intake camshaft.

b. Align the timing marks (2 dot marks) of the camshaft drive and driven gears.

c. Roll down the exhaust camshaft onto the bearing journals while engaging the gears with each other. Install the bearing caps in their proper locations.

d. Apply a light coat of engine oil to the threads and under the heads of the bearing cap bolts. Install the cap bolts.

e. Uniformly tighten the cap bolts in the sequence shown to 12 ft. lbs. (16 Nm).

f. Remove the service bolt from the driven sub-gear. Check that the intake and exhaust camshafts turns smoothly.

g. Align the timing marks (2 dot mark) of the camshaft drive and driven gears by turning the camshaft with a wrench.

9. Install the left intake camshaft as follows:

a. Apply engine oil to the thrust portion of the intake camshaft.

b. Position the intake camshaft at a 90 degree angle of the timing mark (1 dot marks) on the cylinder head.

c. Install the bearing caps in their proper locations. Apply a light coat of engine oil to the threads and under the heads of the bearing cap bolts. Install the cap bolts.

d. Uniformly tighten the cap bolts in the sequence shown to 12 ft. lbs. (16 Nm).

10. Install the left exhaust camshaft as follows:

a. Apply engine oil to the thrust portion of the intake camshaft.

b. Align the timing marks (1 dot marks) of the camshaft drive and driven gears.

c. Roll down the exhaust camshaft onto the bearing journals while engaging the gears with each other. Install the bearing caps in their proper locations.

d. Apply a light coat of engine oil to the threads and under the heads of the bearing cap bolts. Install the cap bolts.

e. Uniformly tighten the cap bolts in the sequence shown to 12 ft. lbs. (16 Nm).

f. Remove the service bolt.

11. Check and adjust the valve clearance.

12. Install the semi-circular plugs.

13. Install the cylinder head covers. Uniformly tighten the bolts in several passes to 53 inch lbs. (6 Nm).

1FZ-FE Engine

➧ See Figures 252, 253, 254, and 255

1. Remove the cylinder head cover.

2. Remove the semi–circular plug from the cylinder head.

3. Remove the spark plugs.

4. Set the No. 1 cylinder to TDC of the compression stroke as follows:

a. Turn the crankshaft pulley and align its groove with the **0** mark on the timing chain cover.

b. Check that the timing marks (one and two dots) of the camshaft drive and driven gears are in straight line on the cylinder head surface. If not, turn the crankshaft one revolution (360 degrees) and align the marks.

5. Remove the chain tensioner.

6. Place matchmarks on the camshaft timing gear and the timing chain and remove the camshaft timing gear, as follows.

a. Hold the intake camshaft with a wrench and remove the bolt and the distributor gear.

b. Remove the camshaft timing gear and chain from the intake camshaft and leave on the slipper and the damper.

➡Since the thrust clearance of the camshaft is small, the camshaft must be kept level while it is being removed. If the camshaft is not kept level, the portion of the cylinder head receiving the shaft thrust may crack or be damaged, causing the camshaft to seize or break. To avoid this, the following steps should be carried out.

7. Remove the exhaust camshaft as follows:

a. Bring the service bolt hole of the driven sub-gear upward by turning the hexagon wrench head portion of the exhaust camshaft with a wrench.

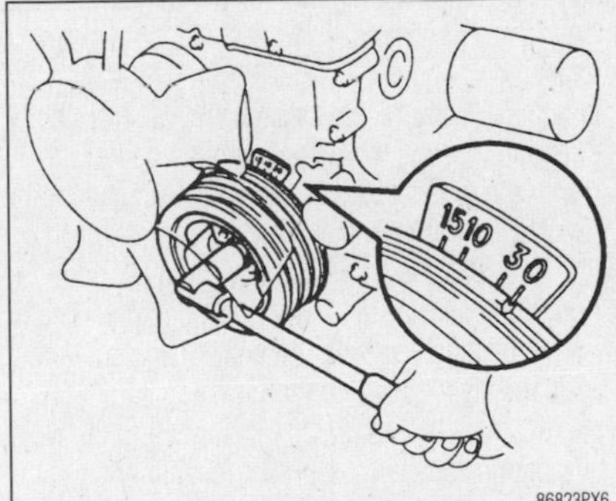

86823PX6

Fig. 252 Turn the crankshaft pulley and align its groove with the 0 mark on the timing chain cover—1FZ-FE engine

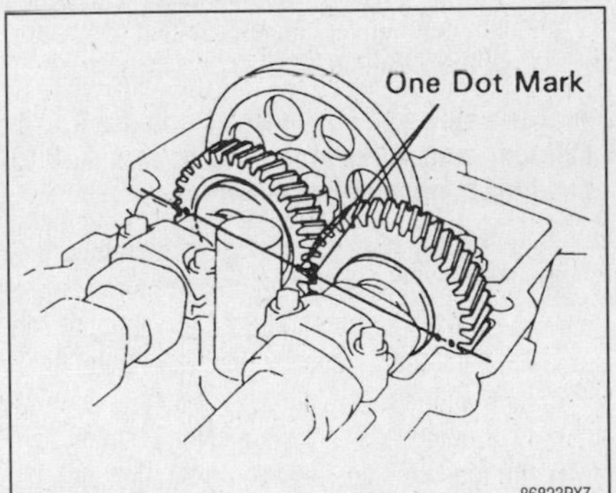

86823PX7

Fig. 253 Check that the marks on the camshaft pulley are aligned—1FZ-FE engine

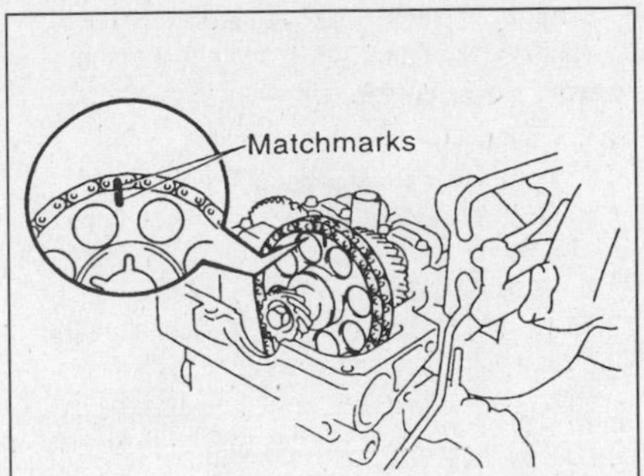

86823PX8

Fig. 254 Matchmark the position of the chain on the gear—1FZ-FE engine

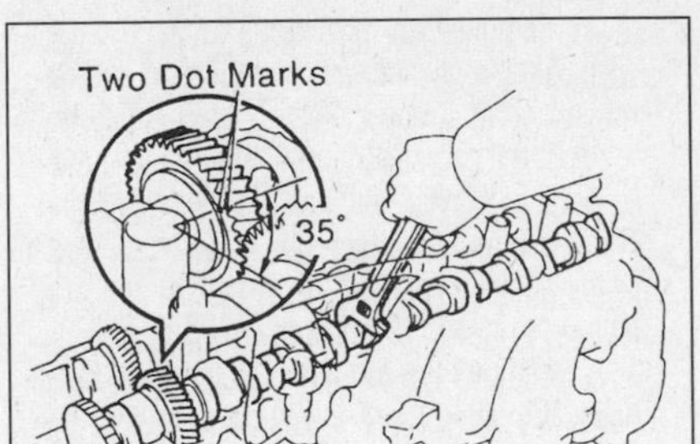

86823PX9

Fig. 255 Turn the camshaft by using the flats provided. Do not use the lobes—1FZ-FE engine

b. Secure the exhaust camshaft sub-gear to the main gear with a service bolt. When removing the camshaft, make sure that the torsional spring force of the sub-gear has been eliminated by the above operation.

c. Set the timing mark (two dot marks) of the camshaft driven gear at approximately a 35 degree angle by turning the hexagon wrench head portion of the intake camshaft with a wrench.

d. Lightly push the camshaft towards the rear without applying excessive force.

e. Loosen and remove the No. 1 bearing cap bolts, alternately loosening the left and right bolts uniformly.

f. Loosen and remove the No. 2, No. 3, No. 5 and the No. 7 bearing cap bolts, alternately loosening the left and right bolts uniformly in several passes, in sequence.

➡Do not remove the No. 4 and No. 6 bearing cap bolts at this stage.

g. Remove the four bearing caps.

h. Alternately and uniformly loosen and remove the No. 4 and the No. 6 bearing cap bolts.

i. If the camshaft is not being lifted out straight and level, retighten the four No. 4 and No. 6 bearing cap bolts. Then reverse the order of the above steps from (g) to (e) and repeat steps from (c) to (h) once again.

j. Remove the two bearing caps and exhaust camshaft. Do not pry on or attempt to force the camshaft with a tool or any other object.

8. Remove the intake camshaft as follows:

a. Set the timing mark (two dot marks) of the camshaft drive gear at approximately a 25 degree angle by turning the hexagon wrench head portion of the intake camshaft with a wrench.

➡This angle allows the No. 1 and the No. 4 cylinder cam lobes of the intake camshaft to push their valve lifters evenly.

b. Lightly push the intake camshaft towards the front without applying excessive force.

c. Loosen and remove the No. 1 bearing cap bolts, alternately loosening the left and the right bolts uniformly.

d. Loosen and remove the No. 3, No. 4, No. 6 and the No. 7 bearing cap bolts, alternately loosening the left and right bolts uniformly in several passes in sequence.

➡Do not remove the No. 2 and No. 5 bearing cap bolts at this stage.

e. Remove the four bearing caps.

f. Alternately and uniformly loosen and remove the No. 2 and the No. 5 bearing cap bolts.

g. If the camshaft is not being lifted out straight and level, retighten the four No. 2 and No. 5 bearing cap bolts. Then reverse the order of the above steps from (e) to (c) and repeat steps from (a) to (f) once again.

h. Remove the two bearing caps and the exhaust camshaft.

To install:

9. Install the intake camshaft as follows:

➡Since the thrust clearance of the camshaft is small, the camshaft must be kept level while it is being installed. If the camshaft is not kept level, the portion of the cylinder head receiving the shaft thrust may crack or be damaged, causing the camshaft to seize or break. To avoid this, the following steps should be carried out.

a. Apply engine oil to the thrust portion of the intake camshaft.

b. Lightly place the intake camshaft on top of the cylinder head so that the No. 1 and the No. 4 cylinder cam lobes face downward.

c. Lightly push the camshaft towards the front without applying excessive force. Place the No. 2 and the No. 5 bearing caps in their proper location.

d. Temporarily tighten these bearing cap bolts uniformly and alternately in several passes until the bearing caps are snug with the cylinder head.

e. Place the No. 3, No. 4, No. 6, and the No. 7 bearing caps in their proper location. Temporarily tighten these bearing cap bolts, alternately tightening the left and right bolts uniformly.

f. Place the No. 1 bearing cap in its proper location. Check that there is no gap between the cylinder head and the contact surface of the bearing cap.

g. Uniformly tighten the 14 bearing cap bolts in several passes to 12 ft. lbs. (16 Nm).

10. Install the exhaust camshaft as follows:

a. Set the timing mark (two dot marks) of the camshaft drive gear at approximately 35 degree angle by turning the hexagon wrench head portion of the intake camshaft with a wrench.

b. Apply engine oil to the thrust portion of the exhaust camshaft. Engage the exhaust camshaft gear to the intake camshaft gear by matching the timing marks (two dot marks) on each gear.

c. Roll down the exhaust camshaft onto the bearing journals while engaging the gears with each other. Lightly push the intake camshaft towards the front without applying excessive force.

d. Install the No. 4 and the No. 6 bearing caps in their proper location. Temporarily tighten these bearing cap bolts, alternately tightening the left and right bolts uniformly.

e. Place the No. 2, No. 3, No. 5, and the No. 7 bearing caps in their proper location. Temporarily tighten these bearing cap bolts, alternately tightening the left and right bolts uniformly.

f. Tighten the 14 bearing cap bolts in several passes to 12 ft. lbs. (16 Nm).

g. Bring the service bolt installed in the driven sub-gear upward by turning the hexagon wrench head portion of the camshaft with a wrench. Remove the service bolt.

h. Check that the intake and the exhaust camshafts turn smoothly.

11. Set the No. 1 cylinder to TDC of the compression stroke as follows:

a. Turn the crankshaft pulley, and align its groove with the timing mark **0** of the timing chain cover. Turn the camshaft so that the timing marks with one and two dots will be in straight line on the cylinder head surface.

12. Install the camshaft timing gear as follows:

a. Check that the matchmarks on the camshaft timing gear and the timing chain are aligned. Place the gear over the straight pin of the intake camshaft.

b. Align the straight pin of the distributor gear with the straight pin groove of the intake camshaft gear.

c. Hold the intake camshaft with a wrench, install and tighten the bolt to 54 ft. lbs. (74 Nm).

13. Install the chain tensioner. Push the tensioner by hand until it touches the head installation surface, then install and tighten the two nuts to 15 ft. lbs. (21 Nm).

14. Check the valve timing as follows:

a. Turn the crankshaft pulley, and align its groove with the timing mark **0** of the timing chain cover. Always turn the crankshaft clockwise.

b. Check that the timing marks (one and two dots) of the camshaft drive and driven gears are in straight line on the cylinder head surface. If not, turn the crankshaft one revolution (360 degrees) and align the marks.

15. Check valve clearance and adjust if necessary.

16. Install the spark plugs.

17. Install the semi-circular plug to the cylinder head.

18. Make sure that the No. 1 cylinder is in TDC of the compression stroke.

19. Install the cylinder head cover.

2UZ-FE Engine

➧ See Figures 256 thru 264

This is a lengthy and complicated procedure requiring careful and precise work.

1. Disconnect the negative battery cable.
2. Drain the engine coolant.
3. Remove the throttle body cover.
4. Disconnect the timing belt from the camshaft pulleys. Please see the timing belt procedure in this section. Use care when working around the timing belt. Do not allow anything to drop inside the timing belt cover. Do not allow the timing belt to come into contact with oil, water or dust.
5. Remove the camshaft timing pulleys. Please see the timing belt procedure in this section.
6. Remove the camshaft position sensor by removing the bolt and stud bolt and then removing the sensor.
7. If necessary, disconnect the power steering pump from the engine.
8. Remove the ignition coils.
9. Remove the three bolts and the stud bolt and remove the left side and right side timing belt rear plates.
10. Disconnect the fuel lines.
11. Tag for identification and detach the following electrical connectors:
   - Throttle Position (TP) sensor
   - Accelerator pedal position sensor connector
   - Throttle control motor connector
   - VSV connector for the EVAP system
   - Eight fuel injector connectors
   - Engine Coolant Temperature (ECT) sensor
   - Water sender gauge connector
   - Eight ignition coil connectors
   - Two heated oxygen sensor connectors.
12. Tag for identification and disconnect the following hoses:
   - The vacuum hose from the fuel pressure regulator.

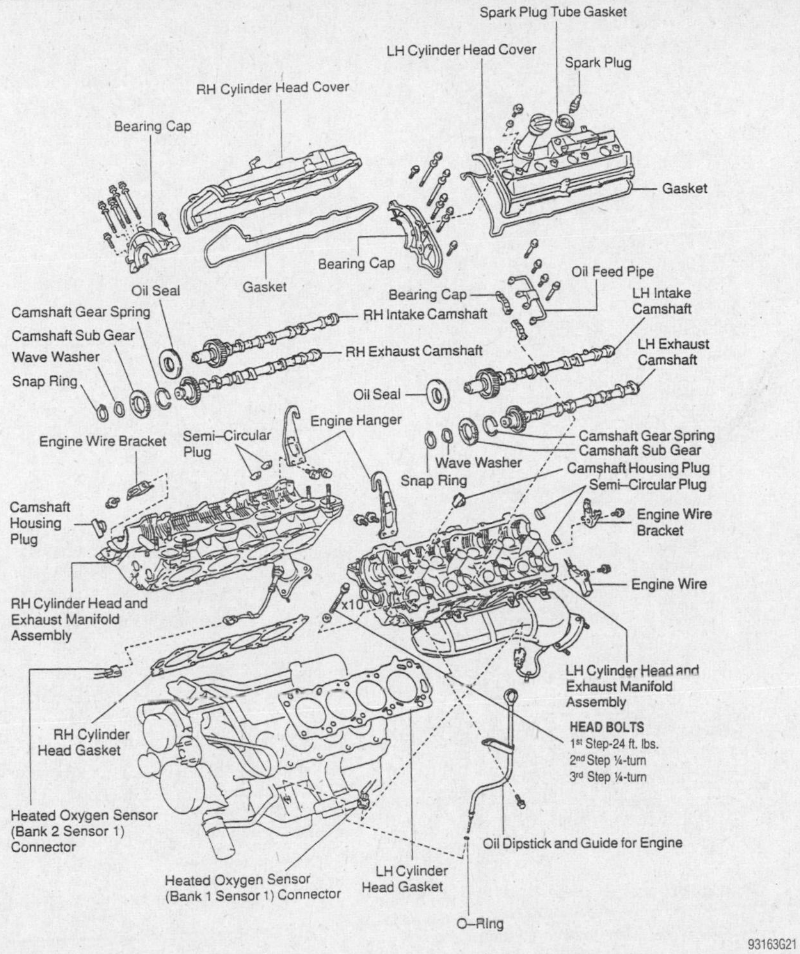

Fig. 256 Cylinder heads, camshafts and related components—2UZ-FE engine

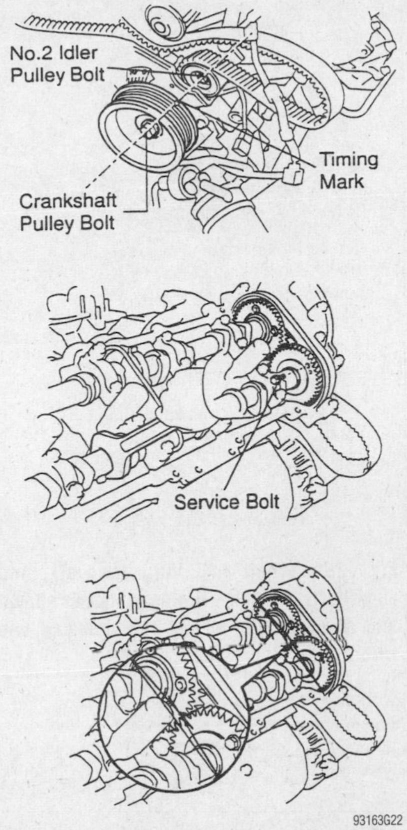

Fig. 257 Setting up the engine and aligning the timing marks before right side camshaft removal. Note the 6mm bolt used to lock together the two-piece cam gear—2UZ-FE engine

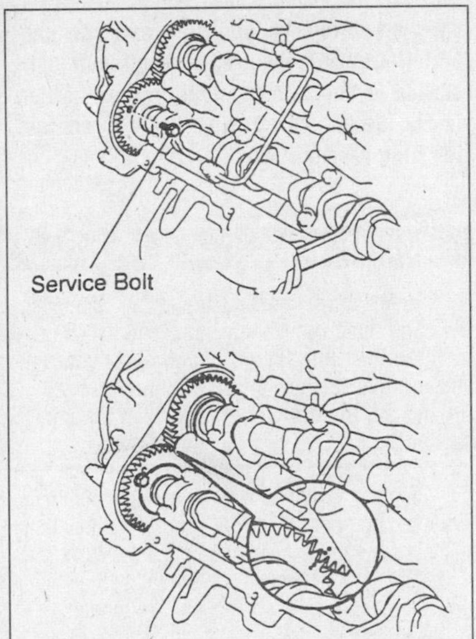

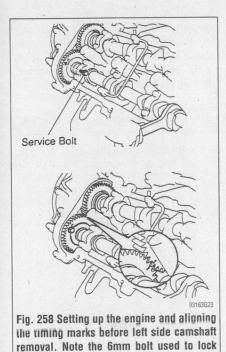

Fig. 258 Setting up the engine and aligning the timing marks before left side camshaft removal. Note the 6mm bolt used to lock together the two-piece cam gear—2UZ-FE engine

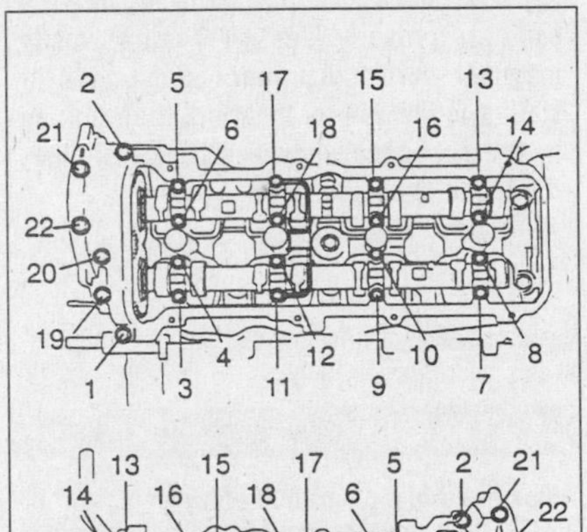

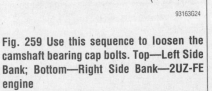

Fig. 259 Use this sequence to loosen the camshaft bearing cap bolts. Top—Left Side Bank; Bottom—Right Side Bank—2UZ-FE engine

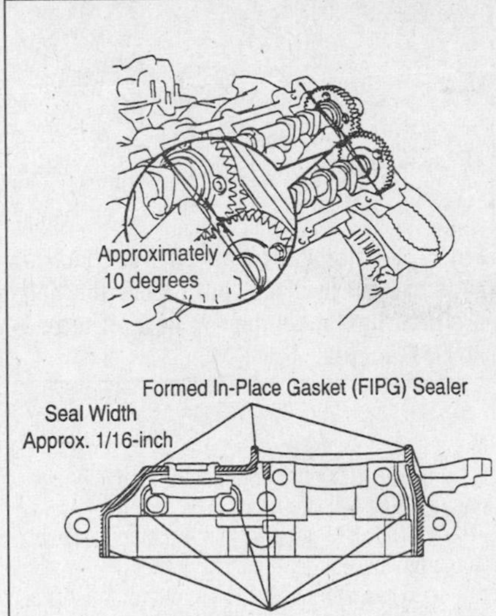

Fig. 260 When installing the right side camshafts, align the timing marks as shown and apply sealer to the front bearing cap where indicated—2UZ-FE engine

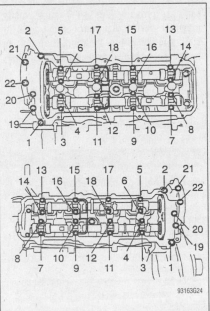

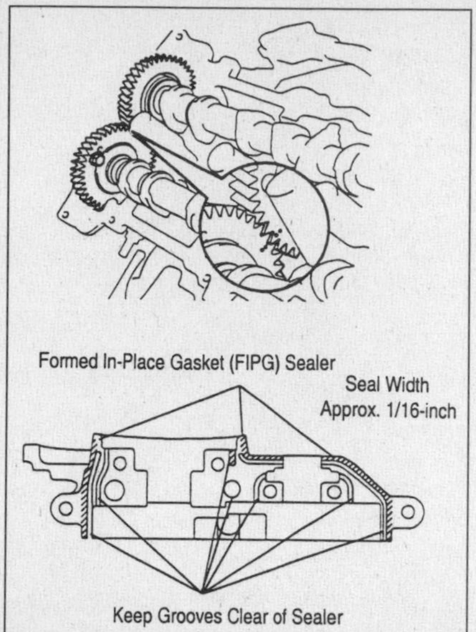

Fig. 261 When installing the left side camshafts, align the timing marks as shown and apply sealer to the front bearing cap where indicated—2UZ-FE engine

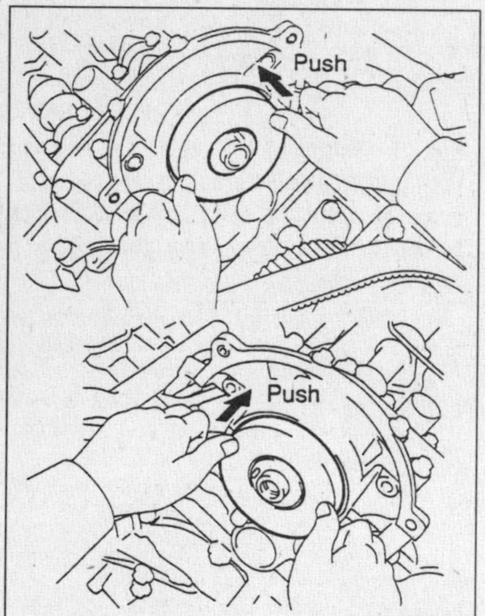

Fig. 262 After the camshaft front bearing caps are set in place, but before the bolts are final-tightened, push in new oil seals—2UZ-FE engine

- The PCV hose from the PCV valve on the left side cylinder head.
- The EVAP hose from the charcoal canister from the VSV for the EVAP system.
- The EVAP hose from the charcoal canister from the EVAP pipe on the intake manifold.
- The power steering vacuum switch lines from the intake manifold.
- The brake booster vacuum line.

13. Remove the upper and lower intake manifolds.

14. Remove the 18 bolts and seal washers from the cylinder head covers and remove the covers and gaskets. If necessary, remove semi-circular plugs and camshaft housing plugs.

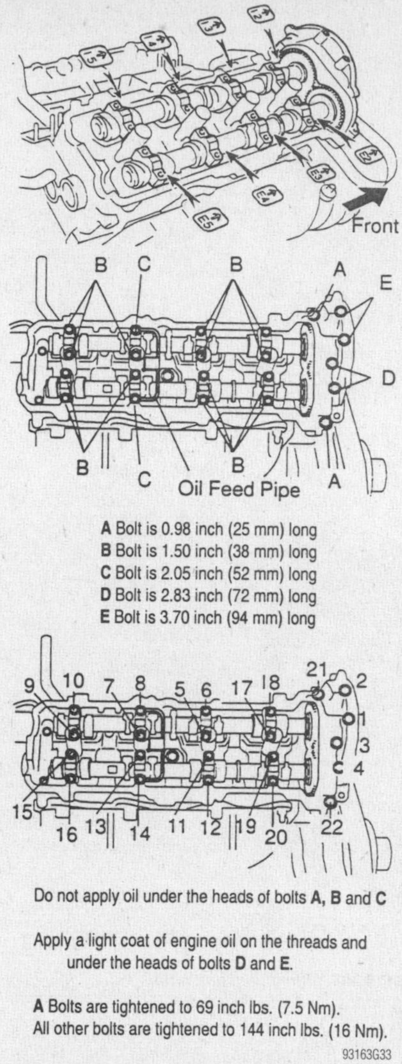

Front
B C B A E
D
B C B Oil Feed Pipe A
A Bolt is 0.98 inch (25 mm) long
B Bolt is 1.50 inch (38 mm) long
C Bolt is 2.05 inch (52 mm) long
D Bolt is 2.83 inch (72 mm) long
E Bolt is 3.70 inch (94 mm) long
Do not apply oil under the heads of bolts A, B and C
Apply a light coat of engine oil on the threads and under the heads of bolts D and E.
A Bolts are tightened to 69 inch lbs. (7.5 Nm).
All other bolts are tightened to 144 inch lbs. (16 Nm).
93163G33

Fig. 263 Make sure the camshaft bearing caps are properly identified and correctly installed. Verify the proper length bolt is installed in the correct location, then tighten in the sequence shown—2UZ-FE engine, right side bank shown

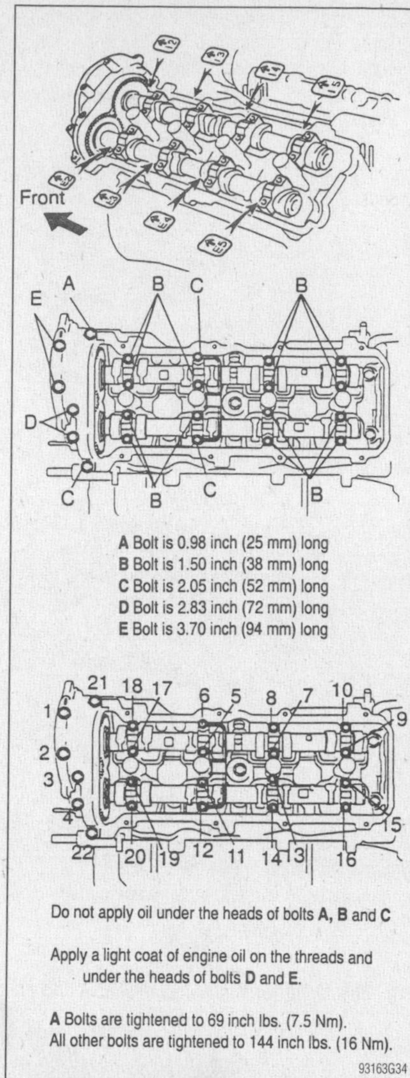

Front
E A B C B
D
C B C B
A Bolt is 0.98 inch (25 mm) long
B Bolt is 1.50 inch (38 mm) long
C Bolt is 2.05 inch (52 mm) long
D Bolt is 2.83 inch (72 mm) long
E Bolt is 3.70 inch (94 mm) long
Do not apply oil under the heads of bolts A, B and C
Apply a light coat of engine oil on the threads and under the heads of bolts D and E.
A Bolts are tightened to 69 inch lbs. (7.5 Nm).
All other bolts are tightened to 144 inch lbs. (16 Nm).
93163G34

Fig. 264 Make sure the camshaft bearing caps are properly identified and correctly installed. Verify the proper length bolt is installed in the correct location, then tighten in the sequence shown—2UZ-FE engine, left side bank shown

WARNING

Since the thrust clearance of the camshaft is small, the camshaft must be kept level while it is being removed. If the camshaft is not kept level, the portion of the head receiving the shaft thrust may crack or be damaged, causing the camshaft to seize or break. To avoid this, the following steps should be carried out.

15. Remove the camshafts using the following procedure.

a. Check the crankshaft pulley position. Check that the timing mark of the crankshaft pulley is aligned with the centers of the crankshaft pulley bolt and the idler pulley.

WARNING

Having the crankshaft pulley at the wrong angle can cause the piston head and valve head to come into contact with each other when you remove the camshaft, causing damage. Always set the crankshaft pulley at the correct angle.

b. Remove the right side camshafts. Bring the service bolt hole of the sub-gear upward by turning the hexagon wrench portion of the exhaust camshaft with a wrench. Secure the sub-gear to the main gear with a bolt 6mm in diameter x 1.0mm thread pitch x 16–20mm long.

WARNING

When removing the camshafts, make sure that the torsion spring force of the sub-gear has been eliminated by the above operation.

c. Set the timing mark (one dot mark) of the camshaft main gear at an angle approximately 10 degrees above horizontal by turning the hexagon wrench portion of the exhaust camshaft with a wrench.

d. Uniformly loosen and remove the 22 bearing cap bolts in several passes, in the sequence illustrated.

e. Remove the oil feed pipe, the bearing caps and the camshafts.

f. Remove the left side camshafts. Bring the service bolt hole of the sub-gear upward by turning the hexagon wrench portion of the exhaust camshaft with a wrench. Secure the sub-gear to the main gear with a bolt 6mm in diameter x 1.0mm thread pitch x 16–20mm long.

⁂ WARNING

When removing the camshafts, make sure that the torsion spring force of the sub-gear has been eliminated by the above operation.

g. Align timing marks (two dot marks) of the camshaft drive gear by turning the hexagon wrench portion of the exhaust camshaft with a wrench.

h. Uniformly loosen and remove the 22 bearing cap bolts in several passes, in the sequence illustrated. Note that there are five different length bearing cap bolts that, at assembly, MUST be returned to their proper locations. Mark these bolts or place in holes punched through cardboard to make sure they will be in the proper location and sequence. Take the time to accurately measure each bolt and mark its length on the cardboard. The reason tor this is that at assembly, certain lengths of bolts are handled differently, and they are identified by length.

i. Remove the oil feed pipe, the bearing caps and the camshafts.

➡Use care to keep the bearing caps in order, in the exact same sequence and direction as originally installed on the engine.

To install:

16. If disassembled, assemble the exhaust camshafts and sprockets using the following procedure:

a. Install the camshaft gear spring, camshaft sub-gear and wave washer. Attach the pins on the gears to the gear spring ends.

b. Install the snapring.

c. Mount the hexagon wrench head portion of the camshaft in a vise. Use care not to damage the camshaft.

d. Using Toyotas Special Service tool or a suitable pin-type spanner, align the holes of the camshaft main gear and sub-gear by turning the camshaft sub-gear counterclockwise, and temporarily install a bolt 6mm in diameter x 1.0mm thread pitch x 16–20mm long. Make sure the teeth of the gears are aligned, then tighten the bolt to secure the assembly.

17. Remove any old sealer from the semi-circular camshaft housing plugs. Apply fresh sealer to the plug grooves and install the camshaft housing plugs to the cylinder heads.

⁂ WARNING

Since the thrust clearance of the camshaft is small, the camshaft must be kept level while it is being installed. If the camshaft is not kept level, the portion of the head receiving the shaft thrust may crack or be damaged, causing the camshaft to seize or break. To avoid this, the following steps should be carried out.

18. Install the right side camshafts using the following procedure:

a. Apply engine assembly lube or multipurpose grease to the thrust portion of the intake and exhaust camshafts.

b. Lay the intake and exhaust camshafts carefully in position.

c. Set the timing mark (one dot mark) of the camshaft main gear at an angle approximately 10 degrees above horizontal by turning the hexagon wrench portion of the exhaust camshaft with a wrench.

d. Remove any old sealer from the front bearing cap. Apply a bead of fresh sealer approximately $^{1}/_{16}$ inch in diameter, to the areas indicated in the illustration. Use care to keep sealer out of the front bearing cap grooves. Assemble the front bearing cap before the sealer has a chance to skin-over (start to cure). Note that installing the front bearing cap will determine the thrust clearance of the camshaft.

e. Install the other bearing caps in the sequence illustrated with the arrow mark facing forward. Align the arrow marks at the front and rear of the cylinder head with the mark on the bearing cap.

f. Install a new camshaft oil seal.

g. Apply a light coat of engine oil on the threads of only two sizes (the two longest) of camshaft bearing cap bolts. These bolts are:

- The 2.83 inch (72mm) bolts (called bolt D).
- The 3.70 inch (94mm) bolts (called bolt E).

h. Do not apply engine oil under the heads of the remaining camshaft bearing cap bolts. These bolts are:

- The 0.98 inch (25mm) bolts (called bolt A).
- The 1.50 inch (38mm) bolts (called bolt B).
- The 2.05 inch (52mm) bolts (called bolt C).

19. Uniformly tighten the 22 bearing cap bolts in several passes, in the sequence illustrated:

a. Torque the shortest bolts (bolt A) to 69 inch lbs. (7.5 Nm).

b. Torque all other bolts to 144 inch lbs. (16 Nm).

c. Bring the service bolt hole of the sub-gear upward by turning the hexagon wrench portion of the exhaust camshaft with a wrench. Remove the bolt. This allows the torsion spring and sub-gear to remove gear backlash.

20. Install the left side camshafts using the same procedure.

21. Turn the camshaft(s) and position so the lobes are upward, and check and adjust the valve clearance, noting the following:

a. Turn the crankshaft pulley and align its groove with the timing mark **0** on the No. 1 timing belt cover.

b. Install the timing belt rear plates.

c. Check that the timing marks of the camshaft timing pulleys and the timing belt rear plates are aligned. If not, turn the crankshaft exactly one revolution (360 degrees) and align the marks.

d. Using a feeler gauge, measure the distance between the valve lifter and camshaft. Clearance should be 0.006–0.010 inch (0.15–0.25mm) on the intake camshaft and 0.010–0.014 inch (0.25–0.35mm) on the exhaust camshaft.

22. Clean all old sealer from the four semi-circular camshaft plugs. Apply a fresh bead of sealer to the center groove of the plugs and install the plugs to the cylinder head.

23. Clean all old sealer from the cylinder head covers. Apply fresh sealer at the joint where the camshaft front bearing cap meets the cylinder head cover sealing surface. Use new cylinder head cover gaskets. Make sure the seal washers under the bolt heads are in good condition. Install the cylinder head covers. Uniformly tighten the bolts in several passes with final torque to 53 inch lbs. (6 Nm).

24. Install the upper and lower intake manifolds using the procedures found in this section. Use care to make sure the lower intake manifold gaskets are properly installed. Factory replacement gaskets should have white paint marks which should be facing upward. Align the port holes of the gasket and the cylinder head.

25. Using the identification tags made at disassembly, connect the following hoses to the intake manifold:

- Vacuum hose to the fuel pressure regulator.
- PCV hose to the PCV valve on the left side cylinder head.
- EVAP hose to the charcoal canister from the VSV for the EVAP system.
- EVAP hose to the charcoal canister from the EVAP pipe on the intake manifold.
- Power steering vacuum switch lines to the intake manifold.
- Brake booster vacuum line.

26. Using the identification tags made at disassembly, attach the following electrical connectors:

- Throttle Position (TP) sensor
- Accelerator pedal position sensor connector
- Throttle control motor connector
- VSV connector for the EVAP system
- Eight fuel injector connectors
- Engine Coolant Temperature (ECT) sensor
- Water sender gauge connector
- Eight ignition coil connectors
- Two heated oxygen sensor connectors

27. Connect the fuel lines.

28. If not done so earlier, install the timing belt rear plates and tighten the bolts to 66 inch lbs. (7.5 Nm).

29. Install the throttle body.

30. Install the ignition coils to their proper spark plug.

31. Install the automatic transmission fluid dipstick and fill tube.

32. Connect the front exhaust pipe.

33. Install the power steering pump.

34. Install the camshaft position sensor.

35. Install the camshaft timing pulleys and the timing belt.

36. An oil and filter change is recommended.

37. Refill the engine with coolant.

38. Check all fluid levels. Start the engine and check for leaks and abnormal noises.

INSPECTION

A dial indicator, micrometer and inside micrometer are all needed to properly measure the camshaft and camshaft housing. If these instruments are available, proceed; if they are not available, have the parts checked at a reputable machine shop. Camshaft specifications are included in the Specifications Chart in this section.

1. Using the micrometer, measure the height of each cam lobe. If a lobe height is less than the minimum specified, the lobe is worn and the cam must be replaced.
2. Place the cam in V-blocks and measure its run-out at the center journal with a dial indicator. Replace the cam if run-out exceeds:
   - 1FZ-FE, 2RZ-FE, 3RZ-FE and 5VZ-FE engines: 0.0024 inch (0.06mm)
   - 2UZ-FE engine: 0.0031 inch (0.08mm)
3. Using the micrometer, measure journal diameter, jot down the readings and compare the readings with those listed in the Specifications chart. Measure the housing bore inside diameter with the inside micrometer, and jot the measurements down. Subtract the journal diameter measurement from the housing bore measurement. If the clearance is greater than the maximum listed under Bearing Clearance in the chart, replace the camshaft and/or the housing.

Rear Crankshaft Oil Seal

REMOVAL & INSTALLATION

Seal Retainer On Engine

See Figures 265, 266, and 267

1. Remove the transmission.
2. Remove the clutch cover assembly and flywheel (manual trans.) or the flexplate (automatic trans.).
3. Use a small, sharp knife to cut off the lip of the oil seal. Take great care not to score any metal with the knife.
4. Use a small prybar to pry the old seal from the retaining plate. Be careful not to damage the plate. Protect the tip of the tool with tape and pad the fulcrum point with cloth.
5. Inspect the crankshaft and seal lip contact surfaces for any sign of damage.

To install:

6. Apply a light coat of multi-purpose grease to the lip of a new oil seal. Loosely fit the seal into place by hand, making sure it is not crooked.
7. Use a seal driver such as (SST 09223-15030 and 09950-70010) of the correct size to install the seal. Tap it into place until the surface of the seal is flush with the edge of the housing.

➡Use the correct tools. Homemade substitutes may install the seal crooked, resulting in oil leaks and premature seal failure.

Seal Retainer Removed

See Figures 268 and 269

1. Support the retainer on two thin pieces of wood.
2. Use a hammer and punch to drive the seal out of the retainer.

To install:

3. Apply a light coat of multi-purpose grease to the lip of a new oil seal. Loosely fit the seal into place by hand, making sure it is not crooked.
4. Use a seal driver such as (SST 09223-15030 and 09950-70010) of the correct size to install the seal. Tap it into place until the surface of the seal is flush with the edge of the housing.

Flywheel and Ring Gear

REMOVAL & INSTALLATION

See Figures 270, 271, 272, 273, and 274

1. If the engine is installed in the vehicle, remove the transmission.

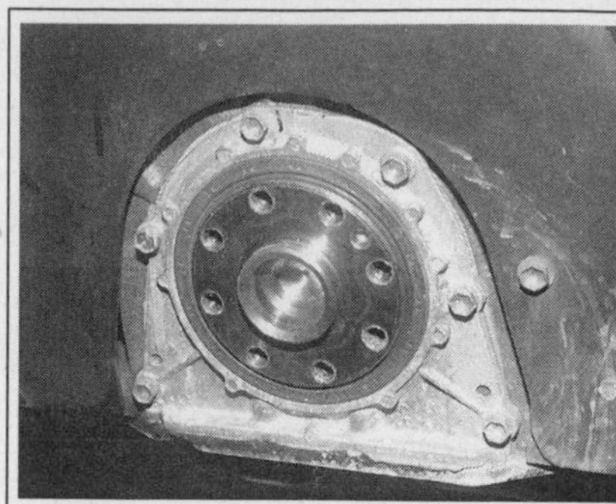
93163ph3
Fig. 265 Installed view of the rear crankshaft oil seal

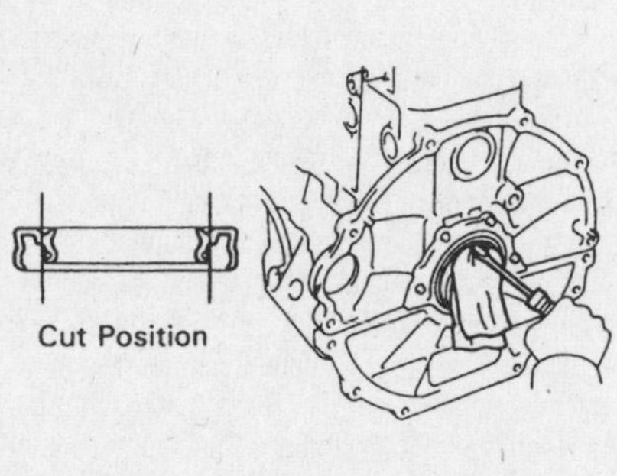

86823PKU
Fig. 266 Cut off the oil seal lip, then pry the seal out of the retaining plate

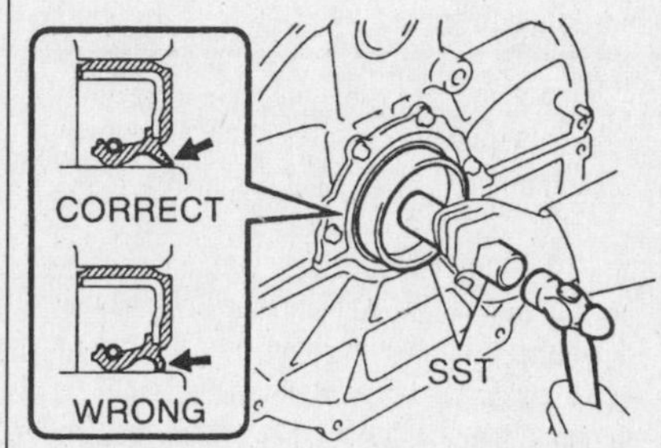

86823PKV
Fig. 267 Tap the new seal into place

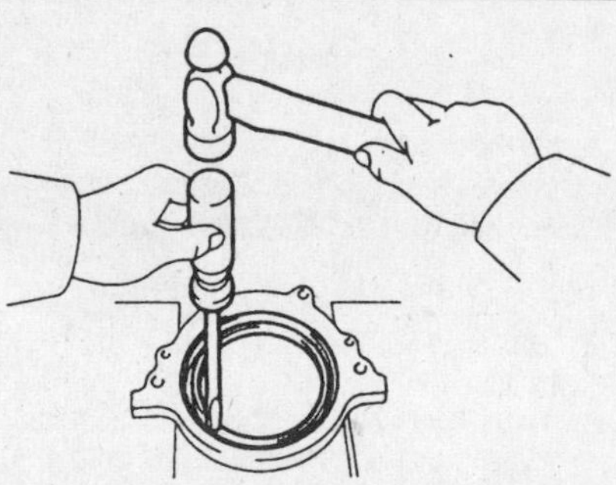
86823PKS
Fig. 268 Carefully tap the old seal from the retainer

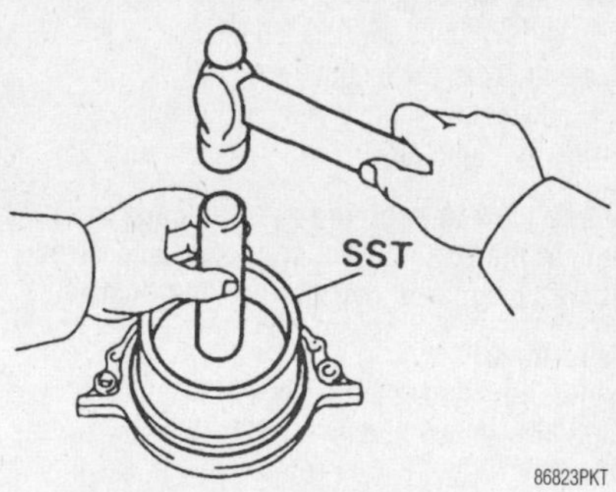

86823PKT
Fig. 269 Use a proper sized driver to seat the seal

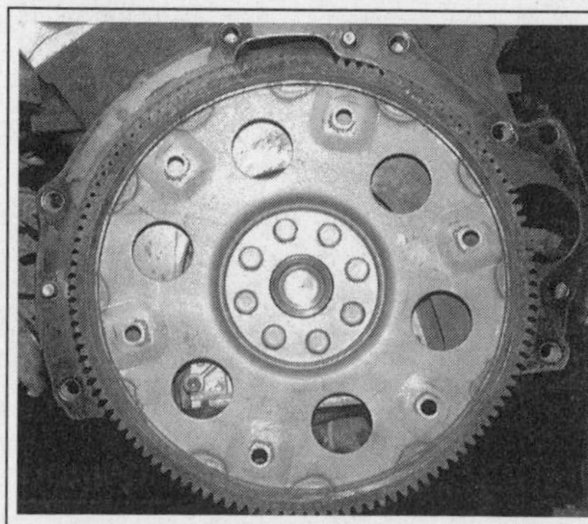
93163pg9
Fig. 270 View of the flywheel bolted to the crankshaft—5VZ-FE engine

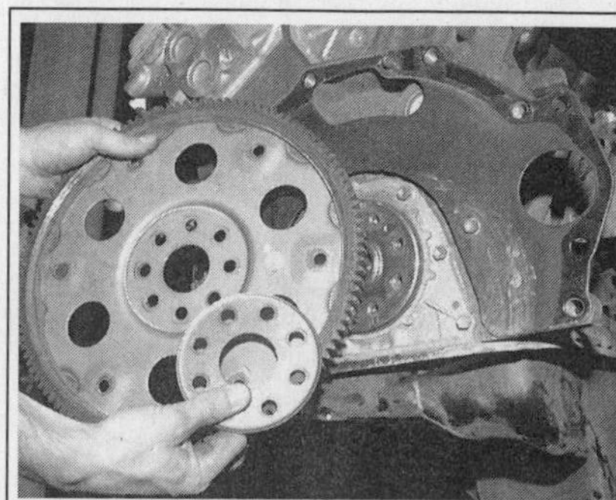
93163pg8
Fig. 271 On automatic transmission equipped vehicles, the flexplate has both front . . .

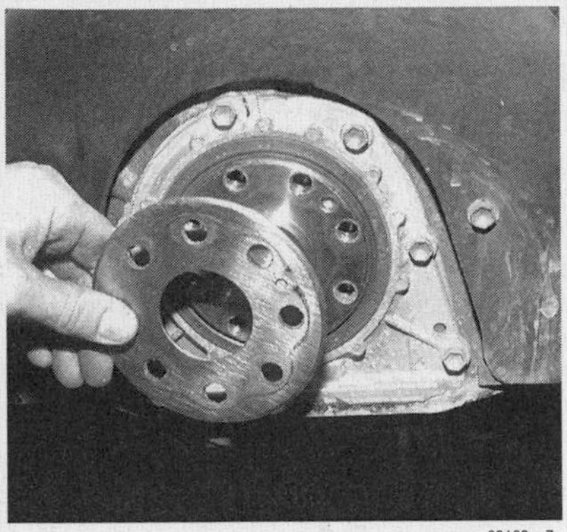

93163pg7

Fig. 272 . . . and rear spacers

86823PMJ

Fig. 273 If a flywheel holding tool is not available, an air gun may be used to loosen the bolts

86823PMI

Fig. 274 Always tighten the bolts with a torque wrench. Note the flywheel holding tool

2. Remove the clutch assembly, if equipped with manual transmission.

3. Make matchmarks on the flywheel and crankshaft end. A pin-punch is suggested since chalk or paint marks may get erased during cleaning.

4. Loosen the bolts holding the flywheel or driveplate a little at a time and in a crisscross pattern. Remove the flywheel. A manual transmission flywheel is heavy so use caution to protect yourself and the vehicles components. Protect the flywheel and ring-gear from damage or impact.

To install:

5. Thoroughly clean the flywheel bolts. Coat the first 3 or 4 threads of each bolt with thread-locking compound. Install the flywheel, aligning the previously made marks. Install the bolts finger-tight.

6. Tighten the bolts in a crisscross pattern and in several passes to the correct tightness:

- 2RZ-FE engine with manual transmission: 65 ft. lbs. (88 Nm)
- 3RZ-FE engine with manual transmission: 1st pass; 19 ft. lbs. (26 Nm), 2nd pass turn 90 degrees ($^1/_4$ turn)
- 2RZ-FE and 3RZ-FE engines with automatic transmissions: 54 ft. lbs. (74 Nm)
- 5VZ-FE engine with automatic transmission: 61 ft. lbs. (83 Nm)
- 5VZ-FE engine with manual transmission: 63 ft. lbs. (85 Nm)
- 1FZ-FE engine with automatic transmission: 74 ft. lbs. (100 Nm)
- 2UZ-FE engine with automatic transmission: 36 ft. lbs. (49 Nm), 2nd pass turn 90 degrees ($^1/_4$ turn)
- 2UZ-FE engine with manual transmission: 63 ft. lbs. (85 Nm)

7. Reinstall the transmission.

EXHAUST SYSTEM

General Information

➡Safety glasses should be worn at all times when working on or near the exhaust system. Older exhaust systems will almost always be covered with loose rust particles which will shower you when disturbed. These particles could injure your eye.

Whenever working on the exhaust system always keep the following in mind:

- Check the complete exhaust system for open seams, holes loose connections, or other deterioration which could permit exhaust fumes to seep into the passenger compartment.
- The exhaust system is usually supported by free-hanging rubber mountings which permit some movement of the exhaust system, but does not permit transfer of noise and vibration into the passenger compartment. Do not replace the rubber mounts with solid ones.
- Before removing any component of the exhaust system, ALWAYS squirt a liquid rust dissolving agent onto the fasteners for ease of removal. It may even be wise to spray the fasteners and allow them to sit overnight.

⁂ CAUTION

Allow the exhaust system to cool sufficiently before spraying a solvent exhaust fasteners. Some solvents are highly flammable and could ignite when sprayed on hot exhaust components.

- Annoying rattles and noise vibrations in the exhaust system are usually caused by misalignment of the parts. When aligning the system, leave all bolts and nuts loose until all parts are properly aligned, then tighten, working from front to rear.
- When installing exhaust system parts, make sure there is enough clearance between the hot exhaust parts and pipes and hoses that would be adversely affected by excessive heat. Also make sure there is adequate clearance from the floor pan to avoid possible overheating of the floor.

Safety Precautions

For a number of reasons, exhaust system work can be the most dangerous type of work you can do on your car. Always observe the following precautions:

- Support the car extra securely. Not only will you often be working directly under it, but you'll frequently be using a lot of force, such as heavy hammer blows, to dislodge rusted parts. This can cause a vehicle that's improperly supported to shift and possibly fall.
- Wear goggles. Exhaust system parts are always rusty. Metal chips can be dislodged, even when you're only turning rusted bolts. Attempting to pry pipes apart with a chisel makes the chips fly even more frequently.
- If you're using a cutting torch, keep it a great distance from either the fuel tank or lines. Stop what you're doing and feel the temperature of the fuel pipes on the tank frequently. Even slight heat can expand and/or vaporize fuel, resulting in accumulated vapor (or even a liquid leak) near your torch.
- Watch where your hammer blows fall and make sure you hit squarely. You could easily tap a brake or fuel line when you hit an exhaust system part with a glancing blow. Inspect all lines and hoses in the area where you've been working.

CAUTION

Be very careful when working on or near the catalytic converter. External temperatures can reach 1,500°F (816°C) and more, causing severe burns. Removal or installation should be performed only on a cold exhaust system.

A number of special exhaust system tools can be rented from auto supply houses or local stores that rent special equipment. A common one is a tail pipe expander, designed to enable you to join pipes of identical diameter.

The exhaust system of Toyota trucks consists of several pieces. At the front of a the first section of pipe connects the exhaust manifold to the catalytic converter. Some vehicles may use a crossover or Y-pipe below the engine to connect the two exhaust manifold ports. The 2UZ-FE V8 engine uses two head pipes, one for each manifold, and each head pipe has its own catalytic converter.

The catalytic converter is a sealed, non-serviceable unit which can be easily unbolted from the system and replaced if necessary.

The exhaust system is attached to the body by several hooks and flexible rubber hangers; these hangers absorb exhaust vibrations and isolate the system from the body of the car. A series of metal heat shields runs along the exhaust piping, protecting the underbody from excess heat.

When inspecting or replacing exhaust system parts, make sure there is adequate clearance from all points on the body to avoid possible overheating of the floorpan. Check the complete system for broken damaged, missing or poorly positioned parts. Rattles and vibrations in the exhaust system are usually caused by misalignment of parts. When aligning the system, leave all the nuts and bolts loose until everything is in its proper place, then tighten the hardware working from the front to the rear. Remember that what appears to be proper clearance during repair may change as the truck moves down the road. The motion of the engine, body and suspension must be considered when replacing parts.

REMOVAL & INSTALLATION

CAUTION

Do NOT perform exhaust repairs with the engine or exhaust hot. Allow the system to cool completely before attempting any work. Exhaust systems are noted for sharp edges, flaking metal and rusted bolts. Gloves and eye protection are required. A healthy supply of penetrating oil and rags is highly recommended.

Complete System

See Figures 275 thru 281

If the entire exhaust system is to be replaced, it is much easier to remove the system as a unit than remove each individual piece. Disconnect the first pipe at the manifold joint and work towards the rear removing brackets and hangers as you go. Separate the rear pipe at the catalytic converter. Remove any retaining brackets and O-rings from the center of exhaust system and back. Then slide the rear section of the exhaust system out from the back the truck. When removed from the vehicle, then you can detach the catalyst from the system, this is usually the one good part. It stays hot enough in normal operation to dry off rust-inducing moisture.

When installing the new assembly, suspend it from the flexible hangers first, then attach the fixed (solid) brackets. Check the clearance to the body and suspension and install the manifold joint bolts, tightening them correctly.

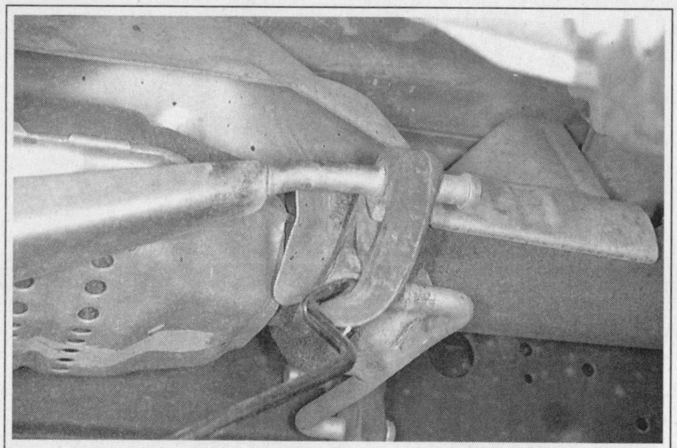

]93163p01

Fig. 275 View of a typical Toyota rubber exhaust hanger

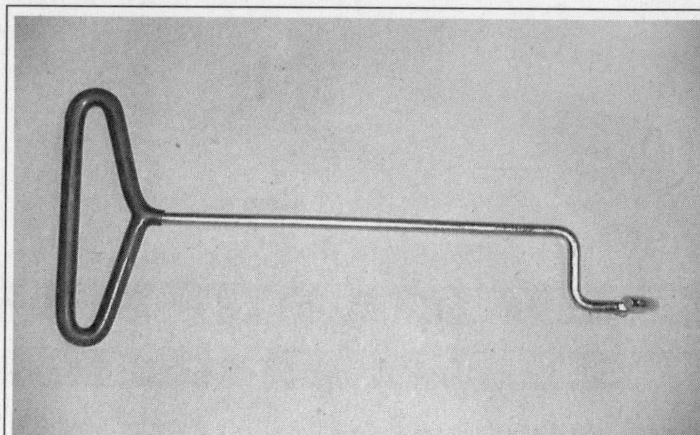

93163p03

Fig. 276 An exhaust hanger tool like this one, makes removal and installation a breeze

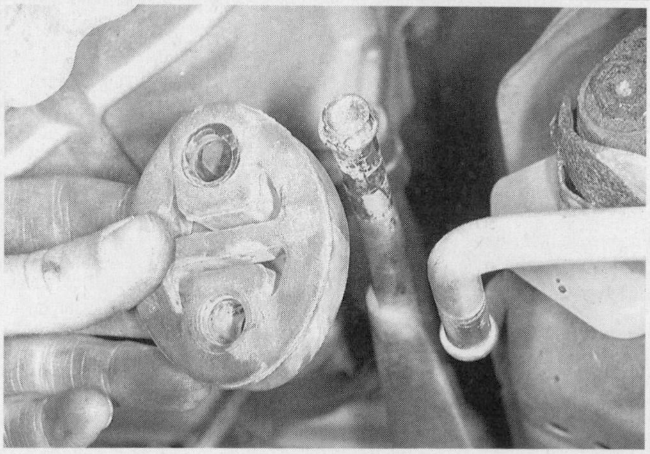

93163p04

Fig. 277 Once loose, pull the exhaust hanger free from the exhaust

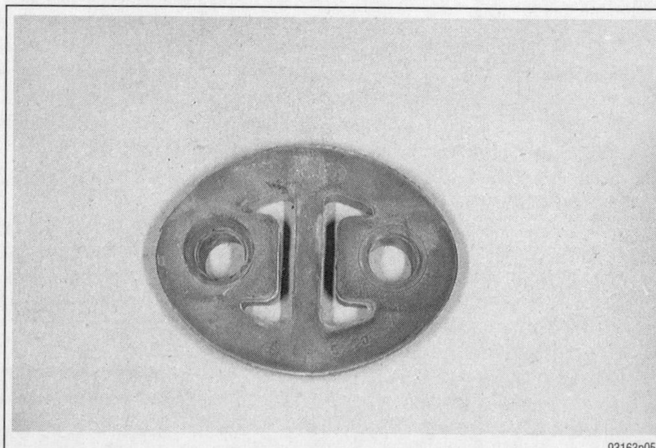

93163p05

Fig. 278 Thoroughly check the rubber exhaust hanger for cracks and replace if necessary

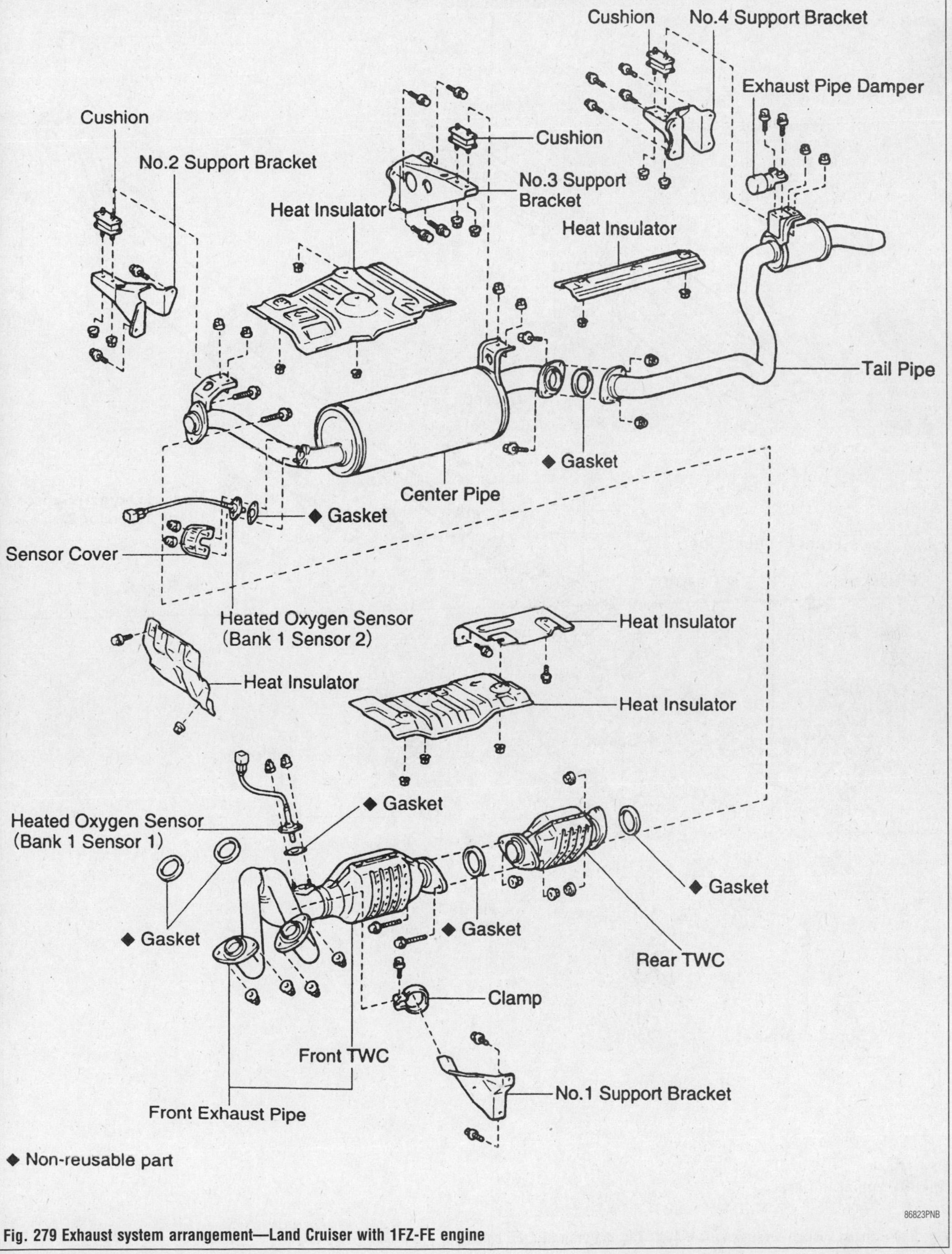

Fig. 279 Exhaust system arrangement—Land Cruiser with 1FZ-FE engine

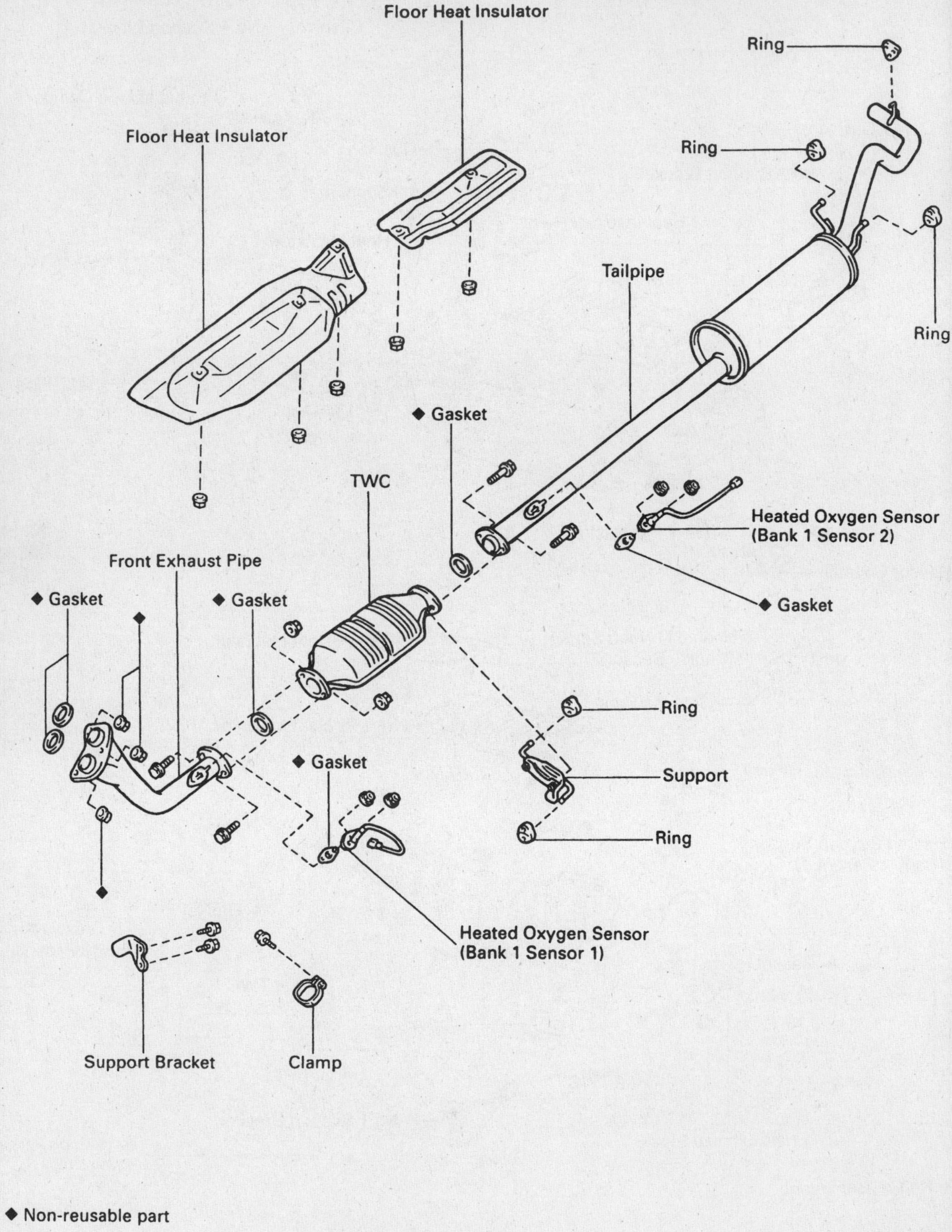

Fig. 280 Exhaust system arrangement—4WD Tacoma with 3RZ-FE engine

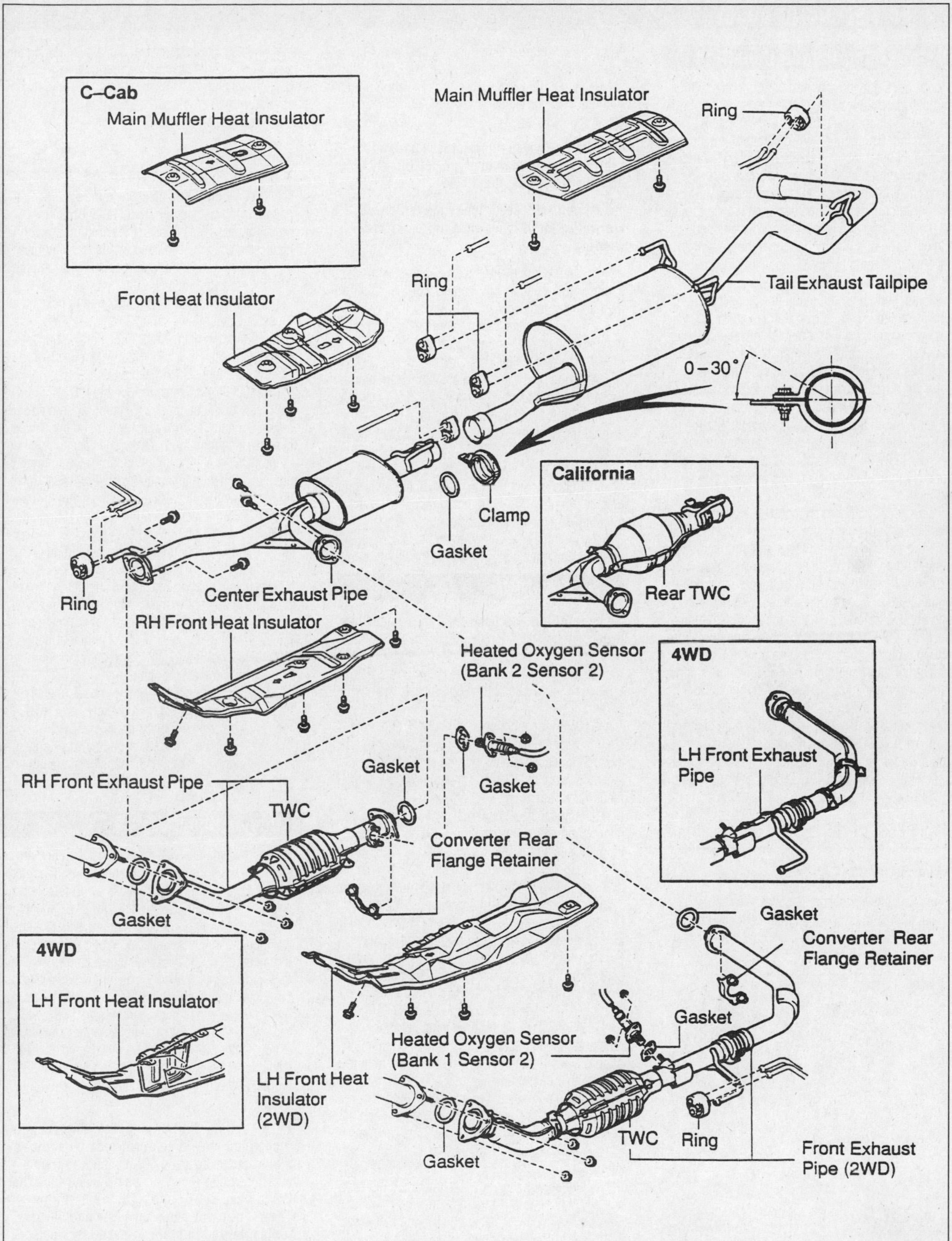

Fig. 281 Exhaust system arrangement—Tundra with 2UZ-FE engine

ENGINE RECONDITIONING

Determining Engine Condition

Anything that generates heat and/or friction will eventually burn or wear out (for example, a light bulb generates heat, therefore its life span is limited). With this in mind, a running engine generates tremendous amounts of both; friction is encountered by the moving and rotating parts inside the engine and heat is created by friction and combustion of the fuel. However, the engine has systems designed to help reduce the effects of heat and friction and provide added longevity. The oiling system reduces the amount of friction encountered by the moving parts inside the engine, while the cooling system reduces heat created by friction and combustion. If either system is not maintained, a break-down will be inevitable. Therefore, you can see how regular maintenance can affect the service life of your vehicle. If you do not drain, flush and refill your cooling system at the proper intervals, deposits will begin to accumulate in the radiator, thereby reducing the amount of heat it can extract from the coolant. The same applies to your oil and filter; if it is not changed often enough it becomes laden with contaminates and is unable to properly lubricate the engine. This increases friction and wear.

There are a number of methods for evaluating the condition of your engine. A compression test can reveal the condition of your pistons, piston rings, cylinder bores, head gasket(s), valves and valve seats. An oil pressure test can warn you of possible engine bearing, or oil pump failures. Excessive oil consumption, evidence of oil in the engine air intake area and/or bluish smoke from the tailpipe may indicate worn piston rings, worn valve guides and/or valve seals. As a general rule, an engine that uses no more than one quart of oil every 1000 miles is in good condition. Engines that use one quart of oil or more in less than 1000 miles should first be checked for oil leaks. If any oil leaks are present, have them fixed before determining how much oil is consumed by the engine, especially if blue smoke is not visible at the tailpipe.

COMPRESSION TEST

See Figure 282

A noticeable lack of engine power, excessive oil consumption and/or poor fuel mileage measured over an extended period are all indicators of internal engine wear. Worn piston rings, scored or worn cylinder bores, blown head gaskets, sticking or burnt valves, and worn valve seats are all possible culprits. A check of each cylinder's compression will help locate the problem.

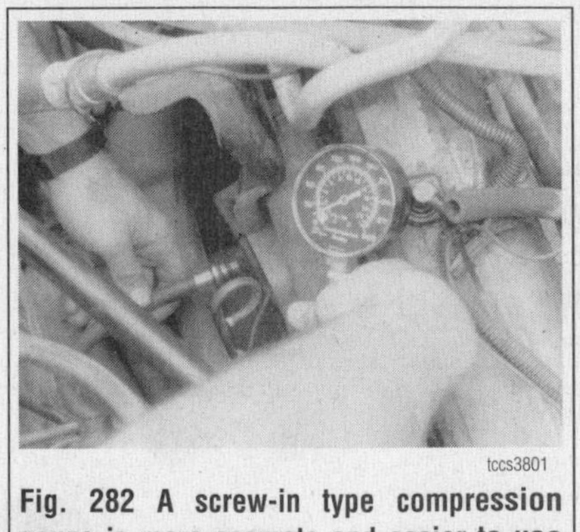

tccs3801

Fig. 282 A screw-in type compression gauge is more accurate and easier to use without an assistant

➡A screw-in type compression gauge is more accurate than the type you simply hold against the spark plug hole.

➡Although it takes slightly longer to use, it's worth the effort to obtain a more accurate reading.

1. Make sure that the proper amount and viscosity of engine oil is in the crankcase, then ensure the battery is fully charged.
2. Warm-up the engine to normal operating temperature, then shut the engine **OFF**.
3. Disable the ignition system.
4. Label and disconnect all of the spark plug wires from the plugs.
5. Thoroughly clean the cylinder head area around the spark plug ports, then remove the spark plugs.
6. Set the throttle plate to the fully open (wide-open throttle) position. You can block the accelerator linkage open for this, or you can have an assistant fully depress the accelerator pedal.
7. Install a screw-in type compression gauge into the No. 1 spark plug hole until the fitting is snug.

✲✲ WARNING

Be careful not to crossthread the spark plug hole.

8. According to the tool manufacturer's instructions, connect a remote starting switch to the starting circuit.
9. With the ignition switch in the **OFF** position, use the remote starting switch to crank the engine through at least five compression strokes (approximately 5 seconds of cranking) and record the highest reading on the gauge.
10. Repeat the test on each cylinder, cranking the engine approximately the same number of compression strokes and/or time as the first.
11. Compare the highest readings from each cylinder to that of the others. The indicated compression pressures are considered within specifications if the lowest reading cylinder is within 75 percent of the pressure recorded for the highest reading cylinder. For example, if your highest reading cylinder pressure was 150 psi (1034 kPa), then 75 percent of that would be 113 psi (779 kPa). So the lowest reading cylinder should be no less than 113 psi (779 kPa).
12. If a cylinder exhibits an unusually low compression reading, pour a tablespoon of clean engine oil into the cylinder through the spark plug hole and repeat the compression test. If the compression rises after adding oil, it means that the cylinder's piston rings and/or cylinder bore are damaged or worn. If the pressure remains low, the valves may not be seating properly (a valve job is needed), or the head gasket may be blown near that cylinder. If compression in any two adjacent cylinders is low, and if the addition of oil doesn't help raise compression, there is leakage past the head gasket. Oil and coolant in the combustion chamber, combined with blue or constant white smoke from the tailpipe, are symptoms of this problem. However, don't be alarmed by the normal white smoke emitted from the tailpipe during engine warm-up or from cold weather driving. There may be evidence of water droplets on the engine dipstick and/or oil droplets in the cooling system if a head gasket is blown.

OIL PRESSURE TEST

Check for proper oil pressure at the sending unit passage with an externally mounted mechanical oil pressure gauge (as opposed to relying on a factory installed dash-mounted gauge). A tachometer may also be needed, as some specifications may require running the engine at a specific rpm.

1. With the engine cold, locate and remove the oil pressure sending unit.
2. Following the manufacturer's instructions, connect a mechanical oil pressure gauge and, if necessary, a tachometer to the engine.
3. Start the engine and allow it to idle.
4. Check the oil pressure reading when cold and record the number. You may need to run the engine at a specified rpm, so check the specifications.
5. Run the engine until normal operating temperature is reached (upper radiator hose will feel warm).
6. Check the oil pressure reading again with the engine hot and record the number. Turn the engine **OFF**.
7. Compare your hot oil pressure reading to that given in the chart. If the reading is low, check the cold pressure reading against the chart. If the cold pressure is well above the specification, and the hot reading was lower than the specification, you may have the wrong viscosity oil in the engine. Change the oil, making sure to use the proper grade and quantity, then repeat the test.

Low oil pressure readings could be attributed to internal component wear, pump related problems, a low oil level, or oil viscosity that is too low. High oil pressure readings could be caused by an overfilled crankcase, too high of an oil viscosity or a faulty pressure relief valve.

Buy or Rebuild?

Now that you have determined that your engine is worn out, you must make some decisions. The question of whether or not an engine is worth rebuilding is largely a subjective matter and one of personal worth. Is the engine a popular one, or is it an obsolete model? Are parts available? Will it get acceptable gas mileage once it is rebuilt? Is the car it's being put into worth keeping? Would it be less expensive to buy a new engine, have your engine rebuilt by a pro, rebuild it yourself or buy a used engine from a salvage yard? Or would it be simpler and less expensive to buy another car? If you have considered all these matters and more, and have still decided to rebuild the engine, then it is time to decide how you will rebuild it.

➡The editors at Chilton feel that most engine machining should be performed by a professional machine shop. Don't think of it as wasting money, rather, as an assurance that the job has been done right the first time. There are many expensive and specialized tools required to perform such tasks as boring and honing an engine block or having a valve job done on a cylinder head. Even in-

specting the parts requires expensive micrometers and gauges to properly measure wear and clearances. Also, a machine shop can deliver to you clean, and ready to assemble parts, saving you time and aggravation. Your maximum savings will come from performing the removal, disassembly, assembly and installation of the engine and purchasing or renting only the tools required to perform the above tasks. Depending on the particular circumstances, you may save 40 to 60 percent of the cost doing these yourself.

A complete rebuild or overhaul of an engine involves replacing all of the moving parts (pistons, rods, crankshaft, camshaft, etc.) with new ones and machining the non-moving wearing surfaces of the block and heads. Unfortunately, this may not be cost effective. For instance, your crankshaft may have been damaged or worn, but it can be machined undersize for a minimal fee.

So, as you can see, you can replace everything inside the engine, but, it is wiser to replace only those parts which are really needed, and, if possible, repair the more expensive ones. Later in this section, we will break the engine down into its two main components: the cylinder head and the engine block. We will discuss each component, and the recommended parts to replace during a rebuild on each.

Engine Overhaul Tips

Most engine overhaul procedures are fairly standard. In addition to specific parts replacement procedures and specifications for your individual engine, this section is also a guide to acceptable rebuilding procedures. Examples of standard rebuilding practice are given and should be used along with specific details concerning your particular engine.

Competent and accurate machine shop services will ensure maximum performance, reliability and engine life. In most instances it is more profitable for the do-it-yourself mechanic to remove, clean and inspect the component, buy the necessary parts and deliver these to a shop for actual machine work.

Much of the assembly work (crankshaft, bearings, piston rods, and other components) is well within the scope of the do-it-yourself mechanic's tools and abilities. You will have to decide for yourself the depth of involvement you desire in an engine repair or rebuild.

TOOLS

The tools required for an engine overhaul or parts replacement will depend on the depth of your involvement. With a few exceptions, they will be the tools found in a mechanic's tool kit (see Section 1 of this manual). More in-depth work will require some or all of the following:

- A dial indicator (reading in thousandths) mounted on a universal base
- Micrometers and telescope gauges
- Jaw and screw-type pullers
- Scraper
- Valve spring compressor
- Ring groove cleaner
- Piston ring expander and compressor
- Ridge reamer
- Cylinder hone or glaze breaker
- Plastigage®
- Engine stand

The use of most of these tools is illustrated in this section. Many can be rented for a one-time use from a local parts jobber or tool supply house specializing in automotive work.

Occasionally, the use of special tools is called for. See the information on Special Tools and the Safety Notice in the front of this book before substituting another tool.

OVERHAUL TIPS

Aluminum has become extremely popular for use in engines, due to its low weight. Observe the following precautions when handling aluminum parts:

- Never hot tank aluminum parts (the caustic hot tank solution will eat the aluminum.
- Remove all aluminum parts (identification tag, etc.) from engine parts prior to the tanking.
- Always coat threads lightly with engine oil or anti-seize compounds before installation, to prevent seizure.
- Never overtighten bolts or spark plugs especially in aluminum threads.

When assembling the engine, any parts that will be exposed to frictional contact must be prelubed to provide lubrication at initial start-up. Any product specifically formulated for this purpose can be used, but engine oil is not recommended as a prelube in most cases.

When semi-permanent (locked, but removable) installation of bolts or nuts is desired, threads should be cleaned and coated with LoctiteR or another similar, commercial non-hardening sealant.

CLEANING

See Figures 283, 284, 285, and 286

Before the engine and its components are inspected, they must be thoroughly cleaned. You will need to remove any engine varnish, oil sludge and/or carbon deposits from all of the components to insure an accurate inspection. A crack in the engine block or cylinder head can easily become overlooked if hidden by a layer of sludge or carbon.

Most of the cleaning process can be carried out with common hand tools and readily available solvents or solutions. Carbon deposits can be chipped away using a hammer and a hard wooden chisel. Old gasket material and varnish or sludge can usually be removed using a scraper and/or cleaning solvent. Extremely stubborn deposits may require the use of a power drill with a wire brush. If using a wire brush, use extreme care around any critical machined surfaces (such as the gasket surfaces, bearing saddles, cylinder bores, etc.). USE OF A WIRE BRUSH IS NOT RECOMMENDED ON ANY ALUMINUM COMPONENTS. Always follow any safety recommendations given by the manufacturer of the tool and/or solvent. You should always wear eye protection during any cleaning process involving scraping, chipping or spraying of solvents.

An alternative to the mess and hassle of cleaning the parts yourself is to drop them off at a local garage or machine shop. They will, more than likely, have the necessary equipment to properly clean all of the parts for a nominal fee.

CAUTION

Always wear eye protection during any cleaning process involving scraping, chipping or spraying of solvents.

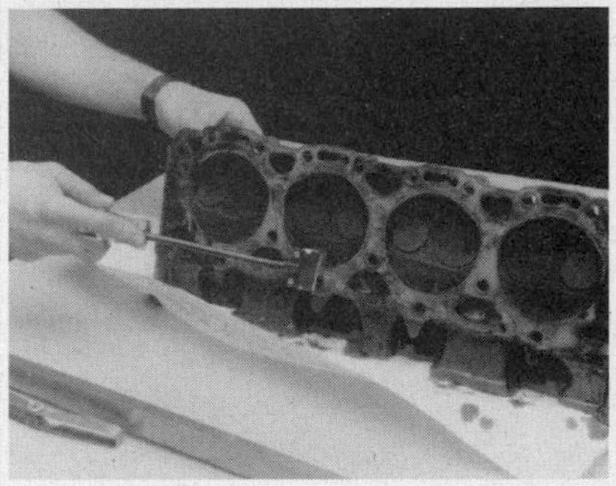

tccs3132

Fig. 283 Use a gasket scraper to remove the old gasket material from the mating surfaces

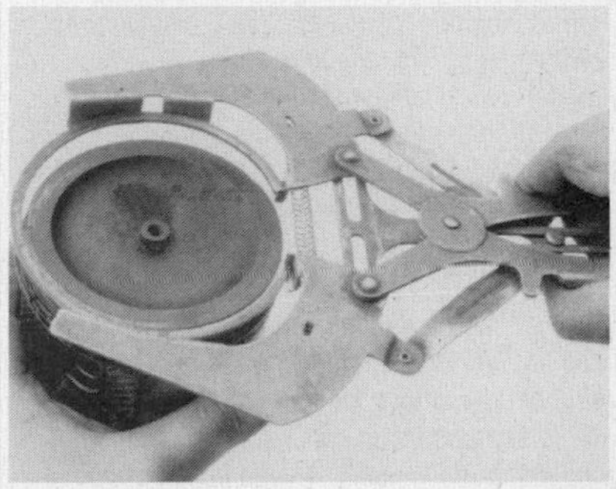

tccs3211

Fig. 284 Use a ring expander tool to remove the piston rings

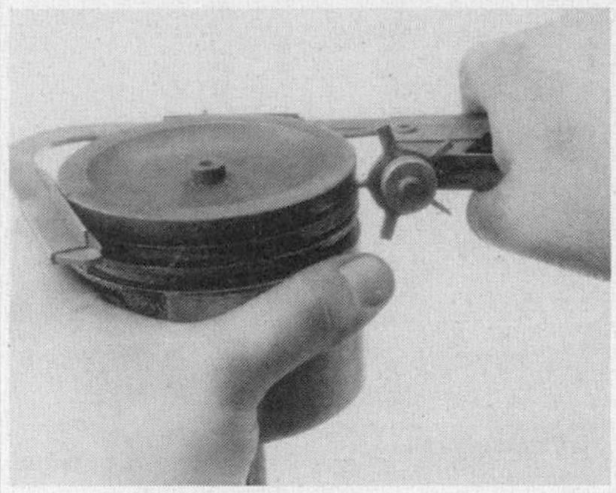

tccs3208

Fig. 285 Clean the piston ring grooves using a ring groove cleaner tool, or . . .

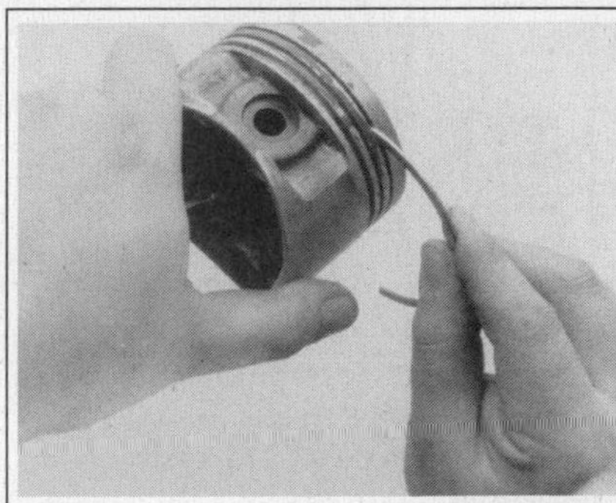

tccs3911

Fig. 286 . . . use a piece of an old ring to clean the grooves. Be careful, the ring can be quite sharp

Remove any oil galley plugs, freeze plugs and/or pressed-in bearings and carefully wash and degrease all of the engine components including the fasteners and bolts. Small parts such as the valves, springs, etc., should be placed in a metal basket and allowed to soak. Use pipe cleaner type brushes, and clean all passageways in the components. Use a ring expander and remove the rings from the pistons. Clean the piston ring grooves with a special tool or a piece of broken ring. Scrape the carbon off of the top of the piston. You should never use a wire brush on the pistons. After preparing all of the piston assemblies in this manner, wash and degrease them again.

⁂ WARNING

Use extreme care when cleaning around the cylinder head valve seats. A mistake or slip may cost you a new seat.

When cleaning the cylinder head, remove carbon from the combustion chamber with the valves installed. This will avoid damaging the valve seats.

REPAIRING DAMAGED THREADS

➧ See Figures 287, 288, 289, 290, and 291

Several methods of repairing damaged threads are available. Heli-Coil® (shown here), Keenserts® and Microdot® are among the most widely used. All involve basically the same principle—drilling out stripped threads, tapping the hole and installing a prewound insert—making welding, plugging and oversize fasteners unnecessary.

Two types of thread repair inserts are usually supplied: a standard type for most inch coarse, inch fine, metric course and metric fine thread sizes and a spark lug type to fit most spark plug port sizes. Consult the individual tool manufacturer's catalog to determine exact applications. Typical thread repair kits will contain a selection of prewound threaded inserts, a tap (corresponding to the outside diameter threads of the insert) and an installation tool. Spark plug inserts usually differ because they require a tap equipped with pilot threads and a combined reamer/tap section. Most manufacturers also supply blister-packed thread repair inserts separately in addition to a master kit containing a variety of taps and inserts plus installation tools.

Before attempting to repair a threaded hole, remove any snapped, broken or damaged bolts or studs. Penetrating oil can be used to free frozen threads. The offending item can usually be removed with locking pliers or using a screw/stud extractor. After the hole is clear, the thread can be repaired, as shown in the series of accompanying illustrations and in the kit manufacturer's instructions.

Engine Preparation

To properly rebuild an engine, you must first remove it from the vehicle, then disassemble and diagnose it. Ideally you should place your engine on an engine stand. This affords you the best access to the engine components. Follow the manufacturer's directions for using the stand with your particular engine. Remove the flywheel or flexplate before installing the engine to the stand.

Now that you have the engine on a stand, and assuming that you have drained the oil and coolant from the engine, it's time to strip it of all but the necessary components. Before you start disassembling the engine, you may want to take a moment to draw some pictures, or fabricate some labels or containers to mark the locations of various components and the bolts and/or studs which fasten them. Modern day engines use a lot of little brackets and clips which hold wiring harnesses and such, and these holders are often mounted on studs and/or bolts that can be easily mixed up. The manufacturer spent a lot of time and money designing your vehicle, and they wouldn't have wasted any of it by haphazardly placing brackets, clips or fasteners on the vehicle. If it's present when you disassemble it, put it back when you assemble, you will regret not remembering that little bracket which holds a wire harness out of the path of a rotating part.

You should begin by unbolting any accessories still attached to the engine, such as the water pump, power steering pump, alternator, etc. Then, unfasten any manifolds (intake or exhaust) which were not removed during the engine removal procedure. Finally, remove any covers remaining on the engine such as the rocker arm, front or timing cover and oil pan. Some front covers may require the vibration damper and/or crank pulley to be removed beforehand. The idea is to reduce the engine to the bare necessities (cylinder head(s), valve train, engine block, crankshaft, pistons and connecting rods), plus any other 'in block' components such as oil pumps, balance shafts and auxiliary shafts.

Finally, remove the cylinder head(s) from the engine block and carefully place on a bench. Disassembly instructions for each component follow later in this section.

Cylinder Head

There are two basic types of cylinder heads used on today's automobiles: the Overhead Valve (OHV) and the Overhead Camshaft (OHC). The latter can also be broken down into two subgroups: the Single Overhead Camshaft (SOHC) and the Dual Overhead Camshaft (DOHC). Generally, if there is only a single camshaft on a head, it is just referred to as an OHC head. Also, an engine with an OHV cylinder head is

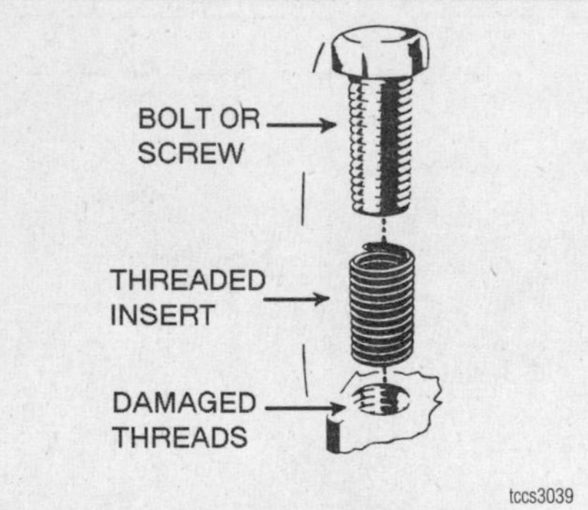

Fig. 287 Damaged bolt hole threads can be replaced with thread repair inserts

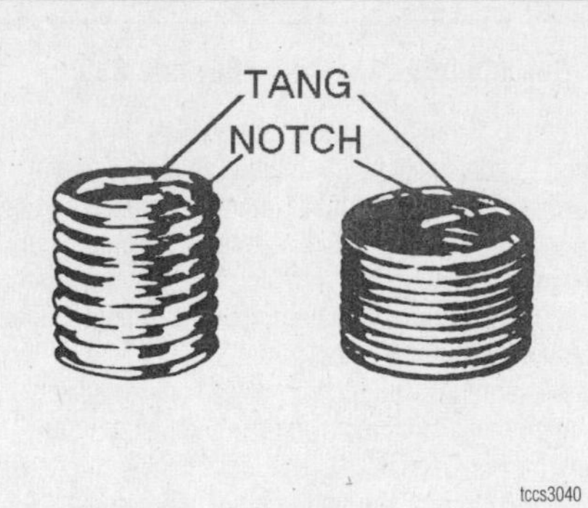

Fig. 288 Standard thread repair insert (left), and spark plug thread insert

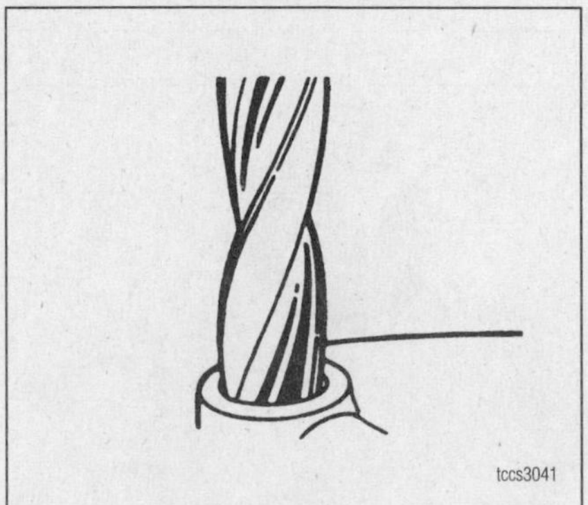

Fig. 289 Drill out the damaged threads with the specified size bit. Be sure to drill completely through the hole or to the bottom of a blind hole

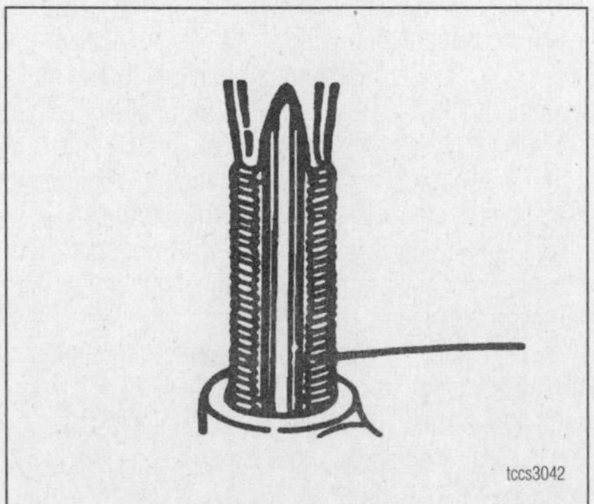

Fig. 290 Using the kit, tap the hole in order to receive the thread insert. Keep the tap well oiled and back it out frequently to avoid clogging the threads

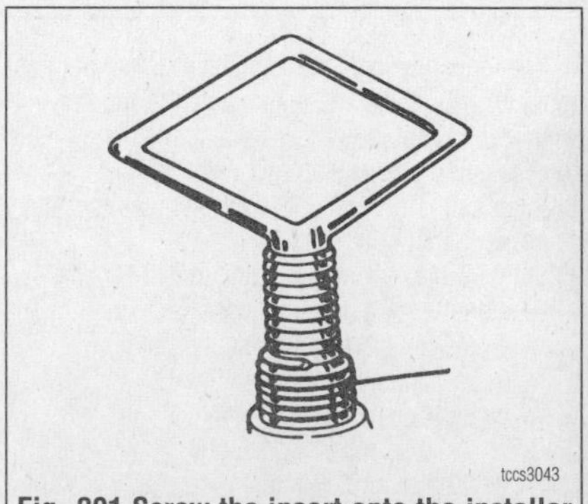

Fig. 291 Screw the insert onto the installer tool until the tang engages the slot. Thread the insert into the hole until it is $^1/_4$–$^1/_2$ turn below the top surface, then remove the tool and break off the tang using a punch

also known as a pushrod engine. All of the vehicles covered by this manual are equipped with Dual Overhead Camshaft (DOHC) engines.

Most cylinder heads these days are made of an aluminum alloy due to its light weight, durability and heat transfer qualities. However, cast iron was the material of choice in the past, and is still used on many vehicles today. Whether made from aluminum or iron, all cylinder heads have valves and seats. Some use two valves per cylinder, while the more hi-tech engines will utilize a multi-valve configuration using 3, 4 and even 5 valves per cylinder. When the valve contacts the seat, it does so on precision machined surfaces, which seals the combustion chamber. All cylinder heads have a valve guide for each valve. The guide centers the valve to the seat and allows it to move up and down within it. The clearance between the valve and guide can be critical. Too much clearance and the engine may consume oil, lose vacuum and/or damage the seat. Too little, and the valve can stick in the guide causing the engine to run poorly if at all, and possibly causing severe damage. The last component all cylinder heads have are valve springs. The spring holds the valve against its seat. It also returns the valve to this position when the valve has been opened by the valve train or camshaft. The spring is fastened to the valve by a retainer and valve locks (sometimes called keepers). Aluminum heads will also have a valve spring shim to keep the spring from wearing away the aluminum.

An ideal method of rebuilding the cylinder head would involve replacing all of the valves, guides, seats, springs, etc. with new ones. However, depending on how the engine was maintained, often this is not necessary. A major cause of valve, guide and seat wear is an improperly tuned engine. An engine that is running too rich, will often wash the lubricating oil out of the guide with gasoline, causing it to wear rapidly. Conversely, an engine which is running too lean will place higher combustion temperatures on the valves and seats allowing them to wear or even burn. Springs fall victim to the driving habits of the individual. A driver who often runs the engine rpm to the redline will wear out or break the springs faster then one that stays well below it. Unfortunately, mileage takes it toll on all of the parts. Generally, the valves, guides, springs and seats in a cylinder head can be machined and re-used, saving you money. However, if a valve is burnt, it may be wise to replace all of the valves, since they were all operating in the same environment. The same goes for any other component on the cylinder head. Think of it as an insurance policy against future problems related to that component.

Unfortunately, the only way to find out which components need replacing, is to disassemble and carefully check each piece. After the cylinder head(s) are disassembled, thoroughly clean all of the components.

DISASSEMBLY

OHC Heads

➧ See Figures 292 and 293

Whether it is a single or dual overhead camshaft cylinder head, the disassembly procedure is relatively unchanged. One aspect to pay attention to is careful labeling of the parts on the dual camshaft cylinder head. There will be an intake camshaft and followers as well as an exhaust camshaft and followers and they must be labeled as such. In some cases, the components are identical and could easily be installed incorrectly. DO NOT MIX THEM UP! Determining which is which is very simple; the intake camshaft and components are on the same side of the head as was the intake manifold. Conversely, the exhaust camshaft and components are on the same side of the head as was the exhaust manifold.

CUP TYPE CAMSHAFT FOLLOWERS

➧ See Figures 294, 295, and 296

Most cylinder heads with cup type camshaft followers will have the valve spring, retainer and locks recessed within the follower's bore. You will need a C-clamp style valve spring compressor tool, an OHC spring removal tool (or equivalent) and a small magnet to disassemble the head.

tcca3p54

Fig. 292 Exploded view of a valve, seal, spring, retainer and locks from an OHC cylinder head

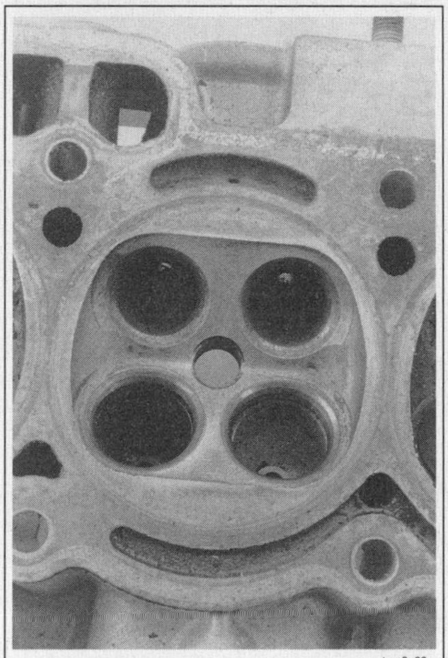

tcca3p62

Fig. 293 Example of a multi-valve cylinder head. Note how it has 2 intake and 2 exhaust valve ports

1. If not already removed, remove the camshaft(s) and/or followers. Mark their positions for assembly.
2. Position the cylinder head to allow use of a C-clamp style valve spring compressor tool.

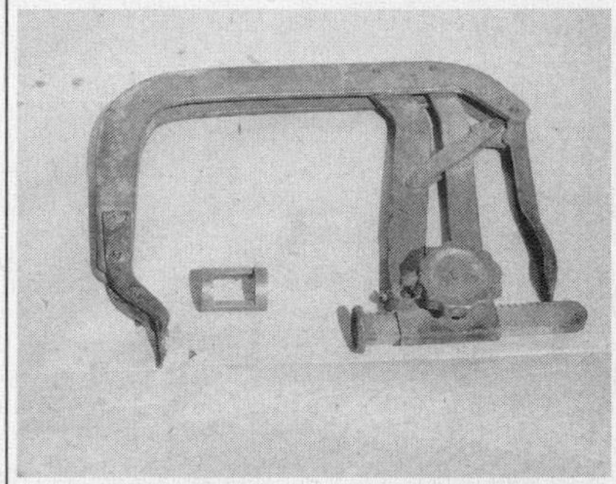

tcca3p51

Fig. 294 C-clamp type spring compressor and an OHC spring removal tool (center) for cup type followers

tcca3p63

Fig. 295 Most cup type follower cylinder heads retain the camshaft using bolt-on bearing caps

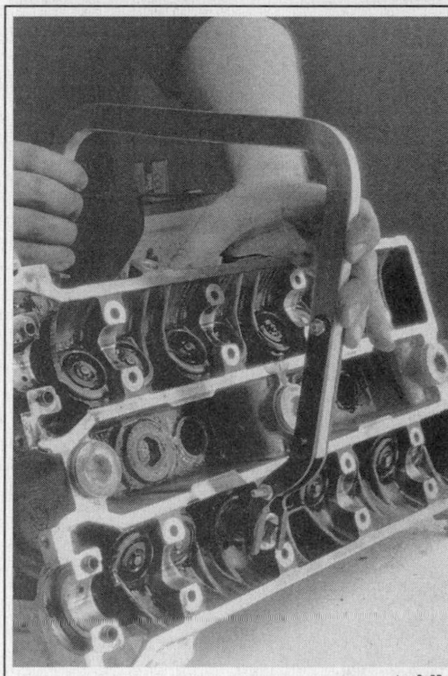

tcca3p65

Fig. 296 Position the OHC spring tool in the follower bore, then compress the spring with a C-clamp type tool

➡It is preferred to position the cylinder head gasket surface facing you with the valve springs facing the opposite direction and the head laying horizontal.

3. With the OHC spring removal adapter tool positioned inside of the follower bore, compress the valve spring using the C-clamp style valve spring compressor.
4. Remove the valve locks. A small magnetic tool or screwdriver will aid in removal.
5. Release the compressor tool and remove the spring assembly.
6. Withdraw the valve from the cylinder head.
7. If equipped, remove the valve seal.

➡Special valve seal removal tools are available. Regular or needlenose type pliers, if used with care, will work just as well. If using ordinary pliers, be sure not to damage the follower bore. The follower and its bore are machined to close tolerances and any damage to the bore will effect this relationship.

8. If equipped, remove the valve spring shim. A small magnetic tool or screwdriver will aid in removal.
9. Repeat Steps 3 through 8 until all of the valves have been removed.

ROCKER ARM TYPE CAMSHAFT FOLLOWERS

See Figures 297 thru 305

Most cylinder heads with rocker arm-type camshaft followers are easily disassembled using a standard valve spring compressor. However, certain models may not have enough open space around the spring for the standard tool and may require you to use a C-clamp style compressor tool instead.

1. If not already removed, remove the rocker arms and/or shafts and the camshaft. If applicable, also remove the hydraulic lash adjusters. Mark their positions for assembly.

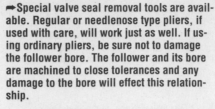

tcca3p53

Fig. 297 Example of the shaft mounted rocker arms on some OHC heads

tcca3p61

Fig. 298 Another example of the rocker arm type OHC head. This model uses a follower under the camshaft

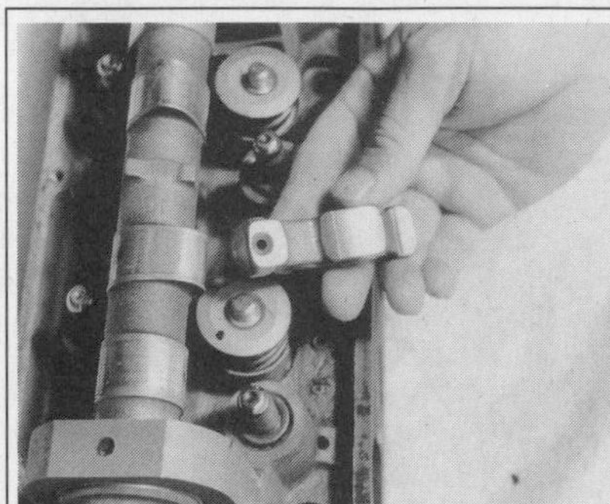
tcca3p60

Fig. 299 Before the camshaft can be removed, all of the followers must first be removed . . .

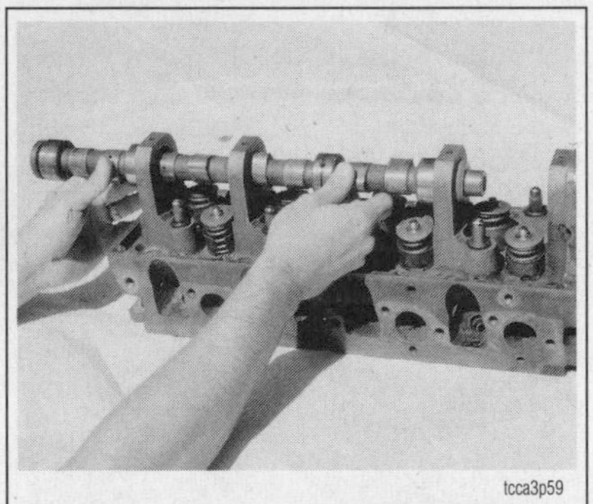
tcca3p59

Fig. 300 . . . then the camshaft can be removed by sliding it out (shown), or unbolting a bearing cap (not shown)

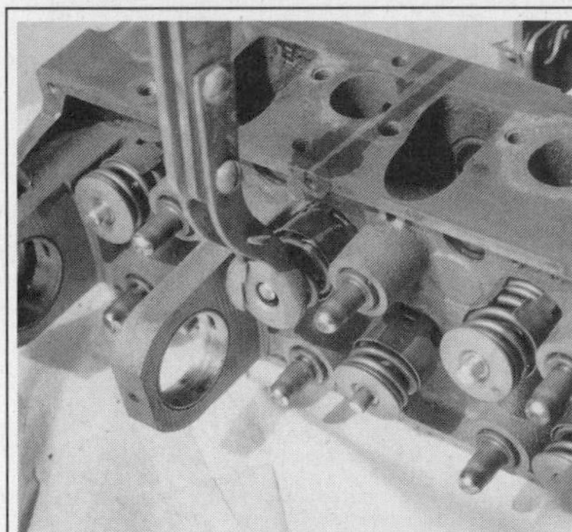
tcca3p57

Fig. 301 Compress the valve spring . . .

tcca3p58

Fig. 302 . . . then remove the valve locks from the valve stem and spring retainer

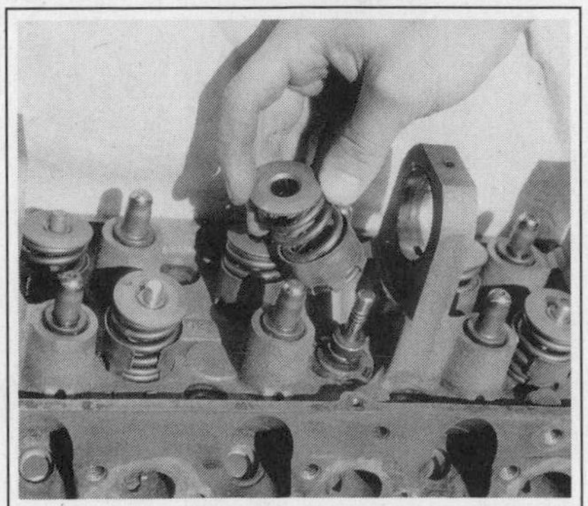
tcca3p56

Fig. 303 Remove the valve spring and retainer from the cylinder head

tcca3p55

Fig. 304 Remove the valve seal from the guide. Some gentle prying or pliers may help to remove stubborn ones

tcca3p52

Fig. 305 All aluminum and some cast iron heads will have these valve spring shims. Remove all of them as well

2. Position the cylinder head to allow access to the valve spring.
3. Use a valve spring compressor tool to relieve the spring tension from the retainer.

➡Due to engine varnish, the retainer may stick to the valve locks. A gentle tap with a hammer may help to break it loose.

4. Remove the valve locks from the valve tip and/or retainer. A small magnet may help in removing the small locks.
5. Lift the valve spring, tool and all, off of the valve stem.
6. If equipped, remove the valve seal. If the seal is difficult to remove with the valve in place, try removing the valve first, then the seal. Follow the steps below for valve removal.
7. Position the head to allow access for withdrawing the valve.

➡Cylinder heads that have seen a lot of miles and/or abuse may have mushroomed the valve lock grove and/or tip, causing difficulty in removal of the valve. If this has happened, use a metal file to carefully remove the high spots around the lock grooves and/or tip. Only file it enough to allow removal.

8. Remove the valve from the cylinder head.
9. If equipped, remove the valve spring shim. A small magnetic tool or screwdriver will aid in removal.
10. Repeat Steps 3 though 9 until all of the valves have been removed.

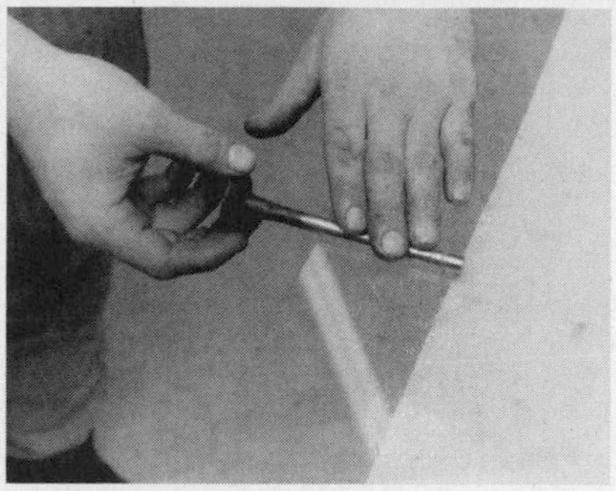

tccs3144

Fig. 306 Valve stems may be rolled on a flat surface to check for bends

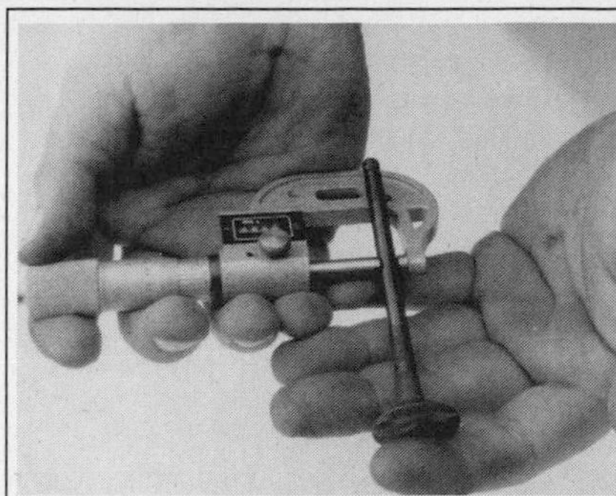

tccs3910

Fig. 307 Use a micrometer to check the valve stem diameter

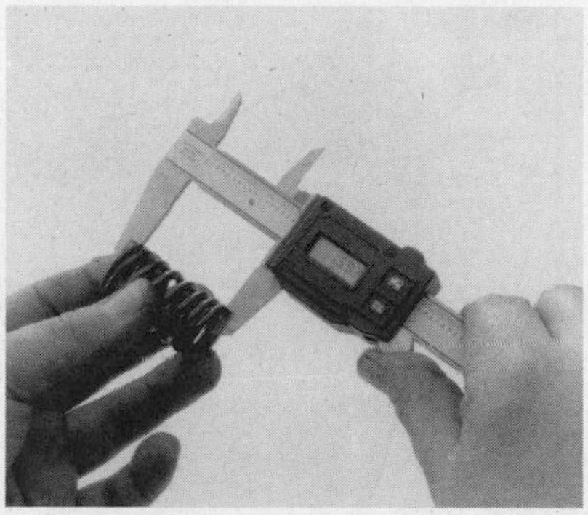

tccs3907

Fig. 308 Use a caliper to check the valve spring free-length

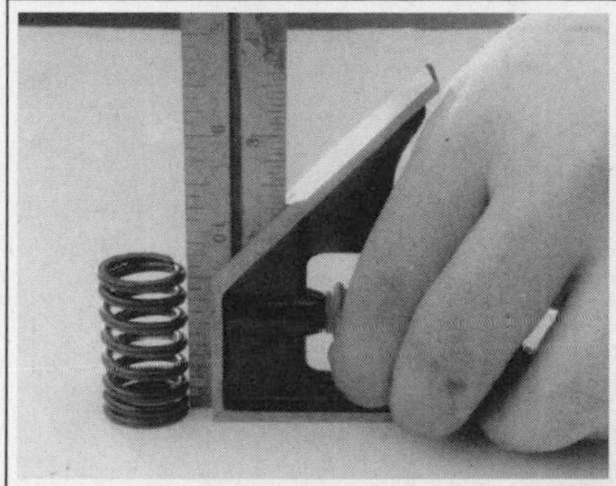

tccs3908

Fig. 309 Check the valve spring for squareness on a flat surface; a carpenter's square can be used

INSPECTION

Now that all of the cylinder head components are clean, it's time to inspect them for wear and/or damage. To accurately inspect them, you will need some specialized tools:

- A 0–1 in. micrometer for the valves
- A dial indicator or inside diameter gauge for the valve guides
- A spring pressure test gauge

If you do not have access to the proper tools, you may want to bring the components to a shop that does.

Valves

➧ See Figures 306 and 307

The first thing to inspect are the valve heads. Look closely at the head, margin and face for any cracks, excessive wear or burning. The margin is the best place to look for burning. It should have a squared edge with an even width all around the diameter. When a valve burns, the margin will look melted and the edges rounded. Also inspect the valve head for any signs of tulipping. This will show as a lifting of the edges or dishing in the center of the head and will usually not occur to all of the valves. All of the heads should look the same, any that seem dished more than others are probably bad. Next, inspect the valve lock grooves and valve tips. Check for any burrs around the lock grooves, especially if you had to file them to remove the valve. Valve tips should appear flat, although slight rounding with high mileage engines is normal. Slightly worn valve tips will need to be machined flat. Last, measure the valve stem diameter with the micrometer. Measure the area that rides within the guide, especially towards the tip where most of the wear occurs. Take several measurements along its length and compare them to each other. Wear should be even along the length with little to no taper. If no minimum diameter is given in the specifications, then the stem should not read more than 0.001 in. (0.025mm) below the unworn area of the valve stem. Any valves that fail these inspections should be replaced.

Springs, Retainers and Valve Locks

➧ See Figures 308 and 309

The first thing to check is the most obvious, broken springs. Next check the free length and squareness of each spring. If applicable, insure to distinguish between intake and exhaust springs. Use a ruler and/or carpenter's square to measure the length. A carpenter's square should be used to check the springs for squareness. If a spring pressure test gauge is available, check each springs rating and compare to the specifications chart. Check the readings against the specifications given. Any springs that fail these inspections should be replaced.

The spring retainers rarely need replacing, however they should still be checked as a precaution. Inspect the spring mating surface and the valve lock retention area for any signs of excessive wear. Also check for any signs of cracking. Replace any retainers that are questionable.

Valve locks should be inspected for excessive wear on the outside contact area as well as on the inner notched surface. Any locks which appear worn or broken and its respective valve should be replaced.

Cylinder Head

There are several things to check on the cylinder head: valve guides, seats, cylinder head surface flatness, cracks and physical damage.

VALVE GUIDES

➧ See Figure 310

Now that you know the valves are good, you can use them to check the guides, although a new valve, if available, is preferred. Before you measure anything, look at the guides carefully and inspect them for any cracks, chips or breakage. Also if the guide is a removable style (as in most aluminum heads),

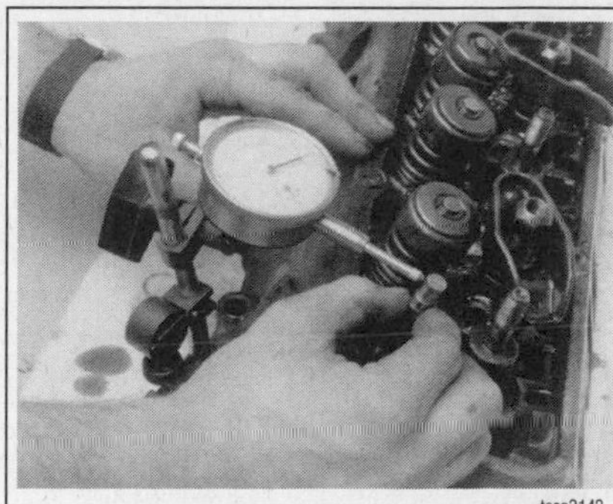

tccs3142

Fig. 310 A dial gauge may be used to check valve stem-to-guide clearance; read the gauge while moving the valve stem

check them for any looseness or evidence of movement. All of the guides should appear to be at the same height from the spring seat. If any seem lower (or higher) from another, the guide has moved. Mount a dial indicator onto the spring side of the cylinder head. Lightly oil the valve stem and insert it into the cylinder head. Position the dial indicator against the valve stem near the tip and zero the gauge. Grasp the valve stem and wiggle towards and away from the dial indicator and observe the readings. Mount the dial indicator 90 degrees from the initial point and zero the gauge and again take a reading. Compare the two readings for a out of round condition. Check the readings against the specifications given. An Inside Diameter (I.D.) gauge designed for valve guides will give you an accurate valve guide bore measurement. If the I.D. gauge is used, compare the readings with the specifications given. Any guides that fail these inspections should be replaced or machined.

VALVE SEATS

A visual inspection of the valve seats should show a slightly worn and pitted surface where the valve face contacts the seat. Inspect the seat carefully for severe pitting or cracks. Also, a seat that is badly worn will be recessed into the cylinder head. A severely worn or recessed seat may need to be replaced. All cracked seats must be replaced. A seat concentricity gauge, if available, should be used to check the seat run-out. If run-out exceeds specifications the seat must be machined (if no specification is given use 0.002 in. or 0.051mm).

CYLINDER HEAD SURFACE FLATNESS

See Figures 311 and 312

After you have cleaned the gasket surface of the cylinder head of any old gasket material, check the head for flatness.

Place a straightedge across the gasket surface. Using feeler gauges, determine the clearance at the center of the straightedge and across the cylinder head at several points. Check along the centerline and diagonally on the head surface. If the warpage exceeds 0.003 in. (0.076mm) within a 6.0 in. (15.2cm) span, or 0.006 in. (0.152mm) over the total length of the head, the cylinder head must be resurfaced. After resurfacing the heads of a V-type engine, the intake manifold flange surface should be checked, and if necessary, milled proportionally to allow for the change in its mounting position.

CRACKS AND PHYSICAL DAMAGE

Generally, cracks are limited to the combustion chamber, however, it is not uncommon for the head to crack in a spark plug hole, port, outside of the head or in the valve spring/rocker arm area. The first area to inspect is always the hottest: the exhaust seat/port area.

A visual inspection should be performed, but just because you don't see a crack does not mean it is not there. Some more reliable methods for inspecting for cracks include Magnaflux®, a magnetic process or Zyglo®, a dye penetrant. Magnaflux® is used only on ferrous metal (cast iron) heads. Zyglo® uses a spray on fluorescent mixture along with a black light to reveal the cracks. It is strongly recommended to have your cylinder head checked professionally for cracks, especially if the engine was known to have

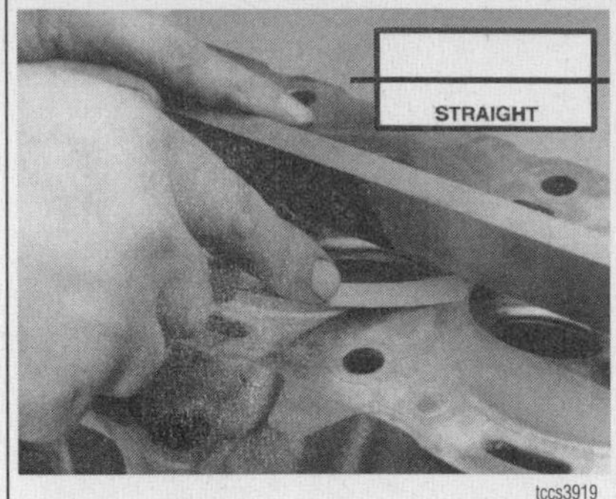

Fig. 311 Check the head for flatness across the center of the head surface using a straightedge and feeler gauge

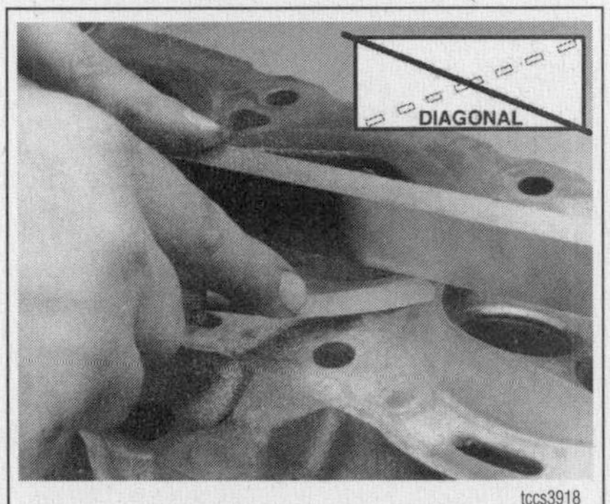

Fig. 312 Checks should also be made along both diagonals of the head surface

overheated and/or leaked or consumed coolant. Contact a local shop for availability and pricing of these services.

Physical damage is usually very evident. For example, a broken mounting ear from dropping the head or a bent or broken stud and/or bolt. All of these defects should be fixed or, if unrepairable, the head should be replaced.

Camshaft and Followers

Inspect the camshaft(s) and followers as described earlier in this section.

REFINISHING & REPAIRING

Many of the procedures given for refinishing and repairing the cylinder head components must be performed by a machine shop. Certain steps, if the inspected part is not worn, can be performed yourself inexpensively. However, you spent a lot of time and effort so far, why risk trying to save a couple bucks if you might have to do it all over again?

Valves

Any valves that were not replaced should be refaced and the tips ground flat. Unless you have access to a valve grinding machine, this should be done by a machine shop. If the valves are in extremely good condition, as well as the valve seats and guides, they may be lapped in without performing machine work.

It is a recommended practice to lap the valves even after machine work has been performed and/or new valves have been purchased. This insures a positive seal between the valve and seat.

LAPPING THE VALVES

➡Before lapping the valves to the seats, read the rest of the cylinder head section to insure that any related parts are in acceptable enough condition to continue.

➡Before any valve seat machining and/or lapping can be performed, the guides must be within factory recommended specifications.

1. Invert the cylinder head.
2. Lightly lubricate the valve stems and insert them into the cylinder head in their numbered order.
3. Raise the valve from the seat and apply a small amount of fine lapping compound to the seat.
4. Moisten the suction head of a hand-lapping tool and attach it to the head of the valve.
5. Rotate the tool between the palms of both hands, changing the position of the valve on the valve seat and lifting the tool often to prevent grooving.
6. Lap the valve until a smooth, polished circle is evident on the valve and seat.
7. Remove the tool and the valve. Wipe away all traces of the grinding compound and store the valve to maintain its lapped location.

WARNING

Do not get the valves out of order after they have been lapped. They must be put back with the same valve seat with which they were lapped.

Springs, Retainers and Valve Locks

There is no repair or refinishing possible with the springs, retainers and valve locks. If they are found to be worn or defective, they must be replaced with new (or known good) parts.

Cylinder Head

Most refinishing procedures dealing with the cylinder head must be performed by a machine shop. Read the sections below and review your inspection data to determine whether or not machining is necessary.

VALVE GUIDE

➡If any machining or replacements are made to the valve guides, the seats must be machined.

Unless the valve guides need machining or replacing, the only service to perform is to thoroughly clean them of any dirt or oil residue.

There are only two types of valve guides used on automobile engines: the replaceable-type (all aluminum heads) and the cast-in integral-type (most cast iron heads). There are four recommended methods for repairing worn guides.

- Knurling
- Inserts
- Reaming oversize
- Replacing

Knurling is a process in which metal is displaced and raised, thereby reducing clearance, giving a true center, and providing oil control. It is the least expensive way of repairing the valve guides. However, it is not necessarily the best, and in some cases, a knurled valve guide will not stand up for more than a short time. It requires a special knurlizer and precision reaming tools to obtain proper clearances. It would not be cost effective to purchase these tools, unless you plan on rebuilding several of the same cylinder head.

Installing a guide insert involves machining the guide to accept a bronze insert. One style is the coil-type which is installed into a threaded guide. Another is the thin-walled insert where the guide is reamed oversize to accept a split-sleeve insert. After the insert is installed, a special tool is then run through the guide to expand the insert, locking it to the guide. The insert is then reamed to the standard size for proper valve clearance.

Reaming for oversize valves restores normal clearances and provides a true valve seat. Most cast-in type guides can be reamed to accept an valve with an oversize stem. The cost factor for this can become quite high as you will need to purchase the reamer and new, oversize stem valves for all guides which were reamed. Oversizes are generally 0.003 to 0.030 in. (0.076 to 0.762mm), with 0.015 in. (0.381mm) being the most common.

To replace cast-in type valve guides, they must be drilled out, then reamed to accept replacement guides. This must be done on a fixture which will allow centering and leveling off of the original valve seat or guide, otherwise a serious guide-to-seat misalignment may occur making it impossible to properly machine the seat.

Replaceable-type guides are pressed into the cylinder head. A hammer and a stepped drift or punch may be used to install and remove the guides. Before removing the guides, measure the protrusion on the spring side of the head and record it for installation. Use the stepped drift to hammer out the old guide from the combustion chamber side of the head. When installing, determine whether or not the guide also seals a water jacket in the head, and if it does, use the recommended sealing agent. If there is no water jacket, grease the valve guide and its bore. Use the stepped drift, and hammer the new guide into the cylinder head from the spring side of the cylinder head. A stack of washers the same thickness as the measured protrusion may help the installation process.

VALVE SEATS

➡Before any valve seat machining can be performed, the guides must be within factory recommended specifications.

➡If any machining or replacements were made to the valve guides, the seats must be machined.

If the seats are in good condition, the valves can be lapped to the seats, and the cylinder head assembled. See the valves section for instructions on lapping.

If the valve seats are worn, cracked or damaged, they must be serviced by a machine shop. The valve seat must be perfectly centered to the valve guide, which requires very accurate machining.

CYLINDER HEAD SURFACE

If the cylinder head is warped, it must be machined flat. If the warpage is extremely severe, the head may need to be replaced. In some instances, it may be possible to straighten a warped head enough to allow machining. In either case, contact a professional machine shop for service.

➡Any OHC cylinder head that shows excessive warpage should have the camshaft bearing journals align bored after the cylinder head has been resurfaced.

WARNING

Failure to align bore the camshaft bearing journals could result in severe engine damage including but not limited to: valve and piston damage, connecting rod damage, camshaft and/or crankshaft breakage.

CRACKS AND PHYSICAL DAMAGE

Certain cracks can be repaired in both cast iron and aluminum heads. For cast iron, a tapered threaded insert is installed along the length of the crack. Aluminum can also use the tapered inserts, however welding is the preferred method. Some physical damage can be repaired through brazing or welding. Contact a machine shop to get expert advice for your particular dilemma.

ASSEMBLY

The first step for any assembly job is to have a clean area in which to work. Next, thoroughly clean all of the parts and components that are to be assembled. Finally, place all of the components onto a suitable work space and, if necessary, arrange the parts to their respective positions.

OHC Engines

➧ See Figure 313

CUP TYPE CAMSHAFT FOLLOWERS

To install the springs, retainers and valve locks on heads which have these components recessed into the camshaft follower's bore, you will need a small screwdriver-type tool, some clean white grease and a lot of patience. You will also need the C-clamp style spring compressor and the OHC tool used to disassemble the head.

1. Lightly lubricate the valve stems and insert all of the valves into the cylinder head. If possible, maintain their original locations.
2. If equipped, install any valve spring shims which were removed.

tcca3p64

Fig. 313 Once assembled, check the valve clearance and correct as needed

3. If equipped, install the new valve seals, keeping the following in mind:
   - If the valve seal presses over the guide, lightly lubricate the outer guide surfaces.
   - If the seal is an O-ring type, it is installed just after compressing the spring but before the valve locks.
4. Place the valve spring and retainer over the stem.
5. Position the spring compressor and the OHC tool, then compress the spring.
6. Using a small screwdriver as a spatula, fill the valve stem side of the lock with white grease. Use the excess grease on the screwdriver to fasten the lock to the driver.
7. Carefully install the valve lock, which is stuck to the end of the screwdriver, to the valve stem then press on it with the screwdriver until the grease squeezes out. The valve lock should now be stuck to the stem.
8. Repeat Steps 6 and 7 for the remaining valve lock.
9. Relieve the spring pressure slowly and insure that neither valve lock becomes dislodged by the retainer.
10. Remove the spring compressor tool.
11. Repeat Steps 2 through 10 until all of the springs have been installed.
12. Install the followers, camshaft(s) and any other components that were removed for disassembly.

ROCKER ARM TYPE CAMSHAFT FOLLOWERS

1. Lightly lubricate the valve stems and insert all of the valves into the cylinder head. If possible, maintain their original locations.
2. If equipped, install any valve spring shims which were removed.
3. If equipped, install the new valve seals, keeping the following in mind:
   - If the valve seal presses over the guide, lightly lubricate the outer guide surfaces.
   - If the seal is an O-ring type, it is installed just after compressing the spring but before the valve locks.
4. Place the valve spring and retainer over the stem.
5. Position the spring compressor tool and compress the spring.
6. Assemble the valve locks to the stem.
7. Relieve the spring pressure slowly and insure that neither valve lock becomes dislodged by the retainer.
8. Remove the spring compressor tool.
9. Repeat Steps 2 through 8 until all of the springs have been installed.
10. Install the camshaft(s), rockers, shafts and any other components that were removed for disassembly.

Engine Block

GENERAL INFORMATION

A thorough overhaul or rebuild of an engine block would include replacing the pistons, rings, bearings, timing belt/chain assembly and oil pump. For OHV engines also include a new camshaft and lifters. The block would then have the cylinders bored and honed oversize (or if using removable cylinder sleeves, new sleeves installed) and the crankshaft would be cut undersize to provide new wearing surfaces and perfect clearances. However, your particular engine may not have everything worn out. What if only the piston rings have worn out and the clearances on everything else are still within factory specifications? Well, you could just replace the rings and put it back together, but this would be a very rare example. Chances are, if one component in your engine is worn, other components are sure to follow, and soon. At the very least, you should always replace the rings, bearings and oil pump. This is what is commonly called a "freshen up".

Cylinder Ridge Removal

See Figures 314 and 315

Because the top piston ring does not travel to the very top of the cylinder, a ridge is built up between the end of the travel and the top of the cylinder bore.

Pushing the piston and connecting rod assembly past the ridge can be difficult, and damage to the piston ring lands could occur. If the ridge is not removed before installing a new piston or not removed at all, piston ring breakage and piston damage may occur.

➡It is always recommended that you remove any cylinder ridges before removing the piston and connecting rod assemblies. If you know that new pistons are going to be installed and the engine block will be bored oversize, you may be able to forego this step. However, some ridges may actually prevent the assemblies from being removed, necessitating its removal.

There are several different types of ridge reamers on the market, none of which are inexpensive. Unless a great deal of engine rebuilding is anticipated, borrow or rent a reamer.

1. Turn the crankshaft until the piston is at the bottom of its travel.
2. Cover the head of the piston with a rag.
3. Follow the tool manufacturers instructions and cut away the ridge, exercising extreme care to avoid cutting too deeply.
4. Remove the ridge reamer, the rag and as many of the cuttings as possible. Continue until all of the cylinder ridges have been removed.

DISASSEMBLY

See Figures 316 thru 327

The engine disassembly instructions following assume that you have the engine mounted on an engine stand. If not, it is easiest to disassemble the engine on a bench or the floor with it resting on the bell housing or transmission mounting surface. You must be able to access the connecting rod fasteners and turn the crankshaft during disassembly. Also, all engine covers (timing, front, side, oil pan, whatever) should have already been removed. Engines which are seized or locked up may not be able to be completely disassembled, and a core (salvage yard) engine should be purchased.

If not done during the cylinder head removal, remove the timing chain/belt and/or gear/sprocket assembly. Remove the oil pick-up and pump assembly and, if necessary, the pump drive. If equipped, remove any balance or auxiliary shafts. If necessary, remove the cylinder ridge from the top of the bore. See the cylinder ridge removal procedure earlier in this section.

Rotate the engine over so that the crankshaft is exposed. Use a number punch or scribe and mark each connecting rod with its respective cylinder number. The cylinder closest to the front of the engine is always number 1. However, depending on the engine placement, the front of the engine could either be the flywheel or damper/pulley end. Generally the front of the engine faces the front of the vehicle. Use a number punch or scribe and also mark the main bearing caps from front to rear with the front most cap being number 1 (if there are five caps, mark them 1 through 5, front to rear).

✻✻ WARNING

Take special care when pushing the connecting rod up from the crankshaft because the sharp threads of the rod bolts/studs will score the crankshaft journal. Insure that special plastic caps are installed over them, or cut two pieces of rubber hose to do the same.

Again, rotate the engine, this time to position the number one cylinder bore (head surface) up. Turn the crankshaft until the number one piston is at the bottom of its travel, this should allow the maximum access to its connecting rod. Remove the number one connecting rods fasteners and cap and place two lengths of rubber hose over the rod bolts/studs to protect the crankshaft from damage. Using a sturdy wooden dowel and a hammer, push the connecting rod up about 1 in. (25mm) from the crankshaft and remove the upper bearing insert. Continue pushing or tapping the connecting rod up until the piston rings are out of the cylinder bore. Remove the piston and rod by hand, put the upper half of the bearing insert back into the rod, install the cap with its bearing insert installed, and hand-tighten the cap fasteners. If the parts are kept in order in this manner, they will

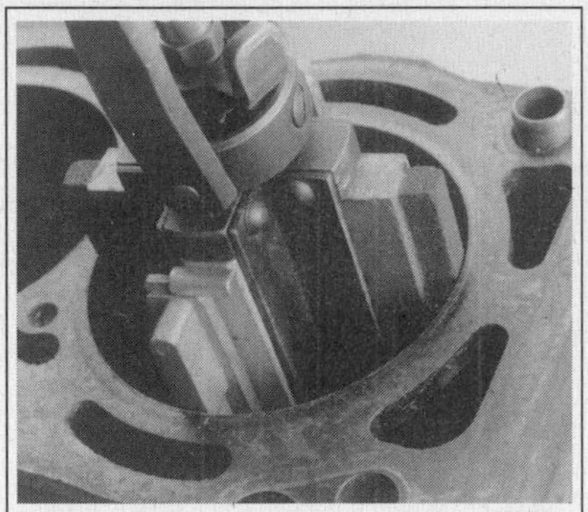

Fig. 314 Use a ridge reamer to remove the ridge from the cylinder bore

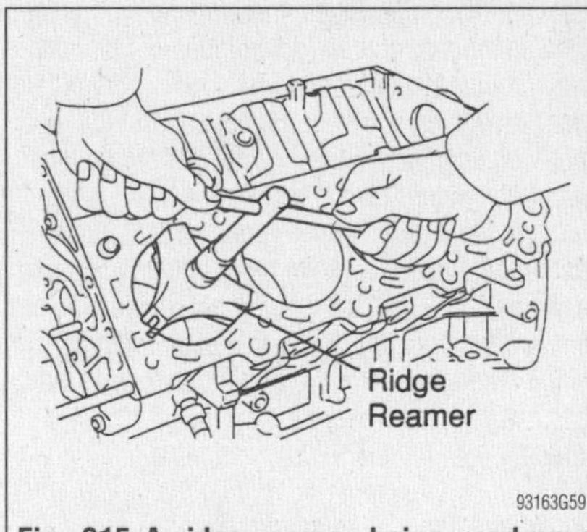

Fig. 315 A ridge reamer being used on a 2UZ-FE V8 engine block—2000 Tundra shown

Fig. 316 Remove the connecting rod bearing cap nuts

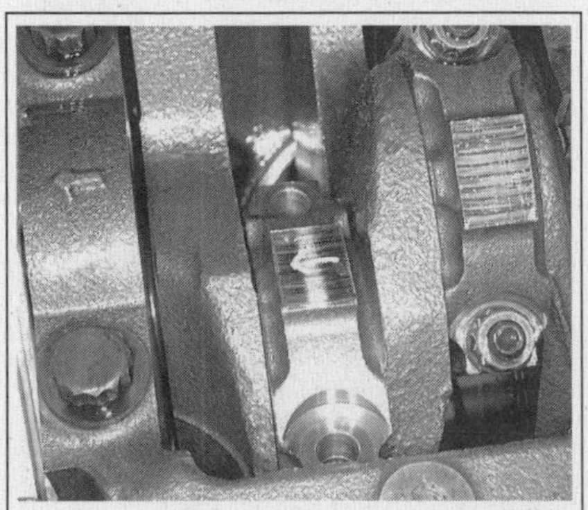

Fig. 317 Mark the direction of the bearing cap with an arrow to prevent re-installing it in the wrong direction

Fig. 318 Remove the connecting rod bearing cap

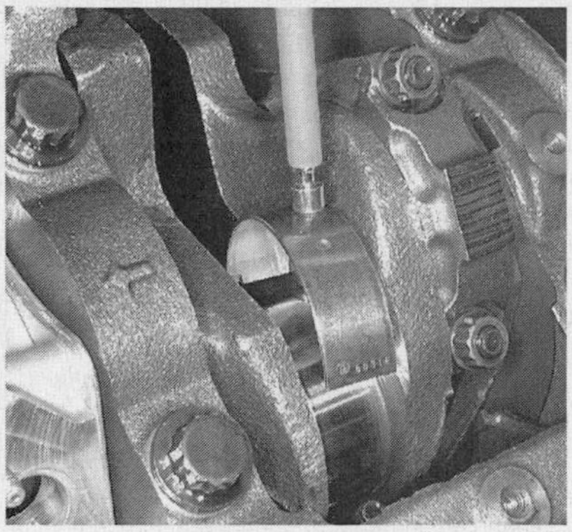

93163pj6

Fig. 319 A magnet is a great aid when removing the connecting rod bearings

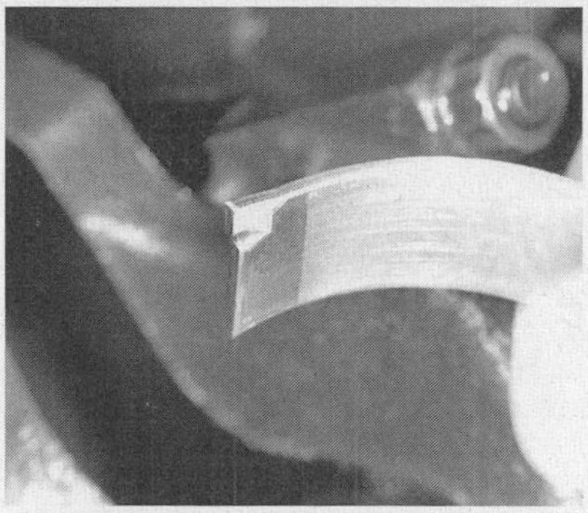

93163pj7

Fig. 320 Toyota connecting rod bearings are usually notched like the one shown. This is to prevent them from spinning

93163pj8

Fig. 321 Place a rubber vacuum cap over the threaded studs on the connecting rod to prevent scratching the crankshaft when removing the piston

93163pj9

Fig. 322 It is best to push the piston through with your fingers . . .

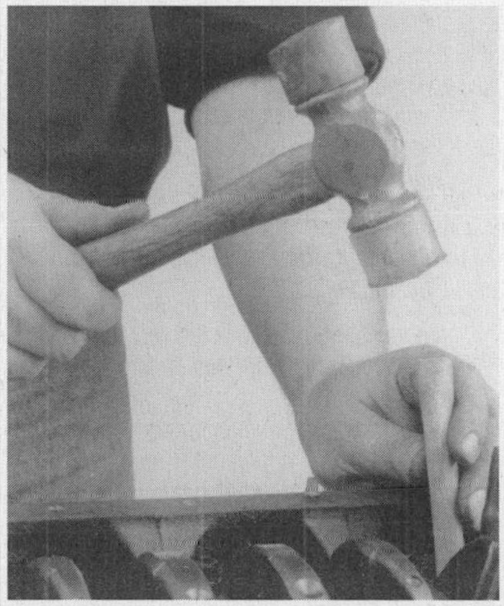

TCCS3804

Fig. 323 . . . or carefully tap the piston out of the bore using a wooden dowel

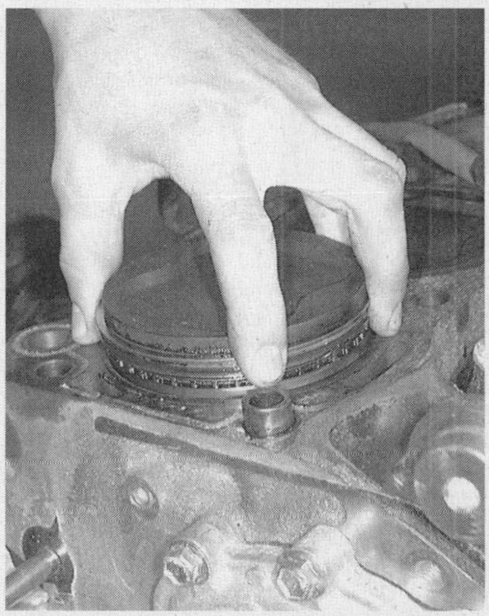

93163pk4

Fig. 324 Grasp the top of the piston

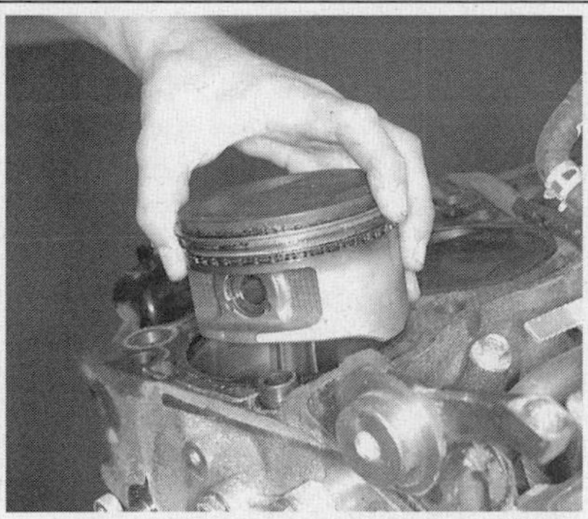

93163pk3

Fig. 325 Pull the piston straight up . . .

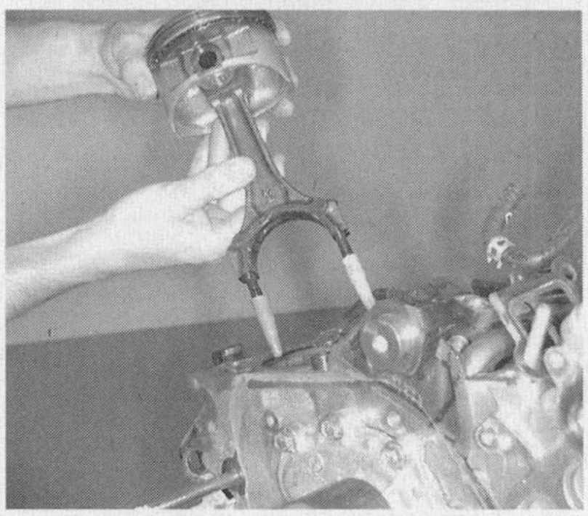

93163pk2

Fig. 326 . . . and out of the bore

93163pk1

Fig. 327 Use care not to scratch the crank journals or the cylinder walls

not get lost and you will be able to tell which bearings came form what cylinder if any problems are discovered and diagnosis is necessary. Remove all the other piston assemblies in the same manner. On V-style engines, remove all of the pistons from one bank, then reposition the engine with the other cylinder bank head surface up, and remove that banks piston assemblies.

The only remaining component in the engine block should now be the crankshaft. Loosen the main bearing caps evenly until the fasteners can be turned by hand, then remove them and the caps. Remove the crankshaft from the engine block. Thoroughly clean all of the components.

INSPECTION

Now that the engine block and all of its components are clean, it's time to inspect them for wear and/or damage. To accurately inspect them, you will need some specialized tools:

- Two or three separate micrometers to measure the pistons and crankshaft journals

- A dial indicator
- Telescoping gauges for the cylinder bores
- A rod alignment fixture to check for bent connecting rods

If you do not have access to the proper tools, you may want to bring the components to a shop that does.

Generally, you shouldn't expect cracks in the engine block or its components unless it was known to leak, consume or mix engine fluids, it was severely overheated, or there was evidence of bad bearings and/or crankshaft damage. A visual inspection should be performed on all of the components, but just because you don't see a crack does not mean it is not there. Some more reliable methods for inspecting for cracks include Magnaflux®, a magnetic process or Zyglo®, a dye penetrant. Magnaflux® is used only on ferrous metal (cast iron). Zyglo® uses a spray on fluorescent mixture along with a black light to reveal the cracks. It is strongly recommended to have your engine block checked professionally for cracks, especially if the engine was known to have overheated and/or leaked or consumed coolant. Contact a local shop for availability and pricing of these services.

Engine Block

ENGINE BLOCK BEARING ALIGNMENT

Remove the main bearing caps and, if still installed, the main bearing inserts. Inspect all of the main bearing saddles and caps for damage, burrs or high spots. If damage is found, and it is caused from a spun main bearing, the block will need to be align-bored or, if severe enough, replacement. Any burrs or high spots should be carefully removed with a metal file.

Place a straightedge on the bearing saddles, in the engine block, along the centerline of the crankshaft. If any clearance exists between the straightedge and the saddles, the block must be align-bored.

Align-boring consists of machining the main bearing saddles and caps by means of a flycutter that runs through the bearing saddles.

DECK FLATNESS

The top of the engine block where the cylinder head mounts is called the deck. Insure that the deck surface is clean of dirt, carbon deposits and old gasket material. Place a straightedge across the surface of the deck along its centerline and, using feeler gauges, check the clearance along several points. Repeat the checking procedure with the straightedge placed along both diagonals of the deck surface. If the reading exceeds 0.003 in. (0.076mm) within a 6.0 in. (15.2cm) span, or 0.006 in. (0.152mm) over the total length of the deck, it must be machined.

CYLINDER BORES

See Figure 328

The cylinder bores house the pistons and are slightly larger than the pistons themselves. A common piston-to-bore clearance is 0.0015–0.0025 in. (0.0381mm–0.0635mm). Inspect and measure the cylinder bores. The bore should be checked for out-of-roundness, taper and size. The results of this inspection will determine whether the cylinder can be used in its existing size and condition, or a rebore to the next oversize is required (or in the case of removable sleeves, have replacements installed).

The amount of cylinder wall wear is always greater at the top of the cylinder than at the bottom. This wear is known as taper. Any cylinder that has a taper of 0.0012 in. (0.305mm) or more, must be rebored. Measurements are taken at a number of positions in each cylinder: at the top, middle and bottom and at two points at each position; that is, at a point 90 degrees from the crankshaft centerline, as well as a point parallel to the crankshaft centerline. The measurements are made with either a special dial indicator or a telescopic gauge and micrometer. If the necessary precision tools to check the bore are not available, take the block to a machine shop and have them mike it. Also if you don't have the tools to check the cylinder bores, chances are you will not have the necessary devices to check the pistons, connecting rods and crankshaft. Take these components with you and save yourself an extra trip.

For our procedures, we will use a telescopic gauge and a micrometer. You will need one of each, with a measuring range which covers your cylinder bore size.

1. Position the telescopic gauge in the cylinder bore, loosen the gauges lock and allow it to expand.

➡Your first two readings will be at the top of the cylinder bore, then proceed to the middle and finally the bottom, making a total of six measurements.

2. Hold the gauge square in the bore, 90 degrees from the crankshaft centerline, and gently tighten the lock. Tilt the gauge back to remove it from the bore.
3. Measure the gauge with the micrometer and record the reading.
4. Again, hold the gauge square in the bore, this time parallel to the crankshaft centerline, and gently tighten the lock. Again, you will tilt the gauge back to remove it from the bore.
5. Measure the gauge with the micrometer and record this reading. The difference between these two readings is the out-of-round measurement of the cylinder.
6. Repeat steps 1 through 5, each time going to the next lower position, until you reach the bottom of the cylinder. Then go to the next cylinder, and continue until all of the cylinders have been measured.

The difference between these measurements will tell you all about the wear in your cylinders. The measurements which were taken 90 degrees from the crankshaft centerline will always reflect the most wear. That is because at this position is where the engine power presses the piston against the cylinder bore the hardest. This is known as thrust wear. Take your top, 90 degree measurement and compare it to your bottom, 90 degree measurement. The difference between them is the taper. When you measure your pistons, you will compare these readings to your piston sizes and determine piston-to-wall clearance.

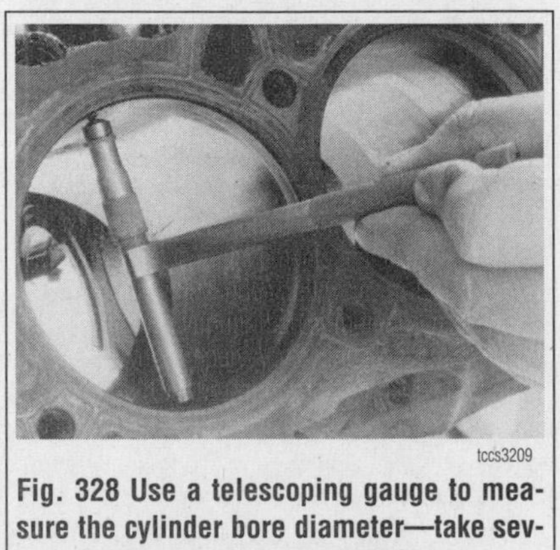

tccs3209

Fig. 328 Use a telescoping gauge to measure the cylinder bore diameter—take several readings within the same bore

Crankshaft

Inspect the crankshaft for visible signs of wear or damage. All of the journals should be perfectly round and smooth. Slight scores are normal for a used crankshaft, but you should hardly feel them with your fingernail. When measuring the crankshaft with a micrometer, you will take readings at the front and rear of each journal, then turn the micrometer 90 degrees and take two more readings, front and rear. The difference between the front-to-rear readings is the journal taper and the first-to-90 degree reading is the out-of-round measurement. Generally, there should be no taper or out-of-roundness found, however, up to 0.0005 in. (0.0127mm) for either can be overlooked. Also, the readings should fall within the factory specifications for journal diameters.

If the crankshaft journals fall within specifications, it is recommended that it be polished before being returned to service. Polishing the crankshaft insures that any minor burrs or high spots are smoothed, thereby reducing the chance of scoring the new bearings.

Pistons and Connecting Rods

PISTONS

See Figure 329

The piston should be visually inspected for any signs of cracking or burning (caused by hot spots or detonation), and scuffing or excessive wear on the skirts. The wrist pin attaches the piston to the connecting rod. The piston should move freely on the wrist pin, both sliding and pivoting. Grasp the connecting rod securely, or mount it in a vise, and try to rock the piston back and forth along the centerline of the wrist pin. There should not be any excessive play evident between the piston and the pin. If there are C-clips retaining the pin in the piston then you have wrist pin bushings in the rods. There should not be any excessive play between the wrist pin and the rod

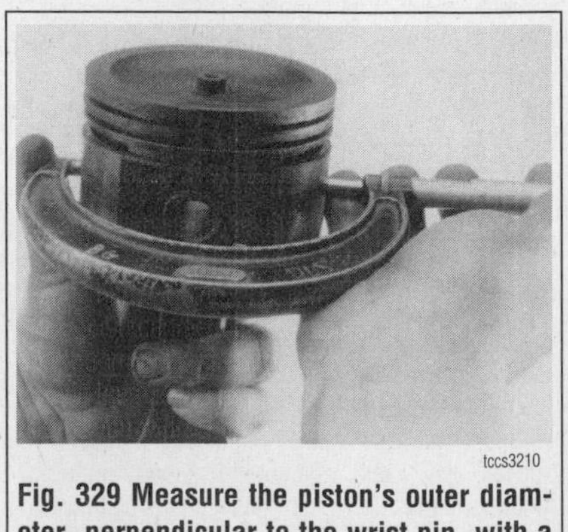

tccs3210

Fig. 329 Measure the piston's outer diameter, perpendicular to the wrist pin, with a micrometer

bushing. Normal clearance for the wrist pin is approx. 0.001–0.002 in. (0.025mm–0.051mm).

Use a micrometer and measure the diameter of the piston, perpendicular to the wrist pin, on the skirt. Compare the reading to its original cylinder measurement obtained earlier. The difference between the two readings is the piston-to-wall clearance. If the clearance is within specifications, the piston may be used as is. If the piston is out of specification, but the bore is not, you will need a new piston. If both are out of specification, you will need the cylinder rebored and oversize pistons installed. Generally if two or more pistons/bores are out of specification, it is best to rebore the entire block and purchase a complete set of oversize pistons.

CONNECTING ROD

You should have the connecting rod checked for straightness at a machine shop. If the connecting rod is bent, it will unevenly wear the bearing and piston, as well as place greater stress on these components. Any bent or twisted connecting rods must be replaced. If the rods are straight and the wrist pin clearance is within specifications, then only the bearing end of the rod need be checked. Place the connecting rod into a vice, with the bearing inserts in place, install the cap to the rod and torque the fasteners to specifications. Use a telescoping gauge and carefully measure the inside diameter of the bearings. Compare this reading to the rods original crankshaft journal diameter measurement. The difference is the oil clearance. If the oil clearance is not within specifications, install new bearings in the rod and take another measurement. If the clearance is still out of specifications, and the crankshaft is not, the rod will need to be reconditioned by a machine shop.

➡You can also use Plastigage® to check the bearing clearances. The assembling section has complete instructions on its use.

Camshaft

Inspect the camshaft and lifters/followers as described earlier in this section.

Bearings

All of the engine bearings should be visually inspected for wear and/or damage. The bearing should look evenly worn all around with no deep scores or pits. If the bearing is severely worn, scored, pitted or heat blued, then the bearing, and the components that use it, should be brought to a machine shop for inspection. Full-circle bearings (used on most camshafts, auxiliary shafts, balance shafts, etc.) require specialized tools for removal and installation, and should be brought to a machine shop for service.

Oil Pump

➡The oil pump is responsible for providing constant lubrication to the whole engine and so it is recommended that a new oil pump be installed when rebuilding the engine.

Completely disassemble the oil pump and thoroughly clean all of the components. Inspect the oil pump gears and housing for wear and/or damage. Insure that the pressure relief valve operates properly and there is no binding or sticking due to varnish or debris. If all of the parts are in proper working condition, lubricate the gears and relief valve, and assemble the pump.

REFINISHING

See Figure 330

Almost all engine block refinishing must be performed by a machine shop. If the cylinders are not to be rebored, then the cylinder glaze can be removed with a ball hone. When removing cylinder glaze with a ball hone, use a light or penetrating type oil to lubricate the hone. Do not allow the hone to run dry as this may cause excessive scoring of the cylinder bores and wear on the hone. If new pistons are required, they will need to be installed to the connecting rods. This should be performed by a machine shop as the pistons must be installed in the correct relationship to the rod or engine damage can occur.

Pistons and Connecting Rods

See Figure 331

Only pistons with the wrist pin retained by C-clips are serviceable by the home-mechanic. Press fit pistons require special presses and/or heaters to remove/install the connecting rod and should only be performed by a machine shop.

All pistons will have a mark indicating the direction to the front of the engine and the must be installed into the engine in that manner. Usually it is a notch or arrow on the top of the piston, or it may be the letter F cast or stamped into the piston.

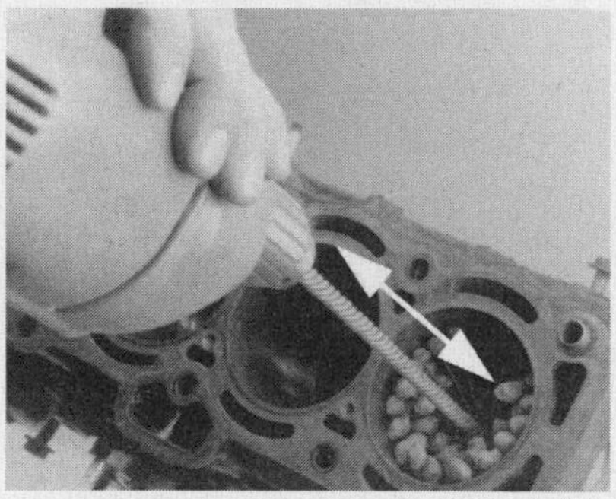
tccs3913

Fig. 330 Use a ball type cylinder hone to remove any glaze and provide a new surface for seating the piston rings

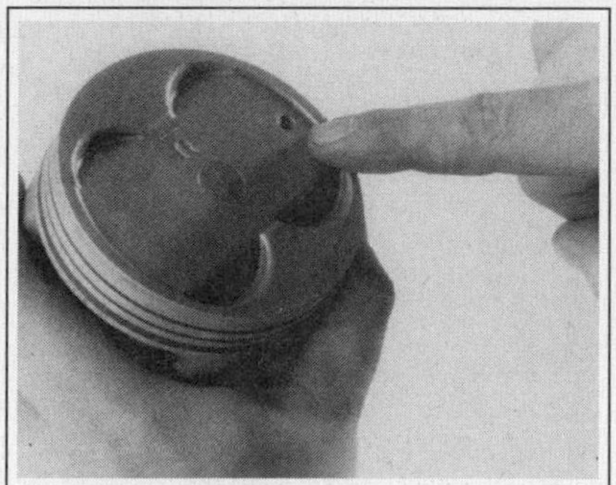
tccs3814

Fig. 331 Most pistons are marked to indicate positioning in the engine (usually a mark means the side facing the front)

C-CLIP TYPE PISTONS

1. Note the location of the forward mark on the piston and mark the connecting rod in relation.
2. Remove the C-clips from the piston and withdraw the wrist pin.

➡Varnish build-up or C-clip groove burrs may increase the difficulty of removing the wrist pin. If necessary, use a punch or drift to carefully tap the wrist pin out.

3. Insure that the wrist pin bushing in the connecting rod is usable, and lubricate it with assembly lube.
4. Remove the wrist pin from the new piston and lubricate the pin bores on the piston.
5. Align the forward marks on the piston and the connecting rod and install the wrist pin.
6. The new C-clips will have a flat and a rounded side to them. Install both C-clips with the flat side facing out.
7. Repeat all of the steps for each piston being replaced.

ASSEMBLY

Before you begin assembling the engine, first give yourself a clean, dirt free work area. Next, clean every engine component again. The key to a good assembly is cleanliness.

Mount the engine block into the engine stand and wash it one last time using water and detergent (dishwashing detergent works well). While washing it, scrub the cylinder bores with a soft bristle brush and thoroughly clean all of the oil passages. Completely dry the engine and spray the entire assembly down with an anti-rust solution such as WD-40® or similar product. Take a clean lint-free rag and wipe up any excess anti-rust solution from the bores, bearing saddles, etc. Repeat the final cleaning process on the crankshaft. Replace any freeze or oil galley plugs which were removed during disassembly.

Crankshaft

See Figures 332 thru 339

1. Remove the main bearing inserts from the block and bearing caps.
2. If the crankshaft main bearing journals have been refinished to a definite undersize, install the correct undersize bearing. Be sure that the bearing inserts and bearing bores are clean. Foreign material under inserts will distort bearing and cause failure.
3. Place the upper main bearing inserts in bores with tang in slot.

➡The oil holes in the bearing inserts must be aligned with the oil holes in the cylinder block.

4. Install the lower main bearing inserts in bearing caps.
5. Clean the mating surfaces of block and rear main bearing cap.
6. Carefully lower the crankshaft into place. Be careful not to damage bearing surfaces.
7. Check the clearance of each main bearing by using the following procedure:
    a. Place a piece of Plastigage® or its equivalent, on bearing surface across full width of bearing cap and about 1/4 in. off center.
    b. Install cap and tighten bolts to specifications. Do not turn crankshaft while Plastigage® is in place.

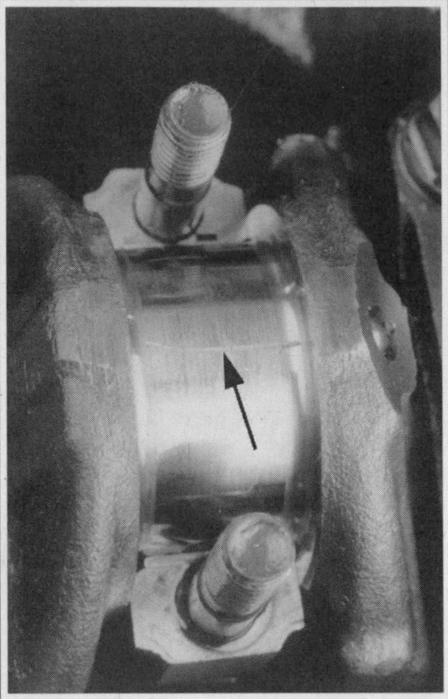

tccs3243

Fig. 332 Apply a strip of gauging material to the bearing journal, then install and torque the cap

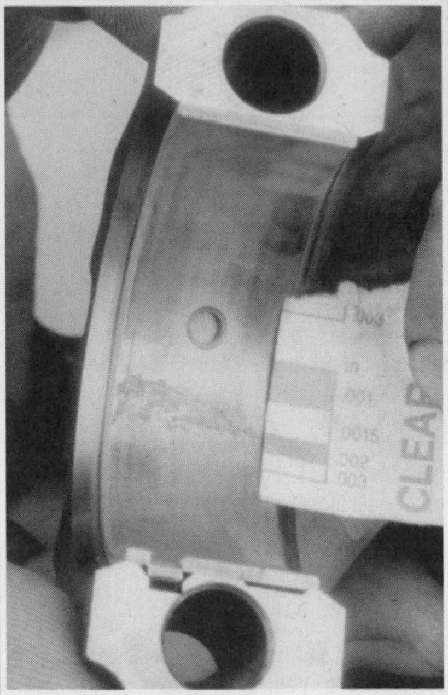

tccs3912

Fig. 333 After the cap is removed again, use the scale supplied with the gauging material to check the clearance

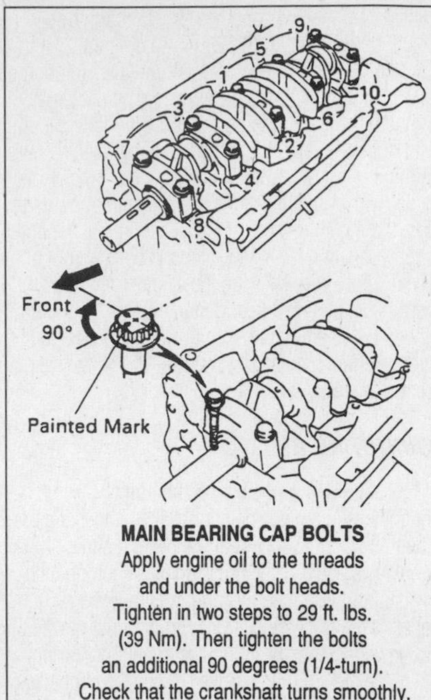

Front
90°
Painted Mark
MAIN BEARING CAP BOLTS
Apply engine oil to the threads and under the bolt heads.
Tighten in two steps to 29 ft. lbs. (39 Nm). Then tighten the bolts an additional 90 degrees (1/4-turn).
Check that the crankshaft turns smoothly.

93163G61

Fig. 334 Main bearing tightening sequence—2RZ-FE and 3RZ-FE engines

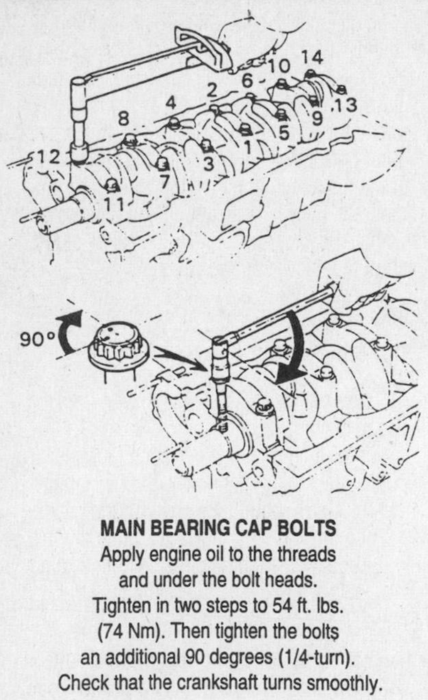

90°
MAIN BEARING CAP BOLTS
Apply engine oil to the threads and under the bolt heads.
Tighten in two steps to 54 ft. lbs. (74 Nm). Then tighten the bolts an additional 90 degrees (1/4-turn).
Check that the crankshaft turns smoothly.

93163G62

Fig. 335 Main bearing tightening sequence—1FZ-FE engine

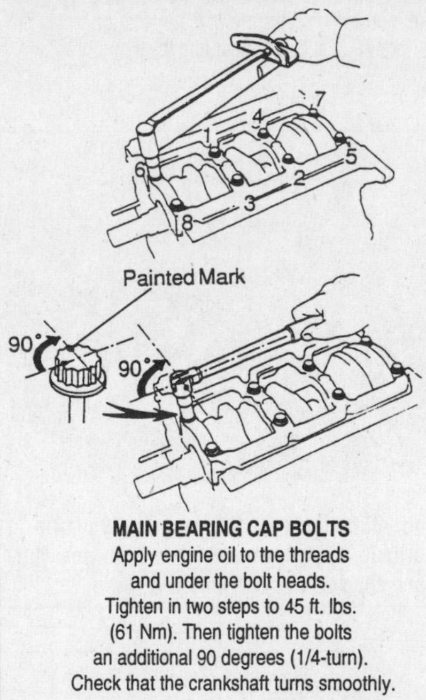

Painted Mark
90°
MAIN BEARING CAP BOLTS
Apply engine oil to the threads and under the bolt heads.
Tighten in two steps to 45 ft. lbs. (61 Nm). Then tighten the bolts an additional 90 degrees (1/4-turn).
Check that the crankshaft turns smoothly.

93163G63

Fig. 336 Main bearing tightening sequence—5VZ-FE engine

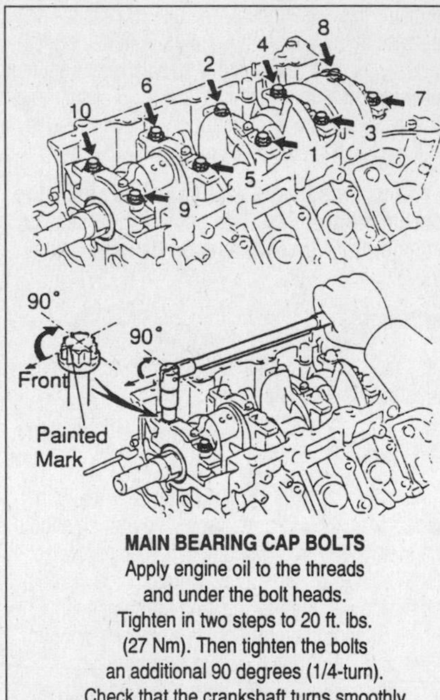

90°
Front
Painted Mark
MAIN BEARING CAP BOLTS
Apply engine oil to the threads and under the bolt heads.
Tighten in two steps to 20 ft. lbs. (27 Nm). Then tighten the bolts an additional 90 degrees (1/4-turn).
Check that the crankshaft turns smoothly.

93163G64

Fig. 337 Main bearing tightening sequence—2UZ-FE engine

c. Remove the cap. Using the supplied Plastigage® scale, check width of Plastigage® at widest point to get maximum clearance. Difference between readings is taper of journal.

d. If clearance exceeds specified limits, try a 0.001 in. or 0.002 in. undersize bearing in combination with the standard bearing. Bearing clearance must be within specified limits. If standard and 0.002 in. undersize bearing does not bring clearance within desired limits, refinish crankshaft journal, then install undersize bearings.

8. Install the rear main seal.

9. After the bearings have been fitted, apply a light coat of engine oil to the journals and bearings. Install the rear main bearing cap. Install all bearing caps except the thrust bearing cap. Be sure that main bearing caps are installed in original locations. Tighten the bearing cap bolts to specifications.

10. Install the thrust bearing cap with bolts finger-tight.

11. Pry the crankshaft forward against the thrust surface of upper half of bearing.

12. Hold the crankshaft forward and pry the thrust bearing cap to the rear. This aligns the thrust surfaces of both halves of the bearing.

13. Retain the forward pressure on the crankshaft. Tighten the cap bolts to specifications.

14. Measure the crankshaft end-play as follows:

a. Mount a dial gauge to the engine block and position the tip of the gauge to read from the crankshaft end.

b. Carefully pry the crankshaft toward the rear of the engine and hold it there while you zero the gauge.

c. Carefully pry the crankshaft toward the front of the engine and read the gauge.

d. Confirm that the reading is within specifications. If not, install a new thrust bearing and repeat the procedure. If the reading is still out of specifications with a new bearing, have a machine shop inspect the thrust surfaces of the crankshaft, and if possible, repair it.

15. Rotate the crankshaft so as to position the first rod journal to the bottom of its stroke.

Pistons and Connecting Rods

See Figures 339 thru 345

1. Before installing the piston/connecting rod assembly, oil the pistons, piston rings and the cylinder walls with light engine oil. Install connecting rod bolt protectors or rubber hose onto the connecting rod bolts/studs. Also perform the following:

a. Select the proper ring set for the size cylinder bore.

b. Position the ring in the bore in which it is going to be used.

c. Push the ring down into the bore area where normal ring wear is not encountered.

d. Use the head of the piston to position the ring in the bore so that the ring is square with the cylinder wall. Use caution to avoid damage to the ring or cylinder bore.

e. Measure the gap between the ends of the ring with a feeler gauge. Ring gap in a worn cylinder is normally greater than specification. If the ring gap is greater than the specified limits, try an oversize ring set.

f. Check the ring side clearance of the compression rings with a feeler gauge inserted between the ring and its lower land according to specification. The gauge should slide freely around the entire ring circumference without binding. Any wear that occurs will form a step at the inner portion of the lower land. If the lower lands have high steps, the piston should be replaced.

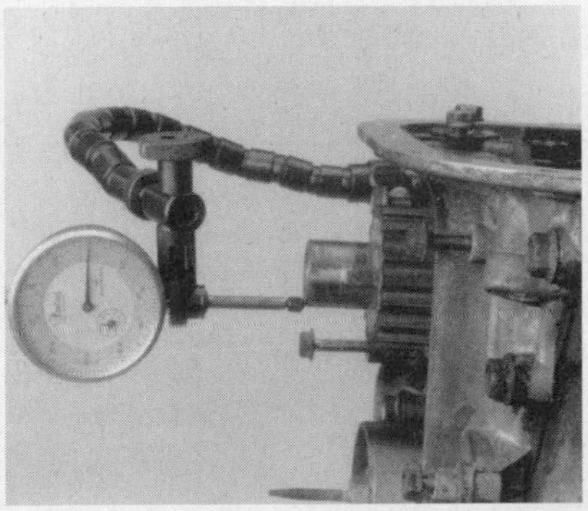

tccs3805

Fig. 338 A dial gauge may be used to check crankshaft end-play

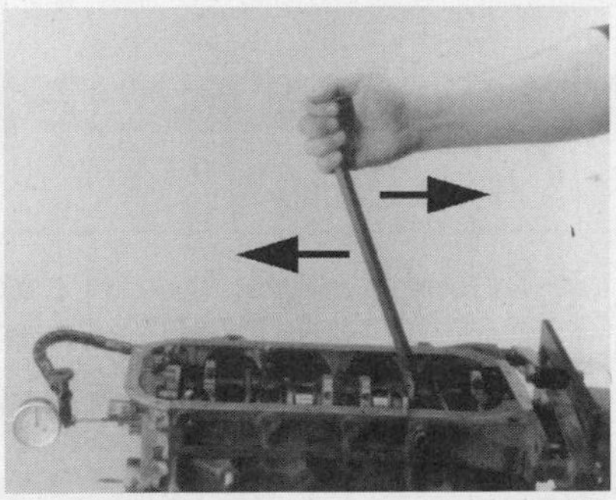

tccs3806

Fig. 339 Carefully pry the crankshaft back and forth while reading the dial gauge for end-play

tccs3923

Fig. 340 Checking the piston ring-to-ring groove side clearance using the ring and a feeler gauge

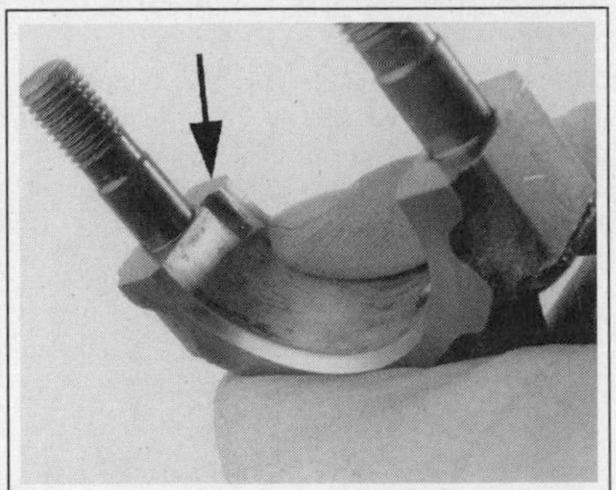

tccs3917

Fig. 341 The notch on the side of the bearing cap matches the tang on the bearing insert

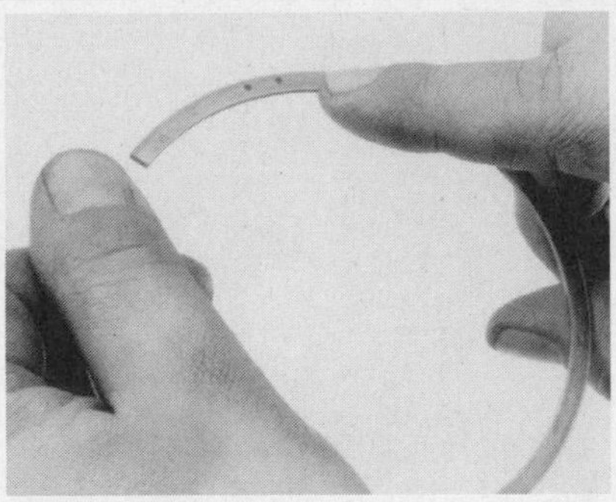

tccs3222

Fig. 342 Most rings are marked to show which side of the ring should face up when installed to the piston

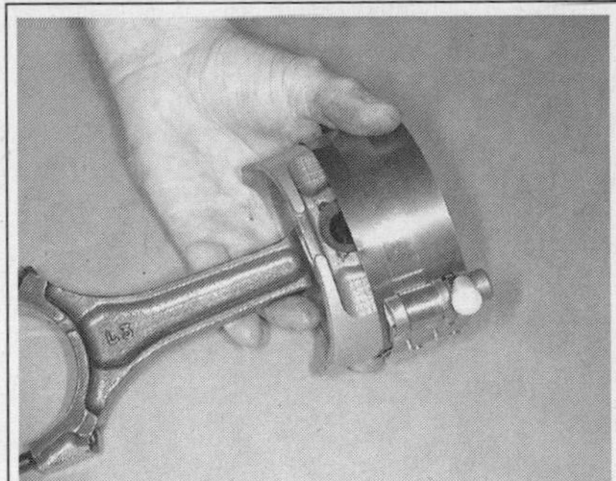

93163pk8

Fig. 343 Install the piston ring compressor on the piston and tighten it until it compresses the rings

86823PFA

Fig. 344 With rubber hoses on the rod bolts, insert the piston into the cylinder

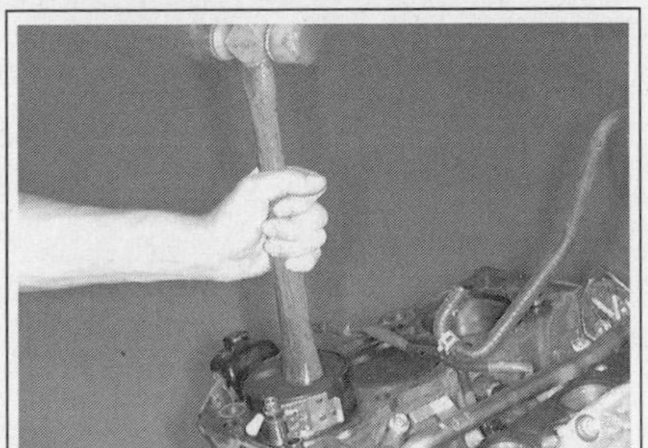

93163pk9

Fig. 345 With a wooden dowel or a hammer shaft, gently insert the piston

93163pk7

Fig. 346 Once the piston has been installed, remove the ring compressor

2. Unless new pistons are installed, be sure to install the pistons in the cylinders from which they were removed. The numbers on the connecting rod and bearing cap must be on the same side when installed in the cylinder bore. If a connecting rod is ever transposed from one engine or cylinder to another, new bearings should be fitted and the connecting rod should be numbered to correspond with the new cylinder number. The notch on the piston head goes toward the front of the engine.

3. Install all of the rod bearing inserts into the rods and caps.

4. Install the rings to the pistons. Install the oil control ring first, then the second compression ring and finally the top compression ring. Use a piston ring expander tool to aid in installation and to help reduce the chance of breakage.

5. Make sure the ring gaps are properly spaced around the circumference of the piston. Fit a piston ring compressor around the piston and slide the piston and connecting rod assembly down into the cylinder bore, pushing it in with the wooden hammer handle. Push the piston down until it is only slightly below the top of the cylinder bore. Guide the connecting rod onto the crankshaft bearing journal carefully, to avoid damaging the crankshaft.

6. Check the bearing clearance of all the rod bearings, fitting them to the crankshaft bearing journals. Follow the procedure in the crankshaft installation above.

7. After the bearings have been fitted, apply a light coating of assembly oil to the journals and bearings.

8. Turn the crankshaft until the appropriate bearing journal is at the bottom of its stroke, then push the piston assembly all the way down until the connecting rod bearing seats on the crankshaft journal. Be careful not to allow the bearing cap screws to strike the crankshaft bearing journals and damage them.

9. After the piston and connecting rod assemblies have been installed, check the connecting rod side clearance on each crankshaft journal.

10. Prime and install the oil pump and the oil pump intake tube.

OHC Engines

CYLINDER HEAD(S)

1. Install the cylinder head(s) using new gaskets.
2. Install the timing sprockets/gears and the belt/chain assemblies.

Engine Covers and Components

Install the timing cover(s) and oil pan. Refer to your notes and drawings made prior to disassembly and install all of the components that were removed. Install the engine into the vehicle.

Engine Start-up and Break-in

STARTING THE ENGINE

Now that the engine is installed and every wire and hose is properly connected, go back and double check that all coolant and vacuum hoses are connected. Check that your oil drain plug is installed and properly tightened. If not already done, install a new oil filter onto the engine. Fill the crankcase with the proper amount and grade of engine oil. Fill the cooling system with a 50/50 mixture of coolant/water.

1. Connect the vehicle battery.
2. Start the engine. Keep your eye on your oil pressure indicator; if it does not indicate oil pressure within 10 seconds of starting, turn the vehicle off.

***** WARNING**

Damage to the engine can result if it is allowed to run with no oil pressure. Check the engine oil level to make sure that it is full. Check for any leaks and if found, repair the leaks before continuing. If there is still no indication of oil pressure, you may need to prime the system.

3. Confirm that there are no fluid leaks (oil or other).
4. Allow the engine to reach normal operating temperature (the upper radiator hose will be hot to the touch).
5. At this point you can perform any necessary checks or adjustments, such as checking the ignition timing.
6. Install any remaining components or body panels which were removed.

BREAKING IT IN

Make the first miles on the new engine, easy ones. Vary the speed but do not accelerate hard. Most importantly, do not lug the engine, and avoid sustained high speeds until at least 100 miles. Check the engine oil and coolant levels frequently. Expect the engine to use a little oil until the rings seat. Change the oil and filter at 500 miles, 1500 miles, then every 3000 miles past that.

KEEP IT MAINTAINED

Now that you have just gone through all of that hard work, keep yourself from doing it all over again by thoroughly maintaining it. Not that you may not have maintained it before, heck you could have had one to two hundred thousand miles on it before doing this. However, you may have bought the vehicle used, and the previous owner did not keep up on maintenance. Which is why you just went through all of that hard work. See?

1FZ-FE ENGINE MECHANICAL SPECIFICATIONS

Component	English Specifications	Metric Specifications
Compression		
At 250 rpm		
Standard	171 psi	1176 kPa
Minimum	128 psi	883 kPa
Difference between each cylinder	14 psi or less	98 kPa
Valve Clearance		
Cold		
Intake	0.006-0.010 in.	0.15-0.25mm
Exhaust	0.010 - 0.014 in.	0.25 - 0.35mm
Cylinder head		
Warpage Maximum	0.059 in.	0.15mm
Valve seat		
Refacing angle	30°, 45°, 60°	
Contacting angle	45°	
Valve guide bushing inside diameter	0.2760 - 0.2768 in.	7.010 -7.030mm
Cylinder head bolt thread inside diameter		
Standard	0.4272-0.4331 in.	10.85-11.00mm
Minimum	0.417 in.	10.60mm
Valve guide bushing		
Inside bore diameter	0.4524-0.4552 in.	11.492-11.513mm
Valve		
Valve overall length		
Standard		
Intake	3.874 in.	98.40mm
Exhaust	3.854 in.	97.90mm
Minimum		
Intake	3.854 in.	97.90mm
Exhaust	3.835 in.	97.40mm
Valve face angle	45.0°	
Stem diameter		
Intake	0.2744-2750 in.	6.970-6.985mm
Exhaust	0.2742-0.2748 in.	6.965-6.980mm
Stem oil clearance		
Standard		
Intake	0.0010-0.0024 in.	0.025-0.060mm
Exhaust	0.0012 - 0.0026 in.	0.030 - 0.065mm
Maximum		
Intake	0.0031 in.	0.08mm
Exhaust	0.0039 in.	0.10mm
Valve spring		
Deviation Maximum	0.079 in.	2.0mm
Free length	1.7299-1.7740 in.	43.94-45.06mm
Installed tension at 35.0mm 1.378 in.	48.1 - 53.4 ft. lbs.	214 - 238 N
Camshaft		
Journal oil clearance		
Standard	0.0010-0.0024 in.	0.025-0.062mm
Maximum	0.0039 in.	0.10mm
Journal diameter	1.0614-1.0620 in.	26.959-26.975mm
Circle runout	0.0024 in.	0.06mm
Cam lobe height		
Standard	1.9925-1.9956 in.	50.61-50.71mm
Minimum	1.9886 in.	50.51 mm
Camshaft gear backlash		
Standard	0.0008 - 0.0079 in.	0.020 - 0.200mm
Maximum	0.0188 in.	0.30mm

93163c01

1FZ-FE ENGINE MECHANICAL SPECIFICATIONS

Component	English Specifications	Metric Specifications
Manifold		
Warpage Maximum		
Intake	0.0118 in.	0.30mm
Exhaust	0.0118 in.	0.30mm
Cylinder block		
Cylinder head surface warpage Maximum	0.0028 in.	0.07mm
Cylinder bore diameter	2.9146 - 2.9149 in.	74.032 - 74.038mm
Piston and piston ring		
Piston diameter Standard	3.9350 - 3.9362 in.	99.950 - 99.980mm
Piston oil clearance		
Standard	0.0016 - 0.0024 in.	0.040 - 0.060mm
Piston ring groove clearance		
No.1	0.0016-0.0031 in.	0.040-0.080mm
No.2	0.0012 - 0.0028 in.	0.030 - 0.070mm
Piston ring end gap		
Standard		
No.1	0.0118-0.0205 in.	0.300-0.520mm
No.2	0.0177 - 0.0264 in.	0.450 - 0.670mm
Oil	0.0059 -0.0205 in.	0.150-0.520mm
Maximum		
No.1	0.0441 in.	1.12mm
No.2	0.0461 in.	1.17mm
Oil	0.0441 in.	1.12mm
Connecting rod		
Thrust clearance		
Standard	0.0063-0.0138 in.	0.160-0.290mm
Maximum	0.0138 in.	0.35mm
Connecting rod oil clearance		
Standard	0.0013-0.0020 in.	0.032-0.050mm
Maximum	0.0039 in.	0.10mm
Piston pin diameter	1.0236 - 1.0241 in.	26.000 - 26.012mm
Crankshaft		
Thrust clearance		
Standard	0.0008-0.0087 in.	0.020-0.220mm
Maximum	0.0118 in.	0.30mm
Thrust washer thickness	0.0961 -0.0980 in.	2.440-2.490mm
Main journal oil clearance Standard	0.0014-0.0021 in.	0.036-0.054mm
Maximum	0.0035 in.	0.075mm
Main journal diameter	2.7161- 2.7163 in.	68.988 - 68.994mm
Circle runout		
Maximum	0.0031 in.	0.08mm
Main journal taper and out-of-round		
Maximum	0.0008 in.	0.02mm
Crank pin taper and out-of-round		
Maximum	0.0008 in.	0.02mm

93163c02

2UZ-FE ENGINE MECHANICAL SPECIFICATIONS

Component	English Specifications	Metric Specifications
Compression		
At 250 rpm		
Standard	192 psi	1,324 kPa
Minimum	142 psi	981 kPa
Difference between each cylinder	14 psi or less	98 kPa
Valve Clearance		
Cold		
Intake	0.006-0.010 in.	0.15-0.25mm
Exhaust	0.010 - 0.014 in.	0.25 - 0.35mm
Cylinder head		
Warpage Maximum	0.039 in.	0.10mm
Valve seat		
Refacing angle	30°, 45°, 60°	
Contacting angle	45°	
Contacting width	0.039 - 0.055 in.	1.0 -1.4mm
Valve guide bushing bore diameter	0.4049 - 0.4057 in.	10.285 -10.306mm
Cylinder head bolt thread inside diameter		
Standard	0.3862 - 0.3921 in.	9.810 - 9.960mm
Minimum	0.3819 in.	9.70mm
Protrusion height		
Intake	0.362-0.386 in.	9.2-9.8mm
Exhaust	0.323-0.346 in.	8.2-8.8mm
Valve guide bushing		
Inside diameter	0.2169 - 0.2374 in.	5.510 - 5.530mm
Valve		
Valve overall length		
Standard		
Intake	3.7421 in.	95.05mm
Exhaust	3.7441 in.	95.1mm
Minimum		
Intake	3.7224 in.	94.55mm
Exhaust	3.7244 in.	94.60mm
Valve face angle	44.5°	
Stem diameter		
Intake	0.2154-0.2159 in.	5.470-5.485mm
Exhaust	0.2152-0.2157 in.	5.465-5.480mm
Stem oil clearance		
Standard		
Intake	0.0010-0.0024 in.	0.025-0.060mm
Exhaust	0.0012 - 0.0026 in.	0.030 - 0.065mm
Maximum		
Intake	0.0031 in.	0.08mm
Exhaust	0.0039 in.	0.10mm
Margin thickness		
Standard		
IN	0.049 in.	1.25mm
EX	0.055 in.	1.4mm
Minimum	0.020 in.	0.5mm
Valve spring		
Deviation Maximum	0.079 in.	2.0mm
Free length	2.130 in.	54.1mm
Installed tension at 35.0mm 1.378 in.	45.9 - 50.7 lbf	204 - 226 N

93163c03

2UZ-FE ENGINE MECHANICAL SPECIFICATIONS

Component	English Specifications	Metric Specifications
Valve lifter		
Lifter diameter	1.2191 -2.2195 in.	30.966-30.976mm
Lifter bore diameter	1.2205 - 1.2211 in.	31.000 - 31.016mm
Oil clearance		
Standard	0.0009-0.0020 in.	0.024-0.050mm
Maximum	0.0028 in.	0.07mm
Camshaft		
Thrust clearance		
Standard		
Intake	0.0016-0.0035 in.	0.040-0.090mm
Exhaust	0.0016-0.0033 in.	0.040-0.085mm
Maximum	0.0047 in.	0.12mm
Journal oil clearance		
Standard	0.0012-0.0026 in.	0.030-0.067mm
Maximum	0.0039 in.	0.10mm
Journal diameter	1.0612 -1.0618 in.	26.954 - 26.970mm
Circle runout	0.0031 in.	0.08mm
Cam lobe height		
Standard		
Intake	1.6512-1.6551 in.	41.94-42.04mm
Exhaust	1.6520-1.6559 in.	41.96-42.06mm
Minimum		
Intake	1.6453 in.	41.79mm
Exhaust	1/6461 in.	41.81mm
Camshaft gear backlash		
Standard	0.0008 - 0.0079 in.	0.020 - 0.200mm
Maximum	0.0188 in.	0.30mm
Camshaft gear spring end free distance	0.712 - 0.740 in.	18.2 - 18.8mm
Manifold		
Warpage Maximum		
Intake	0.0059 in.	0.15mm
Exhaust	0.0197 in.	0.50mm
Cylinder block		
Cylinder head surface warpage Maximum	0.0028 in.	0.07mm
Cylinder bore diameter	3.7009 - 3.7012 in.	94.002 - 94.010mm
Main bearing cap bolt tension portion diameter		
Standard	0.4236 - 0.4319 in.	10.760 -10.970mm
Minimum	0.4094 in.	10.40mm
Piston and piston ring		
Piston diameter Standard	3.6969 - 3.6973 in.	93.902 - 93.912mm
Piston oil clearance		
Standard	0.0035 - 0.0044 in.	0.090 - 0.111mm
Maximum	0.0051 in.	0.13mm
Piston ring groove clearance		
No.1	0.0012-0.0031 in.	0.030-0.080mm
No.2	0.0012 - 0.0028 in.	0.030 - 0.070mm
Piston ring end gap		
Standard		
No.1	0:0118-0.0197 in.	0.300-0.500mm
No.2	0.0157 - 0.0256 in.	0.400 - 0.650mm
Oil	0.0051 -0.0189 in.	0.130-0.480mm
Maximum		
No.1	0.0433 in.	1.10mm
No.2	0.0472 in.	1.20mm
Oil	0.0453 in.	1.15mm

93163c04

2UZ-FE ENGINE MECHANICAL SPECIFICATIONS

Component	English Specifications	Metric Specifications
Connecting rod		
Thrust clearance		
Standard	0.0063-0.0138 in.	0.160-0.290mm
Maximum	0.0138 in.	0.35mm
Connecting rod thickness	0.9008 - 0.9024 in.	22.880 - 22.920mm
Connecting rod oil clearance		
Standard	0.0011 - 0.0021 in.	0.027 - 0.053mm
Maximum	0.0026 in.	0.065mm
Rod bend Maximum per 100mm 3.94 in.	0.0020 in.	0.05mm
Rod twist Maximum per 100mm 3.94 in.	0.0059 in.	0.15mm
Bushing inside diameter	0.8663 - 0.8667 in.	22.005 - 22.014mm
Piston pin diameter	0.8660 - 0.8664 in.	21.997 - 22.006mm
Bushing oil clearance		
Standard	0.0002 - 0.0004 in	0.005 - 0.011mm
Maximum	0.0020 in.	0.05mm
Connecting rod bolt tension portion diameter		
Standard	0.2835-0.2874 in.	7.200-7.300mm
Minimum	0.2756 in.	7.00mm
Crankshaft		
Thrust clearance		
Standard	0.0008-0.0087 in.	0.020-0.220mm
Maximum	0.0118 in.	0.30mm
Thrust washer thickness	0.0961 -0.0980 in.	2.440-2.490mm
Main journal bore diameter on cylinder block with main bearing	2.6372 - 2.6378 in.	66.986 - 67.000mm
Main journal oil clearance Standard	0.0016-0.0023 in.	0.040-0.058mm
Maximum	0.0028 in.	0.070mm
Main journal diameter	2.6373 - 2.6378 in.	66.988 - 67.000mm
Circle runout		
Maximum	0.0031 in.	0.08mm
Main journal taper and out-of-round		
Maximum	0.0008 in.	0.02mm
Crank pin taper and out-of-round		
Maximum	0.0008 in.	0.02mm

93163c05

3RZ-FE ENGINE MECHANICAL SPECIFICATIONS

Description	English Specifications	Metric Specifications
Compression Pressure		
At 250 rpm		
Standard	178 psi	1,230 kPa
Minimum	127 psi	880 kPa
Devation	14 psi	98 kPa
Valve Clearance		
Intake	0.006 - 0.010 in.	0.15 - 0.25mm
Exhaust	0.010 - 0.014 in.	0.25 - 0.35mm
Cylinder head		
Warpage		
Cylinder block side Maximum	0.0020 in.	0.05mm
Manifold side Maximum	0.0039 in.	0.10mm
Valve seat		
Refacing angle Intake	30°, 45°, 60°	
Exhaust	45°, 60°	
Contacting angle	45°	
Contacting width	0.039 - 0.055 in.	1.0 -1.4mm
Cylinder head bolt outside diameter Standard	0.4236 - 0.4319 in.	10.76 -10.97mm
Minimum	0.4094 in.	10.40mm
Valve guide bushing		
Inside diameter		
Outside diameter for repair part	0.2366 - 0.2374 in.	6.010 - 6.030mm
Standard	0.4331 - 0.4341 in.	11.000 - 11.027mm
Protrusion height	0.323-0.339 in.	8.2-8.6mm
Replacing temperature		
Cylinder head side	176 -212°F	80 - 100°C
Valve		
Overall length		
Intake		
Standard	4.0728 in.	103.45mm
Exhaust	4.0787 in.	103.60mm
Intake		
Minimum	4.0531 in.	102.95mm
Exhaust	4.0590 in.	103.10mm
Valve face angle	44.5°	
Stem diameter		
Standard		
Intake	0.2350-0.2356 in.	5.970-5.985mm
Exhaust	0.2348-0.2354 in.	5.965-5.980mm
Stem oil clearance		
Standard		
Intake	0.0010-0.0024 in.	0.025-0.060mm
Exhaust	0.0012 - 0.0026 in.	0.030 - 0.065mm
Maximum		
Intake	0.0031 in.	0.08mm
Exhaust	0.0039 in.	0.10mm
Margin thickness		
Standard	0.039 in.	1.0mm
Minimum	0.020 in.	0.5mm
Valve spring		
Deviation		
Maximum	0.079 in.	2.0mm
Installed tension at 35.7mm 1.406 in.	39.7 - 45.9 lbf	177 - 204 N

93163c06

3RZ-FE ENGINE MECHANICAL SPECIFICATIONS

Description	English Specifications	Metric Specifications
Valve lifter		
Lifter diameter	1.1578 - 1.2195 in.	30.966 - 30.976mm
Lifter bore diameter	1.2205 -1.2211 in.	31.000 - 31.016mm
Oil clearance		
Standard	0.0009-0.0020 in.	0.024-0.050mm
Maximum	0.0028 in.	0.07mm
Manifold		
Warpage Maximum		
Intake	0.0078 in.	0.20mm
Exhaust	0.0197 in.	0.50mm
Camshaft		
Thrust clearance		
Standard	0.0016 - 0.0037 in.	0.040 - 0.095mm
Maximum	0.0047 in.	0.12mm
Journal oil clearance		
Standard	0.0010-0.0024 in.	0.025-0.062mm
Maximum	0.0031 in.	0.08mm
Journal diameter	1.0614- 1.0620 in.	26.959 - 26.975mm
Circle runout Maximum	0.0024 in.	0.06mm
Cam lobe height Intake		
Intake	1.7839-1.7878 in.	45.31 -45.41mm
Exhaust	1.7740 -1.7779 in.	45.06 - 45.16mm
Camshaft gear backlash		
Standard	0.0008 -0.0079 in.	0.020 -0.200mm
Maximum	0.0188 in.	0.30mm
Camshaft gear spring end free distance	0.886- 0.902 in.	22.5 - 22.9mm
Chain and timing gear		
Chain length at 16 links Maximum		
No.1	5.807 in.	147.5mm
No.2	4.866 in.	123.6mm
Camshaft timing gear wear w/ chain		
Minimum	4.480 in.	113.8mm
Crankshaft timing gear wear w/ chain		
Minimum	2.339 in.	59.4mm
Balance shaft drive gear wear w/ chain		
Minimum	2.988 in.	75.9mm
No.2 crankshaft timing sprocket wear w/ chain		
Minimum	3.807 in.	96.7mm
Chain tensioner		
Wear		
Maximum	0.039 in.	1.0mm
Cylinder block		
Cylinder head surface warpage Maximum	0.0020 in.	0.05mm
Cylinder bore diameter		
Standard	3.7400 - 3.7403 in.	94.990 - 95.003mm
Maximum	3.7425 in.	95.06mm
Main bearing bolt outside diameter		
Standard	0.4236 - 0.4319 in.	10.76 - 10.97mm
Minimum	0.4094 in.	10.40mm
Cylinder block main journal bore diameter		
Standard		

93163c07

3RZ-FE ENGINE MECHANICAL SPECIFICATIONS

Description	English Specifications	Metric Specifications
Piston		
Piston diameter		
Standard	3.7375 - 3.7379 in.	94.933 - 94.943mm
Piston oil clearance	0.0019-0.0028 in.	0.047-0.070mm
Piston Ring		
Piston ring groove clearance		
No.1	0.0008-0.0028 in.	0.020-0.070mm
No.2	0.0012 - 0.0028 in.	0.030 - 0.070mm
Piston ring end gap		
No.1	0.0118 -0.0157 in.	0.300 -0.400mm
No.2	0.0157-0.0197 in.	0.400-0.500mm
Piston pin installing temperature	176 -194°F	80 -90°C
Connecting Rod		
Thrust clearance Standard	0.0063-0.0123 in.	0.160-0.312mm
Maximum	0.0138 in.	0.35mm
Connecting rod bearing center wall thickness		
Standard	0.0583 - 0.0585 in.	1.482 -1.485mm
Connecting rod big end inside diameter		
Standard	2.2047 - 2.2050 in.	56.000 - 56.006mm
Connecting rod oil clearance		
Standard	0.0012-0.0022 in.	0.030-0.055mm
Maximum	0.0039 in.	0.10mm
Rod out-of-alignment		
Maximum per 100mm 3.94 in.	0.0020 in.	0.05mm
Rod twist Maximum per 100mm 3.94 in.	0.0059 in.	0.15mm
Bushing inside diameter	0.9452 - 0.9455 in.	24.008 - 24.017mm
Piston pin diameter	0.9449 - 0.9452 in.	24.000 - 24.009mm
Piston pin oil clearance		
Standard	0.0002 - 0.0004 in.	0.005 - 0.011mm
Maximum	0.0006 in.	0.015mm
Connecting rod bolt outside diameter		
Standard	0.3071 - 0.3110 in.	7.80 - 7.90mm
Minimum	0.2992 in.	7.60mm
Crankshaft		
Thrust clearance		
Standard	0.0008 - 0.0087 in.	0.020 - 0.0220mm
Maximum	0.0118 in.	0.30mm
Thrust washer thickness	0.0961 - 0.0980 in.	2.440 - 2.490mm
Main journal oil clearance		
Standard		
No.3	0.0012 - 0.0022 in.	0.030 - 0.055mm
Others	0.0009 - 0.0019 in.	0.024 - 0.049mm
O/S 0.25		
No.3	0.0012-0.0028 in.	0.030-0.070mm
Others	0.0010 - 0.0026 in.	0.025 - 0.065mm
Maximum	0.0039 in.	0.10mm
Main journal diameter		
Standard		
No.3	2.2615 - 2.3620 in.	59.981 - 59.994mm
Others	2.3617-2.3622 in.	59.987-60.000mm
O/S 0.25		
No.3	2.3520 - 2.3524 in.	59.740 - 59.750mm
Others	2.3522 - 2.3526 in.	59.745 - 59.755mm
Main bearing center wall thickness		

93163c08

3RZ-FE ENGINE MECHANICAL SPECIFICATIONS

Description	English Specifications	Metric Specifications
Crankshaft (cont'd)		
Standard		
Mark 1	0.0782 0.0783 in.	1.987 -1.990mm
Mark 2	0.0784-0.0785 in.	1.991 -1.993mm
Mark 3	0.0785 - 0.0786 in.	1.994 - 1.996mm
O/S 0.25	0.0829-0.0831 in.	2.106-2.112mm
Crank pin diameter		
Standard	2.0861 - 2.0866 in.	52.987 - 53.000mm
O/S 0.25	2.0766 - 2.0770 in.	52.745 - 52.755mm
Circle runout Maximum	0.0012 in.	0.03mm
Main journal taper and out-of-round		
Maximum	0.0002 in.	0.005mm
Crank pin taper and out-of-round		
Maximum	0.0002 in.	0.005mm
Balance shaft		
Thrust clearance		
Standard	0.0027 - 0.0051 in.	0.07 - 0.13mm
Maximum	0.0079 in.	0.20mm
Bearing inside diameter	1.4970 -1.4978 in.	38.025 - 38.045mm
No. 1		
No.2	1.4774 - 1.4781 in.	37.525 - 37.545 m m
Journal diameter		
No.1	1.4948 - 1.4955 in.	37.969 - 37.985mm
No.2	1.4744 -1.4750 in.	37.449 - 37.465mm
Journal oil clearance		
Standard		
No 1	0.0016 - 0.0031 in.	0.040 - 0.076mm
No 2	0.0024 - 0.0038 in.	0.060 - 0.096mm
Maximum	0.0059 in.	0.15mm

93163c09

5VZ-FE ENGINE MECHANICAL SPECIFICATIONS

Description	English Specifications	Metric Specifications
Compression		
At 250 rpm		
Standard	174 psi	1,200 kPa
Minimum	145 psi	1,000 kPa
Difference between cylinders	15 psi	100 kPa
Valve clearance		
Cold		
Intake	0.006-0.009 in.	0.13-0.23mm
Exhaust	0.011 -0.014 in.	0.27-0.37mm
Cylinder head		
Warpage Maximum	0.039 in.	0.10mm
Valve seat		
Refacing angle	30°, 45°, 60°	
Contacting angle	45°	
Contacting width	0.039 - 0.055 in.	1.0 -1.4mm
Valve guide bushing bore diameter	0.4325-0.4341 in.	10.985-11.027mm
Valve guide		
Inside diameter	0.2366-0.2374in.	6.010-6.030mm
Bushing		
Outside diameter for repair part		
Standard	0.4344 - 0.4348 in.	11.033 -11.044mm
Valve		
Valve overall length Standard		
Intake	3.7461 in.	95.15mm
Exhaust	3.7362 in.	94.90mm
Valve face angle	44.5°	
Stem diameter		
Intake	0.2350 -0.2356 in.	5.970 -5.985mm
Exhaust	0.2348 - 0.2354 in.	5.965 - 5.980mm
Stem oil clearance Standard		
Intake	0.0010-0.0024 in.	0.025-0.060mm
Exhaust	0.0012 - 0.0026 in.	0.030 - 0.065mm
Margin thickness		
Standard	0.039 in.	1.0mm
Minimum	0.020 in.	0.5mm
Free length	1.7630 in.	44.78mm
Installed tension at 33.3mm (1.311 in.)	41.9-46.31 ft. lbs	186-206 Nm
Lifter diameter	1.2191 -2.2195 in.	30.966-30.976mm
Lifter bore diameter	1.2205 -1.2212 in.	31.000 - 31.018mm
Camshaft		
Oil clearance		
Standard	0.0009-0.0020 in.	0.024-0.052mm
Maximum	0.0031 in.	0.08mm
Thrust clearance		
Standard	0.0013-0.0031 in.	0.033-0.080mm
Maximum	0.0047 in.	0.12mm
Journal oil clearance		
Standard	0.0014-0.0028 in.	0.035-0.072mm
Maximum	0.0039 in.	0.10mm
Journal diameter	1.0610-1.0616 in.	26.949-26.965mm
Circle runout Maximum	0.0024 in.	0.06mm

93163c10

5VZ-FE ENGINE MECHANICAL SPECIFICATIONS

Description	English Specifications	Metric Specifications
Camshaft (cont'd)		
Cam lobe height		
Standard		
Intake	1.6657 -1.6697 in.	42.31 - 42.41mm
Exhaust	1.6520-1.6559 in.	41.96-42.06mm
Minimum		
Intake	1.6598 in.	42.16mm
Exhaust	1.6461 in.	41.81mm
Camshaft gear backlash		
Standard	0.0008-0.0079 in.	0.020- 0.200mm
Maximum	0.0188 in.	0.30mm
Camshaft gear spring end free distance	0.712 - 0.740 in.	18.2 -18.8mm
Warpage Maximum	0.0039 in.	0.10mm
Cylinder head surface warpage Maximum	0.0020 in.	0.05mm
Cylinder block		
Cylinder bore diameter		
Maximum Standard	3.6902 in.	93.730mm
Piston		
Piston diameter Standard	3.6754-3.6758 in.	93.356-93.366mm
Piston oil clearance		
Standard	0.0053 - 0.0060 in.	0.134 - 0.154mm
Maximum	0.0069 in.	0.174mm
Piston ring groove clearance		
Standard		
No.1	0.0016-0.0031 in.	0.040-0.080mm
No.2	0.0012 - 0.0028 in.	0.030 - 0.070mm
Piston ring end gap		
Standard		
No.1	0.0118-0.0197 in.	0.300-0.500mm
No.2	0.0157-0.0236 in.	0.400-0.600mm
Oil	0.0059-0.0217 in.	0.150-0.550mm
Maximum		
No.1	0.0433 in.	1.100mm
No.2	0.0472 in.	1.200mm
Oil	0.0453 in.	1.150mm
Connecting rod		
Thrust clearance		
Standard	0.0059 - 0.0130 in.	0.150 - 0.330mm
Maximum	0.0150 in.	0.380mm
Bearing center wall thickness		
Reference		
Oil clearance		
Standard	0.0009-0.0021 in.	0.024-0.053mm
Maximum	0.0031 in.	0.08mm
Rod bend Maximum per 100mm (3.94 in.)	0.0020 in.	0.05mm
Rod twist Maximum per 100mm (3.94 in.)	0.0059 in.	0.15mm
Bushing inside diameter	0.8663-0.8668 in.	22.005-22.017mm
Piston pin diameter	0.8660-0.8665 in.	21.997-22.009mm
Bushing oil clearance		
Standard	0.0002 - 0.0004 in	0.005 - 0.011mm
Maximum	0.0020 in.	0.05mm

93163c11

5VZ-FE ENGINE MECHANICAL SPECIFICATIONS

Description	English Specifications	Metric Specifications
Connecting rod (cont'd)		
Connecting rod bolt outer diameter		
Standard	0.3094 -0.3150 in.	7.860- 8.000mm
Minimum	0.2992 in.	7.600mm
Thrust clearance		
Standard	0.0008 - 0.0087 in.	0.020 - 0.220mm
Maximum	0.0118 in.	0.300mm
Thrust washer thickness	0.0961 -0.0980 in.	2.440-2.490mm
Main journal oil clearance No.1		
Standard	0.0008-0.0015 in.	0.020-0.038mm
Main journal diameter		
Standard	2.5191 -2.5197 in.	63.985-64.000mm
Main bearing center wall thickness		
Reference No.1	0.0784 -0.0785 in.	1.991 -1.994mm
Others	0.0783 -0.0784 in.	1.989 -1.992mm
Crank pin diameter		
Standard	2.1648-2.1654 in.	54.987-55.000mm
Circle runout Maximum	0.0024 in.	0.06mm
Main journal taper and out-of-round Maximum	0.0008 in.	0.02mm
Crank pin taper and out-of-round Maximum	0.0008 in.	0.02mm

93163c12

1FZ-FE ENGINE TORQUE SPECIFICATIONS

Component	English Specifications (ft. lbs.)	Metric Specifications (Nm)
A/C Compressor-to-cylinder block	36	49
A/C compressor-to-cylinder block, Fan bracket	36	49
Camshaft bearing cap-to-cylinder head		
Bolt C	66 inch lbs.	7.5
Others	12	16
Camshaft timing pulley-to-camshaft timing tube	80	108
Center exhaust pipe-to-front exhaust pipe	30	40
Crankshaft pulley-to-crankshaft	181	245
Cylinder head cover-to-cylinder head	53 inch lbs.	6.0
Drive belt idler pulley-to-fan bracket	27	37
Drive belt tensioner-to-cylinder block	12	16
Drive plate-to-torque converter clutch	35	48
Engine coolant drain union-to-cylinder block	36	49
Engine hanger-to-cylinder head	27	37
Engine mounting bracket-to-cylinder block	27	36
Exhaust manifold-to-cylinder head	33	44
Fan shroud-to-radiator assembly	44 inch lbs.	5
Fluid coupling-to-fan bracket	16	21
Flywheel housing under cover-to-Transmission	13	18
Frame bracket-to-engine mounting bracket	22	30
Frame crossmember-to-body	37	50
Frame crossmember-to-rear engine mounting insulator	55	74
Front exhaust pipe-to-exhaust manifold	46	62
Front water bypass joint, rear water bypass joint-to-cylinder head	13	18
Generator-to-generator bracket	29	39
Heated oxygen sensor (bank 1, 2 sensor 2)-to-front exhaust pipe	14	120
Intake manifold-to-cylinder head	13	18
No.2 front exhaust pipe-to-front exhaust pipe	30	40
No.2 timing belt cover-to-cylinder block	12	16
No.3 timing belt cover-to-cylinder block, cylinder head	66 inch lbs.	7.5
No.i idler pulley, No.2 idler pulley-to-cylinder Block	25	34.5
Power steering pump-to-cylinder head	13	17
Radiator bracket-to-radiator assembly	15	20
Rear oil seal retainer-to-cylinder block	71 inch lbs.	8.0
Timing belt rear plate-to-cylinder head	66 inch lbs.	7.5
Timing belt tensioner-to-oil pump	19	26
Transmission-to-cylinder block	53	72
Transmission-to-No.1 oil pan	27	37
V-bank cover bracket-to-intake manifold	66 inch lbs.	7.5
Water bypass pipe-to-cylinder block	13	18

93163c13

2UZ-FE ENGINE TORQUE SPECIFICATIONS

Components	English Specifications (ft. lbs.)	Metric Specifications (Nm)
A/C Compressor-to-cylinder block	36	49
A/C compressor-to-cylinder block, fan bracket	36	49
Accelerator cable bracket-to-intake manifold	13	18
Camshaft bearing cap-to-cylinder head	66 inch lbs.	7.5
Camshaft timing pulley-to-camshaft timing tube	80	108
Center exhaust pipe-to-front exhaust pipe	30	40
Connecting rod cap-to-connecting rod	18 Turn 90°	24.5 Turn 90°
Crankshaft pulley-to-crankshaft	181	245
Cylinder head cover-to-cylinder head	53 inch lbs.	6.0
Cylinder head-to-cylinder block	24 Turn 90° Turn 90°	32 Turn 90° Turn 90°
Drive belt idler pulley-to-fan bracket	27	37
Drive belt tensioner-to-cylinder block	12	16
Drive plate-to-crankshaft	36 Turn 90°	49 Turn 90°
Drive plate-to-torque converter clutch	35	48
Engine coolant drain union-to-cylinder block	36	49
Engine hanger-to-cylinder head	27	37
Engine rear mounting bracket-to-transmission	48	65
Exhaust manifold-to-cylinder head	33	44
Fan bracket-to-cylinder block 12 mm head	12	16
Fluid coupling-to-fan bracket	21	29
Flywheel housing under cover-to-transmission	13	18
Frame bracket-to-engine mounting bracket	28	38
Frame crossmember-to-body	53	72
Frame crossmember-to-rear engine mounting bracket	13	18
Front exhaust pipe-to-exhaust manifold	46	62
Front water bypass joint, rear water bypass joint-to-cylinder head	13	18
Generator-to-generator bracket	29	39
Heat insulator-to-LH exhaust manifold	66 inch lbs.	7.5
Heat insulator-to-RH exhaust manifold	66 inch lbs.	7.5
Heated oxygen sensor (bank 1, 2 sensor 2)-to-front exhaust pipe	14	20
Intake manifold-to-cylinder head	13	18
Left engine mounting bracket-to-cylinder block	27	36
Main bearing cap-to-cylinder block	20 Turn 90°	27 Turn 90°
No. 1 idler pulley, No.2 idler pulley-to-cylinder Block	25	34.5
No.2 front exhaust pipe-to-front exhaust pipe	30	40
No.2 timing belt cover-to-cylinder block	12	16
No.3 timing belt cover-to-cylinder block, cylinder head	66 inch lbs.	7.5
Power steering pump-to-cylinder head	13	17
Radiator assembly-to-body	9	12
Rear oil seal retainer-to-cylinder block	71 inch lbs.	8.0
Throttle body cover bracket-to-intake manifold	66 inch lbs.	7.5
Timing belt rear plate-to-cylinder head	66 inch lbs.	7.5
Timing belt tensioner-to-oil pump	19	26
Transmission-to-cylinder block	53	72
Transmission-to-No. 1 oil pan	27	37
Water bypass pipe-to-cylinder block	13	18

93163c14

3RZ-FE ENGINE TORQUE SPECIFICATIONS

Components	English Specifications (ft. lbs.)	Metric Specifications (Nm)
Air intake chamber-to-intake manifold	15	21
Balance shaft drive gear-to-balance shaft	18	25
Camshaft bearing cap-to-cylinder head	12	15.5
Camshaft timing gear-to-intake camshaft	54	73.5
Crankshaft pulley-to-crankshaft	193	260
Cylinder head rear cover-to-cylinder head	10	13.5
Cylinder head-to-cylinder block		
1 st	29	39
2nd	Turn 90°	Turn 90°
3rd	Turn 90°	Turn 90°
Cylinder head-to-timing chain cover	15	21
Distributor gear-to-exhaust camshaft	34	46
Drive belt idler pulley for power steering pump-to-cylinder head	14	20
Egr pipe-to-cylinder head	13	18
Egr pipe-to-EGR valve	14	19
Egr pipe-to-exhaust manifold	15	20
Engine hanger-to-cylinder head	30	42
Exhaust manifold-to-cylinder head	36	49
Fuel inlet pipe-to-delivery pipe	22	29
Fuel inlet pipe-to-fuel filter	22	29
Heat insulator-to-exhaust manifold	48 inch lbs.	5.5
Intake air connector-to-cylinder head	13	18
Intake chamber stay-to-air intake chamber	15	20
Intake chamber stay-to-lh engine mounting bracket	15	20
Intake manifold-to-cylinder head	22	29
No. 1 chain tensioner-to-cylinder head	15	21
No. 1 timing chain tensioner slipper-to-cylinder block	20	27
No. 1 vibration damper-to-cylinder block	22	29
No.2 chain tensioner-to-cylinder block	13	18
No.2 crankshaft pulley-to-crankshaft pulley	18	25
No.2 vibration damper-to-cylinder block	20	27
No.3 vibration damper-to-cylinder block	13	18
No.4 vibration damper-to-cylinder block	13	18
Oil dipower steeringtick guide-to-cylinder head	15	20
Power steering pump bracket-to-cylinder head	15	20
Power steering pump bracket-to-power steering pump	43	58
Power steering pump-to-power steering pump pulley	32	43
Spark plug-to-cylinder head	14	19
Timing chain cover mounting bolt	13	18
Timing chain cover-to-cylinder block		
12 mm head		
Bolt A	14	20
Bolt B	18	24.5
14 mm head bolt	32	44
Nut	14	20
Water bypass pipe mounting nut	14	20
Water outlet-to-cylinder head	14	20

93163c15

5VZ-FE ENGINE TORQUE SPECIFICATIONS

Component	English Specifications (ft. lbs.)	Metric Specifications (Nm)
A/C compressor bracket-to-cylinder block	35	47
A/C compressor-to-A/C compressor bracket	18	25
Air intake chamber stay-to-LH cylinder head, air intake chamber	30	40
Air intake chamber-to-intake air connector	13	18
Camshaft bearing cap-to-cylinder head	12	16
Camshaft position sensor-to-RH cylinder head	71 inch lbs.	8
Camshaft timing pulley-to-camshaft	81	110
Connecting rod cap-to-connecting rod		
1 st	18	25
2nd	Turn 90°	Turn 90°
Crankshaft pulley-to-crankshaft	217	295
Cylinder head cover-to-cylinder head	53 inch lbs.	6
Cylinder head-to-cylinder block 12 pointed head bolts		
1st	25	34
2nd	Turn 90°	Turn 90°
3rd	Turn 90°	Turn 90°
Engine coolant drain cock-to-cylinder block	29	39
Engine front mounting insulator-to-frame	28	38
Engine hanger No.2-to-RH cylinder head	30	40
Engine mounting bracket-to-cylinder block	32	44
Engine rear mounting bracket-to-engine rear mounting insulator	13	18
Exhaust crossover pipe-to-exhaust manifold	33	45
Exhaust manifold heat insulator-to-exhaust manifold	71 inch lbs.	8
Exhaust manifold-to-cylinder head	30	40
Fluid coupling-to-fan bracket	48 inch lbs.	5.4
Frame crossmember-to-engine rear mounting bracket	43	58
Generator adjusting bar-to-cylinder block	31	42
Generator bracket-to-LH cylinder head	14	18.5
Intake air connector-to-intake manifold	13	18
Intake manifold, intake manifold stay-to-cylinder head	13	18
Main bearing cap-to-cylinder block		
1st	45	61
2nd	Turn 90°	Turn 90°
No. 1 idler pulley-to-oil pump	26	35
No. 1 timing belt cover-to-oil pump	80 inch lbs.	9
No.2 idler pulley-to-No.2 idler pulley bracket	30	40
No.2 timing belt cover-to-No.3 timing belt cover	80 inch lbs.	9
No.3 timing belt cover-to-cylinder head	80 inch lbs.	9
Oil dipstick guide-to-generator bracket	71 inch lbs.	8
Oil filter union-to-cylinder block	18	25
Oil pressure switch-to-cylinder block	11	15
Ps pump bracket-to-RH cylinder head	14	18.5
Ps pump-to-ps pump bracket	31	43
Rear oil seal retainer-to-cylinder block	71 inch lbs.	8
Rear plate-to-cylinder head	71 inchlbs.	8
Timing belt tensioner-to-oil pump	20	27

93163c16

4

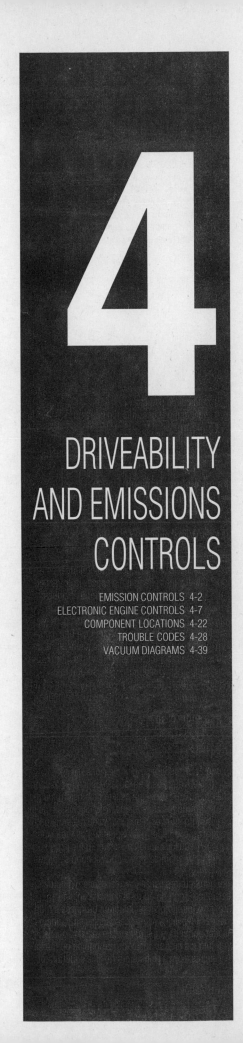

DRIVEABILITY AND EMISSIONS CONTROLS

EMISSION CONTROLS

➧ **See Figures 1, 2, 3, 4, and 5**

Toyota truck emission control systems are installed to reduce the amount of HC, CO and NOx exhausted (Three-Way Catalytic Converter and Sequential Multiport Fuel Injection) from the engine and to prevent the atmospheric release of blow-by gas (Positive Crankcase Ventilation) containing HC and evaporated fuel containing HC from being released from the fuel tank (Evaporative Emission Control).

Positive Crankcase Ventilation System

OPERATION

A closed, positive crankcase ventilation system is employed on all Toyota trucks. This system cycles incompletely burned fuel (which works its way past the piston rings) back into the intake manifold for re-burning with the air/fuel mixture. The oil filler cap is sealed; and the air is drawn from the top of the crankcase into the intake manifold through a valve with a variable orifice.

The recirculation system relies on the integrity of the engine seals. Any air leak around the valve cover, head gasket, oil pan, dipstick, oil filler cap, air intake ducts, vacuum or breather hoses can introduce excess air into the fuel/air mixture, causing rough running or reduced efficiency. Likewise, a plugged hose or passage can cause sludging, stalling and oil leaks.

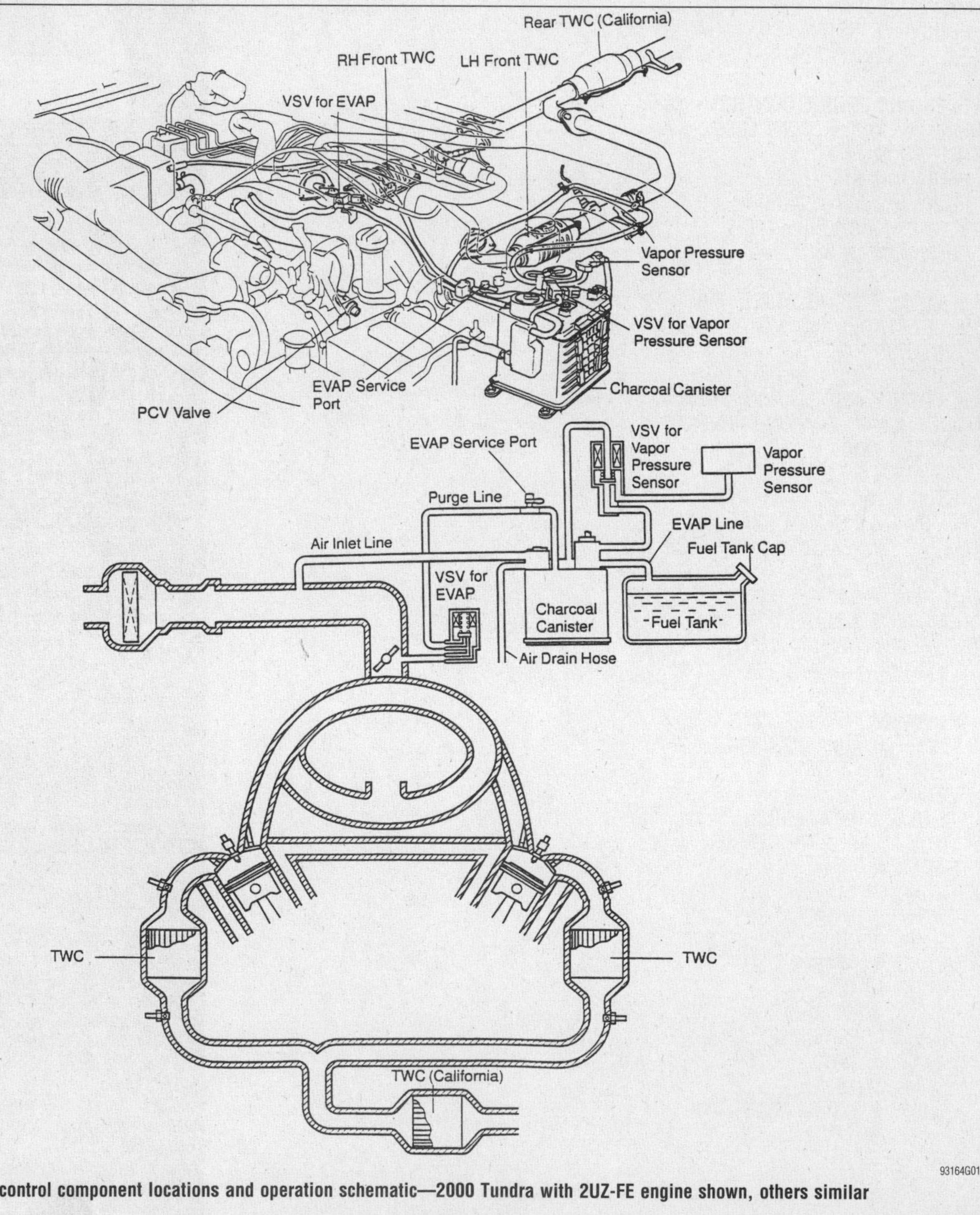

Fig. 1 Emission control component locations and operation schematic—2000 Tundra with 2UZ-FE engine shown, others similar

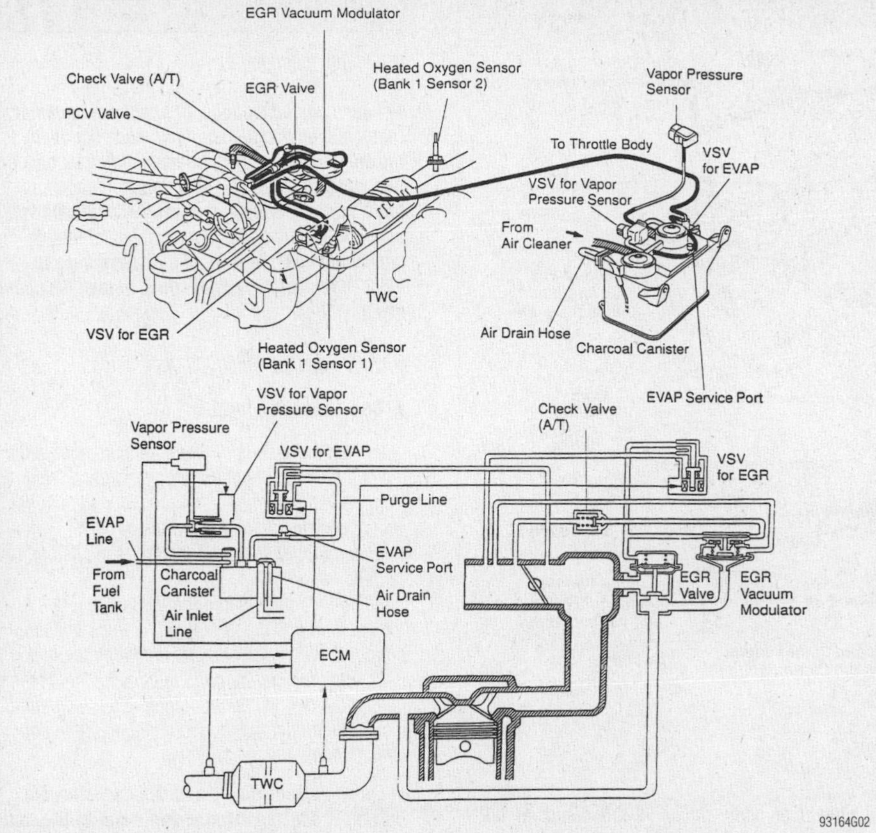

Fig. 2 Emission control component locations and operation schematic—1999 Tacoma with 2RZ-FE, 3RZ-FE engines shown, others similar

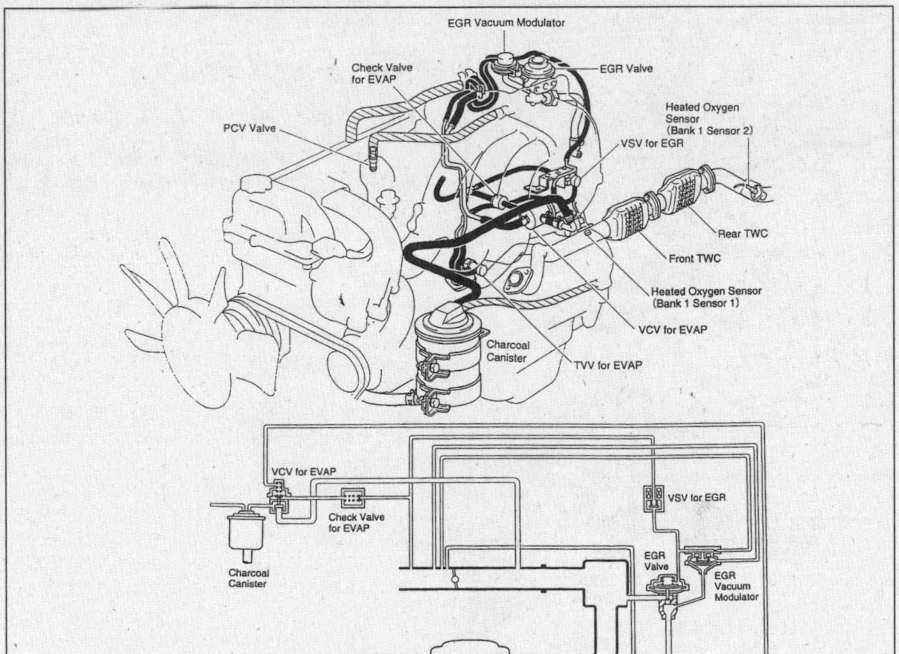

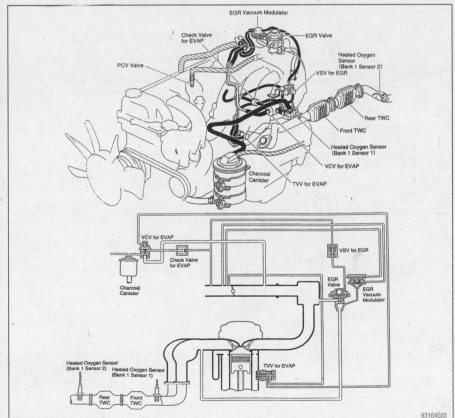

Fig. 3 Emission control component locations and operation schematic—1997 Land Cruiser with 1FZ-FE engine

COMPONENT TESTING

See Figure 6

Inspect the PCV system hoses and connections at each tune-up and replace any deteriorated hoses. Check the PCV valve at every tune-up and replace it at 30,000 mile (48,000 km) intervals.

The PCV valve is easily checked with the engine running at normal idle speed (warmed up).

1. Remove the PCV valve from the valve cover or intake manifold, but leave it connected to its hose.
2. Start the engine.
3. Place your thumb over the end of the valve to check for vacuum. If there is no vacuum, check for plugged hoses or ports. If these are open, the valve is faulty.
4. With the engine **OFF**, remove the valve completely. Shake it end-to-end, listening for the rattle of the needle inside the valve. If no rattle is heard, the needle is jammed (probably due to oil sludge) and the valve should be replaced.

CAUTION

Don't blow directly into the valve; petroleum deposits within the valve can be harmful.

An engine without crankcase ventilation is quickly damaged. It is important to check the PCV at regular intervals. When replacing a PCV valve you must use the correct one for the engine. Many valves look alike on the outside, but have different mechanical values. Putting the incorrect valve on a vehicle can cause a great deal of driveability problems. The engine computer assumes the valve is the correct one and may over adjust the ignition timing or fuel mixture.

REMOVAL & INSTALLATION

See Figure 7

1. Pull the PCV valve from the cylinder head cover or the intake manifold.
2. Remove the hose from the valve.
3. Check the valve for proper operation.
4. Inspect the rubber grommet the PCV valve fits into. If it is in any way deteriorated or oil soaked, replace it.

To install:

5. Insert a new valve into the hose.
6. Push the valve into the rubber grommet. Make sure the valve is firmly into place.

Evaporative Emission Controls

OPERATION

The evaporative emission control system prevents the release of unburned hydrocarbons from the liquid gasoline vapor into the atmosphere. Evaporative fuel vapor from the tank is routed to the charcoal canister located in the engine compartment. The charcoal canister stores the vapor until the engine coolant temperature reaches 129°F (54°C). When the engine coolant temperature is above 129°F (54°C) and the throttle is open, a vacuum switching valve opens to allow vapors trapped in the canister to enter the intake manifold.

A fuel filler cap with a check valve allows air to enter the fuel tank as the fuel is used. This prevents a vacuum build-up in the fuel tank as the engine is running.

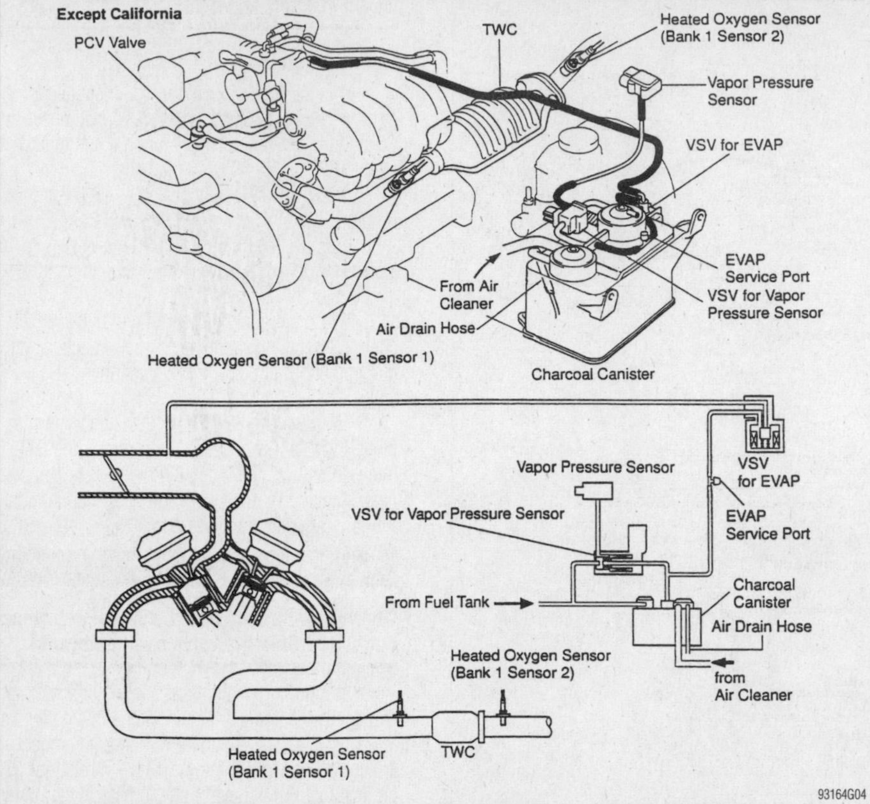

Fig. 4 Emission control component locations and operation schematic—1999 4Runner with 5VZ-FE engine 49-states emissions shown, others similar

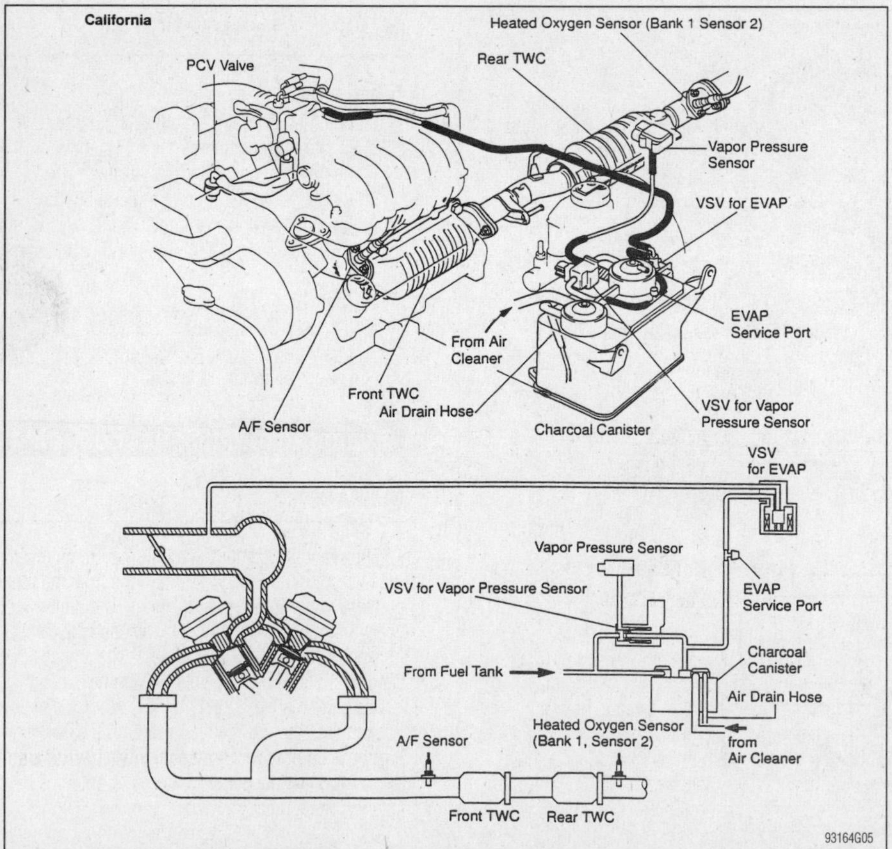

Fig. 5 Emission control component locations and operation schematic—1999 4Runner with 5VZ-FE engine California emissions shown, others similar

COMPONENT TESTING

Charcoal Canister

➡There were two type of charcoal canisters installed on these Toyota trucks. On early model vehicles, the canister only has one or two vacuum hoses. Later model vehicles have canisters with multiple vacuum lines and hoses attached. Regardless of which type your vehicle has, it's always a good idea to tag any vacuum lines before disconnecting them.

EARLY MODEL CANISTERS

▶ See Figures 8 and 9

1. Label and disconnect the vacuum hose at the top of the canister. Remove the charcoal canister from the vehicle.
2. Remove the vacuum switching valve.
3. Look for cracks or damage to the outside of the canister.
4. Using low pressure compressed air ($^1/_2$–1 psi), blow into the tank pipe and check that air flows without any resistance from the other pipes.
5. Blow air into the purge pipe and check that air does not flow from the tank pipe and air flows without resistance from the other pipe. If there is any problems found, replace the canister.

➡Do not attempt to wash the canister. No activated carbon should come out of the canister while cleaning or inspecting the unit. If it does, replace the canister.

6. Install the canister on the vehicle and reconnect the hoses.

LATE MODEL CANISTERS

▶ See Figures 10, 11, 12, 13, and 14

1. Label and disconnect the vacuum hoses at the top of the canister. Remove the charcoal canister from the vehicle.
2. Remove the vacuum switching valve.
3. Look for cracks or damage to the outside of the canister.
4. Install plugs onto ports **A** and **B.**
5. While holding port **C** closed, blow air (about $^1/_4$ psi into port **D** and check that air does not flow from port **F.**
6. Apply vacuum (about 1 in. Hg to port **C,** check that the vacuum does not decrease when port **F** is released.
7. While holding port **F** closed, apply vacuum (about 1 in. Hg) of vacuum to port **D.** Check that the vacuum does not decrease when port **C** is closed, and check that the vacuum decreases when port **C** is released. If a problem occurs, replace the charcoal canister.
8. Remove the plugs.
9. Reinstall the canister.

Exhaust Gas Recirculation (EGR) System

OPERATION

Oxides of nitrogen can be formed under conditions of high pressure and very high temperature. Re-

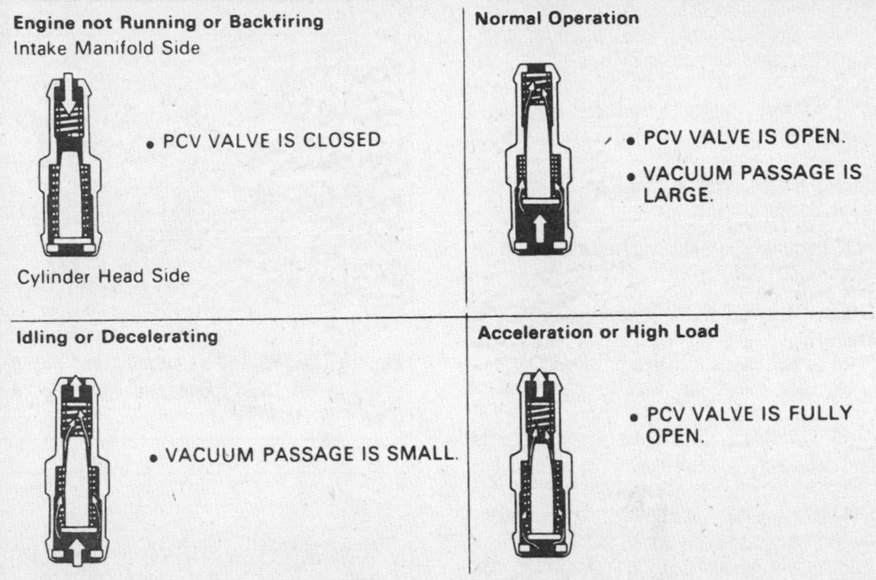

86824P01

Fig. 6 The PCV valve functions differently according to engine operating conditions

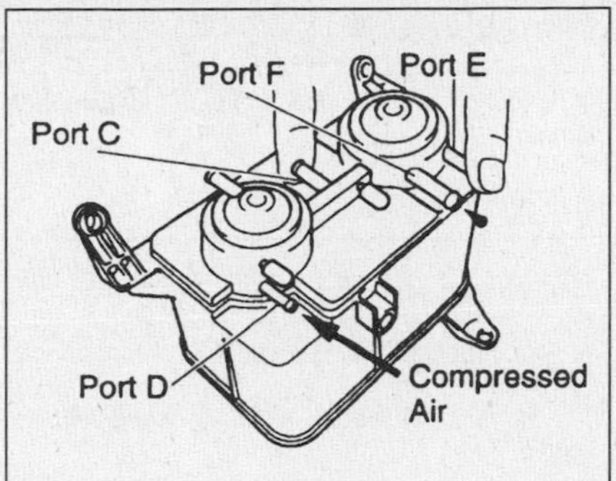

86824P17

Fig. 11 Blow air into port D and check that air does not flow from port F

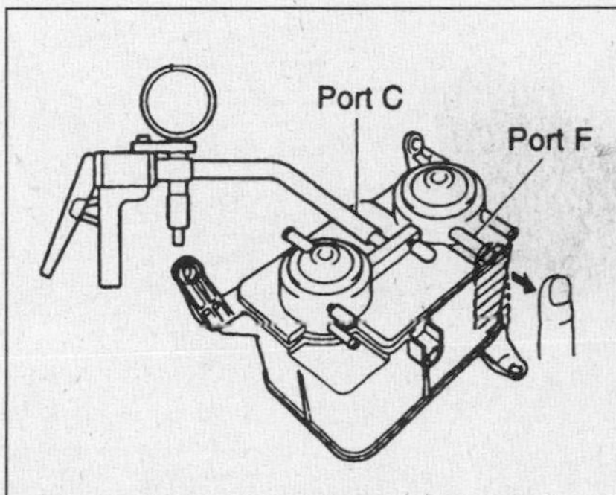

86824P18

Fig. 12 Apply vacuum to port C

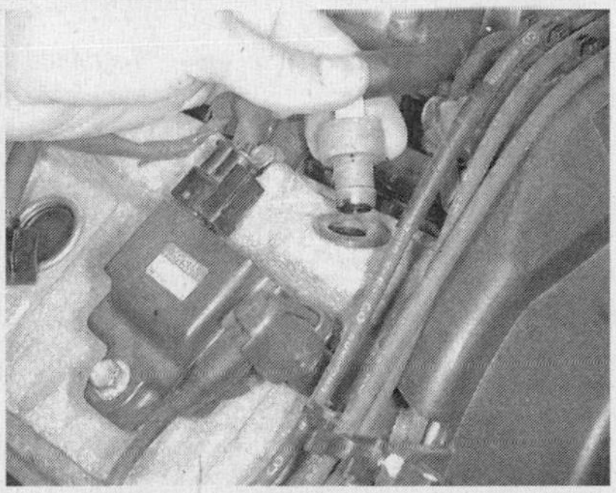

93161pc8

Fig. 7 Pull the PCV valve up and out of the grommet to remove it

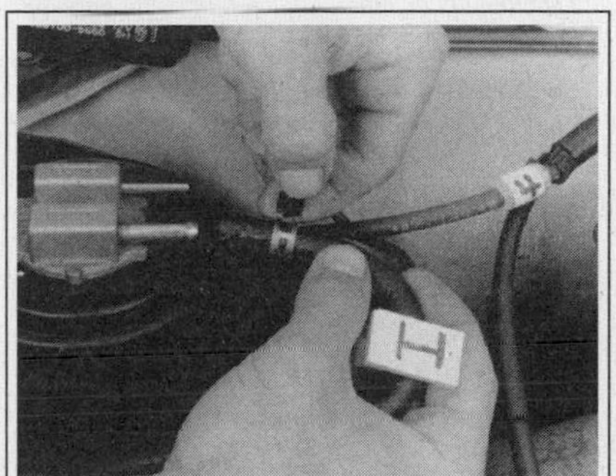

86824P21

Fig. 9 The hoses are easily removed by sliding the clamp off the port end

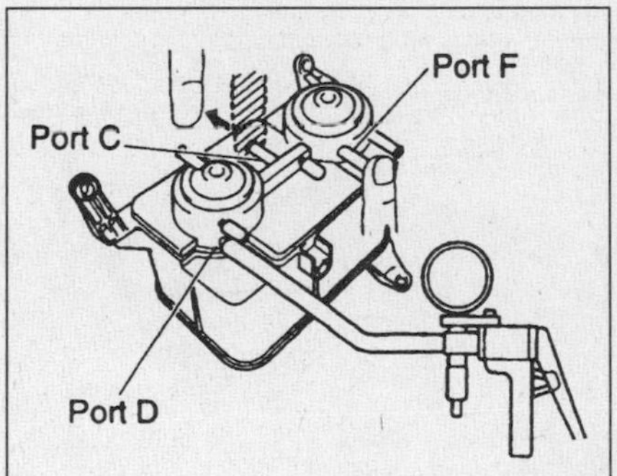

86824P19

Fig. 13 You can use your finger to plug port C

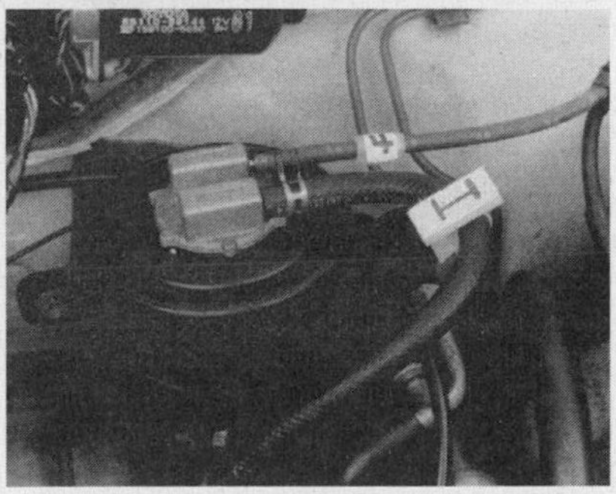

86824P20

Fig. 8 Always label hoses and wires prior to removal—early model charcoal canister shown

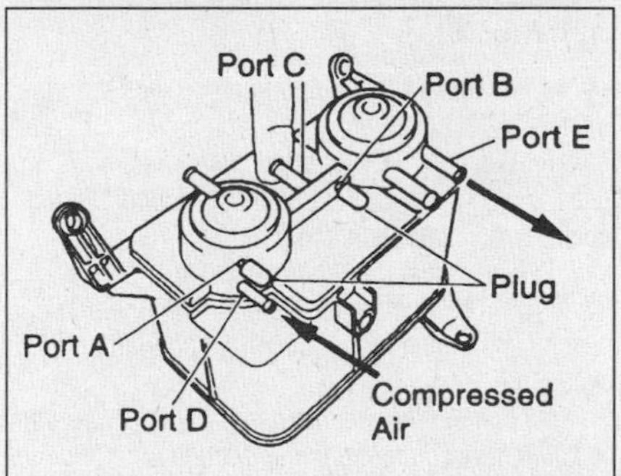

86824P16

Fig. 10 Typical locations of the ports and plugs—3RZ-FE engine shown, 2RZ-FE and 5VZ-FE similar

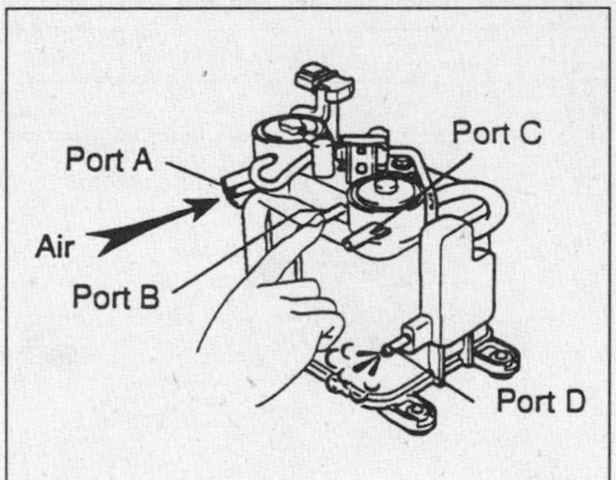

93164G07

Fig. 14 Charcoal canister port identification—2UZ-FE engine

duction of one of these conditions reduces the production of NOx. A reduction of peak combustion temperature is accomplished by recirculating a small amount of exhaust gases into the combustion chamber.

This metering of exhaust gas must be carefully monitored. Too much at the wrong time causes extremely poor driveability; too little and the emissions can increase dramatically. EGR function is overseen by an EGR modulator which controls the flow of vacuum (and therefore the flow of exhaust gasses), limiting it to times when the presence of exhaust gas will not adversely affect the running of the engine. Engines using a Vacuum Solenoid Valve (VSV) have that valve connected to the Engine Control Module (ECM). The computer receives many inputs regarding engine status and temperature; when conditions are favorable, the VSV is activated, allowing EGR function.

Additionally, EGR function is controlled by manifold vacuum so that the valve only operates during periods of high-load or high rpm driving. A binding

EGR valve (either open or closed) can cause stalling, missing or reduced fuel economy.

The 2UZ-FE V8 engine does not use an EGR system.

SYSTEM TESTING

2RZ-FE and 3RZ-FE Engines

➧ See Figures 15, 16, and 17

1. Remove the EGR vacuum modulator cap and filter.
2. Check the filter for damage or contamination.
3. With compressed air, clean the filter.
4. Reinstall the filter and cap. Install the filter with the coarser surface facing the atmospheric side (outwards).
5. Using a 3-way connector, attach a vacuum gauge to the hose between the EGR valve and the EGR vacuum modulator.
6. Start the engine and check that the engine starts and runs at idle.

➡The engine coolant temperature should be below 122°F (20°C).

7. Check that the vacuum gauge indicates zero at 3000 rpm.
8. Check that the EGR pipe is not hot.
9. Remove the 3-way connector with the vacuum hose.
10. Connect the vacuum hose from port **Q** of the EGR modulator to the EGR valve.
11. Plug the hose from the VSV to the EGR.
12. Remove the vacuum gauge, then reconnect the vacuum hoses to their proper locations.
13. Apply vacuum directly to the EGR valve with the engine at idle.
14. Check that the engine now idles rough or stalls.
15. Reconnect the vacuum hoses to their proper locations.

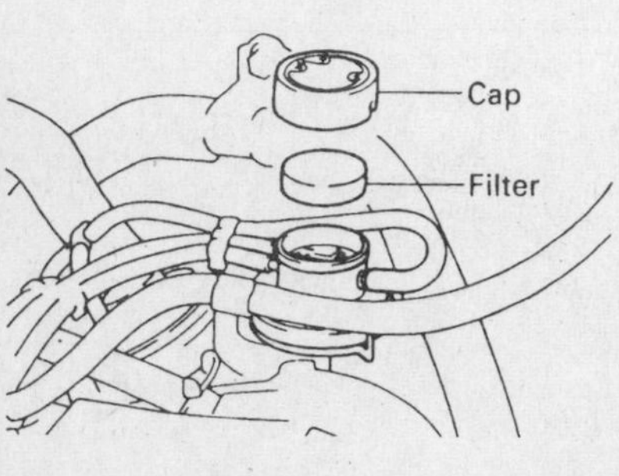

86824P35

Fig. 15 The EGR vacuum modulator filter is directly beneath the cap—2RZ-FE and 3RZ-FE engines

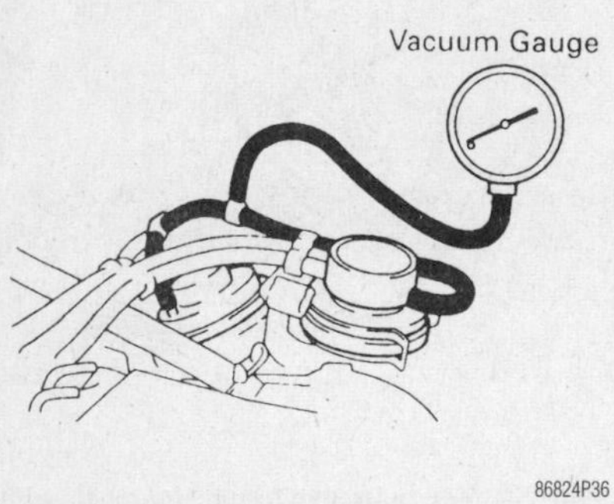

86824P36

Fig. 16 Install a vacuum gauge to the hose between the EGR valve and vacuum modulator—2RZ-FE and 3RZ-FE engines

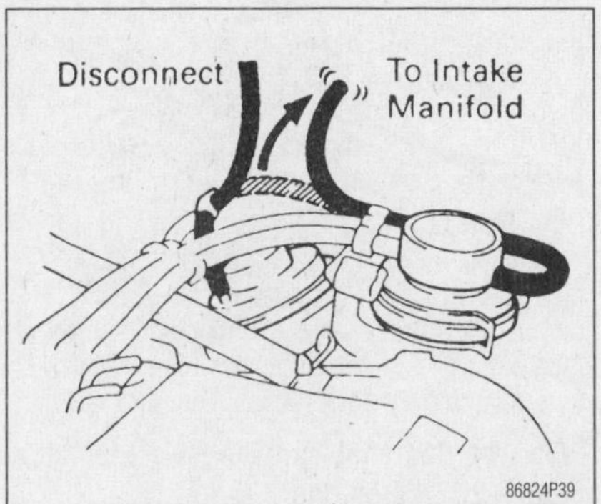

86824P39

Fig. 17 Apply vacuum directly to the EGR valve while the engine is idling—2RZ-FE and 3RZ-FE engines

1FZ-FE Engines

1. Check the filter in the EGR modulator for contamination and clean using compressed air.
2. Using a 3-way connector, connect a vacuum gauge inline between the valve and vacuum pipe. Check that the engine starts and idles smoothly.

➡For accurate system testing, the coolant temperature should be below 117°F (47°C).

3. Accelerate the engine to 2500 rpm and verify that the vacuum gauge reads 0 in. Hg.
4. Check that the EGR pipe is not hot.

➡For accurate test results, the engine coolant temperature must now be above 127°F (53°C)

5. Check that the vacuum gauge reads low vacuum at 2500 rpm.
6. Disconnect the vacuum hose from port **R** of the EGR vacuum modulator and connect port **R** directly to the intake manifold.
7. Check that the vacuum reading is high at 2500 rpm. As large amounts of vacuum enters the engine, the engine idle quality may be adversely affected.
8. Remove the vacuum gauge and reconnect the vacuum hoses in their original locations.
9. Apply vacuum directly to the EGR valve with the engine at idle.
10. If the EGR valve is operating properly, the engine should misfire, run rough and possibly stall. Reconnect the vacuum hoses in their proper locations.

5VZ-FE Engine

➧ See Figures 18 and 19

1. Remove the EGR vacuum modulator cap and filter.
2. Check the filter for damage or contamination.
3. With compressed air, clean the filter.

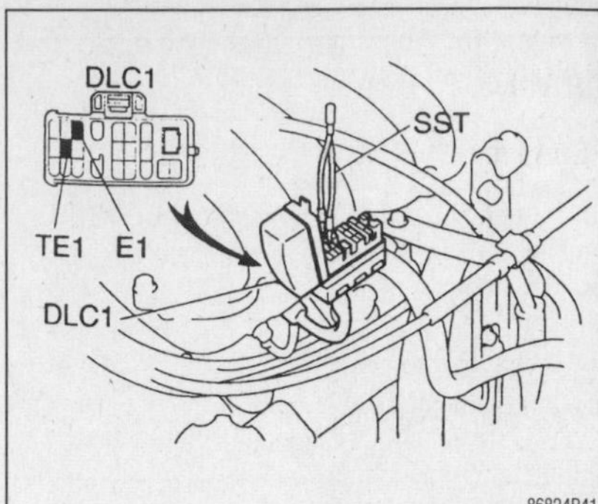

86824P41

Fig. 18 The TE1 and E1 connections are located in the DLC1 connector—5VZ-FE engine

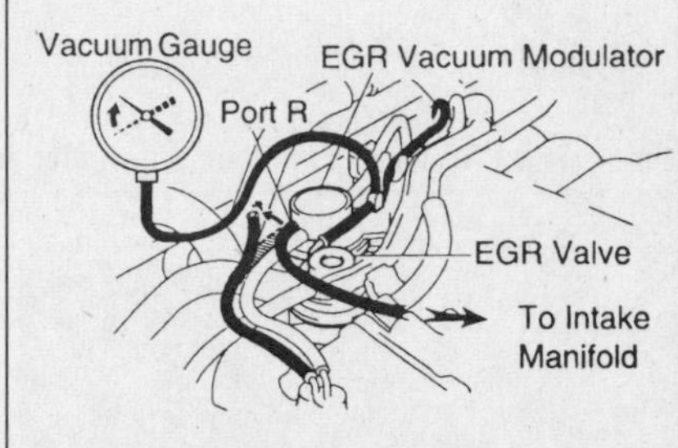

86824P43

Fig. 19 Connect the vacuum gauge as shown—5VZ-FE engine

4. Reinstall the filter and cap. Install the filter with the coarser surface facing the atmospheric side (outwards).
5. Using a 3-way connector, attach a vacuum gauge to the hose between the EGR valve and the VSV.
6. Start the engine and check that the engine starts and runs at idle.
7. Using the SST 09843–18020 or an equivalent jumper wire, connect terminals TE1 and E1 of the DLC1 under the hood.

➡The engine coolant temperature should be below 113°F (45°C).

8. Check that the vacuum gauge indicates zero at 2800 rpm.
9. Check that the EGR pipe is not hot.

➡Allow the engine to run until the coolant temperature is above 176°F (80°C).

10. Check that the vacuum hose gauge reads low vacuum at 2800 rpm.
11. Disconnect the hose from port **R** of the EGR vacuum modulator and connect port **R** directly to the intake manifold with another hose.
12. Check the vacuum gauge, it should read high vacuum at 3500 rpm.
13. Disconnect terminals TE1 and E1 by removing the jumper wire.
14. Remove the vacuum gauge, and reconnect the vacuum hoses to their proper locations.
15. Apply vacuum directly to the EGR valve with the engine at idle.
16. Check that the engine idles rough or stalls.

REMOVAL & INSTALLATION

EGR Valve

See Figures 20 and 21

1. Disconnect the EGR pipe, discard the gasket.
2. Label and disconnect the vacuum hoses, EGR hose, water bypass hoses from the IAC valve and water bypass pipe.
3. Some models have an EGR sensor, remove the screws attaching this if applicable.
4. Remove the 2 nuts holding the valve to the engine. Discard the old gasket.
5. Inspect the valve for sticking and heavy carbon deposits.

To install:

6. With a new gasket, mount the valve to the engine. Tighten the mounting nuts to 14 ft. lbs. (19 Nm).
7. Install the EGR sensor if removed.
8. Attach the EGR pipe with a new gasket.
9. Attach the labeled hoses to their proper locations.
10. Start the vehicle and check for any leaks.

EGR Vacuum Modulator

1. Label and disconnect the hoses attached to the modulator.
2. Loosen and remove the nut holding the tube from the modulator to the EGR valve.
3. Remove the modulator.
4. Check the hoses for signs of deterioration and replace as necessary.

To install:

5. Install the modulator and tighten the nut securely.
6. Connect the vacuum hoses.

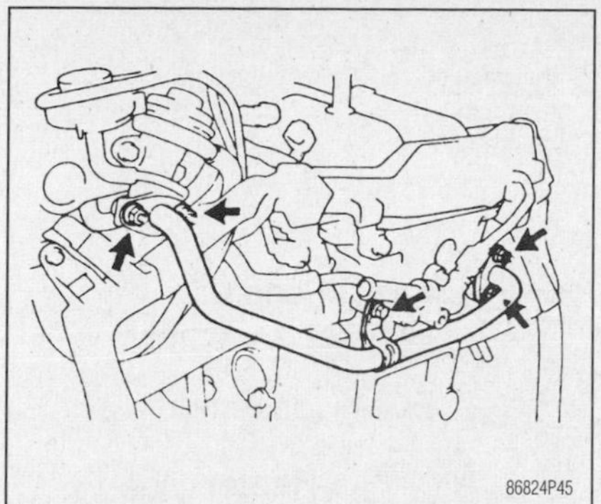

Fig. 20 Detach the EGR pipe from the valve and mounting points on the engine

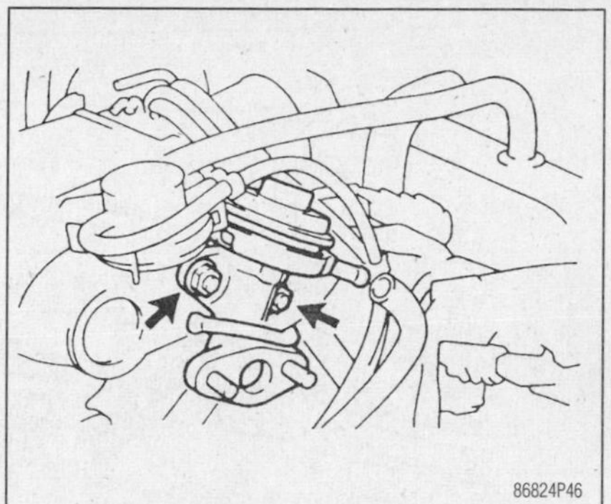

Fig. 21 Remove the two mounting nuts retaining the valve to the engine

Catalytic Converter

OPERATION

The catalytic converter is a muffler-like container built into the exhaust system to aid in the reduction of exhaust emissions. When the exhaust gases come into contact with the catalyst, a chemical reaction occurs which reduces the pollutants into harmless substances such as water and carbon dioxide.

On the Toyota trucks covered by this manual, a three-way catalytic converter is used.

PRECAUTIONS

- Use only unleaded fuel.
- Avoid prolonged idling; the engine should run no longer than 20 min. at curb idle and no longer than 10 min. at fast idle.
- Don't disconnect any of the spark plug leads while the engine is running. If any engine testing procedure requires disconnecting or bypassing a control component, perform the procedure as quickly as possible. A miss-firing engine can overheat the catalyst and damage the oxygen sensor.
- Whenever under the vehicle or around the catalytic converter, remember that it has a very high outside or skin temperature. During operation, the catalyst reach high temperatures to work efficiently. Be very wary of burns, even after the engine has been shut off for a while. Additionally, because of the heat, never park the vehicle on or over flammable materials, particularly dry grass or leaves. Inspect the heat shields frequently and correct any bends or damage.

ELECTRONIC ENGINE CONTROLS

Electronic Control Module (ECM)

OPERATION

The Electronic Control Module (ECM) is the vehicle's on-board computer, the center of the vehicle's electronic control system. The ECM receives signals from various sensors on the engine. The ECM constantly looks at the information from these sensors, processes this information and calculates the correct air/fuel mixture, ignition spark timing and controls the systems that affect vehicle performance.

The ECM also performs the diagnostic function of the system. It can recognize operational problems, alert the driver through the MIL (Malfunction Indicator Lamp, also known as the Service Engine Soon light), and store Diagnostic Trouble Codes (DTCs) which identify the problem areas to aid the technician in making repairs.

Current systems, including the Toyota trucks covered by this manual, use a next-generation system called On Board Diagnostics II (OBD II). This makes available a great deal of information to the service technician. A specialized piece of equipment called a Scan Tool is connected to vehicle's Diagnostic Connector. The scan tool can then read the data stream from the ECM, interrogate the computer for stored DTCs, even obtain a freeze-frame (snapshot) of the vehicle's operating conditions when a DTC is set. While the computer can't tell a technician which component to replace, it can narrow down which system or circuit may require attention, and read real-time operating temperatures, voltages and resistance values of various sensors. A scan tool connected to the vehicle's on-board computer can even take over control of some systems during troubleshooting (fuel pump control, for example).

While an OBD II compliant system may make more information available that can be very helpful when troubleshooting, it also means that traditional methods of troubleshooting have changed. In almost every case, an expensive scan tool is required along with the experience and expertise to interpret the data being presented. This takes most all electronic engine control diagnostics and troubleshooting out of the hands of the non-professional.

The inexperienced and ill-equipped can cause a great deal of damage to any automotive computer controlled system. Due to the very small voltages and resistances involved with the computer and its related sensors and controls, using traditional testing methods such as test lights and voltmeters can cause such a relatively large electrical draw that costly electronic components can and will be damaged. On the other hand, a good circuit producing its designed output voltage (for example, very small voltages, usually in the millivolt range) may not be producing enough voltage to light a test light or move an analog meter needle, giving a false indication of circuit or component failure when it actually is within its operating parameters.

The ECM itself is a relatively fragile and expensive component. Always follow these precautions when servicing the electronic control system.

PRECAUTIONS

- To prevent possible Electrostatic Discharge damage to the ECM, DO NOT touch the connector pins or the soldered components on any circuit board.
- To prevent internal ECM damage, make sure the ignition switch is in the **OFF** position when installing or removing the PCM connectors and disconnecting or reconnecting the power to the ECM (battery cable, ECM wiring, jumper cables, etc.).
- Do not permit parts to receive a severe impact during removal or installation. Always handle all fuel injection parts with care, especially the ECM. DO NOT open the ECM cover!
- Before removing the fuel injected wiring connectors, terminals, or any other electric component, first disconnect the power by either disconnecting the negative battery cable or turning the ignition switch **OFF**.

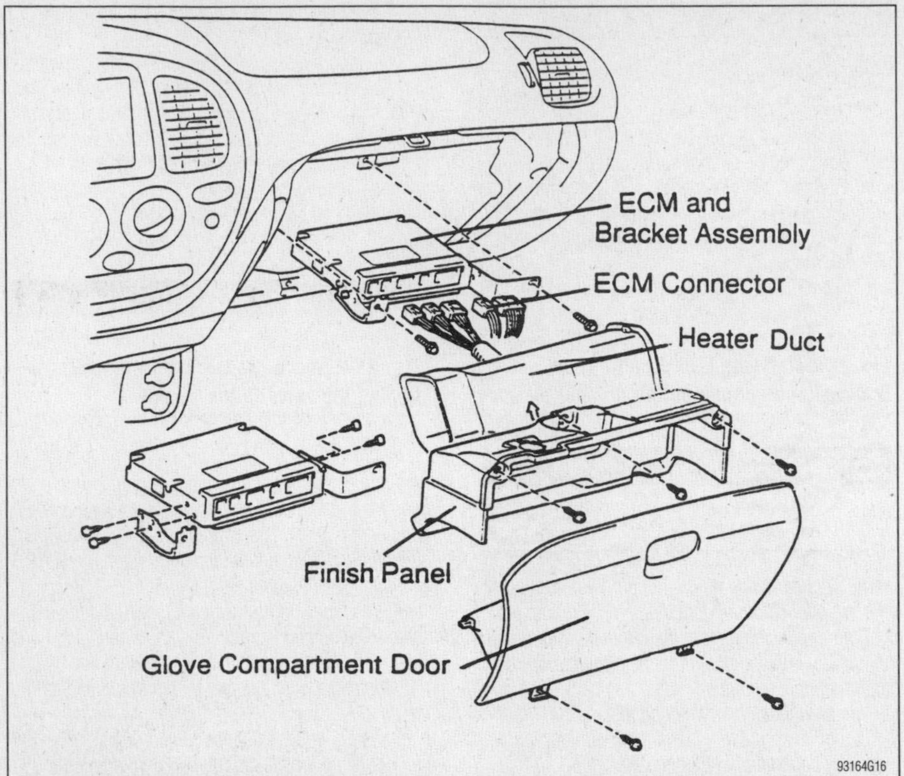

Fig. 22 The ECM is usually found behind the glove box—2000 Tundra shown, others similar

- Do not be careless during troubleshooting. There are numerous transistorized circuits. Even a slight terminal contact can induce a problem into the system.
- Use care when detaching and attaching electrical connectors. Release the lock and pull on the connectors. At assembly, fully insert the connector and check that it is locked.

REMOVAL & INSTALLATION

See Figure 22

1. Disconnect the negative battery cable.
2. Disconnect the negative battery cable.
3. Remove the glove compartment door.
4. Remove the glove compartment frame (Toyota calls it the Lower No. 2 Finish Panel).
5. Some vehicles may have a heater duct or other component that should be removed.
6. Unbolt the ECM from its brackets.
7. Carefully detach the electrical connectors.

To install:

8. Carefully attach the electrical connectors.
9. Install the ECM mounting brackets, as required.
10. Mount the ECM on the vehicle in the proper location.
11. Install the remaining components including the finish panel and glove compartment door.
12. Connect the negative battery cable.

Oxygen Sensor (O2S)

➡Handle any oxygen sensor with care. Protect the end of the sensor from shock. The sensor can be easily damaged by impact or rough handling. Many technicians feel that 'A dropped sensor is a bad sensor.' Additionally, do not allow the sensor to come in contact with water or petroleum products.

OPERATION

See Figure 23

To control emissions of Hydrocarbons (HC), Carbon Monoxide (CO), and Oxides of Nitrogen (NOx), your Toyota truck is equipped with three-way catalytic converters. The catalyst within the converter promotes a chemical reaction which oxidizes the HC and CO present in the exhaust gas, converting them into harmless water vapor and carbon dioxide. The catalyst also reduces NOx, converting it to nitrogen. To get the most efficient operation from the converter, the air-fuel ratio must be precisely controlled so it is always near the ideal air-fuel ratio. The ECM has the ability to monitor this process using the oxygen sensor mounted in front (upstream) of the converter and the oxygen sensor mounted after (downstream) of the converter.

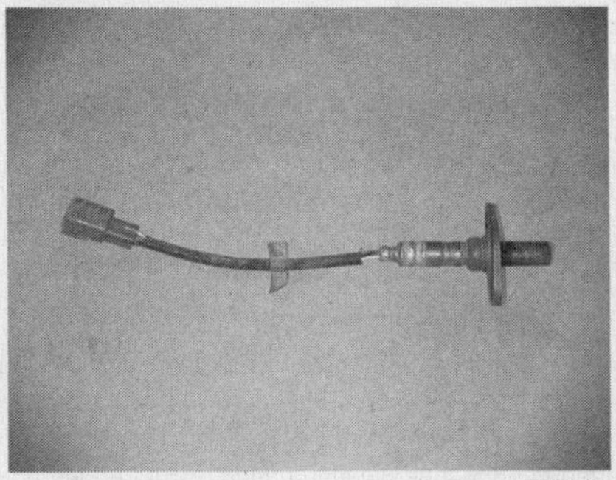

Fig. 23 Common Toyota Oxygen Sensor (O2S)

The oxygen sensor produces an output voltage that varies with the oxygen content of the exhaust stream. A small electrical signal is generated and input to the ECM. This informs the ECM of the oxygen content (air-fuel ratio) in the exhaust. If the air-fuel ratio is lean, the oxygen content in the exhaust increases and the oxygen sensor output will be low (near zero volts). If the air-fuel ratio is richer than ideal, the oxygen content will be less and the oxygen sensor output will be higher (near one volt). The ECM then calculates the proper duration of fuel injector opening. The oxygen sensor voltage can be monitored with a scan tool

The oxygen sensor is a primary input to the ECM. Like most all sensor inputs and outputs on computer controlled engines, the voltages are very small. The components, wiring and especially the connectors must be protected from damage.

Your Toyota truck uses Heated Oxygen Sensors (HO2S). A heater, controlled by the ECM, warms the Zirconia element. This helps the system operate more efficiently at low temperatures when the engine is first started.

Toyota trucks can use up to four HO2S sensors, depending on the engine. Some sensors thread into their mounts, others are retained by two studs and nuts. HO2S sensors are typically installed before and after the catalyst. The front, or upstream sensor produces an output signal which indicates the amount of oxygen present in the exhaust gas entering the three-way converter. The rear (downstream) sensor produces an output signal which indicates the oxygen storage capacity of the catalyst; this, in turn, indicates the catalyst's ability to convert exhaust gases efficiently. If the catalyst is operating efficiently, the upstream signal will be far more active than that produced by the downstream sensor.

The ECM compares the waveform of the sensor before the catalyst (upstream) with the waveform of the sensor after the catalyst (downstream) to determine whether or not the catalyst performance has deteriorated. Air-fuel ratio feedback compensation keeps the waveform of the oxygen sensor before the catalyst repeatedly changing back and forth from rich to lean. If the catalyst is functioning normally, the waveform of the sensor after the catalyst switches back and forth between rich and lean much more slowly than the waveform before the catalyst. If both waveforms change at a similar rate, it indicates that catalyst performance has deteriorated.

A failed HO2S sensor should set a Diagnostic Trouble Code (DTC).

TESTING

1. Start the engine and bring it to normal operating temperature, then run the engine above 1200 rpm for two minutes.
2. Backprobe with a high impedance averaging voltmeter (set to the DC voltage scale) between the Oxygen Sensor (O2S) and battery ground.
3. Verify that the O2S voltage fluctuates rapidly between 0.40–0.60 volts.
4. If the O2S voltage is stabilized at the middle of the specified range (approximately 0.45–0.55 volts) or if the O2S voltage fluctuates very slowly between the specified range (O2S signal crosses 0.5 volts less than 5 times in ten seconds), the O2S may be faulty.
5. If the O2S voltage stabilizes at either end of the specified range, the ECM is probably not able to compensate for a mechanical problem such as a vacuum leak or a leaking fuel injector. These types of

mechanical problems will cause the O2S to sense a constant lean or constant rich mixture. The mechanical problem will first have to be repaired, then the O2S test repeated.

6. Pull a vacuum hose located after the throttle plate. Voltage should drop to approximately 0.12 volts (while still fluctuating rapidly). This tests the ability of the O2S to detect a lean mixture condition. Reattach the vacuum hose.

7. Richen the mixture using a propane enrichment tool. Voltage should rise to approximately 0.90 volts (while still fluctuating rapidly). This tests the ability of the O2S to detect a rich mixture condition.

8. If the O2S voltage is above or below the specified range, the O2S and/or the O2S wiring may be faulty. Check the wiring for any breaks, repair as necessary and repeat the test.

REMOVAL & INSTALLATION

➧ **See Figures 24 thru 32**

1. Disconnect the negative battery cable.
2. Ensure that the engine and exhaust pipes are cold. Locate the oxygen sensor in question. There should be one in front of the catalytic converter and another behind the catalytic converter. Vehicles with dual front pipes will have four oxygen sensors, depending on the engine.
3. Some oxygen sensors thread into the pipe, others mount with two studs and nuts. Spray penetrating oil on the studs to ease removal.
4. Detach the oxygen sensor wiring.
5. Remove the oxygen sensor retaining nuts, if used, or with a suitable wrench, unscrew the sensor if it is the thread-mount type.
6. Remove the oxygen sensor and gasket.

To install:

7. Install the oxygen sensor with a new gasket. If a thread-type sensor, apply an even coat of anti-seize compound only to the threads. If a stud-mount type sensor, apply a coating of anti-seize compound to the mounting studs. Install the nuts and tighten to 14 ft. lbs. (20 Nm).
8. Connect the oxygen sensor wiring.
9. Connect the negative battery cable.

Idle Air Control (IAC) Valve

OPERATION

The purpose of the Idle Air Control (IAC) system is to control engine idle speed while preventing stalls

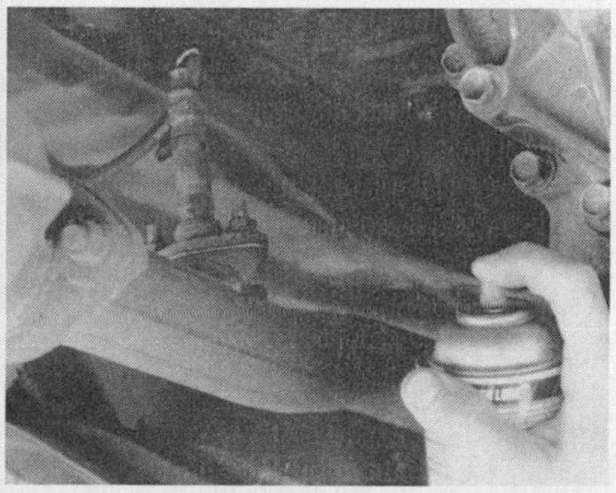

86824P87

Fig. 24 This O2 sensor is mounted with two studs and nuts. Use a penetrating oil to ease the removal of the mounting nuts

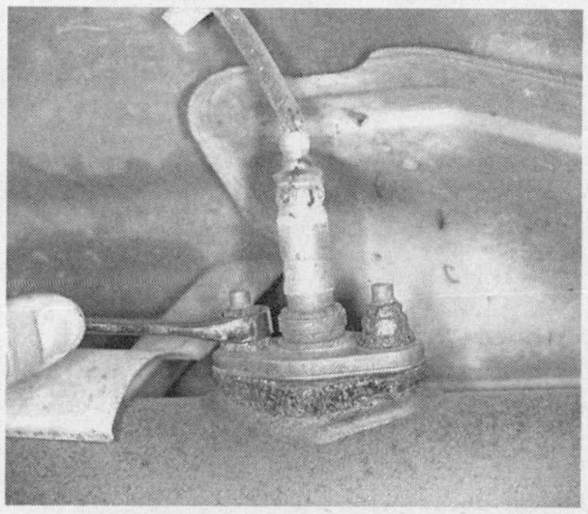

93164p12

Fig. 25 Use a closed end wrench to remove the mounting nuts

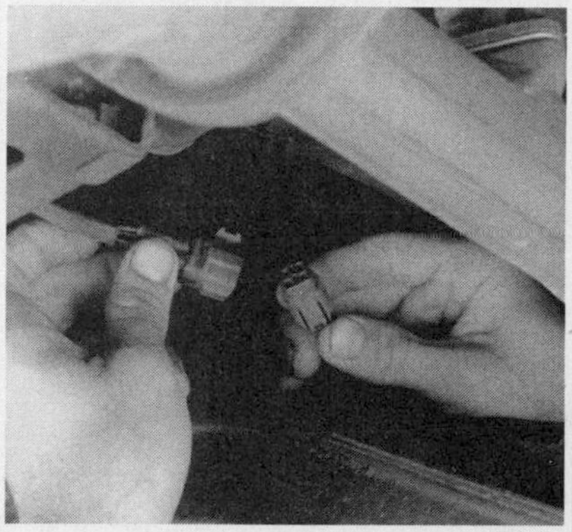

86824P85

Fig. 26 Unplug the O2 sensor harness

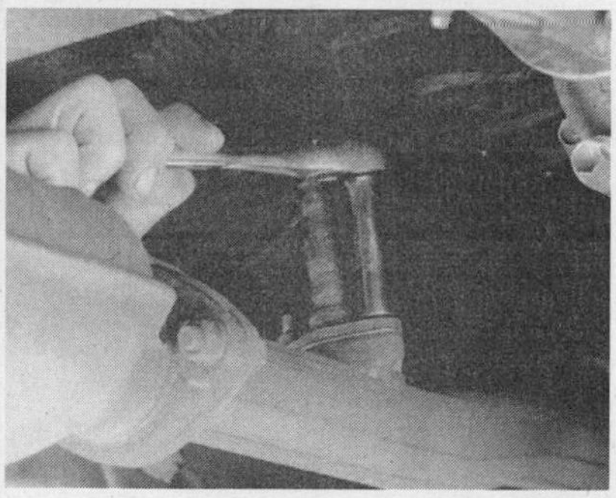

86824p86

Fig. 27 It may be necessary to use a deep socket to remove the mounting nuts

93164p11

Fig. 28 Remove the sensor from the pipe

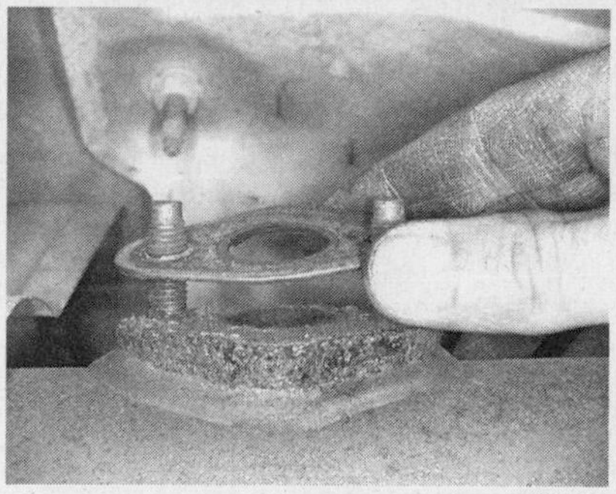

93164p09

Fig. 29 Remove the gasket from the studs . . .

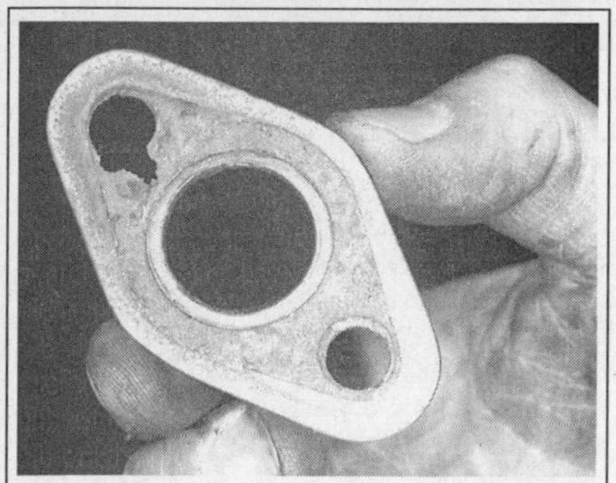

93164p08

Fig. 30 . . then discard the gasket and replace with a new one during installation

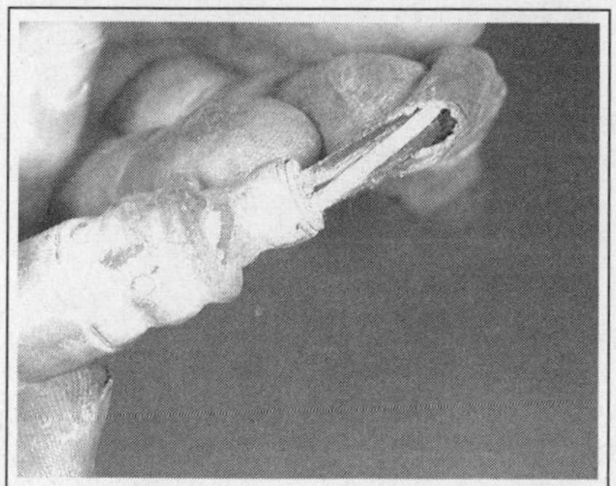

93164p04

Fig. 31 Most Toyota oxygen sensors are of the four wire type

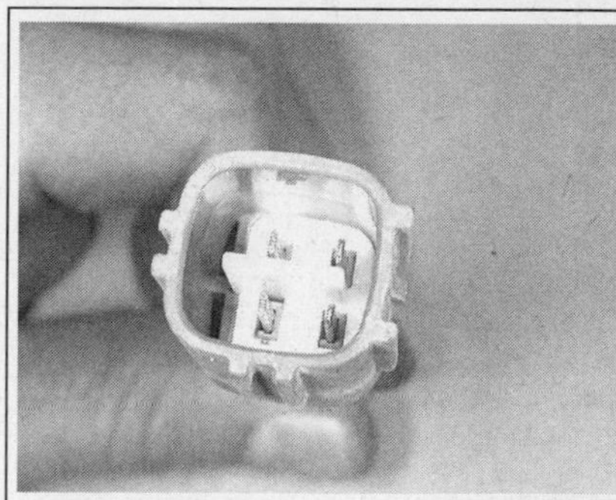

93164p05

Fig. 32 Typical Toyota oxygen sensor wiring harness

due to changes in engine load. The IAC assembly, mounted on the throttle body, controls bypass air around the throttle plate.

During idle, the proper position of the IAC valve is calculated by the ECM based on battery voltage, coolant temperature, engine load, and engine rpm. If the rpm drops below a specified rate, the throttle plate is closed. The ECM will then calculate a new valve position.

The IAC only affects the engine's idle characteristics. If it is stuck fully open, idle speed is too high (too much air enters the throttle bore) If it is stuck closed, idle speed is too low (not enough air entering). If it is stuck somewhere in the middle, idle may be rough, and the engine won't respond to load changes.

On the 1FZ-FE engine, idle air control is by a stepper motor type IAC valve located in front of the air intake chamber. Intake air bypassing the throttle valve is directed to the IAC valve through a passage. The stepper motor consists of four coils, a magnetic rotor, valve shaft and valve. When current flows to the coils due to signals from the ECM, the rotor turns and moves the valve shaft forward or backward, changing the clearance between the valve and the valve seat. In this way, the intake air volume bypassing the throttle valve is regulated, controlling the engine speed. On this engine, there are 125 possible positions to which the valve can be opened.

✱ On the 2RZ-FE, 3RZ-FE and 5VZ-FE engines, a rotary solenoid type IAC valve is located in front of the intake air chamber and intake air bypassing the throttle valve is directed to the IAC valve through a passage, controlling the engine idle speed. The ECM operates only the IAC valve to perform idle-up and provide feedback for the target idling speed.

On the 2UZ-FE engine, the idle speed is controlled by the Electric Throttle Control System (ETCS). It does not use an IAC valve. ETCS is composed of the throttle motor to operate the throttle valve, the magnetic clutch to connect the throttle motor with the throttle valve, the throttle position sensor to detect the opening angle of the throttle valve, the accelerator pedal position sensor to detect the accelerator pedal position, the ECM to control the ETCS and the one valve type throttle body. The ECM controls the throttle motor to make the throttle valve opening angle properly for the target idle speed. If the electric throttle control system malfunctions, the magnetic clutch separates the throttle motor from the throttle valve as a safety disconnect. The ECM shuts down power for the throttle motor and the magnetic clutch and the throttle valve is closed by the return spring. The throttle can still be controlled by the accelerator pedal through the throttle cable.

TESTING

Except 1FZ-FE Engine

➧ See Figures 33 and 34

1. Using an ohmmeter, measure the resistance between terminal +B and other terminals (RSC and RSO). It should read between 17.0–24.5 ohms.
2. Connect the positive lead from the battery to terminal +B and negative lead to RSC, then check that the valve is closed.
3. Connect the positive lead from the battery to terminal +B and negative lead to RSO, then check that the valve is open.

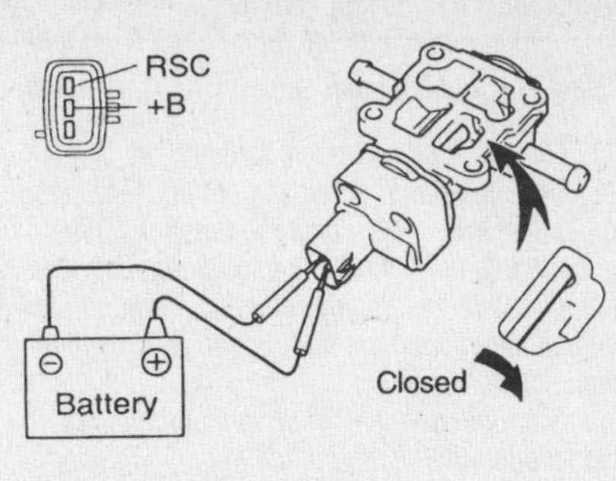

Fig. 33 With battery voltage applied as shown, the valve should be closed

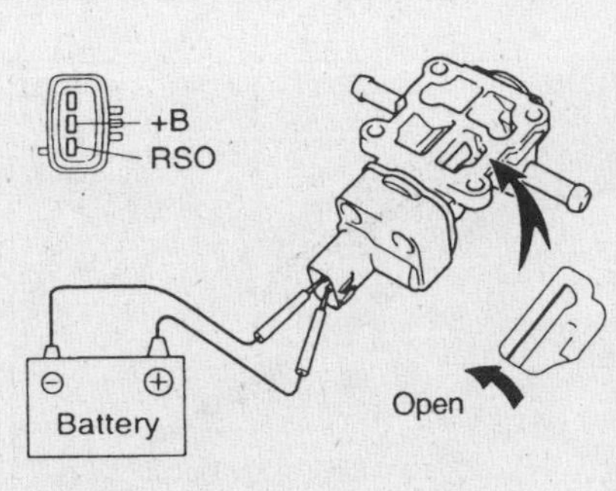

Fig. 34 The valve should open when connected as shown

4. If the valve did not perform as indicated, replace the IAC valve.

1FZ-FE Engine

➧ See Figures 35 and 36

1. Remove the IAC valve.
2. Apply battery voltage to terminals B1 and B2. Then, apply ground to terminals S1, S2, S3, S4 and S1 in sequence. Check that the valve moves towards the closed position.
3. Apply ground to terminals S4, S3, S2, S1 and S4 in sequence. Check that the valve moves towards the open position.
4. If the valve does not function as indicated, it may be necessary to replace the IAC valve.
5. Install the IAC valve.

REMOVAL & INSTALLATION

➧ See Figure 37

1. Drain the coolant to a level below the throttle body.
2. Remove the throttle body.
3. Remove the screws and the IAC valve. Discard the old gasket or O-ring.

To install:

4. Using a new gasket or O-ring, attach the IAC valve and secure the mounting screws.
5. Install the throttle body with new gaskets.
6. Fill the cooling system with the proper water/coolant mixture.
7. Start the engine, top off the cooling system. Check for leaks.

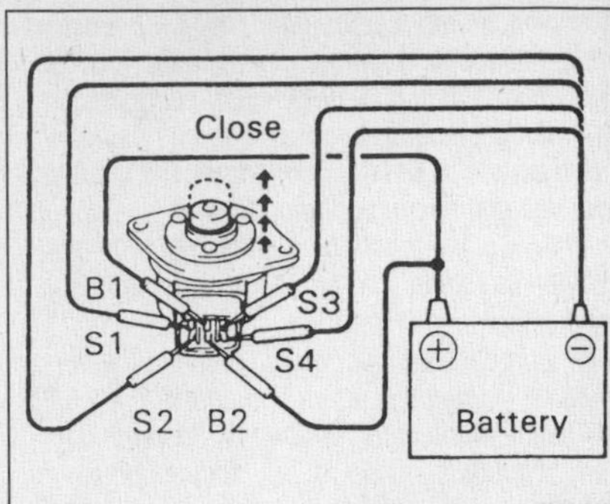

Fig. 35 The valve should close when connected like this—1FZ-FE engine

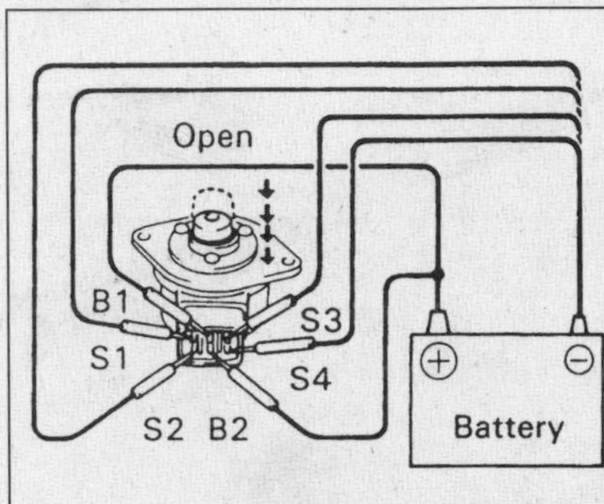

Fig. 36 The valve should open when connected like this—1FZ-FE engine

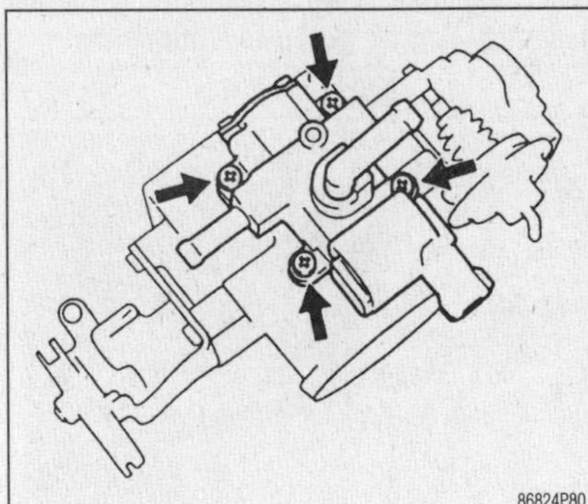

Fig. 37 Remove the screws mounting the IAC valve to the throttle body

Engine Coolant Temperature (ECT) Sensor

OPERATION

The Engine Coolant Temperature (ECT) sensor is a thermistor (a resistor which changes resistance value based on temperature) mounted in the engine coolant stream. As the temperature of the engine coolant changes, the resistance of the coolant sensor changes. Low coolant temperature produces a high resistance: 100,000 ohms at –40°F (–40°C). High temperature causes low resistance: 70 ohms at 284°F (140°C).

The ECM supplies a 5 volt signal to the coolant sensor and measures the voltage that returns. By measuring the voltage change, the ECM determines the engine coolant temperature. The voltage will be high when the engine is cold and low when the engine is hot. This information is used to control fuel management, IAC, spark timing, EGR, canister purge and other engine operating conditions.

TESTING

▸ See Figures 38 and 39

1. Remove the ECT sensor from the engine.
2. Fill a clean container with water and measure its temperature.
3. Place the sensor tip into the water. Measure the resistance of the ECT sensor with an ohmmeter. Compare the resistance with the temperature as per the graph.
4. If it is not within specifications, replace the sensor.
5. Install the ECT sensor.

REMOVAL & INSTALLATION

1FZ-FE, 2RZ-FE and 3RZ-FE Engines

1. Drain the engine cooling system.
2. Disconnect the engine wire protector from the brackets if used.
3. Detach the ECT sensor wiring.
4. Using a deep socket, remove the ECT sensor and gasket.

To install:

5. Using a new gasket and deep socket, install the ECT sensor. Tighten to 14 ft. lbs. (20 Nm).
6. Connect the ECT wiring to the sensor.
7. Install the engine wire protector to the brackets if used.
8. Fill the cooling system, start the engine, top off the system.

5VZ-FE Engine

1. Drain the engine cooling system.
2. Disconnect the upper radiator hose from the water outlet.
3. Disconnect the power steering air hose from the clamp.
4. Disconnect the three cord clamps of the spark plug wires from the belt cover.
5. Remove the mounting bolts for the timing belt cover and gasket.
6. Disconnect the camshaft position sensor harness.
7. Remove the fuel pipe.
8. Disconnect the ECT sensor harness.
9. Using a 19mm deep socket, remove the sensor and gasket.

To install:

10. Using a new gasket and deep socket, install the ECT sensor. Tighten to 14 ft. lbs. (20 Nm).
11. Connect the ECT wiring to the sensor.
12. Reinstall the fuel pipe with four new gaskets, tighten to 25 ft. lbs. (34 Nm).
13. Attach the timing belt cover, tighten to 80 inch lbs. (9 Nm).
14. Reconnect the upper radiator hose to the water outlet.
15. Fill the cooling system, start the engine, top off. Check for leaks.

2UZ-FE Engine

▸ See Figure 40

1. Drain the engine coolant.
2. Remove the cosmetic/acoustic throttle body cover
3. Remove the air intake connector elbow from the throttle body. There are several vacuum hoses which should be tagged for identification before removal, if required.
4. Remove the throttle body from the intake manifolds using the following as a guide:
   a. Disconnect the accelerator cable from the throttle body.
   b. Remove the two bolts and two nuts and separate the throttle body from the intake.
   c. Discard the gasket. A new gasket will be required at assembly.
5. Detach the electrical connector from the ECT. Remove the ECT sensor. It should have an O-ring seal which is discarded. A new seal will be required at assembly.

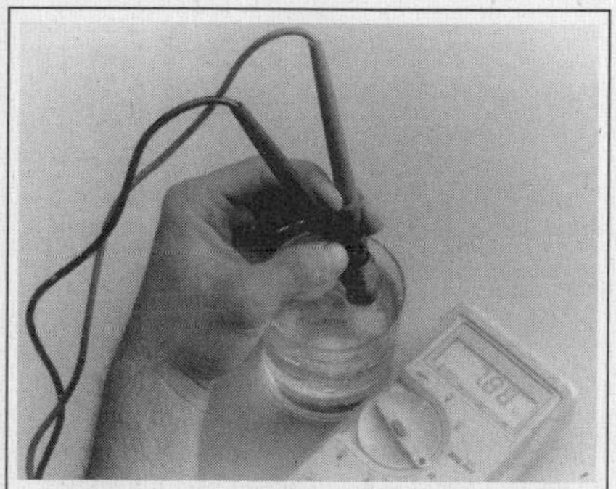

TCCS4P02

Fig. 38 Submerge the end of the temperature sensor in cold or hot water and check resistance

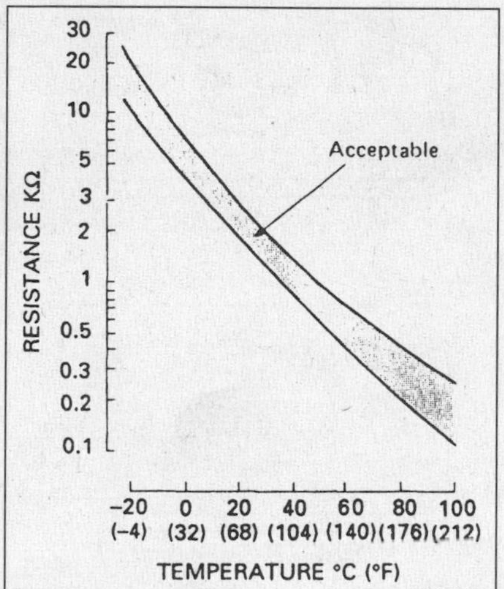

86824P90

Fig. 39 Temperature sensor resistance graph

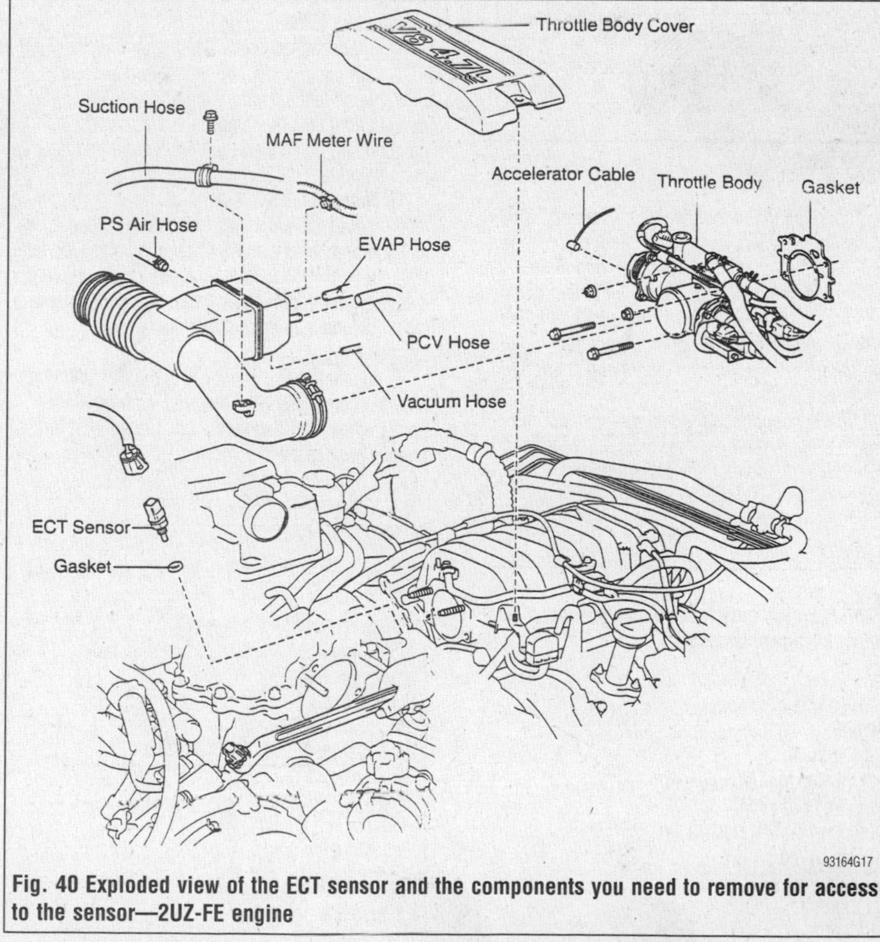

93164G17

Fig. 40 Exploded view of the ECT sensor and the components you need to remove for access to the sensor—2UZ-FE engine

To install:

6. Using a new seal, install the ECT sensor. Tighten to 15 ft. lbs. (20 Nm). Attach the electrical connector.
7. Using a new gasket, install the throttle body to the intake manifold. Tighten the nuts and bolts to 13 ft. lbs. (18 Nm). Connect the throttle cable.
8. Install the intake air connector and attach the vacuum lines that were removed.
9. Refill the cooling system with approved coolant.
10. Install the start the engine and check for leaks.
11. Install the cosmetic/acoustic throttle body cover.

Intake Air Temperature (IAT) Sensor

OPERATION

The Intake Air Temperature (IAT) is a thermistor built into the air flow meter or is mounted on the air cleaner housing. A thermistor is a resistor which changes resistance value based intake air temperature. Low manifold air temperature produces a high resistance: 100,000 ohms at −40°F (–40°C). High temperature cause low resistance: 70 ohms at 284°F (140°C).

The ECM supplies a 5 volt power source voltage to the IAT sensor through a resistor in the ECM and monitors the voltage. The voltage will be high when the manifold air is cold and low when the air is hot. By monitoring the voltage, the ECM calculates the air temperature and uses this data to help determine the fuel delivery and spark advance. A failed IAT sensor should set a Diagnostic Trouble Code (DTC).

TESTING

➧ **See Figure 39**

1. With the IAT sensor exposed, measure the resistance between terminals E2 and THA of the air flow meter or the IAT sensor itself, with an ohmmeter. Check the ambient air temperature with a thermometer. Compare the resistance with the temperature as per the graph. Using a hair dryer or heat gun, carefully warm the air around the sensor and check the resistance again.
2. If it sensor does not come within specifications, replace the sensor. If the sensor is contained inside the air flow meter, the entire unit must be replaced.

REMOVAL & INSTALLATION

➡This applies only for sensors mounted on the air cleaner housing.

1. Detach the electrical harness.
2. Unscrew the sensor and remove it from the housing.

To install:

3. Install the sensor into the housing.
4. Attach the harness.

Volume Air Flow (VAF) Meter

OPERATION

➡This component is used on 1FZ-FE engines.

The Volume Air Flow (VAF) meter measures the amount of air flowing through the intake system. It is used by the ECM to calculate air/fuel mixture.

TESTING

➧ **See Figure 41**

1. Disconnect the wiring from the VAF meter.
2. Using an ohmmeter, measure the resistance between terminals E2 and VS. Resistance should be 200–600 ohms
3. If the test is not within specification, replace the unit.

REMOVAL & INSTALLATION

1FZ-FE Engine

1. Disconnect the negative battery cable.
2. Disconnect the VAF meter electrical connector and wire clamp.
3. Disconnect the cruise control actuator cable.
4. Remove the air cleaner cap, VAF meter and silencer as follows:
   a. Disconnect the air cleaner hose from the VAF meter.
   b. Disconnect the air hose from the air suction reed valve.
   c. Disconnect the 3 clamps, remove the wing nut, air cleaner cap, VAF meter and silencer.
5. Remove the 4 nuts, plate washers, VAF meter, gasket and 4 collars. Remove the 2 screws, bolt and bolt bracket. Disconnect the VAF meter from the air cleaner cap.

To install:

6. Install the VAF meter to the air cleaner cap. Install the bracket to the VAF meter and tighten the fasteners to 43 inch lbs. (5 Nm). Place a new gasket and 4 collars on the VAF meter. Install the VAF meter to the air cleaner cap and tighten retainer nuts to 7 ft. lbs. (10 Nm).
7. Install the air cleaner cap to the air cleaner case with the 3 clips and wing nut. Connect the air hose to the air suction reed valve. Connect the air cleaner hose to the VAF meter.

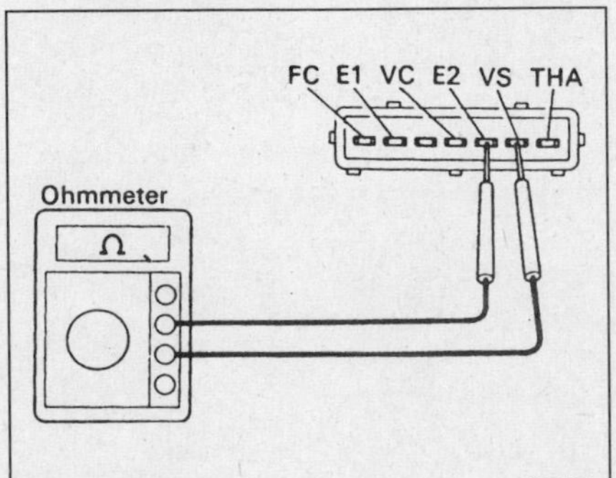

Fig. 41 Attach the ohmmeter to terminals E2 and VS

8. Connect the cruise control actuator cable. Connect the VAF meter connector and wire clamp.
9. Connect the negative battery cable.

Mass Air Flow (MAF) Meter

OPERATION

A Mass Air Flow (MAF) meter is used on all engines. This meter measures the amount of air flowing through the intake system. It is used by the ECM to calculate air/fuel mixture.

The MAF meter, or sensor, has a platinum hot wire, a thermistor and a control circuit, all in a plastic housing. The hot wire and thermistor are located in the intake air bypass of the housing, detecting any changes in the intake air temperature. The hot wire is maintained at the set temperature by controlling the current flow through the hot wire. This current flow is measured as the output voltage of the MAF meter.

A failed MAF meter should set a Diagnostic Trouble Code (DTC).

TESTING

➧ **See Figures 42, 43, and 44**

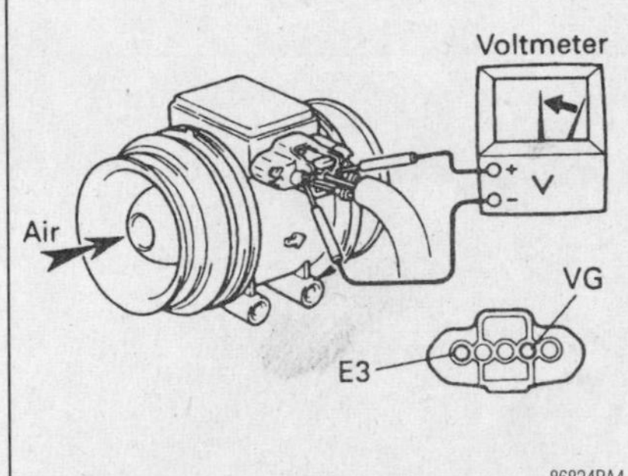

Fig. 42 Testing the Mass Air Flow (MAF) meter E3 and VG circuits—1FZ-FE and 5VZ-FE engines

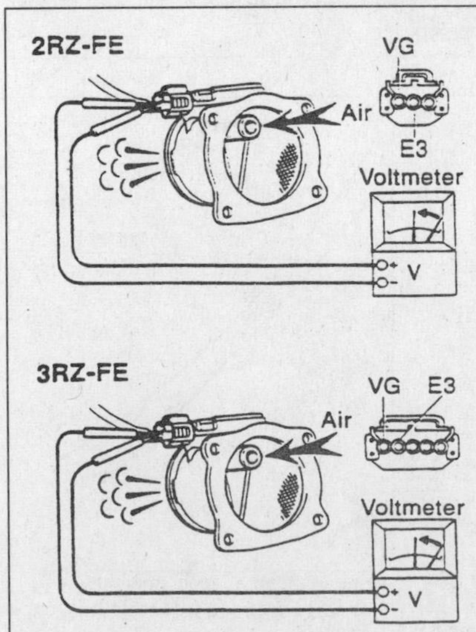

Fig. 43 Testing the Mass Air Flow (MAF) meter E3 and VG circuits—2RZ-FE and 3RZ-FE engines

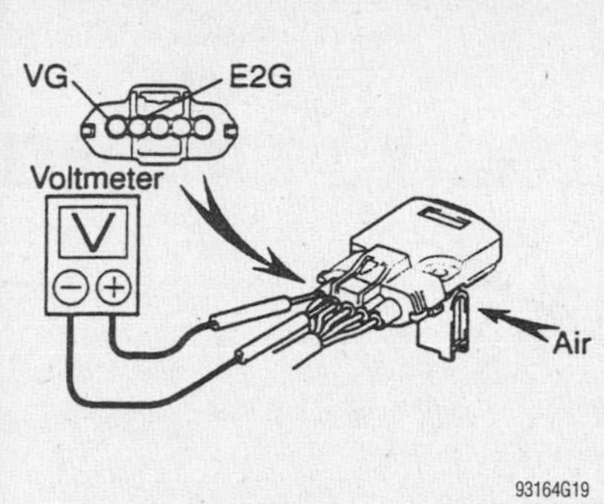

Fig. 44 Testing the Mass Air Flow (MAF) meter E2G and VG circuits—2UZ-FE engine

1. Remove the air intake hose.
2. Turn the ignition switch to the **ON** position.
3. Using a voltmeter, attach the positive terminal probe to the terminal VG, and the negative probe to terminal E3.
4. Blow air into the MAF meter, then check that the voltage fluctuates.
5. Turn the ignition switch to the **OFF** position.
6. Install the air intake hose.

REMOVAL & INSTALLATION

2RZ-FE and 3RZ-FE Engines

➧ **See Figure 45**

1. Disconnect the MAF harness and the IAT harness along with the wire clamps.
2. Loosen the air cleaner hose clamp.
3. On the 3RZ-FE, disconnect the air hose from the air cleaner cap.
4. Loosen the four clips, then the air cleaner cap with the meter attached.
5. Remove the four nuts, MAF meter and gasket from the cap.
6. Discard the gasket.

To install:

7. Place a new gasket on the air cleaner cap.
8. Install the MAF meter and tighten the nuts to 74 inch lbs. (8 Nm).
9. Install the meter and cap assembly on the air cleaner housing.

5VZ-FE Engine

➧ **See Figures 46, 47, 48, 49, and 50**

1. Disconnect the air cleaner cap from the MAF meter.
2. Detach the harness from the meter.
3. Remove the mounting bolts for the meter. Lift off the meter and discard the gasket.

To install:

4. Place a new gasket in position, then tighten the meter to the cap assembly to 61 inch lbs. (7 Nm).
5. Connect the harness to the meter.
6. Attach the meter and cap assembly to the air cleaner housing.

2UZ-FE Engine

➧ **See Figure 51**

1. Disconnect the MAF meter connector.
2. Remove the two retainer screws.
3. Lift off the MAF meter.

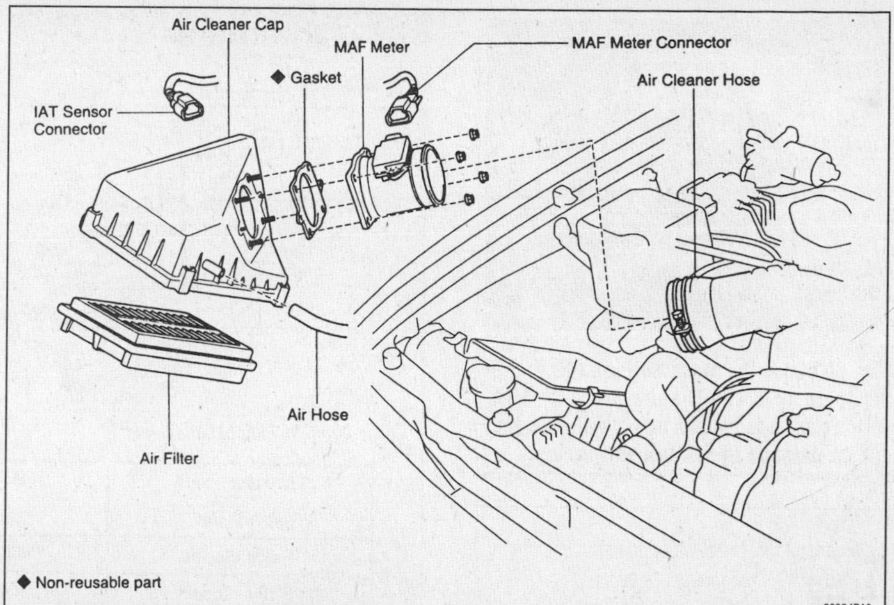

Fig. 45 Exploded view of the MAF meter arrangement—2RZ-FE and 3RZ-FE engines

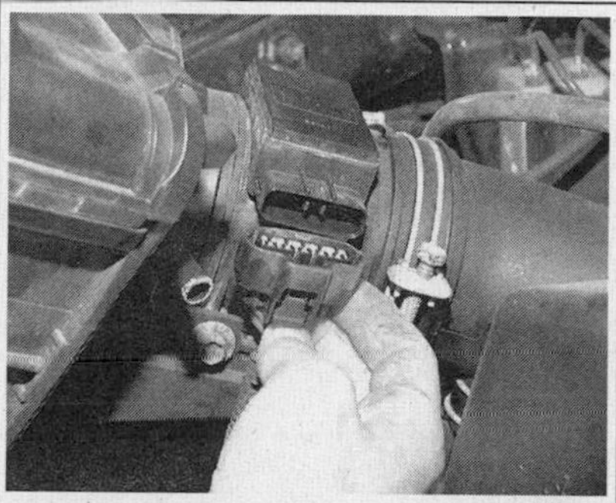

Fig. 46 Detach the electrical connector from the Mass Air Flow (MAF) meter

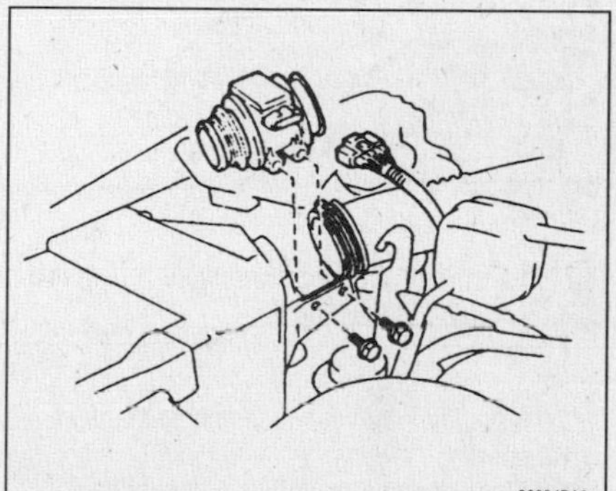

Fig. 47 Remove the bolts securing the meter—5VZ-FE engine

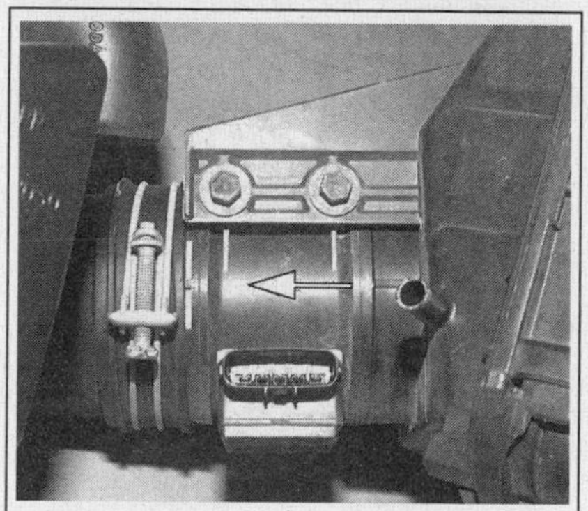

Fig. 48 The Mass Air Flow (MAF) meter must be installed in the correct direction

Fig. 49 Loosen the clamp from the air intake hose and then remove the Mass Air Flow (MAF) meter

4. Installation is the reverse of removal. Verify the electrical connector is secure.

1FZ-FE Engine

1. Disconnect the MAF meter harness and wire clamps.
2. Separate the cruise control actuator cable from the unit.
3. Loosen the air cleaner hose.
4. Disconnect the 3 clips, then remove the wing nut, air cleaner cap and meter assembly.
5. Unbolt the meter from the cap. Discard the gasket.

To install:

6. Secure the MAF meter to the cap with a new gasket.

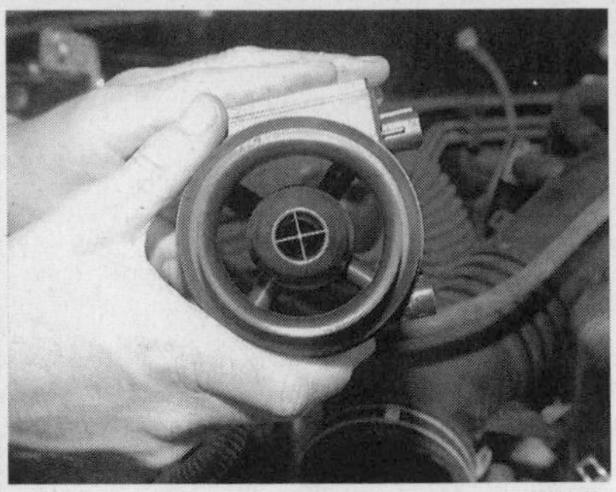

93164p02

Fig. 50 Inside the Mass Air Flow (MAF) meter there is a very fragile piece of wire. Never poke a tool down into the air flow meter for damage to the unit will occur

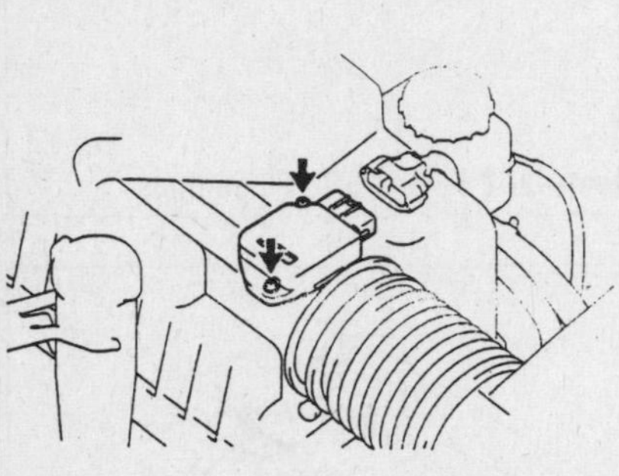

93164G20

Fig. 51 Remove the two screws securing the meter—2UZ-FE Engine

7. Install the cap/meter assembly to the air cleaner housing.
8. Attach the air cleaner hose to the unit.
9. Attach the cruise control actuator cable.
10. Connect the MAF meter harness and wire clamps.

Throttle Position (TP) Sensor

OPERATION

Throttle Position (TP) sensors are usually mounted on the side of the throttle body. The sensor detects the throttle valve opening angle. The voltage of terminal connected to the ECM increases in proportion of the opening angle of the throttle valve. When the throttle valve is fully closed, voltage will be low, usually approximately 0.7 volts. The voltage increases in proportion to the opening angle of the throttle valve and becomes approximately 2.7–5.2 volts when the throttle valve is fully open. The ECM judges the driving conditions from the input signals of the terminals, and uses them as one of the conditions for computing the air/fuel ratio correction, power increases and fuel cut-off control.

TESTING

1FZ-FE Engine

➧ See Figure 52

1. Detach the throttle position sensor connector.
2. Apply vacuum to the throttle opener.

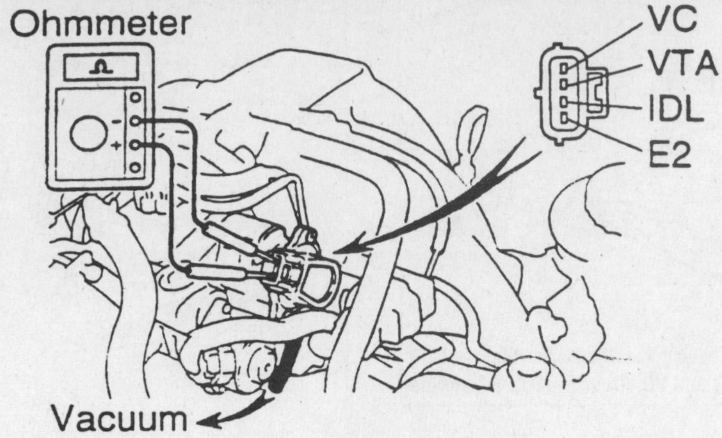

Throttle valve condition	Between terminals	Resistance
Fully closed	VTA – E2	0.2 – 5.7 kΩ
Fully closed	IDL – E2	2.3 kΩ or less
Open	IDL – E2	Infinity
Fully open	VTA – E2	2.0 – 10.2 kΩ
–	VC – E2	2.5 – 5.9 kΩ

93164G21

Fig. 52 Measure the Throttle Position (TP) sensor resistance—1FZ-FE engine

3. Using an ohmmeter, measure the resistance between each terminal.
4. If the resistance is not as specified, replace the throttle position sensor.

2RZ-FE and 3RZ-FE Engines

➧ See Figure 53

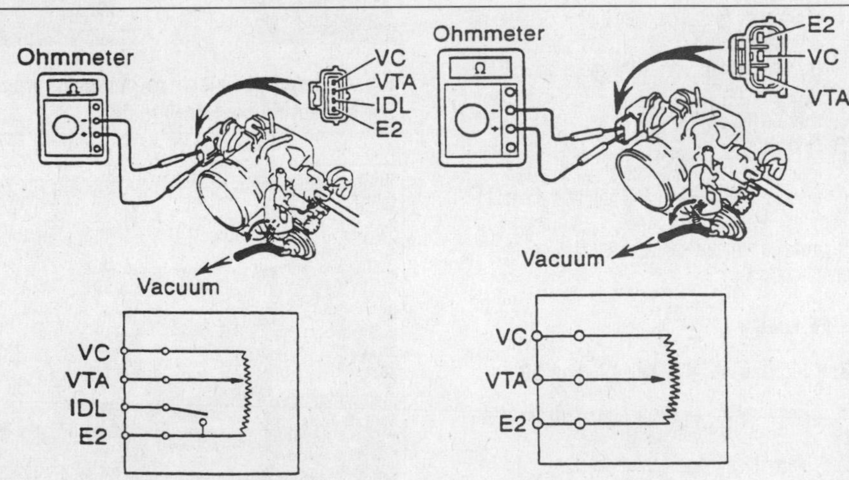

Clearance between lever and stop screw	Between terminals	Resistance
0 mm (0 in.)	VTA – E2	0.2 – 5.7 kΩ
0.57 mm (0.022 in.)*	IDL – E2	2.3 kΩ or less
0.74 mm (0.029 in.)*	IDL – E2	Infinity
Throttle valve fully open	VTA – E2	2.0 – 10.2 kΩ
–	VC – E2	2.5 – 5.9 kΩ

93164G23

Fig. 53 Checking the resistance of the Throttle Position (TP) sensor—2RZ-FE and 3RZ-FE engines

1. Detach the Throttle Position (TP) sensor connector.
2. Apply vacuum to the throttle opener.
3. Confirm that the throttle valve is fully closed.
4. Using an ohmmeter, measure the resistance between each terminal.
5. On 2RZ-FE engines, connect an ohmmeter to terminals IDL and E2. E2 is the bottom terminal, while terminal IDL is positioned directly above it.
   a. Insert a 0.022 in. (0.57mm) thick feeler gauge between the throttle stop screw and lever. Check for continuity between terminals IDL and E2 of the sensor. Resistance should be 2.3 kohms or less.
   b. Insert a 0.029 in. (0.74mm) thick feeler gauge between the throttle stop screw and lever. Check for continuity between terminals IDL and E2 of the sensor. No continuity should be present.
6. If the resistance is not as specified, replace the throttle position sensor.

5VZ-FE and 2UZ-FE Engines

➧ **See Figure 54**

1. Detach the Throttle Position (TP) sensor connector.
2. Apply vacuum to the throttle opener.
3. Using an ohmmeter, measure the resistance between each terminal.
4. Confirm that the throttle valve is fully closed.
5. Connect an ohmmeter to terminals IDL and E2.
6. On 1997 5VZ-FE engines only:
   a. Insert a 0.013 in. (0.32mm) thick feeler gauge between the throttle stop screw and lever. Check for continuity between terminals VTA and E2 of the sensor. Resistance should be 0.2–5.7 kohms.
   b. Insert a 0.021 in. (0.54mm) thick feeler gauge between the throttle stop screw and lever. Check for continuity between terminals VTA and E2 of the sensor. No continuity should be present.
7. On all other model years using the 5VZ-FE engine, simply verify that the throttle valve is either fully closed or fully open to obtain the indicated resistance readings.
8. If the resistance is not as specified, replace the TP sensor.

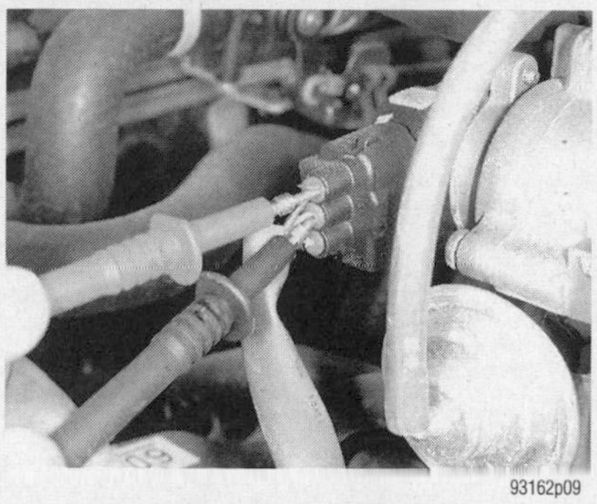

93162p09

Fig. 54 Checking the Throttle Position (TP) sensor—5VZ-FE and 2UZ-FE engines

REMOVAL & INSTALLATION

➧ **See Figures 55, 56, and 57**

1. Disconnect the negative battery cable.
2. Unplug the Throttle Position (TP) sensor electrical connector.
3. Loosen the sensor attaching screws and remove the sensor.

To install:

4. Make sure the tangs to the sensor are in good condition, not bent. Place the sensor on the throttle body.
5. Attach the sensor mounting screws.
6. Connect the negative battery cable.
7. Start the engine and check operation.

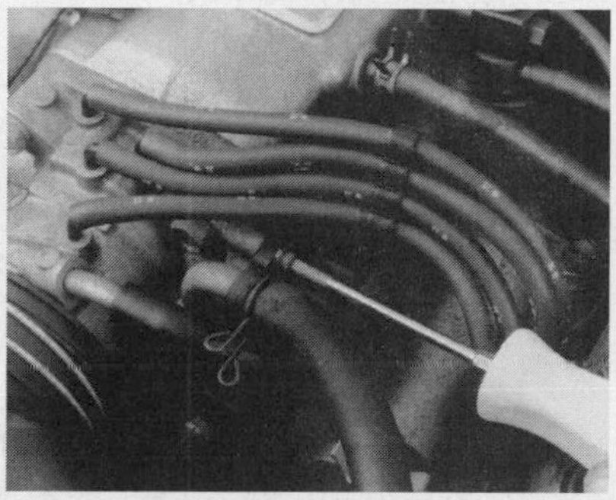

86824G94

Fig. 55 The TP sensor is secured by screws—1FZ-FE engine shown, others similar

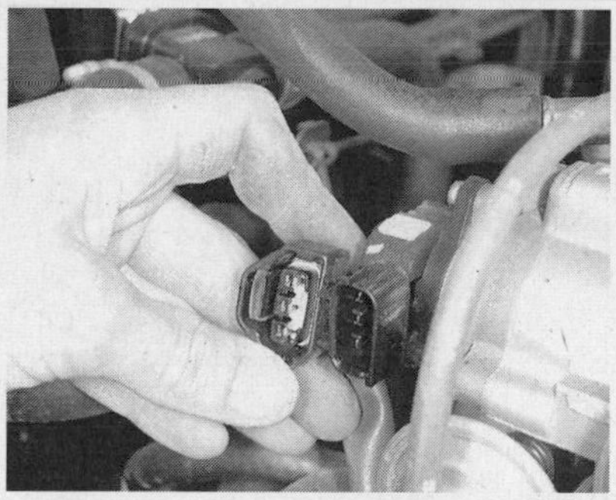

93162p10

Fig. 56 Unplug the throttle position electrical connector

93162p11

Fig. 57 Remove the throttle position sensor from the throttle body

Camshaft Position (CMP) Sensor

OPERATION

Like most Camshaft Position (CMP) sensors in computer-controlled vehicles, these sensors are basically a Hall-Effect switch. A pick-up coil and a toothed piece usually called a reluctor or signal plate, are mounted very close to each other with a small air gap separating them. When a tooth aligns with the pick-up coil a small voltage is induced, then read and interpreted by the ECM so it can compute the proper time to fire the ignition coil and also the fuel injectors. A failed CMP sensor should set a Diagnostic Trouble Code (DTC).

1FZ-FE Engine

The Camshaft Position (CMP) sensor provides the G1 and G2 signals. It consists of a signal plate and a pick-up coil. The G1 and G2 signal plates each have one tooth on the outer circumference and are built into the distributor. When the camshaft rotates, the tooth on the signal plate comes close to the pick-up coil and the air gap on the pick-up coil changes. This causes fluctuations in the magnetic field, generating a small voltage in the pick-up coil. The ECM detects the standard crankshaft angle based on the G1 and G2 signals, detects the actual crankshaft angle and engine speed by the NE signal (generated in a similar manner by the crankshaft position sensor) and even detects misfire by the NE 2 signal.

2RZ-FE and 3RZ-FE Engines

The Camshaft Position (CMP) sensor provides the G signal to the ECM. The rotating signal plate has one tooth on its circumference and is built into the distributor. When the camshafts rotate, the tooth on the signal plate comes close to the pick-up coil and the air gap on the pick-up coil changes. This causes fluctuations in the magnetic field, generating a small voltage in the pick-up coil. At the same time, the crankshaft position sensor signal plate (equipped with 34 teeth and mounted on the crankshaft) generates 34 signals for every engine revolution. The ECM detects the standard crankshaft angle based on the camshaft position sensor G signals and the actual crankshaft angle and engine speed by the NE signals.

5VZ-FE Engine

The Camshaft Position (CMP) sensor is installed on the front of the right cylinder head of the 5VZ-FE engine. The timing rotor has been integrated with the right bank camshaft timing pulley. While the camshaft rotates, the air gap between the protrusion on the timing rotor and the pick-up coil changes. This causes fluctuation in the magnetic field and generates a voltage signal in the pick-up coil.

2UZ-FE Engine

The Camshaft Position (CMP) sensor provides the G signal to the ECM. Like other Toyota CMP sensors, it consists of a magnetic core and a pick-up coil. The signal plate has one tooth and is installed on the left side camshaft timing pulley. When the camshafts rotate, the tooth comes near the pick-up coil. This causes fluctuation in the magnetic field and generates a voltage signal in the pick-up coil.

TESTING

1FZ-FE Engine

See Figure 58

1. Detach the Camshaft Position (CMP) sensor connector.
2. Using an ohmmeter, measure the resistance between terminals 2,3 and 4 of the distributor connector.
3. On a cold engine (coolant temperature up to 122°F.) resistance should be 185–275 ohms.
4. On a hot engine (coolant temperature from 122–212°F.) resistance should be 240–325 ohms.
5. If the resistance is not as specified, replace the camshaft position sensor.

2RZ-FE Engine

See Figure 59

1. Detach the Camshaft Position (CMP) sensor connector.
2. Using an ohmmeter, measure the resistance between terminals G+ and G–.
3. On a cold engine (temperature of the sensors themselves, up to 122°F.) resistance should be 185–275 ohms.
4. On a hot engine (temperature of the sensors themselves, from 122–212°F.) resistance should be 240–325 ohms.
5. If the resistance is not as specified, Toyota recommends that the distributor housing be replaced.
6. The air gap should be checked. Using a feeler gauge, measure the air gap between the signal rotor and the pick-up coil. It should be 0.008–0.016 inch (0.2–0.4mm). If the air gap is not as specified, Toyota recommends that the distributor housing be replaced.

3RZ-FE, 5VZ-FE and 2UZ-FE Engines

See Figures 60, 61, and 62

1. Detach the Camshaft Position (CMP) sensor connector.
2. Using an ohmmeter, measure the resistance between terminals.
3. On a cold engine (temperature of the sensor, up to 122°F.) resistance should be 835–1400 ohms.
4. On a hot engine (temperature of the sensor, from 122–212°F.) resistance should be 1060–1645 ohms.
5. If the resistance is not as specified, replace the camshaft position sensor.

REMOVAL & INSTALLATION

3RZ-FE Engine

See Figure 63

1. Remove the throttle body. The cooling system has to be drained since the throttle body has two water hoses connected to it, to warm the throttle body and prevent icing. Tag for identification all of the vacuum hoses that must be disconnected from the intake air connector and the throttle body.
2. Locate the Camshaft Position (CMP) sensor where it mounts to the left side of the engine. Detach the electrical connector. Remove the sensor hold-down bolt and remove the sensor.

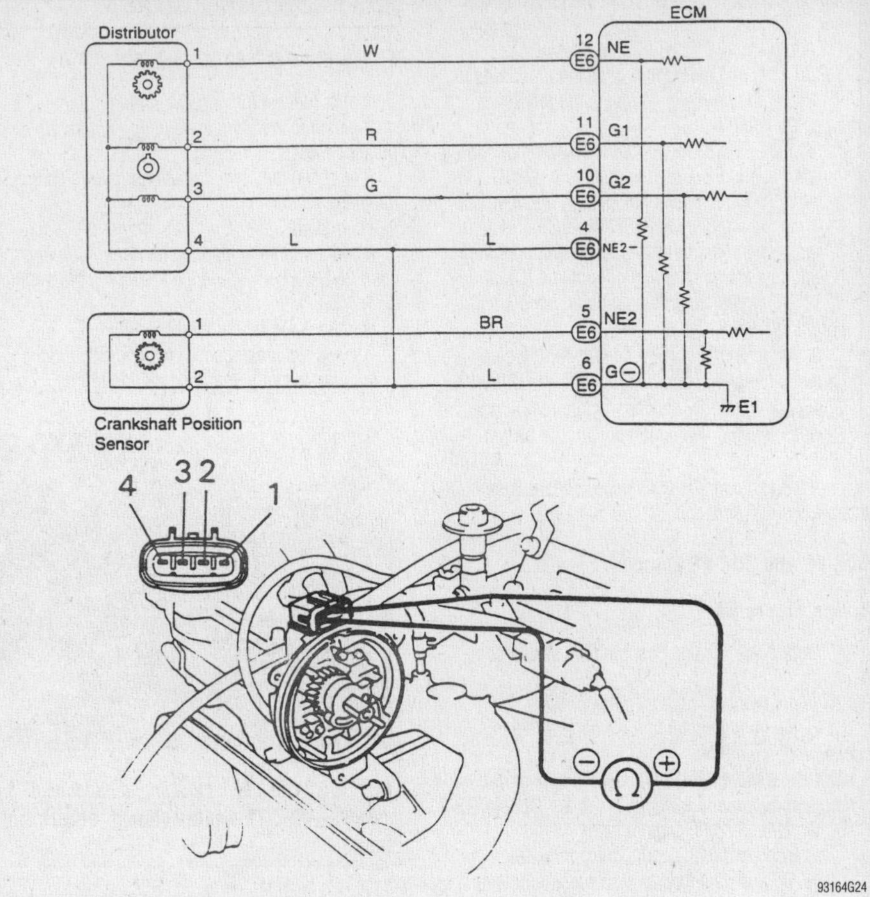

Fig. 58 CMP sensor testing and circuit schematic—1997 1FZ-FE engine

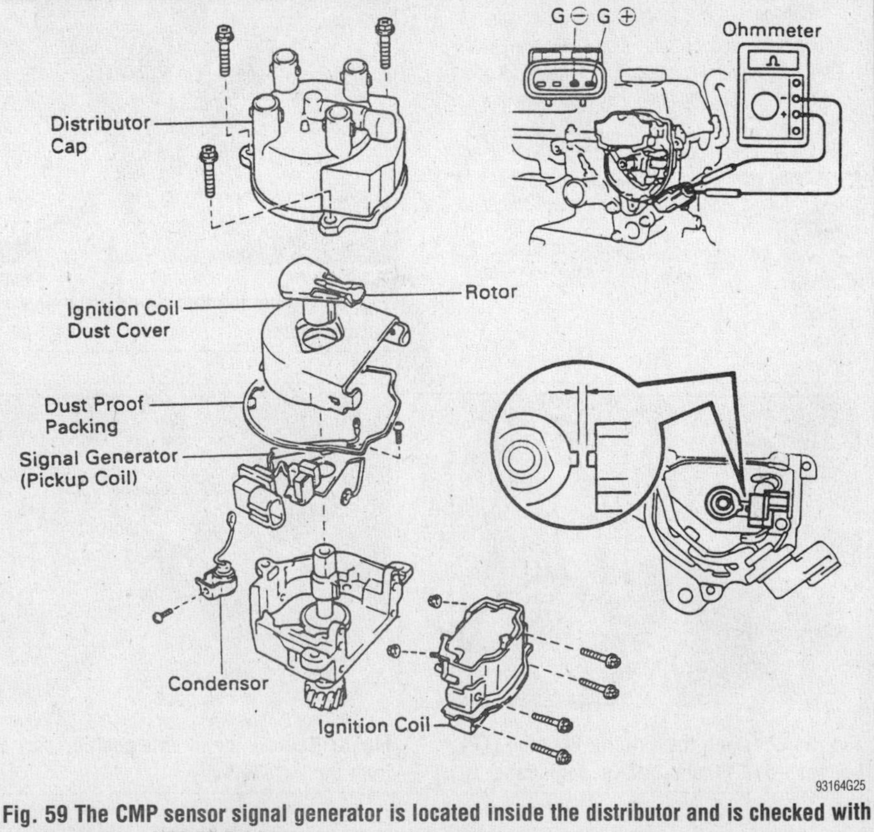

Fig. 59 The CMP sensor signal generator is located inside the distributor and is checked with an ohmmeter—2RZ-FE Engine

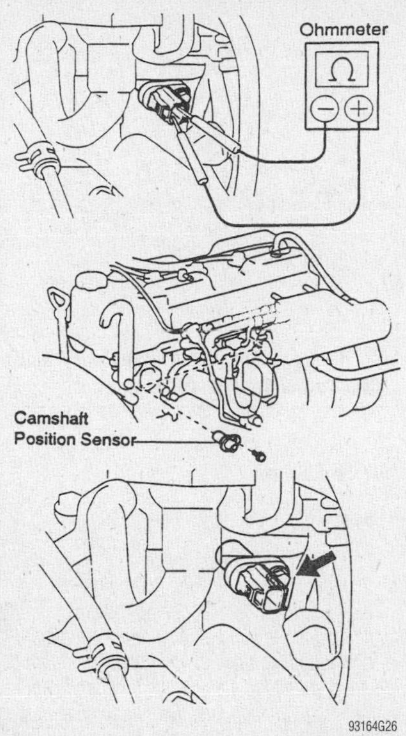

Fig. 60 Camshaft Position (CMP) sensor testing and component location—3RZ-FE engine

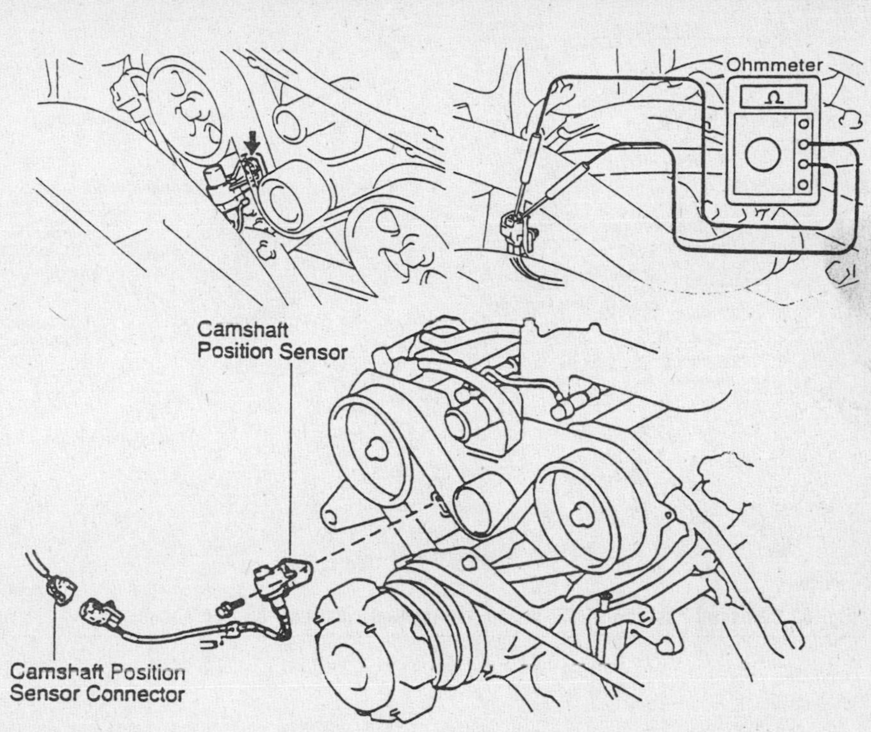

Fig. 61 Camshaft Position (CMP) sensor testing and component location—5VZ-FE engine

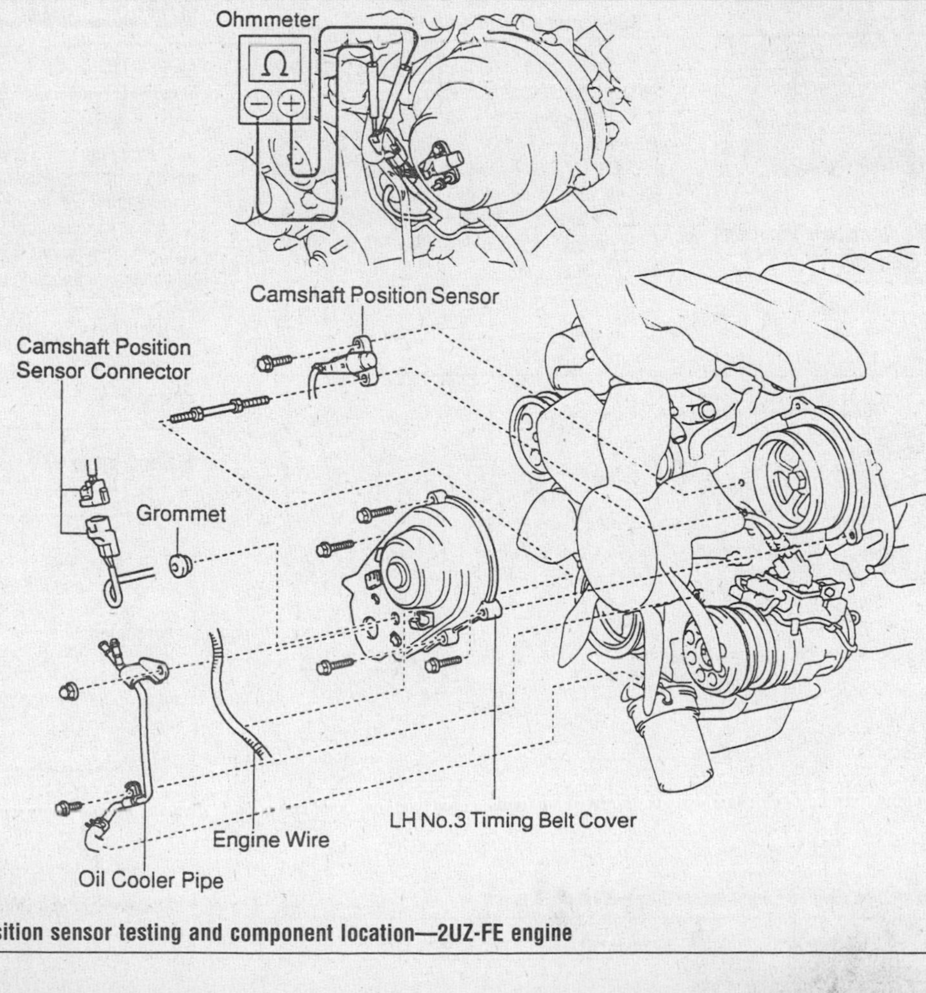

Fig. 62 Camshaft position sensor testing and component location—2UZ-FE engine

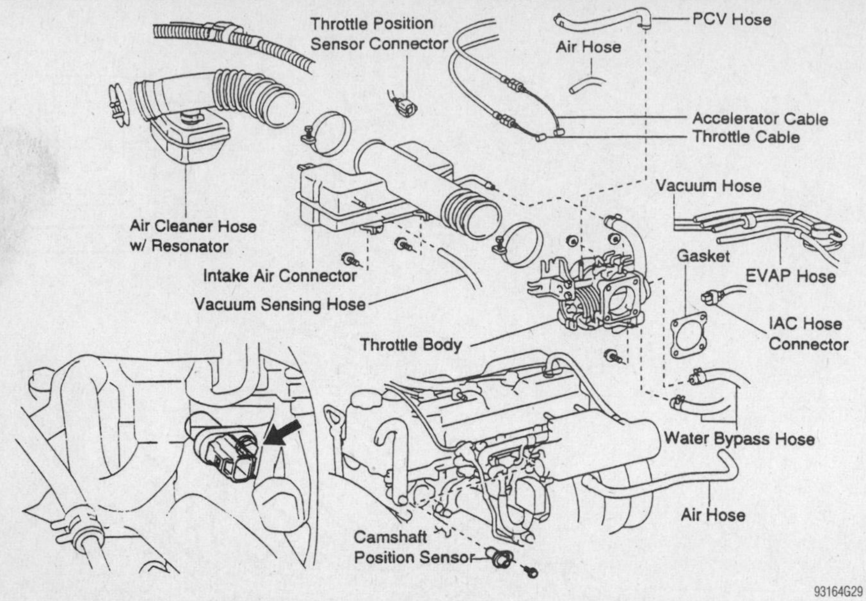

Fig. 63 Camshaft Position (CMP) sensor component location—3RZ-FE engine

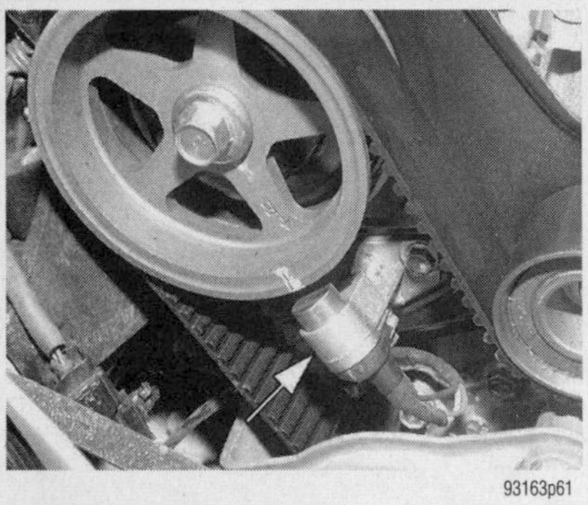

Fig. 64 Location of the Camshaft Position (CMP) sensor—5VZ-FE engine

3. Installation is the reverse of the removal procedure. Tighten the sensor hold-down bolt to 48 inch lbs. (5.4 Nm).

5VZ-FE Engine

➧ See Figures 64 and 65

1. Remove the timing belt cover that goes over the cam drive sprockets.
2. Locate the camshaft position sensor where it mounts to the right side cylinder head. Detach the electrical connector. Remove the sensor hold-down bolt and remove the sensor.
3. Installation is the reverse of the removal procedure. Tighten the sensor hold-down bolt to 69 inch lbs. (7.8 Nm).

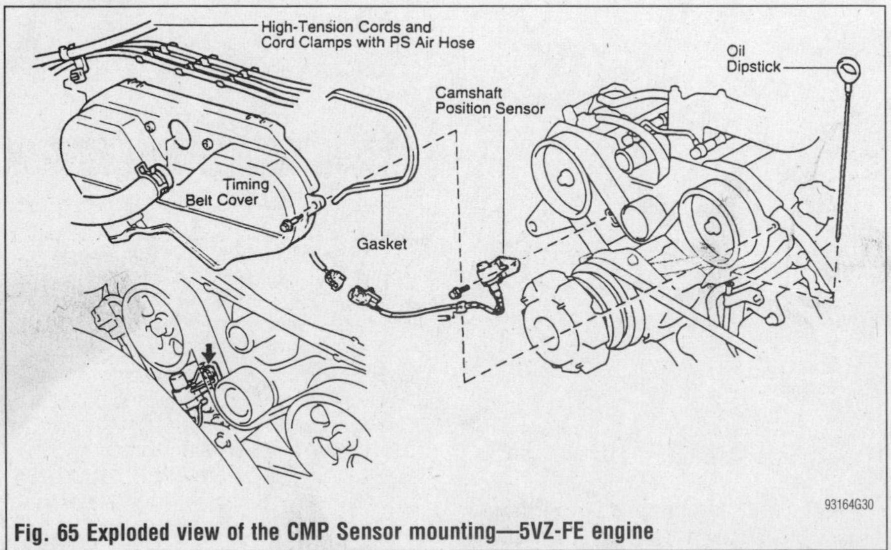

Fig. 65 Exploded view of the CMP Sensor mounting—5VZ-FE engine

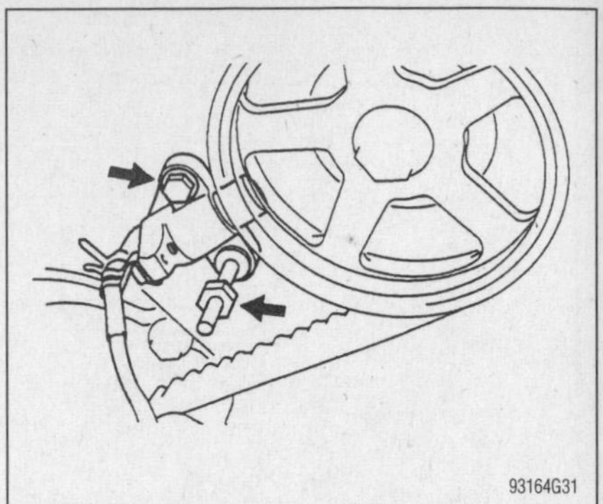

Fig. 66 Location of the Camshaft Position (CMP) sensor—2UZ-FE engine

2UZ-FE Engine

➧ See Figure 66

1. Drain the engine coolant.
2. Remove the accessory drive belt(s).
3. Remove the left side timing belt cover.
4. Locate the camshaft position sensor where it mounts to the left side cylinder head. Detach the electrical connector. Remove the sensor hold-down bolt and the stud bolt. Remove the camshaft position sensor.
5. Installation is the reverse of the removal procedure. Tighten the sensor hold-down bolt to 66 inch lbs. (7.5 Nm).

Crankshaft Position Sensor

OPERATION

The Crankshaft Position (CKP) sensor is essentially a pick-up coil and works in a similar manner to the Camshaft Position (CMP) sensor. While the crankshaft rotates, the air gap between the protrusion (tooth) on the timing rotor and the pick-up coil changes. This causes fluctuation in the magnetic field and generates a varying voltage signal in the pick-up coil. The CKP sensor is used by the ECM to determine crankshaft angle and speed based upon the voltage received.

TESTING

➧ See Figure 67

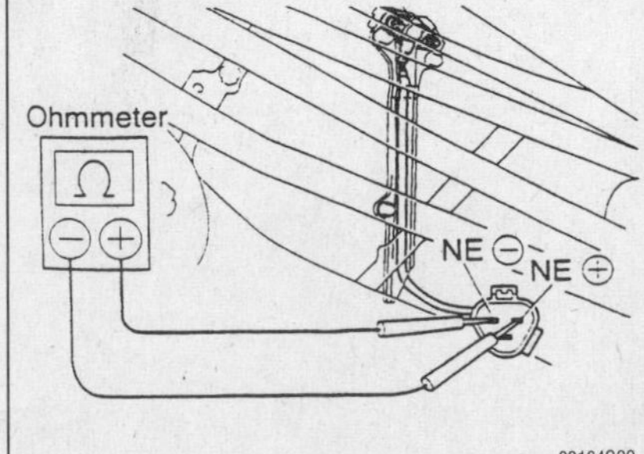

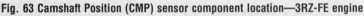

Fig. 67 Crankshaft Position (CKP) sensor testing—1FZ-FE engine shown, others similar

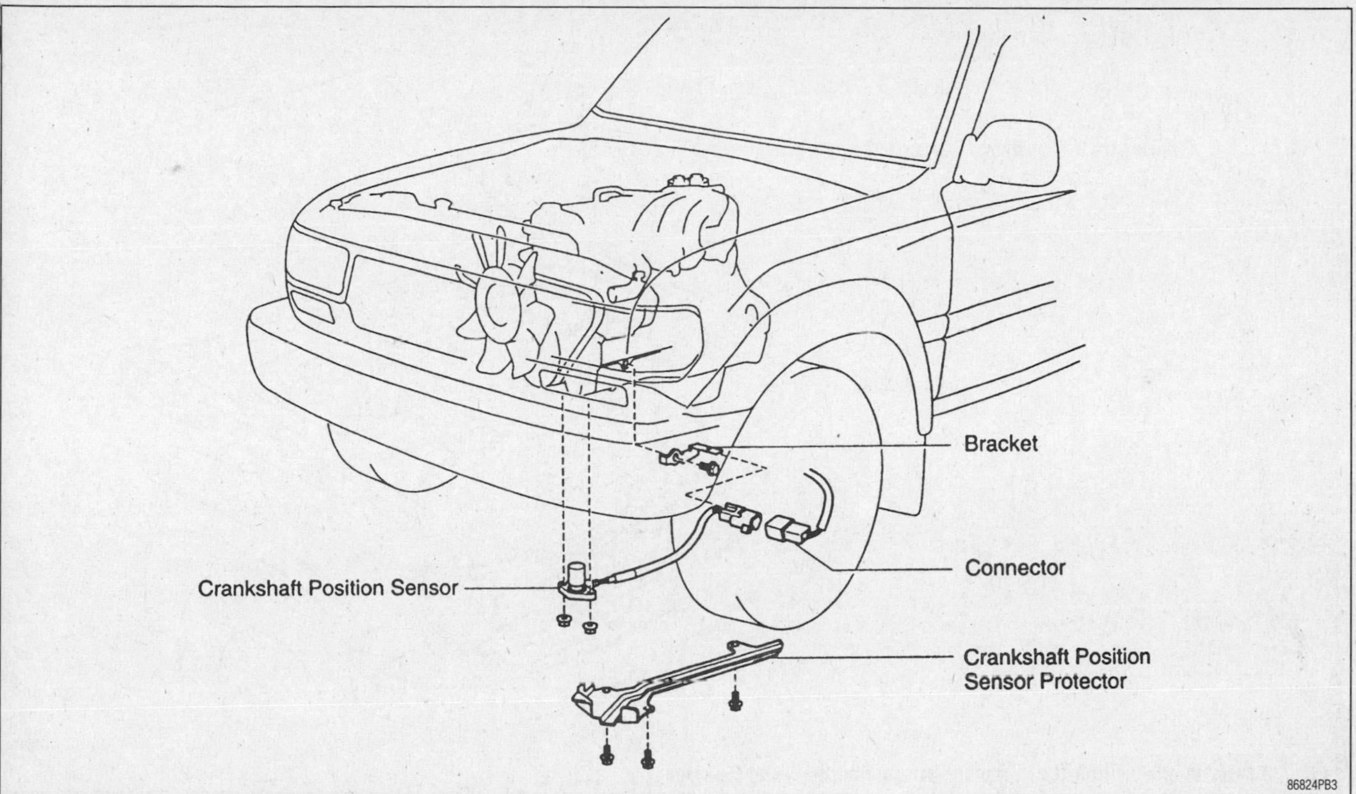

Fig. 68 Exploded view of the CKP sensor and related components—1FZ-FE engine

1. Detach the Crankshaft Position (CKP) sensor connector.
2. Using an ohmmeter, measure the resistance between terminals.
3. On a cold engine (temperature of the sensor, up to 122°F.) resistance should be 1630–2740 ohms.
4. On a hot engine (temperature of the sensor, from 122–212°F.) resistance should be 2065–3225 ohms.
5. If the resistance is not as specified, replace the CKP sensor.

REMOVAL & INSTALLATION

1FZ-FE Engine

➧ **See Figure 68**

1. Remove the engine under cover.
2. Unbolt the sensor protector.
3. Disconnect the Crankshaft Position (CKP) sensor bracket and harness.
4. Remove the bolt, nuts and sensor.

To install:

5. Attach the sensor with the nuts and bolt. Tighten the bolt to 14 ft. lbs. (20 Nm) and the nuts to 78 inch lbs. (9 Nm).
6. Attach the bracket and harness.
7. Install the sensor protector, tighten the mounting bolts to 14 ft. lbs. (20 Nm).
8. Install the engine under cover.

2RZ-FE and 3RZ-FE Engines

➧ **See Figure 69**

1. Remove the engine under cover.
2. Remove the alternator assembly.
3. Remove the alternator bracket.
4. Detach the Crankshaft Position (CKP) sensor harness connector.
5. Remove the two sensor retaining bolts and remove the sensor.
6. Installation is the reverse of the removal process. Use a new O-ring, lightly coated with engine oil at installation. Tighten the retainer bolts to 74 inch lbs. (8.5 Nm).

5VZ-FE Engine

➧ **See Figure 70**

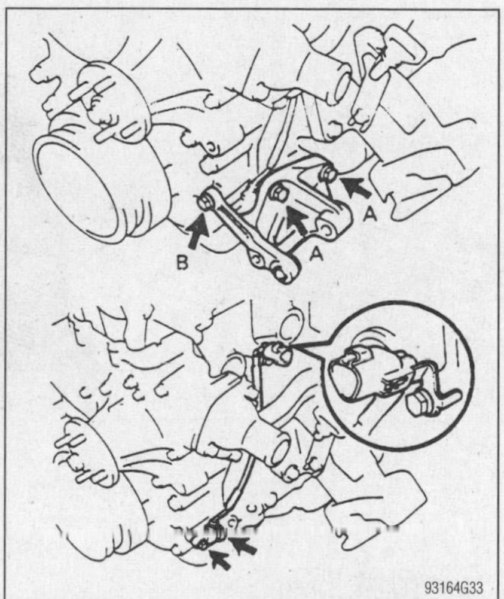

Fig. 69 Remove the alternator bracket to access the Crankshaft Position (CKP) sensor—2RZ-FE engine

1. Disconnect the Crankshaft Position (CKP) sensor harness.
2. Remove the bolt retaining the sensor to the vehicle.
3. Installation is the reverse of the removal process. Tighten the mounting bolt to 69 inch lbs. (8 Nm).

2UZ-FE Engine

➧ **See Figure 71**

1. Remove the engine under cover.
2. Disconnect the Crankshaft Position (CKP) sensor harness.
3. Remove the bolt retaining the sensor to the oil pump body.
4. Installation is the reverse of the removal process. Tighten the mounting bolt to 58 inch lbs. (6.5 Nm).

Knock Sensor (KS)

OPERATION

Located in the engine block or cylinder head, the Knock Sensor (KS) retards ignition timing during a spark knock condition to allow the ECM to maintain maximum timing advance under most conditions. Knock sensors contain a piezoelectric element which generates a voltage when it becomes distorted due to vibration. The ECM reads this voltage and retards the ignition timing slightly. A failed Knock Sensor will set a Diagnostic Trouble Code (DTC). V6 and V8 engines have two Knock Sensors, one for each bank of cylinders.

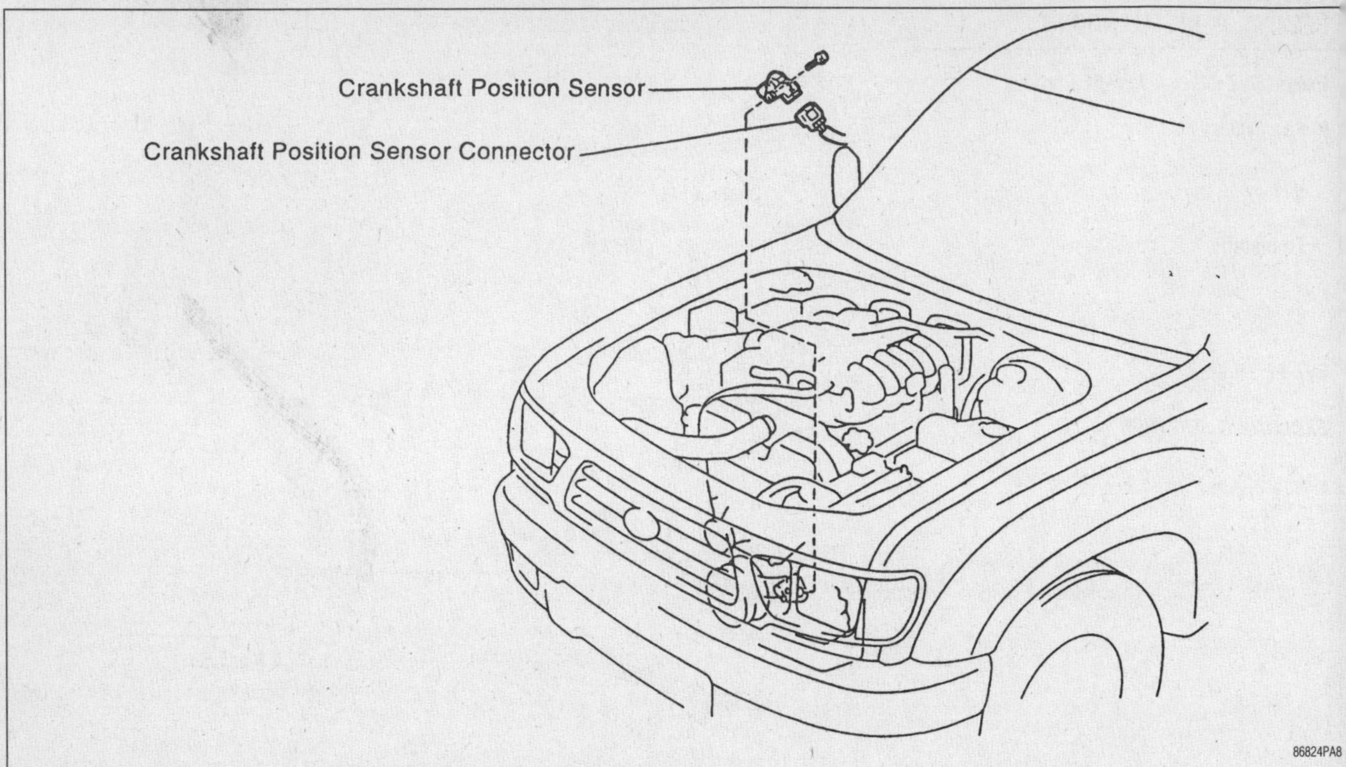

Fig. 70 Crankshaft Position (CKP) sensor arrangement—5VZ-FE engine

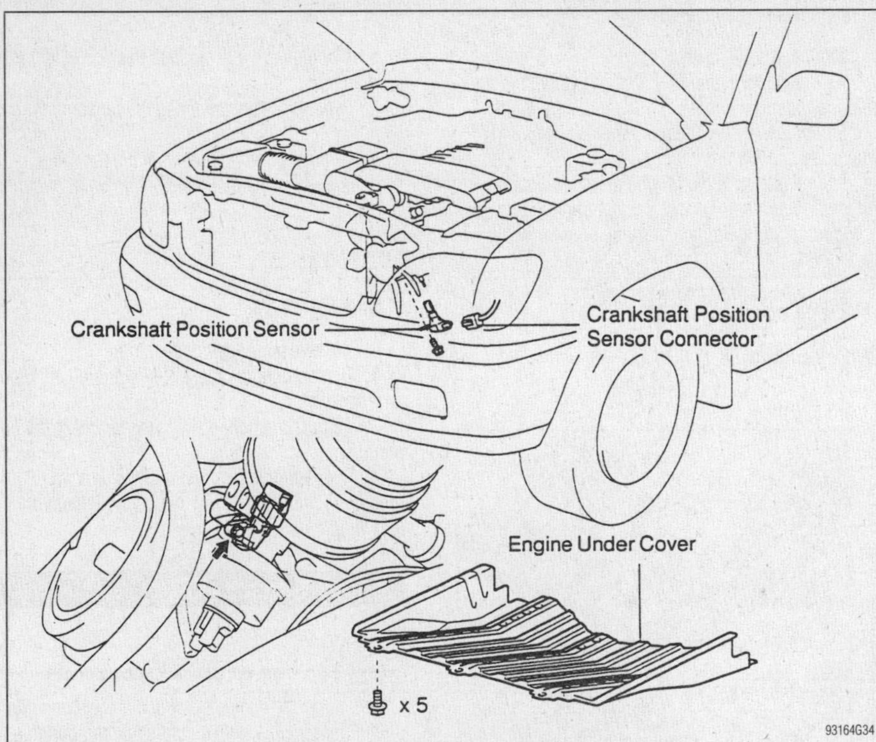

Fig. 71 Exploded view of the CKP sensor—2UZ-FE engine

TESTING

➧ **See Figure 72**

While a scan tool with an oscilloscope display is normally recommended to troubleshoot the knock sensor system, a simple continuity test can be made with an ohmmeter.

1. Remove the knock sensor(s).
2. Using an ohmmeter, check that there is no continuity between the terminal and the body. If there is continuity, replace the sensor.

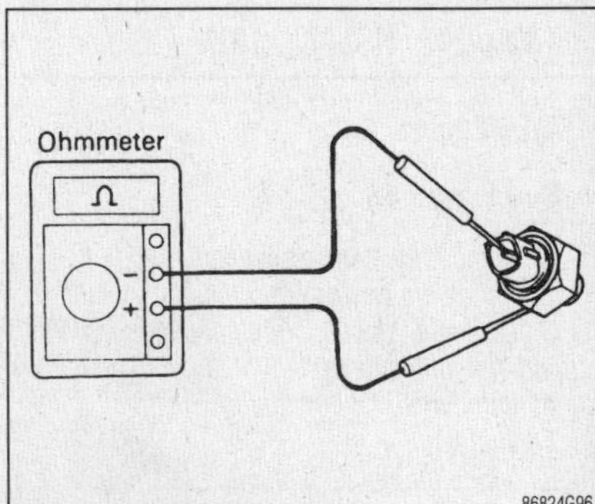

Fig. 72 Checking a knock sensor for continuity with an ohmmeter

REMOVAL & INSTALLATION

Except 5VZ-FE and 2UZ-FE Engines

See Figure 73

1. Disconnect the sensor wire.
2. Remove the sensor. A deep socket may be required.

To install:

3. Install the sensor, tighten to 33 ft. lbs. (44 Nm).
4. Attach the sensor wire.

5VZ-FE Engines

EXCLUDING 4RUNNER

See Figures 74, 75, and 76

1. Drain the engine cooling system.
2. Remove the air cleaner hose.
3. Remove the intake air connector.
4. Remove the spark plug wires and the ignition coils.
5. Unbolt the timing belt and camshaft idler pulleys.
6. Unbolt the timing belt idler.
7. Remove the fuel pressure regulator.
8. Remove the intake manifold assembly.
9. Unbolt and remove the water bypass pipe. Disconnect the knock sensor wire.
10. With the aid of the SST 09816–30010 or equivalent socket, remove the sensor(s).
11. Inspect the sensor(s) for continuity.

To install:

12. Install the sensor(s), tighten to 29 ft. lbs. (39 Nm).
13. Reinstall the water bypass pipe and the knock sensor wires.
14. Attach the intake manifold assembly.
15. Install the fuel pressure regulator.
16. Install the timing belt idler.
17. Attach the camshaft timing pulleys and belt.
18. Install the ignition coils and wires.
19. Attach the intake air connector.
20. Attach the air cleaner hose.
21. Fill the cooling system.
22. Start the engine, top off the cooling system.

4RUNNER

See Figures 74, 75, and 76

1. Drain the engine cooling system.
2. Remove the air cleaner hose.
3. Remove the timing belt cover.
4. Remove the intake air connector.
5. Remove the fuel pressure regulator.
6. Remove the intake manifold.
7. Remove the water bypass pipe and knock sensor wire.
8. Using the appropriate socket, remove the two knock sensors.
9. Inspect the sensors.

To install:

10. Using the sensor tool, install the two sensors. Tighten to 29 ft. lbs. (39 Nm).
11. Attach the water bypass pipe and knock sensor wiring.
12. Install the fuel pressure regulator.
13. Install the intake air connector.
14. Attach the timing belt cover.
15. Attach the air cleaner hose.
16. Refill the engine cooling system.
17. Start the engine, top off the cooling system.

2UZ-FE Engine

The knock sensors are located in the cylinder heads, one on each bank. The intake manifold must be removed for access.

1. Drain the engine coolant.
2. Remove the air cleaner hose.
3. Remove the timing belt cover that goes over the camshaft drive sprockets.
4. Remove the intake air connector.
5. Remove the fuel pressure regulator.
6. Remove the intake manifold.
7. Remove the water bypass pipe and knock sensor wire.
8. Remove the knock sensor(s).

To install:

9. Installation is the reverse of the removal procedure. Thread the knock sensor into the cylinder head and tighten to 29 ft. lbs. (39 Nm).
10. Install the water bypass pipe and knock sensor wire.
11. Install the intake manifold.
12. Install the fuel pressure regulator, the intake air connector and the timing belt cover.
13. Install the intake air connector and refill the system with coolant.

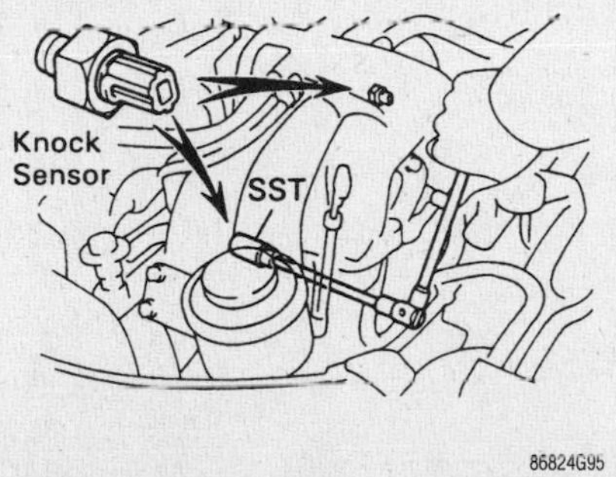

Fig. 73 Remove the sensor with the special tool or a deep socket

Fig. 74 Knock sensor location

Fig. 75 Detach the wiring harness from the knock sensor

Fig. 76 Close up of the knock sensor

COMPONENT LOCATIONS

UNDERHOOD EMISSIONS AND ELECTRONIC ENGINE CONTROL COMPONENT LOCATIONS—5VZ-FE ENGINE

1. Mass Air Flow (MAF) sensor
2. Positive Crankcase Ventilation (PCV) valve
3. Air intake resonator chamber
4. Throttle Position (TP) sensor
5. Camshaft Position (CMP) sensor (not visible)
6. Vacuum Switching Valve (VSV) for vapor pressure sensor
7. Air drain hose
8. Vacuum Switching Valve (VSV) for EVAP
9. Charcoal canister

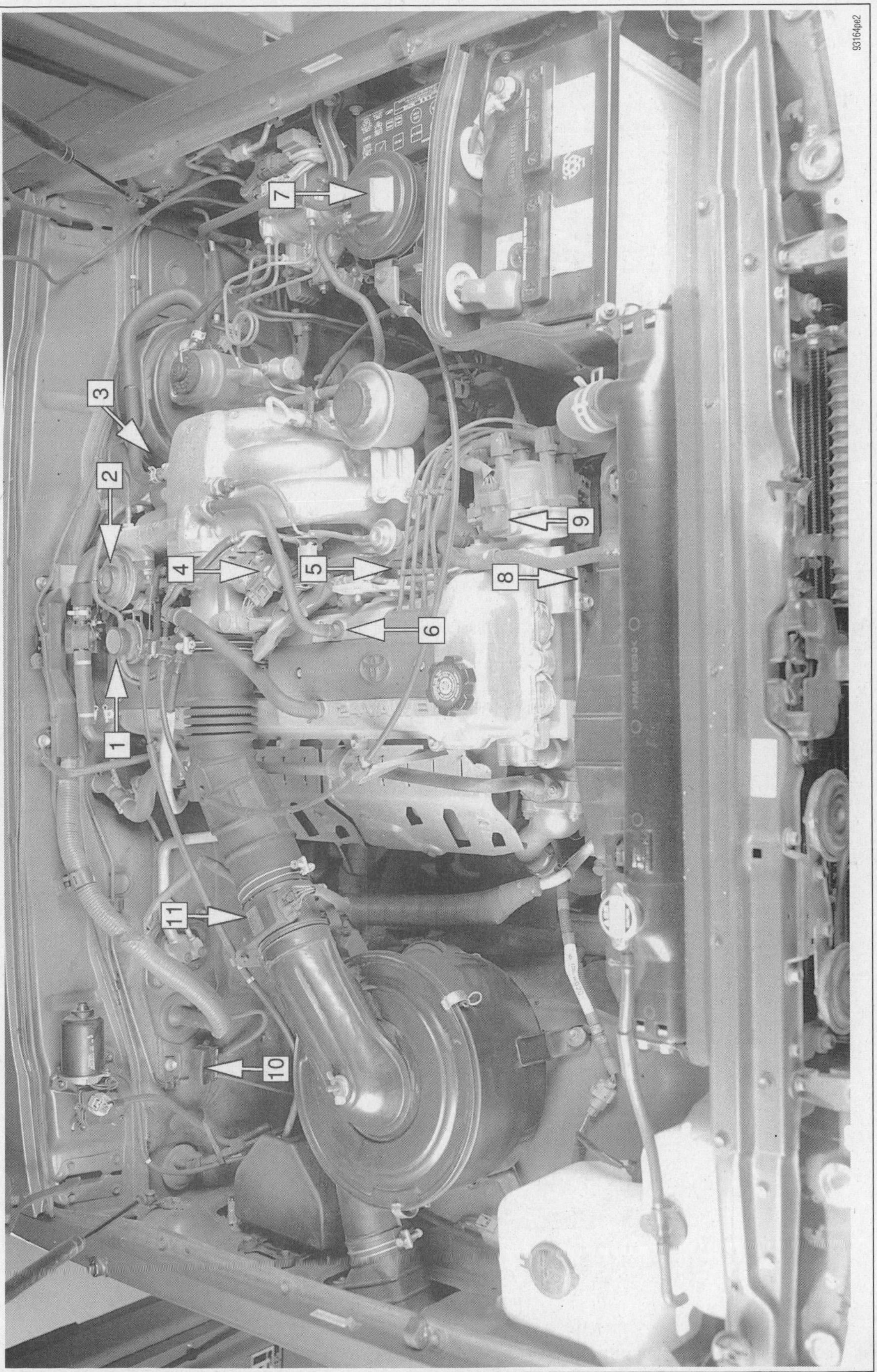

UNDERHOOD EMISSIONS AND ELECTRONIC ENGINE CONTROL COMPONENT LOCATIONS—1FZ-FE ENGINE

1. Exhaust Gas Recirculation (EGR) vacuum modulator
2. EGR valve
3. Vacuum Switching Valve (VSV) for EGR (not visible)
4. Throttle Position (TP) sensor
5. Thermal Vacuum Valve (TVV) for EVAP
6. Positive Crankcase Ventilation (PCV) valve
7. Charcoal canister
8. Crankshaft Position (CKP) sensor (not visible)
9. Ignition Control Module (Igniter)
10. Diagnostic connector
11. Mass Air Flow (MAF) sensor

➧ See Figures 77 thru 84

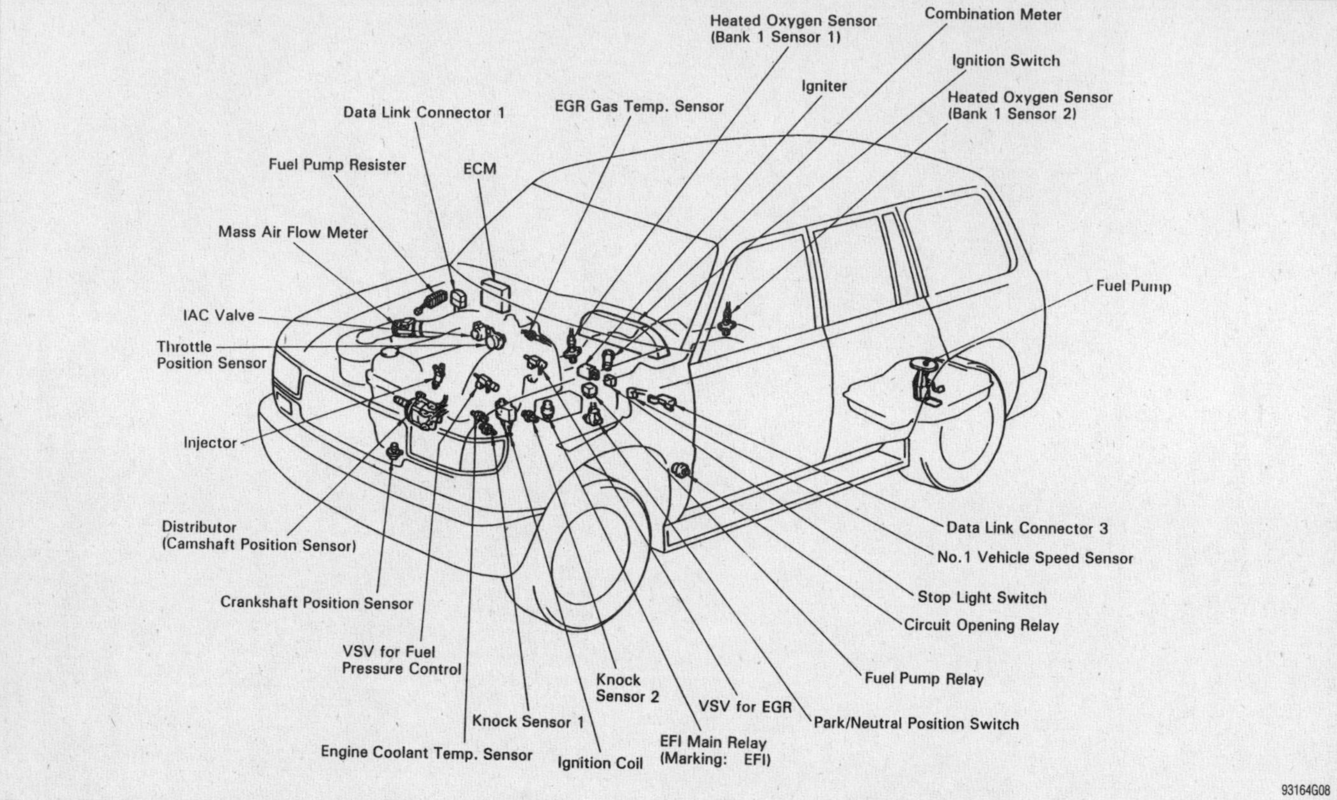

Fig. 77 Electronic engine control system component locations—Land Cruiser with 1FZ-FE engine shown

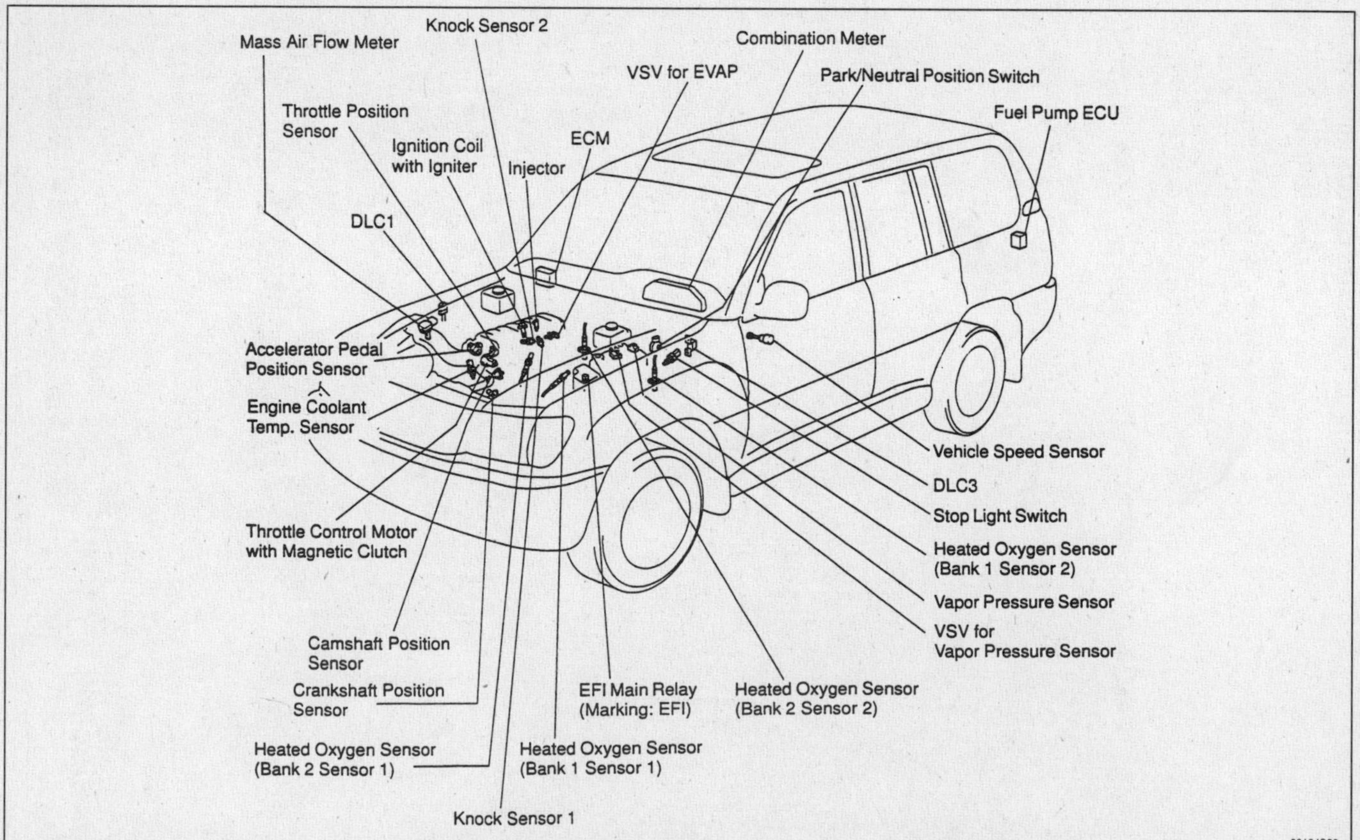

Fig. 78 Electronic engine control system component locations—Land Cruiser with 2UZ-FE engine shown

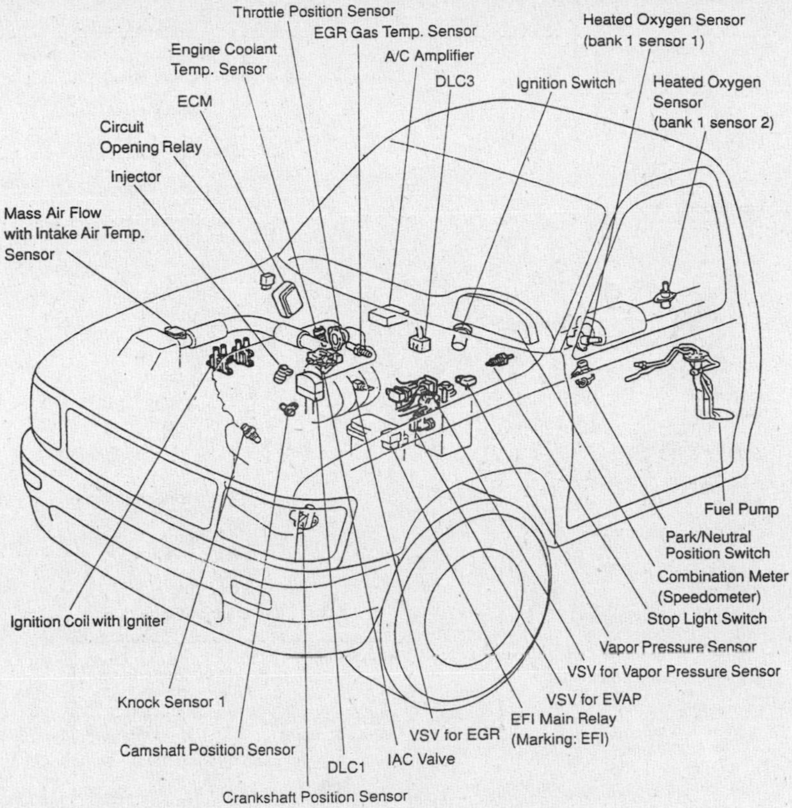

93164G10

Fig. 79 Electronic engine control system component locations—1998 T100 3RZ-FE engine shown

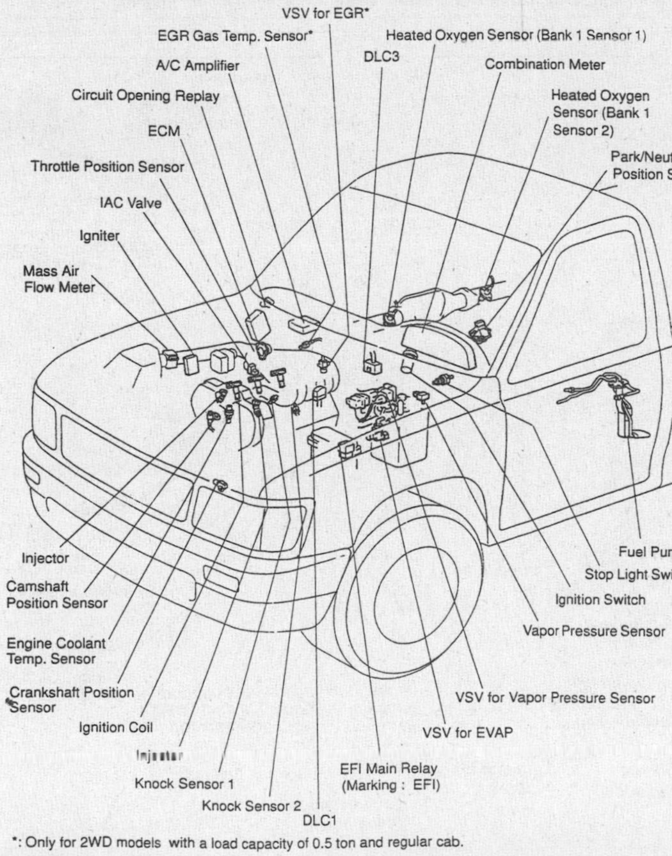

*: Only for 2WD models with a load capacity of 0.5 ton and regular cab.

93164G11

Fig. 80 Electronic engine control system component locations—1998 T100 with 5VZ-FE engine shown

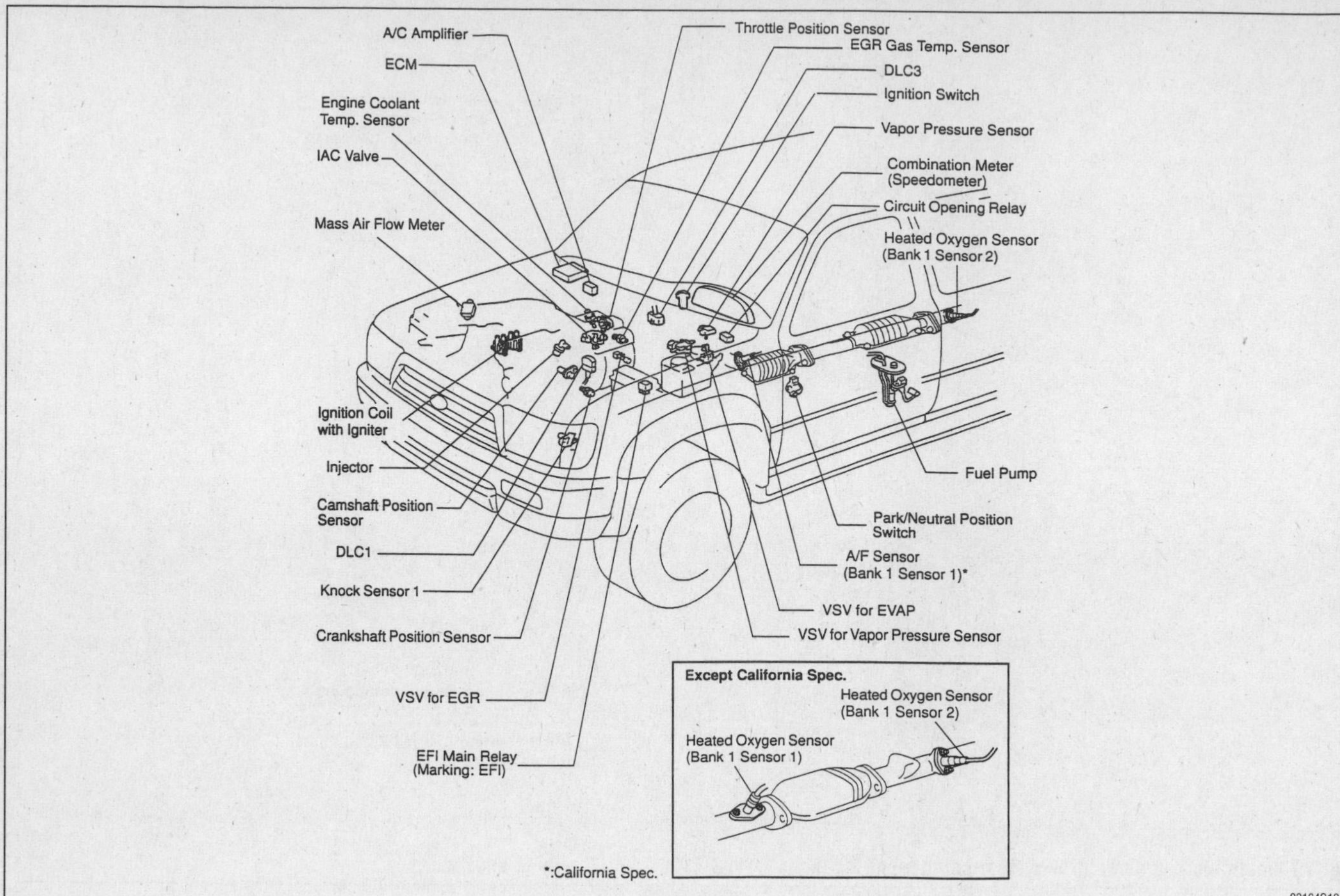

Fig. 81 Electronic engine control system component locations—2000 4Runner with 3RZ-FE engine

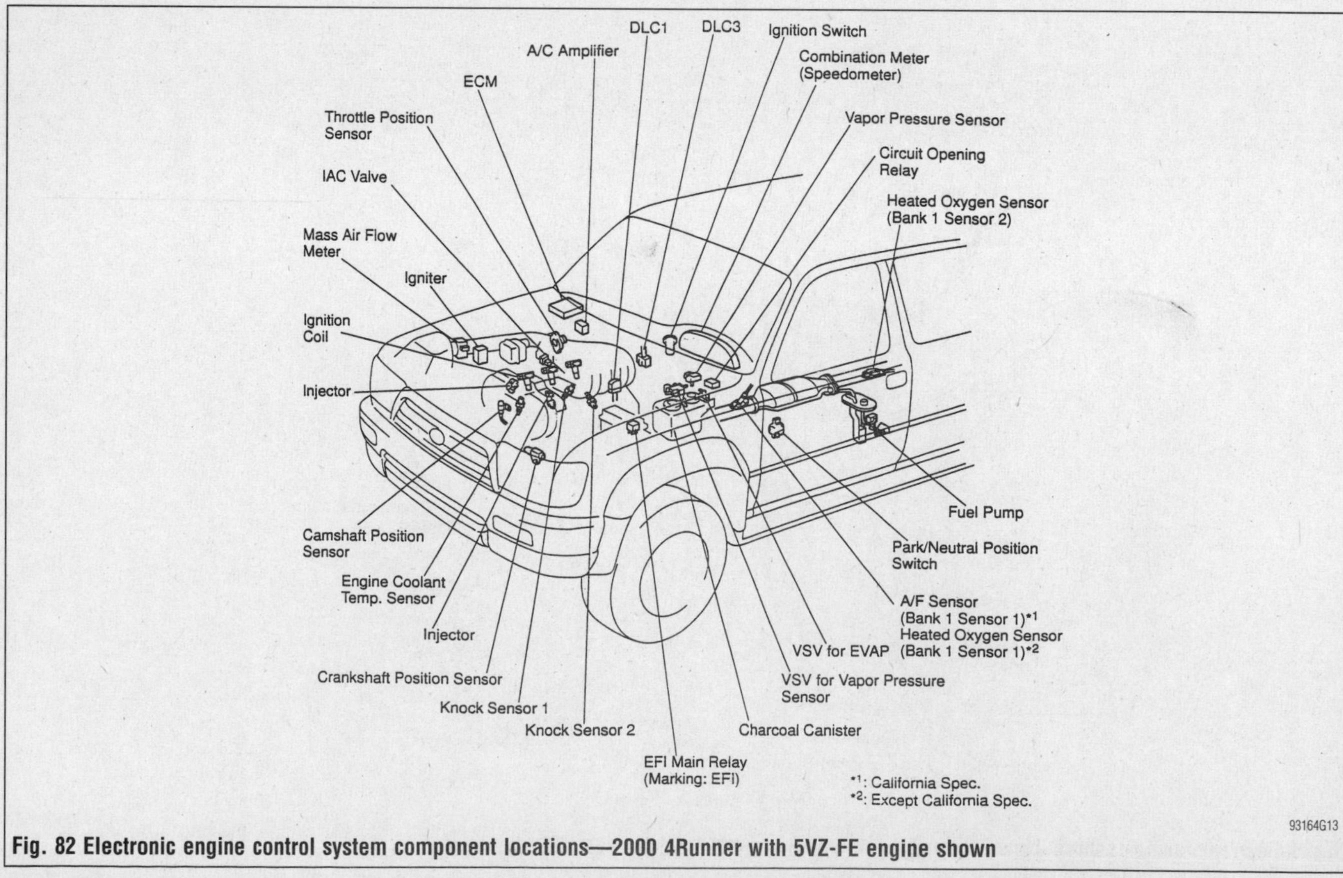

Fig. 82 Electronic engine control system component locations—2000 4Runner with 5VZ-FE engine shown

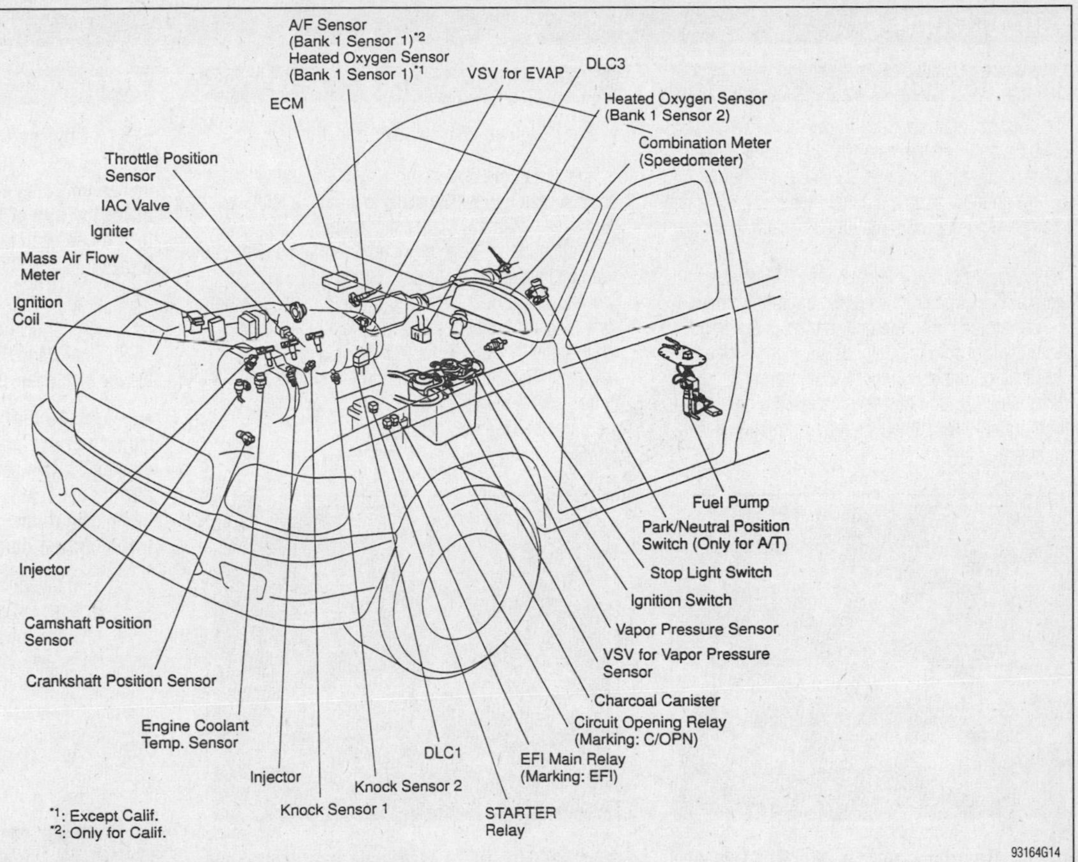

Fig. 83 Electronic engine control system component locations—2000 Tundra with 5VZ-FE engine

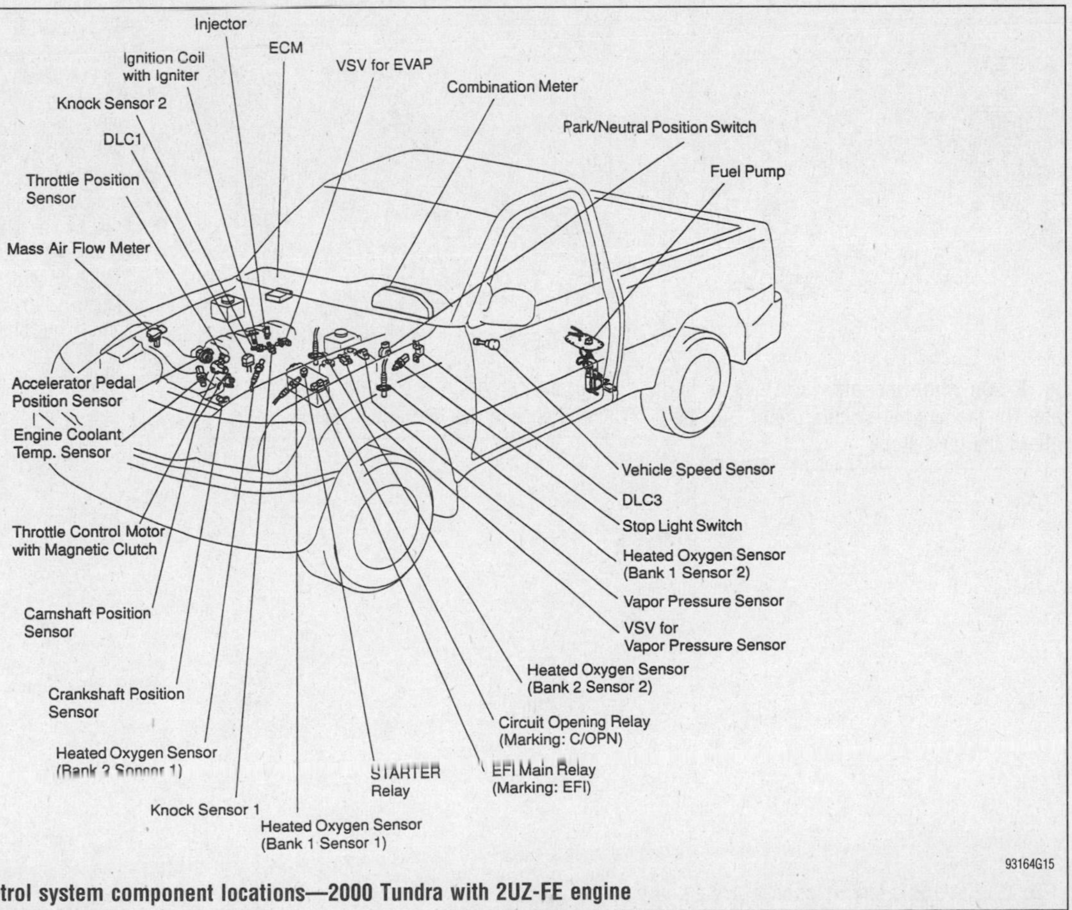

Fig. 84 Electronic engine control system component locations—2000 Tundra with 2UZ-FE engine

TROUBLE CODES

General Information

The ECM contains a built-in, self-diagnosis system which detects troubles within the engine signal network. Once a malfunction is detected, the ECM may turn on the instrument panel Malfunction Indicator Lamp (MIL), if certain malfunction parameters are met.

By analyzing various signals, the ECM detects system malfunctions related to the operating sensors. The ECM stores the failure code associated with the detected failure until the diagnosis system is cleared.

The MIL on the instrument panel informs the driver that a malfunction has been detected. The light will go out automatically once the malfunction has been cleared.

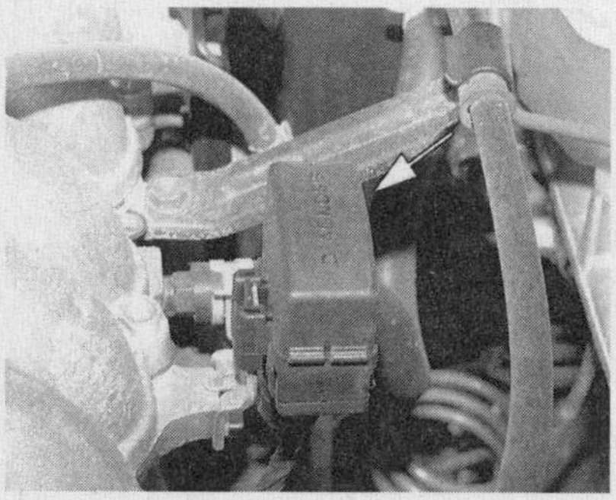

93161p19

Fig. 85 On some models the DLC1 is attached to a bracket on the intake manifold

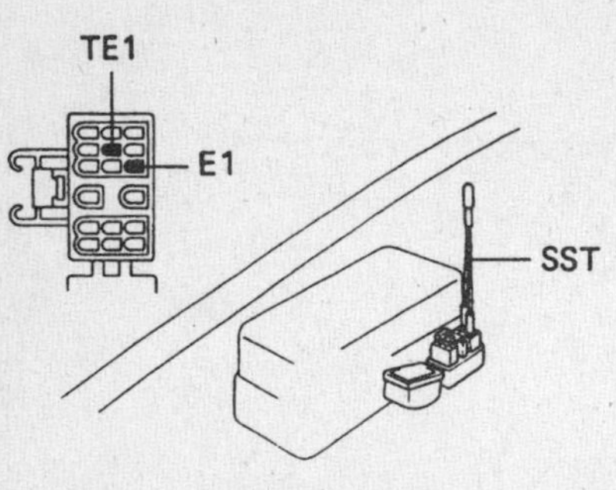

86824PC1

Fig. 87 On some models, the DLC1 is located in the engine compartment, on the side of the fuse block

Data Link Connector

➧ **See Figures 85, 86, 87, and 88**

Two Data Link Connectors (DLC) are normally used. A scan tool is connected to a DLC to read the data stream, capture Diagnostic trouble Codes (DTCs), read real-time operating information and even operate some of the vehicle's systems for testing. Most all modern vehicles will require a scan tool for efficient troubleshooting. The Data Link Connector designated DLC1 is located in the engine compartment. The Data Link Connector designated DLC3 is located in the interior of the vehicle, under the driver's side of the instrument panel.

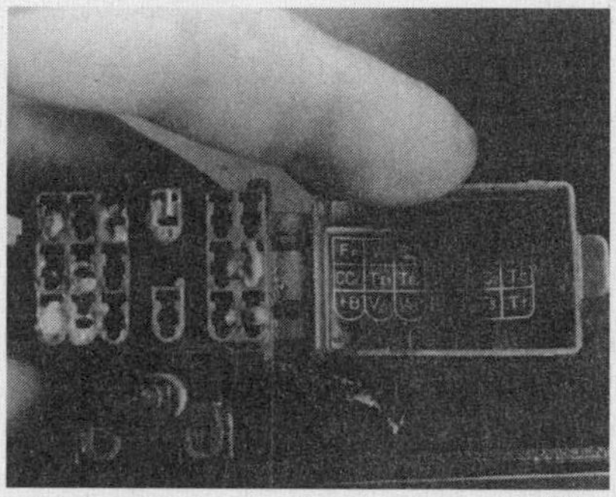

86824G88

Fig. 86 The DLC1 terminals are protected by a lid

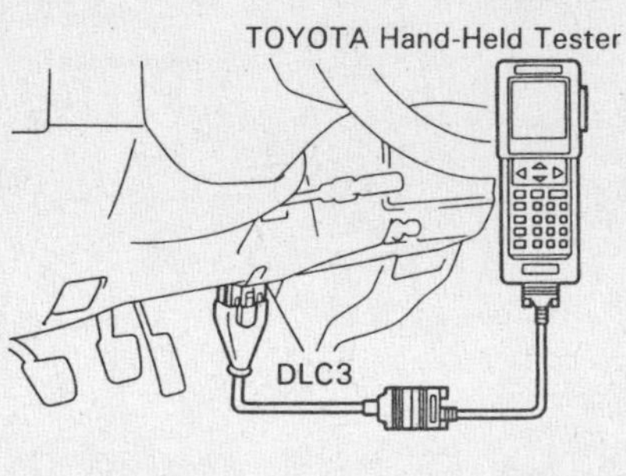

86824PC4

Fig. 88 The DLC3 is located under the driver's side of the instrument panel

Reading Codes

➧ **See Figures 89 thru 99**

➡The vehicles covered by this manual require the use of the Toyota's hand held scan tool or an equivalent OBD II compliant scan tool.

1. Prepare the scan tool according to the manufacturer's instructions.
2. Connect the OBD II scan tool, to the DLC3 under the instrument panel.

➡When the diagnosis system is switched from the normal mode to the check mode, it erases all Diagnostic Trouble Codes (DTC) and freeze frame data recorded. Before switching modes, always check the DTC and freeze frame data and write them down.

3. Turn the ignition switch to the **ON** position and switch the OBD II scan tool switch to on.
4. Use the OBD II scan tool to check the DTC and freeze frame data. Write them down.
5. Compare the codes found to the applicable diagnostic code chart. If necessary, refer to the individual component tests in this section. If the component tests are OK, test the wire harness and connectors for shorts, opens and poor connections.

Clearing Trouble Codes

After repair of the system, the diagnostic code(s) must be removed from the ECM memory. With the ignition turned **OFF,** remove the 15 amp EFI fuse for 30 seconds or more. Once the time period has been observed, reinstall the fuse and check for normal code output.

If the diagnostic code is not erased, it will be retained by the ECM and appear along with a new code in event of future trouble.

Cancellation of the trouble code can also be accomplished by disconnecting the negative battery cable. However, disconnecting the battery cable will erase the other memory systems including the clock and radio settings. If this method is used, always reset these components once the trouble code has been erased.

DIAGNOSTIC TROUBLE CODES

DTC No.	System Detected	Possible Trouble Area	MIL Light Comes On	DTC Retained In Memory
P0100	Mass Air Flow Circuit (MAF) Malfunction	1. Open or Short in MAF circuit 2. Mass Air Flow Meter 3. ECM	YES	YES
P0101	Mass Air Flow Circuit Range/Performance Problem	1. Mass Air Flow Meter	YES	YES
P0110	Intake Air Temp. Circuit Malfunction	1. Open or Short in IAT Circuit 2. IAT Sensor Failure 3. ECM	YES	YES
P0115	Engine Coolant Temp. Circuit Malfunction	1. Open or Short in ECT Circuit 2. ECT Sensor Failure 3. ECM	YES	YES
P0116	Engine Coolant Temp. Circuit Range/ Performance Problem	1. ECT Sensor Failure 2. Cooling System Problem	YES	YES
P0120	Throttle Position Sensor/ Switch A Circuit Malfunction	1. Open or Short in TPS Circuit 2. TPS Sensor Failure 3. ECM	YES	YES
P0121	Throttle Position Sensor/ Switch A Circuit Range/ Performance Problem	1. TPS Sensor Failure	YES	YES
P0125	Insufficient Coolant Temp. for Closed Loop Fuel Control	1. Open or Short in Heated Oxygen Sensor Circuit 2. Heated Oxygen Sensor Failure	YES	YES
P0130	Heated Oxygen Sensor Circuit Malfunction Sensor 1	1. Heated Oxygen Sensor Failure 2. Fuel Trim Malfunction	YES	YES
P0133	Heated Oxygen Sensor Circuit Slow Response Sensor 1	1. Heated Oxygen Sensor Failure	YES	YES
P0135	Heated Oxygen Sensor Heater Circuit Malfunction - Sensor 1	1. Open or Short in Heater Circuit 2. Oxygen Sensor Heater Failure 3. ECM	YES	YES
P0136	Heated Oxygen Sensor Circuit Malfunction Sensor 2	1. Heated Oxygen Sensor Failure	YES	YES
P0141	Heated Oxygen Sensor Heater Circuit Malfunction - Sensor 2	1. Open or Short in Heater Circuit 2. Oxygen Sensor Heater Failure 3. ECM	YES	YES
P0171	System Too Lean (Fuel Trim)	1. Air Intake Hose Loose 2. Fuel Line Pressure, Leak 3. Injector Blockage 4. Oxygen Sensor Malfunction 5. MAF Sensor Problem 6. Engine Coolant Temp. Sensor	YES	YES
P0172	System Too Rich (Fuel Trim)	1. Fuel Line Pressure 2. Injector Leak, Blockage 3. Oxygen Sensor Malfunction 4. MAF Sensor Problem 5. Engine Coolant Temp. Sensor	YES	YES
P0300	Random/Multiple Cylinder Misfire Detected	1. Ignition System Problem 2. Injector Problem 3. Fuel Line Pressure 4. EGR System Problem 5. Compression Pressure Problem 6. Valve Clearance Out Of Spec 7. Valve Timing Problem 8. Mass Air Flow Meter System 9. Engine Coolant Temp. Sensor	YES, or MIL Blinking	YES
P0301 P0302 P0303 P0304 P0305 P0306 P0307	Misfire Detected Cylinder 1 Cylinder 2 Cylinder 3 Cylinder 4 Cylinder 5 Cylinder 6			
P0325	Knock Sensor 1 Circuit Malfunction	1. Open or Short in KS 1 Circuit 2. KS 1 Loose 3. ECM	YES	YES

93164G35

Fig. 89 Diagnostic Trouble Codes (1 of 2)—1FZ-FE engine

DIAGNOSTIC TROUBLE CODES

DTC No.	System Detected	Possible Trouble Area	MIL Light Comes On	DTC Retained In Memory
P0330	Knock Sensor 2 Circuit Malfunction	1. Open or Short in KS 2 Circuit 2. KS 2 Loose 3. ECM	YES	YES
P0335	Crankshaft Position Sensor "A" Circuit Malfunction	1. Open or Short in Sensor Circuit for NE Signal 2. Sensor NE Signal Failure 3. Starter Problem 4. ECM	YES	YES
P0340	Camshaft Position Sensor Circuit Malfunction	1. Open or Short in Sensor Circuit 2. Cam Position Sensor Failure 3. ECM	YES	YES
P0385	Crankshaft Position Sensor "B" Circuit Malfunction	1. Open or Short in Sensor Circuit for NE 2 Signal 2. Sensor NE 2 Signal Failure 3. ECM	YES	YES
P0401	Exhaust Gas Recirculation Flow Insufficient	1. EGR Valve Stuck Closed 2. Short in VSV Circuit for EGR 3. Open EGR Temp Sensor Circuit 4. EGR Hose Disconnected 5. ECM	YES	YES
P0402	Exhaust Gas Recircula. Flow Excessive	1. EGR Valve Stuck Open 2. EGR VSV Open Malfunction 3. Open VSV EGR Circuit 4. Short in EGR Temp. Circuit 5. ECM	YES	YES
P0420	Catalyst System Efficiency Below Threshold	1. 3-Way Cat. Converter Problem 2. Open/Short HO2S Circuit 3. HO2S Failure	YES	YES
P0500	Vehicle Speed Sensor Malfunction	1. Open/Short in VSS Circuit 2. Vehicle Speed Sensor Failure 3. Instrument Cluster Problem 4. ECM	YES	YES
P0505	Idle Control System Malfunction	1. IAC Valve Stuck or Closed 2. Open/Shorted IAC Circuit 3. Open/Shorted A/C Signal Circuit 4. Air Intake Hose Loose	YES	YES
P0510	Closed Throttle Position Switch Malfunction	1. Open in Closed Throttle Position Switch Circuit 2. Closed Throttle Switch Failure 3. ECM	YES	YES
P1300	Igniter Circuit Malfunction	1. Open or Short in IGF or IGT Circuit From Igniter to ECM 2. Igniter Failure 3. ECM	YES	YES
P1335	Crankshaft Position Sensor Circuit Malfunction (during engine running)	1. Open or Short in Crankshaft Position Sensor Circuit for NE Signal 2. Sensor for NE Signal Failure 3. Starter Problem 4. ECM	NO	YES
P1520	Stop Light Switch Signal Malfunction	1. Short in Stop Light Switch Signal Circuit 2. Stop Light Switch Failure 3. ECM	YES	YES
P1600	ECM BATT Malfunction	1. Open in Back Up Power Source Circuit 2. ECM	YES	YES
P1605	Knock Control CPU Malfunction	1. ECM	YES	YES
P1780	Park/Neutral Position Switch Malfunction	1. Short in Park/Neutral Position Switch Circuit 2. Park/Neutral Switch Failure 3. ECM	YES	YES

93164G36

Fig. 90 Diagnostic Trouble Codes (2 of 2)—1FZ-FE engine

DIAGNOSTIC TROUBLE CODES

DTC No.	System Detected	Possible Trouble Area	MIL Light Comes On	DTC Retained In Memory
P0100	Mass Air Flow Circuit (MAF) Malfunction	1. Open or Short in MAF circuit 2. Mass Air Flow Meter 3. ECM	YES	YES
P0101	Mass Air Flow Circuit Range/Performance Problem	1. Mass Air Flow Meter	YES	YES
P0110	Intake Air Temp. Circuit Malfunction	1. Open or Short in IAT Circuit 2. IAT Sensor Failure 3. ECM	YES	YES
P0115	Engine Coolant Temp. Circuit Malfunction	1. Open of Short in ECT Circuit 2. ECT Sensor Failure 3. ECM	YES	YES
P0116	Engine Coolant Temp. Circuit Range/ Performance Problem	1. ECT Sensor Failure 2. Cooling System Problem	YES	YES
P0120	Throttle Position Sensor/ Switch A Circuit Malfunction	1. Open or Short in TPS Circuit 2. TPS Sensor Failure 3. ECM	YES	YES
P0121	Throttle Position Sensor/ Switch A Circuit Range/ Performance Problem	1. TPS Sensor Failure 2. ECM	YES	YES
P0125	Insufficient Coolant Temperature for Closed Loop Fuel Control	1. Open or Short in Heated Oxygen Sensor Circuit 2. Heated Oxygen Sensor Failure 3. Fuel System Problem 4. Injector Problem 5. Ignition System Problem	YES	YES
P0130	Heated Oxygen Sensor Circuit Malfunction Bank 1, Sensor 1	1. Heated Oxygen Sensor Failure 2. Fuel Trim Malfunction	YES	YES
P0133	Heated Oxygen Sensor Circuit Slow Response Sensor 1	1. Heated Oxygen Sensor Failure	YES	YES
P0135	Heated Oxygen Sensor Circuit Slow Response Bank 1, Sensor 1	1. Heated Oxygen Sensor Failure 2. Fuel Trim Malfunction	YES	YES
P0136	Heated Oxygen Sensor Circuit Malfunction Bank 1, Sensor 2	1. Heated Oxygen Sensor Failure	YES	YES
P0141	Heated Oxygen Sensor Heater Circuit Malfun. Bank 1, Sensor 2	1. Open or Short in Heater Circuit 2. Oxygen Sensor Heater Failure 3. ECM	YES	YES
P0150	Heated Oxygen Sensor Circuit Malfunction Bank 2, Sensor 1	1. Heated Oxygen Sensor Failure 2. Fuel Trim Malfunction	YES	YES
P0153	Heated Oxygen Sensor Circuit Slow Response Bank 2, Sensor 1	1. Heated Oxygen Sensor Failure	YES	YES
P0155	Heated Oxygen Sensor Heater Circuit Malfun. Bank 2, Sensor 1	1. Heated Oxygen Sensor Failure 2. Fuel Trim Malfunction	YES	YES
P0156	Heated Oxygen Sensor Circuit Malfunction Bank 2, Sensor 2	1. Heated Oxygen Sensor Failure	YES	YES
P0161	Heated Oxygen Sensor Heater Circuit Malfun. Bank 2, Sensor 2	1. Heated Oxygen Sensor Failure 2. Fuel Trim Malfunction	YES	YES
P0171	System Too Lean (Fuel Trim)	1. Air Intake Hose Loose 2. Fuel Line Pressure, Leak 3. Injector Blockage 4. Oxygen Sensor Malfunction 5. MAF Sensor Problem 6. Engine Coolant Temp. Sensor	YES	YES

93164G37

Fig. 91 Diagnostic Trouble Codes (1 of 4)—2UZ-FE engine

DIAGNOSTIC TROUBLE CODES

DTC No.	System Detected	Possible Trouble Area	MIL Light Comes On	DTC Retained In Memory
P0172	System Too Rich (Fuel Trim)	1. Fuel Line Pressure 2. Injector Leak, Blockage 3. Oxygen Sensor Malfunction 4. MAF Sensor Problem 5. Engine Coolant Temp. Sensor	YES	YES
P0300	Random/Multiple Cylinder Misfire Detected	1. Ignition System Problem 2. Injector Problem 3. Fuel Line Pressure 4. Open/Short in Engine Harness 5. Compression Pressure Problem 6. Valve Clearance Out Of Spec 7. Valve Timing Problem 8. Mass Air Flow Meter System 9. Engine Coolant Temp. Sensor 10. ECM	YES	YES
P0301 P0302 P0303 P0304 P0305 P0306 P0307 P0308 P0309	Misfire Detected Cylinder 1 Cylinder 2 Cylinder 3 Cylinder 4 Cylinder 5 Cylinder 6 Cylinder 7 Cylinder 8			
P0325	Knock Sensor 1 Circuit Malfunction	1. Open or Short in KS 1 Circuit 2. KS 1 Loose 3. ECM	YES	YES
P0330	Knock Sensor 2 Circuit Malfunction	1. Open or Short in KS 2 Circuit 2. KS 2 Loose 3. ECM	YES	YES
P0335	Crankshaft Position Sensor "A" Circuit Malfunction	1. Open or Short in Crankshaft Position Sensor Circuit 2. Crankshaft Sensor Failure 3. Starter Problem 4. ECM	YES	YES
P0340	Camshaft Position Sensor Circuit Malfunction	1. Open or Short in Sensor Circuit 2. Cam Position Sensor Failure 3. Starter Problem 4. ECM	YES	YES
P0420	Catalyst System Efficiency Below Threshold - Bank 1	1. 3-Way Cat. Converter Problem 2. Open/Short HO2S Circuit 3. HO2S Failure	YES	YES
P0430	Catalyst System Efficiency Below Threshold - Bank 2	1. 3-Way Cat. Converter Problem 2. Open/Short HO2S Circuit 3. HO2S Failure	YES	YES
P0440	Evaporative Emission Control System Malfunction	1. Vapor Pressure Sensor 2. Fuel Cap Incorrectly Installed 3. Fuel Cap Cracked or Damaged 4. Vacuum hose loose, damaged 5. EVAP hose loose, cracked 6. Fuel tank damaged 7. Charcoal canister damaged	YES	YES
P0441	Evaporative Emission Control System Incorrect Purge Flow	1. Open, Short in VSV Circuit 2. VSV for Vapor Pressure Sensor 3. Open, Short in Sensor Circuit 4. Vapor Pressure Sensor 5. Open, Short VSV EVAP Circuit 6. VSV for EVAP 7. Vacuum hose loose, damaged 8. Charcoal canister damaged	YES	YES
P0446	Evaporative Emission Control System Vent Control Malfunction			
P0450	EVAP Emission Control System Pressure Sensor Malfunction	1. Open, Short in Vapor pressure Sensor Circuit 2. Vapor Pressure Sensor 3. ECM	YES	YES
P0451	EVAP Emission Control System Pressure Sensor Range/Performance			
P0500	Vehicle Speed Sensor Malfunction	1. Open/Short in No. 1 VSS Circuit 2. No. 1 VSS Failure 3. Instrument Cluster Problem 4. ECM	YES	YES

93164G38

Fig. 92 Diagnostic Trouble Codes (2 of 4)—2UZ-FE engine

DIAGNOSTIC TROUBLE CODES

DTC No.	System Detected	Possible Trouble Area	MIL Light Comes On	DTC Retained In Memory
P0505	Idle Control System Malfunction	1. Electric Throttle Control System 2. Air Intake Hose Loose	YES	YES
P1120	Accelerator Pedal Position Sensor Circuit Malfunction	1. Open or Short in Sensor Circuit 2. Pedal Position Sensor Failure 3. ECM	YES	Yes
P1121	Accelerator Pedal Position Sensor Range/Performance Problem	1. Accelerator Pedal Position Sensor Failure 2. ECM	YES	YES
P1125	Throttle Control Motor Circuit Malfunction	1. Open or Short in Throttle Control Motor Circuit 2. Throttle Control Motor Failure 3. ECM	YES	YES
P1126	Magnetic Clutch Circuit Malfunction	1. Open or Short in Magnetic Clutch Circuit 2. Magnetic Clutch Failure 3. ECM	YES	YES
P1127	ETCS Actuator Power Source Circuit Malfunction	1. Open in ETCS Power Source Circuit 2. ECM	YES	YES
P1128	Throttle Control Motor Lock Malfunction	1. Throttle Control Motor Failure 2. Throttle Body Assembly Problem 3. ECM	YES	YES
P1129	Electric Throttle Control System Malfunction	1. Electric Throttle Control System Failure 2. ECM	YES	YES
P1200	Fuel Pump Relay/ ECU Circuit Malfunction	1. Open/Short in Fuel Pump ECU 2. Fuel Pump ECU Failure 3. ECM Power Source Circuit 4. Fuel Pump Failure 5. ECM	NO	YES
P1300	Igniter Circuit Malfunction (No. 1)	1. Open or Short in IGF1 or IGT1 Circuit From No. 2 Ignition Coil With Igniter to ECM 2. No. 1 Ignition Coil With Igniter 3. ECM	YES	YES
P1305	Igniter Circuit Malfunction (No. 2)	1. Open or Short in IGF2 or IGT2 Circuit From No. 2 Ignition Coil With Igniter to ECM 2. No. 2 Ignition Coil With Igniter 3. ECM	YES	YES
P1310	Igniter Circuit Malfunction (No. 3)	1. Open or Short in IGF2 or IGT3 Circuit From No. 3 Ignition Coil With Igniter to ECM 2. No. 3 Ignition Coil With Igniter 3. ECM	YES	YES
P1315	Igniter Circuit Malfunction (No. 4)	1. Open or Short in IGF1 or IGT4 Circuit From No. 4 Ignition Coil With Igniter to ECM 2. No. 4 Ignition Coil With Igniter 3. ECM	YES	YES
P1320	Igniter Circuit Malfunction (No. 5)	1. Open or Short in IGF2 or IGT5 Circuit From No. 5 Ignition Coil With Igniter to ECM 2. No. 5 Ignition Coil With Igniter 3. ECM	YES	YES
P1325	Igniter Circuit Malfunction (No. 6)	1. Open or Short in IGF1 or IGT6 Circuit From No. 6 Ignition Coil With Igniter to ECM 2. No. 6 Ignition Coil With Igniter 3. ECM	YES	YES

93164G39

Fig. 93 Diagnostic Trouble Codes (3 of 4)—2UZ-FE engine

DIAGNOSTIC TROUBLE CODES

DTC No.	System Detected	Possible Trouble Area	MIL Light Comes On	DTC Retained In Memory
P1330	Igniter Circuit Malfunction (No. 7)	1. Open or Short in IGF1 or IGT7 Circuit From No. 7 Ignition Coil With Igniter to ECM 2. No. 7 Ignition Coil With Igniter 3. ECM	YES	YES
P1335	Crankshaft Position Sensor Malfunction (During Engine Running)	1. Open or Short in Crankshaft Position Sensor Circuit 2. Crankshaft Sensor Failure 3. Starter Problem 4. ECM	NO	YES
P1340	Igniter Circuit Malfunction (No. 8)	1. Open or Short in IGF2 or IGT8 Circuit From No. 8 Ignition Coil With Igniter to ECM 2. No. 8 Ignition Coil With Igniter 3. ECM	YES	YES
P1520	Stop Light Switch Signal Malfunction	1. Short in Stop Light Switch Signal Circuit 2. Stop Light Switch Failure 3. ECM	YES	YES
P1600	ECM BATT Malfunction	1. Open in Back-Up Power Source Circuit 2. ECM	YES	YES
P1633	ECM Malfunction (ETCS Circuit)	1. ECM	YES	YES
P1780	Park/Neutral Position Switch Malfunction	1. Short in P/N Switch Circuit 2. P/N Switch Failure 3. ECM	YES	YES
B2785	Ignition Switch ON Malfunction	1. Ignition Switch Failure 2. Main Relay Failure 3. Wire Harness Problem	NO	YES
B2786	Ignition Switch OFF Malfunction			
B2791	Key Unlock Warning Switch OFF Malfunction	1. Key Warning Switch Failure 2. Main Relay Failure 3. Wire Harness problem	NO	YES
B2795	Unmatch Key Code	1. Key Problem 2. Unregistered Key Inserted Before?	NO	YES
B2796	No Communication in Immobilizer System	1. Key Problem 2. Transponder Key Coil Problem 3. Amplifier Failure 4. Wire Harness Problem 5. ECM	NO	YES
B2797	Communications Malfunction No. 1	1. Communications Contests 2. Unregistered Key Inserted Before?	NO	YES
B2798	Communications Malfunction No. 2	1. Key Problem 2. Transponder Key Coil Problem 3. Amplifier Failure 4. Wire Harness Problem 5. ECM	NO	YES

93164G40

Fig. 94 Diagnostic Trouble Codes (4 of 4)—2UZ-FE engine

DIAGNOSTIC TROUBLE CODES

DTC No.	System Detected	Possible Trouble Area	MIL Light Comes On	DTC Retained In Memory
P0100	Mass Air Flow Circuit (MAF) Malfunction	1. Open or Short in MAF circuit 2. Mass Air Flow Meter 3. ECM	YES	YES
P0101	Mass Air Flow Circuit Range/Performance Problem	1. Mass Air Flow Meter	YES	YES
P0110	Intake Air Temp. Circuit Malfunction	1. Open or Short in IAT Circuit 2. IAT Sensor Failure 3. ECM	YES	YES
P0115	Engine Coolant Temp. Circuit Malfunction	1. Open or Short in ECT Circuit 2. ECT Sensor Failure 3. ECM	YES	YES
P0116	Engine Coolant Temp. Circuit Range/ Performance Problem	1. ECT Sensor Failure 2. Cooling System Problem	YES	YES
P0120	Throttle Position Sensor/ Switch A Circuit Malfunction	1. Open or Short in TPS Circuit 2. TPS Sensor Failure 3. ECM	YES	YES
P0121	Throttle Position Sensor/ Switch A Circuit Range/ Performance Problem	1. TPS Sensor Failure	YES	YES
P0125	Insufficient Coolant Temp. for Closed Loop Fuel Control	1. Open or Short in Heated Oxygen Sensor Circuit 2. Heated Oxygen Sensor Failure	YES	YES
P0130	Heated Oxygen Sensor Circuit Malfunction Bank 1, Sensor 1	1. Heated Oxygen Sensor Failure 2. Fuel Trim Malfunction	YES	YES
P0133	Heated Oxygen Sensor Circuit Slow Response Bank 1, Sensor 1	1. Heated Oxygen Sensor Failure	YES	YES
P0135	Heated Oxygen Sensor Heater Circuit Malfun. Bank 1, Sensor 1	1. Open or Short in Heater Circuit 2. Oxygen Sensor Heater Failure 3. ECM	YES	YES
P0136	Heated Oxygen Sensor Circuit Malfunction Bank 1, Sensor 2	1. Heated Oxygen Sensor Failure	YES	YES
P0141	Heated Oxygen Sensor Heater Circuit Malfun. Bank 1, Sensor 2	1. Open or Short in Heater Circuit 2. Oxygen Sensor Heater Failure 3. ECM	YES	YES
P0171	System Too Lean (Fuel Trim)	1. Air Intake Hose Loose 2. Fuel Line Pressure, Leak 3. Injector Blockage 4. Oxygen Sensor Malfunction 5. MAF Sensor Problem 6. Engine Coolant Temp. Sensor	YES	YES
P0172	System Too Rich (Fuel Trim)	1. Fuel Line Pressure 2. Injector Leak, Blockage 3. Oxygen Sensor Malfunction 4. MAF Sensor Problem 5. Engine Coolant Temp. Sensor	YES	YES
P0300	Random/Multiple Cylinder Misfire Detected	1. Ignition System Problem 2. Injector Problem 3. Fuel Line Pressure 4. EGR System Problem 5. Compression Pressure Problem 6. Valve Clearance Out Of Spec 7. Valve Timing Problem 8. Mass Air Flow Meter System 9. Engine Coolant Temp. Sensor	YES	YES
P0301 P0302 P0303 P0304 P0305	Misfire Detected Cylinder 1 Cylinder 2 Cylinder 3 Cylinder 4			
P0325	Knock Sensor 1 Circuit Malfunction	1. Open or Short in KS 1 Circuit 2. KS 1 Loose 3. ECM	YES	YES
P0335	Crankshaft Position Sensor "A" Circuit Malfunction	1. Open or Short in Sensor Circuit 2. Sensor Failure 3. Starter Problem 4. ECM	YES	YES
P0336 (2RZ-FE)	Crankshaft Position Sensor "A" Circuit Range/Performance	1. Valve Timing Out Of Spec 2. Distributor Improperly Installed 3. ECM	YES	YES
P0340	Camshaft Position Sensor Circuit Malfunction	1. Open or Short in Sensor Circuit 2. Cam Position Sensor Failure 3. Distributor Problem 4. Starter Problem 5. ECM	YES	YES

93164G41

Fig. 95 Diagnostic Trouble Codes (1 of 2)—2RZ-FE and 3RZ-FE engines

DIAGNOSTIC TROUBLE CODES

DTC No.	System Detected	Possible Trouble Area	MIL Light Comes On	DTC Retained In Memory
P0401	Exhaust Gas Recirculation Flow Insufficient	1. EGR Valve Stuck Closed 2. Short in VSV Circuit for EGR 3. Open EGR Temp Sensor Circuit 4. EGR Hose Disconnected 5. ECM	YES	YES
P0402	Exhaust Gas Recirculation Flow Excessive	1. EGR Valve Stuck Open 2. EGR VSV Open Malfunction 3. Open VSV EGR Circuit 4. Short in EGR Temp. Circuit 5. ECM	YES	YES
P0420	Catalyst System Efficiency Below Threshold	1. 3-Way Cat. Converter Problem 2. Open/Short HO2S Circuit 3. HO2S Failure	YES	YES
P0440	EVAP Control System Malfunction (4WD)	1. Vapor Press Sensor Problem 2. Fuel Tank Cap Defective 3. Vacuum Hose Damaged, Loose 4. Fuel Tank Damaged 5. Charcoal Canister Damaged		
P0441	Evaporative Emission Control System Incorrect Purge Flow (2WD)	1. Open, Short in EVAP VSV Circuit 2. EVAP VSV Failure 3. ECM 4. Vacuum hose blocked, off 5. Charcoal Canister Problem	YES	YES
P0441	Evaporative Emission Control System Incorrect Purge Flow (4WD)	1. Open, Short in EVAP VSV Circuit 2. EVAP VSV Failure 3. Open, Short in Sensor Circuit 4. Vapor Pressure Sensor Failure 5. Vacuum Hose Damaged, Loose	YES	YES
P0446	Evaporative Emission Control System Vent Control Malfunction (4WD)	6. Charcoal Canister Problem	YES	YES
P0450	Evaporative Emission Control System Pressure Sensor Malfunction (4WD)	1. Open, Short in Vapor Pressure Sensor Circuit 2. Vapor Pressure Sensor Failure 3. ECM	YES	YES
P0500	Vehicle Speed Sensor (VSS) Malfunction	2. Vehicle Speed Sensor Failure 3. Instrument Cluster Problem 4. ECM 5. Speedometer Cable Problem	YES	YES
P0505	Idle Control System Malfunction	1. IAC Valve Stuck or Closed 2. Open/Shorted IAC Circuit 3. Air Intake Hose Loose	YES	YES
P0510	Closed Throttle Position Switch Malfunction	1. Open in Closed Throttle Position Switch Circuit 2. Closed Throttle Switch Failure 3. ECM	YES	YES
P1300 (2RZ-FE)	Igniter Circuit Malfunction Bank 1	1. Open or Short in IGF or IGT Circuit From Igniter to ECM 2. Igniter Failure 3. ECM	YES	YES
P1300 (3RZ-FE)	Igniter Circuit Malfunction Bank 1	1. Open or Short in IGF or IGT Circuit From Ignition Coil to ECM 2. Igniter Failure 3. ECM	YES	YES
P1335	Crankshaft Position Sensor Circuit Malfunction (during engine running)	1. Open or Short in Crankshaft Position Sensor Circuit 2. Crankshaft Sensor Failure 3. ECM	NO	YES
P1520 (2RZ-FE)	Stop Light Switch Signal Malfunction	1. Short in Stop Light Switch Signal Circuit 2. Stop Light Switch Failure 3. ECM	YES	YES
P1600	ECM BATT Malfunction	1. Open in Back Up PowerSource Circuit 2. ECM	YES	YES
P1780	Park/Neutral Position Switch Malfunction	1. Short in Park/Neutral Position Switch Circuit 2. Park/Neutral Switch Failure 3. ECM	YES	YES

93164G42

Fig. 96 Diagnostic Trouble Codes (2 of 2)—2RZ-FE and 3RZ-FE engines

DIAGNOSTIC TROUBLE CODES

DTC No.	System Detected	Possible Trouble Area	MIL Light Comes On	DTC Retained In Memory
P0100	Mass Air Flow Circuit (MAF) Malfunction	1. Open or Short in MAF circuit 2. Mass Air Flow Meter 3. ECM	YES	YES
P0101	Mass Air Flow Circuit Range/Performance Problem	1. Mass Air Flow Meter	YES	YES
P0110	Intake Air Temp. Circuit Malfunction	1. Open or Short in IAT Circuit 2. IAT Sensor Failure 3. ECM	YES	YES
P0115	Engine Coolant Temp. Circuit Malfunction	1. Open or Short in ECT Circuit 2. ECT Sensor Failure 3. ECM	YES	YES
P0116	Engine Coolant Temp. Circuit Range/ Performance Problem	1. ECT Sensor Failure 2. Cooling System Problem	YES	YES
P0120	Throttle Position Sensor/ Switch A Circuit Malfunction	1. Open or Short in TPS Circuit 2. TPS Sensor Failure 3. ECM	YES	YES
P0121	Throttle Position Sensor/ Switch A Circuit Range/ Performance Problem	1. TPS Sensor Failure	YES	YES
P0125	Insufficient Coolant Temp. for Closed Loop Fuel Control	1. Open or Short in Heated Oxygen Sensor Circuit 2. HO2S Failure, Bank 1, Sensor 1	YES	YES
P0130	Heated Oxygen Sensor Circuit Malfunction Bank 1, Sensor 1	1. Heated Oxygen Sensor Failure 2. Fuel Trim Malfunction	YES	YES
P0133	Heated Oxygen Sensor Circuit Slow Response Bank 1, Sensor 1	1. Heated Oxygen Sensor Failure	YES	YES
P0135	Heated Oxygen Sensor Heater Circuit Malfun. Bank 1, Sensor 1	1. Open or Short in Heater Circuit 2. Oxygen Sensor Heater Failure 3. ECM	YES	YES
P0136	Heated Oxygen Sensor Circuit Malfunction Bank 1, Sensor 2	1. Heated Oxygen Sensor Failure	YES	YES
P0141	Heated Oxygen Sensor Heater Circuit Malfun. Bank 1, Sensor 2	1. Open or Short in Heater Circuit 2. Oxygen Sensor Heater Failure 3. ECM	YES	YES
P0171	System Too Lean (Fuel Trim) (Except California)	1. Air Intake Hose Loose 2. Fuel Line Pressure, Leak 3. Injector Blockage 4. HO2S Failure, Bank 1, Sensor 1 5. MAF Sensor Problem 6. Engine Coolant Temp. Sensor	YES	YES
P0171	System Too Lean (Fuel Trim) (California)	1. Air Induction System Problem 2. Injector Leak, Blockage 3. Mass Air Flow Meter Problem 4. Engine Coolant Temp. Sensor 5. Fuel Pressure Out of Spec 6. Open, Short A/F Sensor or Wire 7. A/F Sensor, Bank 1, Sensor 1 8. ECM	YES	YES
P0172	System Too Rich (Fuel Trim) (Except California)	1. Injector Leak, Blockage 2. Mass Air Flow Meter Problem 3. Engine Coolant Temp. Sensor 4. Ignition System Problem 5. Fuel Pressure Out of Spec 6. Open, Short in HO2S Circuit 7. HO2S Failure, Bank 1, Sensor 1 8. ECM	YES	YES
P0172	System Too Rich (Fuel Trim) (California)	1. Injector Leak, Blockage 2. Mass Air Flow Meter Problem 3. Engine Coolant Temp. Sensor 4. Ignition System Problem 5. Fuel Pressure Out of Spec 6. HO2S Failure, Bank 1 Sensor 1 7. A/F Sensor, Bank 1, Sensor 1 8. ECM	YES	YES

93164G43

Fig. 97 Diagnostic Trouble Codes (1 of 3)—5VZ-FE engine

DIAGNOSTIC TROUBLE CODES

DTC No.	System Detected	Possible Trouble Area	MIL Light Comes On	DTC Retained In Memory
P0300	Random/Multiple Cylinder Misfire Detected	1. Ignition System Problem 2. Injector Problem 3. Fuel Line Pressure 4. EGR System Problem 5. Compression Pressure Problem 6. Valve Clearance Out Of Spec 7. Valve Timing Problem 8. Mass Air Flow Meter System 9. Engine Coolant Temp. Sensor	YES, or MIL Blinking	YES
P0301 P0302 P0303 P0304 P0305 P0306 P0307	Misfire Detected Cylinder 1 Cylinder 2 Cylinder 3 Cylinder 4 Cylinder 5 Cylinder 6			
P0325	Knock Sensor 1 Circuit Malfunction	1. Open or Short in KS 1 Circuit 2. KS 1 Loose 3. ECM	YES	YES
P0330	Knock Sensor 2 Circuit Malfunction	1. Open or Short in KS 2 Circuit 2. KS 2 Loose 3. ECM	YES	YES
P0335	Crankshaft Position Sensor "A" Circuit Malfunction	1. Open or Short in Crankshaft Position Sensor Circuit 2. Crankshaft Sensor Failure 3. Starter Problem 4. ECM	YES	YES
P0340	Camshaft Position Sensor Circuit Malfunction	1. Open or Short in Sensor Circuit 2. Cam Position Sensor Failure 3. Starter Problem 4. ECM 5. RH Camshaft Timing Pulley	YES	YES
P0401	Exhaust Gas Recirculation Flow Insufficient (2WD 1/2 Ton, Reg Cab)	1. EGR Valve Stuck Closed 2. Short in VSV Circuit for EGR 3. Open EGR Temp Sensor Circuit 4. EGR Hose Disconnected 5. ECM	YES	YES
P0402	Exhaust Gas Recirculation Flow Excessive (2WD 1/2 Ton, Reg Cab)	1. EGR Valve Stuck Open 2. EGR VSV Open Malfunction 3. Open VSV EGR Circuit 4. Short in EGR Temp. Circuit 5. ECM	YES	YES
P0420	Catalyst System Efficiency Below Threshold (Except California)	1. 3-Way Cat. Converter Problem 2. Open/Short HO2S Circuit 3. HO2S Failure	YES	YES
P0420	Catalyst System Efficiency Below Threshold (California)	1. 3-Way Cat. Converter Problem 2. Open/Short HO2S Circuit 3. HO2S Failure 4. A/F Sensor, Bank 1, Sensor 1	YES	YES
P0440	Evaporative Emission Control System Malfunction	1. Vapor Pressure Sensor 2. Tank Cap Incorrect, Damaged 3. Vacuum Hose Disconnected 4. EVAP hoses damaged 5. Fuel tank cracked, damaged 6. Charcoal canister damaged	YES	YES
P0441	Evaporative Emission Control System Incorrect Purge Flow	1. Open, Short in Vapor SensorVSV 2. Vapor Sensor VSV Failure 3. Open, Short VSV Circuit 4. Vacuum hoses disconnected 5. Charcoal canister damaged	YES	YES
P0446	Evaporative Emission Control Vent Control Malfunction			
P0450	Evaporative Emission Control System Pressure Sensor Malfunction	1. Open or Short in Vapor Pressure Sensor Circuit 2. Vapor Pressure Sensor Failure 3. ECM	YES	YES
P0451	Evaporative Emission Control System Pressure Sensor Range/Perform.			

93164G44

Fig. 98 Diagnostic Trouble Codes (2 of 3)—5VZ-FE engine

DIAGNOSTIC TROUBLE CODES

DTC No.	System Detected	Possible Trouble Area	MIL Light Comes On	DTC Retained In Memory
P0500	Vehicle Speed Sensor Malfunction	1. Open/Short in VSS Circuit 2. Vehicle Speed Sensor Failure 3. Instrument Cluster Problem 4. ECM	YES	YES
P0505	Idle Control System Malfunction	1. IAC Valve Stuck or Closed 2. Open/Shorted IAC Circuit 3. Open/Shorted A/C Signal Circuit 4. Air Intake Hose Loose	YES	YES
P1300	Igniter Circuit Malfunction	1. Open or Short in IGF or IGT Circuit From Igniter to ECM 2. Igniter Failure 3. ECM	YES	YES
P1335	Crankshaft Position Sensor Circuit Malfunction (during engine running)	1. Open or Short in Crankshaft Position Sensor Circuit 2. Crankshaft Sensor Failure 3. Starter Problem 4. ECM	NO	YES
P1520	Stop Light Switch Signal Malfunction	1. Short in Stop Light Switch Signal Circuit 2. Stop Light Switch Failure 3. ECM	YES	YES
P1600	ECM BATT Malfunction	1. Open in Back Up Power Source Circuit 2. ECM	YES	YES
P1780	Park/Neutral Position Switch Malfunction	1. Short in Park/Neutral Position Switch Circuit 2. Park/Neutral Switch Failure 3. ECM	YES	YES

93164G45

Fig. 99 Diagnostic Trouble Codes (3 of 3)—5VZ-FE engine

VACUUM DIAGRAMS

See Figures 100 thru 117

Following is a listing of vacuum diagrams for most of the engine and emissions package combinations covered by this manual. Because vacuum circuits will vary based on various engine and vehicle options, always refer first to the vehicle emission control information label, if present. Should the label be missing, or should the vehicle be equipped with a different engine from the vehicle's original equipment, refer to the diagrams below for the same or similar configuration.

If you wish to obtain a replacement emissions label, most manufacturers make the labels available for purchase. The labels can usually be ordered from a local dealer.

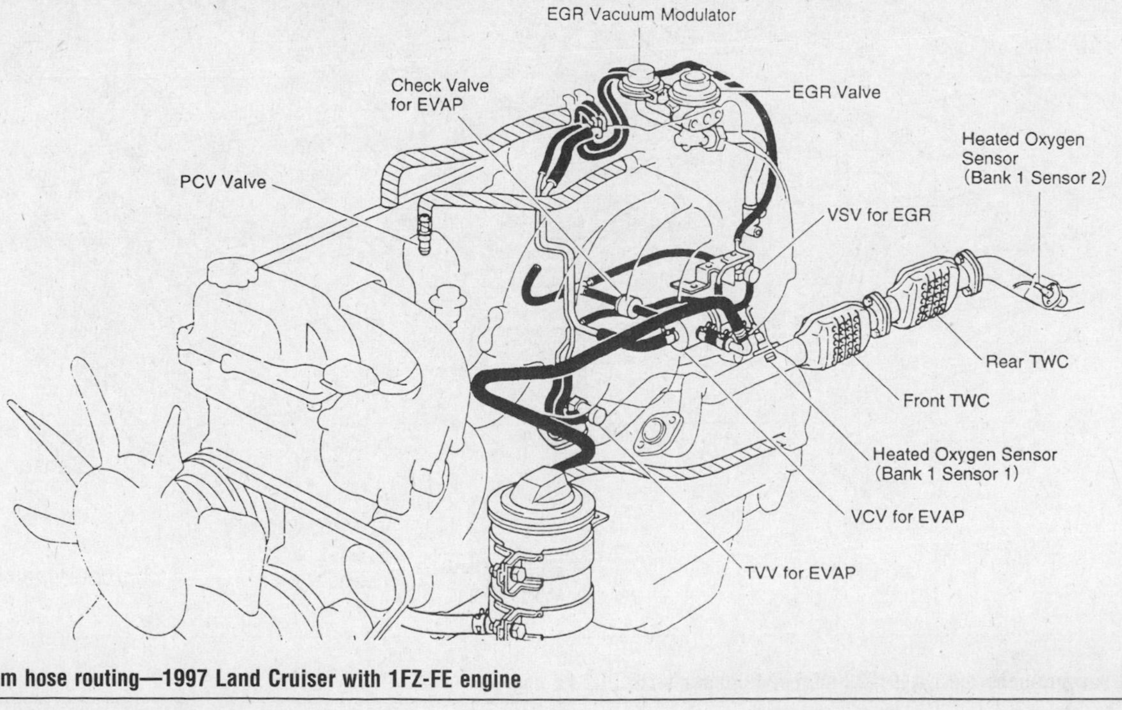

Fig. 100 Vacuum hose routing—1997 Land Cruiser with 1FZ-FE engine

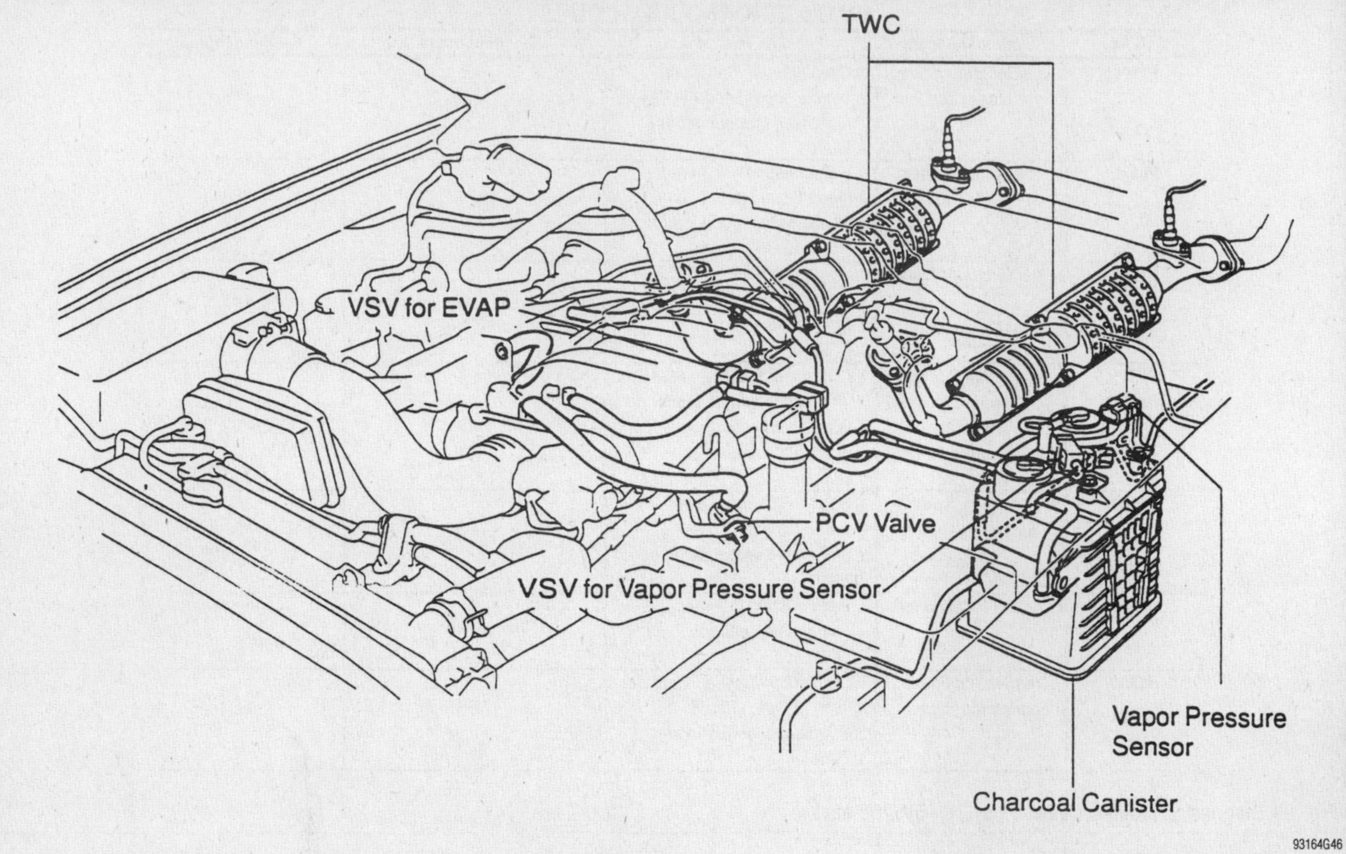

Fig. 101 Vacuum hose routing—1998 Land Cruiser with 2UZ-FE engine

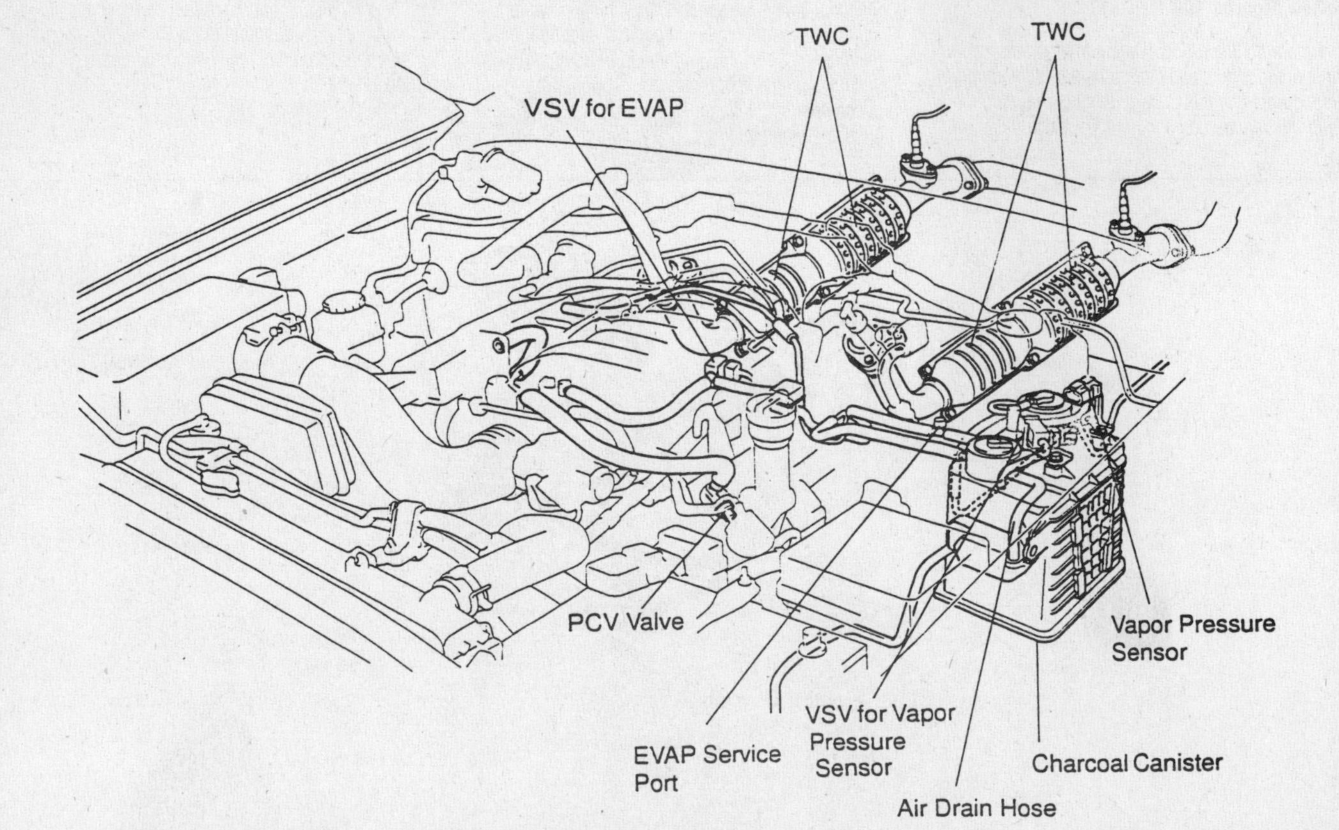

Fig. 102 Vacuum hose routing—1999–00 Land Cruiser with 2UZ-FE engine

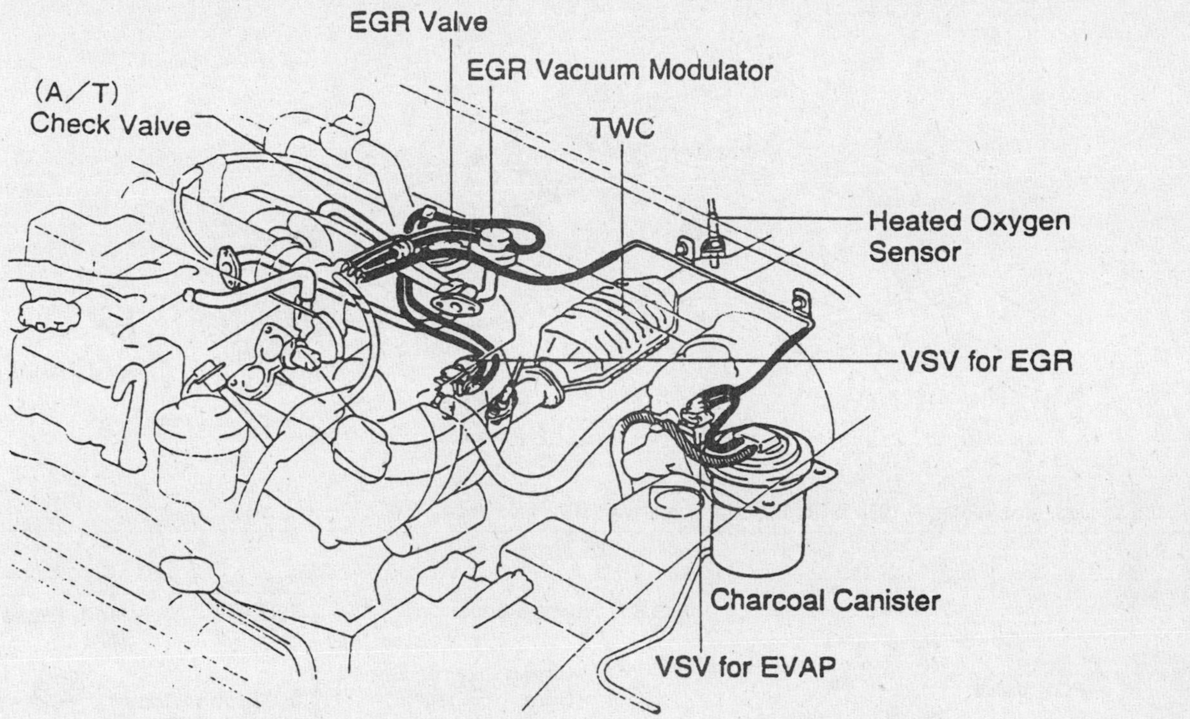

Fig. 103 Vacuum hose routing—1997 T-100 Pick-Up Truck with 3RZ-FE engine

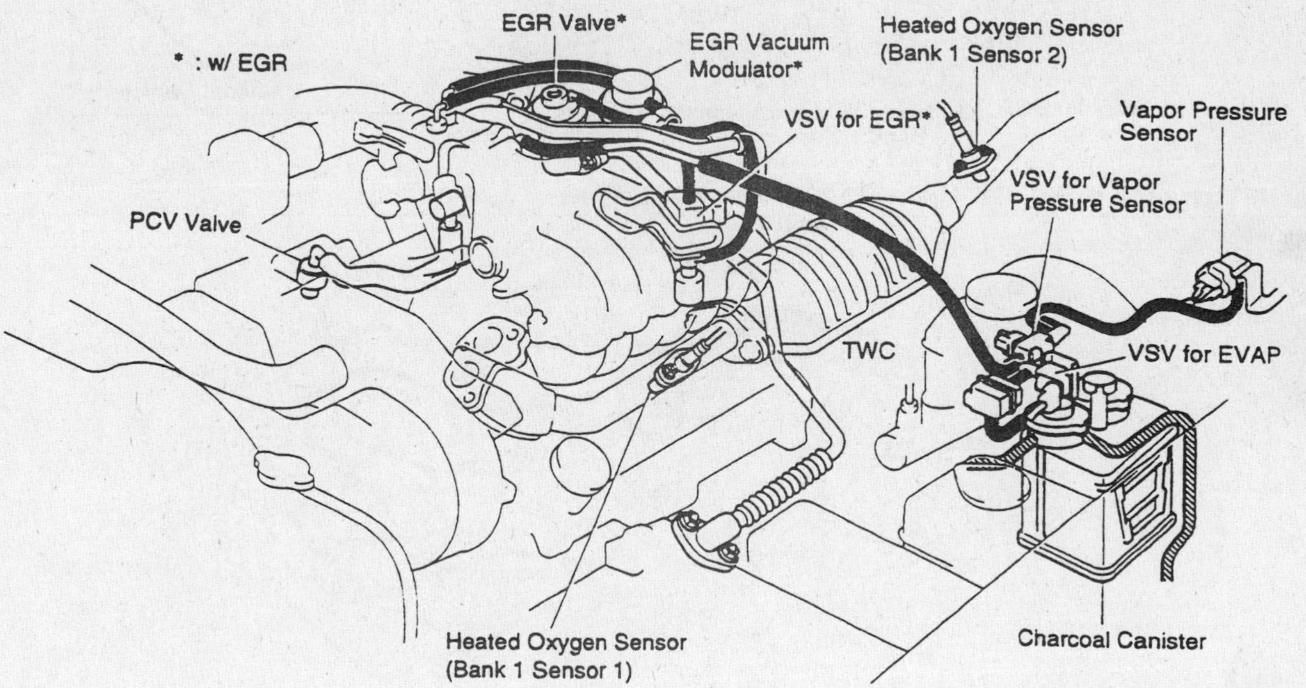

Fig. 104 Vacuum hose routing—1997–98 T-100 Pick-Up Truck with 5VZ-FE engine

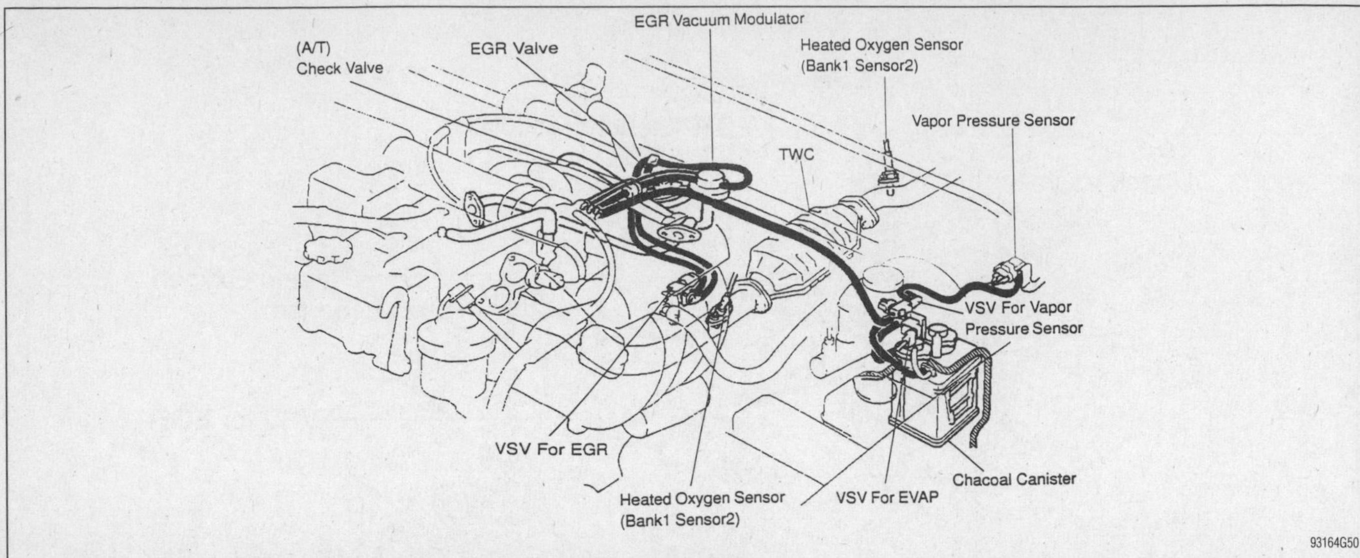

Fig. 105 Vacuum hose routing—1998 T-100 Pick-Up Truck with 3RZ-FE engine

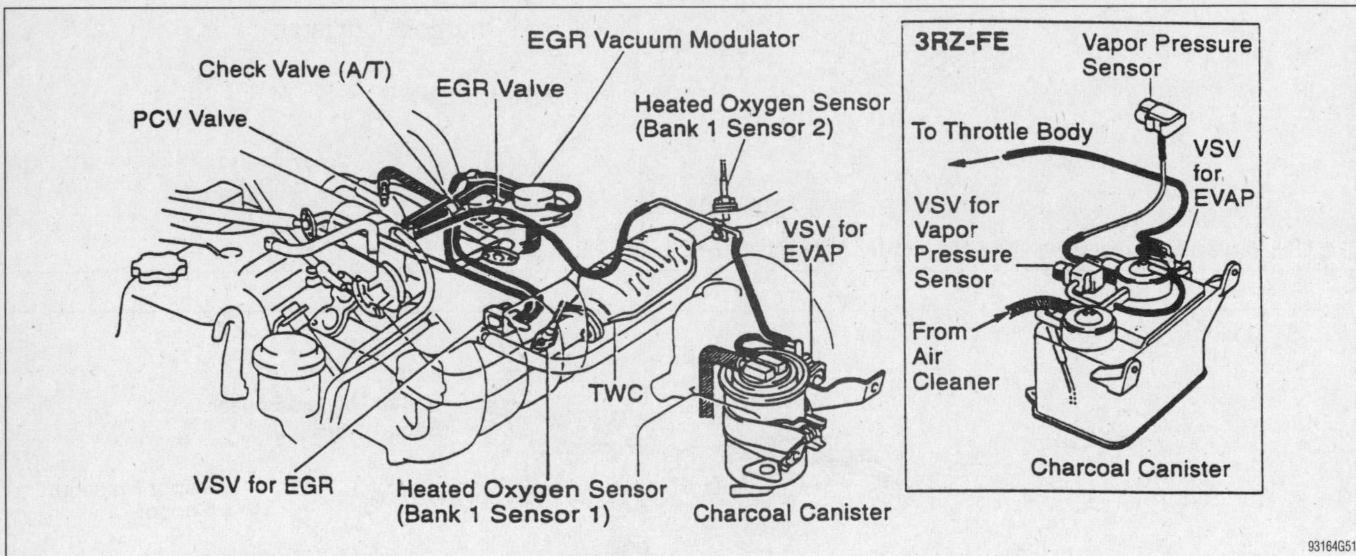

Fig. 106 Vacuum hose routing—1997 Tacoma with 2RZ-FE and 3RZ-FE engines

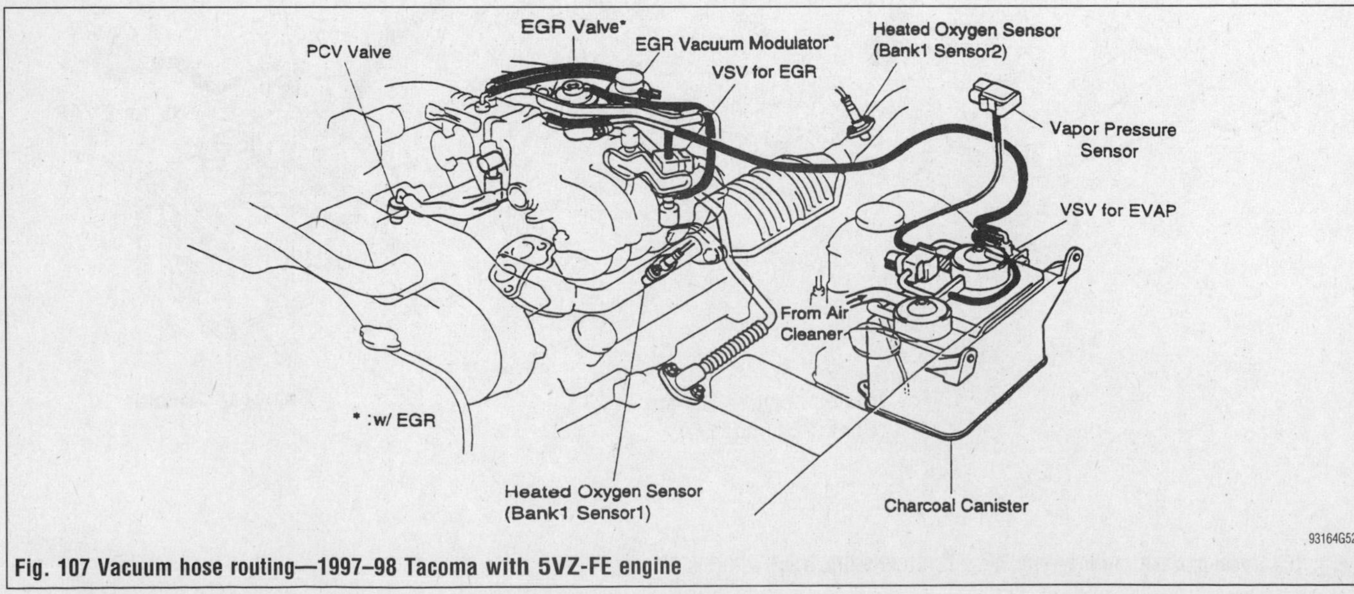

Fig. 107 Vacuum hose routing—1997–98 Tacoma with 5VZ-FE engine

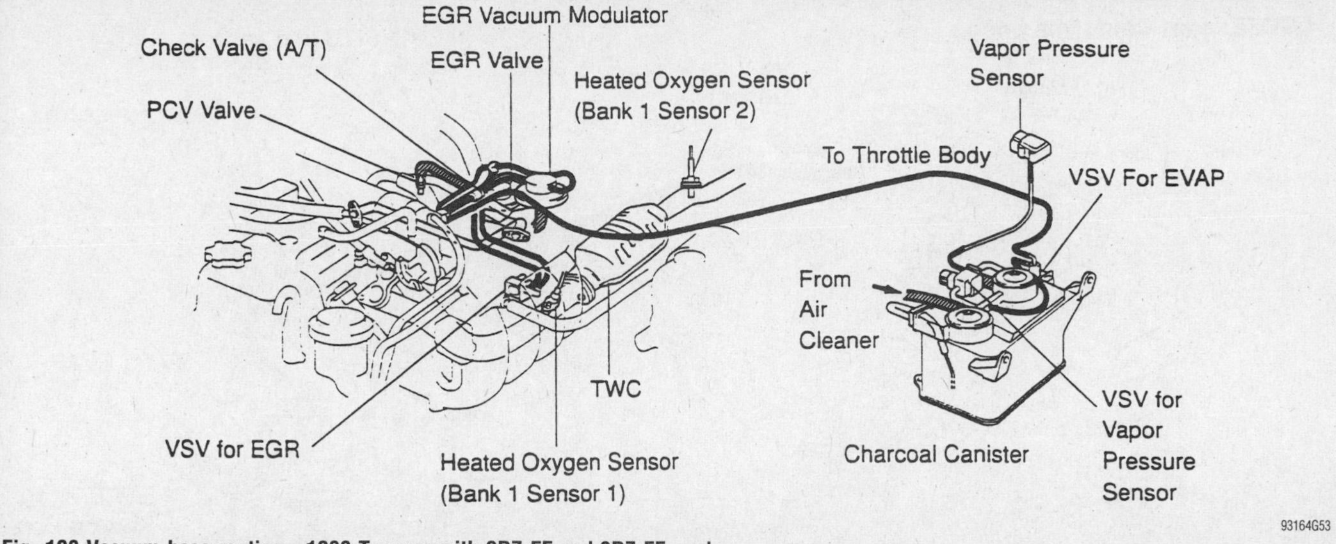

Fig. 108 Vacuum hose routing—1998 Tacoma with 2RZ-FE and 3RZ-FE engines

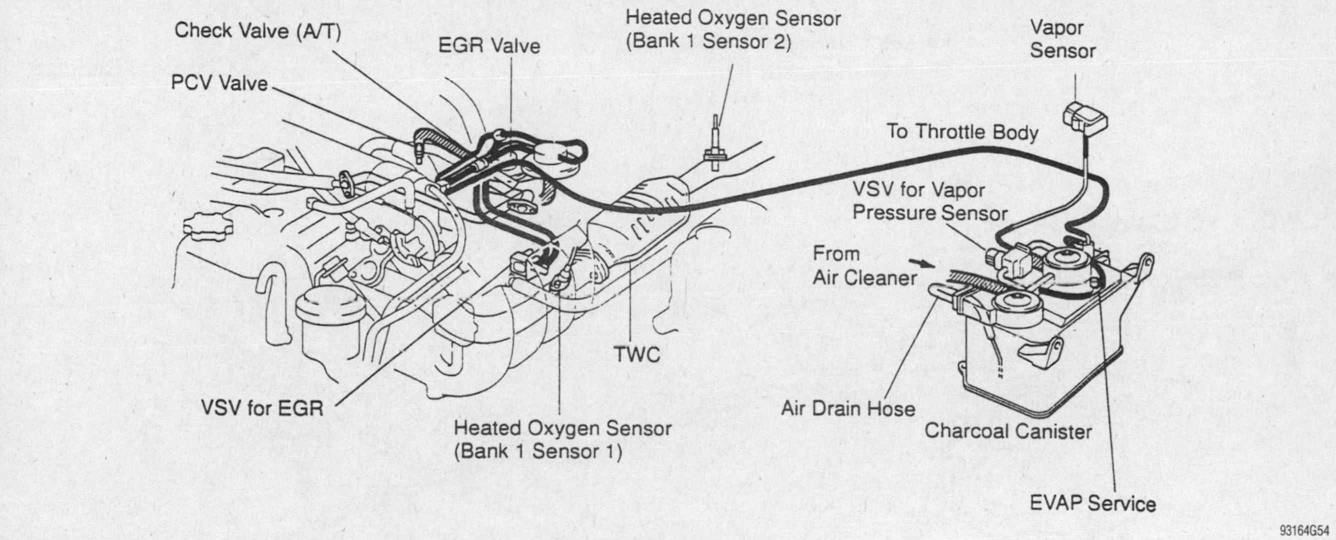

Fig. 109 Vacuum hose routing—1999–00 Tacoma with 2RZ-FE and 3RZ-FE engines

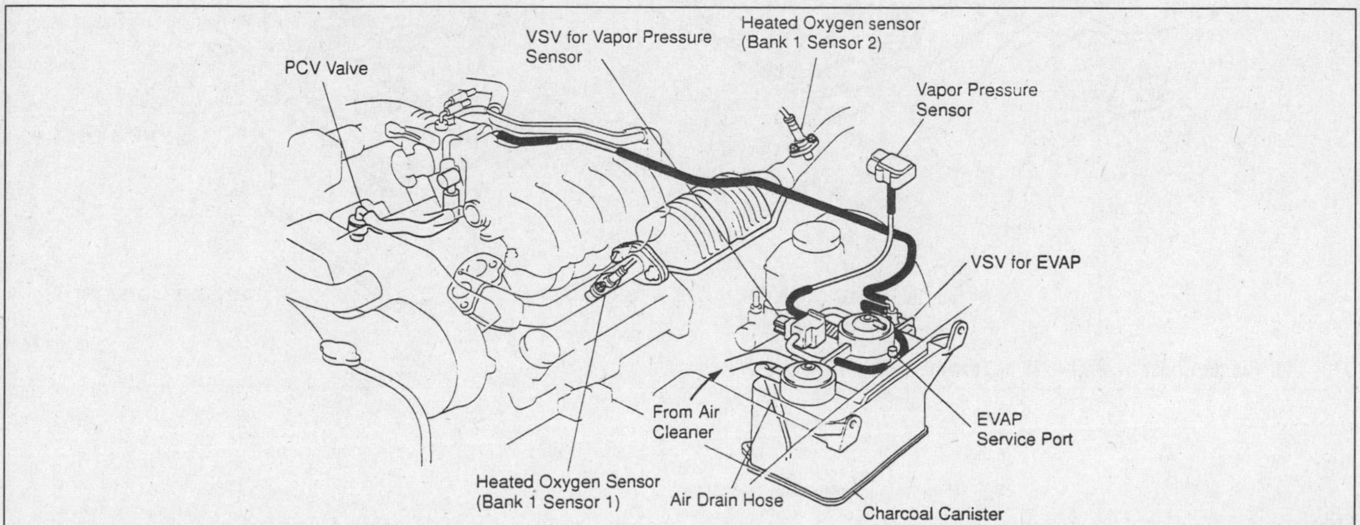

Fig. 110 Vacuum hose routing—1999 Tacoma with 5VZ-FE engine

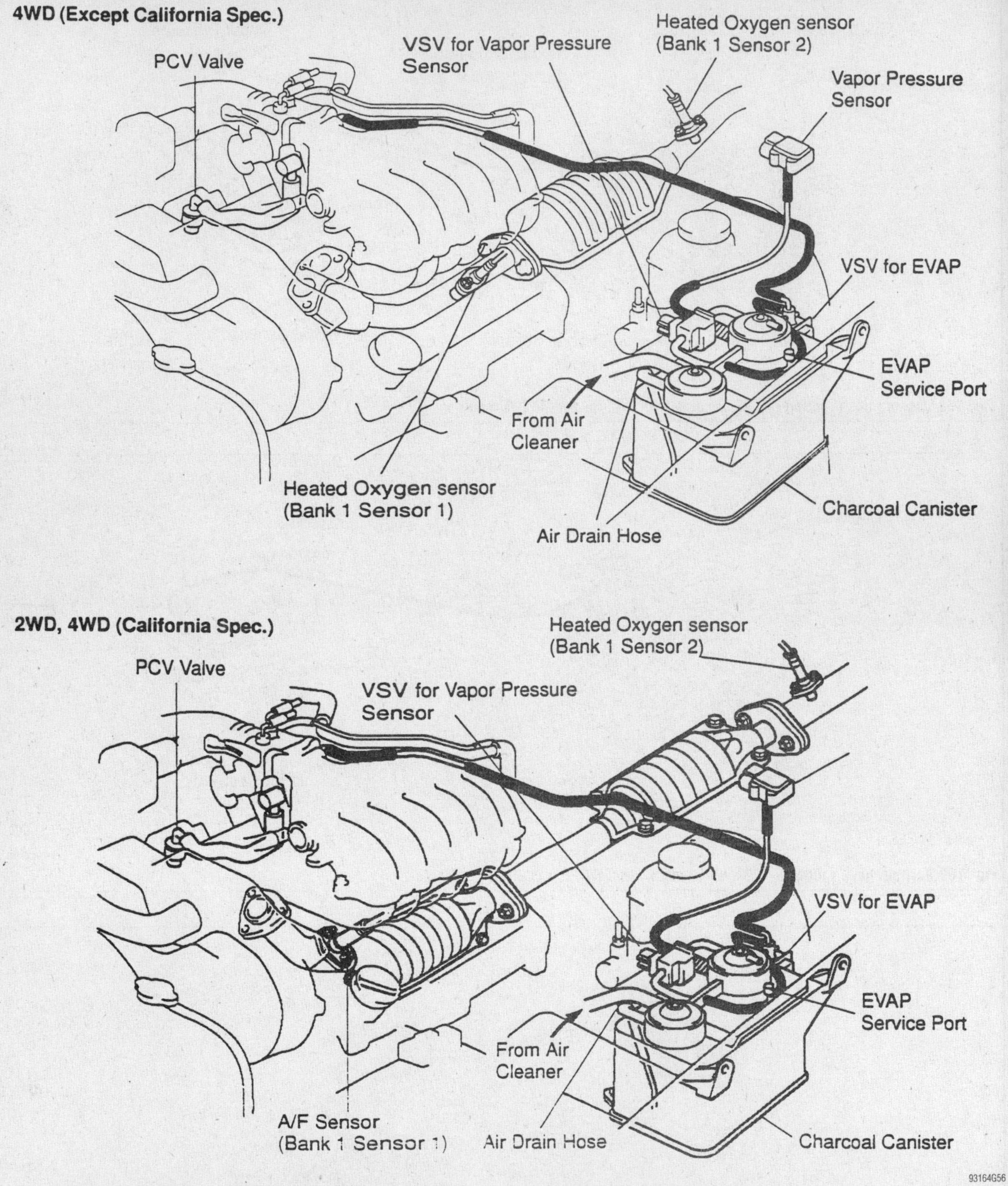

Fig. 111 Vacuum hose routing—2000 Tacoma with 5VZ-FE engine

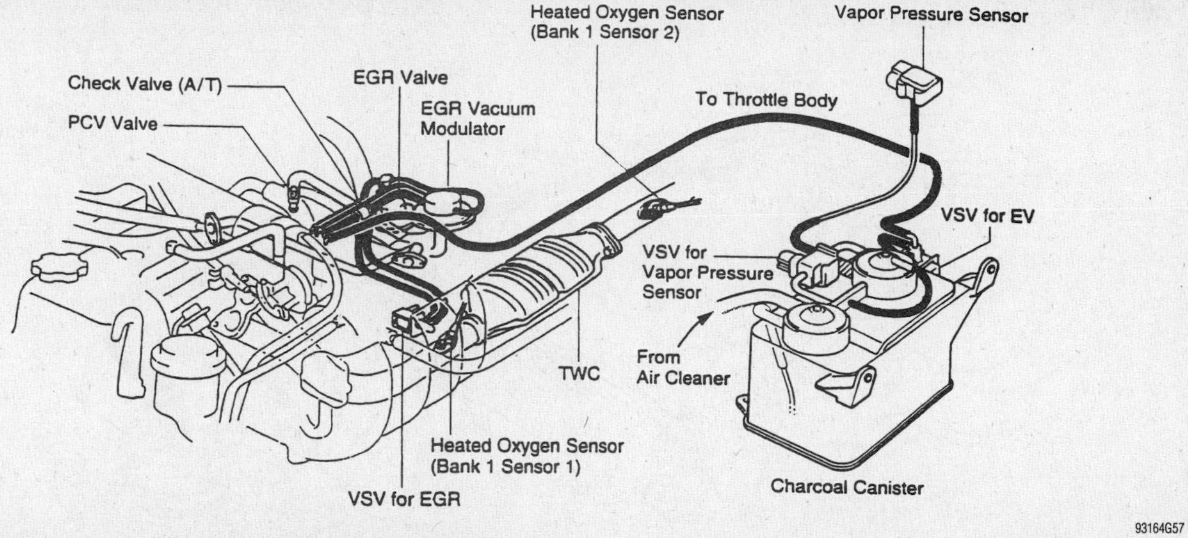

Fig. 112 Vacuum hose routing—1997 4Runner with 3RZ-FE engine

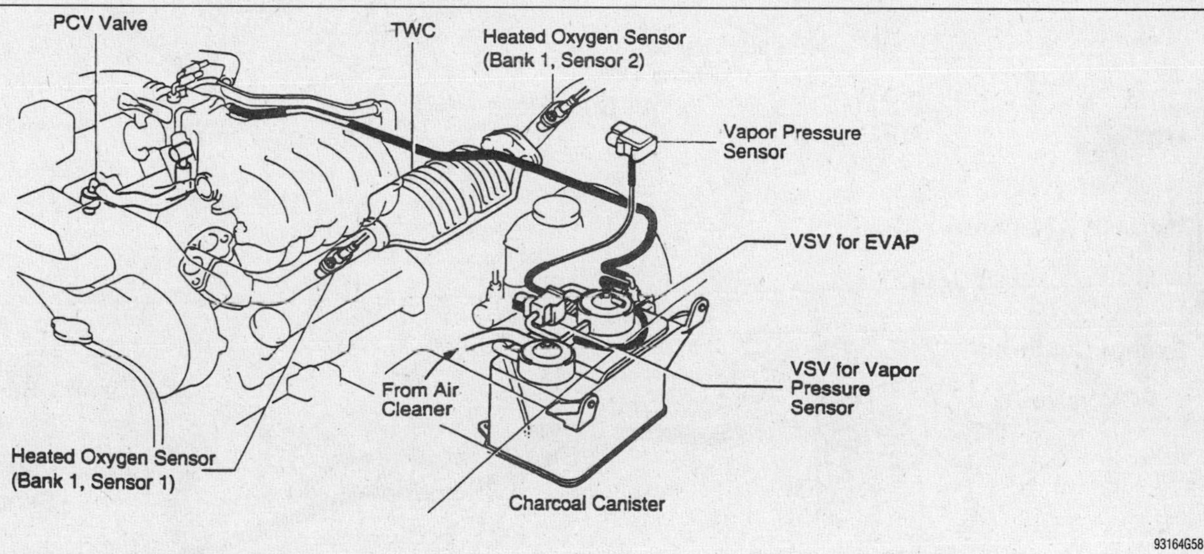

Fig. 113 Vacuum hose routing—1997–98 4Runner with 5VZ-FE engine

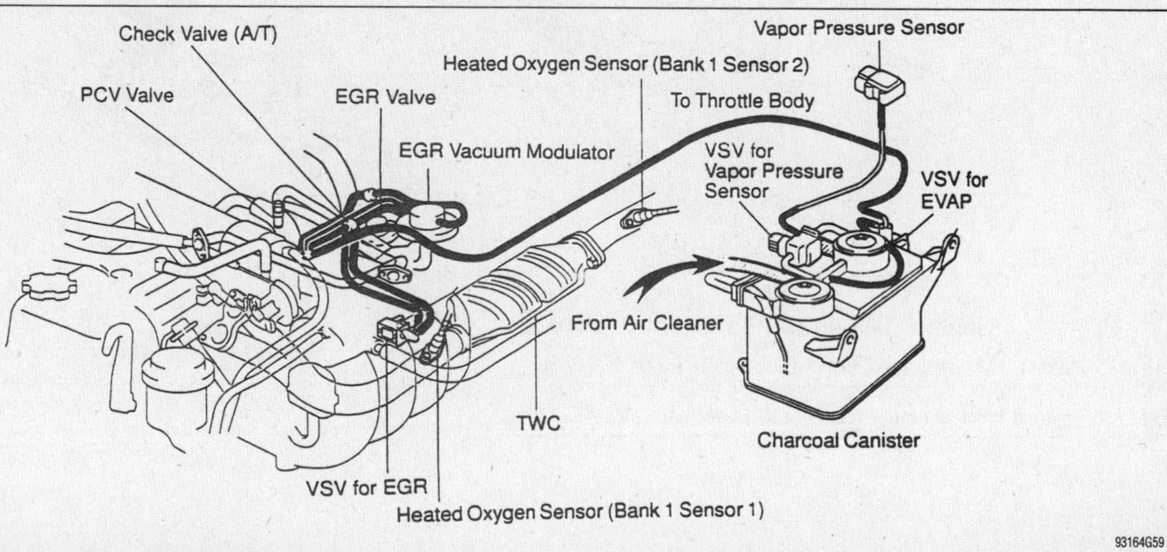

Fig. 114 Vacuum hose routing—1998–99 4Runner with 3RZ-FE engine

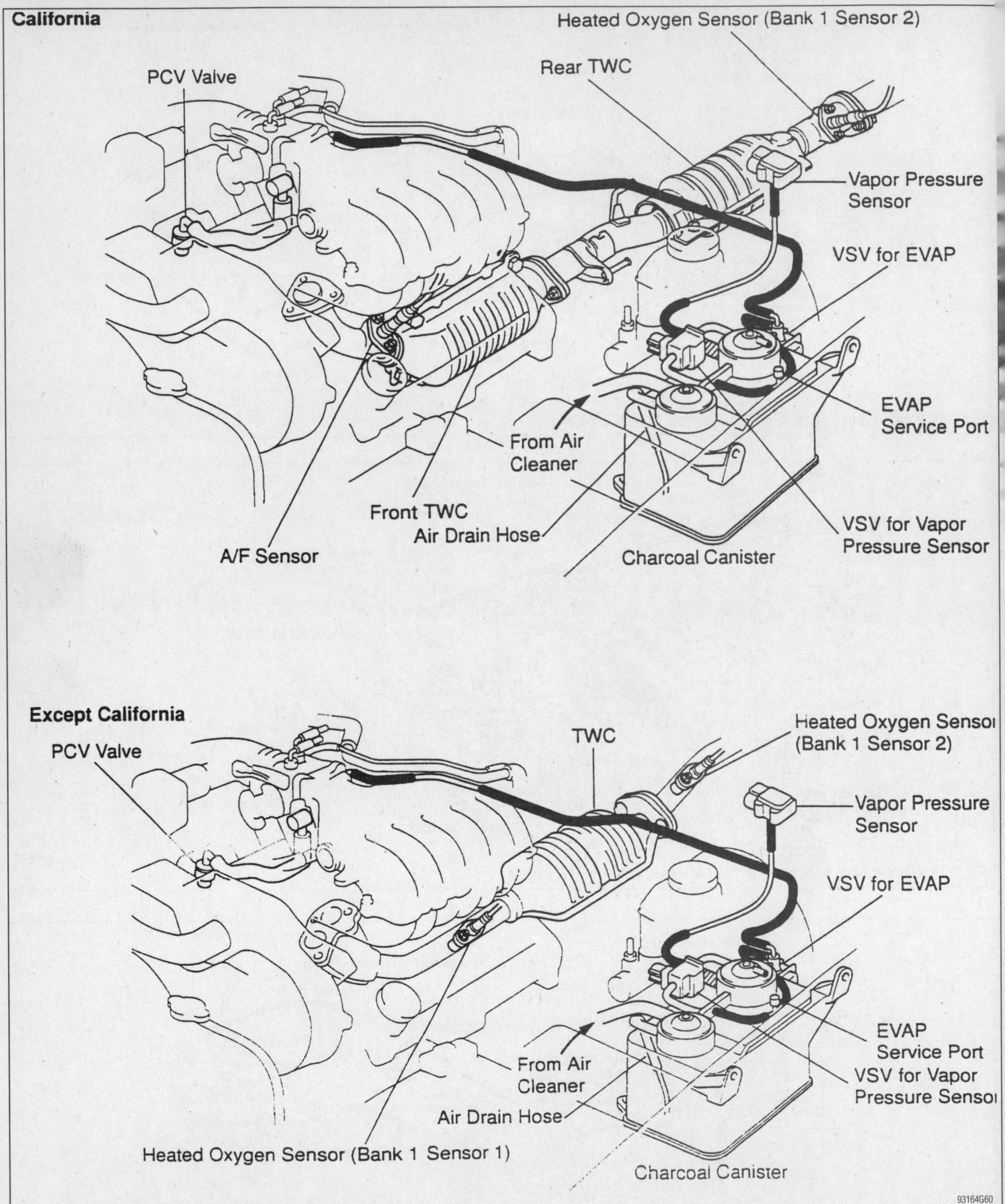

Fig. 115 Vacuum hose routing—1999–00 4Runner with 5VZ-FE engine

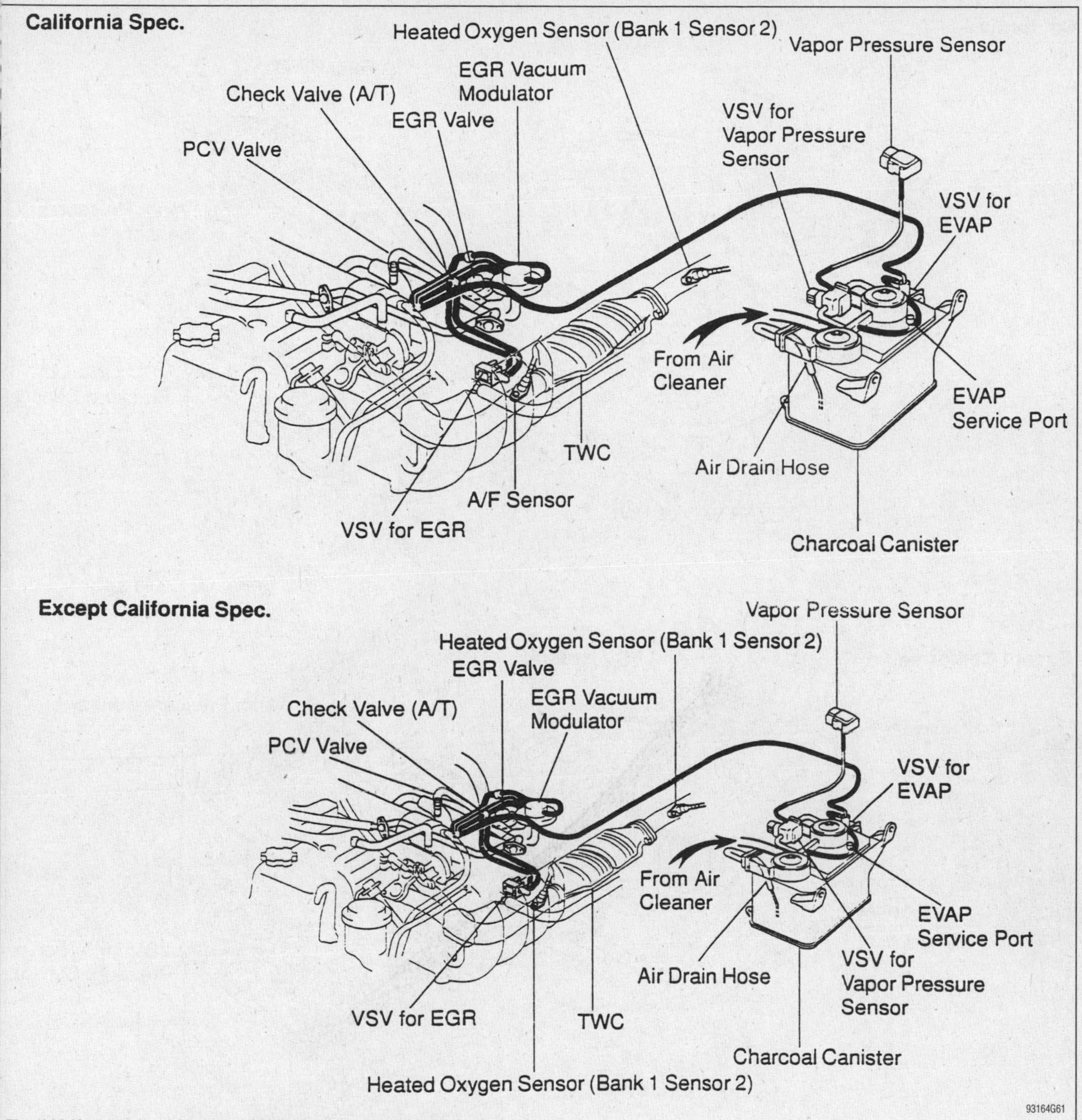

Fig. 116 Vacuum hose routing—2000 4Runner with 3RZ-FE engine

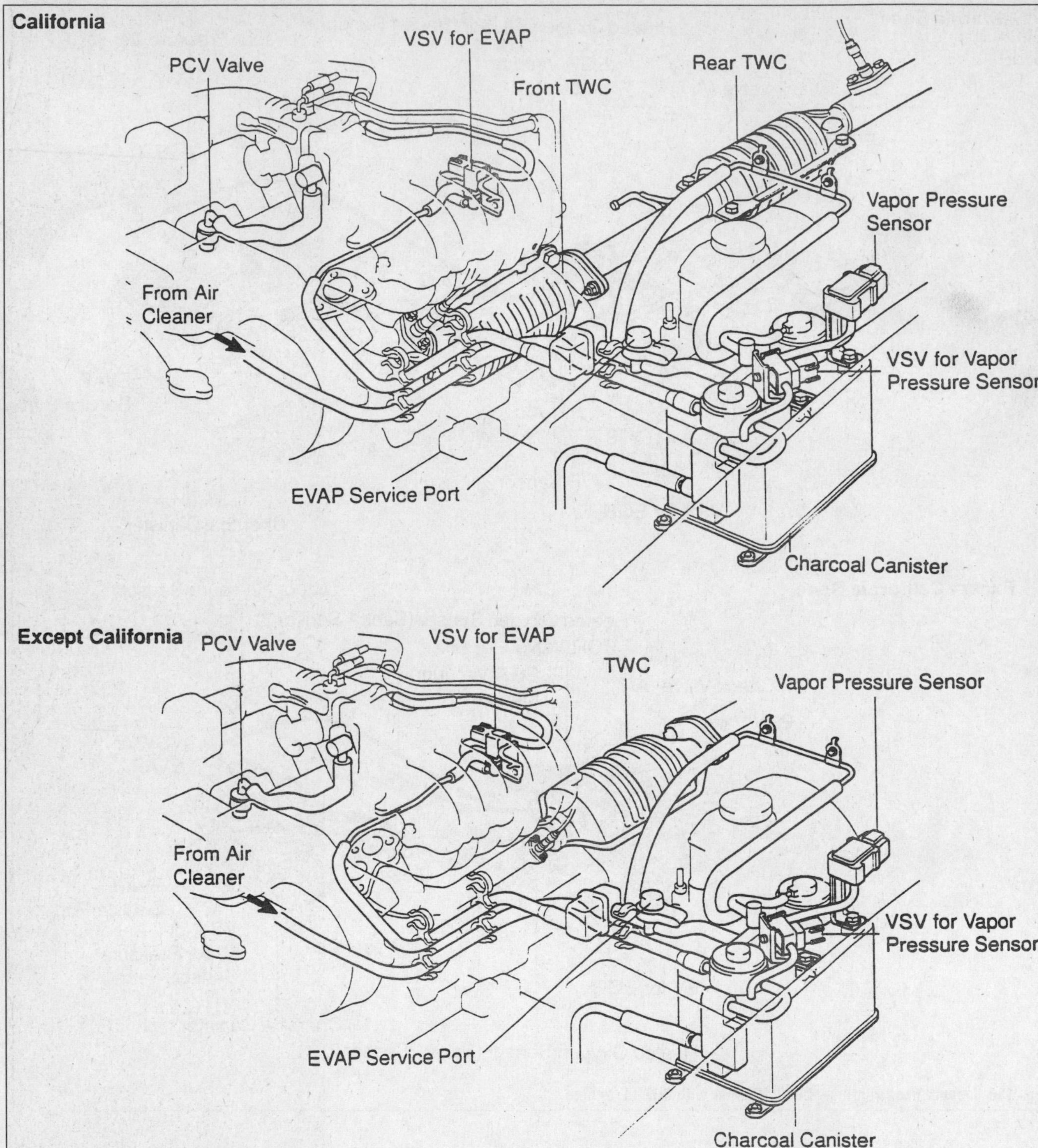

Fig. 117 Vacuum hose routing—2000 Tundra with 2UZ-FE engine

5

FUEL SYSTEM

BASIC FUEL SYSTEM DIAGNOSIS

When there is a problem starting or driving a vehicle, two of the most important checks involve the ignition and the fuel systems. The questions most mechanics attempt to answer first, "is there spark?" and "is there fuel?" will often lead to solving most basic problems. For ignition system diagnosis and testing, please refer to the information on engine electrical components and ignition systems found earlier in this manual. If the ignition system checks out (there is spark), then you must determine if the fuel system is operating properly (is there fuel?).

SEQUENTIAL FUEL INJECTION

General Information

All of the Toyota trucks covered by this manual are equipped with Sequential Fuel Injection (SFI). Sequential Fuel Injection (SFI) is the activating of the fuel injectors according to the engine firing order and is an accurate method of regulating multi-port injection. In this system, the injectors are controlled individually. Each cylinder receives one charge of fuel every two revolutions just before the intake valve opens. Mixture adjustments that can be made almost simultaneously between the firing of one injector and the next. A camshaft signal sensor the ECM when the No. 1 cylinder is on the compression stroke.

PRECAUTIONS

The following precautions should be followed when working on Toyota's SFI system.

- Any Diagnostic Trouble Code retained by the ECM will be erased when the negative battery terminal is disconnected. Use a scan tool to scan for and retrieve trouble codes before disconnecting the negative battery cable.
- Disconnect the negative battery cable before beginning work on the SFI system.
- Do not smoke or work near open flame when working on the fuel system.
- Keep gasoline away from rubber parts.
- After repair work, check that the ignition coil terminals and all other ignition system lines are reconnected securely.
- On sequentially injected fuel injected engines, it is most important that the injector connectors be installed on the proper injector. Always identify and tag the injector connectors before removal. On any connector, release the lock and pull out the connector, not on the wires.
- The entire system depends on the engine being air-tight. If the engine oil dipstick, oil filler cap, PCV valve hose or other component is loose, the engine may run poorly. Similarly, if the gasket between the throttle body and intake manifold is deteriorated or loose, the resulting vacuum leak will cause the engine to run poorly.
- Before removing SFI system wiring connectors, terminals, etc., turn the ignition switch to the **OFF** position. It may also be necessary to disconnect the battery negative terminal.

Relieving Fuel System Pressure

To relieve the fuel pressure, wrap a clean shop cloth around the union bolt (banjo bolt) at the fuel delivery rail. Slowly loosen the bolt holding the fuel line and allow pressurized fuel to escape into the cloth. Do NOT allow fuel to spray from the fitting; always wrap it in a clean cloth.

➡Pressure may also be relieved at the fuel filter, if desired. Tighten the union bolt.

Electric Fuel Pump

All Toyota fuel-injected vehicles are equipped with an electric fuel pump. The pump is located inside the fuel tank. For a fuel injection system to work properly, the pump must develop pressures well above those of a mechanical fuel pump. This high pressure is maintained within the lines even when the engine is not running. Extreme caution must be used to safely release the pressurized fuel before any work is begun.

A quick test for pump operation is to remove the gas cap and listen at the fuel filler opening. Have an assistant turn the ignition switch to the **ON** position. It should be possible to hear the pump run. More information can be found under TESTING in this section.

✻✻ CAUTION

Always relieve the fuel pressure within the system before any work is begun on any fuel component. Failure to safely relieve the pressure may result in fire and/or serious injury.

REMOVAL & INSTALLATION

Except Land Cruiser

➧ See Figure 1

1. Remove the fuel tank from the vehicle. For additional information, please refer to the following topic(s): Fuel Tank Removal and Installation.
2. Remove the fuel pump bracket or assembly from the tank. Disconnect the pump wiring from the clamp as follows:
   a. Remove the 8 mounting bolts and pull the bracket assembly out of the tank.
   b. Remove and discard the gasket on the pump bracket.
3. Pull the lower side of the pump off of the pump bracket. Disconnect the pump wiring, then disconnect the fuel hose from the pump. This should release the pump from the unit.
4. With the aid of a flat-bladed tool, remove the clip retaining the filter to the pump. This will allow the filter to slide off the pump.

To install:

5. Attach filter with the C-clip onto the pump.
6. Push the lower half of the pump into the bracket and attach the wiring. Connect the fuel hose to the pump.
7. With all of the pump parts in place on the bracket, slide the unit into the gas tank with a new gasket. Tighten to 35 inch lbs. (4 Nm).
8. Install the fuel tank.
9. Start the vehicle and check for leaks.

Land Cruiser

➧ See Figures 2 thru 9

✻✻ CAUTION

Observe all applicable safety precautions when working around fuel. Whenever servicing the fuel system, always work in a well ventilated area. Do not allow fuel spray or vapors to come in contact with a spark or open flame. Keep a dry chemical fire extinguisher near the work area. Always keep fuel in a container specifically designed for fuel storage; also, always properly seal fuel containers to avoid the possibility of fire or explosion.

1. Disconnect the negative battery cable.
2. The Land Cruiser has a removable plate in the rear floor, under the carpet, to access the fuel pump. There may be some variation in this procedure as the interior trim components vary between model years. The following should suffice for Land Cruiser fuel pump removal.
3. Remove the rear seats from the Land Cruiser to get to the access plate. The seats use retainer brackets and bolts that go through the brackets and thread into the floorpan. The bolt heads may be covered by a trim cap which can be pried off.
4. Remove the scuff plate, side garnish and step plate.
5. Remove the floor mats.
6. Remove the floor service hole cover.
7. Disconnect the fuel pipe and hose from the fuel pump bracket. Disconnect the pump and sensor gauge connection as follows:
   a. Fuel injection systems use two fuel lines. One is pressure to the engine, the other is excess fuel being returned to the tank. Tag the hoses for identification so they can be returned to their proper locations.
   b. The 1997 Land Cruiser uses union bolts to retain the fuel lines at the fuel pump. Remove the bolts and separate the fittings.
   c. 1998 and newer Land Cruisers no longer use the union bolt and gaskets found in earlier models. Quick-connect connectors are used to secure the lines at the fuel pump. They use horseshoe-shaped clips to retain the hoses to the fuel pump connections. Clean the top of the fuel pump where the connectors are located with a soft bristle brush (paint brush) to clear away dirt and road debris to keep from contaminating the fuel tank.
   d. Spread the horseshoe-shaped clips with your fingers. Toyota specifically advises against using tools to open the clips. Spread the clips slightly and detach both the fuel feed and the fuel return lines. It may be helpful to turn the nylon

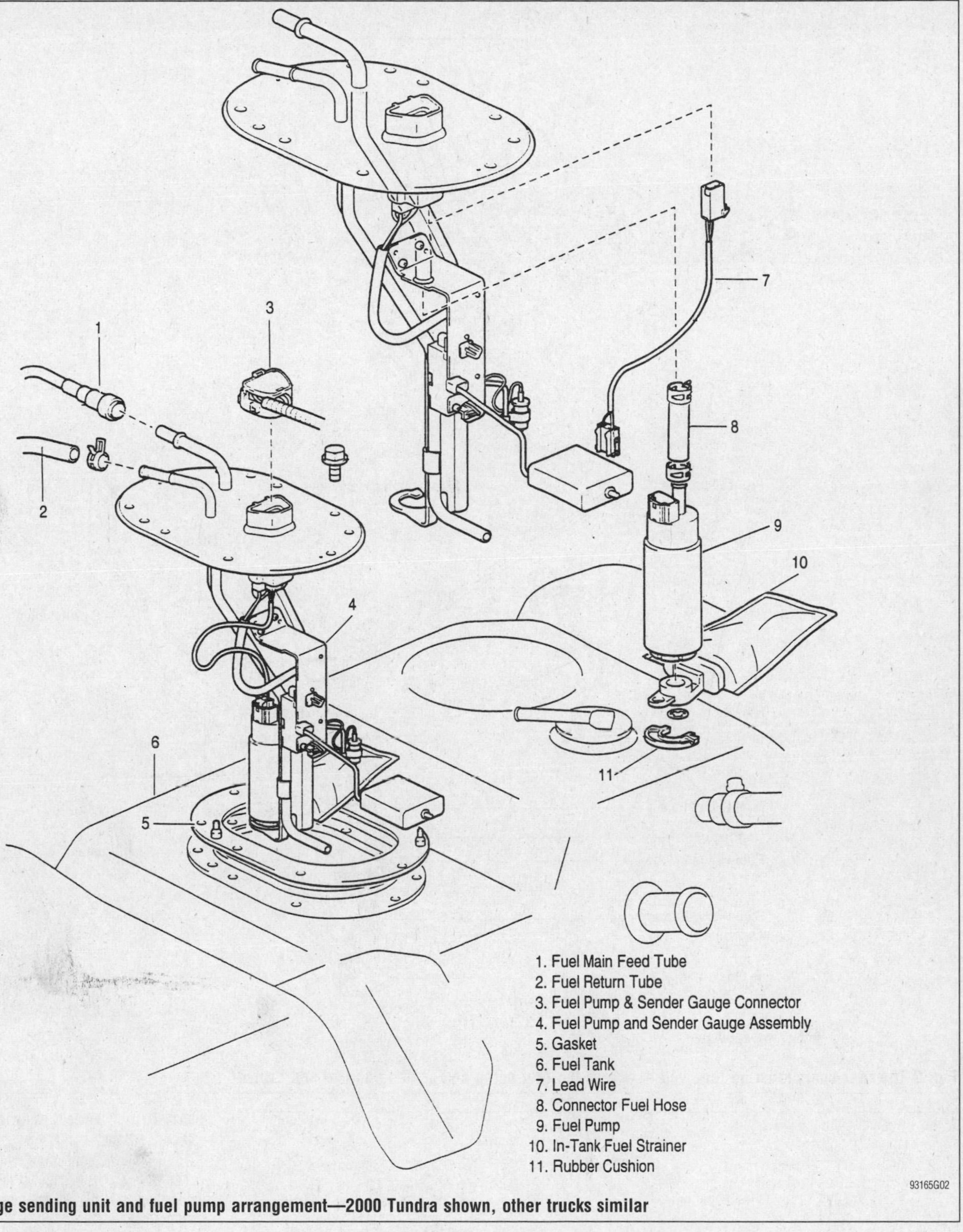

Fig. 1 Fuel gauge sending unit and fuel pump arrangement—2000 Tundra shown, other trucks similar

fuel lines by hand to free them for removal. Toyota recommends plugging the fuel lines to keep out dirt.

8. Remove the pump bracket assembly from the gas tank. There should be eight small screws. Discard the gasket from the pump bracket. Be careful not to bend the arm of the sender gauge.

9. Pull off the lower side of the pump from the pump bracket. Disconnect the pump wiring, then disconnect the fuel hose from the pump. This should release the pump from the unit.

10. With the aid of a flat-bladed tool, remove the clip retaining the in-tank fuel strainer to the pump, allowing the strainer to slide off the pump.

To install:

11. Attach a replacement strainer with the C-clip onto the pump.

12. Push the lower half of the pump into the bracket and attach the wiring. Connect the fuel hose to the pump.

13. With all of the pump parts in place on the bracket, slide the unit into the gas tank with a new gasket. Tighten the eight retaining screws to 35 inch lbs. (4 Nm).

14. On 1997 Land Cruisers, attach the union bolt with new gaskets along with the outlet pipe to the bracket. Tighten to 22 ft. lbs. (29 Nm).

15. On 1998–00 Land Cruisers, before installing the quick-connect clips, make sure no dirt has gotten between the nylon tube and the top of the fuel pump mounting plate. Attach the fuel tube connectors to the ports and insert the clips until you hear a click. After

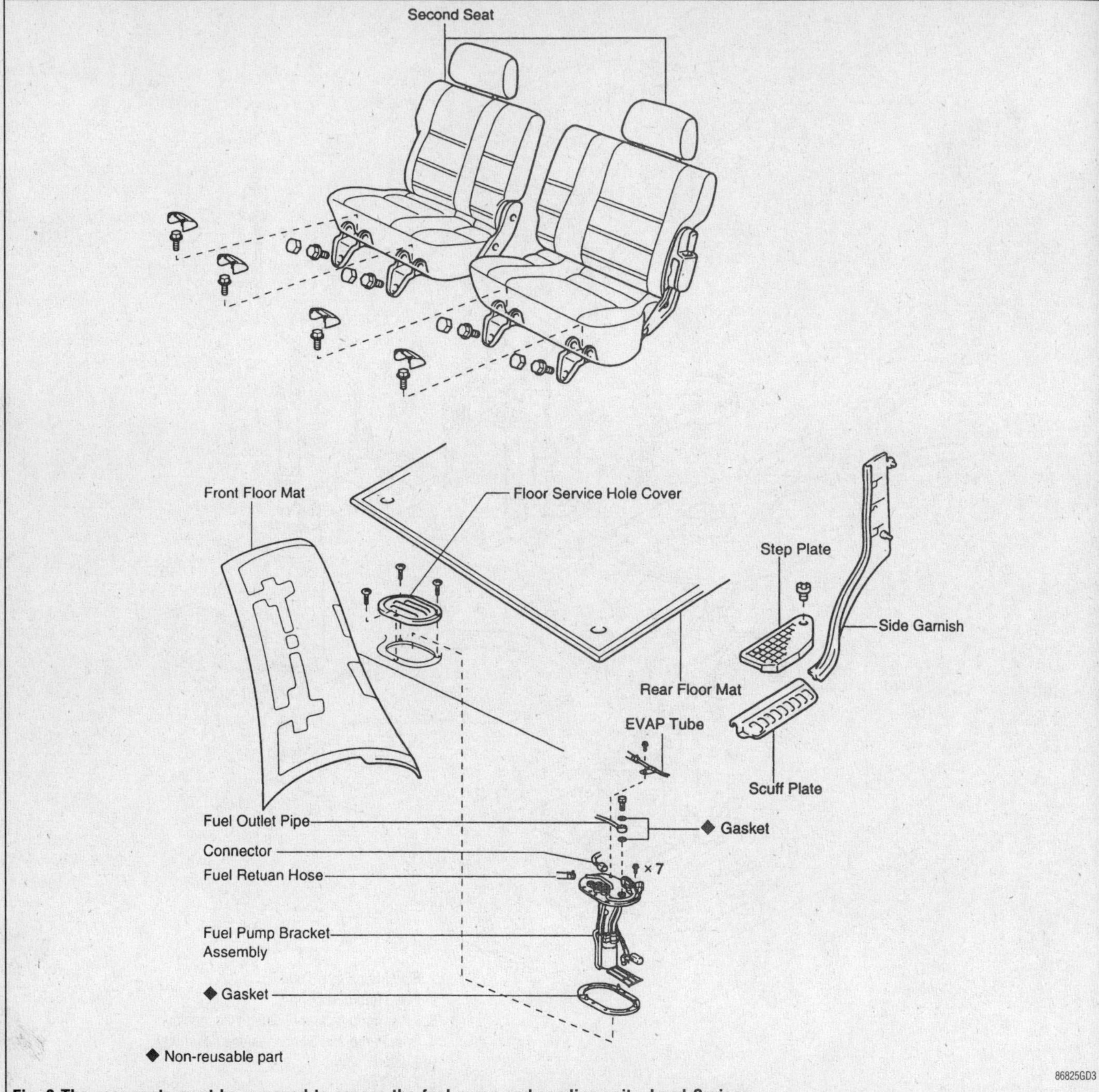

Fig. 2 The rear seats must be removed to access the fuel pump and sending unit—Land Cruiser

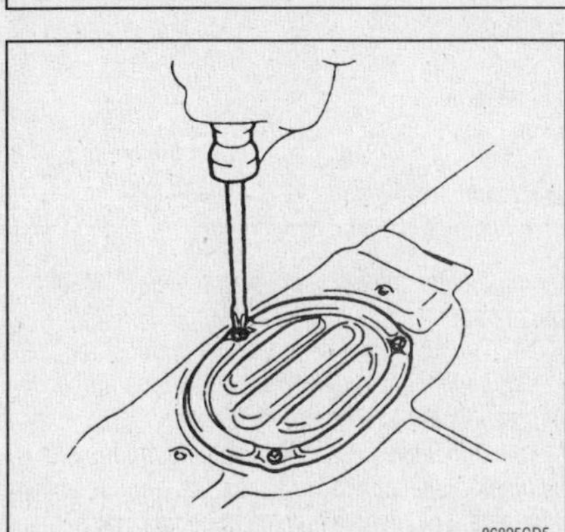

Fig. 3 Loosen and remove the service access panel mounting screws—Land Cruiser

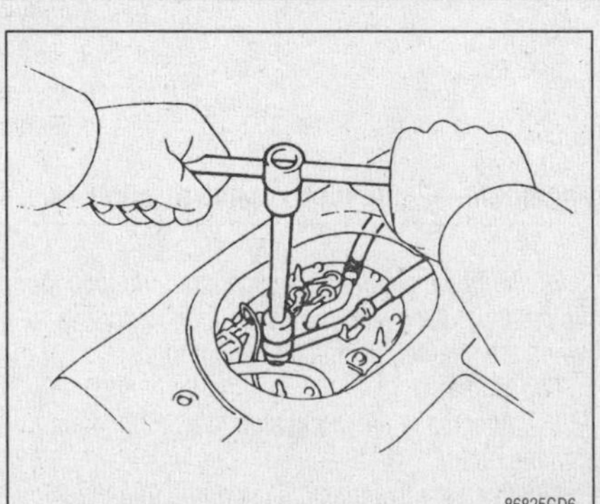

Fig. 4 On 1997 models, remove the union bolt and gaskets, then disconnect the fuel outlet pipe—Land Cruiser

connection, pull on the clips to make sure they are installed securely.

16. Connect the fuel pump wiring.
17. Connect the negative battery cable. Turn the ignition switch to the ON position to pressurize the system. Check for leaks.
18. When satisfied with the installation, double-check that all hoses are secure and that all wiring is intact, then install the service hole cover.
19. Install the floor mats, step plate, side garnish and scuff plate.
20. Install the rear seats, tighten to 29 ft. lbs. (39 Nm).
21. Start the vehicle and check again for leaks.

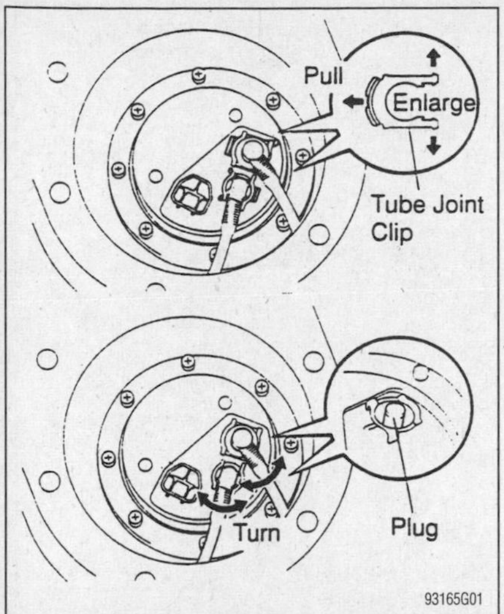

Fig. 5 On 1998 and newer models, quick-connect fittings are used with clips to retain the fuel lines to the fuel pump assembly—Land Cruiser

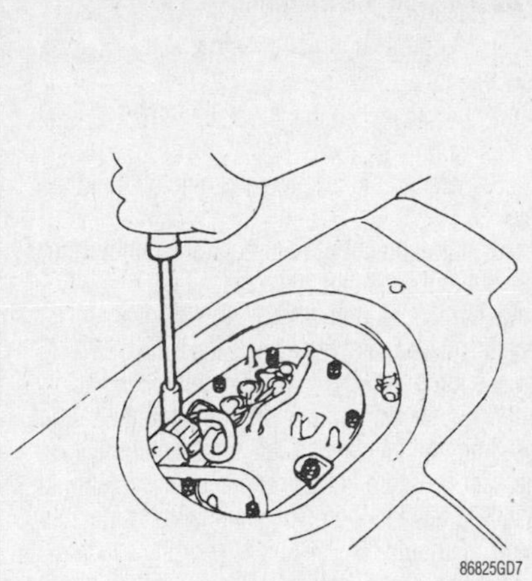

Fig. 6 Remove the 8 bolts holding the fuel pump bracket to the gas tank

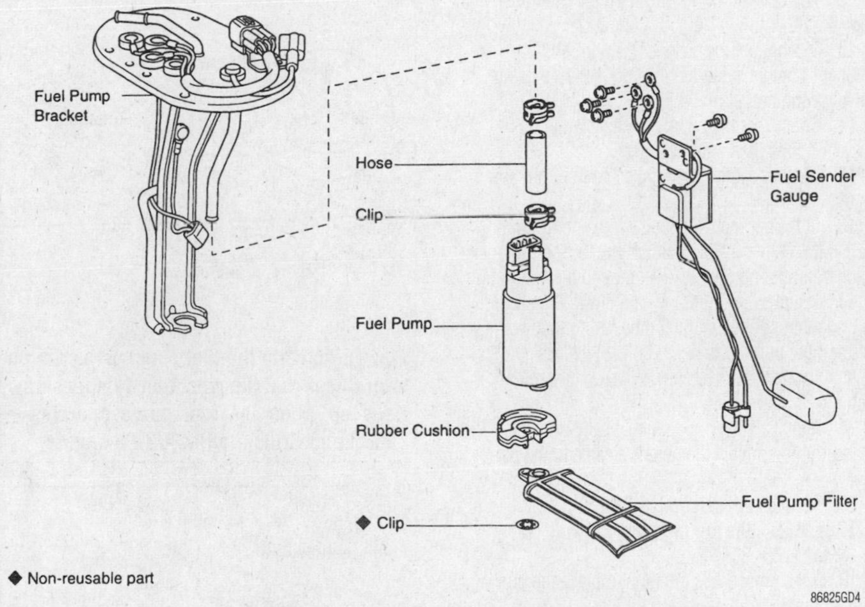

Fig. 7 There are many parts holding the pump, filter and sender to the bracket

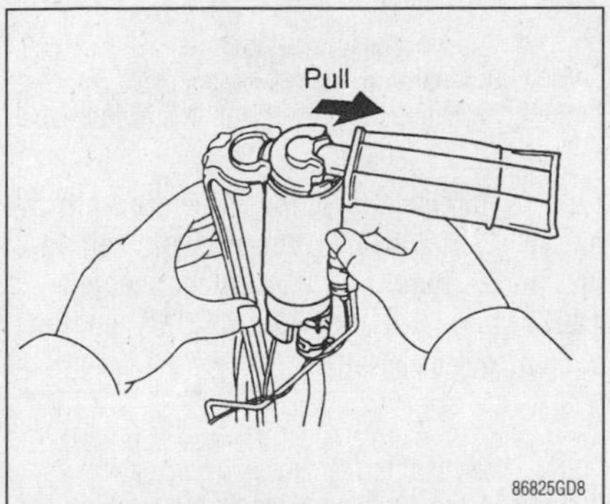

Fig. 8 Pull the pump in an outward motion from the lower side of the bracket

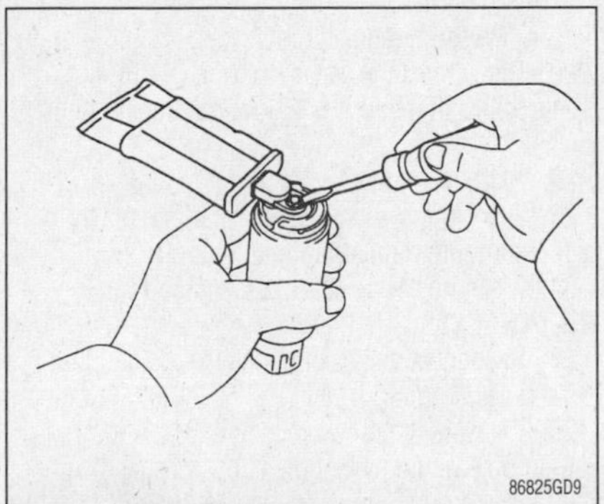

Fig. 9 Carefully release the small C-clip from the in-tank fuel strainer

TESTING

Except Land Cruiser and Tundra

➧ **See Figure 10**

Check the fuel pump operation using the following procedure.

1. Connect a scan tool to the DLC3 diagnostic connector located under the instrument panel

➡**Do not start the engine.**

2. Turn the scan tool on and follow the prompts to turn on the fuel pump from the scan tool.
   a. If you do not have a scan tool, connect the positive and negative leads from a 12V battery to the fuel pump connector.
3. Check that there is pressure in the fuel inlet hose from the fuel filter. If there is pressure, you will hear the sound of fuel flowing.
4. If there is no pressure, check the following:
   - Fuses
   - EFI main relay
   - Fuel pump
   - ECM
   - Wiring connections
5. Turn the ignition switch to LOCK.
6. Disconnect the scan tool from the DLC3.

Check the fuel pressure using the following procedure.

7. Be sure that the battery voltage is above 12V.
8. Disconnect the negative cable from the battery.
9. Remove the bolts, then disconnect the No. 2 timing belt cover.
10. Wrap a shop towel around the delivery pipe, then slowly loosen the union bolt holding the fuel pipe to the delivery pipe and gasket.
11. Install a fuel pressure gauge with adapters to accommodate the fuel line (delivery pipe). Use the two gaskets and the union and union bolt. Tighten to 22 ft. lbs. (29 Nm).

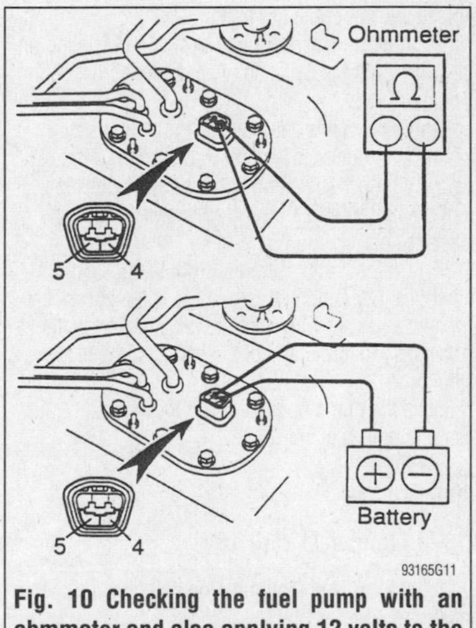

Fig. 10 Checking the fuel pump with an ohmmeter and also applying 12 volts to the connector—2000 4Runner with 5VZ-FE engine shown, 2RZ-FE and 3RZ-FE engines similar

12. Be sure to wipe up any spilled fuel.
13. Reconnect the negative cable to the battery.
14. Start the engine.
15. Measure the fuel pressure, it should read 38–44 psi.
16. If the pressure is too high, replace the pressure regulator.
17. If the pressure is too low, check the following:
- Fuel connections and hoses
- Fuel pump
- Fuel filter
- Pressure regulator
- Vacuum Switching Valve (VSV) for fuel pressure control

18. If removed, install the No. 2 timing belt cover, tighten to 80 inch lbs. (9 Nm).
19. Start the engine.
20. Disconnect the vacuum line from the fuel pressure regulator, then plug the hose end.
21. The fuel pressure at idle should be 38–44 psi.
22. Reconnect the vacuum line to the fuel pressure regulator.
23. The fuel pressure at idle should now be 31–38 psi. If the pressure is not as specified, check the fuel pump, pressure regulator and/or injectors.
24. Stop the engine.
25. Check that the fuel system holds pressure at 21 psi for 5 minutes after the engine has stopped. If the pressure is not as specified, check the pump, pressure regulator and/or injectors.
26. After checking the fuel pressure, disconnect the negative cable from the battery, then carefully remove the fuel pressure gauge and adapters. Use care to prevent gasoline spills.
27. Connect the vehicle's fuel line using new gaskets. Tighten the bolts to 22–25 ft. lbs. (29–34 Nm).
28. Reconnect the negative cable to the battery.
29. Start the engine and check for leaks.

To check the fuel pump electrically, use the following procedure.

30. Remove the fuel tank from the vehicle using all precautions when working around gasoline.
31. At the fuel pump connector. Use an ohmmeter to check the pump's resistance. At room temperature, the resistance should be 0.2–3.0 ohms. If not, replace the fuel pump assembly.
32. A piece of rubber hose should be installed on the pump outlet and placed in an approved gasoline container.
33. Perform this test quickly and limit the run time to 10 seconds to keep from burning out the pump coil. Keep the pump as far away as possible from the battery and always do the switching at the battery side.
34. Connect a jumper wire from the positive terminal of a 12V battery to terminal 4 of the connector. Connect a jumper wire from the negative terminal of a 12V battery to terminal 5 of the connector. The pump should run.
35. If the pump does not meet these tests, replace the fuel pump assembly.

Land Cruiser

➧ **See Figures 11 thru 18**

Check the fuel pump operation using the following procedure.

1. Remove the fuse cover on the instrument panel.
2. Connect a scan tool to the DLC3 diagnostic connector.

➡**Do not start the engine.**

3. Turn the ignition switch **ON** and activate the scan tool.
4. Locate and enable the scan tool's Test Fuel Pump function.
5. Refer to the scan tool's prompts for further details.
6. If you do not have a scan tool, remove the rear seat and carpet as noted in the Fuel Pump Removal procedure. Remove the access cover and connect the positive and negative leads from a 12 volt power source (battery) to the fuel pump connector.
7. Check that there is pressure in the fuel inlet hose from the fuel filter. There are several ways to check for pressure. If there is pressure, you should be able to feel fuel pump pulsations in the fuel inlet line. You should also be able to hear the sound of fuel flowing. Sometimes an assistant listening at the fuel tank fill opening (fuel tank cap off) can verify the pump is running.
8. If there is no pressure, check the following:
- Fusible links (MAIN 2.0L, AM2 0.3P)
- Fuses (EFI 15A, IGN 7.5A)
- EFI main relay
- Fuel pump
- ECM
- Wiring connections

9. Turn the ignition switch to the **LOCK** position.
10. Disconnect the scanner from the DLC3.

Check the fuel system operating pressure using the following procedure.

11. Check that the battery positive voltage is above 12 volts (battery is charged).
12. Disconnect the negative cable from the battery.
13. At the engine's fuel rail, wrap a shop towel around the delivery pipe, then slowly loosen the union bolt holding the fuel inlet pipe to the fuel rail.
14. Install a fuel pressure gauge with the necessary adapters to the fuel inlet pipe, using the two gaskets and the union and union bolt, as necessary. Tighten to 22 ft. lbs. (29 Nm). Wipe up any spilled fuel.
15. Attach a scan tool to the DLC3 diagnostic connector. Reconnect the negative cable to the battery.
16. Turn the ignition switch **ON**.
17. Measure the fuel pressure, it should read 38–44 psi (265–304 kPa).
18. If the pressure is too high, replace the pressure regulator.
19. If the pressure is too low, check the following:
- Fuel connections and hoses
- Fuel pump
- Fuel filter
- Pressure regulator

20. Disconnect the tester from the DLC3.
21. Reinstall the fuse box cover on the instrument panel.
22. Start the engine.
23. Disconnect and plug the vacuum hose from the fuel pressure regulator.
24. Measure the pressure at idle, 38–44 psi (265–304 kPa).
25. Reconnect the vacuum hose to the fuel pressure regulator.
26. Measure the pressure at idle, 31–37 psi (226–255 kPa). If the pressure is not as specified, check the fuel pump, pressure regulator and/or injectors.
27. Stop the engine.

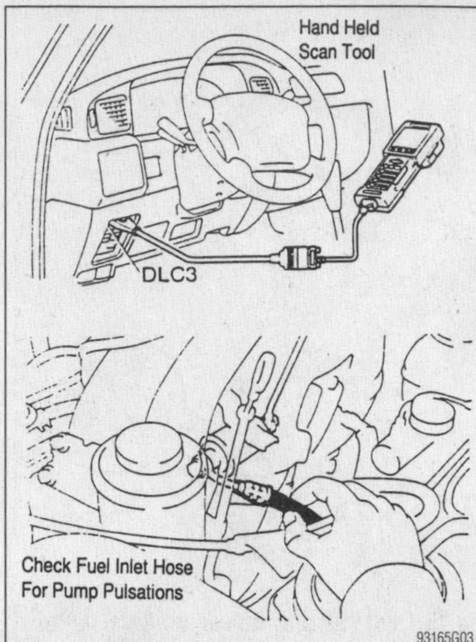

Fig. 11 Activate the fuel pump using a scan tool. Check for pulsations at the fuel inlet line—1997 Land Cruiser with 1FZ-FE engine shown, others similar

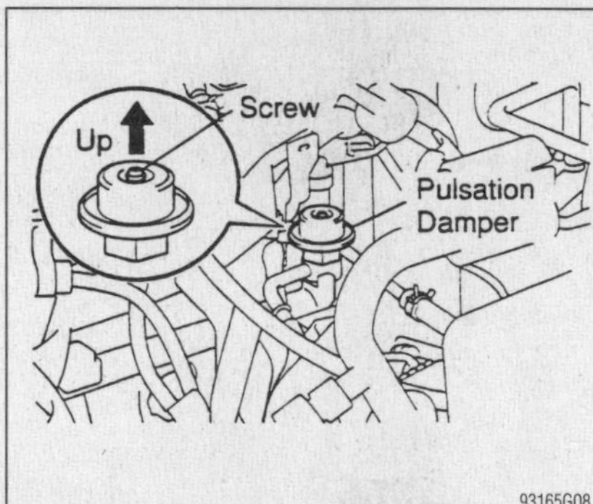

Fig. 12 Activate the fuel pump using a scan tool. Check that the pulsation damper screw rises up when the fuel pump operates—1998 Land Cruiser with 2UZ-FE engine

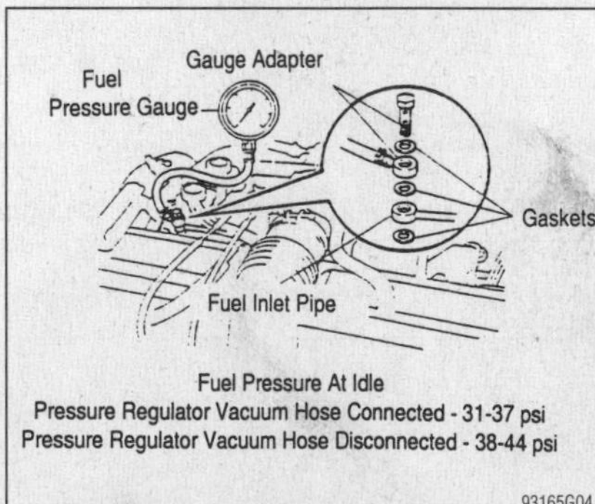

Fig. 13 Check fuel pump pressure with a gauge. Test with the fuel pressure regulator hose attached, then disconnected—1997 Land Cruiser with 1FZ-FE engine shown, others similar

28. Check that the fuel pressure holds at about 21 psi for 5 minutes after engine shutdown. If the system doesn't hold pressure, check the pump, pressure regulator and/or injectors.

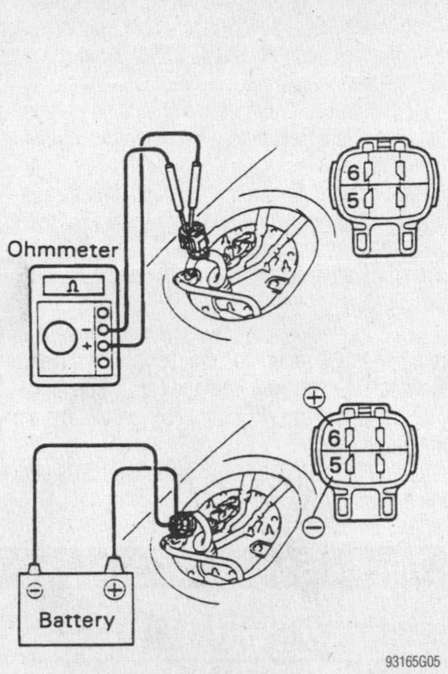

Fig. 14 Checking the fuel pump with an ohmmeter and also applying 12 volts to the connector—1997 Land Cruiser with 1FZ-FE engine shown

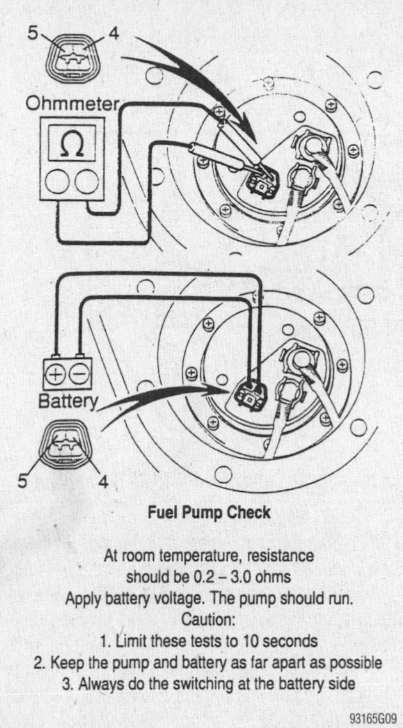

5
4
Ohmmeter
Battery
Fuel Pump Check
At room temperature, resistance
should be 0.2 – 3.0 ohms
Apply battery voltage. The pump should run.
Caution:
1. Limit these tests to 10 seconds
2. Keep the pump and battery as far apart as possible
3. Always do the switching at the battery side
93165G09

Fig. 15 Checking the fuel pump with an ohmmeter and also applying 12 volts to the connector—1998 Land Cruiser with 2UZ-FE engine shown

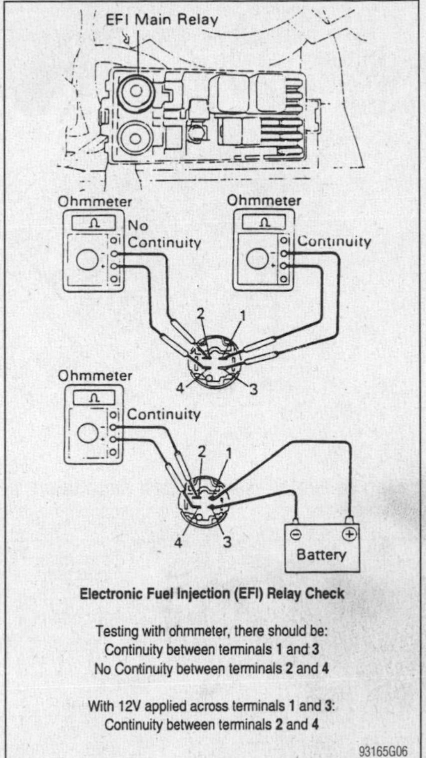

EFI Main Relay
Ohmmeter
No
Continuity
Ohmmeter
Continuity
Ohmmeter
Continuity
Battery
Electronic Fuel Injection (EFI) Relay Check
Testing with ohmmeter, there should be:
Continuity between terminals 1 and 3
No Continuity between terminals 2 and 4
With 12V applied across terminals 1 and 3:
Continuity between terminals 2 and 4
93165G06

Fig. 16 When troubleshooting a fuel pump problem, check the EFI Main Relay—1997 Land Cruiser

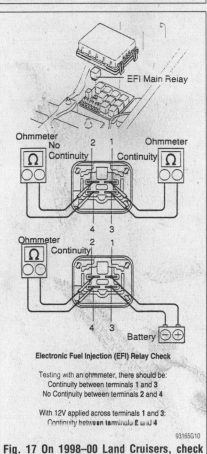

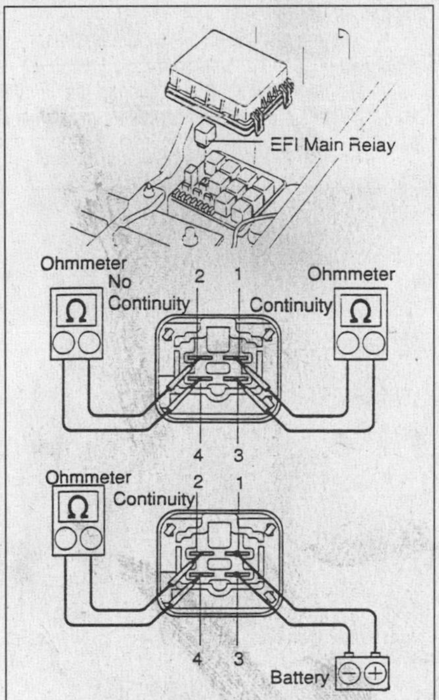

Fig. 17 On 1998–00 Land Cruisers, check the EFI main relay when troubleshooting a fuel pump problem

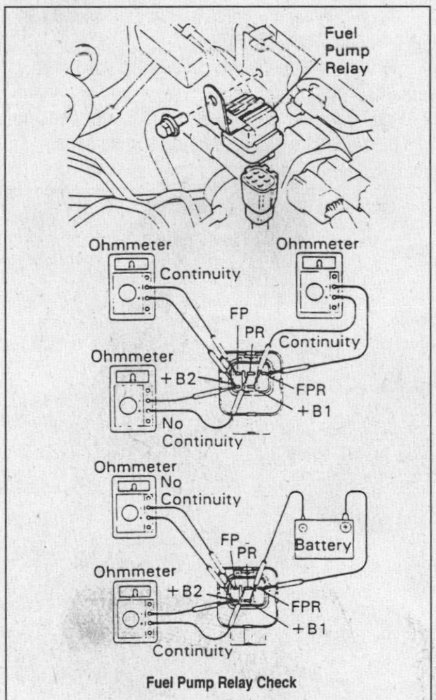

Fig. 18 When troubleshooting a fuel pump problem, check the Fuel Pump Relay—1997 Land Cruiser shown

29. After checking the fuel pressure, disconnect the negative cable from the battery, then carefully remove the fuel pressure gauge and any adapters to prevent fuel spillage.
30. Reinstall the fuel pipe with new gaskets and tighten the union bolts to 22–25 ft. lbs. (29–34 Nm).
31. Reconnect the negative cable to the battery.
32. Check for fuel leaks.

Tundra

See Figures 19 and 20

To check the fuel pump operation, use the following procedure.

1. Connect a scan tool to the underdash diagnostic connector DLC3.
2. Following the tool prompts, activate the fuel pump.

➡Do not start the engine.

3. Locate and check the pulsation damper. The center screw should rise up when the pump operates. If not, check:
   - Fusible links
   - Fuses
   - EFI main relay
   - Fuel pump
   - ECM
   - All related wiring connections

To check the fuel pressure, use the following procedure.

4. Verify that the ignition switch is in the **OFF** position.
5. Verify that the battery is charged.
6. Disconnect the negative battery cable.
7. Remove the front fuel line from the left side fuel rail.

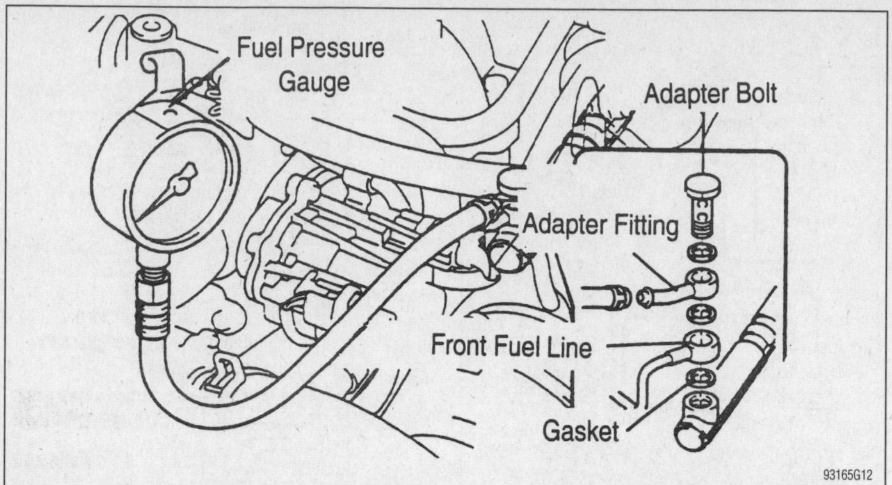

Fig. 19 Fuel pressure gauge installation arrangement—2000 Tundra with 2UZ-FE engine

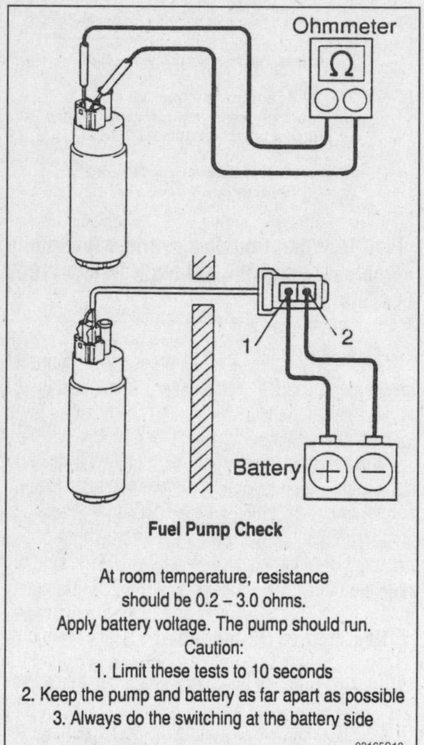

Fig. 20 Checking the fuel pump with an ohmmeter and also applying 12 volts to the connector—2000 Tundra with 2UZ-FE engine

8. Connect a fuel pressure gauge using the appropriate adapters.
9. Clean up any spilled gasoline.
10. Reconnect the negative battery terminal.
11. Connect a scan tool to the underdash diagnostic connector DLC3.
12. Following the tool prompts, activate the fuel pump.
    a. Fuel pressure should be 38–44 psi.
    b. If the pressure is too high, replace the fuel pressure regulator.
    c. If the fuel pressure is too low, check the hoses and connections, fuel pump, fuel filter and fuel pressure regulator.
13. Disconnect the scan tool from DLC3.
14. Start the engine and measure the fuel pressure at idle. Idle fuel pressure should be 38–44 psi.
15. Stop the engine and verify that the system holds fuel pressure of 21 psi or more for five minutes.
    a. If the system does not hold pressure, check the fuel pump, pressure regulator and look for a leaking fuel injector.
16. When all checks are done, disconnect the negative battery cable and remove the fuel pressure gauge and adapters.
17. Reconnect the vehicle's fuel line to the fuel rail.
18. Connect the negative battery cable, start the engine and check for leaks.

To check the fuel pump electrically, use the following procedure.

19. Remove the fuel tank from the vehicle using all precautions when working around gasoline.
20. At the fuel pump connector. Use an ohmmeter to check the pump's resistance. At room temperature, the resistance should be 0.2–3.0 ohms. If not, replace the fuel pump assembly.
21. A piece of rubber hose should be installed on the pump outlet and placed in an approved gasoline container.
22. Perform this test quickly and limit the run time to 10 seconds to keep from burning out the pump coil. Keep the pump as far away as possible from the battery and always do the switching at the battery side.
23. Connect a jumper wire from the positive terminal of a 12V battery to terminal 1 of the connector. Connect a jumper wire from the negative terminal of a 12V battery to terminal 2 of the connector. The pump should run.
24. If the pump does not meet these tests, replace the fuel pump assembly.

Throttle Body

REMOVAL & INSTALLATION

1FZ-FE Engine

See Figure 21

1. Relieve the fuel system pressure.
2. Drain the engine cooling system.
3. Disconnect the PCV and air cleaner hoses.
4. Remove the control cables from the throttle body.
5. Disconnect the Throttle Position (TP) sensor and Idle Air Control (IAC) valve wiring.
6. Tag and disconnect all vacuum and water hoses leading to the throttle body.
7. Remove the bolts and disconnect the throttle body from the air intake chamber (upper intake manifold).

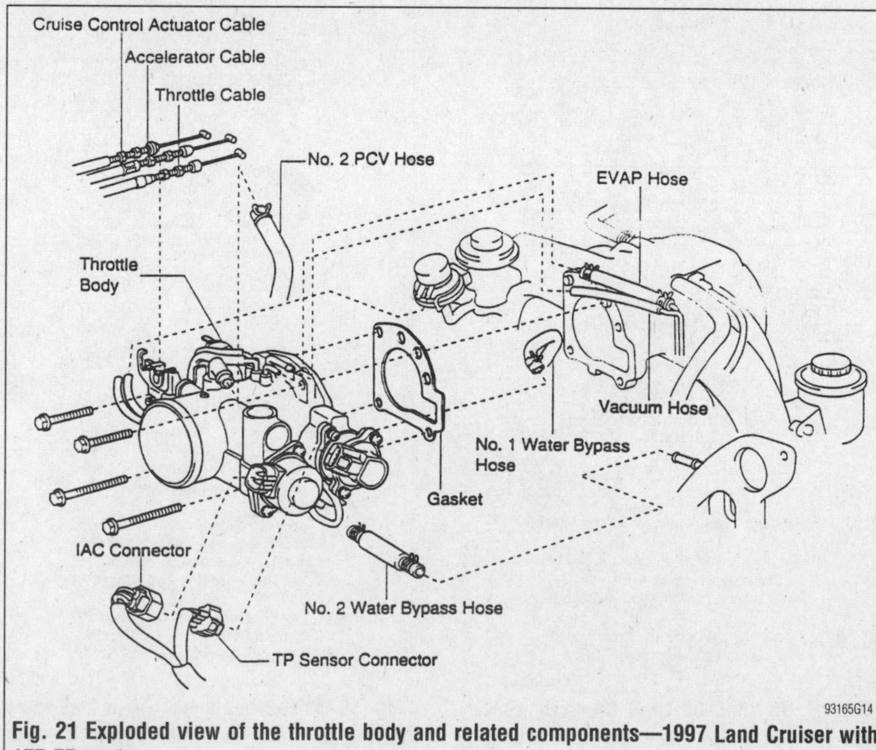

Fig. 21 Exploded view of the throttle body and related components—1997 Land Cruiser with 1FZ-FE engine

8. Remove the throttle body gasket and discard.
9. Disconnect the both of the water bypass hoses from the throttle body, then remove the unit.

To install:

10. Using soft brush and carburetor cleaner, clean the cast aluminum parts. Using compressed air, clean all passages and opening.

✲✲ WARNING

To prevent damaging the parts, do not clean the TP sensor, dashpot or IAC Valve.

11. Apply vacuum to the throttle opener. Check that there is no clearance between the throttle stop screw and throttle lever when the throttle valve is fully closed.
12. Attach the water bypass hoses to the throttle body.
13. Install the throttle body with a new gasket, then tighten to 15 ft. lbs. (21 Nm).
14. Install all of the previously tagged vacuum and water hoses.
15. Attach the Throttle Position (TP) sensor and Idle Air Control (IAC) wiring.
16. Install the control cables to the throttle body.
17. Connect the PCV and air cleaner hoses.
18. Fill the cooling system, start the engine to check for coolant and vacuum leaks. Add coolant, as required.

2RZ-FE and 3RZ-FE Engines

➧ **See Figure 22**

1. Drain the engine coolant.
2. If equipped with a manual transmission, disconnect the accelerator cable from the throttle body.
3. If equipped with an automatic transmission, disconnect the accelerator cable and the throttle cables from the throttle body.
4. Remove the air cleaner hose with the resonator.
5. Tag for identification, then disconnect the air hose from the Idle Air Control (IAC) valve, the vacuum line from the fuel pressure regulator, and the clamp for the engine wiring harness. Remove the two bolts, the hose clamp and remove the intake air intake connector.
6. Disconnect the PCV hose.
7. Tag for identification then disconnect the three vacuum hoses, EVAP hose and, if equipped with power steering, the hose for the power steering idle-up.
8. Detach the Throttle Position (TP) sensor and IAC valve connectors.
9. Remove the two bolts and two nuts and remove the throttle body from the air intake. Discard the gasket.

To install:

10. Using soft brush and carburetor cleaner, clean the cast aluminum parts. Using compressed air, clean all passages and opening.

✲✲ WARNING

To prevent damaging the parts, do not clean the TP sensor or IAC Valve.

11. Apply vacuum to the throttle opener. Check that there is no clearance between the throttle stop screw and throttle lever when the throttle valve is fully closed.
12. Installation is the reverse of the removal procedure. Use a new gasket on the throttle body. Tighten the nuts and bolts to 14 ft. lbs. (20 Nm).
13. Attach the TP sensor and IAC valve wiring.
14. Install the control cables to the throttle body.
15. Install the hoses, noting the identification tags made at removal.
16. Connect the PCV and air cleaner hoses.
17. Fill the cooling system, start the engine to check for coolant and vacuum leaks. Add coolant, as required.

5VZ-FE Engine

➧ **See Figures 23 thru 30**

1. Drain the cooling system.
2. If equipped with cruise control, disconnect the cruise control actuator cable and accelerator cable from the throttle body. If equipped with automatic transmission, disconnect the throttle valve cable from the throttle body.
3. Remove the air cleaner hose.
4. Detach the Throttle Position (TP) sensor connector and Idle Air Control (IAC) valve connectors.
5. Tag and disconnect the water and vacuum hoses from the throttle body.
6. On some vehicles, it may be necessary to disconnect the ignition coil wiring.
7. Unbolt the throttle body and remove and discard the gasket.

To install:

8. Using soft brush and carburetor cleaner, clean the cast aluminum parts. Using compressed air, clean all passages and opening.

✲✲ WARNING

To prevent damaging the parts, do not clean the TP sensor or IAC valve.

9. Installation is the reverse of the removal procedure. Place a new gasket on the air intake chamber facing the tab (protrusion) upwards. Position the throttle body and tighten the fasteners evenly to 13 ft. lbs. (18 Nm).
10. Attach the TP sensor and IAC valve wiring.
11. Install the control cables to the throttle body.
12. Attach the hoses, noting the identification tags made at removal.
13. Connect the PCV and air cleaner hoses.
14. Fill the cooling system, start the engine to check for coolant and vacuum leaks. Add coolant, as required.

2UZ-FE Engine

➧ **See Figure 31**

The throttle body arrangement on Toyota's 2UZ-FE engine is somewhat unique in that although it has a throttle cable, the cable is primarily a back-up. The throttle is electrically controlled. The Throttle Position (TP) sensor is mounted on the throttle body and detects the throttle opening angle. The voltage applied to terminals VTA and VTA2 of the ECM changes between 0 V and 5 V in proportion to the opening angle of the throttle valve. The ECM calculates the current opening angle of the throttle valve from these signal inputs to the ECM and the ECM controls the throttle motor which as a clutch and gear set to control the throttle plate angle to properly position the throttle valve angle in response to the driver's demand. In the event of a component failure, a DTC is set and the ECM shuts down the power for the throttle motor and the electromagnetic clutch, and the throttle valve is closed by the return spring. The throttle valve can still be controlled by the accelerator pedal through the throttle cable.

This system should be handled carefully. Use care not to shock or damage the system in any way. Use care when handling the electrical connectors.

1. Remove the acoustic/cosmetic throttle body cover.
2. Drain the engine coolant.
3. Remove the intake air connector.
4. Disconnect the accelerator cable from the throttle body.
5. Detach the Throttle Position (TP) sensor electrical connector.
6. Detach the throttle control motor electrical connector.

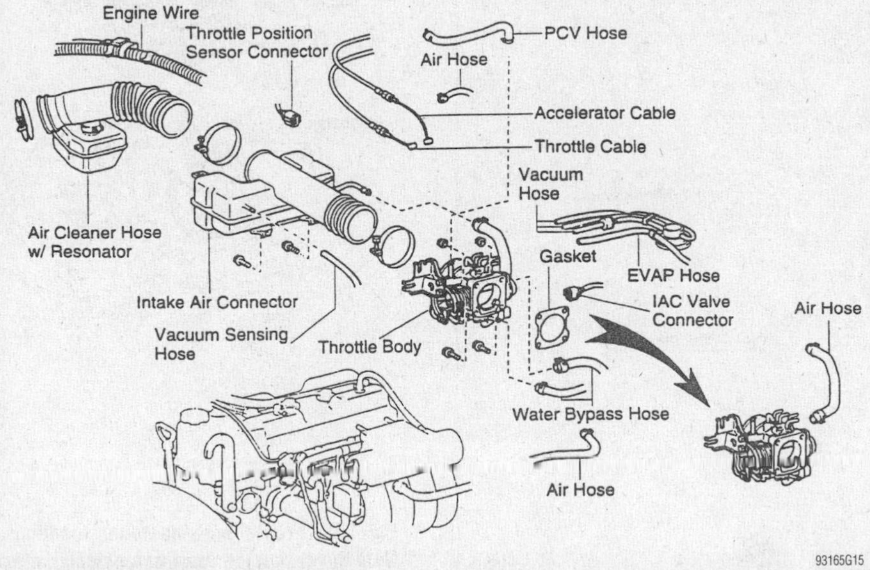

Fig. 22 Throttle body arrangement and related components—2RZ-FE and 3RZ-FE engines

93165p07

Fig. 23 View of the throttle plate in the throttle body

93165p04

Fig. 24 You can use a commercially available spray to clean the throttle body

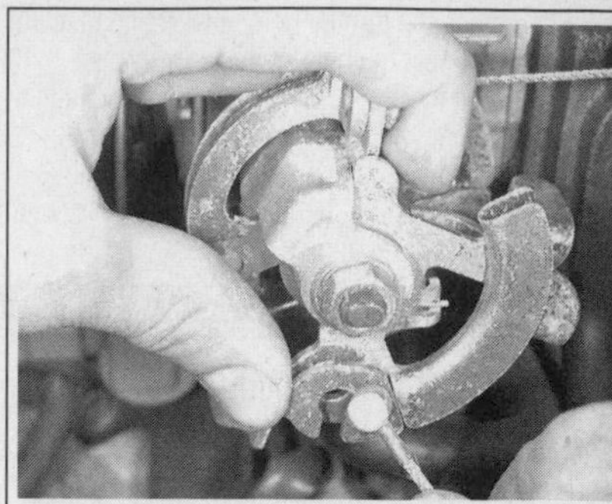

93165p11

Fig. 25 Disconnect the throttle cable from the side of the throttle body

93165p06

Fig. 26 Slide the throttle body straight off the mounting studs

93165p13

Fig. 27 Always use a new gasket when reinstalling the throttle body

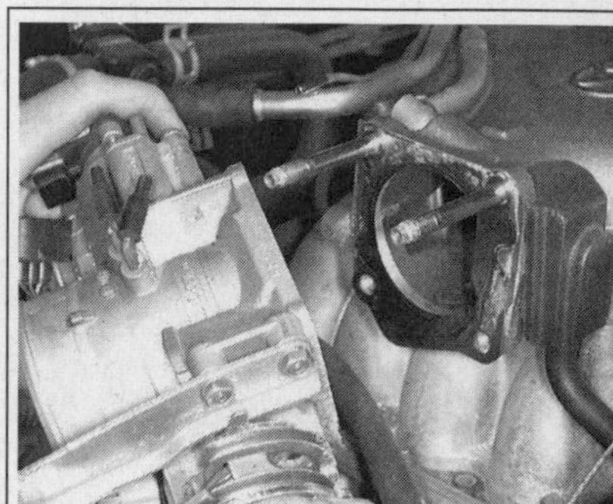

93165p05

Fig. 28 To install, align the throttle body with the studs

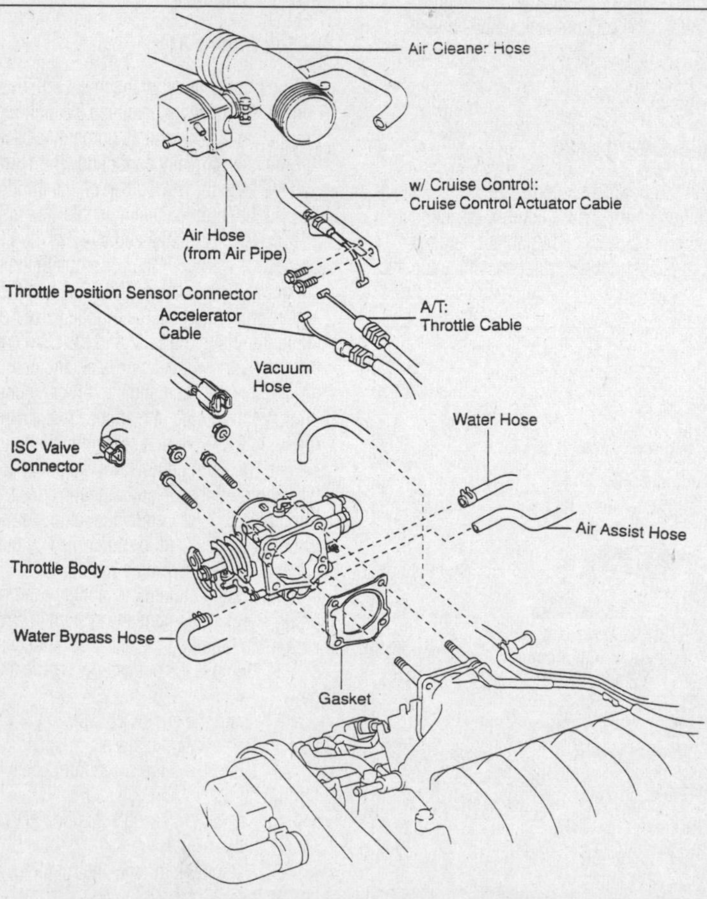

93165G16

Fig. 29 Throttle body arrangement and related components—5VZ-FE engine

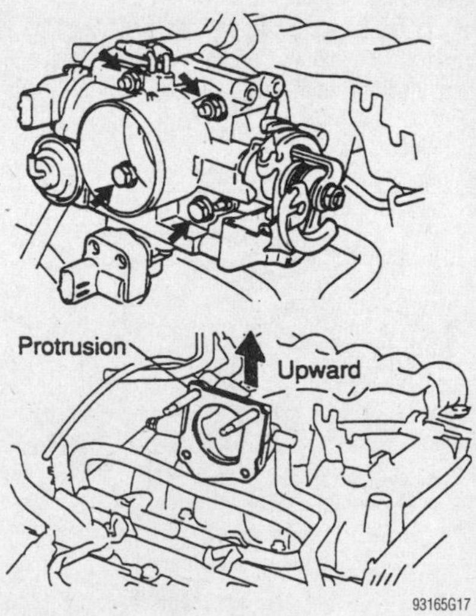

93165G17

Fig. 30 Throttle body fastener locations. Note the gasket tab (protrusion) which must face upward—5VZ-FE engine

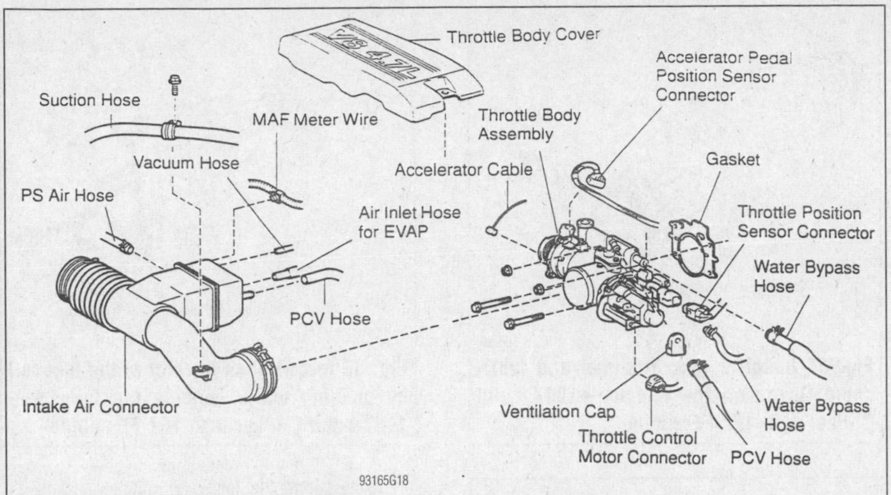

Fig. 31 Throttle body and related components—2UZ-FE engine

7. Disconnect the accelerator pedal position electrical sensor
8. Disconnect the accelerator pedal position sensor wire from the two clamps on the wire bracket.
9. Disconnect the PCV hose and water bypass hose from the throttle body.
10. Remove the ventilation cap.
11. Remove the two bolts and two nuts and remove the throttle body from the intake manifold. Disconnect the water bypass hose from the thermostat on the throttle body and remove the throttle body from the vehicle. Discard the gasket.

To install:

12. Installation is the reverse of the removal procedure. Connect the water bypass hose to the manifold thermostat on the throttle body.
13. Position the throttle body to the intake manifold, using a new gasket. Tighten the two nuts and bolts evenly to 13 ft. lbs. (18 Nm). Install the ventilation cap.
14. Connect the water bypass hose and PCV hose to the throttle body
15. Attach the TP sensor and throttle control motor connectors.
16. Connect the accelerator pedal sensor connector and secure the wire to the clamps on the wire brackets.
17. Connect the accelerator cable to the throttle body and install the air intake connector.
18. Refill the engine with coolant. Start the engine and check for coolant leaks. Install the throttle body cover.

Fuel Rail and Injectors

REMOVAL & INSTALLATION

➡The engines covered by this manual are Sequentially Fuel Injected (SFI). This means the electrical connectors for each injector should be tagged so that they can be installed in their exact original locations. This is extremely important.

1FZ FE Engine

See Figures 32 thru 37

Like most multi-port fuel injected engines, the fuel injectors are mounted on a fuel rail (Toyota calls it a delivery pipe). On this engine, the fuel rail is hidden under the upper half of the intake manifold, which must be removed to access the injectors. At assembly, a new intake manifold gasket will be required. Use care when working around light alloy parts. Numerous hose connections must be detached. Identify and tag these hoses as required.

1. Relieve the fuel system pressure.
2. Drain the engine cooling system.
3. Remove the upper half of the intake manifold. For additional information, please refer to the following topic(s): Engine and Engine Overhaul, Intake Manifold.
4. Remove the 2 union bolts, gaskets and fuel inlet pipe.
5. Remove the delivery pipe and injectors as follows:
   a. Unsecure the 6 injector connectors.
   b. Remove the bolts and delivery pipe together with the 6 injectors. Be careful not to drop the injectors when removing the pipe.
   c. Remove the insulators and spacers on the intake manifold.
   d. Pull the injectors out of the delivery pipe. Remove the O-rings and grommets from each injector.
6. Inspect the injectors.

To install:

7. Install new grommets on each injector, then lubricate the new O-rings with a light coat of gasoline. Install the O-rings to the fuel injectors.
8. While turning the injector left and right to ease it into place, install it to the delivery pipe. Install all 6 injectors.
9. Position the injector connector upwards. Place new insulators and spacers in position on the intake manifold.
10. Temporarily install the bolts holding the delivery pipe to the intake manifold.
11. Check that the injectors rotate smoothly. If they do not, recheck the position of the O-rings, or replace them.
12. Position the injector connector upward, then tighten the bolts holding the delivery pipe to the intake manifold to 15 ft. lbs. (21 Nm).
13. Attach the injector connectors taking note of the identification tags made at removal.

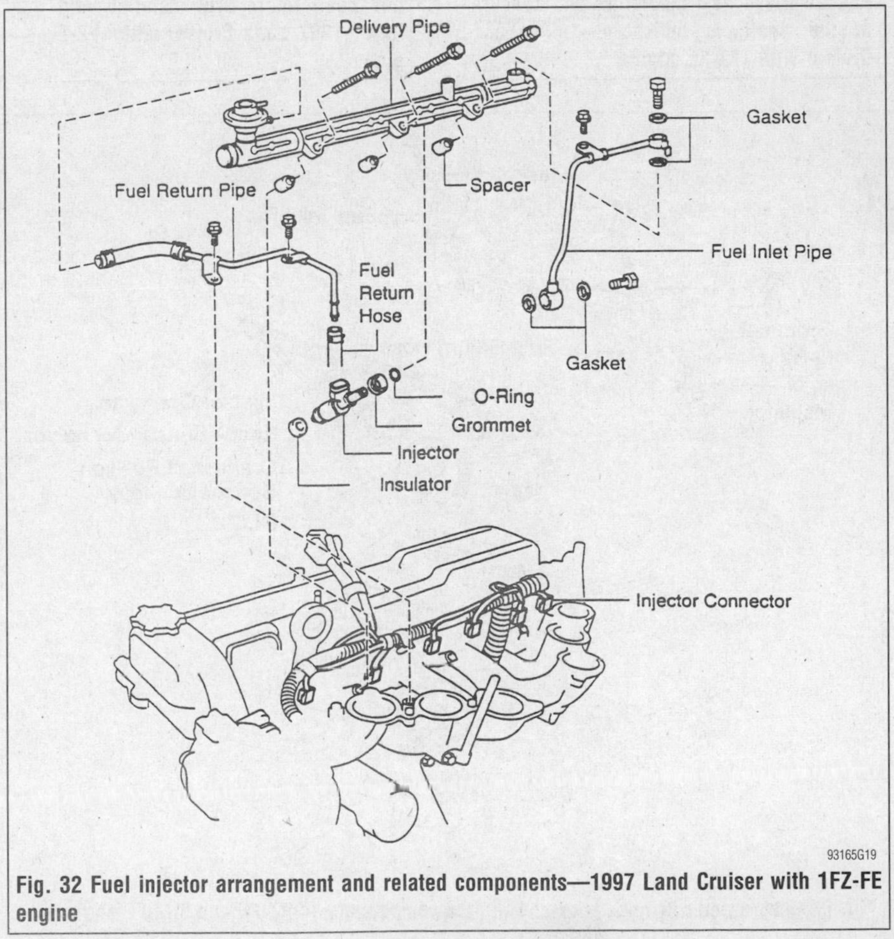

Fig. 32 Fuel injector arrangement and related components—1997 Land Cruiser with 1FZ-FE engine

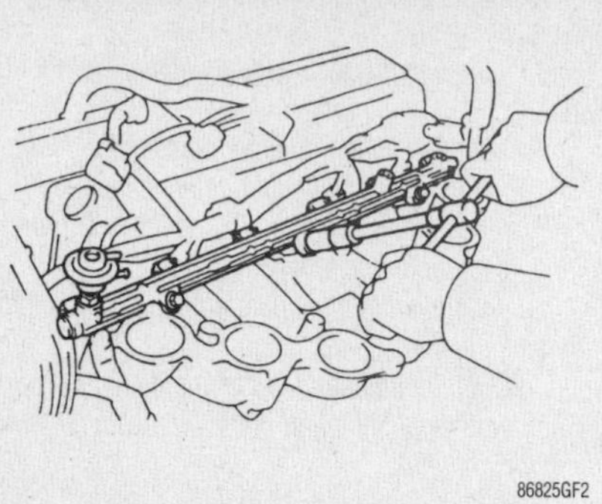

Fig. 33 The injectors are removed with the fuel rail (delivery pipe)—1997 Land Cruiser with 1FZ-FE engine

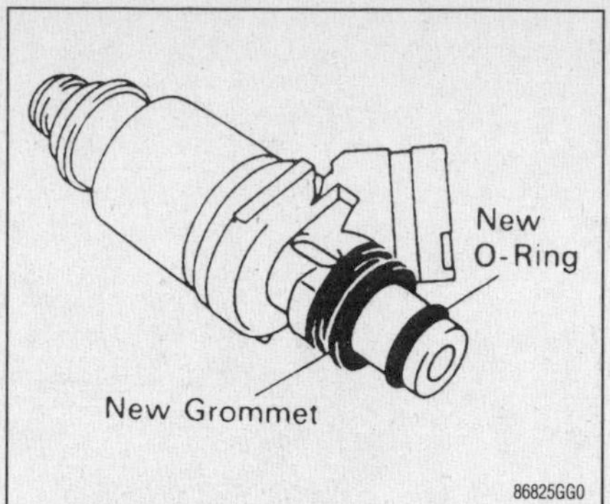

Fig. 34 Install a new grommet and lubricated O-ring on the injector—1997 Land Cruiser with 1FZ-FE engine

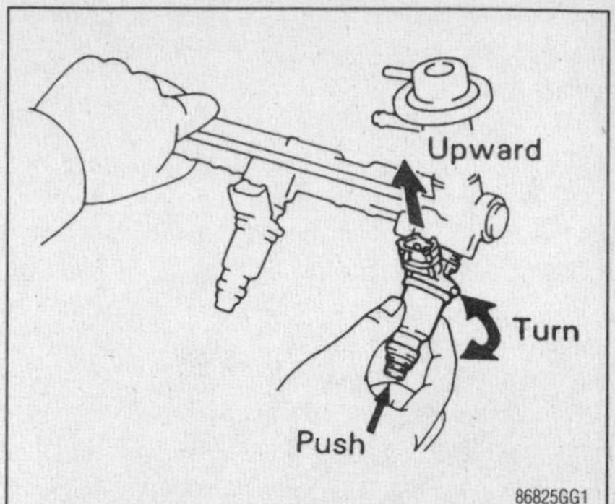

Fig. 35 Install each injector to the fuel rail by pushing while twisting the injector—1997 Land Cruiser with 1FZ-FE engine

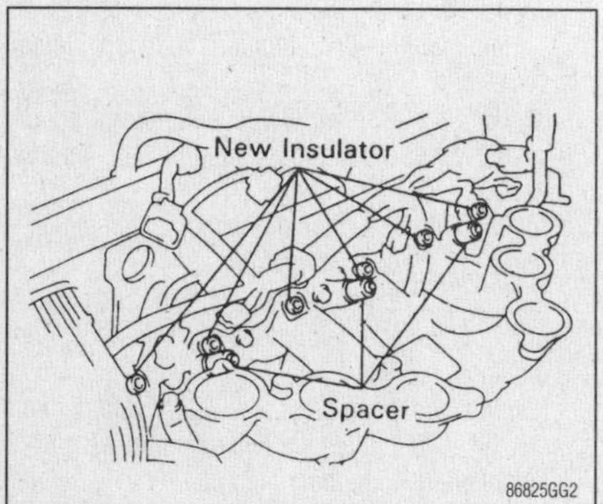

Fig. 36 Place new insulators and spacers in the positions indicated—1997 Land Cruiser with 1FZ-FE engine

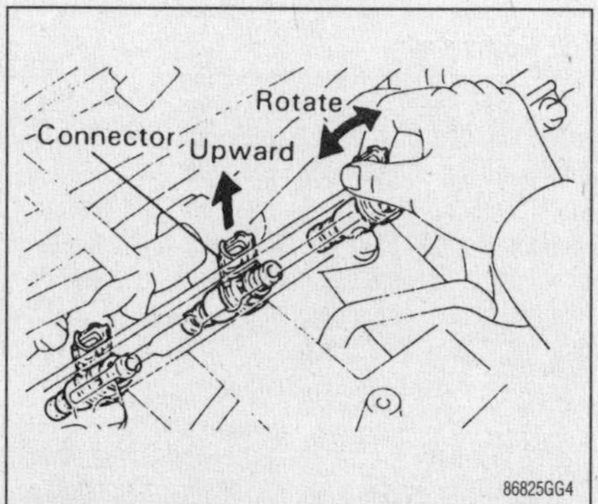

Fig. 37 Rotate the injectors to ensure smooth movement. An injector that binds has been improperly installed and may leak—1997 Land Cruiser with 1FZ-FE engine

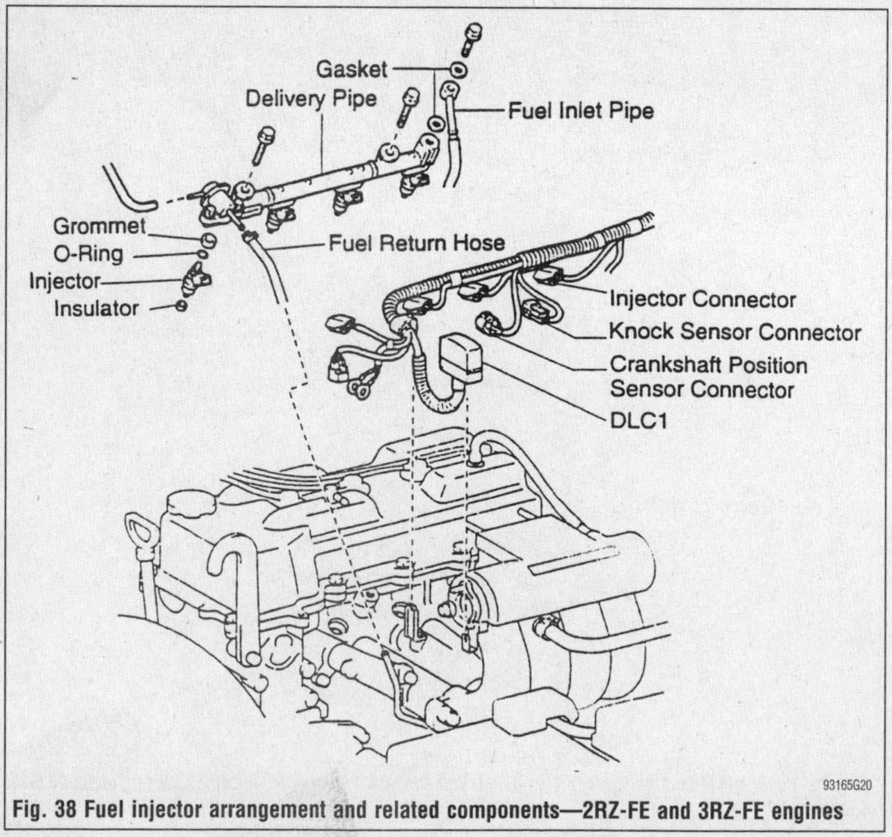

Fig. 38 Fuel injector arrangement and related components—2RZ-FE and 3RZ-FE engines

14. Install the fuel inlet pipe with new gaskets, tighten the union bolt to 22 ft. lbs. (29 Nm) and the bolt to 14 ft. lbs. (20 Nm).
15. Install the fuel return pipe with the bolts and tighten to 14 ft. lbs. (20 Nm).
16. Attach the hose to the pressure regulator.
17. Install the upper intake manifold.
18. Connect the throttle, accelerator and cruise control actuator cables.
19. Attach the air cleaner and PCV hoses.
20. Fill the cooling system with a water/coolant mixture. Start the engine and add coolant as required. Check for coolant, vacuum and fuel leaks.

2RZ-FE and 3RZ-FE Engines

➧ See Figure 38

1. Relieve the fuel system pressure.
2. Remove the throttle body using the procedures found in this section.
3. Tag for identification, then detach the 4 fuel injector electrical connectors, the Crankshaft Position (CKP) sensor connector and the Knock Sensor (KS) connector.
4. Detach the DLC1 diagnostic connector and wire clamp from the brackets.
5. Disconnect the vacuum line from the fuel pressure regulator. Detach the fuel return hose from the pressure regulator.
6. Remove the union bolt and gaskets and disconnect the fuel inlet pipe from the fuel rail (delivery pipe). Expect fuel to run out. Place clean shop cloths under the fuel inlet and loosen the bolt slowly.
7. Remove the two fuel rail hold-down bolts and remove the fuel rail with the injector still attached. The injectors are only retained by their O-rings and will tend to drop out of the fuel rail, so use care. Remove the four insulator from the four spacers.
8. Pull out the injectors from the fuel rail. Discard the O-ring and grommet from each injector.

To install:

9. Install new grommets on each injector, then lubricate the new O-rings with a light coat of gasoline. Install the O-rings to the fuel injectors.
10. While turning the injector left and right to ease it into place, install it to the delivery pipe. Install all 4 injectors.
11. Position the injector connector upwards. Place new insulators and spacers in position on the intake manifold.
12. Temporarily install the bolts holding the delivery pipe to the intake manifold.

13. Check that the injectors rotate smoothly. If they do not, recheck the position of the O-rings, or replace them.

14. Position the injector connector upward, then tighten the bolts holding the delivery pipe to the intake manifold to 15 ft. lbs. (21 Nm).

15. Attach the injector connectors taking note of the identification tags made at removal.

16. Install the fuel inlet pipe with new gaskets, tighten the union bolt to 22 ft. lbs. (29 Nm) and the bolt to 14 ft. lbs. (20 Nm).

17. Install the fuel return pipe to the fuel pressure regulator. Connect the vacuum line to the pressure regulator.

18. Attach all electrical connectors and vacuum lines, as required.

19. Install the throttle body using the procedures found in this section.

5VZ-FE Engine

See Figures 39 thru 44

1. Relieve the fuel system pressure.
2. Remove the air cleaner hose.
3. Remove the upper half of the intake manifold (Toyota calls it the Air Intake Chamber). For additional information, please refer to the following topic(s): Engine and Engine Overhaul, Intake Manifold.
4. Remove the fuel pressure regulator.
5. Disconnect the fuel inlet pipe. Be prepared to collect spilled fuel. Use clean shop cloths under the fuel connection.
6. Tag for identification then detach the fuel injector electrical connections.
7. Unbolt and remove the fuel rail (delivery pipes) together with the injectors.
8. Remove the spacers from the intake manifold.
9. Pull the injectors out of the delivery pipes, then remove the O-rings and grommets from each injector.

To install:

10. Install new grommets and O-rings on each injector. Apply a light coat of gasoline on the O-rings.
11. While turning the injector clockwise and counterclockwise, push it into the delivery pipe. Install all of the injectors in the same manner.
12. Position the injector connector outward.
13. Place the spacers into position on the intake manifold. Temporarily install the bolts to hold the delivery pipes to the intake manifold.
14. Check that the injectors rotate smoothly. If they do not, the O-rings have probably been installed incorrectly. If this has occurred, replace the O-rings with new ones.
15. Position the injector outward, then attach the injector connectors.
16. Install the fuel pipe with new gaskets and union bolts, tighten to 25 ft. lbs. (34 Nm). Tighten the bolts retaining the delivery pipes to the intake manifold to 10 ft. lbs. (13 Nm).
17. Temporarily install the union with new gaskets, then connect the fuel pipe. Install the clamp bolt, tighten to 71 inch lbs. (8 Nm).
18. Install the fuel pressure regulator.
19. Inspect the vacuum lines and connections. Look for any loose connections, sharp bends or damage.
20. Install the intake air cleaner.
21. Attach the air cleaner hose.
22. Start the engine and check for vacuum and fuel leaks.

2UZ-FE Engine

See Figures 45 and 46

1. Remove the acoustic/cosmetic throttle body cover.
2. Remove the intake air connector.
3. Remove the fuel pressure pulsation damper, upper gasket and main fuel hoses and its gasket. Expect fuel to run out. Place a clean shop cloth under the connections before loosening the damper.
4. Remove the accelerator cable then remove the two retaining nuts from the bracket.
5. Disconnect the PCV hose from the PCV valve.
6. Detach the electrical connector from the Vacuum Switch Valve (VSV) for the EVAP system. Disconnect the EVAP hose. Remove the accelerator cable clamp and EVAP VSV from the intake manifold.
7. Disconnect the DLC1 diagnostic connector from the throttle body cover bracket then remove the bolt and cover bracket.
8. Tag for identification as required, then detach the engine wiring harness clamps from the engine brackets.
9. Remove the bolt holding the clamp on the fuel return pipe to the left side delivery pipe. Remove the bolts from the front fuel pipe (crossover fuel line).
10. Tag for identification each fuel injector electrical connector. This is important. This engine is sequentially fuel injected and each injector connector must go on the proper fuel injector. Detach the eight fuel injector connectors.
11. Remove the four nuts holding the fuel rails (Toyota calls them 'delivery pipes') to the lower intake manifold.
12. Remove the fuel rails along with the fuel injectors, the four spacers and eight insulators. Use care. The fuel injectors are retained only by their

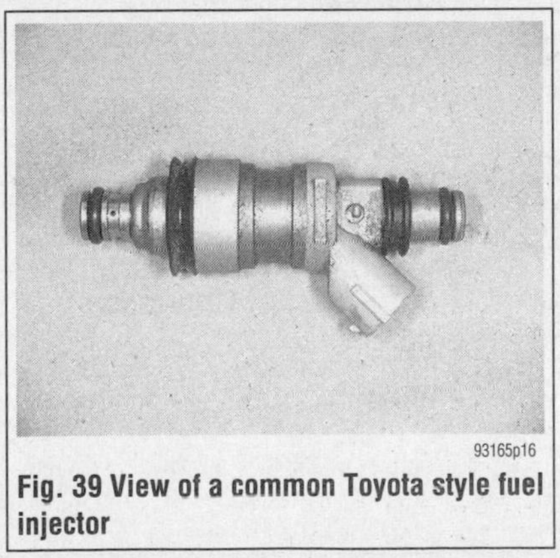

93165p16

Fig. 39 View of a common Toyota style fuel injector

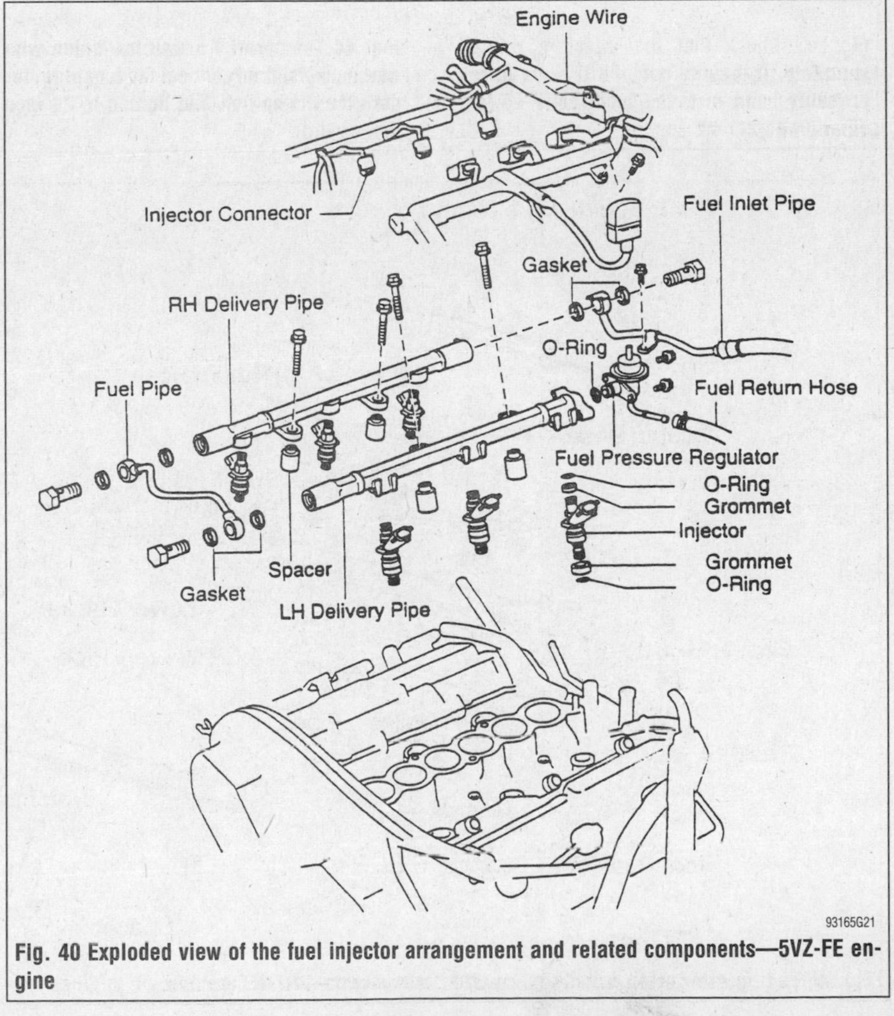

93165G21

Fig. 40 Exploded view of the fuel injector arrangement and related components—5VZ-FE engine

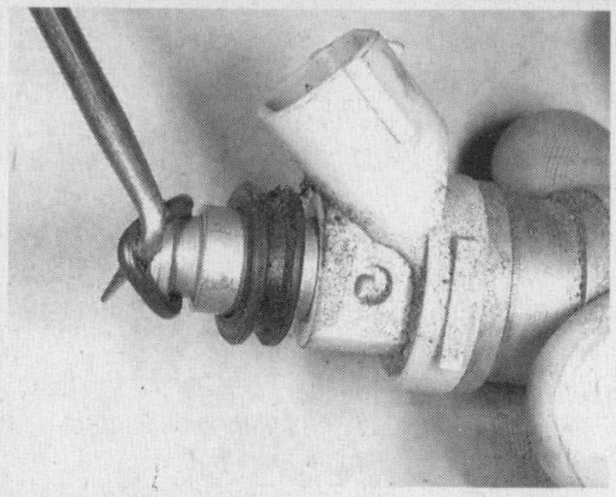
93165p18

Fig. 41 Use a pick to remove the old O-rings. You should always install new O-rings and grommets on each injector prior to installing them

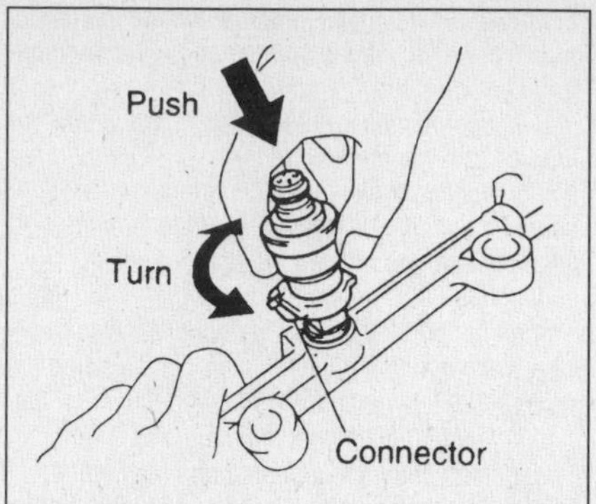

86825GG9

Fig. 42 While twisting the injector clockwise and counterclockwise, push it into its delivery pipe—5VZ-FE engine

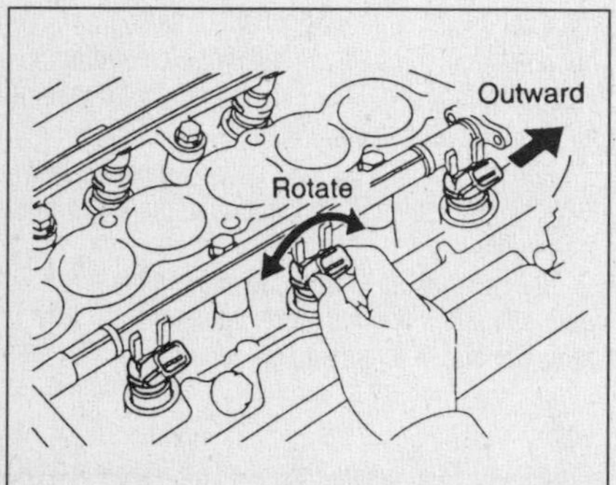

86825GH0

Fig. 43 Check that the injectors rotate smoothly. If they do not, the O-rings have probably been installed incorrectly—5VZ-FE engine

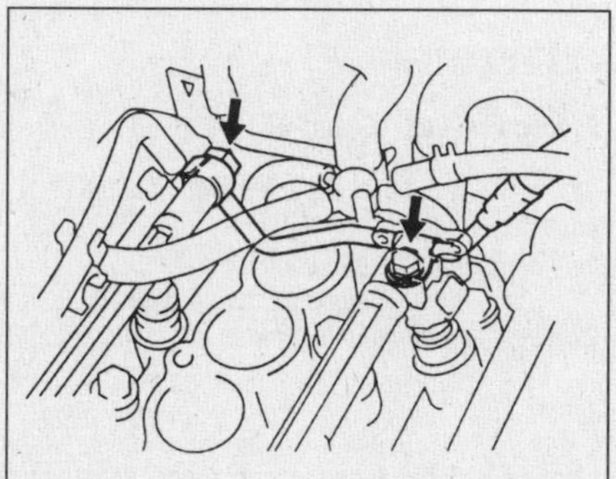
86825GH1

Fig. 44 Temporarily install the union with new gaskets, then connect the fuel pipe. Install the clamp bolt and tighten to 71 inch lbs. (8 Nm)

O-rings and tend to drop out of the fuel rail as it is being removed. Be careful not to drop any injectors.

To install:

13. Install new grommets and O-rings on each injector. Apply a light coat of gasoline on the O-rings.
14. While turning the injector clockwise and counterclockwise, push it into the delivery pipe. Install all eight injectors.
15. Position the injector connector outward so it will match up with the injector harness connectors.
16. Place the four spacers into position on the intake manifold. Temporarily install the four nuts to hold the fuel rails to the intake manifold.
17. Check that the injectors rotate smoothly. If they do not, the O-rings have probably been installed incorrectly. If this has occurred, replace the O-rings with new ones.
18. Attach the injector connectors, noting the identification tags made at removal.
19. Install the front fuel pipe (crossover) with new gaskets and union bolts, tighten the union bolts to 29 ft. lbs. (39 Nm). Tighten the nuts retaining the fuel rails to the intake manifold to 13 ft. lbs. (18 Nm).
20. If removed, install the fuel pressure regulator.
21. Connect the engine wiring harness to its clamps and brackets. Make sure the wire protector is in place.
22. Connect the PCV hose to the PCV valve.
23. Connect the EVAP VSV to the upper intake manifold.
24. Install the throttle body cover bracket and the DLC1 connector.
25. Install the accelerator cable bracket and tighten the nuts to 13 ft. lbs. (18 Nm).
26. Connect the accelerator cable.
27. Thread the fuel pressure pulsation damper into place and tighten to 29 ft. lbs. (39 Nm).

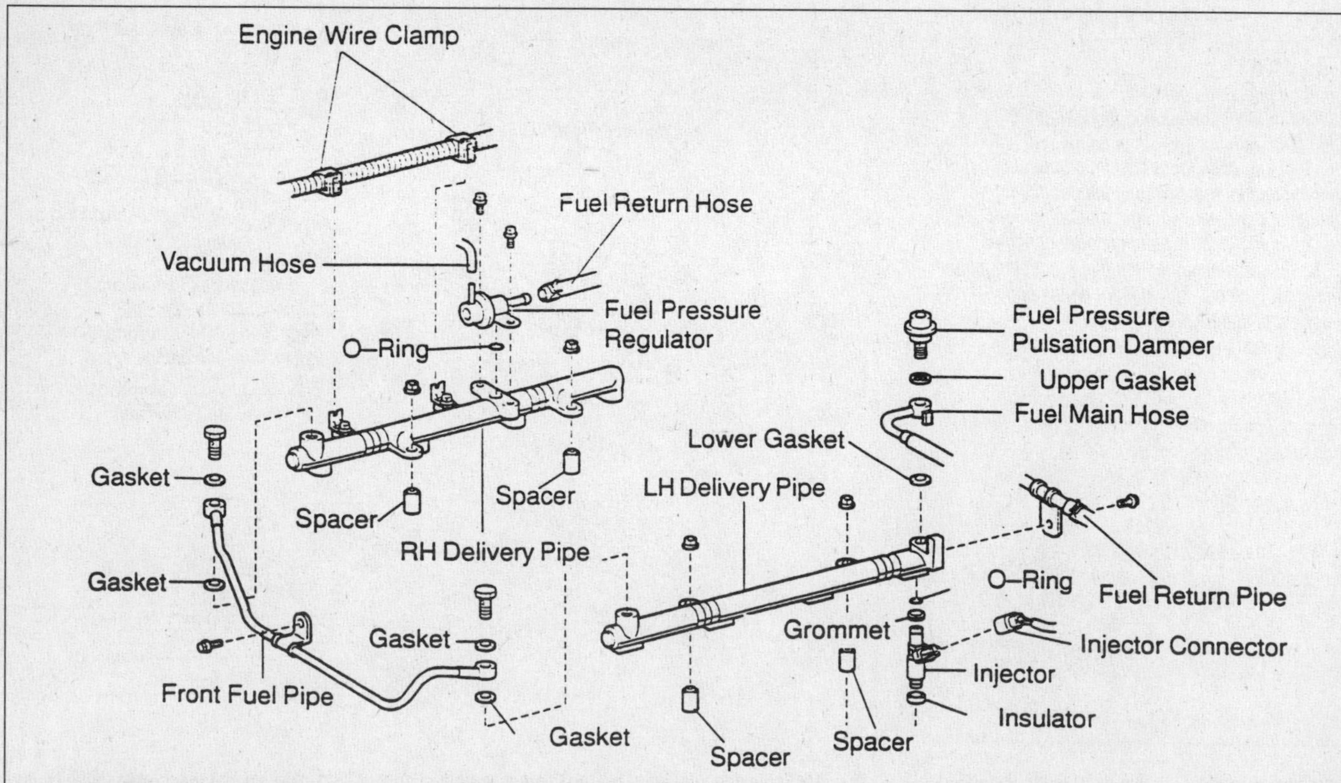

93165G22

Fig. 45 Fuel injector arrangement and related components—2UZ-FE engine

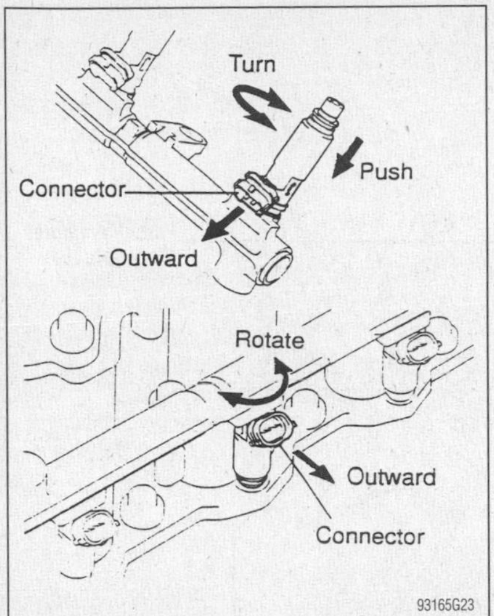

Fig. 46 Install the injectors, twisting slightly to seat them. Align the injector electrical connectors as shown—2UZ-FE engine

28. Install the intake air connector and acoustic/cosmetic throttle body cover.
29. Start the engine and check for vacuum and fuel leaks.

TESTING

See Figures 47, 48, and 49

Correct testing of the fuel injectors requires specific equipment not usually available outside a dealership or a fuel lab. It is recommended that any checking or testing of the injectors, other than that included below, be left to a properly equipped service facility.

Injector operation can be checked with the injectors installed in the engine. A 'sound scope' is needed here. This is a stethoscope-like device available from most auto tool and parts jobbers.

With the engine running or cranking, check each injector for normal operating noise (a clicking, buzzing or humming), which changes in proportion to engine rpm. If a mechanic's stethoscope is not available to you, check injector operation by touching each injector with your finger. It should be buzzing or vibrating indicating the injector solenoid is opening and closing. If no sound or an unusual sound is heard, check the wiring connector, or have the injector checked professionally.

With the engine **OFF**, measure injector resistance by unplugging the wiring connector from the injector, and connecting an ohmmeter across the injector terminals. Check the continuity at both terminals. Resistance at room temperature should be 12–16 ohms. Resistance will vary with injector temperature.

Fuel Pressure Regulator

REMOVAL & INSTALLATION

Fuel injected engines have fuel pumps which produce more pressure than is normally required. A fuel pressure regulator bypasses excess fuel to the fuel tank. A vacuum line (Toyota sometimes calls it a vacuum sensing hose) applies varying amounts of vacuum to the regulator. As the engine changes speed and load, the vacuum also changes. This allows the pressure regulator to vary the fuel pressure to suit the engine's demands.

1FZ-FE Engine

See Figures 50, 51, and 52

1. Relieve the fuel system pressure.
2. Disconnect the vacuum line (sensing hose) from the pressure regulator.
3. Wrap a clean shop cloth around the regulator then disconnect the fuel return hose.
4. Loosen the locknut, then remove the regulator. Discard the O-ring.

To install:

5. Fully loosen the locknut on the regulator.
6. Apply a light coat of gasoline to a new O-ring, then install it onto the regulator.
7. Thread the fuel pressure regulator into the fuel rail all the way by hand. Then turn the regulator counterclockwise until the fuel outlet port faces in the direction proper direction.
8. Tighten the locknut to 18 ft. lbs. (25 Nm).
9. Install the return pipe to the regulator.
10. Connect the vacuum line.
11. Start the engine and check for any fuel leakage.

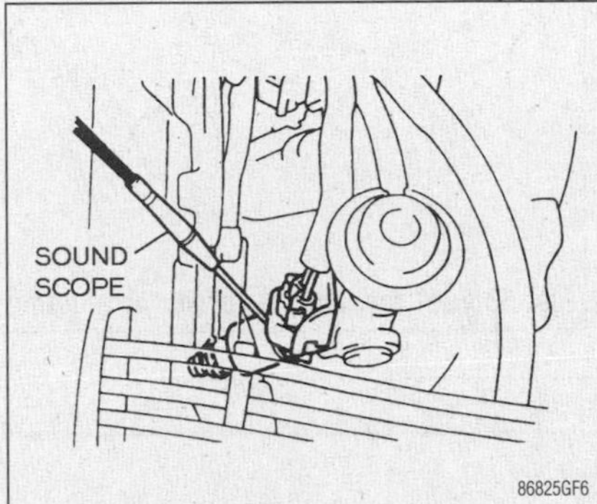

Fig. 47 A 'sound scope' is usually used to inspect injector operation. Listen for a regular clicking sound as the engine is running

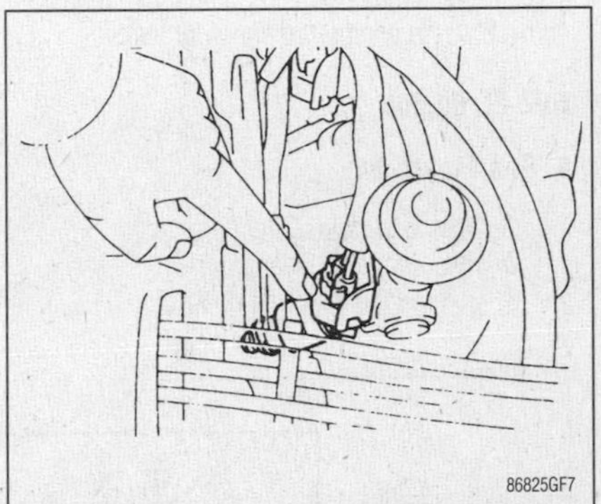

Fig. 48 If a 'sound scope' is not available, check injector operation by feeling for the regular vibrations indicating the injector solenoid is opening and closing

Fig. 49 An ohmmeter is used to check injector resistance

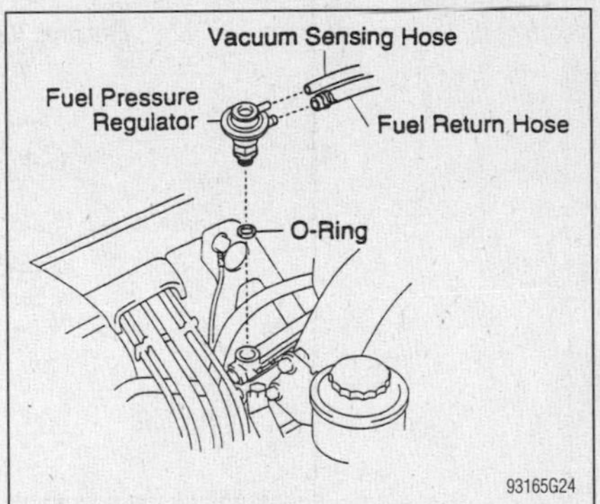

Fig. 50 The fuel pressure regulator threads into the fuel rail—1FZ-FE engine

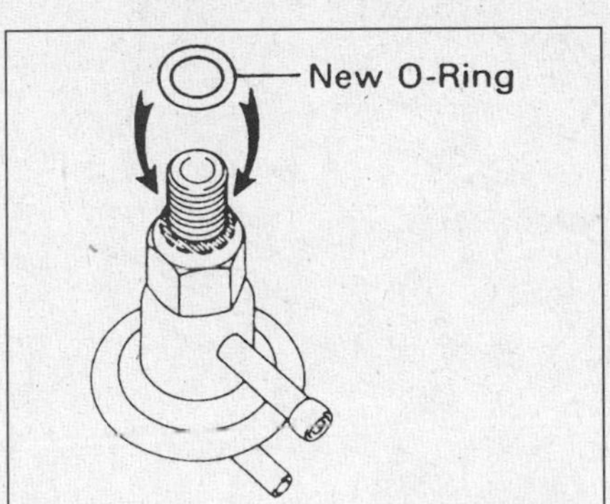

Fig. 51 Install a new O-ring lubricated with a light coat of gasoline—1FZ-FE engine

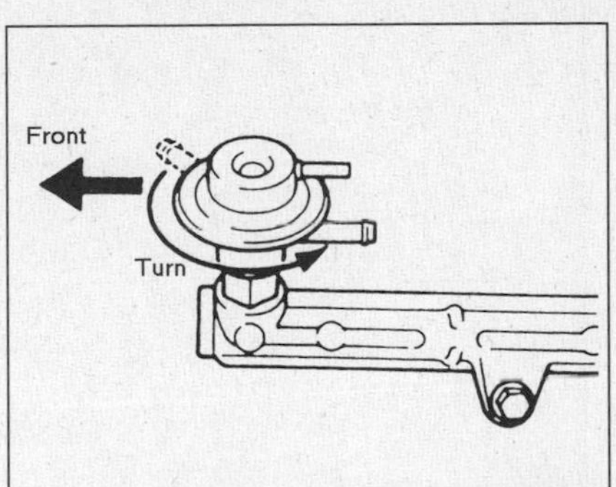

Fig. 52 The regulator must be properly aligned on the fuel rail—1FZ-FE engine

2RZ-FE and 3RZ-FE Engines

➧ See Figure 53

1. Relieve the fuel system pressure.
2. Disconnect the vacuum line from the fuel pressure regulator.
3. Loosen the hose clamp and then remove the fuel return line.
4. Loosen the two retaining bolts. Use clean shop cloths to catch spilled fuel as the bolts are loosened.
5. Remove the bolts and separate the fuel pressure regulator from the fuel rail.

To install:

6. Installation is the reverse of the removal process. Use a new O-ring seal. Apply a light coat of gasoline to a new O-ring, then install it onto the regulator.
7. Tighten the bolts to 78 inch lbs. (8.8 Nm).
8. Start the engine and check for leaks.

5VZ-FE Engine

➧ See Figure 54

1. Relieve the fuel system pressure.
2. Remove the air cleaner hose.
3. Remove the intake air connector.

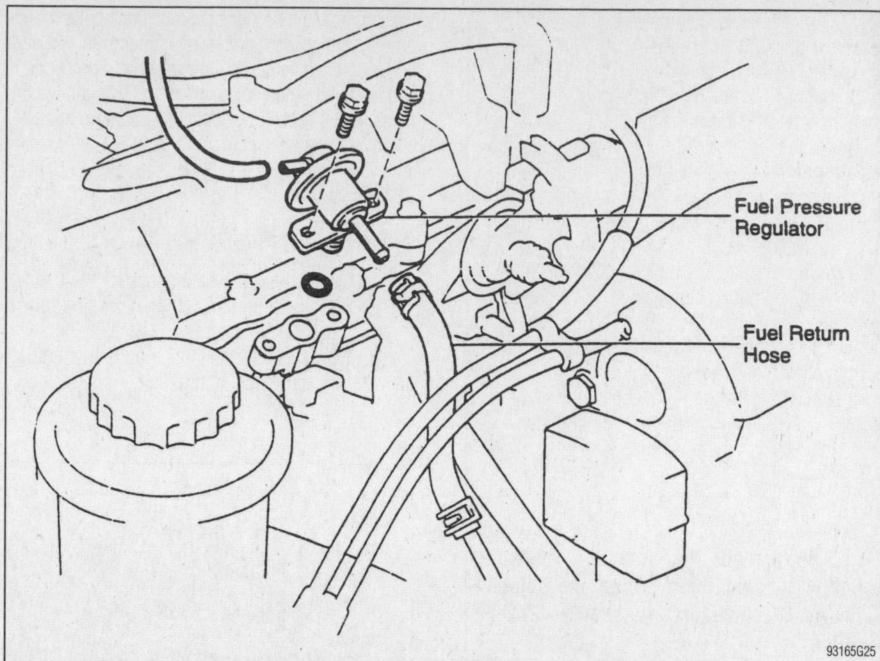

Fig. 53 Fuel pressure regulator arrangement—2RZ-FE and 3RZ-FE engines

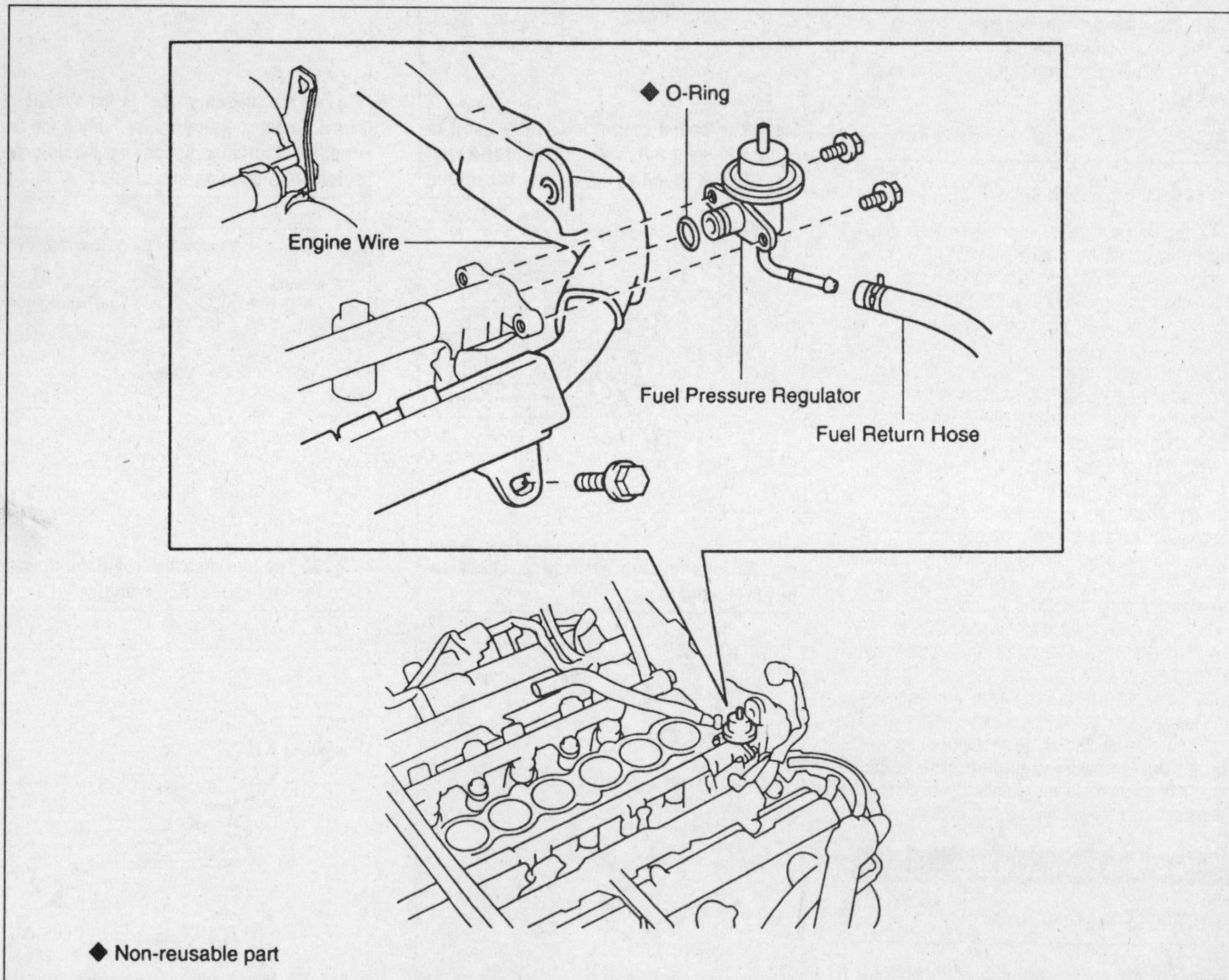

Fig. 54 Fuel pressure regulator arrangement—5VZ-FE engine

4. Disconnect the fuel return hose from the pressure regulator. Place a clean shop cloth under the regulator to catch any leakage.
5. Remove the bolt holding the engine wiring harness to the left-hand valve cover.
6. Disconnect the protector from the bracket on the right side valve cover, then lift up the engine wiring harness.
7. Remove the 2 bolts, then pull out the regulator. Remove and discard the O-ring from the unit.

To install:

8. Apply a light coat of gasoline to the new O-ring, then install it on the regulator.
9. Attach the regulator to the left side fuel rail (Toyota calls it a delivery pipe).
10. Check that the pressure regulator rotates smoothly. If it does not, the O-ring out-of-position may be the cause. Remove the regulator and install a new O-ring.
11. Attach the regulator, then tighten to 71 inch lbs. (8 Nm).
12. Install the engine wire with the bolt.
13. Attach the fuel return hose to the pressure regulator. Be sure to insert the hose up to the stopper and clip it.
14. Install the intake air connector.
15. Install the air cleaner hose.
16. Start the engine and check for leaks.

2UZ-FE Engine

➧ See Figure 55

1. Relieve the fuel system pressure.
2. Disconnect the vacuum line from the fuel pressure regulator.
3. Loosen the hose clamp and then remove the fuel return line.
4. Loosen the two retaining bolts. Use clean shop cloths to catch spilled fuel as the bolts are loosened.
5. Remove the bolts and separate the fuel pressure regulator from the fuel rail.

To install:

6. Installation is the reverse of the removal process. Use a new O-ring seal. Apply a light coat of gasoline to a new O-ring, then install it onto the regulator.
7. Tighten the bolts to 66 inch lbs. (7.5 Nm).
8. Start the engine and check for leaks.

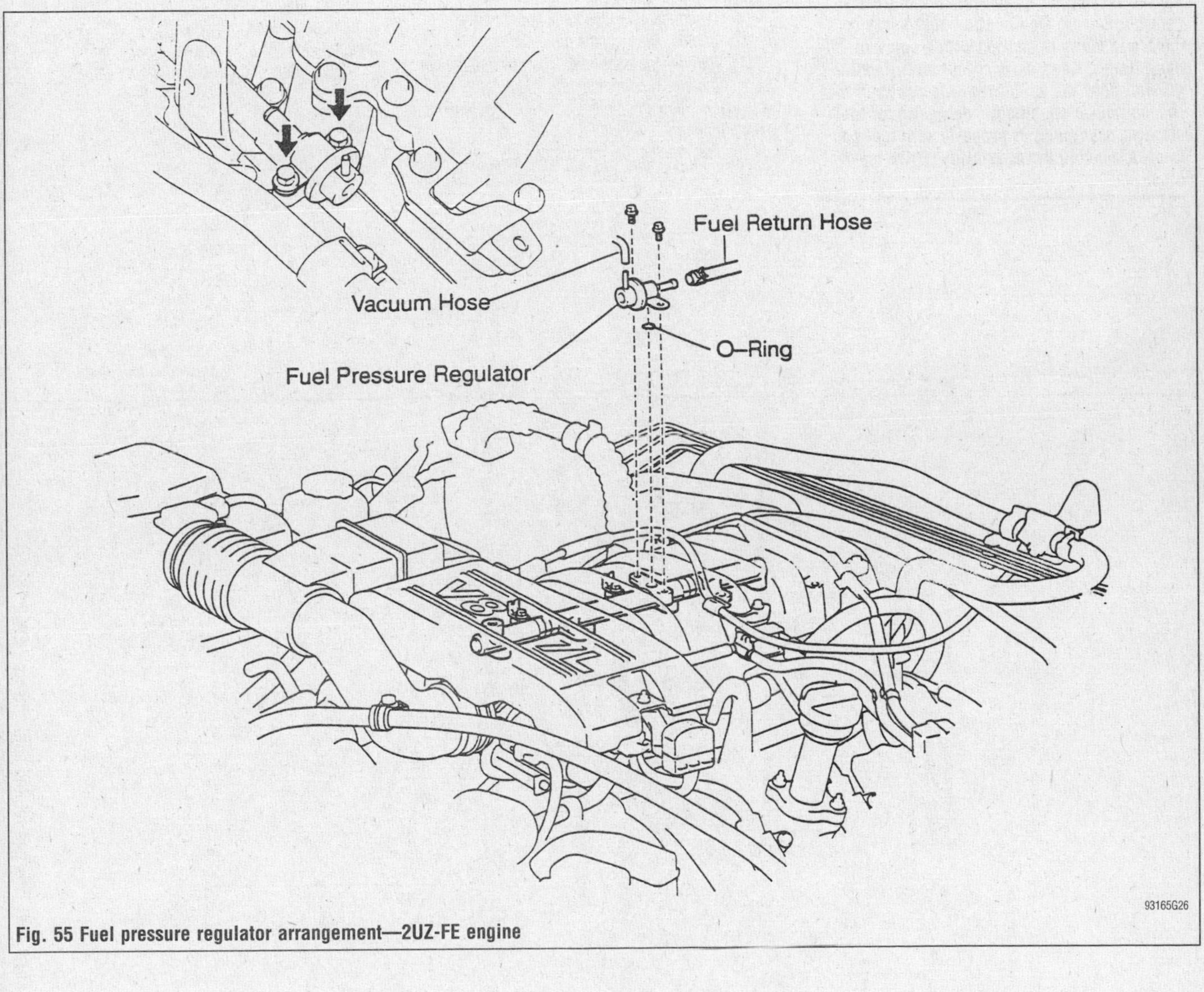

Fig. 55 Fuel pressure regulator arrangement—2UZ-FE engine

FUEL TANK

Tank Assembly

REMOVAL & INSTALLATION

▸ **See Figures 56, 57, 58, and 59**

The gas tanks on all Toyota trucks are mounted basically the same. Each one has a shield, straps, inlet pipe and similar connections. The procedure below is basic, and should apply to most all Toyota trucks.

⁂ CAUTION

Observe all applicable safety precautions when working around fuel. Whenever servicing the fuel system, always work in a well ventilated area. Do not allow fuel spray or vapors to come in contact with a spark or open flame. Keep a dry chemical fire extinguisher near the work area. Always keep fuel in a container specifically designed for fuel storage; also, always properly seal fuel containers to avoid the possibility of fire or explosion.

1. Disconnect the negative battery cable.
2. Raise the vehicle and support it with safety stands.
3. If equipped with a drain plug, remove the drain plug and drain any remaining fuel into a suitable container. If the tank has no drain plug, a siphon pump will be required to remove the fuel. Remember that it is possible to have several gallons in the tank; be prepared with sufficient containers. It is best to run the tank as low on fuel as possible before removing it, but keep in mind that Empty on the gauge may still leave 2 or 3 gallons in the tank.
4. Disconnect the plug from the fuel pump and sending unit assembly. Remove the gravel shield from the tank.
5. Disconnect the fuel lines. Plug all the lines to prevent fuel from leaking.
6. Disconnect the filler neck and vent line.
7. Remove the fuel tank protector.
8. Remove the bolts holding the tank to the vehicle and carefully lower the tank. It is recommended that a jack with a broad piece of lumber be placed to support the tank.
9. Remove the fuel pump assembly.

⁂ CAUTION

Even though the tank has been drained, it still contains highly explosive fuel vapor. Immediately place the tank outside; never store it in the house or garage. Unless the tank is to be immediately reinstalled, use a hose to fill the tank with water as full as possible. This will flush remaining fuel and vapor from the tank and also carry off any dirt which has accumulated.

To install:

10. Make certain the fuel tank is completely dry if it has been flushed. Install the pump assembly.
11. Install the fuel tank. Tighten the tank bolts.
12. Connect the lines and hoses. Make certain the hoses are not crimped or pinched. Make sure the clamps are correctly seated.
13. Connect the negative battery cable.

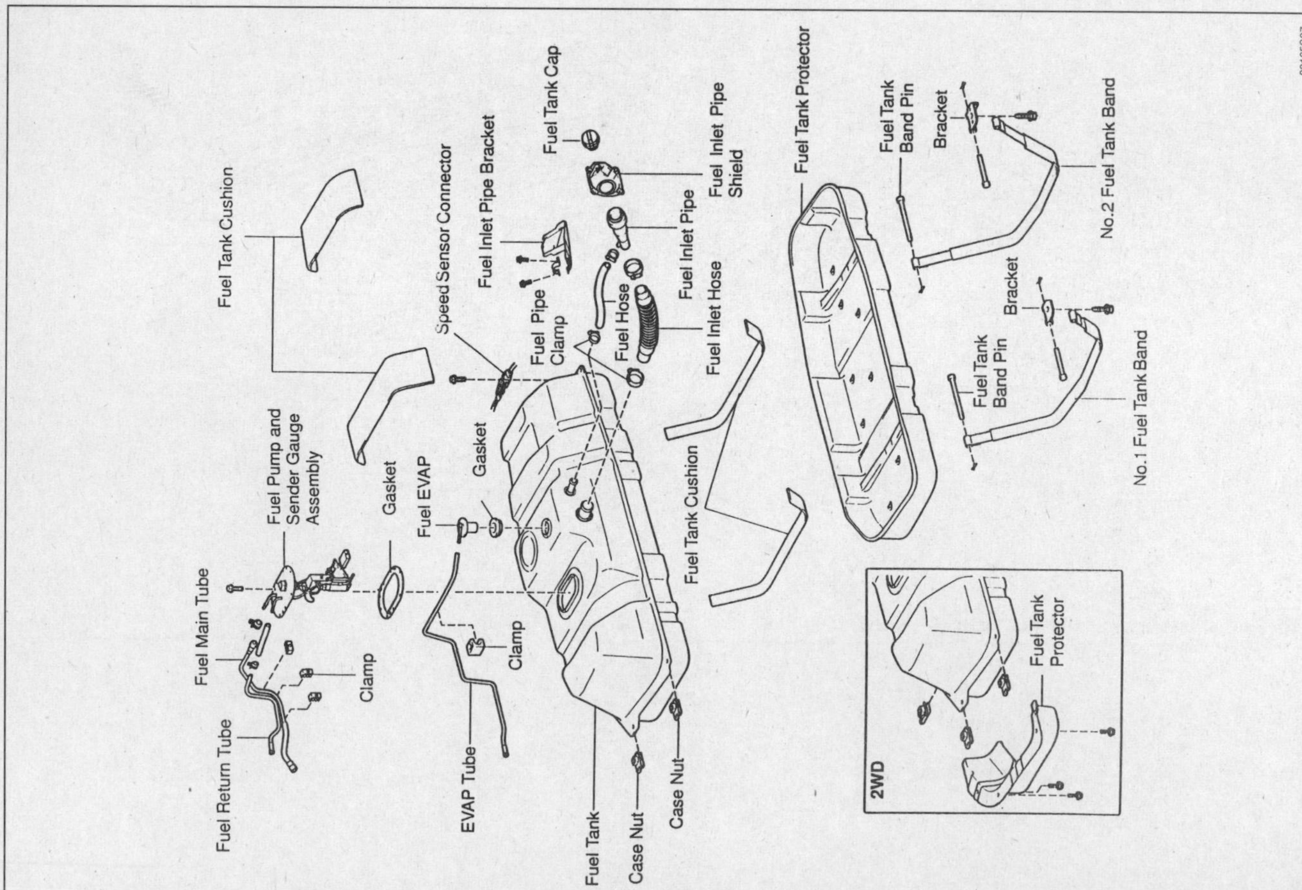

Fig. 56 Exploded view of the fuel tank and related components—2000 Tundra

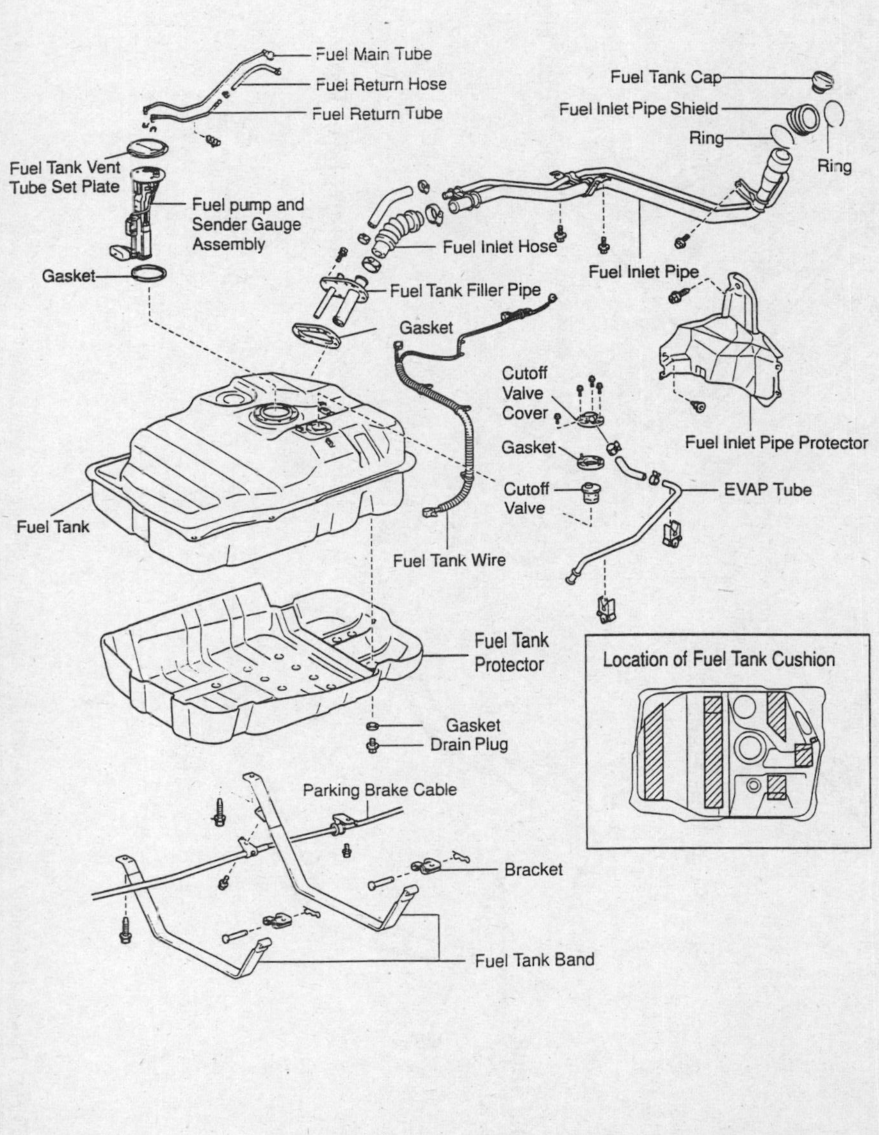

Fig. 57 Fuel tank and related components—2000 Land Cruiser shown, earlier models similar

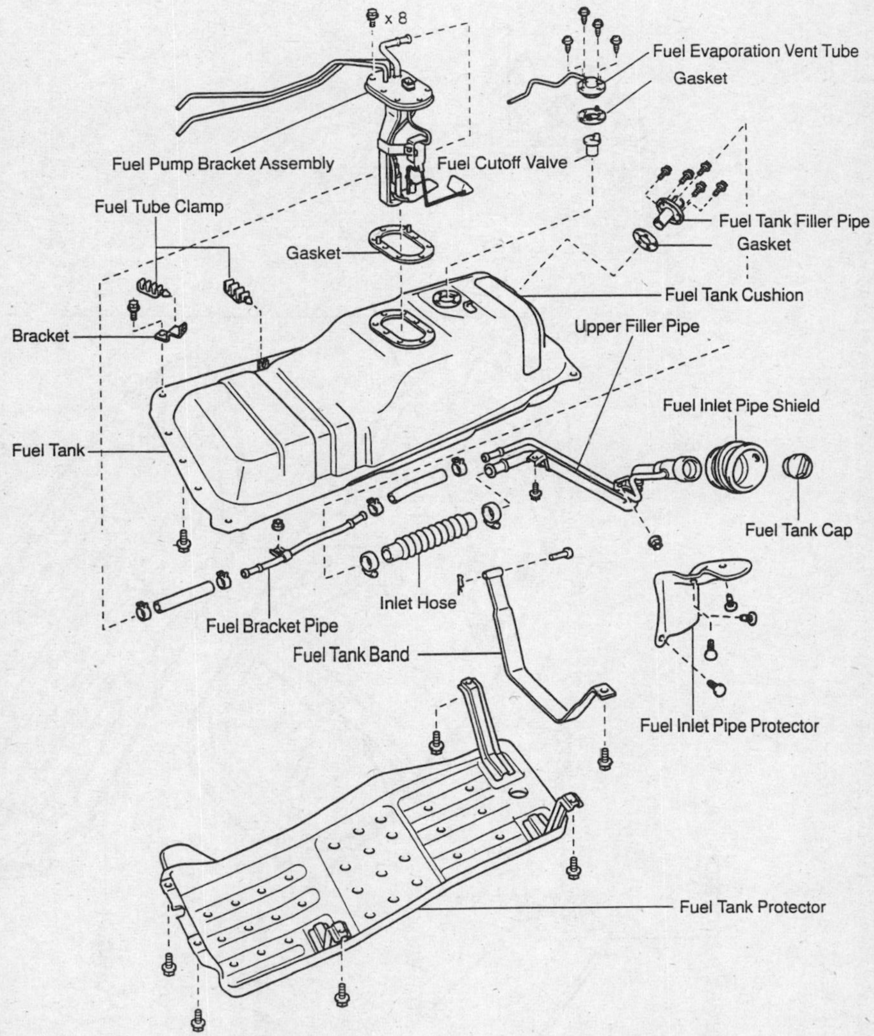

Fig. 58 View of the fuel tank and related components—2000 4Runner shown, earlier models similar

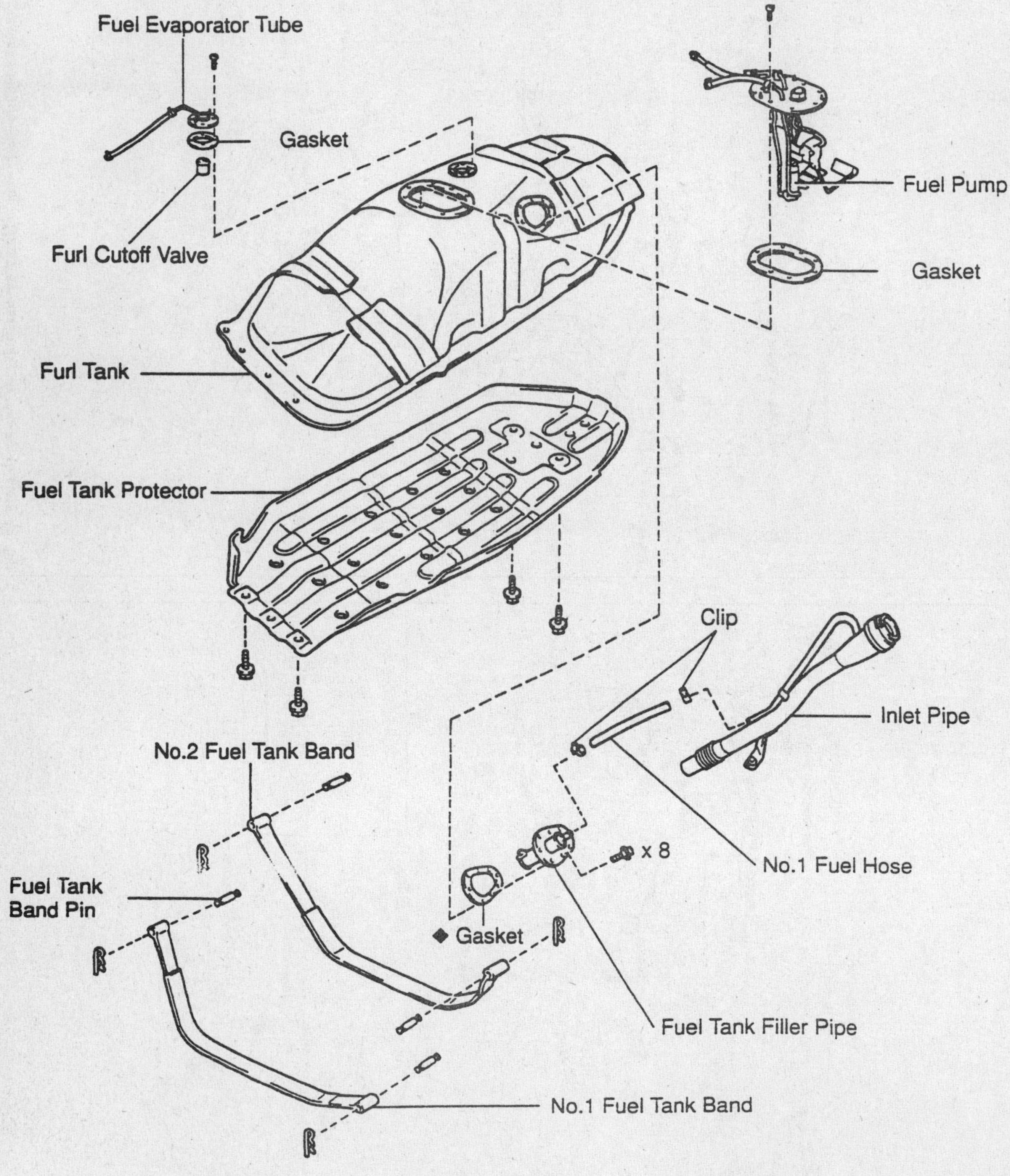

Fig. 59 Fuel tank and related components—2000 Tacoma shown, earlier models similar

6

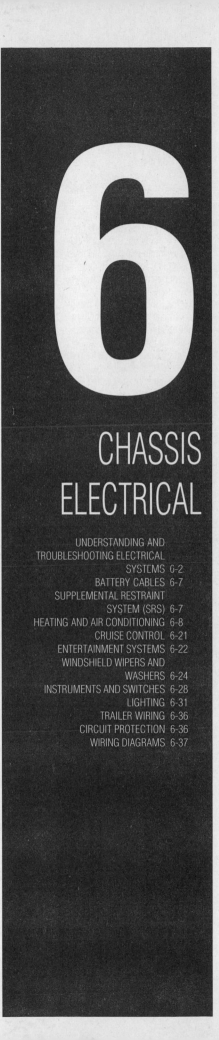

CHASSIS ELECTRICAL

UNDERSTANDING AND TROUBLESHOOTING ELECTRICAL SYSTEMS

Basic Electrical Theory

See Figure 1

For any 12 volt, negative ground, electrical system to operate, the electricity must travel in a complete circuit. This simply means that current (power) from the positive (+) terminal of the battery must eventually return to the negative (-) terminal of the battery. Along the way, this current will travel through wires, fuses, switches and components. If, for any reason, the flow of current through the circuit is interrupted, the component fed by that circuit will cease to function properly.

Perhaps the easiest way to visualize a circuit is to think of connecting a light bulb (with two wires attached to it) to the battery—one wire attached to the negative (-) terminal of the battery and the other wire to the positive (+) terminal. With the two wires touching the battery terminals, the circuit would be complete and the light bulb would illuminate. Electricity would follow a path from the battery to the bulb and back to the battery. It's easy to see that with longer wires on our light bulb, it could be mounted anywhere. Further, one wire could be fitted with a switch so that the light could be turned on and off.

The normal automotive circuit differs from this simple example in two ways. First, instead of having a return wire from the bulb to the battery, the current travels through the frame of the vehicle. Since the negative (-) battery cable is attached to the frame (made of electrically conductive metal), the frame of the vehicle can serve as a ground wire to complete the circuit. Secondly, most automotive circuits contain multiple components which receive power from a single circuit. This lessens the amount of wire needed to power components on the vehicle.

HOW DOES ELECTRICITY WORK: THE WATER ANALOGY

Electricity is the flow of electrons—the subatomic particles that constitute the outer shell of an atom.

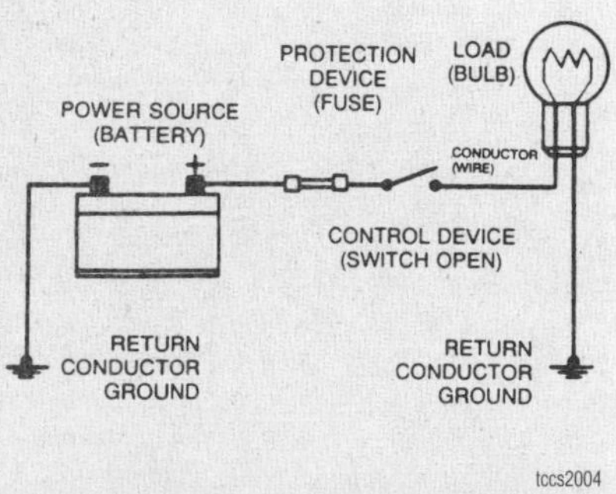

Fig. 1 This example illustrates a simple circuit. When the switch is closed, power from the positive (+) battery terminal flows through the fuse and the switch, and then to the light bulb. The light illuminates and the circuit is completed through the ground wire back to the negative (-) battery terminal. In reality, the two ground points shown in the illustration are attached to the metal frame of the vehicle, which completes the circuit back to the battery

Electrons spin in an orbit around the center core of an atom. The center core is comprised of protons (positive charge) and neutrons (neutral charge). Electrons have a negative charge and balance out the positive charge of the protons. When an outside force causes the number of electrons to unbalance the charge of the protons, the electrons will split off the atom and look for another atom to balance out. If this imbalance is kept up, electrons will continue to move and an electrical flow will exist.

Many people have been taught electrical theory using an analogy with water. In a comparison with water flowing through a pipe, the electrons would be the water and the wire is the pipe.

The flow of electricity can be measured much like the flow of water through a pipe. The unit of measurement used is amperes, frequently abbreviated as amps (a). You can compare amperage to the volume of water flowing through a pipe. When connected to a circuit, an ammeter will measure the actual amount of current flowing through the circuit. When relatively few electrons flow through a circuit, the amperage is low. When many electrons flow, the amperage is high.

Water pressure is measured in units such as pounds per square inch (psi); The electrical pressure is measured in units called volts (v). When a voltmeter is connected to a circuit, it is measuring the electrical pressure.

The actual flow of electricity depends not only on voltage and amperage, but also on the resistance of the circuit. The higher the resistance, the higher the force necessary to push the current through the circuit. The standard unit for measuring resistance is an ohm. Resistance in a circuit varies depending on the amount and type of components used in the circuit. The main factors which determine resistance are:

- Material—some materials have more resistance than others. Those with high resistance are said to be insulators. Rubber materials (or rubber-like plastics) are some of the most common insulators used in vehicles as they have a very high resistance to electricity. Very low resistance materials are said to be conductors. Copper wire is among the best conductors. Silver is actually a superior conductor to copper and is used in some relay contacts, but its high cost prohibits its use as common wiring. Most automotive wiring is made of copper.
- Size—the larger the wire size being used, the less resistance the wire will have. This is why components which use large amounts of electricity usually have large wires supplying current to them.
- Length—for a given thickness of wire, the longer the wire, the greater the resistance. The shorter the wire, the less the resistance. When determining the proper wire for a circuit, both size and length must be considered to design a circuit that can handle the current needs of the component.
- Temperature—with many materials, the higher the temperature, the greater the resistance (positive temperature coefficient). Some materials exhibit the opposite trait of lower resistance with higher temperatures (negative temperature coefficient). These principles are used in many of the sensors on the engine.

OHM'S LAW

There is a direct relationship between current, voltage and resistance. The relationship between current, voltage and resistance can be summed up by a statement known as Ohm's law.

Voltage (E) is equal to amperage (I) times resistance (R): $E=I \times R$

Other forms of the formula are $R=E/I$ and $I=E/R$

In each of these formulas, E is the voltage in volts, I is the current in amps and R is the resistance in ohms. The basic point to remember is that as the resistance of a circuit goes up, the amount of current that flows in the circuit will go down, if voltage remains the same.

The amount of work that the electricity can perform is expressed as power. The unit of power is the watt (w). The relationship between power, voltage and current is expressed as:

Power (w) is equal to amperage (I) times voltage (E): $W=I \times E$

This is only true for direct current (DC) circuits; The alternating current formula is a tad different, but since the electrical circuits in most vehicles are DC type, we need not get into AC circuit theory.

Electrical Components

POWER SOURCE

Power is supplied to the vehicle by two devices: The battery and the alternator. The battery supplies electrical power during starting or during periods when the current demand of the vehicle's electrical system exceeds the output capacity of the alternator. The alternator supplies electrical current when the engine is running. Just not does the alternator supply the current needs of the vehicle, but it recharges the battery.

The Battery

In most modern vehicles, the battery is a lead/acid electrochemical device consisting of six 2 volt subsections (cells) connected in series, so that the unit is capable of producing approximately 12 volts of electrical pressure. Each subsection consists of a series of positive and negative plates held a short distance apart in a solution of sulfuric acid and water.

The two types of plates are of dissimilar metals. This sets up a chemical reaction, and it is this reaction which produces current flow from the battery when its positive and negative terminals are connected to an electrical load. The power removed from the battery is replaced by the alternator, restoring the battery to its original chemical state.

The Alternator

On some vehicles there isn't an alternator, but a generator. The difference is that an alternator supplies alternating current which is then changed to direct current for use on the vehicle, while a generator produces direct current. Alternators tend to be more efficient and that is why they are used.

Alternators and generators are devices that consist of coils of wires wound together making big electromagnets. One group of coils spins within another set and the interaction of the magnetic fields causes a current to flow. This current is then drawn off the coils and fed into the vehicles electrical system.

GROUND

Two types of grounds are used in automotive electric circuits. Direct ground components are grounded to the frame through their mounting points. All other components use some sort of ground wire which is attached to the frame or chassis of the vehicle. The electrical current runs through the chassis of the vehicle and returns to the battery through the ground (-) cable; if you look, you'll see that the battery ground cable connects between the battery and the frame or chassis of the vehicle.

➡It should be noted that a good percentage of electrical problems can be traced to bad grounds.

PROTECTIVE DEVICES

➧ See Figure 2

It is possible for large surges of current to pass through the electrical system of your vehicle. If this surge of current were to reach the load in the circuit, the surge could burn it out or severely damage it. It can also overload the wiring, causing the harness to get hot and melt the insulation. To prevent this, fuses, circuit breakers and/or fusible links are connected into the supply wires of the electrical system. These items are nothing more than a built-in weak spot in the system. When an abnormal amount of current flows through the system, these protective devices work as follows to protect the circuit:

- Fuse—when an excessive electrical current passes through a fuse, the fuse "blows" (the conductor melts) and opens the circuit, preventing the passage of current.
- Circuit Breaker—a circuit breaker is basically a self-repairing fuse. It will open the circuit in the same fashion as a fuse, but when the surge subsides, the circuit breaker can be reset and does not need replacement.
- Fusible Link—a fusible link (fuse link or main link) is a short length of special, high temperature insulated wire that acts as a fuse. When an excessive electrical current passes through a fusible link, the thin gauge wire inside the link melts, creating an intentional open to protect the circuit. To repair the circuit, the link must be replaced. Some newer type fusible links are housed in plug-in modules, which are simply replaced like a fuse, while older type fusible links must be cut and spliced if they melt. Since this link is very early in the electrical path, it's the first place to look if nothing on the vehicle works, yet the battery seems to be charged and is properly connected.

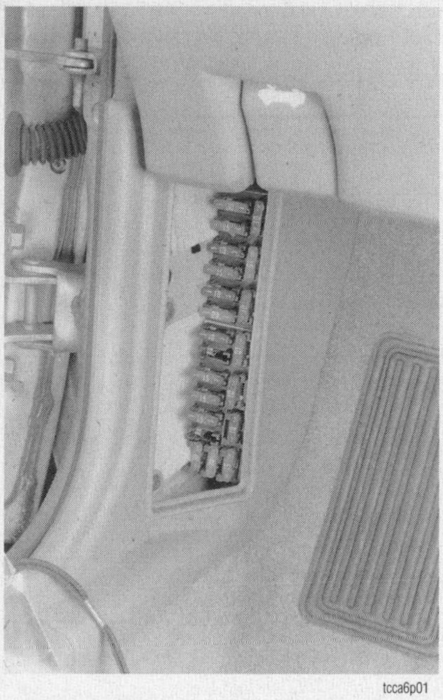

tcca6p01

Fig. 2 Most vehicles use one or more fuse panels. This one is located on the driver's side kick panel

CAUTION

Always replace fuses, circuit breakers and fusible links with identically rated components. Under no circumstances should a component of higher or lower amperage rating be substituted.

SWITCHES & RELAYS

➧ See Figures 3 and 4

Switches are used in electrical circuits to control the passage of current. The most common use is to open and close circuits between the battery and the various electric devices in the system. Switches are rated according to the amount of amperage they can handle. If a sufficient amperage rated switch is not used in a circuit, the switch could overload and cause damage.

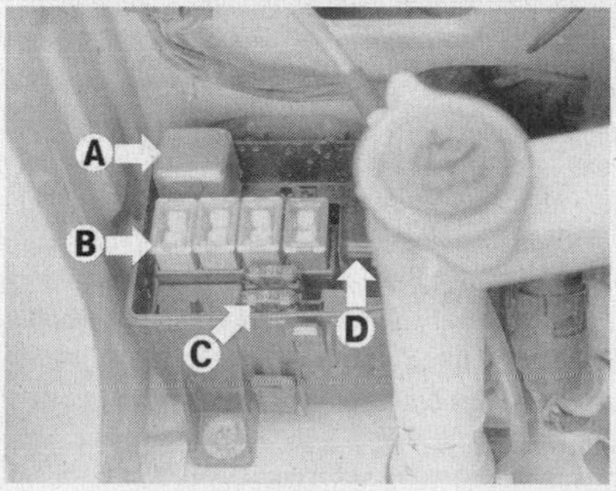

tcca6p02

Fig. 3 The underhood fuse and relay panel usually contains fuses, relays, flashers and fusible links

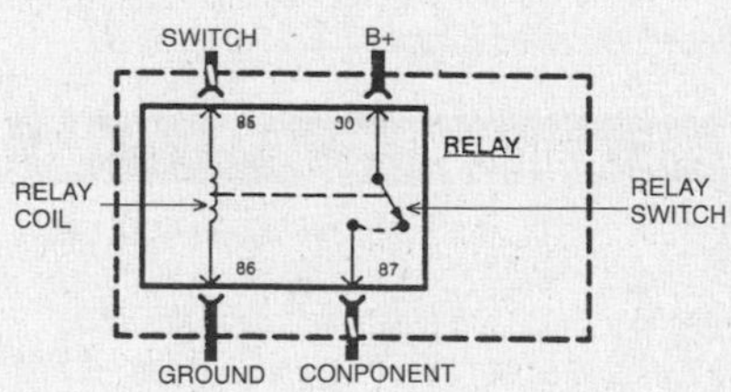

tcca6g02

Fig. 4 Relays are composed of a coil and a switch. These two components are linked together so that when one operates, the other operates at the same time. The large wires in the circuit are connected from the battery to one side of the relay switch (B+) and from the opposite side of the relay switch to the load (component). Smaller wires are connected from the relay coil to the control switch for the circuit and from the opposite side of the relay coil to ground

Some electrical components which require a large amount of current to operate use a special switch called a relay. Since these circuits carry a large amount of current, the thickness of the wire in the circuit is also greater. If this large wire were connected from the load to the control switch, the switch would have to carry the high amperage load and the fairing or dash would be twice as large to accommodate the increased size of the wiring harness. To prevent these problems, a relay is used.

Relays are composed of a coil and a set of contacts. When the coil has a current passed though it, a magnetic field is formed and this field causes the contacts to move together, completing the circuit. Most relays are normally open, preventing current from passing through the circuit, but they can take any electrical form depending on the job they are intended to do. Relays can be considered "remote control switches." They allow a smaller current to operate devices that require higher amperages. When a small current operates the coil, a larger current is allowed to pass by the contacts. Some common circuits which may use relays are the horn, headlights, starter, electric fuel pump and other high draw circuits.

LOAD

Every electrical circuit must include a "load" (something to use the electricity coming from the source). Without this load, the battery would attempt to deliver its entire power supply from one pole to another. This is called a "short circuit." All this electricity would take a short cut to ground and cause a great amount of damage to other components in the circuit by developing a tremendous amount of heat. This condition could develop sufficient heat to melt the insulation on all the surrounding wires and reduce a multiple wire cable to a lump of plastic and copper.

WIRING & HARNESSES

The average vehicle contains meters and meters of wiring, with hundreds of individual connections. To protect the many wires from damage and to keep them from becoming a confusing tangle, they are organized into bundles, enclosed in plastic or taped together and called wiring harnesses. Different harnesses serve different parts of the vehicle. Individual wires are color coded to help trace them through a harness where sections are hidden from view.

Automotive wiring or circuit conductors can be either single strand wire, multi-strand wire or printed circuitry. Single strand wire has a solid metal core and is usually used inside such components as alternators, motors, relays and other devices. Multi-strand wire has a core made of many small strands of wire twisted together into a single conductor. Most of the wiring in an automotive electrical system is made up of multi-strand wire, either as a single conductor or grouped together in a harness. All wiring is color coded on the insulator, either as a solid color or as a colored wire with an identification stripe. A printed circuit is a thin film of copper or other conductor that is printed on an insulator backing. Occasionally, a printed circuit is sandwiched between two sheets of plastic for more protection and flexibility. A complete printed circuit, consisting of conductors, insulating material and connectors for lamps or other components is called a printed circuit board. Printed circuitry is used in place of individual wires or harnesses in places where space is limited, such as behind instrument panels.

Since automotive electrical systems are very sensitive to changes in resistance, the selection of properly sized wires is critical when systems are repaired. A loose or corroded connection or a replacement wire that is too small for the circuit will add extra resistance and an additional voltage drop to the circuit.

The wire gauge number is an expression of the cross-section area of the conductor. Vehicles from countries that use the metric system will typically describe the wire size as its cross-sectional area in square millimeters. In this method, the larger the wire, the greater the number. Another common system for expressing wire size is the American Wire Gauge (AWG) system. As gauge number increases, area decreases and the wire becomes smaller. An 18 gauge wire is smaller than a 4 gauge wire. A wire with a higher gauge number will carry less current than a wire with a lower gauge number. Gauge wire size refers to the size of the strands of the conductor, not the size of the complete wire with insulator. It is possible, therefore, to have two wires of the same gauge with different diameters because one may have thicker insulation than the other.

It is essential to understand how a circuit works before trying to figure out why it doesn't. An electrical schematic shows the electrical current paths when a circuit is operating properly. Schematics break the entire electrical system down into individual circuits. In a schematic, usually no attempt is made to represent wiring and components as they physically appear on the vehicle; switches and other components are shown as simply as possible. Face views of harness connectors show the cavity or terminal locations in all multi-pin connectors to help locate test points.

CONNECTORS

▸ See Figures 5 and 6

Three types of connectors are commonly used in automotive applications—weatherproof, molded and hard shell.

- Weatherproof—these connectors are most commonly used where the connector is exposed to the elements. Terminals are protected against moisture and dirt by sealing rings which provide a weathertight seal. All repairs require the use of a special terminal and the tool required to service it. Unlike standard blade type terminals, these weatherproof terminals cannot be straightened once they are bent. Make certain that the connectors are properly seated and all of the sealing rings are in place when connecting leads.
- Molded—these connectors require complete replacement of the connector if found to be defective. This means splicing a new connector assembly into the harness. All splices should be soldered to insure proper contact. Use care when probing the connections or replacing terminals in them, as it is possible to create a short circuit between opposite terminals. If this happens to the wrong terminal pair, it is possible to damage certain components. Always use jumper wires between connectors for circuit checking and NEVER probe through weatherproof seals.

tcca6p03

Fig. 5 Hard shell (left) and weatherproof (right) connectors have replaceable terminals

tcca6p04

Fig. 6 Weatherproof connectors are most commonly used in the engine compartment or where the connector is exposed to the elements

- Hard Shell—unlike molded connectors, the terminal contacts in hard-shell connectors can be replaced. Replacement usually involves the use of a special terminal removal tool that depresses the locking tangs (barbs) on the connector terminal and allows the connector to be removed from the rear of the shell. The connector shell should be replaced if it shows any evidence of burning, melting, cracks, or breaks. Replace individual terminals that are burnt, corroded, distorted or loose.

Test Equipment

Pinpointing the exact cause of trouble in an electrical circuit is most times accomplished by the use of special test equipment. The following describes different types of commonly used test equipment and briefly explains how to use them in diagnosis. In addition to the information covered below, the tool manufacturer's instructions booklet (provided with the tester) should be read and clearly understood before attempting any test procedures.

JUMPER WIRES

⁂ CAUTION

Never use jumper wires made from a thinner gauge wire than the circuit being tested. If the jumper wire is of too small a gauge, it may overheat and possibly melt. Never use jumpers to bypass high resistance loads in a circuit. Bypassing resistances, in effect, creates a short circuit. This may, in turn, cause damage and fire. Jumper wires should only be used to bypass lengths of wire or to simulate switches.

Jumper wires are simple, yet extremely valuable, pieces of test equipment. They are basically test wires which are used to bypass sections of a circuit. Although jumper wires can be purchased, they are usually fabricated from lengths of standard automotive wire and whatever type of connector (alligator clip, spade connector or pin connector) that is required for the particular application being tested. In cramped, hard-to-reach areas, it is advisable to have insulated boots over the jumper wire terminals in order to prevent accidental grounding. It is also advisable to include a standard automotive fuse in any jumper wire. This is commonly referred to as a "fused jumper". By inserting an in-line fuse holder between a set of test leads, a fused jumper wire can be used for bypassing open circuits. Use a 5 amp fuse to provide protection against voltage spikes.

Jumper wires are used primarily to locate open electrical circuits, on either the ground (-) side of the circuit or on the power (+) side. If an electrical component fails to operate, connect the jumper wire between the component and a good ground. If the component operates only with the jumper installed, the ground circuit is open. If the ground circuit is good, but the component does not operate, the circuit between the power feed and component may be open. By moving the jumper wire successively back from the component toward the power source, you can isolate the area of the circuit where the open is located. When the component stops functioning, or the power is cut off, the open is in the segment of wire between the jumper and the point previously tested.

You can sometimes connect the jumper wire directly from the battery to the "hot" terminal of the component, but first make sure the component uses 12 volts in operation. Some electrical components, such as fuel injectors or sensors, are designed to operate on about 4 to 5 volts, and running 12 volts directly to these components will cause damage.

TEST LIGHTS

▸ See Figure 7

The test light is used to check circuits and components while electrical current is flowing through them. It is used for voltage and ground tests. To use a 12 volt test light, connect the ground clip to a good ground and probe wherever necessary with the pick.

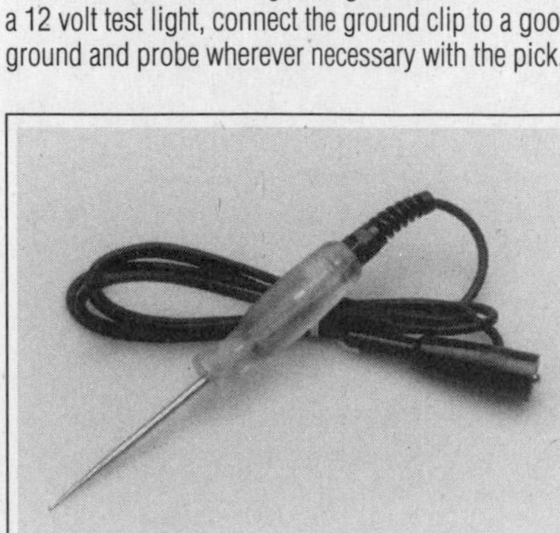

tccs2006

Fig. 7 A 12 volt test light is used to detect the presence of voltage in a circuit

The test light will illuminate when voltage is detected. This does not necessarily mean that 12 volts (or any particular amount of voltage) is present; it only means that some voltage is present. It is advisable before using the test light to touch its ground clip and probe across the battery posts or terminals to make sure the light is operating properly.

WARNING

Do not use a test light to probe electronic ignition, spark plug or coil wires. Never use a pick-type test light to probe wiring on computer controlled systems unless specifically instructed to do so. Any wire insulation that is pierced by the test light probe should be taped and sealed with silicone after testing.

Like the jumper wire, the 12 volt test light is used to isolate opens in circuits. But, whereas the jumper wire is used to bypass the open to operate the load, the 12 volt test light is used to locate the presence of voltage in a circuit. If the test light illuminates, there is power up to that point in the circuit; if the test light does not illuminate, there is an open circuit (no power). Move the test light in successive steps back toward the power source until the light in the handle illuminates. The open is between the probe and a point which was previously probed.

The self-powered test light is similar in design to the 12 volt test light, but contains a 1.5 volt penlight battery in the handle. It is most often used in place of a multimeter to check for open or short circuits when power is isolated from the circuit (continuity test).

The battery in a self-powered test light does not provide much current. A weak battery may not provide enough power to illuminate the test light even when a complete circuit is made (especially if there is high resistance in the circuit). Always make sure that the test battery is strong. To check the battery, briefly touch the ground clip to the probe; if the light glows brightly, the battery is strong enough for testing.

➡A self-powered test light should not be used on any computer controlled system or component. The small amount of electricity transmitted by the test light is enough to damage many electronic automotive components.

MULTIMETERS

Multimeters are an extremely useful tool for troubleshooting electrical problems. They can be purchased in either analog or digital form and have a price range to suit any budget. A multimeter is a voltmeter, ammeter and ohmmeter (along with other features) combined into one instrument. It is often used when testing solid state circuits because of its high input impedance (usually 10 megaohms or more). A brief description of the multimeter main test functions follows:

- Voltmeter—the voltmeter is used to measure voltage at any point in a circuit, or to measure the voltage drop across any part of a circuit. Voltmeters usually have various scales and a selector switch to allow the reading of different voltage ranges. The voltmeter has a positive and a negative lead. To avoid damage to the meter, always connect the negative lead to the negative (-) side of the circuit (to ground or nearest the ground side of the circuit) and connect the positive lead to the positive (+) side of the circuit (to the power source or the nearest power source). Note that the negative voltmeter lead will always be black and that the positive voltmeter will always be some color other than black (usually red).
- Ohmmeter—the ohmmeter is designed to read resistance (measured in ohms) in a circuit or component. Most ohmmeters will have a selector switch which permits the measurement of different ranges of resistance (usually the selector switch allows the multiplication of the meter reading by 10, 100, 1,000 and 10,000). Some ohmmeters are "auto-ranging" which means the meter itself will determine which scale to use. Since the meters are powered by an internal battery, the ohmmeter can be used like a self-powered test light. When the ohmmeter is connected, current from the ohmmeter flows through the circuit or component being tested. Since the ohmmeter's internal resistance and voltage are known values, the amount of current flow through the meter depends on the resistance of the circuit or component being tested. The ohmmeter can also be used to perform a continuity test for suspected open circuits. In using the meter for making continuity checks, do not be concerned with the actual resistance readings. Zero resistance, or any ohm reading, indicates continuity in the circuit. Infinite resistance indicates an opening in the circuit. A high resistance reading where there should be none indicates a problem in the circuit. Checks for short circuits are made in the same manner as checks for open circuits, except that the circuit must be isolated from both power and normal ground. Infinite resistance indicates no continuity, while zero resistance indicates a dead short.

WARNING

Never use an ohmmeter to check the resistance of a component or wire while there is voltage applied to the circuit.

- Ammeter—an ammeter measures the amount of current flowing through a circuit in units called amperes or amps. At normal operating voltage, most circuits have a characteristic amount of amperes, called "current draw" which can be measured using an ammeter. By referring to a specified current draw rating, then measuring the amperes and comparing the two values, one can determine what is happening within the circuit to aid in diagnosis. An open circuit, for example, will not allow any current to flow, so the ammeter reading will be zero. A damaged component or circuit will have an increased current draw, so the reading will be high. The ammeter is always connected in series with the circuit being tested. All of the current that normally flows through the circuit must also flow through the ammeter; if there is any other path for the current to follow, the ammeter reading will not be accurate. The ammeter itself has very little resistance to current flow and, therefore, will not affect the circuit, but it will measure current draw only when the circuit is closed and electricity is flowing. Excessive current draw can blow fuses and drain the battery, while a reduced current draw can cause motors to run slowly, lights to dim and other components to not operate properly.

Troubleshooting Electrical Systems

When diagnosing a specific problem, organized troubleshooting is a must. The complexity of a modern automotive vehicle demands that you approach any problem in a logical, organized manner. There are certain troubleshooting techniques, however, which are standard:

- Establish when the problem occurs. Does the problem appear only under certain conditions? Were there any noises, odors or other unusual symptoms? Isolate the problem area. To do this, make some simple tests and observations, then eliminate the systems that are working properly. Check for obvious problems, such as broken wires and loose or dirty connections. Always check the obvious before assuming something complicated is the cause.
- Test for problems systematically to determine the cause once the problem area is isolated. Are all the components functioning properly? Is there power going to electrical switches and motors. Performing careful, systematic checks will often turn up most causes on the first inspection, without wasting time checking components that have little or no relationship to the problem.
- Test all repairs after the work is done to make sure that the problem is fixed. Some causes can be traced to more than one component, so a careful verification of repair work is important in order to pick up additional malfunctions that may cause a problem to reappear or a different problem to arise. A blown fuse, for example, is a simple problem that may require more than another fuse to repair. If you don't look for a problem that caused a fuse to blow, a shorted wire (for example) may go undetected.

Experience has shown that most problems tend to be the result of a fairly simple and obvious cause, such as loose or corroded connectors, bad grounds or damaged wire insulation which causes a short. This makes careful visual inspection of components during testing essential to quick and accurate troubleshooting.

Testing

OPEN CIRCUITS

➧ **See Figure 8**

This test already assumes the existence of an open in the circuit and it is used to help locate the open portion.

1. Isolate the circuit from power and ground.
2. Connect the self-powered test light or ohmmeter ground clip to the ground side of the circuit and probe sections of the circuit sequentially.
3. If the light is out or there is infinite resistance, the open is between the probe and the circuit ground.

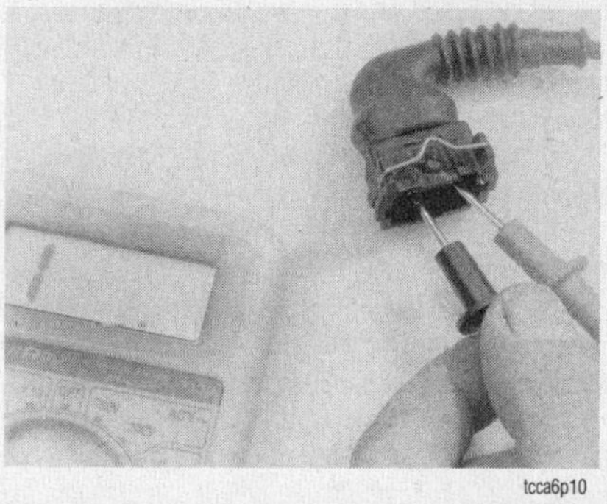

tcca6p10

Fig. 8 The infinite reading on this multimeter indicates that the circuit is open

4. If the light is on or the meter shows continuity, the open is between the probe and the end of the circuit toward the power source.

SHORT CIRCUITS

➡**Never use a self-powered test light to perform checks for opens or shorts when power is applied to the circuit under test. The test light can be damaged by outside power.**

1. Isolate the circuit from power and ground.
2. Connect the self-powered test light or ohmmeter ground clip to a good ground and probe any easy-to-reach point in the circuit.
3. If the light comes on or there is continuity, there is a short somewhere in the circuit.
4. To isolate the short, probe a test point at either end of the isolated circuit (the light should be on or the meter should indicate continuity).
5. Leave the test light probe engaged and sequentially open connectors or switches, remove parts, etc. until the light goes out or continuity is broken.
6. When the light goes out, the short is between the last two circuit components which were opened.

VOLTAGE

This test determines voltage available from the battery and should be the first step in any electrical troubleshooting procedure after visual inspection. Many electrical problems, especially on computer controlled systems, can be caused by a low state of charge in the battery. Excessive corrosion at the battery cable terminals can cause poor contact that will prevent proper charging and full battery current flow.

1. Set the voltmeter selector switch to the 20V position.
2. Connect the multimeter negative lead to the battery's negative (-) post or terminal and the positive lead to the battery's positive (+) post or terminal.
3. Turn the ignition switch **ON** to provide a load.
4. A well charged battery should register over 12 volts. If the meter reads below 11.5 volts, the battery power may be insufficient to operate the electrical system properly.

VOLTAGE DROP

➧ **See Figure 9**

When current flows through a load, the voltage beyond the load drops. This voltage drop is due to the resistance created by the load and also by small resistances created by corrosion at the connectors and damaged insulation on the wires. The maximum allowable voltage drop under load is critical, especially if there is more than one load in the circuit, since all voltage drops are cumulative.

1. Set the voltmeter selector switch to the 20 volt position.
2. Connect the multimeter negative lead to a good ground.
3. Operate the circuit and check the voltage prior to the first component (load).

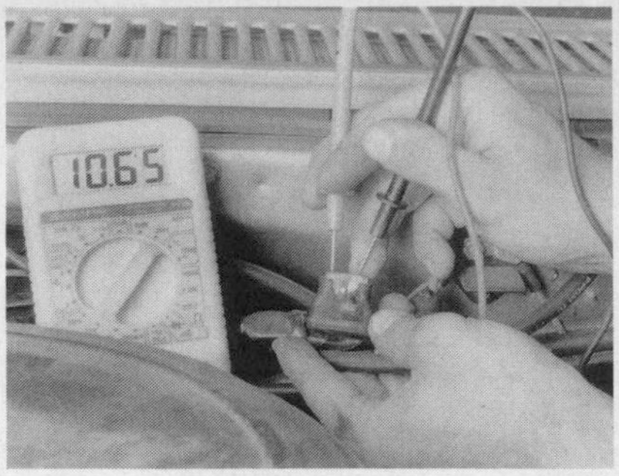

tcca6p07

Fig. 9 This voltage drop test revealed high resistance (low voltage) in the circuit

4. There should be little or no voltage drop in the circuit prior to the first component. If a voltage drop exists, the wire or connectors in the circuit are suspect.
5. While operating the first component in the circuit, probe the ground side of the component with the positive meter lead and observe the voltage readings. A small voltage drop should be noticed. This voltage drop is caused by the resistance of the component.
6. Repeat the test for each component (load) down the circuit.
7. If a large voltage drop is noticed, the preceding component, wire or connector is suspect.

RESISTANCE

➧ **See Figures 10 and 11**

⁂ WARNING

Never use an ohmmeter with power applied to the circuit. The ohmmeter is designed to operate on its own power supply. The normal 12 volt electrical system voltage could damage the meter!

1. Isolate the circuit from the vehicle's power source.
2. Ensure that the ignition key is **OFF** when disconnecting any components or the battery.
3. Where necessary, also isolate at least one side of the circuit to be checked, in order to avoid reading parallel resistances. Parallel circuit resistances will always give a lower reading than the actual resistance of either of the branches.
4. Connect the meter leads to both sides of the circuit (wire or component) and read the actual measured ohms on the meter scale. Make sure the selector switch is set to the proper ohm scale for the circuit being tested, to avoid misreading the ohmmeter test value.

Wire and Connector Repair

Almost anyone can replace damaged wires, as long as the proper tools and parts are available. Wire and terminals are available to fit almost any need. Even the specialized weatherproof, molded and hard shell connectors are now available from aftermarket suppliers.

Be sure the ends of all the wires are fitted with the proper terminal hardware and connectors. Wrapping a wire around a stud is never a permanent solution and will only cause trouble later. Replace wires one at a time to avoid confusion. Always route wires exactly the same as the factory.

➡**If connector repair is necessary, only attempt it if you have the proper tools. Weatherproof and hard shell connectors require special tools to release the pins inside the connector. Attempting to repair these connectors with conventional hand tools will damage them.**

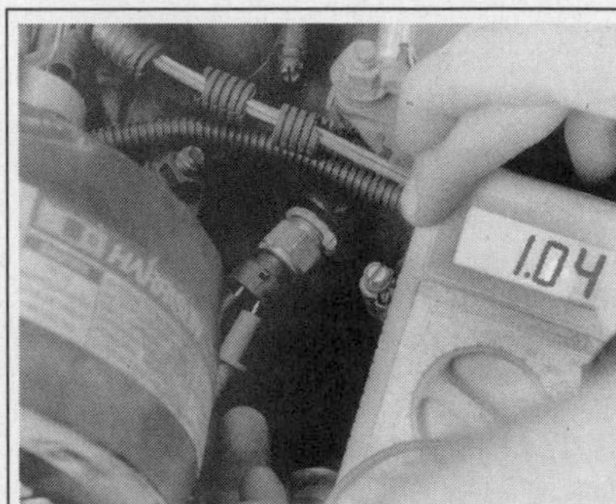

tcca6p08

Fig. 10 Checking the resistance of a coolant temperature sensor with an ohmmeter. Reading is 1.04 kilohms

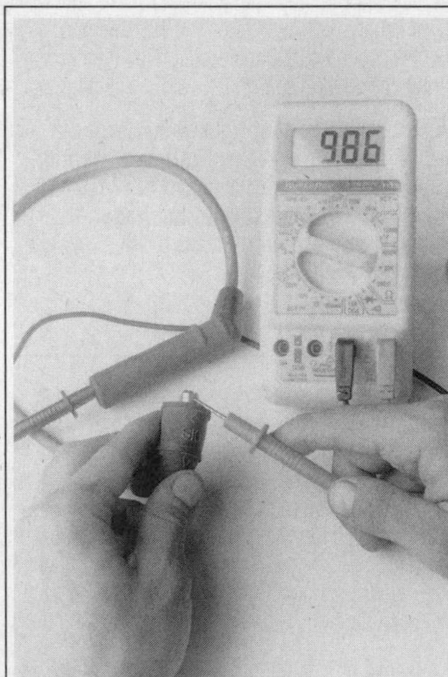

tcca6p09

Fig. 11 Spark plug wires can be checked for excessive resistance using an ohmmeter

BATTERY CABLES

Disconnecting the Cables

When working on any electrical component on the vehicle, it is always a good idea to disconnect the negative (-) battery cable. This will prevent potential damage to many sensitive electrical components such as the Engine Control Module (ECM), radio, alternator, etc.

➡Any time you disengage the battery cables, it is recommended that you disconnect the negative (-) battery cable first. This will prevent your accidentally grounding the positive (+) terminal to the body of the vehicle when disconnecting it, thereby preventing damage to the above mentioned components.

Before you disconnect the cable(s), first turn the ignition to the **OFF** position. This will prevent a draw on the battery which could cause arcing (electricity trying to ground itself to the body of a vehicle, just like a spark plug jumping the gap) and, of course, damaging some components such as the alternator diodes.

When the battery cable(s) are reconnected (negative cable last), be sure to check that your lights, windshield wipers and other electrically operated safety components are all working correctly. If your vehicle contains an Electronically Tuned Radio (ETR), don't forget to also reset your radio stations. Ditto for the clock.

SUPPLEMENTAL RESTRAINT SYSTEM (SRS)

SYSTEM OPERATION

⁂ CAUTION

Many Toyota trucks are equipped with a Supplemental Restraint System (SRS), which is comprised of a driver's and passenger's (on some models) air bag. Failure to carry out the service operations in the correct sequence could cause the SRS to unexpectedly deploy during servicing the SRS may fail to operate when needed. Before servicing, be sure to read the following items carefully.

When a vehicle is involved in a frontal collision in the hatched area and the shock is larger than a predetermined level, the SRS is activated automatically. A safing sensor is designed to tip at a smaller deceleration rate than the air bag sensor. The ignition is caused when a current flows to the squib, which occurs when a safing sensor and the air bag sensor trip simultaneously. When a deceleration force acts on the sensors, two squibs in the driver's air bag and passenger's air bag (if applicable) ignite and generate gas. The gas that discharges into the driver's and passenger's air bags rapidly increases the pressure inside the bags, breaking open the steering wheel pad and (if applicable) instrument panel.

Bag inflation then ends, and the bags deflate as the gas is discharged through the holes at the bag's rear or side.

SYSTEM COMPONENTS

Steering Wheel Air Bag

➧ See Figure 12

The inflator and bag of the SRS are stored in the steering wheel pad and cannot be disassembled. The inflator contains a igniter charge, squib, and gas generator. This inflates the bag when instructed by the center air bag sensor.

Front Passenger Air Bag

➧ See Figure 13

The inflator and bag of the SRS are stored in the instrument panel and cannot be disassembled. The inflator contains a igniter charge, squib, and gas generator. This inflates the bag when instructed by the center air bag sensor.

Spiral Cable

➧ See Figure 14

The spiral cable is located in the combination switch. This cable is used as an electrical joint from the vehicle body side to the steering wheel.

SRS Warning Light

➧ See Figure 15

The SRS warning light is located on the instrument cluster. It turns on to alert the driver of trouble in the system when a malfunction is detected in the air bag sensor assembly. In normal operating conditions when the ignition switch is turned to the **ON** or **ACC** position, the light turns on for about 6 seconds and then turns off.

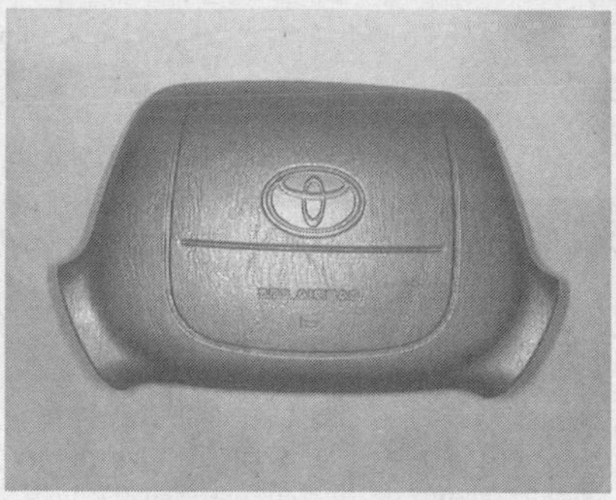

93166p48

Fig. 12 View of the driver's side air bag module removed from the center of the steering wheel

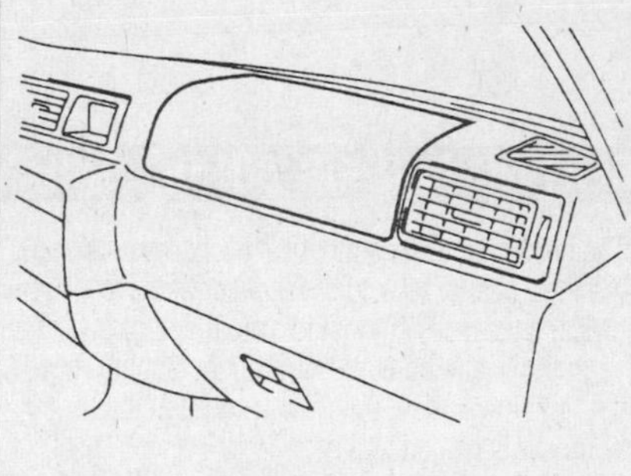

86826g04

Fig. 13 The passenger's air bag is integrated into the instrument panel

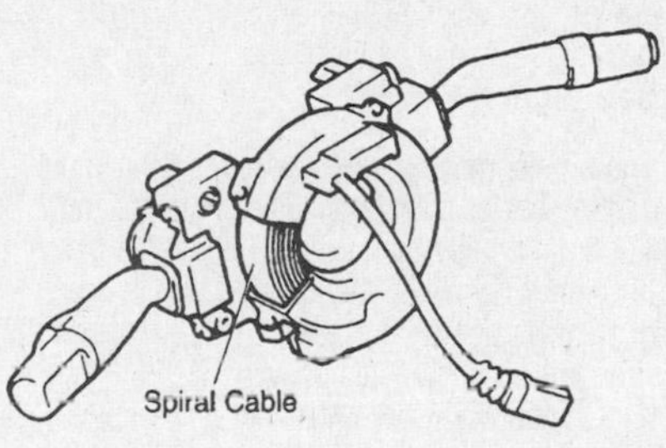

86826g03

Fig. 14 The spiral cable is wrapped in the combination switch

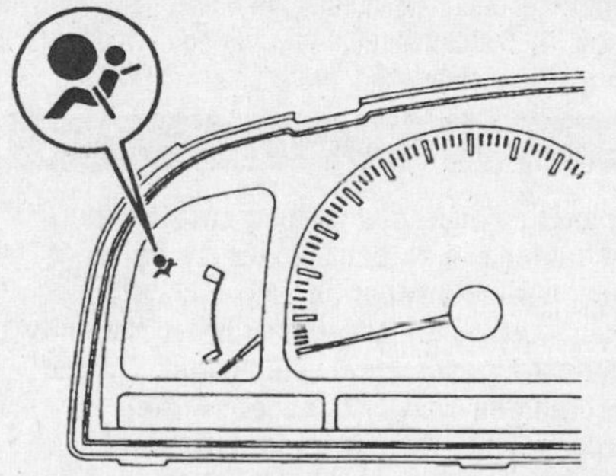

86826g07

Fig. 15 The SRS warning lamp should light for about six seconds with the key ON

Air Bag Sensor Assembly

➧ See Figure 16

The air bag sensor assembly is mounted on the floor inside the console box on Land Cruisers, on the air bag sensor cover on Tacoma and inside each fender on the T100. The air bag sensor assembly consists of an air bag sensor, safing sensor, diagnosis circuit and ignition control. It receives signals from the air bag sensors and judges whether the SRS must be activated or not.

SRS Connectors

All connectors in the SRS are colored yellow to distinguish them from the other connectors. These connectors have special functions are specifically designed for the SRS. These connectors use durable gold-plated terminals.

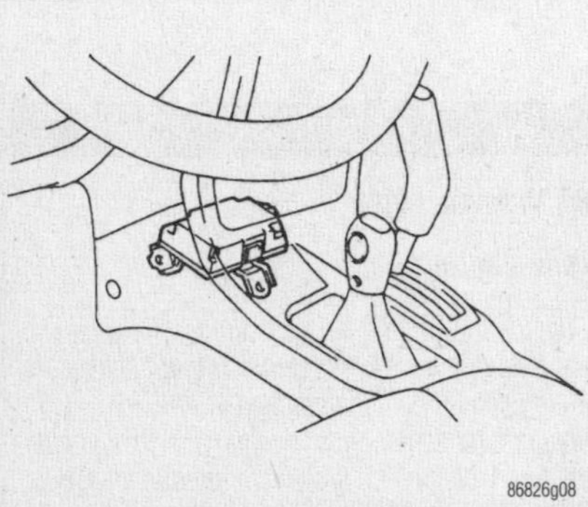

Fig. 16 On Land Cruisers, the air bag sensor is mounted on the floor in the center console

SYSTEM PRECAUTIONS

1. Work must be started after 90 seconds from the time the ignition switch is turned to the **LOCK** position and the negative battery cable has been disconnected. The SRS is equipped with a back-up power source so that if work is started within 90 seconds of disconnecting the negative battery cable, the SRS may deploy. When the negative terminal cable is disconnected from the battery, memory of the clock and radio will be canceled. Before you start working, make a note of the contents memorized by the audio memory system. When you have finished working, reset the audio systems and adjust the clock. Never use a back-up power supply from outside the vehicle.
2. In the event of a minor frontal collision where the air bag does not deploy, the steering wheel pad, front air bag sensors and center air bag sensor assembly should be inspected.
3. Before repairs, remove the air bag sensors if shocks are likely to be applied to the sensors during repairs.
4. Never disassemble and repair the steering wheel pad, front air bag sensors or center air bag sensors.
5. Do not expose the steering wheel pad, front air bag sensors or center air bag sensor assembly directly to flames or hot air.
6. If the steering wheel pad, front air bag sensors or center air bag sensor assembly have been dropped, or there are cracks, dents or other defects in the case, bracket or connectors, have them replaced with new ones.
7. Information labels are attached to the periphery of the SRS components. Follow the instructions of the notices.
8. After arming the system, check for proper operation of the SRS warning light.
9. If the wiring harness in the SRS system is damaged, have the entire harness assembly replaced.

DISARMING THE SYSTEM

Work must be started only after 90 seconds from the time the ignition switch is turned to the **LOCK** position and the negative battery cable has been disconnected. The SRS is equipped with a back-up power source so that if work is started within 90 seconds of disconnecting the negative battery cable, the SRS may deploy. When the negative terminal cable is disconnected from the battery, memory of the clock and radio will be canceled. Before you start working, make a note of the contents memorized by the audio memory system. When you have finished work, reset the audio systems as before and adjust the clock. To avoid erasing the memory of each system, never use a back-up power supply from outside the vehicle.

ARMING THE SYSTEM

Once the negative battery cable is reconnected, the system is armed. Turn the ignition **ON**. Check that the SRS lamp turns off after about 6 seconds.

HEATING AND AIR CONDITIONING

The heater core is a small heat exchanger located inside the truck, similar to the radiator at the front of the truck. Coolant is circulated from the engine through the heater core and back to the engine. The heater fan blows fresh, outside air through the heater core; the air is heated and sent on to the interior of the truck.

About the only time the heater core will need removal is for replacement due to clogging or leaking. Thankfully, this doesn't happen too often; removing the heater core can be a major task. Some are easier than others, but all require working in unusual positions inside the truck and fitting tools into very cramped quarters behind the dashboard. In some cases, the dashboard must be removed during the procedure, another major project.

⁂ CAUTION

On models equipped with air conditioning, the heater and air conditioner are adjacent but completely separate units. Be certain when working under the dashboard that only the heater hoses are disconnected. The air conditioning hoses are under pressure. If disconnected, the escaping refrigerant will freeze any surface with which it comes in contact, including your skin and eyes.

Certain Land Cruiser and 4Runner models may be equipped with an additional heating unit for the rear of the vehicle. These small units contain an additional heater core, fan and blower motor. Coolant hoses or pipes run to either the under-dash heater or the engine piping under the hood. The Land Cruiser unit is located under the right front seat; the 4Runner unit is located at the rear of the center console.

Blower Motor

REMOVAL & INSTALLATION

Front

➧ See Figure 17

The blower motor and fan is mounted in the bottom of the heater case. Depending on model and equipment, it may be possible to remove the blower without removing the heater case. If there is insufficient clearance below the case to get the motor and fan free, the case must be removed.

1. On Land Cruisers with the 1FZ-FE engine you may need to remove the right side scuff plate to gain access to the motor. Remove the linkage on the lower cover, then remove the cover while pushing the locking protrusion.
2. Disconnect the electrical harness from the blower motor.
3. Disconnect the ductwork from the casing if it will interfere with motor removal. The motor may have a smaller, flexible air exchange hose on it; remove it.

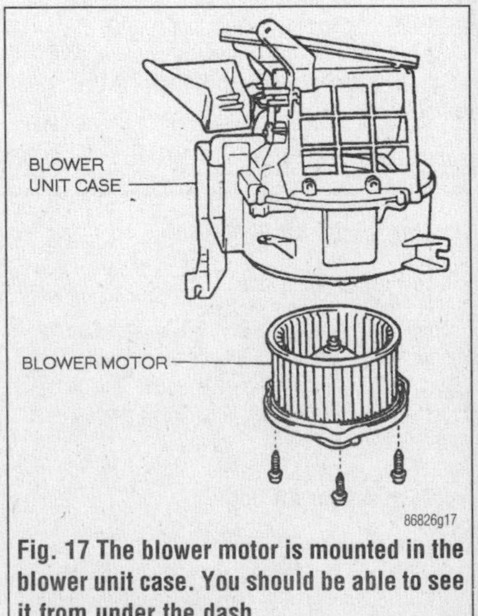

Fig. 17 The blower motor is mounted in the blower unit case. You should be able to see it from under the dash

4. Remove the blower motor fasteners and lower the blower motor out of the heater case.

To install:

5. Install the motor into the inlet duct. Be sure to position the motor so that the flexible tube can be attached to the motor and connect it. Install or connect any ductwork removed from the heater case.
6. Connect the electrical lead.
7. On the 1FZ-FE Land Cruisers, attach the lower cover, linkage and scuff plate.
8. Check the coolant level, add if necessary. Run the heater and check for any leaks.

Rear

LAND CRUISER

See Figures 18, 19, and 20

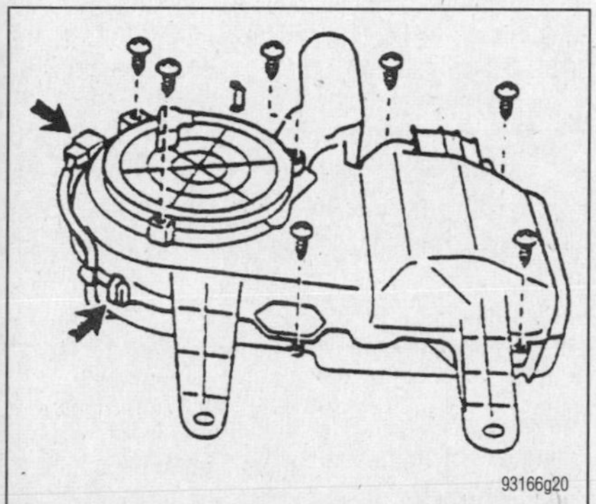

Fig. 18 The rear heater blower motor cover is secured with screws—Land Cruiser

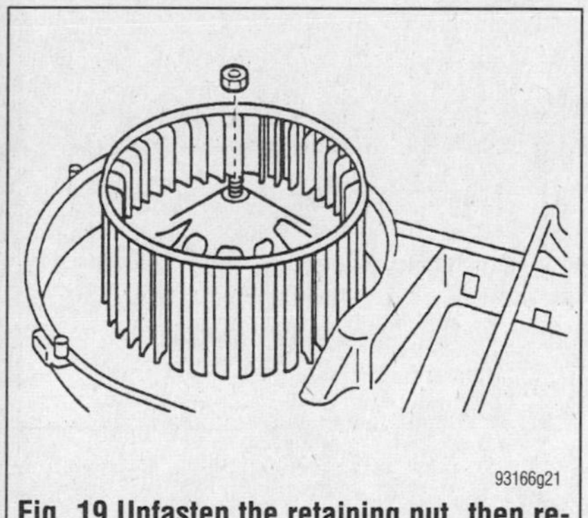

Fig. 19 Unfasten the retaining nut, then remove the blower fan

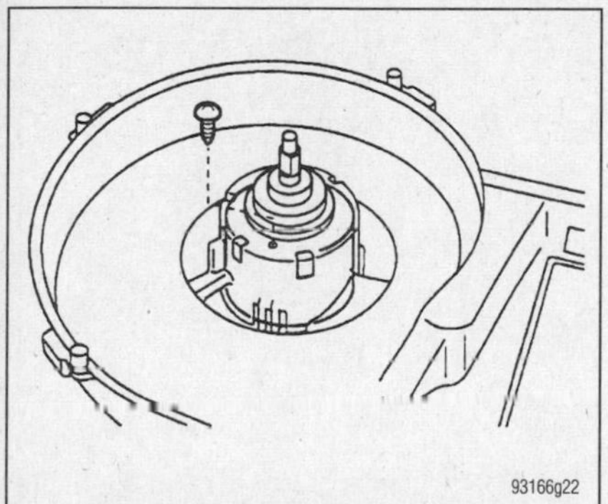

Fig. 20 Remove the screw and blower motor

This procedure requires the removal of the A/C evaporator (called the cooling unit). The A/C system MUST be discharged before you remove the cooling unit. Take the vehicle to a certified A/C repair facility to have the A/C system discharged by qualified repair technician. Once the system has been discharged of the refrigerant you may complete the following steps.

1. Remove the cooling unit.
2. Remove the 3 screws and the motor cover.
3. Remove the 4 screws and the three holding springs and separate the heater cases.
4. Detach the nut and fan blade assembly.
5. Remove the screw and then the blower motor
6. Installation is the reverse of removal.

4RUNNER

See Figures 21, 22, 23, 24, and 25

1. Disconnect the negative battery cable.
2. Remove the rear heater unit from the vehicle.
3. Remove the wire harness clamps.
4. Remove the screws and clamp securing the case halves.

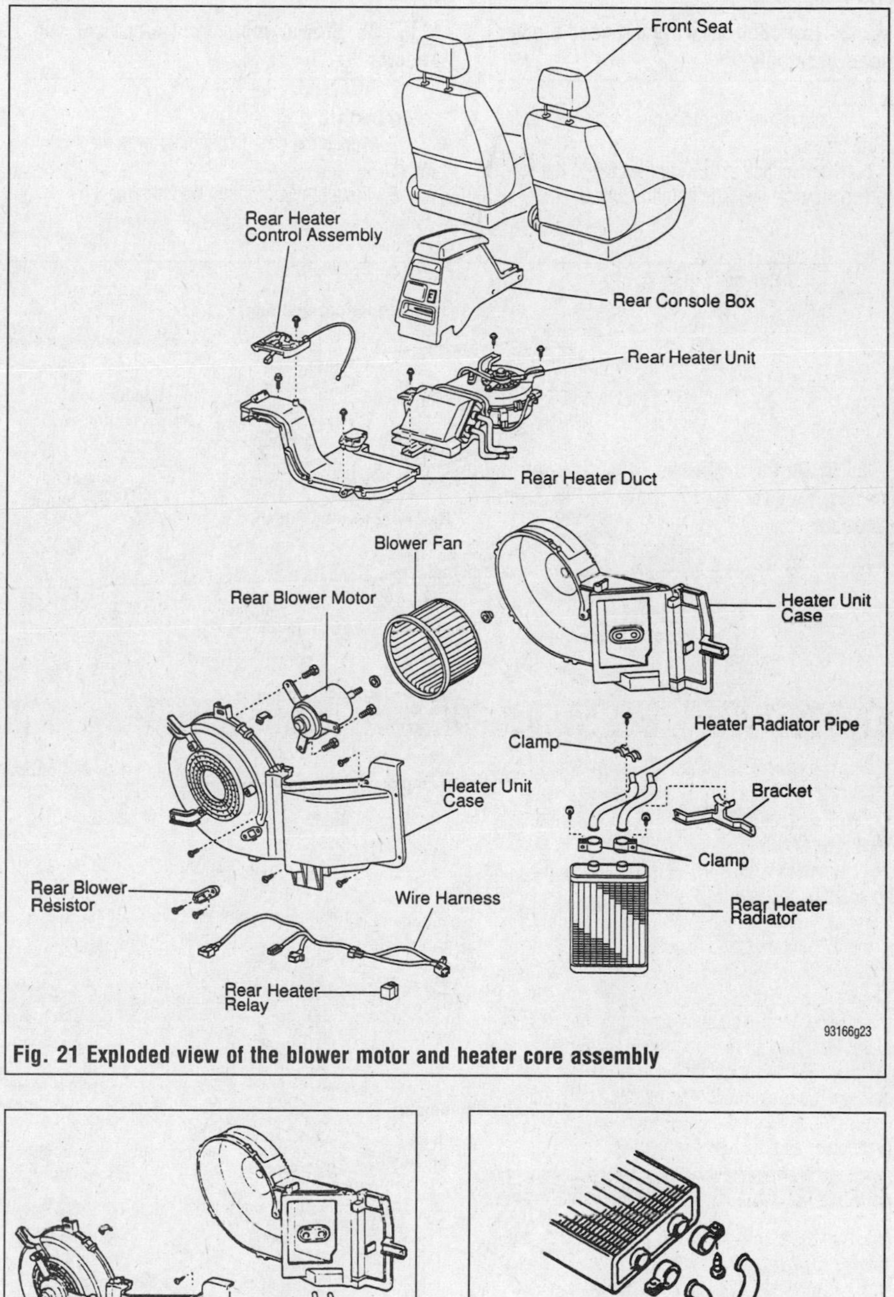

Fig. 21 Exploded view of the blower motor and heater core assembly

Fig. 22 Separate the rear heater case

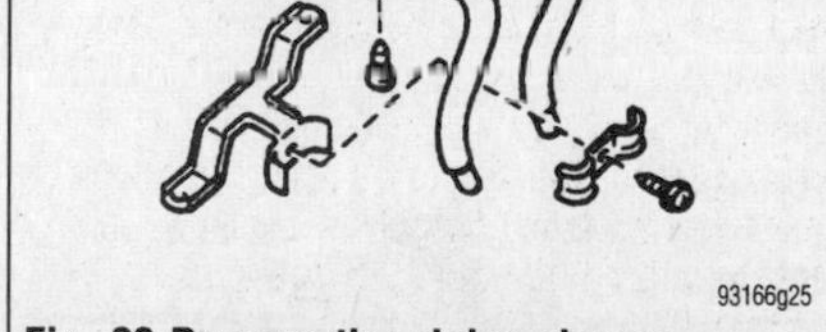

Fig. 23 Remove the piping clamps

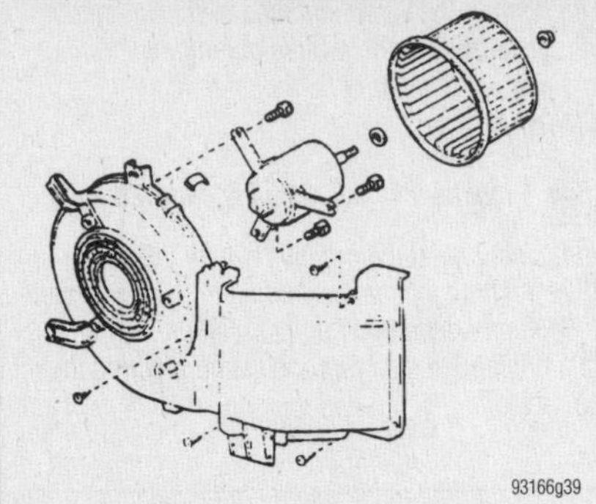

Fig. 24 Exploded view of the rear blower motor assembly

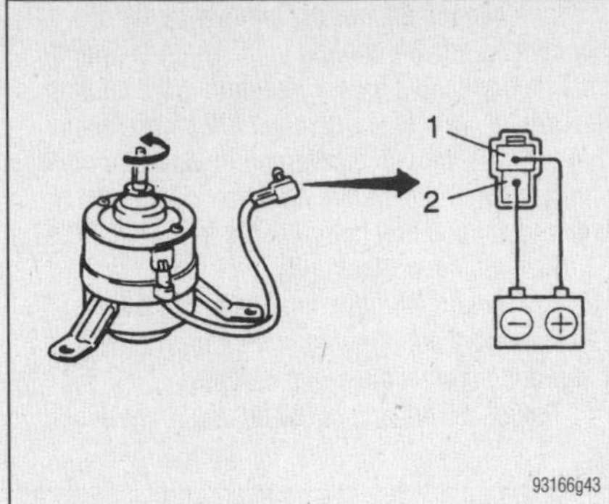

Fig. 25 Blower motor and electrical connector

5. Remove the motor attaching screws, then lift out the motor.
6. Remove the nut holding the cage to the motor, then separate the cage from the unit.

To install:

7. Attach the cage to the motor with the mounting nut.
8. Install the motor into the heater case.
9. Install the heater cases together, then attach the wire harness clamps.
10. Install the rear heater unit into the vehicle.
11. Connect the negative battery cable.
12. Check the operation of the system.

Heater Unit

REMOVAL & INSTALLATION

Front

➧ See Figures 26, 27, and 28

➡Have a lot of towels handy for the leakage of coolant that may spill into your interior.

1. Discharge the A/C system (if applicable), using an approved recovery/recycling machine.
2. Remove the cooling unit (if applicable).
3. Drain the cooling system.

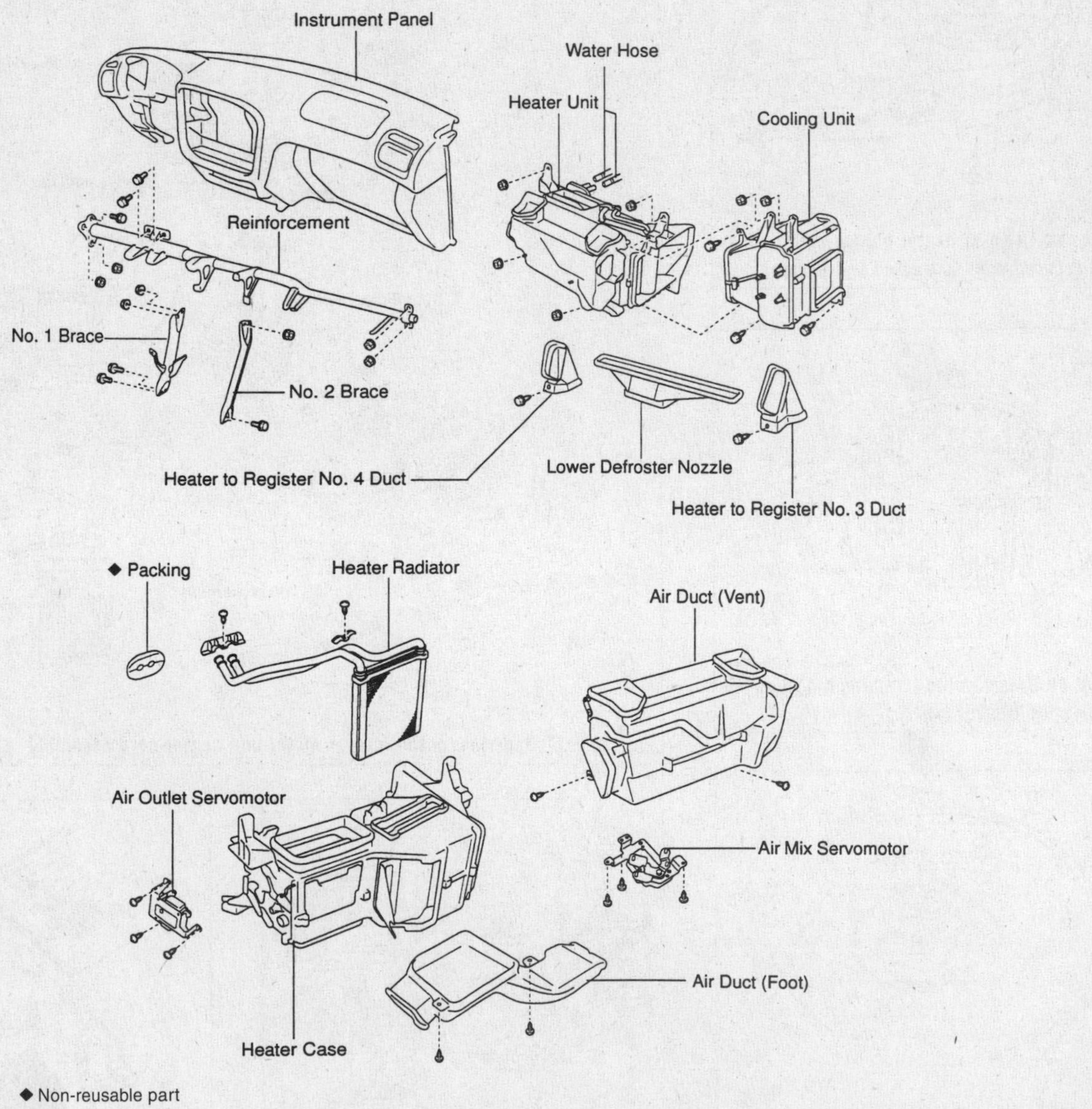

Fig. 26 Front heater unit—Land Cruiser

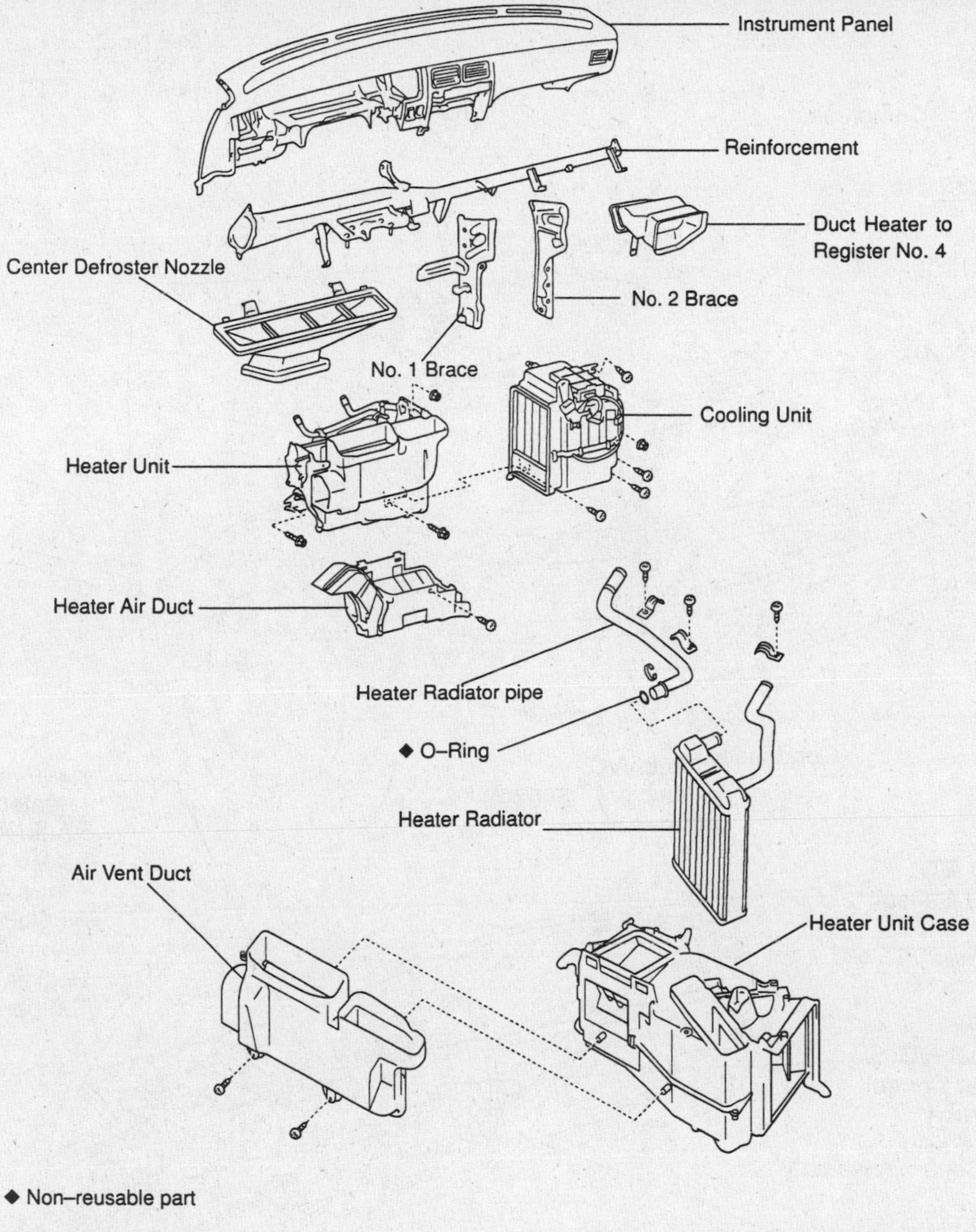

Fig. 27 Heater unit components—T100

CAUTION

When draining engine coolant, keep in mind that cats and dogs are attracted to ethylene glycol antifreeze and could drink any that is left in an uncovered container or in puddles on the ground. This will prove fatal in sufficient quantity. Always drain coolant into a sealable container. Coolant should be reused unless it is contaminated or is several years old.

4. Disconnect the hoses from the heater core. Tag each one so that it may be correctly reinstalled.
5. On some models you will need to remove the glove box assembly. On others, remove the instrument panel and reinforcement.
6. At the heater case under the dash, disconnect the ductwork from the case.
7. Disconnect the heater control cables from the heater case.
8. Lift the spring clip holding the control cable to allow the cable to be manipulated.

➡Don't deform or crimp the cables.

9. Disconnect the wiring harness from the blower fan.
10. Remove the three or four bolts holding the heater case to the dash. Because the inlet tubes project through the firewall, the unit will not fall straight down. It will need to be pulled into the passenger compartment and then brought downward.

To install:

11. Lift the case into position and carefully place the inlet and outlet pipes through the firewall. Install the retaining bolts holding the case to the dash.
12. Connect the wiring harness to the blower fan.
13. Connect the control cables to their linkages. Each must be adjusted so that the motion of the dashboard lever causes the correct corresponding motion in the air door. Both the control lever and the door must reach maximum travel at the same time if full function is to be achieved.
    a. Set the dashboard control to FRESH. Lift the adjustment clip and adjust the air inlet cable towards the heater unit until the linkage is at its maximum travel on Pick-Up and 4Runner. For Land Cruiser, adjust the cable away from the case. Release the adjustment clip.
    b. Set the dashboard control to VENT (Pick-Up) or DEF (4Runner and Land Cruiser). Lift the adjustment clip and adjust the air flow control cable towards the heater unit until the linkage is at its maximum travel. Release the adjustment clip.

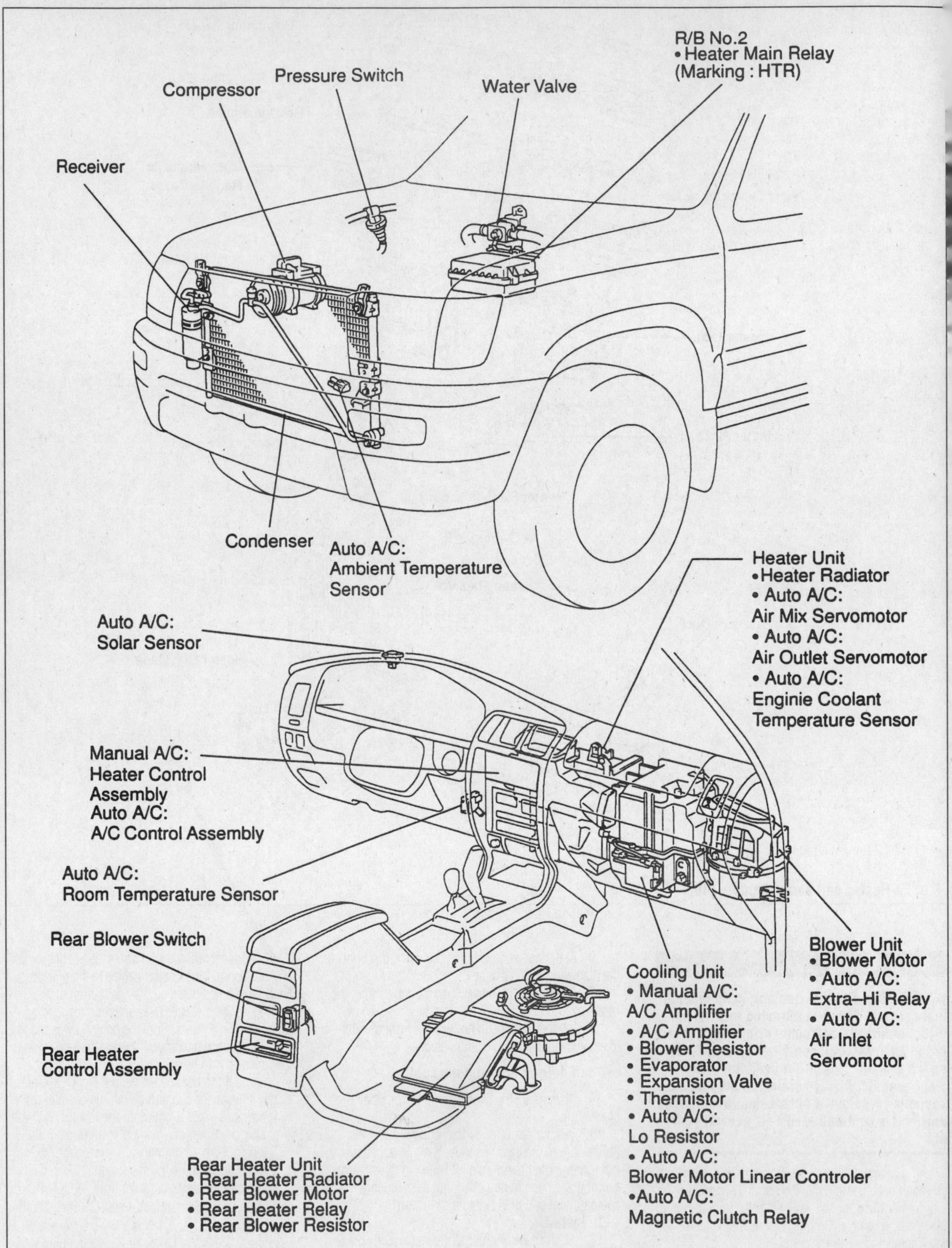
R/B No.2
• Heater Main Relay
(Marking : HTR)
Pressure Switch
Compressor
Water Valve
Receiver
Condenser
Auto A/C:
Ambient Temperature
Sensor
Heater Unit
•Heater Radiator
• Auto A/C:
Air Mix Servomotor
• Auto A/C:
Air Outlet Servomotor
• Auto A/C:
Enginie Coolant
Temperature Sensor
Auto A/C:
Solar Sensor
Manual A/C:
Heater Control
Assembly
Auto A/C:
A/C Control Assembly
Auto A/C:
Room Temperature Sensor
Rear Blower Switch
Blower Unit
• Blower Motor
• Auto A/C:
Extra–Hi Relay
• Auto A/C:
Air Inlet
Servomotor
Cooling Unit
• Manual A/C:
A/C Amplifier
• A/C Amplifier
• Blower Resistor
• Evaporator
• Expansion Valve
• Thermistor
• Auto A/C:
Lo Resistor
• Auto A/C:
Blower Motor Linear Controler
•Auto A/C:
Magnetic Clutch Relay
Rear Heater
Control Assembly
Rear Heater Unit
• Rear Heater Radiator
• Rear Blower Motor
• Rear Heater Relay
• Rear Blower Resistor
93166g05

Fig. 28 Location of the heater unit—4Runner

c. Set the temperature control to COOL. Lift the adjustment clip and adjust the air mix control damper control cable away from the heater case until the linkage is at its maximum travel on. For Land Cruiser, adjust the cable towards the case.
14. Connect or reinstall the ductwork. Make certain each tube is firmly and completely fitted on its port. A light spray of glass cleaner serves as a good lubricant; don't use too much.
15. Install the glove box and/or instrument panel assembly.
16. Connect the heater hoses. Use new clamps.
17. Install the cooling unit (if equipped).
18. Refill the coolant, then charge the A/C system (if equipped).

Rear

LAND CRUISER

➧ See Figures 29 thru 37

1. Drain the engine coolant.
2. Detach the coolant hoses from the heater radiator pipes.
3. Remove the front seats.
4. Detach the heater control assembly.
5. Disconnect the rear console box.
6. Remove the front console box cover.
7. Detach the finish panel from the lower center cluster.
8. Remove the scuff plates from the front door.
9. Detach the cowl side trims.
10. Remove the rear door scuff plates.
11. Detach the center pillar trim.
12. Push the floor carpeting back.
13. Remove the cooler bracket.
14. Remove the heater duct by removing the bolt and screw.
15. Detach the heater unit connector.
16. Remove the bolts from the heater unit.
17. Lift the heater unit out of the vehicle using caution not to spill any antifreeze on the interior of the vehicle.
18. Remove the fasteners and pull the heater radiator out of the case.
19. Installation is the reverse of removal. Remember to push the coolant hoses on to the heater radiator pipe as far as the second ridge.

➡If the heater hoses are not seated properly, they will leak

4RUNNER

➧ See Figures 38 thru 43

1. Drain the engine coolant.
2. Remove the front seats.
3. Remove the center console.
4. Push back the floor carpeting.
5. Detach the coolant hoses.
6. Remove the rear heater duct.
7. Remove the rear heater control assembly.
8. Remove the rear heater duct by removing the three screws.
9. Installation is the reverse of removal. Make sure to install the hose clamps in the proper position.

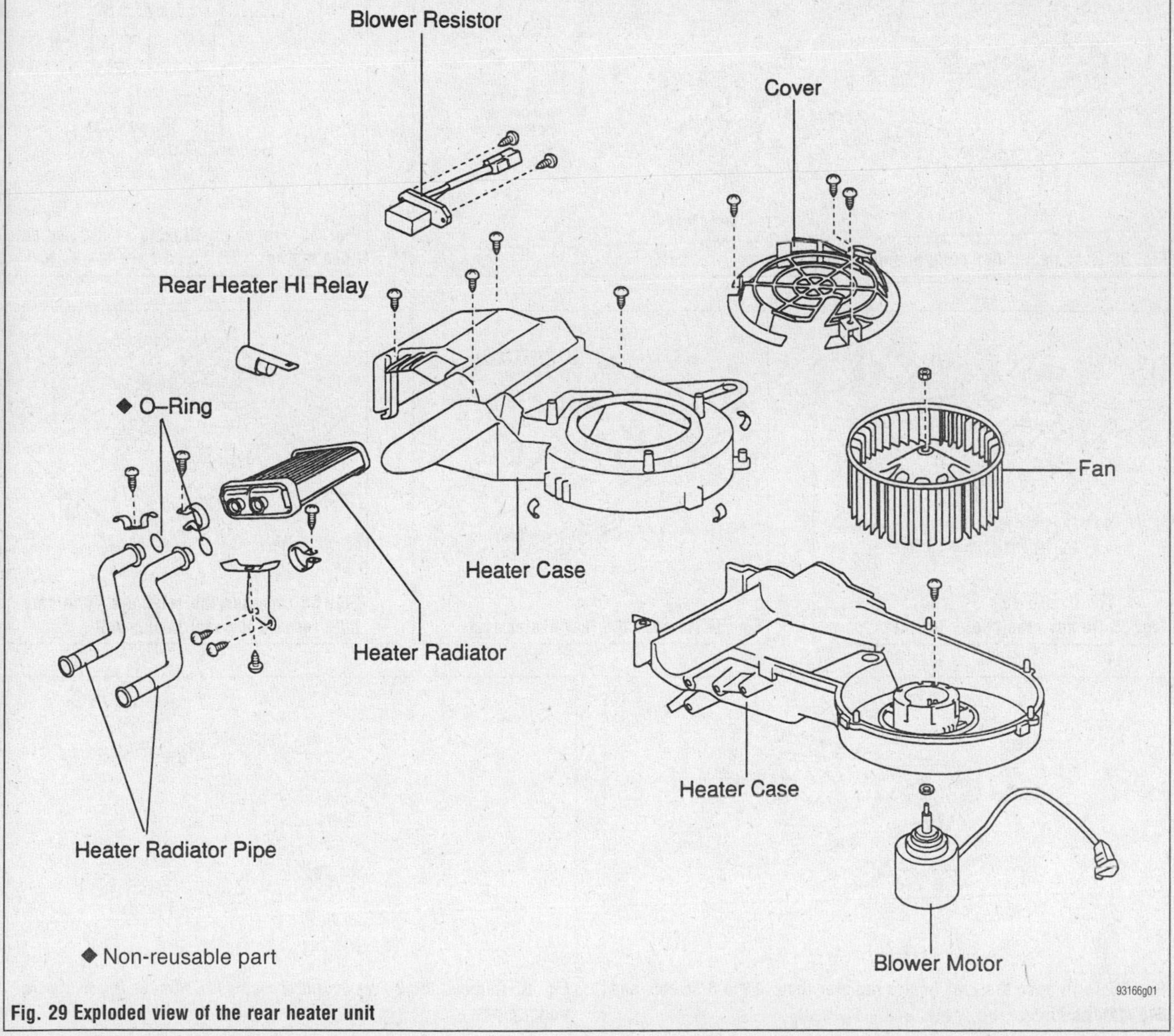

Fig. 29 Exploded view of the rear heater unit

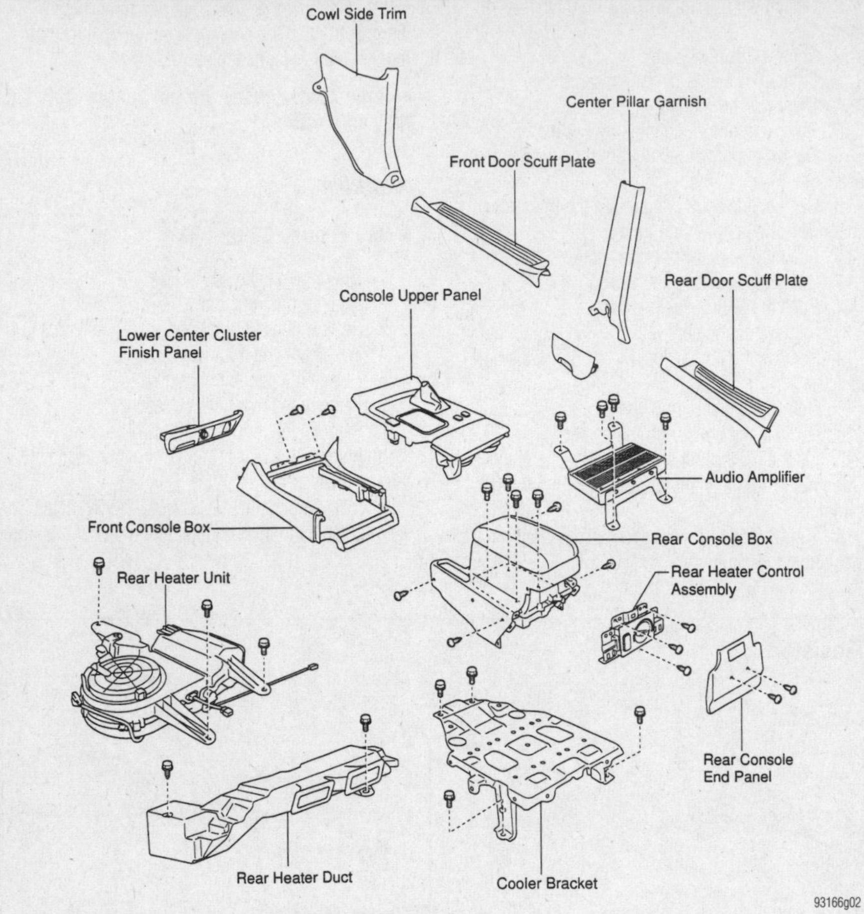

Fig. 30 Rear heater box components—Land Cruiser

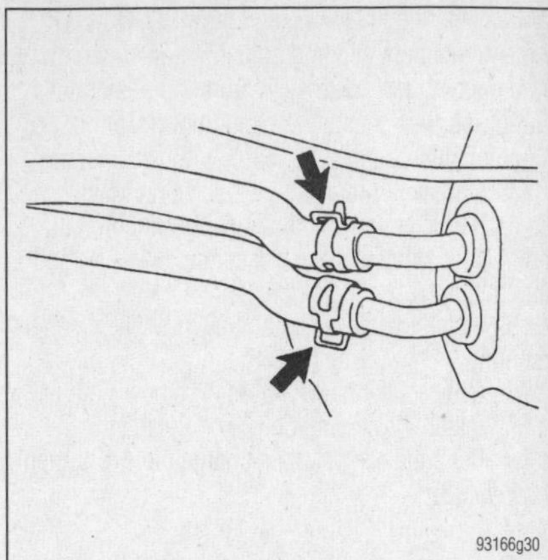

Fig. 31 Location of the coolant hose clamps

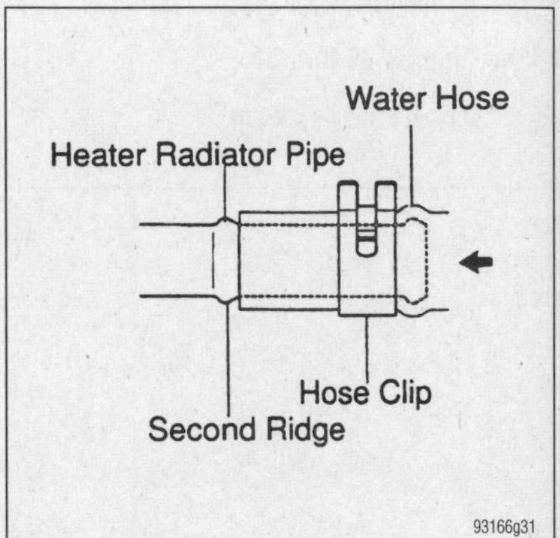

Fig. 32 Proper positioning of the coolant hose clamp

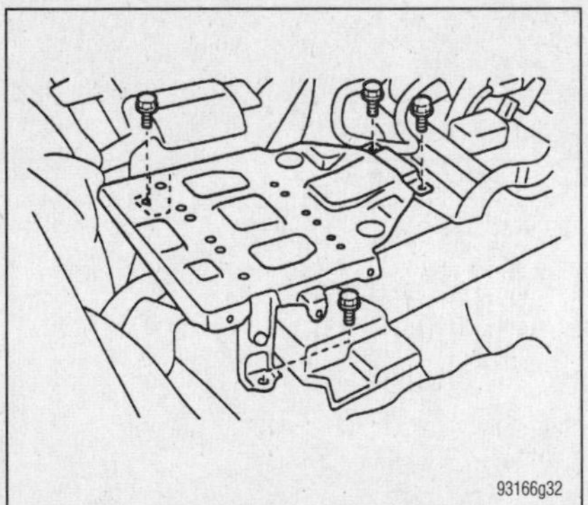

Fig. 33 Remove the cooler bracket

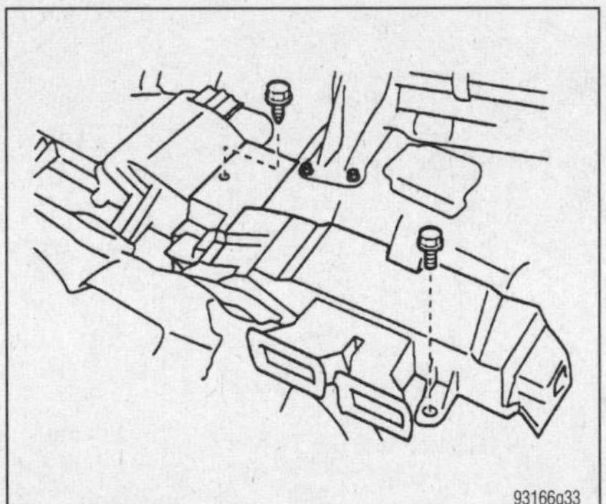

Fig. 34 Remove the rear heater duct

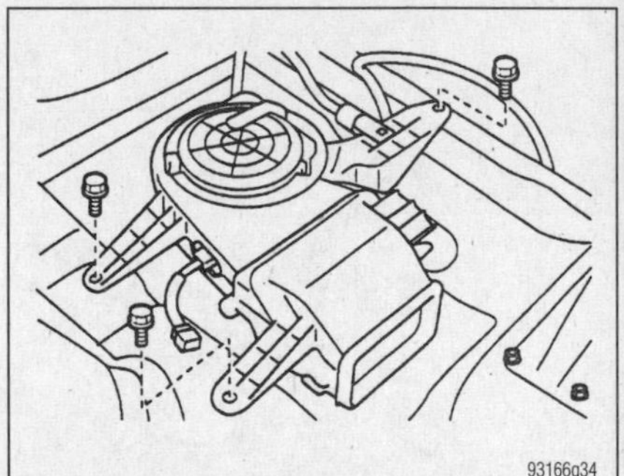

Fig. 35 Unfasten the retainers, then carefully remove the rear heater unit

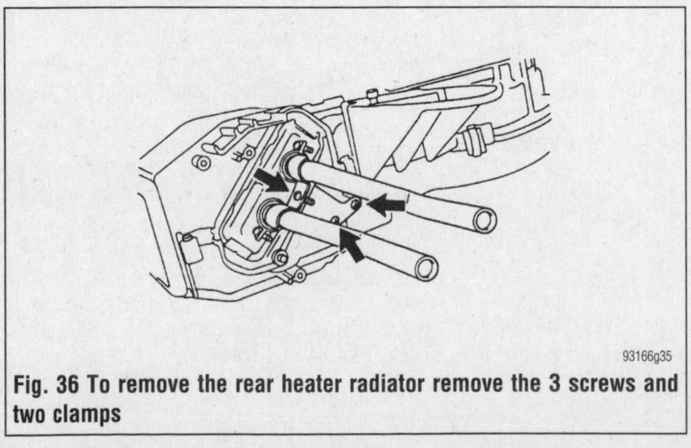

Fig. 36 To remove the rear heater radiator remove the 3 screws and two clamps

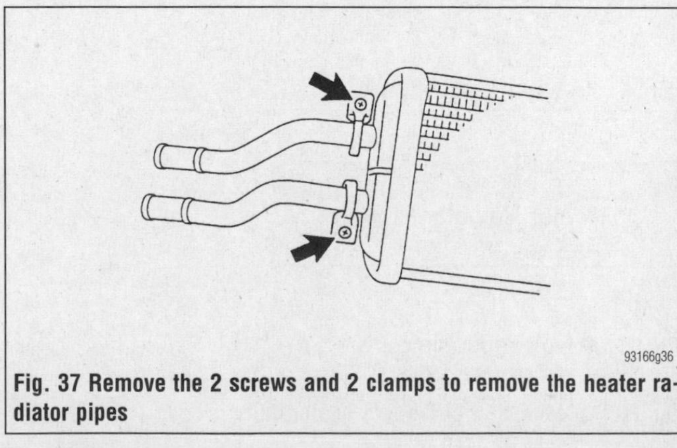

Fig. 37 Remove the 2 screws and 2 clamps to remove the heater radiator pipes

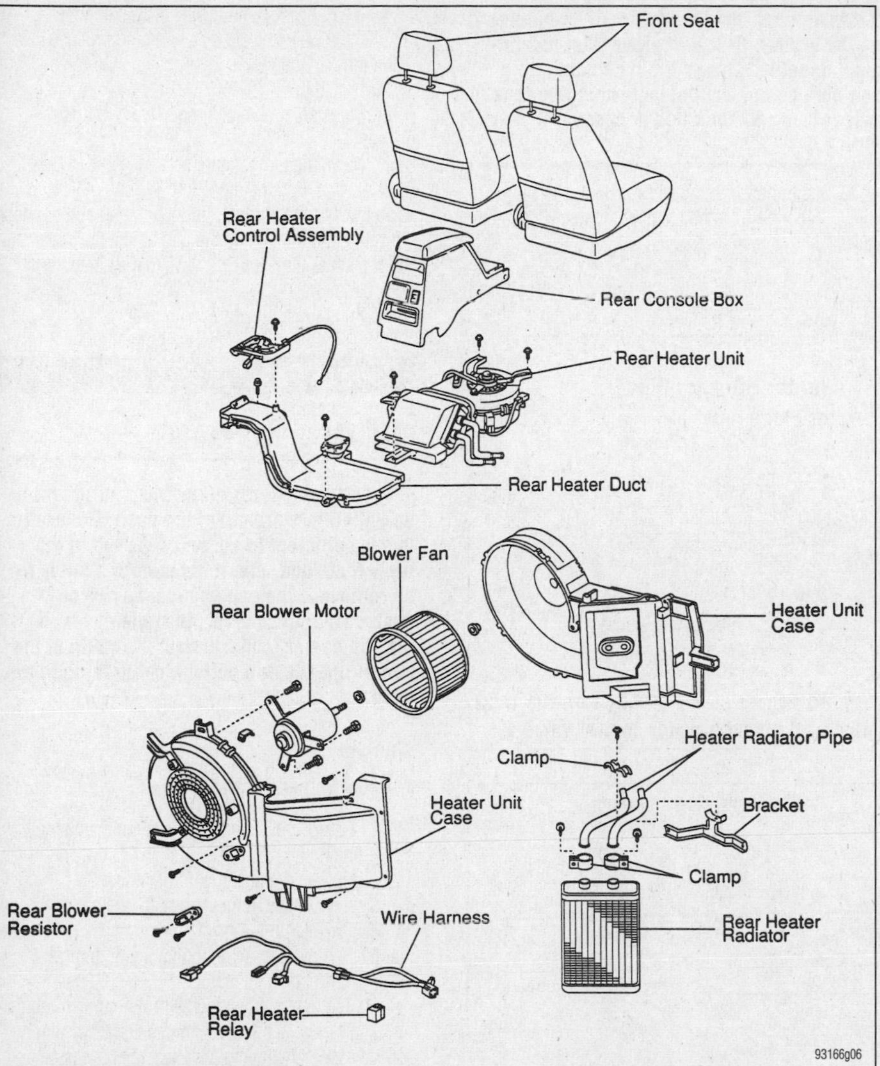

Fig. 38 Rear heater unit—4Runner

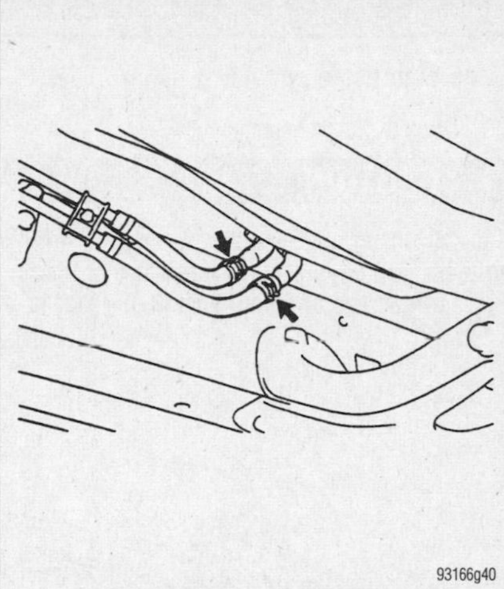

Fig. 39 Disconnect the coolant hoses

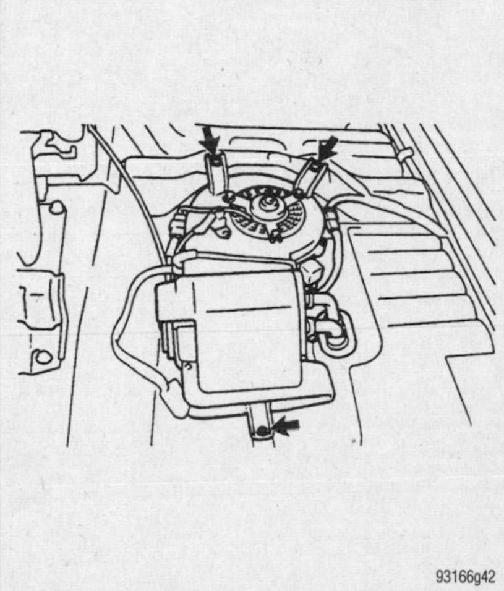

Fig. 40 Remove the 3 screws from the heater unit

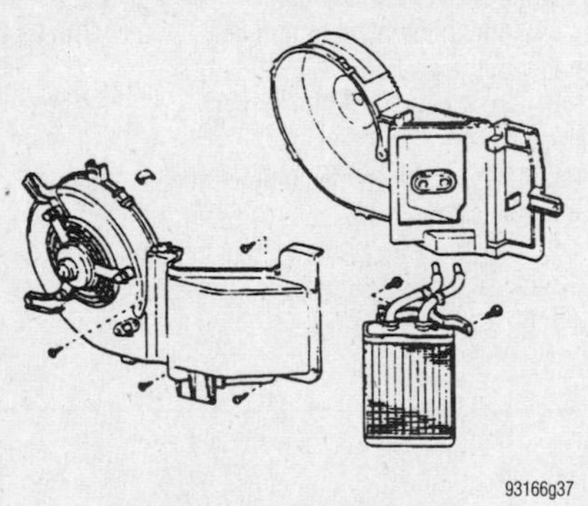

Fig. 41 Heater radiator and case

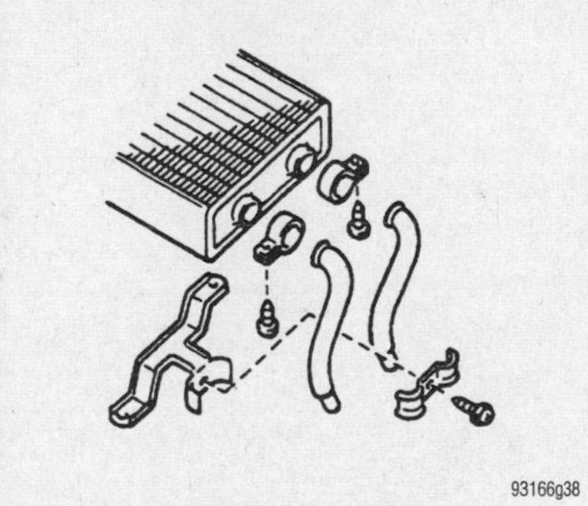

Fig. 42 Heater pipe clamp locations

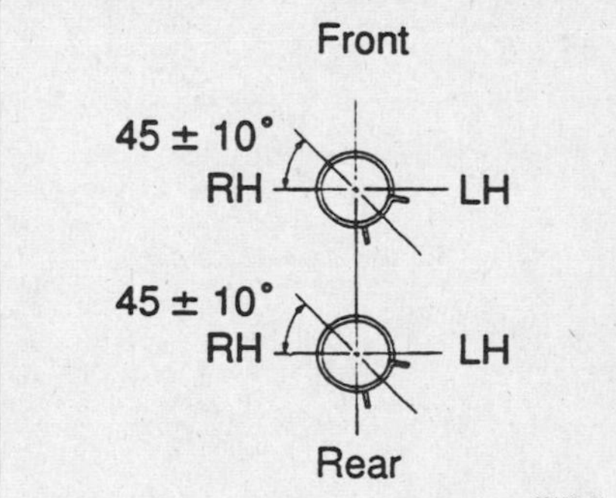

Fig. 43 Proper heater hose clamp positions

Heater Core

REMOVAL & INSTALLATION

Front

1. Drain the cooling system.
2. Remove the heater unit assembly. Have a lot of towels handy for the leakage of coolant that may spill into your interior.
3. Remove the fasteners securing the core to the unit, remove the plates and clamps. Pull upwards to remove the core from the unit.

To install:

4. Inspect the core fins for any blockage. Using compressed air, clean them.
5. Install the core into the unit placing the plates and clamps into position. Tighten the core screws.
6. Install the heater unit into the vehicle.
7. Fill the cooling system.

Heater Water Control Valve

The heater control valve is located under the hood near the firewall. It is operated by a cable connected to the dashboard temperature control lever. The valve is opened to admit hot coolant into the heater core when the operator moves the lever into the warm or hot range.

REMOVAL & INSTALLATION

See Figures 44 and 45

1. Drain the engine coolant.

CAUTION

When draining engine coolant, keep in mind that cats and dogs are attracted to ethylene glycol antifreeze and could drink any that is left in an uncovered container or in puddles on the ground. This will prove fatal in sufficient quantity. Always drain coolant into a sealable container. Coolant should be reused unless it is contaminated or is several years old.

2. Disconnect the control cable from the valve.
3. Disconnect the inlet and outlet hoses from the valve.
4. If equipped, remove the harness connector.
5. If the valve is held by a retaining bolt, remove it and remove the valve.

To install:

6. Reinstall in reverse order. Use new hose clamps.
7. Move the temperature selector lever to COOL. On T100 and Tacoma move it to WARM. Adjust the valve lever to the corresponding position and connect the cable. Lift the spring clip and adjust the cable so that the valve achieves full travel to the closed position.
8. Refill the coolant.

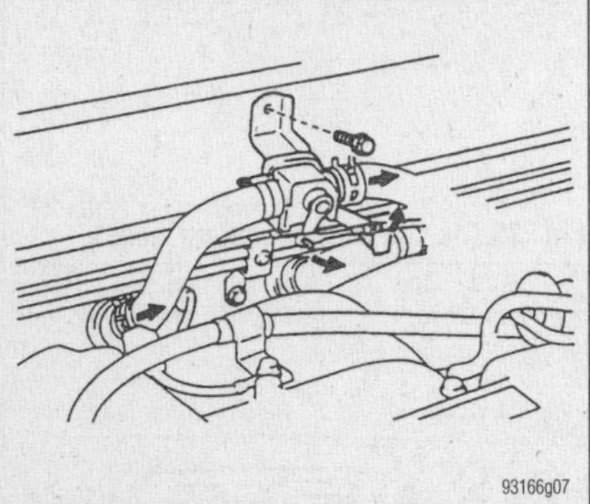

Fig. 44 Location of the heater water control valve

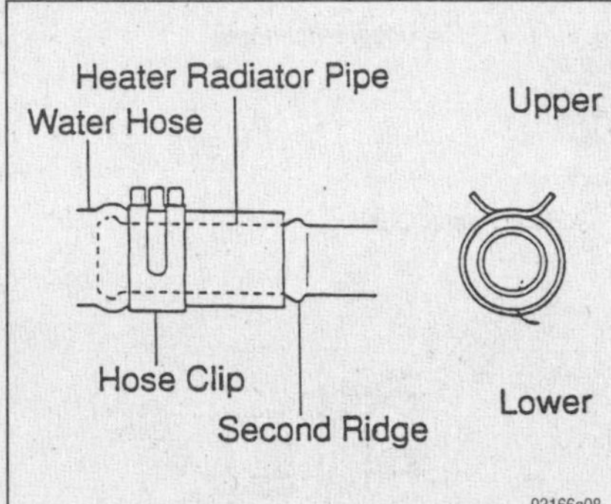

Fig. 45 Proper clamp location on the inlet pipe of the heater water control valve

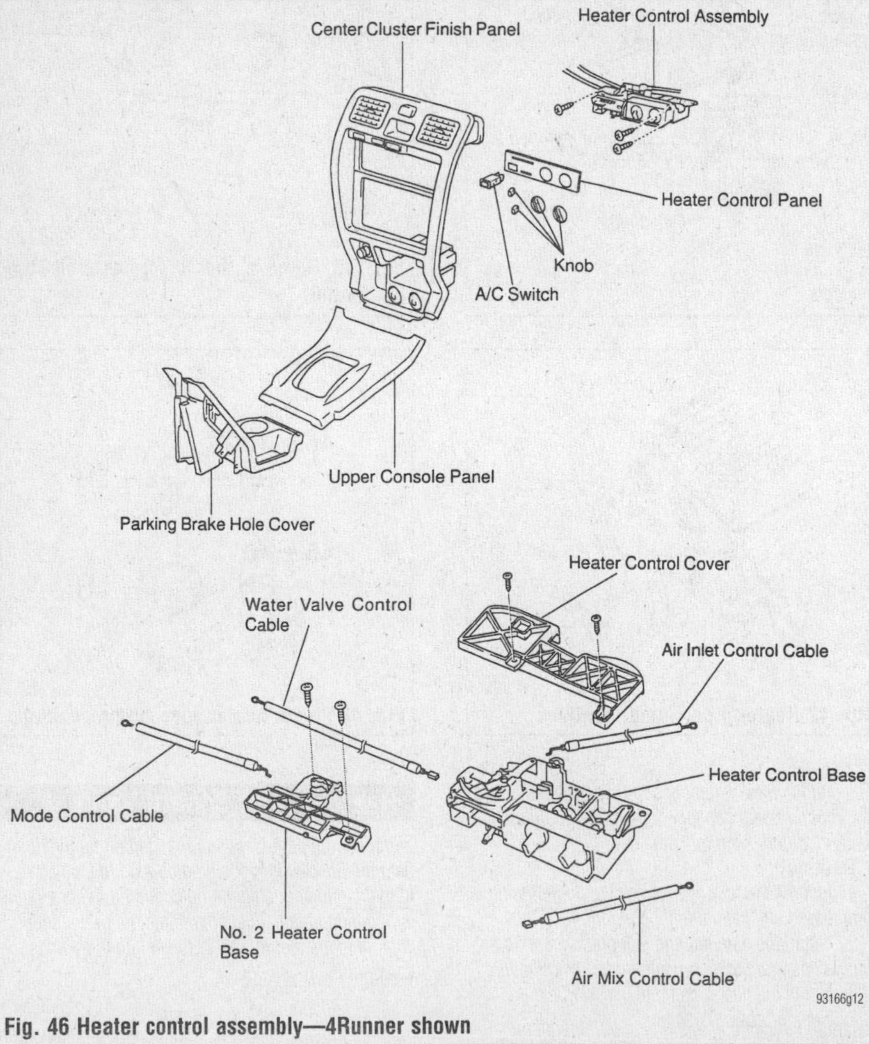

Fig. 46 Heater control assembly—4Runner shown

Control Panel

REMOVAL & INSTALLATION

➡These procedures allow the control unit to be pulled forward out of the dash. Generally, this is sufficient to allow inspection of the lever functions, etc. If the control head is to be removed, the cables must be disconnected from each lever. In some cases, it may be easier to disconnect the cable at the heater linkage and pull the cable through the dash.

4Runner

See Figures 46 and 47

1. Remove the center console cover and the center finish panel.
2. Pull off the heater control knobs.
3. If equipped, remove the A/C switch.
4. Unfasten the control panel screws.
5. Remove the glove compartment door and lower finish panel.
6. Tag and disconnect the heater control cables.
7. Remove the screw and pull out the heater control assembly, then disconnect the harness.

To install:

8. Attach all of the heater cables to their proper locations and adjust if needed.
9. Attach the harness and install the control assembly in the dash.
10. Install the lower finish panel and glove box door.
11. Tighten down the control panel. If equipped, install the A/C switch.
12. Push on the heater knobs, then install the center console cover and center finish panel.

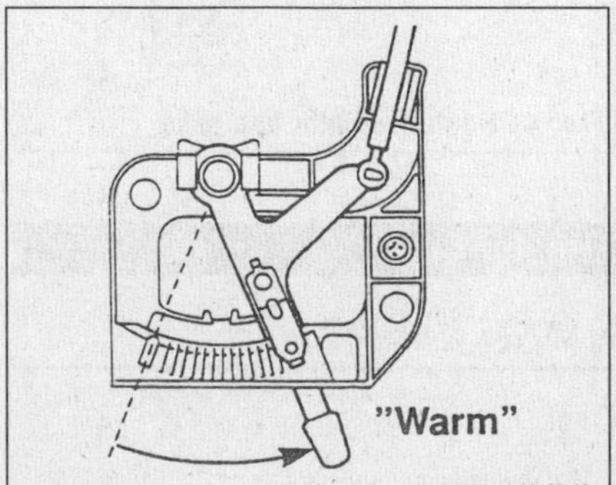

Fig. 47 Close up of the heater control assembly

Tacoma

➧ **See Figure 48**

1. Remove the lower finish panel.
2. Detach the glove box door.
3. Remove the second lower finish panel.
4. Detach the center cluster finish panel
5. Pull out the heater control knobs.
6. Remove the heater control name plate.
7. Remove the two screws
8. Use a screwdriver to remove the four fitting clips and pull out the panel.

➡Tape the end of the screwdriver before you use it to pry out the panel.

9. Detach the connector.

To install:

10. Attach the connector.
11. Install the heater control name plate.
12. Push in the heater control knobs.
13. Install the center cluster finish panel.
14. Install the second lower finish panel.
15. Attach the glove box door.
16. Install the lower finish panel

T100

➧ **See Figures 49 and 50**

1. Remove the instrument panel
2. Detach the heater control cables
3. Remove the two screws and pull out the heater control assembly
4. Detach the connector

To install:

5. Install the connector
6. Install the two screws and tighten securely
7. Attach the control cables to the heater control unit
8. Install the instrument panel

Tundra

➧ **See Figures 51, 52, 53, and 54**

1. Remove the trim panel surrounding the controls.
2. Remove the knobs from the control levers. These knobs do pull off, although often with great effort.
3. If equipped with air conditioning, remove the A/C switch.
4. Use a thin, flat-bladed tool with a protected or taped edge. Carefully work the blade into the area at the bottom of the control unit and pry it out.
5. Gently pull the unit forward. If equipped with a clock in the housing, disconnect the clock. Disconnect the lighting harness and pull the control unit forward.

To install:

6. Install in reverse order, making sure the electrical connections are engage before installing the unit. Install the knobs securely and install the trim panel.

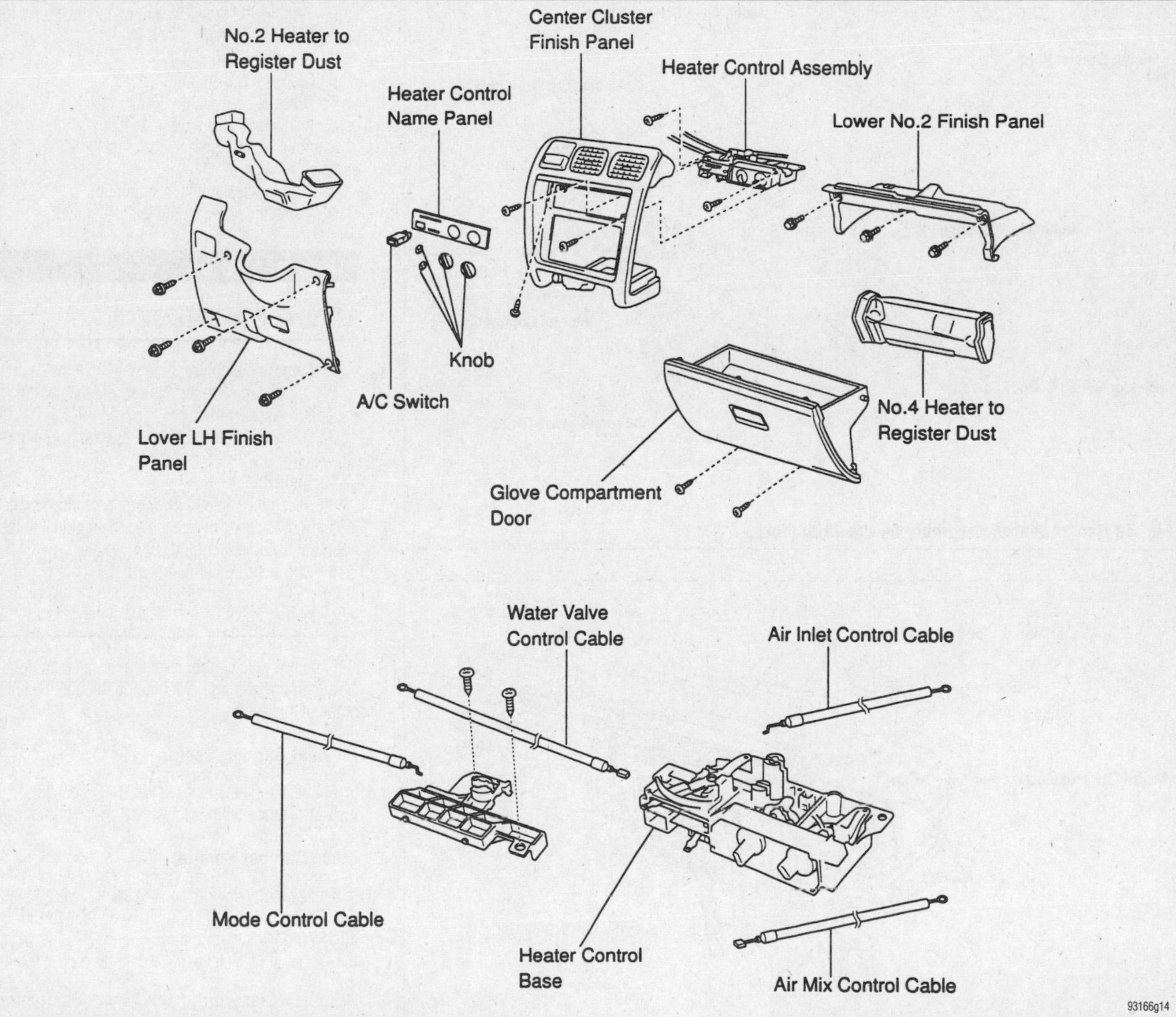

Fig. 48 Exploded view of the heater control assembly—Tacoma

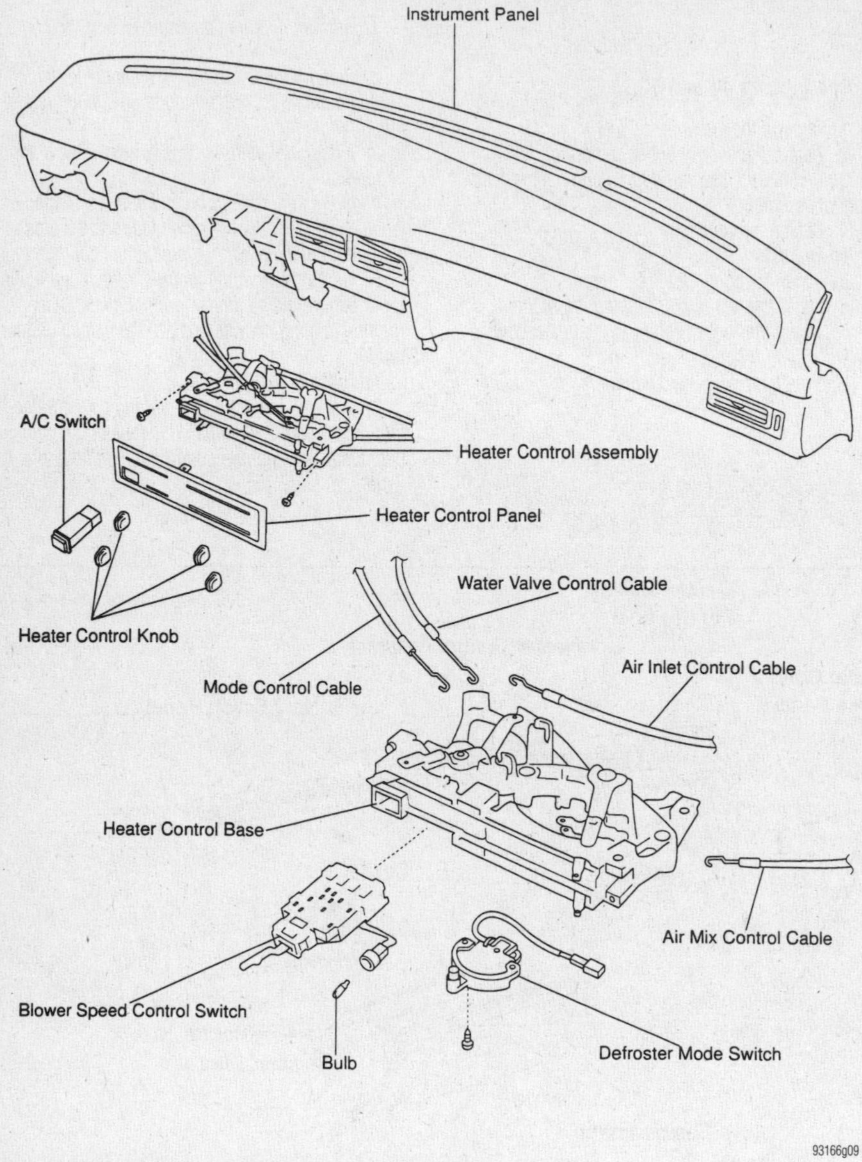

Fig. 49 Heater control assembly on the T100 pickup

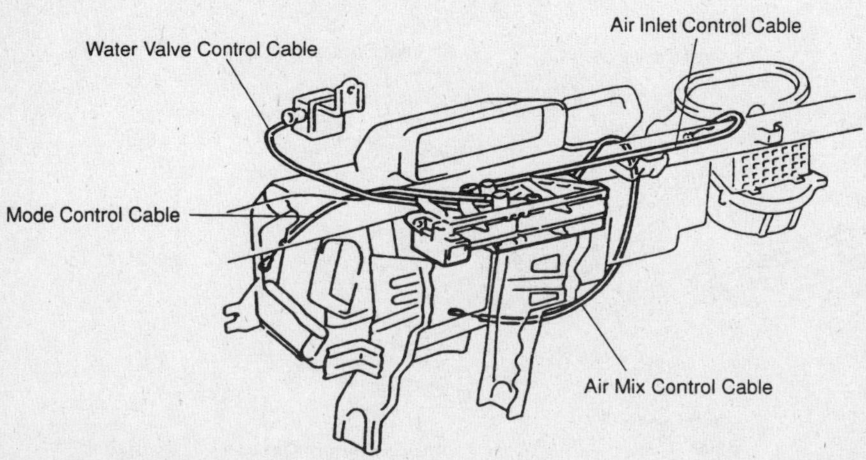

Fig. 50 View of the T100 control cable routing

Land Cruiser

FRONT

➧ **See Figure 55**

1. Using a flat-bladed tool, remove the two claw clips, then remove the cup holder.
2. Remove the ashtray if equipped.
3. Separate the center cluster finish panel from the heater control assembly.
4. Pull out the control assembly, then disconnect the harnesses.

To install:

5. Attach the harness to the back of the control assembly, then install into the dash.
6. Attach the finish panel to the control assembly.
7. Install the ashtray.
8. Install the cup holder.

REAR

➧ **See Figure 56**

1. Remove the rear console end panel door.
2. Turn the heater dial to maximum.
3. Remove the three (3) screws and heater control assembly.
4. Detach the connector.
5. Disconnect the control cable

To install:

6. Install the control cable and connector.
7. Attach the three screws and heater control assembly.
8. Turn the heater dial to maximum.
9. Install the rear console end panel door

Control Cables

REMOVAL & INSTALLATION

1. Remove the control assembly from the dash.
2. Tag and remove the cables from the back of the control assembly.
3. Disconnect the cable from the component it is attached to.

To install:

4. Attach the cable to its appropriate location in the back of the control assembly. Then route it to the appropriate component. Adjust the cable.
5. Check for proper operation.

ADJUSTMENTS

First move the control levers to the left then right. Check for any stiffness and binding through the full range of the levers.

Air Inlet Damper Control

Set the air inlet damper to the FRESH position, then install the control cable and lock the clamp.

Mode Damper Control

Set the mode damper and the control cable to the FACE position on T100 and Tacoma. Set it to DEF on all other models. Clamp the section of the control cable and install the cable to the damper control lever.

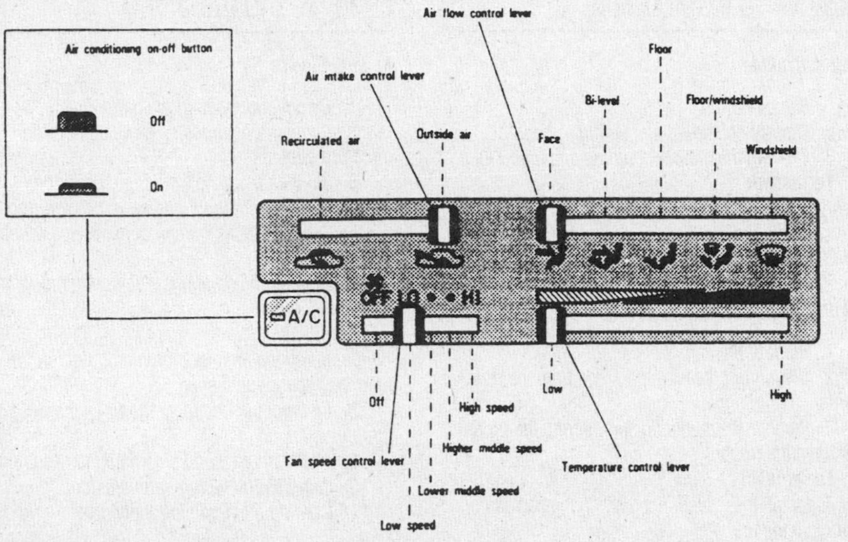

86826g25

Fig. 51 A common heater control panel found on Toyota trucks

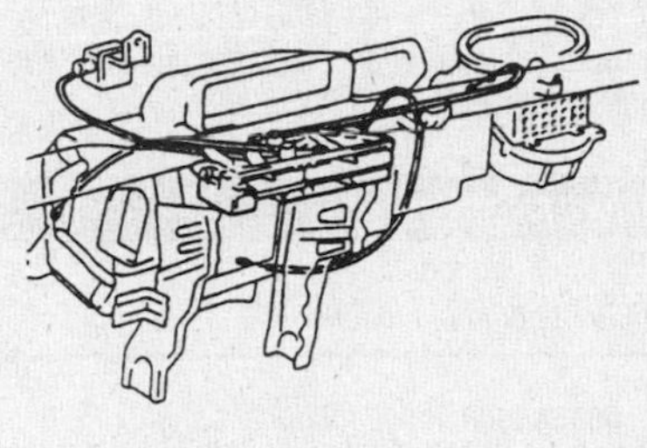

86826g26

Fig. 52 Tag and disconnect the control cables

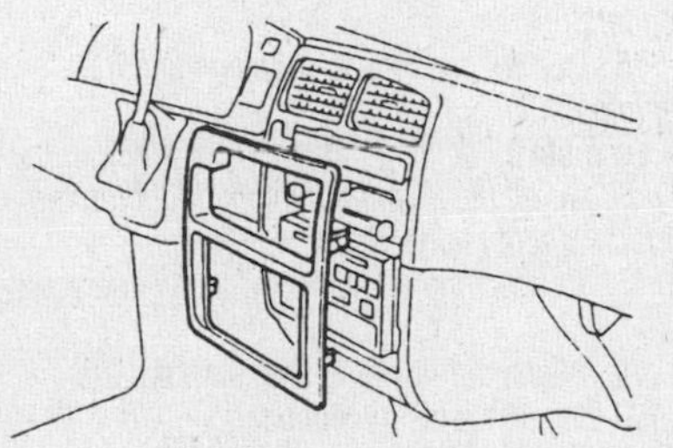

86826g27

Fig. 53 Remove the trim surrounding the control panel

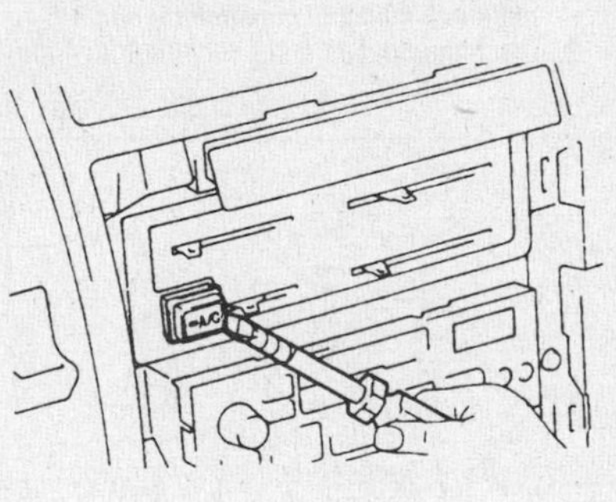

86826g28

Fig. 54 If removing the A/C switch, tape the end of the tool to prevent marring the surface

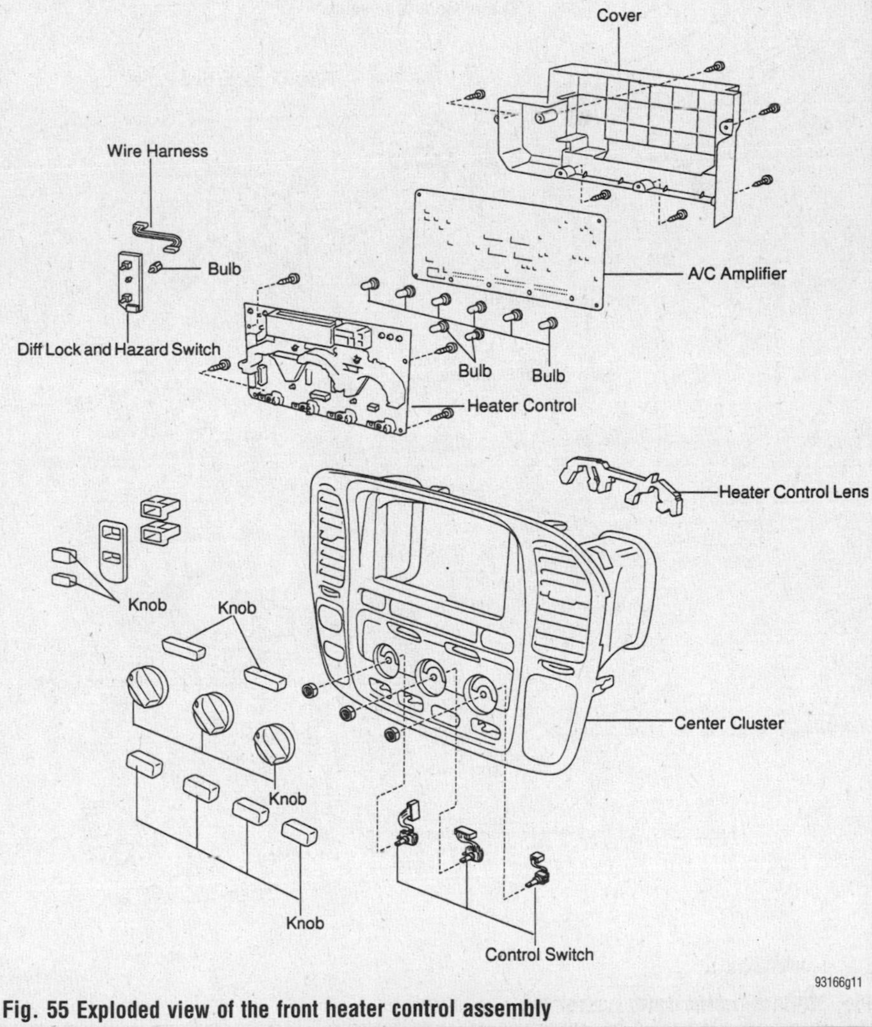

93166g11

Fig. 55 Exploded view of the front heater control assembly

Air Mix Damper Control

Set the air mix damper and the control lever to the COOL position or WARM on the Tacoma and T100. Install the control cable and lock the clamp.

Water Valve Control

Set the water valve in the COOL position or WARM on the Tacoma and T100. While pushing the outer cable in the direction, clamp the outer cable to the water valve bracket.

Blower Switch

REMOVAL & INSTALLATION

1. Remove the heater control assembly.
2. Remove the illumination light from the heater control assembly.
3. Using a flat-bladed tool, pry loose the clip and push out the blower speed control switch to the rear of the heater control assembly.

To install:

4. Push the switch into the heater control assembly.
5. Attach the illumination light, then install the control assembly.

Rear Blower Resistor

REMOVAL & INSTALLATION

Land Cruiser

1. Remove the right front seat.
2. Disconnect the resistor wiring harness.
3. Remove the mounting screws and the resistor.

To install:

4. Install the resistor, then attach the harness wiring to the unit.
5. Install the front seat.

4Runner

1. Remove the console box.
2. Disconnect the wiring harness from the resistor.
3. Remove the mounting screws from the resistor, then the resistor.

To install:

4. Install the resistor, then attach the harness wiring to the unit.
5. Install the console box.

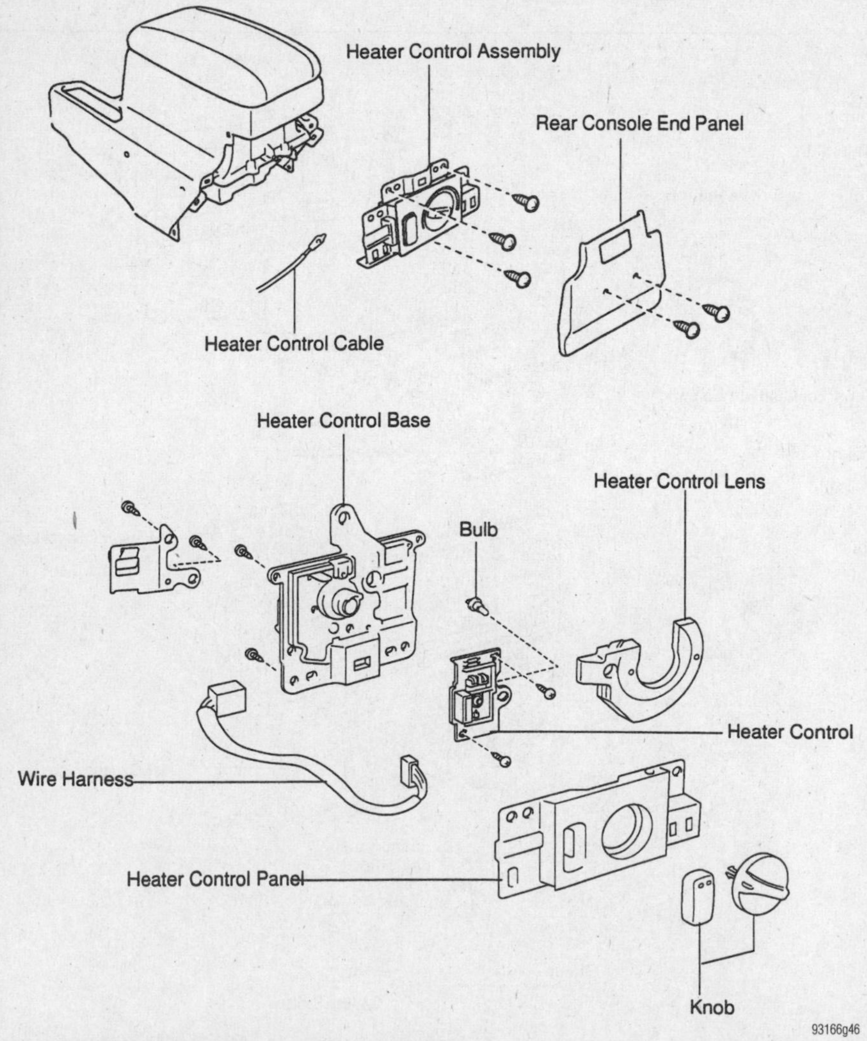

Fig. 56 Rear heater control assembly—Land Cruiser

Air Inlet Servomotor

REMOVAL & INSTALLATION

➧ See Figure 57

1. Disconnect the negative battery cable.
2. Remove the necessary glove box compartment components.
3. Set the damper to the RECIRC position.
4. Disconnect the air inlet servomotor wiring.
5. Disconnect the linkage from the air inlet servomotor.
6. Remove the mounting screws and the air inlet servomotor.

To install:

7. Install the air inlet servomotor, tighten the mounting screws until snug.
8. Connect the linkage to the air inlet servomotor.
9. Attach the air inlet servomotor harness.
10. Install the glove compartment door.
11. Connect the negative battery cable.

Air Mix Servomotor

REMOVAL & INSTALLATION

1. Disconnect the negative battery cable.
2. Remove the instrument panel.
3. Disconnect the air mix servomotor wiring.
4. Disconnect the linkage from the air mix servomotor.
5. Remove the mounting screws and the air mix servomotor.

To install:

6. Install the air mix servomotor, tighten the mounting screws until snug.
7. Connect the linkage to the air mix servomotor.
8. Attach the air mix servomotor harness.
9. Install the instrument panel.
10. Connect the negative battery cable.

Air Outlet Servomotor

REMOVAL & INSTALLATION

➧ See Figure 58

1. Disconnect the negative battery cable.
2. Remove the instrument lower finish panel.
3. Disconnect the air outlet servomotor wiring.

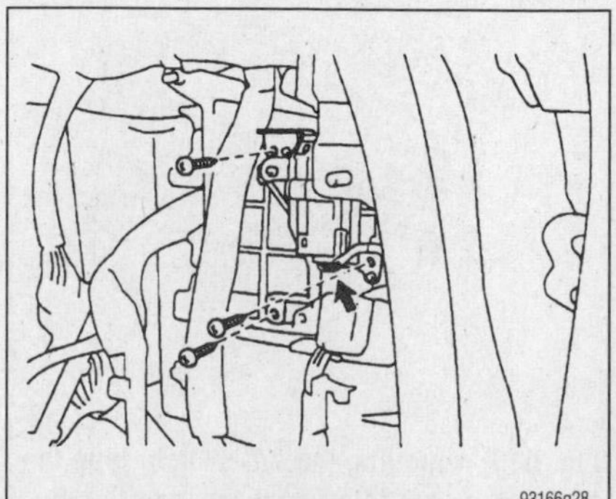

Fig. 57 Air inlet servomotor

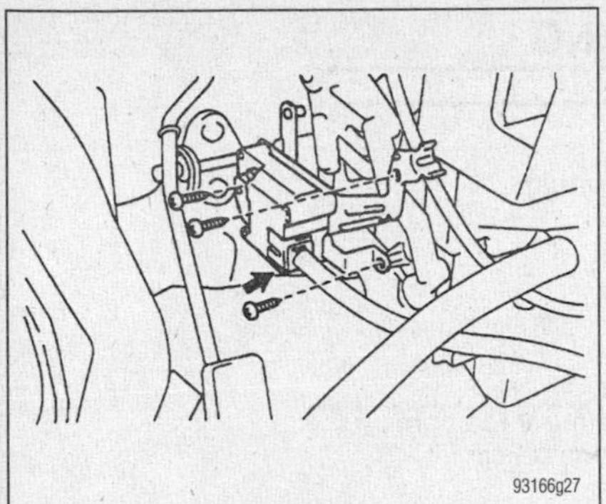

Fig. 58 Air outlet servomotor

4. Disconnect the linkage from the air outlet servomotor.
5. Remove the mounting screws and the air outlet servomotor.

To install:

6. Install the air outlet servomotor, tighten the mounting screws until snug.
7. Connect the linkage to the air outlet servomotor.
8. Attach the air outlet servomotor harness.
9. Install the instrument lower finish panel.
10. Connect the negative battery cable.

Air Conditioning Components

REMOVAL & INSTALLATION

Repair or service of air conditioning components is not covered by this manual, because of the risk of personal injury or death, and because of the legal ramifications of servicing these components without the proper EPA certification and experience. Cost, personal injury or death, environmental damage, and legal considerations (such as the fact that it is a federal crime to vent refrigerant into the atmosphere), dictate that the A/C components on your vehicle should be serviced only by a Motor Vehicle Air Conditioning (MVAC) trained, and EPA certified automotive technician.

CRUISE CONTROL

See Figure 59

The cruise control system is of the electronic stepper type and consists of an Electronic Control Unit (ECU), actuator, control switch and various other switches such as the parking brake switch. The ECU, when signaled by the steering column mounted switch, will command the electronic stepper motor to activate. This will lock the throttle, via a cable, thus holding the speed of the vehicle to the drivers desired setting.

Toyota's cruise control system also has its own diagnostic circuit that monitors and checks for malfunctions. If a malfunction occurs during cruise control driving, the ECU will cancel cruise control, and will blink the cruise control indicator to alert the driver of a problem in the system. At the same time the malfunction is stored in the ECU's memory as a diagnostic trouble code.

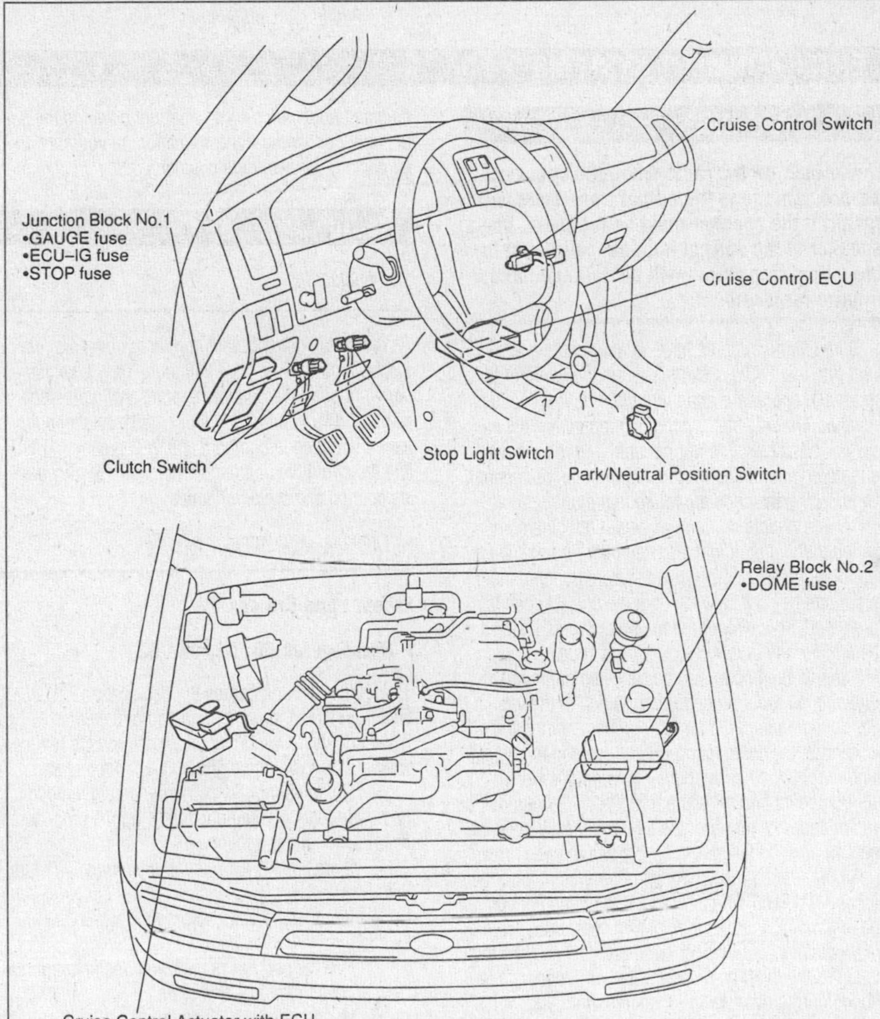

Fig. 59 Typical Toyota cruise control system components

CRUISE CONTROL TROUBLESHOOTING

Problem	Possible Cause
Will not hold proper speed	Incorrect cable adjustment Binding throttle linkage Leaking vacuum servo diaphragm Leaking vacuum tank Faulty vacuum or vent valve Faulty stepper motor Faulty transducer Faulty speed sensor Faulty cruise control module
Cruise intermittently cuts out	Clutch or brake switch adjustment too tight Short or open in the cruise control circuit Faulty transducer Faulty cruise control module
Vehicle surges	Kinked speedometer cable or casing Binding throttle linkage Faulty speed sensor Faulty cruise control module
Cruise control inoperative	Blown fuse Short or open in the cruise control circuit Faulty brake or clutch switch Leaking vacuum circuit Faulty cruise control switch Faulty stepper motor Faulty transducer Faulty speed sensor Faulty cruise control module

Note: Use this chart as a guide. Not all systems will use the components listed.

tcca6co1

ENTERTAINMENT SYSTEMS

** WARNING

Never operate the radio without a speaker; severe damage to the output transistors will result. If the speaker must be replaced, use a speaker of the correct impedance (ohms) or the output transistors will be damaged and require replacement.

Some audio systems have an anti-theft system built into them. The system requires the operator to select and program a code into the unit. If no code is installed, the anti-theft system is inoperative; the audio unit functions as a normal unit, even after power is restored after disconnection. Complete instructions for installing the code are found in the owners manual for the vehicle. As long as power remains connected to the unit, it may be used in the normal fashion. Once power is disconnected from the unit, the audio unit will not function until the correct code is re-entered. This will render the unit useless if stolen; there is no way to retrieve the stored code.

The anti-theft code may be canceled or changed following an exact procedure explained in the vehicles owners manual. If an error is made during the procedure, the designation ERR appears in the digital window. Once 10 errors have occurred, the word HELP appears and the system will not work regardless of codes or power. If the HELP message appears, the unit must be taken to a Toyota dealer to be reset.

All of the units equipped with this system have the words ANTI THEFT SYSTEM visible on the front of the unit, usually on the tape player door. Care must be taken when working on these vehicles anytime the battery cable must be disconnected or if fuses are removed during other test procedures. If it's your vehicle, chances are good that you know the code (if one was installed); if it's a friends vehicle, you could be in trouble. Always check with the owner before beginning any work which could interrupt power to the audio unit. For any further information on your particular unit, see your owners manual.

Radio

TESTING

There may be an occasion where your radio may display a code. This code will most likely be a flashing number on the display. It represents a problem with the unit. Your vehicle's owners manual should have a list of code numbers and their meaning. Before removing the unit for service, consult your owners manual and check for codes.

REMOVAL & INSTALLATION

Except Land Cruiser

➧ **See Figures 60, 61, and 62**

1. If audio unit carries the designation ANTI THEFT SYSTEM, make certain you or the vehicle owner knows the security code. If the code is not re-entered after installation, the unit will not operate.
2. On some models you may need to remove the heater control assembly, following the procedures given earlier in this section.
3. If not already done, carefully remove the trim plate.
4. Remove the bolts holding the audio unit to the dash.
5. Pull the unit out of the lower dash enough to allow access to the rear and sides.
6. Unplug the antenna cable.
7. Detach all wiring connectors.
8. Remove the radio with its bracket.

To install:

9. Fit the audio unit and bracket loosely in place; connect the antenna and wiring connectors.
10. Work the unit gently into position. Be careful not to pinch any wires or lines under or around the unit. Install the retaining screws.
11. If necessary, install the trim plate.
12. Install the heater control assembly.
13. Connect the negative battery cable.
14. Turn the ignition switch to **ACC** or **ON**. Turn the radio on and enter the security code if one is required. Check the system for correct operation.

Land Cruiser

1. Disconnect the negative battery cable. Remove the ashtray. Remove the ashtray holder.
2. Remove the 3 screws holding the lower instrument panel trim. The trim panel is also held by six clips; each must be gently pried loose.

** WARNING

The trim panel is long and thin; it is easily broken by rough handling.

3. Once the panel is loose, unplug the wiring connectors to the switches and remove the panel from the area.
4. Remove the screws holding the audio unit to the dash.
5. Pull the unit outward enough to allow access to the sides and back. Unplug the antenna cable and the electrical connectors. Remove the radio unit.

To install:

6. Loosely fit the unit into place and engage the antenna and electrical connections.
7. Fit the unit into the dash and install the retaining screws.

8. Hold the large dash panel in place and engage the wiring connectors to each switch.
9. Install the trim by aligning all the clips at once and gently pushing each into place. Install the retaining screws.
10. Install the ashtray holder and ashtray.
11. Connect the negative battery cable.
12. Turn the ignition switch to **ACC** or **ON**. Turn the radio on and enter the security code if one is required. Check the system for correct operation.

Speakers

REMOVAL & INSTALLATION

➡Always disconnect the negative battery cable before attempting to remove the speakers.

Dash Mounted

Dash mounted speakers can be accessed after removing the appropriate trim panel. These panels are usually retained by screws and clips. Be sure you have removed all of the attaching screws before prying the panel from the dash. Do not use excessive force on the panel as this will only lead to damage. Once the panel has been removed, loosen the speaker attaching bolts/screws, then pull the speaker from the dash and unplug the electrical connection.

Door Mounted

See Figures 63 thru 68

Door mounted speakers can be accessed after removing the door panel. For additional information on door panel removal, please refer to the following topic(s): Body, Door Panels. These panels are usually retained by screws and clips. Be sure you have removed all of the attaching screws before prying the panel from the door. A special tool can be purchased for this purpose. Do not use excessive force on the panel as this will only lead to damage. Once the panel has been removed, loosen the speaker attaching bolts/screws, then pull the speaker from its mount and unplug the electrical connection.

Rear Speakers

Removing the rear speakers involves basically the same procedure as the front speakers. Remove the appropriate trim panel, then remove the speaker. The rear speakers on some models can be accessed from inside the rear hatch.

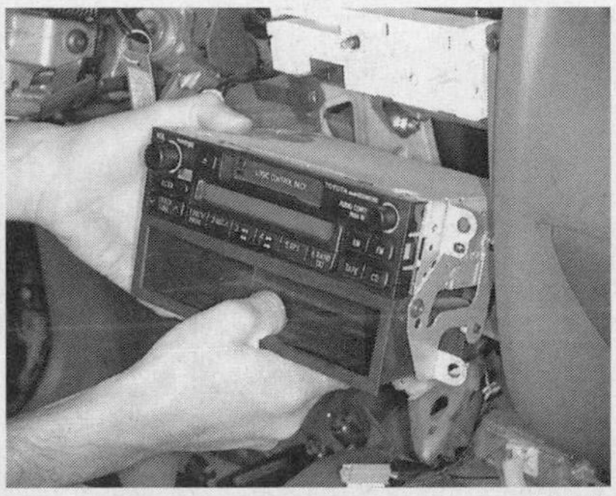

93166p56

Fig. 60 Pull the radio partially out of the dash for access to the antenna and connectors —1998 Tacoma shown

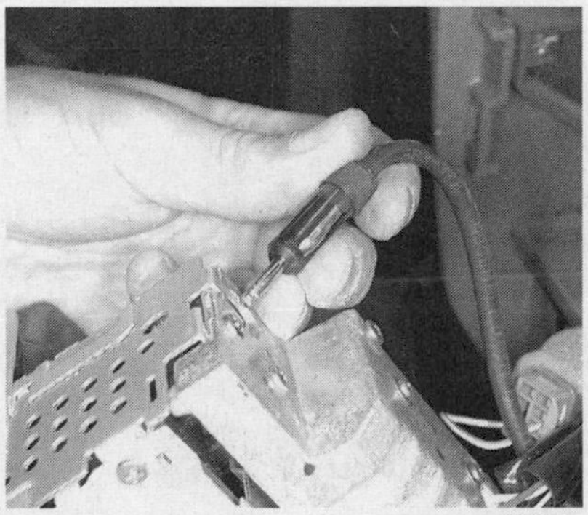

93166p57

Fig. 61 Pull the antenna lead from the rear of the radio

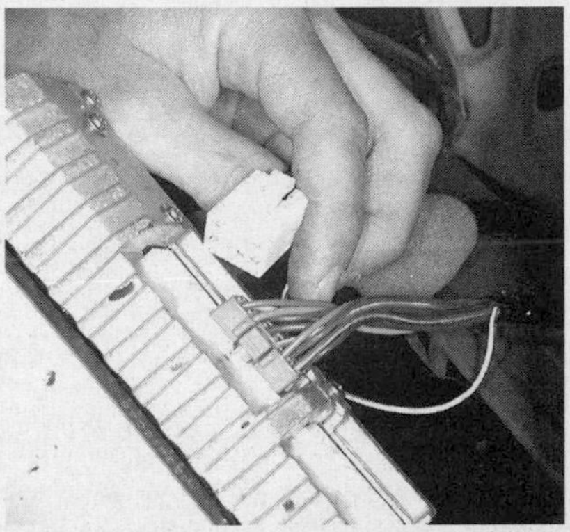

93166p58

Fig. 62 Detach all wiring harnesses

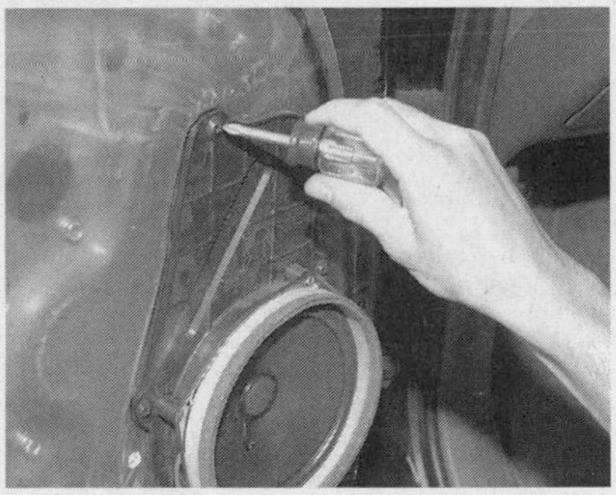

93166p29

Fig. 63 After removing the door panel, unfasten the speaker and mounting plate retaining screws . . .

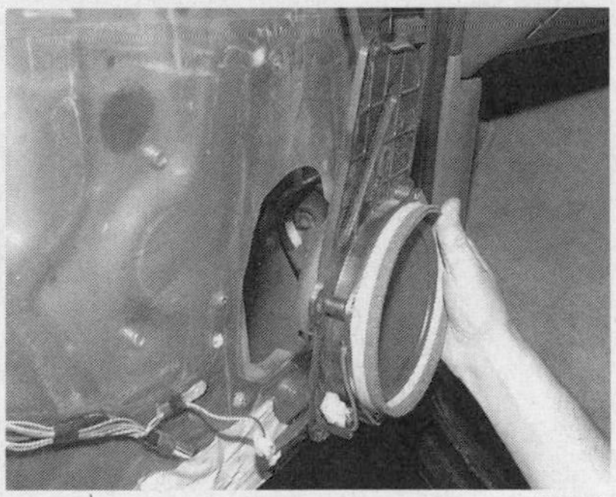

93166p30

Fig. 64 . . . then you can remove the speaker and mounting plate as an assembly

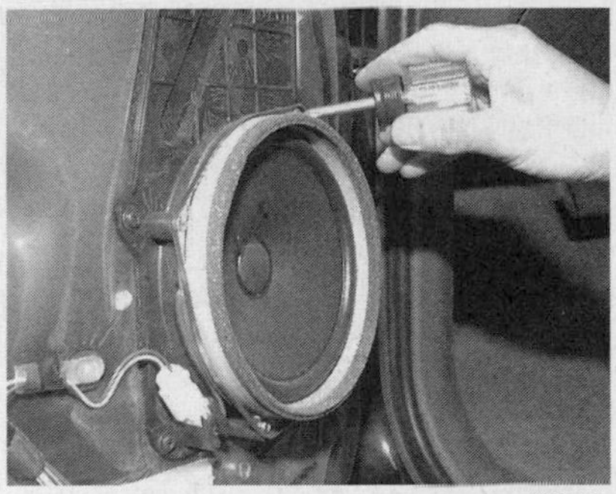

93166p27

Fig. 65 Or, you can remove the speaker from the mounting plate by unscrewing the four fasteners

93166p26

Fig. 66 Carefully pull the speaker from the door . . .

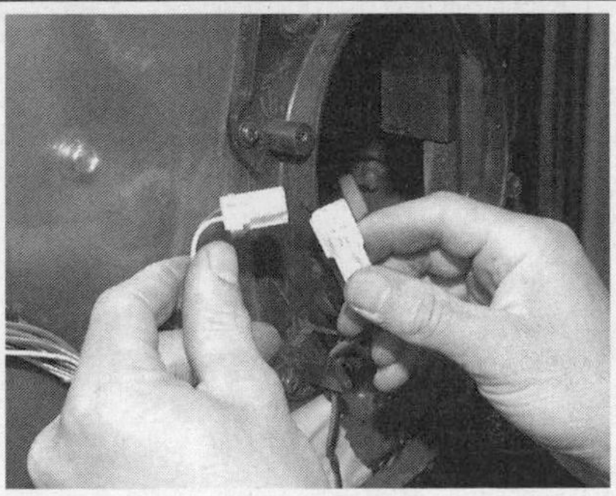

93166p25

Fig. 67 . . . then detach the speaker electrical connector

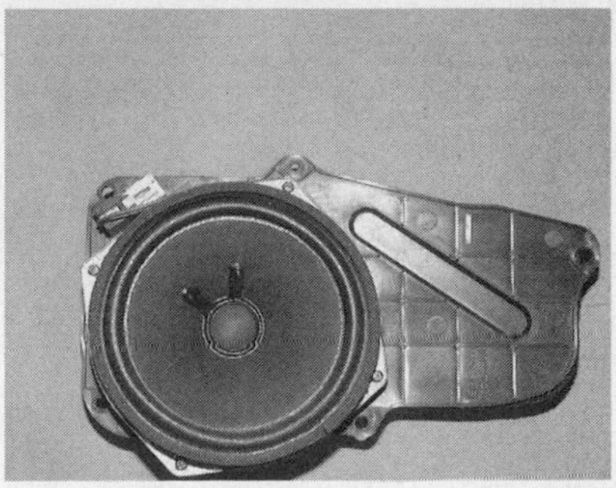

93166p31

Fig. 68 View of the speaker and mounting plate

WINDSHIELD WIPERS AND WASHERS

Windshield Wiper Blade and Arm

REMOVAL & INSTALLATION

See Figures 69 and 70

Wiper blade element replacement is covered in General Information and Maintenance.

Toyota has two types of wiper blades. The screw-on type and the clip-on type.

To remove the clip-on type, lift up the wiper arm from the windshield. Lift up on the spring release tab on the wiper blade-to-wiper arm connector, then pull the blade assembly off the wiper arm.

To remove the screw-on type, lift up the wiper arm from the windshield. Loosen and remove the two screws retaining the blade to the arm, then lift the blade assembly off the wiper arm.

1. There may be a cover over the nut, remove this to access the nut.
2. With the arm in the down position, unscrew the nut which secures it to the pivot.
3. Matchmark the arm to the shaft.
4. Carefully pull the arm upward and off the pivot.

To install:

5. Install the arm by placing the arm onto the linkage shaft. Make sure it is seated correctly; if not correctly aligned, the blade will slap the bodywork at the top or bottom of its stroke. Tighten the nut to approximately 15 ft. lbs. (20 Nm).

If one wiper arm does not move when turned on or only moves a little bit, check the retaining nut at the bottom of the arm. The extra effort of moving snow or wet leaves off the glass can cause the nut to come loose, and as a result, the pivot will move without moving the arm.

Front Windshield Wiper Motor

REMOVAL & INSTALLATION

See Figures 71, 72, 73, and 74

The wiper motor is located in the engine compartment and is secured to the firewall.

1. Disconnect the wiring from the wiper motor.
2. Unbolt the wiper motor and remove it from the firewall.
3. Gently pry the wiper link from the crank arm. Its a ball and socket arrangement, but it may be tight.
4. Remove the motor.

To install:

5. Connect the wiper arm linkage. The socket must be exactly aligned with the ball before snapping them together.
6. Install the motor, tighten the mounting nuts to 47 inch lbs. (6 Nm).
7. Attach the electrical lead.

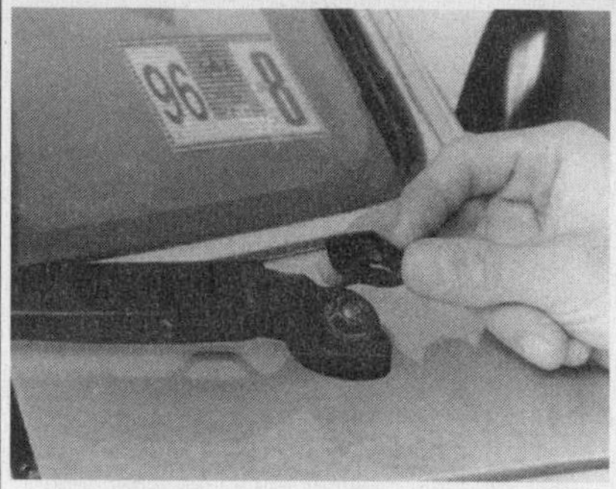

86826p10

Fig. 69 Remove the cover concealing the wiper arm nut

86826p11

Fig. 70 Loosen and remove the wiper arm retaining nut

86826p13

Fig. 71 Unplug the wiring harness from the motor assembly

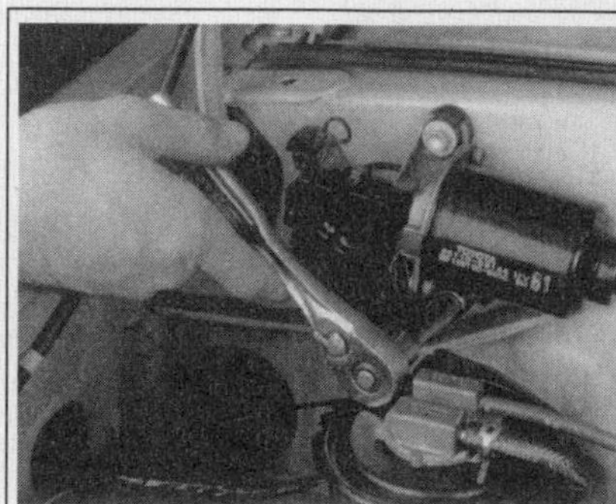

86826p14

Fig. 72 Remove the bolts securing the wiper motor from the firewall

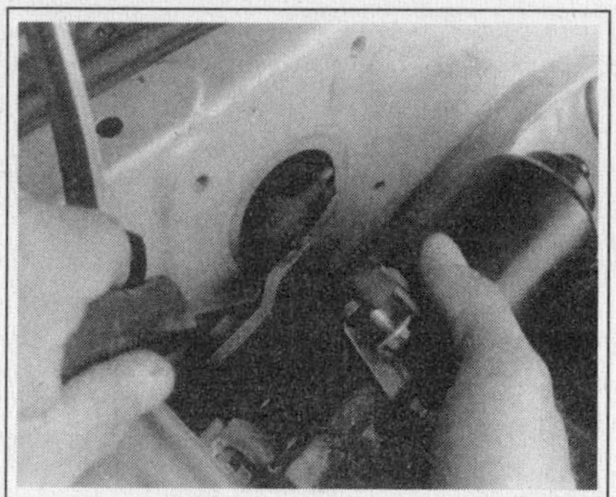

86826p15

Fig. 73 Pull the motor from the firewall, then using a prybar . . .

86826p16

Fig. 74 . . . separate the linkage from the motor

Rear Wiper Motor

REMOVAL & INSTALLATION

4Runner

TOP MOUNTED

See Figure 75

1. Make certain the ignition switch is **OFF**.
2. Pop up the acorn nut cover, remove the nut and pull off the rear wiper.
3. Remove the pivot nut.
4. Inside, above the tailgate, pop out the clips and remove the wiper motor cover.
5. Disconnect the electrical lead and the washer hose, remove the mounting bolts and lift out the wiper motor.

To install:

6. Position the wiper motor and install the mounting bolts.
7. Connect the lead and the washer hose.
8. Position the wiper motor cover over the opening and press in the retaining clips.
9. Install the pivot nut and tighten it to 8 ft. lbs. (11 Nm).
10. Install the wiper arm and tighten the acorn nut to 48 inch lbs. (5 Nm). Snap the cover down.

BOTTOM MOUNTED

See Figures 76 and 77

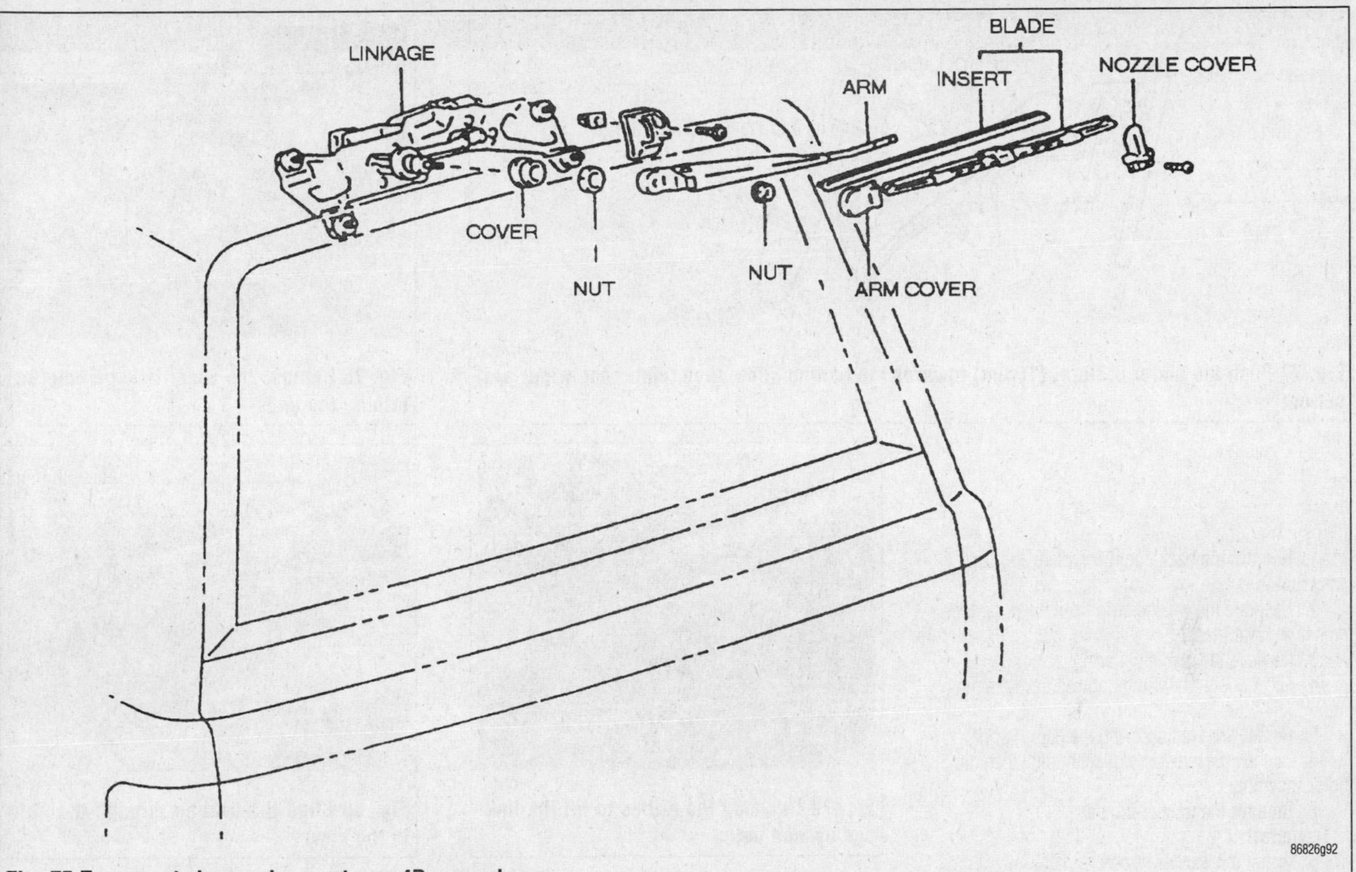

Fig. 75 Top mounted rear wiper system—4Runner shown

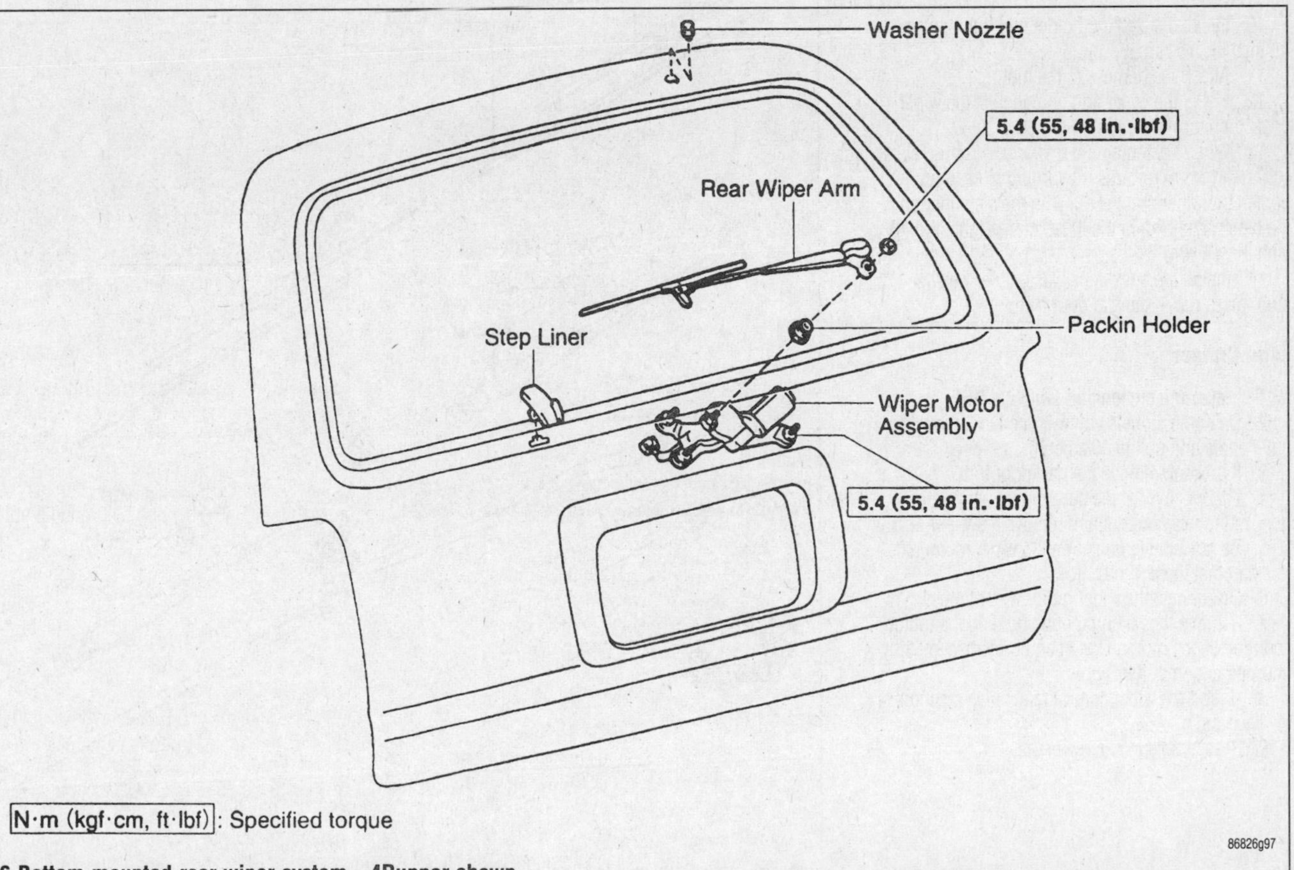

Fig. 76 Bottom mounted rear wiper system—4Runner shown

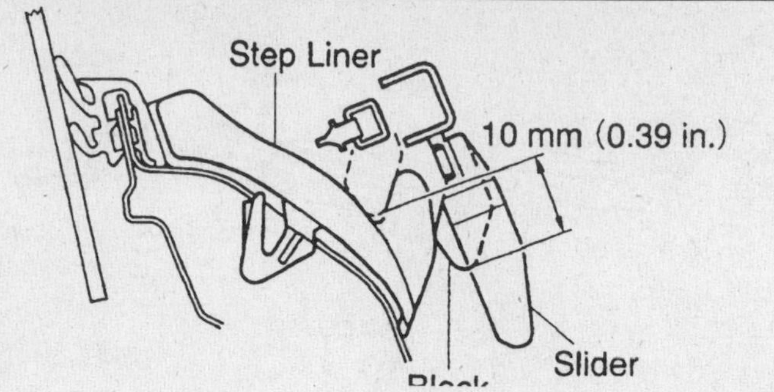

86828gmz

Fig. 77 Push the slider 0.39 in. (10mm) towards the turning slide, then tighten the wiper arm set nut

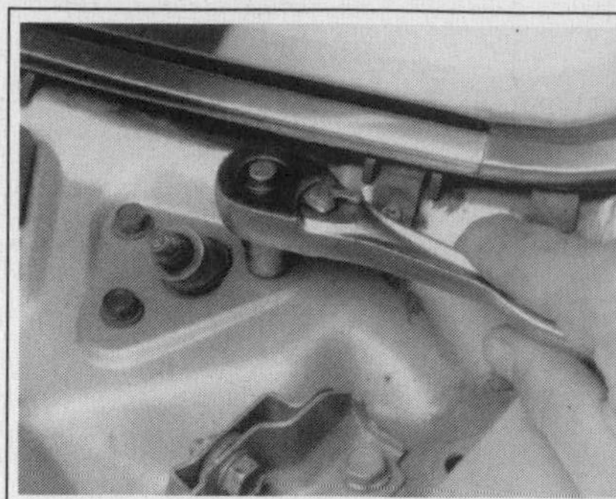

86826p17

Fig. 78 Remove the wiper linkage bolts retaining the ends

1. Remove the back door trim, plate and door glass run.
2. Separate the weatherstrip from the door, then remove the rear glass.
3. Remove the rear wiper arm.
4. Disconnect the wiring harness from the motor.
5. Remove the nut securing the packing holder.
6. Loosen the wiper motor seat bolts, then the motor assembly.
7. Remove the washer nozzle.

To install:

8. Install the washer nozzle.
9. Tighten the wiper motor bolts, then install the motor assembly. Tighten the motor bolts to 48 inch lbs. (5 Nm).
10. Install the packing holder and nut, tighten to 48 inch lbs. (5 Nm).
11. Attach the harness to the motor.
12. Install the wiper arm and operate the wiper once, then turn the wiper switch off.
13. When tightening the rear arm, push the slider 0.39 in. (10mm) towards the turning slide, then tighten the wiper arm set nut with the step liner on the block as shown in the illustration. Tighten to 48 inch lbs. (5 Nm).
14. Install the back door glass, outer weatherstrip, glass run, plate and door trim.

Land Cruiser

1. Make sure the ignition switch is **OFF**.
2. On some models you will need to remove the pull handle and pull handle bezel.
3. If present, remove the backdoor trim.
4. Lift the cover at the base of the rear wiper arm, remove the retaining nut and remove the wiper arm.
5. Remove the large nut on the wiper motor axle (the part that the arm bolts to).
6. Disconnect the wiper motor wire harness.
7. Remove the retaining bolts holding the motor and remove the motor. Don't bend or damage nearby linkages or components.
8. Unbolt the wiper control relay, then disconnect the harness.
9. Reassemble in reverse order.

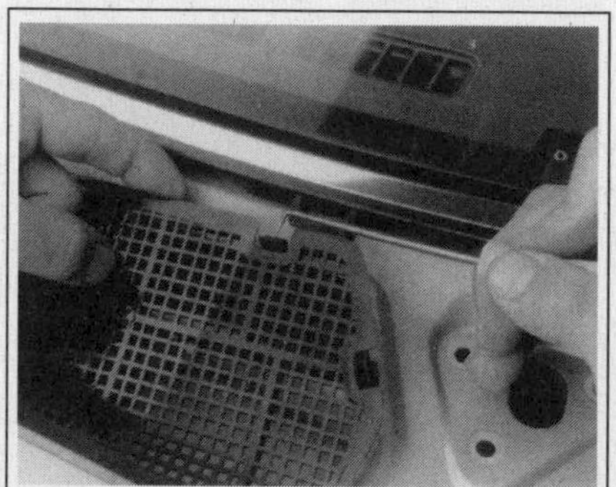

86826p18

Fig. 79 Unclamp the grilles to lift the linkage up and out

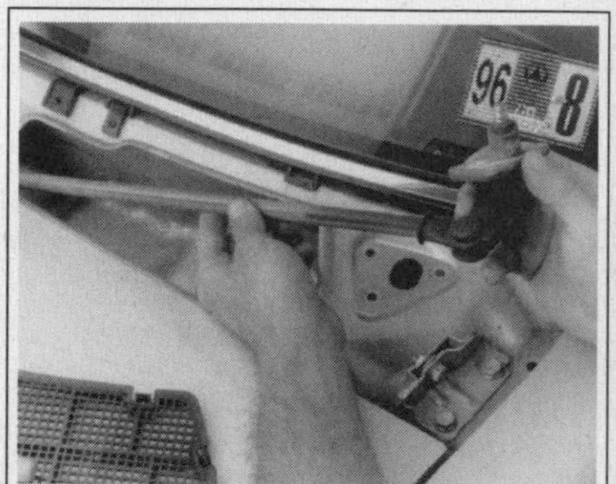

86826p19

Fig. 80 Slide the linkage through the hole in the cowl

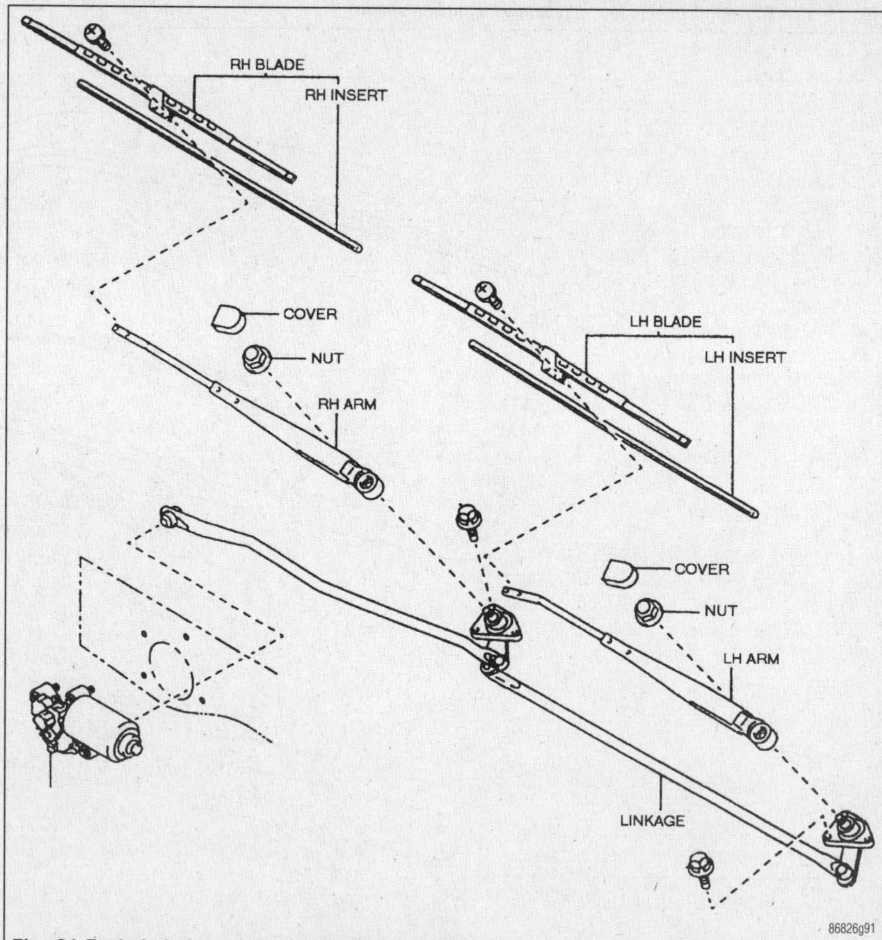

86826g91

Fig. 81 Exploded view of the front wiper linkage

Wiper Linkage

REMOVAL & INSTALLATION

➧ **See Figures 78, 79, 80, and 81**

1. Remove the wiper motor.
2. Separate the wiper arms by removing their retaining nuts and working them off their shafts.
3. Remove the nuts/bolts and spacers holding the wiper shafts.
4. Unclamp the grilles that cover the linkage, then push the shafts down into the body cavity. Pull the linkage out of the cavity through the wiper motor hole.

To install:

5. Insert the wiper linkage through the hole and install the nuts and spacers.
6. Press the wiper arm onto their shafts and install the retaining nuts.
7. Install the wiper motor.

Washer Fluid Reservoir

REMOVAL & INSTALLATION

➧ **See Figures 82 and 83**

1. Unbolt the washer reservoir from the upper radiator support.
2. Lift the unit from the engine compartment, then slide the hose from the unit.
3. Unhook the wiring harness for the pump from the side of the reservoir.
4. Disconnect the wiring harness from the pump, then remove the pump from the reservoir. Check the condition of the grommet that the pump sits on.

To install:

5. Install the pump into the reservoir, ensure the grommet is in good condition.
6. Attach the wiring to the pump, then run the hose for the pump along the side of the reservoir.
7. Seat the reservoir into the engine compartment, secure with the mounting bolt.

Washer Pump

REMOVAL & INSTALLATION

➧ **See Figures 84 thru 89**

1. Remove the washer reservoir from the vehicle.
2. Unhook the wiring harness for the pump from the side of the reservoir.
3. Disconnect the wiring harness from the pump, then remove the pump from the reservoir.

➡Check the condition of the grommet that the pump sits on.

To install:

4. Install the pump into the reservoir, ensure the grommet is in good condition.
5. Attach the wiring to the pump, then run the hose for the pump along the side of the reservoir.
6. Seat the reservoir into the engine compartment. Secure with the mounting bolt.

86826p20

Fig. 82 Unbolt the reservoir bracket from the upper radiator support

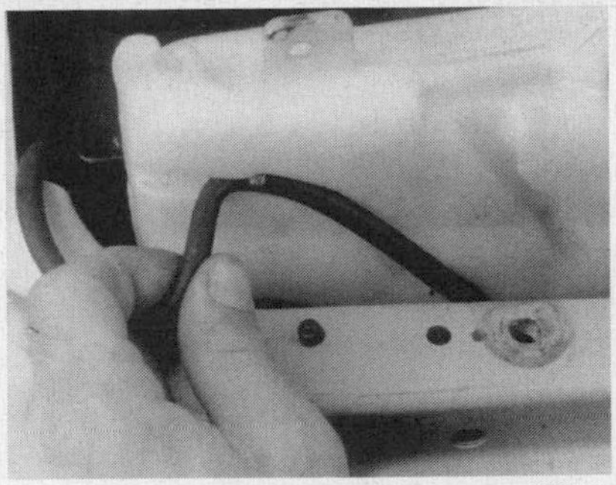

86826p21

Fig. 83 Lift the unit from the engine compartment, then slide the hose from the unit

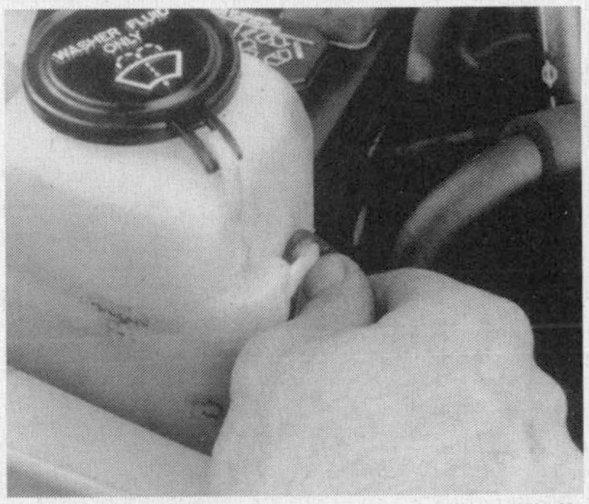

86826p22

Fig. 84 Unhook the wiring harness for the pump from the side of the reservoir

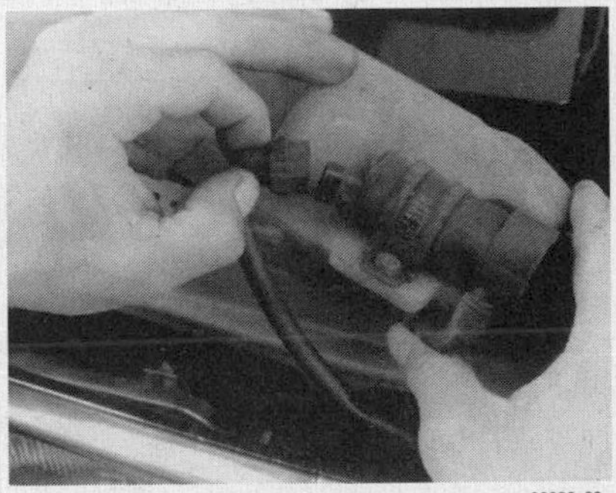

86826p23

Fig. 85 Disconnect the wiring harness from the pump, then remove the pump from the reservoir

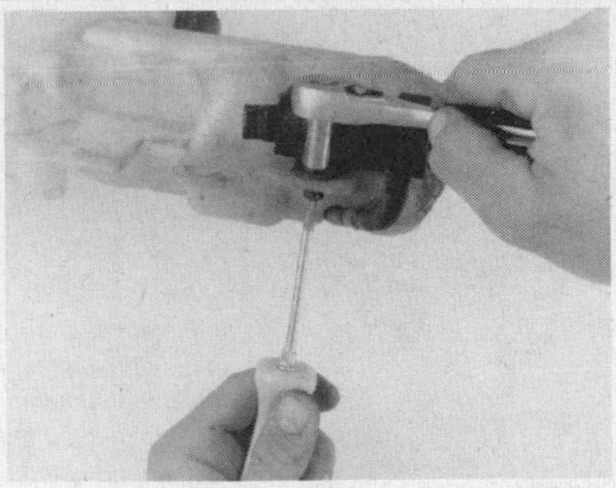

86826p26

Fig. 86 Remove the bolts retaining the pump to the reservoir

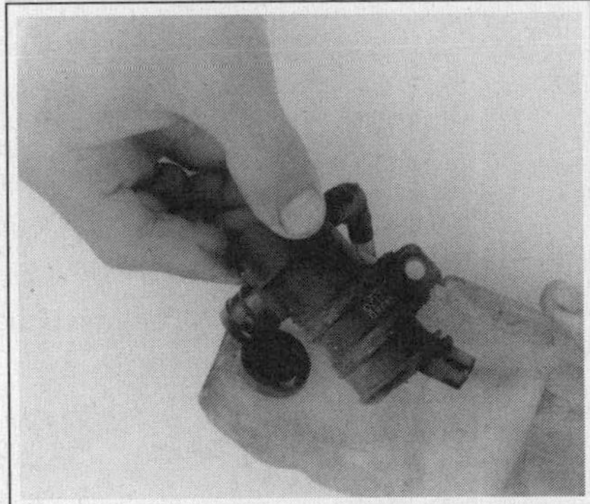

86826p27

Fig. 87 Pull the pump from the grommet

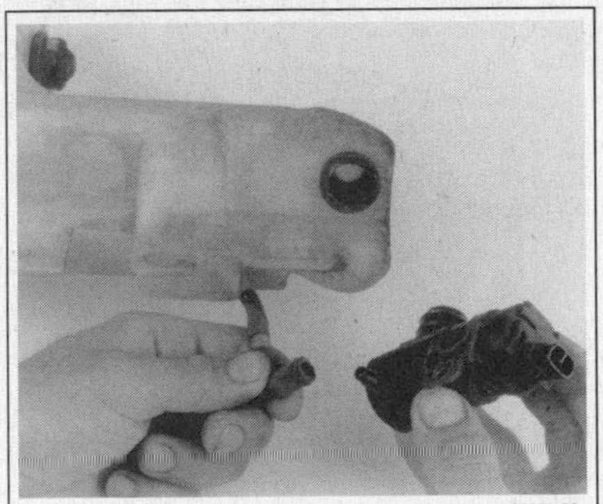

86826p28

Fig. 88 Remove the hose from the pump

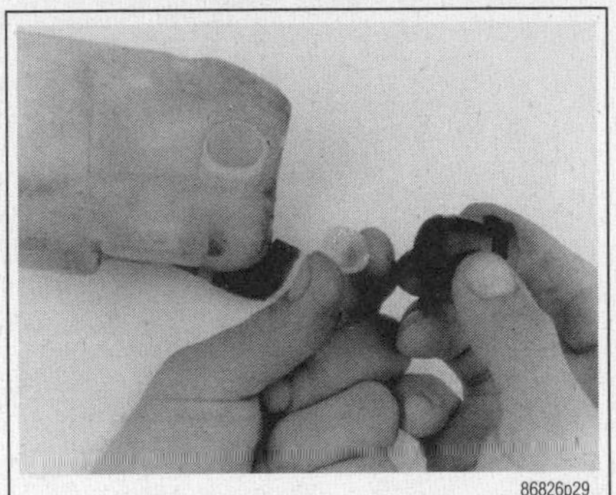

86826p29

Fig. 89 Remove the grommet and screen, then inspect for deterioration

INSTRUMENTS AND SWITCHES

To keep our terms straight, we'll use Toyota's names for various dash components. The instrument panel is what you may call the dashboard; it runs completely across the front of the vehicle. The instrument panel is covered with a soft vinyl surface called the safety pad. The safety pad is the part you see; the instrument panel is the framework under it. All the instruments and warning lamps in front of the driver are contained in the instrument cluster, sometimes called the gauge set or combination meter. The instrument cluster is removed as a unit.

Generally, numbered components use a numbering system with item 1 on the left side of the vehicle. Knowing how many numbered components there are can be helpful, too. For example, if heater ducts Nos. 1, 2 and 3, must be removed, its a fair bet that No. 2 is in the center. If the procedure only refers to Nos. 1 and 2, one may be on the left side and 2 on the right of the passenger compartment.

When disassembling components, always suspect the hidden screw or clip. Much of the fit and finish in the interior is accomplished by using concealed retainers to keep panels in place. Don't force anything during removal; if any resistance is felt, search out the hidden connector. Some of the panels assemble only in the correct order; pay attention. Take note of which bolts and screws go into each retainer; a too-long bolt can damage wiring or components behind the assembly being held.

Finally, understand that this is a lengthy project. Work slowly and carefully so as not to damage anything. Label or mark each electrical connector as it is disconnected; many of the plastic connector shells can be marked with an indelible laundry pen or similar marker. As a panel or component is removed, disconnect the wiring running to switches or components held by the panel. Be careful working around wires and harnesses; most are held by retainers and do not allow a lot of slack.

Instrument Cluster

REMOVAL & INSTALLATION

4Runner and Tundra

See Figures 90 thru 96

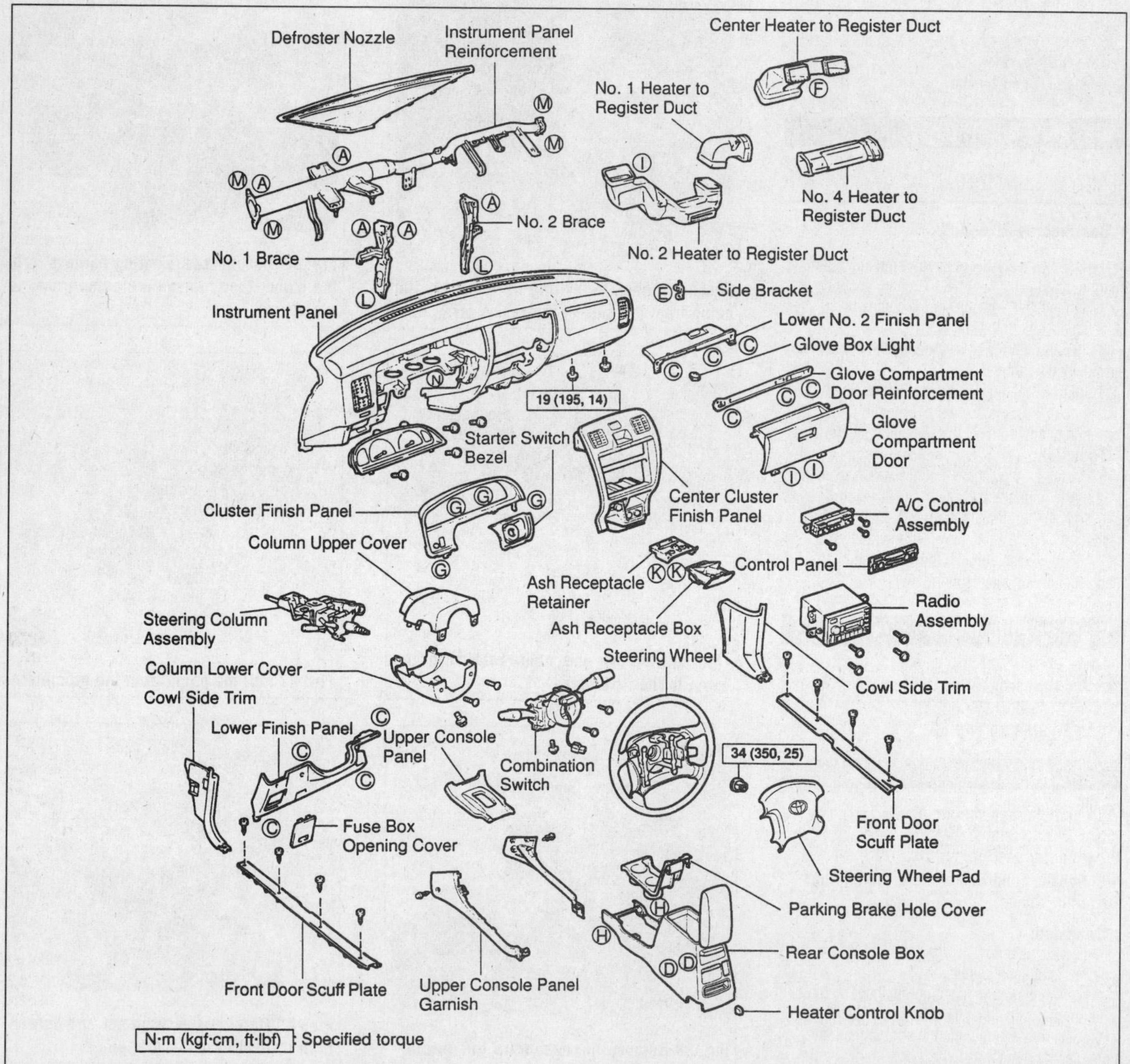

Fig. 90 Exploded view of the instrument panel components

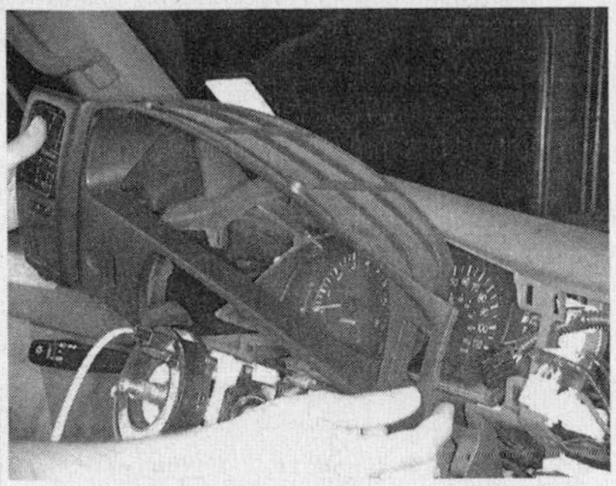

93166p61

Fig. 91 Unfasten all of the screws, then remove the cluster finish panel

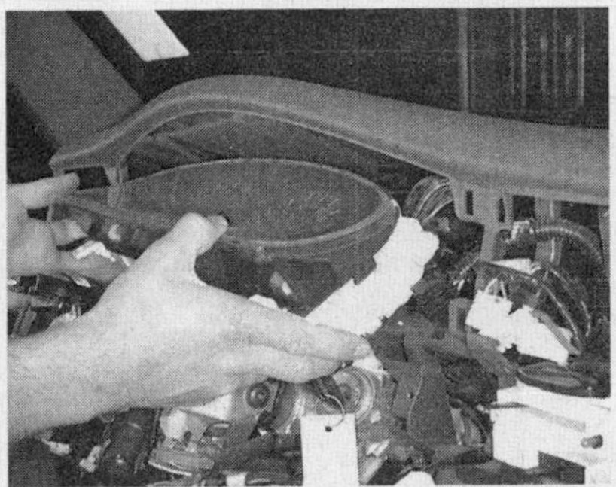

93166p63

Fig. 93 You may have to turn the instrument cluster to remove it

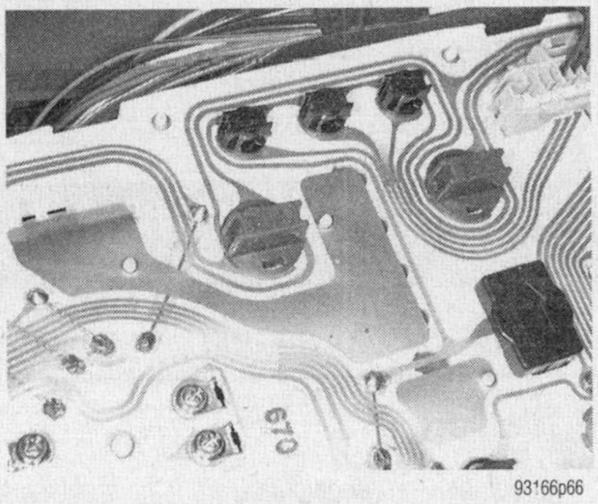

93166p66

Fig. 95 The instrument cluster is powered via a printed circuit board. This grid of etched copper paths supplies the necessary current to all of the gauges

✲✲ CAUTION

Your vehicle may contain an air bag system. Make sure to follow all precautions and use the proper procedure for disarming the system before proceeding.

1. Disable the SRS system.
2. Disconnect the negative battery cable.
3. Remove the steering wheel. For additional information, please refer to the following topic(s): Suspension and Steering, Steering Wheel.
4. Remove the cowl side trim and the front door scuff plate.
5. Remove the retainers securing the lower finish panel, then remove the hood and fuel tank release lever screws.

93166p62

Fig. 92 View of the instrument cluster as it appears in the vehicle

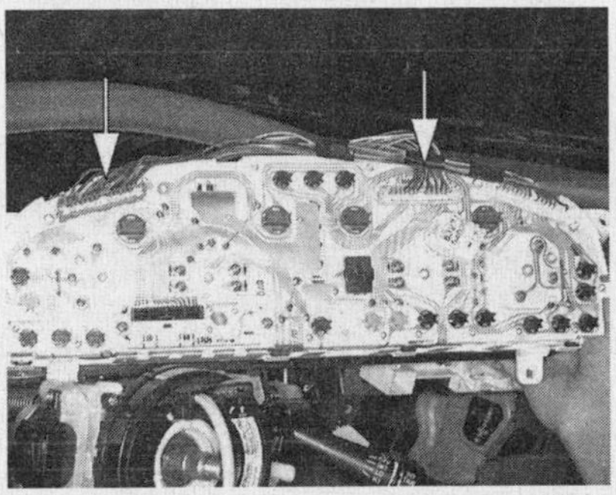

93166p64

Fig. 94 Detach all wiring from the instrument cluster

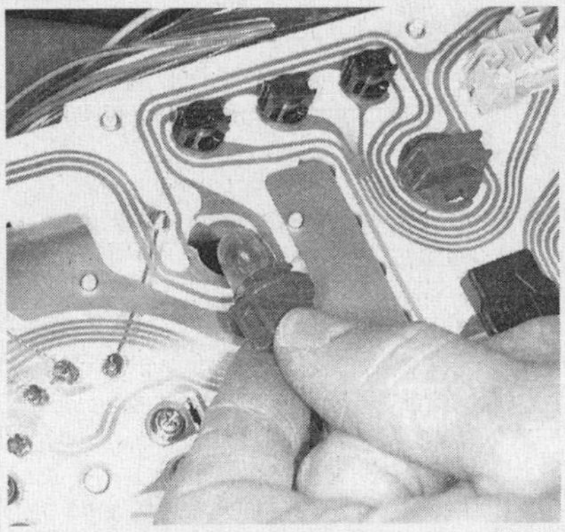

93166p65

Fig. 96 Twist the bulb holder to the left to remove a burned out bulb

6. Remove the ignition switch bezel.
7. Detach the No. 2 and No. 1 heater-to-register duct.
8. Remove the cluster finish panel, then remove.
9. Disconnect the harness for the instrument cluster. Remove the screws securing the meter, then remove it from the vehicle.

To install:

10. Attach the harness to the instrument cluster, then attach to the vehicle.
11. Tighten the cluster finish panel.
12. Attach the No. 2 and No. 1 heater to register duct.
13. Install the ignition switch bezel.
14. Install the lower finish panel, then attach the hood and fuel tank release lever.
15. Install the cowl side trim and the front door scuff plate.
16. Install the steering wheel.
17. Connect the negative battery cable.

Tacoma

✲✲ CAUTION

Your vehicle may contain an air bag system. Make sure to follow all precautions and use the proper procedure for disarming the system before proceeding.

1. Disable the SRS system.
2. Disconnect the negative battery cable.
3. Remove the steering wheel. For additional information, please refer to the following topic(s): Suspension and Steering, Steering Wheel.
4. Remove the following:
   a. Steering column cover
   b. Hood lock release lever
   c. Combination switch
   d. Fuse box cover
5. Remove the lower left hand finish panel.
6. Remove the following parts:
   a. Ignition switch bezel
   b. No. 2 heater-to-register
   c. Steering column
7. Remove the cup holder and the heater control knobs.
8. With the aid of a flat-bladed tool, carefully remove the heater control panel.
9. Disconnect the hazard harness.
10. Remove the mounting screws for the center cluster finish panel.
11. Detach the heater control assembly.
12. Remove the radio.
13. Remove the screws mounting the cluster finish panel, then lower the panel.
14. Remove the instrument cluster screws and the speedometer cable.
15. Disconnect the harness.

To install:

16. Attach the harness to the instrument cluster.
17. Install the speedometer cable, then the instrument cluster.
18. Install the cluster finish panel.
19. Install the radio.
20. Place the heater control assembly in the dash.
21. Reinstall the mounting screws for the center cluster finish panel and tighten.
22. Install the harness for the hazard switch.
23. Place the heater control panel in the dash.
24. Install the cup holder and the heater control knobs.
25. Reattach the following parts:
   a. Ignition switch bezel
   b. No. 2 heater-to-register
   c. Steering column
26. Tighten the lower left hand finish panel.
27. Install the following:
   a. Steering column cover
   b. Hood lock release lever
   c. Combination switch
   d. Fuse box cover
28. Install the steering wheel, then connect the negative battery cable.

T100

✲✲ CAUTION

Your vehicle may contain an air bag system. Make sure to follow all precautions and use the proper procedure for disarming the system before proceeding.

1. Disable the SRS system.
2. Disconnect the negative battery cable.
3. Remove the front pillar garnish.
4. Unscrew the front door scuff plate and the cowl side trims.
5. Remove the steering wheel. For additional information, please refer to the following topic(s): Suspension and Steering, Steering Wheel.
6. Remove the following:
   a. Steering column cover
   b. Disconnect the hood lock release lever
   c. Detach the No. 1 lower finish panel
   d. Remove the combination switch
   e. Remove the glove box door
   f. Detach the No. 2 lower finish panel
   g. Remove the lower center panel
7. Remove the screws retaining the center cluster finish panel, then detach the harness from the unit.
8. Remove the stereo opening cover.
9. Remove the screws securing the meter, then remove the instrument cluster from the dash.

To install:

10. Tighten the instrument cluster into place.
11. Attach the stereo opening cover.
12. Attach the cluster harness, then install and tighten the screws that retain the center cluster finish panel.
13. Install the following:
    a. Steering column cover
    b. Install the hood lock release lever
    c. Attach the No. 1 lower finish panel
    d. Install the combination switch
    e. Install the glove box door
    f. Install the No. 2 lower finish panel
    g. Install the lower center panel
14. Install the steering wheel.
15. Attach, then tighten the front door scuff plate and the cowl side trims.
16. Place the front pillar garnish into position and tighten the screws.
17. Connect the negative battery cable.

Land Cruiser

✲✲ CAUTION

Your vehicle may contain an air bag system. Make sure to follow all precautions and use the proper procedure for disarming the system before proceeding.

1. Disable the SRS system.
2. Disconnect the negative battery cable.
3. Remove the steering wheel. For additional information, please refer to the following topic(s): Suspension and Steering, Steering Wheel.
4. Apply strips of protective tape on the inside of each windshield pillar. This will protect the trim during removal.
5. Remove the upper and lower steering column covers.
6. Remove the hood release and fuel door release levers.
7. Remove the fuse box opening cover.
8. Remove the retaining screws for the lower trim panel below the steering column.
9. Remove the lower instrument panel.
10. Disconnect the No. 2 heater-to-register duct.
11. Loosen the screws and remove the fuse block.
12. Detach the No. 2 center cluster finish panel.
13. Remove the steering column.
14. Detach the cluster finish panel, then the instrument cluster.
15. Remove the center cluster finish panel assembly with the clock attached.
16. With the aid of a taped prytool, take off the 2 claws, then remove the cup holder hole cover.
17. Remove the ashtray.
18. Remove the center cluster finish panel with the heater control assembly, then disconnect the harness.
19. Remove the screws retaining the heater control assembly from the center cluster finish panel.
20. Remove the following:
    a. Radio
    b. Glove compartment door
    c. Speaker panel
    d. Speaker
    e. Front console box
    f. Rear console box
21. Loosen and remove the 5 screws and 9 bolts holding the instrument panel.
22. Remove the lower instrument panel reinforcement, then the No. 1 brace and the instrument panel.

To install:

23. Attach the No. 1 brace and lower instrument panel, then the instrument panel reinforcement.
24. Tighten the 5 screws and 9 bolts holding the instrument panel.
25. Install the following:
    a. Radio
    b. Glove compartment door
    c. Speaker panel
    d. Speaker
    e. Front console box
    f. Rear console box
26. Tighten the screws retaining the heater control assembly to the center cluster finish panel.
27. Connect the harness to the heater control, then attach the center cluster finish panel with the heater control assembly.
28. Reinstall the ashtray.
29. Place the cup holder hole cover into position.
30. Install the center cluster finish panel assembly with the clock attached.
31. Install the instrument cluster.
32. Attach the cluster finish panel.
33. Install the steering column.
34. Attach the No. 2 center cluster finish panel.
35. Install the fuse block.
36. Insert and attach the No. 2 heater-to-register duct.
37. Install and tighten down the lower instrument panel.
38. Place the lower trim panel below the steering column, then tighten.
39. Attach the fuse box opening cover.
40. Place into position, then tighten down the hood release and fuel door release levers.
41. Attach the upper and lower steering column covers.
42. Install the steering wheel.
43. Connect the negative battery cable.

Speedometer, Tachometer and Gauges

REMOVAL & INSTALLATION

➧ See Figure 97

1. Remove the gauge cluster from the dashboard.
2. Remove the lens covering the gauges.
3. Remove the printed circuit board from the back of the cluster. This can be done by removing any attaching screws and by removing the bulbs from the unit.
4. Remove the gauge attaching screws.
5. Installation is the reverse of removal.

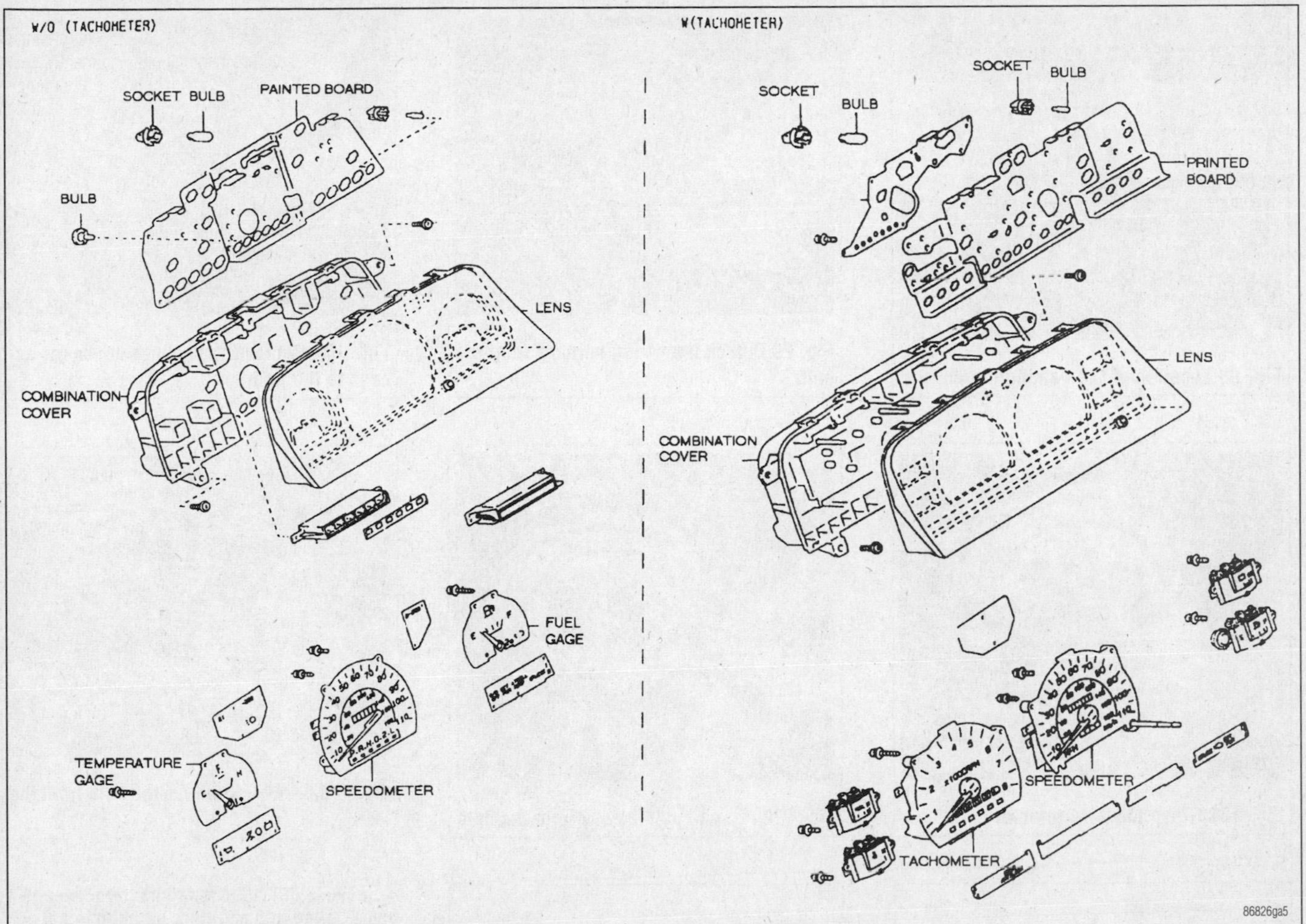

Fig. 97 Exploded view of the instrument cluster assembly

LIGHTING

Headlights

There are two general styles of headlamps, the sealed beam and replaceable bulb type. The sealed beam type of headlamps are used on older vehicles that were built through the 1980s. The sealed beam is so named because it includes the lamp (filament), the reflector and the lens in one sealed unit. Sealed beams are available in several sizes and shapes.

The replaceable bulb is the newer technology. All vehicles covered by this manual use the replaceable bulb, or composite headlight bulb. Using a small halogen bulb, only the lamp is replaced, while the lens and reflector are part of the body of the car. This is generally the style found on wrap-around or "European" lighting systems. While the replaceable bulbs are more expensive than sealed beams, they generally produce more and better light. The fixed lenses and reflectors can be engineered to allow better frontal styling and better light distribution for a particular vehicle.

It is quite possible to replace a headlight of either type without affecting the alignment (aim) of the light. Sealed beams mount into a bracket (bucket) to which springs are attached. The adjusting screws control the position of the bucket which in turn aims the light. Replaceable bulbs simply fit into the back of the reflector. The lens and reflector unit are aimed by separate adjusting screws.

Take a moment before disassembly to identify the large adjusting screws (generally two for each lamp, one above and one at the side) and don't change their settings.

REMOVAL & INSTALLATION

See Figures 98 thru 105

1. With the ignition switch **OFF** and the headlamp switch OFF, raise and prop the hood.
2. Locate the headlight bulb, then unplug the connector for the bulb.
3. Turn the plastic cover counterclockwise, then remove it.
4. Remove the rubber cover.
5. Release the bulb retaining spring, then carefully remove the bulb from the headlight lens.

To install:

6. Align the tabs of the bulb with the cutout of the mounting hole and install the bulb.
7. Install the retaining spring, then attach the rubber cover. Make sure the rubber cover is snug on the connector and the headlight body.
8. Install the plastic cover with the ON mark facing upwards. Turn it clockwise, then insert the connector.
9. Aiming is usually not necessary after replacing these types of bulbs.

93166p01

Fig. 98 Location of the headlight bulb

93166p07

Fig. 99 Detach the wiring harness from the bulb

93166p09

Fig. 100 Remove the rubber cover for access to the bulb

93166p10

Fig. 101 Grasp the wire retainer . . .

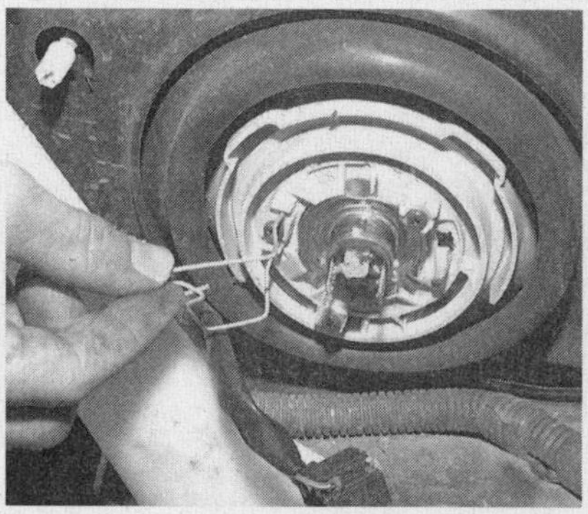

93166p11

Fig. 102 . . . and pull it away from the bulb

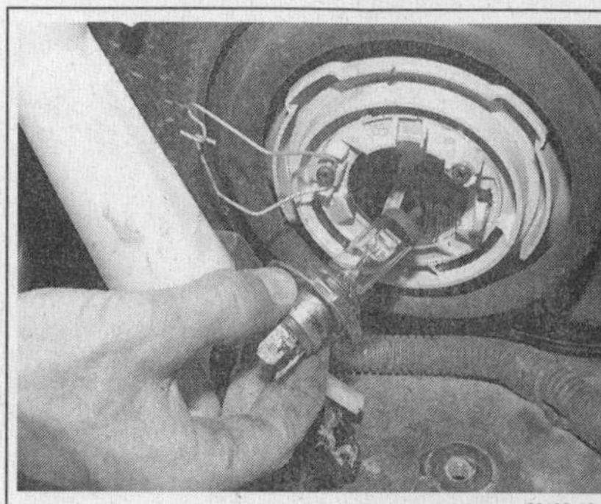

93166p12

Fig. 103 Carefully remove the bulb from the lens

86826gc1

Fig. 104 Make sure the rubber cover is snug on the connector and the headlight body

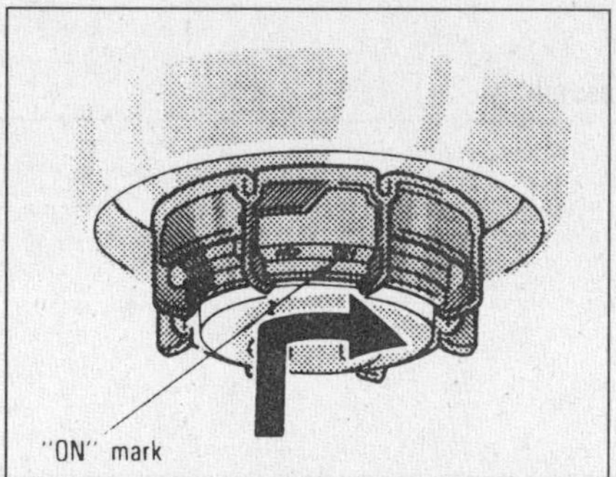

86826gc2

Fig. 105 Install the plastic cover with the ON mark facing upwards. Turn it clockwise, then insert the connector

AIMING THE HEADLIGHTS

➧ **See Figures 106, 107, 108, and 109**

The headlights must be properly aimed to provide the best, safest road illumination. The lights should be checked for proper aim and adjusted as necessary. Certain state and local authorities have requirements for headlight aiming; these should be checked before adjustment is made.

CAUTION

About once a year, when the headlights are replaced or any time front end work is performed on your vehicle, the headlight should be accurately aimed by a reputable repair shop using the proper equipment. Headlights not properly aimed can make it virtually impossible to see and may blind other drivers on the road, possibly causing an accident. Note that the following procedure is a temporary fix, until you can take your vehicle to a repair shop for a proper adjustment.

Headlight adjustment may be temporarily made using a wall, as described below, or on the rear of another vehicle. When adjusted, the lights should not glare in oncoming car or truck windshields, nor should they illuminate the passenger compartment of vehicles driving in front of you. These adjustments are rough and should always be fine-tuned by a repair shop which is equipped with headlight aiming tools. Improper adjustments may be both dangerous and illegal.

➡Because the composite headlight assembly is bolted into position, no adjustment should be necessary or possible. Some applications, however, may be bolted to an adjuster plate or may be retained by adjusting screws. If so, follow this procedure when adjusting the lights, BUT always have the adjustment checked by a reputable shop.

Before removing the headlight bulb or disturbing the headlamp in any way, note the current settings in order to ease headlight adjustment upon reassembly. If the high or low beam setting of the old lamp still works, this can be done using the wall of a garage or a building:

1. Park the vehicle on a level surface, with the fuel tank about $^1/_2$ full and with the vehicle empty of all extra cargo (unless normally carried). The vehicle should be facing a wall which is no less than 6 feet (1.8m) high and 12 feet (3.7m) wide. The front of the vehicle should be about 25 feet from the wall.
2. If aiming is to be performed outdoors, it is advisable to wait until dusk in order to properly see the headlight beams on the wall. If done in a garage, darken the area around the wall as much as possible by closing shades or hanging cloth over the windows.
3. Turn the headlights **ON** and mark the wall at the center of each light's low beam, then switch on the brights and mark the center of each light's high beam. A short length of masking tape which is visible from the front of the vehicle may be used. Although marking all four positions is advisable, marking one position from each light should be sufficient.
4. If neither beam on one side is working, and if another like-sized vehicle is available, park the sec-

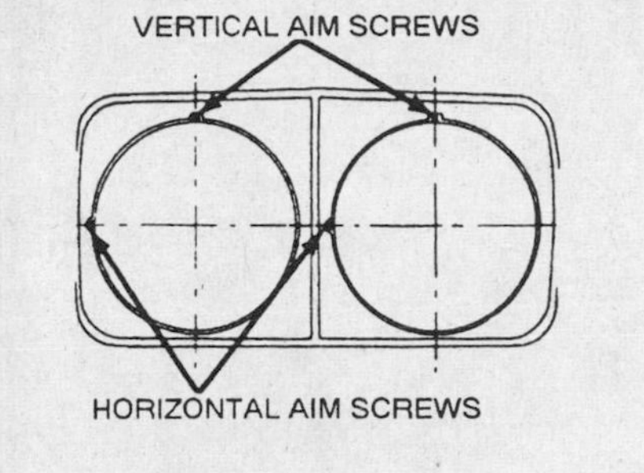

Fig. 106 Dual headlight adjustment screw locations—one side shown here (other side should be mirror image)

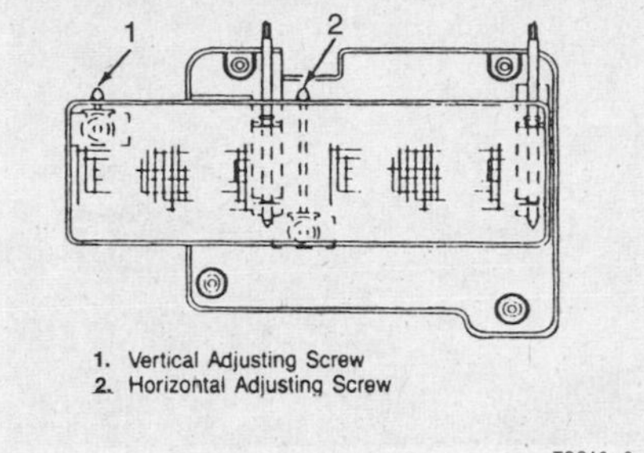

Fig. 107 Example of headlight adjustment screw location for composite headlamps

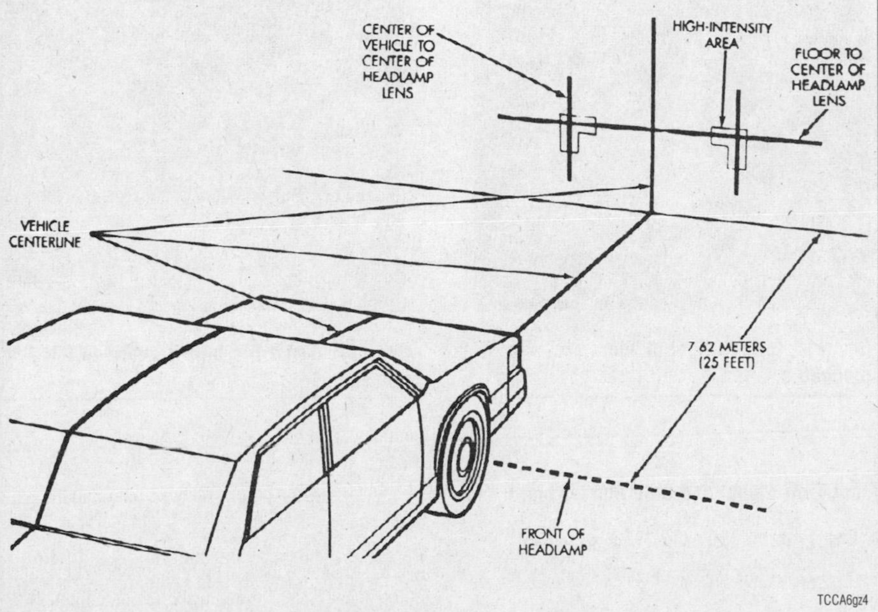

Fig. 108 Low-beam headlight pattern alignment

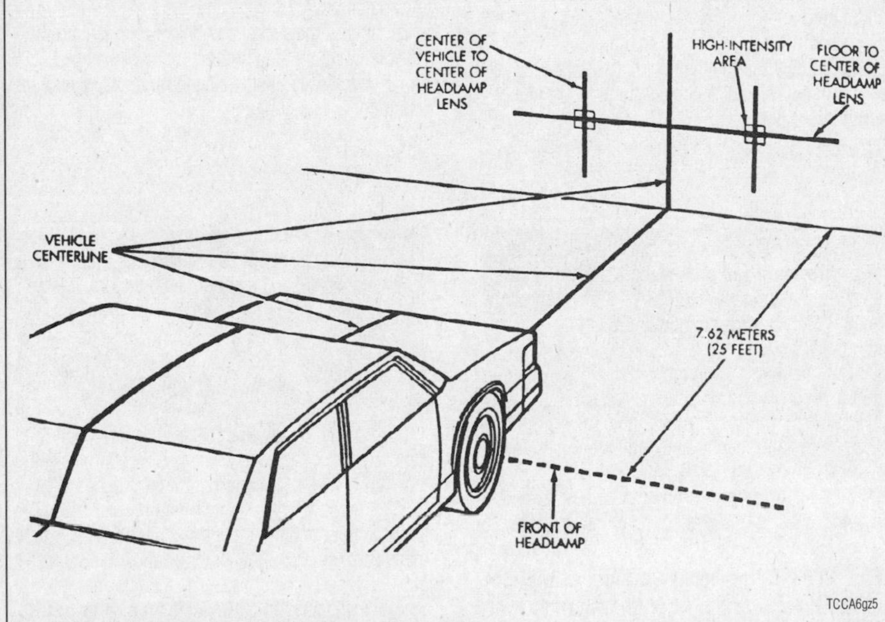

Fig. 109 High-beam headlight pattern alignment

ond one in the exact spot where the vehicle was and mark the beams using the same-side light. Then switch the vehicles so the one to be aimed is back in the original spot. It must be parked no closer to or farther away from the wall than the second vehicle.

5. Perform any necessary repairs, but make sure the vehicle is not moved, or is returned to the exact spot from which the lights were marked. Turn the headlights **ON** and adjust the beams to match the marks on the wall.

6. Have the headlight adjustment checked as soon as possible by a reputable repair shop.

Signal, Marker and Interior Lamps

REMOVAL & INSTALLATION

On these types of lights, the lens is usually removed to allow access to the bulb. External lenses usually have a rubber gasket around them to keep dust and water out of the housing; the gasket must be present and in good condition at reinstallation. Exterior lenses and the larger interior ones are held by one or more screws which must be removed. Once the lens is removed from the body, the bulb is removed from the socket and replaced. For the rear lamps, front marker lamps and some front turn signals, the socket and bulb is removed from the lens with a counterclockwise turn.

Smaller interior lenses usually fit in place with plastic clips and must be pried or popped out of place. A small, flat, plastic tool is ideal for this job; if other tools are used, care must be taken not to break the lens or the clip.

The bulbs used on Toyota trucks are all US standard and may be purchased at any auto store or dealer. Because of the variety of lamps used on any vehicle, it's a good idea to take the old one with you when shopping for the replacement.

On some models the lens can be replaced separately. On others, you have to replace the lens with the plastic backing attached.

Rear Turn Signal and Brake Lights

See Figures 110 thru 115

1. Depending on the vehicle and bulb application, either unscrew and remove the lens or disengage the bulb and socket assembly from the rear of the lens housing.

2. To remove a light bulb with retaining pins from its socket, grasp the bulb, then gently depress and twist it 1/8 turn counterclockwise, and pull it from the socket.

To install:

3. Before installing a light bulb into the socket, ensure that all electrical contact surfaces are free of corrosion or dirt.

➡Before installing the light bulb, note the positions of the two retaining pins on the bulb. They will likely be at different heights on the bulb, to ensure that the bulb is installed correctly. If, when installing the bulb, it does not turn easily, do not force it. Remove the bulb and rotate it 180 degrees from its former position, then reinsert it into the bulb socket.

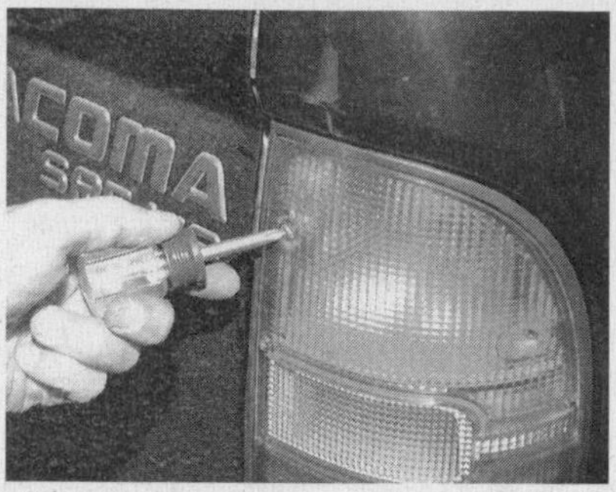

93166p18

Fig. 110 Remove the screws from the tail light assembly . . .

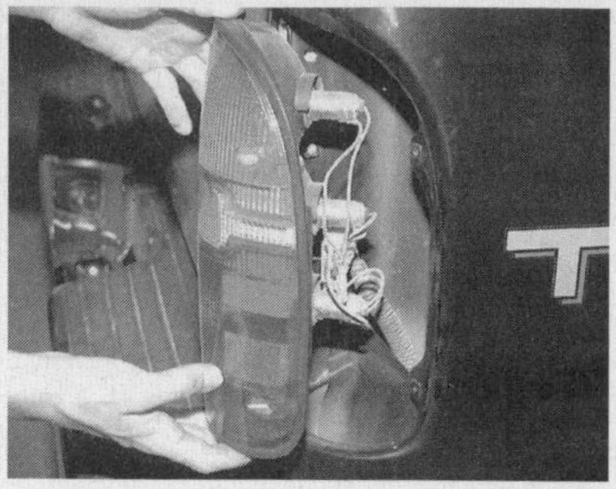

93166p19

Fig. 111 . . . then remove the tail light assembly

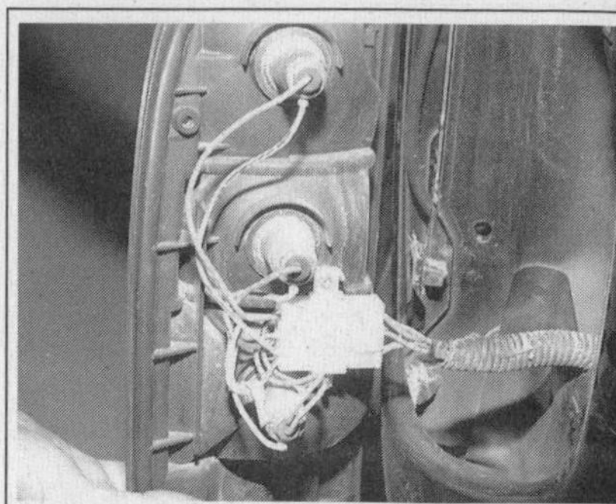

93166p24

Fig. 112 View of the wiring harnesses at the rear of the tail light assembly

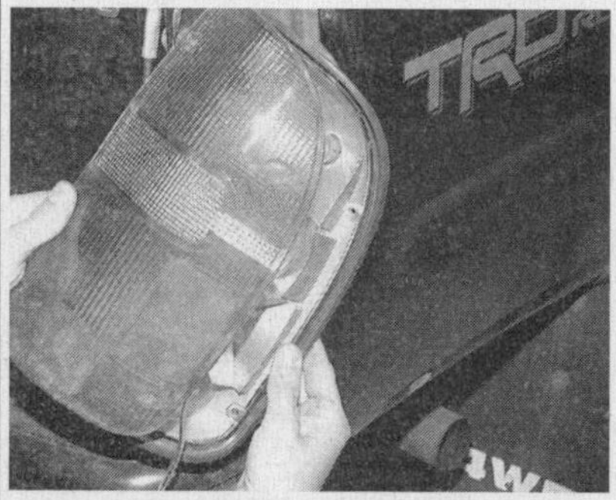

93166p21

Fig. 113 The tail light lens can be separated from the assembly

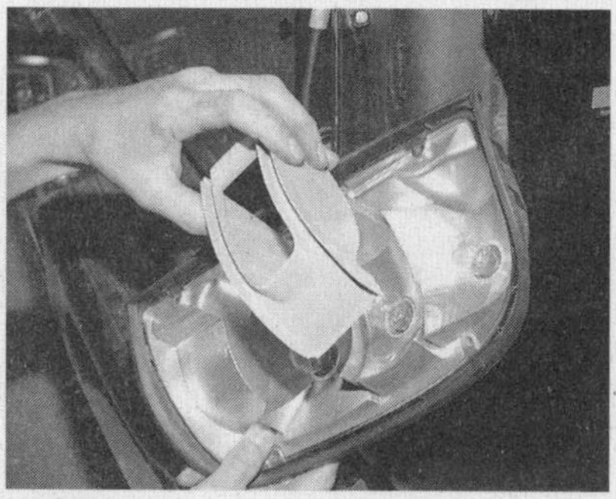

93166p20

Fig. 114 The tail light dividers are also replaceable

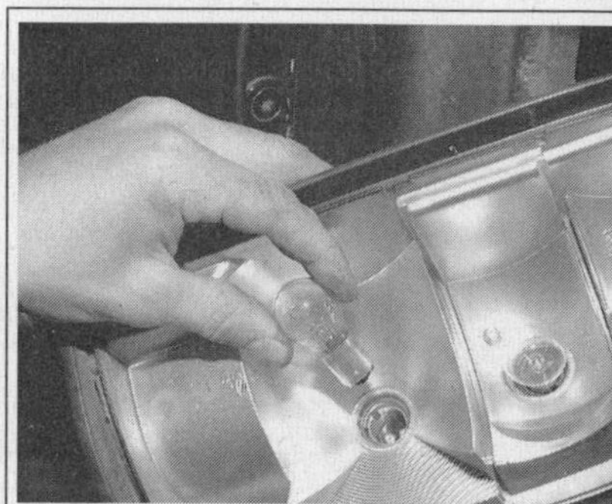

93166p23

Fig. 115 Twist the bulb $^{1}/_{8}$ turn to the left to remove it

4. Insert the light bulb into the socket and, while depressing the bulb, twist it 1/8 turn clockwise until the two pins on the light bulb are properly engaged in the socket.

5. To ensure that the replacement bulb functions properly, activate the applicable switch to illuminate the bulb which was just replaced. If the replacement light bulb does not illuminate, either it too is faulty or there is a problem in the bulb circuit or switch. Correct if necessary.

6. If applicable, install the socket and bulb assembly into the rear of the lens housing; otherwise, install the lens over the bulb.

Front Turn Signal and Side Marker Light

See Figures 116, 117, 118, and 119

1. If necessary, unfasten the retainers and remove the lens.

2. Disengage the bulb and socket assembly from the lens housing.

3. Gently grasp the light bulb and pull it straight out of the socket.

To install:

4. Before installing the light bulb into the socket, ensure that all electrical contact surfaces are free of corrosion or dirt.

5. Line up the base of the light bulb with the socket, then insert the light bulb into the socket until it is fully seated.

6. To ensure that the replacement bulb functions properly, activate the applicable switch to illuminate the bulb which was just replaced. If the replacement light bulb does not illuminate, either it too is faulty or there is a problem in the bulb circuit or switch. Correct as necessary.

7. Install the socket and bulb assembly into the lens housing.

8. If removed, install the lens and secure with the retainers.

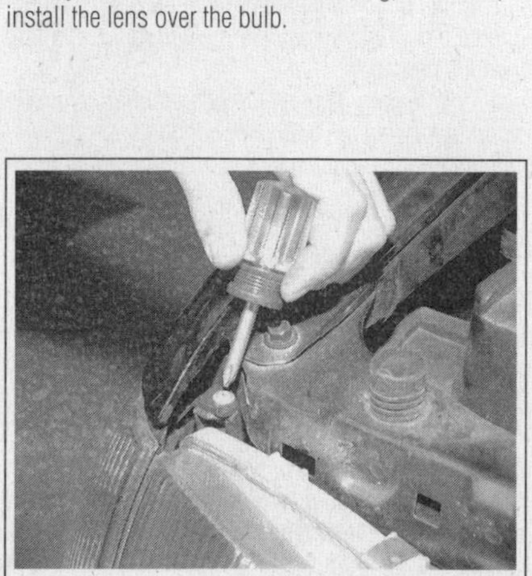

93166p02

Fig. 116 Removing the mounting screw from the front side marker lens—1998 Tacoma

93166p03

Fig. 117 Pull the bottom tab out of the slot at the bottom of the front side marker lens assembly—1998 Toyota Tacoma

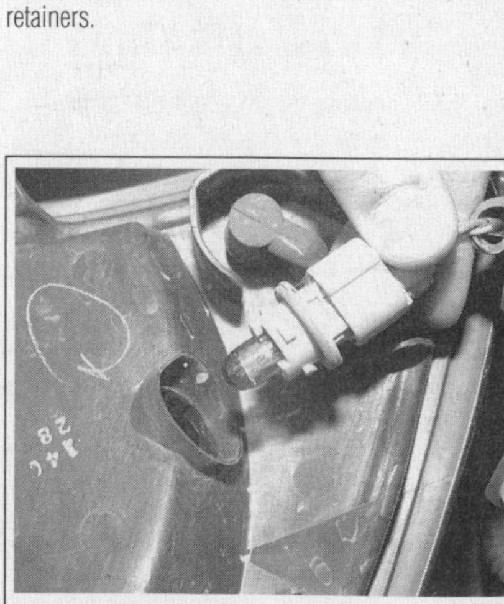

93166p04

Fig. 118 Twist to unlock, then gently pull to remove the bulb and socket

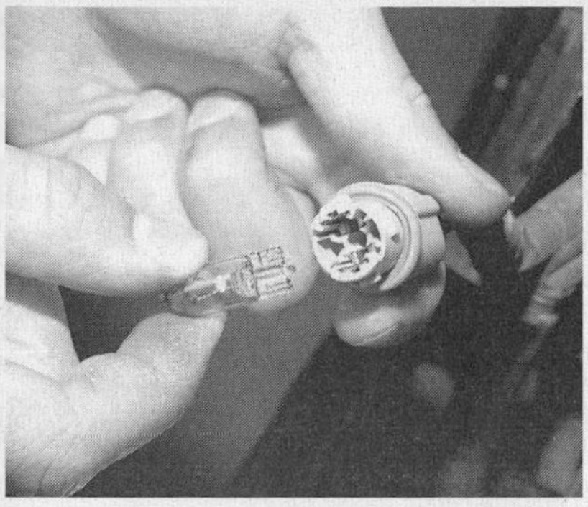

93166p05

Fig. 119 Pull the bulb straight out of the holder

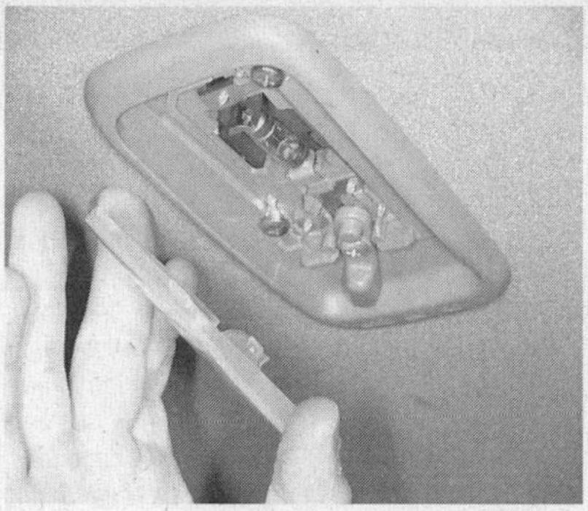

93166p72

Fig. 120 Detach the dome light lens from the assembly

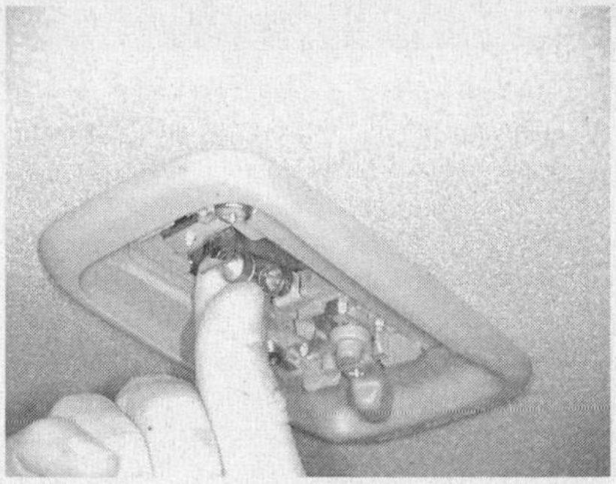

3166p71

Fig. 121 Disengage the spring clip which retains one tapered end of this dome light bulb, then withdraw the bulb

Dome Light

➧ **See Figures 120 and 121**

1. Using a small prytool, carefully remove the cover lens from the lamp assembly.
2. Remove the bulb from its retaining clip contacts. If the bulb has tapered ends, gently depress the spring clip/metal contact and disengage the light bulb, then pull it free of the two metal contacts.

To install:

3. Before installing the light bulb into the metal contacts, ensure that all electrical conducting surfaces are free of corrosion or dirt.
4. Position the bulb between the two metal contacts. If the contacts have small holes, be sure that the tapered ends of the bulb are situated in them.
5. To ensure that the replacement bulb functions properly, activate the applicable switch to illuminate the bulb which was just replaced. If the replacement light bulb does not illuminate, either it is faulty or there is a problem in the bulb circuit or switch. Correct as necessary.
6. Install the cover lens until its retaining tabs are properly engaged.

High-Mount Brake Light

➧ **See Figures 122, 123, and 124**

1. Remove the lens cover fastening screws.
2. Pull the lens cover away from the high-mount brake light assembly.
3. Remove the bulbs by pulling them straight out of the holders.
4. Installation is the reverse of removal.

License Plate Light

➧ **See Figures 125, 126, and 127**

The license plate light is mounted in the rear bumper of most Toyota trucks.

1. Locate the light in the bumper.
2. Remove the socket and bulb assembly by twisting it a quarter turn to the left and then pulling it straight out.
3. On some models you will have to twist the bulb one quarter turn to the left while slightly pushing in to release it from the holder. Other bulbs are of the blade type and will simply require you to pull the bulb straight out of the socket.
4. Installation is the reverse of removal

93166p70

Fig. 122 Location of the high-mount brake lens cover screws—1998 Tacoma shown

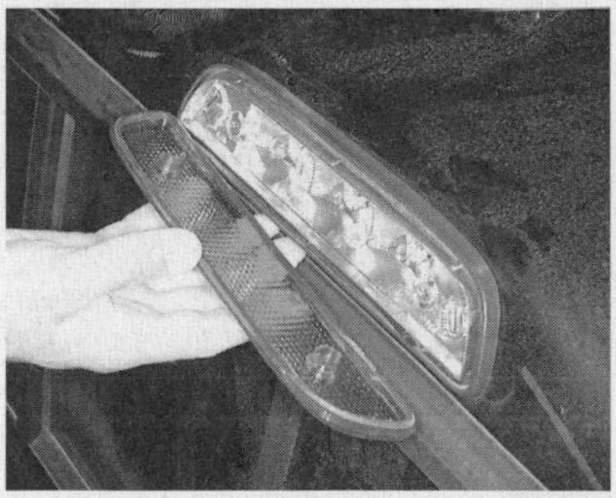

93166p69

Fig. 123 Once all mounting hardware has been removed, pull the lens away for access to the bulbs

93166p68

Fig. 124 Pull the bulbs straight out of the holders

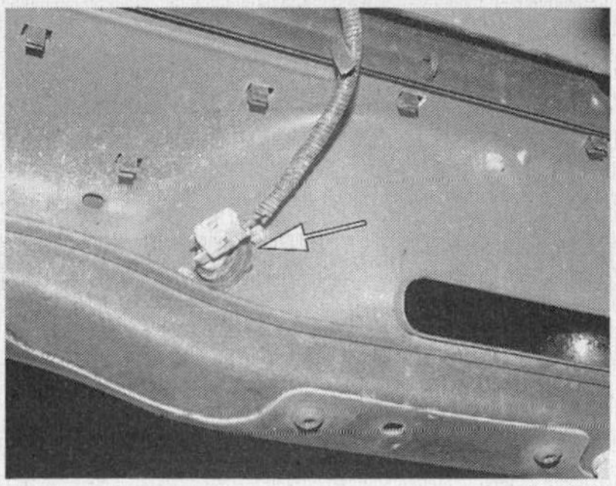

93166p16

Fig. 125 Location of the bumper-mounted license plate bulb holder

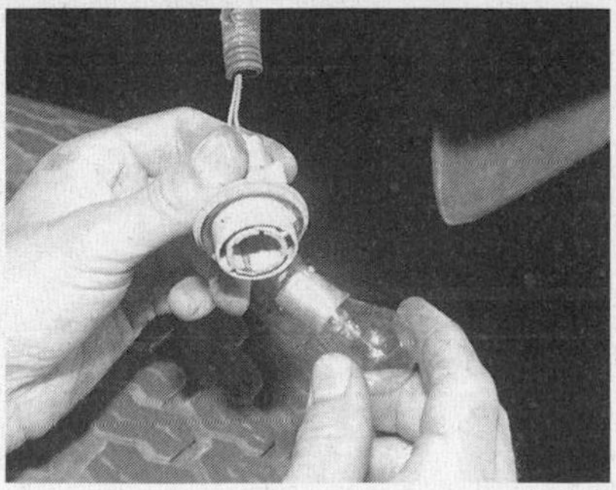

93166p15

Fig. 126 View of the twist style bulb and holder

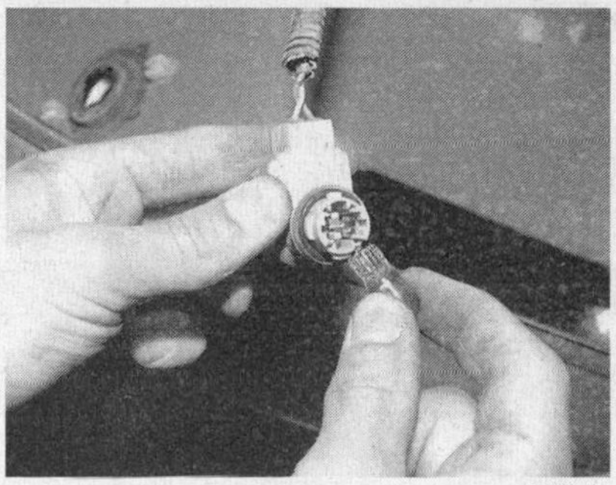

93166p17

Fig. 127 Some vehicles are equipped with the blade style, pull-type bulb and holder

TRAILER WIRING

Wiring the vehicle for towing is fairly easy. There are a number of good wiring kits available and these should be used, rather than trying to design your own.

All trailers will need brake lights and turn signals as well as tail lights and side marker lights. Most areas require extra marker lights for overwide trailers. Also, most areas have recently required back-up lights for trailers, and most trailer manufacturers have been building trailers with back-up lights for several years.

Additionally, some Class I, most Class II and just about all Class III and IV trailers will have electric brakes. Add to this number an accessories wire, to operate trailer internal equipment or to charge the trailer's battery, and you can have as many as seven wires in the harness.

Determine the equipment on your trailer and buy the wiring kit necessary. The kit will contain all the wires needed, plus a plug adapter set which includes the female plug, mounted on the bumper or hitch, and the male plug, wired into, or plugged into the trailer harness.

When installing the kit, follow the manufacturer's instructions. The color coding of the wires is usually standard throughout the industry. One point to note: some domestic vehicles, and most imported vehicles have separate turn signals. On most domestic vehicles, the brake lights and rear turn signals operate with the same bulb. For those vehicles without separate turn signals, you can purchase an isolation unit so that the brake lights won't blink whenever the turn signals are operated.

One, final point, the best kits are those with a spring loaded cover on the vehicle mounted socket. This cover prevents dirt and moisture from corroding the terminals. Never let the vehicle socket hang loosely; always mount it securely to the bumper or hitch.

CIRCUIT PROTECTION

Fuses

REPLACEMENT

➧ See Figure 128

The fuse block is located below the left side of the instrument panel on all vehicles. Additional fuses are found on the underhood relay board. The radio or audio unit is protected by an additional fuse in the body of the unit. In the event that anything electrical isn't working, the fuse should be the first item checked.

The underdash or underhood fusebox contains a fuse puller which can be used to grip and remove the fuse. The fuse cannot be checked while in the fuseblock; it must be removed. View the fuse from the side, looking for a broken element in the center. Sometimes the break is hard to see; if you can't check the fuse with an ohmmeter for continuity, replace the fuse.

If a fuse should blow, turn **OFF** the ignition switch and also the circuit involved. Replace the fuse with one of the same amperage rating, and turn on the switches. If the new fuse immediately blows out, the circuit should be tested for shorts, broken insulation, or loose connections.

➡Do not use fuses of a higher amperage than recommended.

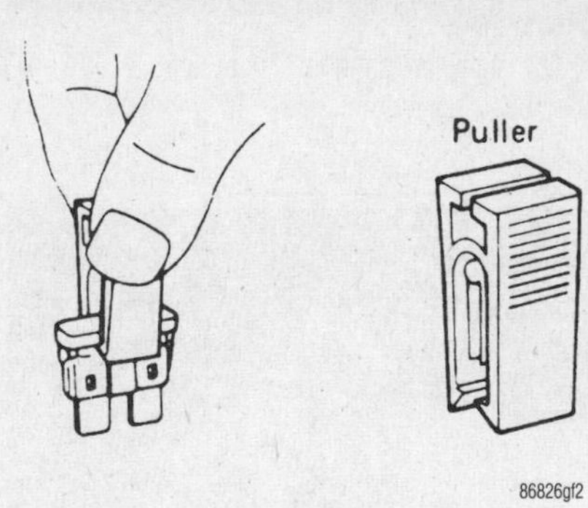

Fig. 128 A fuse puller can make replacement easier

Circuit Breakers

REPLACEMENT

➧ See Figure 129

Many circuits, particularly high amperage ones, are protected by resetable circuit breakers. Much like the circuit breakers in a household system, these units will trip when too much current attempts to pass through. On Toyota vehicles, the breaker may not automatically reset, but may be reset manually.

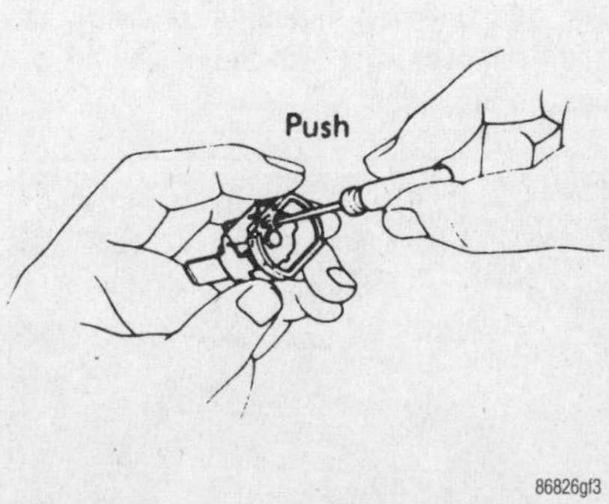

Fig. 129 Reset the circuit breaker with a small probe

To reset the breaker:

1. Disconnect the negative battery cable.
2. Remove the circuit breaker.
3. Use a needle probe or other thin tool to reach into the reset hole and push the reset button.
4. Once reset, use an ohmmeter to check for continuity at the pins of breaker. If no continuity is present, the breaker did not reset.
5. Reinstall the circuit breaker and connect the negative battery cable.

Relays

REPLACEMENT

As vehicles rely more and more on electronic systems and electrically operated options, the number of relays grows steadily. Many relays are located in logical positions on the relay and fuse board under the dash or in the engine compartment. However, many relays are located throughout the vehicle, often near the component they control. During diagnosis of a circuit, always suspect a failed relay until proven otherwise.

Flashers

REPLACEMENT

The turn signal flasher is usually located in the convenience center, under the dash, on the left side kick panel. In all cases, replacement is made by unplugging the old unit and plugging in a new one.

WIRING DIAGRAMS

INDEX OF WIRING DIAGRAMS

93166w01

INDEX OF WIRING DIAGRAMS

93166w02

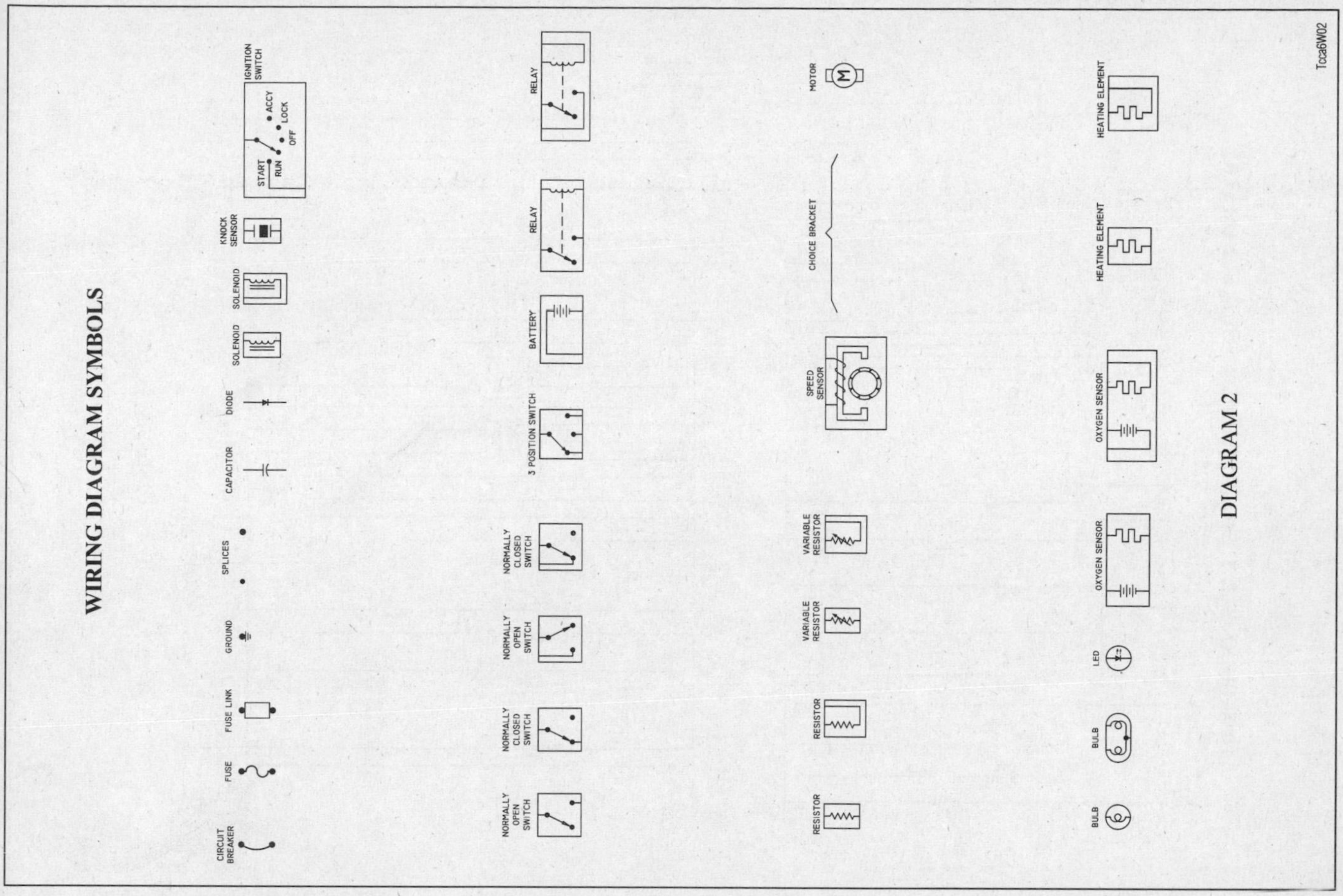
WIRING DIAGRAM SYMBOLS
CIRCUIT BREAKER
FUSE
FUSE LINK
GROUND
SPLICES
CAPACITOR
DIODE
SOLENOID
SOLENOID
KNOCK SENSOR
START
RUN
OFF
LOCK
ACCY
IGNITION SWITCH
NORMALLY OPEN SWITCH
NORMALLY CLOSED SWITCH
NORMALLY OPEN SWITCH
NORMALLY CLOSED SWITCH
3 POSITION SWITCH
BATTERY
RELAY
RELAY
RESISTOR
RESISTOR
VARIABLE RESISTOR
VARIABLE RESISTOR
SPEED SENSOR
CHOICE BRACKET
MOTOR
BULB
BULB
LED
OXYGEN SENSOR
OXYGEN SENSOR
HEATING ELEMENT
HEATING ELEMENT
DIAGRAM 2
TCCA6W02

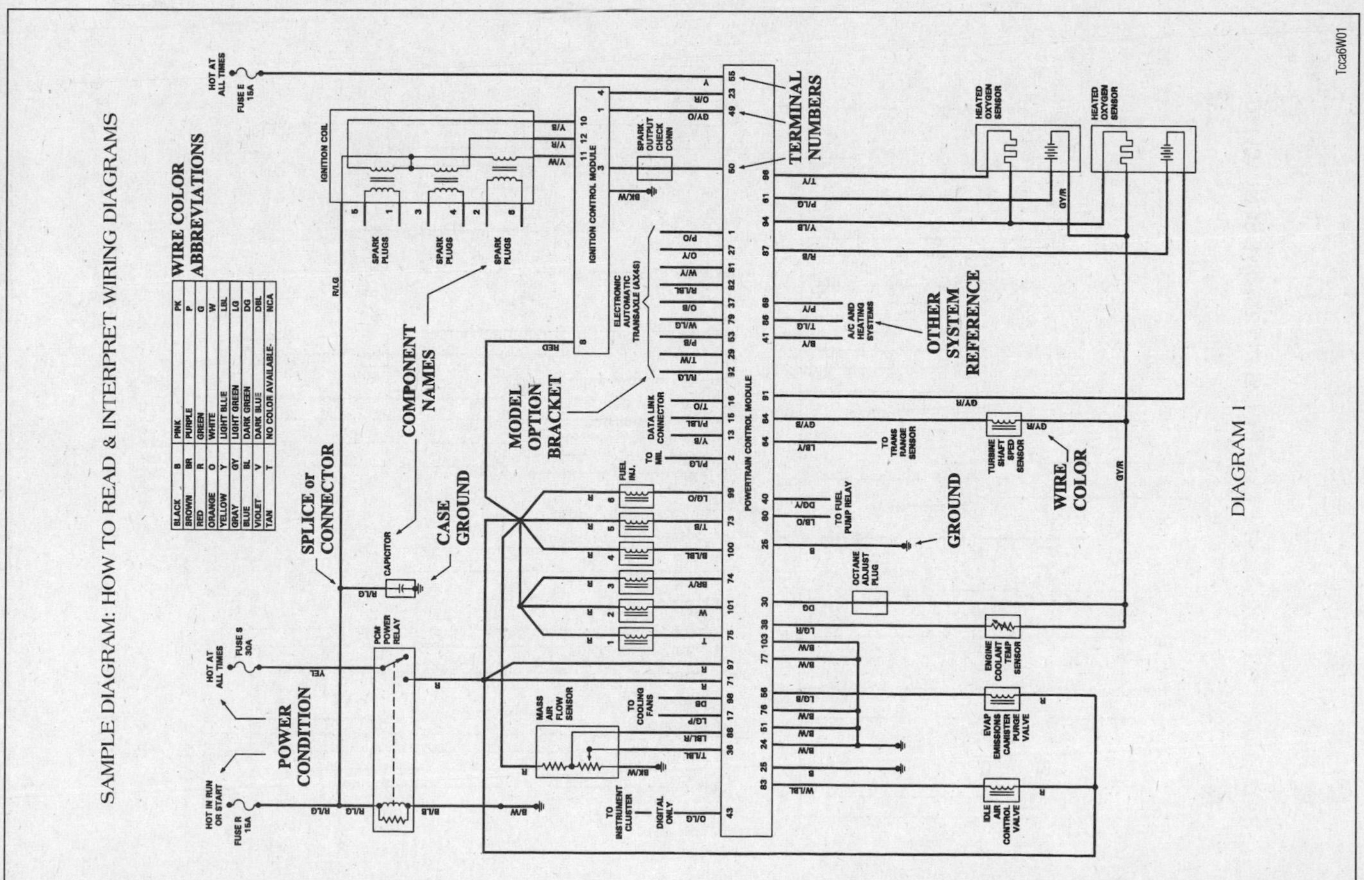
SAMPLE DIAGRAM: HOW TO READ & INTERPRET WIRING DIAGRAMS
WIRE COLOR ABBREVIATIONS
BLACK B
BROWN BR
RED R
ORANGE O
YELLOW Y
GRAY GY
BLUE BL
VIOLET V
TAN T
PINK PK
PURPLE P
GREEN G
WHITE W
LIGHT BLUE LBL
LIGHT GREEN LG
DARK GREEN DG
DARK BLUE DBL
NO COLOR AVAILABLE- NCA
POWER CONDITION
SPLICE or CONNECTOR
CASE GROUND
COMPONENT NAMES
MODEL OPTION BRACKET
TERMINAL NUMBERS
OTHER SYSTEM REFERENCE
GROUND
WIRE COLOR
POWERTRAIN CONTROL MODULE
IGNITION CONTROL MODULE
IGNITION COIL
SPARK PLUGS
DIAGRAM 1
TCCA6W01

2000 4RUNNER 2.7L (3RZ-FE CALIF.) ENGINE SCHEMATIC

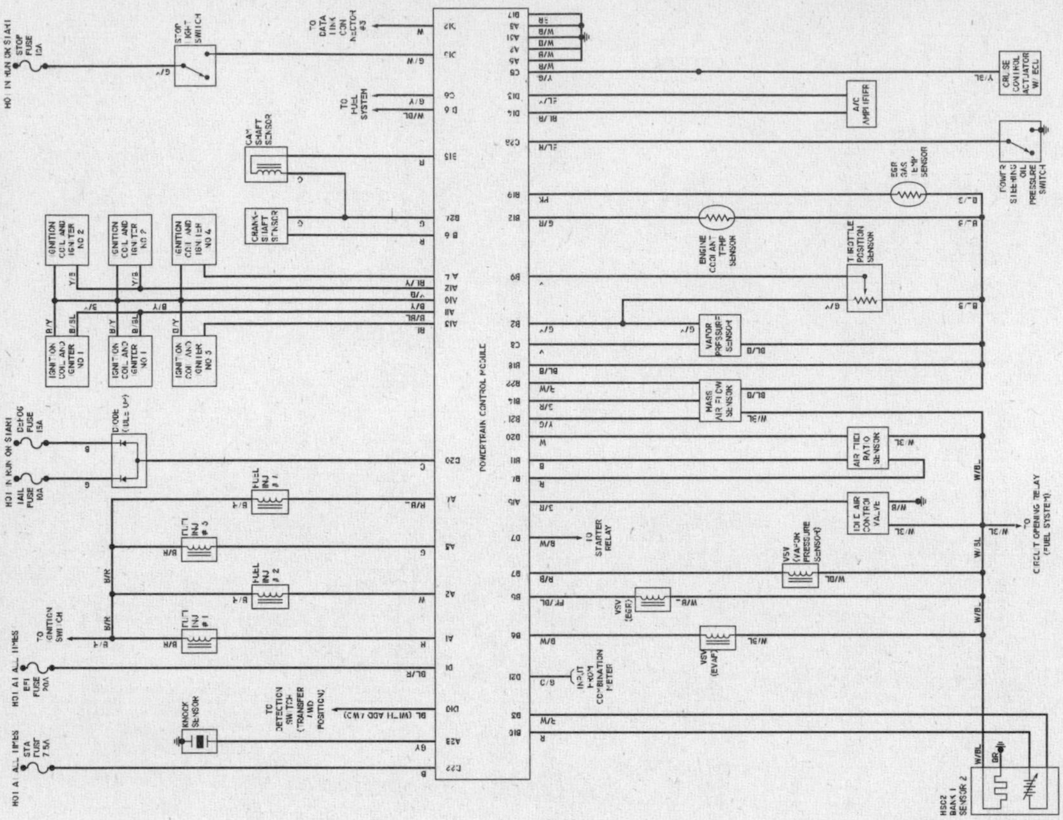

DIAGRAM 4

93166E11

1997-00 4RUNNER 2.7L (3RZ-FE EXCEPT CALIF.) ENGINE SCHEMATIC

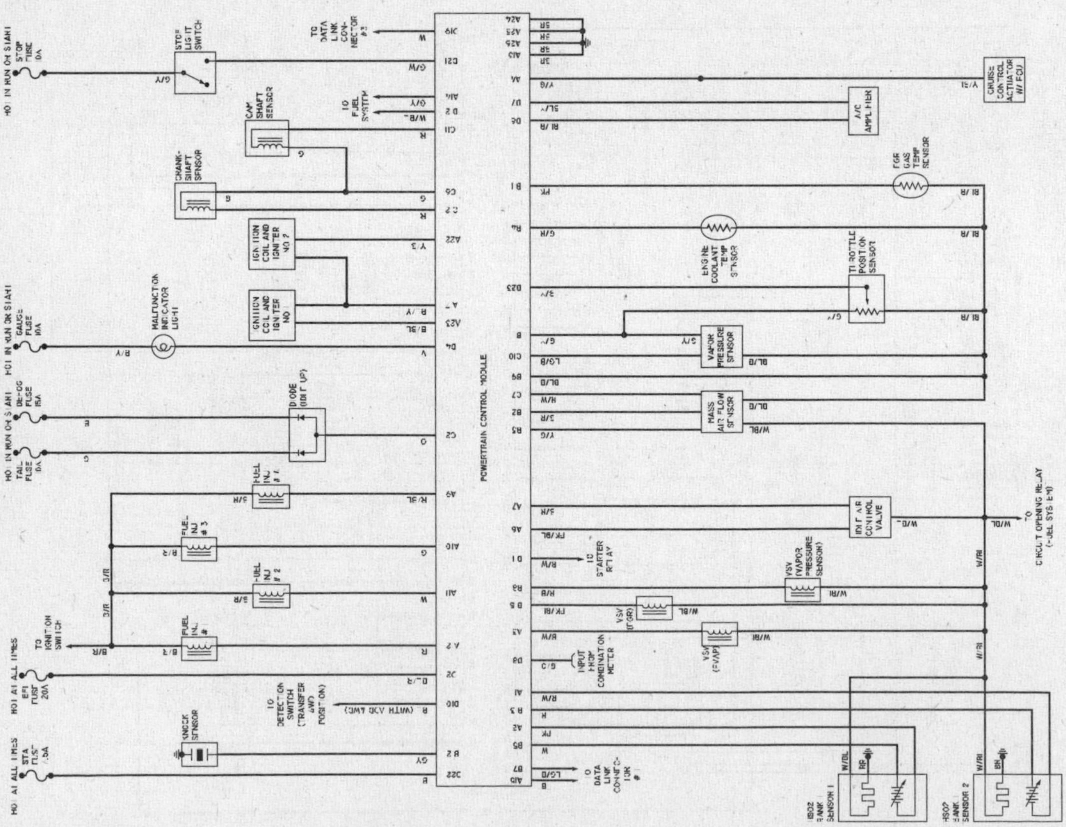

DIAGRAM 3

93166E02

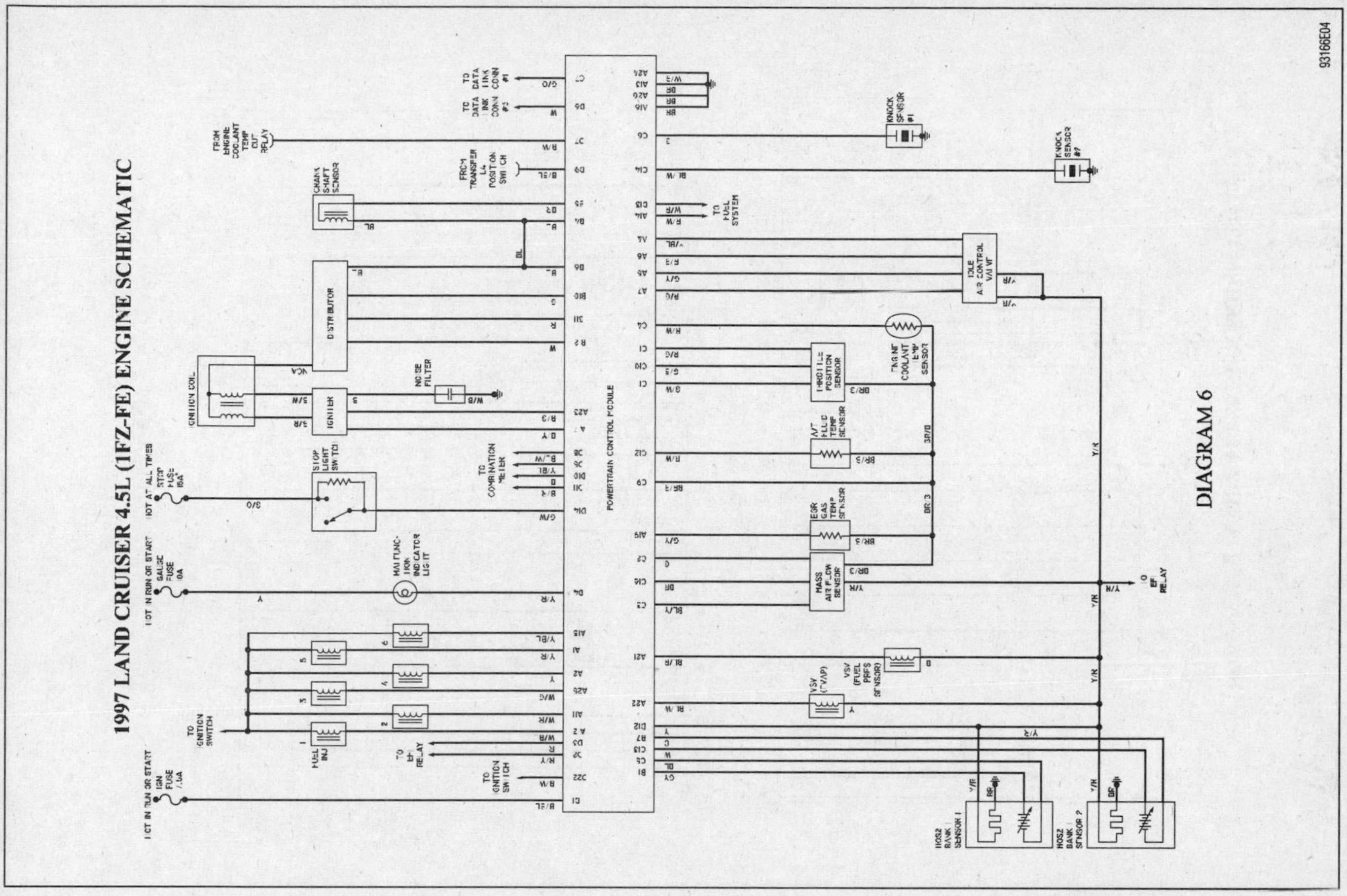
1997 LAND CRUISER 4.5L (1FZ-FE) ENGINE SCHEMATIC
POWERTRAIN CONTROL MODULE
DIAGRAM 6
93166E04

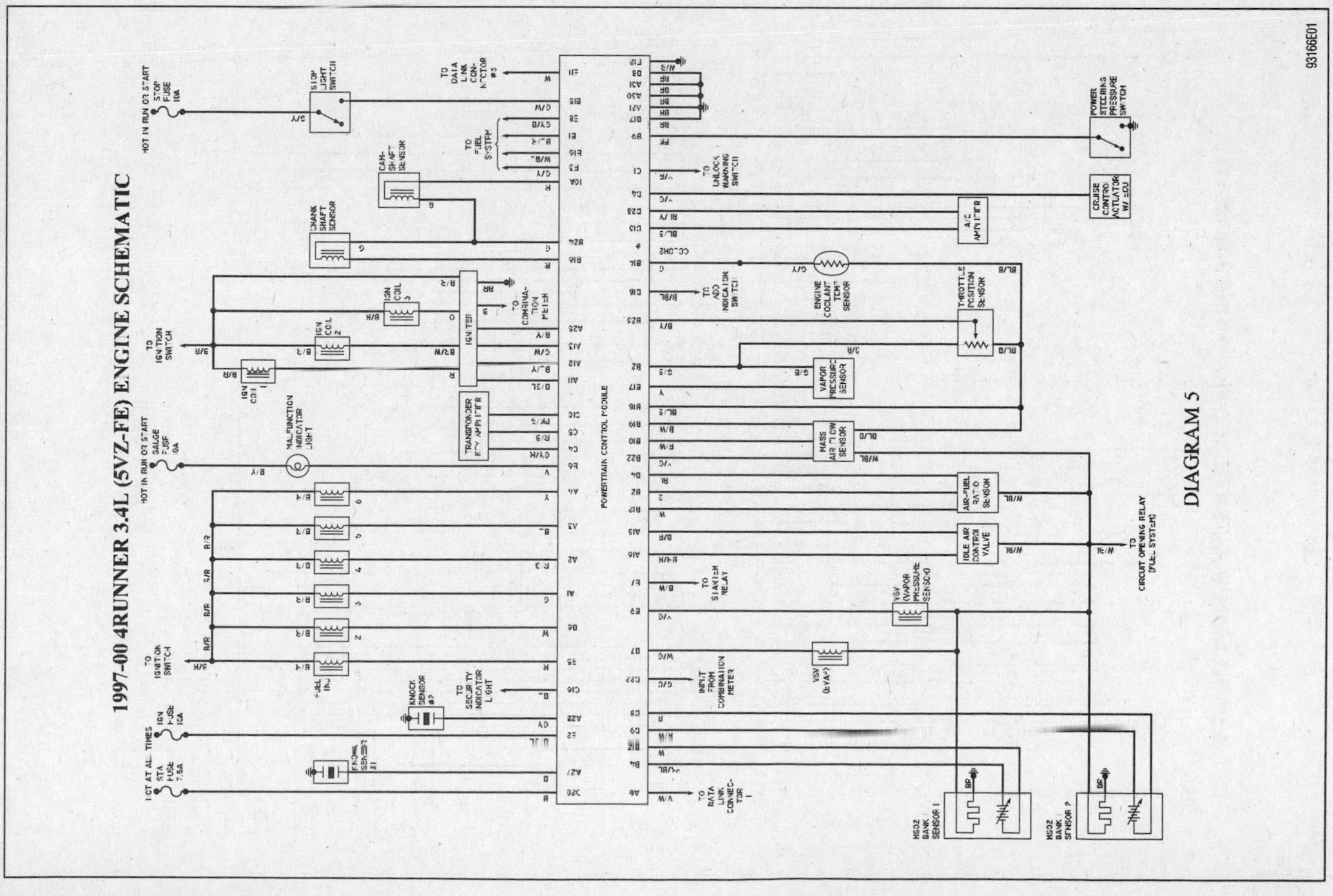
1997-00 4RUNNER 3.4L (5VZ-FE) ENGINE SCHEMATIC
POWERTRAIN CONTROL MODULE
DIAGRAM 5
93166E01

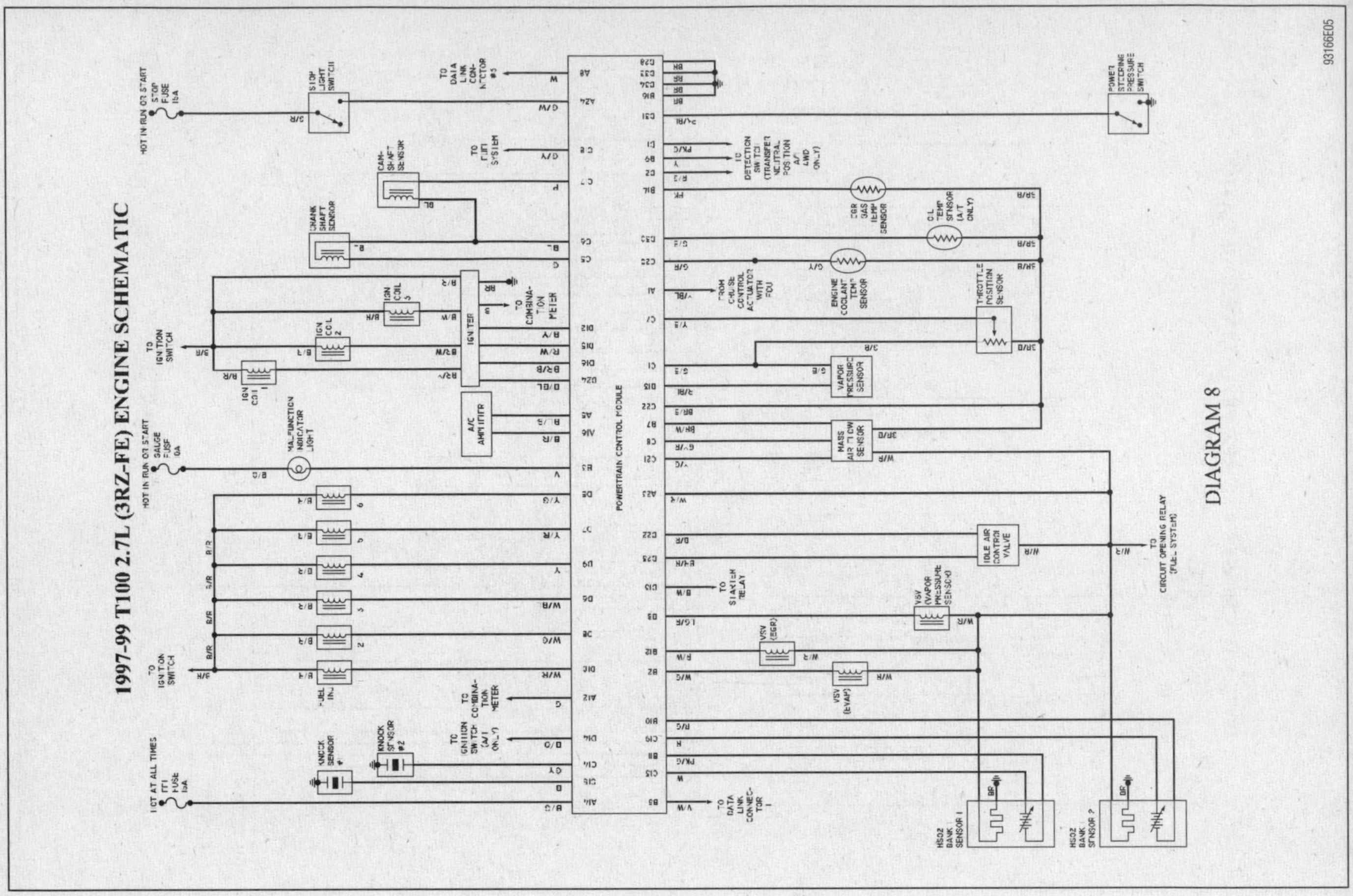
1997-99 T100 2.7L (3RZ-FE) ENGINE SCHEMATIC
DIAGRAM 8
93166E05

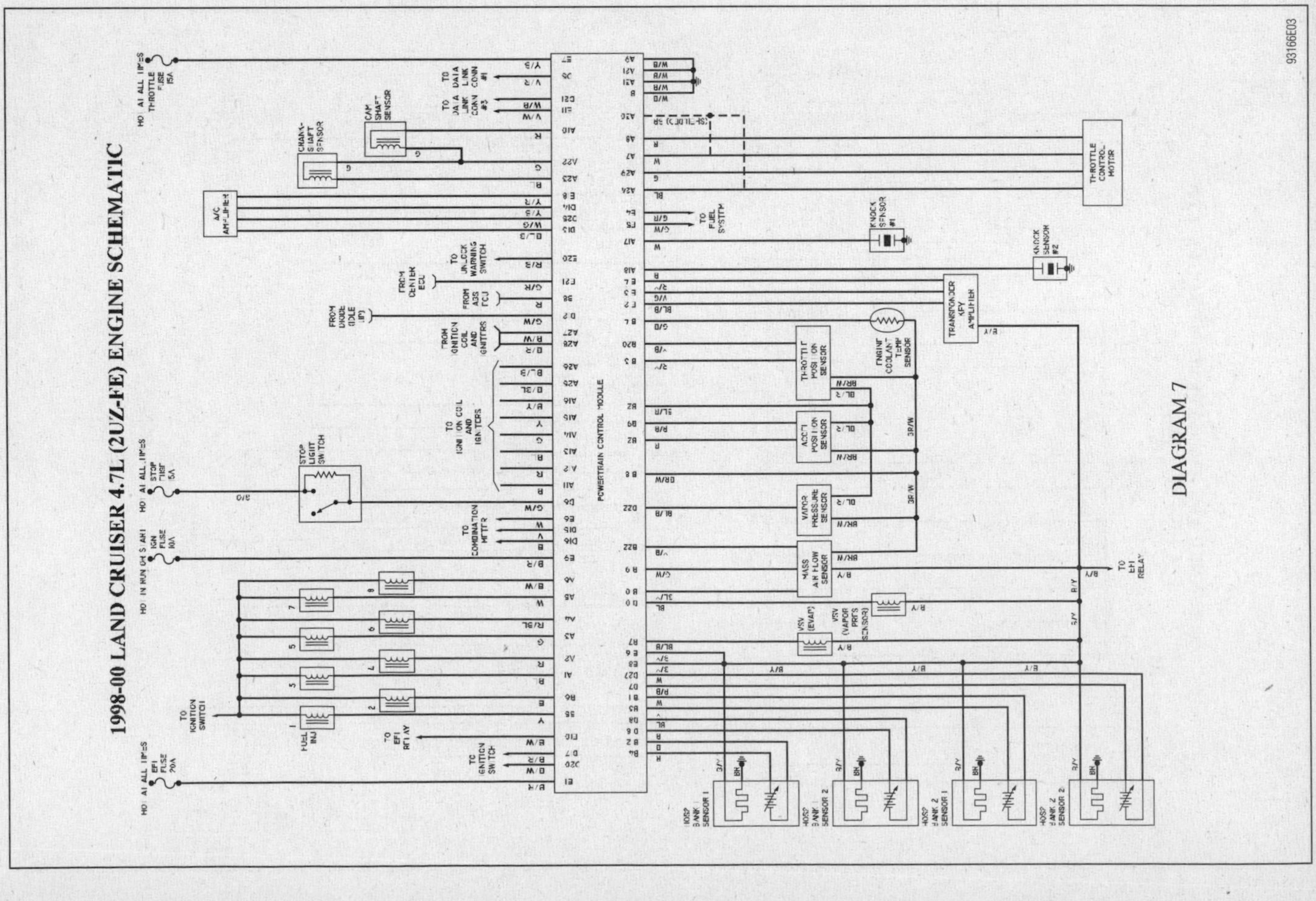
1998-00 LAND CRUISER 4.7L (2UZ-FE) ENGINE SCHEMATIC
DIAGRAM 7
93166E03

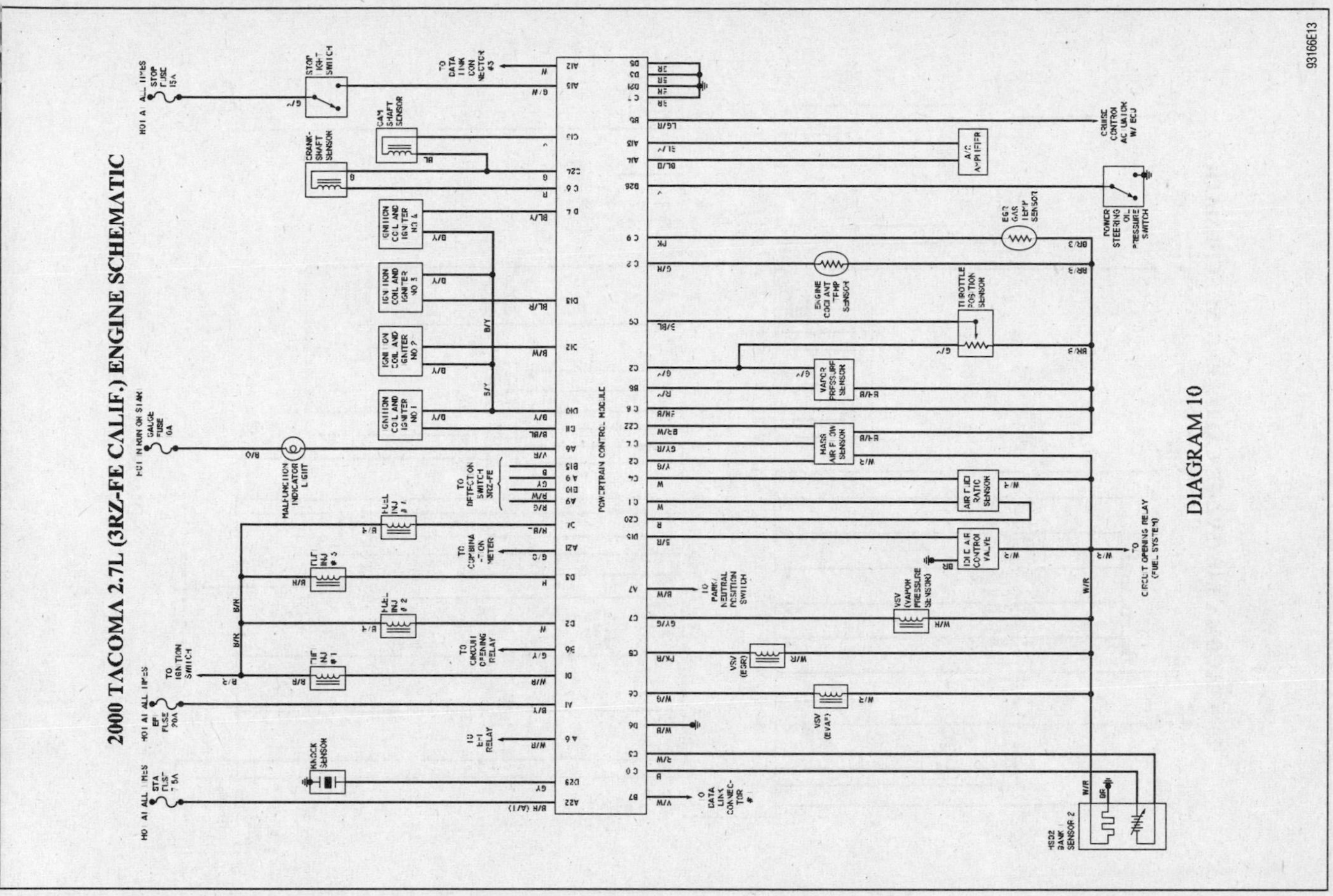

2000 TACOMA 2.7L (3RZ-FE CALIF.) ENGINE SCHEMATIC

DIAGRAM 10

93166E13

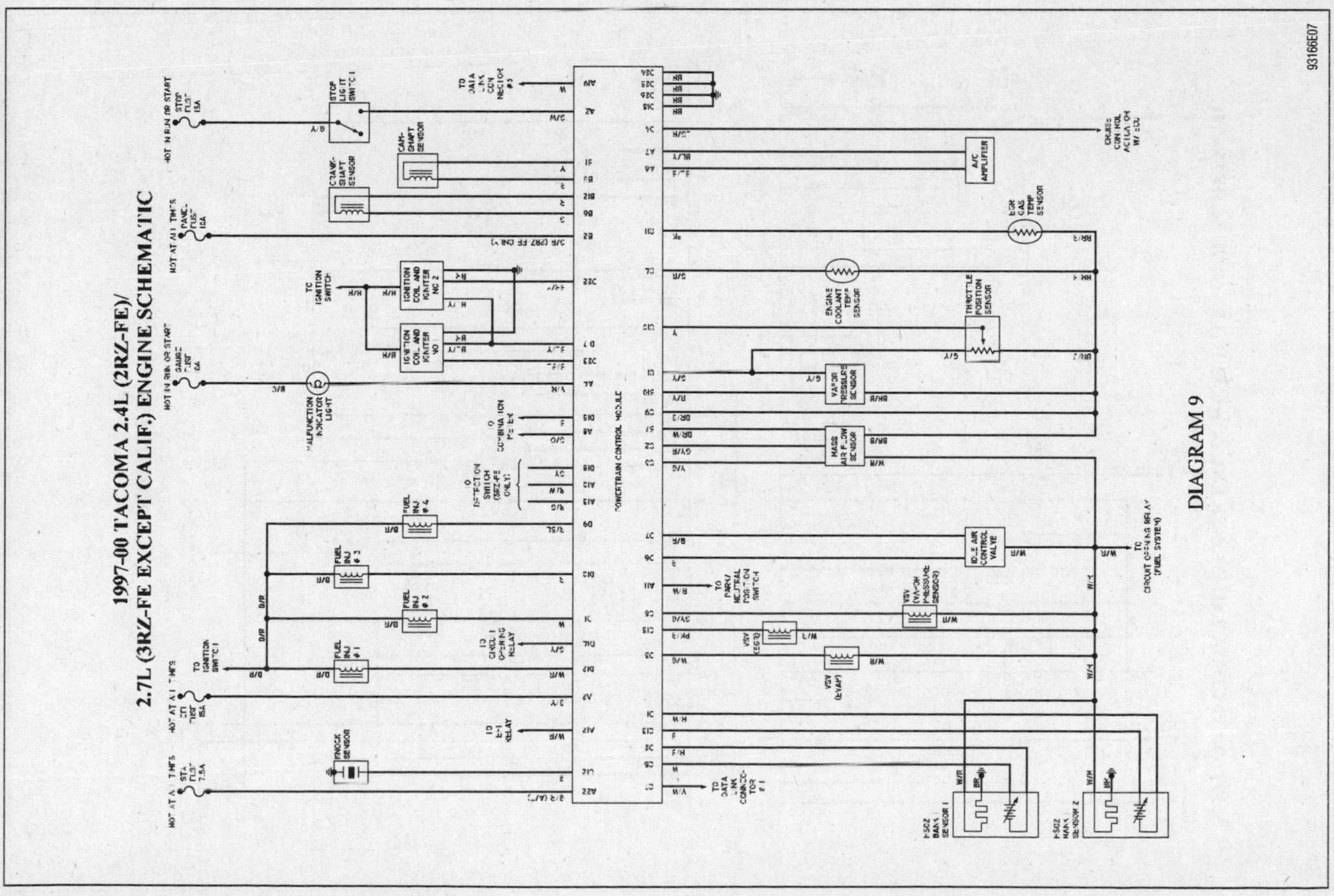

1997-00 TACOMA 2.4L (2RZ-FE)/ 2.7L (3RZ-FE EXCEPT CALIF.) ENGINE SCHEMATIC

DIAGRAM 9

93166E07

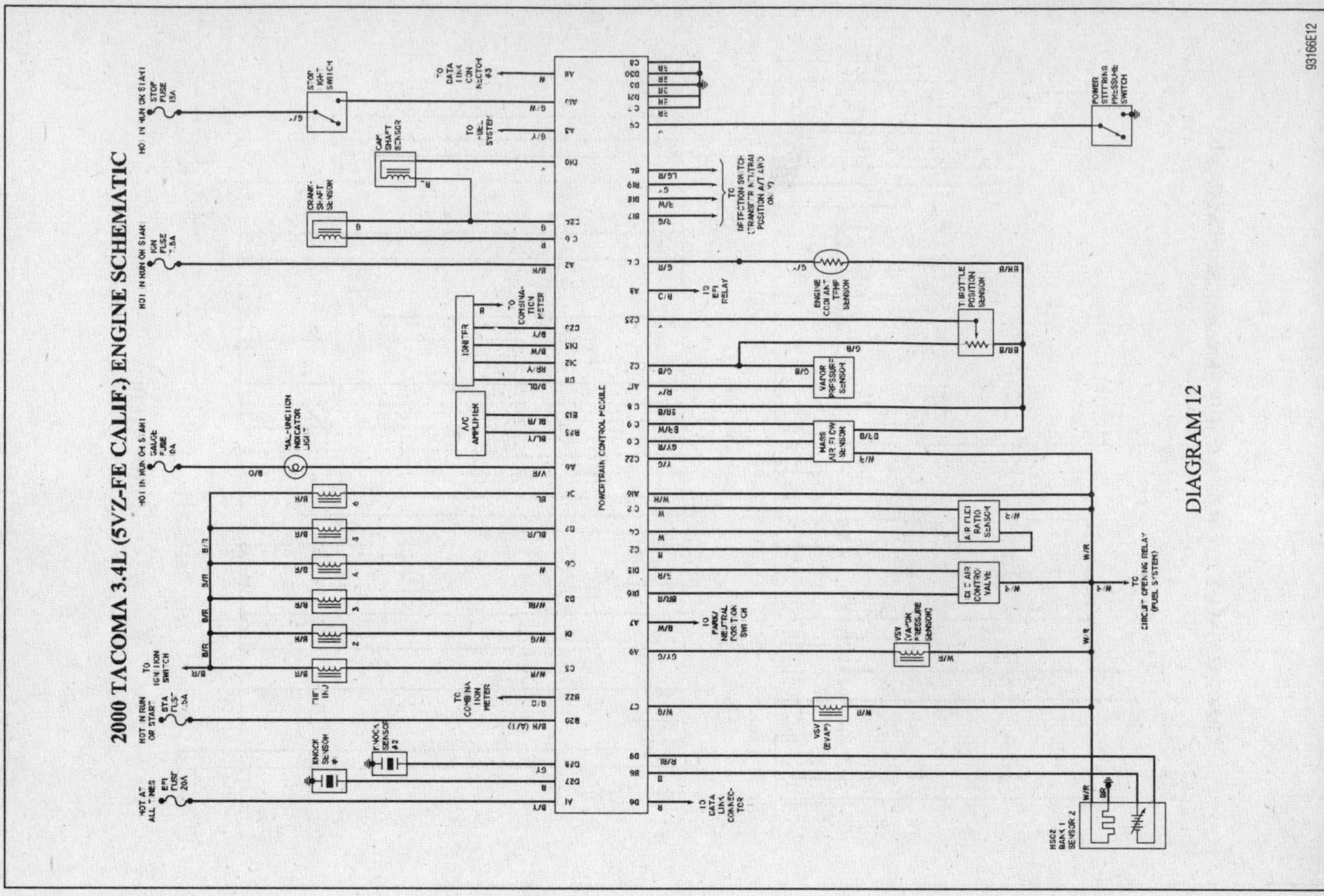
2000 TACOMA 3.4L (5VZ-FE CALIF.) ENGINE SCHEMATIC
POWERTRAIN CONTROL MODULE
DIAGRAM 12
93166E12

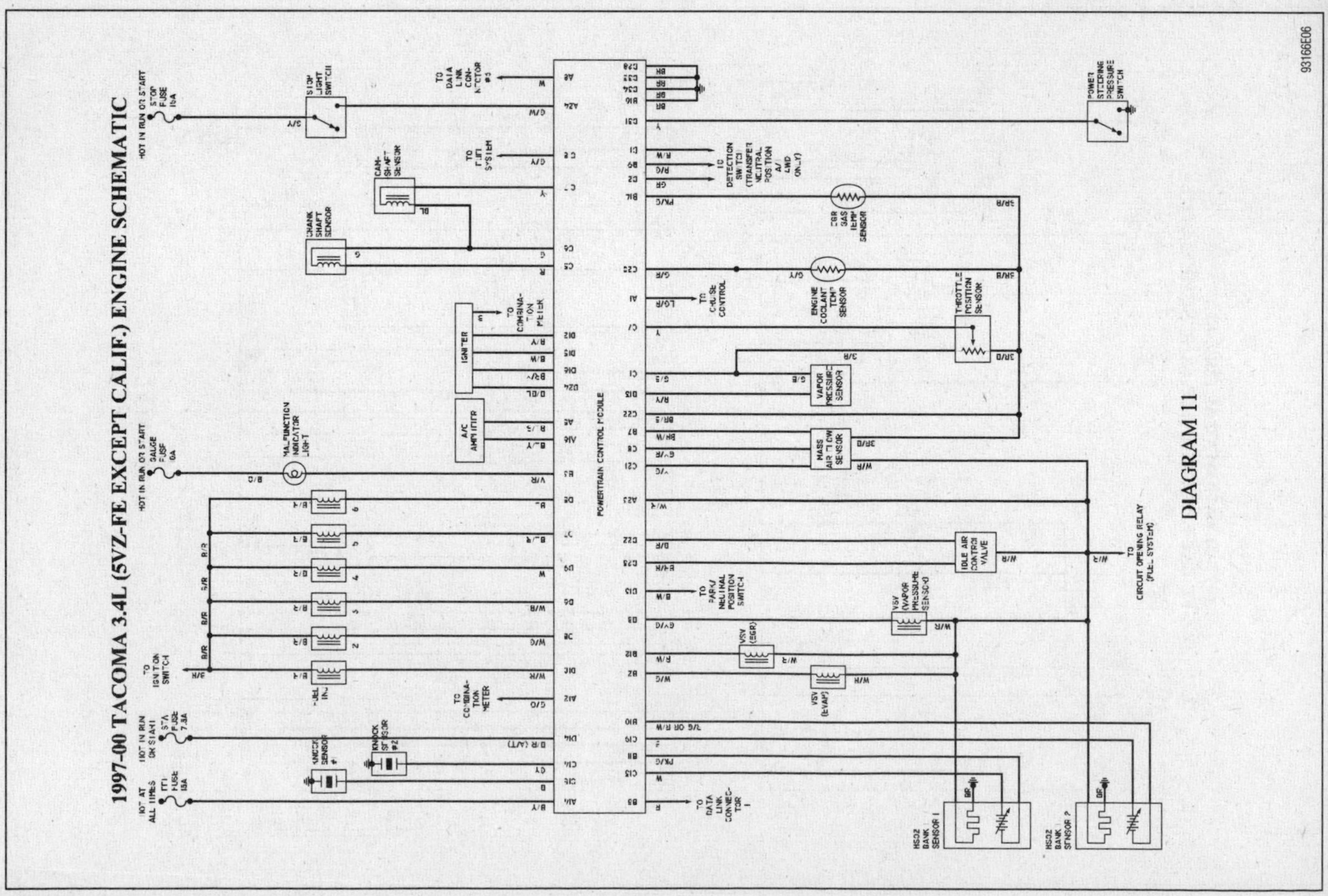
1997-00 TACOMA 3.4L (5VZ-FE EXCEPT CALIF.) ENGINE SCHEMATIC
POWERTRAIN CONTROL MODULE
DIAGRAM 11
93166E06

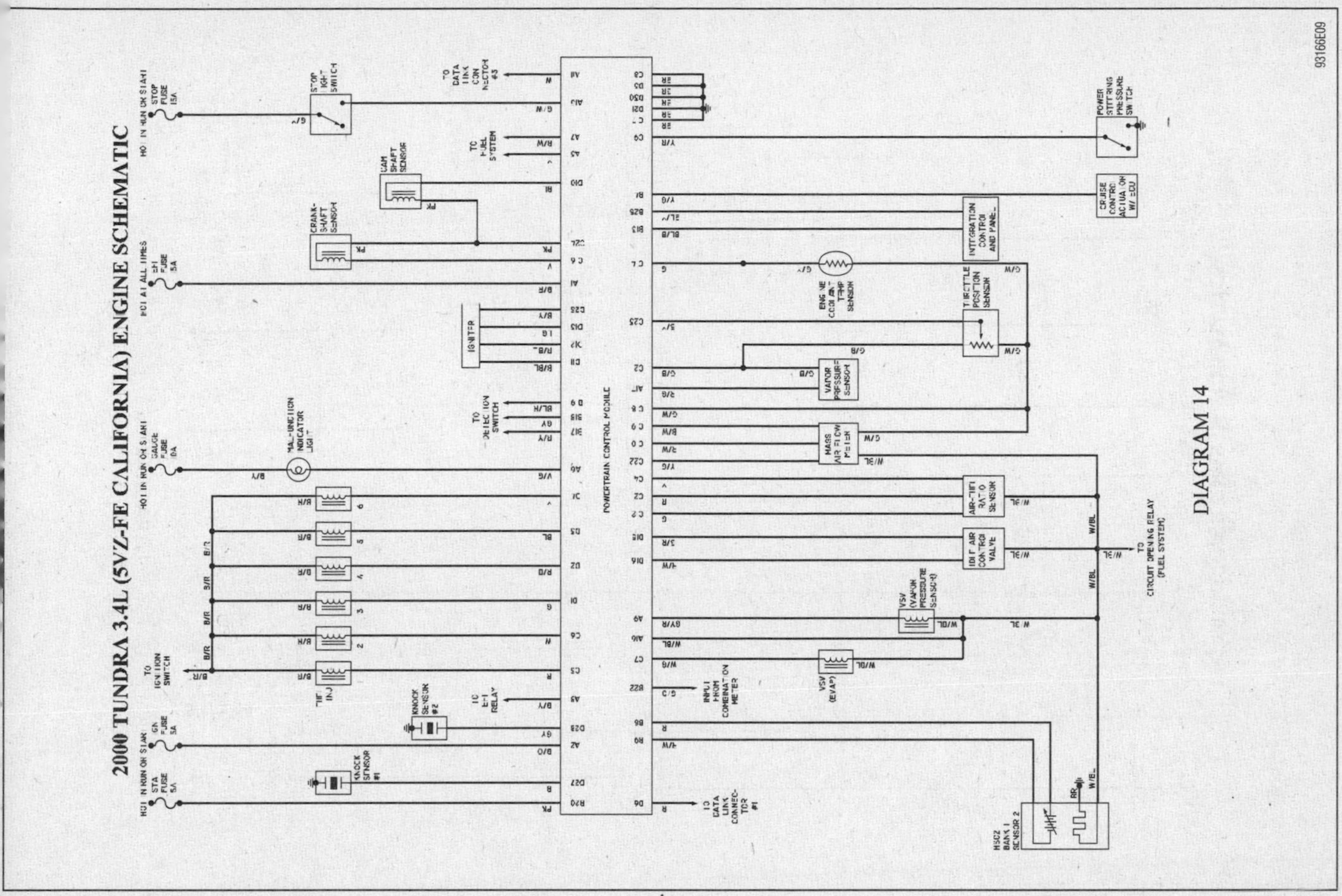
2000 TUNDRA 3.4L (5VZ-FE CALIFORNIA) ENGINE SCHEMATIC
DIAGRAM 14
93166E09
POWERTRAIN CONTROL MODULE

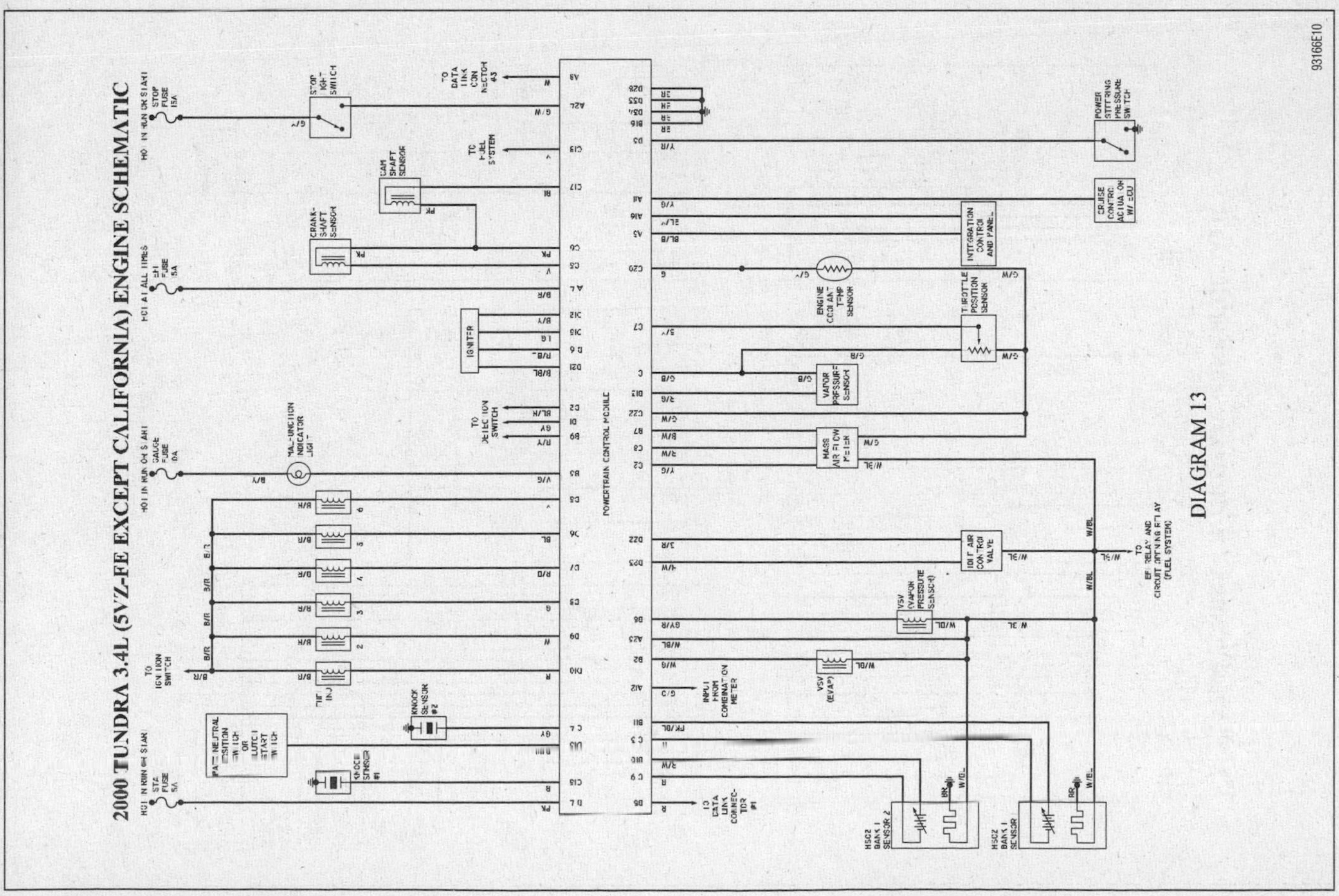
2000 TUNDRA 3.4L (5VZ-FE EXCEPT CALIFORNIA) ENGINE SCHEMATIC
DIAGRAM 13
93166E10
POWERTRAIN CONTROL MODULE

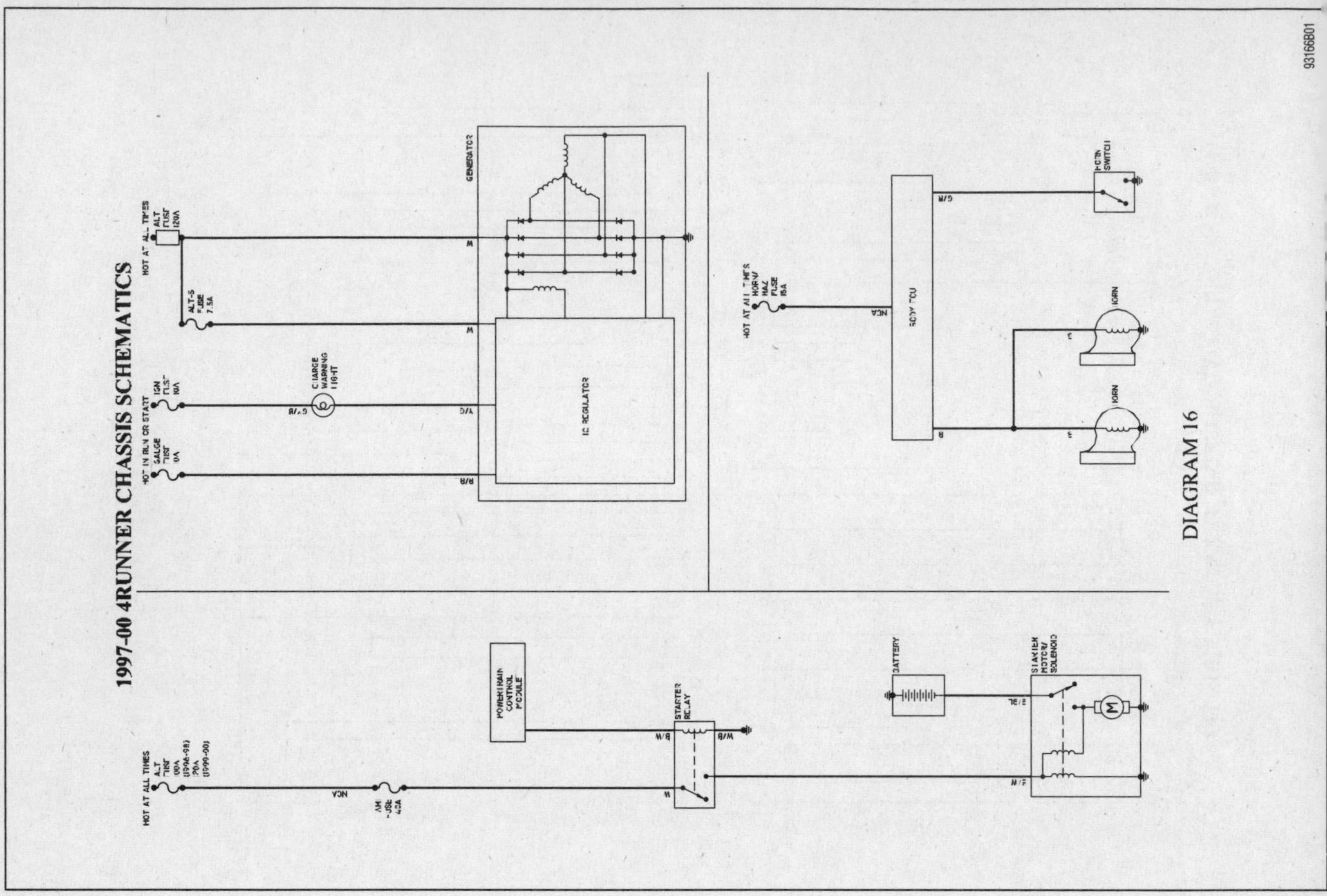
1997-00 4RUNNER CHASSIS SCHEMATICS
DIAGRAM 16
93166B01

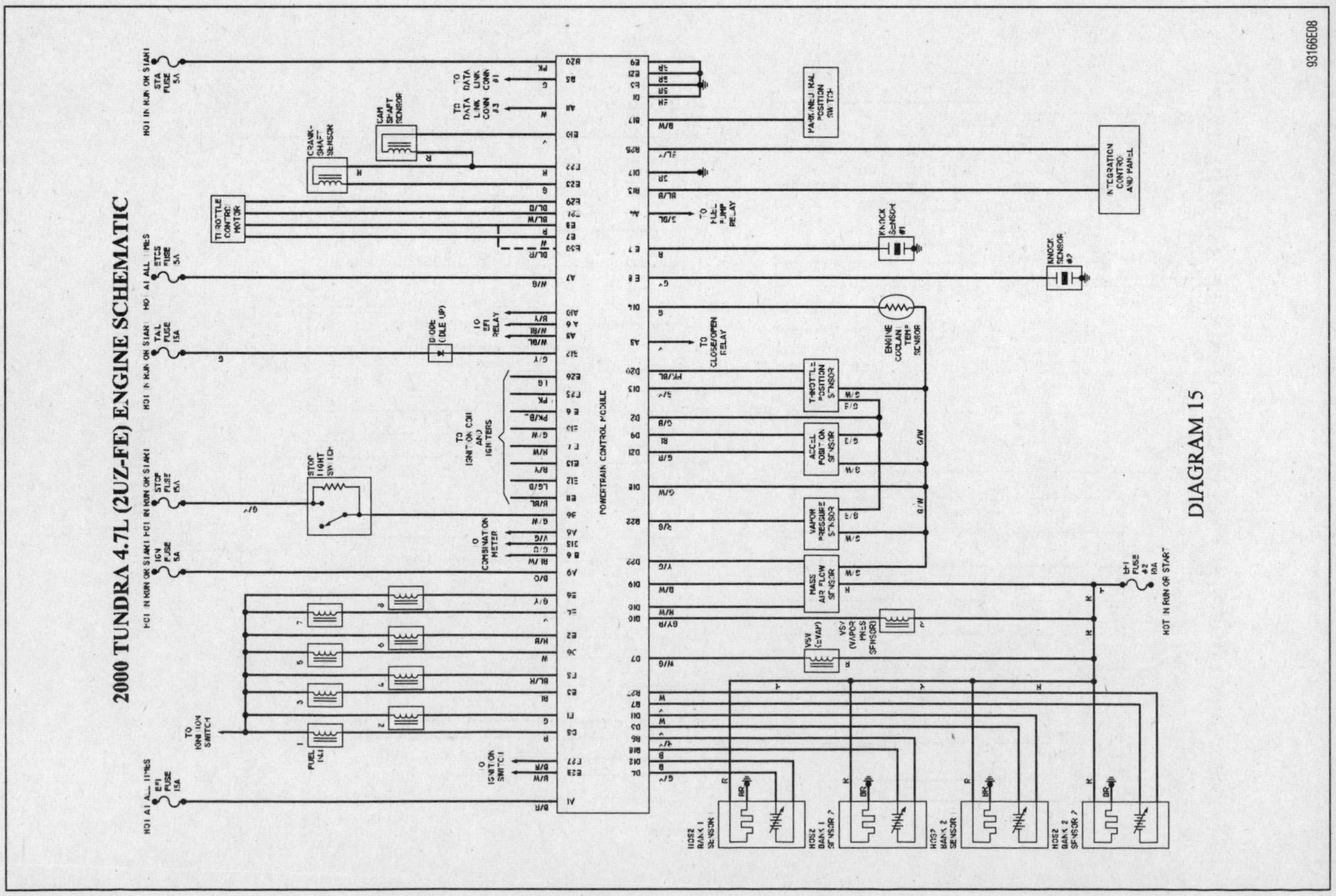
2000 TUNDRA 4.7L (2UZ-FE) ENGINE SCHEMATIC
DIAGRAM 15
93166E08

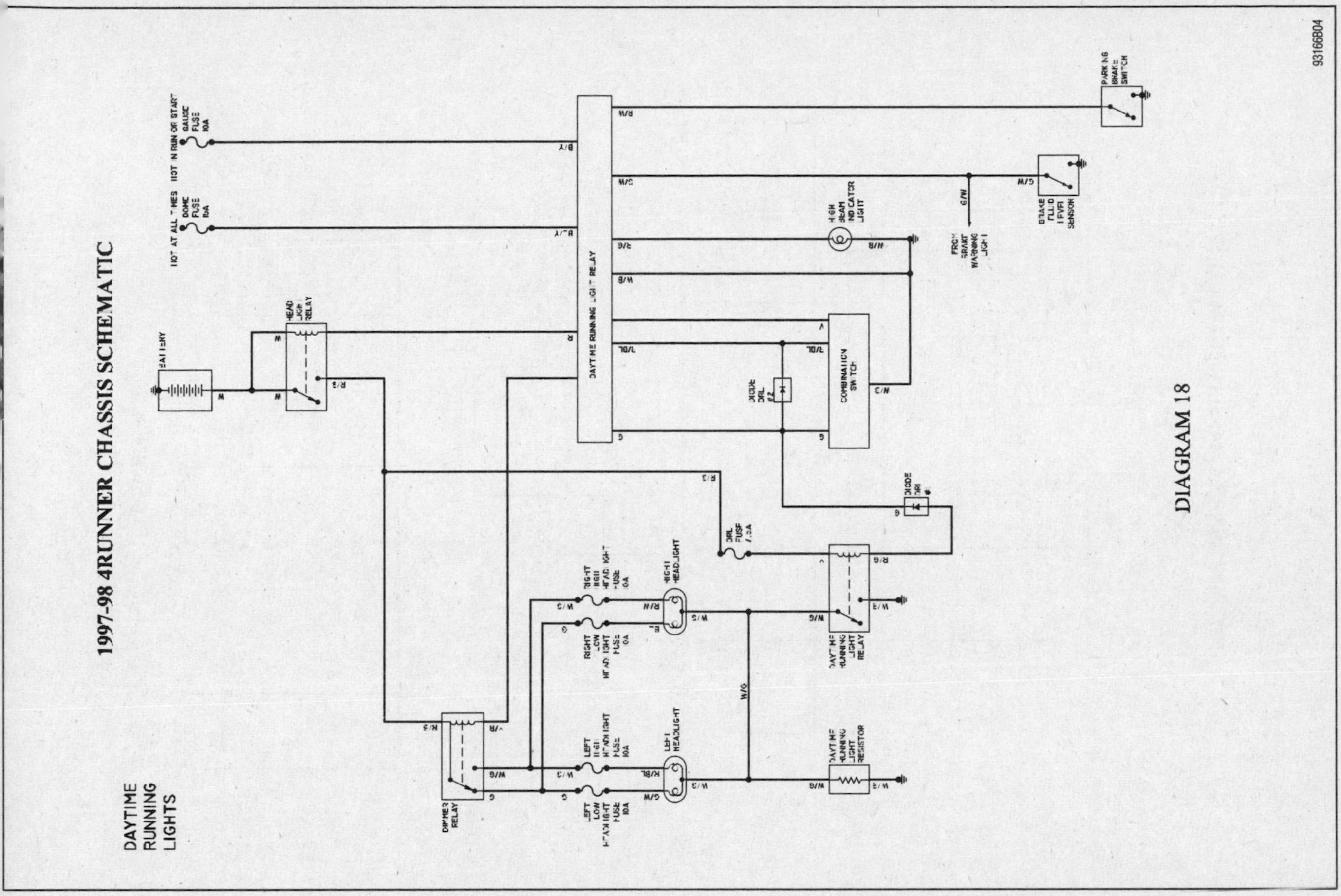
1997-98 4RUNNER CHASSIS SCHEMATIC
DAYTIME RUNNING LIGHTS
DIAGRAM 18
93166804

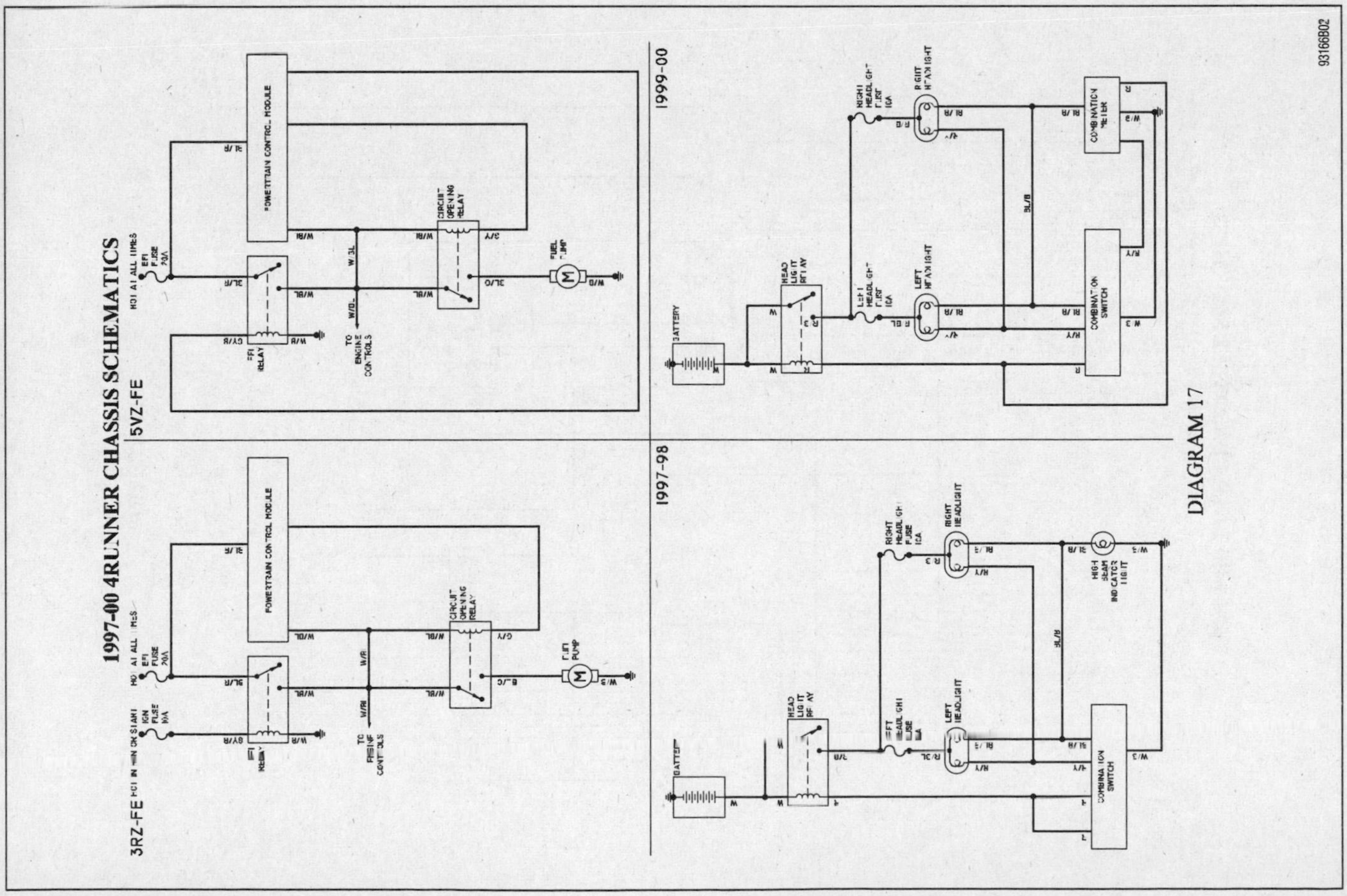
1997-00 4RUNNER CHASSIS SCHEMATICS
3RZ-FE
5VZ-FE
1997-98
1999-00
DIAGRAM 17
93166802

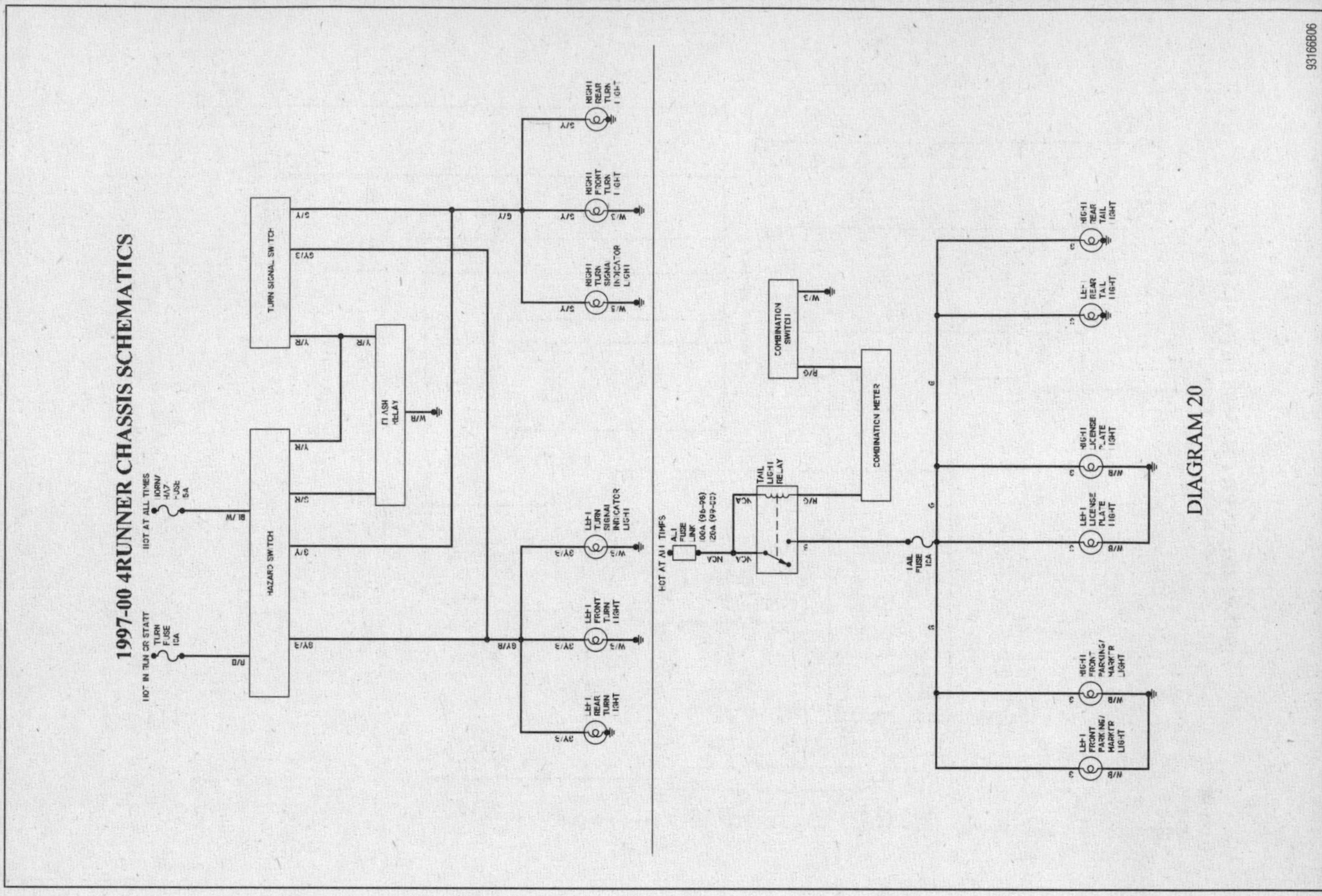
1997-00 4RUNNER CHASSIS SCHEMATICS
DIAGRAM 20
93166806

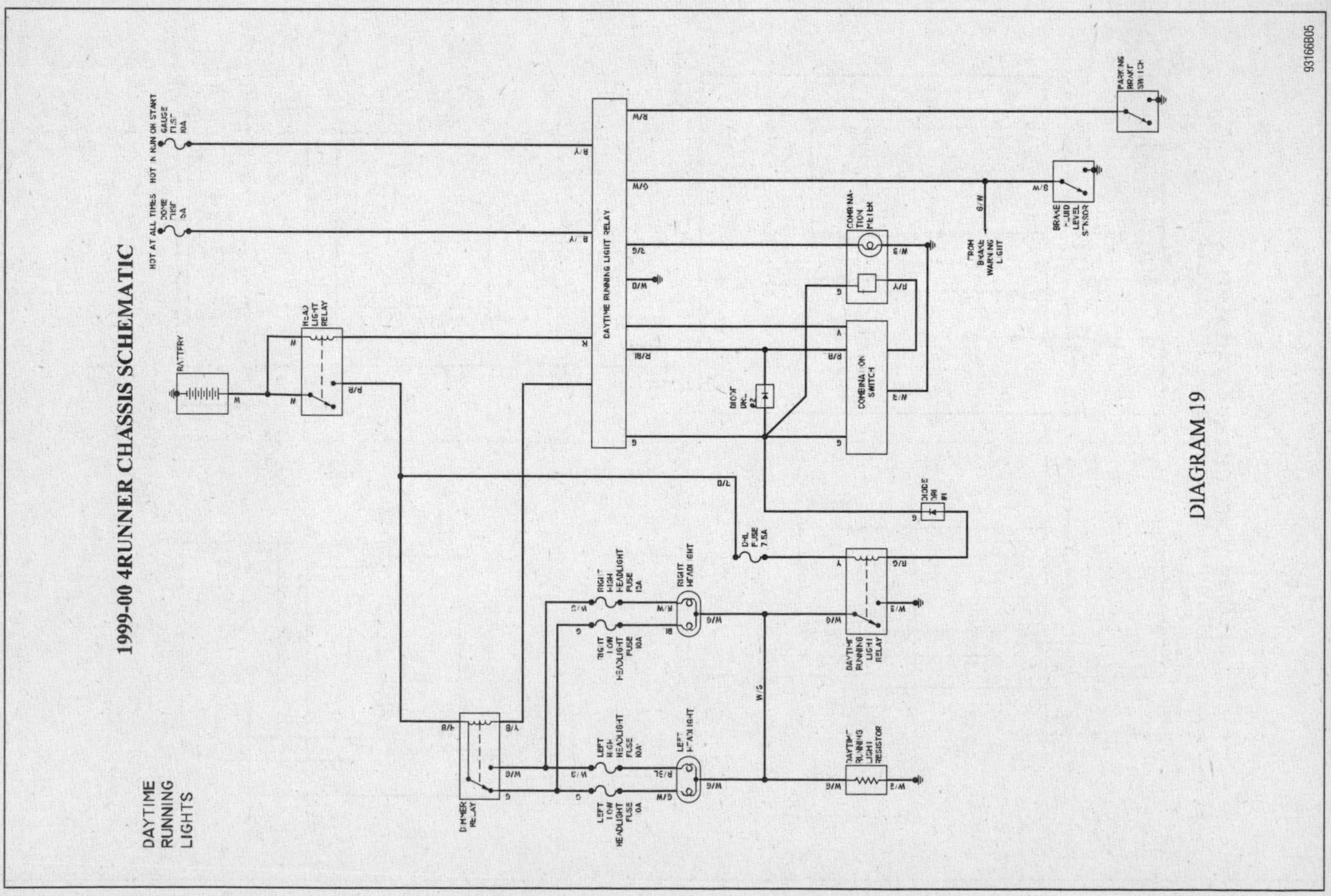
1999-00 4RUNNER CHASSIS SCHEMATIC
DAYTIME RUNNING LIGHTS
DIAGRAM 19
93166805

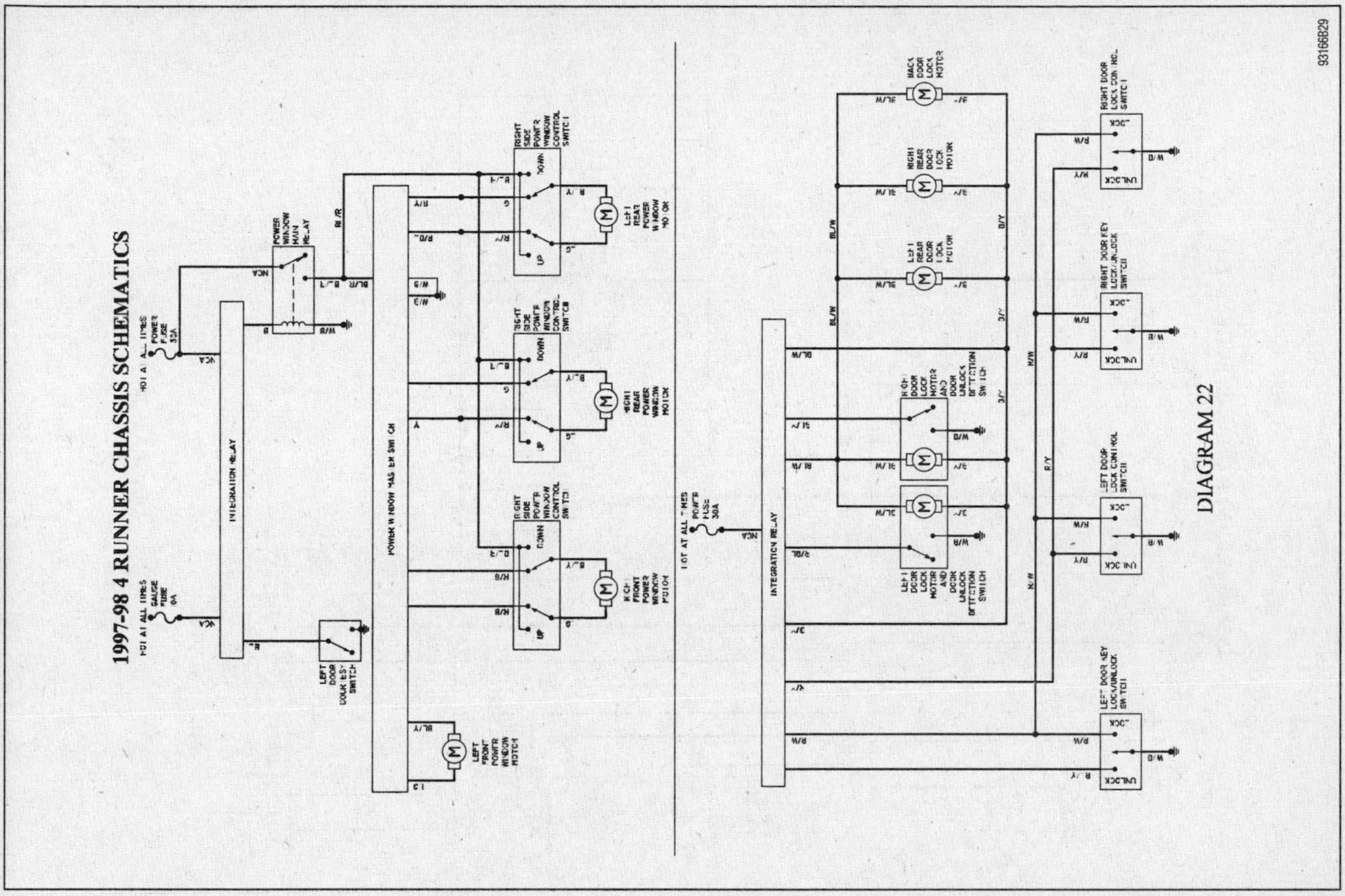

1997-98 4 RUNNER CHASSIS SCHEMATICS

DIAGRAM 22

93166829

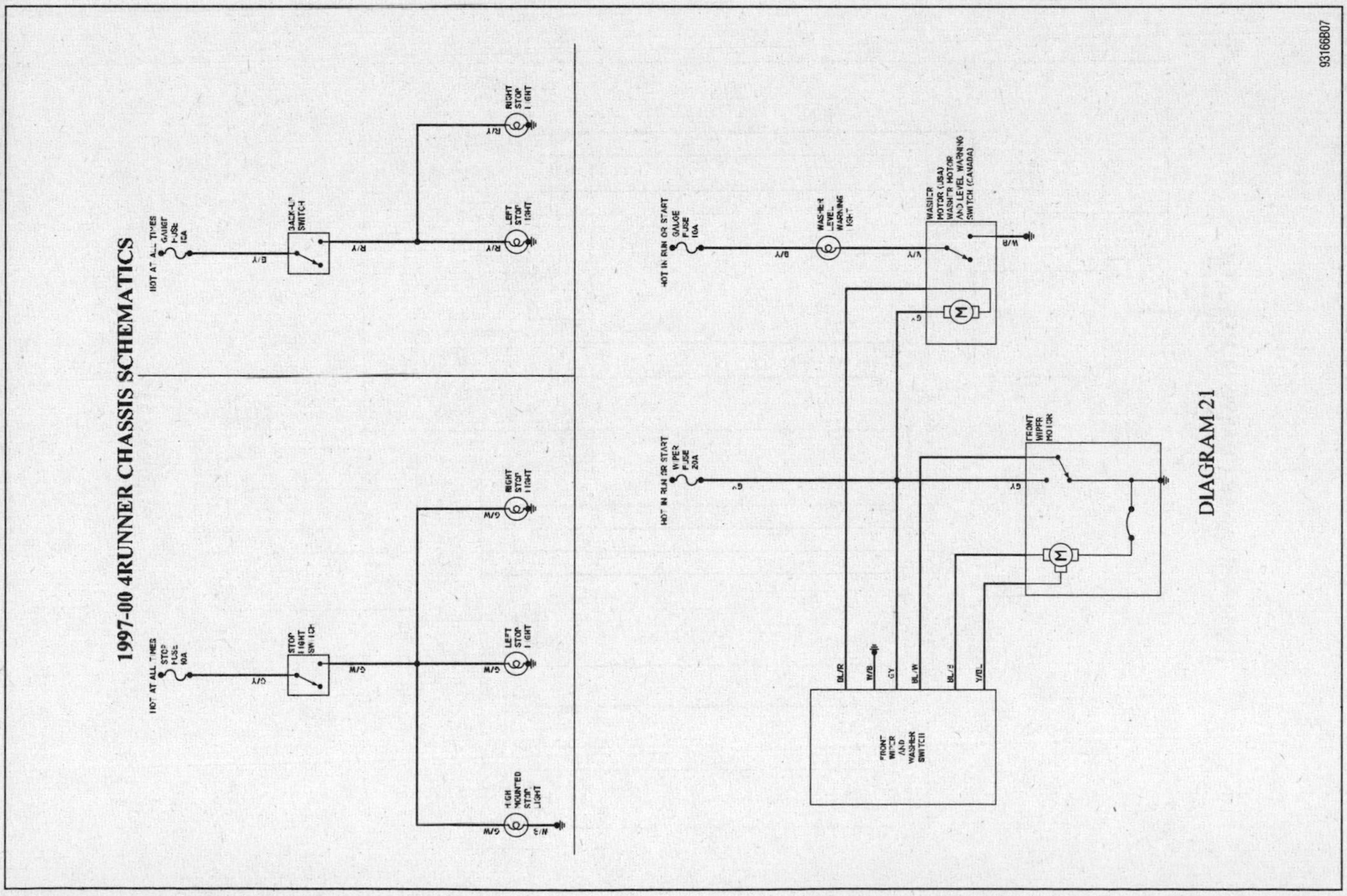

1997-00 4RUNNER CHASSIS SCHEMATICS

DIAGRAM 21

93166807

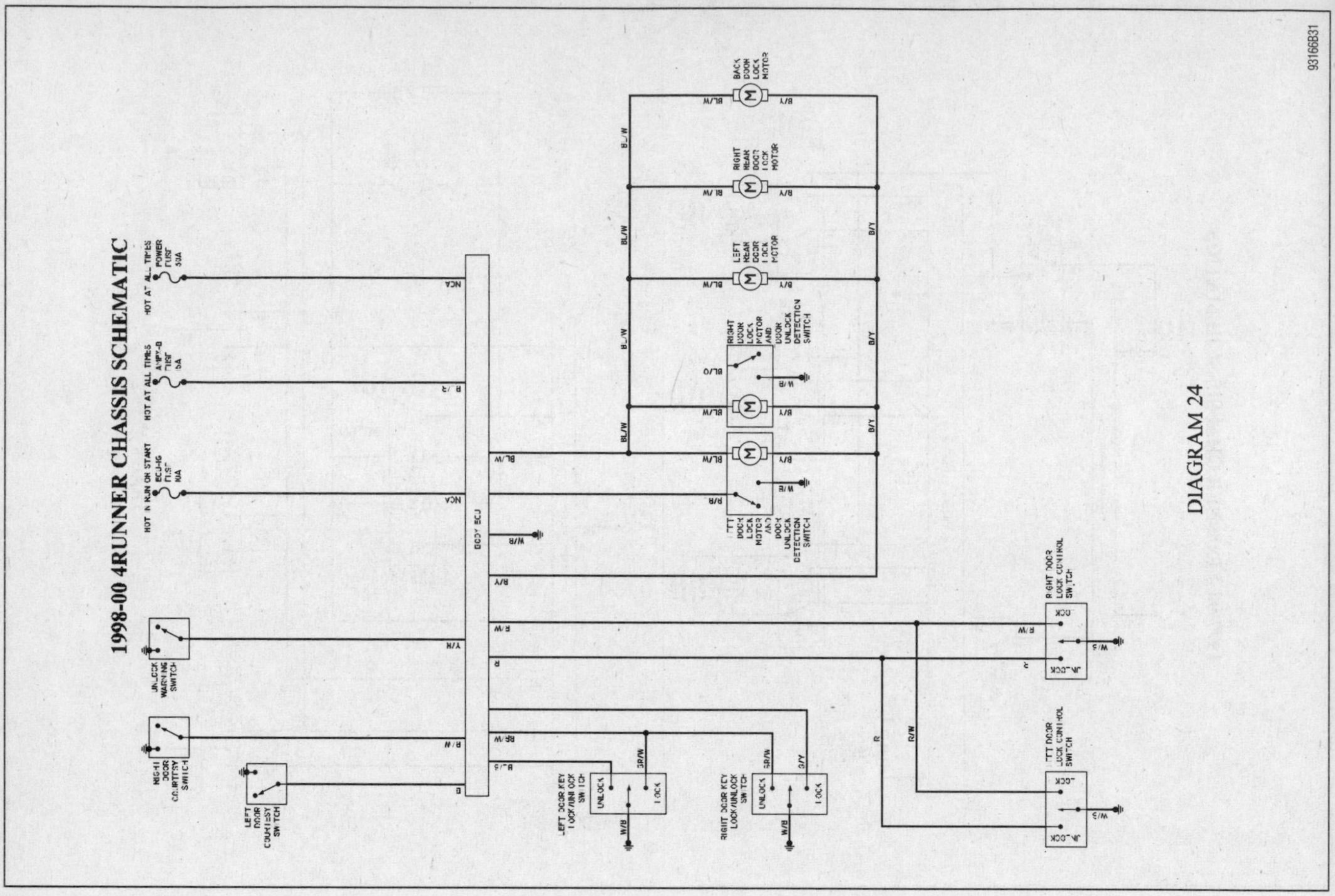
1998-00 4RUNNER CHASSIS SCHEMATIC
DIAGRAM 24
93166831

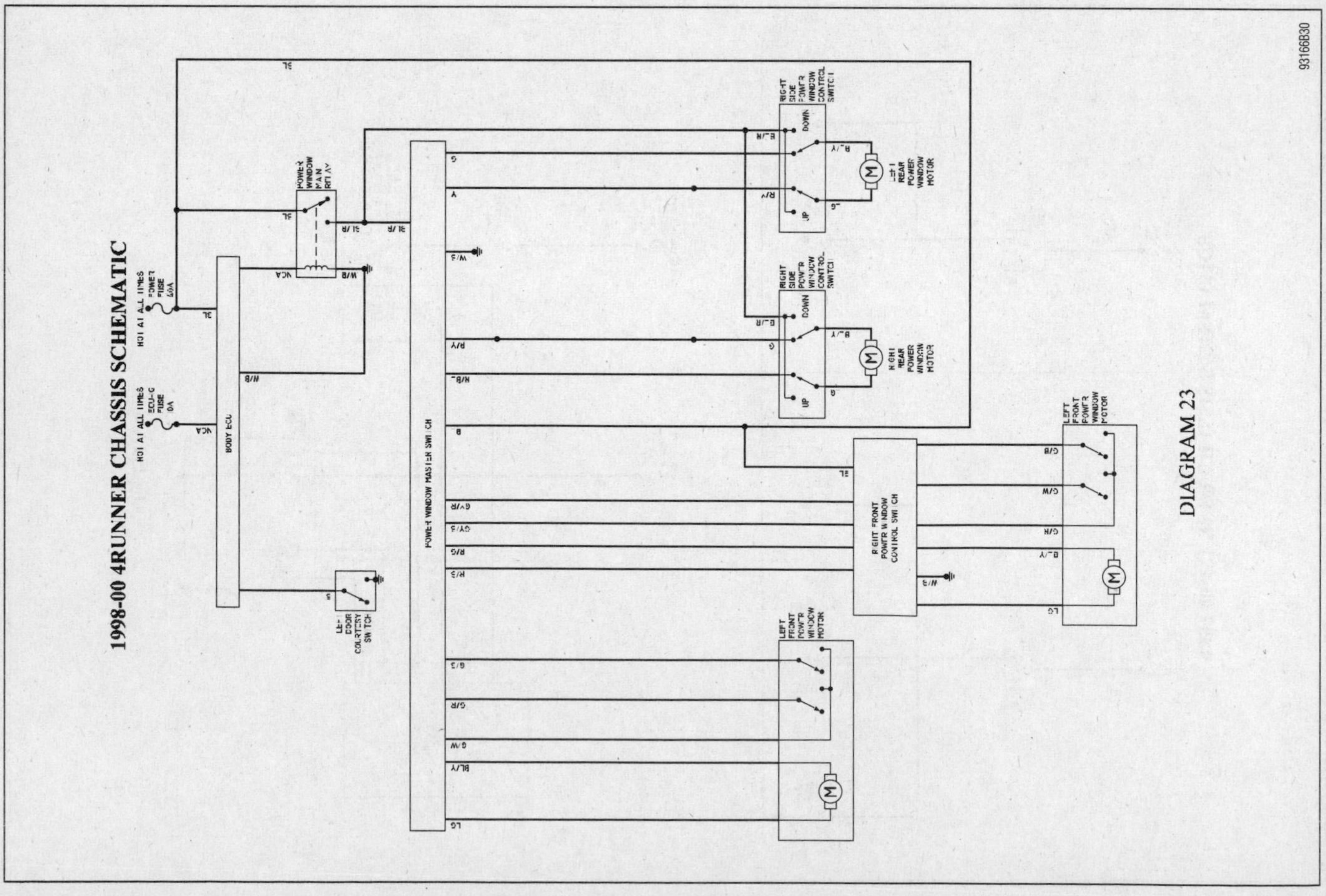
1998-00 4RUNNER CHASSIS SCHEMATIC
DIAGRAM 23
93166830

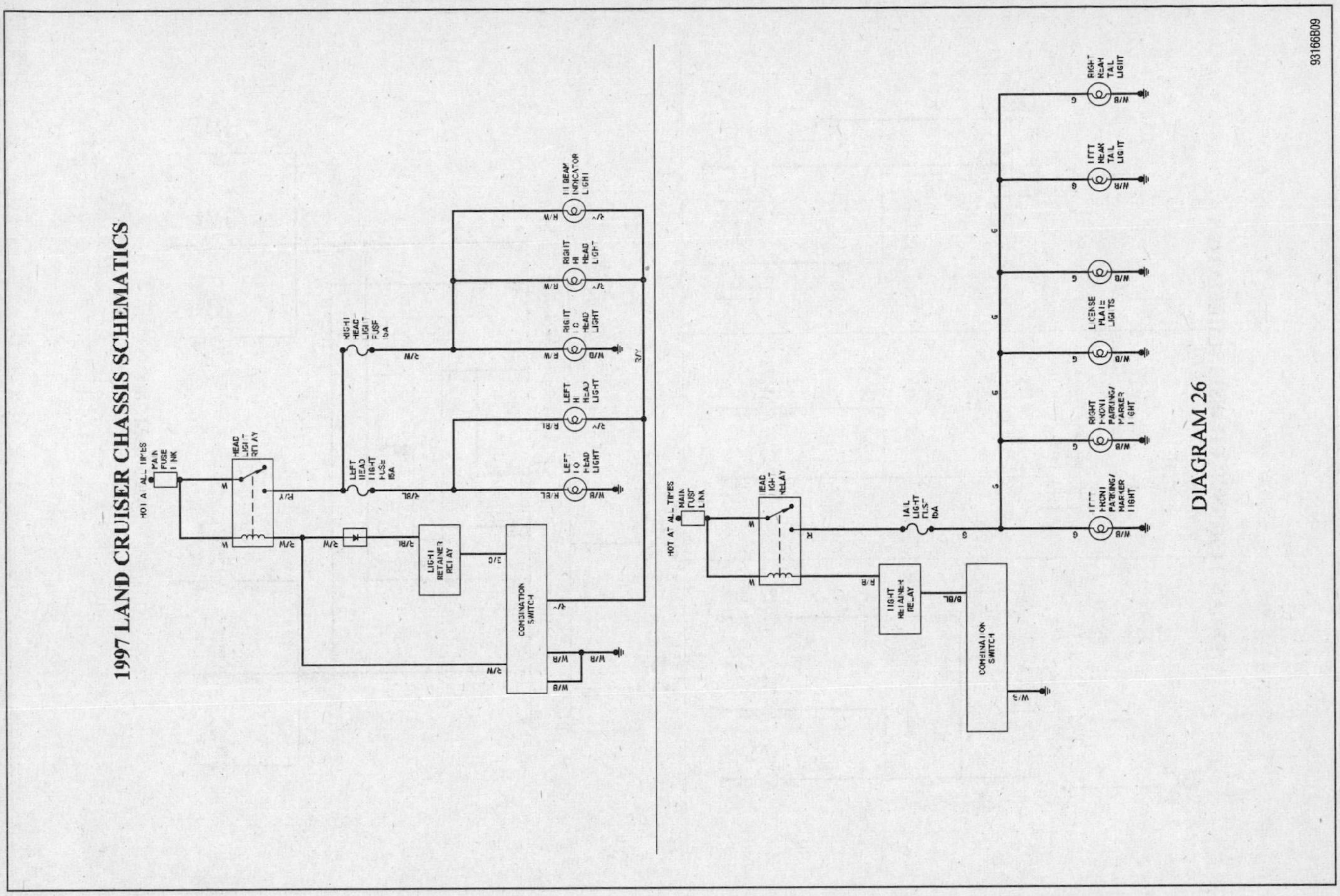
1997 LAND CRUISER CHASSIS SCHEMATICS
DIAGRAM 26
93166B09

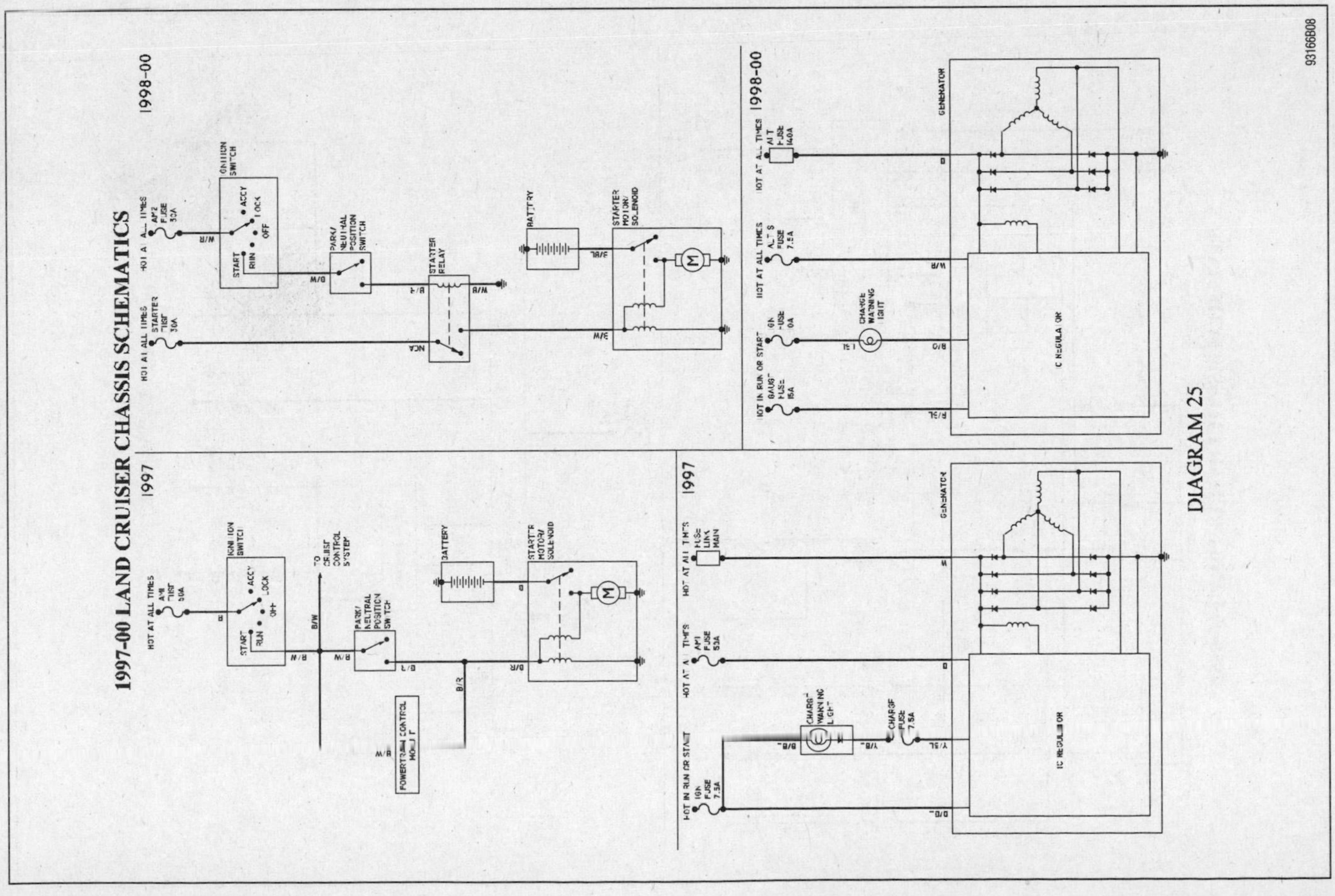
1997-00 LAND CRUISER CHASSIS SCHEMATICS
1997
1998-00
DIAGRAM 25
93166B08

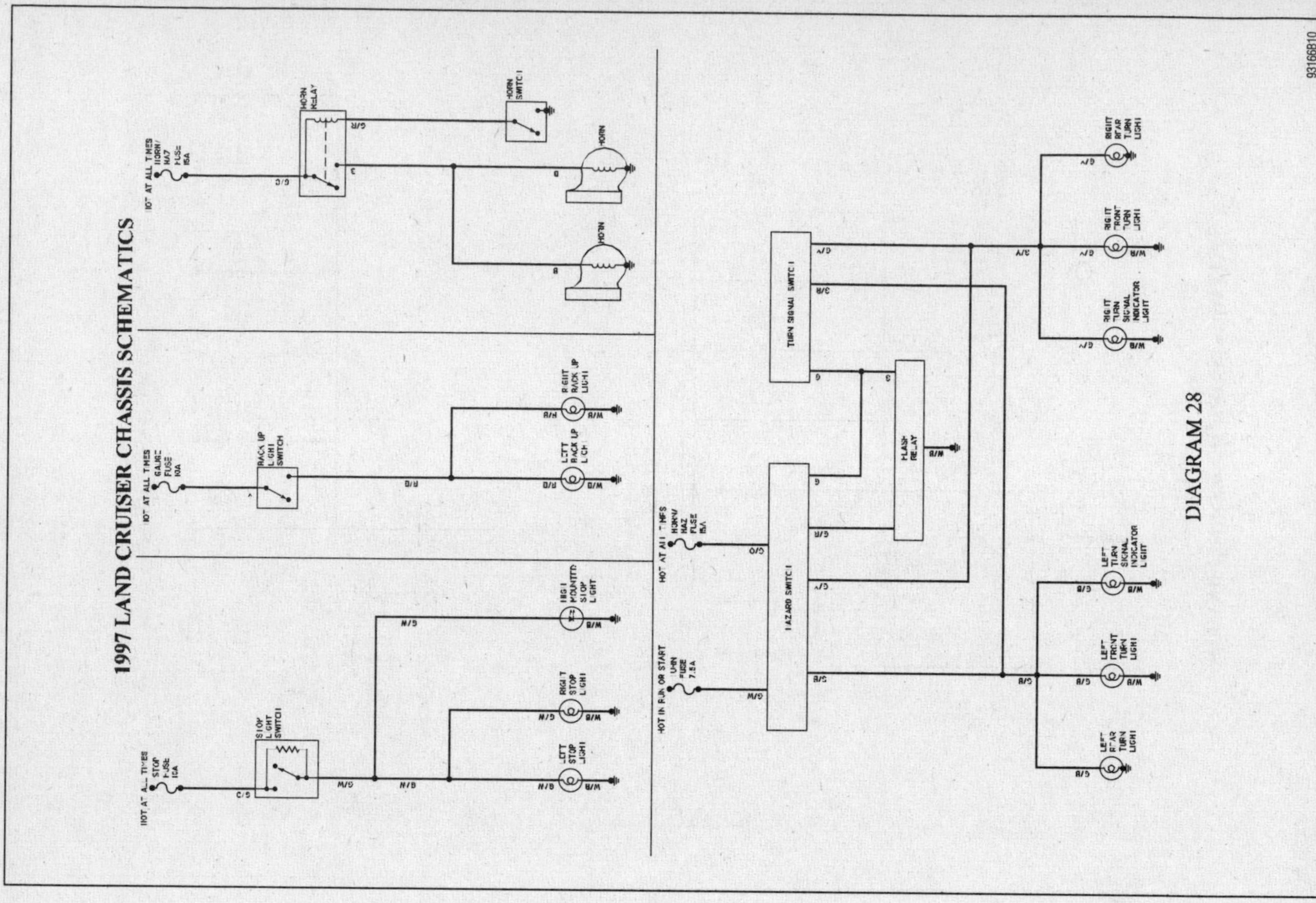
1997 LAND CRUISER CHASSIS SCHEMATICS
DIAGRAM 28
93166810

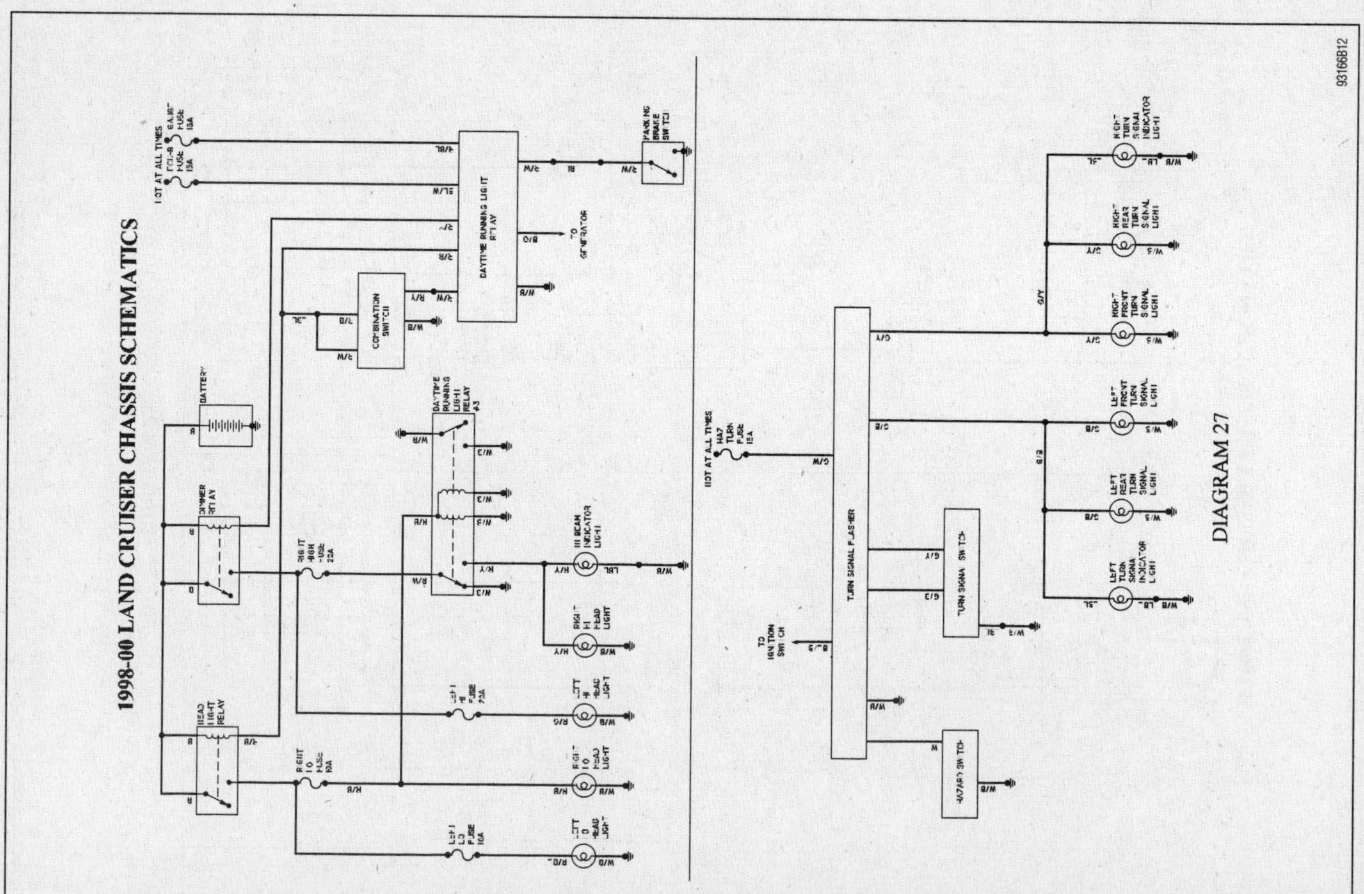
1998-00 LAND CRUISER CHASSIS SCHEMATICS
DIAGRAM 27
93166812

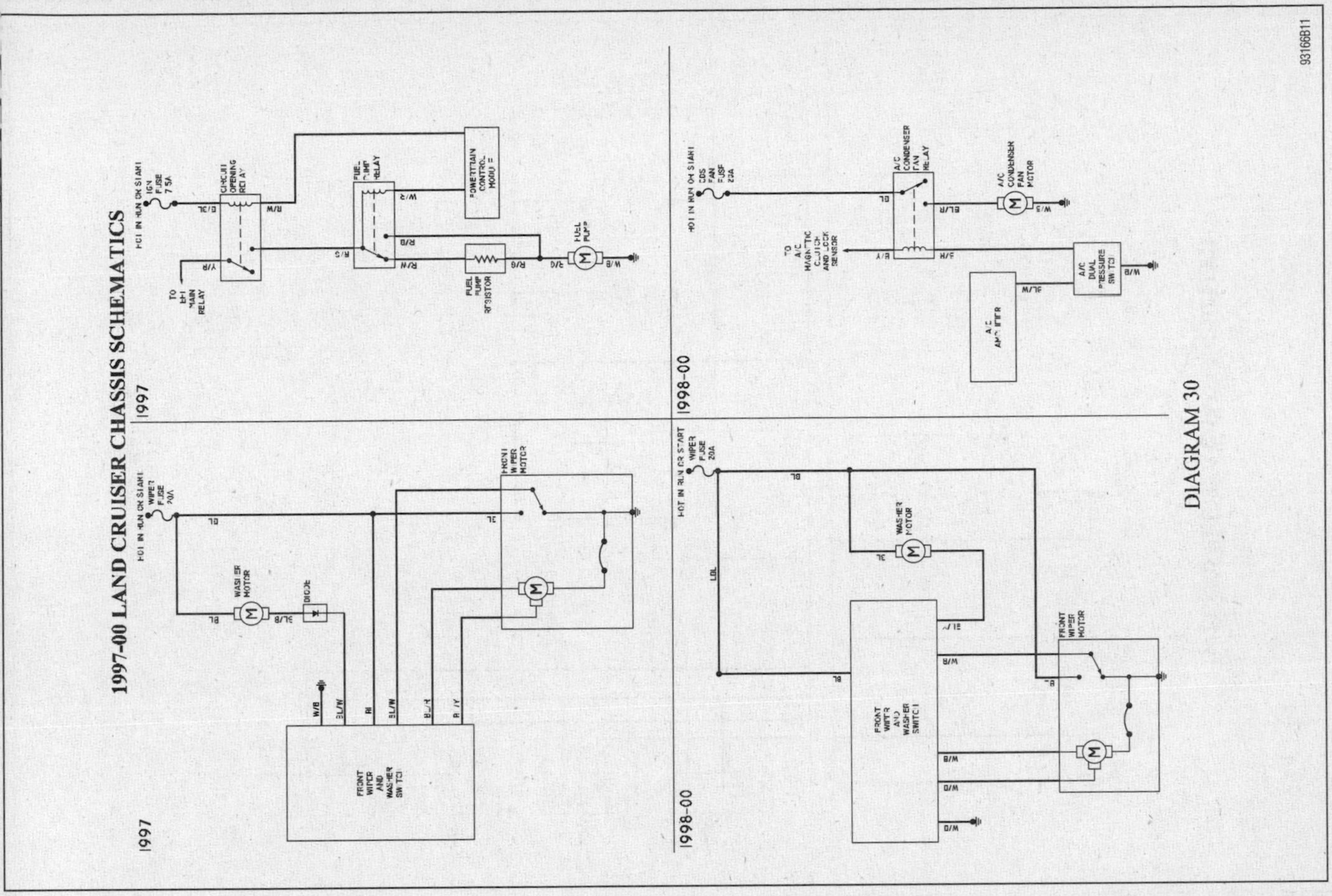

DIAGRAM 30

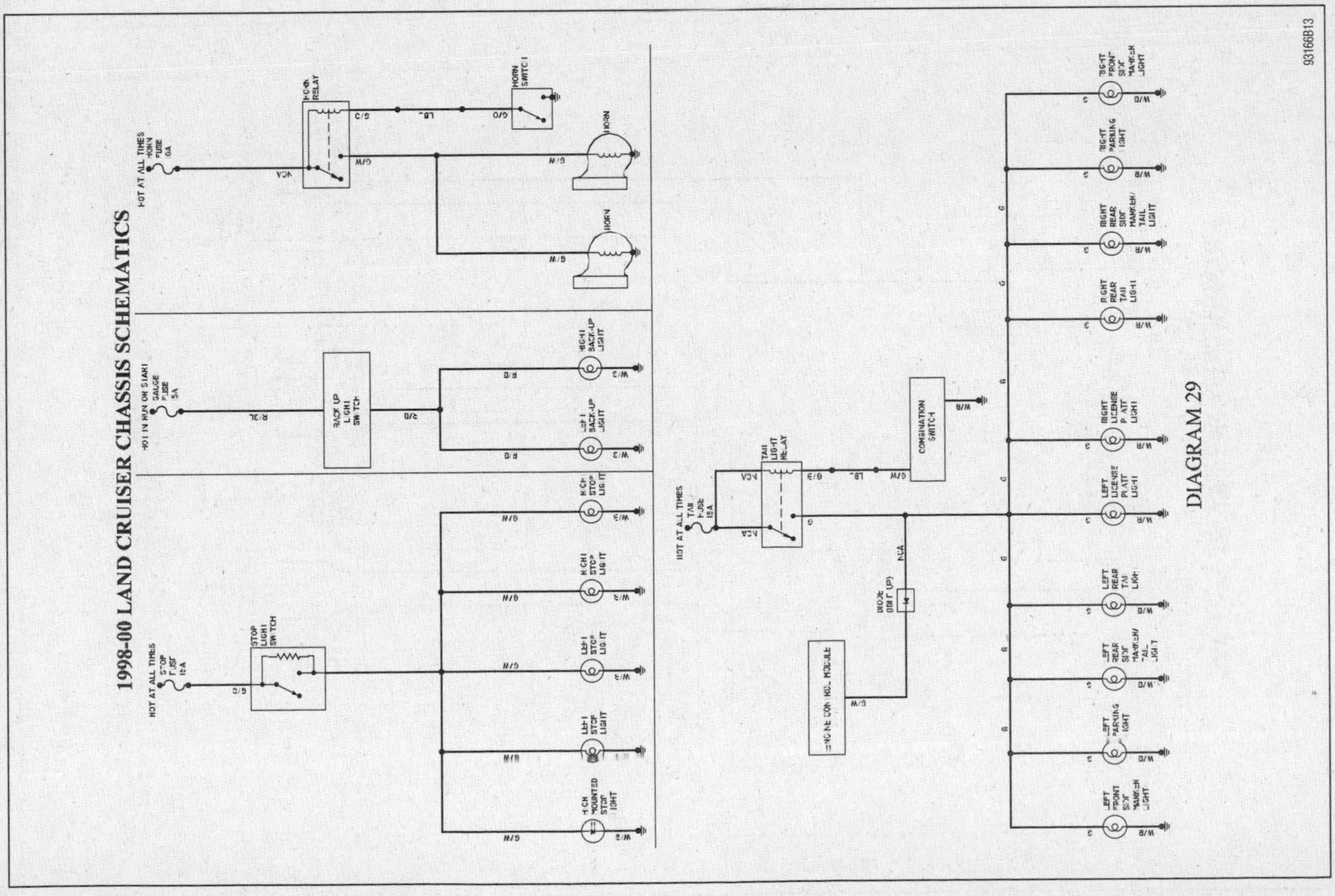

DIAGRAM 29

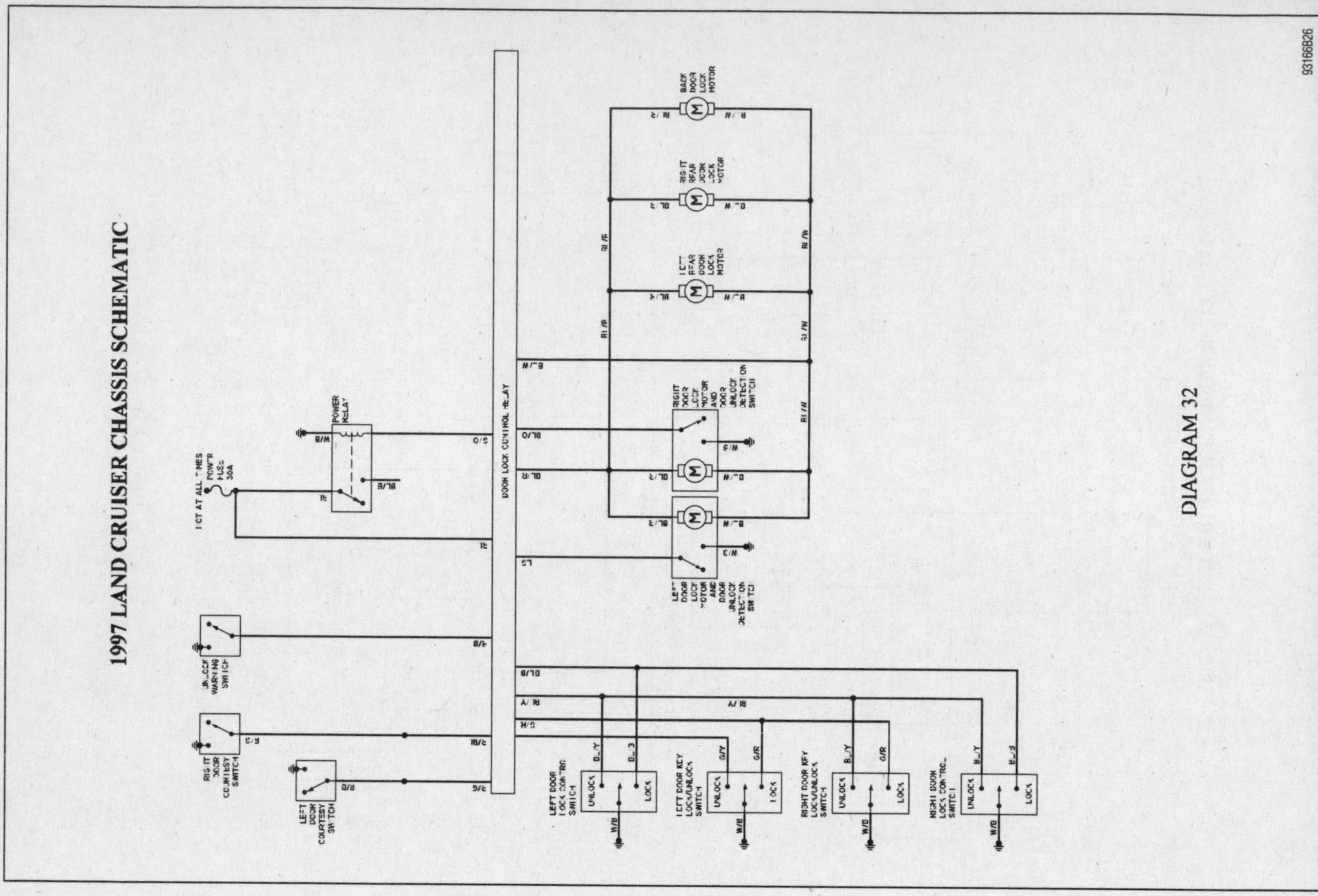
1997 LAND CRUISER CHASSIS SCHEMATIC
DOOR LOCK CONTROL RELAY
DIAGRAM 32
93166B26

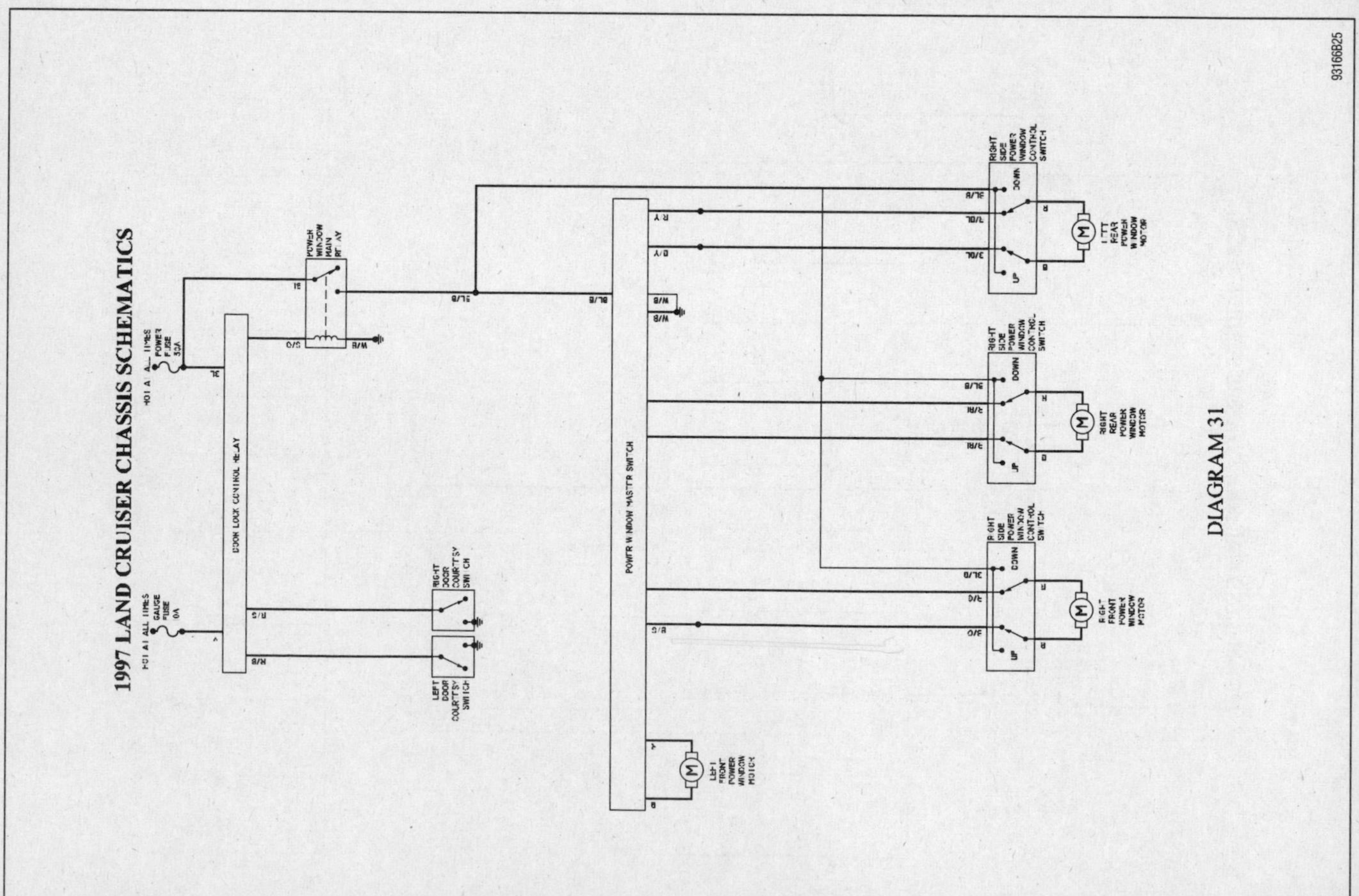
1997 LAND CRUISER CHASSIS SCHEMATICS
DOOR LOCK CONTROL RELAY
POWER WINDOW MASTER SWITCH
DIAGRAM 31
93166B25

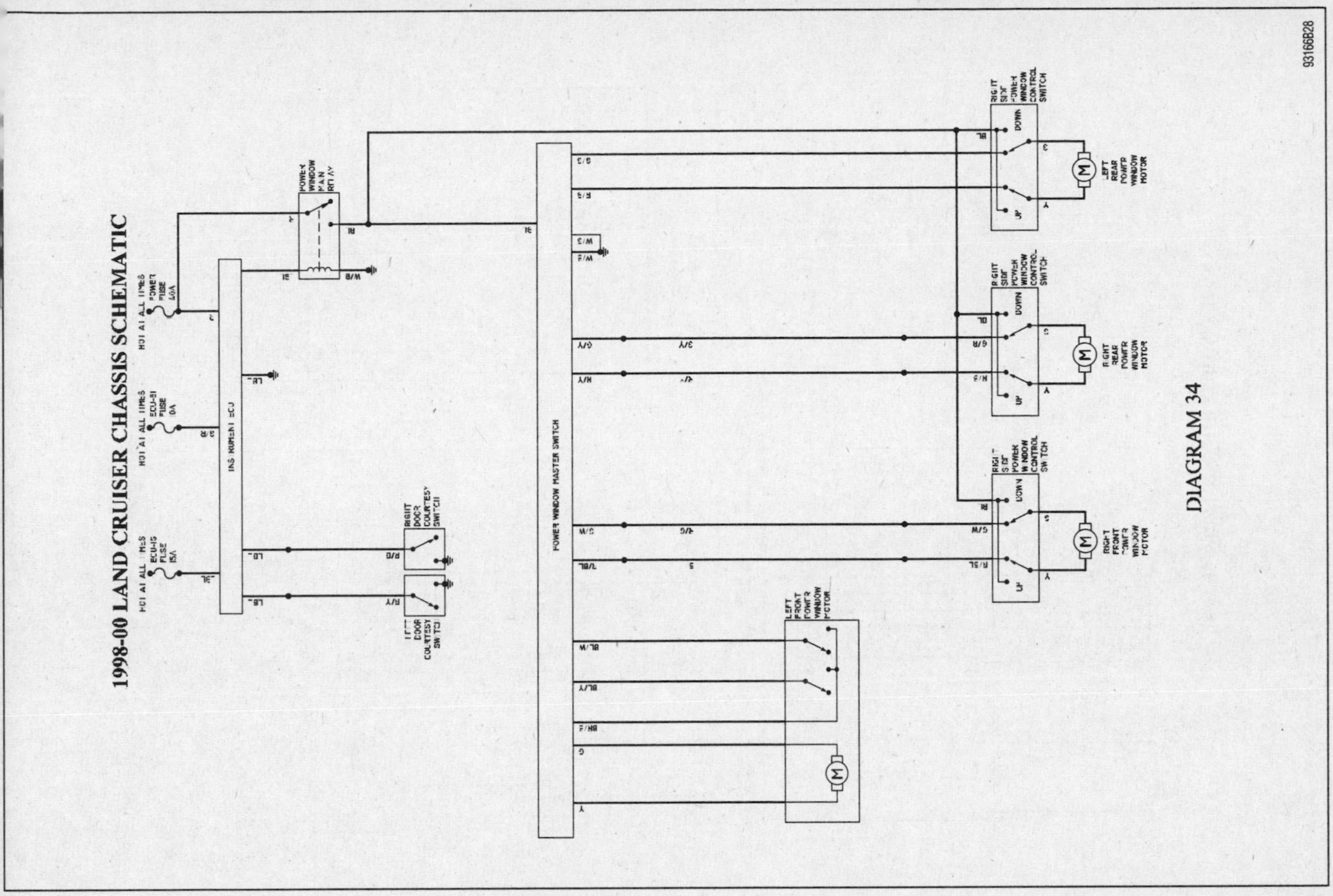
1998-00 LAND CRUISER CHASSIS SCHEMATIC
POWER WINDOW MASTER SWITCH
DIAGRAM 34
93166B28

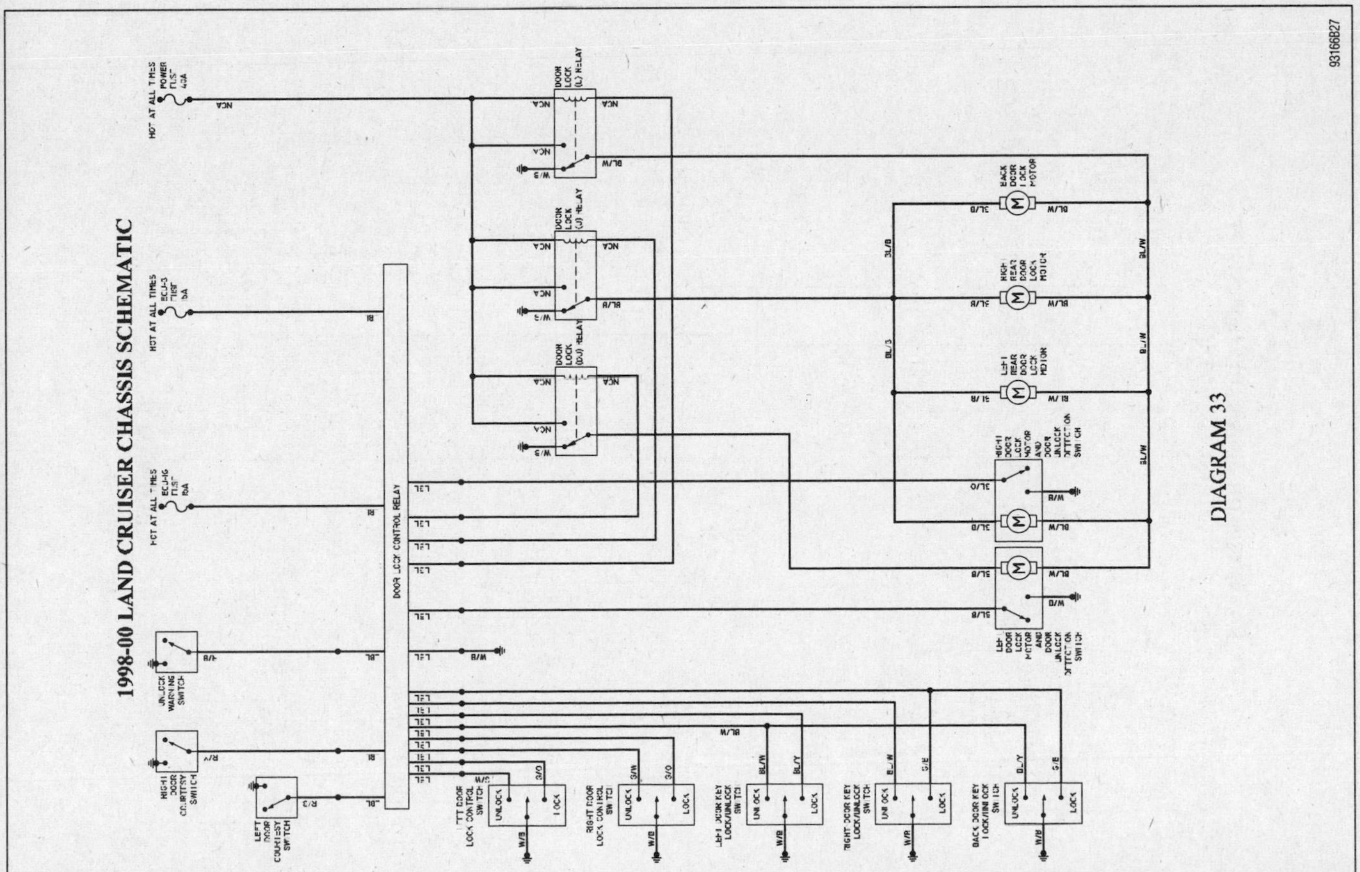
1998-00 LAND CRUISER CHASSIS SCHEMATIC
DOOR LOCK CONTROL RELAY
DIAGRAM 33
93166B27

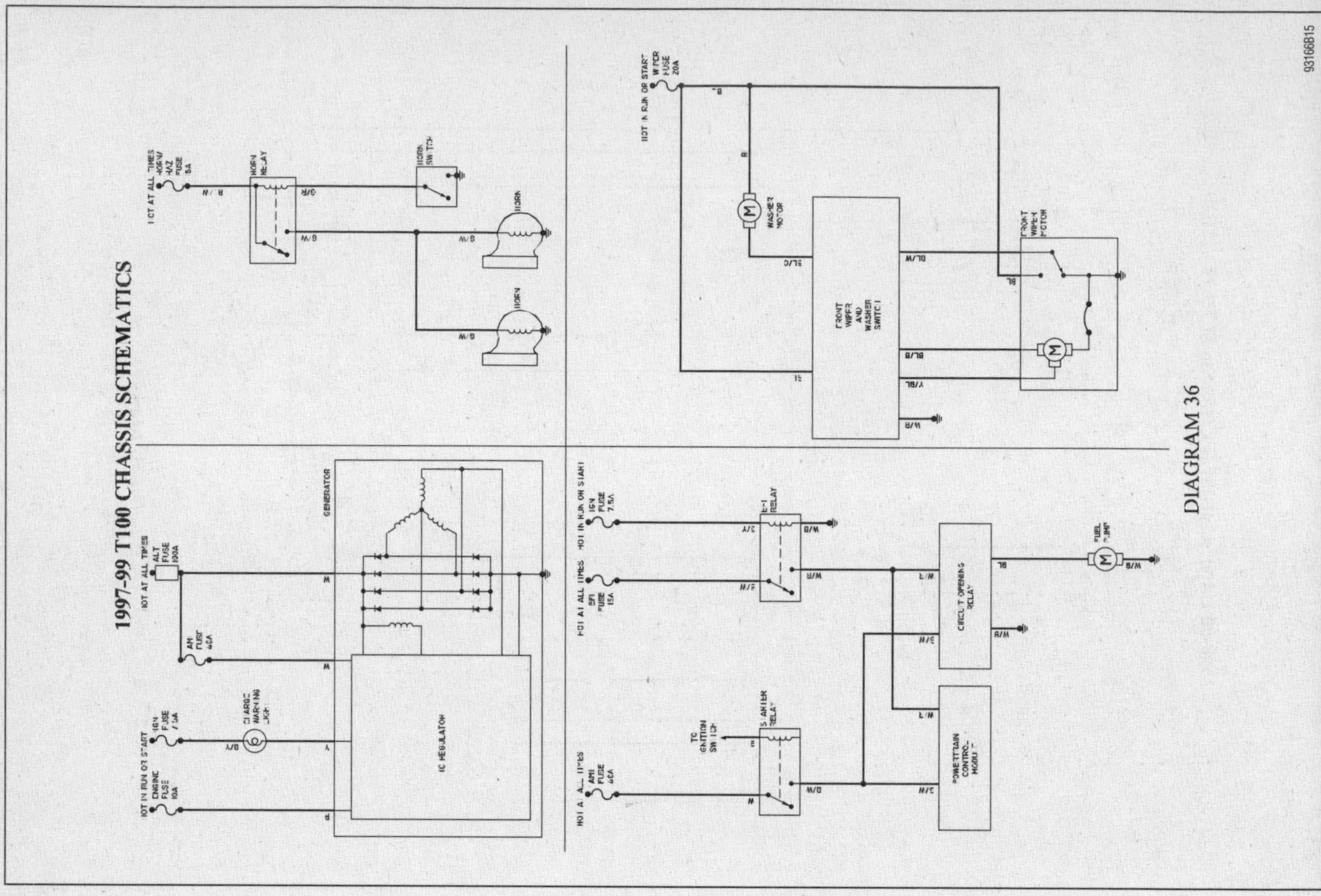
1997-99 T100 CHASSIS SCHEMATICS
DIAGRAM 36
93166B15
GENERATOR
IC REGULATOR
FRONT WIPER AND WASHER SWITCH
CIRCUIT OPENING RELAY
POWERTRAIN CONTROL MODULE

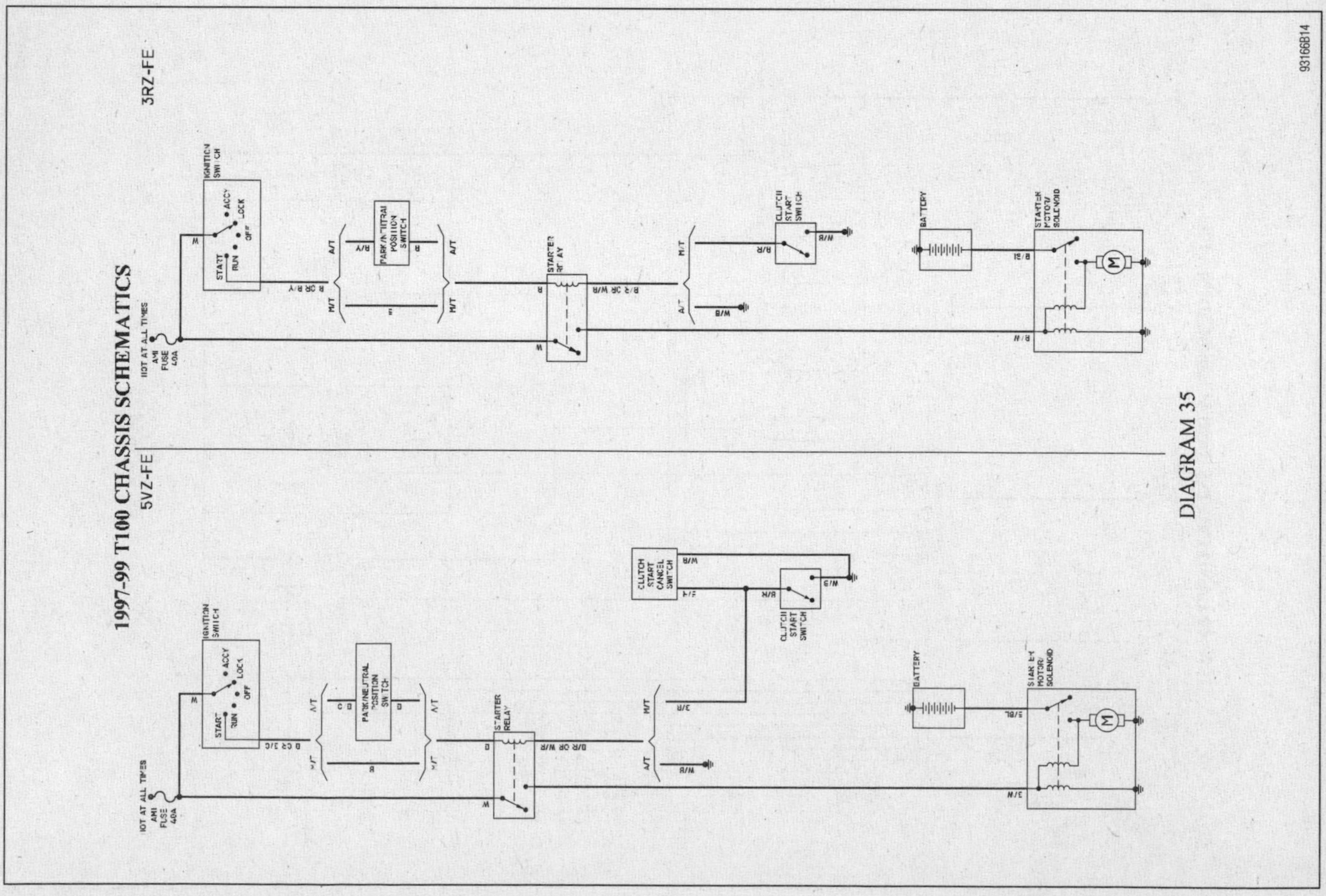
1997-99 T100 CHASSIS SCHEMATICS
3RZ-FE
5VZ-FE
DIAGRAM 35
93166B14
IGNITION SWITCH
STARTER RELAY
BATTERY

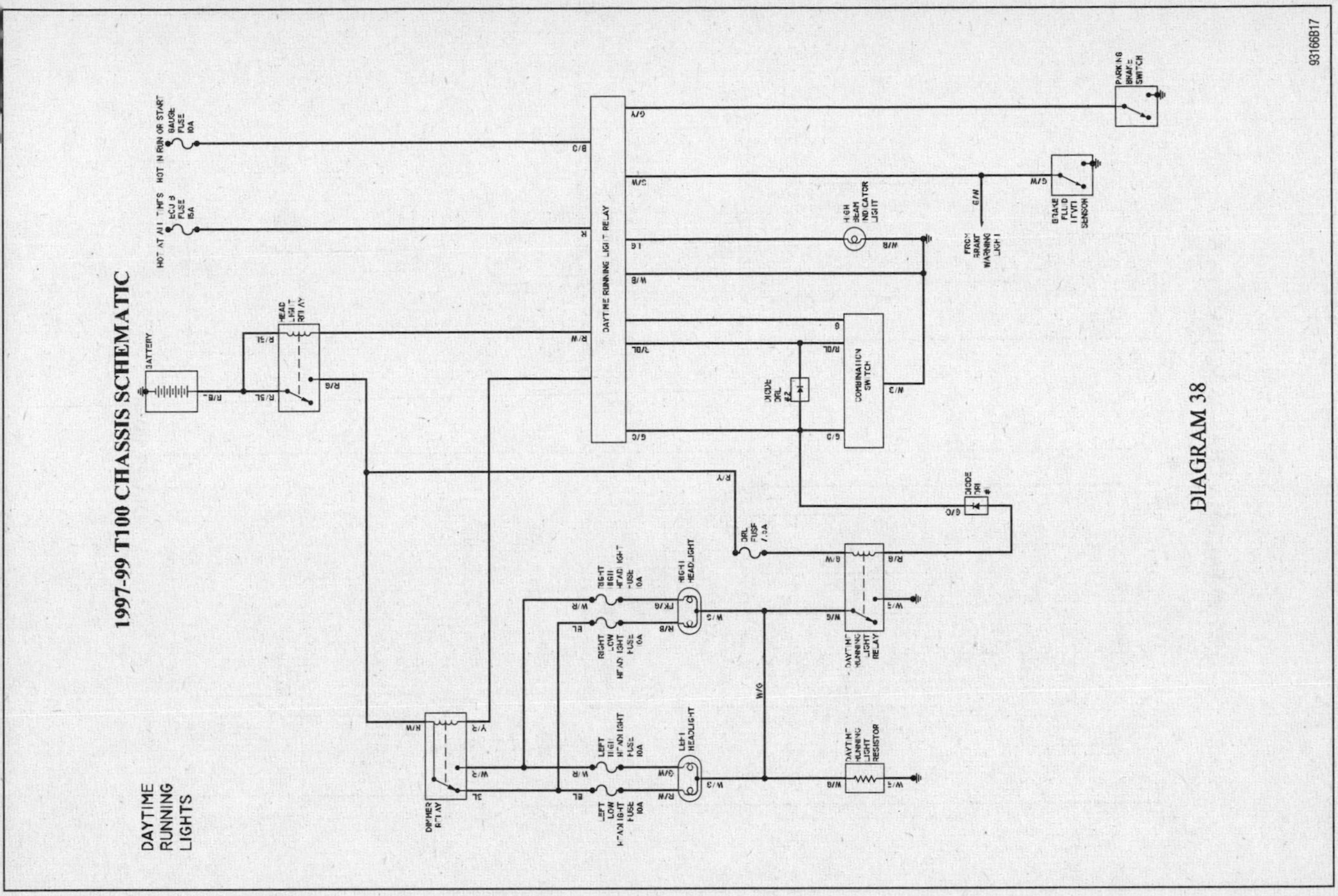
1997-99 T100 CHASSIS SCHEMATIC
DAYTIME RUNNING LIGHTS
DIAGRAM 38
93166817

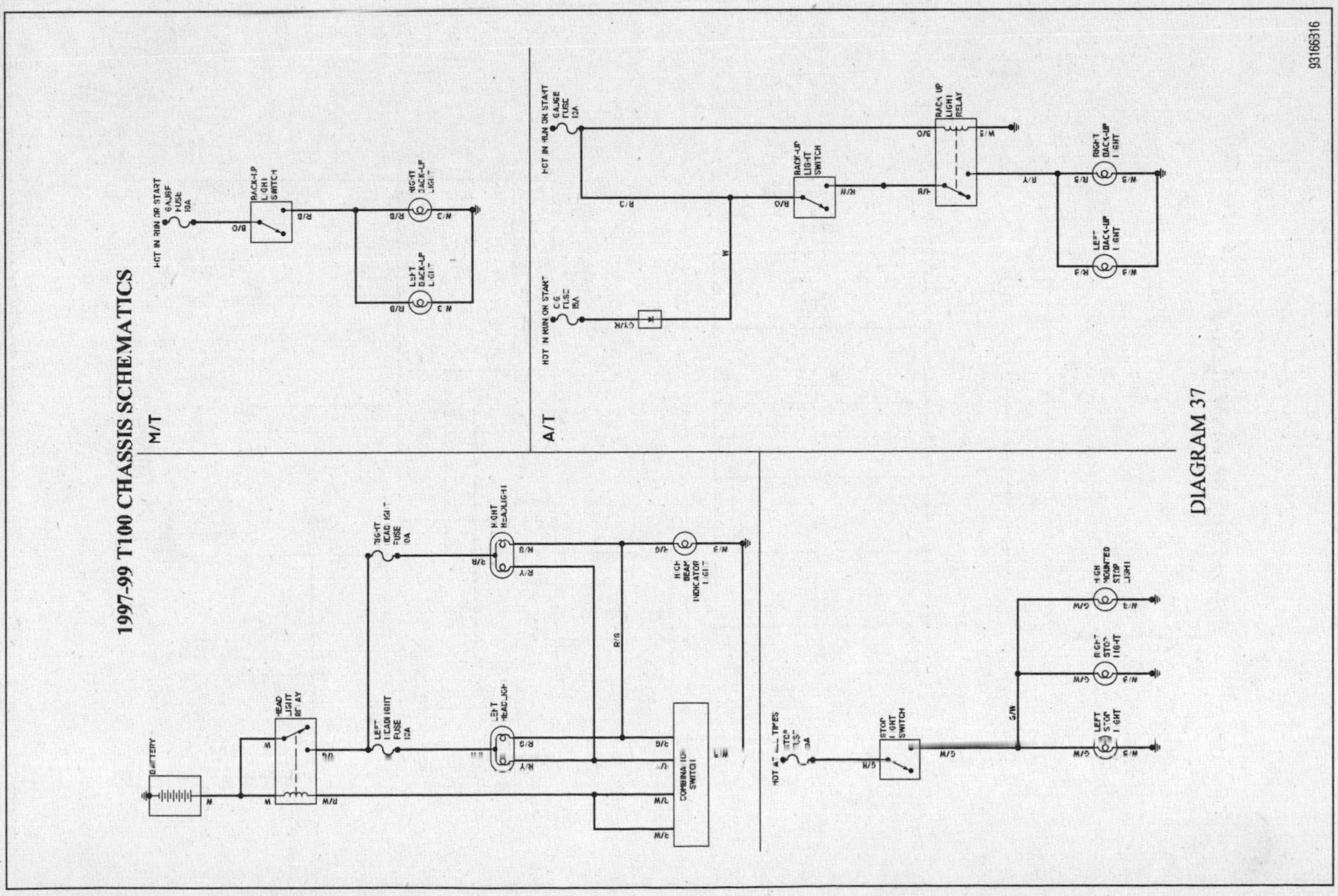
1997-99 T100 CHASSIS SCHEMATICS
M/T
A/T
DIAGRAM 37
93166316

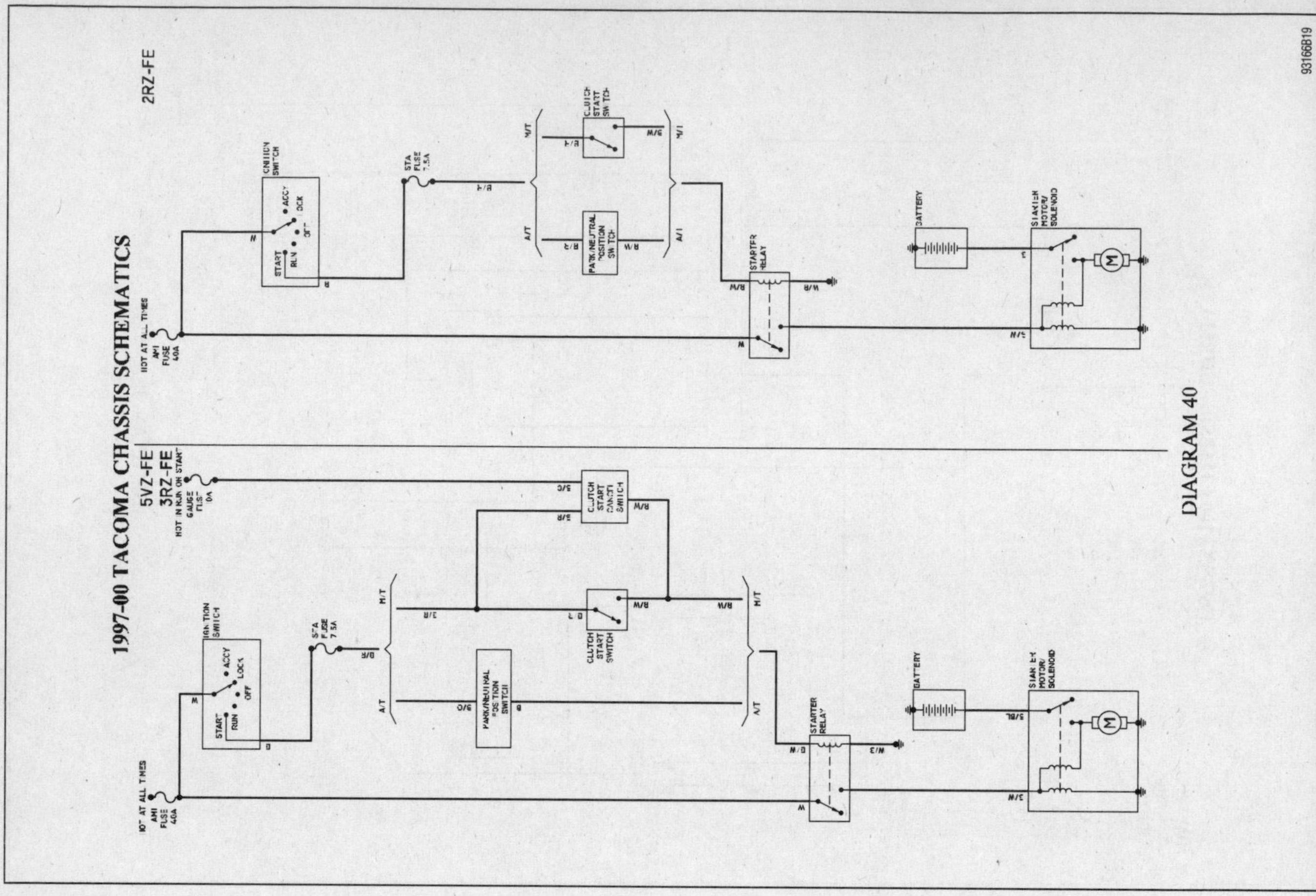
1997-00 TACOMA CHASSIS SCHEMATICS
2RZ-FE
5VZ-FE
3RZ-FE
DIAGRAM 40
93166819

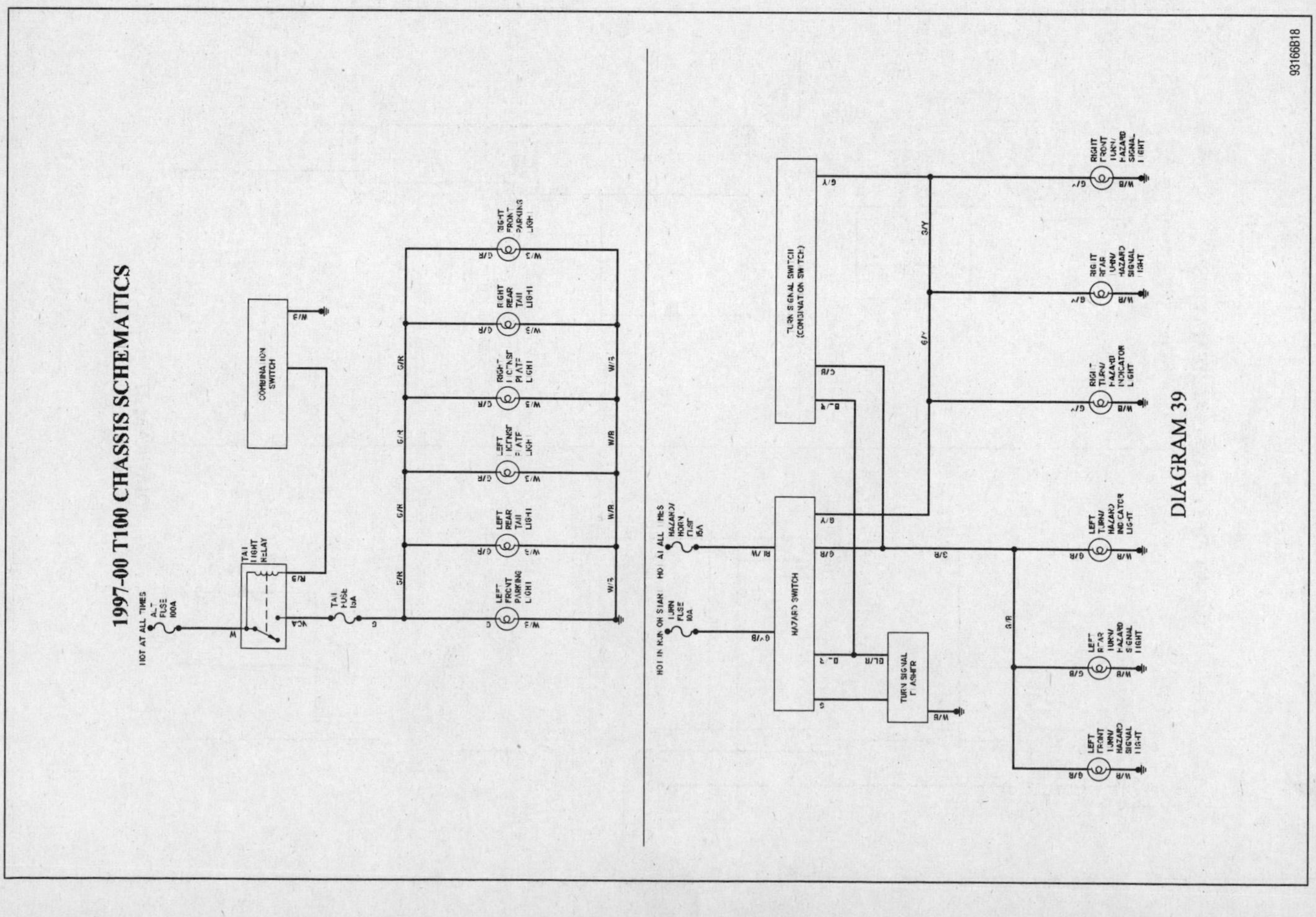
1997-00 T100 CHASSIS SCHEMATICS
DIAGRAM 39
93166818

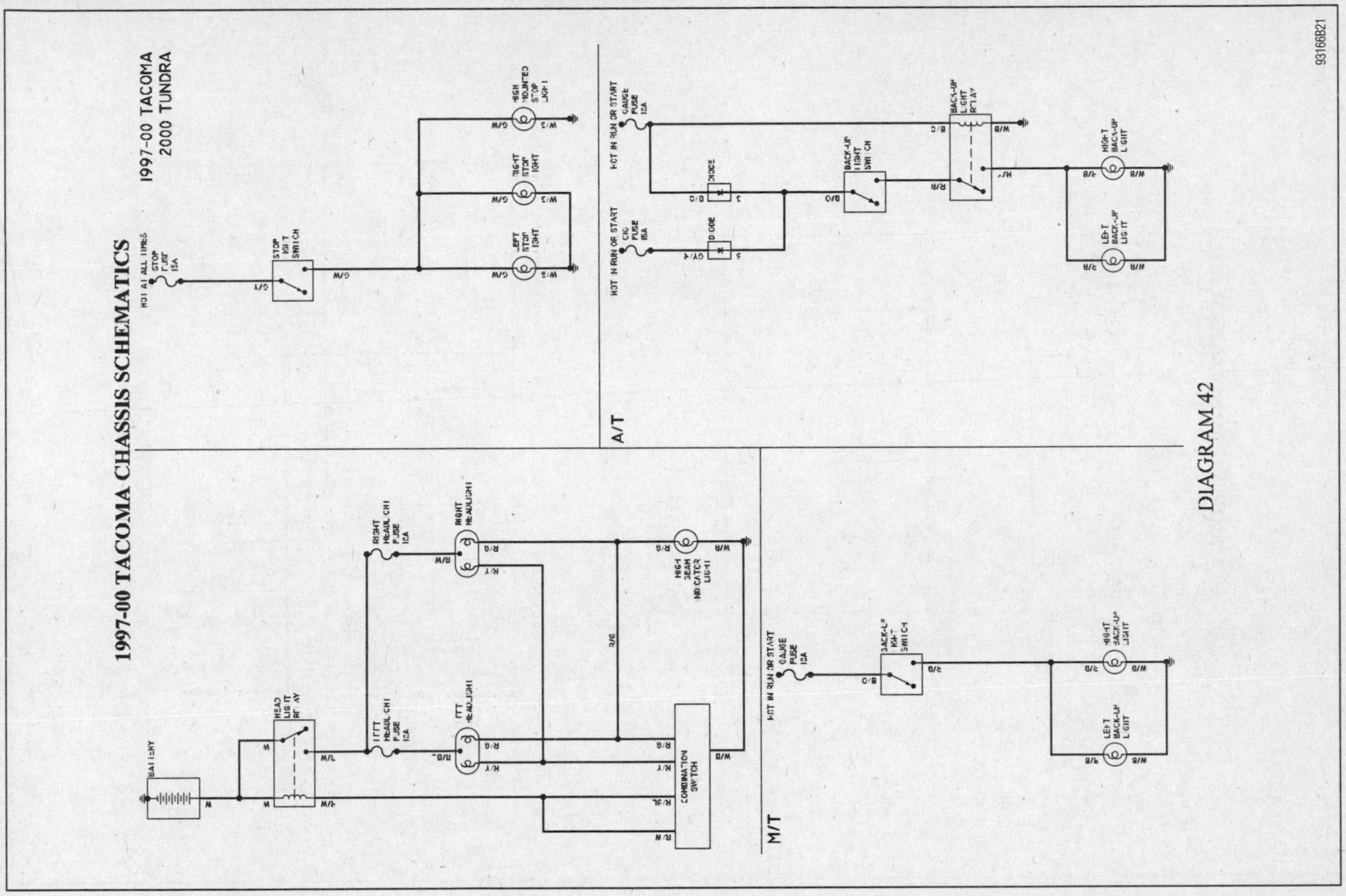
1997-00 TACOMA CHASSIS SCHEMATICS
1997-00 TACOMA
2000 TUNDRA
HOT AT ALL TIMES STOP FUSE 15A
STOP LIGHT SWITCH
LEFT STOP LIGHT
RIGHT STOP LIGHT
HIGH MOUNTED STOP LIGHT
HOT IN RUN OR START GAUGE FUSE 10A
HOT IN RUN OR START CIG FUSE 15A
DIODE
BACK-UP LIGHT SWITCH
BACK-UP LIGHT RELAY
LEFT BACK-UP LIGHT
RIGHT BACK-UP LIGHT
A/T
BATTERY
HEAD LIGHT RELAY
LEFT HEADLIGHT
RIGHT HEADLIGHT
HIGH BEAM INDICATOR LIGHT
COMBINATION SWITCH
M/T
DIAGRAM 42
93166B21

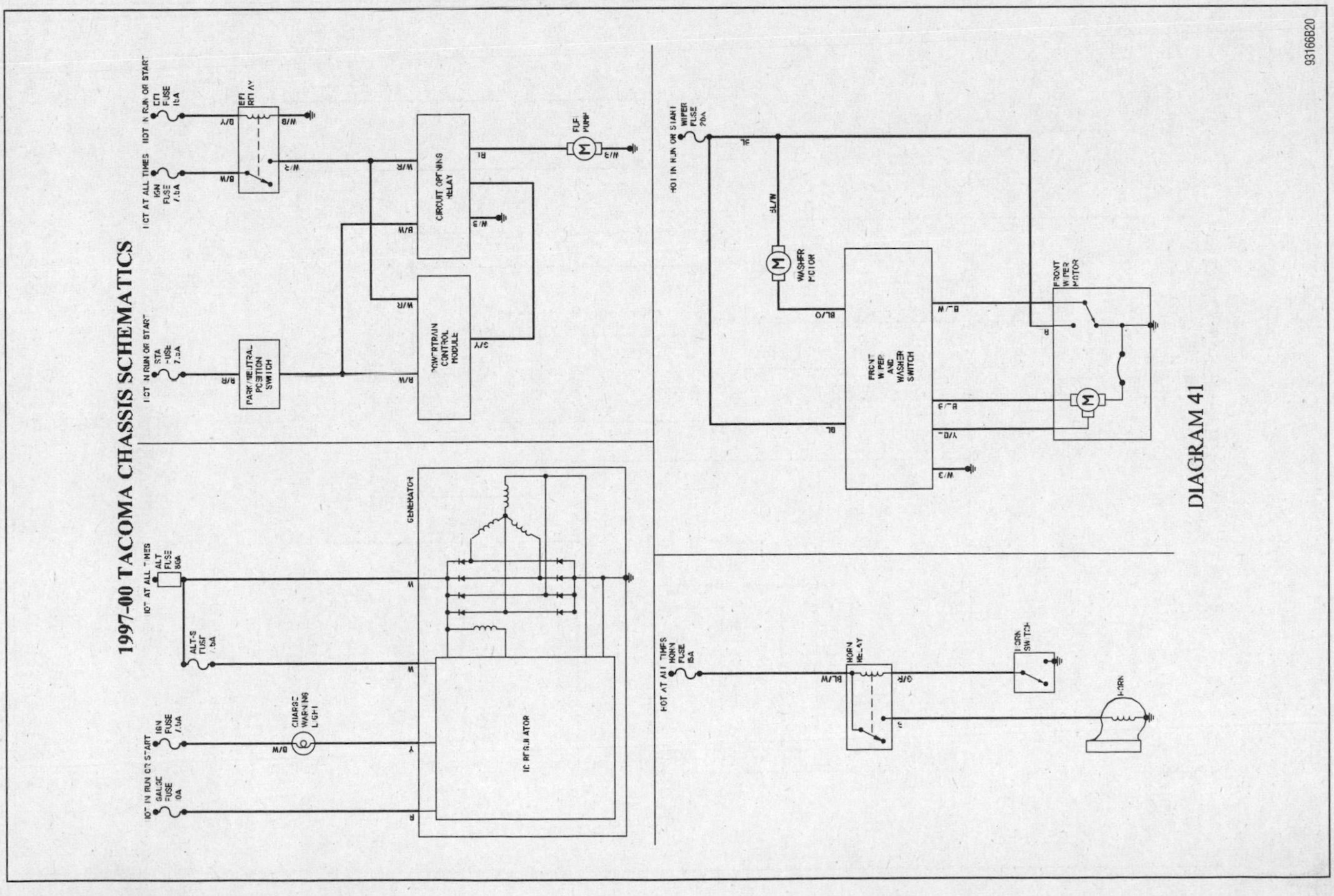
1997-00 TACOMA CHASSIS SCHEMATICS
HOT AT ALL TIMES ALT FUSE
GENERATOR
IC REGULATOR
CHARGE WARNING LIGHT
HOT IN RUN OR START STA FUSE 7.5A
PARK/NEUTRAL POSITION SWITCH
POWERTRAIN CONTROL MODULE
CIRCUIT OPENING RELAY
EFI RELAY
FUEL PUMP
HOT IN RUN OR START WIPER FUSE 20A
WASHER MOTOR
FRONT WIPER AND WASHER SWITCH
FRONT WIPER MOTOR
HOT AT ALL TIMES HORN FUSE
HORN RELAY
HORN SWITCH
HORN
DIAGRAM 41
93166B20

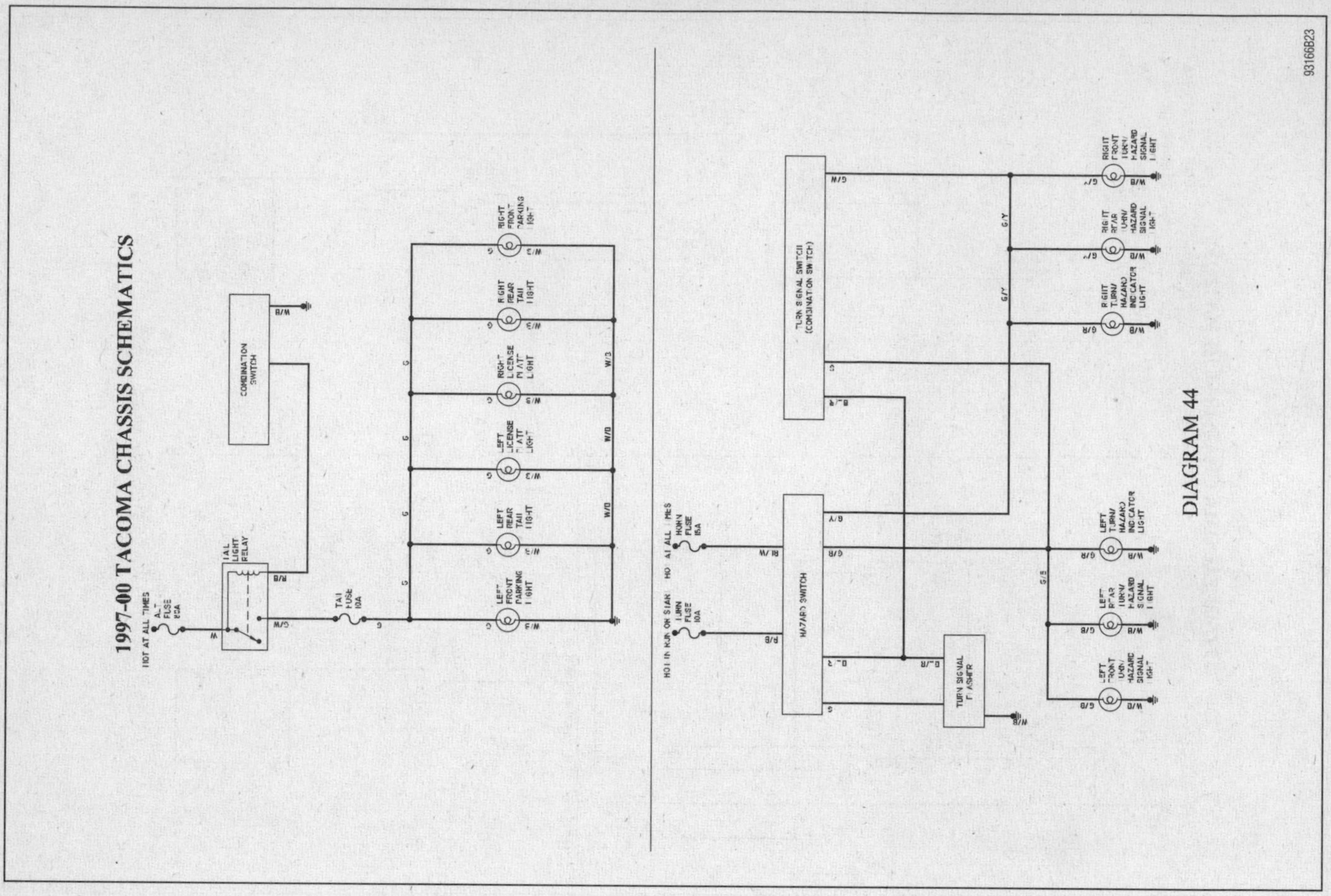
1997-00 TACOMA CHASSIS SCHEMATICS
DIAGRAM 44
93166B23

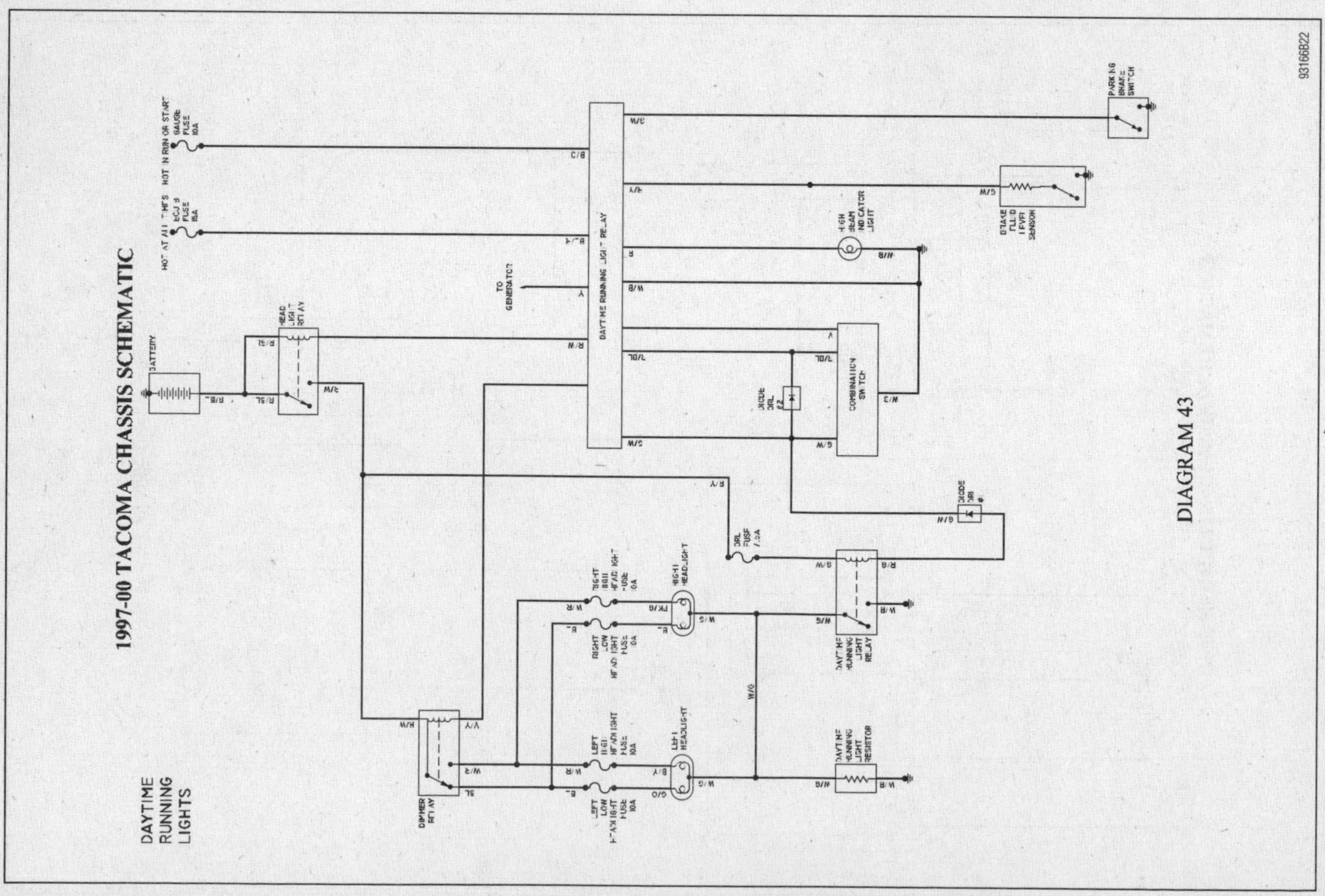
1997-00 TACOMA CHASSIS SCHEMATIC
DAYTIME RUNNING LIGHTS
DIAGRAM 43
93166B22

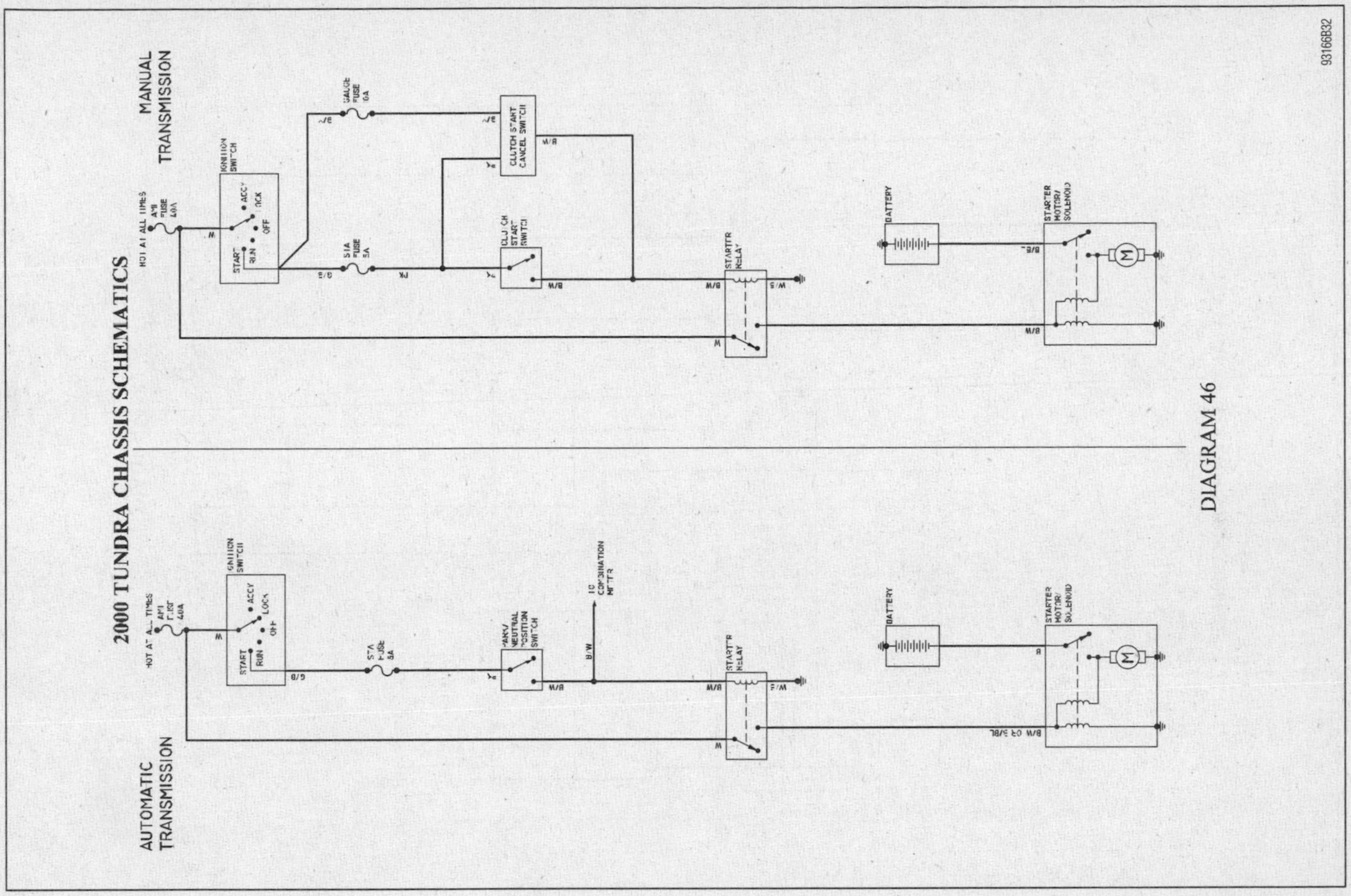

2000 TUNDRA CHASSIS SCHEMATICS

MANUAL TRANSMISSION

AUTOMATIC TRANSMISSION

DIAGRAM 46

93166832

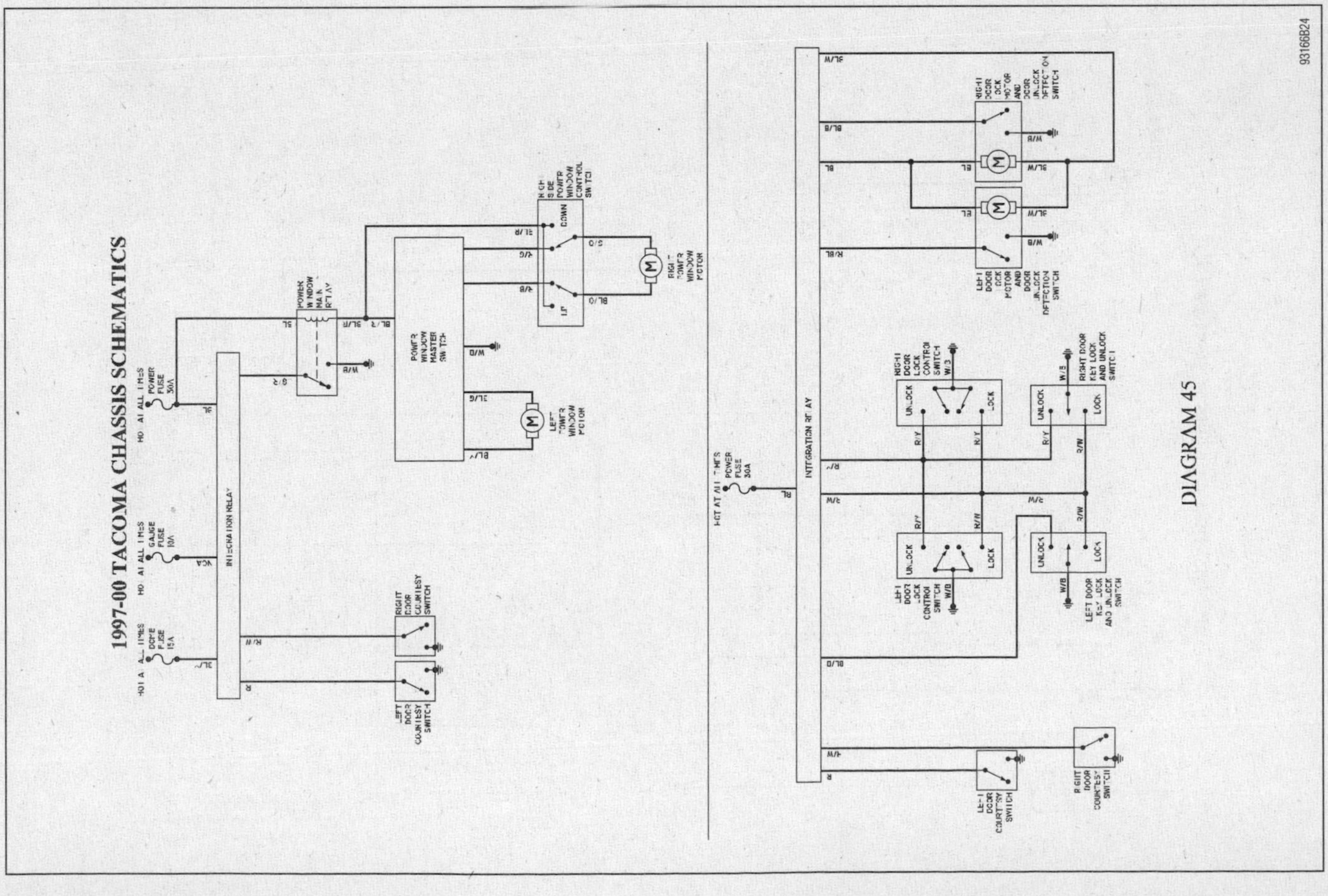

1997-00 TACOMA CHASSIS SCHEMATICS

DIAGRAM 45

93166824

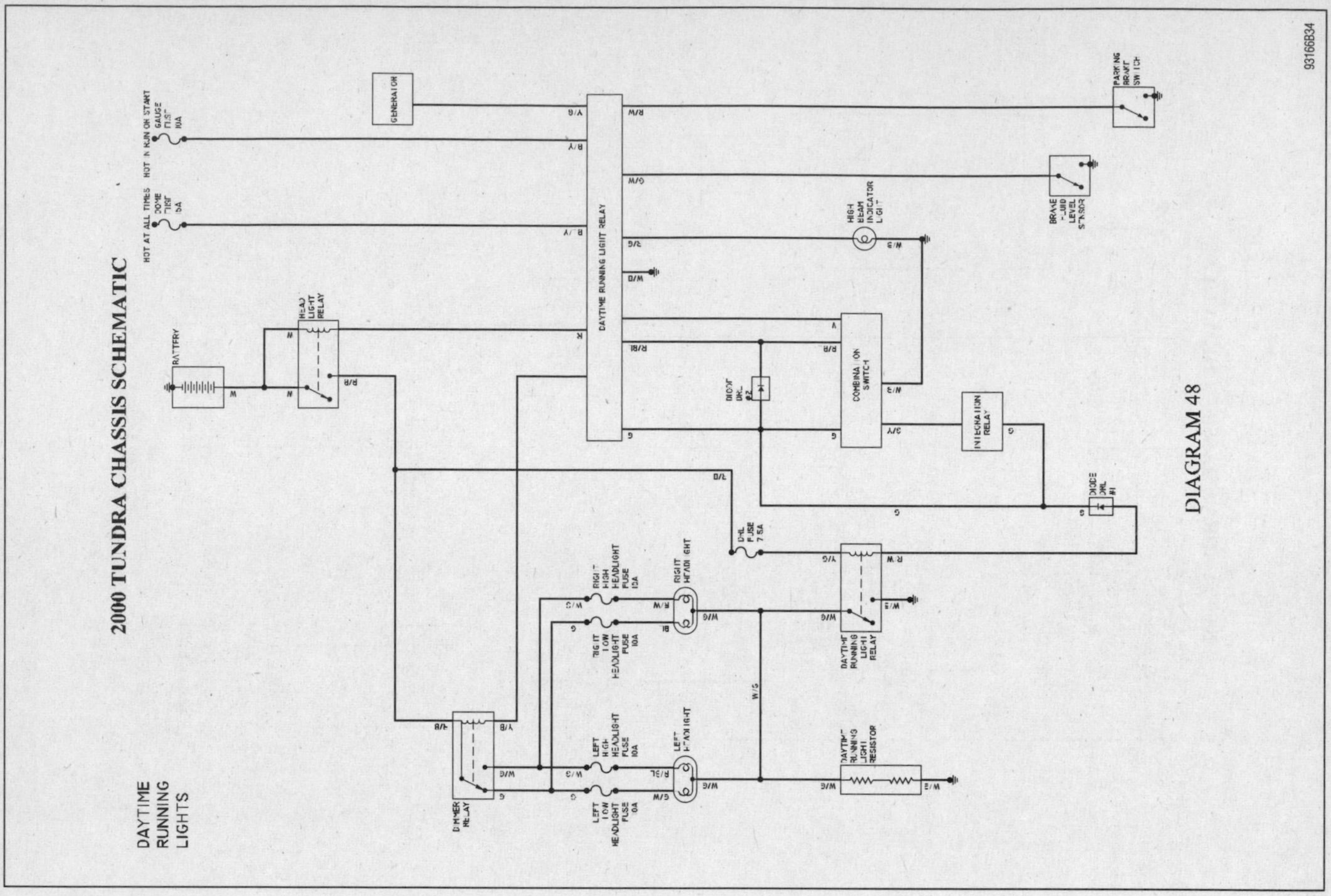
2000 TUNDRA CHASSIS SCHEMATIC
DAYTIME RUNNING LIGHTS
DIAGRAM 48
93166B34

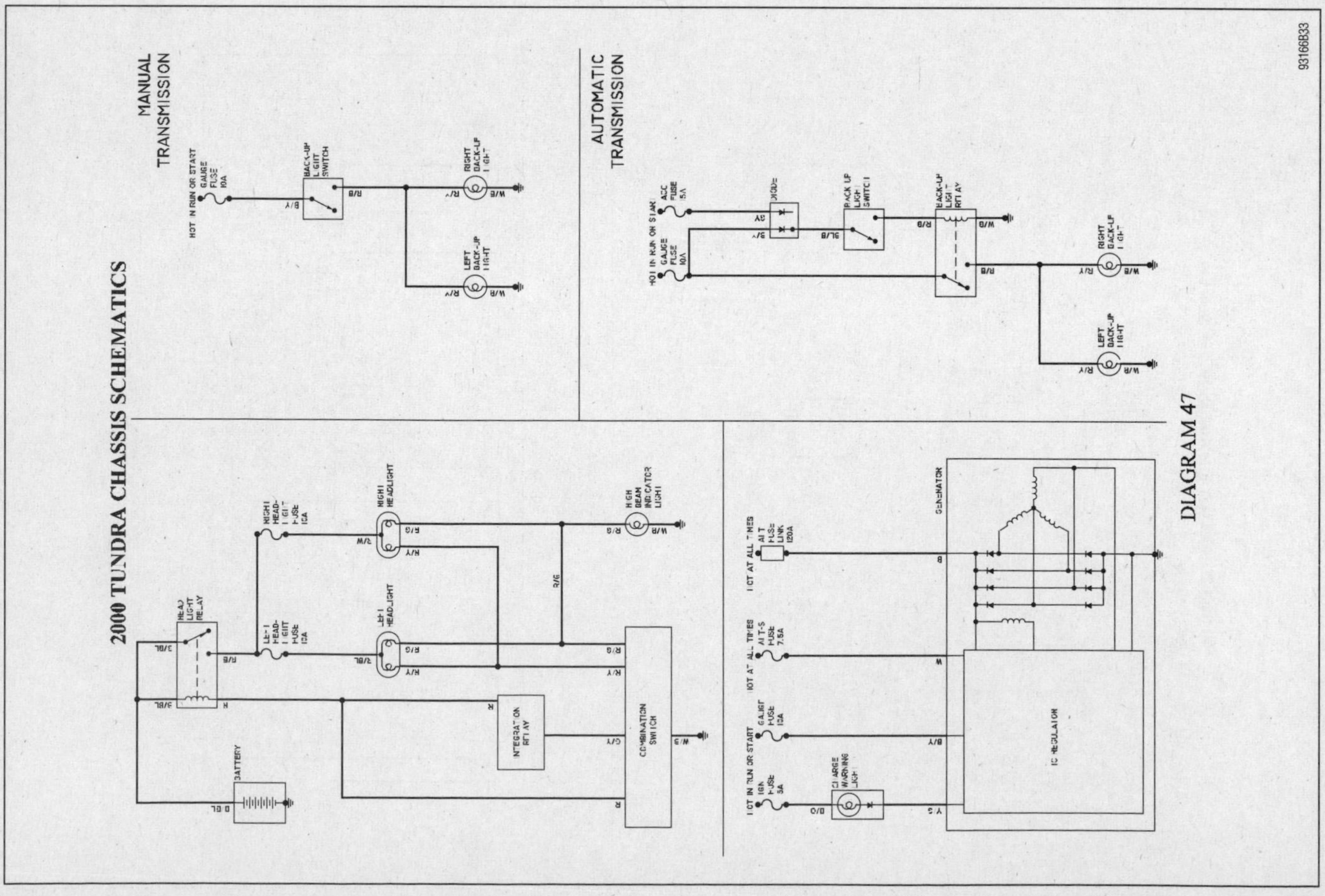
2000 TUNDRA CHASSIS SCHEMATICS
MANUAL TRANSMISSION
AUTOMATIC TRANSMISSION
DIAGRAM 47
93166B33

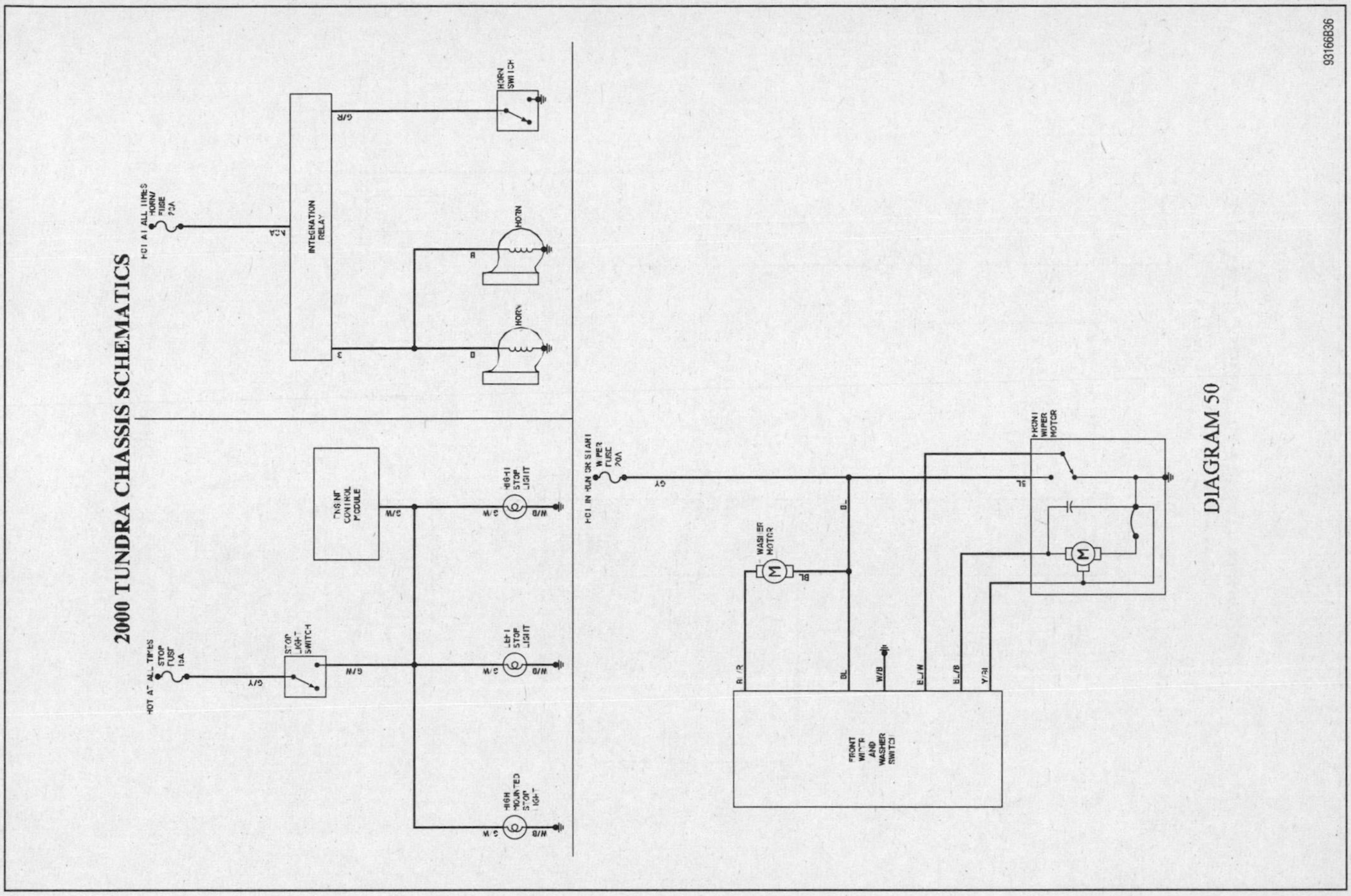
2000 TUNDRA CHASSIS SCHEMATICS
DIAGRAM 50
93166836

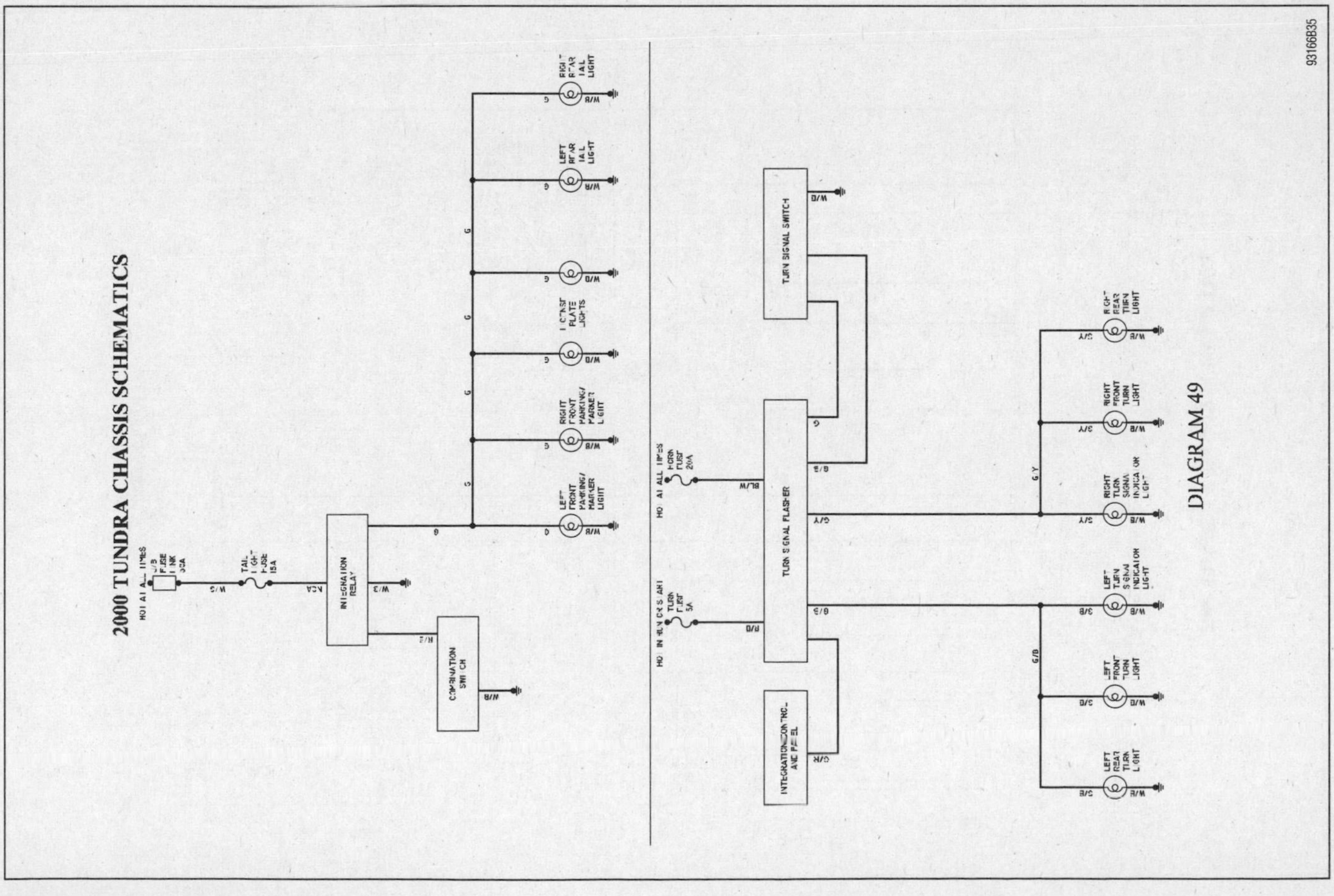
2000 TUNDRA CHASSIS SCHEMATICS
DIAGRAM 49
93166835

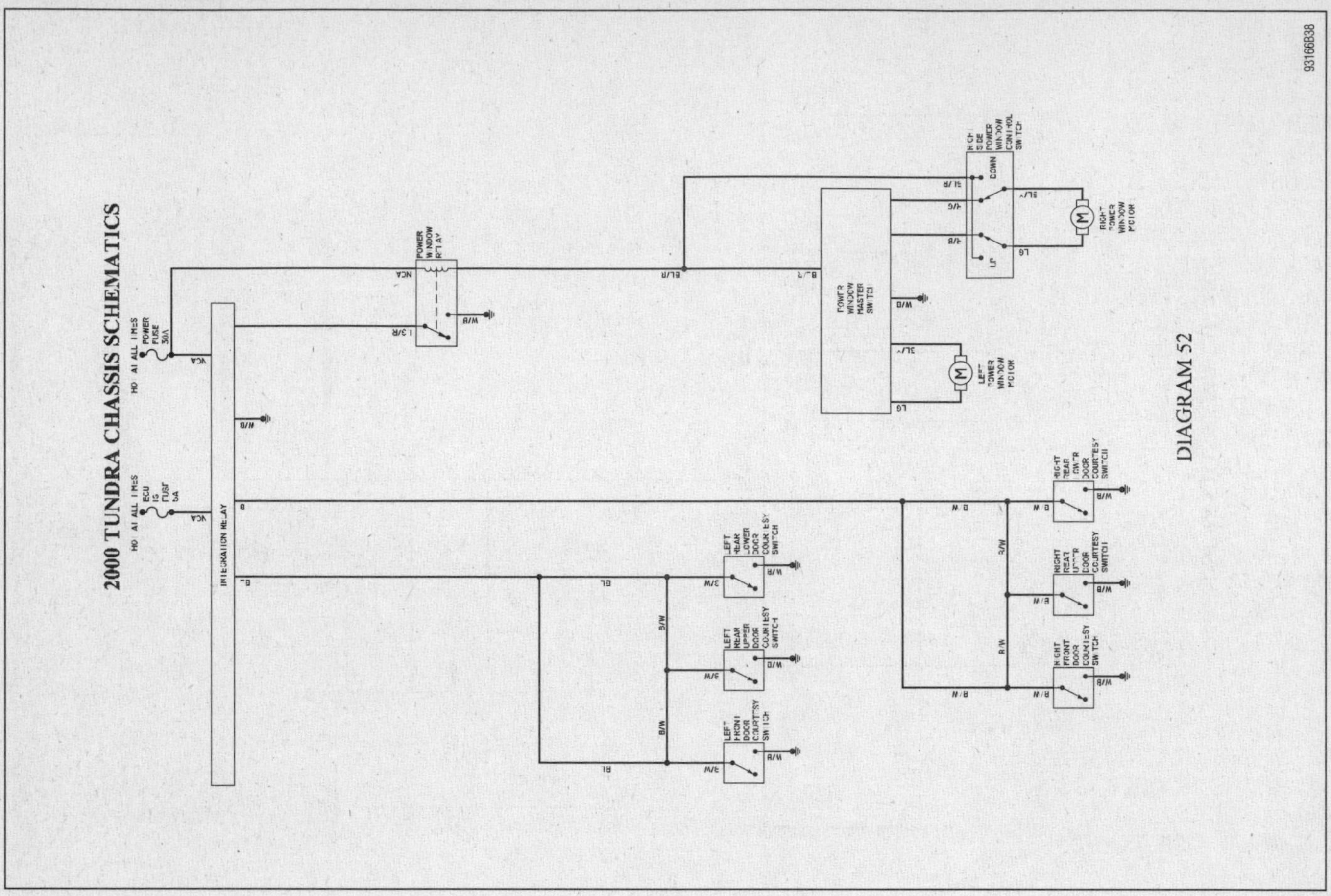
2000 TUNDRA CHASSIS SCHEMATICS
INTEGRATION RELAY
POWER WINDOW RELAY
POWER WINDOW MASTER SWITCH
LEFT POWER WINDOW MOTOR
RIGHT POWER WINDOW MOTOR
DIAGRAM 52
93166B38

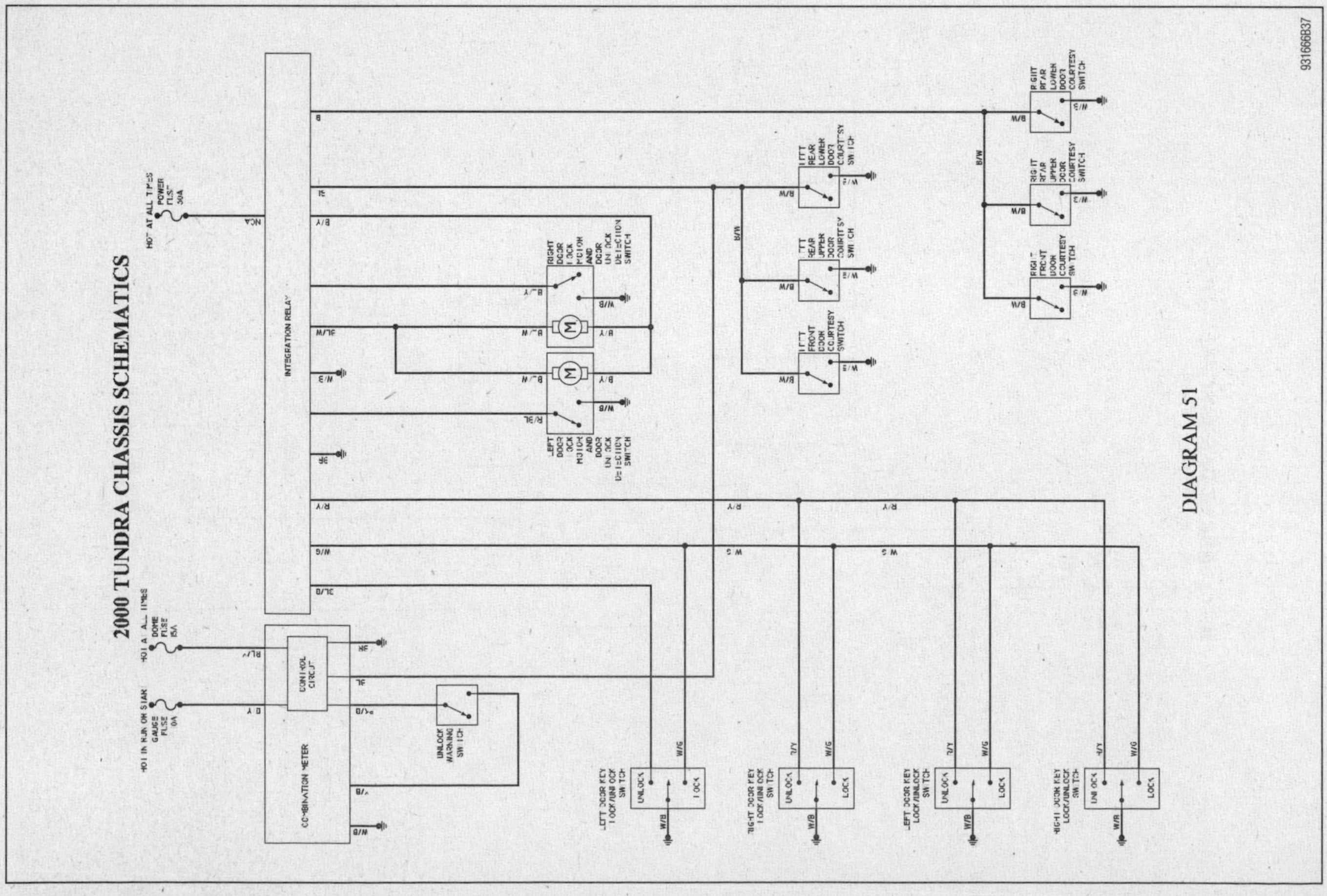
2000 TUNDRA CHASSIS SCHEMATICS
INTEGRATION RELAY
COMBINATION METER
UNLOCK WARNING SWITCH
DIAGRAM 51
93166B37

7

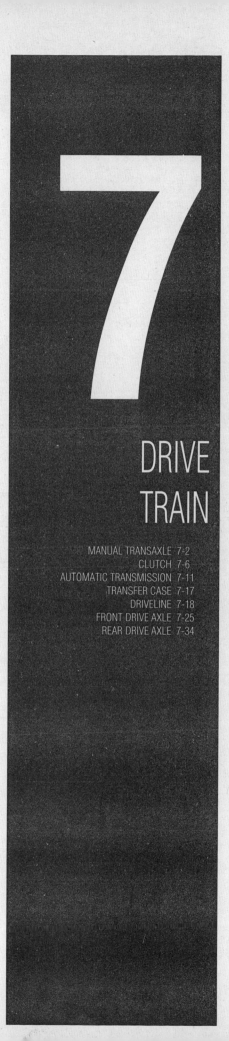

DRIVE TRAIN

MANUAL TRANSMISSION

Identification

➧ **See Figures 1 and 2**

The manual transmissions found in Tacomas, Tundra's, T100s and 4Runners are denoted by their Toyota model designations: W59, R150 and R150F. The W59 and R150F are used in 4WD applications and are connected to the transfer case. See Section 1 for more information on models.

Adjustments

All models utilize a floor-mounted shifter and an internally-mounted shift linkage. No external adjustments are either necessary or possible.

Shift Lever

REMOVAL & INSTALLATION

4Runner, Tacoma, and T100

1. Remove the front console box.

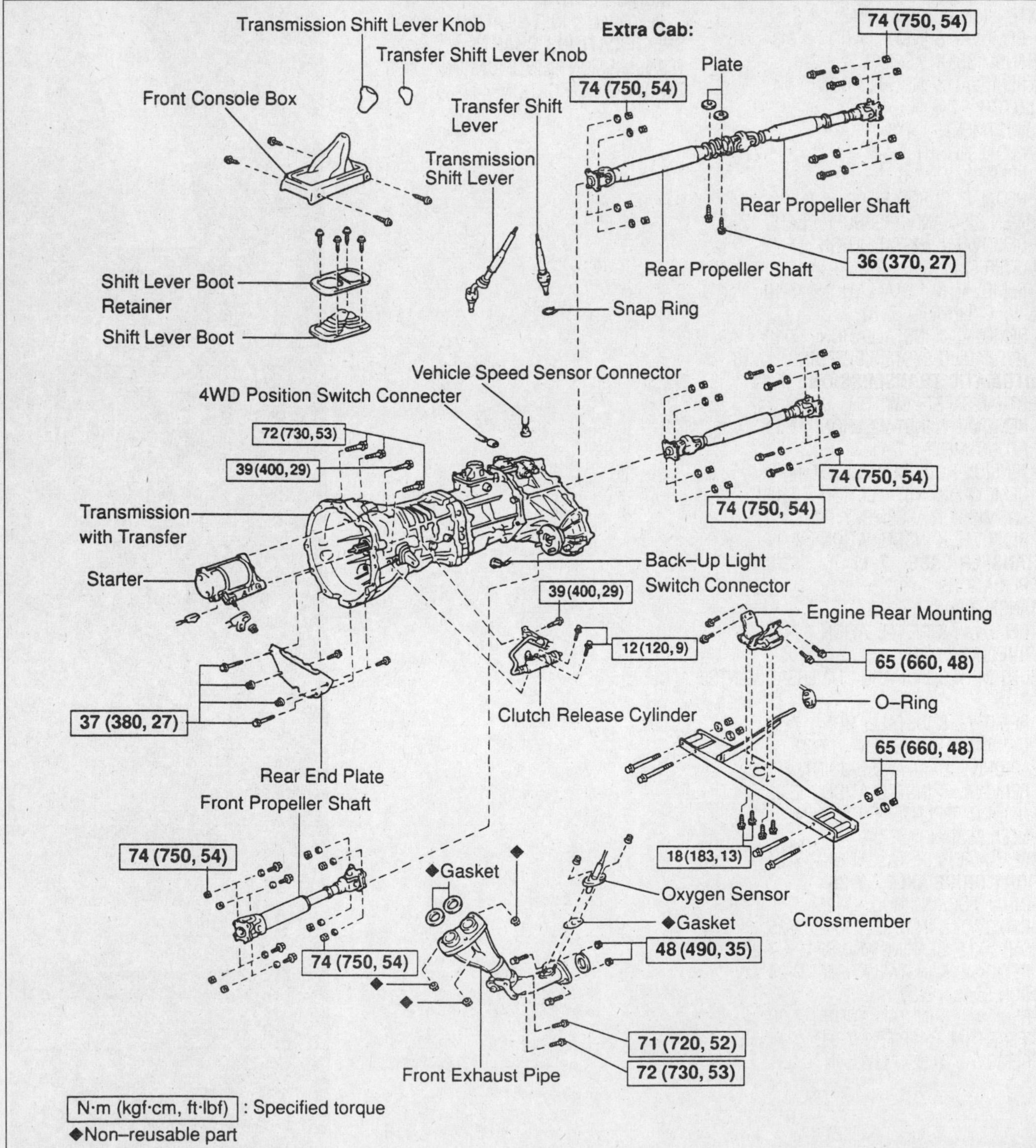

Fig. 1 Manual transmission—4WD

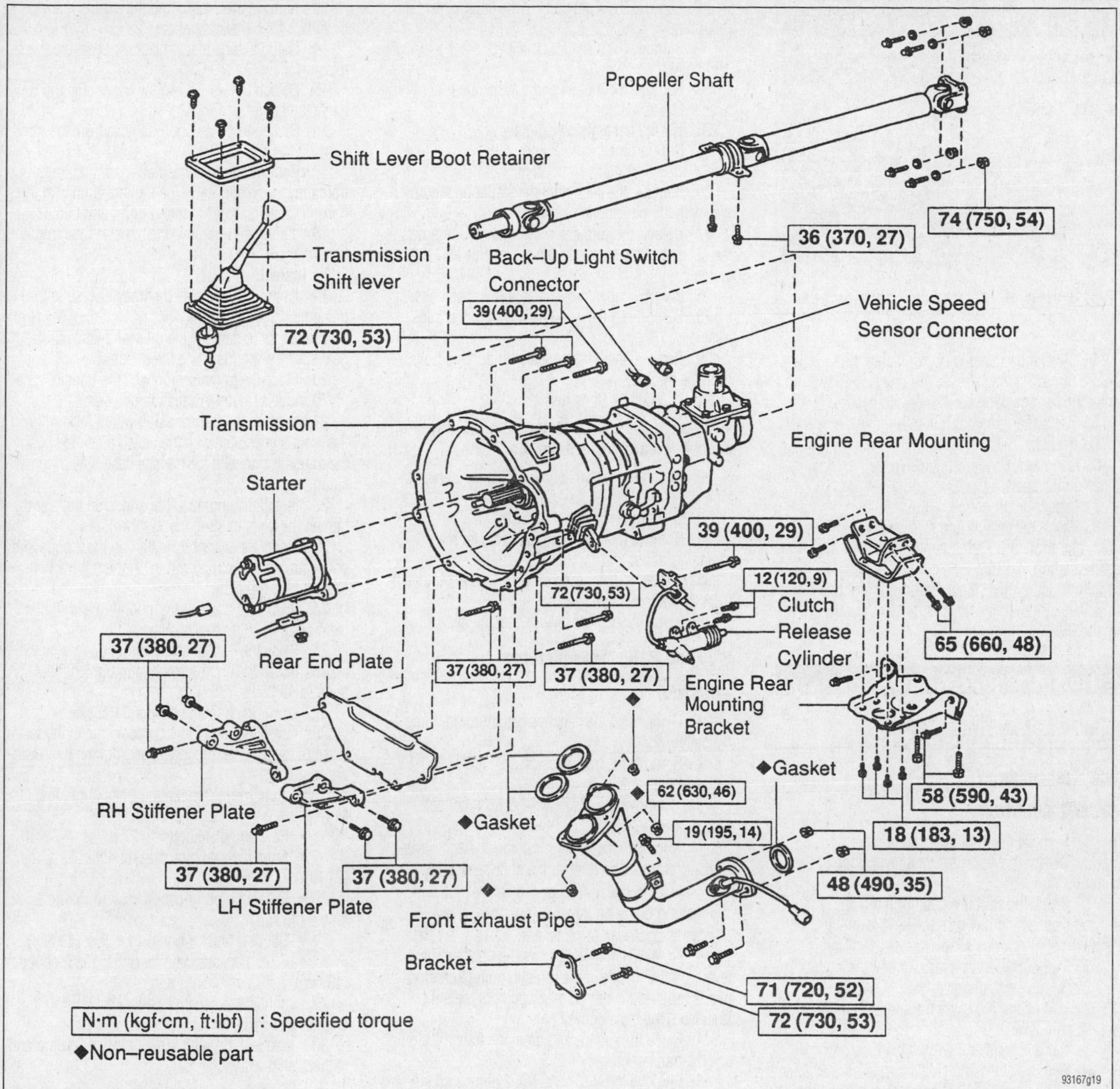

Fig. 2 Manual transmission—2WD

2. Remove the four screws and then the shift lever and retainer.
3. Use a shop rag to cover the shifter lever cap.
4. Press down on the shift lever cap and turn it counterclockwise to remove it.
5. Pull out the shift lever.
6. Installation is the reverse of removal. Apply multi-purpose grease to the end of the shift lever.

Tundra

1. Remove the transmission shift lever knob.
2. Remove the 4 bolts and the shift lever boot retainer.
3. Detach the transmission shift lever boot.
4. Turn over the dust boot.
5. Using a shop towel, cover the shift lever cap.
6. Apply pressure to the shift lever cap while rotating it counterclockwise to remove.
7. Pull out the shift lever.
8. Installation is the reverse of removal. Apply multi-purpose grease to the end of the shift lever.

Back-Up Light Switch

REMOVAL & INSTALLATION

1. Position the shift lever in Neutral.
2. Raise the truck and support it on safety stands.
3. Unplug the electrical connector at the switch.
4. Unscrew the back-up light switch from the extension housing.

To install:

5. Screw the new switch into the housing and tighten it to 60 inch lbs. (7 Nm).
6. Connect the wire and lower the truck.

Extension Housing Seal

REMOVAL & INSTALLATION

➧ **See Figure 3**

1. Elevate and safely support the vehicle.
2. Position a catch pan below the work area to contain spilled fluid.
3. Remove the driveshaft.

93167p37
Fig. 3 View of an extension housing seal

4. Clean the extension housing area thoroughly before removing the seal. No dirt must be allowed to enter the transmission during replacement.
5. Use a seal extractor tool to remove the seal.

To install:

6. Use a seal driver tool to drive the new seal into place until it seats.
7. Install the driveshaft.
8. Lower the vehicle and start the engine. With the brake applied, shift the transmission through each position, pausing long enough to allow the gear to fully engage. Place the selector in **P** and check the fluid level, topping the fluid as needed. Do NOT overfill the fluid.

Transmission Assembly

REMOVAL & INSTALLATION

W59 Transmission

EXCEPT 4RUNNER

1. Remove the front console box.
2. Detach the 4 screws, shift lever boot and retainer.
3. Cover the shift lever cap with a cloth.
4. Depressing down on the shift lever cap and rotate it counterclockwise to remove.
5. Pull out the shift lever.
6. Remove transfer shift lever.
7. Use pliers to remove the snapring and pull out the shift lever.
8. Raise vehicle and drain transmission oil.
9. Remove No. 1 and No. 2 engine undercovers
10. Disconnect the front and rear propeller shafts
11. Detach the vehicle speed sensor, back-up light switch and 4WD position switch connectors.
12. If your vehicle has an Antilock Braking System (ABS) and/or a differential lock, detach the connector from the switch.
13. Remove the 2 bolts and disconnect the clutch release cylinder.
14. Detach the front exhaust pipe.
15. Remove the ring, and remove the 2 bolts and support bracket.
16. Detach the 2 nuts, oxygen sensor and gasket.
17. Detach the 2 set bolts of the front exhaust pipe bracket.
18. Remove the 3 nuts, front exhaust pipe and 2 gaskets.
19. Remove the 4 bolts, 2 nuts and rear end plate.
20. Support the rear of the transmission.
21. Remove the 4 set bolts of the engine rear mounting.
22. Remove the mounting bracket from the rear of the engine.
23. Remove the 4 bolts and engine rear mounting from the transmission.
24. Lift the transmission slightly.
25. Support the transmission using a suitable device.
26. Remove the set bolt of the starter on the lower side with the clutch line bracket.
27. Detach the connector and wire, and remove the set bolt of the starter on the upper side and starter.
28. Remove the transmission with transfer case.
29. Disconnect the wire harness from the transmission.
30. Remove the 3 transmission mounting bolts from the engine.
31. Pull out the transmission.

➡Remove the transmission with the transfer case down and toward the rear.

32. Separate the transfer case from the transmission.
33. Disconnect the breather hose
34. Remove the 8 transfer case adapter rear mounting bolts.
35. Lift the transfer case straight up and remove it from the transmission.
36. Installation is the reverse of removal.

W59 and R150 Transmissions

4RUNNER

1. Disconnect the negative battery cable from the battery.
2. Remove the transmission shift lever from the inside of the vehicle, as follows:
   a. Remove the 4 screws and front console box.
   b. Remove the screws holding the shift lever boot retainer and remove the shift lever boot.
   c. Cover the shift lever cap with a cloth. Pressing down on the shift lever cap, rotate it counterclockwise to remove it.
3. On 4WD models, remove the transfer shift lever from the inside of the vehicle. Using snapring pliers, remove the snapring and pull out the shift lever from the transfer case.
4. Raise the vehicle and drain the transmission and the transfer oil.
5. Remove the No. 1 and No. 2 engine undercover.
6. Disconnect the front and rear driveshafts.
7. Detach the vehicle speed sensor, back-up light switch, and the 4WD position switch connectors.
8. If equipped with ABS and/or differential lock: Detach the L4 position switch connector.
9. Remove the 2 bolts holding the clutch release cylinder and lay it along side the engine. Do not disconnect the clutch line.
10. Remove the exhaust pipe bracket.
11. Remove the rear end plate by removing the nuts and 2 bolts.
12. Remove the crossmember.
    a. Support the transmission rear side.
    b. Remove the 4 bolts from the engine rear mounting.
    c. Remove the 4 bolts, nuts and the crossmember.
13. Remove the 4 bolts and the engine rear mounting from the transfer case.
14. Using a transmission jack, support the transmission.
15. Detach the wiring and the connector and remove the starter.
16. Disconnect the wiring harness from the transmission.
17. Remove the transmission mounting bolts from the engine and lower the transmission with the transfer case (on 4WD models) down and to the rear.
18. If equipped, remove the transfer case from the transmission.

To install:

19. If applicable, install the transfer case to the transmission. Tighten the bolts to 17 ft. lbs. (24 Nm). Be careful not to damage the oil seal by the input gear spline when installing the transfer.
20. Place the transmission with the transfer case (4WD models) at the installation position.
21. Support the transmission with a jack. Align the input shaft spline with the clutch disc, and push the transmission with the transfer case fully into position.
22. Install the engine to transmission bolts and tighten the bolts to 53 ft. lbs. (72 Nm)
23. Install the starter by installing the 2 bolts and connecting the electrical wiring. Tighten the 2 bolts to 29 ft. lbs. (39 Nm).
24. Install the engine rear mounting and tighten the 4 bolts to 48 ft. lbs. (65 Nm).
25. Raise the transmission slightly with a jack.
26. Install the crossmember and tighten the 4 bolts to 48 ft. lbs. (65 Nm).
27. Lower the transmission and transfer.
28. Install the remaining components in the reverse of the removal procedure and tighten the retainers as follows:
    - 4 engine rear mounting bolts: 14 ft. lbs. (19 Nm)
    - Rear end plate bolts: to 27 ft. lbs. (37 Nm)
    - Front exhaust pipe bracket bolts: 52 ft. lbs. (71 Nm)
    - Exhaust pipe-to-catalytic converter bolts: 35 ft. lbs. (48 Nm)
    - Support bracket bolts: 14 ft. lbs. (19 Nm)
    - Clutch release cylinder bolts: 108 inch lbs. (13 Nm)
29. Connect the negative battery cable, start the engine, and check for leaks.
30. Road test the vehicle for proper operation and recheck all the fluid levels.

R150 and R150F Transmission

2WD T100 MODELS

➧ See Figure 4

➡On these models, the transmission is removed with the engine.

1. Turn the ignition switch **OFF**. Disconnect the battery cables, negative cable first.
2. Matchmark the hood hinges and remove the hood.
3. Remove the battery and battery tray.
4. Drain the engine oil, transmission oil and cooling system.
5. Remove the expansion tank.
6. Remove the radiator.
7. Remove the air cleaner cap, Mass Air Flow (MAF) meter and resonator. Remove the air cleaner case.

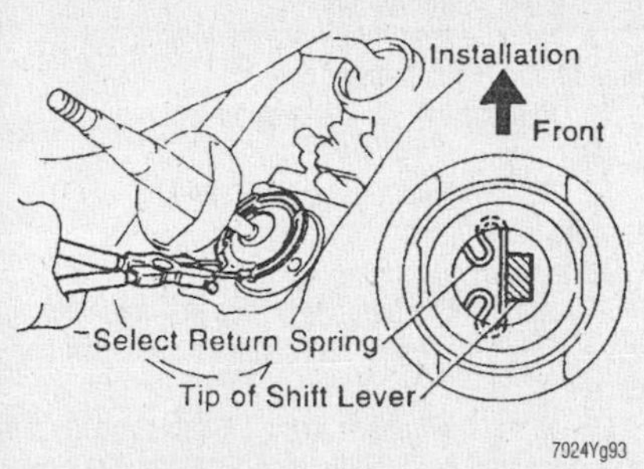

Fig. 4 Removing the transfer shift lever—Tacoma, 4Runner and T-100 with R150 and R150F transmissions

8. Disconnect the accelerator cable from the throttle body.
9. Remove the intake air connector.
10. If equipped with air conditioning, remove the air conditioning compressor and bracket. Position the compressor aside with the air conditioning lines attached.
11. Disconnect the heater hoses at the cowl panel.
12. Disconnect the following hoses:
  - Brake booster vacuum hose
  - Evaporator Emissions (EVAP) hose
  - 2 power steering hoses
  - Fuel return hose
  - Fuel inlet hose
13. Remove the power steering pump.
14. Disconnect the alternator wires from the alternator.
15. Disconnect the Engine Control Module (ECM) wiring from the ECM.
16. Disengage the engine wiring harness and connectors from the vehicle as follows:
  a. Disengage the igniter connector.
  b. Disconnect the ground strap from the cowl top panel.
  c. Disconnect the 4 engine wiring harness clamps.
  d. Pull out the engine wiring harness from the vehicle.
17. Remove the shift lever assembly as follows:
  a. Remove the shift lever knob.
  b. Remove the 4 screws and shift lever boot.
  c. Remove the 6 bolts, shift lever assembly and baffle.
18. Remove the sway bar.
19. Remove the driveshaft from the vehicle.
20. Disconnect the speedometer cable from the transmission.
21. Disconnect the front exhaust pipe from the exhaust manifold and catalytic converter.
22. Remove the clutch release cylinder.
23. Disconnect the wires at the starter.
24. Position a jack and wooden block under the transmission and remove the rear engine mounting bracket.
25. Attach a suitable engine hoist to the engine hangers.
26. Remove the nuts and bolts from the engine mounts.
27. Carefully lift the engine/transmission assembly out of the vehicle.
28. Safely support the engine/transmission assembly.
29. Remove the rear end plate by removing the nuts and 4 bolts.
30. Remove the starter by removing the 2 bolts.
31. Remove the transmission from the engine by removing the 6 mounting bolts from the engine.
32. Pull out the transmission toward the rear.
33. Remove the transmission mount by removing the 4 bolts.

To install:

34. Install the transmission mount by installing the 4 bolts. Tighten the bolts to 18 ft. lbs. (25 Nm).
35. Connect the transmission to the engine by installing the 6 bolts. Tighten the bolts to 53 ft. lbs. (72 Nm).
36. Install the starter and tighten the 2 bolts to 29 ft. lbs. (39 Nm).
37. Install the rear end plate and tighten the 4 nuts and bolts to 27 ft. lbs. (37 Nm).
38. Attach the engine hoist to the engine hangers. Carefully lower the engine/transmission assembly into the vehicle. Keep the engine level, while aligning the engine mounts.
39. Install the engine mount fasteners, but do not fully tighten.
40. Position a jack and wooden block under the transmission and install the rear engine mounting bracket. Tighten the bolts to the frame to 42 ft. lbs. (58 Nm) and the bolts to the mount to 13 ft. lbs. (18 Nm).
41. Remove the jack and engine hoist. Tighten the engine mounts to 28 ft. lbs. (38 Nm).
42. Install the remaining components in the reverse of the removal procedure. Tighten the exhaust pipe-to-manifold bolts to 46 ft. lbs. (62 Nm), the support bracket bolts and the exhaust pipe-to-catalytic converter bolts to 29 ft. lbs. (39 Nm), and the exhaust pipe clamp nuts to 14 ft. lbs. (19 Nm).
43. Fill the engine oil, engine coolant, and transmission oil.
44. Connect the negative and positive cables to the battery.
45. Start the engine and check for leaks.
46. Install the engine undercover. Install the hood.
47. Road test the vehicle and check all fluids.

4WD T100 MODELS

1. Disconnect the negative battery cable from the battery.
2. Remove the transmission shift lever from the inside of the vehicle, as follows:
  a. Remove the 4 screws and front console box.
  b. Remove the screws holding the shift lever boot retainer and remove the shift lever boot.
  c. Cover the shift lever cap with a cloth. Pressing down on the shift lever cap, rotate it counterclockwise to remove it.
3. Remove the transfer shift lever from the inside of the vehicle. Using snapring pliers, remove the snapring and pull out the shift lever from the transfer case.
4. Raise the vehicle and drain the transmission and the transfer oil.
5. Disconnect the driveshafts from the vehicle.
6. Detach the speedometer cable, back-up light switch connector and the transfer indicator switch connector.
7. Remove the 2 bolts holding the clutch release cylinder and lay it along side the engine. Do not disconnect the clutch line.
8. Remove the exhaust pipe bracket.
9. Remove the starter by disconnecting the starter wires and removing the 2 bolts.
10. Remove the stiffener plate by removing the 4 bolts.
11. Remove the rear end plate by removing the nuts and 2 bolts.
12. Remove the stabilizer bar from the suspension.
13. Using a transmission jack, support the transmission.
14. Remove the frame crossmember from the side frame as follows:
  a. Remove the 4 bolts from the engine rear mounting.
  b. Remove the 8 bolts and the frame crossmember from the side frame.
15. Remove the 6 transmission mounting bolts from the engine.
16. Disconnect the 3 wire clamps from the transmission.
17. Remove the transmission with the transfer toward the rear of the vehicle.
18. Remove the 4 bolts and the engine rear mounting from the transfer case.
19. Remove the transfer adapter rear mounting bolts.
20. Pull the transfer straight up and remove it from the transmission.

To install:

21. Apply multi-purpose grease to the adapter oil seal and shift the 2 shift fork shafts to the high 4 position.
22. Install the transfer to the transmission. Install the bolts and tighten the bolts to 27 ft. lbs. (37 Nm). Be careful not to damage the oil seal by the input gear spline when installing the transfer.
23. Install the engine rear mounting and tighten the 4 bolts to 18 ft. lbs. (25 Nm).
24. Place the transmission with the transfer at the installation position.
25. Support the transmission with a jack. Align the input shaft spline with the clutch disc, and push the transmission with the transfer fully into position.
26. Install the engine to transmission bolts. Tighten the bolts to 53 ft. lbs. (72 Nm)
27. Install the No. 2 frame crossmember, as follows:
  a. Raise the transmission slightly with a jack.
  b. Install the No. 2 frame crossmember to the side frame and tighten the 8 bolts to 70 ft. lbs. (95 Nm).
  c. Lower the transmission and transfer.
  d. Install the 4 mounting bolts to the engine rear mounting and tighten the bolts to 108 inch lbs. (13 Nm).
28. Install the stabilizer bar.
29. Install the rear end plate by installing the 2 bolts and nuts. Tighten to 27 ft. lbs. (37 Nm).
30. Install the stiffener plate with the 4 bolts. Tighten the bolts to 27 ft. lbs. (37 Nm).
31. Install the remaining components in the reverse order of removal.
32. Install the transmission shift lever, as follows:
  a. Apply MP grease to the transmission shift lever.
  b. Align the groove of the shift lever cap and the pin part of the case cover. Cover the shift lever cap with a cloth. Pressing down on the shift lever cap, rotate it clockwise to install.
  c. Install shift lever boot retainer with the 4 screws.
  d. Install the front console box with the 4 screws.

33. Connect the negative battery cable. Start the engine and check for leaks.
34. Road test the vehicle for proper operation. Recheck all fluid levels.

2WD TACOMA MODELS

1. Disconnect the negative battery cable from the battery.
2. Remove the shift lever (see 4WD Tacoma models).
3. Raise the vehicle and support it securely on jackstands.
4. Drain the transmission oil.
5. Remove the driveshaft.
6. Detach the front exhaust pipe from the exhaust manifold.
7. Disconnect all electrical connectors from the transmission.
8. Unbolt the clutch release cylinder from the transmission. Hang the cylinder out of the way with a piece of wire. Don't push on the clutch pedal while the release cylinder is removed.
9. Remove the starter (see Chapter 2).
10. Unbolt the rear end plate from the transmission.
11. Support the transmission with a jack. If available, use a transmission jack. Raise the transmission slightly.
12. Support the engine with a floor jack. Place a piece of wood on the jack head so as not to damage the oil pan.
13. Remove the transmission mounting bracket and mount.
14. Remove the transmission mounting bolts.
15. Pull the transmission to the rear, guiding the rear of the transmission over the crossmember. Turn the transmission clockwise 90-degrees and move it to the rear a little more, then lower the front of the transmission and maneuver it to the floor.

To install:

16. Installation is the reverse of removal, noting the following points:
    a. Tighten the transmission mounting bolts to 53 ft. lbs. (72 Nm).
    b. Tighten the transmission mount-to-transmission bolts to 13 ft. lbs. (18 Nm).
    c. Tighten the mount-to-crossmember bolts to 43 ft. lbs. (58 Nm).
    d. Refill the transmission with the proper type of oil (see Chapter 1).

4WD TACOMA MODELS

1. Disconnect the negative battery cable from the battery.
2. Remove the transmission shift lever from the inside of the vehicle, as follows:
    a. Remove the 4 screws and front console box.
    b. Remove the screws holding the shift lever boot retainer and remove the shift lever boot.
    c. Cover the shift lever cap with a cloth. Pressing down on the shift lever cap, rotate it counterclockwise to remove it.
3. Remove the transfer shift lever from the inside of the vehicle. Using snapring pliers, remove the snapring and pull out the shift lever from the transfer case.
4. Raise the vehicle and drain the transmission and the transfer oil.
5. Disconnect the front and rear driveshafts.
6. Detach the speedometer cable and the back-up light switch connector.
7. On the standard cab, disconnect the 4WD position switch connector.
8. On the extra cab, disconnect the L4 position switch connector.
9. Remove the 2 bolts holding the clutch release cylinder and lay it along side the engine. Do not disconnect the clutch line.
10. Remove the exhaust pipe bracket.
11. Remove the starter by disconnecting the starter wires and removing the 2 bolts.
12. Remove the rear end plate by removing the nuts and 2 bolts.
13. Remove the crossmember.
    a. Support the transmission rear side.
    b. Remove the 4 bolts from the engine rear mounting.
    c. Disconnect the O-ring and remove the 4 bolts, nuts and the crossmember.
14. Using a transmission jack, support the transmission.
15. Remove the 6 transmission mounting bolts from the engine.
16. Disconnect the 3 wire clamps from the transmission.
17. Remove the transmission with the transfer toward the rear of the vehicle.
18. Remove the 4 bolts and the engine rear mounting from the transfer case.
19. Remove the transfer adapter rear mounting bolts.
20. Pull the transfer straight up and remove it from the transmission.

To install:

21. Apply multi-purpose grease to the adapter oil seal and shift the 2 shift fork shafts to the high 4 position.
22. Install the transfer to the transmission. Install the bolts and tighten the bolts to 17 ft. lbs. (24 Nm). Be careful not to damage the oil seal by the input gear spline when installing the transfer.
23. Place the transmission with the transfer at the installation position.
24. Support the transmission with a jack. Align the input shaft spline with the clutch disc, and push the transmission with the transfer fully into position.
25. Install the engine to transmission bolts. Tighten the bolts to 53 ft. lbs. (72 Nm)
26. Install the engine rear mounting and tighten the 4 bolts to 48 ft. lbs. (65 Nm).
27. Install the crossmember, as follows:
    a. Raise the transmission slightly with a jack.
    b. Install the crossmember and tighten the 4 bolts to 48 ft. lbs. (65 Nm).
    c. Lower the transmission and transfer.
    d. Install the remaining components in the reverse of the removal procedure, making sure to note the following tightening specifications:
        - 4 engine rear mounting bolts: 14 ft. lbs. (19 Nm)
        - Rear end plate bolts: 13 ft. lbs. (18 Nm) on R150 and R150F transmissions, or to 27 ft. lbs. (37 Nm) on W59 transmissions
        - Starter bolts: 29 ft. lbs. (39 Nm)
        - Front exhaust pipe-to-manifold bolts: 46 ft. lbs. (62 Nm)
        - Exhaust bracket bolts: 33 ft. lbs. (44 Nm)
        - Exhaust pipe-to-catalytic converter bolts: 35 ft. lbs. (48 Nm)
        - Clutch release cylinder bolts: 108 inch lbs. (13 Nm)
28. Refill the transmission to the correct level.
29. Connect the negative battery cable. Start the engine and check for leaks.
30. Road test the vehicle for proper operation. Recheck all fluid levels.

CLUTCH

Adjustments

PEDAL HEIGHT

▸ See Figure 5

The pedal height measurement is gauged from the angled section of the floorboard to the center of the clutch pedal pad. If necessary, adjust the pedal height by loosening the locknut and turning the pedal stop bolt which is located above the pedal toward the driver's seat. Tighten the locknut after the adjustment.

1. The pedal height from the floor panel is as follows:
    - 4Runner: 6.889–7.283 in. (175.0–185.0mm)
    - T100: 6.087–6.480 in (154.6–164.6mm)
    - Tacoma: 6.692–7.086 in (170.0–180.0mm)
    - Tundra: 6.303–6.697 in. (160.1–170.1mm)

FREE-PLAY

▸ See Figure 6

Check the pedal free-play to see if it is correct, push in on until the beginning of the clutch resistance is felt. To adjust, loosen the locknut and turn the pushrod until the free-play is correct. Tighten the locknut. After adjusting the free-play, check the pedal height.

1. Pedal free play should be as follows:
    - 4Runner: 0.197–0.591 in. (5.0–15.0mm)
    - T100: 0.197–0.591 in. (5.0–15.0mm))
    - Tacoma: 0.197–0.591 in. (5.0–15.0mm)
    - Tundra: 0.197–0.591 in. (5.0–15.0mm)

PEDAL PUSHROD PLAY

The pedal pushrod play is the distance between the clutch master cylinder piston and the pedal pushrod located above the pedal towards the firewall. Since it is nearly impossible to measure this distance at the source, it must be measured at the pedal pad.

If necessary, adjust the pedal play by loosening the pedal pushrod locknut and turning the pushrod.

1. Pedal push rod free play should be as follows:
    - 4Runner: 0.0039–0.197 in. (1.0–5.0mm)
    - T100: 0.0039–0.197 in. (1.0–5.0mm)
    - Tacoma: 0.0039–0.197 in. (1.0–5.0mm)
    - Tundra: 0.0039–0.197 in. (1.0–5.0mm)

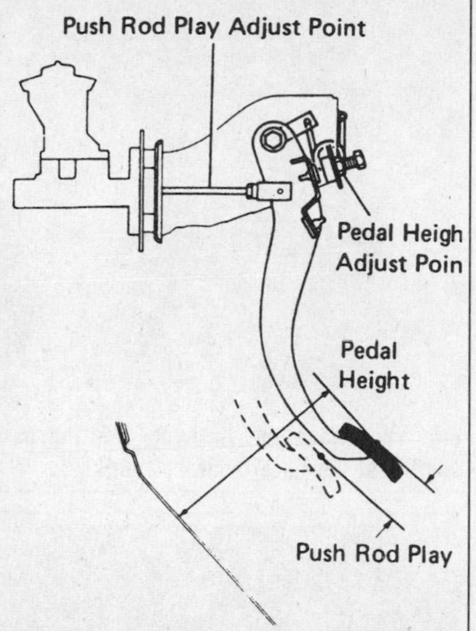

86827g14

Fig. 5 Pedal height and pushrod play adjustments

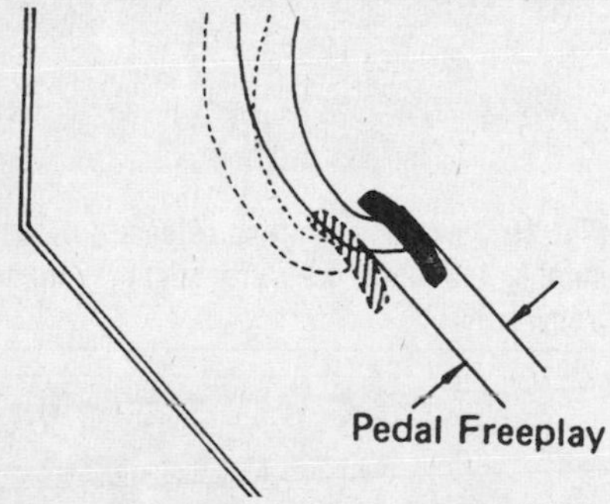

86827g15

Fig. 6 Free-play is the amount of pedal movement before the clutch engages

Driven Disc and Pressure Plate

REMOVAL & INSTALLATION

See Figures 7 thru 33

CAUTION

The clutch driven disc may contain asbestos, which has been determined to be a cancer causing agent. Avoid inhaling any dust from any clutch surface! When cleaning clutch surfaces, use a commercially available brake cleaning fluid. Never clean clutch surfaces with compressed air.

1. Remove the transmission.
2. Matchmark the clutch cover (pressure plate) and flywheel, indicating their relationship.
3. Loosen the clutch cover-to-flywheel retaining bolts one turn at a time in a crisscross pattern. The pressure on the clutch disc must be released GRADUALLY.
4. Remove the clutch cover-to-flywheel bolts. Remove the clutch cover and the clutch disc.
5. If the clutch throwout bearing is to be replaced, do so at this time as follows:
   a. Remove the bearing retaining clip(s) and remove the bearing and hub.
   b. Remove the release fork and the boot.
   c. The bearing is press fit to the hub. Turn the bearing by hand while placing it under some pressure; check for freedom of motion and lack of grinding or resistance. The bearing is permanently lubricated and cannot be disassembled or greased.
   d. Clean all parts; lightly grease the input shaft splines and all of the contact points.
   e. Install the bearing/hub assembly, fork, boot, and retaining clip(s) in their original locations.

TCCS7115

Fig. 7 View of the clutch and pressure plate assembly

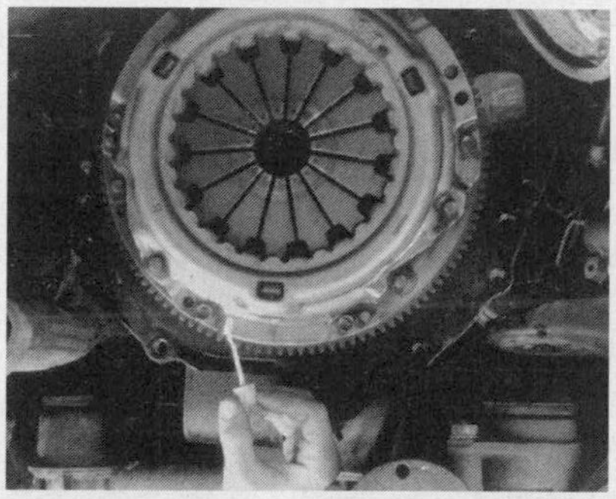

86827p09

Fig. 8 Matchmark the pressure plate and flywheel

TCCS7116

Fig. 9 Remove the clutch and pressure plate bolts

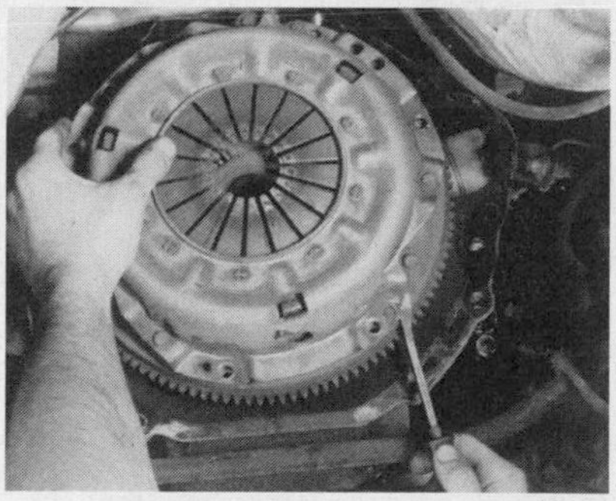

TCCS7117

Fig. 10 Carefully pry the clutch and pressure plate assembly away from the flywheel

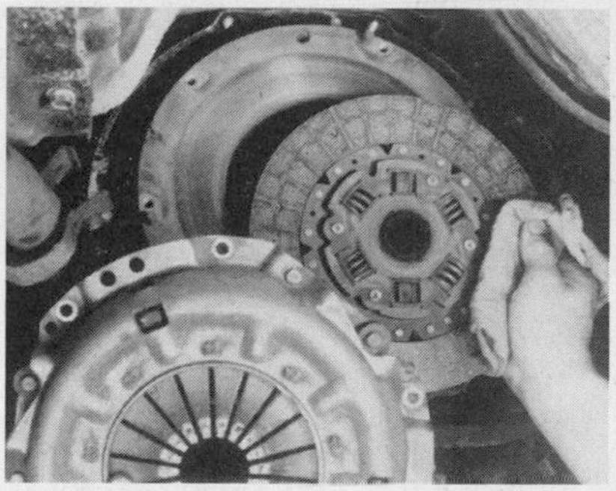

TCCS7118

Fig. 11 Remove the clutch and pressure plate

TCCS7119

Fig. 12 View of the flywheel once the clutch assembly is removed

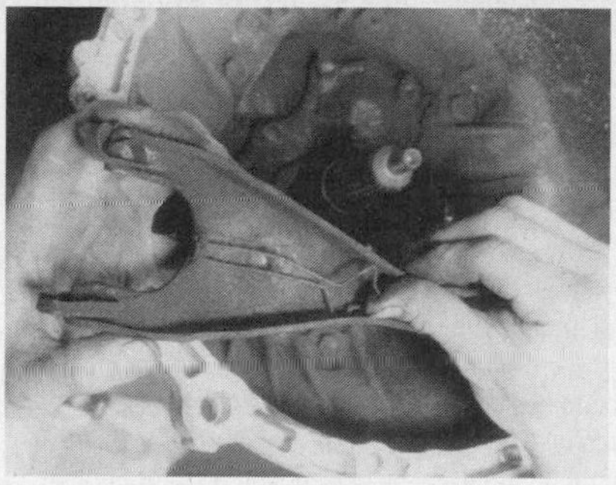

TCCS7135

Fig. 13 View of the clutch release fork; check it for signs of damage

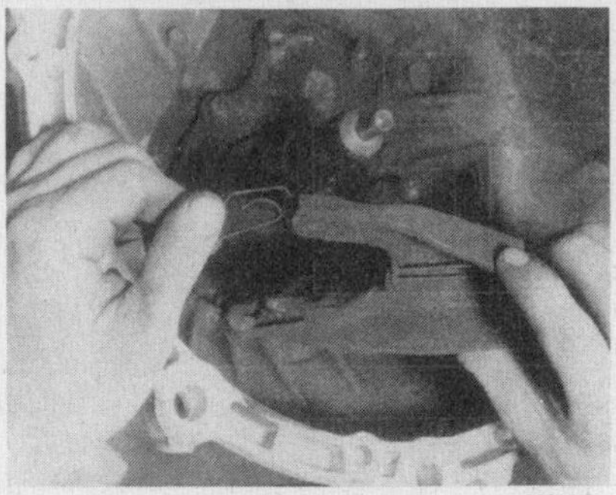

TCCS7136

Fig. 14 View of the clutch release fork bearing clips; make sure these are not bent or broken

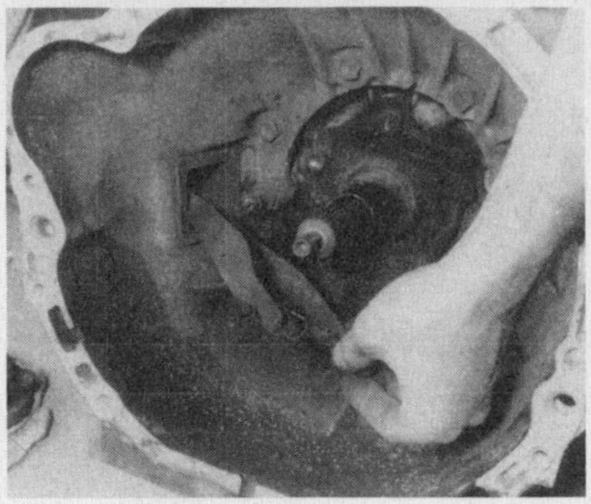

TCCS7137

Fig. 15 Removing the clutch release fork bearing clips

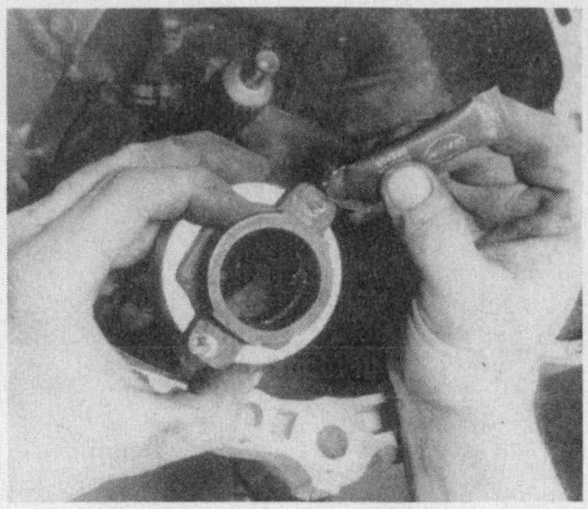

TCCS7138

Fig. 16 Grease the throwout bearing assembly at the outer contact points

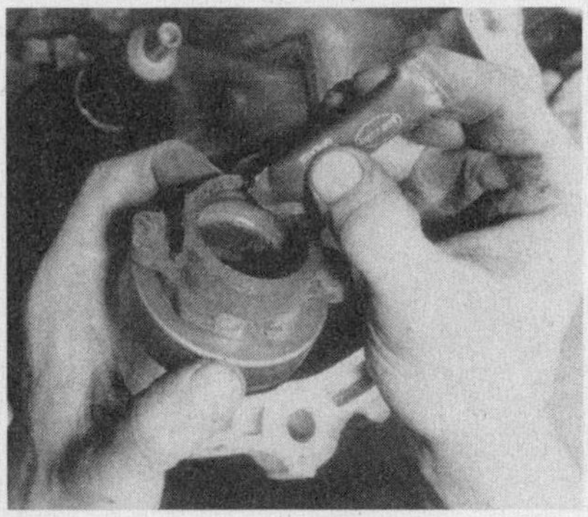

TCCS7139

Fig. 17 Grease the throwout bearing assembly at the inner contact points

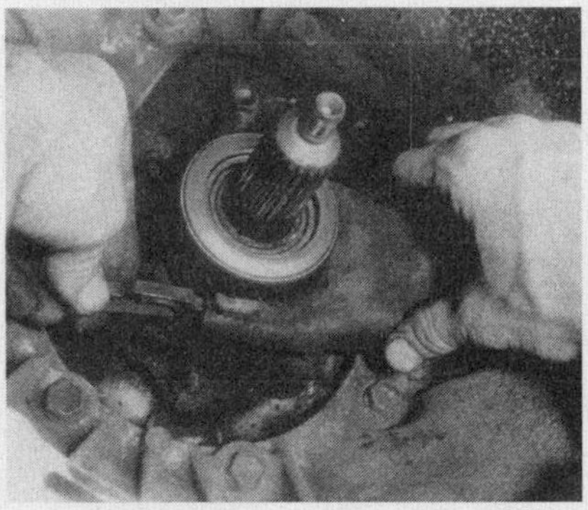

TCCS7140

Fig. 18 Installing the clutch release fork bearing clip

TCCS7141

Fig. 19 View of the clutch release fork assembly installed; be sure all parts move freely

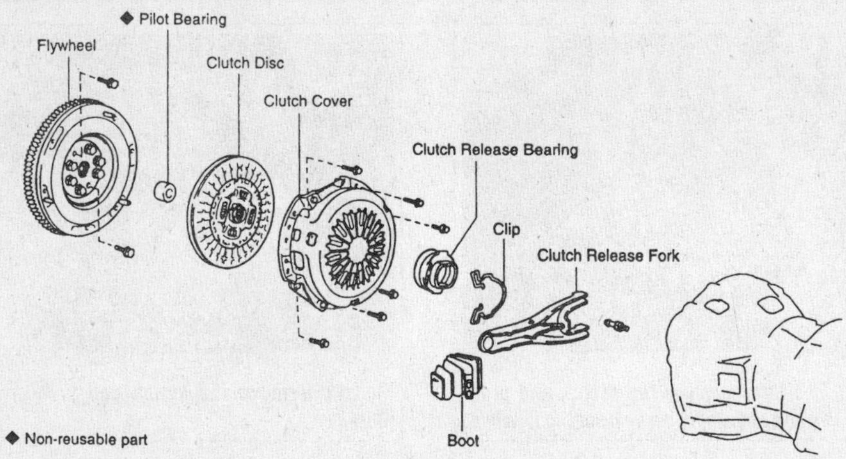

Fig. 20 Exploded view of the common clutch set-up

TCCS7121

Fig. 21 Lock the flywheel in place, then remove the flywheel bolts

6. Inspect the flywheel surface for cracks, heat scoring (blue marks), and warpage. If oil is present on the flywheel surface, this indicates that either the engine rear oil seal or the transmission front oil seal is leaking. If necessary, replace the seal(s). If in doubt concerning the condition of the flywheel, consult an automotive machine shop.

7. Before installing any new parts, make sure that they are clean. During installation, do not get grease or oil on any of the components, as this will shorten clutch life considerably. Grease or fingerprints may be cleaned with an evaporative cleaner such as the type used on brake linings.

To install:

8. Position the clutch disc against the flywheel. The long side of the splined section faces the flywheel.

9. Install the clutch cover over the disc and install the bolts loosely. Align the matchmarks made. If a new or rebuilt clutch cover assembly is installed, use the matchmark on the old cover assembly as a reference.

➡Whenever the clutch disc is replaced, replacement of the pressure plate (clutch cover) and release bearing is highly recommended.

10. Align the clutch disc with the flywheel using a clutch aligning tool. These handy tools are available in many auto parts stores at a reasonable price. Do NOT attempt to align the clutch disc by eye; use an alignment tool.

11. With the clutch aligning tool installed, tighten the clutch cover bolts gradually in a star pattern, as is done with lug nuts. Final tighten the bolts to 14 ft. lbs. (19 Nm).

12. Apply molybdenum disulfide grease or multipurpose grease to the release fork contact points, the pivot and the clutch disc splines. Install the boot, fork, and bearing on the transmission input shaft.

13. Install the transmission.

TCCS7122

Fig. 22 Removing the flywheel from the crankshaft

TCCS7123

Fig. 23 Add a threadlocking agent to the flywheel bolts upon installation

TCCS7124

Fig. 24 Be sure that the flywheel surface is clean, before installing the clutch

TCCS7125

Fig. 25 Place a straightedge across the flywheel surface, then use a feeler gauge to check for warpage

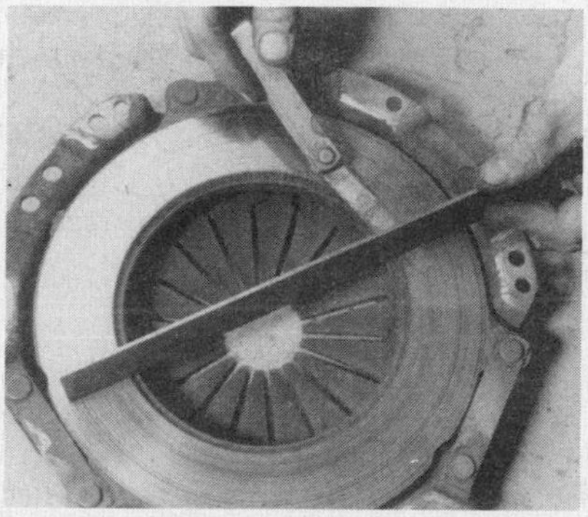
TCCS7126

Fig. 26 Checking the pressure plate for excessive wear

TCCS7127

Fig. 27 Install a clutch alignment arbor, to align the clutch assembly during installation

TCCS7128

Fig. 28 Clutch plate installed with the arbor in place

TCCS7129

Fig. 29 Clutch plate and pressure plate installed with the alignment arbor in place

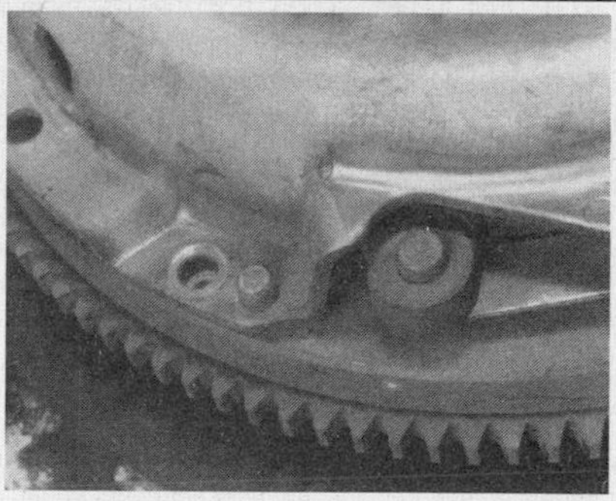
TCCS7130

Fig. 30 Pressure plate-to-flywheel bolt holes should align

TCCS7131

Fig. 31 Apply locking agent to the clutch assembly bolts

TCCS7133

Fig. 32 Be sure to use a torque wrench to tighten all bolts in a star pattern

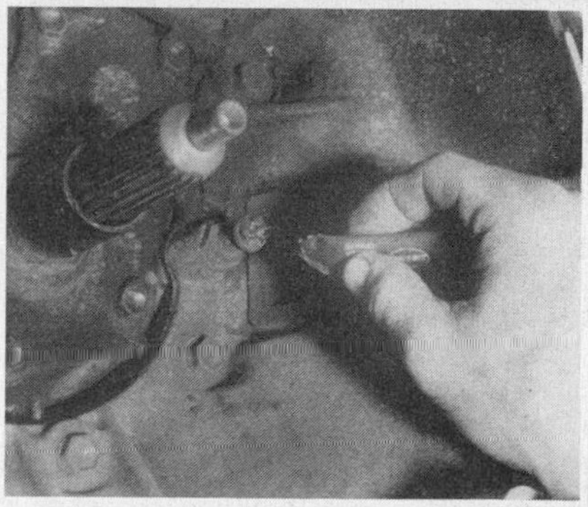
TCCS7134

Fig. 33 Grease the clutch release fork ball

Master Cylinder

REMOVAL & INSTALLATION

➧ **See Figure 34**

1. Remove the clip and pin on the clutch pedal arm; disconnect the master cylinder pushrod from the clutch pedal.
2. Have a container handy to catch any spillage of fluids. Remove the hydraulic line from the master cylinder, being careful not to damage the fitting.
3. Remove the two bolts holding the master cylinder to the engine compartment.

**** WARNING**

Brake fluid dissolves paint. Do not allow it to drip onto the body when removing the master cylinder.

To install:

4. Install the master cylinder. Partially tighten the hydraulic line, then tighten the cylinder mounting bolts to 9 ft. lbs. (13 Nm).
5. Connect the pushrod to the clutch pedal.
6. Bleed the system. Adjust the clutch pedal.

Slave Cylinder

REMOVAL & INSTALLATION

➧ **See Figure 35**

1. Jack up the front of the truck and support it on jackstands.
2. Remove the tension spring on the clutch fork.
3. Remove the hydraulic line from the slave cylinder. Be careful not to damage the fitting.
4. Remove the mounting bolts and withdraw the cylinder.

To install:

5. Place the cylinder in position, then install the bolts. Tighten to 9 ft. lbs. (13 Nm).
6. Install the hydraulic line from the master cylinder.
7. Bleed the system.

HYDRAULIC SYSTEM BLEEDING

This operation must be performed any time the clutch master or slave cylinder has been removed or if any of the hydraulic lines have been opened.

**** WARNING**

Do not spill brake fluid on the bodywork of the vehicle; it will destroy the paint. If fluid is spilled, immediately wash the surface with plenty of clean water.

1. Fill the master cylinder reservoir with brake fluid.
2. Remove the cap on the bleeder screw on the clutch slave cylinder. Install a clear vinyl hose on the fitting; place the other end submerged in a clear glass jar partially filled with brake fluid.
3. Have an assistant pump the clutch pedal slowly several times. After several pumps, hold the pedal down and open the bleeder, allowing fluid to flow into the jar. Close the bleeder valve almost immediately after opening it. Release the pedal only after the bleeder is closed.
4. Repeat the process until the fluid in the hose contains no air bubbles. tube. When there are no more air bubbles in the system, tighten the plug fully with the pedal depressed. Replace the plastic cap.
5. Fill the clutch master cylinder reservoir to the correct level with brake fluid.
6. Check the system for leaks.

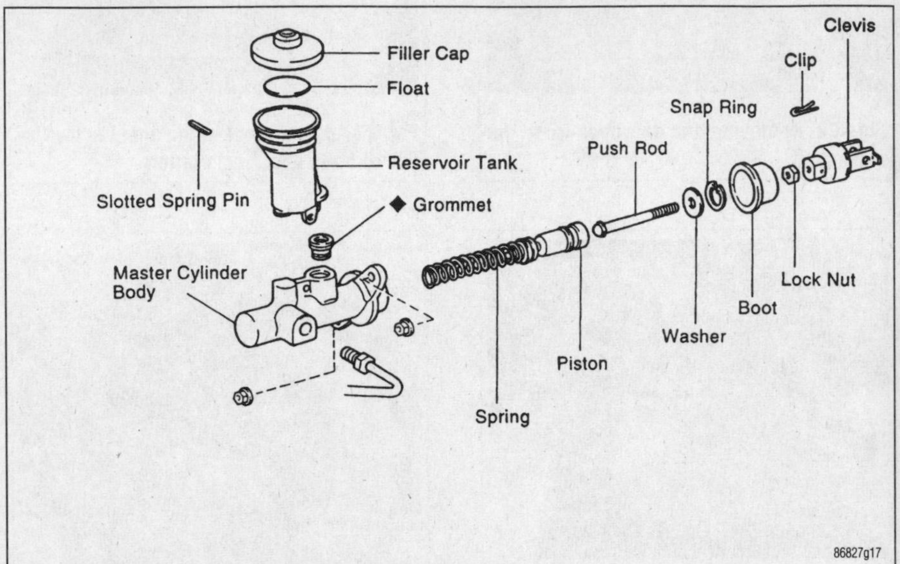

Fig. 34 Exploded view of the clutch master cylinder

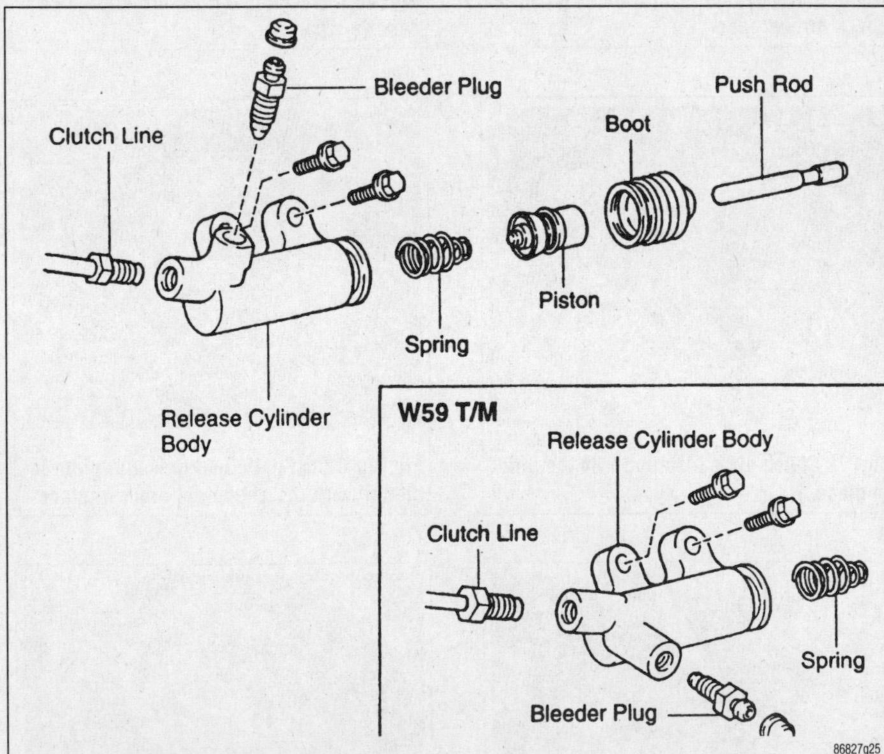

Fig. 35 Exploded view of the clutch slave cylinder

AUTOMATIC TRANSMISSION

Neutral Safety Switch

The neutral safety switch prevents the vehicle from starting unless the gearshift selector is in either the **P** or **N** positions. If the vehicle will start in any other positions, adjustment or replacement of the switch is required.

REMOVAL & INSTALLATION

Vehicles with A340E and A340F Transmissions

➧ See Figure 36

➡On some models it will be necessary to remove the oil cooler pipes for access.

1. Disconnect the harness for the neutral safety switch.
2. Pry off the washer and remove the nut, then remove the bolt for the switch.

To install:

3. Attach the switch to the vehicle with the bolt, tighten to 9 ft. lbs. (13 Nm).
4. Install a new lock plate and nut. Tighten the nut to 35 inch lbs. (4 Nm).
5. Stake the nut with the lock plate.
6. Adjust the neutral safety switch.
7. Attach the harness to the switch.
8. Attach the oil cooler pipes.

Vehicles with A43D Transmission

➧ See Figures 37 and 38

1. Unstake the lockwasher.
2. Remove the nut and bolt, then the lockwasher and grommet.
3. Slide the neutral safety switch off the manual lever shaft.

To install:

4. Insert the neutral safety switch onto the manual lever shaft, then temporarily tighten the adjusting bolt.
5. Install the grommet and a new lockwasher. Install and tighten the nut to 35 inch lbs. (4 Nm).
6. Using the control shaft lever, turn the manual valve lever shaft forwards and return two notches. It is now in neutral.
7. Align the switch basic line and the switch groove, then tighten the adjusting bolt. Tighten to 48 inch lbs. (5 Nm).
8. Bend the tabs of the lockwasher over the nut.

ADJUSTMENT

1. Loosen the neutral start switch bolt.
2. Place the gearshift selector lever in the **N** position.
3. Align the shaft groove of the switch with the neutral basic line. Hold the switch in this position and tighten the switch bolts on the A43D transmission to 48 inch lbs. (6 Nm) and all others to 9 ft. lbs. (13 Nm).
4. With the parking brake set and the brake pedal fully applied, attempt to start the engine in each shifter range. The engine should only start in **N** or **P**.

Extension Housing Seal

REMOVAL & INSTALLATION

➧ See Figures 39 and 40

Removal of the extension housing seal is only possible on the A43D and A340E transmissions.

1. Elevate and safely support the vehicle.
2. Position a catch pan below the work area to contain spilled fluid.
3. Remove the driveshaft.
4. Clean the extension housing area thoroughly before removing the seal. No dirt must be allowed to enter the transmission during replacement.
5. Using a seal extractor such as tool 09308–10010 or equivalent, remove the seal.

To install:

6. Use a seal driver such as tool 09325–20010 or equivalent. Drive the new seal into place until it seats.
7. Install the driveshaft.
8. Lower the vehicle and start the engine. With the brake applied, shift the transmission through each position, pausing long enough to allow the gear to fully engage. Place the selector in **P** and check the fluid level, topping the fluid as needed. Do NOT overfill the fluid.

Transmission Assembly

REMOVAL & INSTALLATION

1997–99 4Runner

A340D, A340E AND A340H TRANSMISSIONS

➡The transfer case and the transmission should be removed as an assembly.

1. Disconnect the negative battery cable.
2. If required, remove the air cleaner assembly.
3. Disconnect the transmission throttle cable from the throttle body.
4. Raise and safely support the vehicle.
5. Remove the engine undercover.
6. Drain the transmission and transfer case (if applicable) fluid.
7. Detach the wiring connectors from the transmission and transfer case (if applicable).

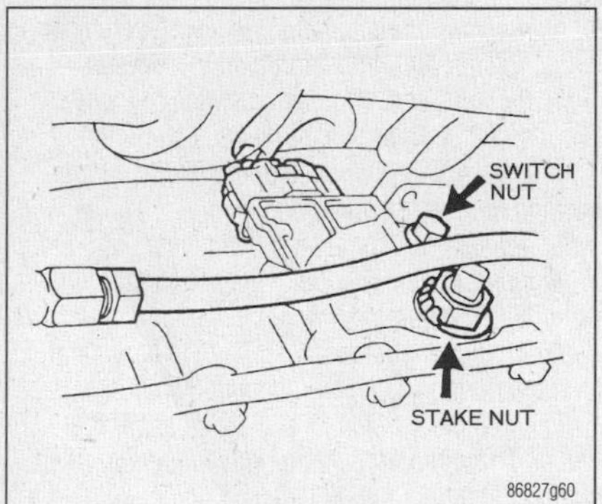

Fig. 36 Neutral safety switch nut locations

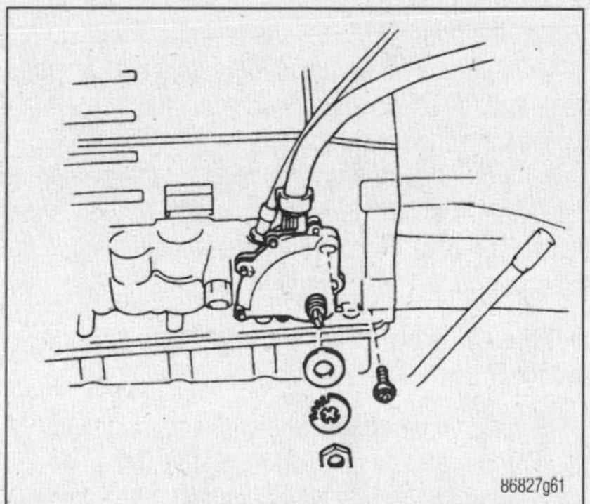

Fig. 37 Exploded view of neutral safety switch mounting

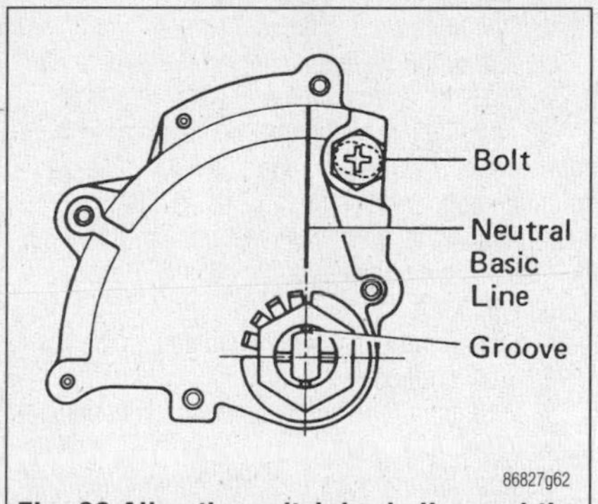

Fig. 38 Align the switch basic line and the switch groove, then tighten the adjusting bolt to 48 inch lbs. (5 Nm)

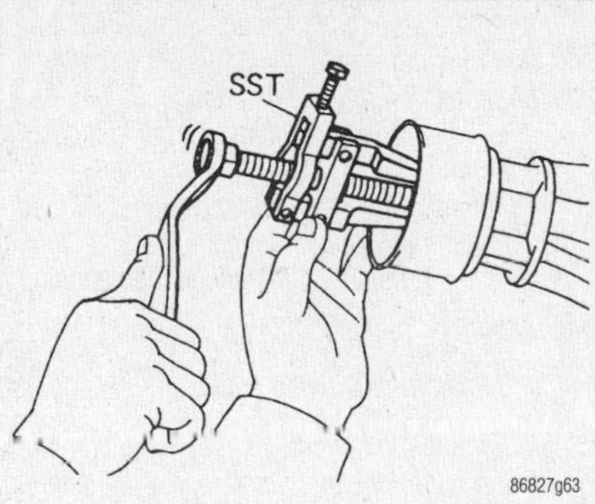

Fig. 39 Use SST 09308–10010 or equivalent to remove the extension housing seal

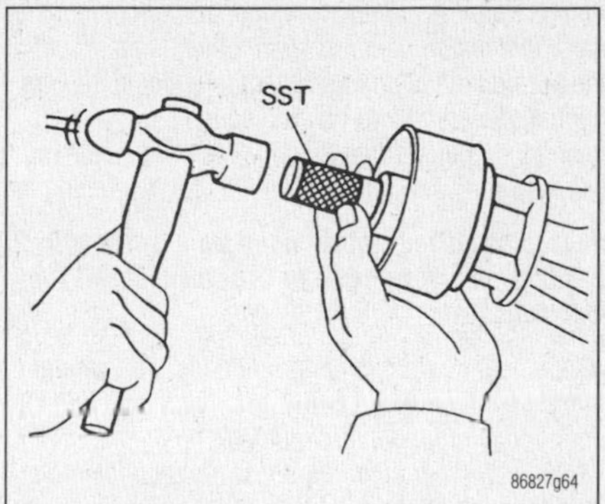

Fig. 40 Upon replacement, tap on the seal driver to insert the seal as far as it will go

8. Disconnect the starter wiring at the starter. Remove the mounting bolts and the starter from the engine.

9. Make matchmarks on the front and rear driveshaft flanges and the differential pinion flanges. These marks must be aligned during installation.

10. Unbolt the front and rear driveshaft flanges. If the vehicle has a 2 piece driveshaft, remove the center bearing bracket bolts. Remove the driveshaft from the vehicle.

11. Disconnect the speedometer cable.

12. Remove the front exhaust pipe and the bracket.

13. Disconnect the transmission oil cooler lines at the transmission.

14. Disconnect the oil cooler lines bracket and remove the transmission oil filler tube, as required.

15. Support the transmission, using a jack with a wooden block placed between the jack and the transmission pan. Raise the transmission, just enough to take the weight off of the rear mount.

16. Remove the rear engine mount with the bracket, the rear crossmember, and the transfer case (if applicable) undercover.

17. Remove the dynamic damper (regular cab only) and the No. 2 cross-shaft bracket.

18. Place a wooden block(s) between the engine oil pan and the front frame crossmember.

19. Slowly, lower the transmission until the engine rests on the wooden block(s).

20. Remove the torque converter cover at the rear of the engine in order to gain access to the converter bolts.

21. Rotate the crankshaft to access the bolts through the service holes and remove the torque converter bolts.

22. Remove the stiffener plates from the transmission.

23. Disconnect the shift control rod and the transfer case shift lever.

24. For the A340H transmissions, perform the following:

a. Remove the cross-shaft and the No. 2 shifting rod.

b. Remove the front stabilizer bar.

c. Support the front differential with a jack and remove the differential mounting bolts.

d. Slowly lower the front differential so there is enough clearance to remove the transmission and transfer case (if applicable). If enough clearance can't be obtained, remove the differential from the vehicle.

25. Remove the stabilizer bar, if equipped, the auxiliary frame crossmember.

26. For A340D transmissions, obtain a bolt of the same dimensions as the torque converter bolts. Cut the head off of the bolt and hacksaw a slot in the bolt opposite the threaded end. Thread the guide pin into one of the torque converter bolt holes. The guide pin will help keep the converter with the transmission.

➡This modified bolt is used as a guide pin. 2 guide pins are needed to properly install the transmission.

27. Remove the transmission bolts, then carefully move the transmission rearward by prying on the dowel pins through the service hole.

28. Pull the transmission rearward and lower it out of the vehicle.

29. Separate the transfer case from the transmission

To install:

30. Connect the transfer case to the transmission.

31. Apply a coat of multi-purpose grease to the torque converter stub shaft and the corresponding pilot hole in the flexplate.

32. Install the torque converter into the front of the transmission. Push inward on the torque converter while rotating it to completely couple the torque converter to the transmission.

33. To be sure the converter is properly installed, measure the distance between the torque converter mounting lugs and the front mounting face of the transmission. The proper distance is 0.71 in. (18mm) for the A340H transmission, or 0.79 in. (20mm) for the A340D, A340E and A340F transmissions.

34. For A340D transmissions, install guide pins into 2 opposite mounting lugs of the torque converter.

35. Raise the transmission to the engine and align the transmission with the dowel pins.

36. Install and tighten the transmission mounting bolts to 47 ft. lbs. (63 Nm).

37. Rotate the crankshaft and install the torque converter mounting bolts. Evenly, tighten the converter mounting bolts to 30 ft. lbs. (41 Nm) for the A340H, A3430D and A340E transmissions, or to 20 ft. lbs. (27 Nm) for the A340F transmission.

38. Install the torque converter access cover.

39. Raise the transmission slightly and remove the wood block(s) from under the engine oil pan.

40. Install the transmission crossmember. Tighten the crossmember bolts to 70 ft. lbs. (95 Nm).

41. Install the rear mount and the mounting bracket. Tighten the bracket mounting bolts to 43 ft. lbs. (58 Nm) and tighten the bracket to the rear mount bolts to 108 inch lbs. (13 Nm).

42. Lower the transmission onto the crossmember and install the transmission to mount bolts. Tighten the bolts to 18 ft. lbs. (25 Nm).

43. Remove the wooden blocks from between the frame and the engine. Remove the support from under the transmission.

44. For the A340H transmission, install the front differential. Tighten the 2 rear mounting bolts to 123 ft. lbs. (167 Nm). Tighten the front mounting through-bolt to 108 ft. lbs. (147 Nm).

➡If the differential oil was drained, refill it at this time.

45. Install the remaining components in the reverse of the removal procedure, making sure to note the following tightening specifications:

- Stiffener plate bolts: 27 ft. lbs. (37 Nm)
- Dynamic damper mounting bolts: 27 ft. lbs. (37 Nm)
- Oil cooler line fittings: 25 ft. lbs. (34 Nm)
- Front and rear driveshaft-to-pinion flange bolts: 54 ft. lbs. (74 Nm).

46. Refill the transmission and the transfer case (if applicable).

47. Connect the negative battery cable.

48. Start the engine and check for leaks.

49. Road test the vehicle for proper operation.

50. Recheck all fluid levels.

A340F TRANSMISSION

1. Disconnect the negative battery cable.

2. Disconnect the throttle cable from the engine compartment.

3. Remove the ATF level gauge.

4. On the 3RZ-FE engine, remove the oil filler pipe upper side bolt.

5. On the 5VZ-FE engine, remove the oil filler pipe.

6. Remove the transmission shift lever assembly and transfer shift lever.

a. Remove the rear console upper panel and disconnect the connectors.

b. Pull off the heater control knobs.

c. Remove the center cluster finish panel and disconnect the connectors.

d. Without 2-4 selector: Remove the transfer shift lever knob.

e. With 2-4 selector: Remove the bolt and disconnect the transfer shift lever knob.

f. Remove the front console upper panel.

g. If equipped, disconnect the 2-4 selector connector and remove the transfer shift lever knob.

h. Remove the shift control rod.

i. Remove the connector and remove the eight screws and the transmission shift lever assembly.

j. Using pliers, remove the snapring and pull out the shift lever from the transfer case.

7. Remove the engine undercover.

8. Remove the front and rear driveshafts.

9. Remove the exhaust pipe.

10. On the 3RZ-FE engine, remove the oil filler pipe.

11. Disconnect the following connectors from the transmission:

- No. 2 vehicle speed sensor connector
- Solenoid connector
- ATF temperature sensor connector
- Park/neutral position switch connector

12. Detach the following connectors from the transfer case:

- No. 1 vehicle speed sensor connector (3RZ-FE engine)
- Transfer neutral position switch connector
- Transfer L4 position switch connector
- Transfer 4WD position switch connector
- Actuator connector (2-4 selector only)

13. Separate the wiring harness from the transmission and the transfer case.

14. Disconnect the 2 oil cooler pipes.

15. Remove the rear end plate and torque converter clutch mounting bolt.

16. Support the transmission with a jack stand and remove the engine rear mounting bolts.

17. Remove the 4 bolts and the crossmember.

18. Disconnect the starter wire and remove the starter.

19. Remove the transmission.

To install:

20. Install the transmission in the vehicle. Tighten the bolts to 53 ft. lbs. (71 Nm).

21. Install the starter and tighten the bolts to 29 ft. lbs. (39 Nm). Connect the wiring for the starter.

22. Install the crossmember and tighten the 4 bolts to 48 ft. lbs. (65 Nm). Install the 4 engine rear mounting bolts and tighten to 14 ft. lbs. (19 Nm).

23. Install the clutch converter bolts by installing the green colored bolt before the other 5. Tighten them to 30 ft. lbs. (41 Nm).

24. Install the rear end plate and tighten the bolts to 13 ft. lbs. (18 Nm).

25. Install the 2 oil cooler pipes and tighten to 25 ft. lbs. (34 Nm).

26. Install the 3 bolts for the oil cooler pipe clamps and tighten to:

- 10mm head bolt: 48 inch lbs. (5 Nm)
- 12mm head bolt: 108 inch lbs. (13 Nm)

27. Connect the harness from the transmission and the transfer.
28. Install the remaining components in the reverse order of removal.
29. Fill the transmission and transfer case with transmission fluid.
30. Connect the throttle cable to the cable clamps in the engine compartment.
31. Connect the negative battery cable.

2000 4Runner

A340E TRANSMISSION

1. Loosen the 2 nuts and disconnect the throttle cable.
2. Disconnect the throttle cable from cable clamps in the engine compartment.
3. Remove the automatic transmission dipstick.
4. Detach the oil filler pipe.
5. Unscrew the bolt and oil filler pipe with O-ring.
6. Detach the two engine undercovers.
7. Remove the propeller shaft.
8. Remove the front exhaust pipe.
9. Disconnect the transmission control rod.
10. Detach the No. 1 vehicle speed sensor connector from the transmission.
11. Detach the No. 2 vehicle speed sensor connector from the transmission.
12. Disconnect the solenoid wire connector from the transmission.
13. Detach the automatic transmission fluid temperature sensor connector from the transmission.
14. Disconnect the park/neutral position switch connector from the transmission.
15. Separate the wire harness from the transmission.
16. Remove the 3 bolts and oil cooler pipe clamps.
17. Disconnect the 2 oil cooler pipes.
18. Remove rear end plate and torque converter clutch mounting bolt.
19. On vehicles equipped with the 3RZ-FE engine, remove the 2 nuts, 4 bolts and rear end plate.
20. On vehicles equipped with the 5VZ-FE engine perform the following:
    a. Remove the 4 bolts and rear end plate.
    b. Turn the crankshaft to gain access and remove the 6 bolts with holding the crankshaft pulley set bolt by a wrench.
21. Using a transmission jack, support the transmission.
22. Remove No. 3 crossmember by performing the following steps:
    a. Remove the 4 set bolts of the engine rear mounting.
    b. Remove the 4 bolts, nuts and No. 3 crossmember.
23. Remove engine rear mounting by detaching the 4 bolts and engine rear mounting from the transmission.
24. Remove the nut and disconnect the starter wire and connector.
25. Remove the 2 bolts and starter.
26. On vehicles equipped with the 3RZ-FE engine, remove the 3 bolts and transmission.
27. On vehicles equipped with the 5VZ-FE engine, remove the 6 bolts and transmission.

To install:

28. Check torque converter clutch installation.
29. Using calipers and a straight edge, measure the distance from the installed surface of the transmission housing to the installed surface of the torque converter clutch.
30. The distance should be as follows:
    - 3RZ-FE engine: More than 1.2500 in. (31.75mm)
    - 5VZ-FE engine: More than 0.7067 in. (7.95mm)
31. Installation is in the reverse order of removal

➡After installation, adjust the shift lever position and throttle cable

32. Fill and check fluid levels.

A340F TRANSMISSION

1. Loosen the 2 nuts and disconnect the throttle cable.
2. Disconnect the throttle cable from cable clamps in the engine compartment.
3. Remove Automatic Transmission Fluid (ATF) dipstick.
4. On 3RZ-FE engine, remove oil filler pipe upper side bolt.
5. On 5VZ-FE engine, remove the bolt and oil filler pipe with O-ring.
6. If your vehicle does not have a 2-4 selector, remove the transfer shift lever knob.
7. If you vehicle is equipped with 2-4 selector, remove the screw and disconnect the transfer shift lever knob.
8. Remove the front console upper panel.
9. If your vehicle is equipped with 2-4 selector, detach the 2-4 selector connector and remove the transfer shift lever knob.
10. Detach the 2 clips, screws and front console box.
11. Remove the nut and washer and disconnect the shift control rod.
12. Disconnect the connector and remove the 8 bolts and transmission shift lever assembly.
13. Using pliers, remove the snapring and pull out the transfer shift lever from the transfer case.
14. Remove 2 engine undercovers.
15. Detach front and rear propeller shaft.
16. Remove front exhaust pipe.
17. On the 3RZ-FE engine, remove the bolt and oil filler pipe with O-ring.
18. Detach no. 2 vehicle speed sensor connector from transmission.
19. Detach the solenoid connector from transmission.
20. Disconnect the Automatic Transmission Fluid (ATF) temperature sensor connector from transmission.
21. Detach the park/neutral position switch connector from transmission.
22. On the 3RZ-FE engine, detach No.1 vehicle speed sensor connector from transfer.
23. Disconnect the transfer neutral position switch connector from the transfer case.
24. Disconnect the transfer 4WD position switch connector from the transfer case.
25. If your vehicle is equipped with a 2-4 selector, disconnect actuator connector from transfer case.
26. Separate wire harness from transmission and transfer case.
27. Remove the 3 bolts and oil cooler pipe clamps.
28. Disconnect the 2 oil cooler pipes.
29. On the 3RZ-FE engine, remove the 2 nuts, 4 bolts and rear end plate.
30. On the 5VZ-FE engine, remove the 4 bolts and rear end plate.
31. Turn the crankshaft to gain access and remove the 6 bolts with holding the crankshaft pulley set bolt by a wrench.
32. Remove No. 3 crossmember
33. Support the transmission rear side with a support stand.
34. Remove the 4 set bolts of the engine rear mounting.
35. Remove the 4 bolts, nuts and No. 3 crossmember.
36. Remove the 4 bolts and engine rear mounting from the transmission.
37. On the 5VZ-FE engine (VF3AM type transfer), remove the 4 bolts, nuts and No. 4 crossmember.
38. Support the transmission with a transmission jack.
39. Remove a support stand from the transmission rear side.
40. Remove the nut and disconnect the starter wire and connector.
41. Remove the 2 bolts and starter.
42. On the 3RZ-FE engine, remove the 3 bolts and transmission.
43. On the 5VZ-FE engine, disconnect the stabilizer bar
44. On the 5VZ-FE engine, remove the 6 bolts and transmission.

To install:

45. Check torque converter clutch installation.
46. Using calipers and a straight edge, measure the distance from the installed surface of the transmission housing to the installed surface of the torque converter clutch.
47. The correct distance should be:
    - 3RZ-FE engine: More than 1.2500 in. (31.75mm)
    - 5VZ-FE engine: More than 0.7067 in. (17.95mm)
48. Install the transmission in the reverse order of removal.

➡After installation, adjust the shift lever position and throttle cable.

49. Fill and check fluid level.

T-100

A340E TRANSMISSION—3RZ-FE ENGINE

1. Turn the ignition switch **OFF.** Disconnect the battery cables; negative cable first.
2. Matchmark the hood hinges and remove the hood.
3. Remove the battery and battery tray.
4. Drain the engine oil, transmission oil, and the cooling system.
5. Remove the expansion tank.
6. Remove the radiator.
7. Remove the air cleaner cap, Mass Air Flow (MAF) meter, and the resonator. Remove the air cleaner case.
8. Disconnect the accelerator and throttle cables from the throttle body.
9. Remove the intake air connector.
10. If equipped with air conditioning, remove the air conditioning compressor and bracket. Position the compressor aside with the air conditioning lines attached.
11. Disconnect the heater hoses at the cowl panel.
12. Disconnect the following hoses:
    - Brake booster vacuum hose
    - Evaporator Emissions (EVAP) hose

- 2 power steering hoses
- Fuel return hose
- Fuel inlet hose

13. Remove the power steering pump.
14. Disconnect the alternator wires from the alternator.
15. Disconnect the Engine Control Module (ECM) wiring from the ECM.
16. Remove the engine wiring harness and connectors from the vehicle as follows:
    a. Remove the igniter connector.
    b. Disconnect the ground strap from the cowl top panel.
    c. Disconnect the 4 engine wiring harness clamps.
    d. Pull out the engine wiring harness from the vehicle.
17. Remove the sway bar.
18. Remove the driveshaft from the vehicle.
19. Disconnect the speedometer cable from the transmission.
20. Disconnect the front exhaust pipe from the exhaust manifold and catalytic converter.
21. Remove the cross-shaft as follows:
    a. Remove the clip and disconnect the No. 2 gear shifting rod.
    b. Remove the nut, washer, 4 bolts, and the cross-shaft.
22. Disconnect the wires at the starter.
23. Position a jack and wooden block under the transmission and remove the rear engine mounting bracket.
24. Attach a suitable engine hoist to the engine hangers.
25. Remove the nuts and bolts from the engine mounts.
26. Be sure all connectors, wires, and hoses are disconnected and away from the engine and transmission.
27. Carefully lift the engine/transmission assembly out of the vehicle.
28. Remove the rear end plate by removing the 2 nuts and 4 bolts.
29. Turn the crankshaft to gain access to the torque converter bolts.
30. Remove the torque converter bolts.
31. Remove the starter by removing the 2 bolts.
32. Remove the 3 mounting bolts from the engine.
33. Pull out the transmission toward the rear.

To install:

34. Connect the engine to the transmission. Install the 3 bolts and tighten the bolts to 53 ft. lbs. (71 Nm).
35. Install the torque converter bolts to the torque converter. Tighten the bolts to 30 ft. lbs. (41 Nm).
36. Install the rear end plate and tighten the nuts and bolts to 27 ft. lbs. (37 Nm).
37. Connect the starter and bolts. Tighten the bolts to 29 ft. lbs. (39 Nm).
38. Attach the engine hoist to the engine hangers. Carefully lower the engine/transmission assembly into the vehicle. Keep the engine level, while aligning the engine mounts.
39. Install the engine mount fasteners, but do not fully tighten.
40. Position a jack and wooden block under the transmission and install the rear engine mounting bracket. Tighten the bolts to the frame to 42 ft. lbs. (58 Nm) and the bolts to the mount to 13 ft. lbs. (18 Nm).
41. Remove the jack and engine hoist. Tighten the engine mounts to 28 ft. lbs. (38 Nm).
42. Connect the starter wires to the starter.
43. Install the cross-shaft.
44. Install the remaining components in the reverse order of removal. Tighten the fasteners as follows:
    - Exhaust pipe-to-exhaust manifold nuts: 46 ft. lbs. (62 Nm)
    - Exhaust pipe support bracket bolts: 29 ft. lbs. (39 Nm)
    - Exhaust pipe clamp nuts: 14 ft. lbs. (19 Nm)
    - Exhaust pipe-to-catalytic converter bolts: 29 ft. lbs. (39 Nm)
    - Sway bar mounting bolts: 22 ft. lbs. (30 Nm)
    - Power steering pump-to-bracket bolts: 43 ft. lbs. (58 Nm)
    - Air conditioning compressor bracket-to-engine bolts: 32 ft. lbs. (44 Nm)
    - Air conditioning compressor-to-bracket bolts: 18 ft. lbs. (25 Nm).
45. Fill the engine oil, engine coolant, and the transmission oil.
46. Connect the negative and positive cables to the battery.
47. Start the engine and check for leaks.
48. Check the ignition timing.
49. Install the engine undercover.
50. Install the hood.
51. Road test the vehicle and check all fluids.

A340E TRANSMISSION—5VZ-FE ENGINE

1. Remove the hood.
2. Disconnect the battery and remove it from the vehicle.
3. Raise and safely support the vehicle.
4. Remove the engine undercovers.
5. Drain the engine coolant.
6. Drain the engine oil.
7. Remove the radiator from the vehicle.
8. Remove the power steering pump drive belt.
9. If equipped with air conditioning, remove the air conditioning drive belt by loosening the idler pulley nut and adjusting bolt.
10. Loosen the lockbolt, pivot bolt, and the adjusting bolt. Remove the alternator drive belt.
11. Remove the fan with the fluid coupling and fan pulleys.
12. Disconnect the power steering pump from the engine and set aside. Do not disconnect the lines from the pump.
13. If equipped with air conditioning, disconnect the compressor from the engine and set aside. Do not disconnect the lines from the compressor.
14. Remove the air cleaner cap, Mass Air Flow (MAF) meter, and the resonator.
15. Remove the air cleaner case and filter.
16. Disconnect the following cables:
    - If equipped with cruise control, the actuator cable with the bracket.
    - Accelerator cable
    - Throttle cable
17. Disconnect the heater hoses.
18. Disconnect the following hoses:
    - Brake booster vacuum hose
    - Evaporator Emissions (EVAP) hose
    - Fuel return hose
    - Fuel inlet hose
19. Remove the starter wire and connectors.
20. Disconnect the alternator connector and wire.
21. Remove the engine wiring harness and connectors as follows:
    a. Remove the 4 screws to the right front door scuff plate. Remove the scuff plate from the vehicle.
    b. Remove the cowl panel side trim by removing the clip.
    c. Remove the Engine Control Module (ECM) electrical connectors.
    d. Remove the 2 connectors from the cowl wire.
    e. Remove the igniter connector.
    f. Disconnect the ground strap.
    g. Disconnect the 6 engine wiring harness clamps.
    h. Pull out the engine wiring harness from the vehicle.
22. Remove the stabilizer bar.
23. Remove the driveshaft from the transmission.
24. Disconnect the speedometer cable.
25. Remove the front exhaust pipe.
26. Remove the cross-shaft.
27. Place a jack under the transmission.
28. Remove the transmission rear mounting bracket by removing the 8 bolts.
29. If equipped with air conditioning, remove the bolt and disconnect the air conditioning compressor wire clamp.
30. If necessary, install a No. 2 engine hanger with 2 bolts. Tighten the 2 bolts to 30 ft. lbs. (40 Nm).
31. Attach the engine hoist chain to the 2 engine hangers.
32. Remove the 4 bolts and nuts holding the engine front mounting insulators to the frame.
33. Lift the engine and transmission out of the vehicle.
34. Remove the starter by removing the 2 bolts.
35. Remove the transmission 6 mounting bolts from the engine.
36. If equipped, remove the rear end plate by removing the 4 bolts and 4 nuts.
37. Turn the crankshaft to gain access to the torque converter bolts.
38. Remove the torque converter bolts.
39. Pull out the transmission toward the rear.
40. Remove the 3 mounting bolt from the engine.
41. Pull out the transmission toward the rear.

To install:

42. Connect the engine to the transmission. Install the 3 bolts and tighten the bolts to 53 ft. lbs. (71 Nm).
43. Install the torque converter bolts to the torque converter. Tighten the bolts to 30 ft. lbs. (41 Nm).
44. Install the rear end plate and tighten the nuts and bolts to 27 ft. lbs. (37 Nm).
45. Connect the starter and bolts. Tighten the bolts to 29 ft. lbs. (39 Nm).
46. Install the transmission to the engine and install the 6 mounting bolts. Tighten the bolts to 53 ft. lbs. (71 Nm).
47. Install the starter and install the 2 bolts. Tighten the bolts to 29 ft. lbs. (39 Nm).
48. Install the engine assembly to the vehicle. Attach the engine mounts to the body mounts. Install the bolts and nuts but do not tighten at this time.
49. Remove the engine chain hoist the No. 2 engine hanger.
50. If equipped with air conditioning, connect the air conditioning wire with the bolt.
51. Raise the transmission slightly and install the transmission mounting bracket. Tighten the bolts to

the frame to 43 ft. lbs. (58 Nm) and the bolts to the mounting insulator to 13 ft. lbs. (18 Nm).

52. Tighten the engine mounting nuts and bolts to 28 ft. lbs. (38 Nm).
53. Install the cross-shaft.
54. Install the remaining components in the reverse order of removal. Make certain to tighten the exhaust pipe-to-exhaust manifold bolts to 46 ft. lbs. (62 Nm), the exhaust pipe support bracket bolts to 33 ft. lbs. (44 Nm), the exhaust pipe-to-catalytic converter bolts to 35 ft. lbs. (48 Nm) and the cooling fan-to-fluid clutch nuts to 48 inch lbs. (5 Nm).
55. Fill the engine with oil and fill the transmission with fluid.
56. Fill the engine and radiator with coolant.
57. Install the engine undercover.
58. Install the battery and connect the cables.
59. Start the engine and check for leaks.
60. Install the hood.

A340F TRANSMISSION

1. Disconnect the negative battery cable.
2. Disconnect the transmission throttle cable and clamp from the throttle body.
3. Raise and safely support the vehicle.
4. Remove the engine undercover.
5. Drain the transmission fluid.
6. Remove the transfer shift lever front the inside of the vehicle as follows:
   a. Remove the shift lever knob.
   b. Remove the 4 screws and the boot.
   c. Using pliers, remove the snapring, and pull out the shift lever from the transfer case.
7. Remove the transmission oil filler tube.
8. Remove the front and rear driveshafts.
9. Remove the front exhaust pipe.
10. Disconnect the speedometer cable.
11. Remove the No. 2 vehicle speed sensor connector.
12. Remove the solenoid connector by removing the electrical connector and bolt.
13. Disconnect the transfer case neutral position switch.
14. Disconnect the transfer case L4 position switch.
15. Remove the clip and disconnect the No. 2 gear shifting rod.
16. Remove the nut, 4 bolts, and the cross-shaft.
17. Disconnect the starter wires.
18. Remove the oil cooler pipe by removing the bolts and clamps.
19. Remove the Automatic Transmission Fluid (ATF) temperature sensor connector.
20. Remove the park/neutral position switch connector.
21. Remove the starter from the engine by removing the 2 bolts.
22. Remove the stiffener plate and rear end plate by removing the 8 bolts.
23. Remove the sway bar.
24. Support the transmission, using a jack with a wooden block placed between the jack and the transmission pan. Raise the transmission just enough to take the weight off of the rear mount.
25. Remove the rear engine mounting bracket.
26. Remove the rear support member by removing the 8 bolts.
27. Rotate the crankshaft to access the torque converter bolts. Remove the 6 bolts from the torque converter.
28. Disconnect or remove any component that will get in the way of removing the transmission.
29. Remove the transmission bolts, then carefully move the transmission rearward.
30. Pull the transmission rearward and lower it out of the vehicle.

To install:

31. Raise the transmission into place and install the bolts. Tighten the transmission bolts to 53 ft. lbs. (71 Nm).
32. Install the torque converter bolts and tighten the bolts to 30 ft. lbs. (41 Nm).
33. Install the rear support member and tighten the 8 bolts to 70 ft. lbs. (97 Nm).
34. Install the rear mounting bracket and install the 4 bolts. Tighten the bolts to 13 ft. lbs. (18 Nm).
35. Install the dynamic damper with the 2 bolts. Tighten the bolts to 44 ft. lbs. (61 Nm).
36. Remove the jack supporting the transmission.
37. Install the sway bar.
38. Install the stiffener plate and rear end plate and tighten the bolts to 27 ft. lbs. (37 Nm).
39. Install the starter and tighten the bolts to 29 ft. lbs. (39 Nm).
40. Attach the park/neutral position switch connector.
41. Attach the ATF temperature sensor connector.
42. Install the oil cooler pipes and clamps. Tighten the 2 oil cooler pipes to 25 ft. lbs. (34 Nm).
43. Connect the starter wires.
44. Install the cross-shaft with the 4 bolts, washer, and nut. Tighten the nut to 108 inch lbs. (13 Nm) and the bolts as follows:
    - Transmission side: 108 inch lbs. (13 Nm)
    - Frame side: 21 ft. lbs. (28 Nm)
45. The balance of installation is the reverse of the removal procedure.
46. Fill the transmission with the proper fluid.
47. Connect the negative battery cable to the battery.
48. Road test the vehicle and check for leaks.
49. Check all fluids.

Tacoma

A340F TRANSMISSION

1. Remove the automatic transmission fluid (ATF) level gauge.
2. Remove the engine undercover.
3. Drain the transmission fluid.
4. Disconnect the throttle cable.
5. Remove the No. 1 fan shroud.
6. Remove the transmission shift lever assembly and the transfer shift lever, as follows:
   a. Remove the 2 bolts and the 4 screws and remove the rear console box.
   b. Remove the front console box with the transfer shift lever knob.
   c. Disengage the connectors.
   d. Remove the nut and washer and disconnect the shift control rod.
   e. Remove the connector and remove the 8 screws and the transmission shift lever assembly.
   f. Using snapring pliers, remove the snapring and pull out the shift lever from the transfer case.
7. Remove the oil filler pipe with the O-ring.
8. Remove the front and rear driveshaft.
9. Remove the exhaust pipe.
10. Disconnect the speedometer cable.
11. Remove the No. 2 vehicle speed sensor connector.
12. Remove the solenoid connector.
13. Remove the transfer neutral position switch connector.
14. Remove the transfer L4 position switch connector.
15. Disconnect the transfer indicator switch.
16. Disconnect the oil cooler pipe, as follows:
    a. Remove the 3 bolts and clamps.
    b. Loosen the 2 union nuts and disconnect the 2 oil cooler pipes.
17. Disengage the ATF temperature sensor connector.
18. Remove the park/neutral position switch connector.
19. Remove the connector and remove the starter.
20. Remove the 4 stabilizer bar bracket mounting bolts.
21. Remove the torque converter clutch mounting bolt, as follows:
    a. Remove the nuts and bolts and the flywheel housing undercover.
    b. While turning the crankshaft to gain access, remove the 6 bolts.
22. Remove the front differential rear mounting cushion, as follows:
    a. Using a hexagon wrench, remove the nut.
    b. Lift up the front differential. Be careful not to touch the torque converter clutch housing and the front differential companion flange.
    c. Remove the 2 rear mounting cushion mounting bolts.
23. Remove the crossmember.
    a. Support the transmission rear side.
    b. Remove the 4 engine rear mounting bolts.
    c. Supporting the transmission with a jack, remove the 4 nuts, bolts and the crossmember.
24. Lower the transmission rear side, separate the wiring harness and remove the bolts and the transmission.

To install:

25. Install the transmission to the engine and install the transmission to engine bolts. Tighten the bolts to 53 ft. lbs. (71 Nm).
26. Install the crossmember and tighten the bolts to 48 ft. lbs. (65 Nm).
27. Install the engine rear mounting bolts and tighten to 14 ft. lbs. (19 Nm).
28. Install the front differential rear mounting cushion and tighten the nut to 64 ft. lbs. (41 Nm).
29. Install the torque converter clutch mounting bolt. First install the green colored bolt, then the 5 others. Tighten to 30 ft. lbs. (41 Nm).
30. Install the flywheel housing undercover and tighten to:
    - 5VZ-FE engine: 13 ft. lbs. (18 Nm)
    - 3RZ-FE engine: 27 ft. lbs. (37 Nm)
31. Install the 4 stabilizer bar bracket mounting bolts and tighten to 19 ft. lbs. (25 Nm).
32. Install the starter and tighten the bolts to 29 ft. lbs. (39 Nm). Connect the connector and terminal.
33. Install the remaining components in the reverse order of removal.
34. Install the ATF level gauge.
35. Fill and check the fluid level.
36. Test drive and check for proper shifting.

A340D AND A340E TRANSMISSIONS

1. Remove the transmission with the engine. For additional information, please refer to the following topic(s): Engine Mechanical, Engine Removal and Installation.
2. Place the engine/transmission assembly on a stand.
3. Remove the bolts, 2 stiffener plates and rear end plate.

4. Turn the crankshaft to gain access to the torque converter bolts. Remove the torque converter bolts.
5. Remove the starter by removing the 2 bolts.
6. Remove the transmission mounting bolts from the engine.
7. Pull out the transmission toward the rear and separate the engine from the transmission.

To install:

8. Connect the transmission to the engine and install the bolts. Tighten the bolts to 53 ft. lbs. (71 Nm).
9. Install the starter with the 2 bolts. Tighten the bolts to 29 ft. lbs. (39 Nm).
10. Install the torque converter bolts and tighten to 30 ft. lbs. (41 Nm).
11. Install the stiffener plate and rear end plate with the bolts. Tighten the bolts to 27 ft. lbs. (37 Nm).
12. Connect the starter wires to the starter.
13. Install the transmission with the engine.

Land Cruiser

1997 MODELS

1. Disconnect the battery cables and remove the battery and the battery tray.
2. Loosen the fan shroud of the cooling fan to avoid damage to the fan.
3. Disconnect the throttle cable.
4. Raise and support the vehicle.
5. Drain the transmission and transfer case fluid.
6. Remove the upper starter mounting bolt.
7. Remove the transmission select lever and the transfer shift lever.
   a. Remove the clip, washer and the wave washer and disconnect the link.
   b. Remove the nut and washer and disconnect the link.
   c. Remove the transfer shift lever knob.
   d. Remove the console and the transfer shift lever boot.
   e. Remove the center console box and disconnect the three connectors.
   f. Remove the transmission shift lever assembly and the transfer shift lever.
8. Disconnect the No. 1 and No. 2 vehicle speed sensors, the park/neutral switch, the solenoid connector and the A/T fluid temperature sensor.
9. Detach the connectors and hoses from the transfer.
10. Remove the front and rear propeller (drive) shaft.
11. Remove the oil lever gauge, the upper side mounting bolt and the filler pipe.
12. Loosen the two oil cooler pipe union nuts.
13. Remove the four stabilizer bar bracket mounting bolts.
14. Remove the engine undercover.
15. Remove the torque converter clutch mounting bolts.
   a. Remove the converter hole plug.
   b. Turn the crankshaft to gain access to each bolt.
   c. Hold the crankshaft pulley nut with a wrench and remove the bolts.
16. Remove the front exhaust pipe assembly.
   a. Loosen the clamp bolt and disconnect the clamp from the No. 1 support bracket.
   b. Remove the No. 1 support bracket.
17. Disconnect the wiring and remove the starter.
18. Place a jack under the transmission and remove the crossmember.
19. Lower the rear end of the transmission.
20. Separate the wiring harness from the transmission and the transfer case.
21. Remove the oil cooler pipe mounting bolts from the torque converter clutch housing and disconnect the two oil cooler pipes from the elbows.
22. Remove the ten bolts and remove the transmission.
23. Remove the transfer case from the transmission.

To install:

24. Install the transfer case to the transmission. Install the transmission and tighten the bolts to 53 ft. lbs. (72 Nm).
25. Install the remaining components in the reverse of the removal procedure, making sure to note the following tightening specifications.
   - Crossmember bolts: 45 ft. lbs. (61 Nm)
   - Crossmember nuts: 54 ft. lbs. (74 Nm)
   - Starter bolt: 29 ft. lbs. (39 Nm)
   - No. 1 support bracket bolts: 29 ft. lbs. (39 Nm)
   - No. 1 support bracket clamp bolt: 14 ft. lbs. (19 Nm)
   - Front exhaust pipe bolts: 29 ft. lbs. (39 Nm)
   - Torque converter clutch mounting bolts: 40 ft. lbs. (55 Nm)

➡First install the gray colored bolt, then the five other bolts.

   - Engine undercover bolts: 21 ft. lbs. (28 Nm)
   - Stabilizer bar bracket mounting bolts: 13 ft. lbs. (18 Nm)
   - Shift lever bolts: 13 ft. lbs. (18 Nm)
26. Lower the vehicle and fill the transfer case and transmission with the proper fluid.
27. Connect the throttle cable.
28. Tighten the fan shroud of the cooling fan.
29. Install the battery tray and the battery. Connect the battery cables.
30. Test drive the vehicle and check the shifting operation.

1998–00 MODELS

1. Disconnect the negative cable first, then the positive cable. Remove the battery.
2. Remove the air cleaner assembly, drive belt, fan assembly, shroud and reservoir.
3. Remove the upper mounting bolt on the oil dipstick tube.
4. Remove the knob, console panel and the boot from the transfer case shift lever.
5. Raise and safely support the vehicle.
6. Remove the engine undercovers.
7. Disconnect the front exhaust pipes from the manifolds.
8. Place a drain pan under the rear of the transmission. Matchmark, then remove the front and rear driveshafts.
9. Remove the oil dipstick tube.
10. Disconnect the shift linkage from the transmission and transfer case.
11. Detach the following connectors:
   - No. 1 and No. 2 vehicle speed sensors
   - O/D direct clutch speed sensor
   - Solenoid
   - ATF temperature sensor
   - P/N position switch
   - Center differential lock indicator switch
   - Motor actuator
   - L4 position switch
   - Neutral position switch
12. Remove the inspection cover, then remove the six bolts attaching the torque converter to the flexplate.
13. Disconnect the fluid cooler lines from the transmission.
14. Support the transmission assembly with a jack, then remove the crossmember. Be sure to place a block of wood between the jack and transmission.

⁂ CAUTION

The torque converter will fall out of the transmission if the transmission is tilted forward.

15. Carefully lower the transmission to gain access to the mounting bolts. Remove the mounting bolts and slowly lower the transmission from the vehicle.

To install:

16. If removed, install the torque converter into the transmission. Slowly rotate the converter while gently pushing it towards the transmission until it is fully seated. When the torque converter is fully seated, the distance from the mounting surface of the transmission to the mounting boss for the flexplate mounting bolts should be 0.673 inch (17.1mm) or more.
17. Raise and position the transmission assembly on the rear of the engine. Install the mounting bolts and tighten them to 53 ft. lbs. (72 Nm).
18. Install the crossmember. Tighten the bolts to 37 ft. lbs. (50 Nm). Tighten the nuts to 54 ft. lbs. (74 Nm).
19. Connect the fluid cooler lines to the transmission, tighten the union nuts to 24 ft. lbs. (32 Nm).
20. Install the six torque converter-to-flexplate bolts. Install the green bolt first, then the remaining bolts. Turn the crankshaft pulley bolt to gain access to the bolt holes. Tighten the bolts to 35 ft. lbs. (48 Nm).
21. Install the remaining components in the reverse of the removal procedure.
22. Refill the transmission with the correct amount of fluid. First check the level, then add fluid as needed. Be sure not to overfill the transmission.
23. Check for leaks and road test the vehicle.

TRANSFER CASE

Applications

Toyota Pick-Ups, 4Runners, T100's and Tacomas use either the RF1A or VF1A transfer case. The RF1A uses a countergear reduction scheme. The VF1A transfer case is a planetary gear reduction unit. It is found in the T100, Pick-Up, and 4Runner.

The Tundra uses the VF2A or VF2BM transfer case.

The Land Cruiser employs the HF2A or HF2AV transfer case, used with the A440F and A343F transmissions for full time 4WD application.

Transfer Case

REMOVAL & INSTALLATION

Tacoma and 4Runner

➧ See Figure 41

1. Disconnect the negative battery cable.
2. Raise and safely support the vehicle.
3. Drain the transmission and the transfer case.
4. Remove the transfer case with the transmission.
5. If equipped with an automatic transmission, disconnect the breather hose from the transfer upper cover and the transmission control retainer.
6. Remove the rear engine mounting.
7. Remove the dynamic damper.
8. Remove the driveshaft upper dust cover and the transfer from the transmissions follows:
   a. Remove the dust cover bolt from the bracket.
   b. Remove the transfer adapter rear mounting bolts.
   c. Pull the transfer straight up and remove it from the transmission. Be careful not to damage the adapter rear oil seal with the transfer input gear spline.

To install:

9. Install the transfer and the driveshaft upper dust cover to the transmission with a new gasket as follows:
   a. Shift the 2 shift fork shafts to the high 4 position.
   b. Apply MP grease to the adapter oil seal.
   c. Place a new gasket to the transfer adapter.
   d. Install the transfer to the transmission. Take care not to damage the oil seal by the input gear spline.
   e. Install the transfer adapter rear mounting bolts and tighten the bolts to 27 ft. lbs. (37 Nm).
   f. Install the dust cover bolt to the bracket. Tighten the bolt to 17 ft. lbs. (23 Nm).
10. Install the engine rear mounting and tighten the bolts to 19 ft. lbs. (25 Nm).
11. Install the dynamic damper and tighten the bolts to 27 ft. lbs. (37 Nm).
12. If equipped with an automatic transmission, install the breather hose.
13. Install the transfer case with the transmission to the engine.
14. Fill the transmission and the transfer case with oil.
15. Test drive the vehicle and check the abnormal noise and smooth operation.
16. Recheck the fluid levels.

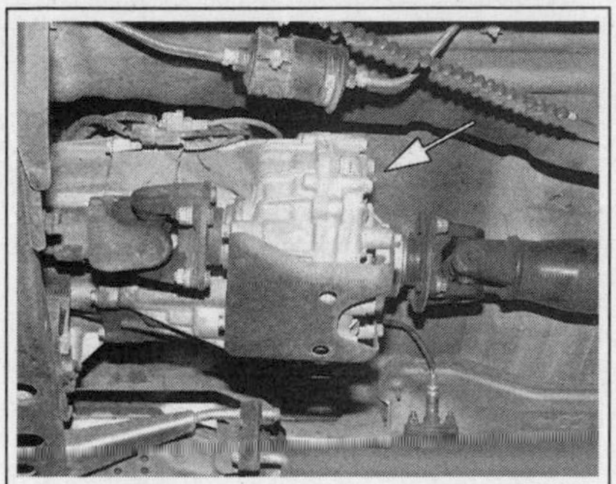

93167p08

Fig. 41 The transfer case is mounted on the end of the transmission—Tacoma shown, other models similar

T100

1. If the vehicle is equipped with a manual transmission remove the following:
   - 4 screws and front console box.
   - Remove the 4 screws and shift lever boot retainer.
   - Using snapring pliers, remove the snapring and pull out the shift lever.

➡You may need to shift the transfer shift lever to the "H4" position.

2. If the vehicle is equipped with a automatic transmission remove the transfer shift lever by;
   - Remove the 4 screws and the boot.
   - Using pliers, remove the snapring and pull out the shift lever from the transfer case.

➡You may need to shift the transfer shift lever to the "H4" position.

3. Disconnect the breather hose from transfer upper cover and also from the transmission control retainer.
4. Raise the vehicle.
5. Drain the transfer case oil.
6. Disconnect and remove the front and rear propeller shafts.
7. Remove the damper by removing the 2 bolts.
8. Support the rear side of the transmission.
9. Remove the 3 bolts and transfer undercover.
10. Unscrew the 2 bolts and then remove the dynamic damper.
11. Remove the 4 set bolts of the engine rear mounting.
12. Unscrew the 8 bolts and remove the crossmember.
13. Remove the 4 bolts and rear engine mounting from the transmission.
14. Disconnect vehicle speed sensor and transfer case indicator switch connectors.
15. Remove the 9 bolts of the transfer adapter mounting.
16. To remove the transfer case, pull it out, then down and toward the rear.

➡Be careful not to damage the adapter rear oil seal with the transfer input gear spline.

To install:

➡Upon installation, be careful not to damage the adapter rear oil seal with the transfer input gear spline.

17. To install the transfer case, push it in, then up and toward the front.
18. Install the 9 bolts of the transfer case adapter mounting. Torque them to 27 ft. lbs. (37 Nm).
19. Install the 4 bolts and rear engine mounting from the transmission. Torque them to 46 ft. lbs. (63 Nm).
20. Attach the 8 bolts and then install the crossmember. Torque the bolts to 70 ft. lbs. (95 Nm).
21. Install the 4 set bolts of the engine rear mounting. Torque the fasteners to 13 ft. lbs. (18 Nm).
22. Attach the 2 bolts and then attach the dynamic damper. Torque the bolts to 44 ft. lbs. (61 Nm).
23. Install the 3 bolts and transfer undercover. Torque the bolts to 13ft.lb (18 Nm).
24. Attach the damper by installing the 2 bolts. Torque to 27 ft. lbs. (37 Nm).
25. Install the front and rear propeller shafts.
26. Fill the transfer case with oil having a grade of API GL-4 or GL-5, and a viscosity of SAE 75W-90. The capacity is approximately 1.2 qts. (1.1) liters.
27. Lower the vehicle.
28. The remainder of the installation process is the reverse of removal.

Tundra

VF2A TRANSFER CASE

This transfer case is used with the 3.4L engine.

1. Drain the transfer case oil.
2. Shift the transfer shift lever into the **H4** position.
3. Remove or disconnect the following:
   - Transfer case shift lever knob
   - 4 screws, transfer case shift lever boot retainer and the shift lever boot
   - Snapring from the transfer case shift lever and the lever
   - Breather hose from the transfer case
   - Front and rear driveshafts
   - Dynamic damper from the transfer case
   - Crossmember from the rear of the transmission
   - 4 bolts and the engine rear mount from the transfer case adapter
   - Vehicle Speed Sensor (VSS) connector
   - Transfer Detection Switch (TDS) connector
4. Support the transfer case
5. Remove the 8 transfer case-to-transfer adapter bolts, then remove the transfer case.

To install:

6. Install the transfer case and secure with the transfer case-to-transfer adapter bolts. Torque the 8 bolts to 17 ft. lbs. (24 Nm).
7. Install the remaining components in the reverse order of removal, making sure to note the following tightening specifications:
   - Engine rear mount-to-transfer case adaptor bolts: 48 ft. lbs. (65 Nm)
   - Crossmember-to-transmission nuts/bolts to 53 ft. lbs. (72 Nm)
   - Crossmember-to-chassis bolts: 13 ft. lbs. (18 Nm)

• Dynamic damper-to-transfer case bolts: 28 ft. lbs. (38 Nm)

8. Refill the transfer case to the correct level.
9. Test drive the vehicle.

VF2BM TRANSFER CASE

1. Turn the touch select 4WD selector switch ON.
2. Disconnect the breather hose from the transfer case.
3. Raise the vehicle and drain transfer case oil.
4. Remove left and right front exhaust pipes
5. Detach the front and rear propeller shafts
6. Support the rear side of the transmission with a transmission jack.
7. Remove the 4 bolts, nuts and crossmember.
8. Remove the 4 bolts and engine rear mounting from the transfer adapter.
9. Disconnect vehicle speed sensor, transfer case detection switches and motor actuator connectors.
10. Support the transfer case with another transmission jack.
11. Remove the 8 transfer case mounting bolts.
12. Pull out the transfer from the transfer case adapter down and toward the rear.

To install:

13. Support the transfer case with a transmission jack.
14. Install the transfer case.
15. Install the 8 transfer case mounting bolts.
16. Attach the vehicle speed sensor, transfer case detection switches and motor actuator connectors.
17. Install the 4 bolts and engine rear mounting from the transfer adapter.
18. Install the 4 bolts, nuts and crossmember.
19. Attach the front and rear propeller shafts
20. Install the left and right front exhaust pipes
21. Lower the vehicle and fill the transfer case with oil.
22. Disconnect the breather hose from the transfer case.
23. Turn the touch select 2-4 switch OFF.

Land Cruiser

1. Raise the vehicle.

➡Make sure that the vehicle is securely supported.

2. Remove transfer case protector.
3. Remove the 3 bolts and transfer case protector.
4. Drain transfer case oil.
5. Remove front and rear propeller shafts.
6. Disconnect transfer shift lever rod assembly.
7. Remove the clip, plate washer, wave washer and bushing, and disconnect the transfer shift lever rod assembly.
8. Disconnect ground cable.
9. Remove the bolt and disconnect the ground cable from the transfer case.
10. Support the transmission, as shown.

➡Use a wooden block so as not to damage the transmission oil pan.

11. Remove the 8 bolts, 2 nuts and crossmember.
12. Disconnect breather hose.

➡At the time of installation, assemble the clip to the position shown in the illustration.

13. Disconnect no. 1 vehicle speed sensor, 3 transfer indicator switch and motor actuator connectors
14. Jack up transfer slightly.
15. Using a transmission jack, support the transfer.
16. Disconnect the wire harness from the transfer case.
17. Remove the 6 transfer adapter rear mounting bolts.
18. Pull out the transfer down and toward the rear.

To install:

19. Install transfer case protector.
20. Install the 3 bolts and transfer case protector. Torque the bolts to 21 ft. lbs. (28 Nm).
21. Fill the transfer case with the proper oil.
22. The transfer case oil must meet the following specifications:

• Oil grade: API GL-4 or GL-5
• Viscosity: SAE 75 W-90
• Approximate capacity: 1.3 liters (1.4 US qts, 1.1 Imp. qts)

23. Install the 3 bolts and transfer case protector. Torque them to 21 ft. lbs. (28 Nm).
24. Pull out the transfer down and toward the rear.
25. Install the 6 transfer adapter rear mounting bolts. Torque them to 51 ft. lbs. (69 Nm).
26. Attach the wire harness to the transfer case.
27. Using a transmission jack, support the transfer case.
28. Use the jack to raise the transfer slightly.
29. Attach the No. 1 vehicle speed sensor, the transfer indicator switch and motor actuator connectors.

➡At the time of installation, assemble the clip to the proper position.

30. Disconnect breather hose.
31. Install the 8 bolts, 2 nuts and crossmember. Torque the bolts to 37 ft. lbs. (50 Nm). Tighten the nut to 54 ft. lbs.(74 Nm).

➡Use a wooden block so as not to damage the transmission oil pan.

32. Support the transmission, as shown.
33. Install the bolt and disconnect the ground cable from the transfer case.
34. Disconnect ground cable.
35. Install the clip, plate washer, wave washer and bushing, and disconnect the transfer shift lever rod assembly.
36. Disconnect transfer shift lever rod assembly.
37. Install front and rear propeller shafts.

DRIVELINE

Front Driveshaft and Universal Joints

REMOVAL & INSTALLATION

➧ See Figures 42 thru 51

1. Jack up the front of the vehicle and support with jackstands.
2. Place matchmarks on the flanges. Remove the nuts and bolts.
3. Remove the front driveshaft dust cover. Some types are equipped with 2 bolts, while others use 4.
4. Remove the driveshaft dust cover subassembly. The three bolts are two different sizes.

➡The driveshaft dust cover is located around the outer portion of the U-joint. On some models you may have an upper and lower cover.

5. Suspend the front side of the driveshaft.
6. Place matchmarks on the flanges. Remove the nuts and bolts.
7. Remove the front driveshaft.

To install:

8. Align the matchmarks on the rear flanges, then connect the flanges with the nuts and/or bolts. Tighten to 54 ft. lbs. (74 Nm).

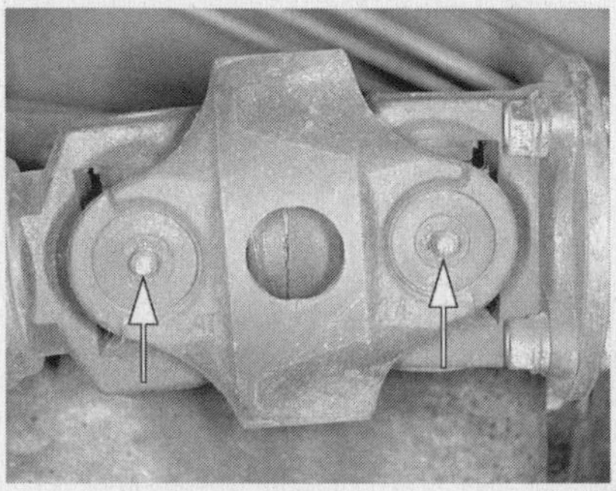

93167p05

Fig. 42 Many universal joints have grease fittings to extend their service life through better lubrication

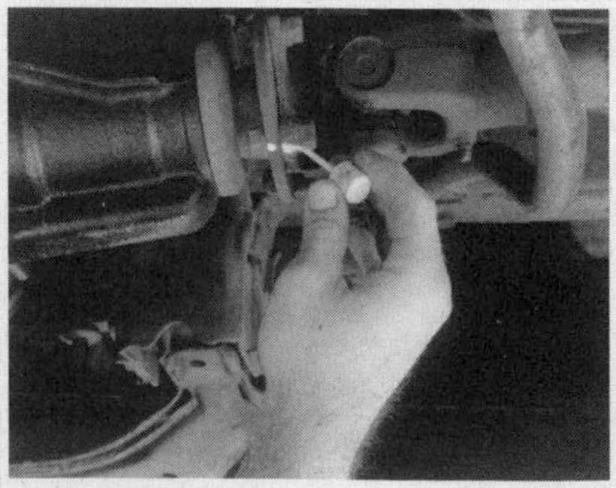

86827p10

Fig. 43 ALWAYS matchmark with paint prior to separating the driveshaft from the vehicle

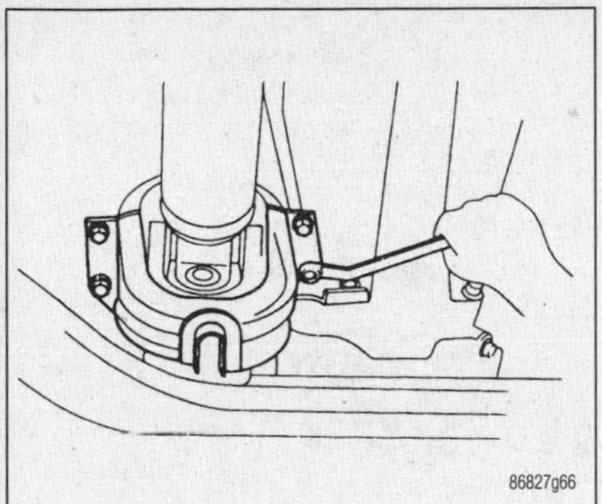

Fig. 44 Remove the front dust cover retaining bolts

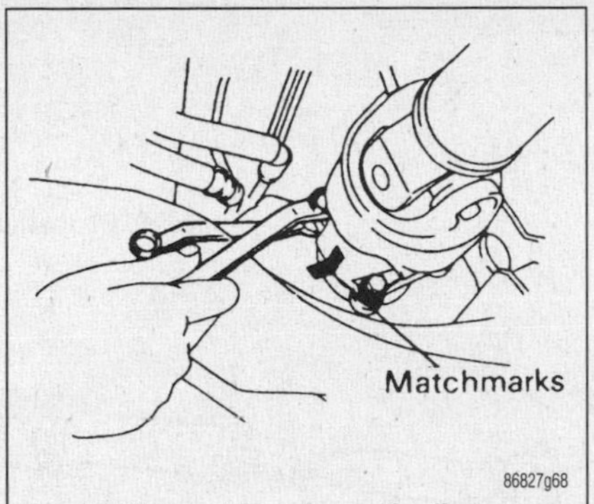

Fig. 45 The matchmarks on the flanges are helpful in installation for lining things up correctly

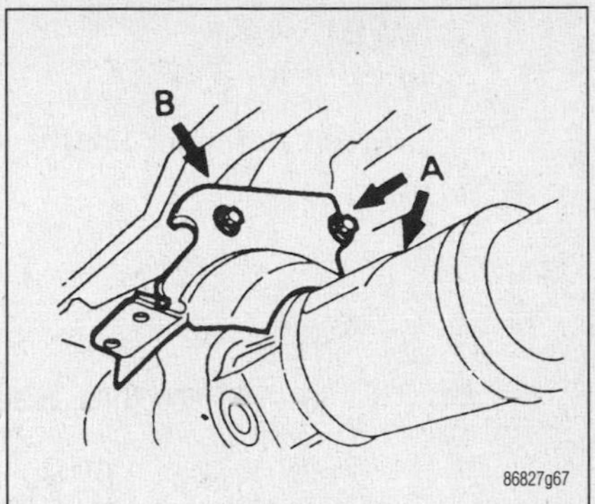

Fig. 46 Tighten bolt A to 27 ft. lbs. (36 Nm) and B to 17 ft. lbs. (23 Nm)

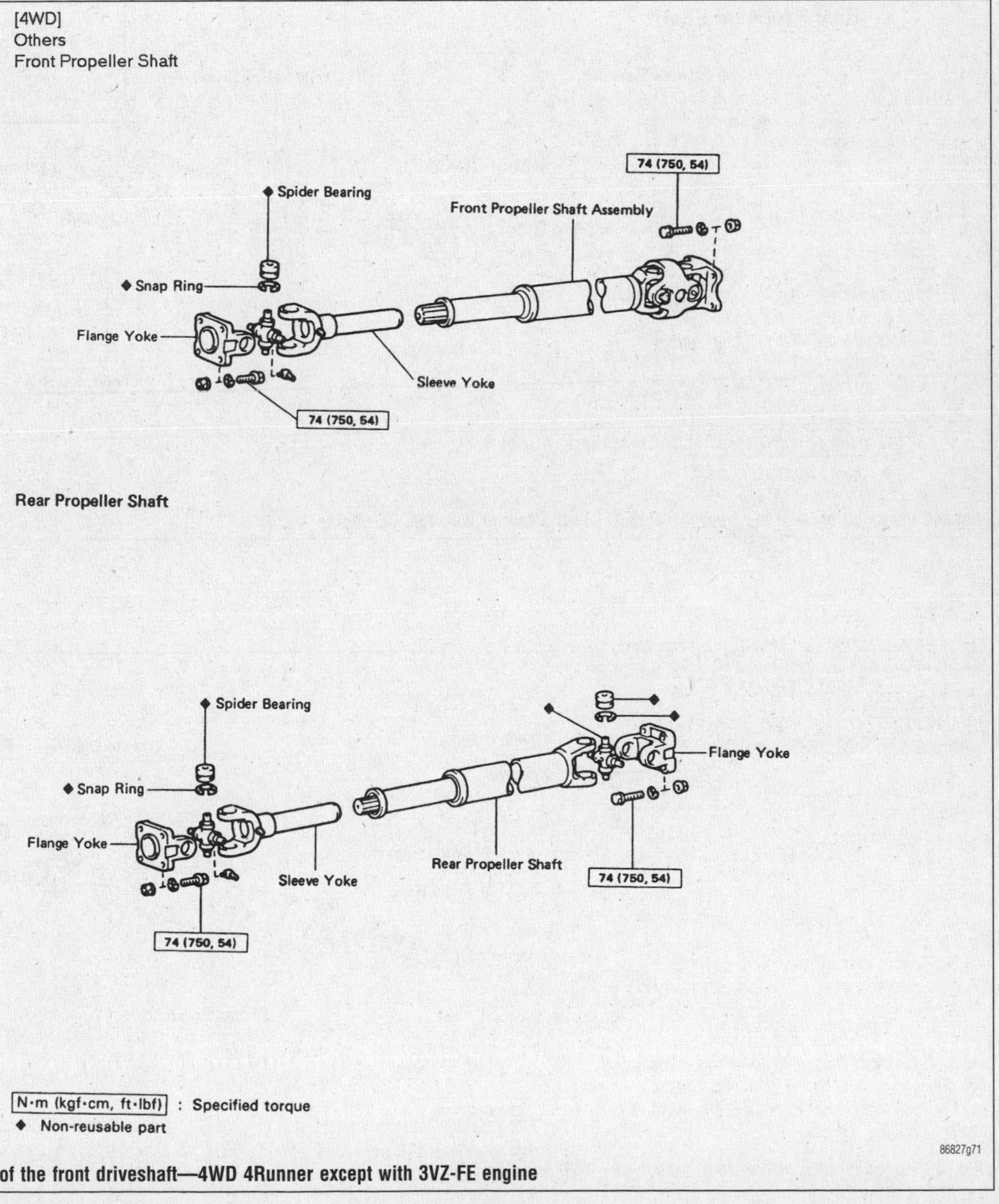

Fig. 47 Exploded view of the front driveshaft—4WD 4Runner except with 3VZ-FE engine

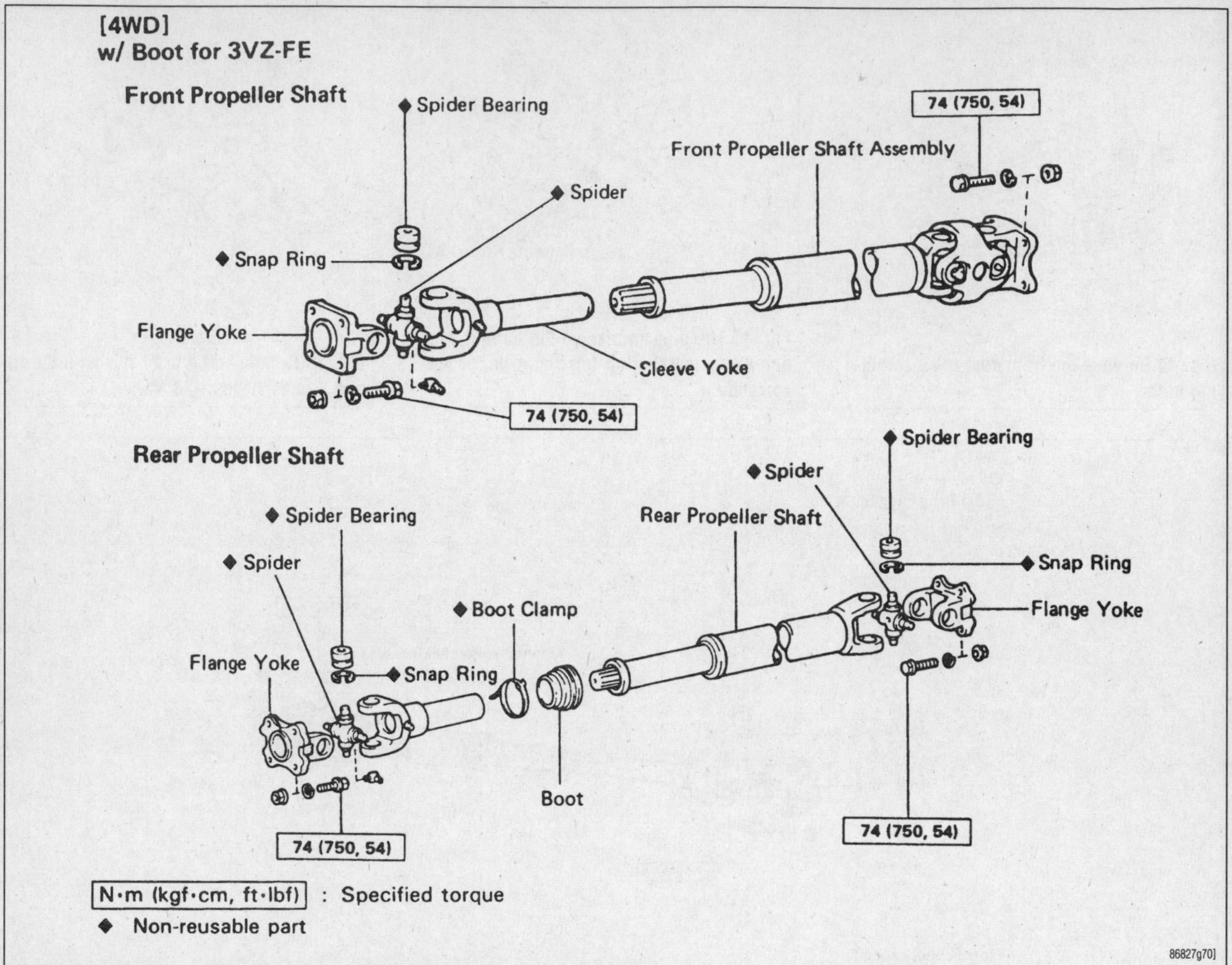

Fig. 48 Exploded view of the front driveshaft—4WD 4Runner with 3VZ-FE engine

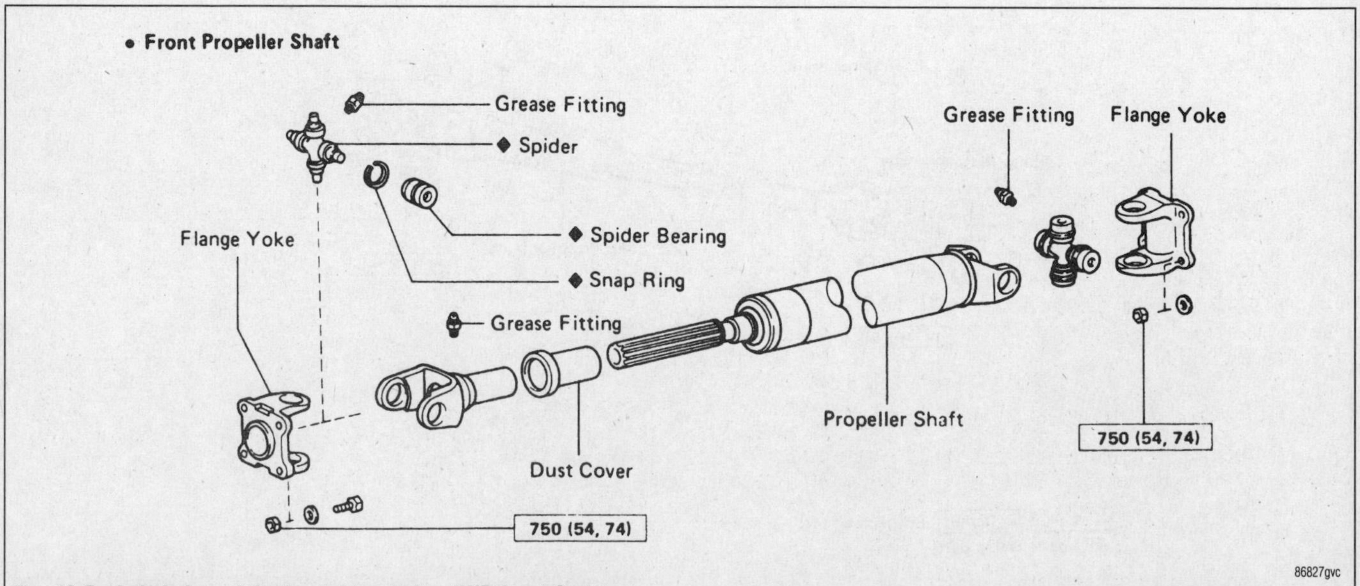

Fig. 49 Exploded view of the front driveshaft—4WD Land Cruiser

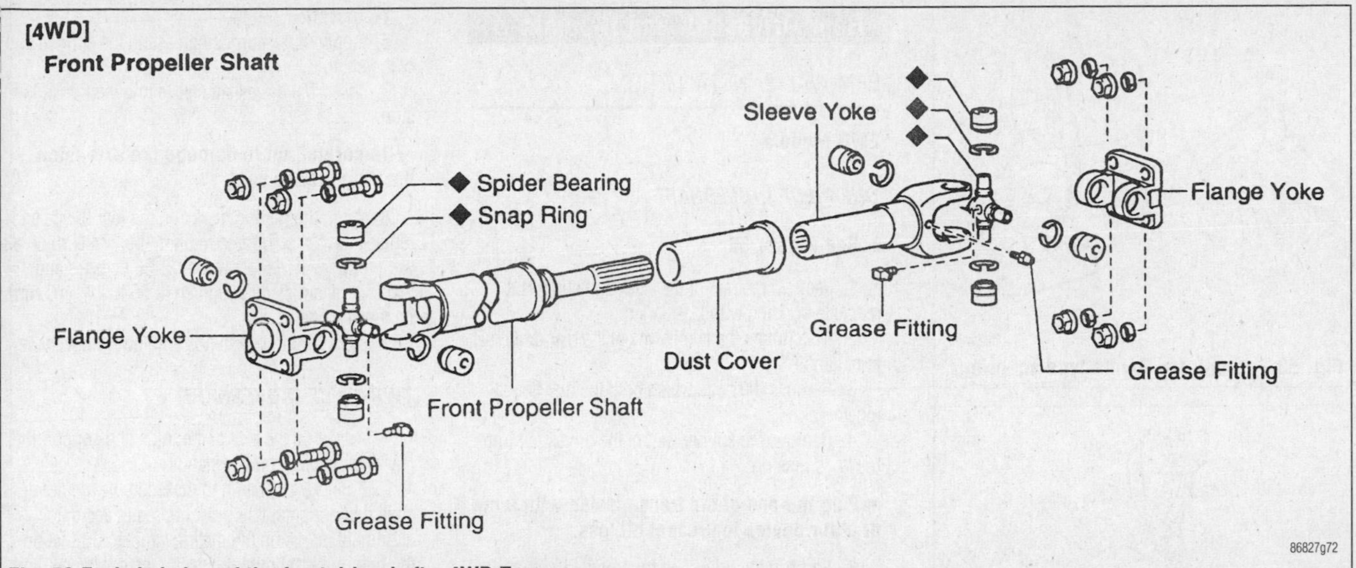

Fig. 50 Exploded view of the front driveshaft—4WD Tacoma

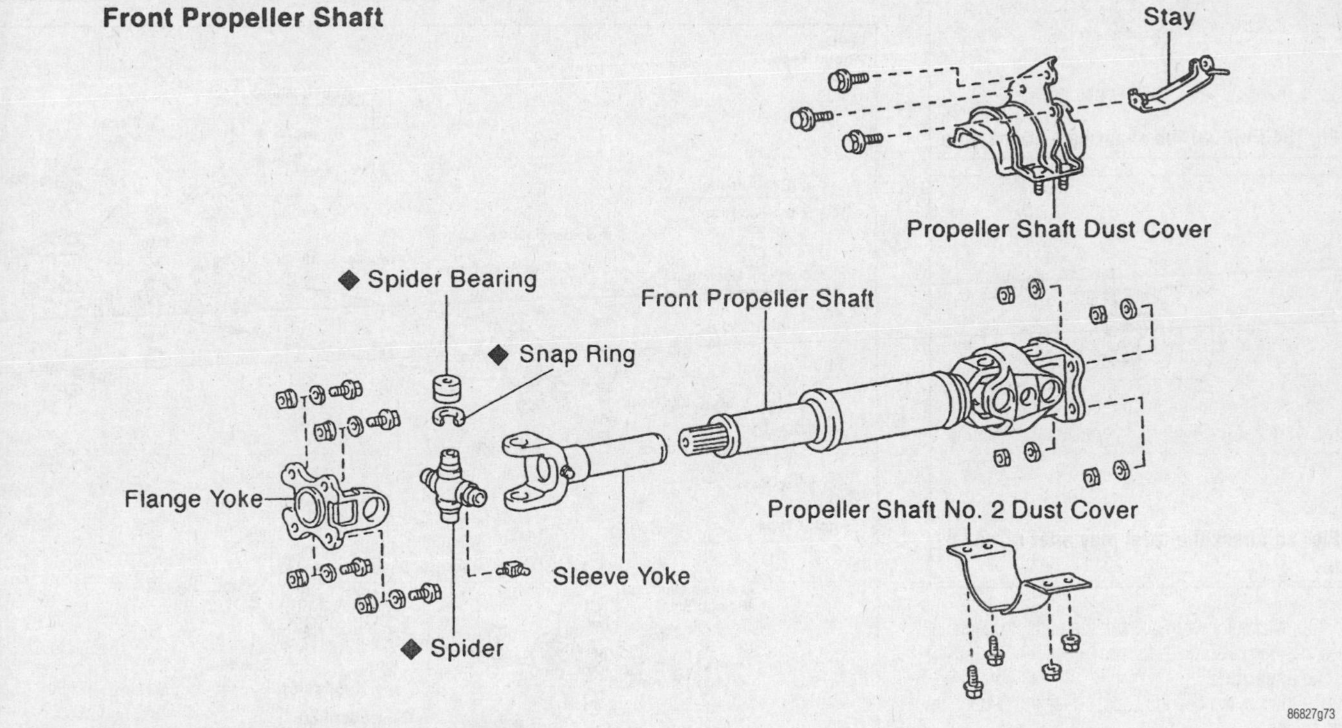

Fig. 51 Exploded view of the front driveshaft—4WD T100

9. Install the front driveshaft dust cover sub-assembly. Tighten bolts A to 27 ft. lbs. (36 Nm) and B to 17 ft. lbs. (23 Nm).

10. Align the matchmarks on the front flanges, then connect the flanges with the bolts and nuts. Tighten to 54 ft. lbs. (74 Nm).

11. Install the front driveshaft dust cover. Tighten the bolts to 13 ft. lbs. (17 Nm) and the nuts to 10 ft. lbs. (13 Nm).

12. Attach the rear driveshaft flange to the companion flange on the transfer case. Align the matchmarks on the flanges, then connect the flanges with the bolts and nuts. Tighten to 54–56 ft. lbs. (74–76 Nm).

13. Lower the vehicle and road test it.

U-JOINT REPLACEMENT

➧ **See Figures 52, 53, 54, and 55**

1. Raise and support the vehicle.
2. Remove the driveshaft.
3. Matchmark the yoke and the driveshaft.
4. Remove the snaprings from the bearings. There are two types of snaprings; Toyota and Dana.
5. Position the yoke on vise jaws. Using a bearing remover and a hammer, gently tap the remover until the bearing is driven out of the yoke about 1 in. (25mm).
6. Place the tool in the vise and drive the yoke away from the tool until the bearing is removed.
7. Repeat Steps 4 and 5 for the other bearings.

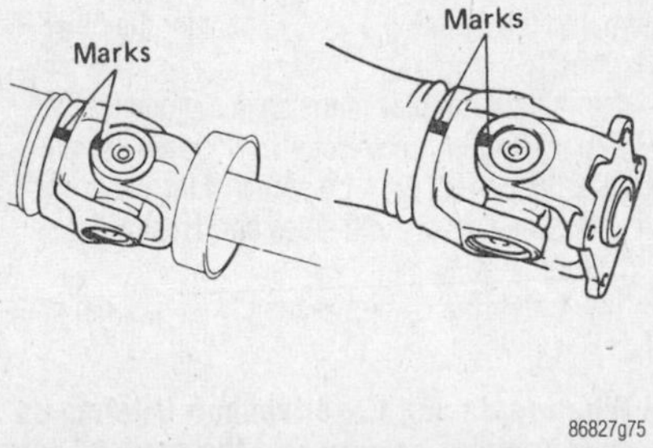

Fig. 52 Always place matchmarks on the spider and yoke

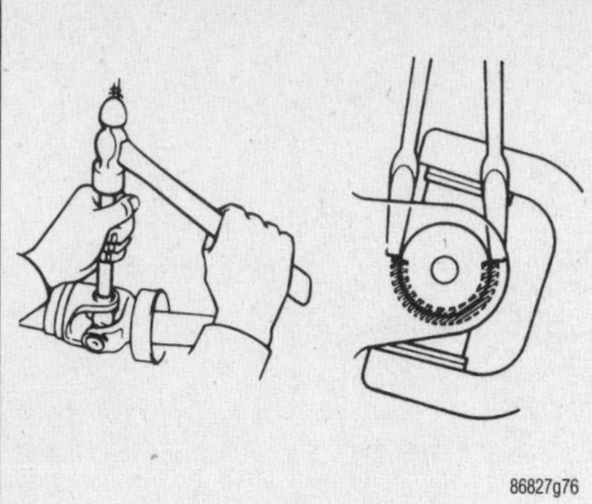

Fig. 53 Tap out the Toyota type snaprings

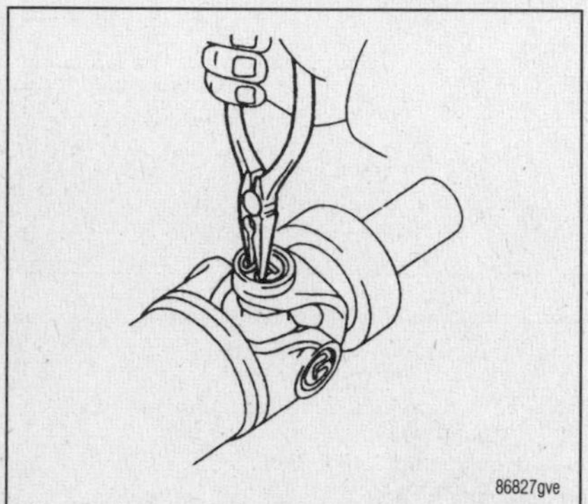

Fig. 54 Pull out the snaprings—Dana type

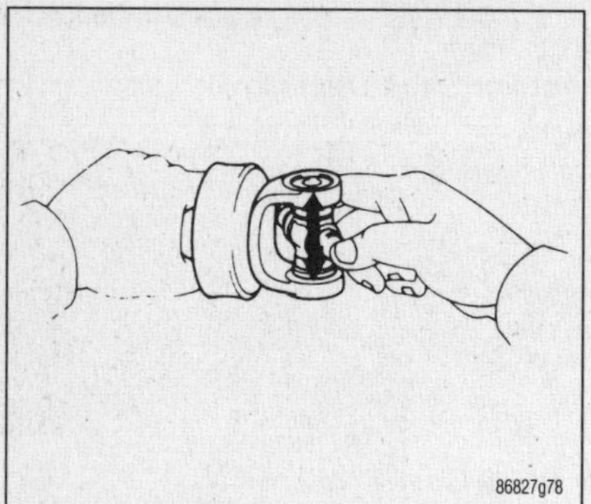

Fig. 55 Check the axial play after reassembly

8. Check for worn or damaged parts. Inspect the bearing journal surfaces for wear.

To assemble:

9. Install the bearing cups, seals, and O-rings in the spider.
10. Apply multi-purpose grease to a new spider and bearings. Be careful not to apply too much grease.
11. Position the spider into the yoke.
12. Start the bearings in the yoke, then press them into place, using a vise. Repeat for the other bearings.
13. If the axial play of the spider is greater than 0.0020 in. (0.05mm), select snaprings which will provide the correct play. Be sure that the snaprings are the same size on both sides or driveshaft noise and vibration will result.
14. Check the U-joint assembly for smooth operation.

➡When replacing the driveshaft U-joints on a 4WD vehicle, be sure that the grease fitting is accessible after the joint is assembled.

Rear Driveshaft and U-Joints

REMOVAL & INSTALLATION

2WD Models

ONE-PIECE DRIVESHAFT

➧ See Figure 56

1. Jack up the rear of the truck and support the rear axle housing with jackstands.
2. Matchmark the two halves of the rear universal joint flange.
3. Remove the bolts which hold the rear flange together.
4. Remove the splined end of the driveshaft from the transmission.

➡Plug the end of the transmission with a rag or other device to prevent oil loss.

5. Remove the driveshaft from under the truck.

To install:

6. Apply multi-purpose grease to the splined end of the shaft.
7. Insert the driveshaft sleeve into the transmission.

➡Be careful not to damage the extension housing grease seal.

8. Align the mating marks on the rear flange and replace the bolts. Tighten to 54 ft. lbs. (74 Nm) on all vehicles except models with 3VZ-FE engines and manual transmissions. Tighten to 56 ft. lbs. (76 Nm) on these models.
9. Remove the jackstands and lower the vehicle.

TWO-PIECE DRIVESHAFT

1. Jack up the rear of the truck and support the rear axle housing on jackstands.
2. Before you begin to disassemble the driveshaft components, you must first paint accurate alignment marks on the mating flanges. Do this on the rear universal joint flange, the center flange, and on the transmission flange.

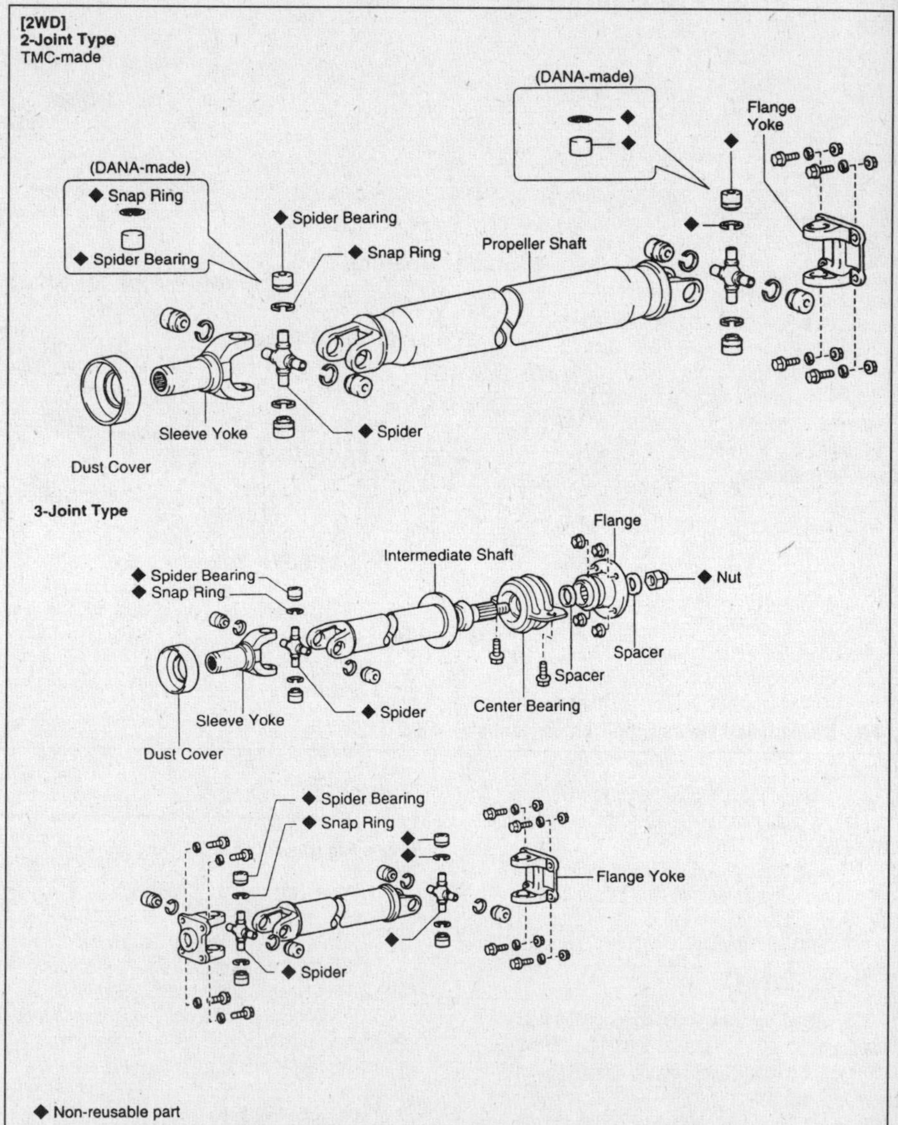

Fig. 56 Exploded view of one and two-piece rear driveshaft—2WD Tacoma shown

3. Remove the bolts attaching the rear universal joint flange to the drive pinion flange.
4. Drop the rear section of the shaft slightly and pull the unit out of the center bearing sleeve yoke.
5. Remove the center bearing support from the crossmember.
6. Separate the transmission output flange and remove the front half of the driveshaft together with the center bearing assembly.

To install:

7. Connect the output flange of the transmission to the flange on the front half of the shaft.
8. Install the center bearing support to the crossmember, but do not fully tighten the bolts.
9. Install the rear section of the shaft making sure that all mating marks are aligned.
10. Tighten all flange bolts to 22–36 ft. lbs. (30–49 Nm).

4WD Models

EXCEPT LAND CRUISER

See Figures 57 thru 62

1. Raise and support the vehicle with jackstands.
2. Matchmark all driveshaft flanges BEFORE removing any bolts.
3. Disconnect the driveshaft flange at the companion flange on the differential.
4. Remove the center bearing from the frame crossmember.
5. Disconnect the front flange at the companion flange on the rear of the transfer case and remove the driveshaft.
6. Separate the front portion of the shaft at the intermediate shaft flange.
7. Disconnect the rear of the driveshaft at the center bearing flange.
8. Using a hammer and chisel, loosen the staked portion of the center bearing nut, then remove the nut. Matchmark the flange to the intermediate shaft, then pull the bearing off the shaft.

To install:

9. If equipped, install the center bearing on the intermediate shaft. Tighten the nut to 134 ft. lbs. (181 Nm), then loosen the nut, and retighten again to 51 ft. lbs. (69 Nm). Stake the nut.
10. Connect the front portion of the driveshaft to the intermediate shaft and the rear portion to the center flange. Make sure the marks all line up, then tighten the bolts to 54 ft. lbs. (74 Nm).
11. Connect the rear flange to the differential flange and tighten the bolts to 54 ft. lbs. (74 Nm).
12. Connect the front flange to the transfer case flange and tighten the bolts to 54 ft. lbs. (74 Nm).
13. Mount the center bearing on the crossmember and tighten the mounting bolts to 27 ft. lbs. (36 Nm).
14. Lower the vehicle and road test.

LAND CRUISER

See Figure 63

1. Raise the vehicle and support it with jackstands.
2. Matchmark all driveshaft flanges BEFORE removing the bolts.
3. Unfasten the bolts which secure the universal joint flange to the differential pinion flange.

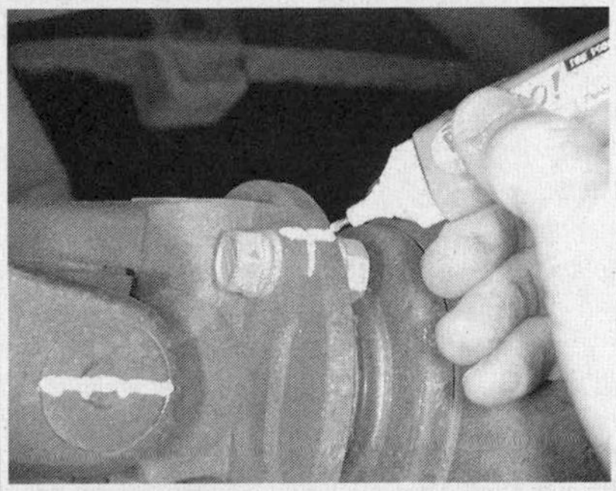
93167p15
Fig. 57 Matchmark the driveshaft to the flange

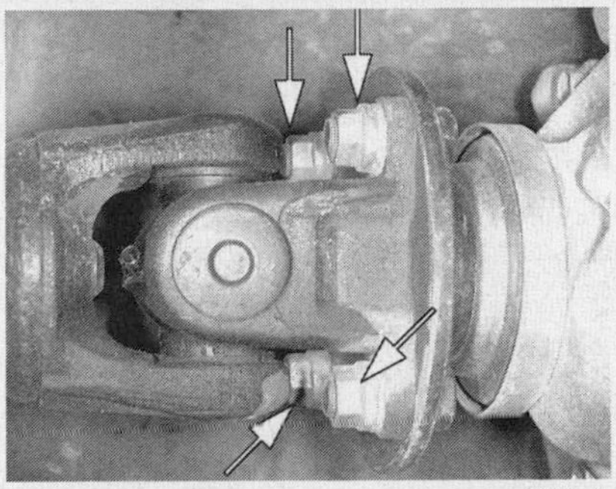
93167p03
Fig. 58 Typically four bolts hold the driveshaft to the flange

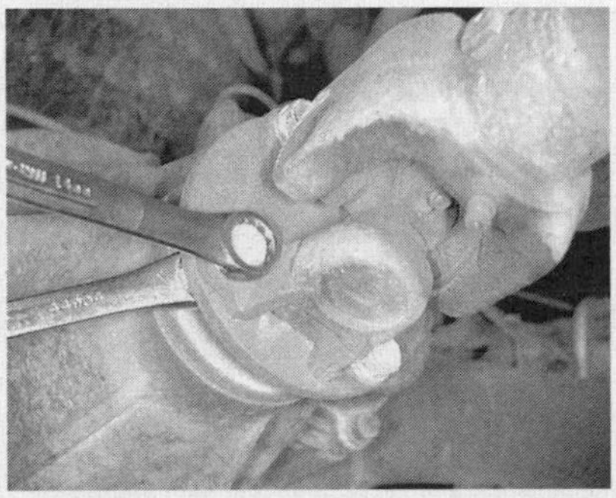
93167p07
Fig. 59 Use a closed end wrench to remove the bolts from the driveshaft

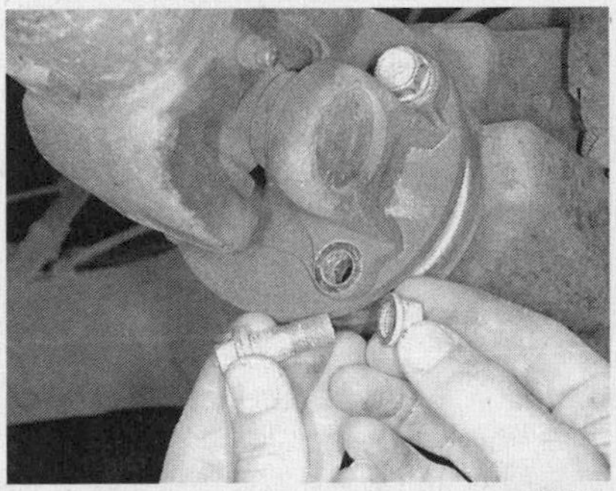
93167p18
Fig. 60 View of a driveshaft-to-flange nut and bolt

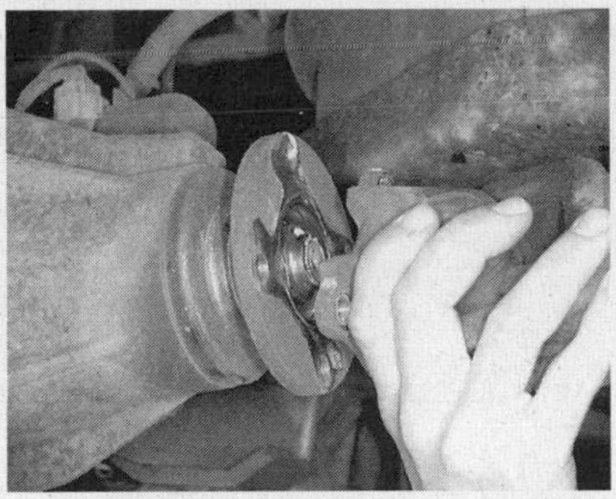
93167p19
Fig. 61 Once all of the bolts have been removed, pull the driveshaft away from the flange on the differential

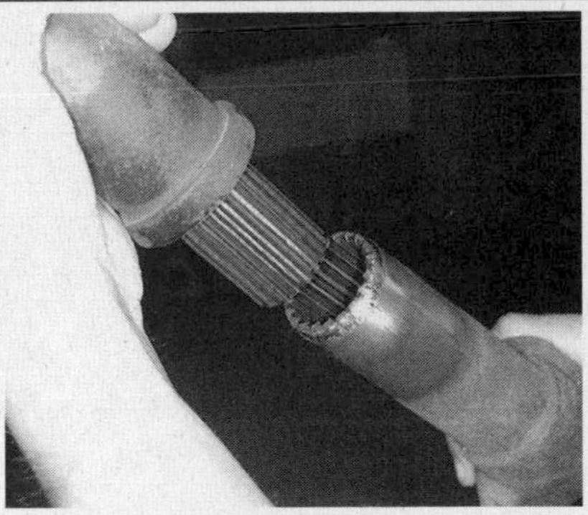
93167p20
Fig. 62 Slide the driveshaft off the end of the transmission output shaft

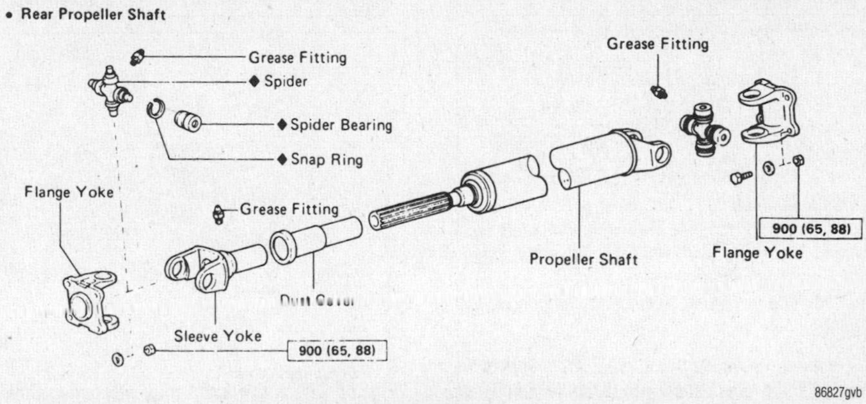

86827gvb
Fig. 63 Exploded view of rear driveshaft—Land Cruiser

4. Matchmark all of the flanges for the joint-to-transfer case flange bolts.
5. Withdraw the driveshaft from beneath the vehicle.

To install:

➡Lubricate the U-joints and sliding joints with multi-purpose grease before installation.

6. Position the driveshaft so that all marks line up, then tighten the flange bolts to 65 ft. lbs. (88 Nm).
7. Lower the vehicle and road test it.

U-JOINT REPLACEMENT

➧ See Figures 64, 65, 66, 67, and 68

1. Raise and support the vehicle.
2. Remove the driveshaft.
3. Matchmark the yoke and the driveshaft.
4. Remove the snaprings from the bearings. There are two types of snaprings: Toyota and Dana.
5. Position the yoke on vise jaws. Using a bearing remover and a hammer, gently tap the remover until the bearing is driven out of the yoke about 1 in. (25mm).
6. Place the tool in the vise and drive the yoke away from the tool until the bearing is removed.
7. Repeat Steps 4 and 5 for the other bearings.
8. Check for worn or damaged parts. Inspect the bearing journal surfaces for wear.

To assemble:

9. Install the bearing cups, seals, and O-rings in the spider.
10. Apply multi-purpose grease to a new spider and bearings. Be careful not to apply too much grease.
11. Position the spider into the yoke.
12. Start the bearings in the yoke, then press them into place, using a vise.
13. Repeat Step 5 for the other bearings.
14. If the axle play of the spider is greater than 0.0020 in. (0.05mm), select snaprings which will provide the correct play. Be sure that the snaprings are the same size on both sides or driveshaft noise and vibration will result.
15. Check the U-joint assembly for smooth operation.

Center Bearing

REMOVAL & INSTALLATION

➧ See Figure 69

The center support bearing is a sealed unit which requires no periodic maintenance. The following procedure should be used if it becomes necessary to replace the bearing. Toyota does not supply individual parts for the bearing replacement only the assembly. See your local jobber if necessary.

1. Remove the intermediate driveshaft and the center support bearing assembly.
2. Paint mating marks on the universal joint flange and the intermediate driveshaft.
3. Remove the cotter pin and castle nut from the intermediate driveshaft; the nut will be staked. Remove the universal joint flange from the driveshaft using a press.
4. Remove the center support bearing assembly from the driveshaft.
5. Remove the two bolts from the bearing housing and remove the housing.
6. Remove the dust deflectors from both sides of the bearing cushion. Remove the dust deflectors from either side of the bearing.
7. Remove the snaprings from each side of the bearing. This is easy to do if you have a snapring tool which fits the holes in the ring, and very difficult otherwise. Remove the bearing.

To assemble:

8. Install the new bearing into the cushion and fit a snapring on each side.
9. Apply a coat of multi-purpose grease to the dust deflectors and put them in their respective places on each side of the bearing. The single deflector with a slightly larger diameter goes on the rear of the bearing.
10. Press the dust deflector onto each side of the cushion. The water drain holes in the deflectors should be in the same position on each side of the cushion. The water drain holes should face the bottom of the housing.
11. Press the support bearing assembly firmly onto the intermediate driveshaft, with the seal facing front.
12. Match the mating marks painted earlier, and install the universal joint flange to the driveshaft. Install the center bearing on the intermediate shaft and tighten the nut to 134 ft. lbs. (181 Nm). Loosen the nut and then retighten it to 51 ft. lbs. (69 Nm). Stake the nut.

➡Check to see if the center support bearing assembly will rotate smoothly around the driveshaft.

13. When reinstalling the driveshaft, be certain to match up the marks on both the front transmission flange and the flange on the sleeve yoke of the rear driveshaft.

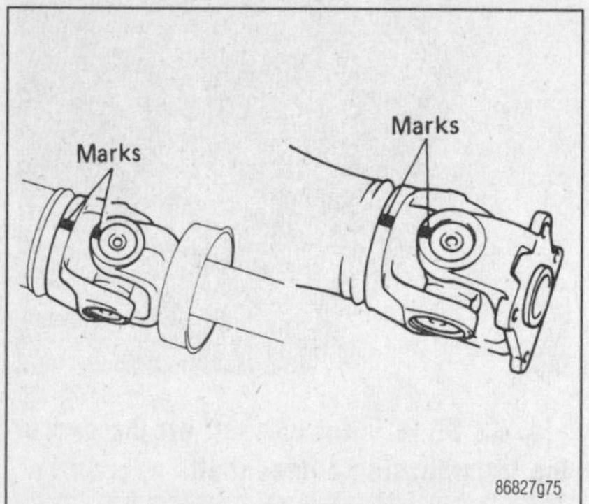

Fig. 64 Always place matchmarks on the spider and yoke

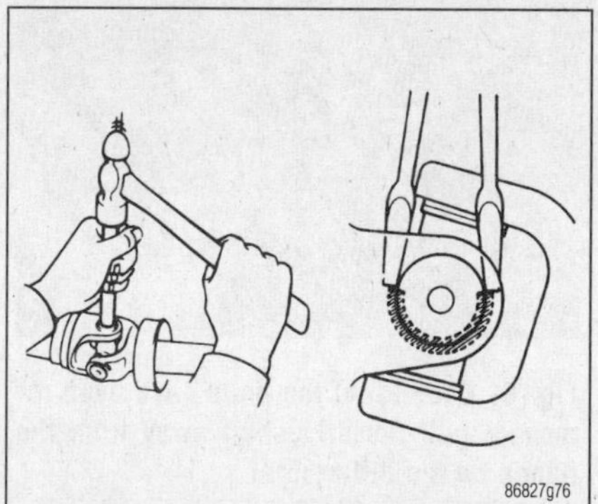

Fig. 65 Tap out the Toyota type snaprings

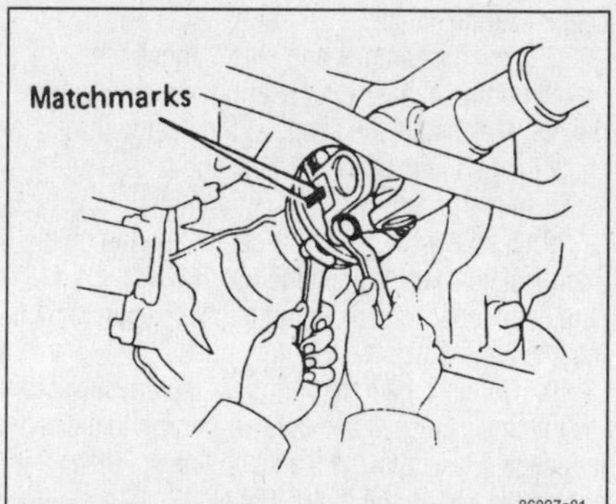

Fig. 66 Place matchmarks on the flanges, then loosen and remove the bolts

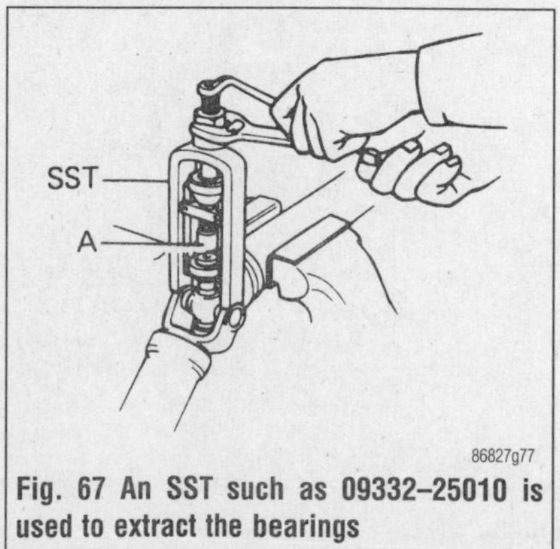

Fig. 67 An SST such as 09332–25010 is used to extract the bearings

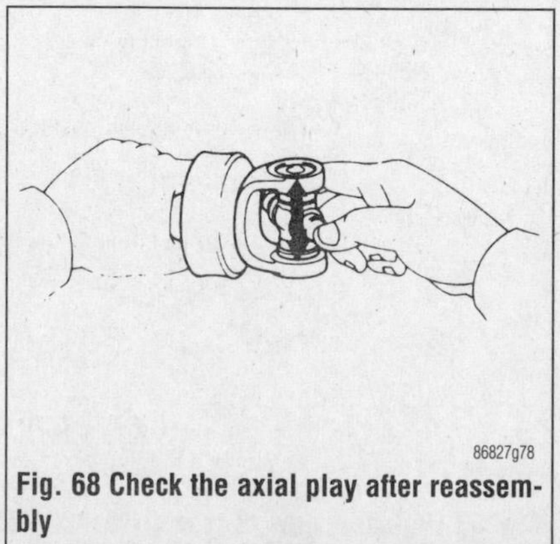

Fig. 68 Check the axial play after reassembly

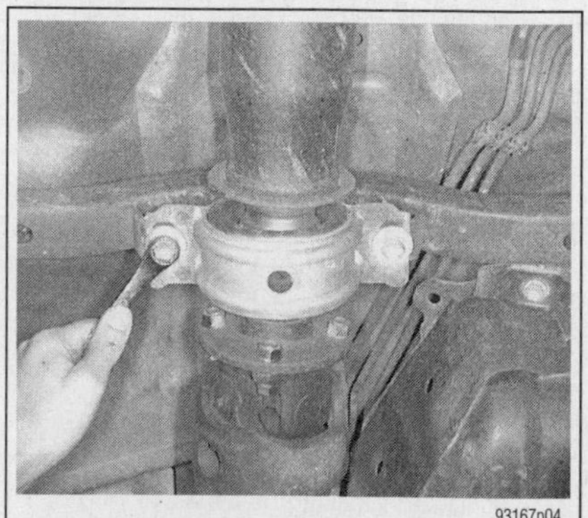

Fig. 69 View of the center bearing

FRONT DRIVE AXLE

Manual Locking Hub

REMOVAL & INSTALLATION

➧ **See Figures 70 thru 80**

1. Remove the hub cover. Set the control handle to free.
2. Remove the cover mounting bolts, then pull off the cover. Remove and discard the gasket.
3. Remove the bolt with washer.
4. Remove the mounting nuts and washers.
5. Using a brass bar and hammer, tap on the bolt ends, then remove the cone washers.
6. Pull off the hub body.
7. Remove and discard the gasket.

To install:

8. Place a new gasket into position on the front axle hub. Install the free wheeling hub body with the cone washers and nuts. Tighten the nuts to 23 ft. lbs. (31 Nm).
9. Install the bolt with washer, tighten to 13 ft. lbs. (18 Nm).
10. Apply multi-purpose grease to the inner hub splines.
11. Set the control handle and clutch to the free position.
12. Place a new gasket into position on the cover.
13. Install the cover to the body with the follower pawl tabs aligned with the non toothed portions of the body.
14. Tighten the cover mounting bolts to 7 ft. lbs. (10 Nm).

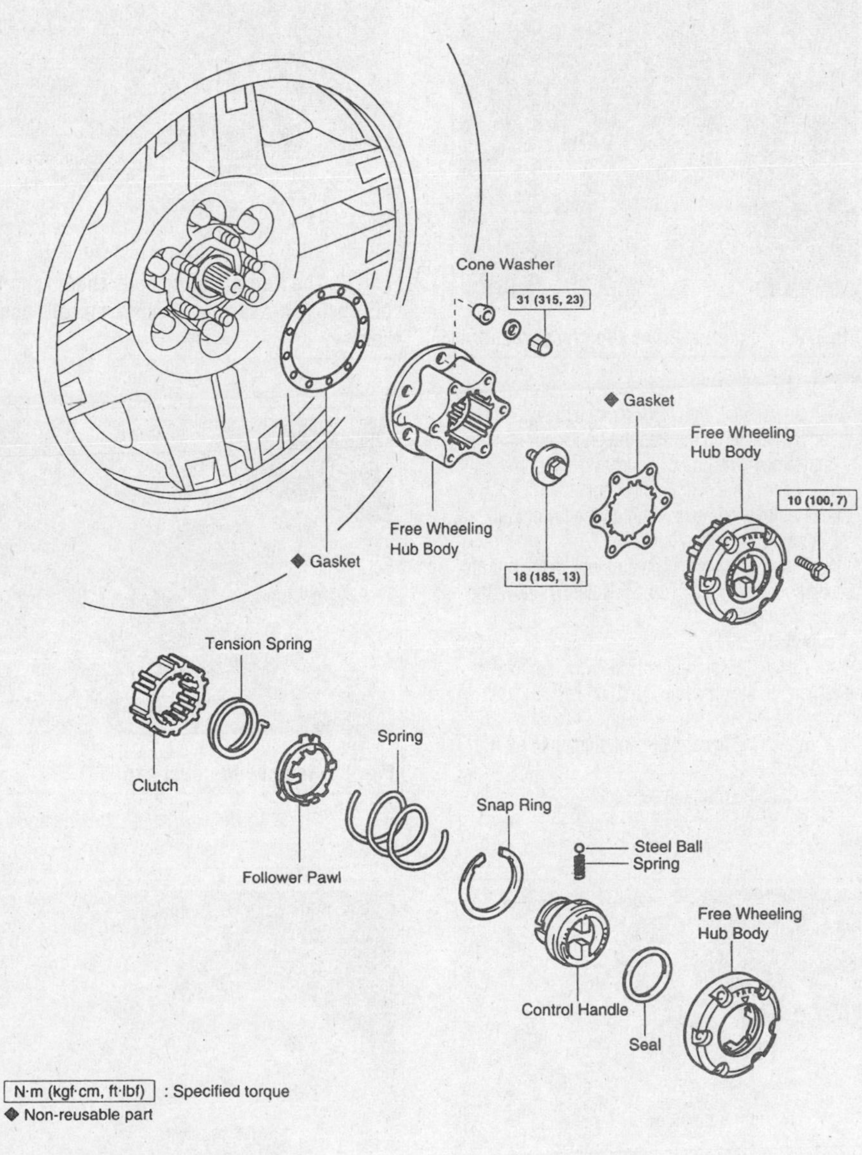

Fig. 70 Exploded view of the free wheeling hub

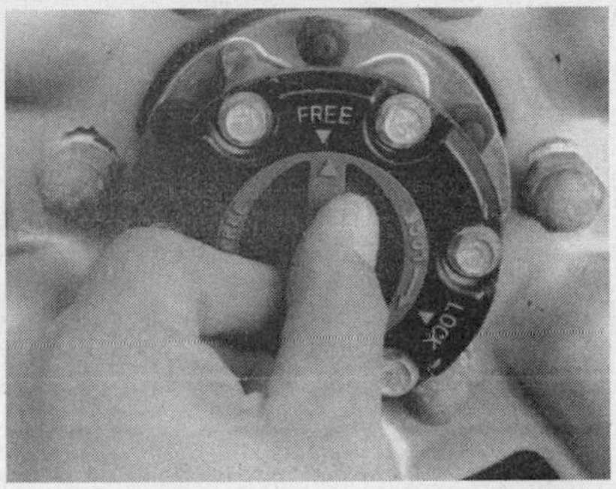

Fig. 71 Turn the handle with your hand to the free position

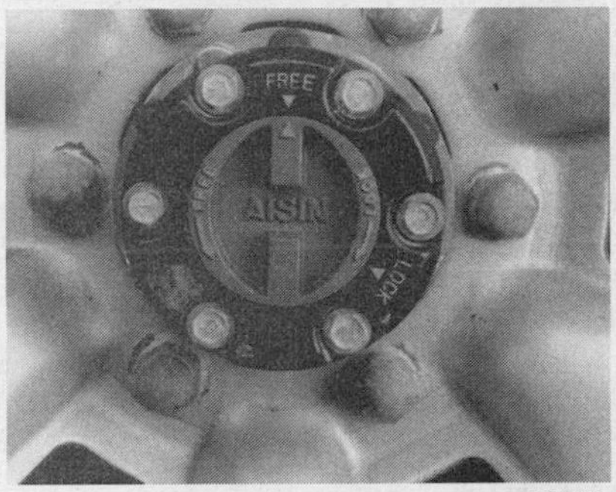

Fig. 72 Note the directions in which you can turn the handle: left—free, right—lock

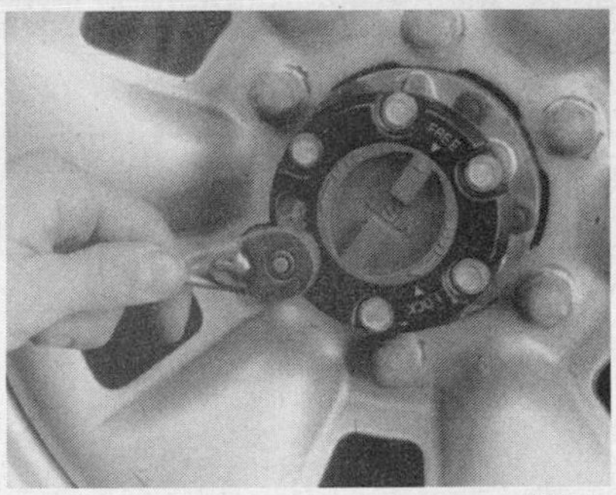

Fig. 73 With the handle in the free position, remove the six hub cover bolts

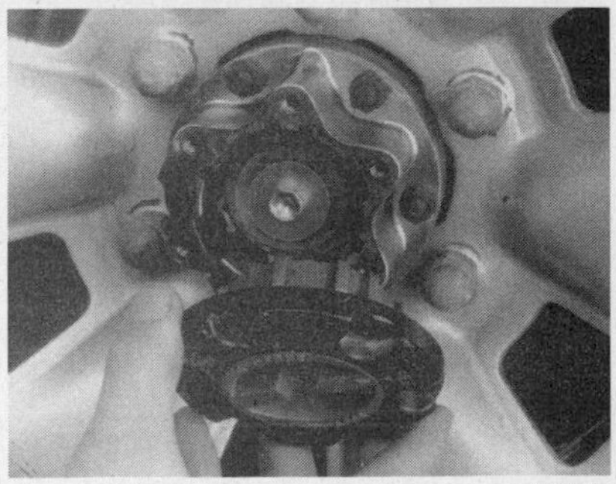

Fig. 74 Pull the cover off

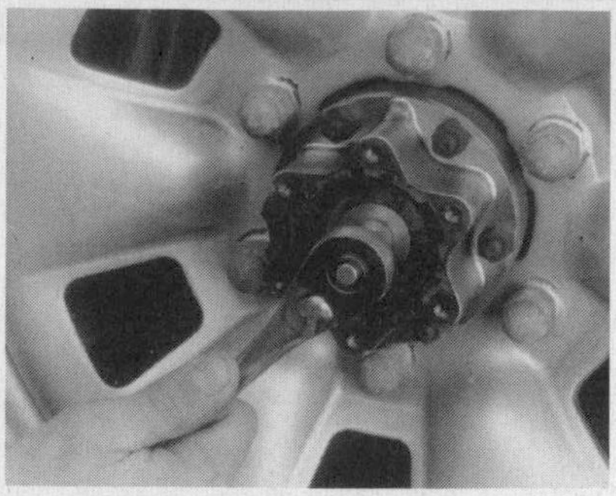

86827p13

Fig. 75 Using the correct size wrench, loosen . . .

86827p14

Fig. 76 . . . then remove the center bolt and washer

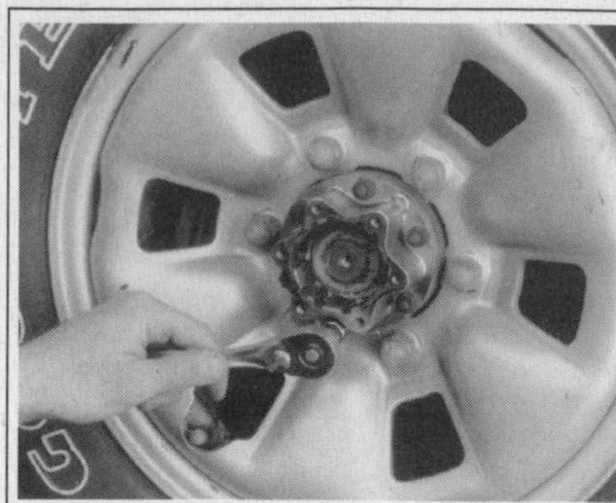

86827p15

Fig. 77 Next, remove the outside mounting nuts and washers

86827p16

Fig. 78 Using a brass bar and hammer, tap on the bolt ends . . .

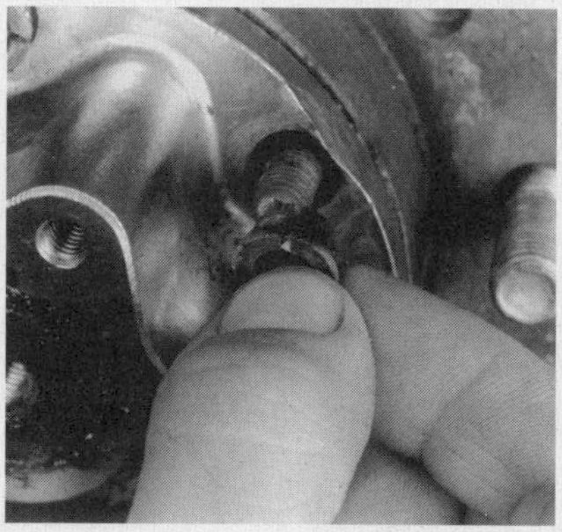

86827p17

Fig. 79 . . . then remove the cone washers

86827p18

Fig. 80 The free wheeling body should come off easily; be sure to discard the old gaskets

Front Axle, Bearing and Seal

REMOVAL & INSTALLATION

T100 and 1997–99 Tacoma and 4Runner

➧ See Figures 81 thru 87

1. Loosen the lug nuts.
2. Raise and support the vehicle.
3. Remove the front wheels.
4. Remove the shock absorber.
5. Pull off the grease cap.
6. Disconnect the driveshaft. Remove the cotter pin and lock cap.
7. With a helper applying the brakes, remove the locknut.
8. On vehicles with ABS, remove the speed sensor and harness from the steering knuckle.
9. Remove the brake line from the knuckle.
10. Remove the caliper and rotor.
11. Remove the bolts retaining the lower ball joint, separate from the knuckle.
12. Remove the cotter pin and loosen the nut on the axle hub. Using a SST or equivalent, remove the steering knuckle.

To install:

13. Attach the steering knuckle with hub axle to the vehicle, tighten the hub nut to 80 ft. lbs. (108 Nm).
14. Attach the lower ball joint, tighten to 59 ft. lbs. (80 Nm).
15. Install the disc and caliper.

93168p13

Fig. 81 Remove the dust cap

93168p12

Fig. 82 Remove the cotter pin

93168p15

Fig. 83 Once removed, discard the cotter pin . . .

93168p16

Fig 84 . . . then remove the nut lock cap

93168p17

Fig. 85 Remove the axle shaft nut by hand once it has been loosened with a breaker bar—4WD models

93168p18

Fig. 86 On 4WD models, the front axle shaft may get stuck in the hub assembly. If this occurs, thread the nut back on and gently tap it with a (preferably plastic) hammer

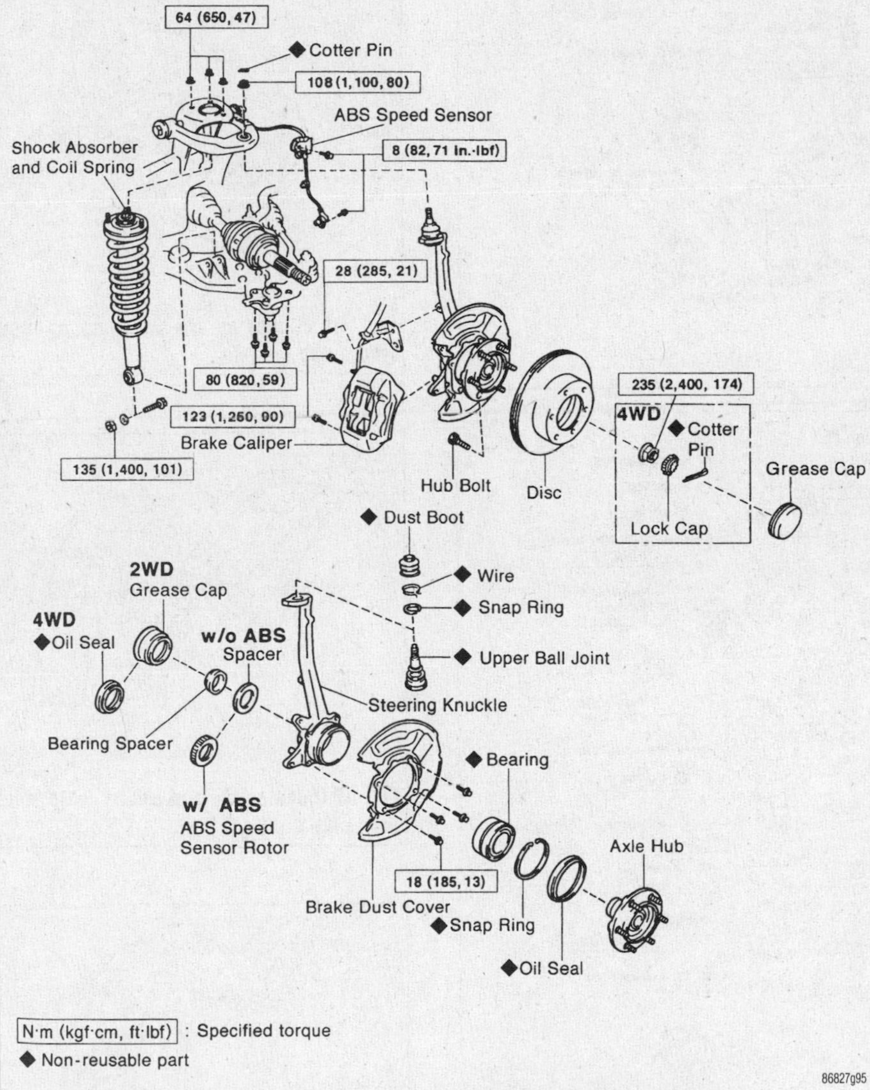

Fig. 87 Exploded view of the front axle hub and components—4Runner shown

16. Place the brake line bracket on the steering knuckle, tighten to 21 ft. lbs. (28 Nm).
17. Install the ABS sensor (if equipped) and harness.
18. Install the driveshaft. Tighten the locknut to 174 ft. lbs. (235 Nm).
19. Install the grease cap.
20. Install the shock absorber.
21. Install the wheel, lower the vehicle, tighten the lug nuts.

2000 Tacoma, 4Runner and Tundra

See Figures 88 thru 104

1. Remove the front wheel.
2. Detach the shock absorber.
3. Disconnect the driveshaft by removing the grease cap and pulling out the cotter pin and lock cap.
4. Apply the brakes to hold the axle from spinning and remove the lock nut.
5. If the vehicle is equipped with antilock brakes, detach the speed sensor and wiring harness clamp from the steering knuckle.
6. Remove the banjo bolt and 2 gaskets from the caliper.
7. Detach the flexible brake hose from the caliper.
8. Remove the brake caliper and then the rotor.
9. Properly hang the brake caliper.
10. Detach the lower ball joint.
11. Remove the steering knuckle.
12. Clamp the axle hub in a soft jaw vise.

➡Close the vise until it holds the hub bolts.

13. Using the proper seal puller or prytool, remove the oil seal.
14. On vehicles equipped with a free wheel hub and on the Pre Runner, use a chisel and hammer to loosen the staked part of the lock nut.
15. Remove the lock nut. A special service tool may be required.
16. Remove the Antilock Brake System (ABS) speed sensor rotor/spacer.

➡Do not scratch the speed sensor rotor.

17. Detach the bolts to the dust shield and shift the shield towards the outside of the hub.
18. Remove the axle from the steering knuckle, a special service tool may be required.
19. Remove the dust cover from the steering knuckle.
20. On vehicles without a free wheeling hub, that are 4WD only, remove the bearing spacer and ABS speed sensor rotor spacer.
21. Remove the outside seal by prying it out with a seal puller.
22. Remove the bearing from the steering knuckle by removing the snapring with a pair of snapring pliers.
23. Press the bearing from the steering knuckle.

To install:

24. Install the new bearing.
25. Install a new oil seal.
26. Install the axle hub to the steering knuckle. Torque the bolts to 13 ft. lbs. (18 Nm).
27. Re-install the ABS speed sensor rotor.
28. On vehicles that are equipped with a free wheel hub, install the bearing spacer.
29. On four wheel drive models, install a new inside oil seal.
30. On the Pre-Runner, install the grease cap.
31. The remainder of the installation procedure is the reverse of removal.

Land Cruiser

1. Remove the front wheel.
2. Remove the front brake caliper.
3. Using a flat bladed tool and a hammer, remove the grease cap from the flange.
4. Using a snapring expander, remove the snapring.

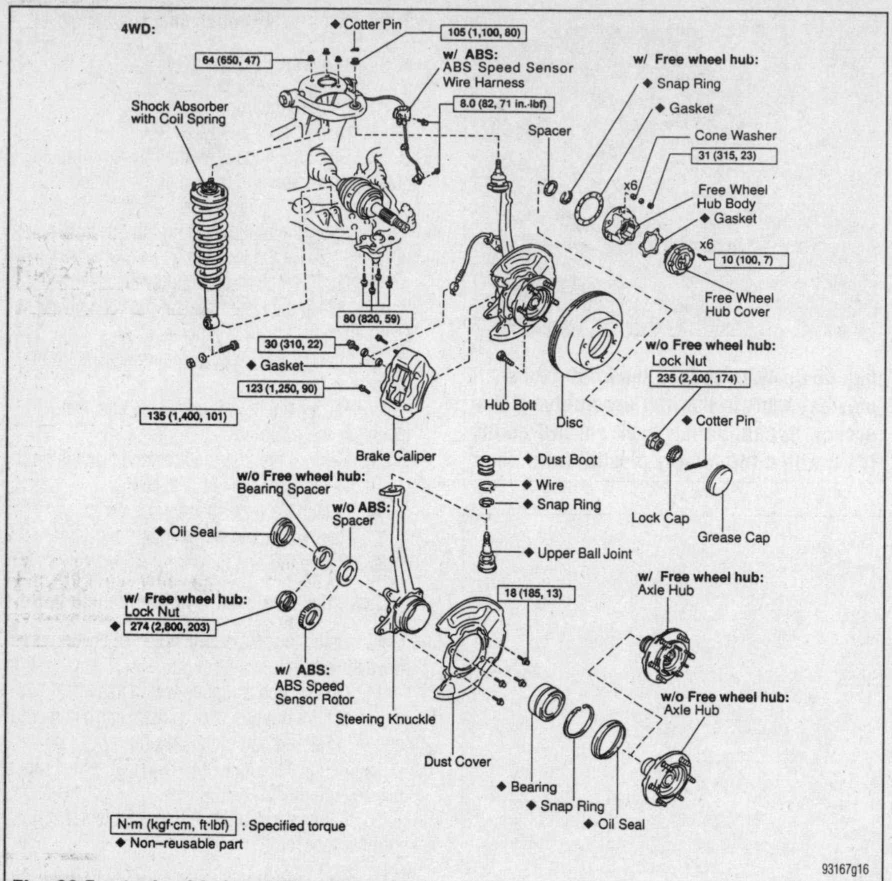

Fig. 88 Front wheel hub—4WD components

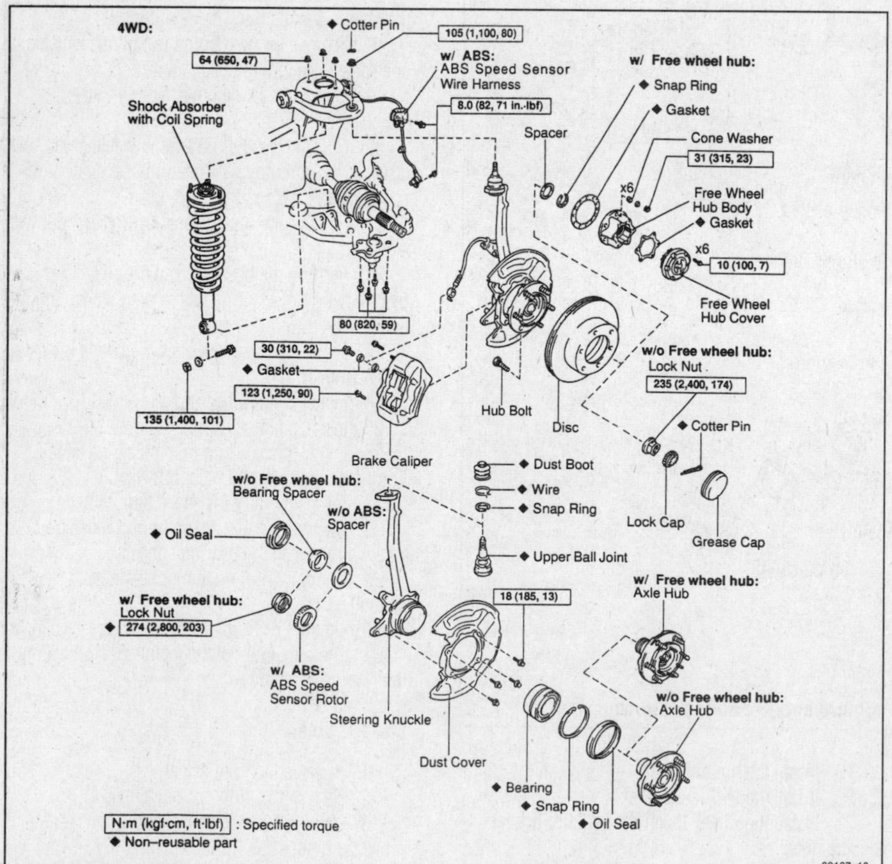

Fig. 89 Front wheel hub—Pre Runner

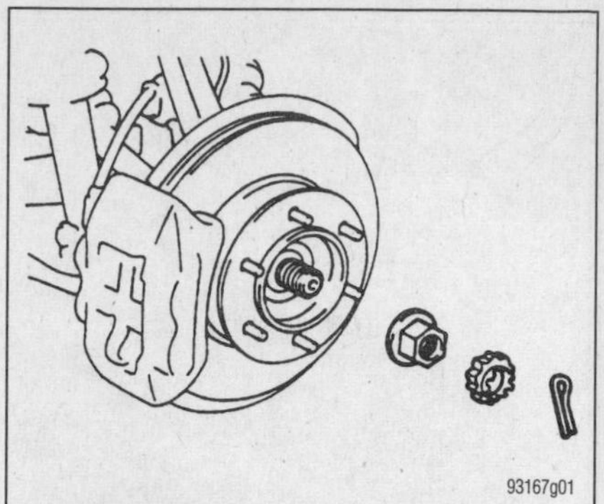

Fig. 90 Exploded view of the hub nut, locking ring and cotter pin

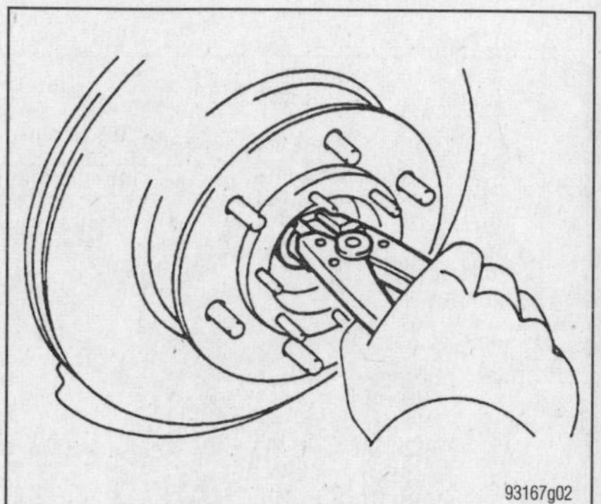

Fig. 91 Removing the snapring on free wheel hub models

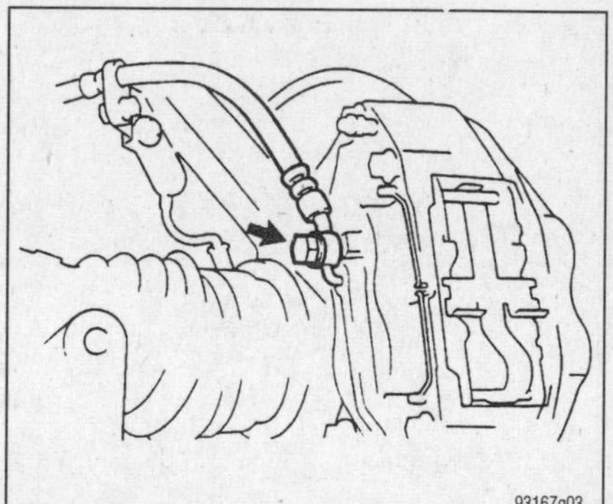

Fig. 92 Unfasten the brake hose banjo bolt, then plug the line

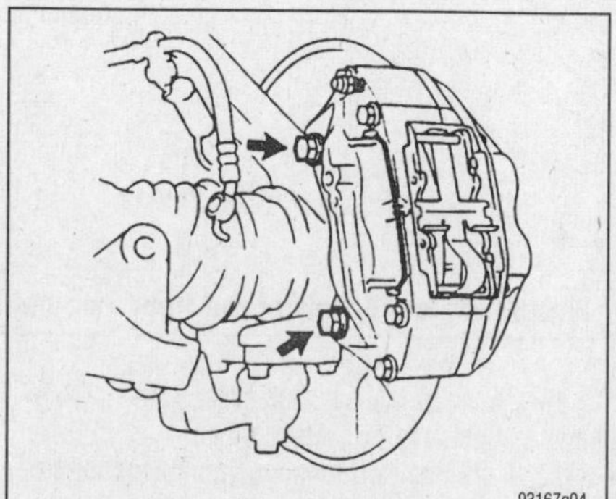

Fig. 93 Remove the brake caliper mounting bolts, then remove the caliper

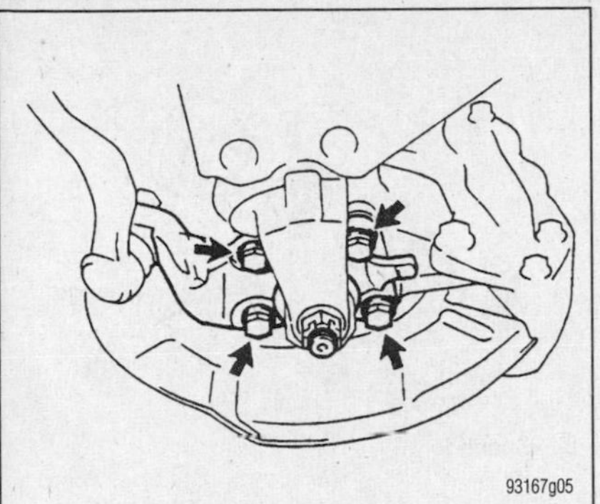

Fig. 94 Unfasten the lower ball joint bolts, then separate the lower ball joint

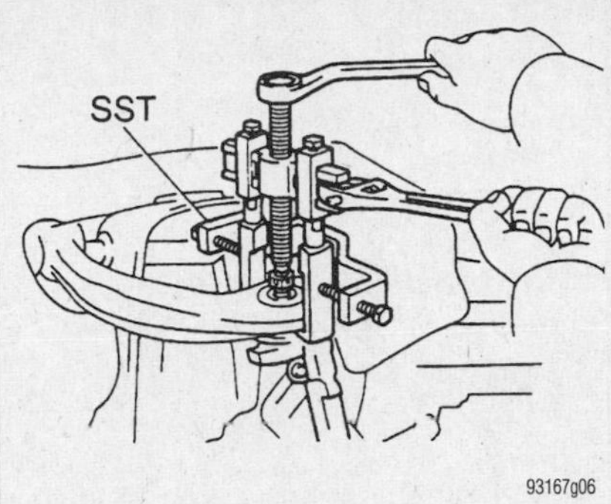

Fig. 95 You must use a special tool to separate the ball joint from the upper control arm

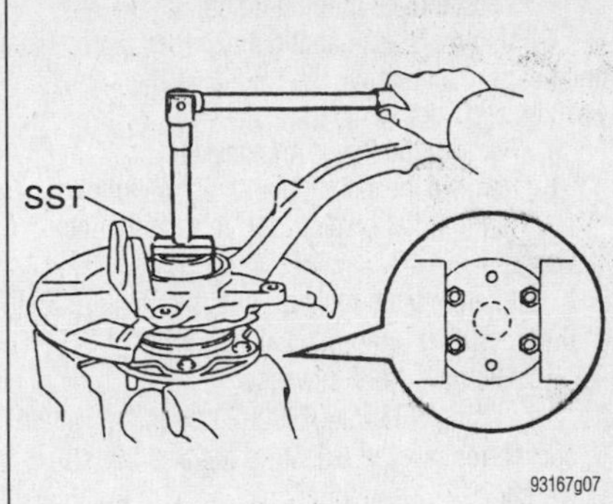

Fig. 96 Removing the lock nut with the Special Service Tool (SST)

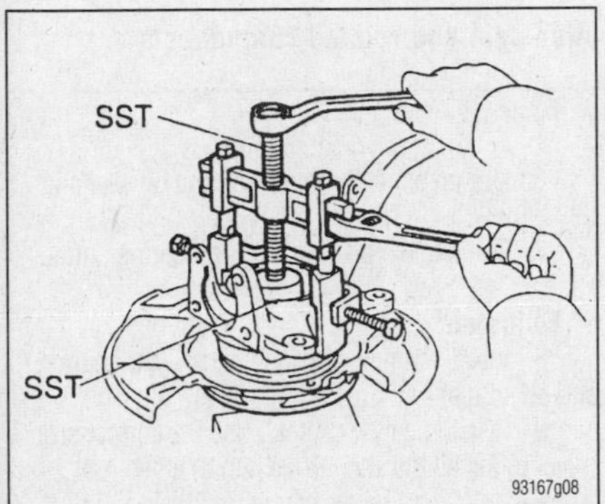

Fig. 97 Removing the axle hub from the steering knuckle

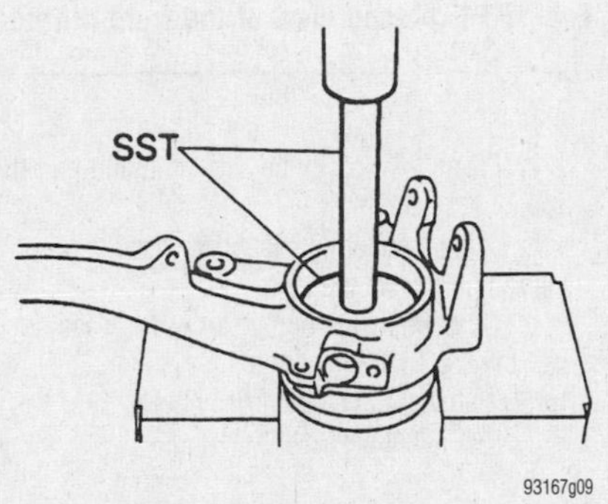

Fig. 98 Using a press to release the bearing from the knuckle assembly

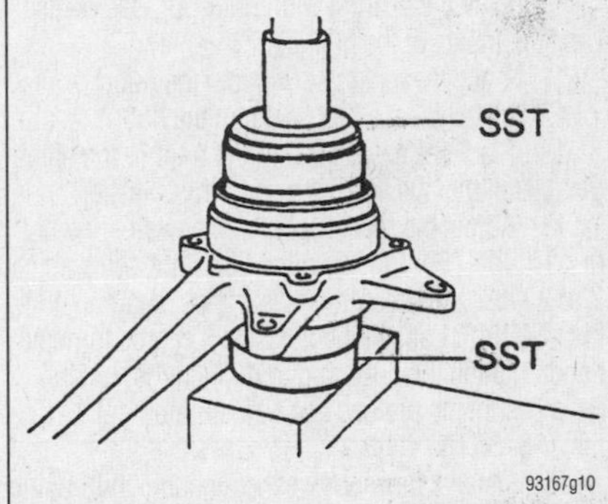

Fig. 99 Press the new bearing into the steering knuckle

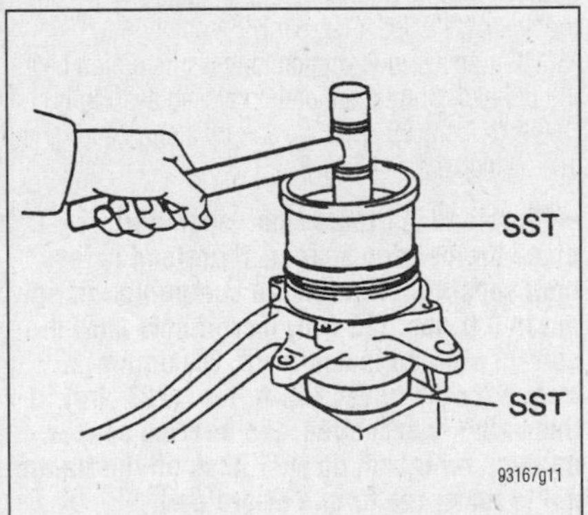

Fig. 100 Using a plastic hammer, install the new seal

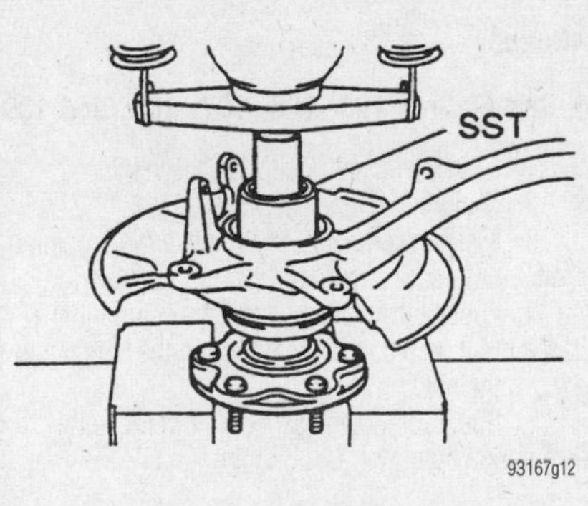

Fig. 101 A Special Service Tool (SST) may be required to install the ABS speed sensor

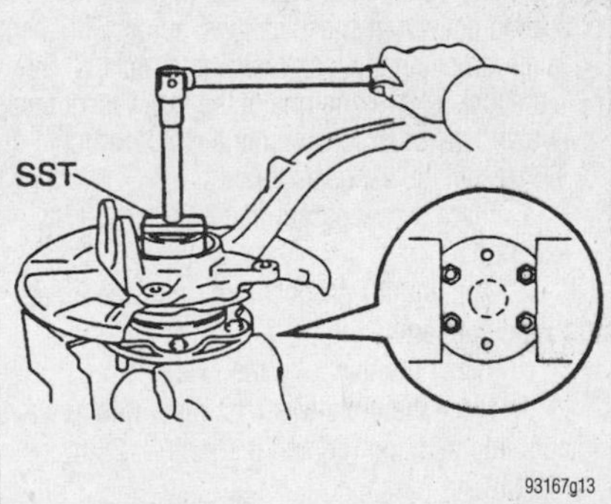

Fig. 102 Install a new lock nut into the hub assembly and tighten to 203 ft. lbs. (274 Nm)

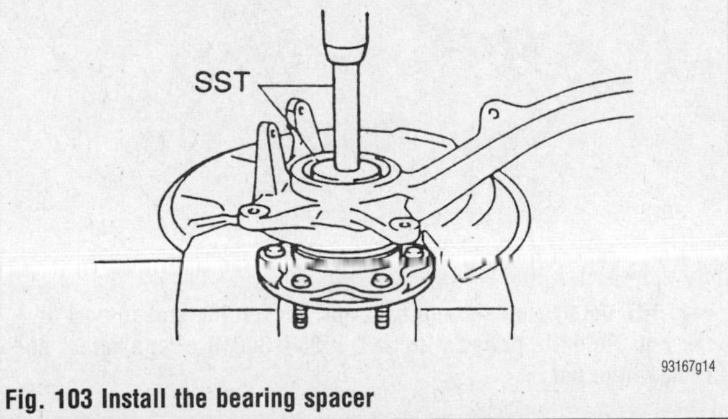

Fig. 103 Install the bearing spacer

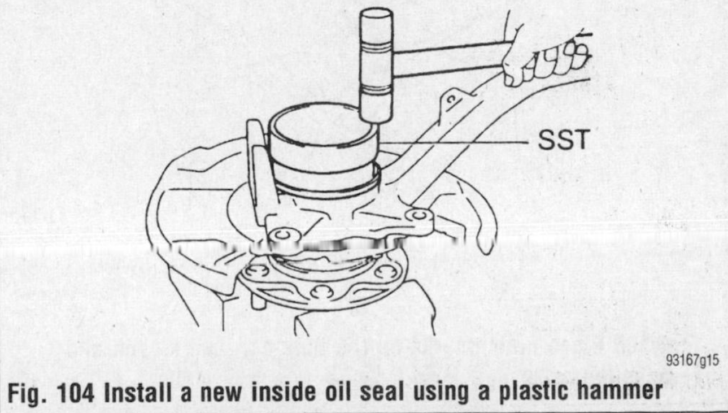

Fig. 104 Install a new inside oil seal using a plastic hammer

5. Loosen the 6 mounting nuts.
6. Using a brass bar and a hammer, tap on the bolt heads, then remove the 6 cone washers, plate washers and nuts.
7. Remove the flange and gasket.
8. Remove the axle hub and disc as follows:
a. With a flat bladed tool, release the lockwasher.
b. Remove the locknut, this may require SST 09607-60020 or an equivalent socket.
c. Remove the lockwasher.
d. Using SST 09607-60020 or an equivalent socket, remove the adjusting nut and thrust washer.
e. Remove the hub and rotor together with the outer bearing.
9. Remove the oil seal and inner bearing from the hub.

To install:

10. Pack the bearing with multi-purpose grease. Coat the inside of the hub also.
11. Place the inner bearing into the hub.
12. Install the new oil seal into the hub.
13. Place the axle hub with the rotor to the spindle. Install the outer bearing and thrust washer.
14. Adjust the preload, tighten the adjusting nut to 43 ft. lbs. (59 Nm). Turn the hub right and then left 2 or 3 times. Tighten the adjusting nut again to 43 ft. lbs. (59 Nm). Loosen the nut until it can be turned by hand. Tighten the nut again to 48 inch lbs. (5 Nm). Re-measure the preload again. It should be 6.4–12.6 lbs. (28–56 N).
15. Install a new lock washer and lock nut. Using SST 09607-60020, tighten the lock nut to 47 ft. lbs. (64 Nm). Check that the axle hub turns smoothly and the bearing has no play.
16. Using a spring tension gauge, measure the preload. It should be 6.4–12.6 lbs. (28–56 N). If the preload is not within specifications, adjust with the nut after removing the lockwasher and locknut. Secure the locknut by hand one of the lockwasher teeth inward and the other lockwasher teeth outward.
17. Install the flange as follows:
a. Place a new gasket into position on the axle hub.
b. Apply multi-purpose grease to the inner flange splines.
c. Install the flange to the axle hub.
d. Place the cone washers, plate washers and nuts into position, tighten the nuts to 26 ft. lbs. (35 Nm).

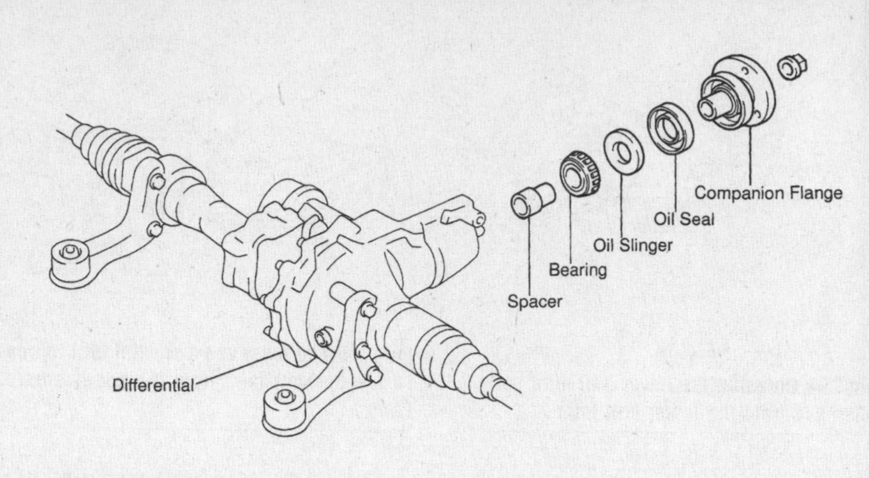

Fig. 105 Exploded view of the front differential pinion seal and related components

e. Install the bolt in the axle shaft and pull it out.
f. Using a snapring expander, install a new snapring. Remove the bolts.
g. Coat the inside of the cap with grease. Install the cap to the flange.
18. Install the caliper and front wheel.
19. Bleed the brake system.

Pinion Seal

REMOVAL & INSTALLATION

4Runner

See Figures 105, 106, 107, 108, and 109

1. Elevate and safely support the vehicle.
2. Drain the differential oil.
3. Make matchmarks and remove the propeller shaft.
4. Loosen the staked part of the companion flange nut. Use a counterhold tool on the flange and remove the nut.
5. Use a screw-type extractor to remove the companion flange.
6. Use an extractor to remove the oil seal and oil slinger.
7. Remove the bearing spacer, bearing and oil slinger.

To install:

8. Install the new bearing spacer, rear bearing and oil slinger.
9. Install the new oil seal. Use the correct size driver to install the seal. Drive it in to a depth of 0.059 in. (1.5mm) below the lip.
10. Apply a coat of multi-purpose grease to the inner lip of the seal. Install the companion flange.
11. Coat the threads of a NEW nut with multi-purpose grease. Counterhold the flange and tighten the nut to 89 ft. lbs. (120 Nm).
12. Use a torque wrench to measure pinion bearing preload. Correct preload on a used bearing is 5–9 inch lbs. (0.6–1.0 Nm) and on a new bearing is 10–17 inch lbs. (1–2 Nm).

➡If preload is greater than specified, replace the bearing spacer. If preload is less than specified, tighten the companion flange nut in 9 ft. lbs. (13 Nm) increments until the correct preload is achieved. Maximum torque for the nut is 165 ft. lbs. (223 Nm). If this value is exceeded, the bearing spacer must be replaced; do NOT back off the flange nut to lower the torque or preload.

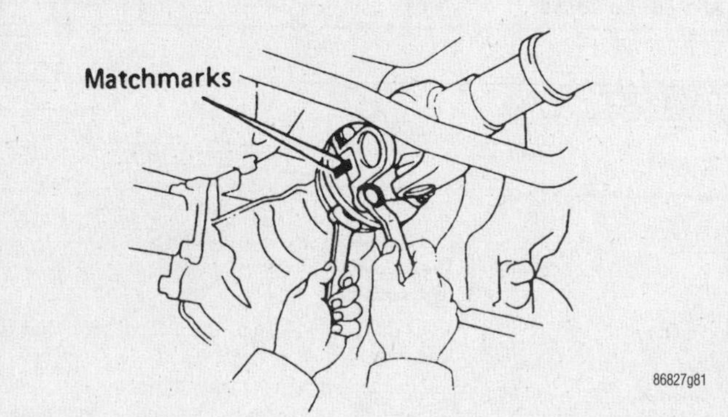

Fig. 106 Place matchmarks on the flanges, then loosen and remove the bolts

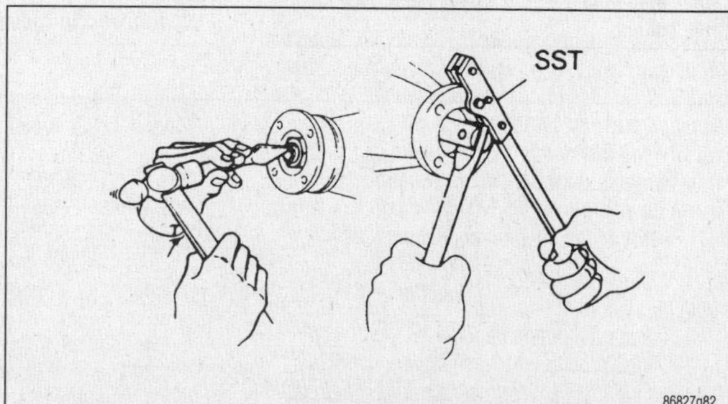

Fig. 107 Using a chisel and hammer, loosen the staked part of the nut. Hold the flange with SST 09950–30010 or equivalent and remove the nut

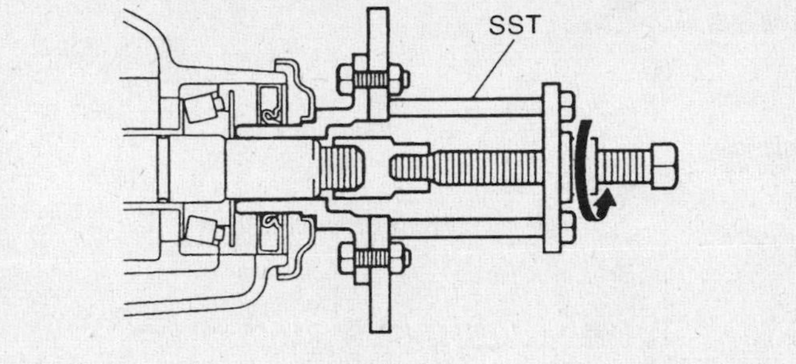

Fig. 108 This is a screw-type extractor from Toyota—Tool 09950-30010

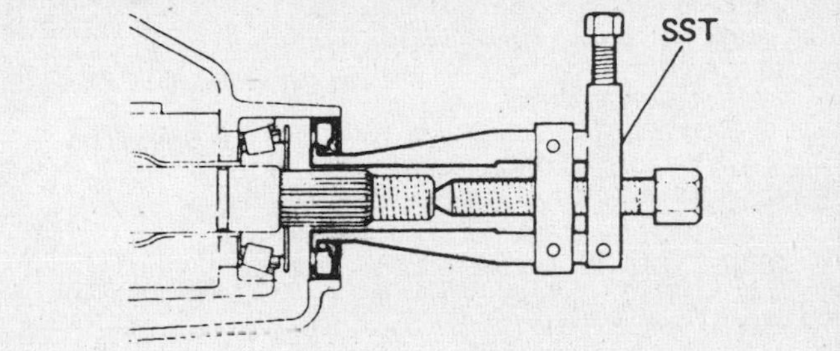

Fig. 109 The extractor fits into Seal Removal Tool 09308-10010 as shown

13. Check the run-out at the companion flange; maximum allowable run-out is 0.003 in. (0.10mm).
14. Stake the pinion flange nut.
15. Fill the differential with the correct amount of fluid.
16. Install the front propeller shaft.
17. Lower the vehicle to the ground.

T100 and Tacoma

1. Remove the engine undercover.
2. Drain the differential fluid.
3. Remove the front driveshaft.
4. Using a chisel and hammer, loosen the staked part of the nut. Hold the flange and remove the nut, then the flange.
5. With a seal extractor, remove the oil seal and slinger.
6. Pull the bearing from the drive pinion, then extract the spacer.

To install:

7. Install the new bearing spacer, rear bearing and oil slinger.
8. Install the new oil seal. Use the correct size driver to install the seal. Drive it in to a depth of 0.059 in. (1.5mm) below the lip.
9. Apply a coat of multi-purpose grease to the inner lip of the seal. Install the companion flange.
10. Coat the threads of a NEW nut with multi-purpose grease. Counterhold the flange and tighten the nut to 89 ft. lbs. (120 Nm).
11. Use a torque wrench to measure pinion bearing preload. Correct preload on a used bearing is 5–9 inch lbs. (0.6–1.0 Nm) and on a new bearing is 10–17 inch lbs. (1–2 Nm).

➡If preload is greater than specified, replace the bearing spacer. If preload is less than specified, tighten the companion flange nut in 9 ft. lbs. (13 Nm) increments until the correct preload is achieved. Maximum torque for the nut is 173 ft. lbs. (235 Nm). If this value is exceeded, the bearing spacer must be replaced; do NOT back off the flange nut to lower the torque or preload.

12. Check the run-out at the companion flange; maximum allowable run-out is 0.003 in. (0.10mm).
13. Stake the pinion flange nut.
14. Install the front driveshaft.
15. Fill the differential with the correct amount of fluid.
16. Install the front propeller shaft.
17. Lower the vehicle to the ground.

Land Cruiser

1. Elevate and safely support the vehicle.
2. Make matchmarks and disconnect the front propeller shaft.
3. Loosen the staked part of the companion flange nut. Use a counterhold tool on the flange and remove the nut.
4. Use screw type extractor to remove the companion flange.
5. Use an extractor to remove the oil seal and oil slinger.

To install:

6. Install the oil slinger and a new seal. Use the correct size driver to install the seal; drive it in to a depth of 0.04 in. (1.0mm) below the lip.
7. Apply a coat of multi-purpose grease to the inner lip of the seal. Install the companion flange.
8. Coat the threads of a NEW nut with multi-purpose grease. Counterhold the flange and tighten the nut to 145 ft. lbs. (196 Nm).
9. Use a torque wrench to measure pinion bearing preload. Correct preload is 4.3–6.9 inch lbs. (0.5–0.8 Nm).
10. If preload is greater than specified, replace the bearing spacer. If preload is less than specified, tighten the companion flange nut in 9 ft. lbs. (13 Nm.) increments until the correct preload is achieved. Maximum torque for the nut is 253 ft. lbs. (343 Nm). If this value is exceeded, the bearing spacer must be replaced; do NOT back off the flange nut to lower torque or preload.
11. Check the run-out at the companion flange; maximum allowable run-out is 0.02 in. (0.10mm).
12. Stake the pinion flange nut.
13. Fill the differential with the correct amount of fluid.
14. Install the front propeller shaft.
15. Lower the vehicle to the ground.

Differential Carrier

REMOVAL & INSTALLATION

4Runner

➧ See Figure 110

1. Remove the engine undercover.
2. Drain the differential oil.
3. Disconnect the front driveshaft.
4. Place matchmarks on the driveshaft, then remove the 4 nuts, washers and bolts. Disconnect the driveshaft.
5. Remove the front differential as follows:
   a. With Automatic Disconnecting Differential (ADD), disconnect the vacuum hoses, breather hose, ADD switch harness and oil TEMP sensor connector with 2-4 selector.
   b. Without ADD, disconnect the breather hose. Remove the 2 bolts and tube from the differential.
6. Support the front differential with a suitable jack.
7. Remove the rear mounting nut and front mounting bolts.
8. Lower the jack, then remove the front differential assembly.
9. Remove the front and rear mounting cushions.

To install:

10. Attach the front and rear mounting cushions, tighten the rear to 80 ft. lbs. (108 Nm) and the front to 116 ft. lbs. (157 Nm).
11. Raise and support the differential assembly into position.
12. Install the rear mounting nut and front mounting bolts. Tighten the nuts to 64 ft. lbs. (87 Nm) and the bolts to 101 ft. lbs. (137 Nm).
13. On vehicles without ADD, attach the tube to the differential, tighten the mounting bolts to 9 ft. lbs. (13 Nm). Install the breather hose.
14. On vehicles with ADD, attach the vacuum hoses, breather hose, ADD switch harness and oil TEMP sensor connector with 2-4 selector. Attach the tube to the differential, then tighten the mounting bolts to 9 ft. lbs. (13 Nm).
15. Attach the front driveshaft, tighten to 54 ft. lbs. (74 Nm).
16. Install the driveshafts.
17. Install the drain plug if it was removed or double check its tightness. Install the proper amount of gear oil.
18. Install the engine undercover.
19. Test drive the vehicle.

T100

1. Remove the engine undercover.
2. Drain the differential oil.
3. Disconnect the front driveshaft.
4. Place matchmarks on the driveshaft and remove the 6 nuts holding the driveshaft and side gear shaft. Remove the driveshaft nuts.
5. Disconnect the vacuum hoses and the 4WD indicator switch harness.
6. Remove the crossmember.
7. Loosen and remove the mounting bolt and nut for the differential.
8. Support the front differential with a suitable jack.

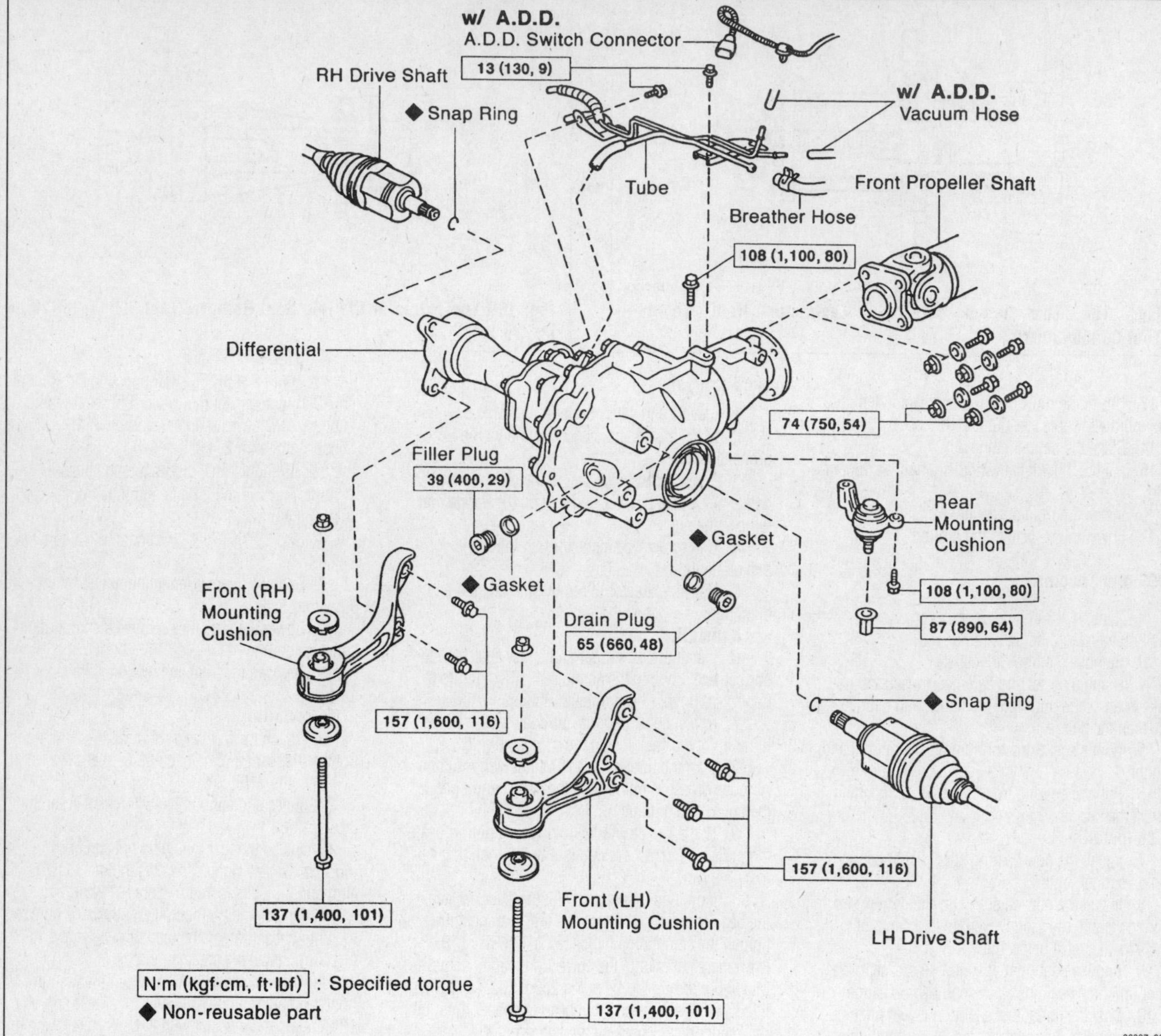

Fig. 110 Front differential mounting details—4Runner

9. Remove the right and left rear mounting bolts. Lower the jack, then remove the differential assembly.

To install:

10. Support the differential with a jack and raise into position. Install and tighten the right and left mounting bolts to 123 ft. lbs. (167 Nm).
11. Attach the front mounting bolt and nut, tighten to 108 ft. lbs. (147 Nm).
12. Install and attach the crossmember, tighten to 93 ft. lbs. (126 Nm).
13. Attach the vacuum hoses and the 4WD indicator harness.
14. Install and tighten the driveshaft nuts to 61 ft. lbs. (83 Nm).
15. Attach the front driveshaft.
16. Install the drain plug if it was removed or double check its tightness. Install the proper amount of gear oil.
17. Install the engine undercover.
18. Test drive the vehicle.

Tacoma

See Figure 111

1. Remove the engine undercover.
2. Drain the differential oil.
3. Disconnect the front driveshaft.
4. Place matchmarks on the driveshaft, then remove the 4 nuts, washers and bolts. Disconnect the driveshaft.
5. Remove the front differential as follows:
   a. With Automatic Disconnecting Differential (ADD), disconnect the vacuum hoses, breather hose, ADD switch harness and oil TEMP sensor connector with 2-4 selector.
   b. Without ADD, disconnect the breather hose. Remove the 2 bolts and tube from the differential.
6. Support the front differential with a suitable jack.
7. Remove the rear mounting nut and front mounting bolts.
8. Lower the jack, then remove the front differential assembly.
9. Remove the front and rear mounting cushions.

To install:

10. Attach the front and rear mounting cushions, tighten the rear to 80 ft. lbs. (108 Nm). and the front to 116 ft. lbs. (157 Nm).
11. Raise and support the differential assembly into position.
12. Install the rear mounting nut and front mounting bolts. Tighten the nuts to 64 ft. lbs. (87 Nm) and the bolts to 101 ft. lbs. (137 Nm).
13. On vehicles without ADD, attach the tube to the differential, tighten the mounting bolts to 9 ft. lbs. (13 Nm). Install the breather hose.

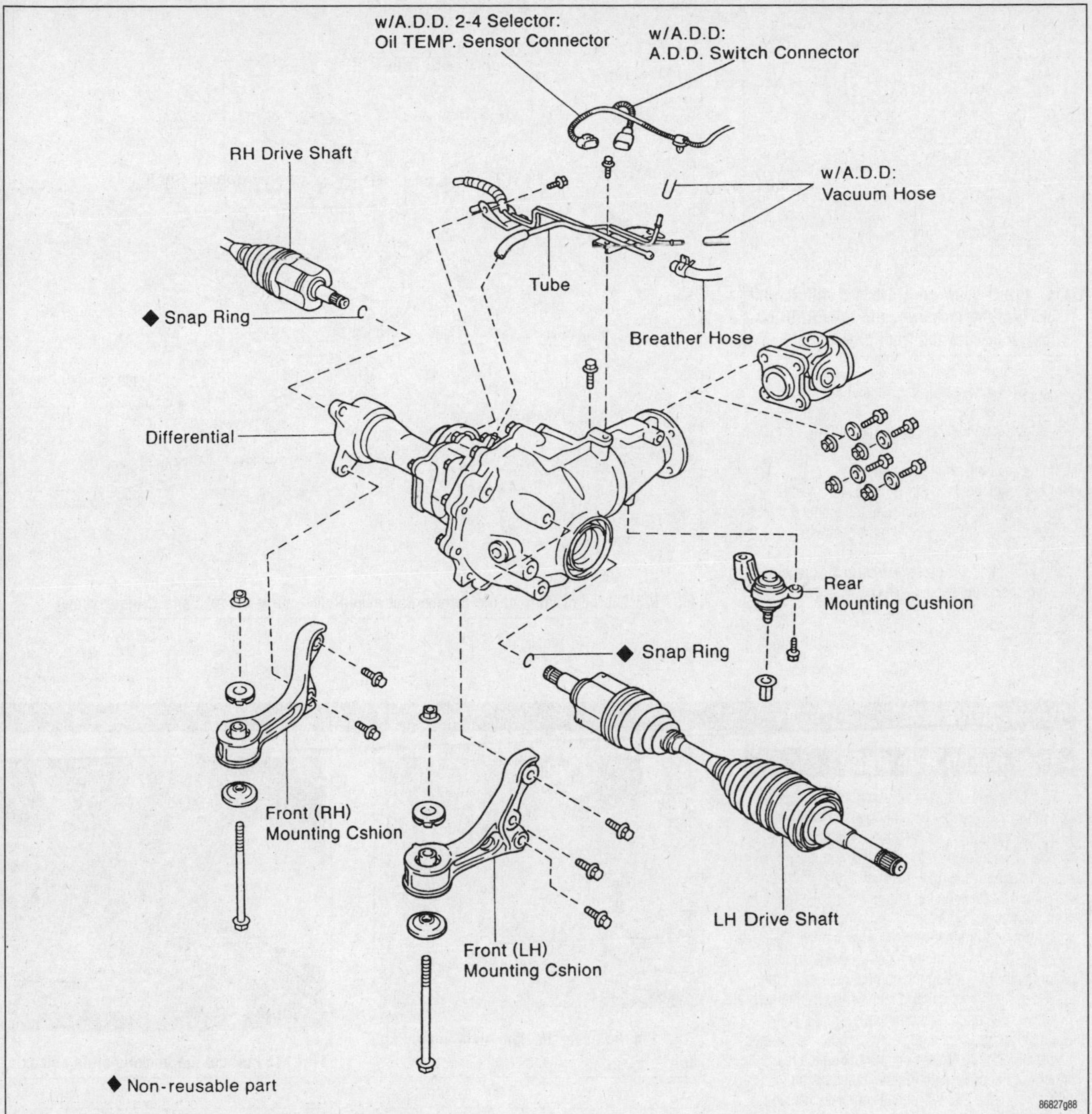

Fig. 111 Front differential mounting details—Tacoma

14. On vehicles with ADD, attach the vacuum hoses, breather hose, ADD switch harness and oil TEMP sensor connector with 2-4 selector. Attach the tube to the differential, then tighten the mounting bolts to 9 ft. lbs. (13 Nm).
15. Attach the front driveshaft, tighten to 54 ft. lbs. (74 Nm).
16. Install the driveshafts.
17. Install the drain plug if it was removed or double check its tightness. Install the proper amount of gear oil.
18. Install the engine undercover.
19. Test drive the vehicle.

Land Cruiser

➧ **See Figures 112 and 113**

Before removal on vehicles with a differential lock, turn the ignition switch to the **ON** position. Turn the lock switch to the FR/RR position, then lock the front differential. Disconnect the negative battery cable.

1. Elevate and safely support the vehicle on stands. Double check the security and placement of the stands.
2. Drain the differential oil.
3. Remove the front axle shafts.
4. Remove the cotter pin and castle nut from each end of the steering tie rod. Use a ball joint separator (NEVER a hammer) to separate the tie rod joints; remove the tie rod.
5. Disconnect the front shaft. Make matchmarks first. On vehicles with differential lock, disconnect the harness and tube.
6. Remove the ring of nuts holding the carrier and remove the carrier assembly. Do not scratch the machined surfaces during removal.

To install:

7. Place a new gasket in position on the housing. Fit the carrier into the axle and install the nuts. Tighten the nuts to 18–20 ft. lbs. (25–27 Nm).

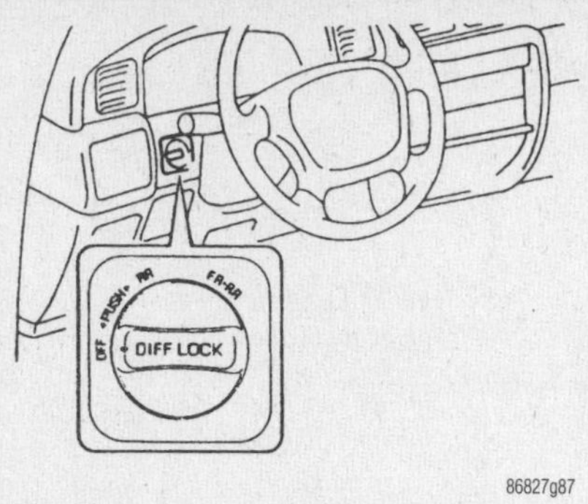

Fig. 112 If your vehicle has a differential lock, turn the lock switch to the FR/RR position, then lock the front differential

8. On vehicles with differential lock, attach the harness and tube.
9. Connect the front driveshaft.
10. Install the tie rod.
11. Install the front driveshafts.
12. Install the drain plug if it was removed or double check its tightness. Install the proper amount of gear oil. Lower the vehicle to the ground.
13. Test drive the vehicle.
14. Check that the bleeder plug at the point of the bleeder (inside the engine area) is not damaged or worn.

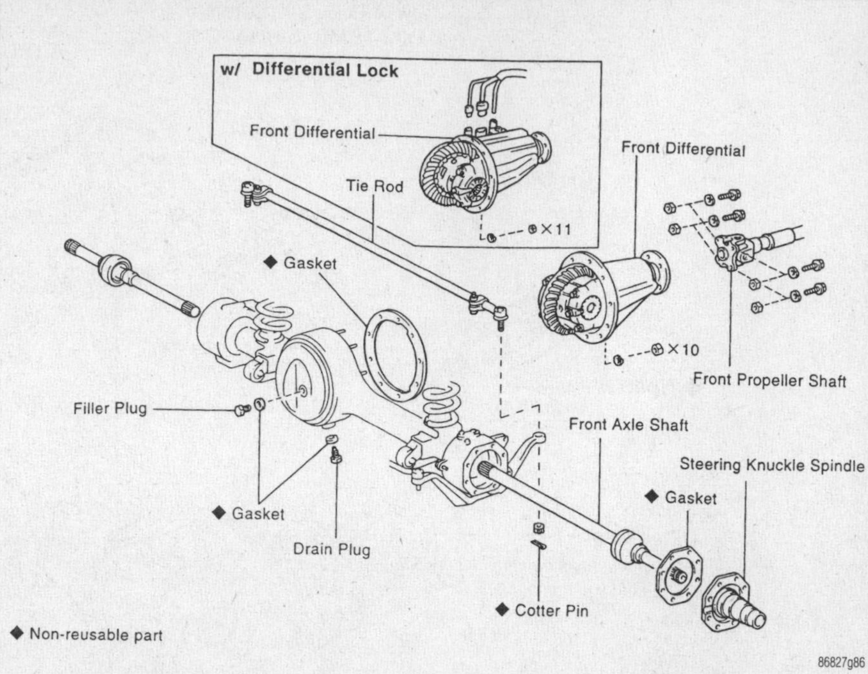

Fig. 113 Exploded view of the differential assembly—early model Land Cruiser shown

REAR DRIVE AXLE

Determining Axle Ratio

The drive axle of a vehicle is said to have a certain axle ratio. This number (usually a whole number and a decimal fraction) is actually a comparison of the number of gear teeth on the ring gear and the pinion gear. For example, a 4.11 rear means that, in theory, there are 4.11 teeth on the ring gear and one tooth on the pinion gear or, put another way, the driveshaft must turn 4.11 times to turn the wheels once. There might be 37 teeth on the ring gear and 9 teeth on the pinion gear. By dividing the number of teeth on the ring gear, the numerical axle ratio (4.11) is obtained.

Another method of determining gear ratio is to jack up and support the truck so that both rear wheels are off the ground. Make a chalk mark on the rear wheel and the driveshaft. Put the transmission in neutral. Turn the rear wheel one complete turn and count the number of turns that the driveshaft makes. The number of turns that the driveshaft makes in one complete revolution of the rear wheel is an approximation of the rear axle ratio.

Axle Shaft, Bearing and Seal

REMOVAL & INSTALLATION

Pick-Ups, 4Runner, T100 and Tacoma

➧ See Figures 114 thru 120

1. Loosen the lug nuts on the rear wheel.
2. Raise and support the vehicle, then remove the wheel.
3. Remove the brake drum.

Fig. 114 Remove the four axle mounting bolts

Fig. 115 Pull out the backing plate and axle

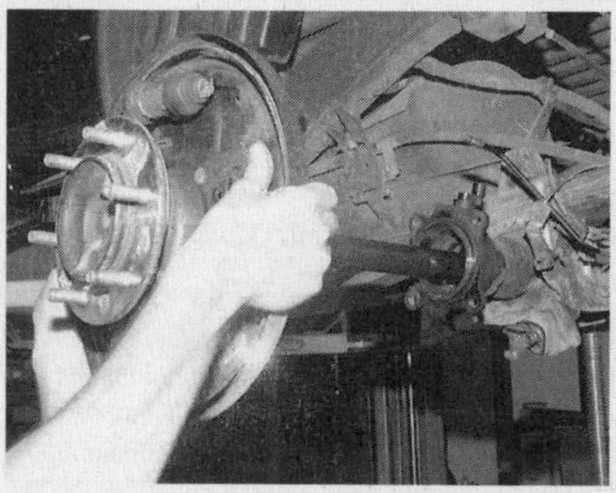

Fig. 116 The rear hub and axle assembly are heavy. Be sure you have a firm grasp on the axle when removing it

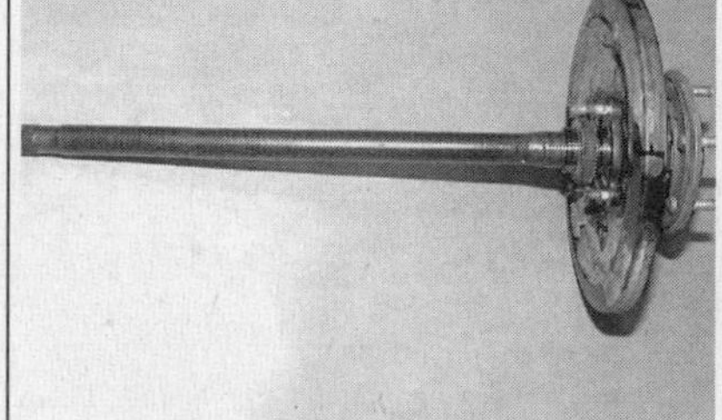

Fig. 117 View of the axle shaft and brake backing plate removed from the vehicle

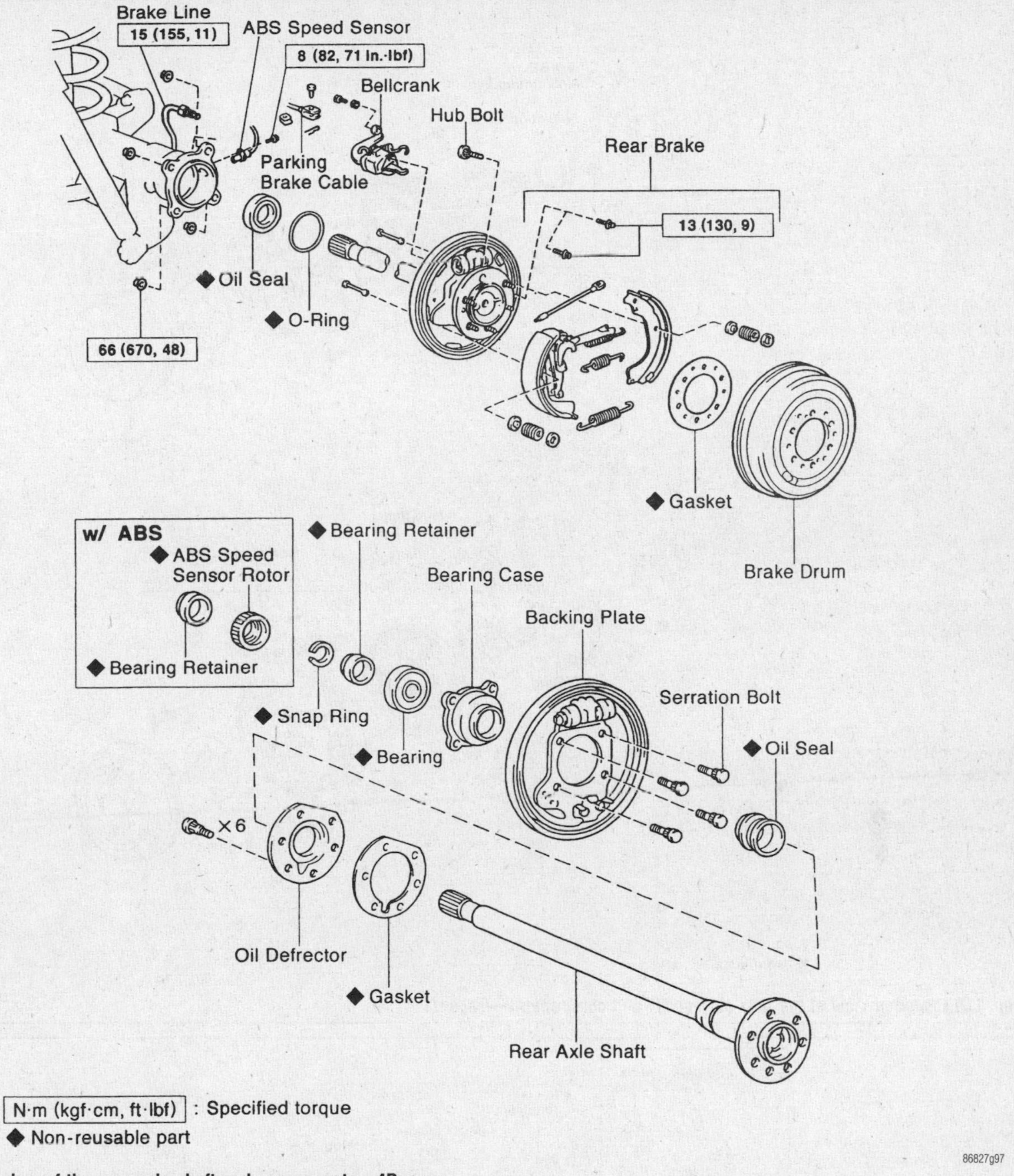

Fig. 118 Exploded view of the rear axle shaft and components—4Runner

4. Check the bearing backlash and axle shaft deviation as follows:
   a. Using a dial indicator, check that the backlash in the bearing shaft direction. The maximum is 0.027 in. (0.7mm).
   b. If the backlash exceeds the maximum, replace the bearing.
   c. Using a dial indicator, check the deviation at the surface of the axle shaft outside the hub bolt. Maximum is 0.0039 in. (0.1mm).
   d. If the deviation exceeds the maximum, replace the axle shaft.
5. On models with ABS, remove the ABS speed sensor from the axle housing.
6. Remove the axle shaft assembly by unfastening the 4 nuts from the backing plate. Pull out the shaft assembly from the rear axle housing.
7. Remove the O-ring from the axle housing.
8. On ABS models, remove the bearing and retainer (differential side) and ABS speed sensor rotor.
9. Remove the snapring from the axle shaft.
10. Remove the rear axle shaft from the backing plate. Inspect the axle shaft run-out. Shaft run-out should be 0.079 in. (2.0mm) and the flange run-out should be 0.004 in. (0.1mm).
11. Remove the outer seal. Using a suitable bearing removal tool, separate the bearing from the axle shaft.

To install:

12. Install a new bearing to the axle shaft.
13. Install a new outer seal onto the axle shaft.
14. Replace the inner side oil seal.
15. Apply multi-purpose grease to the oil seal lip. Press the axle shaft into the backing plate. Install a new snapring.
16. On ABS models, install the ABS speed sensor rotor and bearing retainer on the differential side.
17. Attach a new O-ring on the axle housing.
18. Install the axle assembly attach the 4 mounting bolts to the backing plate. Tighten to 48 ft. lbs. (66 Nm).
19. Install the rear brake assembly.

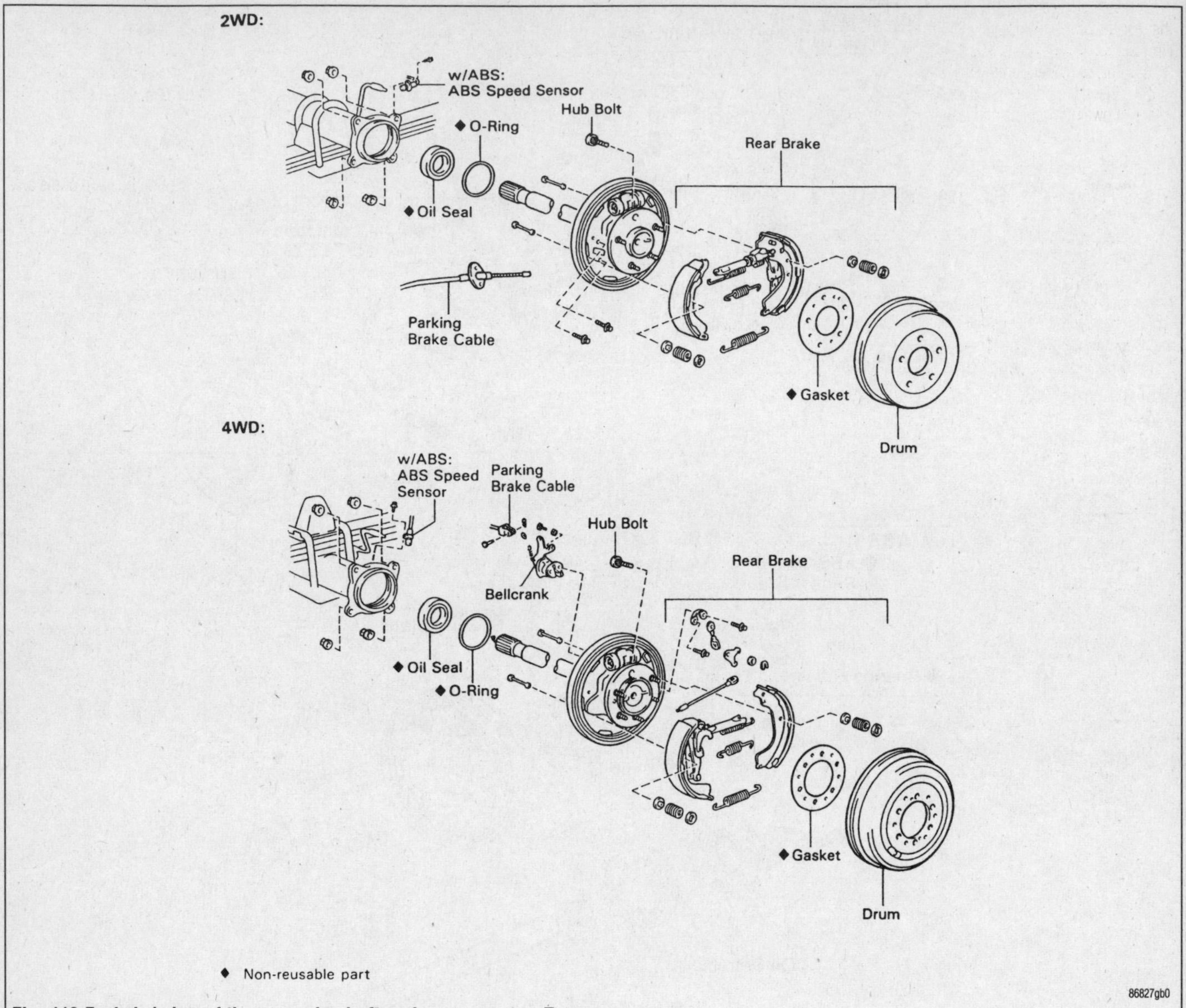

Fig. 119 Exploded view of the rear axle shaft and components—Tacoma

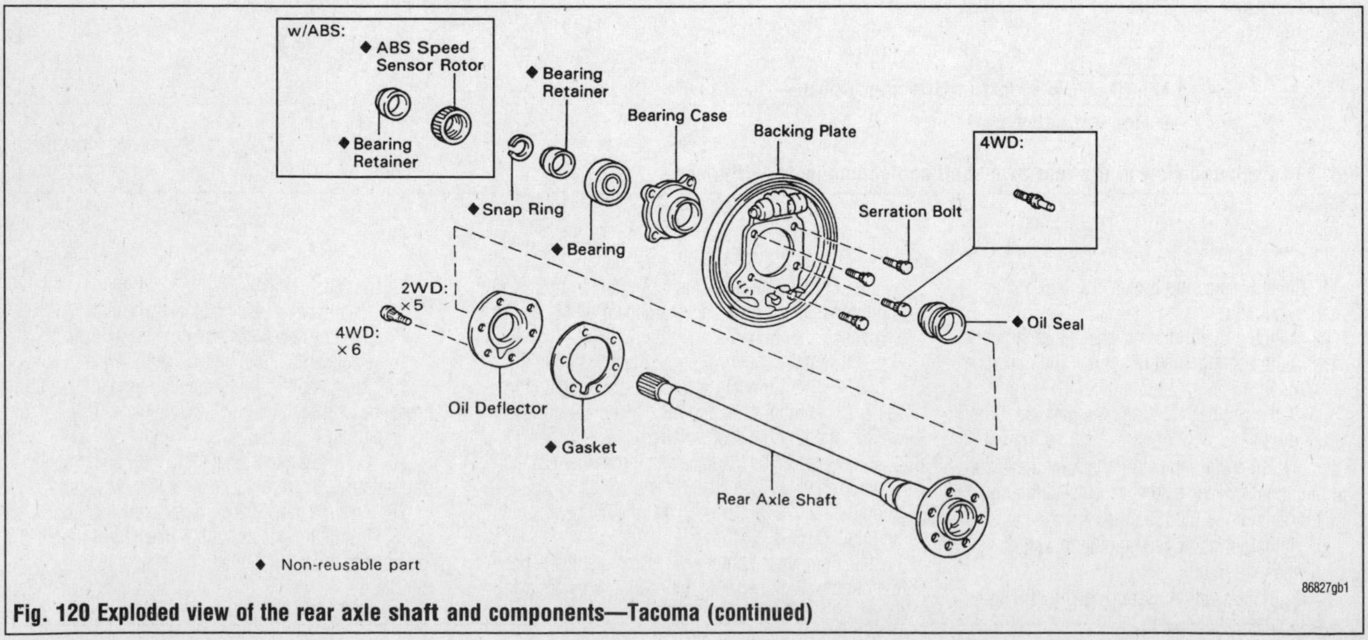

Fig. 120 Exploded view of the rear axle shaft and components—Tacoma (continued)

20. On vehicles with ABS, install the sensor to the rear housing assembly, tighten to 71 inch lbs. (8 Nm).
21. Install the rear drum and wheel.
22. Bleed the brake system and check for leaks.
23. Lower the vehicle and test drive.

Land Cruiser

See Figures 121, 122, 123, and 124

1. Loosen the lug nuts on the rear wheel. Raise and support the vehicle.
2. Remove the wheel.
3. Remove the 6 nuts and plate washers. Using a brass bar and hammer, strike the center part of the axle shaft to remove the cone washers.
4. Install 2 bolts into the axle holes. Gradually tighten the bolts evenly, then pull the axle shaft. Remove the bolts from the shaft. Remove the shaft and discard the gasket.
5. Remove the brake caliper and rotor.
6. Disconnect the ABS speed sensor.
7. Remove the two mounting screws from the rear axle bearing locknut. Remove the locknut, a SST 09509-25011 or an equivalent socket may be used.
8. Pull out the rear axle hub, locknut plate and outer bearing. Remove the axle hub.
9. Once the hub is removed, with a seal puller, remove the oil seal and inner bearing from the unit.
10. Using a brass bar and hammer, tap out the outer bearing races.

To install:

11. Using a special tool and a press, install the new outer races.
12. Pack multi-purpose grease into the bearing until it oozes out from the other side.
13. Coat the inside of the hub with grease.
14. Install the inner bearing and oil seal as follows:
    a. Place the inner bearing into the hub.
    b. Tap the seal into place with the seal installer.
    c. Apply multi-purpose grease to the oil seal lip.
15. Clean the hub installation position of the axle housing and apply clean lubricant (thinly).
16. Place the hub into position Be careful not to damage the axle seal.
17. Install the outer bearing.
18. Place the locknut plate on the axle housing, making sure the tongue lines up with the key groove. Temporarily install the locknut.
19. Install the rotor to the hub.

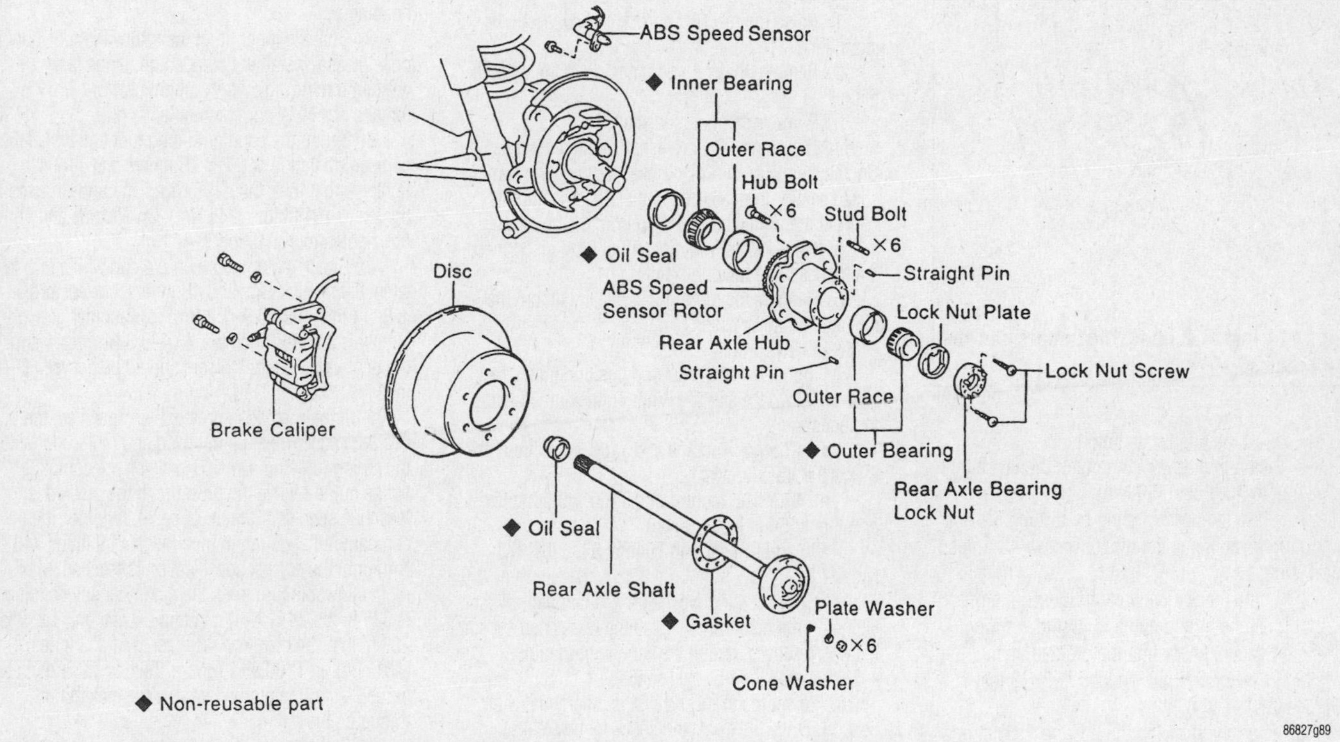

Fig. 121 Exploded view of the rear axle hub and components—Land Cruiser

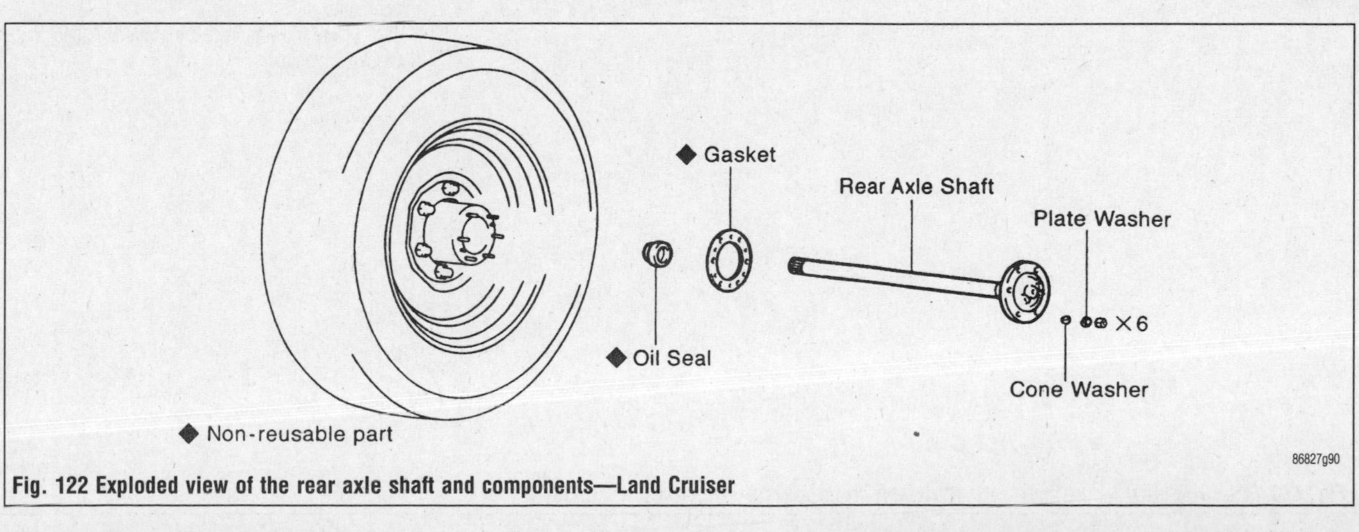

Fig. 122 Exploded view of the rear axle shaft and components—Land Cruiser

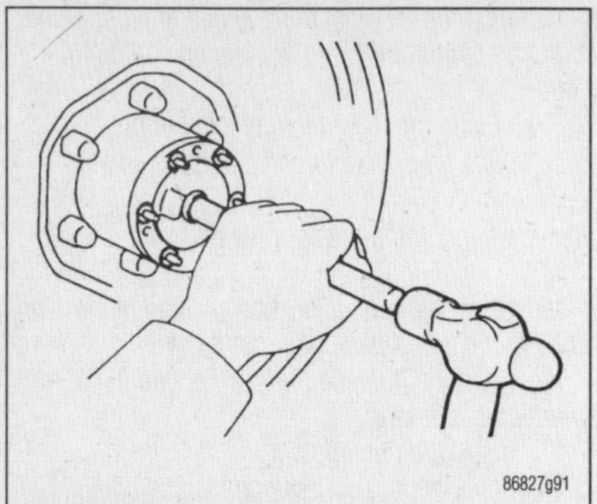

Fig. 123 Remove the 6 set nuts and plate washers. Using a brass bar and hammer, strike the center part of the axle hub to remove the cone washers

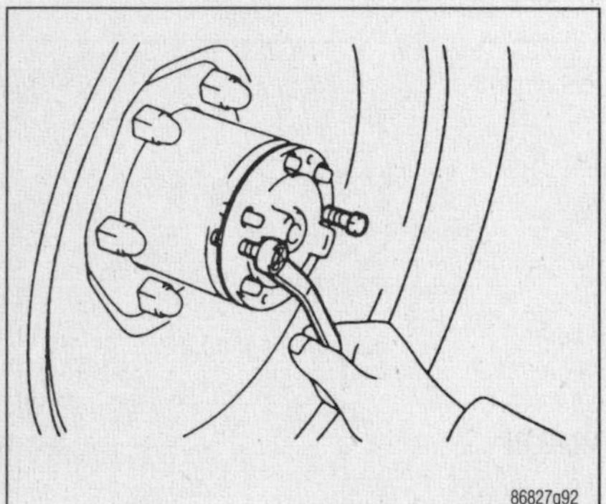

Fig. 124 Install 2 bolts 180° apart into the axle holes

20. Adjust the preload as follows:
   a. Use a torque wrench tighten the bearing locknut to 43 ft. lbs. (59 Nm).
   b. Make the bearing snug by turning the hub several times. Retighten the locknut to 43 ft. lbs. (59 Nm).
   c. Using the torque wrench, loosen the nut until it can be turned by hand. Using a spring tension gauge, check that the preload, then tighten the nut until the preload is 6–13 lbs. (26–57 N).
   d. Align the mark on the bearing locknut and tip of the axle housing under the above preload range.
   e. Check the distance between the top surface of the axle housing and the locknut. It should be 0.0079–0.0354 in. (0.2–0.9mm) below the surface of the axle housing. If the distance is greater than specified, reassemble the locknut plate.
   f. Check that the hub with the rotor rotates smoothly and the hub has no axle play.
21. Install the bearing locknut screw, tighten to 48 inch lbs. (5 Nm).
22. Attach the ABS speed sensor, tighten to 13 ft. lbs. (18 Nm).
23. Install the caliper, rear axle shaft and wheel.
24. Tighten the lug nuts on steel wheels to 109 ft. lbs. (147 Nm) and on aluminum wheels to 76 ft. lbs. (103 Nm).

Differential Carrier

REMOVAL & INSTALLATION

1. Raise the rear of the truck and support it on jackstands.
2. Remove the drain plug and drain the differential oil.
3. Remove the rear axle shafts.
4. Disconnect the driveshaft at the differential. On vehicles with anti-lock brakes, remove the rear speed sensor from the differential housing and disconnect the wiring harness clip from the housing.
5. On vehicles with differential lock, disconnect the harness and tube.
6. Remove the mounting bolts and lift out the differential carrier assembly.

To install:

7. Install a new gasket and position the carrier assembly into the axle housing. Tighten the mounting bolts to:
   - 4Runner, Tacoma and T100 with differential lock: 18 ft. lbs. (25 Nm)
   - 4Runner, Tacoma and T100 without differential lock: 54 ft. lbs. (73 Nm)
   - Land Cruiser and Tundra: 54 ft. lbs. (73 Nm)
8. Connect the driveshaft to the companion flange on the differential. Install the rear speed sensor if it was removed; install the wire harness clips.
9. Install the rear axle shafts.
10. Lower the truck and fill the differential with gear oil. Drive the truck and check for any leaks.

Pinion Seal

REMOVAL & INSTALLATION

1. Elevate and safely support the vehicle.
2. Matchmark the flanges on the driveshaft and pinion. Disconnect the driveshaft from the differential.
3. Use a hammer and small chisel to loosen the staking on the companion flange bolt. Attach a counterholding tool to the companion flange and remove the nut. Use the proper threaded extractor to remove the companion flange.
4. Use an extractor to remove the oil seal and oil slinger from the housing.

To install:

5. Make certain the new seal faces in the correct direction. Install the new seal with a driver or seal installation tool of the correct diameter. Drive the new seal in until it is recessed 0.039 in. (1.0mm) in the housing.
6. Coat the inner lip of the seal with multi-purpose grease. Install the companion flange (and washer, if removed). Apply a light coat of oil to the threads of a NEW companion flange nut.
7. Set up the counterholding tool and install the companion flange nut. For 4Runners and T100s, tighten it to 145 ft. lbs. (196 Nm). On Land Cruisers, tighten to 181 ft. lbs. (245 Nm). On Tacoma and Tundra, tighten to 109 ft. lbs. (147 Nm).
8. Check the drive pinion preload with a torque wrench. For Pick-Ups and 4Runners, correct torque is 8–11 inch lbs. (0.9–1.2 Nm) for 2-spider gear differentials and 4–7 inch lbs. (0.4–0.8 Nm) for 4-spider gear units. Land Cruisers should be between 6–9 inch lbs. (0.6–1.0 Nm).
9. If the preload is greater than specified, the bearing spacer must be removed and replaced inside the pinion housing. Do NOT back off the companion flange nut to relieve the pressure. If the preload is less than specified (the usual case), retighten the companion flange nut in increments of 9 ft. lbs. (13 Nm) until the correct specification is reached. Maximum allowable torque on the nut under any condition is 325 ft. lbs. (441 Nm) on Land Cruiser and Tacoma, 253 ft. lbs. (343 Nm) on 4Runner, and 333 ft. lbs. (451 Nm) on T100 and Tundra. Take great care not to exceed either the preload limit or the maximum torque on the nut.
10. Stake the drive pinion nut.
11. Connect the rear propeller shaft, aligning the matchmarks.
12. Lower the vehicle to the ground; inspect the fluid level in the axle.

TRANSMISSION IDENTIFICATION CHART

Year	Model	Manual Transmission	Automatic Transmission
1997	Land Cruiser	—	A343F
	T100	R150,R150F,W59	A340E,A340F
	T100	R150,R150F,W59	A340E,A340F
	Tacoma	R150,R150F,W59	A43D,A340E,A340F
	Tacoma	R150,R150F,W59	A43D,A340E,A340F
	Tacoma	R150,R150F,W59	A43D,A340E,A340F
	4Runner	W59,R150F	A340E,A340F
	4Runner	W59,R150F	A340E,A340F
1998	Land Cruiser	—	A343F
	T100	R150,R150F,W59	A340E,A340F
	T100	R150,R150F,W59	A340E,A340F
	Tacoma	R150,R150F,W59	A43D,A340E,A340F
	Tacoma	R150,R150F,W59	A43D,A340E,A340F
	Tacoma	R150,R150F,W59	A43D,A340E,A340F
	4Runner	W59,R150F	A340E,A340F
	4Runner	W59,R150F	A340E,A340F
1999	Land Cruiser	—	A343F
	T100	R150,R150F	A340E,A340F
	T100	R150,R150F	A340E,A340F
	Tacoma	W59,R150,R150F	A43D,A340E,A340F
	Tacoma	W59,R150,R150F	A43D,A340E,A340F
	Tacoma	W59,R150,R150F	A43D,A340E,A340F
	4Runner	W59,R150F	A340E,A340F
	4Runner	W59,R150F	A340E,A340F
2000	Land Cruiser	—	A343F
	Tundra	R150,R150F	A340E,A340F
	Tundra	R150,R150F	A340E,A340F
	Tacoma	W59,R150,R150F	A43D,A340E,A340F
	Tacoma	W59,R150,R150F	A43D,A340E,A340F
	Tacoma	W59,R150,R150F	A43D,A340E,A340F
	4Runner	W59,R150F	A340E,A340F
	4Runner	W59,R150F	A340E,A340F

93167C01

TORQUE SPECIFICATIONS — LAND CRUISER AND TUNDRA

Components	English Specifications (ft. lbs.)	Metric Specifications (Nm)
Automatic Transmission		
ATF temperature sensor to oil cooler elbow	11	15
Detent spring to valve body	7	10
Drain plug to oil pan	15	20
Oil pan to transmission case	65 inch lbs.	7.4
Park/neutral position switch	9	13
Parking lock pawl bracket to transmission case	65 inch lbs.	7.4
Shift solenoid valve and valve body	8	11
Transmission control shaft lever to control rod	9	13
Transmission control shaft lever to park/neutral switch	12	16
Valve body to transmission case	7	10
Vehicle speed sensor lock plate to transfer case	12	16
Vehicle speed sensor to transmission case	48 inch lbs.	5.4
Transfer Case		
Case cover to rear case	27	37
Crossmember to engine rear mounting	74	54
Crossmember to the frame	37	50
Crossmember to transfer case protector	21	28
Filler and drain plug	27	37
Front case to rear case	27	37
Front extension housing to front case	27	37
Front propeller shaft to front differential	59	80
Lever lock pin	9	12
Motor actuator to front case	13	18
Oil pump cover to rear extension housing	43 inch lbs.	4.9
Oil pump plate and rear extension housing	43 inch lbs.	4.9
Oil receiver to front case	9	12
Oil strainer to rear case	43 inch lbs.	4.9
Rear extension housing to rear case	27	37
Rear extension housing to retainer	29	39
Rear propeller shaft to rear differential	78	106
Screw plug to front case	14	19
Screw plug to rear extension housing	22	29
Speed sensor driven gear	8	11
Transfer control shift lever retainer to transmission	14	19
Transfer indicator switch (center diff. lock)	27	37
Transfer indicator switch (low switch)	27	37
Transfer indicator switch (neutral switch)	27	37
Transfer shift lever rod assembly to shift outer lever	10	14
Transfer to front propeller shaft	59	80
Transfer to rear propeller shaft	78	106
Transfer to the transmission	51	69

93167C02

TORQUE SPECIFICATIONS — 4RUNNER AND TACOMA

Components	English Specifications (ft. lbs.)	Metric Specifications (Nm)
Front differential		
(A.D.D.) Actuator-to-(A.D.D.) Clutch case	15	21
(A.D.D.) Clutch case-to-differential	58	78
(A.D.D.) Clutch case-to-differential tube	58	78
(A.D.D.) Switch-to-clutch case cover	30	40
Differential carrier-to-differential tube w/o (A.D.D.)	77	105
Differential carrier-to-side bearing retainer	51	69
Differential front mounting cushion-to-differential	116	157
Differential front mounting cushion-to-frame	101	137
Differential rear mounting cushion-to-differential	80	108
Differential rear mounting cushion-to-frame	64	87
Differential-to-front propeller shaft	54	74
Drain plug	48	65
Drive pinion-to-companion flange	80	108
Filler plug	129	39
Ring gear-to-differential case	71	97
Screw plug-to-(A.D.D.) Actuator	9	13
Screw plug-to-clutch case cover	14	20
Rear differential		
ABS speed sensor-to-axle housing	8.0	71 inch lbs.
Adjusting nut lock-to-bearing cap	13	9
Adjusting nut lock-to-bearing cap	13	9
Axle housing-to-backing plate	68	50
Brake line union nut	15	11
Differential carrier-to-axle housing	25	18
Differential carrier-to-axle housing	73	54
Differential carrier-to-axle housing	25	18
Differential carrier-to-bearing cap	85	63
Differential carrier-to-bearing cap	113	83
Differential carrier-to-bearing cap	78	58
Differential carrier-to-diff. Lock indicator switch	40	31
Differential carrier-to-shaft retainer	24	17
Differential case-to-ring gear	97	71
Differential case-to-ring gear	125	92
Differential case-to-ring gear	97	71
Differential LH case-to-differential RH case	47	35
Differential RH case-to-differential LH case	47	35
Differential-to-propeller shaft	74	56
Differential-to-propeller shaft	74	56
Differential-to-propeller shaft	74	56
Drain plug, filler plug	49	36
Drain plug, filler plug	49	36
Drive pinion-to-companion flange (standard)	108	80
Hub nut	110	83
H-bolt-to-spring seat	123	90
Leaf spring center bolt	44	33
Leaf spring hanger pin bolt-to-frame	157	116
Parking brake cable set bolt 2WD	26	19
Parking brake cable-to-backing plate 2WD	9.3	82 inch lbs.
Shackle pin-to-frame	92	67
Shackle pin-to-leaf spring	92	67
Shock absorber-to-frame 2WD	26	19
Shock absorber-to-frame 4WD	71	53
Shock absorber-to-spring seat 2WD	26	19
Shock absorber-to-spring seat 4WD	71	53
Spring bumper-to-frame 2WD only	29	22

(A.D.D.): Automatic Disconnecting Differential

ABS: Antilock Brake System

93167C03

TORQUE SPECIFICATIONS — T100

Components	English Specifications (ft. lbs.)	Metric Specifications (Nm)
A.D.D. Indicator switch-to-clutch case cover	30	40
ABS speed sensor wire harness	44 inch lbs.	5.0
ABS speed sensor wire harness-to-upper suspension arm	44 inch lbs.	5.0
ABS speed sensor-to-rear axle housing	71 inch lbs.	8.0
ABS speed sensor-to-steering knuckle	71 inch lbs.	8.0
Actuator-to-clutch case cover	15	21
Axle drain plug	36	49
Axle filler plug	29	39
Axle hub bearing lock nut	35	47
Bearing cap-to-differential carrier	83	113
Bracket-to-pump assembly (5VZ-FE engine)	32	43
Brake line	11	15
Carrier cover-to-oil deflector	65 inch lbs.	7.4
Clutch case cover-to-clutch case	15	21
Clutch case-to-differential carrier	500	78
Clutch case-to-tube	58	78
Companion flange-to-front differential assembly	80	108
Compression spring set bolt	69 inch lbs.	7.8
Control shaft lever-to-control shaft assembly	26	35
Control valve housing-to-rack housing	13	18
Control valve shaft-to-intermediate shaft	35	26
Cross shaft adjusting screw set nut (4WD)	46	34
Crossmember-to-frame	93	126
Differential carrier cover-to-differential carrier	34	47
Differential carrier-to-axle housing	54	73
Differential carrier-to-bearing cap	58	78
Differential-to-front propeller shaft	54	74
Differential-to-propeller shaft	56	76
Disc-to-axle hub	47	64
Dust cover-to-steering knuckle	14	19
Flange-to-axle hub	23	31
Flange-to-front drive shaft	13	18
Front drive shaft-to-side gear shaft	61	83
Hub nut	76	103
Idler arm assembly-to-frame	142	105
Idler arm-to-idler arm bracket	78	58
Intermediate shaft-to-control valve assembly (2WD)	26	35
Intermediate shaft-to-worm gear valve assembly (4WD)	26	35
Knuckle stopper bolt lock nut	35	47
Leaf spring center bolt	33	44
Lower ball joint-to-strut bar	55	75
Lower suspension arm shaft nut	152	206
Lower suspension arm-to-frame	145	196
Lower suspension arm-to-lower ball joint	55	75
Lower suspension arm-to-shock absorber	13	18
Lower suspension arm-to-shock absorber (4WD)	101	137
Lower suspension arm-to-stabilizer bar	9	13
Main shaft assembly-to-sliding w/shaft york sub-assembly	26	35
Mount bracket-to-suspension crossmember	88	65
Oil reservoir set bolt front	9	13
Oil seal-to-dust cover	13	18
Parking brake set bolt	19	25
Pitman arm-to-cross shaft	177	130
Pitman arm-to-cross shaft (4WD)	177	130

93167C04

TORQUE SPECIFICATIONS — LAND CRUISER

Components	English Specifications (ft. lbs.)	Metric Specifications (Nm)
ABS speed sensor wire clamp-to-steering knuckle	71 inch lbs.	8.0
ABS speed sensor wire clamp-to-upper suspension arm	71 inch lbs.	8.0
ABS speed sensor-to-steering knuckle	71 inch lbs.	8.0
Axle hub bearing lock nut (w/ Free wheel hub)	203	274
Axle hub-to-disc	47	64
Drive shaft-to-axle hub (w/o Free wheel hub)	174	235
Flexible hose-to-brake caliper	22	30
Free wheel hub body-to-axle hub	23	31
Free wheel hub cover-to-free wheel hub body	7	10
Hub nut	83	110
Lower suspension arm No.3-to-lower ball joint	80	110
Lower suspension arm-to-frame	148	200
Lower suspension arm-to-frame	96	130
Lower suspension arm-to-lower ball joint	103	140
Lower suspension arm-to-lower suspension arm No.3	111	150
Lower suspension arm-to-No.i, No.2 spring bumper	23	31
Lower suspension arm-to-spring bumper	32	43
Lower suspension arm-to-stabilizer bar link	29	39
Lower suspension arm-to-strut bar	111	150
Shock absorber-to-frame	18	25
Stabilizer bar bracket-to-frame	22	29
Steering knuckle-to-brake caliper	80	108
Steering knuckle-to-brake caliper	90	123
Steering knuckle-to-dust cover	74 inch lbs.	8.3
Steering knuckle-to-dust cover	13	18
Steering knuckle-to-knuckle arm	135	183
Steering knuckle-to-lower ball joint	116	160
Steering knuckle-to-lower ball joint	59	80
Steering knuckle-to-upper ball joint	80	110
Strut bar-to-frame	221	300
Tie rod end lock nut	40	54
Tie rod end lock nut	41	55
Tie rod end-to-lower ball joint	53	72
Tie rod end-to-lower ball joint	67	90
Upper suspension arm shaft-to-frame	94	130
Upper suspension arm shaft-to-upper suspension arm	92	125
Upper suspension arm-to-shock absorber	29	39
Upper suspension arm-to-upper ball joint	29	39
Upper suspension arm-to-upper ball joint	80	105

93167C05

8

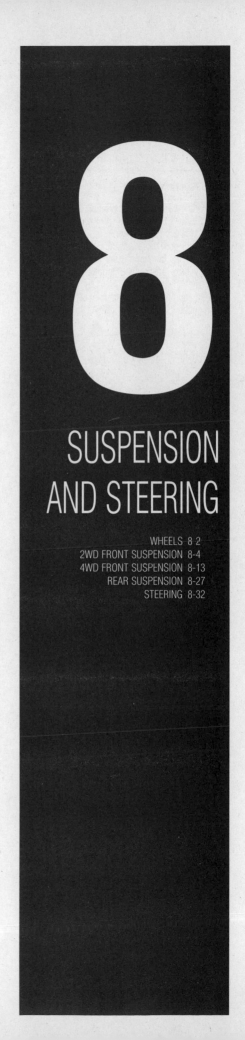

SUSPENSION AND STEERING

WHEELS

Wheels

REMOVAL & INSTALLATION

See Figures 1 thru 7

1. Park the vehicle on a level surface.
2. Remove the jack, tire iron and, if necessary, the spare tire from their storage compartments.
3. Check the owner's manual or refer to General Information and Maintenance for the jacking points on your vehicle. Then, place the jack in the proper position.
4. If equipped with lug nut trim caps, remove them by either unscrewing or pulling them off the lug nuts, as appropriate. Consult the owner's manual, if necessary.

tcca8p00

Fig. 1 Place the jack at the proper lifting point on your vehicle

5. If equipped with a wheel cover or hub cap, insert the tapered end of the tire iron in the groove and pry off the cover.
6. Apply the parking brake and block the diagonally opposite wheel with a wheel chock or two.

➡Wheel chocks may be purchased at your local auto parts store, or a block of wood cut into wedges may be used. If possible, keep one or two of the chocks in your tire storage compartment, in case any of the tires has to be removed on the side of the road.

7. If equipped with an automatic transmission, place the selector lever in **P** or Park; with a manual transmission, place the shifter in Reverse.
8. With the tires still on the ground, use the tire iron/wrench to break the lug nuts loose.

➡If a nut is stuck, never use heat to loosen it or damage to the wheel and bearings may occur. If the nuts are seized, one or two heavy hammer blows directly on the end of the bolt usually loosens the rust. Be careful, as continued pounding will likely damage the brake drum or rotor.

9. Using the jack, raise the vehicle until the tire is clear of the ground. Support the vehicle safely using jackstands.
10. Remove the lug nuts, then remove the tire and wheel assembly.

To install:

11. Make sure the wheel and hub mating surfaces, as well as the wheel lug studs, are clean and free of all foreign material. Always remove rust from the wheel mounting surface and the brake rotor or drum. Failure to do so may cause the lug nuts to loosen in service.
12. Install the tire and wheel assembly and hand-tighten the lug nuts.
13. Using the tire wrench, tighten all the lug nuts, in a crisscross pattern, until they are snug.
14. Raise the vehicle and withdraw the jackstand, then lower the vehicle.
15. Using a torque wrench, tighten the lug nuts in a crisscross pattern, as follows:
    a. 1997 Land Cruiser with steel wheels: 109 ft. lbs. (147 Nm)
    b. 1997 Land Cruiser with aluminum wheels: 76 ft. lbs. (103 Nm)
    c. 1998–00 Land Cruiser: 97 ft. lbs. (131 Nm)
    d. T100: 76 ft. lbs. (103 Nm)
    e. 4Runner, Tacoma & Tundra: 83 ft. lbs. (110 Nm)

WARNING

Do not overtighten the lug nuts, as this may cause the wheel studs to stretch or the brake disc (rotor) to warp.

16. If so equipped, install the wheel cover or hub cap. Make sure the valve stem protrudes through the

tcca8p01

Fig. 2 Before jacking the vehicle, block the diagonally opposite wheel with one or, preferably, two chocks

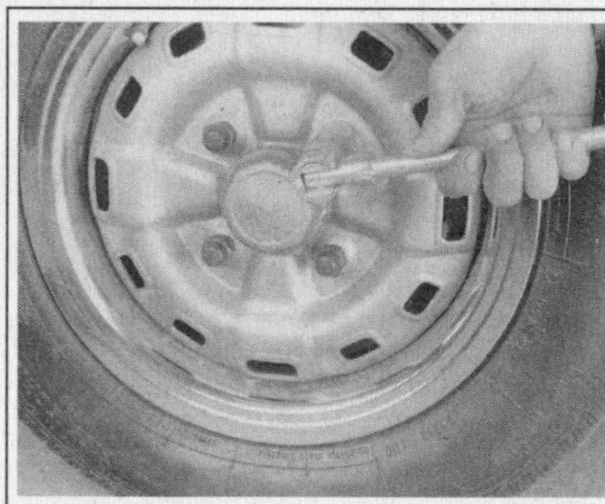

tcca8p02

Fig. 3 With the vehicle still on the ground, break the lug nuts loose using the wrench end of the tire iron

tcca8p03

Fig. 4 After the lug nuts have been loosened, raise the vehicle using the jack until the tire is clear of the ground

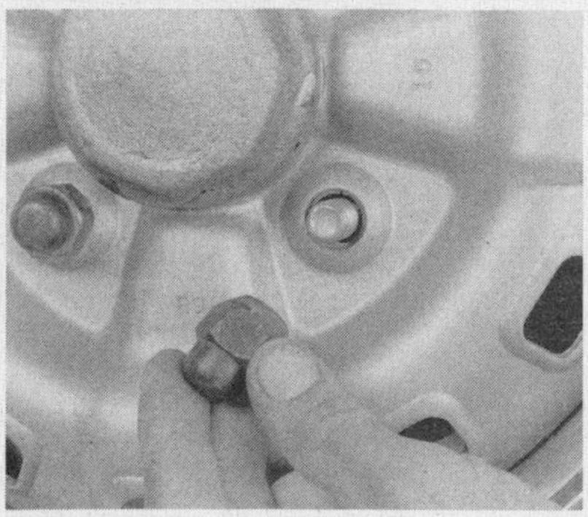

tcca8p04

Fig. 5 Remove the lug nuts from the studs

tcca8p05

Fig. 6 Remove the wheel and tire assembly from the vehicle

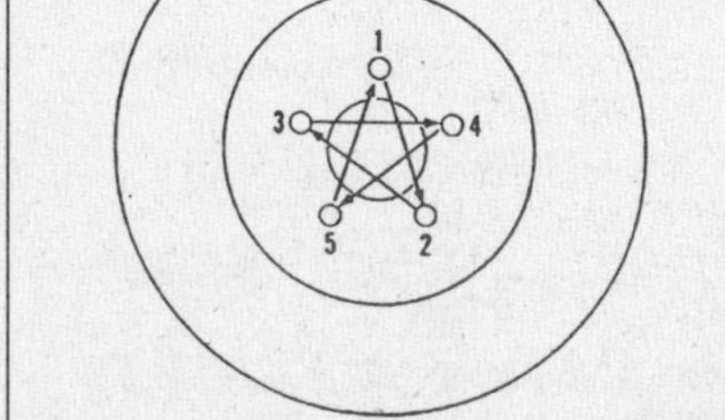

tcca8g04

Fig. 7 Typical wheel lug tightening sequence

proper opening before tapping the wheel cover into position.

17. If equipped, install the lug nut trim caps by pushing them or screwing them on, as applicable.

18. Remove the jack from under the vehicle, and place the jack and tire iron/wrench in their storage compartments. Remove the wheel chock(s).

19. If you have removed a flat or damaged tire, place it in the storage compartment of the vehicle and take it to your local repair station to have it fixed or replaced as soon as possible.

INSPECTION

Inspect the tires for lacerations, puncture marks, nails and other sharp objects. Repair or replace as necessary. Also check the tires for treadwear and air pressure as outlined in Section 1 of this manual.

Check the wheel assemblies for dents, cracks, rust and metal fatigue. Repair or replace as necessary.

Wheel Lug Studs

REMOVAL & INSTALLATION

With Disc Brakes

➧ **See Figures 8, 9, 10, 11, and 12**

1. Raise and support the appropriate end of the vehicle safely using jackstands, then remove the wheel.
2. Remove the brake pads and caliper. Support the caliper aside using wire or a coat hanger. For additional information, please refer to the following topic(s): Brakes, Caliper and Brake Pads.
3. Remove the outer wheel bearing and lift off the rotor.
4. Properly support the rotor using press bars, then drive the stud out using an arbor press.

➥If a press is not available, CAREFULLY drive the old stud out using a blunt drift. MAKE SURE the rotor is properly and evenly supported or it may be damaged.

To install:

5. Clean the stud hole with a wire brush and start the new stud with a hammer and drift pin. Do not use any lubricant or thread sealer.
6. Finish installing the stud with the press.

➥If a press is not available, start the lug stud through the bore in the hub, then position about 4 flat washers over the stud and thread the lug nut. Hold the hub/rotor while tightening the lug nut, and the stud should be drawn into position. MAKE SURE THE STUD IS FULLY SEATED, then remove the lug nut and washers.

7. Install the rotor and adjust the wheel bearings.
8. Install the brake caliper and pads.
9. Install the wheel, then remove the jackstands and carefully lower the vehicle.
10. Tighten the lug nuts to the proper torque.

With Drum Brakes

➧ **See Figures 13, 14, and 15**

1. Raise the vehicle and safely support it with jackstands, then remove the wheel.

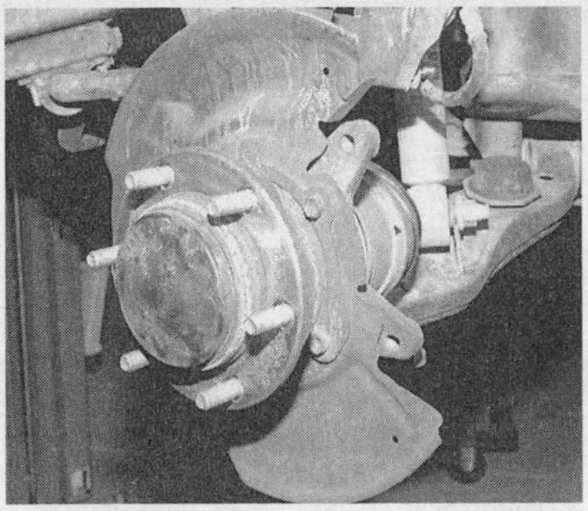

93168p07

Fig. 8 Typical Toyota hub

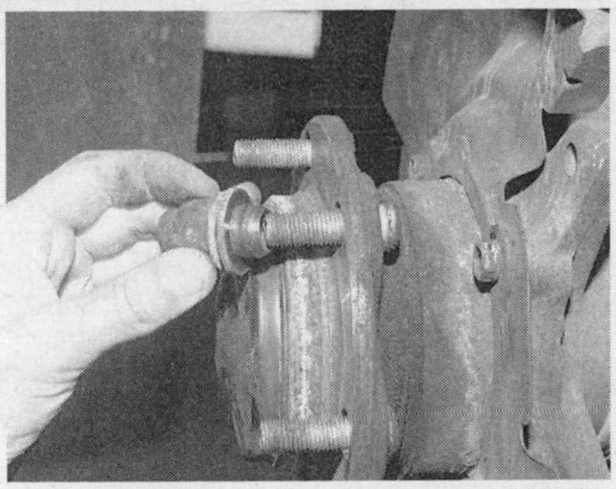

93168p10

Fig. 9 Thread a lug nut over the stud to be removed

93168p08

Fig. 10 Use a hammer to drive the stud out of the hub

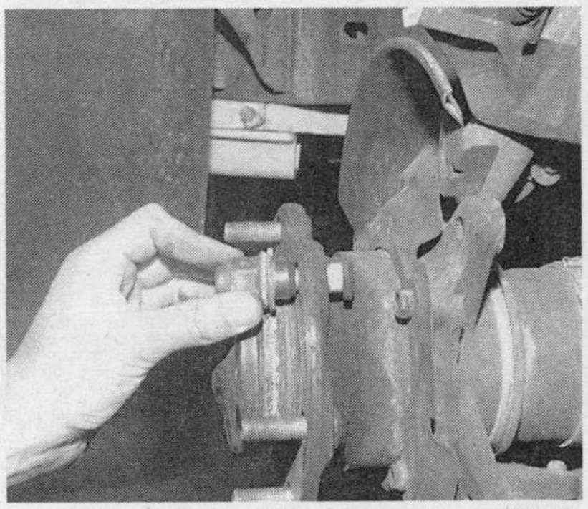

93168p09

Fig. 11 Remove the lug nut . . .

93168p11

Fig. 12 . . . and then pull the stud out from the rear

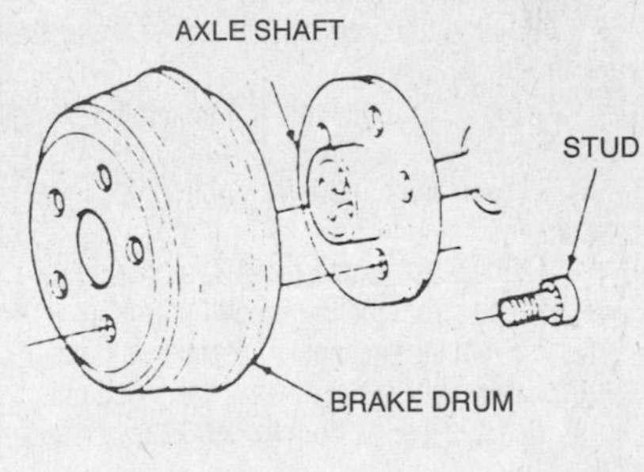

tcca8g08

Fig. 13 Exploded view of the drum, axle flange and stud

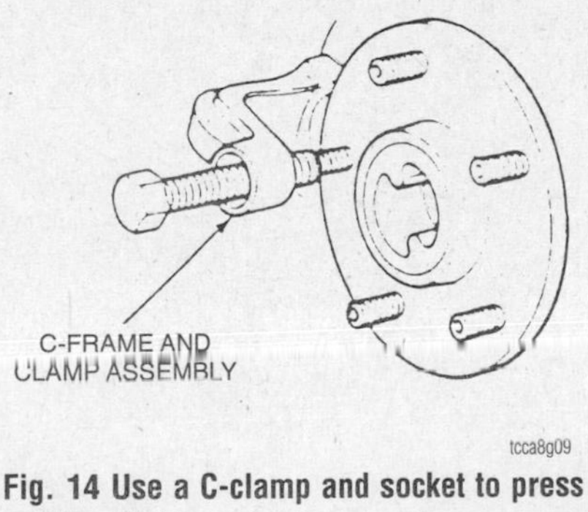

tcca8g09

Fig. 14 Use a C-clamp and socket to press out the stud

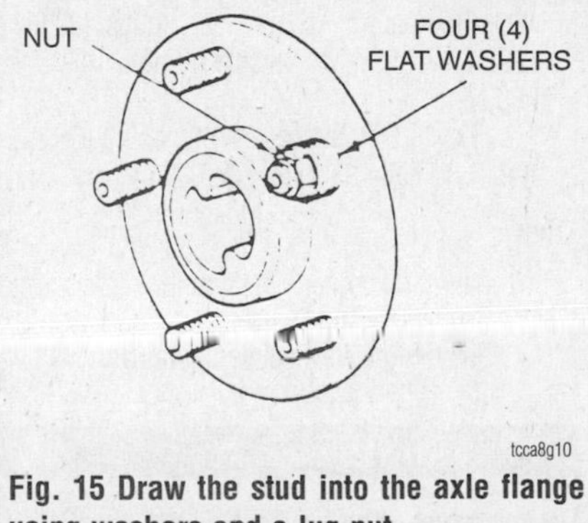

tcca8g10

Fig. 15 Draw the stud into the axle flange using washers and a lug nut

2. Remove the brake drum.
3. If necessary to provide clearance, remove the brake shoes. For additional information, please refer to the following topic(s): Brakes, Brake Shoes.
4. Using a large C-clamp and socket, press the stud from the axle flange.
5. Coat the serrated part of the stud with liquid soap and place it into the hole.

To install:

6. Position about 4 flat washers over the stud and thread the lug nut. Hold the flange while tightening the lug nut, and the stud should be drawn into position. MAKE SURE THE STUD IS FULLY SEATED, then remove the lug nut and washers.
7. If applicable, install the brake shoes.
8. Install the brake drum.
9. Install the wheel, then remove the jackstands and carefully lower the vehicle.
10. Tighten the lug nuts to the proper torque.

2WD FRONT SUSPENSION

After you work on your truck's suspension, it is advisable to have the alignment checked at a reputable repair facility. This will ensure that the front end is in order after repairs.

Coil Spring

REMOVAL & INSTALLATION

4Runner

Please refer to the procedure for 4 Wheel Drive (4WD) vehicles.

Tacoma

1. Raise and properly support the vehicle.
2. Remove the front wheel.
3. Detach the shock absorber lower mount by removing the two bolts.
4. Remove the retainer nut, retainer, cushion and shock absorber.
5. Detach the cushion retainer from the shock absorber.
6. Compress the coil spring with a commercially available spring compressor.
7. Detach the stabilizer bar.
8. Support the upper suspension arm and steering knuckle securely.
9. Remove the cotter pin from the lower balljoint nut.
10. Loosen and remove the nut from the lower balljoint.
11. Using a ball joint removal tool, detach the lower ball joint from the lower control arm.
12. Loosen the suspension arm set bolt.
13. Remove the suspension arm set bolt nut.
14. Remove the nut from the strut bar front set bolt.
15. Pull out both set bolts.
16. Remove the lower suspension arm and coil spring.

To install:

17. Installation is the reverse of removal. Note the following torque specifications:
    a. Strut bar front set bolt: 221 ft. lbs. (300 Nm)
    b. Lower suspension arm set bolt: 148 ft. lbs. (200 Nm)
    c. Lower ball joint nut: 80 ft. lbs. (110 Nm)
    d. Lug nuts: 83 ft. lbs. (110 Nm).

Tundra

1. Raise and properly support the vehicle.
2. Remove the front wheel.
3. Remove the shock absorber nut and washer from the lower control arm.

⁂ WARNING

Do not remove the bolt at this time.

4. While slowly lowering the front suspension, remove the lower bolt from the shock absorber assembly.
5. Support the shock absorber assembly.
6. Remove the three nuts from the top of the shock tower.
7. Lower the assembly out of the wheel well.
8. Remove the coil spring by compressing the spring with a commercially available spring compressor.
9. Compress the coil spring until it is clear of the shock assembly at both ends.
10. Remove the center nut from the shock.
11. Detach the retainers, cushions, suspension support and coil spring.

To install:

12. Compress the coil spring.
13. Install the coil spring on to the shock absorber.

➡Fit the lower end of the coil spring into the gap of the spring seat of the shock absorber.

14. Install the cushions, retainers, and suspension support to the rod.
15. Install and snug the center nut of the shock.
16. Align the top of the assembly so that two (2) of the bolts are parallel with the direction of the lower shock bushing.
17. Remove the spring compressor.
18. Torque the center nut to 22 ft. lbs. (29Nm).
19. The remainder is the reverse of removal. Please note the following torque specifications:
    - Torque the 3 upper mount to body nuts: 47 ft. lbs. (64 Nm).
    - Torque the lower shock absorber mounting bolt to 101 ft. lbs. (135 Nm).
    - Wheel lug nuts: 83 ft. lbs. (110 Nm).

Torsion Bar

REMOVAL & INSTALLATION

T100

➧ See Figures 16, 17, 18, and 19

1. Raise and properly support the vehicle.

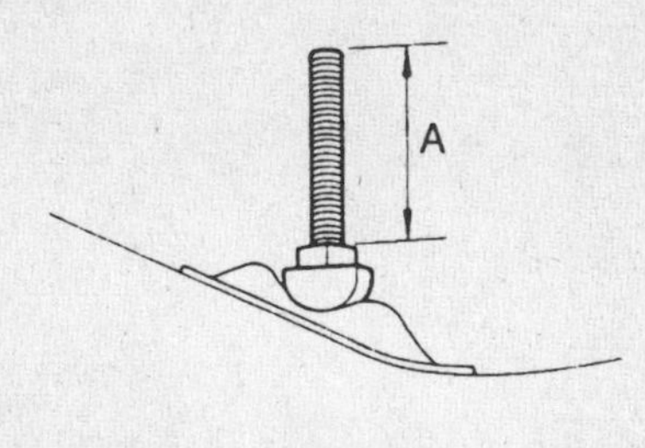

93168g10

Fig. 16 Measure the length of the threaded bolt end and use the measurement as a reference when installing the torsion bar

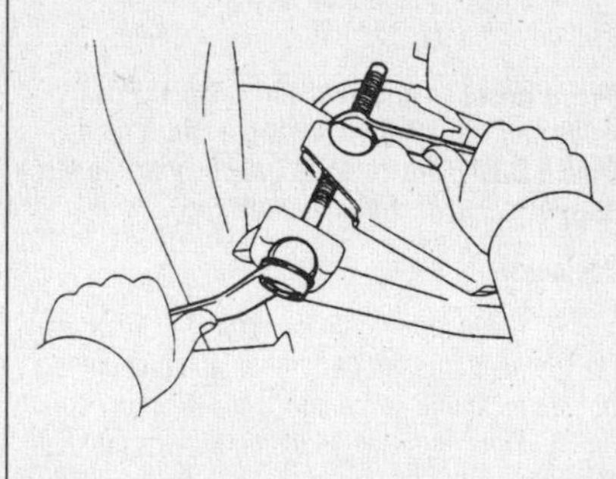

93168g11

Fig. 17 Loosing the adjuster nut and anchor arm

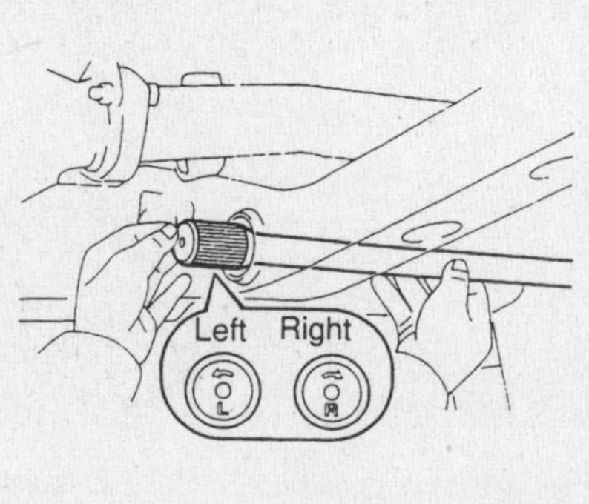

93168g12

Fig. 18 Removing the torsion bar spring

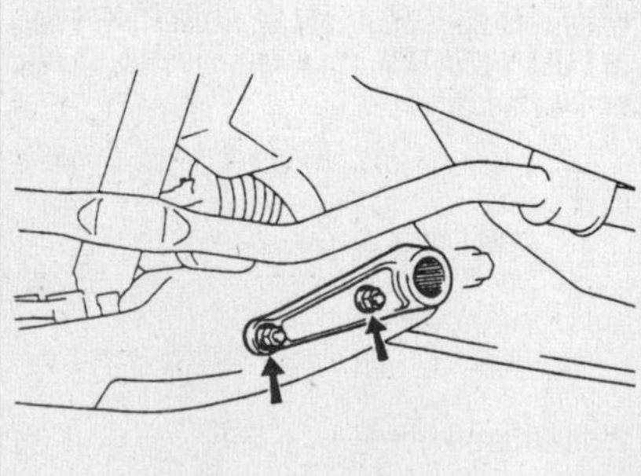

93168g13

Fig. 19 Unfasten the torque arm mounting bolts

2. Remove the front wheel.
3. Measure the length of the threaded bolt end. Use this measurement as a reference during installation.
4. Loosen the adjusting nut and remove the anchor arm.
5. Remove the torsion bar spring only after all tension has been removed from it.
6. Remove the torque arm.

To install:

7. Installation is the reverse of removal. Please note the following torque specifications:
   - Torque arm bolts: 64 ft. lbs. (87 Nm)
   - Lug nuts: 76 ft. lbs. (103 Nm)

Shock Absorbers

REMOVAL & INSTALLATION

T100

1. Raise and properly support the vehicle.
2. Remove the front wheel.
3. Detach the shock absorber lower mount by removing the two bolts.
4. Remove the retainer nut, retainer, cushion and shock absorber.
5. Detach the cushion retainer from the shock absorber.
6. Remove the shock absorber assembly.

To install:

7. Installation is the reverse of removal. Note the following torque specifications:
   - Lower shock bolt: 101 ft. lbs. (135 Nm)
   - Upper mounting nuts: 47 ft. lbs. (64 Nm)

TESTING

See Figure 20

The purpose of the shock absorber is simply to limit the motion of the spring during compression and rebound cycles. If the vehicle is not equipped with these motion dampers, the up and down motion would multiply until the vehicle was alternately trying to leap off the ground and to pound itself into the pavement.

Contrary to popular rumor, the shocks do not affect the ride height of the vehicle. This is controlled by other suspension components such as springs and tires. Worn shock absorbers can affect handling; if the front of the vehicle is rising or falling excessively, the "footprint" of the tires changes on the pavement and steering is affected.

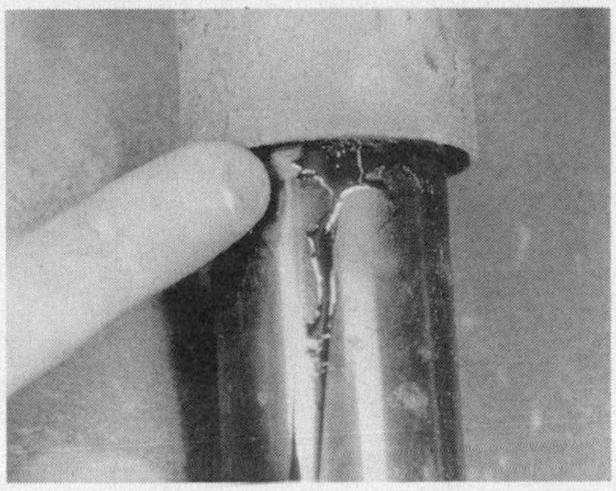

tcca8p73

Fig. 20 When fluid is seeping out of the shock absorber, it's time to replace it

The simplest test of the shock absorber is simply push down on one corner of the unladen vehicle and release it. Observe the motion of the body as it is released. In most cases, it will come up beyond it original rest position, dip back below it and settle quickly to rest. This shows that the damper is controlling the spring action. Any tendency to excessive pitch (up-and-down) motion or failure to return to rest within 2-3 cycles is a sign of poor function within the shock absorber. Oil-filled shocks may have a light film of oil around the seal, resulting from normal breathing and air exchange. This should NOT be taken as a sign of failure, but any sign of thick or running oil definitely indicates failure. Gas filled shocks may also show some film at the shaft; if the gas has leaked out, the shock will have almost no resistance to motion.

While each shock absorber can be replaced individually, it is recommended that they be changed as a pair (both front or both rear) to maintain equal response on both sides of the vehicle. Chances are quite good that if one has failed, its mate is weak also.

Shock Absorber/Coil Spring Assembly

REMOVAL & INSTALLATION

Tacoma, Tundra, 4 Runner and Pre Runner

See Figures 21, 22, 23, and 24

1. Raise and properly support the vehicle.
2. Remove the front wheel.
3. Remove the shock absorber nut and washer from the lower control arm.

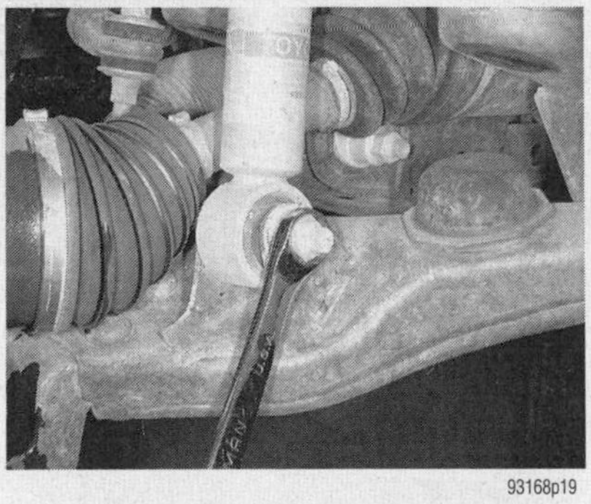

93168p19

Fig. 21 Use a closed end wrench to remove the lower shock mounting nut and bolt

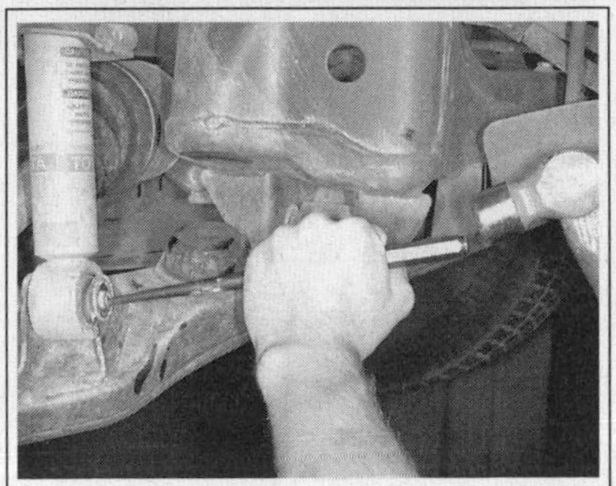

93168p22

Fig. 23 Use a punch and a small hammer to knock the bolt through the lower strut mount

WARNING

Do not remove the bolt at this time.

4. While slowly lowering the front suspension, remove the lower bolt from the shock absorber assembly.
5. Support the shock.
6. Remove the three nuts from the top of the shock tower.
7. Lower the assembly out of the wheel well.

To install:

8. The remainder of installation is the reverse of removal. Please note the following torque specifications:
   - 3 upper mount to body nuts: 47 ft. lbs. (64 Nm)
   - Lower shock absorber mounting bolt: 101 ft. lbs. (135 Nm)
   - Wheel lug nuts: 83 ft. lbs. (110 Nm)

Upper Ball Joint

INSPECTION

See Figure 25

1. Flip the ball joint stud back and forth 5 times.
2. Install the nut.
3. Turn the nut, with a torque wrench, one turn (continuously) each 2–4 seconds.
4. Take the torque reading on the 5th turn.

93168p21

Fig. 22 Nut, washer, and bolt

93168p23

Fig. 24 Removing the lower strut mounting bolt

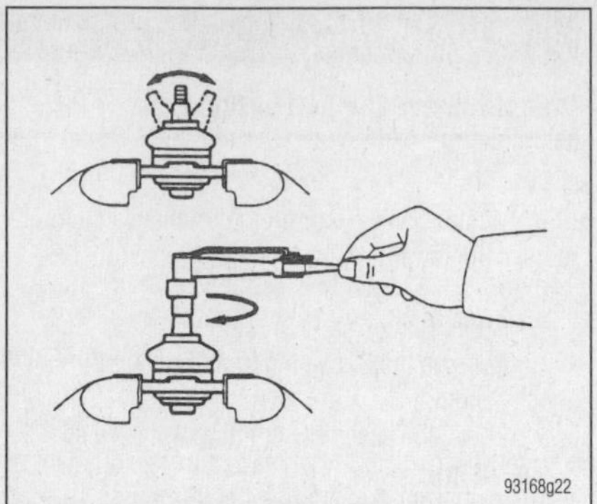

Fig. 25 Use a torque wrench to check the ball joint

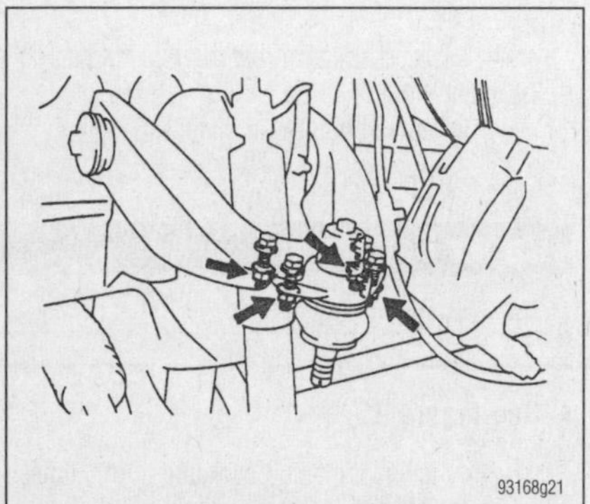

Fig. 26 Remove the four (4) bolts from the upper ball joint

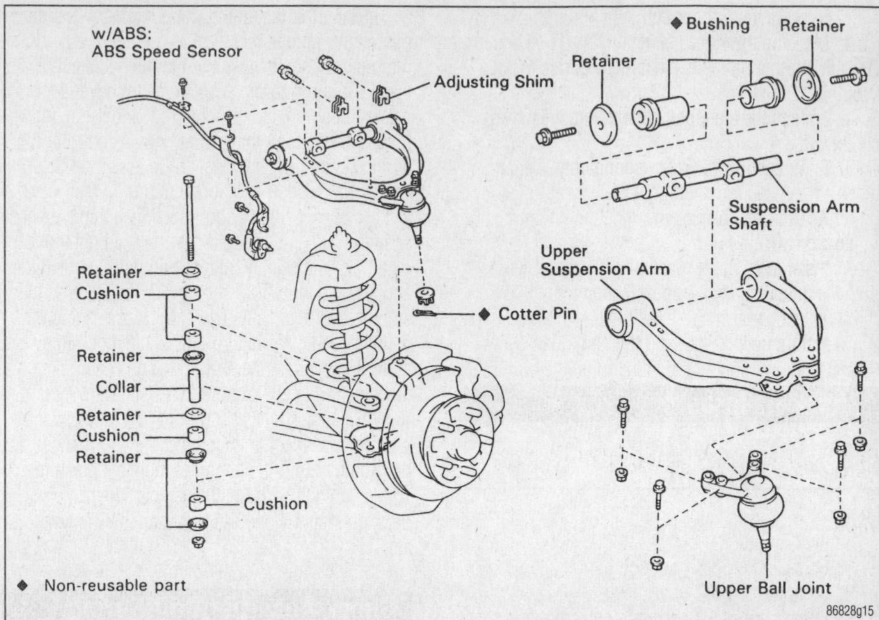

Fig. 27 Exploded view of the upper ball joint and associated components—Tacoma shown

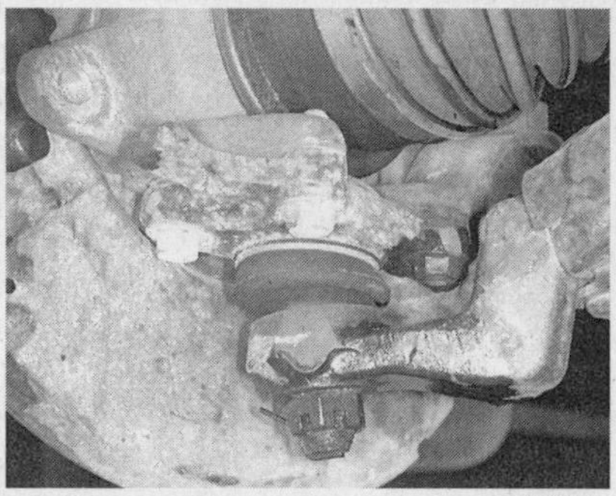

Fig. 28 Inspect the lower ball joint dust boot for cracks

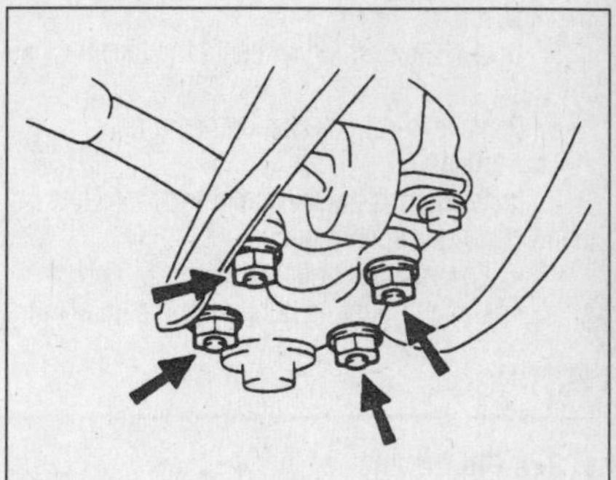

Fig. 29 Remove the four (4) mounting bolts from the lower ball joint

5. Turning torque should be 6–39 inch lbs. (0.7–4.4 Nm).

REMOVAL & INSTALLATION

T100

➧ See Figure 26

1. Raise and support the vehicle on jackstands.
2. Remove the front tire and wheel assembly.
3. Detach the steering knuckle.
4. Remove 4 nuts and bolts from the upper ball joint.
5. Remove the upper ball joint from the suspension arm.
6. Installation is the reverse of removal.

4Runner

Please refer to the procedure for 4 Wheel Drive (4WD) vehicles.

Tacoma and Tundra

➧ See Figure 27

1. Remove the front wheel.
2. Remove the steering knuckle with the axle hub.
3. Separate the upper ball joint as follows:
   a. Remove the wire and boot.
   b. Using a snapring expander, remove the snapring.
   c. With a ball joint remover and a deep socket, remove the upper ball joint.

To install:

4. With the aid of the ball joint installer and a socket wrench, install the ball joint.
5. Using a snapring expander, install a new snapring.
6. Apply multi-purpose grease, then install a new boot. Fix it with a new wire.
7. Install the steering knuckle with the axle hub.
8. Install the front wheel, lower the vehicle and tighten the lug nuts.
9. Have the alignment checked at a reputable repair facility.

Lower Ball Joint

INSPECTION

➧ See Figure 28

To check the lower ball joint for wear, jack up the front of the vehicle and support it with stands. Remove excess play from the other suspension parts (wheel bearings, tie rods, etc.). Have an assistant press the brake pedal; Move the lower suspension arm up and down, checking that the lower ball joint has minimal play, if any. The maximum allowable vertical play is 0.079 in. (2.3mm). If the play is greater, replace the ball joint. The upper ball joint is subject to the same limit on trucks; the 4Runner upper ball joint must have no play at all. The upper ball joint is tested by moving the wheel and tire up and down.

REMOVAL & INSTALLATION

Tundra

➧ See Figure 29

1. Raise and support the vehicle on jack stands.
2. Remove the front wheel.
3. Detach the steering knuckle.
4. Remove the 4 bolts to the lower ball joint.
5. Remove the lower ball joint.
6. Installation is the reverse of removal.

4Runner and Tacoma

1. Raise and properly support the vehicle with jackstands.
2. Remove the front wheel.
3. Detach the tie rod end.
4. Support the lower control arm with a suitable jack.
5. On the lower ball joint, separate the tie rod end from the steering knuckle. Throw out the old cotter pin.

6. Remove the cotter pin and nut from the lower ball joint. Discard the cotter pin.
7. With a ball joint remover, separate the ball joint from the lower control arm.
8. Remove the 4 bolts that mount the lower ball joint to the lower control arm.
9. While lifting up the upper control arm, remove the lower ball joint.
10. Securely support the upper control arm and steering knuckle.

To install:

11. Install the ball joint with the mounting nuts and bolts.
12. Tighten the nut to 80 ft. lbs. (108 Nm) on the Tacoma or to 105 ft. lbs. (142 Nm) on the 4Runner. Install a new cotter pin in the hole.
13. Attach the tie rod end tightening the nut to 53 ft. lbs. (72 Nm) on the Tacoma or to 66 ft. lbs. (90 Nm) on the 4Runner.
14. Install a new cotter pin.
15. Tighten the lower ball joint set bolts to 116 ft. lbs. (160 Nm) on the Tacoma or to 59 ft. lbs. (80 Nm) on 4Runner.
16. Remove the jack slowly, making sure everything is secure and in place.
17. Install the wheel, lower the vehicle and tighten the lug nuts.
18. Check the ABS speed sensor signal and front wheel alignment.

T100

1. Raise the vehicle and support it with jackstands.
2. Remove the front wheel.
3. Support the lower control arm with a floor jack and remove the steering knuckle.
4. Loosen the mounting bolts and remove the lower ball joint from the lower control arm.

To install:

5. Attach the lower ball joint and tighten the nut to 55 ft. lbs. (75 Nm).
6. Install the steering knuckle.
7. Install the wheels and lower the truck.
8. Check the ABS speed sensor signal and front wheel alignment.

Strut Bar

REMOVAL & INSTALLATION

T100

1. Remove the wheels, raise the truck and support it on safety stands.
2. On some models it will be necessary to remove the engine undercover.
3. Paint matchmarks on the strut bar and retaining nut.
4. Remove the retaining nut from the front of the bar.
5. Remove the nuts holding the bar to the lower control arm and lift out the strut bar.

To install:

6. Position the bar and install the front nut so that the matchmarks line up.
7. Slide the washer and bushing onto the bar and install it to the bracket at the rear.
8. Install the collar, bushing and washer to the other side and then connect the rear of the bar to the control arm. Tighten the mounting nut to 55 ft. lbs. (75 Nm).
9. Lower the truck and bounce it several times to set the suspension.
10. Tighten the front nut to 90 ft. lbs. (123 Nm) and check the alignment.

Tacoma

➧ See Figure 30

1. Remove the front wheel.
2. Remove the shock absorber.
3. Compress the spring using a spring compressor, according to the tool manufacturer's instructions.
4. Disconnect the stabilizer bar as follows:
   a. Remove the nut and stabilizer bar link from the lower control arm.
   b. Remove the 2 stabilizer bar bracket set bolts.
5. Remove the lower control arm and strut bar as follows:
   a. Support the upper control arm and steering knuckle securely.
   b. Support the upper control arm and steering knuckle assembly.
   c. Remove the cotter pin and nut.
   d. Using a ball joint extractor, disconnect the lower ball joint from the lower control arm.
   e. Loosen the lower control arm set bolt and remove the nut.
   f. Loosen the strut bar front set bolt, then remove the nut.
   g. Pull out the bolts and remove the lower control arm along with the strut bar.

To install:

6. Install the lower control arm and strut bar as follows:
   a. Attach the strut bar front set bolt, tighten to 221 ft. lbs. (300 Nm) make sure the suspension is stabilized prior to tightening the bolt.
   b. Install the lower control arm set bolt and nut, tighten to 148 ft. lbs. (200 Nm). Make sure the suspension is stabilized prior to tightening the bolt.
   c. Install the lower ball joint with a ball joint installer tool. Install the nut and cotter pin. Tighten the nut to 80 ft. lbs. (110 Nm).
7. Attach the stabilizer bar bracket set bolts, tighten to 22 ft. lbs. (29 Nm).
8. Install the stabilizer link to the lower control arm, tighten to 29 ft. lbs. (39 Nm).

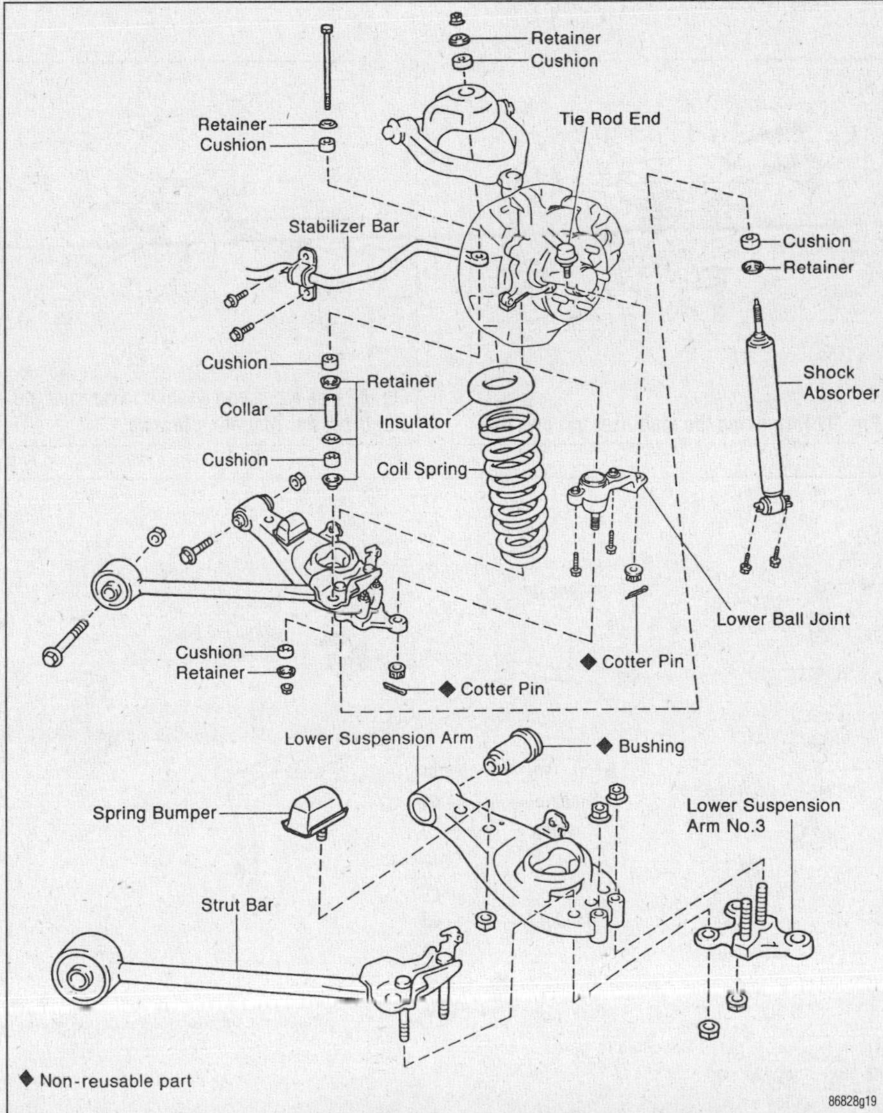

Fig. 30 Exploded view of the strut bar and associated components—Tacoma

9. Remove the spring compressing tool.
10. Install the shock absorber.
11. Install the wheel, lower the truck and tighten the lug nuts.
12. Have the alignment checked at a reputable repair facility.

Stabilizer (Sway) Bar

REMOVAL & INSTALLATION

T100

➧ **See Figures 31 and 32**

1. Raise and support the vehicle on jackstands.
2. Remove the front wheel.
3. Loosen and remove the nut, three retainers, and two cushions from the stabilizer bar end link.
4. Lower the stabilizer bar from the lower suspension arm.
5. Remove the nut, cushions, retainers and detach the stabilizer bar.
6. Repeat the same steps to remove the stabilizer bar from the other side of the vehicle.
7. Remove the 4 bolts, brackets, bushings, and then remove the stabilizer bar from the vehicle.

To install:

8. Installation is the reverse of removal.
9. Torque the stabilizer bar bracket bolts to 22 ft. lbs. (30 Nm).
10. Torque the end link bolts and nuts to 9 ft. lbs. (13 Nm).

Tacoma and Tundra

1. Remove the front wheels.
2. Hold the bolt with a wrench, then remove the nut, retainer, collar and cushion from the lower control arm.
3. Remove the bolts and stabilizer bar with the cushions and brackets.
4. Remove the brackets and cushions from the stabilizer bar.

To install:

5. Install the cushions to the inside of the paint mark. Attach the bar with the brackets, tighten the bracket bolts to 22 ft. lbs. (29 Nm).
6. Tighten the nut holding the lower control arm components to 29 ft. lbs. (39 Nm).
7. Install the wheel, lower the vehicle.
8. Tighten the lug nuts.
9. Have the alignment checked at a reputable repair facility.

4Runner

➧ **See Figure 33**

1. Remove the front wheels.
2. Disconnect the stabilizer bar links as follows:
   a. Remove the nuts and disconnect the stabilizer bar links from the lower control arm.
   b. Hold the link with a wrench, then remove the nut, retainers, cushions and link.
3. Remove the bolts and stabilizer bar with cushions and brackets.

To install:

4. Place the stabilizer bar into position, then install the both bar cushions and brackets to the frame. Temporarily install the bolts. Tighten to 19–22 ft. lbs. (25–29 Nm).
5. Hold the stabilizer bar link with a wrench, then install the link onto the lower control arm with a new nut. Tighten the nut to 14–19 ft. lbs. (19–25 Nm).
6. Using a hexagon wrench, connect the stabilizer bar on both sides to the links with new nuts, tighten to 55–70 ft. lbs. (69–95 Nm).
7. Install the front wheels.
8. Have the alignment checked at a reputable repair facility.

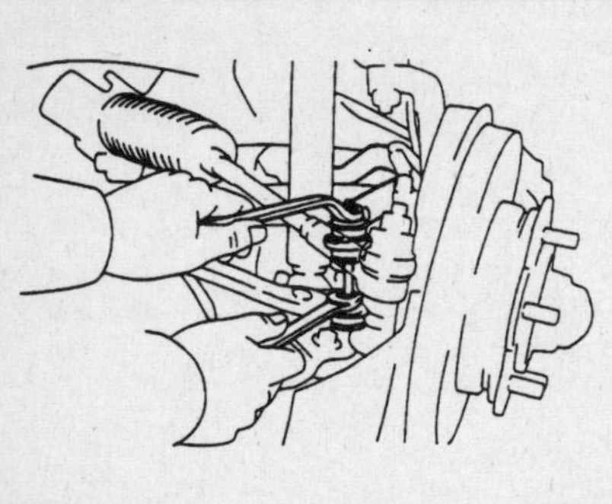

Fig. 31 Removing the stabilizer bar end link

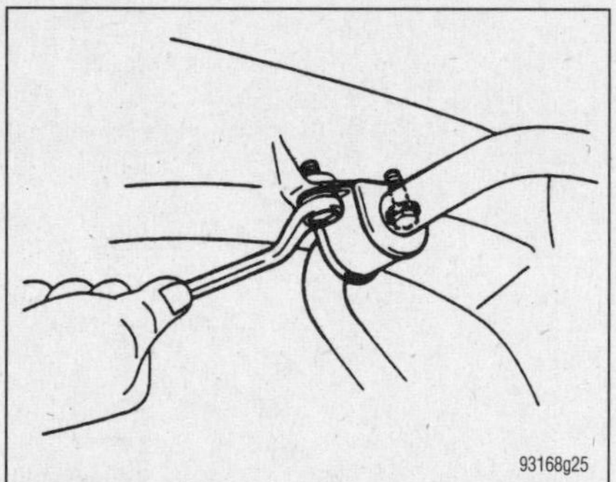

Fig. 32 Use a box end wrench to remove the stabilizer bar mounting bracket

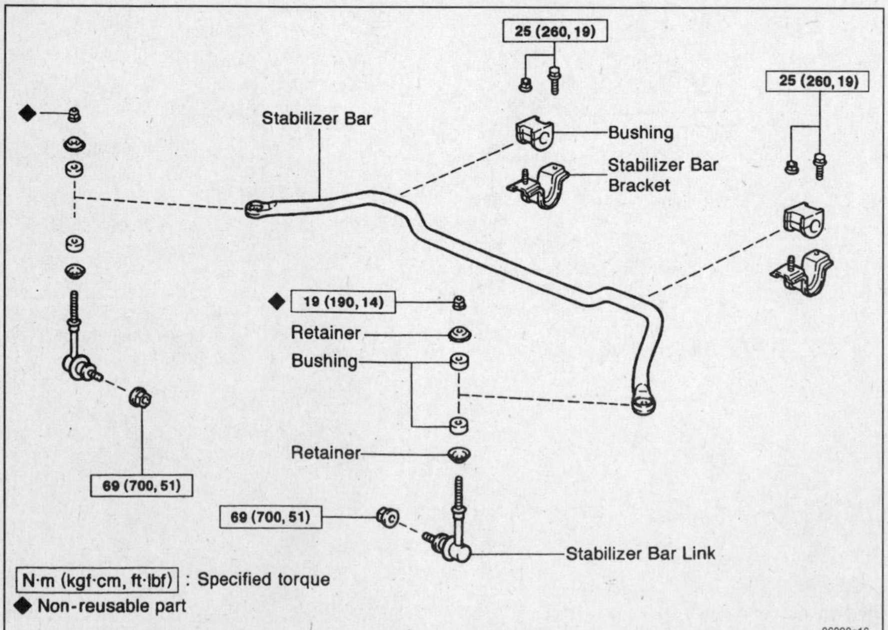

Fig. 33 Exploded view of the front stabilizer bar components—4Runner shown

Upper Control Arm

REMOVAL & INSTALLATION

Tacoma and Tundra

1. Raise and support the vehicle.
2. Remove the front wheel.
3. On the Tundra, remove the fender apron seal to gain better access to the upper control arm.
4. Removed the ABS speed sensor and wire harness.
5. On the Tundra, remove the brake and fuel line clamp.
6. Remove the stabilizer bar link.
7. Disconnect the steering knuckle from the upper bar joint.
8. Loosen the 2 bolts, then remove the front and rear alignment adjusting shims.
9. Make note of the number and thickness of the front and rear shims.
10. Unbolt the upper control arm.
11. Remove the bolts, nuts and upper ball joint from the arm.

To install:

12. Attach the ball joint to the arm, tighten to 29 ft. lbs. (39 Nm).

➡Do not lose the camber adjusting shims. Record the position and thickness of the camber shims so that these can be reinstalled to their original locations. Install the equal number and thickness of shims into their locations.

13. Install the arm to the vehicle, with the shims, then tighten the mounting bolts to 94 ft. lbs. (130 Nm).
14. Attach the steering knuckle to the upper ball joint.
15. Install the stabilizer bar link.
16. Install the ABS speed sensor and wire harness.
17. Place the wheel into position, hand tighten the lug nuts.

18. Lower the vehicle, tighten the lug nuts to 83 ft. lbs. (110 Nm).
19. Have the alignment checked at a reputable repair facility.

T100

1. Raise and support the vehicle.
2. Remove the front wheel(s).
3. Remove the front brake caliper.
4. On models with ABS, disconnect the ABS speed sensor wire from the upper control arm.
5. Support the lower control arm with a jack. Remove the nuts and disconnect ball joint from the upper control arm.
6. Remove the bolts and camber adjusting shims.
7. Remove the upper control arm.

➡Do not lose the camber adjusting shims. Record the position and thickness of the camber shims so that these can be reinstalled to their original locations. Install the equal number and thickness of shims into their locations.

To install:

8. Attach the upper control arm with the shims in there correct positions.
9. Tighten the bolts to 71 ft. lbs. (96 Nm).
10. Install the nuts to the upper control arm, tighten to 23 ft. lbs. (31 Nm).
11. Attach the ABS speed sensor and harness to the upper control arm.
12. Install the brake caliper.
13. Install the wheel, lower the vehicle.
14. Tighten the lug nuts to 76 ft. lbs. (103 Nm).
15. Bleed the brake system.
16. Have the alignment checked at a reputable repair facility.

CONTROL ARM BUSHING REPLACEMENT

➧ See Figures 34 and 35

1. Use a chisel and hammer to pry up the flange of the bushing.
2. Use a press to remove the bushing.

To install:

3. Install the bushing with a press.
4. Make sure that the bushing is fully seated against the control arm.

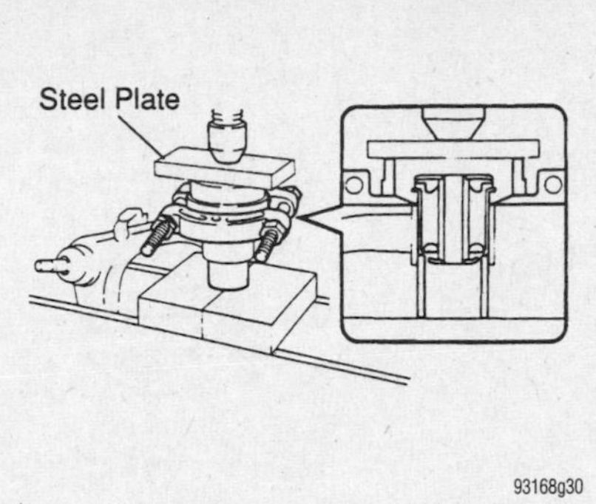

Fig. 34 Using a press to remove the control arm bushing

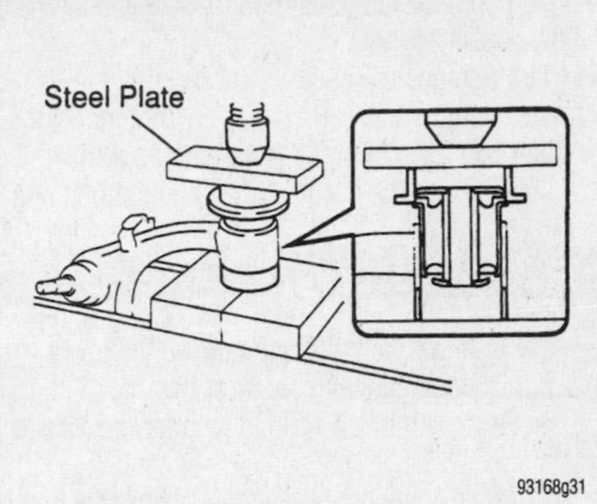

Fig. 35 Using a steel plate to press in the new control arm bushing

Lower Control Arm

REMOVAL & INSTALLATION

T100

➧ See Figure 36

1. Remove the front wheel.
2. Detach the engine undercover.
3. Remove the torsion bar spring.
4. Remove the shock from the lower control arm.
5. Disconnect the stabilizer bar from the lower control arm.
6. Remove the strut bar from the lower control arm.
7. Detach the lower ball joint from the lower control arm.
8. Remove nut from the mounting bolt to the lower control arm and then pull out the bolt(s).

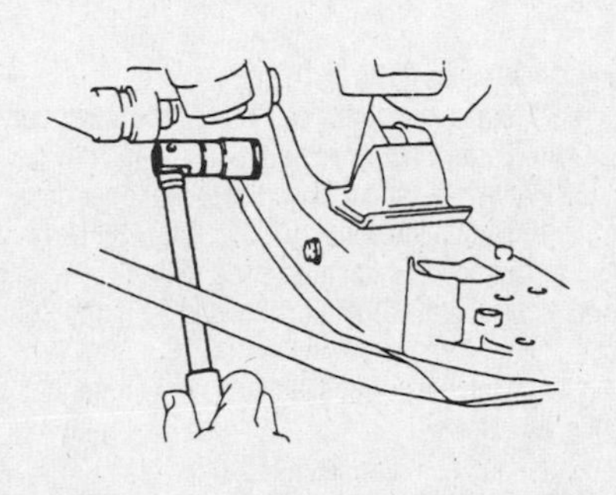

Fig. 36 Lower control arm mounting bolt

9. Remove the lower control arm from the vehicle.

To install:

10. Attach the lower control arm but do not tighten yet.
11. Attach the lower ball joint, strut bar and stabilizer bar to the control arm.
12. Tighten the lower control arm bolt to 152 ft. lbs. (206 Nm).
13. Install the shock to the control arm.
14. Attach the torsion spring bar.
15. Install the engine undercover.
16. Install the wheel, lower the truck and tighten the lug nuts to 76 ft. lbs. (103 Nm).
17. Have the alignment checked at a reputable repair facility.

4Runner

➧ See Figure 37

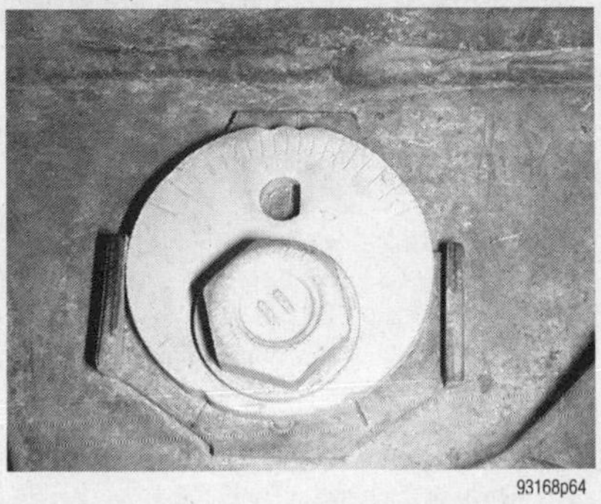

Fig. 37 Lower control arm camber adjusting cam

1. Remove the front wheel.
2. Remove the steering gear assembly.
3. Disconnect the stabilizer bar link.
4. Unbolt the shock absorber from the lower control arm.
5. Support the upper control arm and the steering knuckle securely.
6. Remove the cotter pin and nut from the lower ball joint.
7. Using a ball joint remover, disconnect the lower ball joint from the control arm.
8. Place matchmarks on the front and rear adjusting cams. Remove the bolts, nuts, adjusting cams and lower control arm.
9. Using tool SST 09922–10010 or equivalent, remove the 2 spring bumpers.
10. Install in the reverse order. Tighten the spring bumpers to 17 ft. lbs. (23 Nm), the lower control arm to 96 ft. lbs. (130 Nm), and the lower ball joint nut to 105 ft. lbs. (142 Nm).

Tacoma

➧ See Figure 38

1. Remove the front wheel.
2. Remove the shock absorber.
3. Compress the spring using a spring compressor, following the manufacturer's instructions.
4. Disconnect the stabilizer bar as follows:
   a. Remove the nut and stabilizer bar link from the lower control arm.
   b. Remove the 2 stabilizer bar bracket set bolts.
5. Remove the lower control arm and strut bar as follows:

➡Be sure to support the upper control arm and steering knuckle securely.

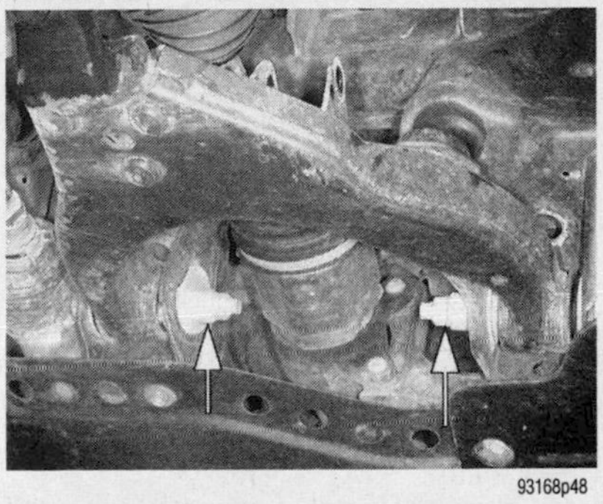

Fig. 38 Lower control arm bolts

a. Support the upper control arm and steering knuckle assembly.
b. Remove the cotter pin and nut.
c. Using a ball joint extractor, disconnect the lower ball joint from the lower control arm.
d. Loosen the lower control arm set bolt and remove the nut.
e. Loosen the strut bar front set bolt, then remove the nut.
f. Pull out the bolts and remove the lower control arm along with the strut bar.
6. Remove the coil spring compressor tool and coil.
7. Remove the nuts and strut bar from the lower control arm. Separate the nut and spring bumper.
8. Remove the lower suspension arm No. 3.

To install:

9. Attach the lower suspension arm No. 3 to the vehicle, tighten the mounting bolts to 111 ft. lbs. (150 Nm).
10. Install the spring bumper, tighten to 32 ft. lbs. (43 Nm) and the strut bar to the lower control arm 111 ft. lbs. (150 Nm).
11. Place each end of the coil spring and lower control arm seat in contact when applying the coil spring expander.
12. Install the lower control arm and strut bar as follows:
a. Attach the strut bar front set bolt, tighten to 221 ft. lbs. (300 Nm) make sure the suspension is stabilized prior to tightening the bolt.
b. Install the lower control arm set bolt and nut, tighten to 148 ft. lbs. (200 Nm). Make sure the suspension is stabilized prior to tightening the bolt.
c. Install the lower ball joint with a ball joint installer tool. Install the nut and cotter pin. Tighten the nut to 80 ft. lbs. (110 Nm).
13. Attach the stabilizer bar bracket set bolts, tighten to 22 ft. lbs. (29 Nm).
14. Install the stabilizer link to the lower control arm, tighten to 29 ft. lbs. (39 Nm).
15. Remove the spring compressing tool.
16. Install the shock absorber.
17. Install the wheel, lower the truck and tighten the lug nuts.
18. Have the alignment checked at a reputable repair facility.

Tundra

1. Raise and safely support the vehicle with jackstands.
2. Remove the right and left front wheels.
3. Detach the tie rod ends from the knuckle spindle assembly on each side.
4. Remove the power steering gear set bolts and nuts.
5. Disconnect the stabilizer bar end links from the lower control arm.
6. Detach the shock absorber from the lower control arm.
7. Disconnect the ball joint from the lower control arm.
8. Matchmark the front and rear cam plates to the chassis.
9. Remove the bolts, and cam plates while slightly shifting the power steering gear towards the rear.

To install:

10. Install the lower suspension arm. Torque the bolts to 96 ft. lbs. (130 Nm).
11. Connect the lower ball joint to the lower control arm. Torque the nut to 103 ft. lbs. (140 Nm).
12. Attach the shock absorber to the lower control arm. Torque the bolts to 100 ft. lbs. (135 Nm).
13. Connect the stabilizer bar end link to the lower control arm. Torque the bolts to 51 ft. lbs. (69 Nm).
14. Install the power steering gear. Torque the bolts, as follows:
- Bolt A: 122 ft. lbs. (165 Nm)
- Nut B: 96 ft. lbs. (130 Nm)
- Nut and bolt C: 122 ft. lbs. (165 Nm)
15. Install the tie rod ends.
16. Install the wheels.
17. Have the alignment checked by a qualified repair facility.

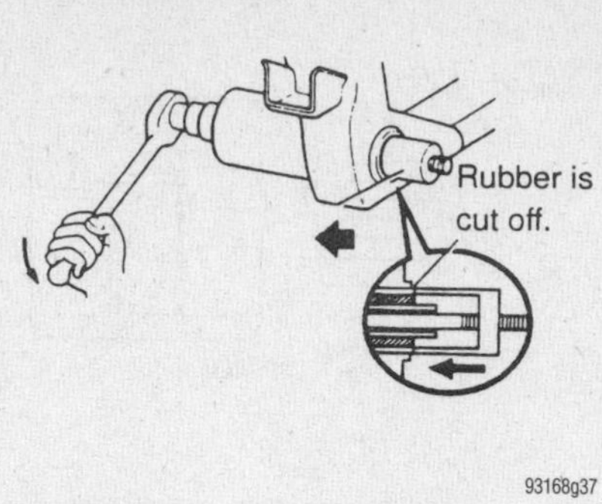

Fig. 39 Lower control arm bushing

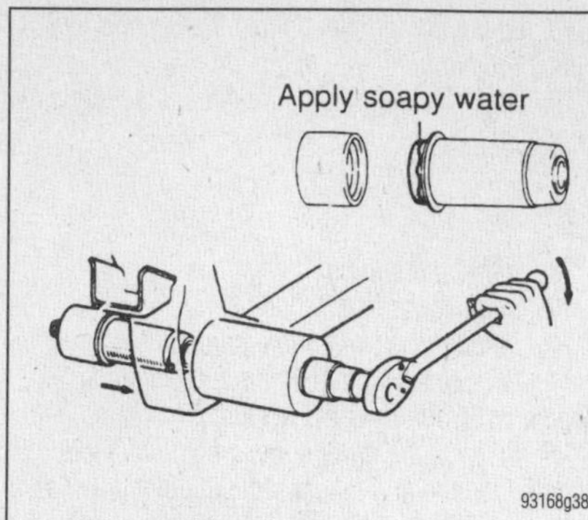

Fig. 40 Installing the new bushing

CONTROL ARM BUSHING REPLACEMENT

See Figures 39 and 40

1. Cut off the rubber lip on the outside of the bushing. This may require a commercially available special service tool.
2. Push the bushing out of the control arm.

A press may be required to remove the bushing.

To install:

The same special service tool may be required to install the bushing.

3. Apply soap water to the new bushing.
4. Install the new bushing into the control arm.

Knuckle and Spindle

REMOVAL & INSTALLATION

4Runner

1. Remove the front wheel.
2. Detach the shock absorber.
3. Remove the grease cap.
4. Remove the ABS wheel speed sensor wire from the steering knuckle.
5. Disconnect the brake line bracket from the steering knuckle.
6. Remove the brake caliper.
7. Remove the front brake rotor.
8. Detach the lower ball joint.
9. Remove the cotter pin from the upper ball joint.
10. Loosen the nut from the upper ball joint.
11. Remove the nut and the steering knuckle.
12. Installation is the reverse of removal.

T100

See Figure 41

1. Remove the front wheel.
2. On models with ABS, remove the speed sensor from the steering knuckle.
3. Remove the caliper.
4. Check the axle hub bearing backlash as follows:
a. Remove the cap, cotter pin and lock cap.
b. Place a dial indicator near the center of the axle hub and check that the backlash in the bearing shaft direction.
c. The maximum is 0.0020 in. (0.05mm). If the backlash is not within specifications, replace the bearing.
5. Remove the hub with the rotor.
6. Remove the oil seal and inner bearing.
7. Remove the dust cover.
8. Unbolt the knuckle arm from the steering knuckle.
9. Support the lower control arm with a suitable jack.
10. Remove the upper and lower cotter pins.
11. Remove the upper and lower nuts.
12. With a ball joint remover, separate the steering knuckle from the upper and lower ball joints.
13. Remove the knuckle.

To install:

14. Support the lower control arm with a jack.
15. Install the steering knuckle to the upper ball joint and nut. Push down the upper control arm and steering knuckle to the lower ball joint and nut. Tighten the upper ball joint nut to 80 ft. lbs. (108 Nm).
16. Tighten the lower ball joint nut to 105 ft. lbs. (142 Nm).
17. Install new cotter pins.
18. Attach the knuckle arm to the steering knuckle as follows:
a. Clean the threads of the bolts and steering knuckle with trichloroethylene.
b. Apply sealant to the bolt threads such as Three Bond 1324 or equivalent. Tighten the bolts to 135 ft. lbs. (183 Nm).

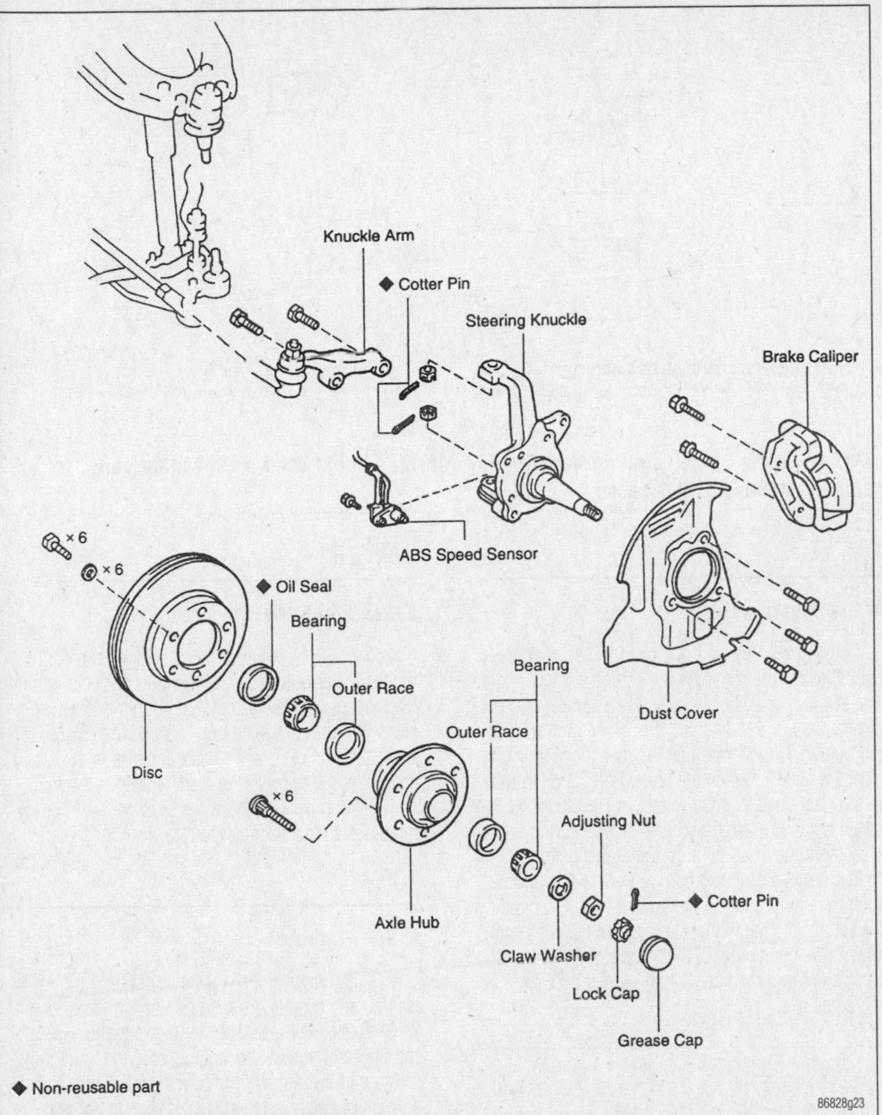

Fig. 41 Exploded view of the front hub and steering knuckle and other suspension components—T100

19. Install the dust cover, tighten the bolts to 14 ft. lbs. (19 Nm).
20. Pack the bearings with multi-purpose grease and coat the inside of the hub and cap.
21. Install the inner bearing and oil seal.
22. Install the hub and rotor assembly.
23. Adjust the preload.
24. Install the lock cap, cotter pin and grease cap.
25. Attach the brake caliper.
26. On models with ABS, connect the ABS speed sensor to steering knuckle, tighten to 71 inch lbs. (8 Nm).
27. Install the front wheel.
28. Lower the vehicle, tighten the lug nuts.
29. Check the front end alignment.
30. On ABS vehicles, check the ABS speed sensor signal.
31. Bleed the brake system.

Tacoma

1. Remove the front wheel.
2. On models with ABS, remove the speed sensor from the steering knuckle.
3. Remove the caliper.
4. Check the axle hub bearing backlash as follows:
   a. Remove the cap, cotter pin and lock cap.
   b. Place a dial indicator near the center of the axle hub and check that the backlash in the bearing shaft direction.
   c. The maximum is 0.0020 in. (0.05mm). If the backlash is not within specifications, replace the bearing.
5. Remove the hub with the rotor.
6. Remove the oil seal and inner bearing.
7. Remove the dust cover.
8. Remove the stabilizer bar link.
9. Support the lower control arm with a jack.
10. Loosen the ball joint set bolts. Remove the cotter pin and discard it, then loosen the nut.
11. With a special tool 09628–62011 or its equivalent, remove the ball joint from the steering knuckle.
12. Remove the ball joint set bolts, then the nut and steering knuckle.

To install:

13. Install the steering knuckle to the upper ball joint and nut.
14. Push down the upper control arm and steering knuckle to the lower ball joint and nut. Tighten the upper ball joint nut to 80 ft. lbs. (110 Nm).
15. Tighten the lower ball joint nut to 116 ft. lbs. (160 Nm).
16. Install new cotter pins.
17. Install the dust cover, tighten the bolts to 14 ft. lbs. (19 Nm).
18. Install the stabilizer bar link.
19. Pack the bearings with multi-purpose grease and coat the inside of the hub and cap.
20. Install the inner bearing and oil seal.
21. Attach the knuckle arm to the steering knuckle as follows:
   a. Clean the threads of the bolts and steering knuckle with trichloroethylene.
   b. Apply sealant to the bolt threads such as Three Bond 1324 or equivalent. Tighten the bolts to 135 ft. lbs. (183 Nm).
22. Install the hub and rotor assembly.
23. Adjust the preload.
24. Install the lock cap, cotter pin and grease cap.
25. Attach the brake caliper.
26. On models with ABS, connect the ABS speed sensor to steering knuckle, tighten to 71 inch lbs. (8 Nm).
27. Install the front wheel.
28. Lower the vehicle, tighten the lug nuts.
29. Check the front end alignment.
30. On ABS vehicles, check the ABS speed sensor signal.
31. Bleed the brake system.

Tundra

1. Raise and properly support the vehicle on jackstands.
2. Remove the front wheel.
3. Remove the grease cap.
4. On vehicles with ABS, remove the wheel speed sensor and wiring harness clamp.
5. Remove the brake caliper.
6. Remove the brake rotor.
7. Loosen the bolts to the shock absorber and then remove it from the vehicle.
8. Detach the lower ball joint.
9. Remove the cotter pin and then loosen the nut to the ball joint.
10. Remove the ball joint nut and then the steering knuckle.

To install:

11. Install the steering knuckle back onto the vehicle.
12. Connect the lower ball joint and torque the nut to 77 ft. lbs. (105 Nm). Torque the four bolts to 59 ft. lbs. (80 Nm).
13. Install the shock absorber.
14. Install the brake rotor and then the caliper.
15. Attach the ABS speed sensor wire harness clamp.
16. Install the driveshaft lock nut and tighten it while applying the brakes.
17. Install the grease cap and then the front wheel.
18. Depress the brakes several times.
19. Have the front alignment checked.
20. Check the ABS speed sensor signal.

Front Axle Hub and Bearing

REMOVAL & INSTALLATION

1. Raise the front of the truck and support with safety stands.
2. Remove the wheels.
3. Remove the brake caliper and suspend it with wire, out of the way.
4. Remove the caliper mount bracket (torque plate).
5. Remove the axle end cap and then remove the cotter pin, nut lock and nut. Discard the cotter pins.
6. Pull the hub/disc assembly off the spindle with the outer bearing. Don't let the bearing fall out.
7. Pry the inner oil seal out and remove the inner bearing from the hub.
8. Clean the bearings and outer races and inspect them for wear or cracks.

To install:

9. Using a brass drift and a hammer, drive out the bearing outer race. Press a new one into position.
10. Pack the bearings with grease until it oozes out the other side. Coat the inside of the hub and cap with grease.
11. Position the inner bearing into the hub, coat the oil seal with grease and press it into the hub.
12. Press the hub assembly onto the spindle and install the outer bearing and thrust washer.
13. Install the hub nut and tighten. Turn the hub a few times to seat the bearings, then loosen the nut until there is no more than 0.02 in. (0.5mm) play. Using a spring tension gauge, check that the preload is 1.3–4.0 lbs.
14. Install the locknut, new cotter pin and hub grease cap.
15. Install the brake torque plate to the knuckle.
16. Install the brake caliper.
17. Bleed the brake system.
18. Install the wheels and lower the vehicle.

Wheel Alignment

If the tires are worn unevenly, if the vehicle is not stable on the highway or if the handling seems uneven in spirited driving, the wheel alignment should be checked. If an alignment problem is suspected, first check for improper tire inflation and other possible causes. These can be worn suspension or steering components, accident damage or even unmatched tires. If any worn or damaged components are found, they must be replaced before the wheels can be properly aligned. Wheel alignment requires very expensive equipment and involves minute adjustments which must be accurate; it should only be performed by a trained technician. Take your vehicle to a properly equipped shop.

Following is a description of the alignment angles which are adjustable on most vehicles and how they affect vehicle handling. Although these angles can apply to both the front and rear wheels, usually only the front suspension is adjustable.

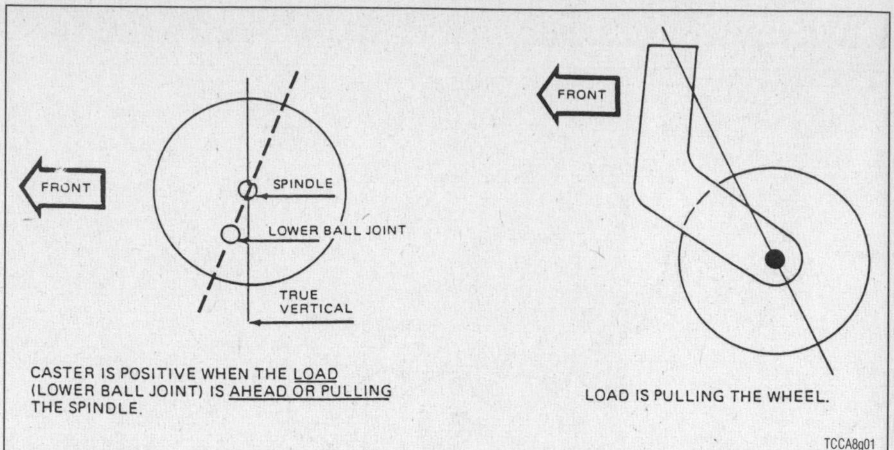

Fig. 42 Caster affects straight-line stability. Caster wheels used on shopping carts, for example, employ positive caster

CASTER

➧ See Figure 42

Looking at a vehicle from the side, caster angle describes the steering axis rather than a wheel angle. The steering knuckle is attached to a control arm or strut at the top and a control arm at the bottom. The wheel pivots around the line between these points to steer the vehicle. When the upper point is tilted back, this is described as positive caster. Having a positive caster tends to make the wheels self-centering, increasing directional stability. Excessive positive caster makes the wheels hard to steer, while an uneven caster will cause a pull to one side. Overloading the vehicle or sagging rear springs will affect caster, as will raising the rear of the vehicle. If the rear of the vehicle is lower than normal, the caster becomes more positive.

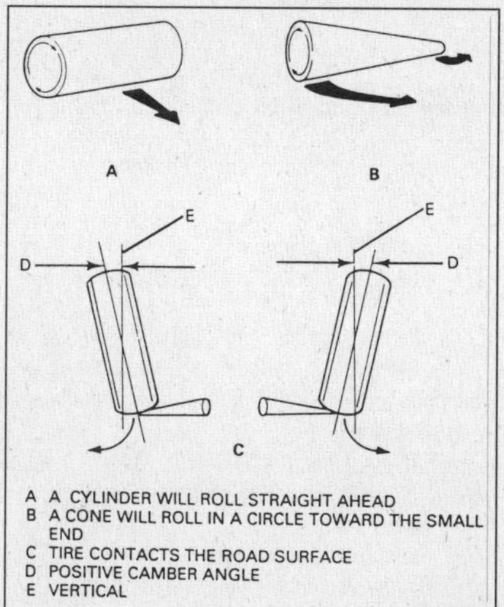

Fig. 43 Camber influences tire contact with the road

CAMBER

➧ See Figure 43

Looking from the front of the vehicle, camber is the inward or outward tilt of the top of wheels. When the tops of the wheels are tilted in, this is negative camber; if they are tilted out, it is positive. In a turn, a slight amount of negative camber helps maximize contact of the tire with the road. However, too much negative camber compromises straight-line stability, increases bump steer and torque steer.

TOE

➧ See Figure 44

Looking down at the wheels from above the vehicle, toe angle is the distance between the front of the wheels, relative to the distance between the back of the wheels. If the wheels are closer at the front, they are said to be toed-in or to have negative toe. A small amount of negative toe enhances directional stability and provides a smoother ride on the highway.

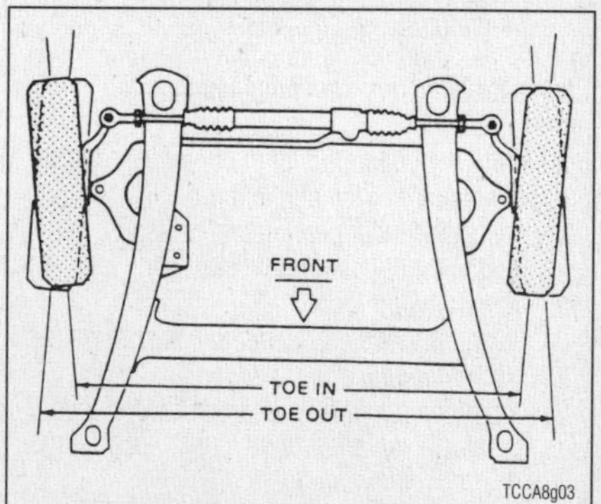

Fig. 44 With toe-in, the distance between the wheels is closer at the front than at the rear

4WD FRONT SUSPENSION

FRONT SUSPENSION COMPONENTS—4WD TACOMA

1. Upper ball joint
2. Shock absorber/coil spring assembly
3. Wheel bearing
4. Outer tie rod end
5. Rack and pinion steering unit
6. Stabilizer bar
7. Inner tie rod end dust (bellows) boot
8. Lower control arm
9. Upper control arm
10. Coil spring
11. Knuckle spindle
12. Lower ball joint

FRONT SUSPENSION COMPONENTS—EARLY MODEL LAND CRUISER

1. Steering damper
2. Relay rod end
3. Relay rod
4. Leading arm
5. Tie rod end
6. Stabilizer bar cushion and bracket
7. Axle assembly
8. Tie rod tube
9. Stabilizer bar
10. Shock absorber
11. Coil spring
12. Front axle hub

After you work on your truck's suspension, it is advisable to have the alignment checked at a reputable repair facility. This will ensure that front end is in order after repairs.

Coil Spring

REMOVAL & INSTALLATION

Except Land Cruiser

1. Raise and properly support the vehicle.
2. Remove the front wheel.
3. Remove the strut absorber nut and washer from the lower control arm.

WARNING

Do not remove the bolt at this time.

4. While slowly lowering the front suspension, remove the lower bolt from the shock absorber assembly.
5. Support the shock absorber.
6. Remove the three nuts from the top of the shock tower.
7. Lower the assembly out of the wheel well.
8. Remove the coil spring by compressing the spring with a commercially available spring compressor.
9. Compress the coil spring until it is clear of the assembly at both ends.
10. Remove the center nut from the shock.
11. Detach the retainers, cushions, suspension support and coil spring.

To install:

12. Compress the coil spring.
13. Install the coil spring on to the shock absorber.

➡Fit the lower end of the coil spring into the gap of the spring seat of the shock absorber.

14. Install the cushions, retainers, and suspension support to the rod.
15. Install and snug the center nut of the shock.
16. Align the top of the shock so that two (2) of the bolts are parallel with the direction of the lower shock bushing.
17. Remove the spring compressor.
18. Torque the center nut to 22 ft. lbs. (29Nm).
19. The remainder of installation is the reverse of the removal procedure. Please note the following torque specifications:
   - 3 upper mount to body nuts: 47 ft. lbs. (64 Nm)
   - Lower shock absorber mounting bolt: 101 ft. lbs. (135 Nm)
   - Wheel lug nuts: 83 ft. lbs. (110 Nm)

Land Cruiser

See Figures 45, 46, 47, 48, and 49

1. Elevate and safely support the vehicle. Make certain the jackstands are securely placed under the frame rails.
2. Use a floor jack to slightly jack and support the front axle housing. Hold the piston rod of the shock absorber and remove the upper mounting nut. Hold the shock and remove the lower mounting nut, the cushions and the retainer.
3. Disconnect the stabilizer bar from the axle housing.

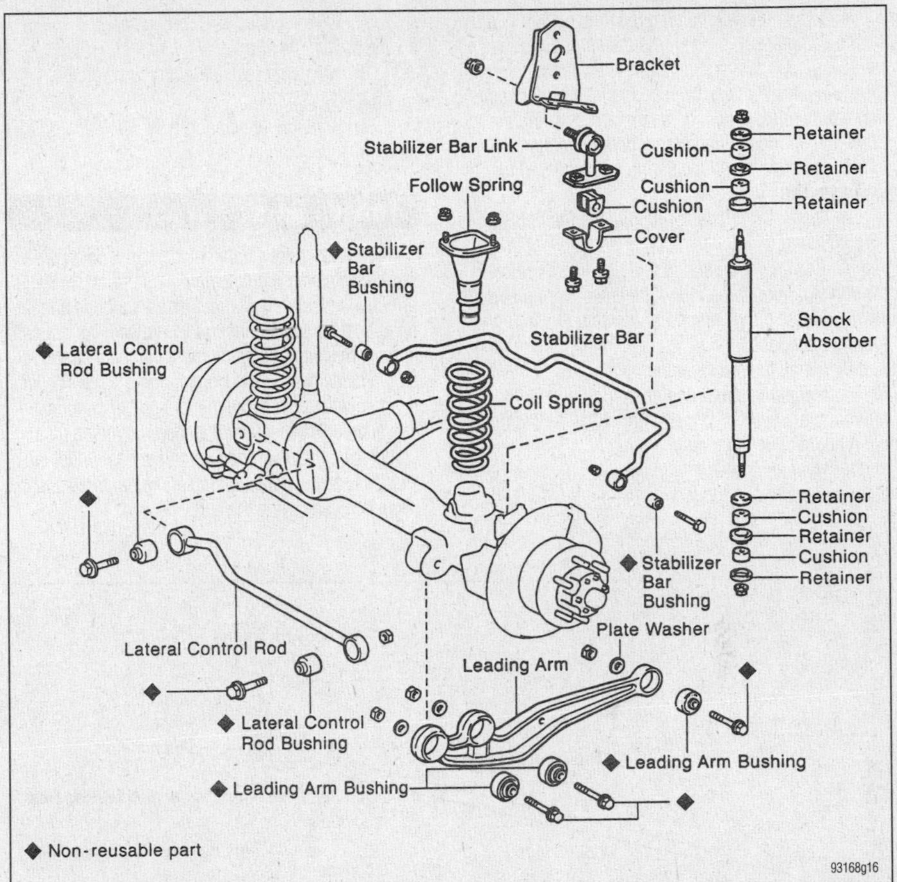

Fig. 45 Exploded view of the front suspension, including the coil springs—1997 Land Cruiser shown

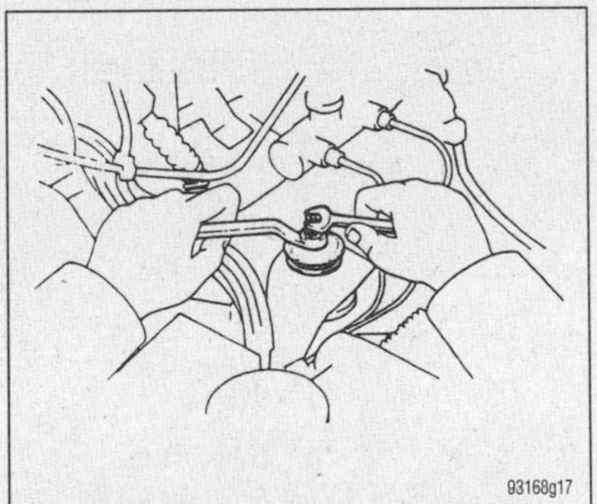

Fig. 46 Removing the upper shock nut

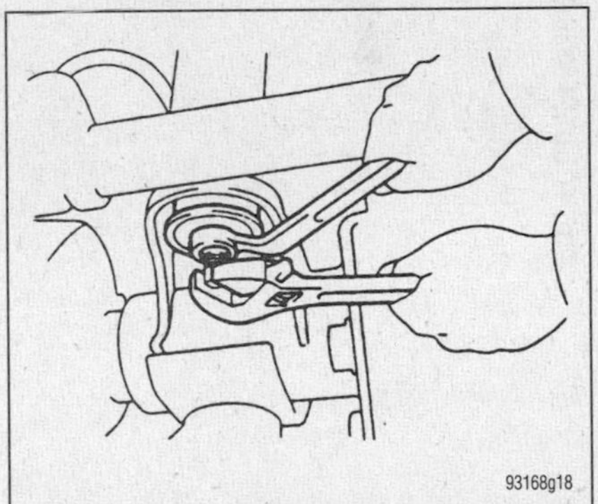

Fig. 47 Lower shock absorber mounting nut

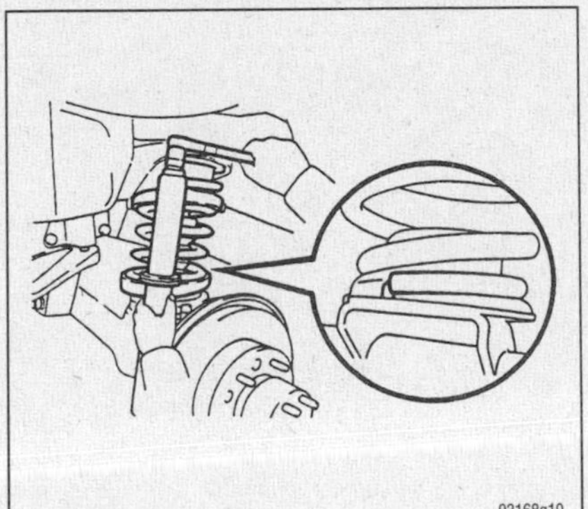

Fig. 48 Compressing the coil spring with a spring compressor

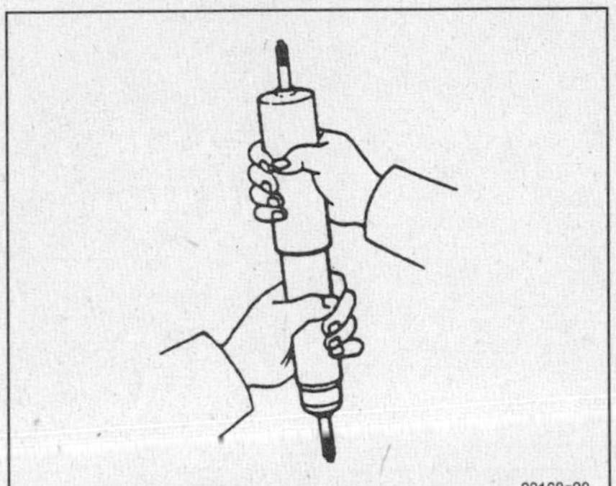

Fig. 49 Check the shock absorber for smooth operation before re-installing it. If it binds during its travel, replace it

4. Lower the jack holding the front axle. Use a spring compressor to compress the spring. Remove the spring, still compressed, from the vehicle. Place the spring, facing away from you, on the work bench and slowly release the tension on the compressor. When the spring is fully extended, remove the tool.
5. Remove the follow spring nuts and spring.

To install:

6. Install the follow spring, tighten the nuts to 82 inch lbs. (9 Nm).
7. Compress the spring and fit it into position in the vehicle. Align the end with the lower spring seat; slowly release the compressor, allowing the spring to expand into place.
8. Install the stabilizer bar.
9. Install the shock absorber. Tighten the lower mounting nut to 51 ft. lbs. (69 Nm) and then the upper mount to the same value.
10. Lower the vehicle to the ground. Tighten the lug nuts as follows:
   a. 1997 vehicles with steel wheels: 109 ft. lbs. (147 Nm)
   b. 1997 vehicles with aluminum wheels: 76 ft. lbs. (103 Nm).
   c. 1998–00 vehicle lug nuts: 97 ft. lbs. (131 Nm)

Torsion Bars

Torsion bars are used in place of coil springs on some trucks. While employing the same torsional principal as a spring, the torsion bars are installed parallel to the ground instead of vertically as is a coil spring. This allows a much more compact suspension arrangement, lower front end styling and better suspension control since the torsion bar need not move through the greater distances traversed by a compression spring. The torsion bars are under tension as is any installed spring and great care must be taken when removing the bars.

REMOVAL & INSTALLATION

**** WARNING**

Great care must be taken to make sure torsion bars are not mixed after removal, it is strongly suggested that before removal; each be marked with paint, showing the front and rear of spring and from which side of the truck it was taken. If they are installed backward or on the wrong sides of the truck, they could fracture. New units are marked L or R with an arrow showing direction of flex.

Land Cruiser

➧ **See Figures 50, 51, 52, 53, and 54**

1. Raise and properly support the vehicle.

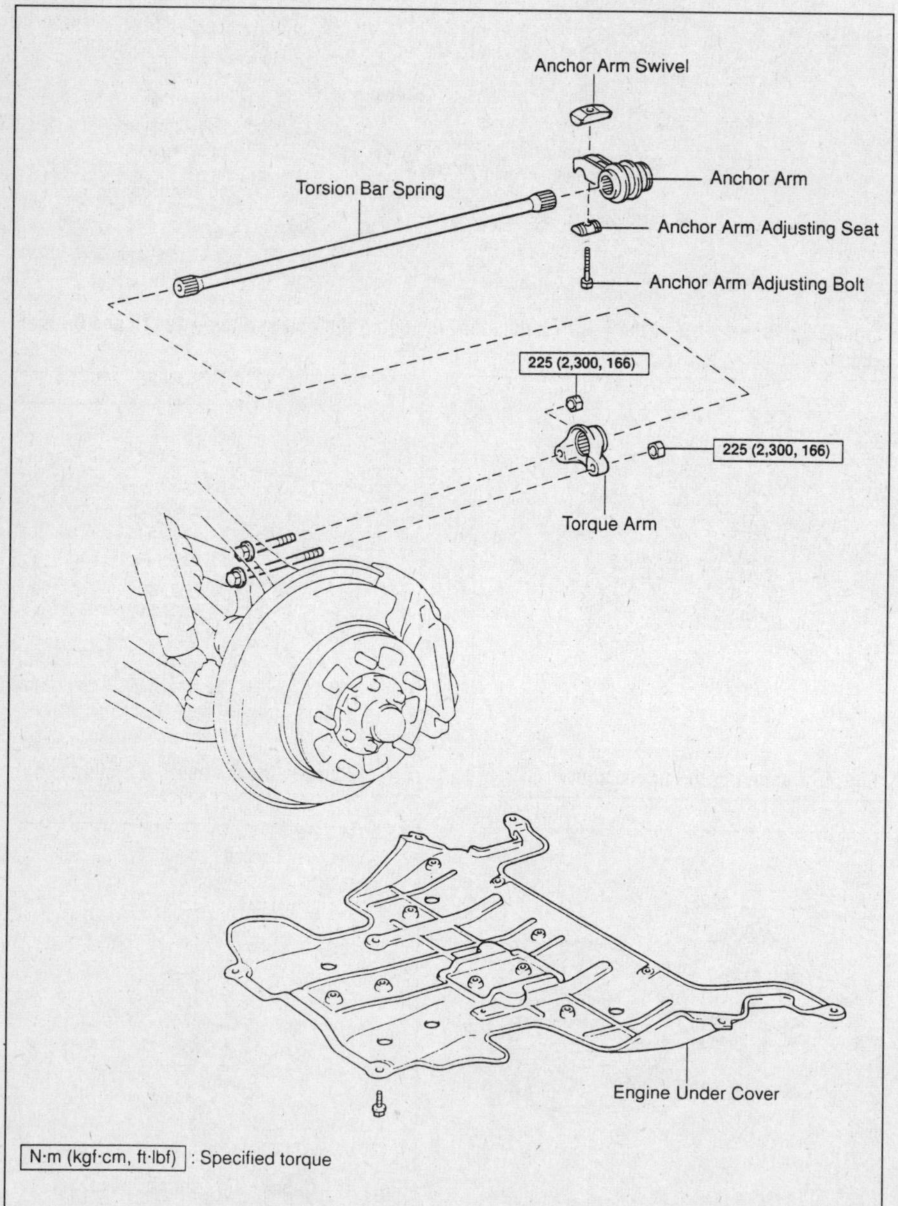

Fig. 50 Front torsion bar suspension—Land Cruiser shown

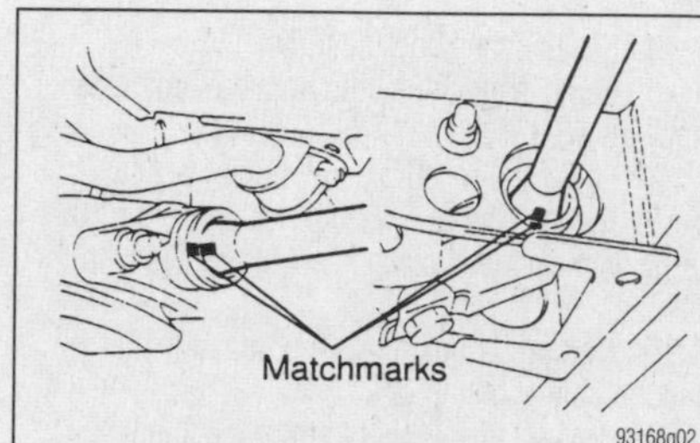

Fig. 51 Matchmark the position of the torsion bar before removing it

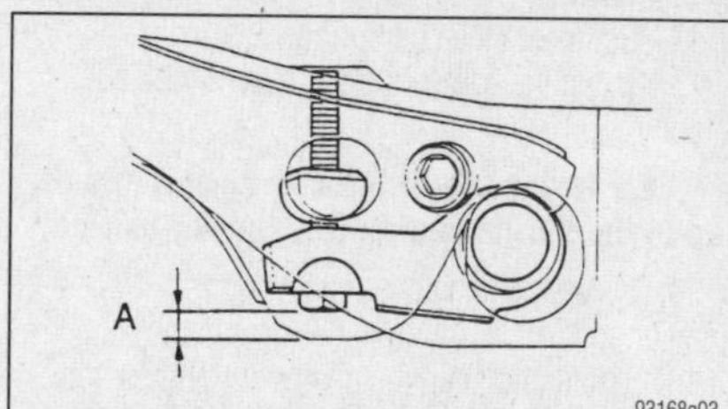

Fig. 52 Measure the height of "A". Use this measurement as a reference upon installation

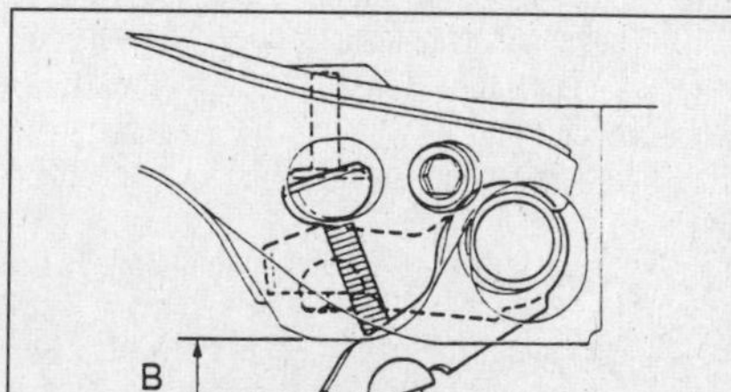

Fig. 53 Measure the height of "B" to aid you when re-installing the anchor arm

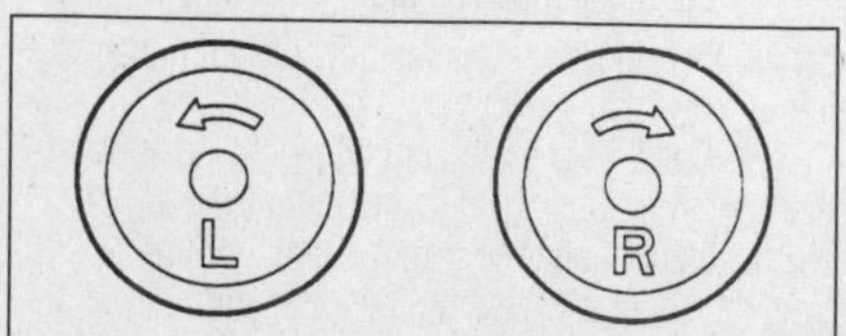

Fig. 54 Proper direction of rotation of the torsion bar

2. Remove the front wheel.
3. Detach the engine undercover.
4. Matchmark the torsion bar spring, anchor arm, and torque arm.
5. Measure the dimension "A" between the anchor arm adjusting bolt and the end of the frame. This measurement can be used as a reference point when installing the anchor arm.
6. Loosen the anchor arm until the spring is free of all tension.
7. Measure the anchor arm bolt "B". Again, this measurement can be used as a reference point for installation.
8. Remove the adjusting bolt from the anchor arm.
9. Remove the anchor arm swivel and anchor arm adjusting seat.
10. Remove the torsion bar spring with the anchor arm.
11. Detach the anchor arm from the torsion bar spring.
12. Remove the 2 nuts and bolts, then remove the torque arm.

To install:

13. Install the bolt, torque arm and the 2 nuts. Torque the bolts to 166 ft. lbs. (225 Nm).

➡The torsion bars are marked left and right on the ends. There are also arrows that show the proper direction of travel.

14. Install the anchor arm to a new torsion bar spring.
15. Assemble the torsion bar spring and the anchor arm.
16. Install the anchor arm to the torque arm.
17. Assemble the anchor arm adjusting seat, anchor arm swivel, and anchor arm adjusting bolt.
18. Check the length of the anchor arm adjusting bolt end is close to your measurement from the removal process.
19. Tighten the anchor arm adjusting bolt to the following specifications:
    - Left: 0.315–0.984 in. (8–25mm)
    - Right: 0.079–0.709 in. (2–18mm)
20. If you are installing a used torsion bar spring, perform the following:
    - Install the torsion bar spring and anchor.
    - Align the matchmarks, you made earlier in the removal procedure, on the torsion bar spring and anchor arm.
    - Install the torsion bar spring into the anchor arm.
    - Align the matchmarks you made on the torsion bar spring and torque arm. Once they line up, install them.
21. Tighten the anchor arm adjusting bolt so that the dimension "A" is the same as the dimension measured before you removed the bar.
22. Install the engine undercover.
23. Install the front wheel and torque the lug nuts to 97 ft. lbs. (131 Nm).
24. Check the vehicle ride height.

T100

➧ See Figures 55, 56, and 57

1. Raise and properly support the vehicle.
2. Remove the front wheel
3. Measure the length of the threaded bolt end. Use this measurement as a reference during installation.

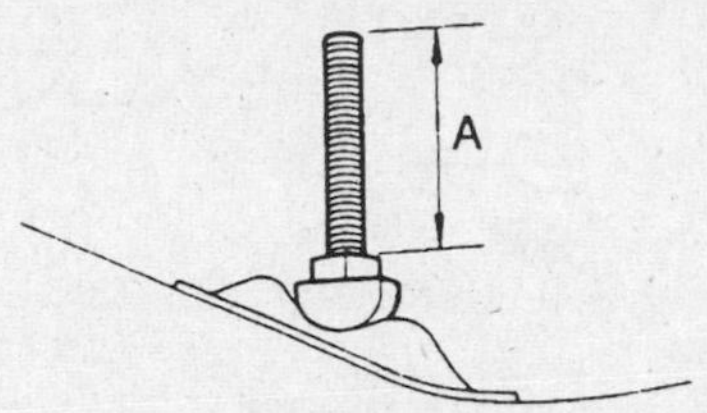

93168g10

Fig. 55 Measure the length of the threaded bolt end and use the measurement as a reference when installing the torsion bar

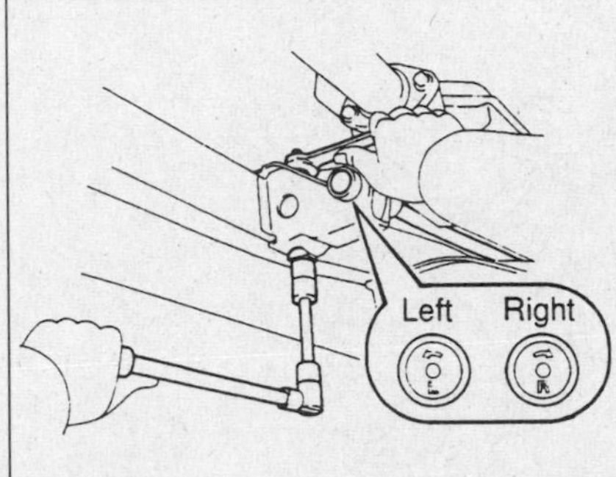

93168g14

Fig. 56 Loosening the adjuster nut and anchor arm

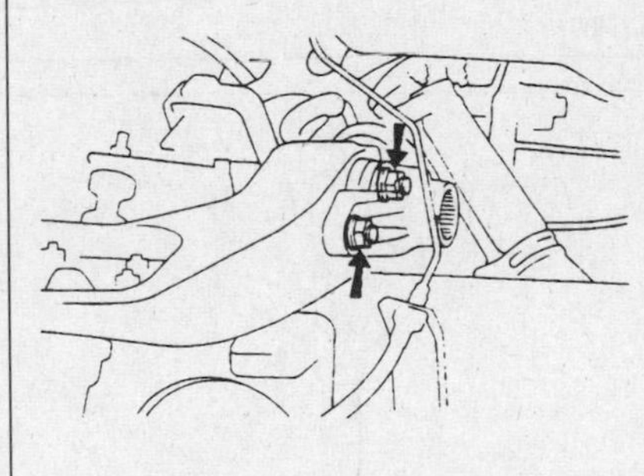

93168g15

Fig. 57 Torque arm mounting bolts

4. Loosen the adjusting nut and remove the anchor arm.
5. Remove the torsion bar spring only after all tension has been removed from it.
6. Remove the torque arm.

To install:

7. Installation is the reverse of removal. Please note the following torque specifications:
    - Torque arm bolts: 64 ft. lbs. (87 Nm).
    - Lug nuts: 76 ft. lbs. (103 Nm).

Shock Absorber

REMOVAL & INSTALLATION

➧ See Figures 58, 59, and 60

1. Loosen the lug nuts.
2. Raise front of the truck and support it with safety stands.
3. Remove the wheel.
4. Unfasten the double nuts at the top end of the shock absorber.
5. Remove the cushions and cushion retainers.
6. Remove the bolt(s) which secure the lower end of the shock absorber to the lower control arm.
7. Remove the shock absorber.

To install:

8. Place the parts on the shock in the correct order and positions: Retainer, cushion, retainer.
9. Install the shock absorber, then tighten the lower mounting on the Land Cruiser to nuts/bolt to 100 ft. lbs. (135 Nm). Tighten the upper mounting nut to 50 ft. lbs. (68 Nm).
10. Install the wheels and lower the truck.

TESTING

➧ See Figure 61

The purpose of the shock absorber is simply to limit the motion of the spring during compression (bump) and rebound cycles. If the vehicle were not equipped with these motion dampers, the up and down motion of the vehicle would multiply until the vehicle was alternately trying to leap off the ground and to pound itself into the pavement.

Contrary to popular rumor, the shocks do not affect the ride height of the vehicle, nor do they affect the ride quality except for limiting the pitch or bounce. These factors are controlled by other suspension components such as springs and tires. Worn shock absorbers can affect handling; if the front of the vehicle is rising or falling excessively, the "footprint" of the tires changes on the pavement and steering response is affected. The simplest test of the shock absorbers is simply to push down on one corner of the unladen vehicle and release it.

Observe the motion of the body as it is released. In most cases, it will come up beyond its original rest position, dip back below it and settle quickly to rest. This shows that the damper is slowing and controlling the spring action. Any tendency to excessive pitch (up-and-down) motion or failure to return to rest within 2–3 cycles is a sign of poor function within the shock absorber.

While each shock absorber can be replaced individually, it is recommended that they be changed as a pair (both front or both rear) to maintain equal response on both sides of the vehicle. Chances are quite good that if one has failed, its mate is weak also.

INSPECTION

Once removed, the shock should be carefully inspected for any signs of leakage. Oil-filled shocks may have a light film of oil around the seal, resulting from normal breathing and air exchange. This should NOT be taken as a sign of failure, but any sign of thick or running oil definitely indicates failure. Gas filled shocks may also show some film at the shaft; if the gas has leaked out, the shock will have almost no resistance to motion.

Hold the shock firmly in each hand and compress it; compression should be reasonably even and smooth. Release the piston end; it should return smoothly and at an even pace. Stretch the shock, checking again for smooth motion and any abnormal resistance.

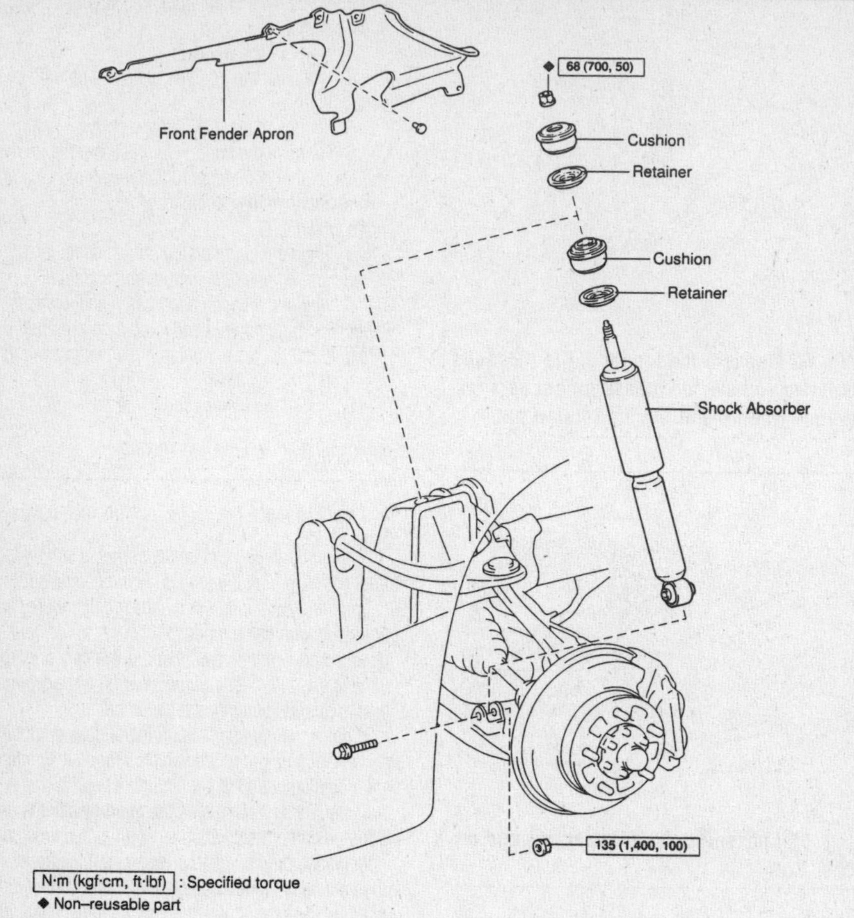

93168g09

Fig. 58 Front shock absorber assembly—Land Cruiser

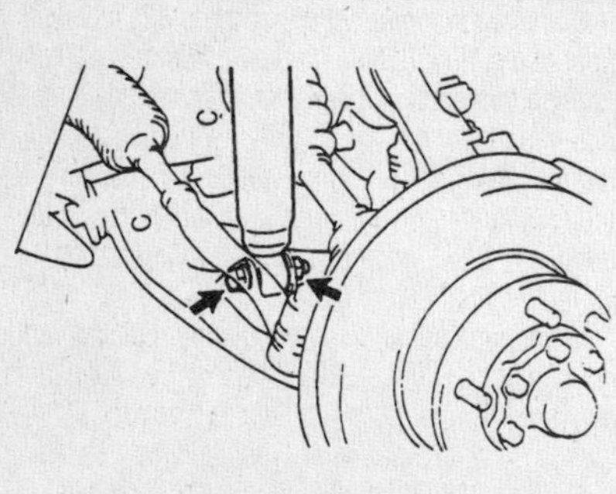

93168g06

Fig. 59 Location of the lower shock bolt—Land Cruiser

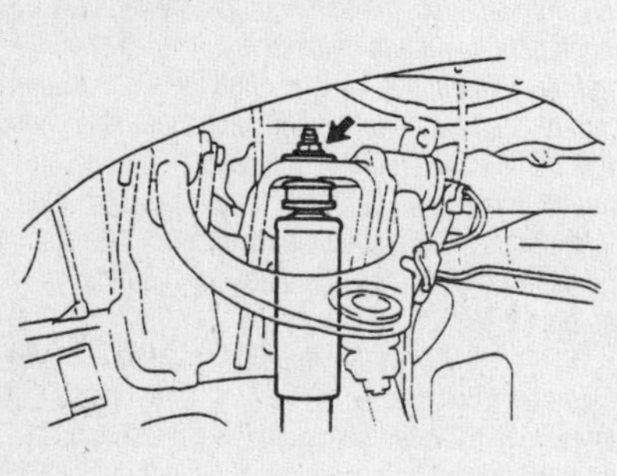

93168g07

Fig. 60 Upper shock mount bolt

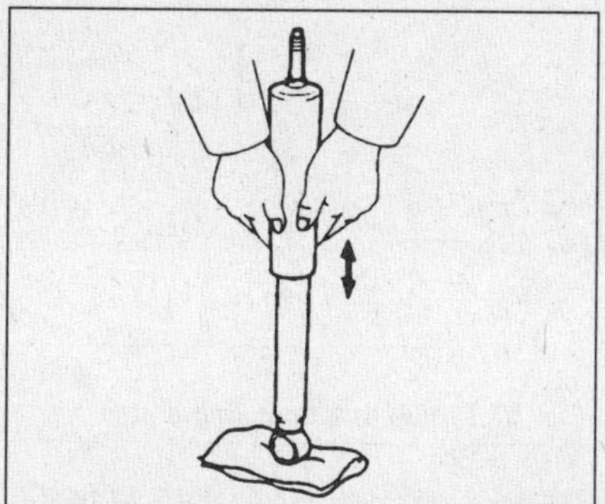

93168g08

Fig. 61 Depress the shock to test it. Check for smooth travel of the piston assembly. If any inconsistencies are detected, replace the shock absorber

DISPOSAL OF GAS-FILLED SHOCK ABSORBERS

The factory installed gas shocks found on some vehicles contain nitrogen. The gas is under pressure, even with the shock removed from the vehicle. To eliminate the possibility of explosion after disposal, the shock case must be drilled to release the gas.

Drill a 0.079–0.118 in. (2–3mm) hole at a point 1.18 in. (30mm) above the base of the shock case. Drill a second hole 1.97 in. (50mm) below the edge of the piston cover (with the shock compressed).

CAUTION

Although nitrogen is non-toxic and non-flammable, the escaping gas may carry metal chips from the drill; always wear eye or full-face protection when drilling.

Once the gas is released, the shock absorber may be safely discarded.

Shock Absorber/Coil Spring Assembly

REMOVAL & INSTALLATION

Tacoma, Tundra, 4 Runner and Pre Runner

See Figures 62, 63, 64, and 65

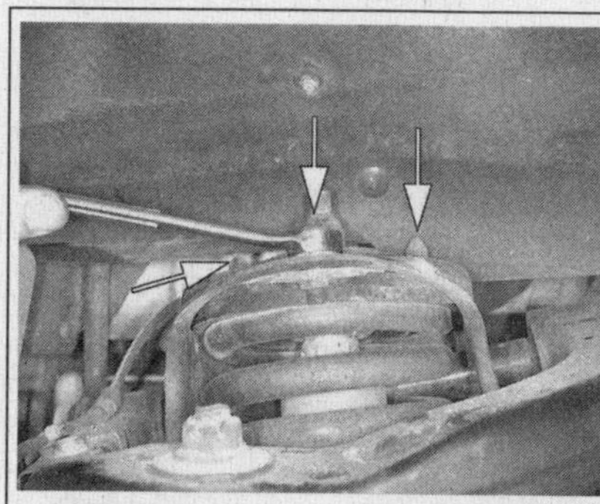

93168p25

Fig. 62 Remove the three nuts at the top of the shock tower

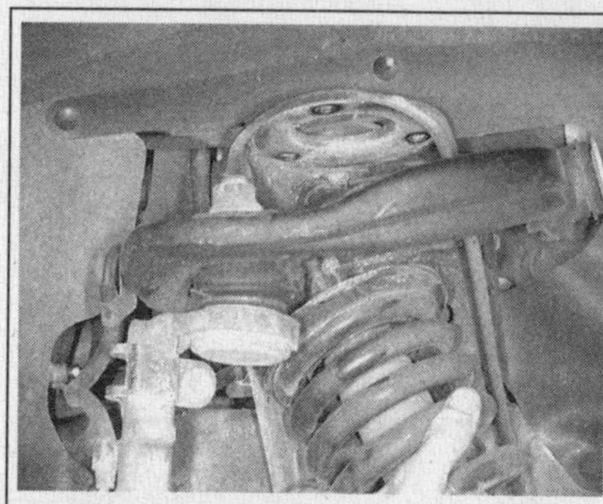

93168p27

Fig. 63 Pull the assembly down to remove it from the vehicle

93168p26

Fig. 64 View of the shock upper mount

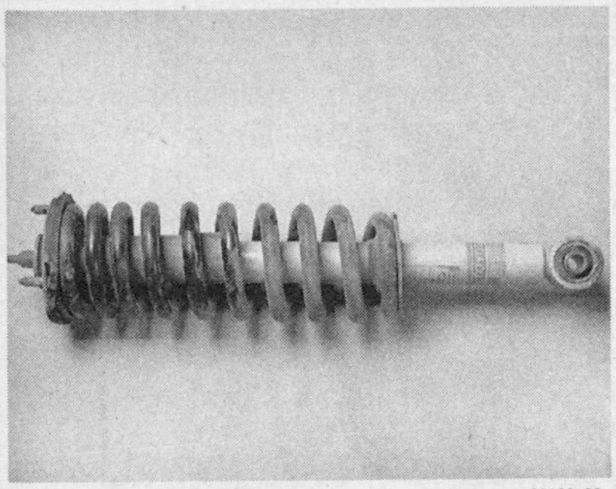

Fig. 65 Shock absorber and coil spring assembly

1. Raise and properly support the vehicle.
2. Remove the front wheel.
3. Remove the shock absorber nut and washer from the lower control arm.

WARNING

Do not remove the bolt at this time.

4. While slowly lowering the front suspension, remove the lower bolt from the shock absorber assembly.
5. Support the shock.
6. Remove the three nuts from the top of the shock tower.
7. Lower the assembly out of the wheel well.

To install:

8. Installation is the reverse of the removal procedure. Please note the following torque specifications:
   - 3 upper mount to body nuts: 47 ft. lbs. (64 Nm)
   - Lower shock absorber mounting bolt: 101 ft. lbs. (135 Nm)
   - Lug nuts: 83 ft. lbs. (110 Nm).

Upper Ball Joint

REMOVAL & INSTALLATION

Land Cruiser

1. The upper ball joint is an integral part of the upper control arm and can not be replaced separately. If the ball joint fails, the entire control arm must be replaced.

T100

See Figure 66

1. Remove the front wheel.
2. Disconnect the upper ball joint from the steering knuckle.
3. Remove the upper ball joint 4 mounting nuts. Separate the ball joint from the upper control arm.

To install:

4. Attach the ball joint mounting nuts, tighten to 25 ft. lbs. (33 Nm).
5. Attach the ball joint to the steering knuckle.
6. Install the front wheel, lower the vehicle and tighten the lug nuts.
7. Have the alignment checked at a reputable repair facility.

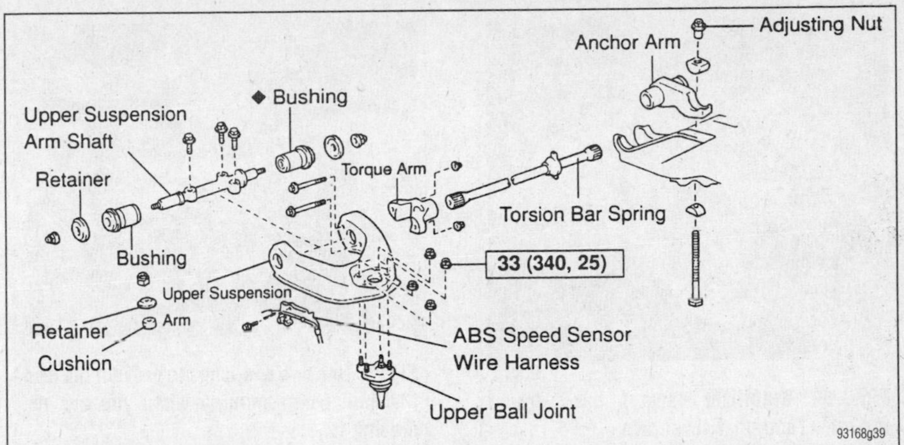

Fig. 66 Exploded view of the upper ball joint and related suspension components

Tacoma, Tundra, and 4Runner

See Figure 67

1. Remove the front wheel.
2. Remove the steering knuckle with the axle hub.
3. Separate the upper ball joint as follows:
   a. Remove the wire and boot.
   b. Using a snapring expander, remove the snapring.
   c. With a ball joint remover and a deep socket, remove the upper ball joint.

To install:

4. With the aid of the ball joint installer and a socket wrench, install the ball joint.
5. Using a snapring expander, install a new snapring.
6. Apply multi-purpose grease, then install a new boot. Fix it with a new wire.
7. Install the steering knuckle with the axle hub.
8. Install the front wheel, lower the vehicle and tighten the lug nuts.
9. Have the alignment checked at a reputable repair facility.

Lower Ball Joint

REMOVAL & INSTALLATION

Land Cruiser

1. The lower ball joint is an integral part of the lower control arm and can not be replaced separately. If the ball joint fails, the entire control arm must be replaced.

T100

1. Remove the front wheel.
2. Disconnect the lower ball joint from the steering knuckle.
3. Remove the cotter pin and nut.
4. With the aid of a ball joint separator, disconnect the joint from the steering knuckle.

To install:

5. Attach the ball joint to the knuckle with the special installer tool.
6. Attach the ball joint to the steering knuckle, tighten the nut to 105 ft. lbs. (142 Nm). Use a new cotter pin.
7. Install the front wheel, lower the vehicle and tighten the lug nuts.
8. Have the alignment checked at a reputable repair facility.

Tacoma, Tundra, and 4Runner

See Figure 68

1. Remove the front wheel.
2. Support the lower control arm with a suitable jack.
3. Loosen the four bolts attaching the lower ball joint. Do not remove them. Remove the cotter pin and nut from the tie rod end. Throw out the old cotter pin. With special tool 09610–20012 or equivalent, disconnect the tie rod end from the steering knuckle.

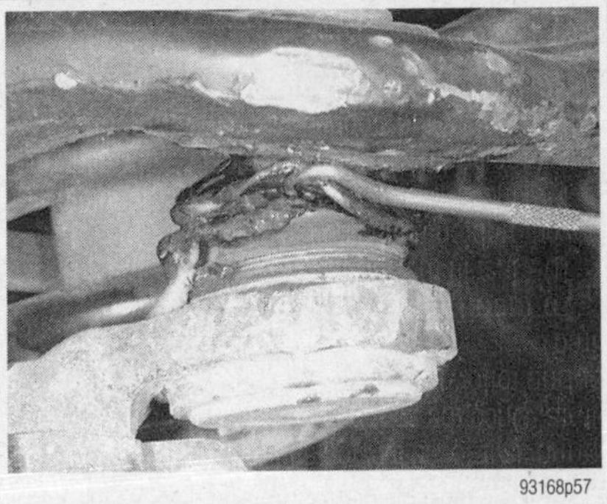

Fig. 67 This upper ball joint boot has cracked. Grease has escaped and moisture and dirt have entered the joint

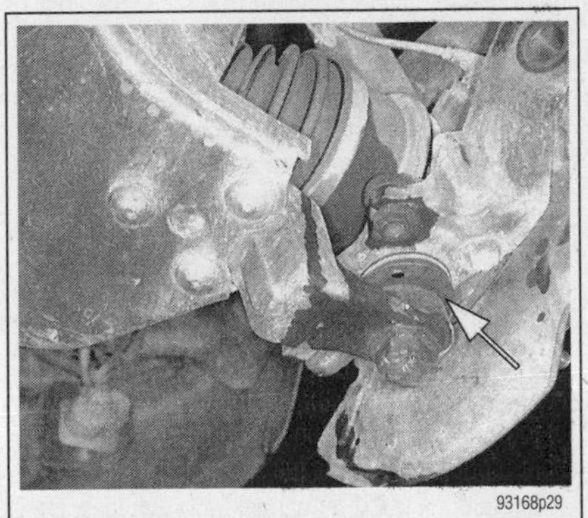

Fig. 68 View of the lower ball joint—Tacoma TRD shown

93168p33

Fig. 69 Stabilizer (sway) bar-to-frame mount—Tacoma TRD shown

93168p24

Fig. 70 Use two wrenches to prevent the end link bolt from spinning when you are removing it

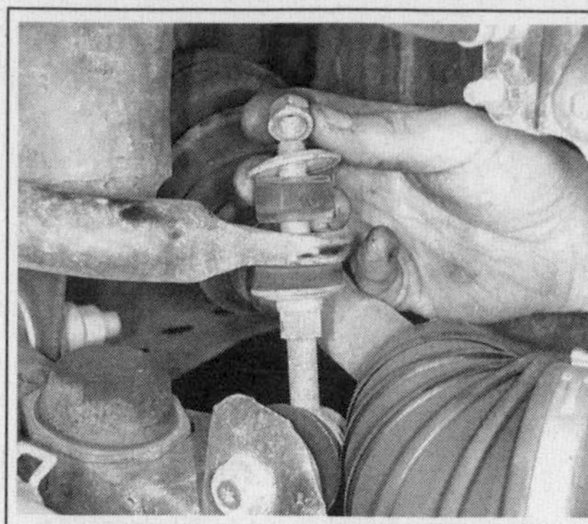

93168p45

Fig. 71 Removing the nuts, washers and bolt from the stabilizer bar end links

4. Remove the cotter pin and nut from the lower ball joint. Discard the cotter pin.
5. With a ball joint remover such as tool 09628–62011 or equivalent, separate the ball joint from the lower control arm.
6. Remove the four mounting bolts. When lifting the upper control arm and steering knuckle, remove the ball joint. After the ball joint is removed, support the upper control arm and knuckle securely.

To install:

7. Install the ball joint with the mounting nut and bolts.
8. Tighten the nut to 112 ft. lbs. (152 Nm) on the Tacoma, to 105 ft. lbs. (142 Nm) on the 4Runner, or to 103 ft. lbs. (140 Nm) on the Tundra. Install a new cotter pin in the hole.
9. Attach the tie rod end tightening the nut to 67 ft. lbs. (91 Nm). Install a new cotter pin.
10. Tighten the lower ball joint set bolts to 59 ft. lbs. (80 Nm) on the 4Runner and Tundra, or to 83 ft. lbs. (113 Nm) on the Tacoma.
11. Remove the jack slowly, making sure everything is secure and in place.
12. Install the wheel, lower the vehicle and tighten the lug nuts.
13. Check the ABS speed sensor signal.
14. Have the alignment checked at a reputable repair facility.

Stabilizer Bar (Sway Bar)

REMOVAL & INSTALLATION

Except Land Cruiser

➧ See Figures 69, 70, and 71

1. Remove the front wheels.
2. Remove the nuts and disconnect the stabilizer bar links from the lower control arm.
3. Hold the link with a wrench, then remove the nut, retainers, cushions and link.
4. Remove the bolts and stabilizer bar with cushions and brackets.

To install:

5. Place the stabilizer bar into position, then install both the bar cushions and brackets to the frame. Temporarily install the bolts. Tighten to 19–22 ft. lbs. (25–29 Nm).
6. Hold the stabilizer bar link with a wrench, then install the link onto the lower control arm with a new nut. Tighten the nut to 14–19 ft. lbs. (19–25 Nm).
7. On models with the links using a hexagon wrench, connect the stabilizer bar on both sides to the links with new nuts, tighten to 55–70 ft. lbs. (69–95 Nm).
8. Install the front wheels.
9. Have the alignment checked at a reputable repair facility.

Land Cruiser

➧ See Figures 72, 73, 74, and 75

1. Raise the truck and support it on safety stands.
2. Remove the wheels.
3. If necessary, remove the engine undercover.
4. Remove the nut, then disconnect the stabilizer bar with the link from the bracket.
5. Disconnect the bar from the axle housing. Remove the stabilizer bar. Remove the 2 bolts and remove the bracket from the bar.

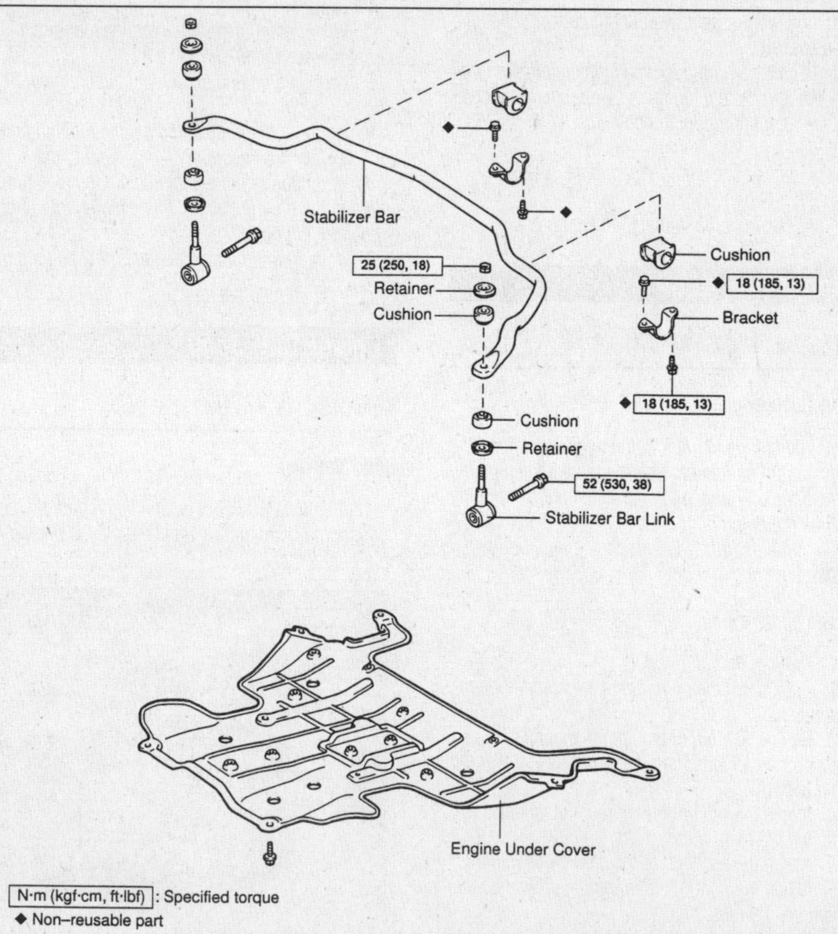

93168g26

Fig. 72 You may have to remove the engine undercover for access to the front stabilizer bar—Land Cruiser

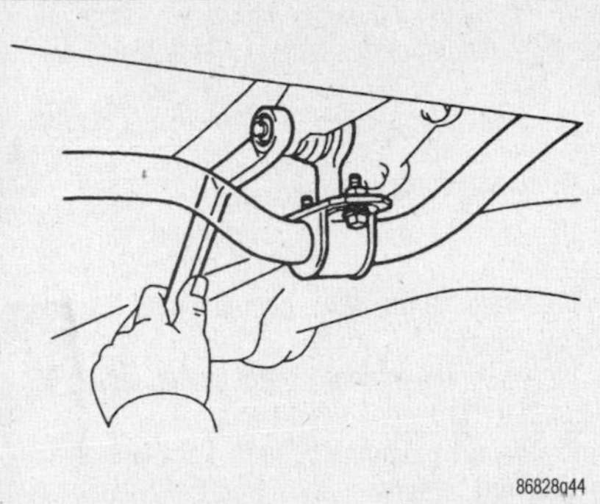
86828g44

Fig. 73 Remove the nut, then disconnect the stabilizer bar and link from the bracket

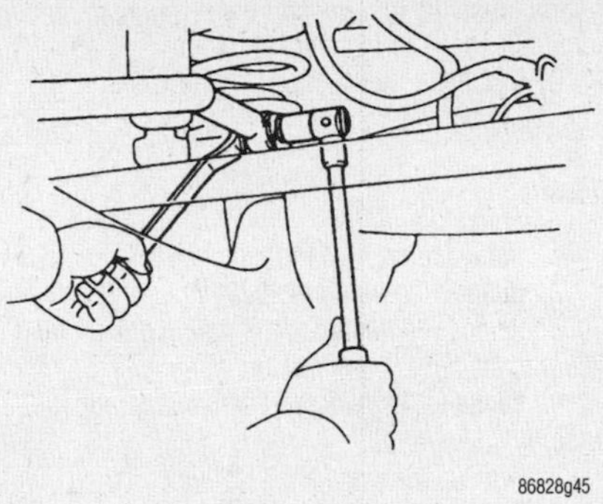
86828g45

Fig. 74 Two wrenches will be needed to remove the through-bolt

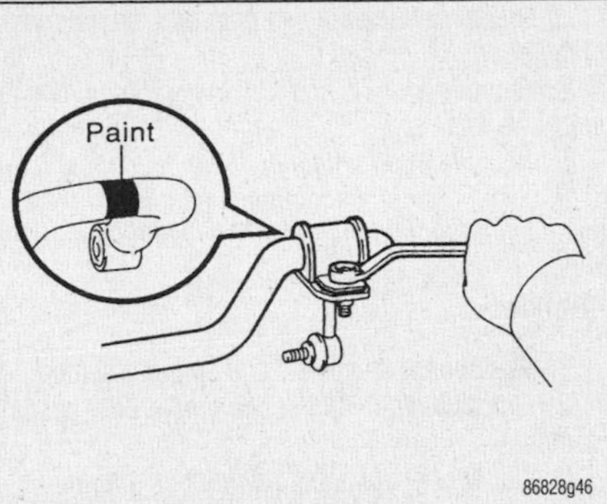

86828g46

Fig. 75 Reassemble the cushions and cover over the painted mark on the bar

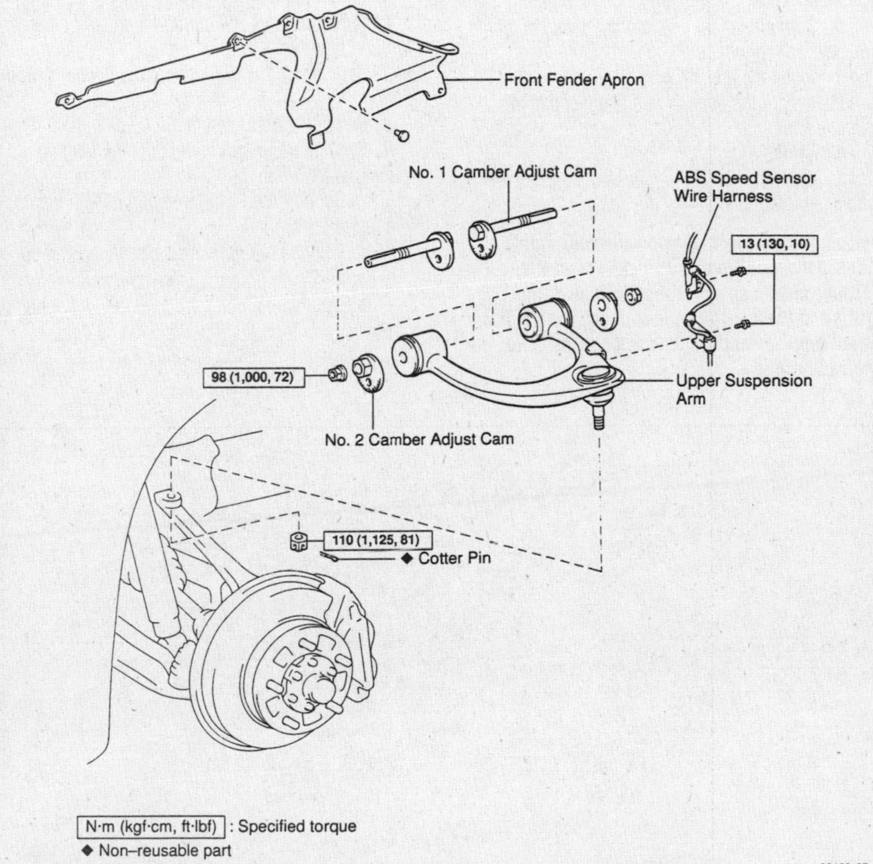

93168g27

Fig. 76 Exploded view of the front upper control arm and related components

➡Examine the rubber bushings very carefully for any splits or deformation. Clean the inner and outer surfaces of the bushings before reinstallation. Failed or dirty bushings can create a chorus of odd noises under the vehicle, particularly during cornering.

To install:

6. Reassemble the cushions and cover onto the painted mark on the bar.
7. Tighten the bar-to-bracket bolts to 13 ft. lbs. (18 Nm). Mount the bar, tightening the fittings just snug.
8. Install the wheels and lower the vehicle to the ground. Bounce the front end several times to stabilize the suspension.
9. Tighten the bolts at the axle tube to 19 ft. lbs. (25 Nm). Tighten the nuts at the top of the small link to 13 ft. lbs. (18 Nm).
10. Have the alignment checked at a reputable repair facility.

Upper Control Arm

REMOVAL & INSTALLATION

Land Cruiser

➧ **See Figures 76, 77, 78, and 79**

1. Raise and safely support the vehicle on jackstands.
2. Remove the front wheel.
3. Detach the front fender apron.
4. Detach the ABS speed sensor wire.
5. Disconnect the steering knuckle from the upper control arm.

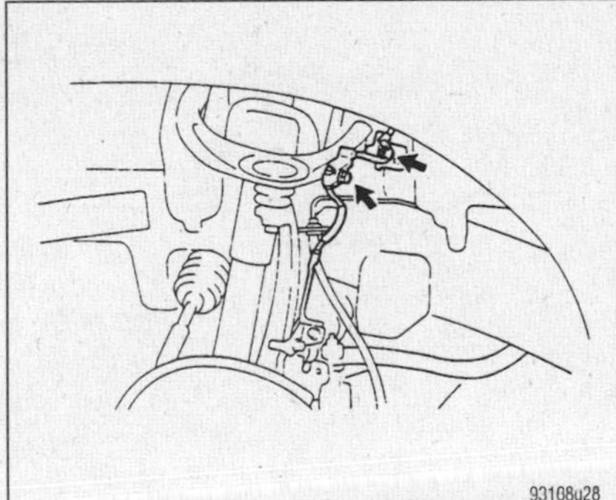
93168g28

Fig. 77 Wheel speed sensor wire mounting positions

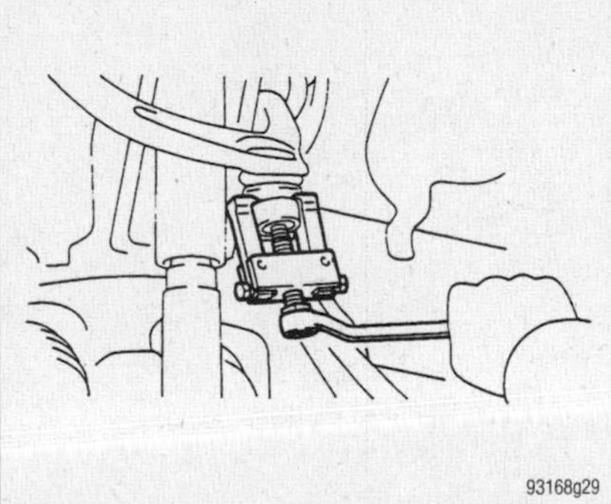
93168g29

Fig. 78 There is a special tool available to remove the upper ball joint

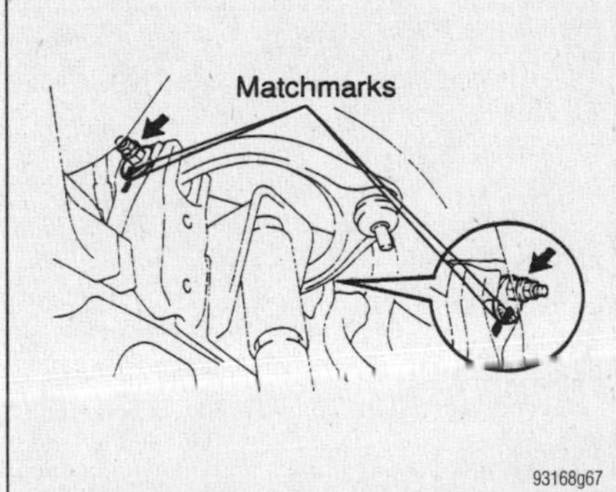

93168g67

Fig. 79 Matchmark the front and rear adjustment cams to the body

6. Matchmark the front and rear adjustment cams to the body.
7. Remove the nuts and then the No. 1 and No. 2 adjustment cams.
8. Remove the upper control arm.
9. Installation is the reverse of removal. Torque the upper control arm bolts to 72 ft. lbs. (98 Nm).

4Runner

1. Remove the shock and coil spring assembly.
2. Disconnect the ABS speed sensor wire harness clamp.
3. Disconnect the upper ball joint as follows:
   a. Remove the cotter pins and loosen the nut.
   b. Using a ball joint separator, disconnect the upper ball joint from the control arm.
   c. Support the steering knuckle securely.
   d. Remove the nut.
4. Detach the control arm, by removing the nut, bolt, washers and lowering the arm.

To install:

5. Attach the upper control arm with the washer, bolt and nut. Make sure the arm is stabilized, then tighten the nut to 87 ft. lbs. (115 Nm).
6. Attach the upper ball joint to the control arm. Tighten the mounting nut to 80 ft. lbs. (105 Nm). Install a new cotter pin.
7. Attach the ABS speed sensor wire harness clamp, tighten to 71 inch lbs. (8 Nm).
8. Install the shock and coil spring assembly.
9. Check the alignment.

Tacoma

See Figure 80

1. Remove the front wheel.
2. Remove the shock and coil spring assembly.
3. Disconnect the ABS speed sensor wire harness clamp.
4. Disconnect the upper ball joint as follows:
   a. Remove the cotter pins and loosen the nut.
   b. Using a ball joint separator, disconnect the upper ball joint from the control arm.
   c. Support the steering knuckle securely.
   d. Remove the nut.
5. Detach the control arm, by removing the nut, bolt, washers and lowering the arm.

To install:

6. Attach the upper control arm with the washer, bolt and nut. Make sure the arm is stabilized, then tighten the nut to 87 ft. lbs. (115 Nm).
7. Attach the upper ball joint to the control arm. Tighten the mounting nut to 80 ft. lbs. (105 Nm). Install a new cotter pin.
8. Attach the ABS speed sensor wire harness clamp, tighten to 71 inch lbs. (8 Nm).
9. Install the shock and coil spring assembly.
10. Check the alignment.

Tundra

1. Raise and support the vehicle.
2. Remove the front wheel.
3. Remove the fender apron seal to gain better access to the upper control arm.
4. Removed the ABS sped sensor and wire harness.
5. Remove the brake and fuel line clamp.
6. Remove the stabilizer bar link.
7. Disconnect the steering knuckle from the upper bar joint.
8. Loosen the 2 bolts, then remove the front and rear alignment adjusting shims.
9. Make note of the number and thickness of the front and rear shims.
10. Unbolt the upper control arm.
11. Remove the bolts, nuts and upper ball joint from the arm.

To install:

12. Attach the ball joint to the arm, tighten to 29 ft. lbs. (39 Nm).

➡Do not lose the camber adjusting shims. Record the position and thickness of the camber shims so that these can be reinstalled to their original locations. Install the equal number and thickness of shims into their locations.

13. Install the arm to the vehicle, with the shims, then tighten the mounting bolts to 94 ft. lbs. (130 Nm).
14. Attach the steering knuckle to the upper ball joint.
15. Install the stabilizer bar link.
16. Install the ABS speed sensor and wire harness.
17. Place the wheel into position, hand tighten the lug nuts.
18. Lower the vehicle, tighten the lug nuts to 83 ft. lbs. (110 Nm).
19. Have the alignment checked at a reputable repair facility.

T100

See Figures 81, 82, and 83

1. Raise the truck and support it on safety stands. Remove the wheels.
2. Disconnect the ABS speed sensor wire harness clamp.
3. Remove the torsion bar.
4. Remove upper ball joint out of the steering knuckle as follows:
   a. Support the lower control arm with a suitable jack.
   b. Remove the nuts, then disconnect the upper control arm from the steering knuckle.
   c. Remove the bolts, then remove the upper control arm from the frame.

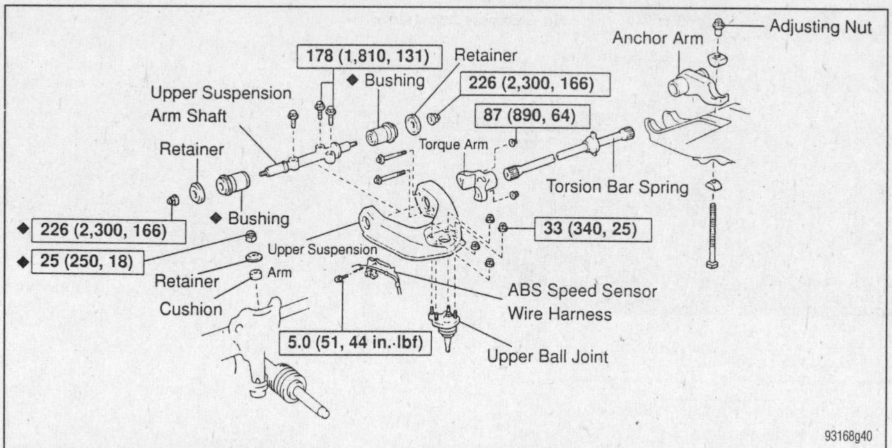

Fig. 81 Exploded view of the upper control arm—4WD T100 shown

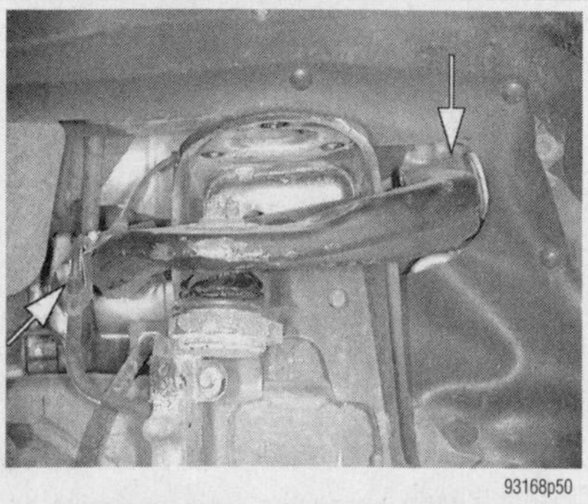

Fig. 80 Upper control arm mounting bolt locations

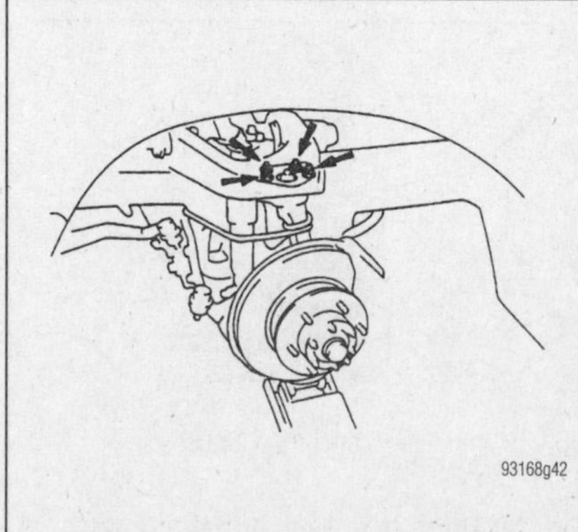

Fig. 82 Upper ball joint bolt locations

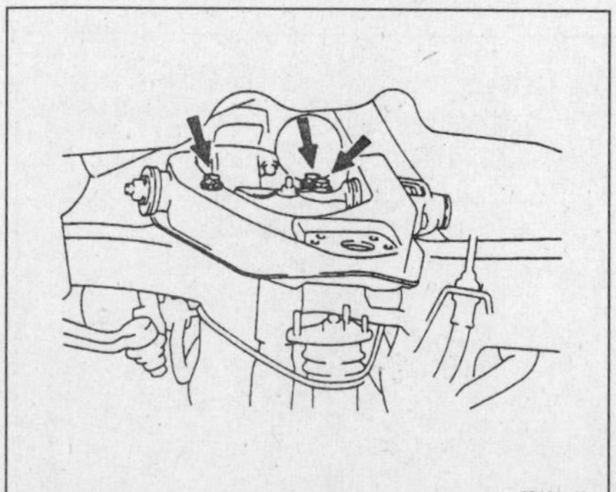

Fig. 83 Remove the three bolts and remove the upper control (suspension) arm from the frame

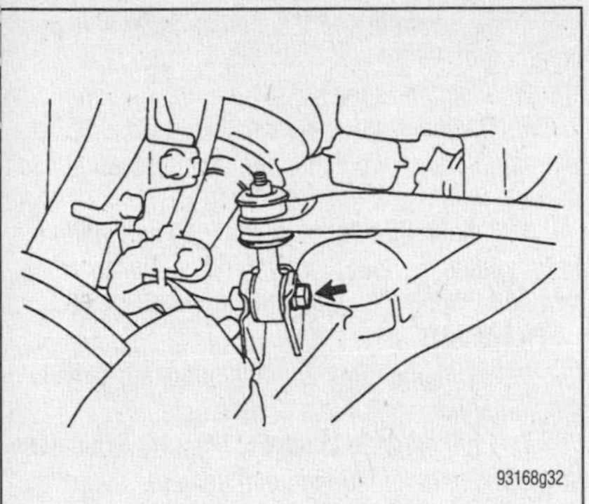

Fig. 84 Location of the stabilizer end link

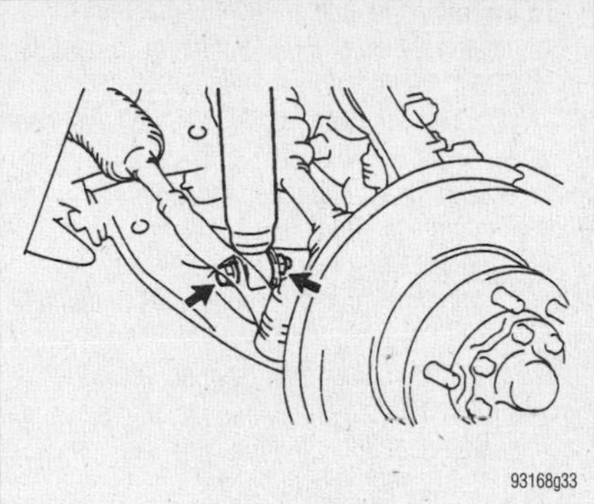

Fig. 85 Lower shock mounting bolt location

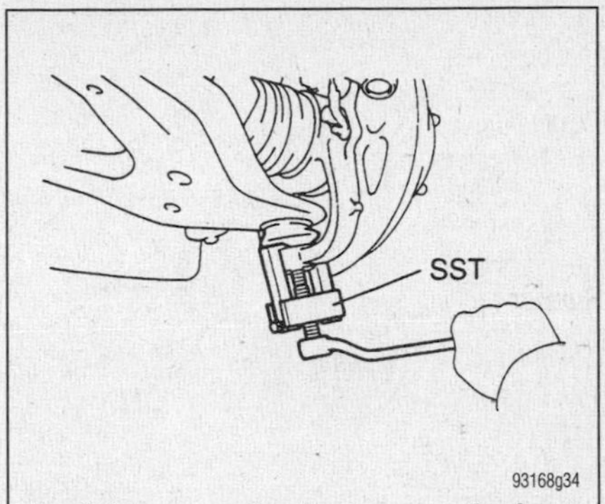

Fig. 86 Use a puller to separate the lower ball joint

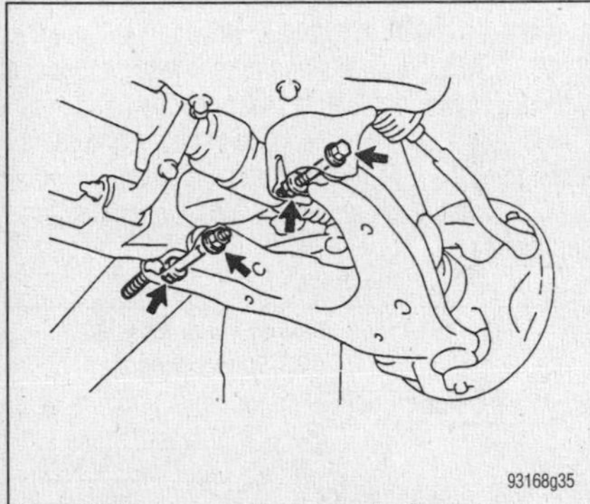

Fig. 87 Lower control arm bolts

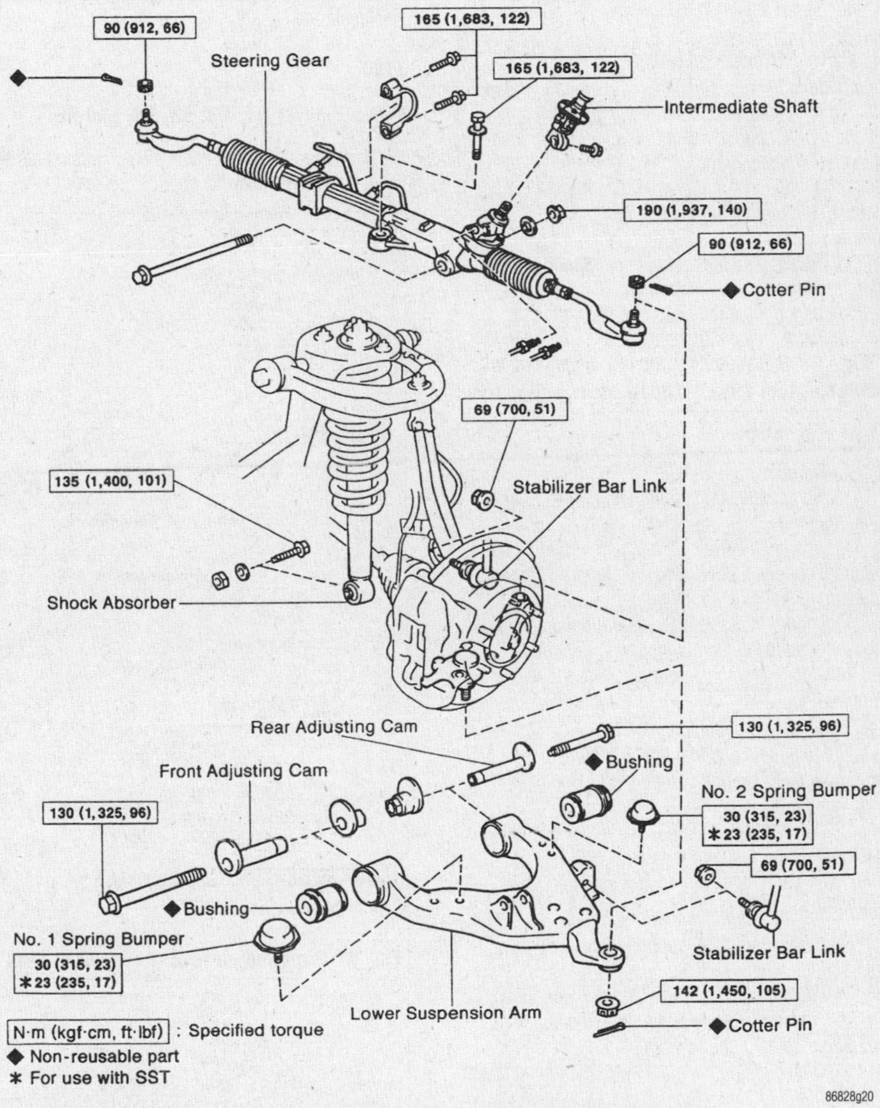

Fig. 88 Exploded view of the lower control arm and associated components

To install:

5. Install the upper arm and tighten the mounting bolts to 131 ft. lbs. (178 Nm).
6. Connect the upper ball joint to the steering knuckle, then tighten the nut to 25 ft. lbs. (33 Nm).
7. Install the torsion bar.
8. Install the wheel(s) and lower the vehicle.
9. Have the alignment checked and adjusted at a reputable repair facility.

Lower Control Arm

REMOVAL & INSTALLATION

Land Cruiser

See Figures 84, 85, 86, and 87

1. Remove the front wheel.
2. Detach the engine undercover.
3. Remove the torsion bar.
4. Disconnect the stabilizer bar end link. Also, unbolt the shock absorber from the lower control arm.
5. Detach the steering knuckle from the lower control arm.
6. Remove the nuts, bolts, and then the lower control arm.
7. Installation is the reverse of removal. Torque the lower suspension arm bolts to 170 ft. lbs. (230 Nm).

4Runner and Tacoma

See Figures 88, 89, and 90

1. Remove the front wheel.
2. Remove the steering gear assembly.
3. Disconnect the stabilizer bar link.
4. Disconnect the shock absorber from lower control arm.
5. Support the upper control and steering knuckle securely.
6. Remove the cotter pin and nut from the lower ball joint.
7. With a ball joint remover, disconnect the ball joint from the lower control arm
8. Place matchmarks on the front and rear adjusting cams.
9. Remove the 2 bolts, nuts, adjusting cams and lower control arm.
10. Remove the spring bumpers with a special tool 09922–10010 or its equivalent.

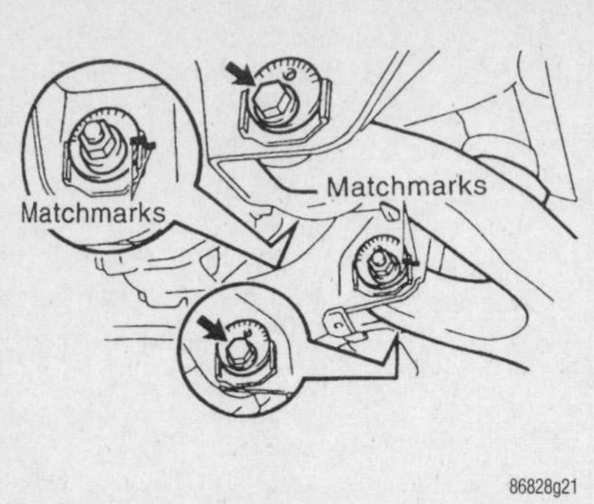

86828g21
Fig. 89 Place matchmarks on the front and rear adjusting cams

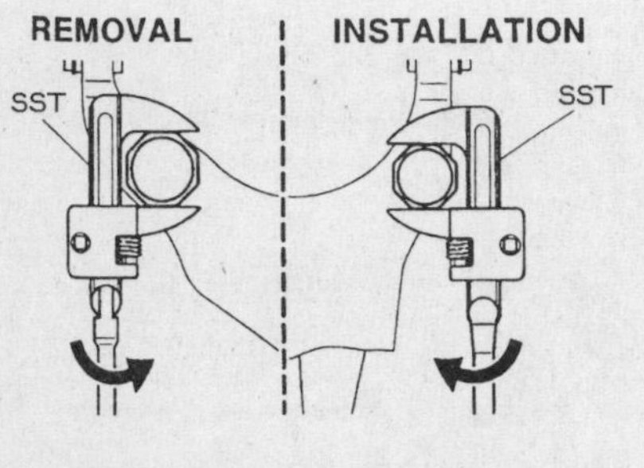

86828g22
Fig. 90 Remove the spring bumpers with special tool 09922–10010 or its equivalent

To install:

11. Attach the spring bumpers, tighten to 17 ft. lbs. (23 Nm).
12. Attach the lower control arm, placing it in the appropriate position with the matchmarks. Tighten the arm to 96 ft. lbs. (130 Nm).
13. Attach the lower ball joint with the correct tool, tighten the nut to 105 ft. lbs. (142 Nm).
14. Attach the shock absorber to the lower control arm.
15. Install the stabilizer bar link.
16. Install the steering gear assembly.
17. Install the front wheel, lower the vehicle. Tighten the lug nuts.
18. Have the alignment checked at a reputable repair facility.

Tundra

1. Raise and safely support the vehicle with jackstands.
2. Remove the right and left front wheels.
3. Detach the tie rod ends from the knuckle spindle assembly on each side.
4. Remove the power steering gear set bolts and nuts.
5. Disconnect the stabilizer bar end links from the lower control arm.
6. Detach the strut from the lower control arm.
7. Disconnect the ball joint from the lower control arm.
8. Matchmark the front and rear cam plates to the chassis.
9. Remove the bolts, and cam plates while slightly shifting the power steering gear towards the rear.

To install:

10. Install the lower suspension arm. Torque the bolts to 96 ft. lbs. (130 Nm).
11. Connect the lower ball joint to the lower control arm. Torque the nut to 103 ft. lbs. (140 Nm).
12. Attach the strut to the lower control arm. Torque the bolts to 100 ft. lbs. (135 Nm).
13. Connect the stabilizer bar end link to the lower control arm. Torque the bolts to 51 ft. lbs. (69 Nm).
14. Install the power steering gear. Torque the bolts as follows:
    - Bolt A: 122 ft. lbs. (165 Nm).
    - Nut B: 96 ft. lbs. (130 Nm).
    - Nut and bolt C: 122 ft. lbs. (165 Nm).
15. Install the tie rod ends.
16. Install the wheels.
17. Have the alignment checked by a qualified repair facility.

T100

➧ **See Figures 91, 92, 93, 94, and 95**

1. Raise the front of the truck and support it with safety stands. Remove the wheels.
2. Remove the shock absorber from the lower control arm.
3. Disconnect the stabilizer bar at the lower arm.
4. Disconnect the lower ball joint from the control arm. Remove the cotter pin, then discard. Loosen the nut.
5. Paint matchmarks on the front and rear adjusting cams, remove them and lift out the control arm.

To install:

6. Install the lower arm and adjusting cams to the frame. Temporarily tighten the nuts.
7. Connect the ball joint to the arm. Tighten the nut to 105 ft. lbs. (142 Nm) and install a new cotter pin.
8. Connect the stabilizer bar and tighten the nuts.
9. Install the shock absorber to the lower control arm, tighten to 101 ft. lbs. (137 Nm).
10. Install the wheels and lower the truck. Bounce the truck several times to set the suspension.
11. Align the matchmarks on the adjusting cams and tighten the nuts to 145 ft. lbs. (196 Nm).
12. Have the alignment checked at a reputable repair facility.

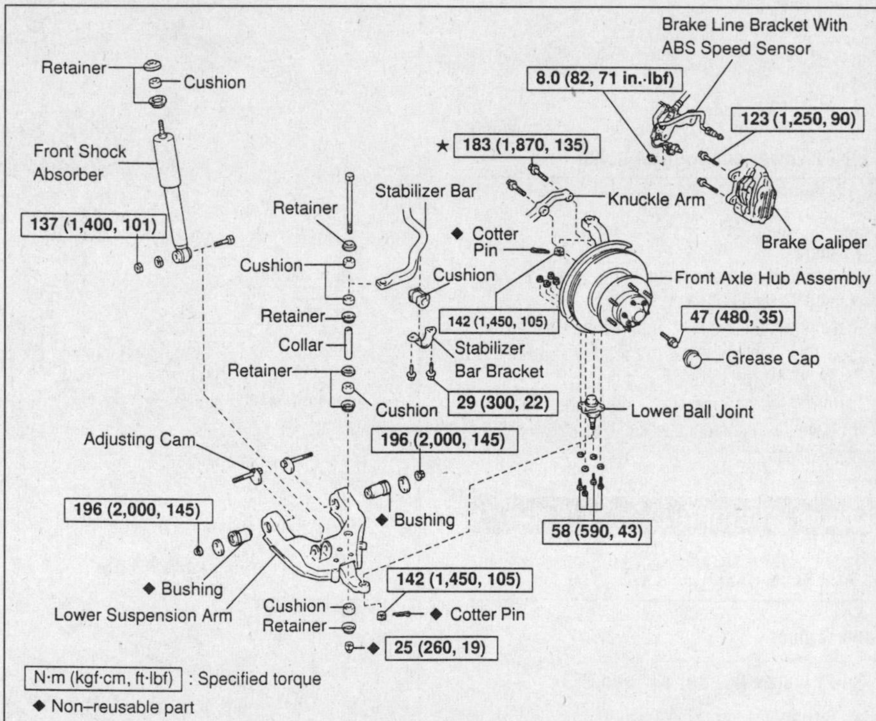

93168g44
Fig. 91 Exploded view of the lower control arm and related components

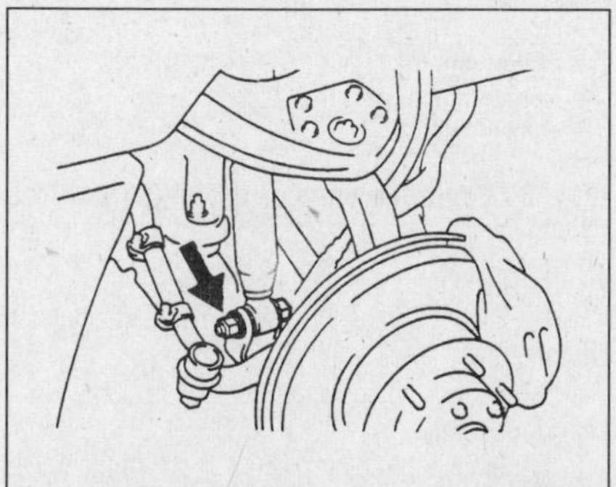
93168g45
Fig. 92 Lower shock absorber bolt location

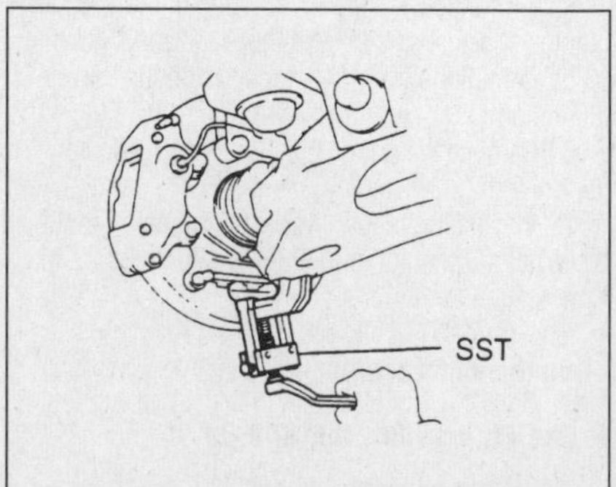

93168g46
Fig. 93 Remove the lower ball joint

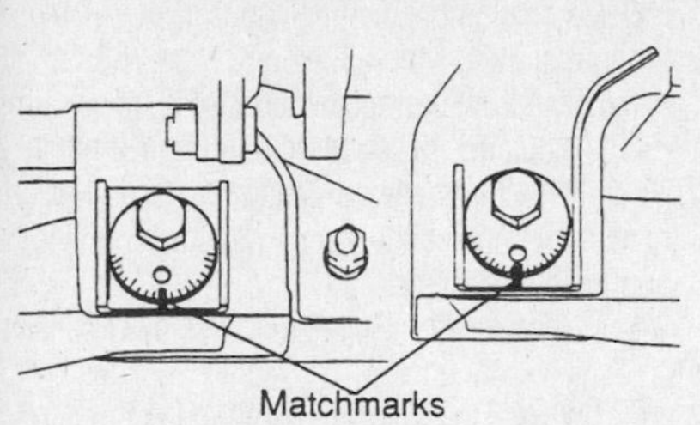

93168g47

Fig. 94 Matchmark the front and rear adjusting cam plates

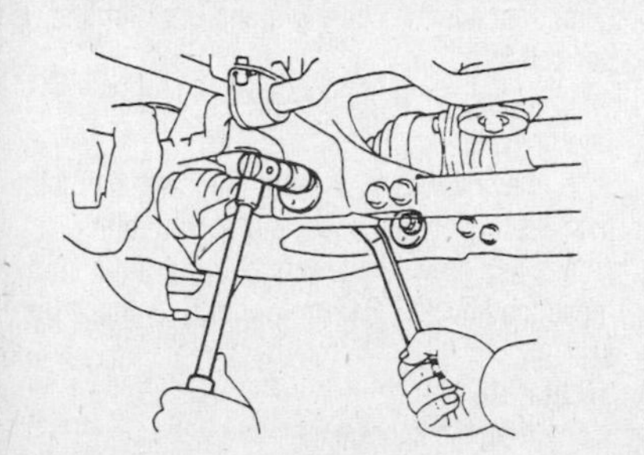

93168g48

Fig. 95 Remove the bolt and nut, then remove the lower control arm

Steering Knuckle and Spindle

REMOVAL & INSTALLATION

Land Cruiser

1997 VEHICLES

1. Remove the front axle hub.

CAUTION

Brake pads and shoes may contain asbestos, which has been determined to be a cancer causing agent. Never clean the brake surfaces with compressed air. Avoid inhaling any dust from brake surfaces. When cleaning brakes, use commercially available brake cleaning fluids.

2. Remove the knuckle spindle mounting bolts.
3. Remove the dust seal and dust cover (splash shield).
4. Tap the knuckle spindle gently and remove it from the steering knuckle.
5. Turn the axle so that one flat part of the outer shaft faces upward; pull out the axle shaft.
6. Use a separator to disconnect the tie rod end from the knuckle arm.
7. Remove the oil seal and retainer.
8. Remove the knuckle arm bearing and bearing cap nuts. Lightly tap the slits of the washers and remove them. Push out the knuckle arm and shims from the steering knuckle. Don't lose the shims.
9. Remove the steering knuckle and bearing. Mark the removed adjusting shims and bearings by position for reassembly.

To install:

10. Install a new oil seal if it was removed from the axle housing. Install a new oil seal set (felt dust seal, rubber seal and steel ring, in that order).
11. Place the bearings in position on the knuckle and axle housing. Place the knuckle onto the housing.
12. Support the upper bearing inner race on the knuckle arm. Install the arm over the shims, making sure the shims are in their exact original location. Tap the knuckle arm into the inner race.
13. Support the lower bearing inner race. Install the bearing cap over the shims, making sure the shims are in their exact original location. Tap the bearing cap into the inner race.
14. Remove the race supports. Install the cone washers to the third arm and tighten the nuts to 71 ft. lbs. (96 Nm). Install the cone washers to the knuckle arm and tighten the nuts to the same value.
15. Use a spring tension gauge to measure the bearing preload. Correct preload is 6.6–13.2 lbs. (19–59 N).
16. Connect the tie rod to the knuckle arm. Tighten the castle nut to 67 ft. lbs. (91 Nm). Install a new cotter pin.
17. Install the oil seal set to the knuckle.
18. Install the axle shaft.
19. Pack the knuckle about $^3/_4$ full with molydisulfide grease.
20. Place a new gasket on the knuckle and install the spindle. Install the gasket, dust cover and dust seal on the spindle. Tighten the spindle mounting bolts to 34 ft. lbs. (47 Nm).
21. Install the axle hub.
22. Have the alignment checked at a reputable repair facility.

1998–00 VEHICLES

1. Remove the axle hub assembly.
2. Detach the oil seal.
3. Remove the gasket and dust cover.
4. Detach the ABS wheel speed sensor wiring harness.
5. Remove the outer tie rod end from the steering knuckle.
6. Support the lower control arm with a floor jack. Detach the lower control arm from the steering knuckle.
7. Remove the cotter pin and nut.
8. Disconnect the steering knuckle from the upper control arm.
9. Remove the steering knuckle from the lower control arm.
10. Installation is the reverse of removal.

4Runner

1. Remove the front wheel.
2. Unbolt the shock absorber from the lower control arm.
3. Remove the grease cap.
4. On models with ABS, remove the ABS speed sensor and wire harness clamp from the steering knuckle.
5. Remove the brake line bracket from the steering knuckle.
6. Remove the caliper and rotor.
7. Disconnect the lower ball joint.
8. Remove the steering knuckle with hub as follows:
   a. Remove the cotter pin and loosen the nut.
   b. Using a special tool 09950–40010 or equivalent, disconnect the steering knuckle.
   c. Remove the nut and knuckle.

To install:

9. Attach the steering knuckle and tighten the nut to 80 ft. lbs. (108 Nm). Install a new cotter pin.
10. Attach the lower ball joint, tighten the four mounting bolts to 59 ft. lbs. (80 Nm).
11. Attach the caliper and rotor.
12. Install the brake line bracket to the steering knuckle, tighten to 21 ft. lbs. (28 Nm).
13. Attach the ABS speed sensor and wire harness clamp if removed, tighten to 71 inch lbs. (8 Nm).
14. Install the grease cap.
15. Install the shock absorber.
16. Attach the wheel, lower the vehicle.
17. Tighten the lug nuts, the bleed the brake system.
18. Have the alignment checked at a reputable repair facility.

Tacoma

➧ **See Figures 96 and 97**

1. Remove the front wheel.
2. Unbolt the shock absorber from the lower control arm.
3. Disconnect the driveshaft as follows:
   a. Without a freewheeling hub, use a flat-bladed tool to remove the grease cap.
   b. Remove the cotter pin and lock cap.
   c. Have an assistant apply the brakes, then remove the locknut.
   d. With free wheeling hubs, remove the free wheel hub.
   e. Using a snapring expander, removed the snapring.
   f. Remove the spacer.
4. On models with ABS, remove the ABS speed sensor and wire harness clamp from the steering knuckle.
5. Remove the caliper and rotor.
6. Disconnect the lower ball joint.
7. Remove the steering knuckle with hub as follows:
   a. Remove the cotter pin and loosen the nut.
   b. Using a special tool 09950–40010 or equivalent, disconnect the steering knuckle.
   c. Remove the nut and knuckle.

To install:

8. Attach the steering knuckle and tighten the nut to 80 ft. lbs. (108 Nm). Install a new cotter pin.
9. Attach the lower ball joint, tighten the four mounting bolts to 59 ft. lbs. (80 Nm).
10. Attach the caliper and rotor.
11. Attach the ABS speed sensor and wire harness clamp if removed, tighten to 71 inch lbs. (8 Nm).

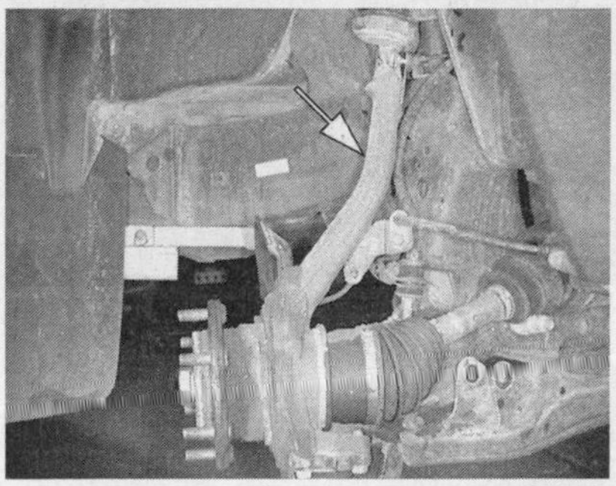

93168p49

Fig. 96 Installed view of the knuckle spindle assembly—Tacoma TRD shown

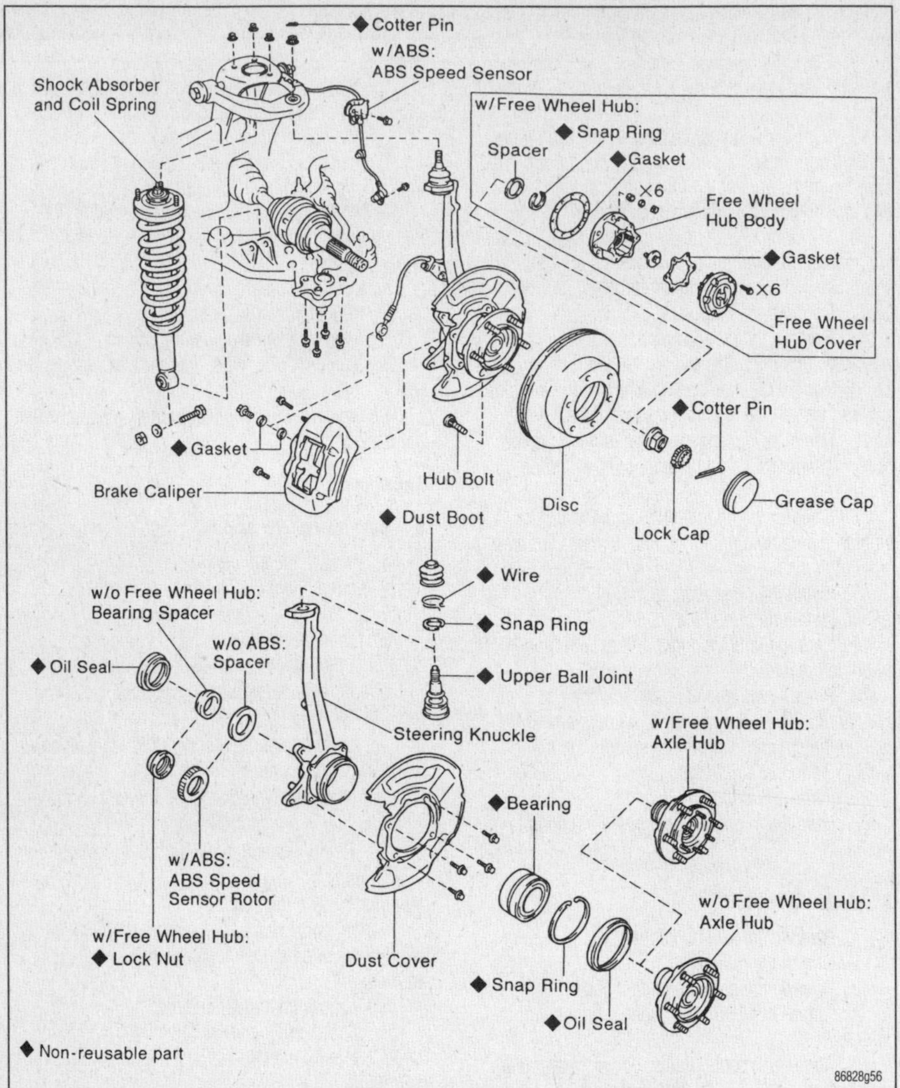

Fig. 97 Exploded view of the steering knuckle and hub—Tacoma shown

12. Attach the driveshaft.
13. Install the shock absorber.
14. Attach the wheel, lower the vehicle.
15. Tighten the lug nuts, then bleed the brake system.
16. Have the alignment checked at a reputable repair facility.

Tundra

1. Raise and properly support the vehicle on jackstands.
2. Remove the front wheel.
3. Remove the grease cap.
4. On 4WD models, disconnect the driveshaft.
5. On vehicles with ABS, remove the wheel speed sensor and wiring harness clamp.
6. Remove the brake caliper.
7. Remove the brake rotor.
8. Loosen the bolts to the shock absorber and then remove it from the vehicle.
9. Detach the lower ball joint.
10. Remove the cotter pin and then loosen the nut to the ball joint.
11. Remove the ball joint nut and then the steering knuckle.

To install:

12. Install the steering knuckle back onto the vehicle.
13. Connect the lower ball joint and torque the nut to 77 ft. lbs. (105 Nm). Torque the four bolts to 59 ft. lbs. (80 Nm).
14. Install the shock absorber.
15. Install the brake rotor and then the caliper.
16. Attach the ABS speed sensor wire harness clamp.
17. Install the driveshaft lock nut and tighten it while applying the brakes.
18. Install the grease cap and then the front wheel.
19. Depress the brakes several times.
20. Have the front alignment checked.
21. Check the ABS speed sensor signal.

T100

1. Remove the front wheels.
2. Remove the caliper and front axle hub.
3. Measure the steering knuckle bushing thrust clearance as follows:
   a. Install a bolt in the driveshaft.
   b. Using a feeler gauge, measure the driveshaft thrust clearance between the steering knuckle outside bushing and spacer, by pulling the bolt and applying a load of 22 lbs. (98 N).
   c. Standard clearance: 0.0039–0.0197 in. (0.10–0.50mm). Maximum 0.039 in. (1.0mm).
   d. If the thrust clearance is more than the maximum, replace the steering knuckle outside and inside bushings.
4. Detach the front shock from the lower control arm.
5. Separate the stabilizer bar from the lower control arm.
6. Remove the steering knuckle as follows:
   a. Using a pair of snapring pliers, remove the ring and spacer.
   b. Support the lower control arm with a jack.
   c. Remove the cotter pin and nut from the upper ball joint.
   d. Using a ball joint separator, detach the joint from the knuckle.
   e. Remove the bolts from the lower ball joint, then disconnect the knuckle from the joint.
   f. Push down the lower control arm, then remove the knuckle. Be careful not to damage the seal.

To install:

7. Install the knuckle as follows:
   a. Apply synthetic oil and lithium soap base chassis grease NLGI No. 1 or equivalent to the driveshaft.
   b. Push down on the lower control arm, then install the steering knuckle.
   c. Connect the lower ball joint to the steering knuckle, tighten the nut to 105 ft. lbs. (142 Nm).
   d. Install a new cotter pin.
   e. Install a spacer to the driveshaft.
   f. Using a pair of snapring pliers, install the ring.

➡If you replace the knuckle bushing, recheck the clearance of the driveshaft thrust.

   g. Using a feeler gage, measure the driveshaft thrust clearance between the knuckle and the outside bushing and spacer, by pulling the bolt and applying a load of 22 lbs. (98 N).
   h. Standard clearance should be 0.0039–0.0197 in. (0.10–0.50mm).
   i. If the clearance is not within specifications, replace the spacer.
8. Connect the stabilizer bar to the lower control arm, tighten the nut to 19 ft. lbs. (25 Nm).
9. Attach the front shock to the lower control arm, tighten the nut to 101 ft. lbs. (137 Nm).
10. Install the dust cover and new seal, tighten to 13 ft. lbs. (18 Nm).
11. Install the front axle hub and caliper.
12. Install the wheel, lower the vehicle. Depress the brake pedal several times.
13. Tighten the lug nuts. Check the front end alignment.
14. Check the ABS speed sensor signal.

Front Axle Hub and Bearing

Hub and bearing removal and installation procedures for these models can be found under Drivetrain.

Wheel Alignment

For information on Wheel Alignment, please refer to the section under 2WD Front Suspension.

REAR SUSPENSION

REAR SUSPENSION COMPONENTS—TACOMA

1. Shock absorber
2. Differential assembly
3. Leaf spring
4. Spring plate and U-bolts
5. Axle assembly
6. Rear leaf spring shackle-to-body mounting
7. Lower shock absorber bushing and retainer

93168prs

93168pr1

REAR SUSPENSION COMPONENTS—EARLY MODEL LAND CRUISER

1. Lower control arm
2. Upper control arm
3. Coil spring
4. Stabilizer bar cushion and bracket
5. Stabilizer bar
6. Axle assembly
7. Upper control arm bushing
8. Shock absorber
9. Stabilizer bar bushing
10. Lower shock absorber bushing and retainer

Leaf Springs

REMOVAL & INSTALLATION

See Figure 98

1. Loosen the rear wheel lug nuts.
2. Raise the rear of the vehicle. Support the vehicle with jackstands placed under the frame. Support the rear axle with a floor jack.
3. Remove the lug nuts and the wheel.
4. Remove the cotter pin, nut, and washer from the lower end of the shock absorber.
5. Detach the shock absorber from the spring seat.
6. Remove the parking brake cable clamp.

➡Remove the parking brake equalizer, if necessary.

7. Unfasten the U-bolt nuts and remove the spring seat assemblies.
8. Adjust the height of the rear axle housing so that the weight of the rear axle is removed from the rear springs.
9. Unfasten the spring shackle retaining nuts. Withdraw the spring shackle inner plate. Carefully pry out the spring shackle with a bar.
10. Remove the spring bracket pin from the front end of the spring hanger and remove the rubber bushing.
11. Remove the spring. Use care not to damage the hydraulic brake line or the parking brake cable.

To install:

12. Install the rubber bushing in the eye of the spring.
13. Align the eye of the spring with the spring hanger bracket and drive the pin through the bracket holes and rubber bushings.

➡Use soapy water or glass cleaner as a lubricant, if necessary, to aid in pin installation. Never use oil or grease.

14. Finger-tighten the spring hanger nuts and/or bolts.
15. Install the rubber bushing in the spring eye at the opposite end of the spring.
16. Raise the free end of the spring. Install the spring shackle through the bushing and the bracket.
17. Install the shackle inner plate and finger-tighten the retaining nuts.
18. Center the bolt head in the hole which is provided in the spring seat on the axle housing.
19. Fit the U-bolts over the axle housing. Install the lower spring seat.
20. Tighten the U-bolt nuts to:
    - T100—97 ft. lbs. (132 Nm)
    - Tacoma—90 ft. lbs. (120 Nm)
21. Install the parking brake cable and clamp. Install the equalizer, if it was removed.
22. Tighten the hanger pin and shackle nuts. Install the shock absorber bushings and washers. Tighten, and install the cotter pins.
23. Install the stabilizer link and hand tighten its retaining nuts.
24. Install the wheels, remove the stands, and lower the vehicle to the ground.
25. Bounce the truck several times to set the suspension and then tighten the shock absorber bolt. Tighten the hanger pin nut or bolt to:
    - Tacoma—115 ft. lbs. (120 Nm)
    - T100—19 ft. lbs. (26 Nm)
26. Tighten the shackle pin to 67 ft. lbs. (91 Nm) for all vehicles.

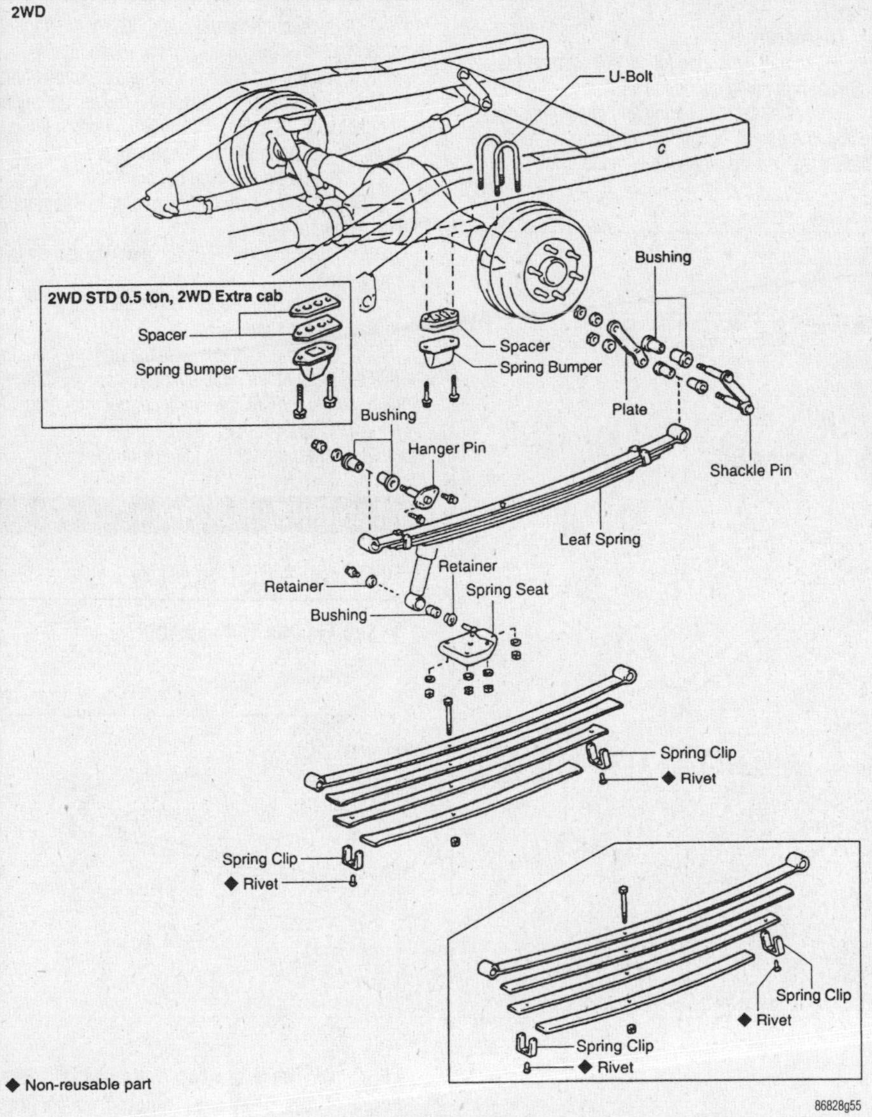

Fig. 98 Exploded view of the rear leaf spring and related components—2WD Tacoma shown

Coil Springs and Shock Absorbers

REMOVAL & INSTALLATION

See Figures 99, 100, 101, 102, and 103

1. Elevate and safely support the vehicle on jackstands placed under the frame rails. Place a floor jack under the rear axle housing and set the jack to hold the axle in place.

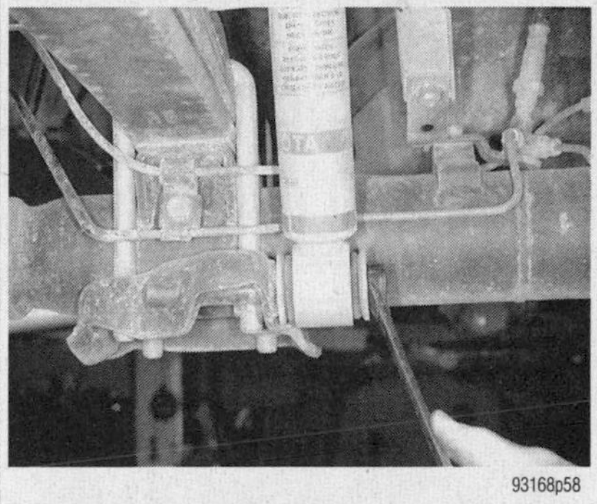

Fig. 99 Remove the lower shock absorber mounting bolt

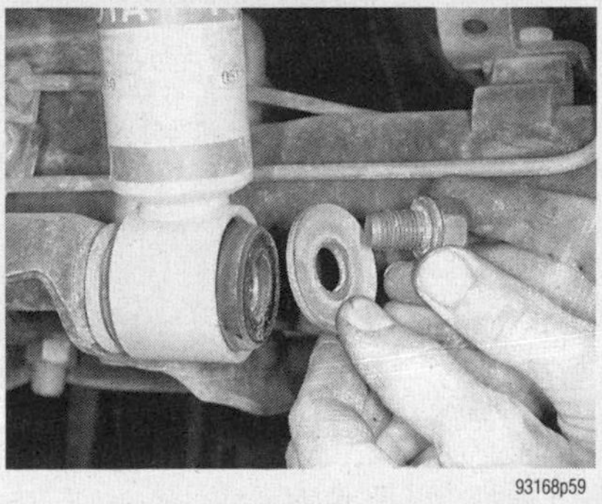

Fig. 100 Lower shock absorber mount bolt and washer

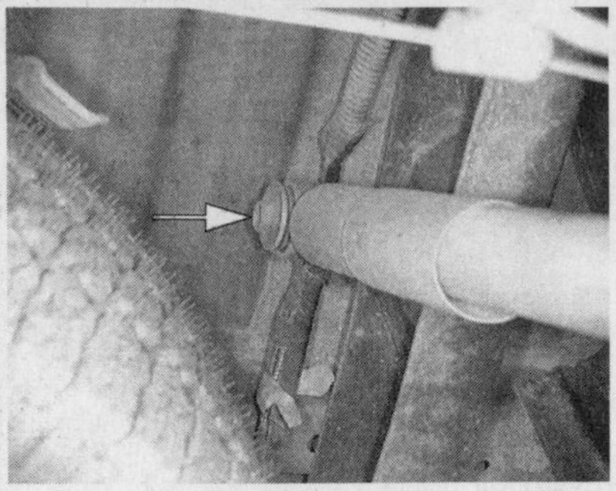
93168p60

Fig. 101 Upper shock absorber mounting bolt

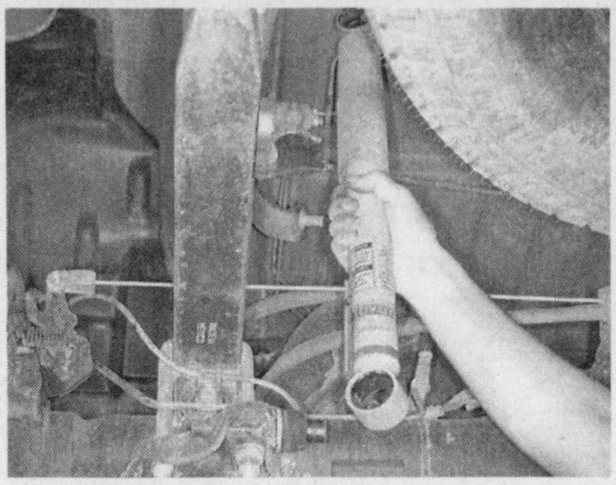
93168p61

Fig. 102 Slide the shock absorber off the upper mounting stud

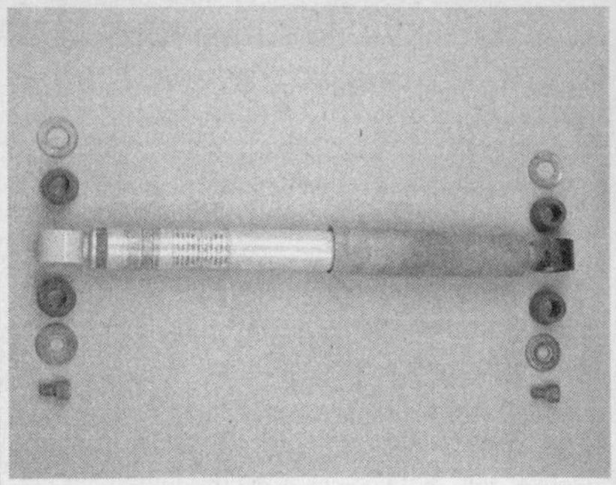
93168p62

Fig. 103 Exploded view of a typical Toyota rear shock absorber

2. Remove the wheel(s).
3. Remove the parking brake cable bracket from the rear axle housing.
4. Remove the lower shock absorber mount bolt. If the shock is to be replaced, disconnect the upper mount and remove the shock. If the shock is not to be removed, the upper mount may be left connected during spring removal. If only the shock is to be replaced (removal of the spring not required, skip to Step 13 for reinstallation. Refer to Inspection and/or Disposal of Shock Absorbers in the Front Suspension part of this Section.
5. Disconnect the stabilizer bar brackets from the rear axle housing.
6. Disconnect the right shock absorber lower mount.
7. Remove the bolt(s) holding the lateral control arm to the frame.
8. Very carefully begin to lower the jack holding the axle housing. Use extreme caution not to snap the brake lines and/or parking brake cable.
9. While lowering the axle, remove the coil spring as it loses tension and remove the upper insulators. Once the spring is removed, the bump stop (spring follow) may be unbolted from the frame if desired.

To install:

10. Install the spring follow to the frame if removed, tightening the bolt to 11 ft. lbs. (15 Nm).
11. Install the coil spring and upper insulators. Check the end of the spring; it must be correctly installed against the stopper on the lower mount.
12. Once the spring is in place, jack the axle housing enough to hold it but no more.

CAUTION

Do not compress the spring beyond the point reasonably necessary to hold it in place. Severe injury can occur if the spring comes loose.

13. Connect the lateral control rod to the frame, inserting the bolt from the front or shock absorber side. Install the nut but do NOT tighten it at this time.
14. Install the shock absorber. Tighten the upper mount to 14–18 ft. lbs. (20–25 Nm). Tighten the lower mount bolt to 47 ft. lbs. (64 Nm).
15. Attach the stabilizer bar brackets.
16. Attach the parking brake cable bracket to the rear axle housing.
17. Install the wheel(s) and lower the vehicle to the ground.
18. Bounce the rear of the vehicle several times to stabilize the suspension.
19. Use a floor jack to raise the rear axle housing (not the body of the vehicle) and support the axle with stands. Tighten the lateral control rod nut to 64–101 ft. lbs. (86–137 Nm).
20. Lower the vehicle to the ground.

Lateral Control Rod

REMOVAL & INSTALLATION

➧ **See Figures 104 and 105**

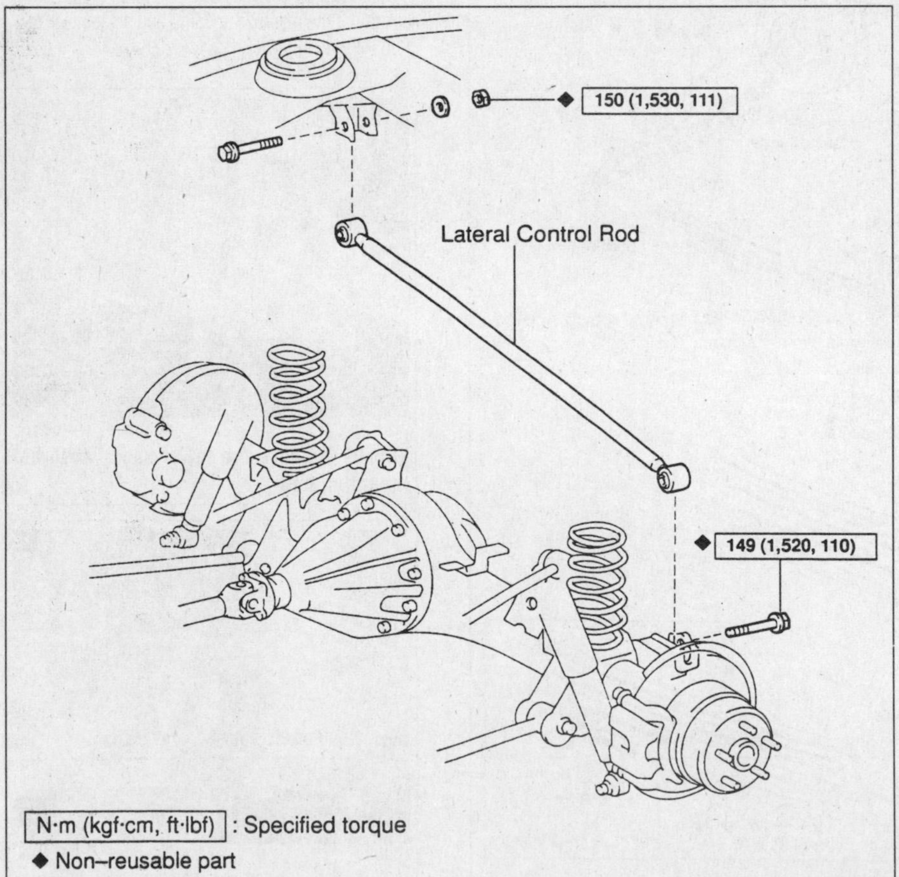

93168g49

Fig. 104 Lateral control rod—Land Cruiser

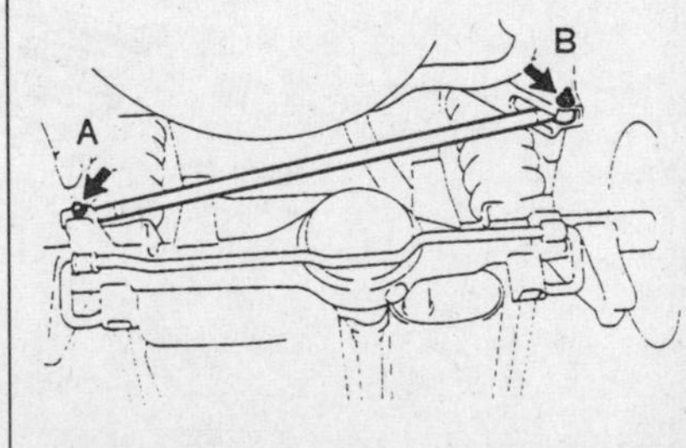

93168g50

Fig. 105 There are two bolts to the lateral control rod. They are depicted as "A" and "B"—Land Cruiser

1. Raise the rear of the vehicle and support it securely on jackstands placed under the frame rails. Support the rear axle with a floor jack.
2. Remove the bolts, nuts and washers.
3. Detach the lateral control rod.
4. Installation is the reverse of removal. Tighten the lateral control rod mounting bolts A to 110 ft. lbs. (149 Nm) and bolts B to 111 ft. lbs. (150 Nm).

Upper and Lower Control Arms

REMOVAL & INSTALLATION

See Figures 106, 107, and 108

1. Raise the rear of the vehicle and support it securely on jackstands placed under the frame rails. Support the rear axle with a floor jack.
2. Remove the rear wheel.
3. Detach the ABS speed sensor wiring harness.
4. Remove the bolt and then detach the heat insulator.
5. Loosen and remove the nuts, washers, and bolts to the lower control arm.
6. Remove the lower control arm.

To install:

7. Installation is the reverse of removal.
8. Torque the control arm mounting bolts to 111 ft. lbs. (150 Nm).

Anti-Sway (Stabilizer) Bar

REMOVAL & INSTALLATION

See Figures 109, 110, and 111

1. Raise the rear of the vehicle and support it securely on jackstands. Remove the rear wheels.
2. Loosen and remove the nuts and bolts to the left and right anti-sway bar end links.
3. Remove the anti-sway bar to rear axle housing mount bolts.
4. Lower the anti-sway bar.
5. Installation is the reverse of removal. Tighten the anti-way bar mounting brackets and end link bolts, 13 ft. lbs. (18 Nm).

Rear Wheel Bearings

REMOVAL & INSTALLATION

1. Before servicing the vehicle, refer to the precautions in the beginning of this section.
2. Raise the rear of the vehicle and support it securely on jackstands. Remove the rear wheel, and rear brakes.
3. If equipped, remove the Antilock Brake Sensor (ABS) from the rear axle assembly.
4. Disconnect the brake line and parking brake cable.
5. Remove the 4 backing plate mounting nuts and pull the axle shaft from the housing.
6. Remove the bearing retainer and antilock brake sensor rotor (differential side) by threading a nut over the bolts and lightly tapping with a hammer.

➡Do not reuse the nuts removed from the vehicle.

7. Grind the ABS sensor retainer and rotor surfaces, then chisel them out.
8. Place washers and 4 new nuts over the serration bolts and tighten the bolts to install the serration bolts to the backing plate.
9. Remove the 4 bolts from the serration bolts.
10. Remove the snapring.
11. Remove the axle shaft from the backing plate.
12. A special service tool (SST) (part number 09521-25011) will be needed to remove the rear axle shaft and bearing retainer from the backing plate. After the axle is removed, disconnect the service tool.
13. Remove the outer oil seal.
14. Remove the rear axle bearing.
15. Remove the inner oil seal.

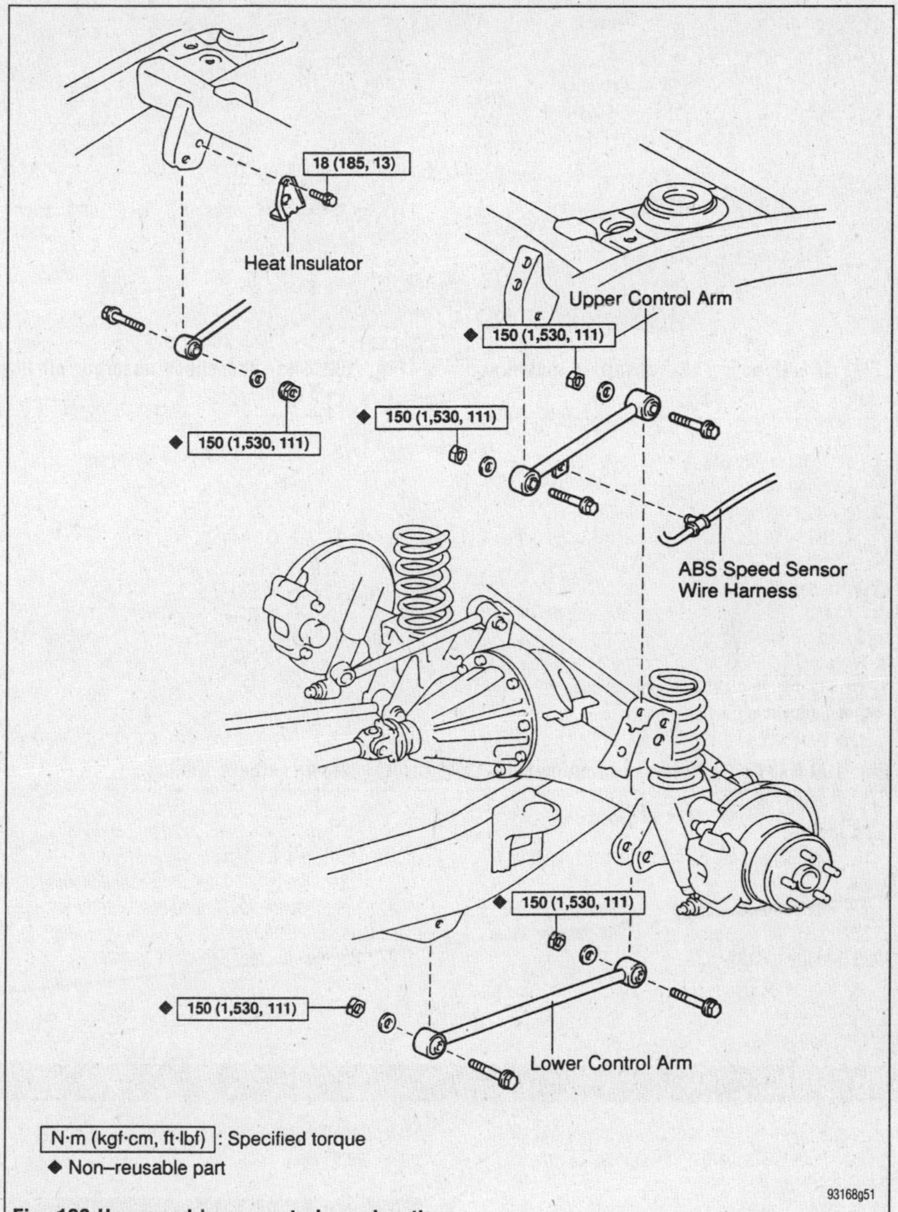

Fig. 106 Upper and lower control arm locations

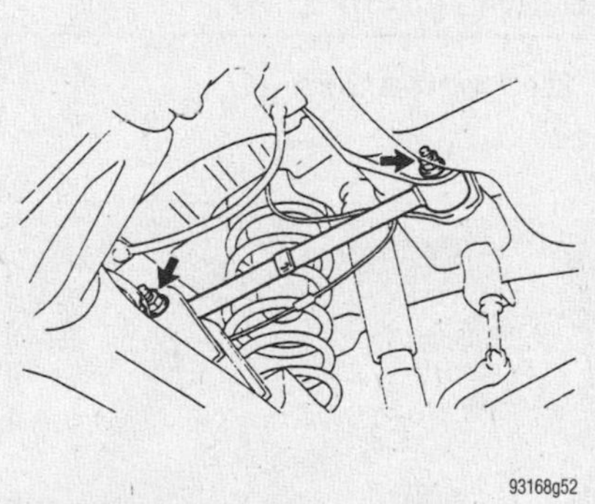

Fig. 107 Upper control arm bolts

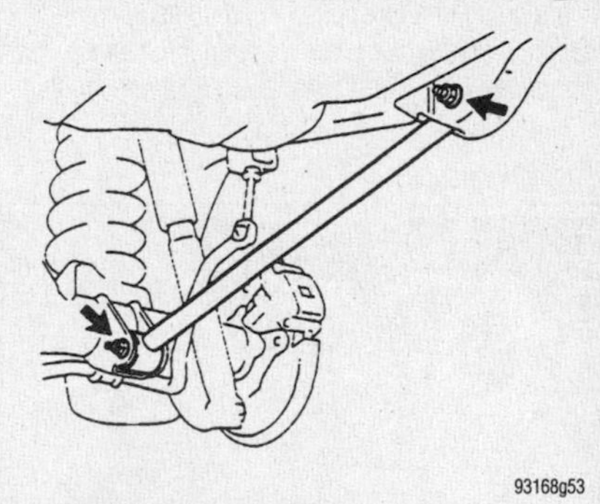

Fig. 108 Lower control arm bolts

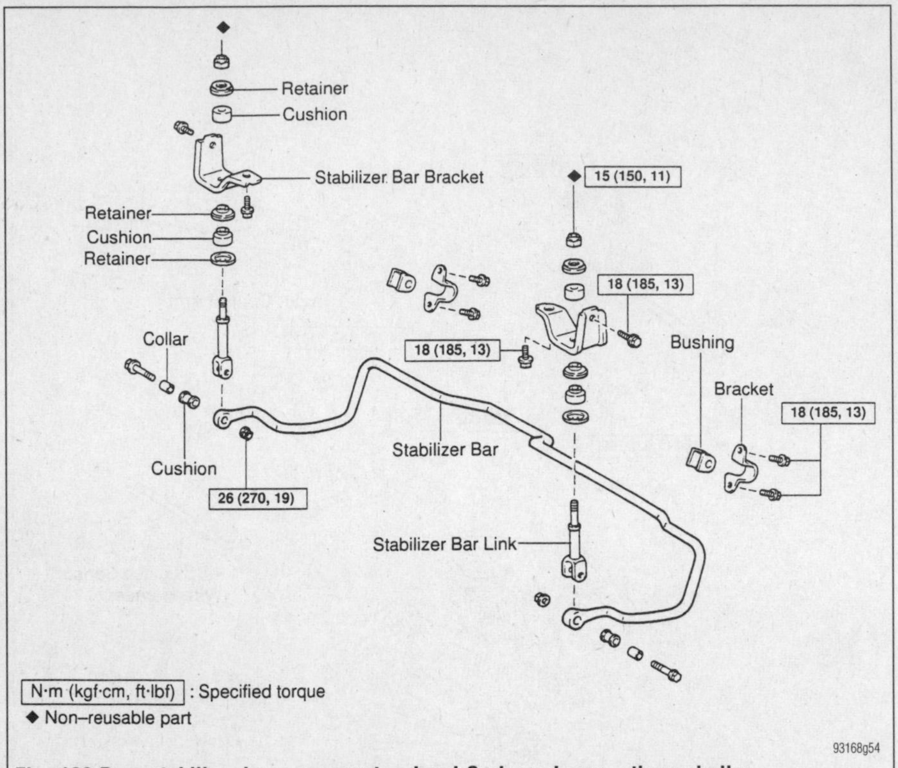

Fig. 109 Rear stabilizer bar components—Land Cruiser shown, others similar

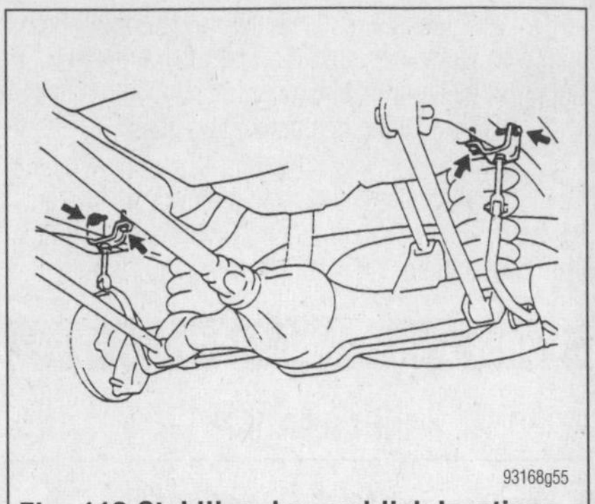

Fig. 110 Stabilizer bar end link locations

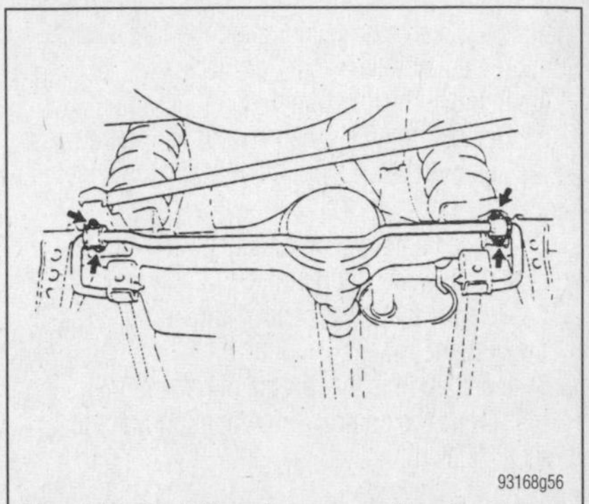

Fig. 111 Stabilizer bar mounting locations

To install:

16. Install the inner oil seal with the proper seal driver.
17. Install the rear axle bearing and outer seal.
18. Place the axle shaft and a new bearing retainer into the backing plate.
19. Replace the snapring.
20. Bleed the braking system and check for leaks.
21. Install a new ABS speed sensor rotor and retainer (differential side).
22. Replace the rear axle shaft assembly.
23. Connect brake line and parking brake cable.
24. Install the ABS sensor into the rear axle housing.
25. Install the rear brake assembly.
26. Replace the brake drum and rear wheel.

STEERING

Toyota offers two types of power steering on their trucks. There is standard and Progressive Power Steering (PPS).

On the PPS, the vehicle speed is detected by a speed sensor and fluid pressure acting on the piston is varied accordingly. When the truck is stopped or when moving at a low speed, fluid pressure is increased to lighten the force required for steering. At high speeds, the pressure is reduced to lessen the amount of assist and provide appropriate steering wheel response.

Steering Wheel

REMOVAL & INSTALLATION

➧ **See Figures 112 thru 117**

✻✻ CAUTION

Work must not begin until at least 90 seconds after the ignition switch is turned to the LOCK position and the negative battery cable is disconnected from the battery. The SRS is equipped with a back-up power source so that if the work is started within the 90 seconds of disconnecting the negative terminal, the SRS may be deployed.

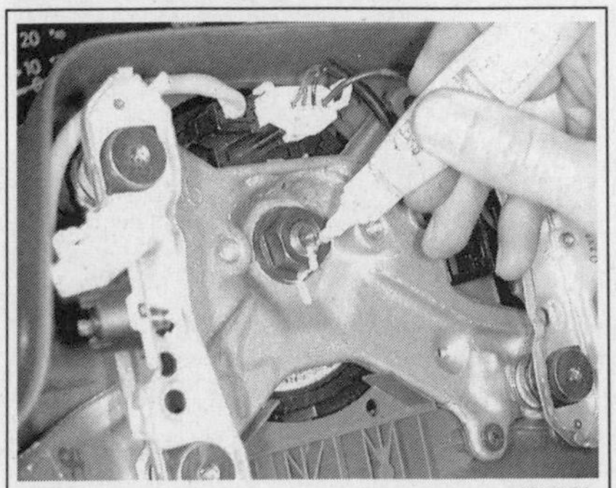

Fig. 112 Matchmark the steering wheel to the splined steering column shaft

Fig. 113 Use a deep socket and a breaker bar to remove the steering wheel nut

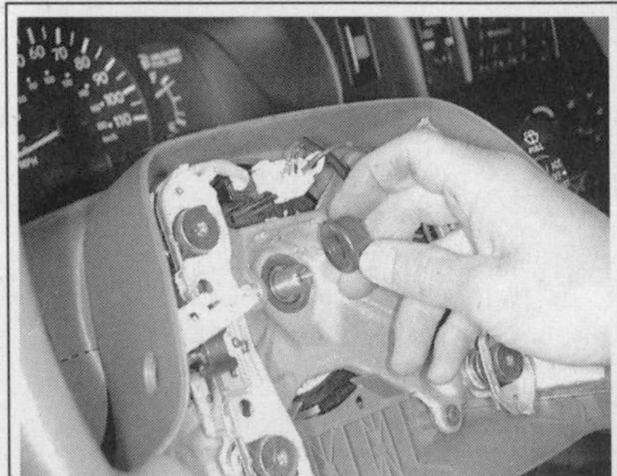

Fig. 114 Once loose, remove the nut by hand

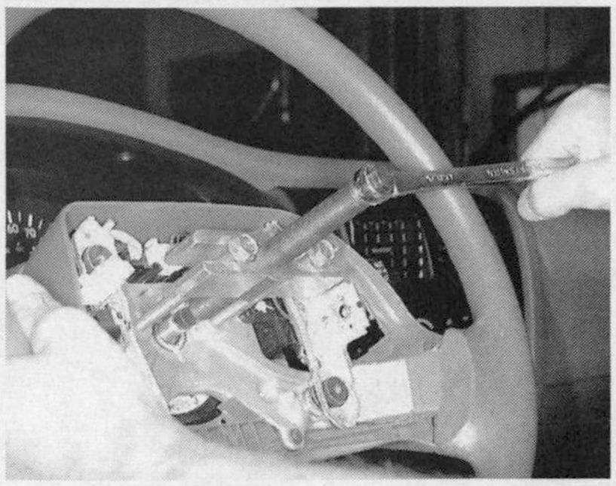

93168p03

Fig. 115 You may have to use a steering wheel puller to extract the wheel from the shaft

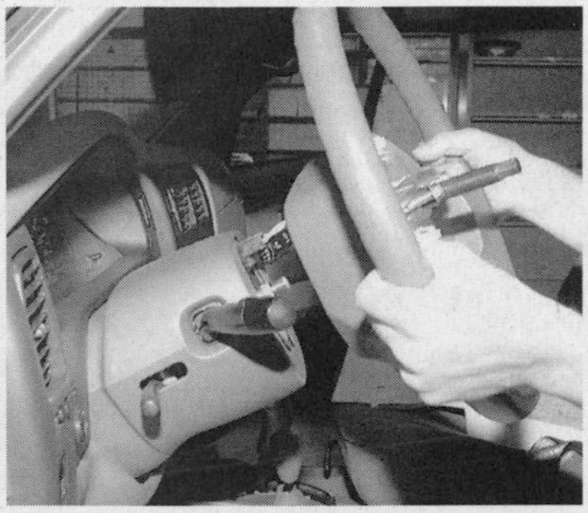

93168p02

Fig. 116 Using both hands, pull the wheel straight off the steering column

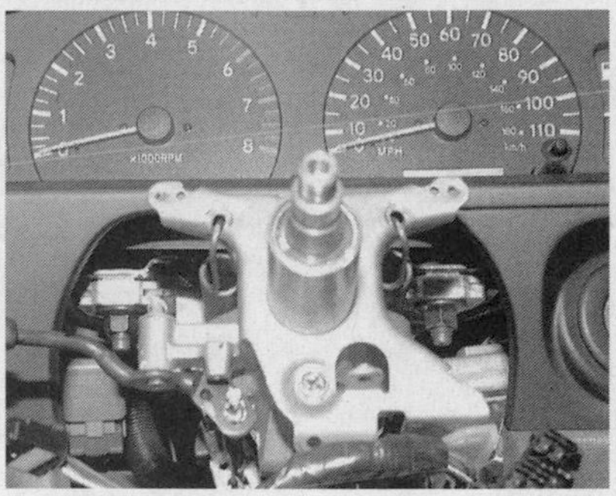

93168p01

Fig. 117 View of the steering column with the wheel removed

1. Disarm the SRS system. For additional information, please refer to the following topic(s): Chassis Electrical, SRS System.
2. On models without tilt steering, proceed as follows:
   a. Place the front wheels facing straight ahead.
   b. Remove the 2 steering wheel lower covers. Using a Torx® driver, loosen the Torx® screws until the groove along the screw circumference catches on the screw case.
   c. Pull out the wheel pad from the steering wheel, then detach the air bag connector.
3. Remove the steering wheel set nut. A special wheel puller may be needed. Place matchmarks on the steering wheel and mainshaft assembly. Remove the wheel.
4. Unplug the harness.

To install:

5. Align the matchmarks on the wheel and the mainshaft. Tighten the wheel set nut to 25 ft. lbs. (34 Nm).
6. Attach the harness.
7. Attach the air bag harness, then install the wheel pad after confirming that the circumference groove of the Torx® screw is caught on the screw case.
8. Using a Torx® driver, tighten the screws to 78 inch lbs. (9 Nm).
9. Install the steering wheel covers.
10. Check the steering wheel center point.

Turn Signal (Combination) Switch

REMOVAL & INSTALLATION

➧ **See Figures 118, 119, and 120**

The individual switches within the combination switch are individually replaceable after the combination assembly is removed and disassembled. It is not difficult but is exacting, requiring careful removal of wire terminals from the multi-pin connector.

1. Insure the ignition is switched **OFF**.
2. Remove the steering wheel pad and remove the steering wheel. Use of a steering wheel puller is strongly recommended. Always scribe matchmarks on the wheel hub and the steering column so the wheel can be reinstalled straight.
3. Remove the upper and lower steering covers. Remove the retaining screws holding the combination switch to the column.
4. Trace the harness down the column, then unplug the connector. Release the harness from the harness clamp(s).
5. Remove the combination switch from the column and place it on the workbench.
6. Disconnect the air bag harness (if equipped).
7. On the newer models, you will be able to remove the two mounting screws retaining the arm (wiper etc.) to replace.
8. Otherwise, identify the component to be replaced. Identify each wire color running from the switch (to be replaced) to the connector. These wires (only) will need to be removed so the new ones can be installed.
9. On all but 1989–90 Land Cruiser, the cover on the back of the connector must be raised to allow the wire terminal to be removed.
10. Diagram each wire and terminal to be removed. The new wiring must be installed exactly as original. From the front or plug end, insert a small pick or probe between the locking lug and the wire terminal. Pry down the locking lug with the tool and pull the terminal out from the rear. Repeat the procedure for each wire from the switch to be replaced.

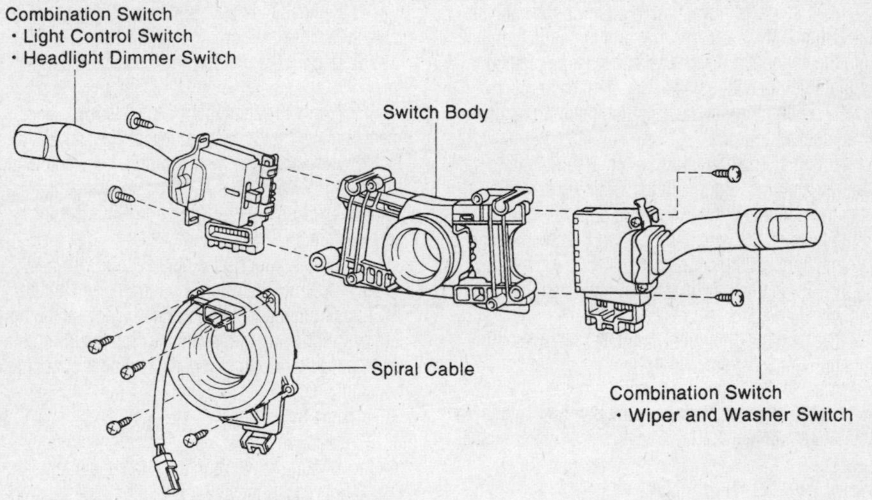

86826ga0

Fig. 118 The switches are secured to the switch body with screws

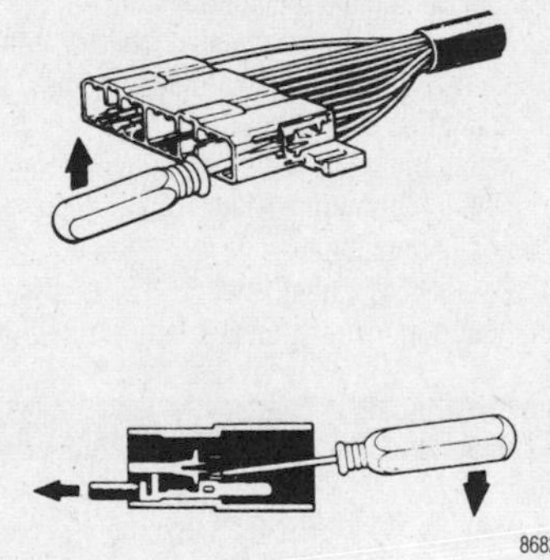

86826ga6

Fig. 119 From the front or plug end, insert a small pick or probe between the locking lug and the wire terminal

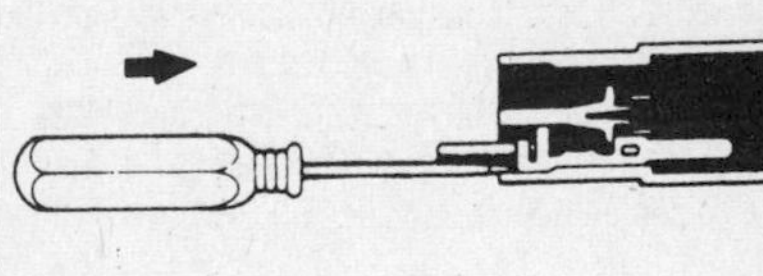

86826ga8

Fig. 120 Each terminal must be pushed in until it overrides the locking lug

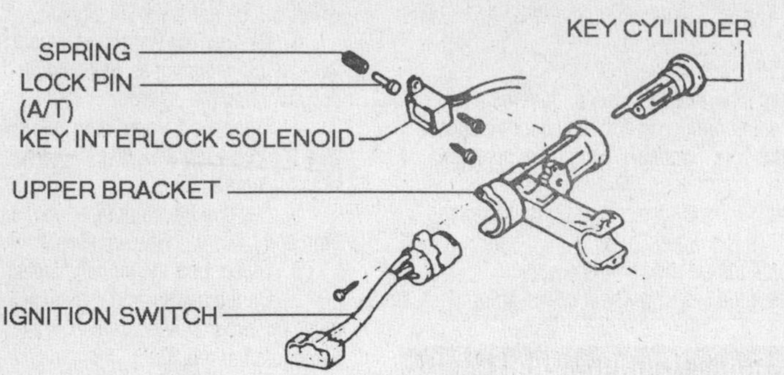

Fig. 121 Exploded view of the ignition switch assembly

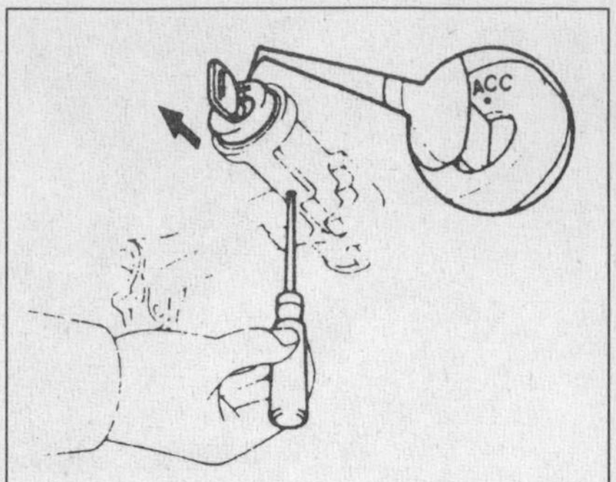

Fig. 122 Insert a thin rod in the hole at the bottom of the housing and press the stop tab inward. While holding the tab in, pull the cylinder out of the housing

11. With the wires free, remove the retaining screws holding the switch to be changed and remove it. The lighting control stalk has a spring and small ball with it; don't lose them.

To install:

12. Assemble the new component(s) onto the switch. Retaining screws should be tight enough to hold but not over tight. Components with cracked plastic won't stay in place.
13. Track the new wires into the harness and place each wire loosely in its correct terminal socket.
14. Use the removal tool to push on the back of the terminal (NOT on the wire) and force the terminal into the connector. Each terminal must be pushed in until it overrides the locking lug. Test each one by gently pulling the wire backwards; it should be positively locked in place.
15. Fit the combination switch assembly onto the steering column and install the retaining screws. Install the upper and lower steering column covers.
16. Install the wire harness into the clips and retainers; connect the connectors.
17. Align the matchmarks and reinstall the steering wheel and pad.
18. Turn the ignition switch **ON** and check the function of each control item.

Ignition Switch

REMOVAL & INSTALLATION

See Figures 121 and 122

Both the electrical portion of the ignition switch and the key/lock portion may be replaced without removing the housing or bracket holding them. The bracket holding the ignition switch assembly is held to the column by bolts whose heads were intentionally broken off at installation. About the only time the bracket must be removed would be if the steering column or tube must be replaced. In the event that the bracket must be removed, the headless bolts must be center-punched, drilled and removed with a screw extracting tool.

CAUTION

Work must be started after 90 seconds from the time the ignition switch is turned to the LOCK position and the negative battery cable is disconnected from the battery. The SRS is equipped with a back-up power source so that if the work is started within the 90 seconds of disconnecting the negative terminal, the SRS may be deployed.

1. Disarm the SRS system.
2. Turn the ignition **OFF** and remove the key from the ignition.
3. Remove the steering wheel pad and remove the steering wheel.
4. Remove the upper and lower steering column covers. Remove the combination switch.
5. Unplug the ignition wiring harness connector.
6. If only the electrical switch needs replacement, remove the retaining screw at the back of the lock housing and remove the switch. If the automatic transmission interlock relay must be changed, it may be unbolted from the housing; don't lose the spring and lock pin.
7. If the key lock assembly is to be changed, place the key in the switch and turn the key to the **ACC** position. Insert a thin rod in the hole at the bottom of the housing and press the stop tab inward. While holding the tab in, pull the cylinder out of the housing.

To install:

8. Install the new lock cylinder if necessary, making certain the key is in the **ACC** position before installation. Insert the cylinder and be sure the stop tab engages the hole. Once installed, turn the switch **OFF** and remove the key.
9. Align the electrical switch with the back of the key cylinder. Install the retaining screw.
10. Attach the wiring harness connector. Make certain the harness is correctly routed and held by its clamps and clips.
11. Install the combination switch.
12. Install the steering wheel. Install the upper and lower steering column covers.
13. Operate the ignition switch in all positions, checking for correct function and lack of binding.

Ignition Lock Cylinder

REMOVAL & INSTALLATION

Please follow the ignition switch removal procedure.

Steering Linkage

REMOVAL & INSTALLATION

4WD T100 Models

➡Before working on any of the following steering linkage components, disconnect the battery cable, raise the front of the truck and support it with safety stands.

PITMAN ARM

1. Remove the strut bar.
2. Loosen the pitman arm nut.
3. Using a tie rod end puller or similar tool, disconnect the pitman arm from the sector shaft.
4. Using a tie rod end puller or similar tool, disconnect the pitman arm from the relay rod.

To install:

5. Align the marks on the pitman arm and sector shaft and connect them. Tighten the nut to 90 ft. lbs. (123 Nm).
6. Connect the arm to the relay rod and tighten the nut to 67 ft. lbs. (90 Nm).
7. Install the strut bar.

TIE ROD

1. Using a tie rod end puller, disconnect the tie rod from the relay rod.
2. Using a tie rod end puller, disconnect the tie rod from the knuckle arm.
3. Remove the tie rod and remove the tie rod ends.

To install:

4. Screw the tie rod ends onto the tie rod. The tie rod length should be approximately (314.5mm). The remaining length of threads on both ends should always be equal.
5. Turn the tie rod ends so they cross at about 90°. Tighten the clamp nuts to 19 ft. lbs. (25 Nm).
6. Connect the tie rod to the knuckle arm and relay rod and tighten the mounting nuts to 67 ft. lbs. (90 Nm).

RELAY ROD

1. Disconnect the tie rod ends from the relay rod.

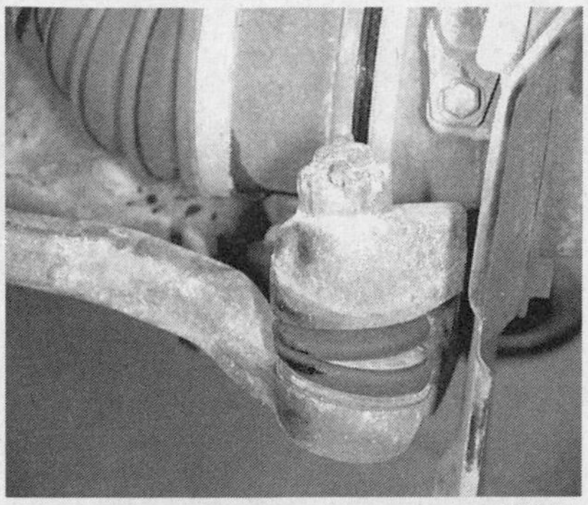

93168p41

Fig. 125 View of the outer tie rod end

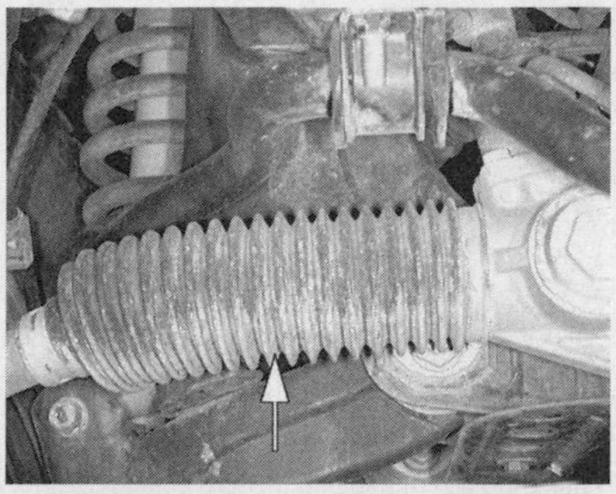

93168p32

Fig. 126 Inspect the dust boot for cracks. Replace as necessary

93168p44

Fig. 127 Use needlenose pliers to straighten the ends of the cotter pin

93168p43

Fig. 128 Pull on the cotter pin while wiggling it back and forth . . .

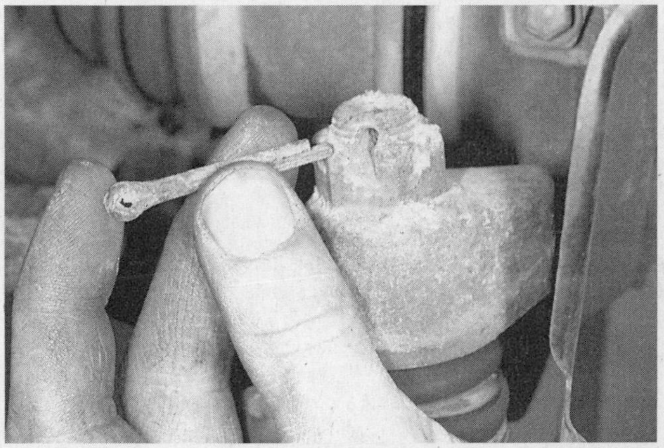

93168p40

Fig. 129 . . . to remove the pin. Discard the cotter pin after it is removed

2. Using a tie rod end puller, disconnect the pitman arm from the relay rod.
3. Using a tie rod end puller, disconnect the idler arm from the relay rod.
4. Remove the rod and inspect it for cracks or other damage.

To install:

5. Connect the relay rod to the idler arm to the relay rod and tighten the nut 43 ft. lbs. (59 Nm).
6. Connect the relay rod to the pitman arm, then tighten the nut to 67 ft. lbs. (90 Nm).
7. Connect the tie rod ends to the relay rod, then tighten the nuts to 67 ft. lbs. (90 Nm).

KNUCKLE ARM

1. Remove the front axle hub.
2. Separate the tie rod at the knuckle arm, then remove the arm.
3. Inspect the arm for cracks or other damage.

To install:

4. Install the arm to the steering knuckle and tighten the nut to 80 ft. lbs. (108 Nm).
5. Connect the tie rod to the knuckle arm, then tighten the nut to 67 ft. lbs. (90 Nm).
6. Install the front axle hub.

STEERING DAMPER

1. Separate the steering damper at the relay rod.
2. Disconnect the damper at the frame, then remove the damper with all washers and cushions.

To install:

3. Install the damper to the frame bracket and tighten the nut to 9 ft. lbs. (13 Nm).
4. Connect the other end of the steering damper to the relay rod, then tighten the nut to 43 ft. lbs. (59 Nm).

IDLER ARM

1. Separate the relay rod from the idler arm.
2. Remove the 3 mounting bolts and remove the idler arm bracket with the arm attached.

To install:

3. Position the bracket and arm on the frame and tighten the bolts to 48–58 ft. lbs. (65–78 Nm).
4. Connect the idler arm to the relay rod, then tighten the nut to 43 ft. lbs. (59 Nm).

All models

OUTER TIE ROD END

See Figures 125 thru 135

1. Raise and safely support the vehicle.
2. Remove the front wheel/tire assembly.
3. Matchmark the tie rod end to the threaded shaft.
4. Remove the cotter pin and castle nut from the outer tie rod end threaded spindle, and using a tie rod end removal tool, remove the tie rod from the steering knuckle.

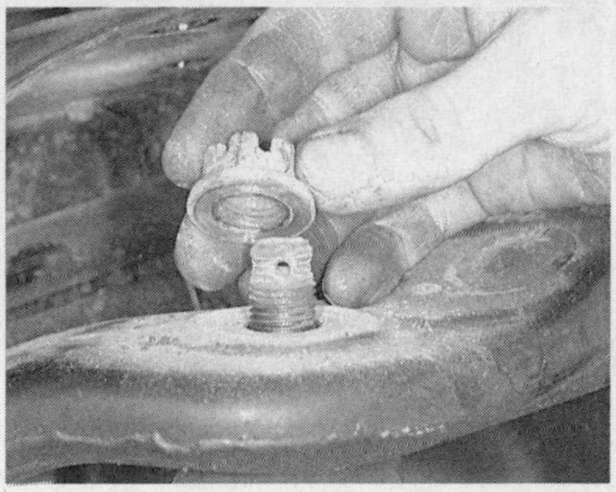

93168p42

Fig. 130 Remove the nut

5. Remove the tie rod and remove the tie rod ends.

To install:

6. Screw the tie rod ends onto the tie rod. The tie rod length should be approximately 47.51 in. (121cm). The remaining length of threads on both ends should always be equal.
7. Turn the tie rod ends so they point in the same direction. Tighten the clamp nuts to 27 ft. lbs. (37 Nm).
8. Connect the tie rod to the knuckle arms, then tighten the mounting nuts to 67 ft. lbs. (90 Nm). Install a new cotter pin.
9. Install the front wheel and tire assembly, then carefully lower the vehicle.

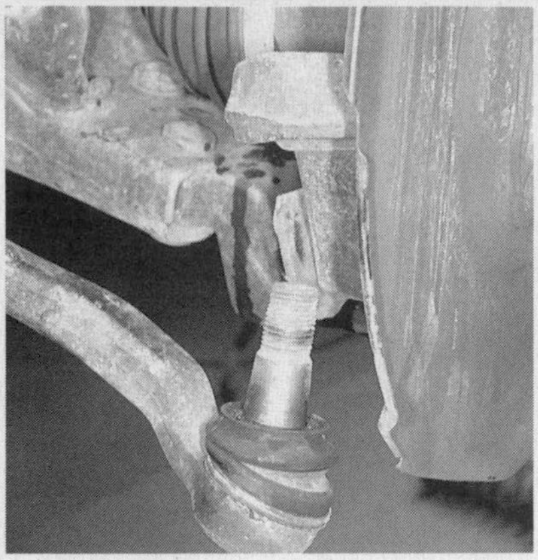

93168p37

Fig. 131 Pull down on the tie rod end to remove it from the knuckle spindle. Use a puller as necessary

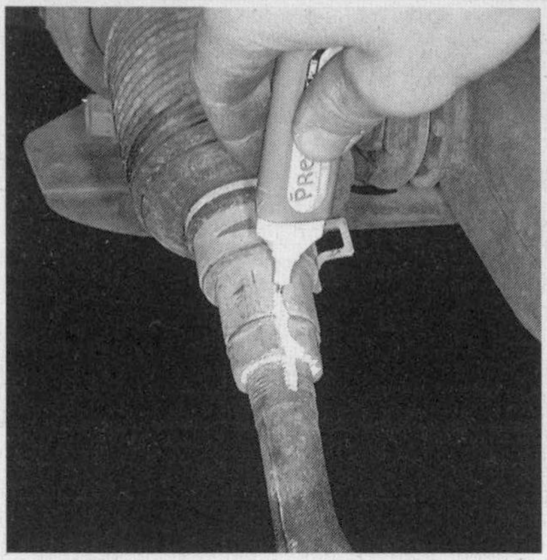

93168p53

Fig. 132 Use a paint marker or equivalent to matchmark the outer tie rod end's position to the tie rod

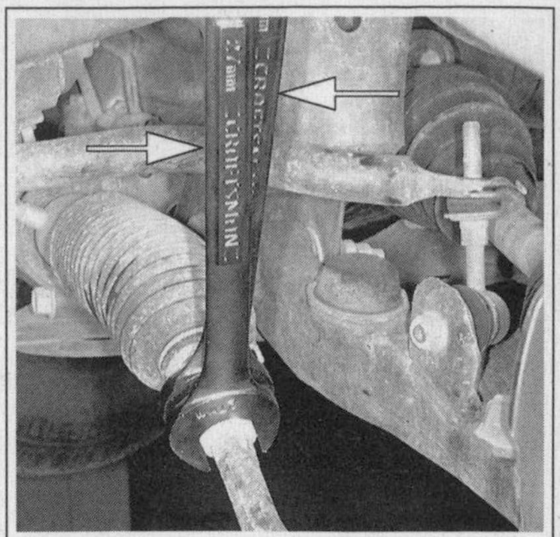

93168p36

Fig. 133 The tie rod may be secured with a double set of nuts to prevent it from coming loose. You must use two wrenches, one to hold and one to turn, to prevent damage to the inner tie rod

Land Cruiser (1997)

See Figure 136

Before working on any of the following steering linkage components, raise the front of the truck and support it with safety stands.

PITMAN ARM

1. Remove the pitman arm set nut and washer.

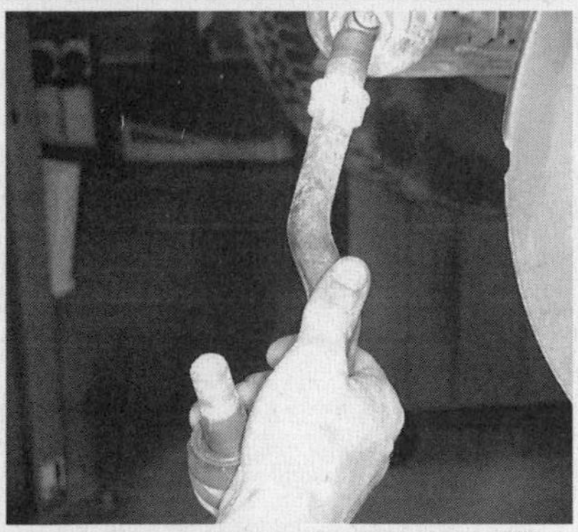

93168p35

Fig. 134 Unthread the tie rod to remove it. It's a good idea to count the number of turns it takes to remove the tie rod end

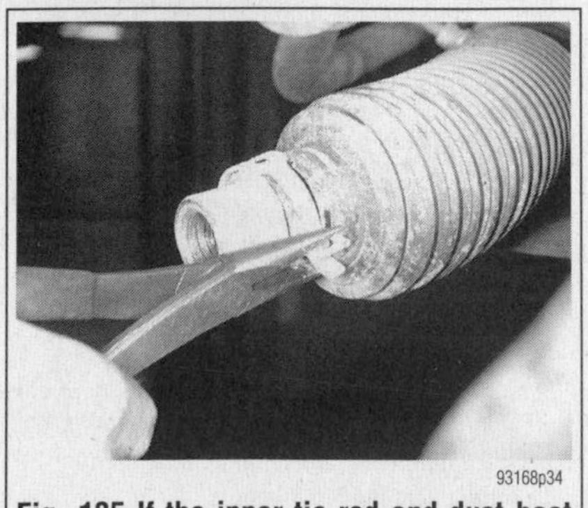

93168p34

Fig. 135 If the inner tie rod end dust boot (bellows) is damaged, replace it at this time

2. Using a tie rod end puller or similar tool, disconnect the pitman arm from the sector shaft.
3. Using a tie rod end puller or similar tool, disconnect the pitman arm from the relay rod.

To install:

4. To install, align the marks on the pitman arm and sector shaft and connect them. Tighten the nut to 130 ft. lbs. (177 Nm).
5. Connect the arm to the relay rod, then tighten the nut to 67 ft. lbs. (90 Nm). Install a new cotter pin.

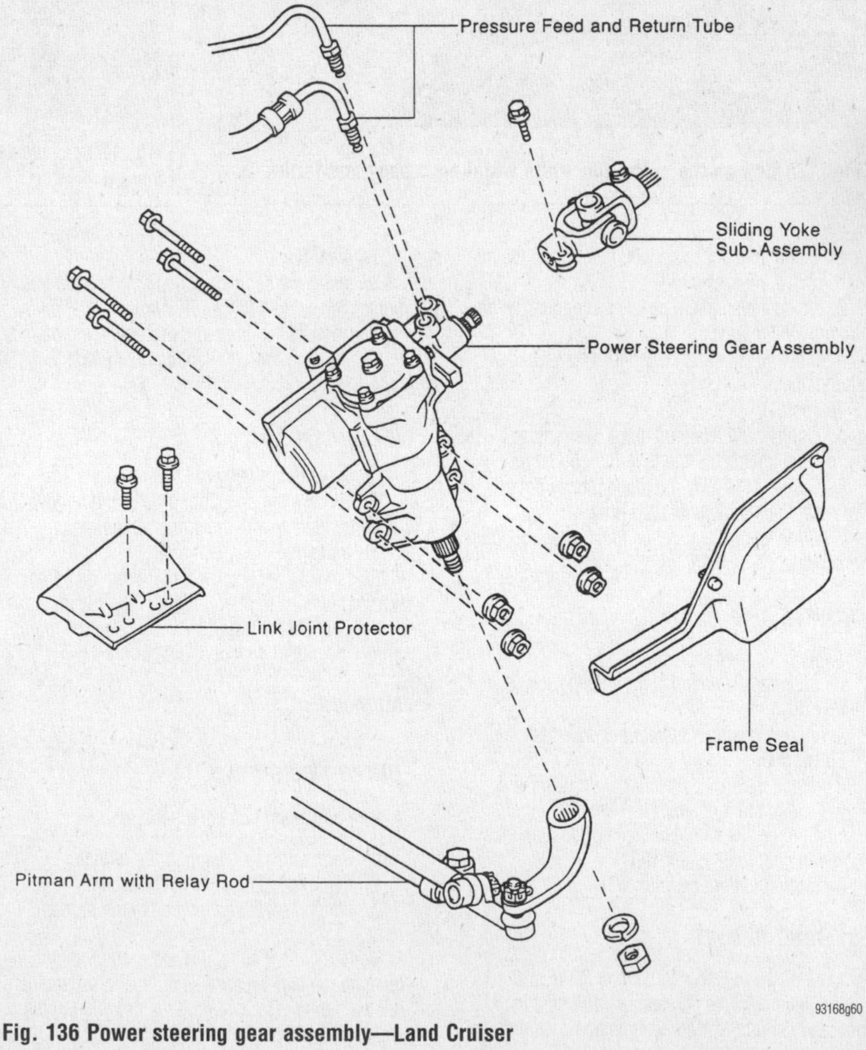

Fig. 136 Power steering gear assembly—Land Cruiser

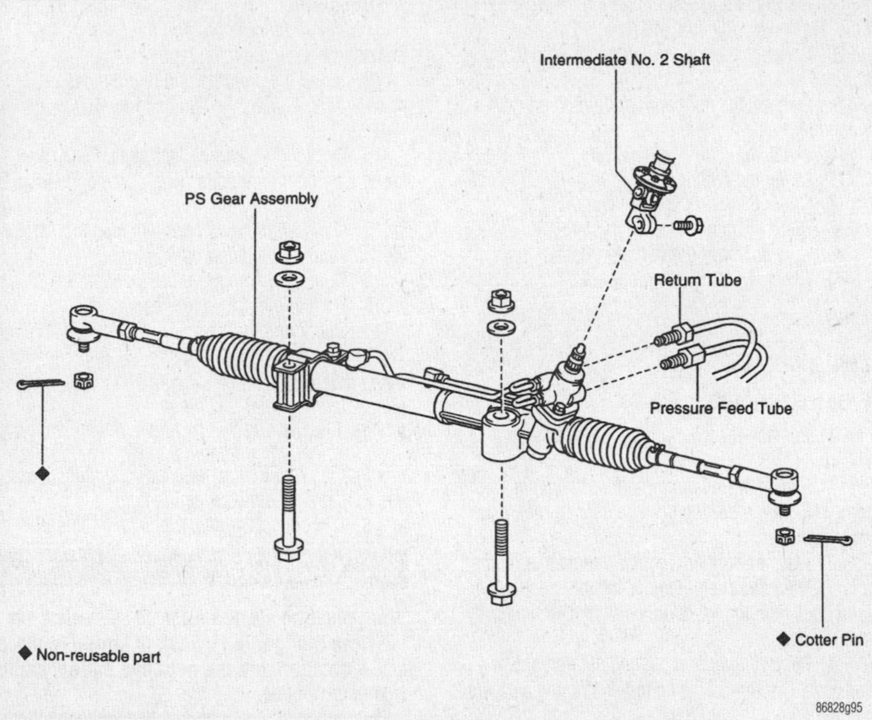

Fig. 137 Exploded view of the power steering gear—2WD Tacoma shown

TIE ROD

1. Using a tie rod end puller, disconnect the tie rod from the knuckle arms.
2. Remove the tie rod and remove the tie rod ends.

To install:

3. Screw the tie rod ends onto the tie rod. The tie rod length should be approximately 47.51 in. (121cm). The remaining length of threads on both ends should always be equal.
4. Turn the tie rod ends so they point in the same direction. Tighten the clamp nuts to 27 ft. lbs. (37 Nm).
5. Connect the tie rod to the knuckle arms, then tighten the mounting nuts to 67 ft. lbs. (90 Nm).

RELAY ROD

1. Separate the relay rod from the pitman arm.
2. Using a tie rod end puller, disconnect the pitman arm from the relay rod.
3. Disconnect the steering damper from the relay rod.
4. Separate the relay rod from the knuckle arm. Always use a joint separator tool.
5. Remove the rod and inspect it for cracks or other damage.

To install:

6. The relay rod ends are to be replaced, install them and set the length to approximately 42.34 in. (108cm). The amount of threads projecting from each side of the rod must be equal.
7. Set the rod ends so that the end for pitman arm (with the flange for the steering damper) faces up and the knuckle end points down. Tighten the clamp bolts to 27 ft. lbs. (37 Nm).
8. Install the rod loosely in position at the pitman arm and knuckle arm.
9. Tighten the pitman arm nut and the knuckle rod to 67 ft. lbs. (90 Nm). Install a new cotter pin in each fitting.
10. Connect the steering damper to the relay rod, then tighten the nut to 43 ft. lbs. (50 Nm). Install a new cotter pin.

KNUCKLE ARM

1. Disconnect the tie rod at the knuckle arm and remove the arm.
2. Inspect the arm for cracks or other damage.

To install:

3. Install the arm to the steering knuckle and tighten the nut to 71 ft. lbs. (96 Nm).
4. Connect the tie rod to the knuckle arm and tighten the nut to 67 ft. lbs. (90 Nm).

STEERING DAMPER

1. Separate the steering damper at the relay rod.
2. Disconnect the damper at the bracket, then remove the damper with all washers and cushions.

To install:

3. Install the damper to the bracket and tighten the nut to 54 ft. lbs. (74 Nm).
4. Connect the other end of the steering damper to the relay rod. Tighten the nut to 54 ft. lbs. (74 Nm).

Power Steering Gear

REMOVAL & INSTALLATION

4Runner, Tacoma, Tundra and 1998 and later Land Cruiser

2WD MODELS

▸ See Figure 137

1. Place the front wheels facing straight ahead.
2. Disconnect the negative battery cable.

✱✱ CAUTION

Work must be started after 90 seconds from the time the ignition switch is turned to the LOCK position and the negative battery cable is disconnected.

3. Raise and safely support the vehicle.
4. Disconnect the right and left tie rod ends from the knuckle.
5. Disconnect the intermediate No. 2 shaft from the steering rack.
6. Using SST 09631–22020 or equivalent, remove the pressure feed and the return tubes.
7. Remove the power steering rack.

To install:

8. Install the power steering rack, then tighten the bolts to 148 ft. lbs. (201 Nm).
9. Install a new O–ring and install the pressure feed tube, then tighten to 33 ft. lbs. (45 Nm). Install the return tube, then tighten to 36 ft. lbs. (49 Nm).
10. Connect the intermediate No. 2 shaft to the steering rack.
11. Connect the right and left tie rod ends to the steering knuckle. Tighten the castle nuts to specification and install new cotter pins.
12. Lower the vehicle.
13. Connect the negative battery cable.
14. Check the steering wheel center point.
15. Bleed the power steering system.
16. Check the front wheel alignment. Tighten the tie rod end locknuts to 67 ft. lbs. (90 Nm)

4WD MODELS

▸ See Figures 138 and 139

1. Place the front wheels facing straight ahead.
2. Disconnect the negative battery cable.

✱✱ CAUTION

Work must be started after 90 seconds from the time the ignition switch is turned to the LOCK position and the negative battery cable is disconnected.

3. Raise and safely support the vehicle.
4. Remove the engine undercover.
5. Disconnect the right and left tie rod ends from the steering knuckle.
6. Disconnect the intermediate No. 2 shaft from the steering rack.

Fig. 138 Power steering fluid line-to-rack and pinion steering gear connection locations—Tacoma TRD

Fig. 139 The rack and pinion steering coupler as it appears from beneath the vehicle—Tacoma TRD

7. Disconnect the pressure feed tube and return tube.
8. Remove the power steering rack assembly.
9. Remove the bracket and grommet.

To install:

10. Install the bracket and grommet.
11. Install the power steering rack assembly then tighten the bolts to:
    - Rack assembly bolt: 123 ft. lbs. (167 Nm)
    - Rack assembly nut and bolt: 141 ft. lbs. (191 Nm)
    - Nut and bolt to the bracket: 123 ft. lbs. (167 Nm)
12. Connect the pressure feed tube and the return tube. Tighten to 29 ft. lbs. (40 Nm).
13. Connect the intermediate No. 2 shaft to the steering rack.
14. Connect the right and left tie rod ends to the steering knuckle.
15. Install the engine undercovers.
16. Lower the vehicle.
17. Check the steering wheel center point.
18. Bleed the power steering system.
19. Connect the negative battery cable.
20. Check the front end alignment.

T100

2WD MODELS

See Figure 140

1. Position the front wheels facing straight ahead.
2. Secure the steering wheel so that it does not turn. The driver's seat belt can be used to secure the steering wheel.
3. Place matchmarks on the intermediate shaft and control valve shaft. Remove the lower and upper joint bolts from the intermediate shaft. Disconnect the shaft.
4. Remove the cotter pin and nut from the tie rod ends. Disconnect the tie rod ends using a separator tool.
5. Disconnect the pressure and return pipes using flare nut wrenches.
6. Remove the bracket bolts and grommets.
7. Remove the steering rack assembly from the vehicle.

To install:

8. Install the gear housing then tighten the mounting bolts to 65 ft. lbs. (88 Nm).
9. Install the pressure and return tubes using new O-rings. Tighten the fittings to 15 ft. lbs. (20 Nm).
10. Connect the intermediate shaft. Install the lower and upper joint bolts. Tighten the bolts to 26 ft. lbs. (35 Nm).
11. Connect the tie rod ends, tighten to 67 ft. lbs. (90 Nm) and install a new cotter pin.
12. Connect the negative battery cable.
13. Fill and bleed the steering system.
14. Check and adjust toe-in.

4WD MODELS

See Figure 141

1. Place the front wheels facing straight ahead.
2. Drain the power steering fluid.
3. Disconnect the negative battery cable.

CAUTION

Work must be started after 90 seconds from the time the ignition switch is turned to the LOCK position and the negative battery cable is disconnected.

4. Raise and safely support the vehicle.
5. Remove the pitman arm set nut and the spring washer. Using SST 09628–62011, or equivalent, disconnect the pitman arm from the gear assembly.

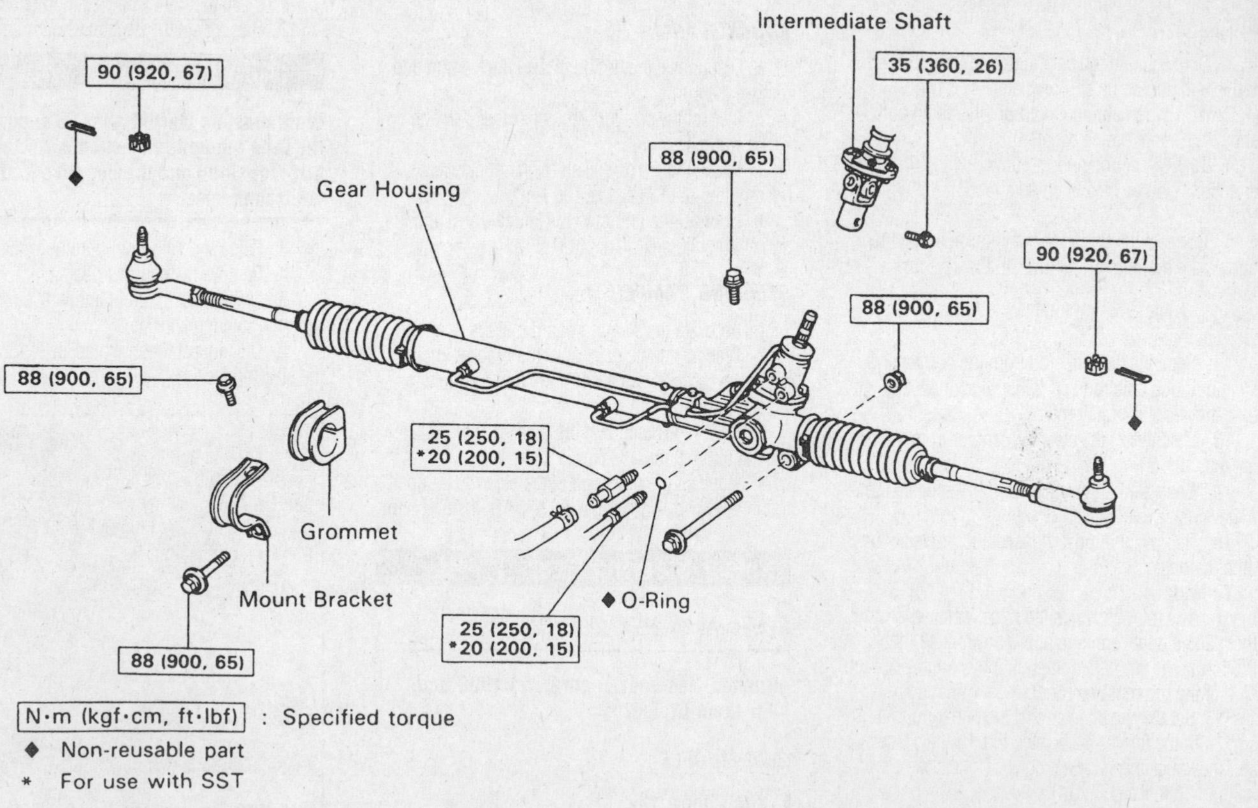

Fig. 140 Exploded view of the power steering gear—2WD T100 shown

6. Disconnect the pressure feed tube and return tube.
7. Make matchmarks and disconnect the intermediate shaft from the steering gear.
8. Remove the power steering gear mounting bolts and remove the gear assembly.

To install:

9. Install the power steering gear assembly, then tighten the bolts to 105 ft. lbs. (142 Nm).
10. Align the matchmarks and connect the intermediate shaft to the steering gear.

➡If installing a new gear assembly, be sure the gear box and the steering wheel are centered.

11. Connect the pressure feed tube and the return tube. Tighten the line fittings to 26 ft. lbs. (36 Nm).
12. Align the alignment marks on the cross shaft and the pitman arm and connect the pitman arm. Install the spring washer and the pitman arm set nut, then tighten to 130 ft. lbs. (177 Nm).
13. Lower the vehicle.
14. Check the steering wheel center point.
15. Fill and bleed the power steering system.
16. Connect the negative battery cable.

1997 Land Cruiser

See Figure 142

1. Drain the power steering fluid.
2. Disconnect the negative battery cable.

CAUTION

Work must be started after 90 seconds from the time the ignition switch is turned to the LOCK position and the negative battery cable is disconnected.

3. Raise and safely support the vehicle.
4. Remove the frame seal.
5. Remove the link joint protector.
6. Remove the pitman arm set nut and spring washer. Using SST 09628-62011, or equivalent, disconnect the pitman arm from the gear assembly.
7. Using SST 09631-22020, or equivalent, disconnect the pressure feed and the return tubes.
8. Separate the sliding yoke sub-assembly from the steering gear.
9. Remove the mounting bolts and the power steering gear assembly.

To install:

10. Install the power steering gear assembly, then tighten the bolts to 105 ft. lbs. (142 Nm).
11. Connect the sliding yoke sub–assembly to the steering gear.
12. Connect the pressure feed and the return tubes. Tighten the tube fittings to 26 ft. lbs. (36 Nm).
13. Connect the pitman arm and align the alignment marks on the cross shaft and the pitman arm. Install the spring washer and the pitman arm set nut. Tighten the nut to 130 ft. lbs. (177 Nm).
14. Refill and bleed the power steering system.
15. Install the link joint protector.
16. Install the frame seal.
17. Lower the vehicle.
18. Connect the negative battery cable.
19. Test drive the vehicle. Check the steering wheel center point.

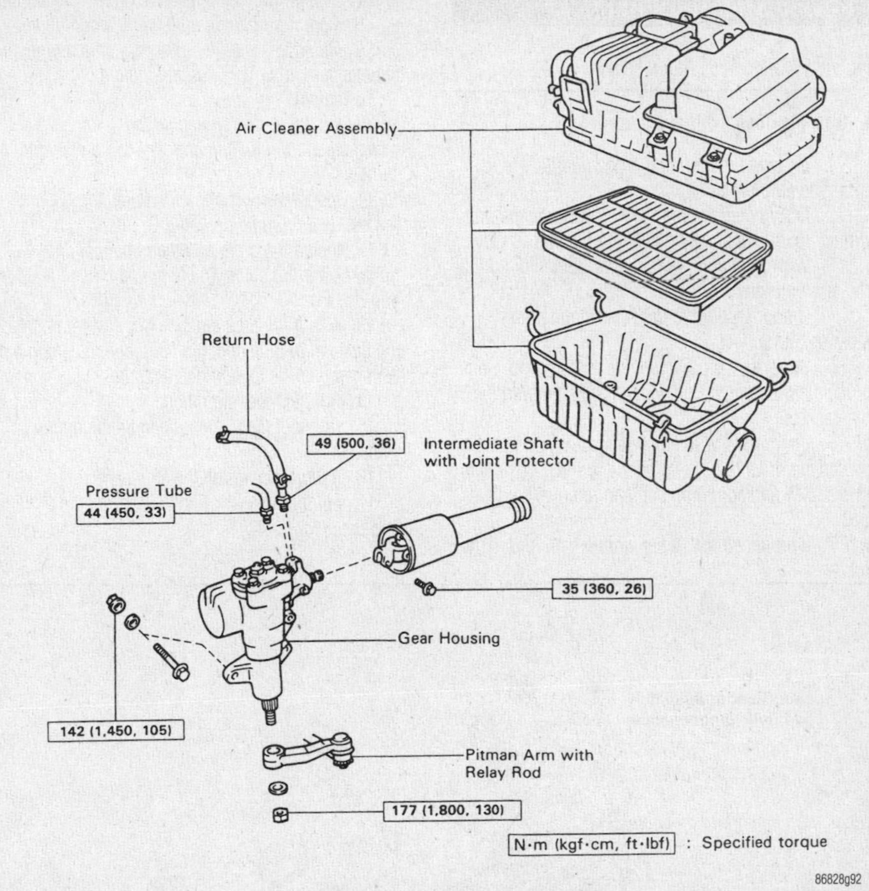

Fig. 141 Exploded view of the power steering gear—4WD T100 shown

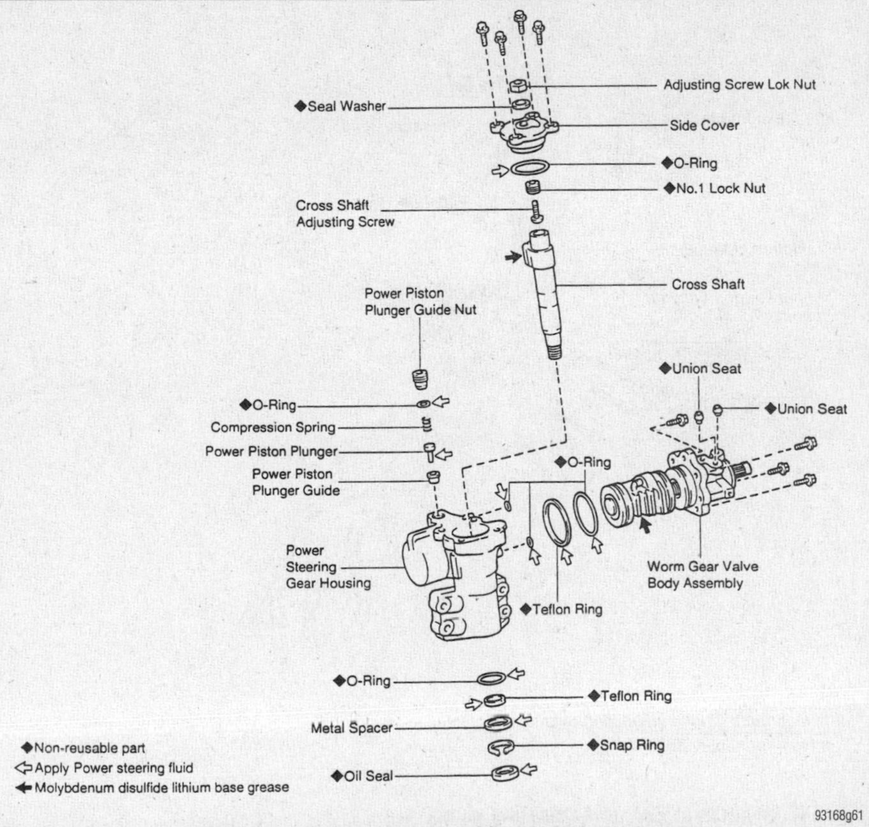

Fig. 142 Exploded view of the steering gear assembly—1997 Land Cruiser

Power Steering Pump

REMOVAL & INSTALLATION

See Figures 143, 144, and 145

1. On some models it will be necessary to remove the air cleaner.
2. Disconnect the high tension lines at the distributor, then disconnect the air lines at the air valve.
3. With a suitable device, suck some fluid out of the reservoir tank.
4. Disconnect the return hose at the power steering pump.
5. Separate the pressure line at the pump. Some models have a union bolt with gaskets. Discard the old gaskets.
6. If equipped with a power steering pump belt, loosen the drive belt pulley retaining nut. Loosen the idler pulley and adjusting bolt and remove the drive belt.
7. If equipped with a serpentine belt, loosen the tensioner to relieve belt tension, then remove the belt.
8. Remove the drive pulley and Woodruff key.
9. Remove the power steering pump. Some models have an O-ring, discard the old O-ring.

To install:

10. On the O-ring type, coat the O-ring with power steering fluid, then install it to the pump assembly.
11. Install the pump in its bracket, then tighten the nuts to 27–29 ft. lbs. (36–39 Nm).
12. Install the drive pulley and belt. Tighten the pulley bolt to 32 ft. lbs. (43 Nm) and check the drive belt tension.
13. Attach the pressure line to the pump; tighten the flare nut to 33 ft. lbs. (45 Nm), and the union bolt with new gaskets to 42 ft. lbs. (56 Nm).
14. Connect the return hose.
15. Connect the air hoses and the high tension leads.
16. If removed, install the air cleaner.
17. Fill the reservoir with fluid, bleed the system and check for leaks.

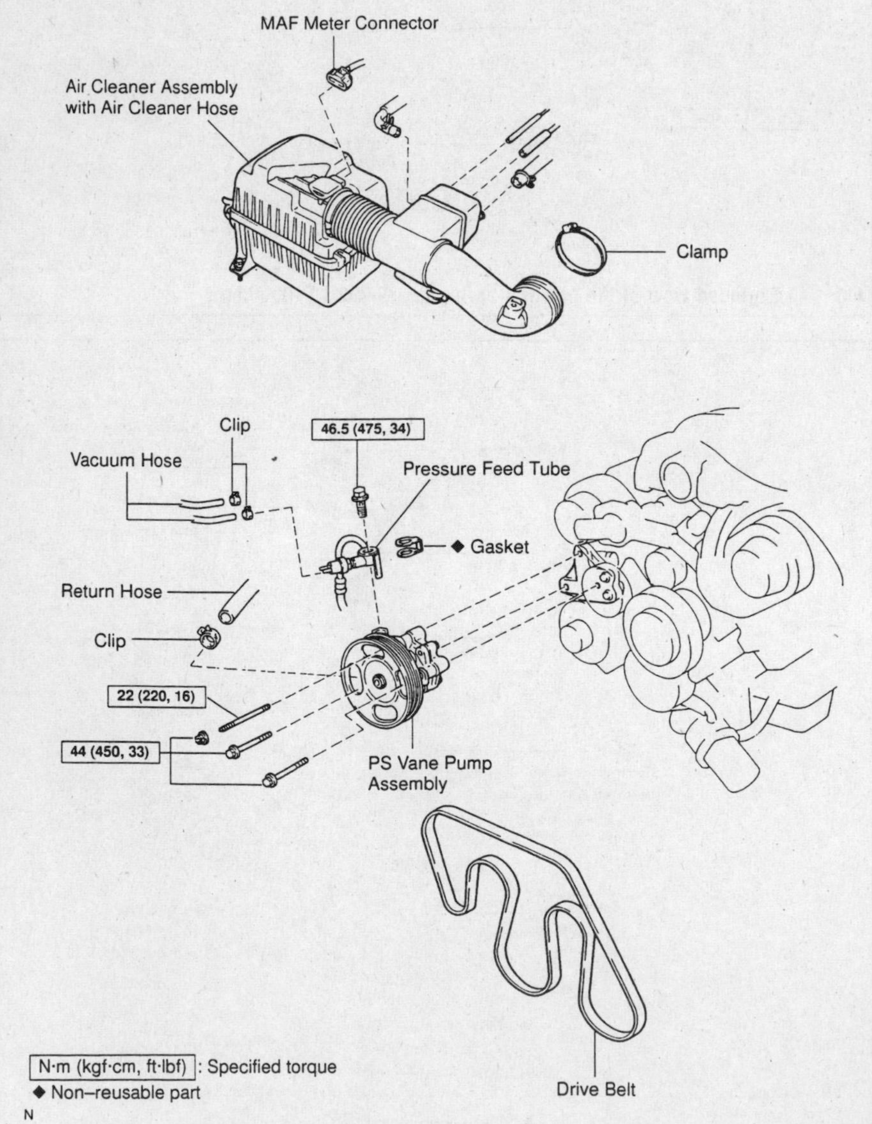

Fig. 143 Location of the power steering pump

BLEEDING

⁂ WARNING

Vehicles equipped with Rear Wheel Anti-Lock (RWAL) brakes use a different bleeding procedure than those not so equipped. Bleeding the RWAL system requires the use of an electronic brake tester, an expensive unit usually found only at dealers.

Without RWAL System

1. Check the fluid level in the reservoir. It should be at the correct level (HOT or COLD) depending on engine temperature.
2. Start the engine and run it below 1000 rpm.
3. Turn the steering wheel from lock-to-lock 3 or 4 times.
4. Shut the engine **OFF**. Connect a clear plastic tube to the bleeder port on the steering gearbox. Place the other end of the tube in a container of power steering fluid. Make sure the end is immersed in the fluid.
5. Start the engine again. Turn the wheel lock-to-lock 3–4 times and return the steering wheel to the centered position.
6. Loosen the bleeder plug. Observe the tubing; when no air bubbles are seen, close the bleeder plug.

⁂ CAUTION

Do not allow the tubing to come off the bleed port. The power steering fluid is under high pressure and may be very hot.

7. Inspect the fluid level with the engine running; the fluid should not be foamy or cloudy. Shut the engine **OFF** and check the fluid level. If level rises too much, try re-bleeding the system. If the problem persists, repair the power steering system.

With RWAL System

The RWAL system uses power steering fluid pressure to maintain control pressures in the brake system. While the fluids never mix, air in the power steering system can render the rear anti-lock brakes ineffective.

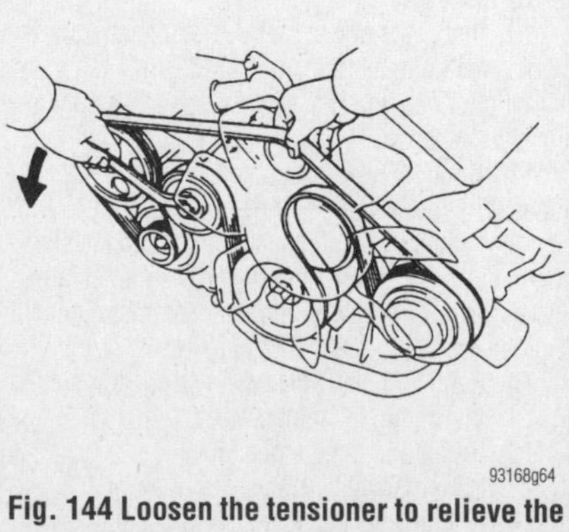

Fig. 144 Loosen the tensioner to relieve the tension from the serpentine belt—2UZ-FE engine

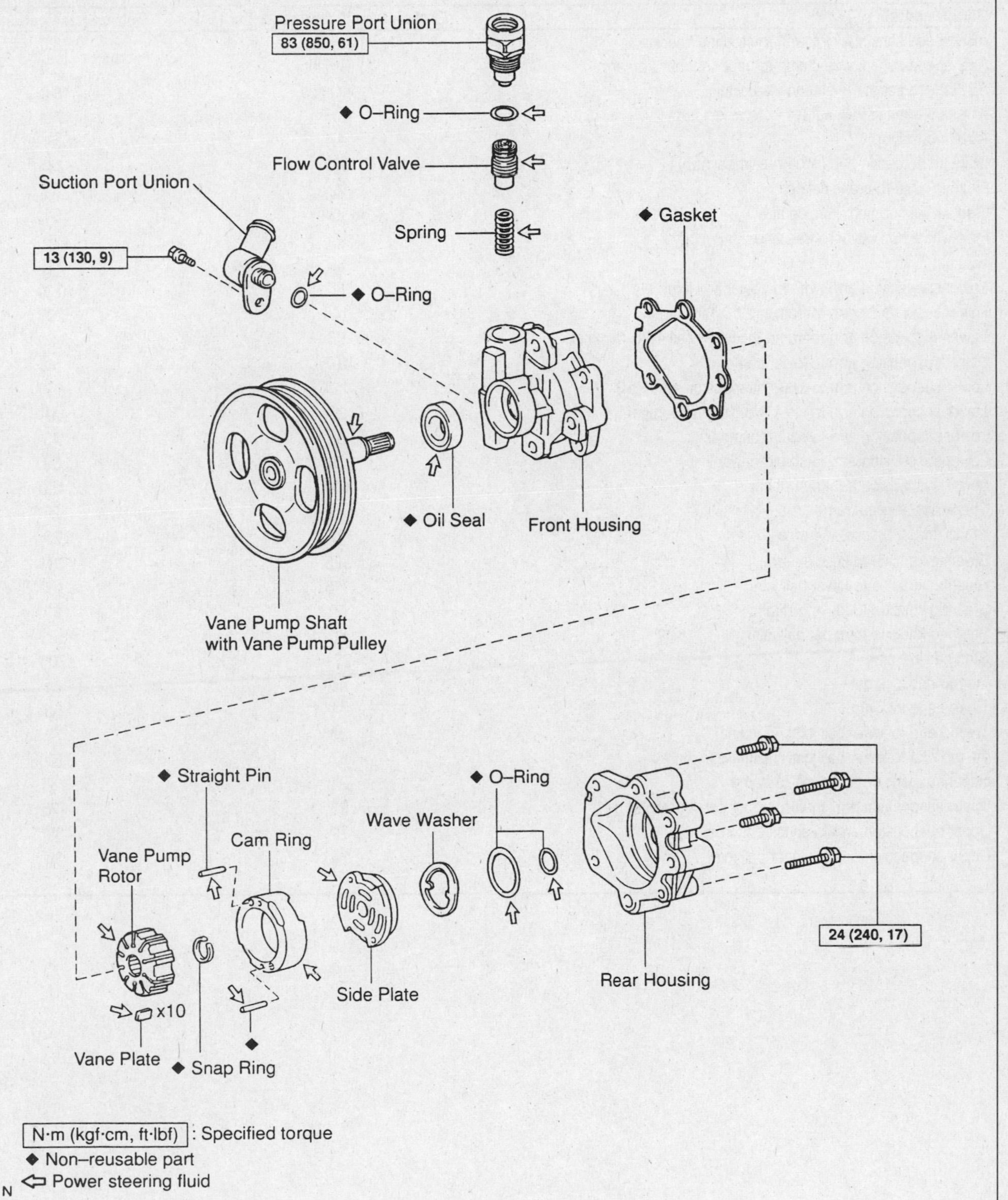

Fig. 145 Exploded view of a typical power steering pump

If the any of the lines or components in the power steering system are loosened or removed, the brake system must be bled as well. Preliminary bleeding of both the power steering and brake systems will eliminate most of the air, but the vehicle MUST be taken to a dealer to have the systems properly bled using the Toyota ABS Checker. Be warned that until this is done, the rear wheel anti-lock brake function may be impaired.

TORQUE SPECIFICATIONS — 4RUNNER & TACOMA

Components	English Specifications (ft. lbs.)	Metric Specifications (Nm)
ABS speed sensor wire clamp-to-steering knuckle	71 inch lbs.	8.0
ABS speed sensor wire clamp-to-upper suspension arm	71 inch lbs.	8.0
ABS speed sensor-to-steering knuckle	71 inch lbs.	8.0
Axle hub bearing lock nut (w/ Free wheel hub)	203	274
Axle hub-to-Disc	47	64
Drive shaft-to-axle hub (w/o Free wheel hub)	174	235
Flexible hose-to-brake caliper	22	30
Free wheel hub body-to-axle hub	23	31
Free wheel hub cover-to-free wheel hub body	7	10
Hub nut	83	110
Lower suspension arm No.3-to-Lower ball joint	80	110
Lower suspension arm-to-frame (2WD Tacoma)	148	200
Lower suspension arm-to-frame (4Runner and 4WD Tacoma)	96	130
Lower suspension arm-to-lower ball joint	103	140
Lower suspension arm-to-lower suspension arm No.3	111	150
Lower suspension arm-to-No.1, No.2 spring bumper	23	31
Lower suspension arm-to-spring bumper	32	43
Lower suspension arm-to-stabilizer bar link	29	39
Lower suspension arm-to-strut bar	111	150
Shock absorber-to-frame	18	25
Stabilizer bar bracket-to-frame	22	29
Steering knuckle-to-knuckle arm	135	183
Steering knuckle-to-lower ball joint	116	160
Steering knuckle-to-lower ball joint	59	80
Steering knuckle-to-upper ball joint	80	105
Strut bar-to-frame	221	300
Tie rod end lock nut	40	54
Tie rod end lock nut	41	55
Tie rod end-to-lower ball joint (Tacoma)	53	72
Tie rod end-to-lower ball joint (4Runner)	67	90
Upper suspension arm shaft-to-frame	94	130
Upper suspension arm shaft-to-upper suspension arm	92	125
Upper suspension arm-to-shock absorber	29	39
Upper suspension arm-to-upper ball joint	29	39

93168c01

TORQUE SPECIFICATIONS — T100

Components	English Specifications (ft. lbs.)	Metric Specifications (Nm)
A.D.D. Indicator switch-to-clutch case cover	30	40
Axle hub bearing lock nut	35	47
Bracket-to-pump assembly (5VZ-FE engine)	32	43
Compression spring set bolt	69 inch lbs.	7.8
Control shaft lever-to-control shaft assembly	26	35
Control valve housing-to-rack housing	13	18
Control valve shaft-to-intermediate shaft	35	26
Cross shaft adjusting screw set nut (4WD)	46	34
Crossmember-to-frame	93	126
Disc-to-axle hub	47	64
Dust cover-to-steering knuckle	14	19
Flange-to-axle hub	23	31
Flange-to-front drive shaft	13	18
Front drive shaft-to-side gear shaft	61	83
Hub nut	76	103
Idler arm assembly-to-frame	142	105
Idler arm-to-idler arm bracket	78	58
Intermediate shaft-to-control valve assembly	26	35
Knuckle stopper bolt lock nut	35	47
Leaf spring center bolt	33	44
Lower ball joint-to-strut bar	55	75
Lower suspension arm shaft nut	152	206
Lower suspension arm-to-frame	145	196
Lower suspension arm-to-lower ball joint	55	75
Lower suspension arm-to-shock absorber	13	18
Lower suspension arm-to-shock absorber (4WD)	101	137
Lower suspension arm-to-stabilizer bar	9	13
Main shaft assembly-to-sliding w/shaft york sub-assembly	26	35
Mount bracket-to-suspension crossmember	88	65
Oil reservoir set bolt front	9	13
Oil seal-to-dust cover	13	18
Parking brake set bolt	19	25

93168c03

TORQUE SPECIFICATIONS — T100

Components	English Specifications (ft. lbs.)	Metric Specifications (Nm)
Pitman arm-to-cross shaft	130	177
Pitman arm-to-relay rod	67	90
Plunger guide nut (4WD)	15	20
Pressure feed tube-to-control valve housing	14	19
Pressure feed tube-to-PS gear assembly (4WD)	26	36
Pressure port union-to-pump housing	61	83
PS gear assembly set bolt and nut (2WD)	65	88
PS gear assembly-to-body (4WD)	105	142
Rack housing cap	51	69
Rack-to-rack end	45	61
Rear axle housing-to-rear brake assembly	51	69
Rear housing set bolt	17	24
Rear mounting bolt	123	167
Rear shock absorber-to-frame	19	26
Rear shock absorber-to-spring seat	19	26
Relay rod-to-idler arm assembly	43	59
Relay rod-to-steering damper	43	59
Return tube-to-control valve housing	14	19
Return tube-to-PS gear assembly (4WD)	26	36
Screw plug-to-clutch case cover	14	20
Self-locking nut	18	25
Shackle pin-to-leaf spring	67	91
Shock absorber-to-frame	18	25
Shock absorber-to-frame	18	25
Side cover-to-gear housing (4WD)	45	61
Sliding w/shaft york sub-assembly-to-intermediate shaft	26	35
Spring bumper seat set bolt	22	30
Stabilizer bar bracket-to-frame	22	30
Stabilizer bar link set nut	9	13
Steering column assembly set bolt and nut	19	25
Steering damper set bolt and nut	19	25
Steering knuckle arm-to-steering knuckle	135	183
Steering knuckle-to-brake caliper	80	108
Steering knuckle-to-brake caliper (4WD)	90	123
Steering knuckle-to-lower ball joint	43	58
Steering knuckle-to-lower ball joint (4WD)	105	142
Steering knuckle-to-steering knuckle arm	135	183
Steering knuckle-to-upper ball joint	80	108
Steering knuckle-to-upper ball joint (4WD)	105	142
Steering wheel pad set screw (torx screw)	78 inch lbs.	9.0
Steering wheel set nut	26	35
Strut bar-to-frame	90	123
Tie rod assembly-to-knuckle arm	67	90
Tie rod assembly-to-relay rod	67	90
Tie rod clamp bolt	16	22
Tie rod clamp bolt	16	22
Tie rod end lock nut	41	56
Tie rod end lock nut	41	56
Tie rod end-to-steering knuckle	67	90

93168c04

TORQUE SPECIFICATIONS — T100

Components	English Specifications (ft. lbs.)	Metric Specifications (Nm)
Tilt lever assembly set bolt	17 inch lbs.	2
Tilt lever retainer set nut	11	15
Tilt sub lever side pawl set bolt-to-nut	52 inch lbs.	5.9
Torque arm-to-lower suspension arm	36	49
Tube-to-bearing retainer	9	12
Turn pressure tube union nut	7	10
Turn signal bracket set bolt	69 inch lbs.	7.8
U-bolt-to-spring seat	97	132
Union bolt-to-pressure feed tube	34	47
Upper suspension arm shaft lock nut	166	226
Upper suspension arm shaft-to-frame (2WD)	71	96
Upper suspension arm shaft-to-frame (4WD)	131	178
Upper suspension arm shaft-to-upper suspension arm	93	126
Upper suspension arm-to-torque arm	64	87
Upper suspension arm-to-upper ball joint (2WD)	23	31
Upper suspension arm-to-upper ball joint (4WD)	25	33
Vane pump assembly set bolt (3RZ-FE engine)	29	39
Vane pump assembly with bracket set bolt and nut (5VZ-FE engine)	29	39
Vane pump pulley set nut	32	43
Worm gear valve body assembly-to-gear housing (4WD)	45	61
Worm gear valve body assembly-to-intermediate shaft (4WD)	26	35

(A.D.D.): Automatic Disconnecting Differential

ABS: Antilock Brake System

93168c05

TORQUE SPECIFICATIONS — TUNDRA

Components	English Specifications (ft. lbs.)	Metric Specifications (Nm)
Axle hub bearing lock nut (2WD)	203	274
Brake line clamp-to-steering knuckle	21	28
Brake line union nut	11	15
Column housing support-to-column tube assembly	14	19
Column upper tube-to-column tube assembly	14	19
Control valve housing set bolt	13	18
Control valve shaft-to-No. 2 intermediate shaft assembly	26	35
Control valve shaft-to-No. 2 intermediate shaft assembly	26	35
Drive shaft lock nut	173	235
Leaf spring center bolt	33	44
Leaf spring front side set nut	125	170
Leaf spring-to-shackle	125	170
Lower suspension arm-to-chassis frame	96	130
Lower suspension arm-to-lower ball joint	103	140
Lower suspension arm-to-shock absorber	100	135
Lower suspension arm-to-stabilizer bar link	51	69
No. 2 intermediate shaft assembly-to-No. 2 universal joint assembly	26	35
No. 2 universal joint assembly-to-main shaft assembly	26	35

93168c06

TORQUE SPECIFICATIONS — TUNDRA

Components	English Specifications (ft. lbs.)	Metric Specifications (Nm)
Piston rod-to-suspension support	18	25
Pressure port union	61	83
Pressure port union-to-pump housing	61	83
PS gear assembly set bolt	123	165
PS gear assembly set bolt and nut	96	130
PS vane pump assembly set bolt and nut	33	44
PS vane pump assembly set stud bolt	16	22
Rack housing cap	43	59
Shackle-to-chassis frame	125	170
Shift lever housing-to-column housing support A/T	9	12
Shift lever set bolt A/T	13	18
Shock absorber-to-axle housing	64	87
Shock absorber-to-chassis frame	15	20
Stabilizer bar bracket-to-chassis frame	19	25
Stabilizer bar-to-stabilizer bar link	14	19
Steering column assembly set nut	19	26
Steering knuckle-to-brake caliper	90	123
Steering knuckle-to-dust cover	13	18
Steering knuckle-to-lower ball joint	59	80
Steering wheel pad set screw (Torx screw)	78 inch lbs.	8.8
Steering wheel set nut	26	35
Suction port union set bolt	9	13
Suspension support-to-chassis frame	47	64
Tie rod end lock nut	41	55
Tie rod end lock nut	41	55
Tie rod end-to-lower ball joint	67	91
Tube with wire harness assembly clamp-to-differential carrier	9	13
Turn signal bracket-to-column upper tube	65 inch lbs.	7.5
Turn signal bracket-to-steering column housing	65 inch lbs.	7.5
U-bolt-to-spring seat	98	133
Union bolt-to-pressure feed tube	34	46.5
Union bolt-to-pressure feed tube	34	46.5
Upper suspension arm-to-chassis frame	72	98
Upper suspension arm-to-upper ball joint	77	105
Vane pump assembly with bracket set bolt and nut	33	44

93168c07

Notes

9 BRAKES

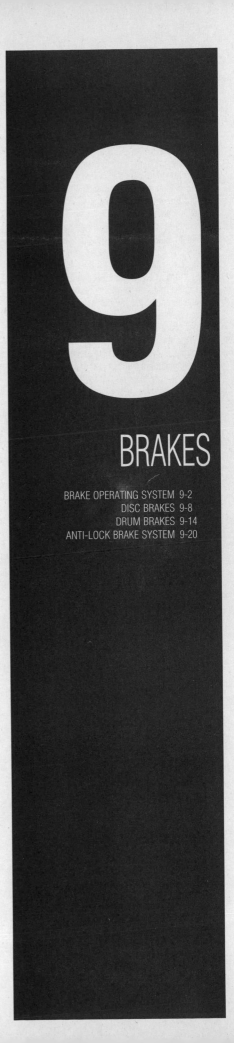

BRAKE OPERATING SYSTEM

Basic Operating Principles

Hydraulic systems are used to actuate the brakes of all modern automobiles. The system transports the power required to force the frictional surfaces of the braking system together from the pedal to the individual brake units at each wheel. A hydraulic system is used for two reasons.

First, fluid under pressure can be carried to all parts of an automobile by small pipes and flexible hoses without taking up a significant amount of room or posing routing problems.

Second, a great mechanical advantage can be given to the brake pedal end of the system, and the foot pressure required to actuate the brakes can be reduced by making the surface area of the master cylinder pistons smaller than that of any of the pistons in the wheel cylinders or calipers.

The master cylinder consists of a fluid reservoir along with a double cylinder and piston assembly. Double type master cylinders are designed to separate the front and rear braking systems hydraulically in case of a leak. The master cylinder converts mechanical motion from the pedal into hydraulic pressure within the lines. This pressure is translated back into mechanical motion at the wheels by either the wheel cylinder (drum brakes) or the caliper (disc brakes).

Steel lines carry the brake fluid to a point on the vehicle's frame near each of the vehicle's wheels. The fluid is then carried to the calipers and wheel cylinders by flexible tubes in order to allow for suspension and steering movements.

In drum brake systems, each wheel cylinder contains two pistons, one at either end, which push outward in opposite directions and force the brake shoe into contact with the drum.

In disc brake systems, the cylinders are part of the calipers. At least one cylinder in each caliper is used to force the brake pads against the disc.

All pistons employ some type of seal, usually made of rubber, to contain pressure within its cylinder. A rubber dust boot seals the outer end of the cylinder against dust and dirt. The boot fits around the outer end of the piston on disc brake calipers, and around the brake actuating rod on wheel cylinders.

The hydraulic system operates as follows: When at rest, the entire system, from the piston(s) in the master cylinder to those in the wheel cylinders or calipers, is full of brake fluid. Upon application of the brake pedal, fluid trapped in front of the master cylinder piston(s) is forced through the lines to the wheel cylinders. Here, it forces the pistons outward, in the case of drum brakes, and inward toward the disc, in the case of disc brakes. The motion of the pistons is opposed by return springs mounted outside the cylinders in drum brakes, and by spring seals, in disc brakes.

Upon release of the brake pedal, a spring located inside the master cylinder immediately returns the master cylinder pistons to the normal position. The pistons contain check valves and the master cylinder has compensating ports drilled in it. These are uncovered as the pistons reach their normal position. The piston check valves allow fluid to flow toward the wheel cylinders or calipers as the pistons withdraw. Then, as the return springs force the brake pads or shoes into the released position, the excess fluid returns to the reservoir through the compensating ports.

Dual circuit master cylinders employ two pistons, located one behind the other, in the same cylinder. The primary piston is actuated directly by mechanical linkage from the brake pedal through the power booster. The secondary piston is actuated by fluid trapped between the two pistons. If a leak develops in front of the secondary piston, it moves forward until it bottoms against the front of the master cylinder, and the fluid trapped between the pistons will operate the rear brakes. If the rear brakes develop a leak, the primary piston will move forward until direct contact with the secondary piston takes place, and it will force the secondary piston to actuate the front brakes. In either case, the brake pedal moves farther when the brakes are applied, and less braking power is available.

All dual circuit systems use a switch to warn the driver when only half of the brake system is operational. This switch is usually located in a valve body which is mounted on the firewall or the frame below the master cylinder. A hydraulic piston receives pressure from both circuits, each circuit's pressure being applied to one end of the piston. When the pressures are in balance, the piston remains stationary. When one circuit has a leak, however, the greater pressure in that circuit during application of the brakes will push the piston to one side, closing the switch and activating the brake warning light.

In disc brake systems, this valve body also contains a metering valve and, in some cases, a proportioning valve. The metering valve keeps pressure from traveling to the disc brakes on the front wheels until the brake shoes on the rear wheels have contacted the drums, ensuring that the front brakes will never be used alone. The proportioning valve controls the pressure to the rear brakes to lessen the chance of rear wheel lock-up during very hard braking.

Warning lights may be tested by depressing the brake pedal and holding it while opening one of the wheel cylinder bleeder screws. If this does not cause the light to go on, substitute a new lamp, make continuity checks, and, finally, replace the switch as necessary.

The hydraulic system may be checked for leaks by applying pressure to the pedal gradually and steadily. If the pedal sinks very slowly to the floor, the system has a leak. This is not to be confused with a springy or spongy feel due to the compression of air within the lines. If the system leaks, there will be a gradual change in the position of the pedal with a constant pressure.

Check for leaks along all lines and at wheel cylinders. If no external leaks are apparent, the problem is inside the master cylinder.

DISC BRAKES

Instead of the traditional expanding brakes that press outward against a circular drum, disc brake systems utilize a disc (rotor) with brake pads positioned on either side of it. An easily-seen analogy is the hand brake arrangement on a bicycle. The pads squeeze onto the rim of the bike wheel, slowing its motion. Automobile disc brakes use the identical principle but apply the braking effort to a separate disc instead of the wheel.

The disc (rotor) is a casting, usually equipped with cooling fins between the two braking surfaces. This enables air to circulate between the braking surfaces making them less sensitive to heat buildup and more resistant to fade. Dirt and water do not drastically affect braking action since contaminants are thrown off by the centrifugal action of the rotor or scraped off the by the pads. Also, the equal clamping action of the two brake pads tends to ensure uniform, straight line stops. Disc brakes are inherently self-adjusting. There are three general types of disc brake:

1. A fixed caliper.
2. A floating caliper.
3. A sliding caliper.

The fixed caliper design uses one or more pistons mounted on either side of the rotor (in each side of the caliper). The caliper is mounted rigidly and does not move.

The sliding and floating designs are quite similar. In fact, these two types are often lumped together. In both designs, the pad on the inside of the rotor is moved into contact with the rotor by hydraulic force. The caliper, which is not held in a fixed position, moves slightly, bringing the outside pad into contact with the rotor.

DRUM BRAKES

Drum brakes employ two brake shoes mounted on a stationary backing plate. These shoes are positioned inside a circular drum which rotates with the wheel assembly. The shoes are held in place by springs. This allows them to slide toward the drums (when they are applied) while keeping the linings and drums in alignment. The shoes are actuated by a wheel cylinder which is mounted at the top of the backing plate. When the brakes are applied, hydraulic pressure forces the wheel cylinder's actuating links outward. Since these links bear directly against the top of the brake shoes, the tops of the shoes are then forced against the inner side of the drum. This action forces the bottoms of the two shoes to contact the brake drum by rotating the entire assembly slightly (known as servo action). When pressure within the wheel cylinder is relaxed, return springs pull the shoes back away from the drum.

Most modern drum brakes are designed to self-adjust themselves during application when the vehicle is moving in reverse. This motion causes both shoes to rotate very slightly with the drum, rocking an adjusting lever, thereby causing rotation of the adjusting screw. Some drum brake systems are designed to self-adjust during application whenever the brakes are applied. This on-board adjustment system reduces the need for maintenance adjustments and keeps both the brake function and pedal feel satisfactory.

POWER BOOSTERS

Virtually all modern vehicles use a vacuum assisted power brake system to multiply the braking force and reduce pedal effort. Since vacuum is always available when the engine is operating, the system is simple and efficient. A vacuum diaphragm is located on the front of the master cylinder and assists the driver in applying the brakes, reducing both the effort and travel he must put into moving the brake pedal.

The vacuum diaphragm housing is normally connected to the intake manifold by a vacuum hose. A check valve is placed at the point where the hose enters the diaphragm housing, so that during periods of low manifold vacuum brakes assist will not be lost.

Depressing the brake pedal closes off the vacuum source and allows atmospheric pressure to enter on one side of the diaphragm. This causes the master cylinder pistons to move and apply the brakes. When the brake pedal is released, vacuum is applied to both sides of the diaphragm and springs return the diaphragm and master cylinder pistons to the released position.

If the vacuum supply fails, the brake pedal rod will contact the end of the master cylinder actuator rod and the system will apply the brakes without any power assistance. The driver will notice that much higher pedal effort is needed to stop the car and that the pedal feels harder than usual.

Vacuum Leak Test

1. Operate the engine at idle without touching the brake pedal for at least one minute.
2. Turn off the engine and wait one minute.
3. Test for the presence of assist vacuum by depressing the brake pedal and releasing it several times. If vacuum is present in the system, light application will produce less and less pedal travel. If there is no vacuum, air is leaking into the system.

System Operation Test

1. With the engine **OFF**, pump the brake pedal until the supply vacuum is entirely gone.
2. Put light, steady pressure on the brake pedal.
3. Start the engine and let it idle. If the system is operating correctly, the brake pedal should fall toward the floor if the constant pressure is maintained.

Power brake systems may be tested for hydraulic leaks just as ordinary systems are tested.

**** WARNING**

Clean, high quality brake fluid is essential to the safe and proper operation of the brake system. You should always buy the highest quality brake fluid that is available. If the brake fluid becomes contaminated, drain and flush the system, then refill the master cylinder with new fluid. Never reuse any brake fluid. Any brake fluid that is removed from the system should be discarded.

Brake Light Switch

REMOVAL & INSTALLATION

➧ **See Figure 1**

1. Disconnect the electrical harness at the switch.
2. Remove the locknut (closest to the pedal).
3. Remove the switch from the brake pedal.

To install:

4. Insert the new switch and loosely install the locknut.
5. Adjust the switch so that plunger at the tip of the switch is held in by the pedal in its at-rest position.

➡**Remember that the pedal holds the switch off; the brake lamps come on when the pedal moves away from the switch.**

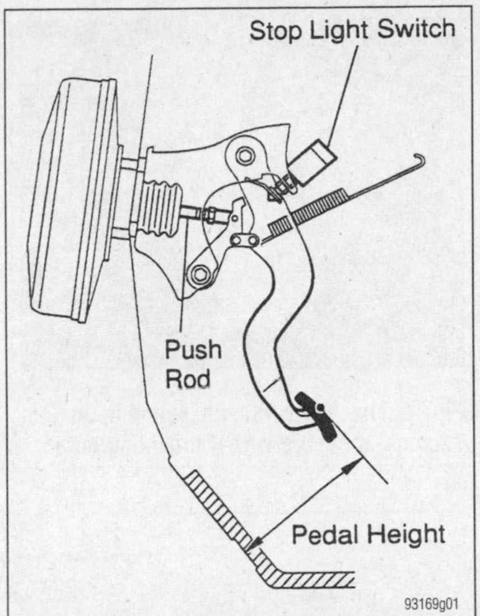

Fig. 1 Location of the brake stop light switch

6. Once positioned, tighten the locknut and connect the wiring.
7. Check the switch function by pressing the pedal. Have an assistant observe the brake lamps for proper operation.

Master Cylinder

REMOVAL & INSTALLATION

➧ **See Figures 2 thru 13**

93169p73

Fig. 2 Use a clean rag to wipe away any dirt or debris from the master cylinder reservoir cap . . .

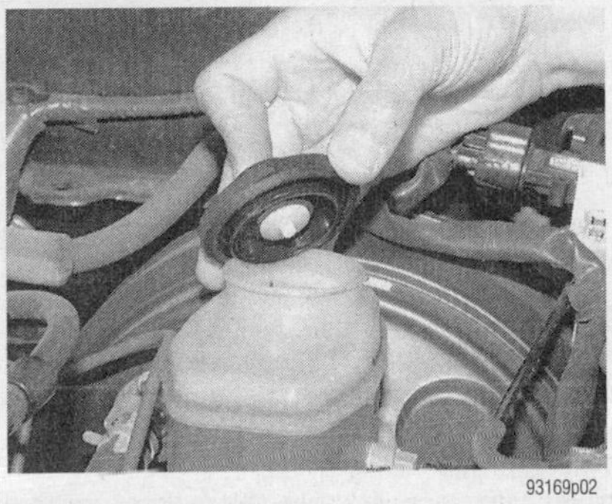

93169p02

Fig. 3 . . . then remove the cap from the master cylinder

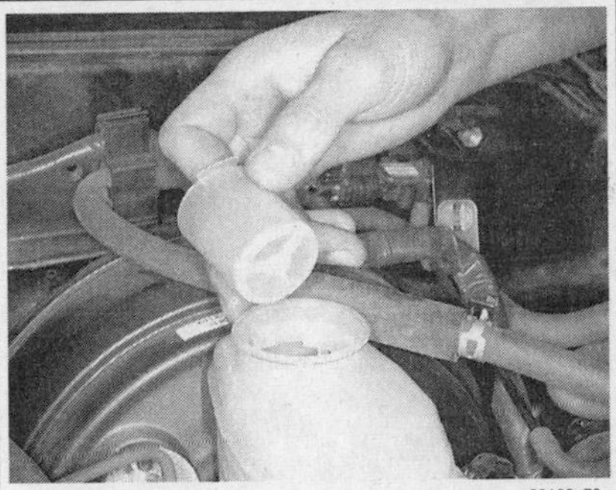

93169p76

Fig. 4 Remove the screen from the master cylinder

93169p75

Fig. 5 Siphon all brake fluid from the reservoir

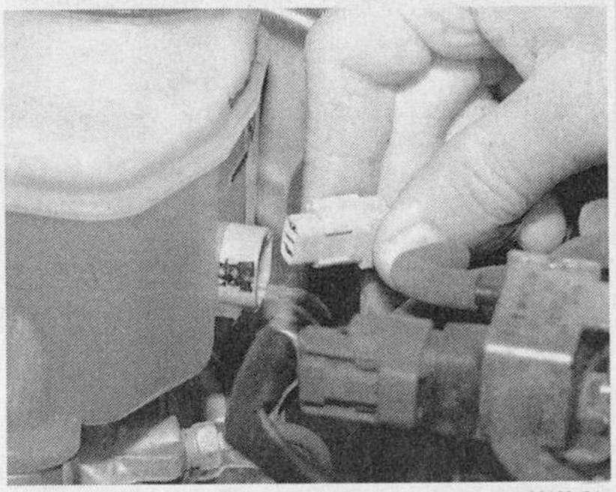

93169p01

Fig. 6 Detach the fluid level sender connector from the side of the master cylinder

93169p74

Fig. 7 Use a flare nut or line wrench to loosen the brake fluid lines

Fig. 8 Once loosened, pull the line up and out of the top of the master cylinder

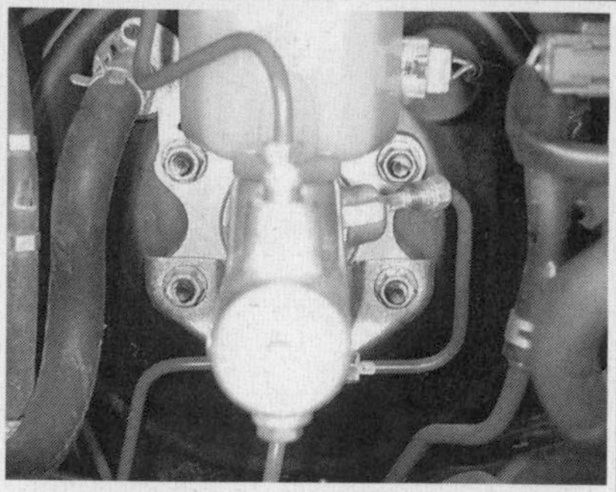

Fig. 9 The brake master cylinder on this Tacoma is secure with 4 mounting nuts

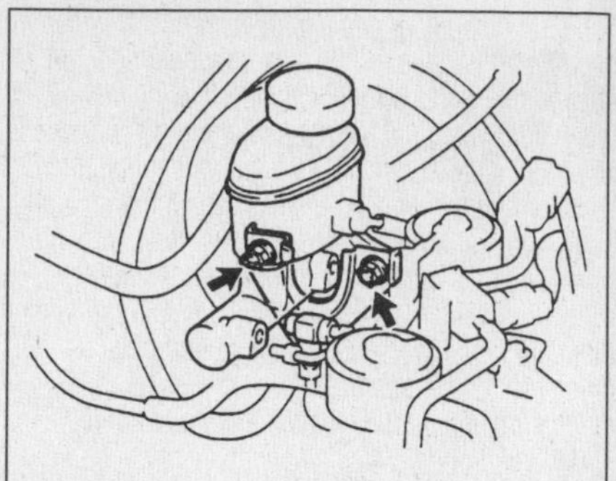

Fig. 10 Brake master cylinder mounting bolt locations

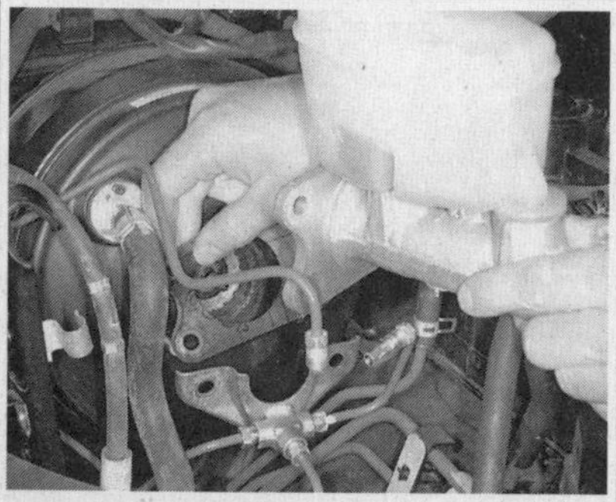

Fig. 11 Removing the master cylinder may require the temporary re-routing of a few lines and hoses

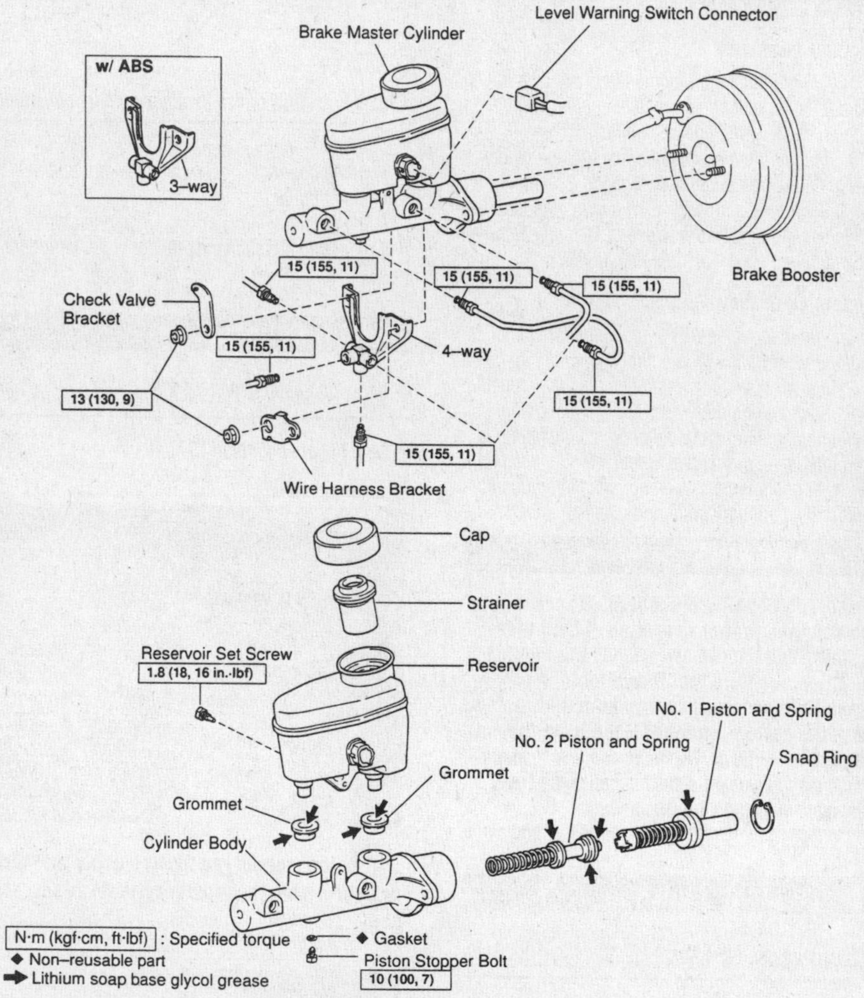

Fig. 13 Exploded view of the brake master cylinder

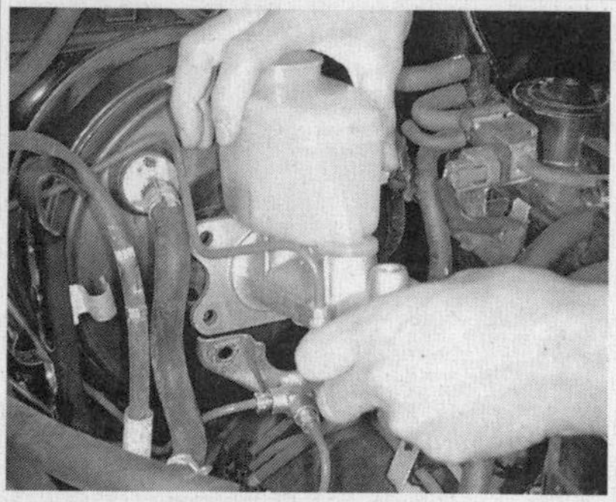

Fig. 12 Pull the master cylinder out and away from the brake booster—Tacoma

✲✲ WARNING

Be careful not to spill brake fluid on the painted surfaces. It will damage the paint. If a spill occurs, flush the area with plenty of fresh water.

1. Thoroughly clean all dirt and debris from the master cylinder cap and the area surrounding the cap.
2. Unplug the fluid level warning switch connector.
3. Use a syringe or similar tool to remove as much fluid as possible from the reservoir.
4. Carefully disconnect the brake lines at the master cylinder.

✲✲ WARNING

To prevent line damage, use a line wrench. Regular open-end wrenches are NOT recommended. Take great care not to bend or deform the lines. Plug the lines to keep dirt from entering.

5. Remove the nuts holding the master cylinder to the booster. Unbolt the 3-way or 4-way union.

➡When removing the cylinder, take care to recover the clamps, gaskets, etc.

To install:

6. Using a new gasket, install the master cylinder onto the brake booster. Tighten the mounting nuts to 9 ft. lbs. (13 Nm).
7. Attach the union. Carefully connect the brake tubes, initially threading them into place by hand. Once properly engaged, tighten the fittings to 11 ft. lbs. (15 Nm).

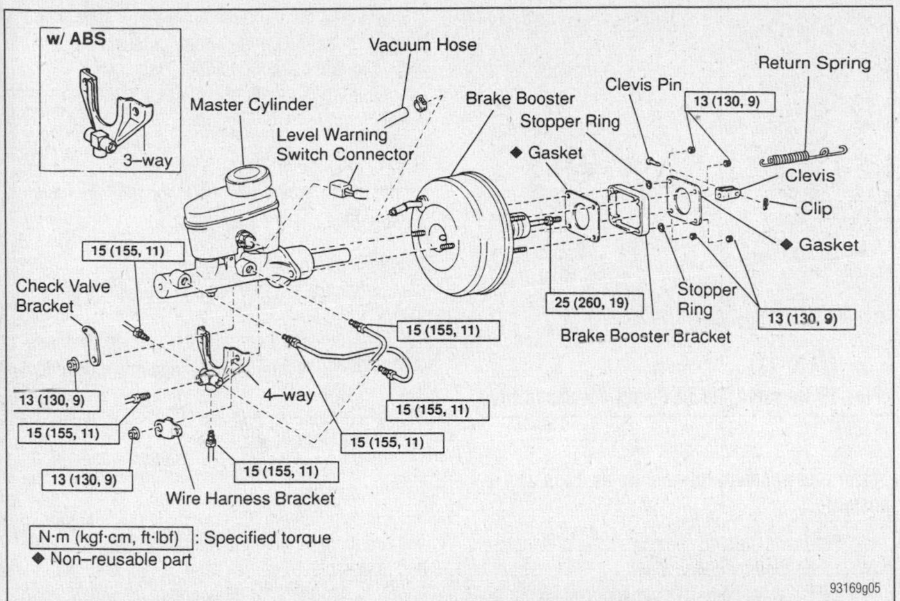

Fig. 14 You must remove the master cylinder first in order to remove the booster

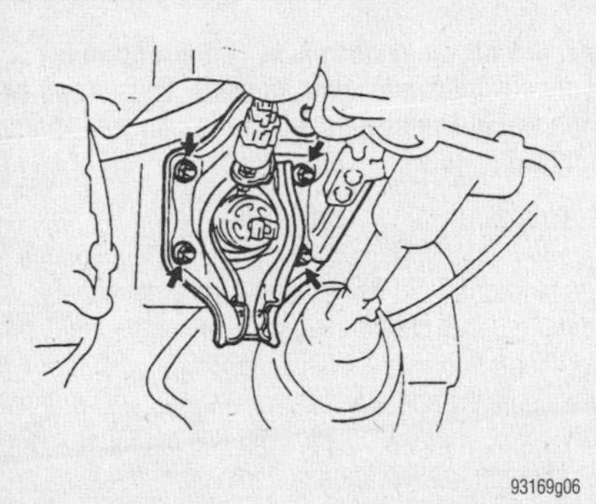

Fig. 15 Brake booster mounting bolt locations

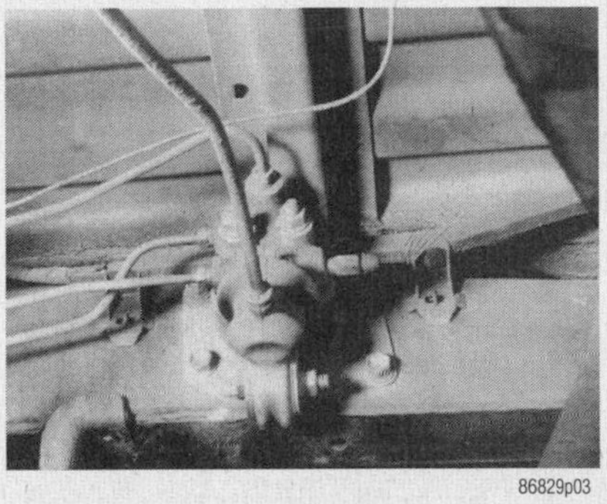

Fig. 16 The load sensing valve can usually be found secured to the frame rail

8. Connect the wiring harness for the brake fluid switch.
9. Fill the brake fluid reservoir with fluid to the MAX line. Check the leakage.
10. Bleed the brake system. Check again for any leakage.
11. Check and adjust the brake pedal.

Power Brake Booster

REMOVAL & INSTALLATION

▸ See Figures 14 and 15

1. Remove the master cylinder.
2. At the brake pedal, remove the clip and separate the clevis from the pedal.
3. Remove the pedal return spring.
4. Disconnect the vacuum hose from the booster.
5. Loosen the four nuts, then pull out the vacuum booster, bracket and gasket.

➡Some models employ a spacer and additional gaskets at the firewall.

To install:

6. Using a new gasket, install the booster, then tighten the mounting bolts to 9 ft. lbs. (13 Nm).
7. Install the clevis pin to the clevis through the brake pedal. Secure the pin with the clip.
8. Install the pedal return spring.
9. Adjust the length of the booster pushrod as follows:
   a. Install the gasket to the master cylinder.
   b. Set the SST 09737–00010 or equivalent on the gasket, then lower the pin until its tip slightly touches the piston.
   c. Turn the tool upside down and position it on the booster.
   d. Measure the clearance between the booster pushrod and the pin head. There should be zero clearance.
   e. Adjust the booster pushrod length until the pushrod lightly touches the pin head. While doing this depress the brake pedal enough so that the pushrod sticks out.
10. Install the master cylinder.
11. Attach the vacuum hose to the booster.
12. Fill the reservoir with brake fluid, then bleed the system.
13. Check for leakage.
14. Check and adjust the brake pedal.

Load Sensing Proportioning (LSP) and Bypass Valve (BV)

The purpose of this valve is to control the fluid pressure applied to the brakes to prevent rear wheel lock-up during weight transfer at high speed stops.

REMOVAL & INSTALLATION

▸ See Figures 16, 17, 18, and 19

1. Disconnect the shackle from the bracket.
2. Remove the cotter pin, then the nut and cushion retainer.
3. Disconnect the shackle and remove the cushions and collar.

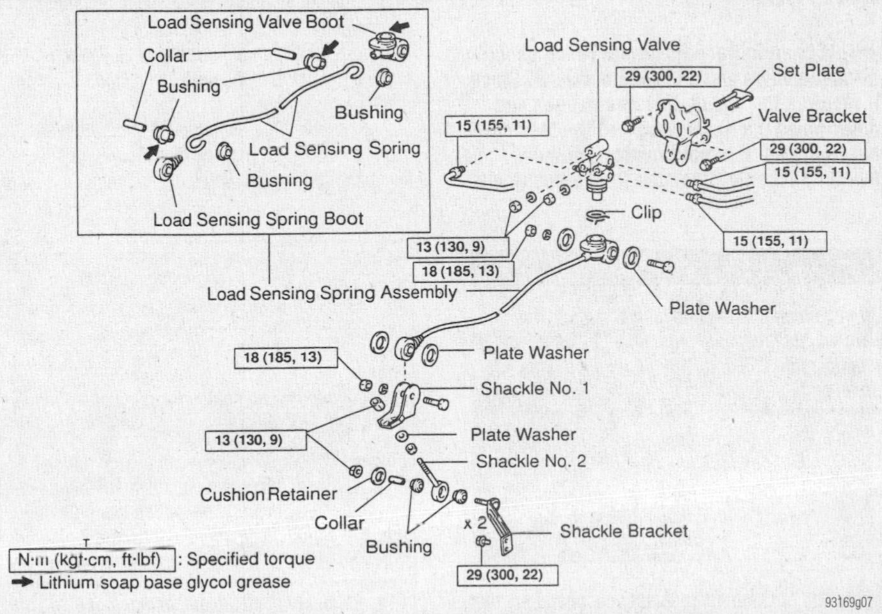

Fig. 17 Exploded view of the load sensing valve and its related components

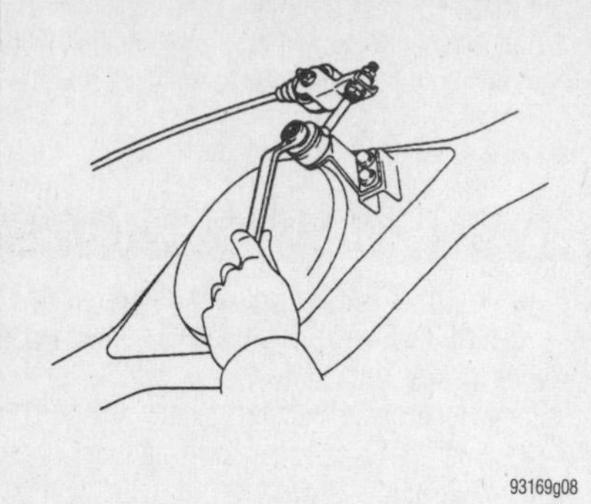

Fig. 18 Remove the shackle from the bracket

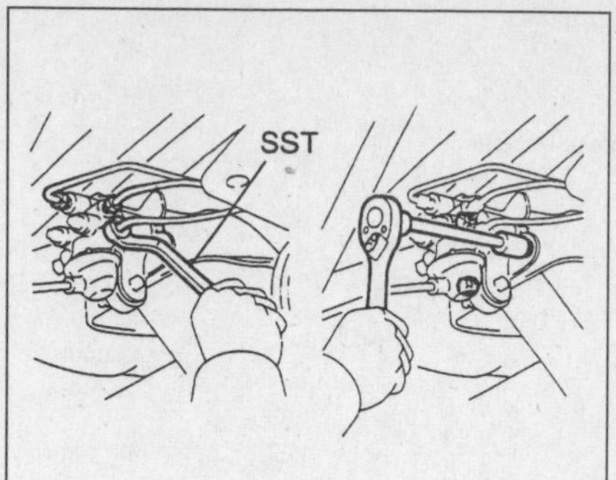

Fig. 19 Remove the LSP and BV assembly

4. Disconnect the brake lines attached to the valve. Plug the lines to keep dirt from entering.
5. Remove the mounting bolt, if used, and remove the valve.

To install:

➡This valve cannot be rebuilt. If it fails, the valve must be replaced.

6. Install the LSP and BV assembly to the frame, tighten to 19–22 ft. lbs. (25–29 Nm).
7. Install the shackle to the load sensing spring.
8. Attach the shackle to the shackle bracket, tighten to 9 ft. lbs. (13 Nm).
9. Install a new cotter pin.
10. Attach the brake lines, tighten to 11 ft. lbs. (15 Nm).
11. Set the valve body as follows:
    a. When pulling the load sensing spring, confirm that the valve piston moves down slowly.
    b. Position the valve body so that the valve piston lightly contacts the load sensing spring.
    c. Tighten the valve body mounting nuts to 9 ft. lbs. (13 Nm).
12. Bleed the brake system.

ADJUSTMENT

➧ See Figure 20

➡This is an initial adjustment which should bring the valve close to specifications. Since it requires the use of pressure gauges and determines the exact weight of the load on the rear axle, it is not practical for the owner/mechanic. Have the final adjustments performed at a reputable shop as soon as possible.

1. Pull down the load sensing spring to determine that the piston moves slowly.
2. Set the valve body so that the piston lightly touches the load sensing spring.
3. Tighten the mounting bolts.
4. Adjust the length of the shackle. Lengthening the distance between the centers lowers the pressure; shortening the distance raises the pressure. One full turn of the nut increases pressure about 20 psi. on Land Cruiser or about 11–14 psi (75–96 kPa) on all other vehicles. Initial length of this link should be:
   - 4Runner and Tundra: 3.54 inches (90mm)
   - Land Cruiser: 3.54 inches (90mm)
   - T100: 4.72 inches (120mm)
   - Tacoma 2WD: 3.07 inches (78mm)
   - Tacoma 4WD: 4.72 inches (120mm)
5. If the initial distance is correct, fluid metering should be very close to specification.

Brake Hoses and Lines

Metal lines and rubber brake hoses should be checked frequently for leaks and external damage. Metal lines are particularly prone to crushing and kinking under the vehicle. Any such deformation can restrict the proper flow of fluid and therefore impair braking at the wheels. Rubber hoses should be checked for cracking or scraping; such damage can create a weak spot in the hose and it could fail under pressure.

Any time the lines are removed or disconnected, extreme cleanliness must be observed. Clean all joints and connections before disassembly (use a stiff bristle brush and clean brake fluid); be sure to plug the lines and ports as soon as they are opened. New lines and hoses should be flushed clean with brake fluid before installation to remove any contamination.

REMOVAL & INSTALLATION

➧ See Figures 21 and 22

1. Disconnect the negative battery cable.
2. Raise and safely support the vehicle on jackstands.
3. Remove any wheel and tire assemblies necessary for access to the particular line you are removing.
4. Thoroughly clean the surrounding area at the joints to be disconnected.
5. Place a suitable catch pan under the joint to be disconnected.
6. Using two wrenches (one to hold the joint and one to turn the fitting), disconnect the hose or line to be replaced.
7. Disconnect the other end of the line or hose, moving the drain pan if necessary. Always use a back-up wrench to avoid damaging the fitting.
8. Disconnect any retaining clips or brackets holding the line and remove the line from the vehicle.

➡If the brake system is to remain open for more time than it takes to swap lines, tape or plug each line and port to keep contaminants out and fluid in.

To install:

9. Install the new line or hose, starting with the end farthest from the master cylinder. Connect the other end, then confirm that both fittings are correctly threaded and turn smoothly using finger pressure. Make sure the new line will not rub against any other part. Brake lines must be at least 1/2 in. (13mm) from the steering column and other moving parts. Any protective shielding or insulators must be reinstalled in the original location.

⁂ WARNING

Make sure the hose is NOT kinked or touching any part of the frame or suspension after installation. These conditions may cause the hose to fail prematurely.

10. Using two wrenches as before, tighten each fitting.
11. Install any retaining clips or brackets on the lines.

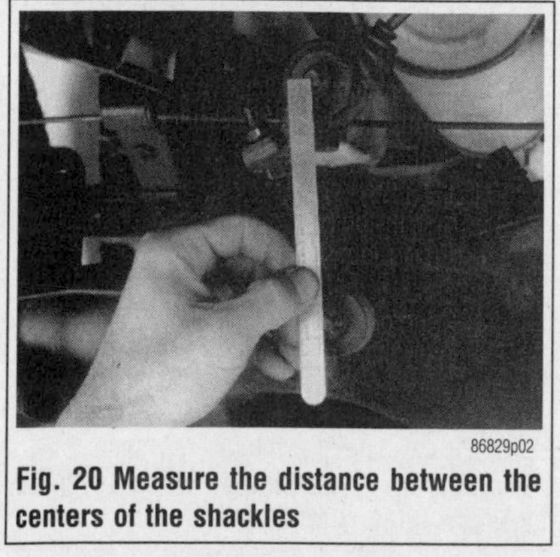

Fig. 20 Measure the distance between the centers of the shackles

Fig. 21 View of the front brake hose to line fitting—Tacoma

Fig. 22 Removing the brake hose mounting bolt

12. If removed, install the wheel and tire assemblies, then carefully lower the vehicle to the ground.
13. Refill the brake master cylinder reservoir with clean, fresh brake fluid, meeting DOT 3 specifications. Properly bleed the brake system.
14. Connect the negative battery cable.

Bleeding Brake System

See Figure 23

It is necessary to bleed the hydraulic system any time the system has been opened or has trapped air within the fluid lines. It may be necessary to bleed the system at all four brakes if air has been introduced through a low fluid level or by disconnecting brake pipes at the master cylinder.

If a line is disconnected at one wheel only, generally only that brake needs bleeding. If lines are disconnected at any fitting between the master cylinder and the brake, the system served by the disconnected pipe must be bled.

WARNING

Do not allow brake fluid to splash or spill onto painted surfaces; the paint will be damaged. If spillage occurs, flush the area immediately with clean water.

MASTER CYLINDER

If the master cylinder has been removed, the lines disconnected or the reservoir allowed to run dry, the cylinder must be bled before the lines are bled.

1. Check the level of the fluid in the reservoir. If necessary, fill with fluid.
2. Disconnect the brake lines from the master cylinder. Plug the lines to keep dirt from entering.
3. Place a pan or rags under the cylinder.
4. Have an assistant slowly depress the brake pedal and hold it down.
5. Block off the outlet ports with your fingers. Be sure to wear gloves. Have the assistant release the pedal. Make a tight seal with your fingers; do not allow the cylinder to ingest air when the pedal is released.
6. Repeat three or four times.
7. Connect the brake lines to the master cylinder and top off the fluid in the master cylinder reservoir.

LINES AND WHEEL CIRCUITS

See Figures 24, 25, 26, 27, and 28

1. Fill the master cylinder to the maximum level with the proper brake fluid.

An assistant will be needed to properly bleed the brake system.

2. Raise and safely support the vehicle.
3. Remove the protective caps from the bleeder screws and bleed the brakes using the following bleeding sequence. Always start with the brake unit farthest from the master cylinder. The proper bleeding sequence is:
   - Right rear
   - Left rear
   - Right front
   - Left front.
4. Insert a tight fitting clear plastic tube over the bleeder screw on the caliper and the other end of the tube in a transparent container partially filled with clean brake fluid.

WARNING

When bleeding do not allow the system to run dry, otherwise the entire procedure must be repeated.

5. Have an assistant slowly pump the brake pedal several times. On the last pump, have the assistant hold the pedal fully depressed. While the pedal is depressed, open the bleeder plug until fluid starts to run out, then close the plug.

If the brake pedal is pumped too fast, small air bubbles will form in the brake fluid which will be very difficult to remove.

6. Repeat this procedure until no air bubbles are visible in the hose. Close the bleeder port.

Constantly replenish the brake fluid in the master cylinder reservoir, so that it does not run out during bleeding.

7. If bleeding the entire system, repeat the procedure at the left rear wheel, the right front wheel and the left front wheel in that order.
8. Bleed the load sensing proportioning and bypass valve.

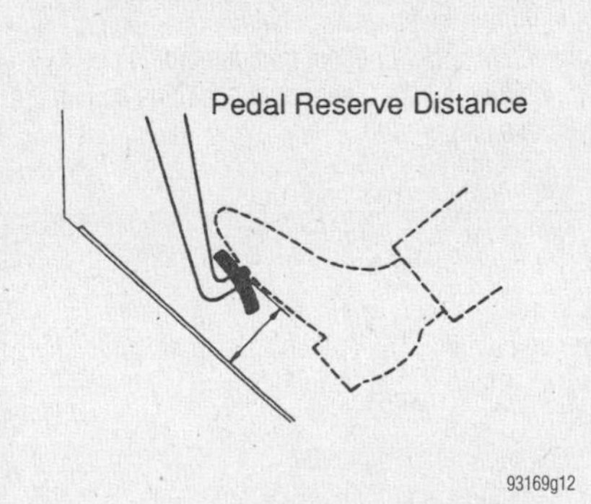

Fig. 23 If excessive pedal travel is detected, air may be trapped in the lines

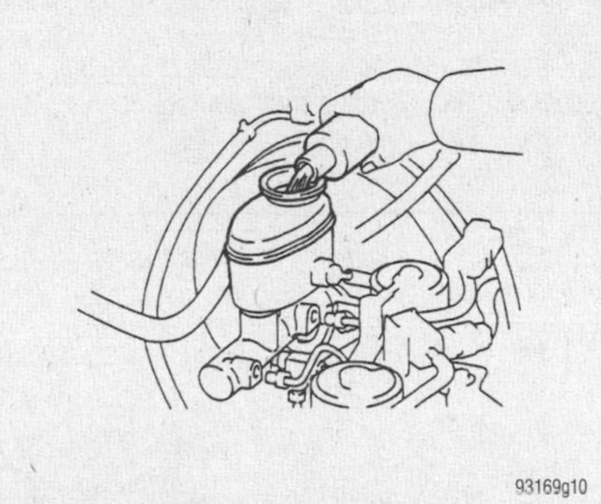

Fig. 24 Always keep the fluid in the brake master cylinder at the proper level when bleeding the system

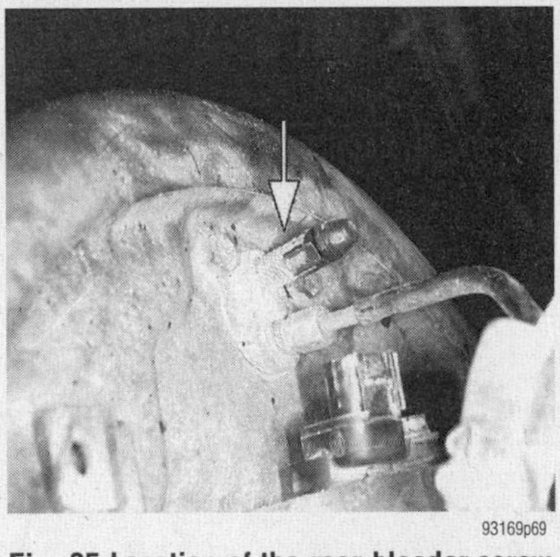

Fig. 25 Location of the rear bleeder screw

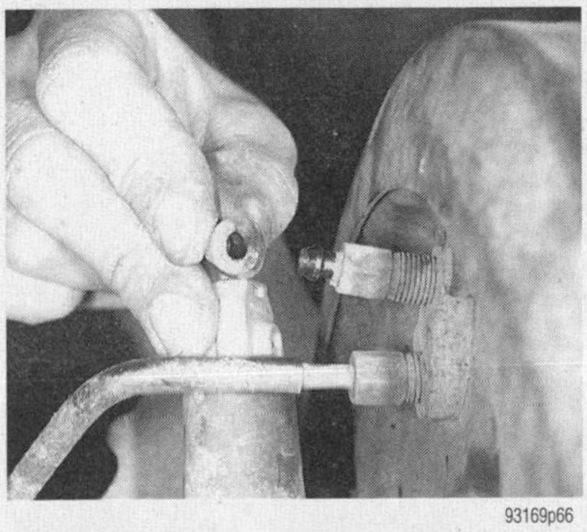

Fig. 26 Remove the bleeder screw dust cap

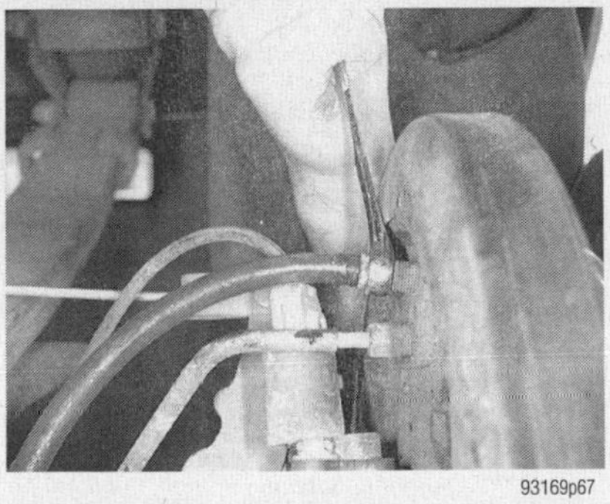

Fig. 27 Loosen the bleeder screw with a box-end wrench

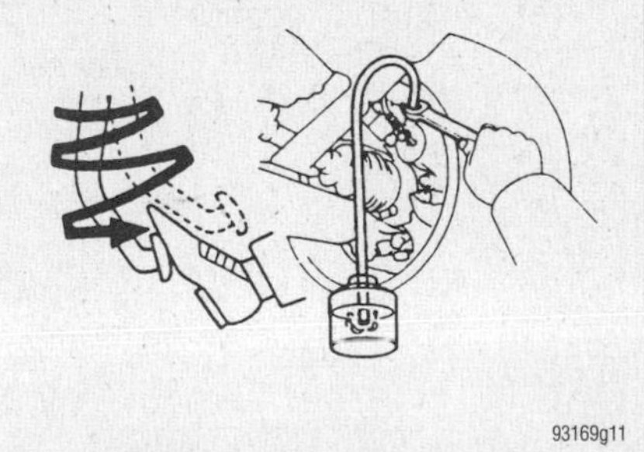

Fig. 28 Using a vinyl tube submerged in a container of brake fluid to bleed the brake system

DISC BRAKES

➧ See Figure 29

✻✻ CAUTION

Older brake pads or shoes may contain asbestos, which has been determined to be a cancer causing agent. Never clean the brake surfaces with compressed air! Avoid inhaling any dust from any brake surface! When cleaning brake surfaces, use a commercially available brake cleaning fluid.

Brake Pads

WEAR INDICATORS

The front disc brake pads may be equipped with a metal tab which will come into contact with the rotor after the friction surface material has worn near its usable minimum. The wear indicators make a constant, distinct metallic sound that should be easily heard. The sound has been described as similar to either fingernails on a blackboard or a field full of crickets. The key to recognizing that it is the wear indicators and not some other brake noise is that the sound is heard when the vehicle is being driven WITHOUT the brakes applied. It may or may not be present under braking and is heard during normal driving.

It should also be noted that any disc brake system, by its design, cannot be made to work silently under all conditions. Each system includes various shims, plates, cushions and brackets to suppress brake noise, but no system can completely silence all noises. Some brake noise, either high or low frequency, can be controlled and perhaps lessened, but cannot be totally eliminated.

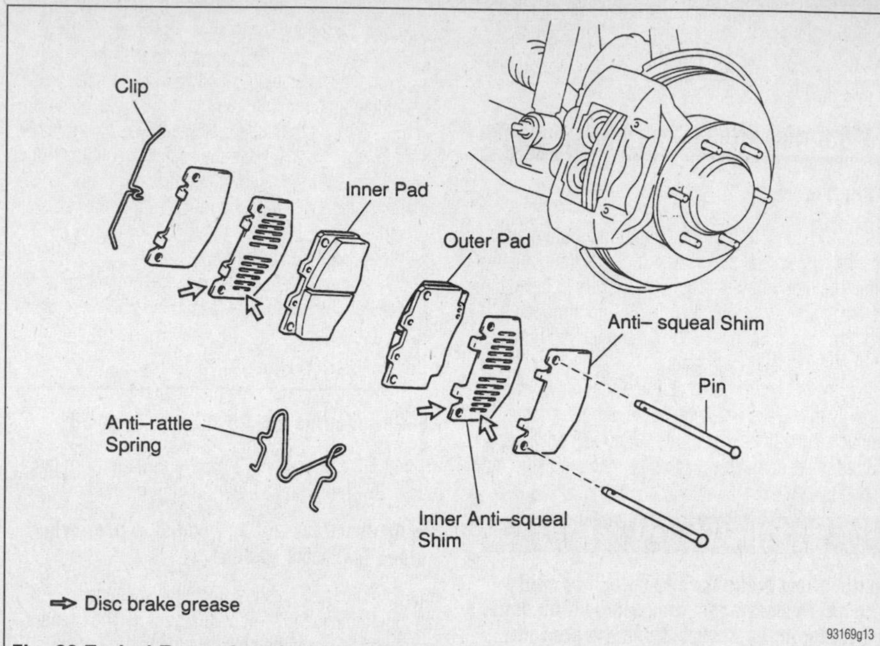

Fig. 29 Typical Toyota front brake components

REMOVAL & INSTALLATION

2WD Vehicles (except Pre-Runner)

PD60 AND 66 TYPE BRAKES

➧ See Figure 30

1. Remove a small amount of fluid from the reservoir, using a syringe or similar tool.
2. Raise the front of the truck and safely support it with jackstands.
3. Remove the lug nuts and the wheel.
4. Remove the lower caliper-to-torque plate bolt. The torque plate is the framework that holds the caliper.
5. Pivot the caliper assembly upwards and suspend it from the suspension with a wire. Do NOT disconnect the brake line, but take care not to stretch it.
6. Remove the 2 anti-squeal springs and lift out the brake pads.

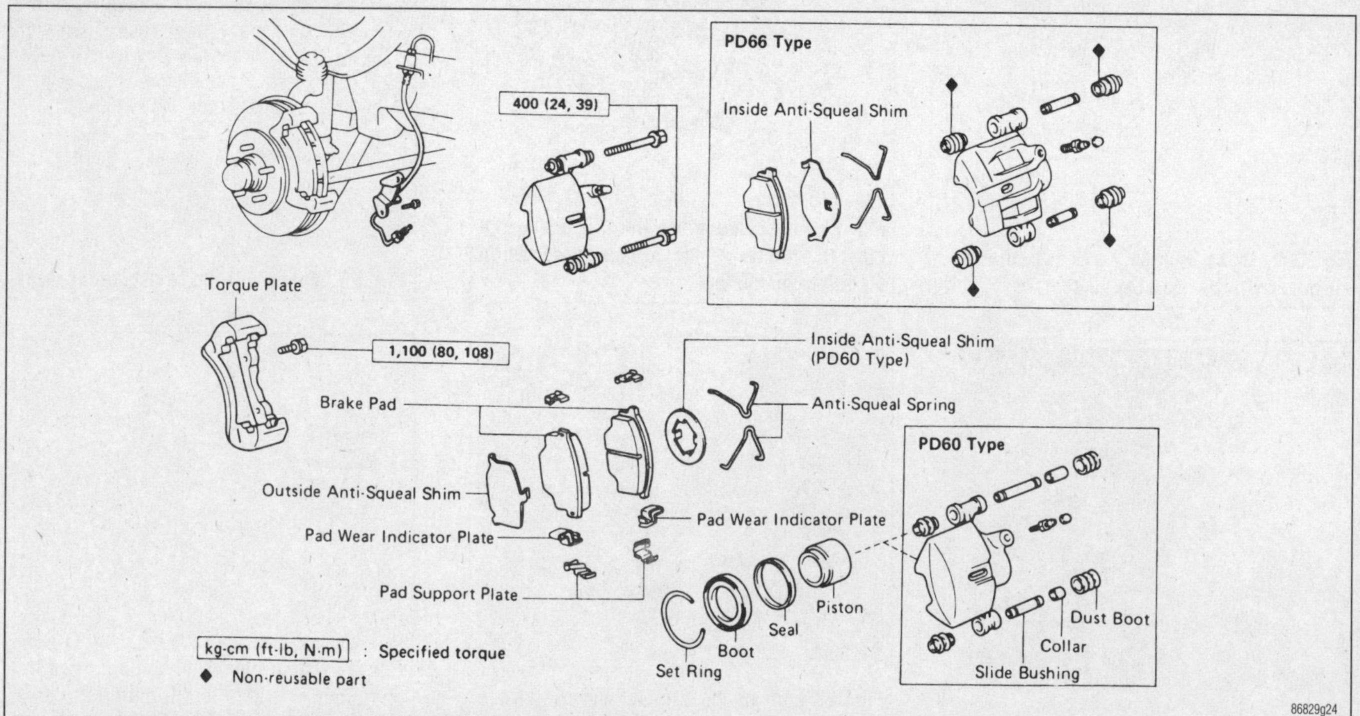

Fig. 30 Exploded view of the PD60 and 66 type brake components

7. Remove the 2 anti-squeal shims and the 4 pad support plates. Pull the 2 pad wear indicators off the pads.

8. Check the pad thickness and replace the pads if they are less than 0.039 in. (1mm) thick. New pads measure approximately 0.374–0.472 in. (9.6–12.0mm) thick depending on the vehicle.

➡This minimum thickness measurement may disagree with your state inspection laws.

To install:

9. Install the 4 pad support plates into the torque plate.

10. Install a new pad wear indicator plate to each pad.

11. Install the large anti-squeal shim to the back of the outer pad (PD 60) or to the back of each pad (PD 66) and then position both pads into the torque plate. Install the anti-squeal springs in place.

➡When installing new brake pads, make sure your hands are clean. Do not allow any grease or oil to touch the contact face of the pads or the brakes may not stop the truck properly.

12. Use a C-clamp or hammer handle and press the caliper piston back into the housing.

⁂ WARNING

Never press the piston into the caliper when the pads are out on both sides of the truck. The opposite piston may pop completely out of the caliper. This may spoil your afternoon.

13. For PD 60 types, press the round anti-squeal shim over the caliper piston; position the caliper over the torque plate so the dust boot is not pinched.

14. Swing the caliper down and fit the lower bolt. Tighten it to 29 ft. lbs. (39 Nm).

15. Install the wheel and lower the truck. Check the brake fluid level in the reservoir and fill to the max line if necessary. (The level should have risen when the piston was pushed back.)

16. Apply the parking brake and put the vehicle in Park or Neutral. Step on the brake pedal two or three times. The first pedal application will be due to the pistons being pushed back. The pedal travel should be normal after two or three pumps. Do NOT drive the vehicle until the pedal has a normal feel. If necessary, bleed the brakes to remove pedal sponginess.

➡Braking should be moderate for the first 5 miles (8 km) or so until the new pads seat correctly. The new pads will bed best if put through several moderate heating and cooling cycles. Avoid hard braking until the brakes have experienced several long, slow stops with time to cool in between. Taking the time to properly bed the brakes will yield quieter operation, more efficient stopping and contribute to extended brake life.

FS17 AND 18 TYPE BRAKES

➧ See Figure 31

1. Remove the hub cap and loosen the lug nuts.

2. Raise the front of the truck and safely support it with jackstands.

3. Remove the lug nuts and the wheel.

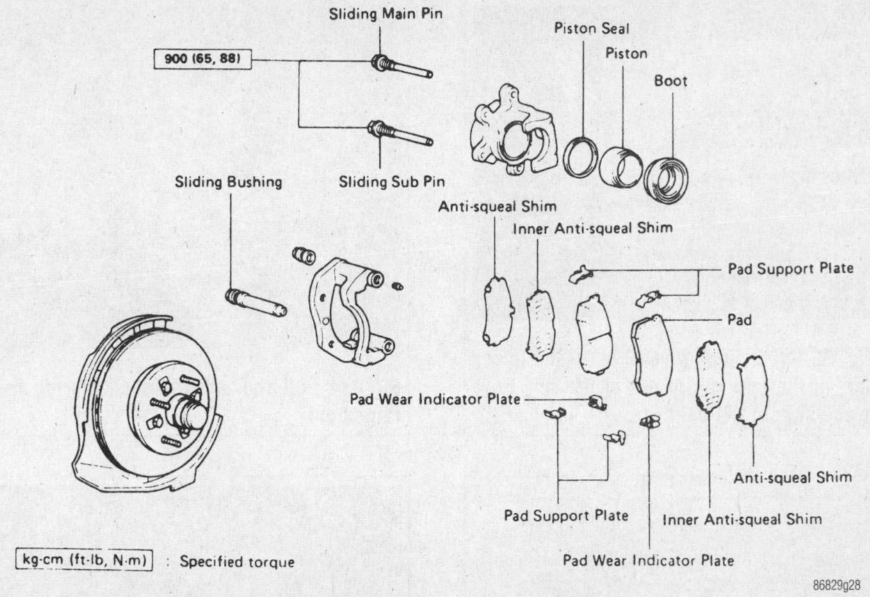

Fig. 31 Exploded view of the FS17 and FS18 type brake components

4. Remove the caliper slide pin on the sub-pin (lower) side.

5. Swivel the caliper up and away from the torque plate. Tie the caliper to a suspension member so it is out of the way. Do not disconnect the brake line.

6. Lift the 2 brake pads out of the torque plate. Remove the anti-squeal shim.

7. Remove the 4 pad support plates. Pull the 2 pad wear indicator plates off the pads.

8. Check the pad thickness and replace the pads if they are less than 0.03 in. (1mm) thick. New pads measure approximately 0.374 in. (9.6mm) thick.

➡This minimum thickness measurement may disagree with your state inspection laws.

To install:

9. Install the 4 pad support plates into the torque plate.

10. Install a new pad wear indicator plate to the bottom of each pad.

11. Install the anti-squeal shim to the back of the outer pad and then position both pads into the torque plate.

⁂ WARNING

When installing new brake pads, make sure your hands are clean. Do not allow any grease or oil to touch the contact face of the pads or the brakes will not stop the truck properly.

12. Use a syringe or similar tool to remove some fluid from the reservoir. Use a C-clamp or hammer handle and press the caliper piston back into the housing.

13. Untie the caliper and swivel it back into position over the torque plate so that the dust boot is not pinched. Install the slide pin and tighten it to 65 ft. lbs. (88 Nm).

14. Check the condition of the cylinder side bushing boot.

15. Install the wheel and lower the truck.

16. Check the brake fluid level in the reservoir and fill to the max line if necessary. (The level should have risen when the piston was pushed back.)

17. Apply the parking brake and put the vehicle in Park or Neutral. Step on the brake pedal two or three times. The first pedal application will be due to the pistons being pushed back. The pedal travel should be normal after two or three pumps. Do NOT drive the vehicle until the pedal has a normal feel. If necessary, bleed the brakes to remove pedal sponginess.

➡Braking should be moderate for the first 5 miles (8 km) or so until the new pads seat correctly. The new pads will bed best if put through several moderate heating and cooling cycles. Avoid hard braking until the brakes have experienced several long, slow stops with time to cool in between. Taking the time to properly bed the brakes will yield quieter operation, more efficient stopping and contribute to extended brake life.

4WD Vehicles and Pre-Runner

➧ See Figures 32 thru 44

1. Raise the front of the truck, support it on jackstands, and remove the front wheel.

93169p18

Fig. 32 View of the caliper with the brake pads installed—Tacoma shown

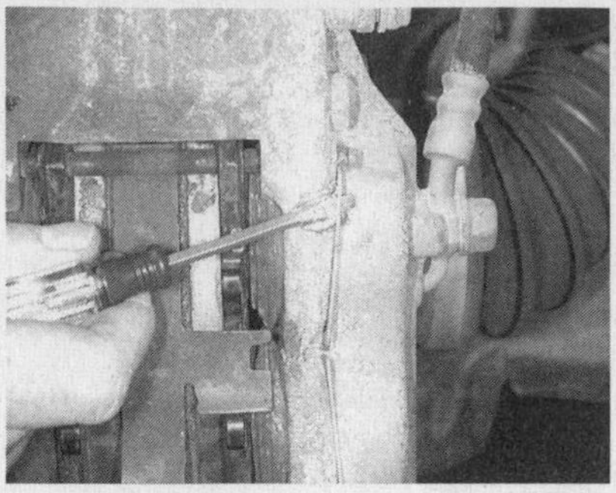

Fig. 33 Use a small prytool to lift the lower part of the spring clip out of the tiny hole in the side of the caliper

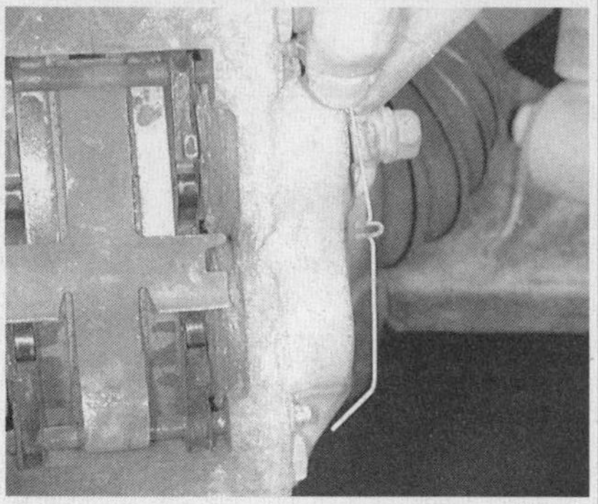

Fig. 34 Pull the anti-rattle clip/spring retainer out

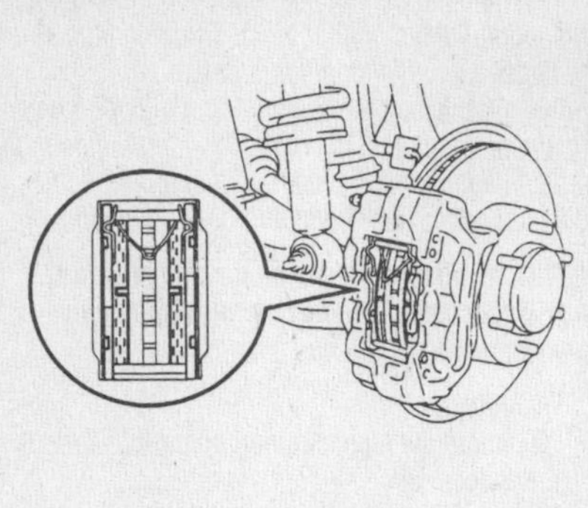

Fig. 35 View of the anti-rattle spring on a Tundra

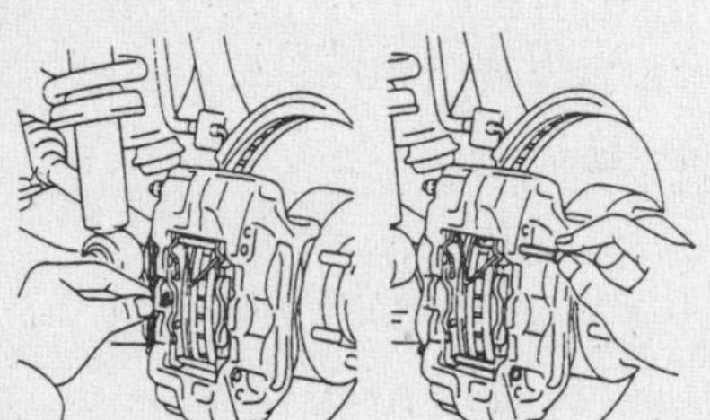

Fig. 36 Remove the pad pins—Tundra

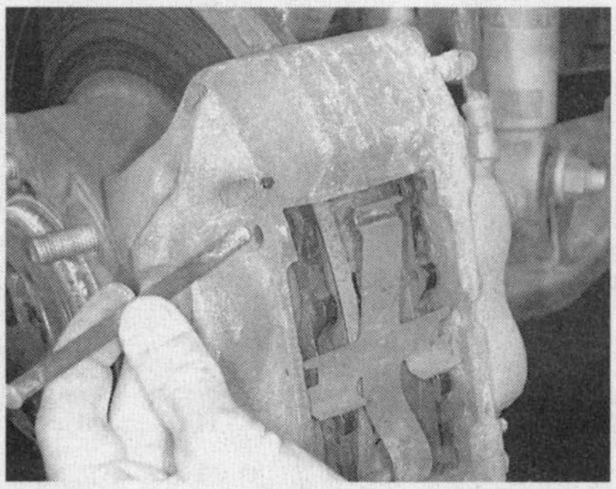

Fig. 37 Pull out the upper brake pad retaining pin . . .

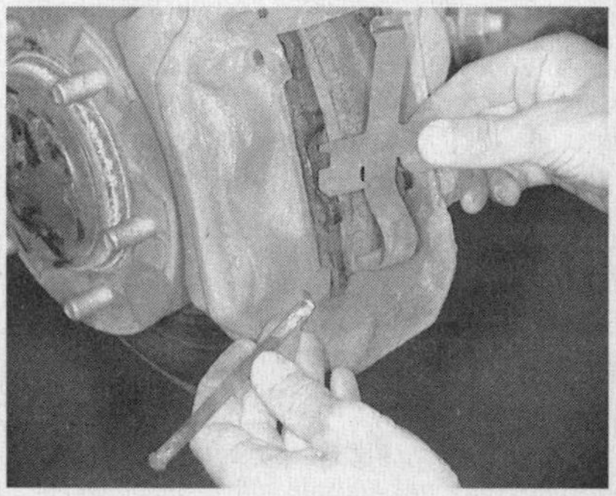

Fig. 38 . . . then remove the lower brake pad retaining pin

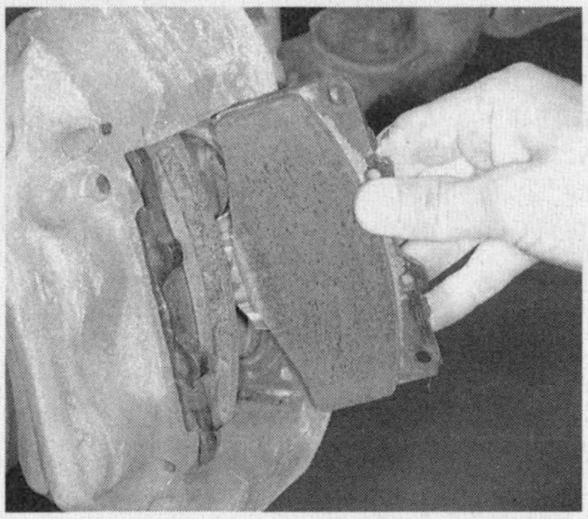

Fig. 39 Pull out the inner pad . . .

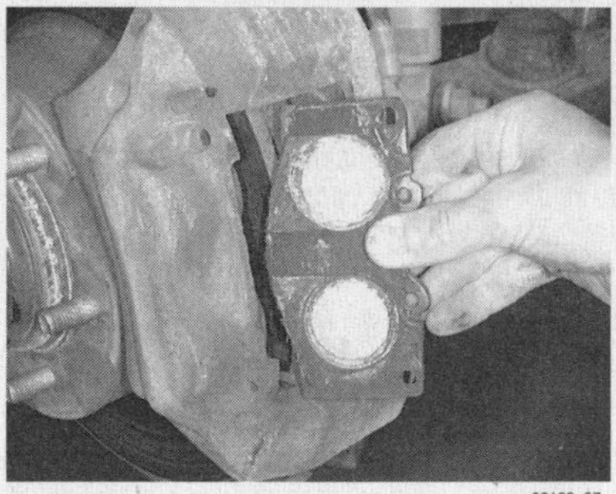

Fig. 40 . . . and the outer pad

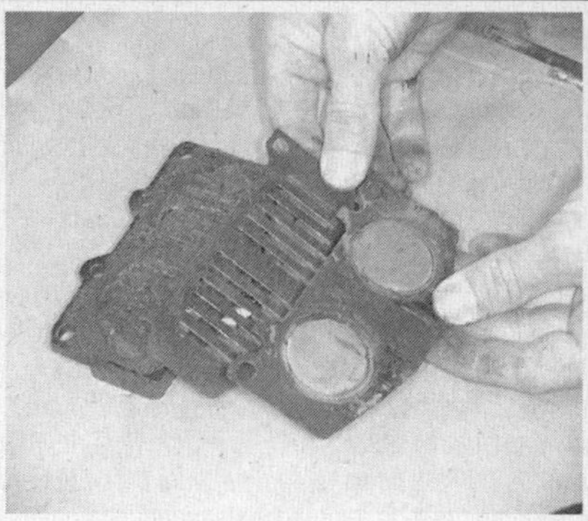

Fig. 41 Remove the pad shims

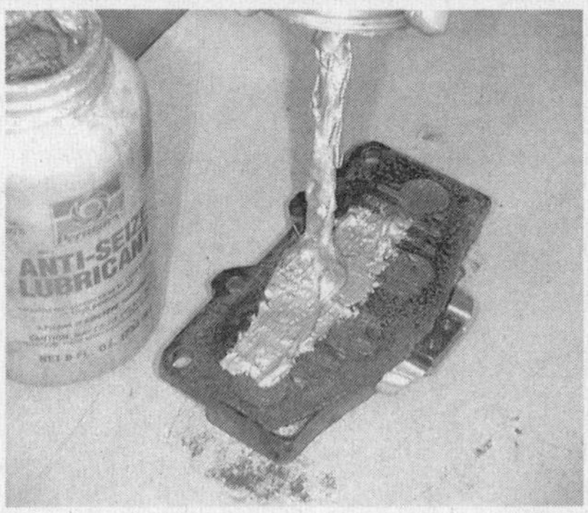

Fig. 42 Apply a suitable anti-seize lubricant to the pad's metal backing plate

Fig. 43 Install a pad shim on to the back of the brake pad and then coat it with a thin layer of anti-seize

Fig. 44 Do not apply anti-seize to the rear of the final brake pad shim to be installed

2. Pull out the wire clip at the ends of the pad pins.

3. Remove the pins. Remove the anti-rattle spring (W-shaped on older trucks), the brake pads and the four anti-squeal shims.

4. Check the pad thickness and replace the pads if they are less than 0.03 in. (1mm) thick. New pads measure approximately 0.374 in. (9.6mm) thick.

➡This minimum thickness measurement may disagree with your state inspection laws.

5. Check the pins for straightness and wear, and replace if necessary.

To install:

6. Use a syringe or similar tool to remove a small amount of fluid from the master cylinder reservoir.

7. Use a C-clamp and press the caliper pistons back into the housing.

➡Never press the pistons into the caliper when the pads are out on both sides of the truck.

8. Install the 4 anti-squeal shims so that the black shims are between the silver shims and the brake pad.

9. Install the brake pads. Be very careful not to get grease or oil on the inner surfaces of the pads.

10. Install the anti-rattle spring.

11. Slide the 2 pad retaining pins through the caliper and pads and install the retaining clip.

12. Install the wheel and lower the truck. Bleed the brakes and road test the vehicle.

13. Check the brake fluid level in the reservoir and fill to the max line if necessary. (The level should have risen when the piston was pushed back.)

14. Apply the parking brake and put the vehicle in Park or Neutral. Step on the brake pedal two or three times. The first pedal application will be due to the pistons being pushed back. The pedal travel should be normal after two or three pumps. Do NOT drive the vehicle until the pedal has a normal feel. If necessary, bleed the brakes to remove pedal sponginess.

➡Braking should be moderate for the first 5 miles (8 km) or so until the new pads seat correctly. The new pads will bed best if put through several moderate heating and cooling cycles. Avoid hard braking until the brakes have experienced several long, slow stops with time to cool in between. Taking the time to properly bed the brakes will yield quieter operation, more efficient stopping and contribute to extended brake life.

INSPECTION

➧ See Figure 45

The front brake pads may be inspected without removal. With the front end elevated and supported, remove the wheel(s). Unlock the steering column lock and turn the wheel so that the brake caliper is out from under the fender.

View the pads, inner and outer, through the cutout in the center of the caliper. Remember to look at the thickness of the pad friction material (the part that actually presses on the disc) rather than the thickness of the backing plate which does not change with wear.

Keep in mind that you are looking at the profile of the pad, not the whole thing. Brake pads can wear on

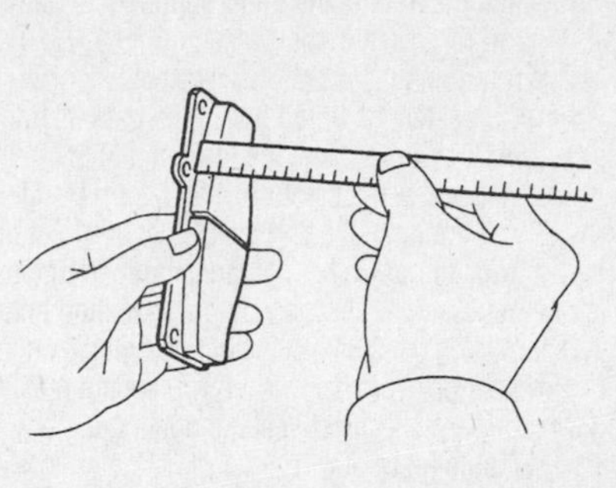

93169g19

Fig. 45 Measuring brake pad thickness

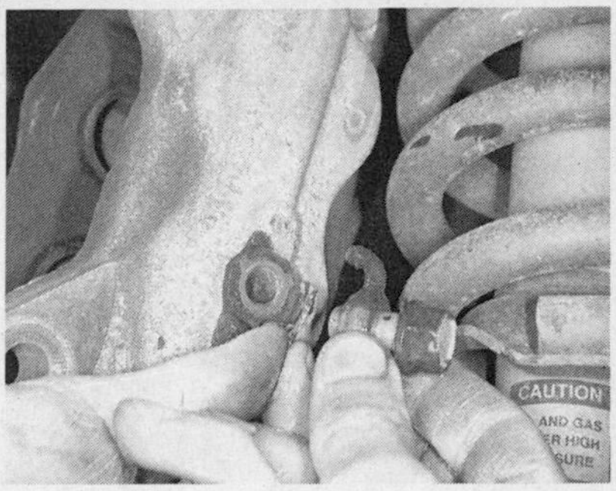

93169p70

Fig. 46 To remove the brake hose, unthread the banjo bolt from the caliper

a taper which may not be visible through the window. It is also not possible to check the contact surface for cracking or scoring from this position. This quick check can be helpful only as a reference; detailed inspection requires pad removal.

Brake Caliper

REMOVAL & INSTALLATION

2WD Vehicles

➧ See Figure 46

1. Elevate and safely support the vehicle.

2. Remove the wheel.

3. If removing the caliper from the vehicle for overhaul or replacement, disconnect the brake line from the caliper, then plug the line and port. If not, it is not necessary to disconnect the fluid line.

4. Remove the bolts holding the caliper to the torque plate.

5. Remove the caliper from the torque plate. If not replacing or overhauling the caliper, suspend it from a suspension component with a piece of wire. Never let the caliper hang by the brake hose.

6. If necessary, remove the pads and shims.

To install:

7. If removed, install the pads and shims.

8. Fit the caliper into position. Install the two retaining or slide bolts, then tighten as follows:

- FS17 or 18 brakes: 65 ft. lbs. (88 Nm)
- PD60 or 66 brakes: 29 ft. lbs. (39 Nm)
- T100 $^1/_2$ ton: 27 ft. lbs. (36 Nm)
- T100 1 ton: 29 ft. lbs. (39 Nm)

9. Install the brake line, tightening the fitting to 11–22 ft. lbs. (15–30 Nm).

10. Install the wheel.

11. Lower the vehicle to the ground. Bleed the brakes and road test the vehicle.

4WD Vehicles

➧ See Figures 47, 48, 49, 50, and 51

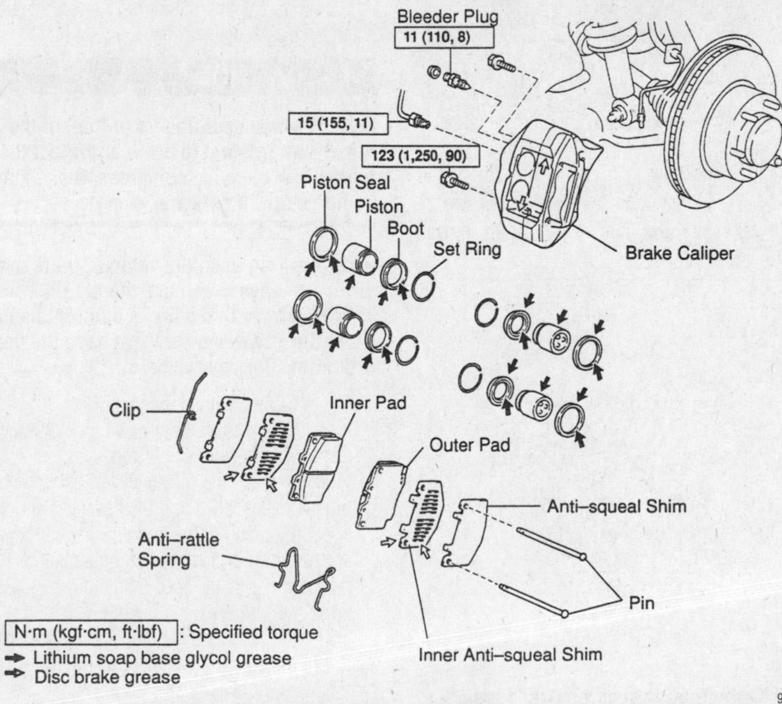

93169g16

Fig. 47 Exploded view of the front brake caliper assembly

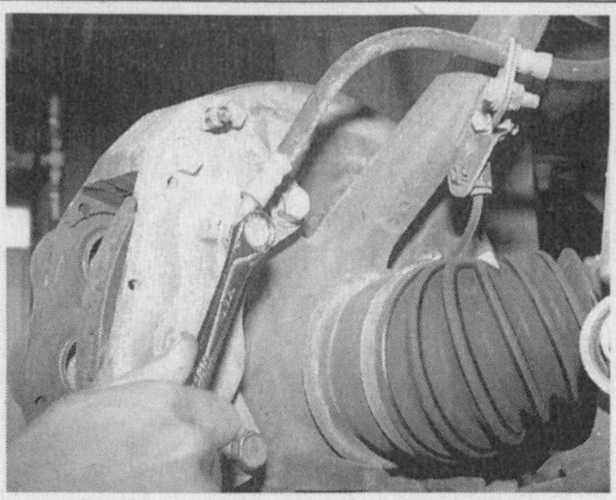
93169p25

Fig. 48 Use a closed-end wrench to remove the banjo bolt from the brake hose

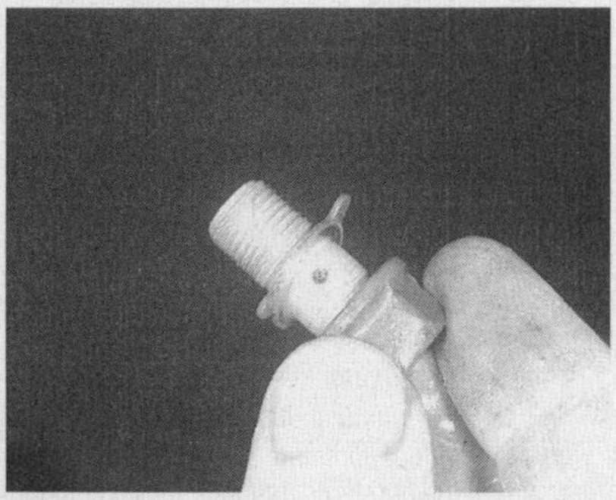
93169p31

Fig. 49 Close up view of a brake hose banjo bolt

93169g17

Fig. 50 Remove the hydraulic brake line from the caliper

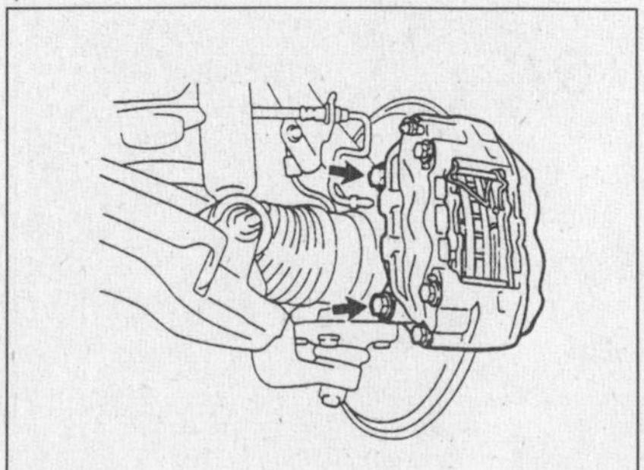
93169g18

Fig. 51 The caliper is secured with 2 mounting bolts

1. Raise the front of the truck, support it on jackstands, and remove the front wheel.
2. If removing the caliper for replacement or overhaul, unfasten the union bolt and 2 gaskets from the caliper, then disconnect the brake fluid hoses from the caliper, being careful not to deform the fittings. If you are not replacing the caliper, and just removing it for rotor or other component replacement, it is not necessary to disconnect the brake fluid line.
3. Unfasten the 2 caliper mounting bolts, then remove the caliper from the rotor. If you are not replacing the caliper, you can suspend it out of the way with a suitable piece of wire.
4. If necessary, remove the following:
   a. Pull out the two wire clips at the ends of the pad pins.
   b. Pull out the pads and anti-rattle spring.
   c. Remove the brake pads, and the anti-squeal shims.

To install:

5. If removed, install the brake pads.
6. Position the caliper over the rotor and install the mounting bolts. Tighten the caliper mounting bolts to 90 ft. lbs. (123 Nm). Be certain to position the shims correctly.

➡Make sure to install the flexible brake hose lock securely in the lock hole in the caliper.

7. If disconnected, attach the brake line to the caliper. Tighten the union bolt to 22 ft. lbs. (30 Nm).
8. Install the wheel and lower the truck. Bleed the brakes and road test the vehicle.

OVERHAUL

See Figures 52 thru 59

➡Some vehicles may be equipped dual or four-piston calipers. The procedure to overhaul the caliper is essentially the same with the exception of multiple pistons, O-rings and dust boots.

1. Remove the caliper from the vehicle and place on a clean workbench.

CAUTION

NEVER place your fingers in front of the pistons in an attempt to catch or protect the pistons when applying compressed air. This could result in personal injury!

➡Depending upon the vehicle, there are two different ways to remove the piston from the caliper. Refer to the brake pad replacement procedure to make sure you have the correct procedure for your vehicle.

2. The first method is as follows:
   a. Stuff a shop towel or a block of wood into the caliper to catch the piston.
   b. Remove the caliper piston using compressed air applied into the caliper inlet hole. Inspect the piston for scoring, nicks, corrosion and/or worn or damaged chrome plating. The piston must be replaced if any of these conditions are found.
3. For the second method, you must rotate the piston to retract it from the caliper.
4. If equipped, remove the anti-rattle clip.
5. Use a prytool to remove the caliper boot, being careful not to scratch the housing bore.

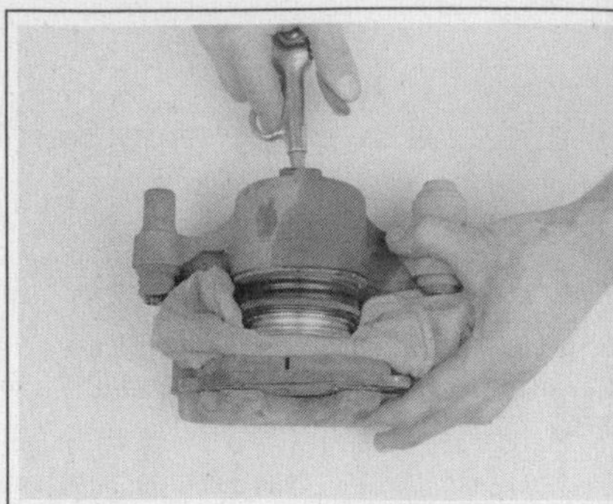
TCCA9p01

Fig. 52 For some types of calipers, use compressed air to drive the piston out of the caliper, but make sure to keep your fingers clear

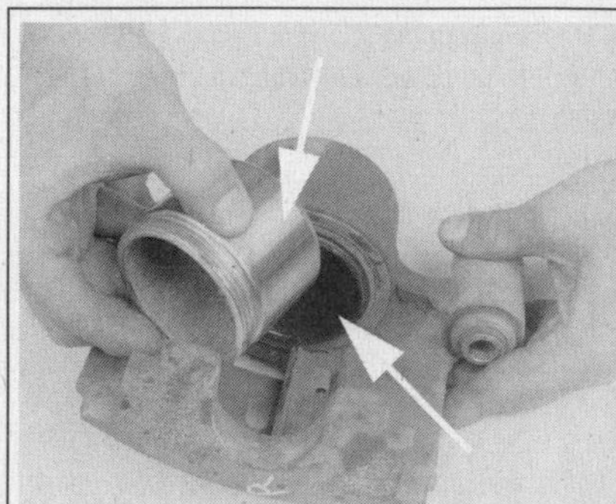
TCCA9p02

Fig. 53 Withdraw the piston from the caliper bore

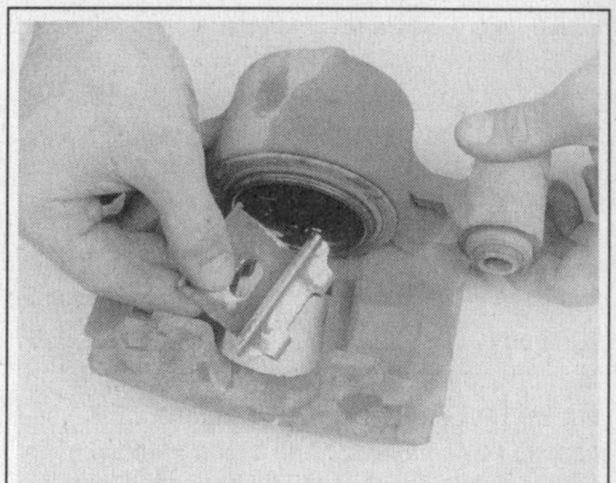
TCCA9p03

Fig. 54 On some vehicles, you must remove the anti-rattle clip

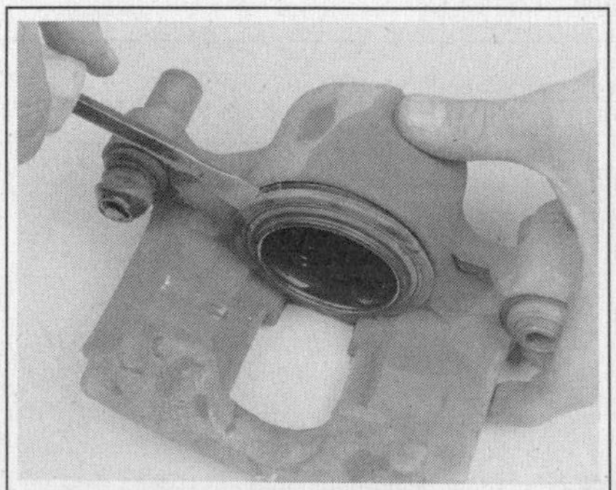
TCCA9p04

Fig. 55 Use a prytool to carefully pry around the edge of the boot . . .

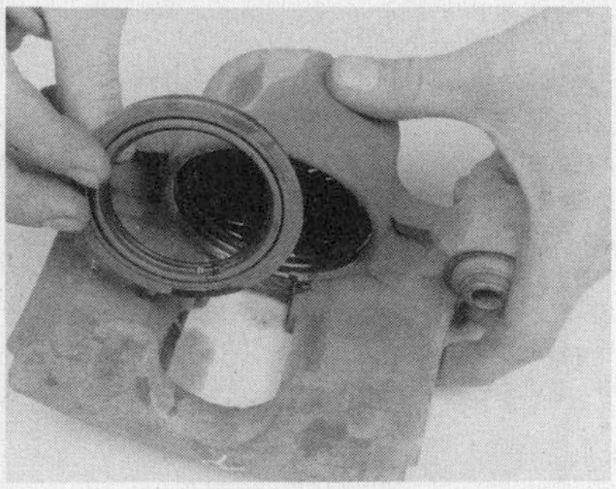

TCCA9p05

Fig. 56 . . . then remove the boot from the caliper housing, taking care not to score or damage the bore

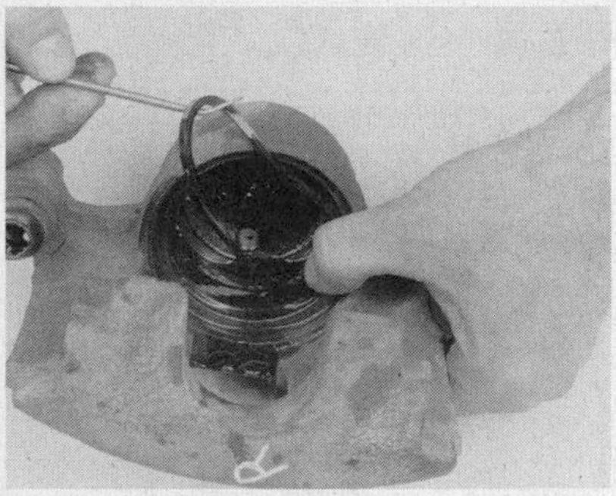

TCCA9p06

Fig. 57 Use extreme caution when removing the piston seal; DO NOT scratch the caliper bore

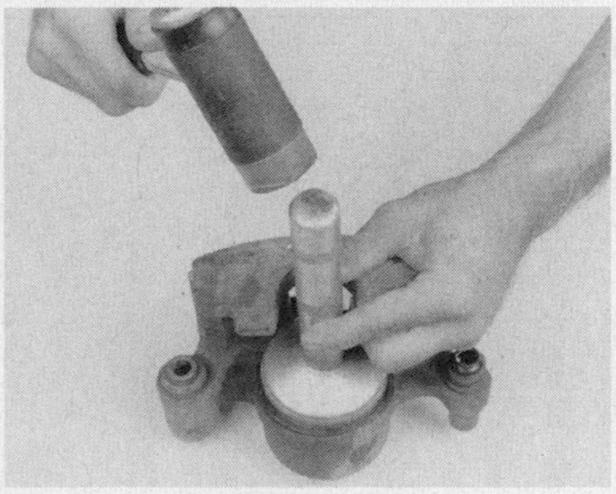

TCCA9p07

Fig. 58 Use the proper size driving tool and a mallet to properly seal the boots in the caliper housing

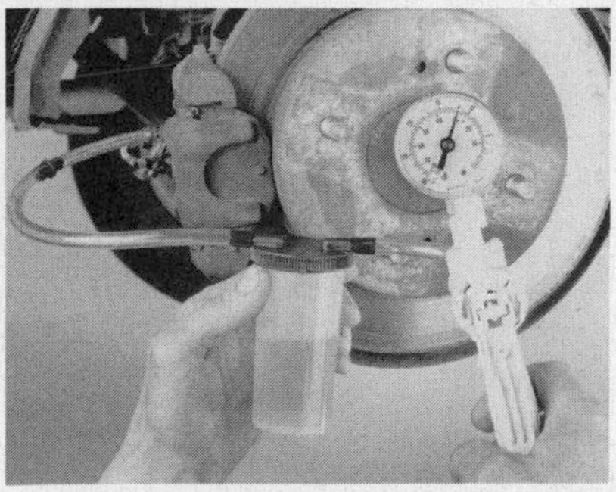

TCCA9p08

Fig. 59 There are tools, such as this Mighty-Vac, available to assist in proper brake system bleeding

6. Remove the piston seals from the groove in the caliper bore.
7. Carefully loosen the brake bleeder valve cap and valve from the caliper housing.
8. Inspect the caliper bores, pistons and mounting threads for scoring or excessive wear.
9. Use crocus cloth to polish out light corrosion from the piston and bore.
10. Clean all parts with denatured alcohol and dry with compressed air.

To assemble:

11. Lubricate and install the bleeder valve and cap.
12. Install the new seals into the caliper bore grooves, making sure they are not twisted.
13. Lubricate the piston bore.
14. Install the pistons and boots into the bores of the calipers and push to the bottom of the bores.
15. Use a suitable driving tool to seat the boots in the housing.
16. Install the caliper in the vehicle.
17. Install the wheel and tire assembly, then carefully lower the vehicle.
18. Properly bleed the brake system.

Brake Disc (Rotor)

REMOVAL & INSTALLATION

See Figures 60 and 61

1. Raise and safely support the vehicle.
2. Remove the wheel and tire assembly.
3. Disconnect the ABS speed sensor from the knuckle, if equipped.
4. Remove the brake pads and the caliper. On some models the rotor can be slid off the hub at this point. On these models, reinstall the lug nuts to hold the rotor to the hub for the next step.
5. Check the disc run-out at this point. Make a note of the results for use during installation. Refer to the inspection procedure.
6. On 2WD models where the rotor is bolted to the hub, remove the grease cap from the hub. Remove the cotter pin and the castellated nut. Remove the wheel hub with the brake rotor attached. The rotor can now be separated from the hub by removing the bolts.
7. On 4WD models where the rotor is bolted to the hub, remove the hub/rotor assembly (see Chapter 7), then unbolt the rotor from the hub.
8. Perform the rotor inspection procedure.

To install:

9. Coat the hub oil seal lip with multi-purpose grease and install the disc/hub assembly.
10. Adjust the wheel bearings.
11. Using a dial indicator, measure the disc run-out. Check it against the specifications in the Brake Specifications chart and the figures noted earlier.

➡If the wheel bearing nut is improperly tightened, disc run-out will be affected.

12. Install the remainder of the components as outlined in the appropriate sections.
13. Bleed the brake system.
14. Road test the truck.

93169p32

Fig. 60 4WD brake rotor, shown removed from vehicle

93169p30

Fig. 61 Install the brake rotor onto the hub, as shown

INSPECTION

See Figures 62, 63, and 64

Examine the disc. If it is worn, warped or scored, it must be replaced. Check the thickness of the rotor

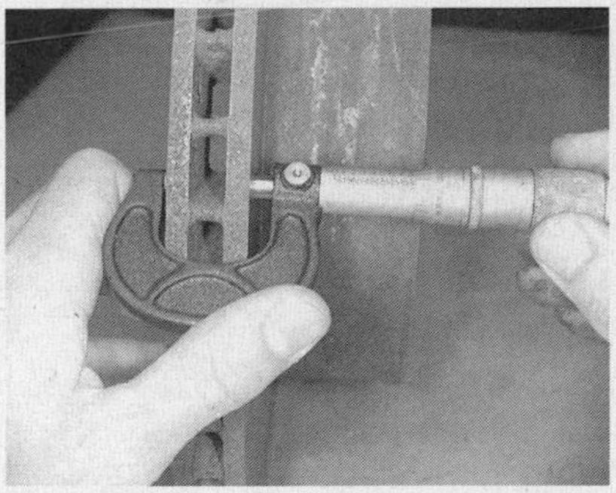

93169p38

Fig. 62 Use a micrometer to measure the thickness of the brake rotor. A one to two inch micrometer will work on most Toyota truck rotors

93169p40

Fig. 63 If the brake rotor is below specifications, replace it with a new one

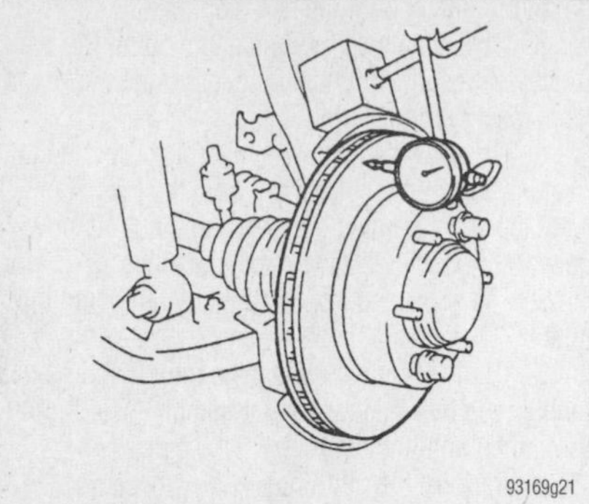

Fig. 64 Measuring brake rotor runout with a dial indicator

against the specifications given in the Brake Specifications chart. If below specifications, replace it. Use a micrometer to measure the thickness. Because the allowable wear from new thickness to minimum thickness is only approx. 0.078 in. (2mm), resurfacing the discs is not recommended.

The disc run-out should be measured before the rotor is removed and again, after the rotor is installed. Use a dial indicator mounted on a stand to determine run-out. If run-out exceeds the maximum specification, replace the disc. Maximum runout is as follows:

- T100, Tacoma, Tundra and 4Runner: 0.0028 in. (0.07mm)
- Land Cruiser: 0.0059 in. (0.015mm)

➡Be sure that the wheel bearing nut is properly tightened. If it is not, an inaccurate run-out reading may be obtained. If different run-out readings are obtained with the same disc, between removal and installation, this is probably the cause.

DRUM BRAKES

✲✲ CAUTION

Older brake pads or shoes may contain asbestos, which has been determined to be a cancer causing agent. Never clean the brake surfaces with compressed air! Avoid inhaling any dust from any brake surface! When cleaning brake surfaces, use a commercially available brake cleaning fluid.

Brake Drums

REMOVAL & INSTALLATION

See Figures 65 thru 71

1. Remove the hub cap (if used) and loosen the lug nuts. Release the parking brake.
2. Block the front wheels, raise the rear of the truck, and support it with jackstands.
3. Remove the rear wheels.
4. Unfasten the brake drum retaining screws, if used. Not all models have them.
5. Tap the drum lightly with a mallet in order to free it.

Fig. 65 Lubricate the threaded holes in the drum with a light amount of penetrating oil

Fig. 66 To press a stuck drum off the hub, insert bolts into the threaded holes in the drum

Fig. 67 Tighten the bolts evenly until they press the drum off the hub

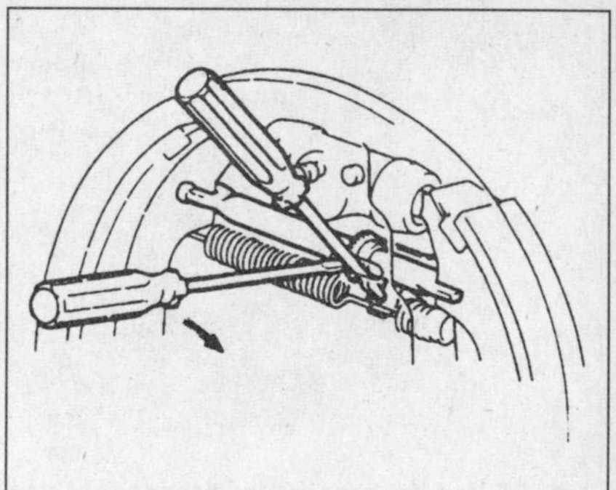

Fig. 68 You may need to back the self-adjuster off a few turns if the drum becomes lodged on the brake shoes during removal

Fig. 69 With both hands, pull the drum straight off the hub

Fig. 70 There may be a thin paper gasket stuck to the drum

Fig. 71 Typical Toyota drum

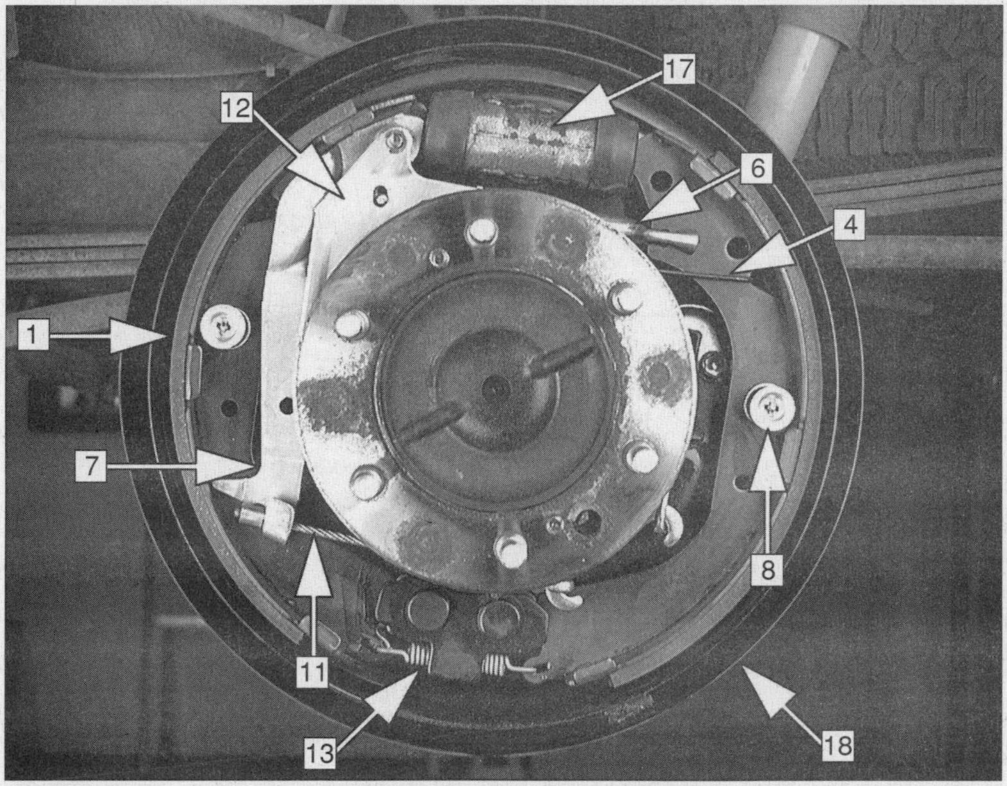

REAR DRUM BRAKE COMPONENTS

1) Brake shoe
2) Pin
3) C-Washer
4) Return spring
5) Adjuster star wheel
6) Adjuster assembly
7) Parking brake lever
8) Shoe hold-down spring
9) Wave washer
10) C-Washer
11) Parking brake cable
12) Automatic adjusting lever
13) Anchor spring
14) Automatic adjusting lever spring
15) Parking brake bellcrank, part 2
16) Parking brake bellcrank, part 1
17) Wheel cylinder
18) Backing plate

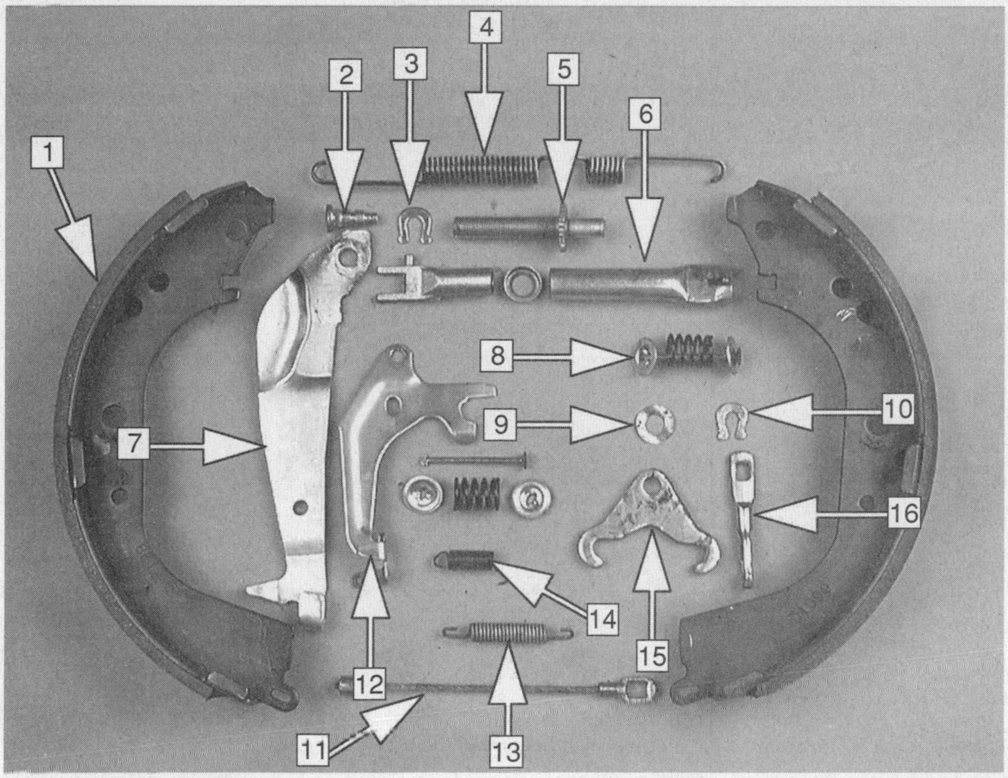

93169pbr

6. If the drum cannot be removed easily, try one or both of the following steps:

a. Thread two 8 x 1.25mm bolts into the threaded holes two turns at a time to lift the drum off the hub.

b. Insert a screwdriver into the hole in the backing plate and hold the automatic adjusting lever away from the adjusting bolt. Using another flat-bladed tool, relieve the brake shoe tension by turning the adjusting bolt clockwise. If the drum still will not come off, use a puller, but first make sure that the parking brake is fully released.

⁂ WARNING

Do not press the brake pedal with the brake drum removed.

To install:

7. Inspect the brake drum for any wear or deterioration. Check the inside diameter of the drum with the Brake Specifications chart. Replace if necessary.

8. To install the drum, simply place the drum on the axle and tighten the retaining screw, if used. Adjust the brakes.

9. Install the wheels and lower the truck. Road test the vehicle checking for correct function.

INSPECTION

See Figures 72 and 73

1. Clean the drum.

2. Inspect the drum for scoring, cracks, grooves and out-of-roundness. Replace the drum or have it "turned" at a machine or brake specialist shop, as required. Light scoring may be removed by dressing the drum with fine emery cloth.

3. Measure the inside diameter of the drum. A tool called an H-gauge caliper is used. See the Brake Specifications chart for your vehicle.

Brake Shoes

INSPECTION

See Figures 74, 75, 76, and 77

The brake shoes can be inspected without removing the brake drum if necessary. Remove the inspection hole plug in the backing plate. Check the shoe lining thickness through the hole. If they are less than the minimum of 0.039 in. (1.0mm), replace the shoes.

REMOVAL & INSTALLATION

➡Drum brakes require the use of two common brake tools to make the job easier. A brake spring wrench and a spring removing tool can be purchased at almost any automotive outlet for low cost. These are two of the handiest special tools you can own; they can generally be used on any vehicle with drum brakes.

2WD Vehicles

LEADING-TRAILING BRAKES

See Figure 78

1. Raise the rear of the truck and support it with jackstands. Remove the wheels.

2. Remove the brake drum.

3. Using a brake tool, remove the return spring.

4. Remove the hold-down spring and pin and pull out the rear shoe.

5. Remove the parking brake cable from the lever.

6. Remove the E-clip and spread the C-washer to remove it from the parking brake lever. Remove the adjusting lever spring.

To install:

7. Apply high temperature grease to the contact surface of the brake backing plate and to the threads and end of the adjuster bolt.

8. Pull the parking brake cable out, then attach it to the lever.

9. Connect the strut and return spring to the lever.

10. Position the rear shoe so that the upper end of the shoe is in the wheel cylinder and the lower end is in the anchor plate. Install the pin and hold-down spring.

11. Connect the anchor spring to the rear shoe and then stretch it onto the front shoe.

12. Position the front shoe so the upper end is in the wheel cylinder and the lower end is in the strut. Install the pin and hold-down spring.

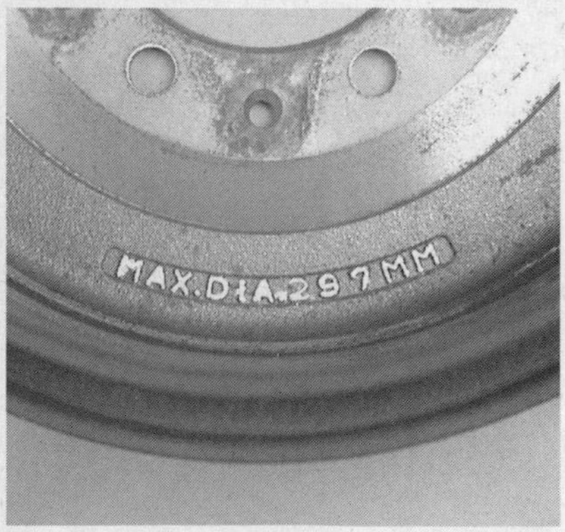

93169p51

Fig. 72 The maximum diameter is usually stamped on the outside surface of the drum

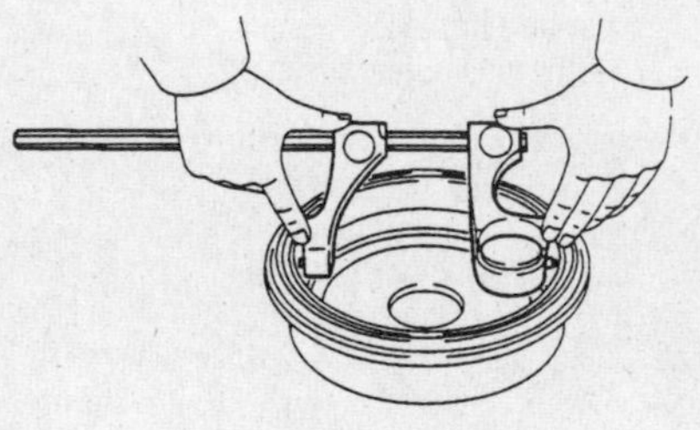

93169g32

Fig. 73 Measuring the inside diameter of the brake drum

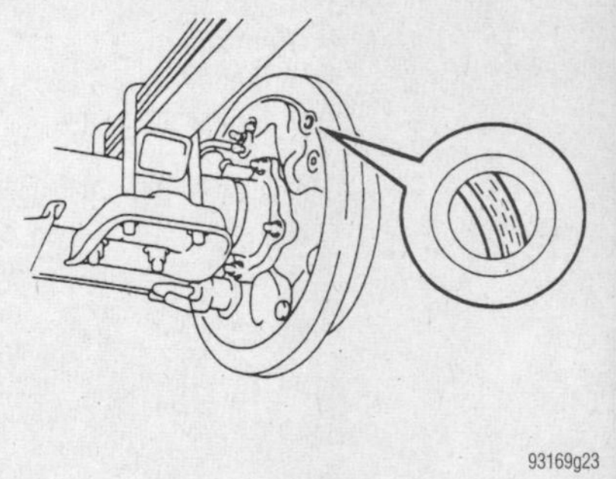

93169g23

Fig. 74 You can view the condition and thickness of the brake shoes on most Toyota trucks through an inspection hole in the backing plate

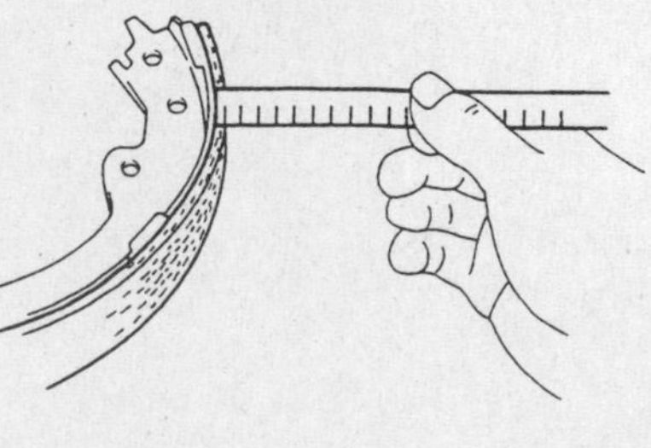

93169g33

Fig. 75 Using a ruler to measure the thickness of the brake shoe lining

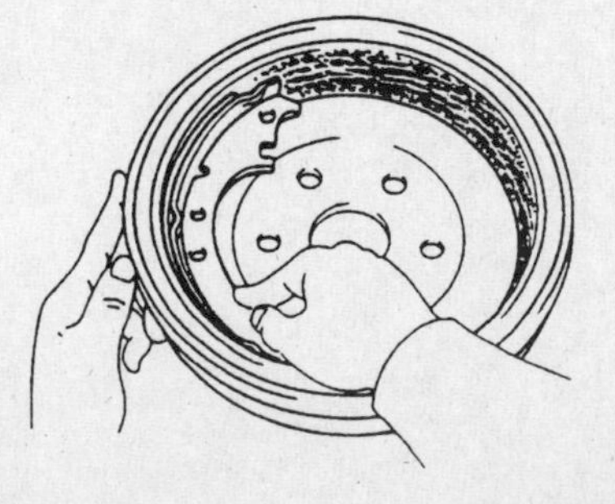

93169g34

Fig. 76 Check for proper contact between the brake shoe lining and the inside of the drum

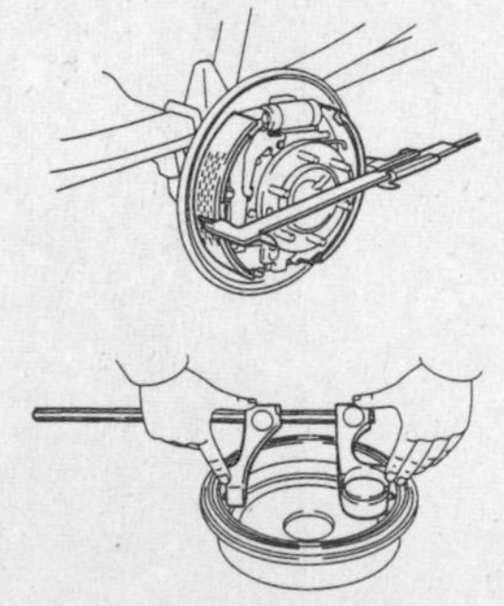

93169g35

Fig. 77 Measure the inside diameter of the brake drum and the brake shoes to ensure proper clearance of 0.020 inches (0.5mm)

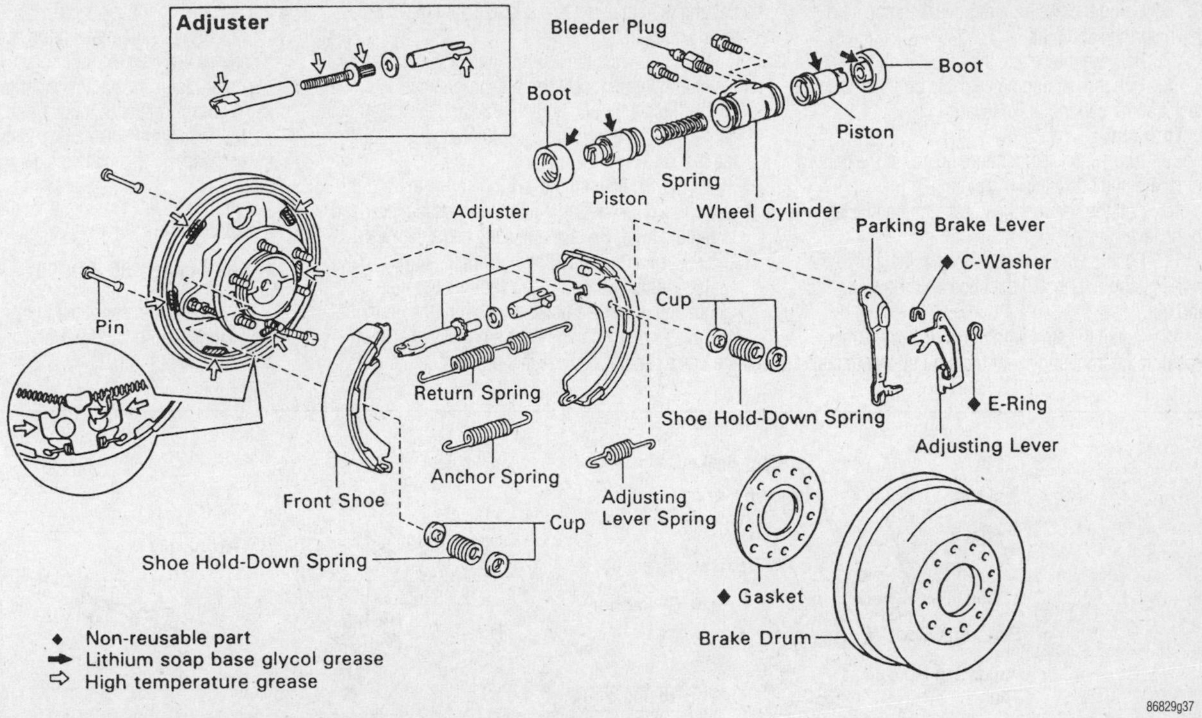

Fig. 78 Exploded view of the 2WD rear brake components with leading-trailing brakes

13. Install the return spring.

14. Check that the adjuster bolt turns while pulling up on the brake lever. Adjust the strut to the shortest possible length and install the brake drum. Pull the parking brake lever (inside the truck) out until the clicks stop.

15. Remove the brake drum and check that the difference between the inner brake drum diameter and the outer brake shoe diameter is no more than 0.024 in. (0.6mm). Adjust or replace parts as needed.

16. Install the brake drum. Install the wheels and lower the truck. Bleed the brakes and road test the vehicle.

DUO-SERVO BRAKES

➧ See Figure 79

1. Raise the rear of the truck and support it with jackstands. Remove the wheels.

2. Remove the brake drum.

3. Using a brake tool, remove the 2 return springs.

4. Push up on the brake adjusting lever and remove the cable, shoe guide plate and cable guide. Disconnect the springs at the brake lever and remove them both.

5. Using needle-nose pliers, remove the 2 tension springs.

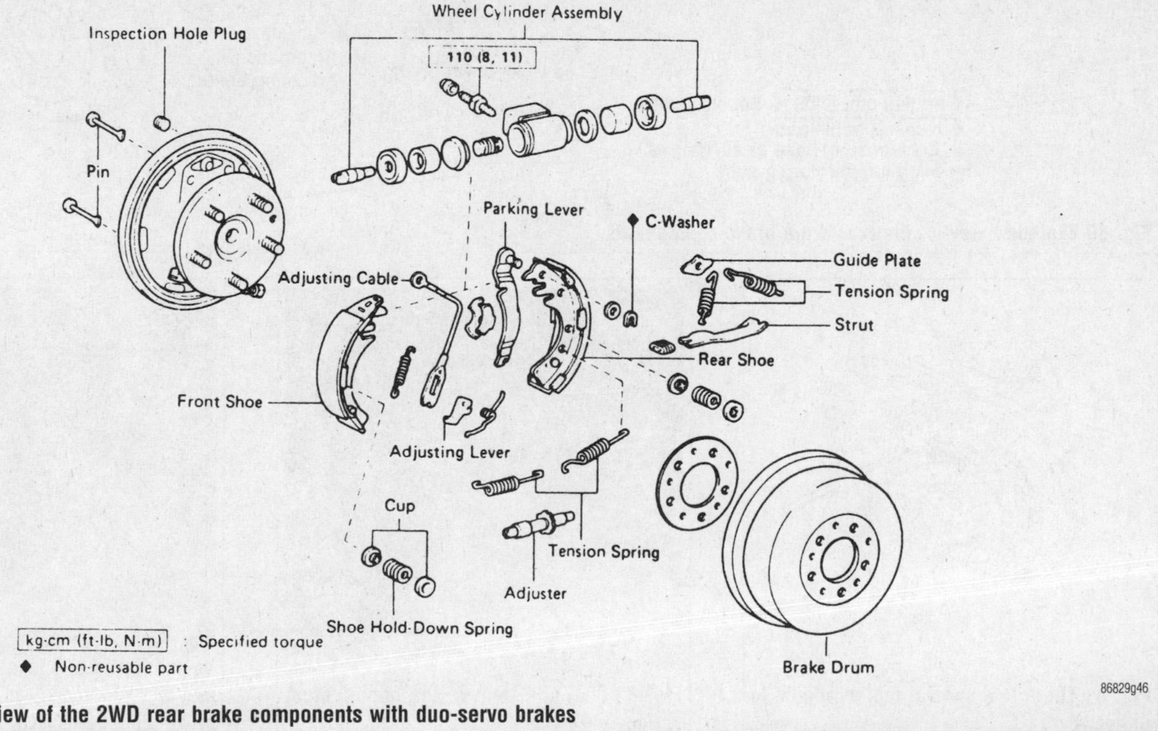

Fig. 79 Exploded view of the 2WD rear brake components with duo-servo brakes

6. Using a brake tool, remove the shoe hold-down springs and pins.

7. Remove the shoes, the adjuster and the strut.

8. Pull the parking brake cable out, then disconnect it at the parking brake lever.

To install:

9. Apply high-temperature grease to the contact surface of the brake backing plate.

10. Pull the parking brake cable out and attach it to the lever.

11. Position the rear shoe so that its upper end is in the piston rod. Install the shoe hold-down spring and pin.

12. Install the strut with the spring to the rear. Position the front shoe over the strut so that the upper end is in the piston rod. Install the hold-down spring and pin.

13. Grease the threads and end of the brake adjuster and install it between the brake shoes.

14. Install the shoe guide plate and the adjusting cable. Install the front return spring and then install the rear one.

15. While holding the tension spring against the rear shoe, hook the cable into the adjusting lever and install the lever. Pull the adjusting cable backward and release it; the adjusting bolt should turn.

16. Adjust the strut to the shortest possible length and install the brake drum. Turn the drum in the reverse direction and have an assistant step on the brake pedal. Continue this process until the clicking noise is no longer heard.

17. Remove the brake drum and check that the difference between the inner brake drum diameter and the outer brake shoe diameter is no more than 0.024 in. (0.6mm). Adjust or replace parts as needed.

18. Install the brake drum. Install the wheels and lower the truck. Bleed the brakes and road test the vehicle.

4WD Vehicles

➧ See Figures 80 thru 90

1. Raise the rear of the truck and support it with jackstands. Remove the wheels.

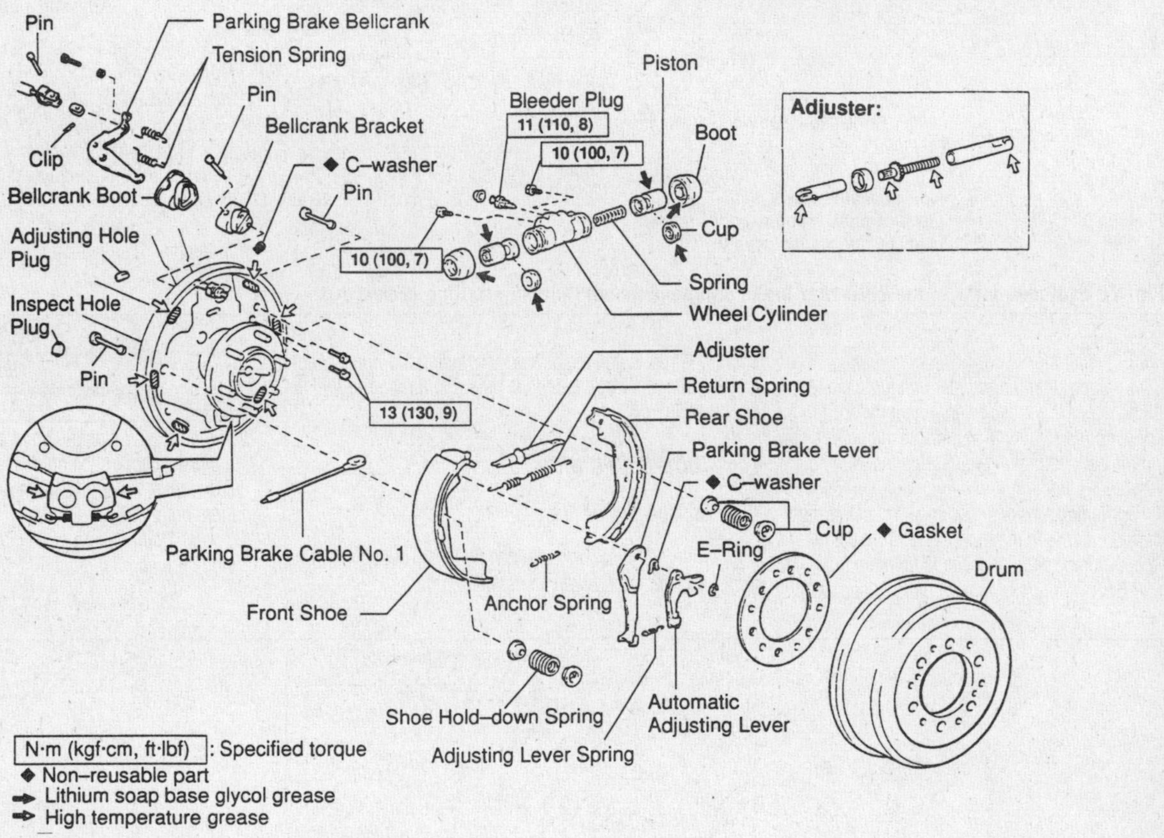

Fig. 80 Exploded view of the rear drum brake components

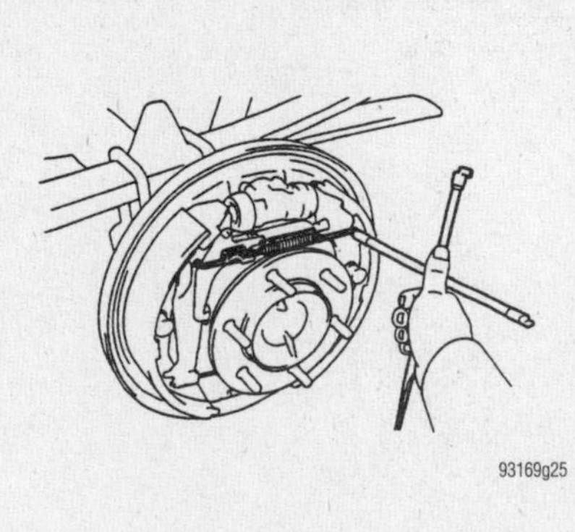

Fig. 81 There is a special tool available to unhook . . .

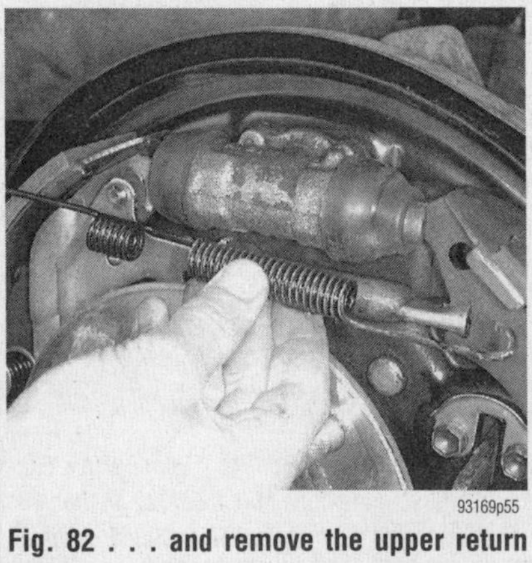

Fig. 82 . . . and remove the upper return spring

Fig. 83 A tool such as the one shown can be purchased at a local automotive retailer and will greatly aid in the removal of the brake shoe hold-down spring

2. Remove the brake drum.
3. Remove the tension spring.
4. Remove the rear shoe hold-down spring and pin and then lift out the rear shoe and anchor spring.
5. Remove the front shoe hold-down spring and pin. Disconnect the parking brake cable at the bellcrank.
6. Remove the automatic adjusting lever and parking brake lever as follows:
   a. Remove the E-clip.
   b. Remove the automatic adjusting lever.
   c. Spread and remove the C-washer.
   d. Remove the parking brake lever.
7. Remove the front shoe with the strut. Disconnect the other parking brake cable.
8. Disconnect the adjusting lever spring and remove the adjuster from the front shoe.

To install:

9. Assemble and install the parking brake bellcrank as follows:
   a. Apply grease to the rotating parts of the bellcrank.
   b. Install the parking brake bellcrank to the bellcrank bracket.
   c. Install the pin with a new C-clip and tighten it.
   d. Install the bellcrank boot to the parking brake bracket.
   e. Install the parking brake bellcrank and dust cover on the backing plate.
10. Apply high-temperature grease to the brake backing plate contact surfaces and the threads of the adjuster.
11. Position the parking brake lever and the automatic adjuster. Use new clips and tighten the C-clip.
12. Connect the parking brake cable to the shoe lever. Attach the other side of the cable to the bellcrank. Position the front shoe so the upper end is in the piston rod and install the hold-down spring and pin.
13. Connect the anchor spring to the front shoe, then stretch it onto the rear shoe. Position the rear shoe and install the hold-down spring and pin.
14. Install the tension spring. Lightly pull the bellcrank in direction **A** until there is no slack at **B**. Turn the adjusting bolt so that **C** will be 0.02–0.03 in. (0.4–0.8mm) on all models excluding 4Runner which is 0.016–0.031 in. (0.4–0.8mm). Lock the adjusting bolt with the locknut.
15. Connect the parking brake cable to the bellcrank and install the tension spring.
16. Check that the parking brake lever (inside the truck) travel is correct and that the adjuster turns while pulling the lever.
17. Turn the adjuster to the shortest possible length and install the brake drum. Pull the parking brake lever out until the clicks stop.
18. Remove the brake drum and check that the difference between the inner brake drum diameter and the outer brake shoe diameter is no more than 0.024 in. (0.6mm).
19. Install the brake drum. Install the wheels and lower the truck. Bleed the brakes and road test the vehicle.

Wheel Cylinders

REMOVAL & INSTALLATION

➧ See Figures 91 and 92

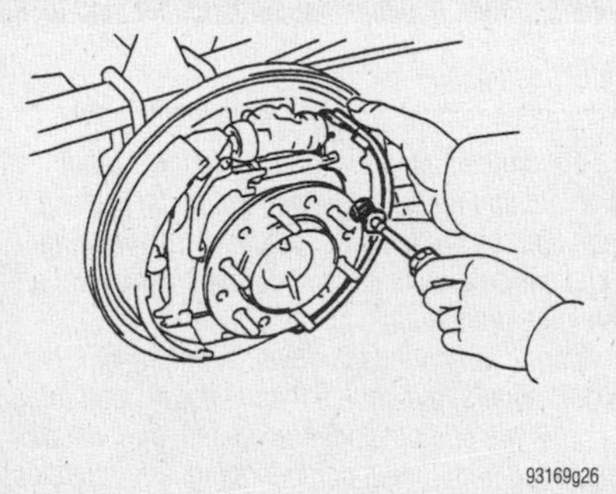

Fig. 84 Remove the brake shoe hold-down spring and retainer

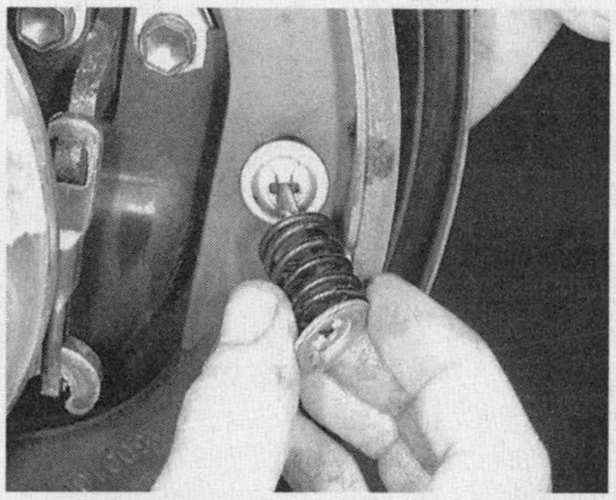

Fig. 85 Note the order of the spring and retainer ring assembly

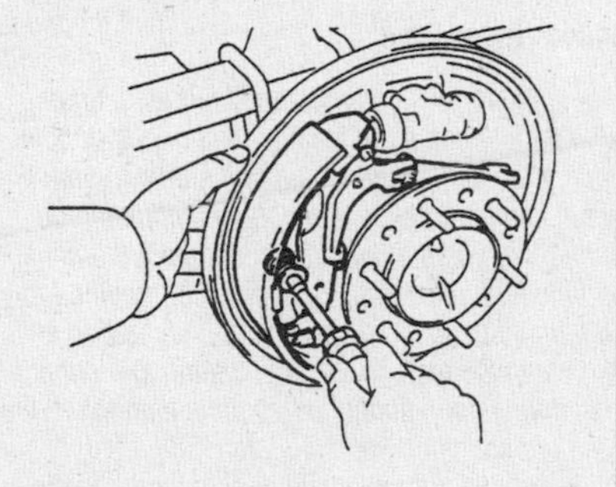

Fig. 86 Remove the front shoe by releasing the hold-down spring

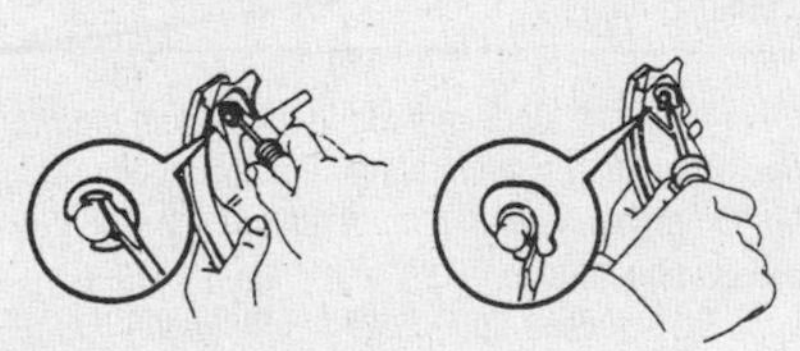

Fig. 87 Detach the C-clip from the parking brake lever

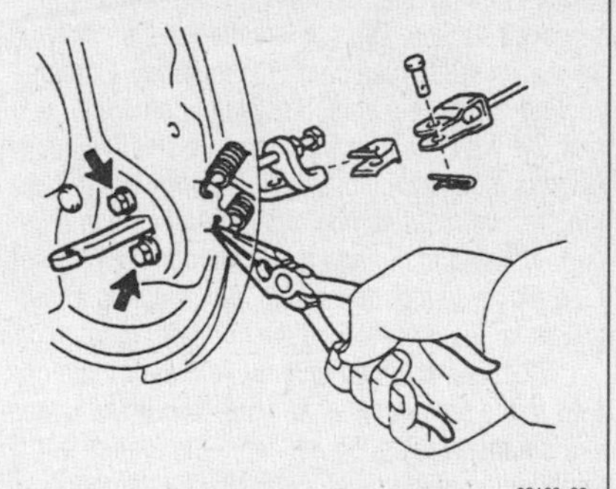

Fig. 88 Use a pair of needlenose pliers to disconnect the tension springs

Fig. 89 To remove the bell crank boot, remove the C-clip

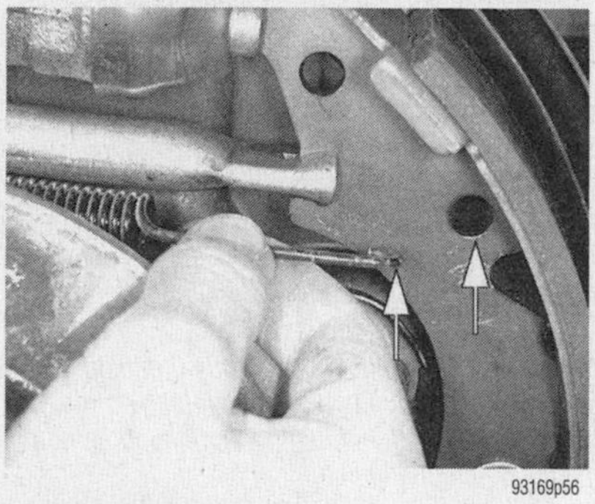

Fig. 90 When installing the upper return spring, ensure that the hook at the end of the spring is firmly seated in the hole in the brake shoe

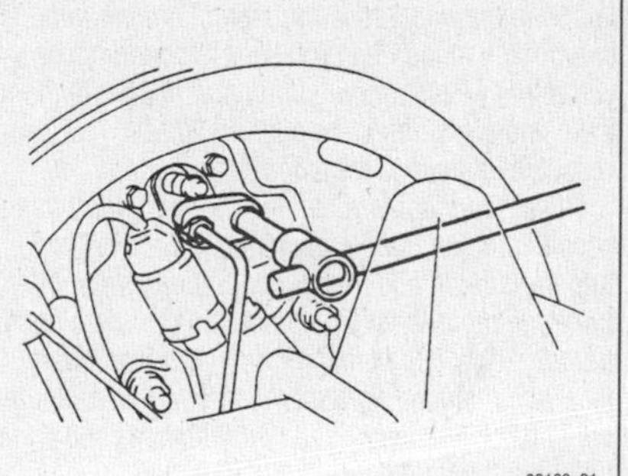

Fig. 91 Using a crow's foot style line wrench to remove the hydraulic line from the wheel cylinder

93169p60

Fig. 92 Typical wheel cylinder

1. Remove the brake drums and shoes.
2. Working from behind the backing plate, disconnect the hydraulic line from the wheel cylinder. You may find it helpful to use a crow's foot line wrench to access and loosen the line fitting. Plug the line to prevent fluid loss.
3. Unfasten the bolts retaining the wheel cylinder and withdraw the cylinder.

To install:

4. Position the cylinder and install the bolts; tighten them to 7 ft. lbs. (10 Nm).
5. Connect the brake line, tightening it to 11 ft. lbs. (15 Nm).
6. Install the shoes and drums.
7. Bleed the brake system.

ANTI-LOCK BRAKE SYSTEM

General Information

Anti-lock Brake Systems (ABS) are designed to prevent locked-wheel skidding during hard braking or during braking on slippery surfaces. The front wheels of a vehicle cannot apply steering force if they are locked and sliding; the vehicle will continue in the previous direction of travel. The 4-wheel ABS system used on Toyota trucks holds the wheels just below the point of locking, thereby allowing some steering response and preventing the rear of the vehicle from sliding sideways.

There are conditions for which the ABS system provides no benefit. Hydroplaning is possible when the tires ride on a film of water, losing contact with the paved surface. This renders the vehicle totally uncontrollable until road contact is regained. Extreme steering maneuvers at high speed or cornering beyond the limits of tire adhesion can result in skidding which is independent of vehicle braking. For this reason, the system is named anti-lock rather than anti-skid. Wheel spin during acceleration on slippery surfaces may also fool the system into detecting a system failure and entering the fail-safe mode.

Under normal conditions, the ABS system functions in the same manner as a standard brake system and is transparent to the operator. The system is a combination of electrical and hydraulic components, working together to control the flow of brake fluid to the wheels when necessary.

The Electronic Control Unit (ECU) is the electronic brain of the system, receiving and interpreting signals from the wheel speed sensors. The unit will enter anti-lock mode when it senses impending wheel lock at any wheel, and will immediately control the brake line pressures to the affected wheel(s) by issuing output signals to the actuator assembly.

The actuator contains solenoids which react to the signals from the ECU. Each solenoid controls brake fluid pressure to one wheel. The solenoids allow brake line pressure to build according to brake pedal pressure, hold (by isolating the system from the pedal and maintaining current pressure) or decrease (by isolating the pedal circuit and bleeding some fluid from the line).

The decisions regarding these functions are made very rapidly, as each solenoid can be cycled up to 10 times per second.

The operator may feel a pulsing in the brake pedal and/or hear popping or clicking noises when the system engages. These sensations are due to the valves cycling and the pressures being changed rapidly within the brake system. While completely normal and not a sign of system failure, these sensations can be disconcerting to an operator unfamiliar with the system.

Although the ABS system prevents wheel lock-up under hard braking, as brake pressure increases, wheel slip is allowed to increase as well. This slip will result in some tire chirp during ABS operation. The sound should not be interpreted as lock-up but rather as an indication of the system holding the wheel(s) just outside the locking point.

Diagnosis and Testing

PRECAUTIONS

- Certain components within the system are not intended to be serviced or repaired individually. Only those components with removal and installation procedures should be serviced.
- Do not use rubber hoses or other parts not specifically specified for the anti-lock system. When using repair kits, replace all parts included in the kit.
- Use only DOT 3 or equivalent brake fluid from an unopened container.
- If any hydraulic component (either power steering or brake) is removed or replaced, it may be necessary to bleed the entire system.
- A clean repair area is essential. Always clean the reservoir and cap thoroughly before removing the cap. The slightest amount of dirt in the fluid may plug an orifice and impair the system function. Perform repairs after components have been thoroughly cleaned; use only denatured alcohol to clean components. Do not allow components to come into contact with any substance containing mineral oil; this includes used shop rags.
- The ECU is a microprocessor similar to other computer units in the vehicle. Insure that the ignition switch is **OFF** before removing or installing controller harnesses. Avoid static electricity discharge at or near the controller.
- If any arc welding is to be done on the vehicle, the ECU should be disconnected before welding operations begin.
- If the vehicle is to be baked after paint repairs, remove the ECU from the vehicle.

INSPECTION

If a malfunction occurs, the system will identify the problem and the computer will assign and store a fault code for the fault(s). The dashboard warning lamp will be illuminated to inform the driver that a fault has been found.

During diagnostics, the system will transmit the stored code(s) by flashing the dashboard warning lamp. If two or more codes are stored, they will be displayed from lowest number to highest, regardless of the order of occurrence. The system does not display the diagnostic codes while the vehicle is running.

Visual Inspection

Before diagnosing an apparent anti-lock brake system problem, make absolutely certain that the normal braking system and power steering systems are in correct working order. Many common problems (dragging parking brake, seepage, etc.) will affect the ABS system. A visual check of specific system components may reveal problems creating an apparent ABS malfunction. Performing this inspection may reveal a simple failure, thus eliminating extended diagnostic time.

- Inspect the brake fluid level in the reservoir.
- Inspect lines, hoses, master cylinder assembly, brake calipers and cylinders for leakage. Inspect the power steering system and components for the same conditions.
- Visually check lines and hoses for excessive wear, heat damage, punctures, contact with other parts, missing clips or holders, blockage or crimping.
- Check the calipers or wheel cylinders for rust or corrosion. Check for proper sliding action if applicable.
- Check the caliper and wheel cylinder pistons for freedom of motion during application and release.
- Inspect the speed sensor for proper mounting and correct connection.
- Confirm the fault occurrence. Certain driver induced faults, such as not releasing the parking brake fully, will set a fault code and trigger the dash warning light. Excessive wheel spin on low-traction surfaces, high speed acceleration or riding the brake pedal may also set fault codes and trigger a warning lamp. These induced faults are not system failures

ut examples of vehicle performance outside the parameters of the control unit.

- Many system shut-downs are due to loss of sensor signals to or from the controller. The most common cause is not a failed sensor but a loose, corroded or dirty connector. Check harness and component connectors carefully.

Reading Codes

1. Turn the ignition switch **OFF**. Check battery condition; approximately 12 volts is required to operate the system.
2. Turn the ignition switch **ON** and check that the ABS dashboard warning lamp comes on for 3 seconds. If the lamp does not come on, repair the fuse, bulb or wiring.
3. Use a jumper wire to attach terminals Tc and E1 of the Data Link Connector (DLC1). Turn the ignition **ON**.
4. If a fault code has been set, the dashboard warning lamp will begin to blink 4 seconds later. The number of flashes corresponds to the first digit of a 2-digit code; after a 1.5 second pause, the second digit is transmitted. If a second code is stored, it will be displayed after a 2.5 second pause. Once all codes have been displayed, the entire series will repeat after a 4 second pause. If no codes have been stored, the warning lamp will flash continuously every 1/2 second with no variation.
5. Turn the ignition switch **OFF**.
6. Check or repair the system as indicated by the fault code.
7. After repairs are completed, clear the codes from the memory. If the battery is disconnected during repairs, the controller memory will be erased of all stored codes.
8. Remove the jumper wire if one was used and reattach the service connector at the actuator.

Clearing Codes

1. Detach the service connector at the actuator.
2. Use the jumper wire to connect terminals Tc and E1 of the Data Link Connector (DLC1). Turn the ignition **ON**.
3. Clear the diagnostic trouble codes stored in the ECU by depressing the brake pedal 8 or more times within 3 seconds.
4. After the rapid pedal application, the dash warning lamp should display constant flashing, indicating a normal system. If codes are still displayed, make certain the repairs made to the system are correct. Also inspect the brake light switch at the brake pedal for any binding or sticking.
5. Once the codes are cleared, disconnect the jumper wire. The dash warning lamp should go out.

Speed Sensor

SYSTEM TEST

▸ **See Figure 93**

➡The following procedures require driving the vehicle while it is in the diagnostic mode. The anti-lock system will be disabled; only normal braking function will be available.

1. If working on a 4WD vehicle, make certain it is only in 2WD. Check the battery voltage with the engine **OFF**; voltage should be approximately 12 volts.
2. With the ignition switch **ON**, make certain the ABS warning lamp comes on for about 3 seconds and then goes out. Turn the ignition switch **OFF**.
3. Using a 3-way jumper, connect terminals Tc, Ts and E1 at the Data Link Connector (DLC1).
4. Pull the parking brake on securely and start the motor without stepping on the brake pedal. Depressing the brake pedal will either void the test or cause the system to enter a different diagnostic mode.
5. The dashboard warning lamp should flash evenly about 4 times per second. If, instead, a code is flashed, repairs must be made and the code(s) cleared before continuing. If the light does not flash, check the parking brake switch, the DLC1 connector and the wiring to the ABS controller.
6. To check the sensor signal level, release the parking brake and drive the vehicle straight ahead at low speed. Once a speed of 2–5 mph (3–8 km) is reached, the warning lamp should turn off. Once the light has gone off, it should begin to blink as the vehicle leaves the speed range. This blinking is normal and indicates the speed sensor is operating correctly. If no blinking occurs, the system is defective.
7. Check the sensor signal change by driving the vehicle on the road. Once a speed of 25–31 mph (40–50 km) is achieved, the warning lamp should come on after a one second pause. As before, the lamp should blink evenly as the vehicle leaves the speed range; failure to blink indicates a system fault.

➡While the warning lamp is off, do not subject the vehicle to any shocks or impact such as shifting, acceleration, deceleration or road impact.

8. Stop the vehicle in a safe location and apply the parking brake fully. Read and record any stored codes which are displayed.
9. Turn the ignition switch **OFF**; remove the jumper wire from the DLC1 connector.

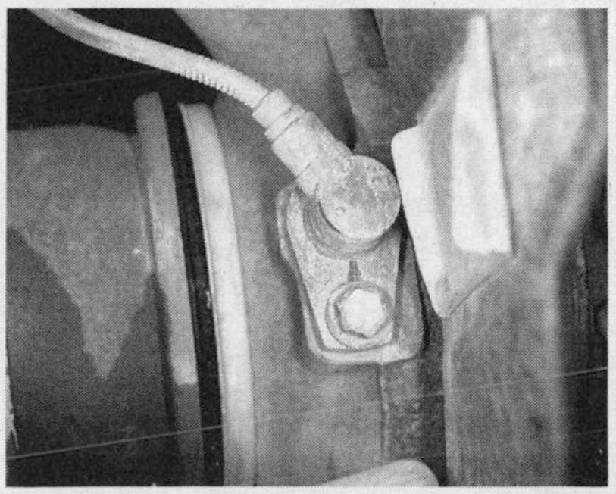
93169p35

Fig. 93 Typical Toyota wheel speed sensor

COMPONENT TEST

Front Sensor

▸ **See Figure 94**

1. Unplug the speed sensor connector.
2. Measure the resistance between terminals 1 and 2. The resistance should be as follows:
   - 4Runner, Tacoma and Tundra: 1.4–1.8 kohms
   - T100: 0.6–1.8 kohms
   - Land Cruiser: 0.97–1.77 kohms
3. If the resistance is not as specified, replace the sensor.
4. Check that there is no continuity between each terminal and the sensor body. If there is continuity, replace the sensor.
5. Attach the speed sensor harness.
6. Check the installation of the sensor. If the mounting bolt is loose, tighten it to 69 inch lbs. (8 Nm).
7. Remove the axle hub with the rotor. Inspect the sensor rotor serrations for scratches, cracks, warping or missing teeth. Replace if necessary.

➡To prevent from damaging the serrations, do not strike the axle hub with the rotor.

8. Reconnect the speed sensor to the harness.

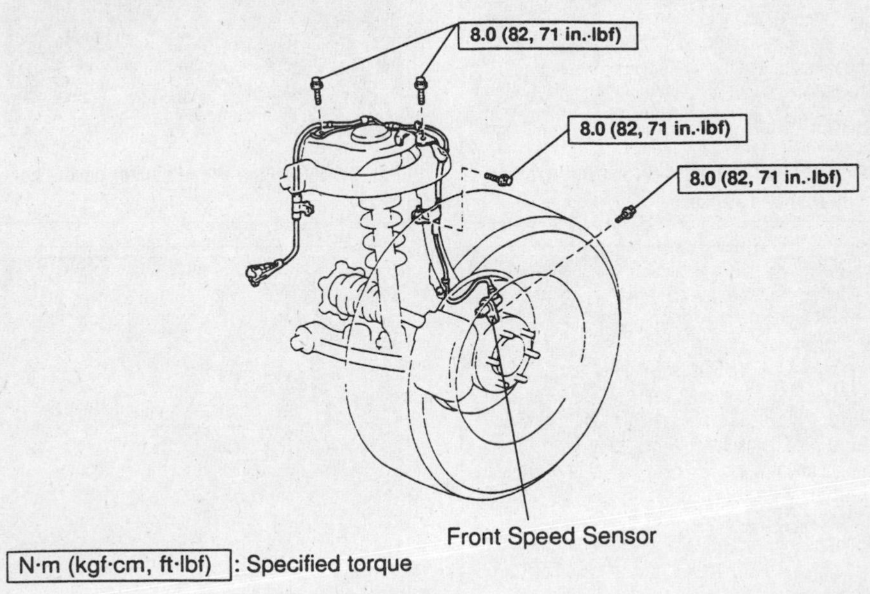

93169g40

Fig. 94 Components of the front speed sensor

Rear Sensor

➧ See Figure 95

1. Unplug the speed sensor connector.
2. Measure the resistance between the terminal 1 and 2. The resistance should be as follows:
   - 4Runner, Tacoma and Tundra: 1.0–1.4 kohms
   - T100: 0.6–2.05 kohms
   - Land Cruiser: 0.5–1.6 kohms
3. If the resistance is not as specified, replace the sensor.
4. Check that there is no continuity between each terminal and the sensor body. If there is continuity, replace the sensor.
5. Attach the speed sensor harness.
6. Check the installation of the sensor. If the mounting bolt is loose, tighten it to 69 inch lbs. (8 Nm).
7. Remove the axle hub with the rotor. Inspect the sensor rotor serrations for scratches, cracks, warping or missing teeth.

➡To prevent from damaging the serrations, do not strike the axle hub with the rotor.

REMOVAL & INSTALLATION

Front

➧ See Figures 94, 96 thru 101

1. Unplug the speed sensor harness from the unit.
2. On 4WD vehicles, remove the clamp bolts and clips holding the sensor harness from the frame, upper arm and steering knuckle.
3. On 2WD vehicles, remove the clamp bolts and clips holding the sensor harness to the frame and upper arm.

➡Discard the old clips.

4. Remove the sensor from the knuckle.

To install:

5. Attach the sensor to the steering knuckle, tighten to 69–71 inch lbs. (7–8 Nm).
6. Attach the harness along the upper arm and frame with new clips. Tighten the mounting bolts to 48–71 inch lbs. (5–8 Nm).
7. Engage the sensor harness to the unit.

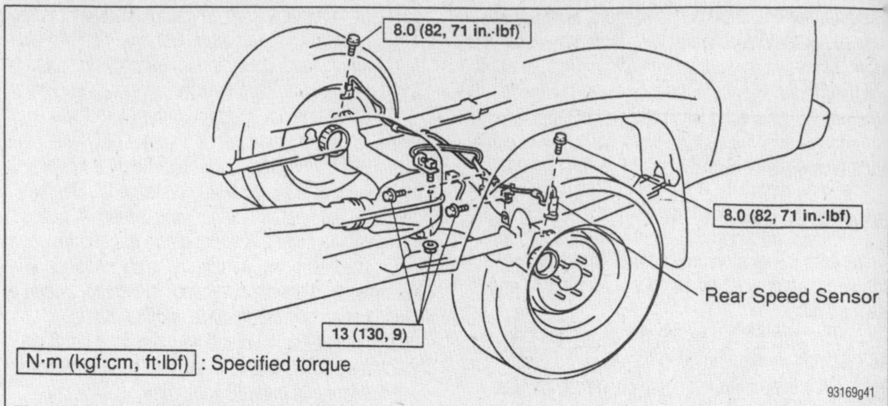

Fig. 95 Rear speed sensor location

Rear

➧ See Figure 95

1. Unplug the speed sensor harness from the unit.
2. Remove the clamp bolts and nuts holding the sensor harness from the frame, upper arm, axle housing and fuel tank (if attached).

➡Discard the old clips.

3. Remove the sensor from the axle.

To install:

4. Attach the sensor to the axle, tighten to 69–71 inch lbs. (7–8 Nm).
5. Attach the harness along the appropriate areas, then tighten the mounting bolts to 48–71 inch lbs. (5–8 Nm). Be sure to used all new clips, and install them in the same angle of the removed ones.
6. Engage the sensor harness to the unit.

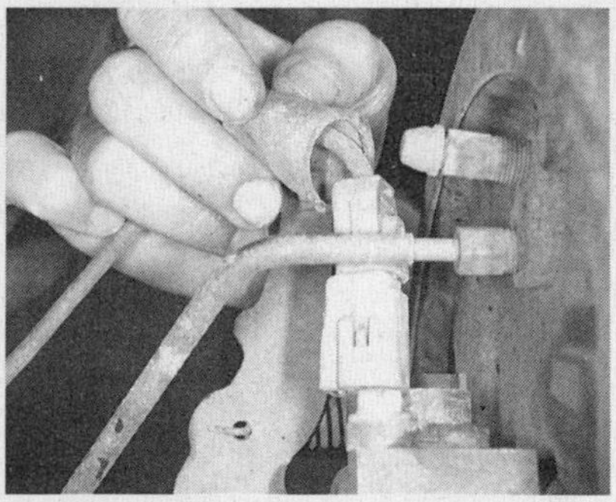

Fig. 96 Pull the dust boot away from the wheel speed sensor

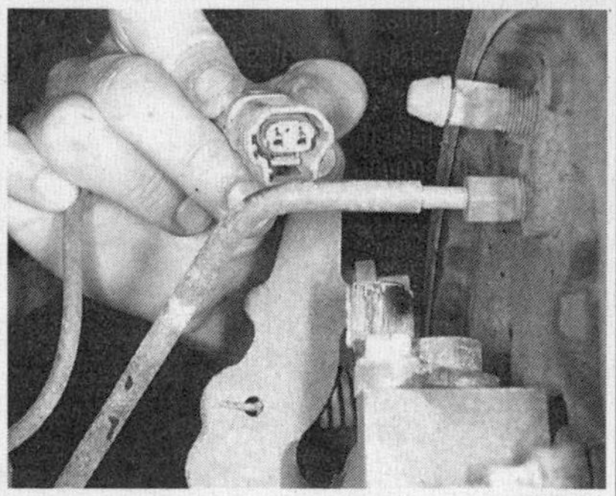

Fig. 97 Detach the speed sensor wiring harness

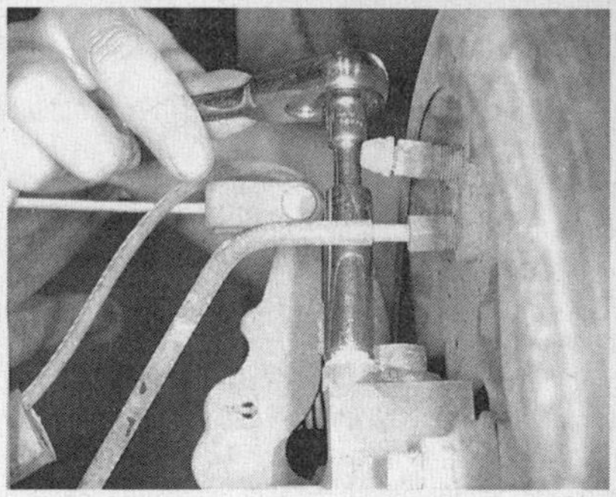

Fig. 98 Use a ratchet to loosen and remove the speed sensor retaining bolt . . .

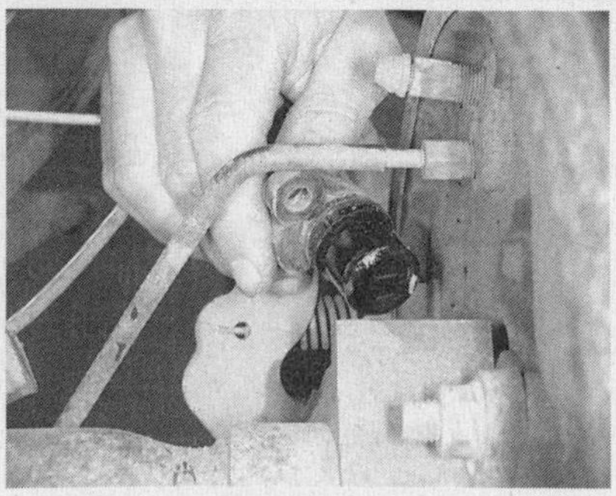

Fig. 99 . . . then remove the sensor from the hub

Fig. 100 Once the sensor is removed, you can see the reluctor wheel

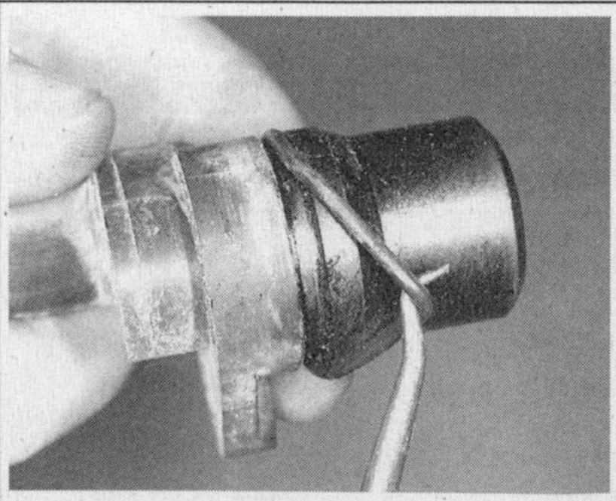

Fig. 101 Inspect the condition of the sealing O-ring, and replace if necessary

Deceleration Sensor

COMPONENT TESTING

➡The following procedures require driving the vehicle while it is in the diagnostic mode. The anti-lock system will be disabled; only normal braking function will be available.

1. Check the battery voltage with the engine **OFF**; voltage should be approximately 12 volts.
2. With the ignition switch **ON**, make certain the ABS warning lamp comes on for about 2 seconds and then goes out. Turn the ignition switch **OFF**.
3. Use a jumper wire to attach terminals Ts and E1 at the Data Link Connector (DLC1).
4. Apply the parking brake fully, depress the brake pedal and start the engine.
5. After a short delay, the dashboard warning lamp should flash about 4 times every second. Stop the vehicle on a level surface for about one second.
6. Drive the vehicle straight ahead at 28 mph (45 kph) or greater speed for several seconds. The warning light should be off when it works normally.
7. Stop the vehicle, then the light will begin to blink. Attach the jumper wire to terminals Tc and E1 of the DLC1. Read the number of blinks of the ABS light.
8. The light blinks about 2 times ever second. If 2 or more blinks are indicated at the same time, the smallest numbered code will be displayed first.
9. Repair any malfunctioning parts. Be sure the ignition switch is in the **OFF** position.
10. Remove the jumper wire from the Tc, Ts and E1 terminals of the DLC1.

Actuator

REMOVAL & INSTALLATION

➧ See Figures 102, 103, 104, 105, and 106

1. Disconnect and plug the brake lines.
2. Unplug the ABS connectors from the actuator.
3. Remove the bolts and nuts to release the assembly from the vehicle.
4. Unbolt the unit from the bracket.

To install:

5. Attach the ABS actuator to the bracket, tighten the mounting nuts to 48 inch lbs. (5 Nm).
6. Install the actuator with bracket to the vehicle, tighten the mounting bolts to 14 ft. lbs. (19 Nm).
7. Attach the brake lines to the actuator, tighten them to 11 ft. lbs. (15 Nm).

93169p72

Fig. 102 ABS actuator—Tacoma TRD

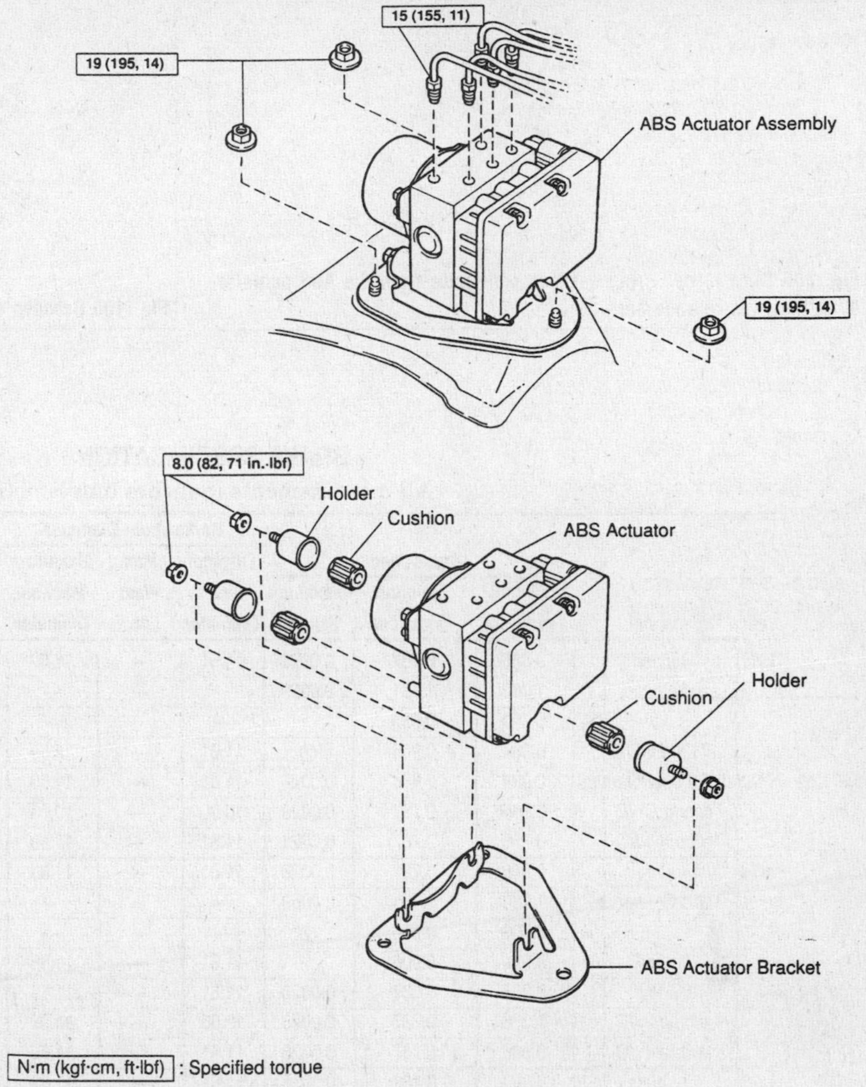

93169g36

Fig. 103 Exploded view of the ABS actuator assembly

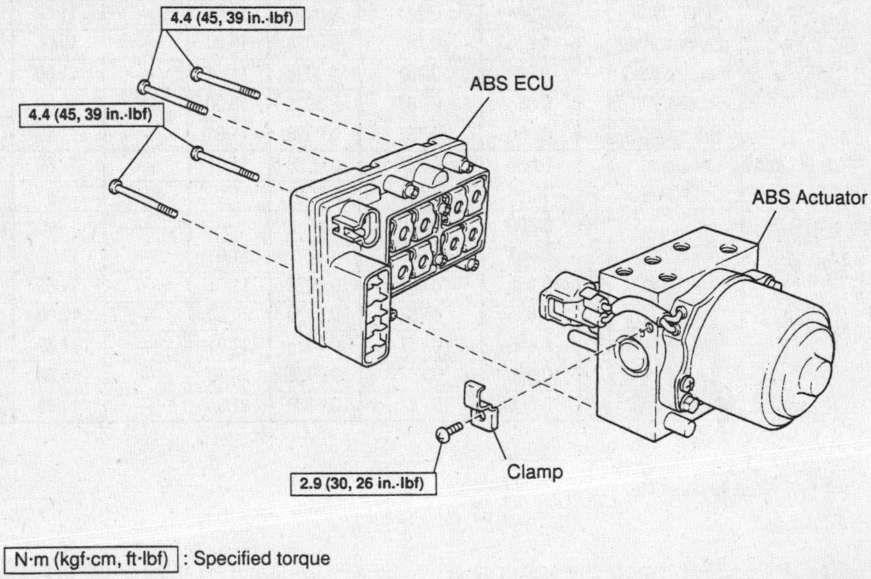

93169g37

Fig. 104 View of the ABS actuator as it is mounted on the ABS ECU

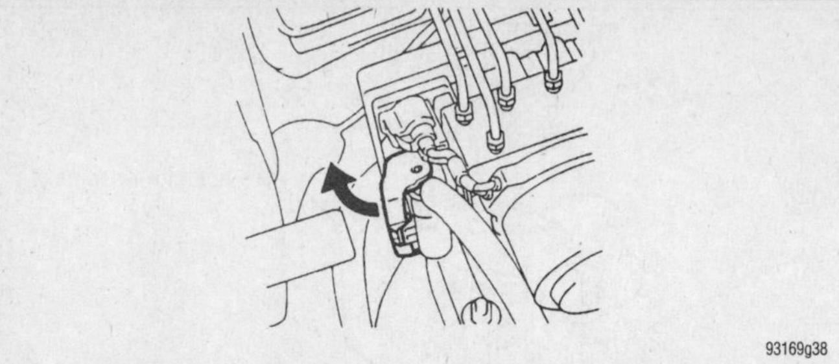

93169g38

Fig. 105 Detach the wiring harness connector from the ABS actuator by pulling the release bar

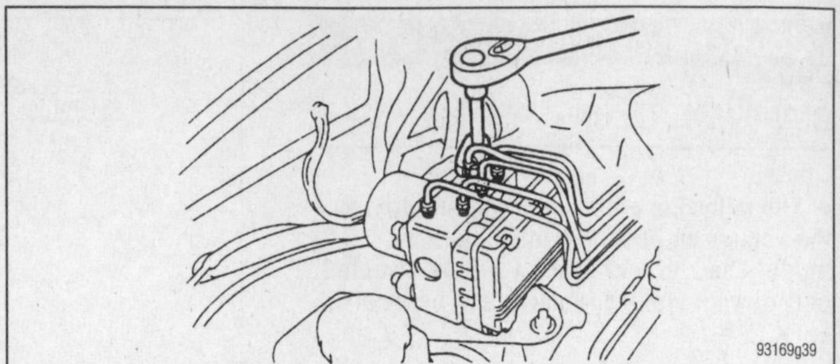

93169g39

Fig. 106 Remove the brake lines from the ABS actuator

BRAKE SPECIFICATIONS

All measurements in inches unless noted

			Brake Disc			Brake Drum Diameter			Minimum Lining Thickness		Brake Caliper	
Year	Model		Original Thickness	Minimum Thickness	Maximum Runout	Original Inside Diameter	Max. Wear Limit	Maximum Machine Diameter	Front	Rear	Mounting Bolts (ft.-lbs.)	Bracket-to-Steering Knuckle Bolts (ft.lbs.)
1997	4Runner		0.866	0.787	0.0028	11.61	—	11.69	0.039	0.039	—	90
	Land Cruiser	F	1.260	1.181	0.0059	—	—	—	0.039	—	—	90
		R	0.709	0.630	—	—	—	—	—	①	65	76
	T100 2WD		0.984	0.906	②	11.61	—	11.69	0.039	0.039	29	80
	T100 4WD		0.984	0.984	0.0028	11.61	—	11.69	0.039	0.039	—	90
	Tacoma 2WD		0.866	0.787	0.0028	10.00	—	10.08	0.039	—	65	80
	Tacoma 4WD		0.866	0.787	0.0028	11.61	—	11.69	—	0.039	—	90
1998	4Runner		0.866	0.787	0.0028	11.61	—	11.69	0.039	0.039	—	90
	Land Cruiser	F	1.260	1.181	0.0059	—	—	—	0.039	—	—	90
		R	0.709	0.630	②	—	—	—	—	①	65	76
	T100 2WD		0.984	0.906		11.61	—	11.69	0.039	0.039	29	80
	T100 4WD		0.984	0.984	0.0028	11.61	—	11.69	0.039	0.039	—	90
	Tacoma 2WD		0.866	0.787	0.0028	10.00	—	10.08	0.039	—	65	80
	Tacoma 4WD		0.866	0.787	0.0028	11.61	—	11.69	—	0.039	—	90
1999	4Runner		0.866	0.787	0.0028	11.61	—	11.69	0.039	0.039	—	90
	Land Cruiser	F	1.260	1.181	0.0059	—	—	—	0.039	—	—	90
		R	0.709	0.630	—	—	—	—	—	①	65	76
	T100 2WD		0.984	0.906	④	11.61	—	11.69	0.039	0.039	29	80
	T100 4WD		0.984	0.984	0.0028	11.61	—	11.69	0.039	0.039	—	90
	Tacoma 2WD		0.866	0.787	0.0028	10.00	—	10.08	0.039	—	65	80
	Tacoma 4WD		0.866	0.787	0.0028	11.61	—	11.69	—	0.039	—	90
	Tundra 2WD		0.866	0.787	0.0028	10.00	—	10.08	0.039	—	65	90
	Tundra 4WD		0.866	0.787	0.0028	11.61	—	11.69	—	0.039	—	90
2000	4Runner		0.866	0.787	0.0028	11.61	—	11.69	0.039	0.039	—	90
	Land Cruiser	F	1.260	1.181	0.0059	—	—	—	0.039	—	—	90
		R	0.709	0.630	—	—	—	—	—	①	65	76
	T100 2WD		0.984	0.906	②	11.61	—	11.69	0.039	0.039	29	80
	T100 4WD		0.984	0.984	0.0028	11.61	—	11.69	0.039	0.039	—	90
	Tacoma 2WD		0.866	0.787	0.0028	10.00	—	10.08	0.039	—	65	80
	Tacoma 4WD		0.866	0.787	0.0028	11.61	—	11.69	—	0.039	—	90
	Tundra 2WD		0.866	0.787	0.0028	10.00	—	10.08	0.039	—	65	80
	Tundra 4WD		0.866	0.787	0.0028	11.61	—	11.69	—	0.039	—	90

NA - Not Available

① Brake shoe lining: 0.059
Disc pad lining: 0.039

② 1 ton: 0.0035
1/2 ton: 0.0028

93169c01

10

BODY AND TRIM

EXTERIOR

Doors

REMOVAL & INSTALLATION

➧ See Figure 1

1. Matchmark the hinge-to-body and hinge-to-door locations.

➡Either support the door on jackstands or have somebody hold it for you.

2. On models with a center door check, push in on the claw and pull out the stopper pin.

3. Unbolt the door check from the door.

➡Depending on equipment, it may be necessary to disconnect various wires running into the door.

4. Remove the lower hinge-to-door bolts.

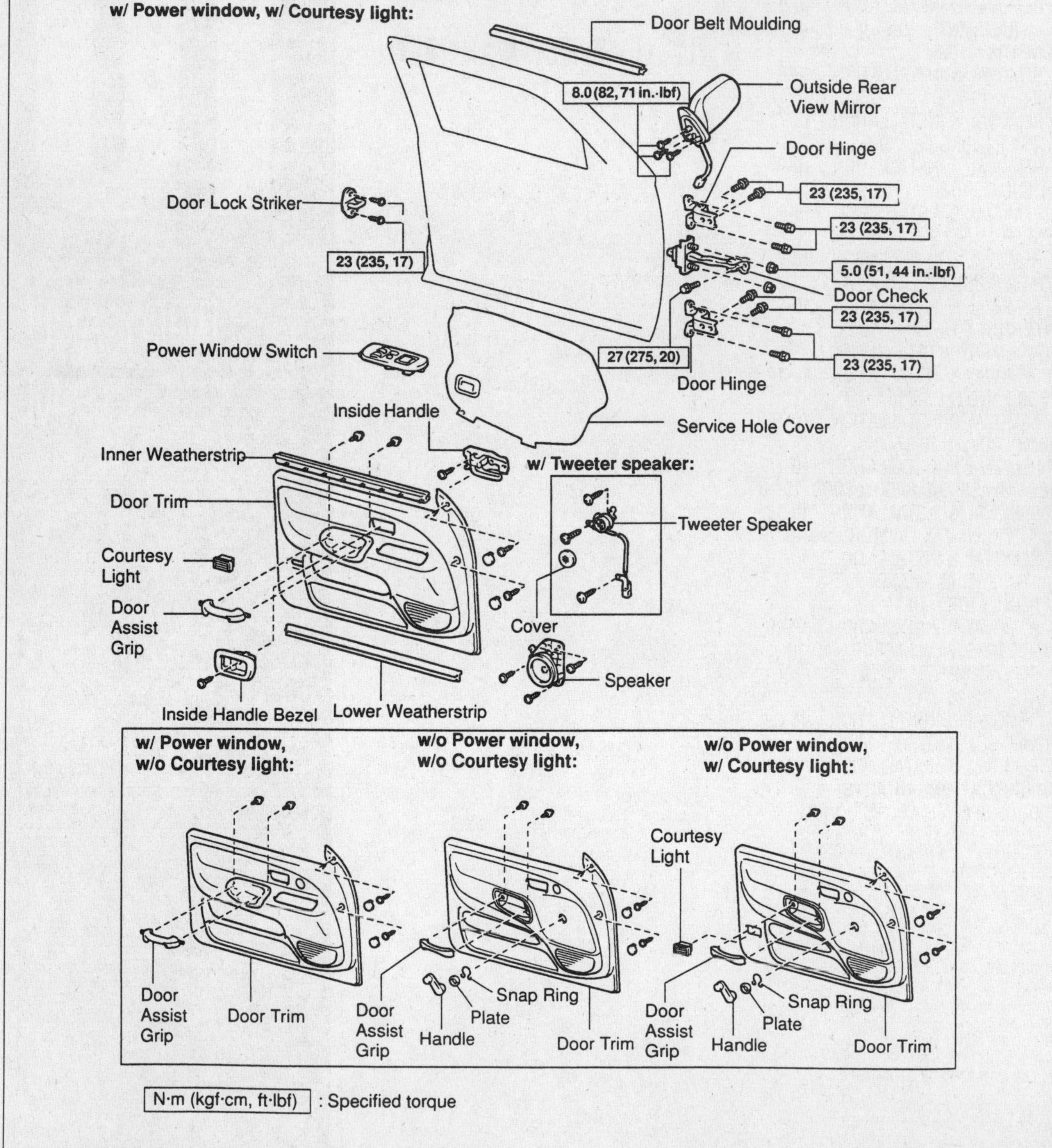

Fig. 1 Exploded view of a typical Toyota door and trim components

5. Remove the upper hinge-to-door bolts and lift the door off the hinges.
6. If the hinges are being replaced, remove them from the door pillar.

To install:

7. Install the door and hinges with the bolts finger-tight.
8. Adjust the door and tighten the hinge bolts to 15–22 ft. lbs. (20–30 Nm).
9. Install the door check.

ADJUSTMENT

When checking door alignment, look carefully at each seam between the door and body. The gap should be constant and even all the way around the door. Pay particular attention to the door seams at the corners farthest from the hinges; this is the area where errors will be most evident. Additionally, the door should pull against the weatherstrip when latched to seal out wind and water. The contact should be even all the way around and the stripping should be about half compressed.

The position of the door can be adjusted in three dimensions: fore and aft, up and down, in and out. The primary adjusting points are the hinge-to-body bolts. Apply tape to the fender and door edges to protect the paint. Two layers of common masking tape works well. Loosen the bolts (using SST 09812-00010 if necessary) just enough to allow the hinge to move. With the help of an assistant, position the door and retighten the bolts. Inspect the door seams carefully and repeat the adjustment until correctly aligned.

The in-out adjustment (how far the door "sticks out" from the body) is adjusted by loosening the hinge-to-door bolts. Again, move the door into place, then retighten the bolts. This dimension affects both the amount of crush on the weatherstrips and the amount of "bite" on the striker.

Further adjustment for closed position and smoothness of latching is made at the latch plate or striker. This piece is located at the rear edge of the door and is attached to the bodywork; it is the piece the latch engages when the door is closed.

Although the striker size and style may vary between models or from front to rear, the method of adjusting it is the same:

1. Loosen the large cross-point screw(s) holding the striker. Know in advance that these bolts will be very tight; an impact screwdriver is a handy tool to have for this job. Make sure you are using the proper size bit.
2. With the bolts just loose enough to allow the striker to move if necessary, hold the outer door handle in the released position and close the door. The striker will move into the correct location to match the door latch. Open the door and tighten the mounting bolts. The striker may be adjusted towards or away from the center of the car, thereby tightening or loosening the door fit. The striker can be moved up and down to compensate for door position, but if the door is correctly mounted at the hinges this should not be necessary.

➡Do not attempt to correct height variations (sag) by adjusting the striker.

3. Additionally, some models may use one or more spacers or shims behind the striker. These shims may be removed or added in combination to adjust the reach of the striker.
4. After the striker bolts have been tightened, open and close the door several times. Observe the motion of the door as it engages the striker; it should continue its straight-in motion and not deflect up or down as it hits the striker.
5. Check the feel of the latch during opening and closing. It must be smooth and linear, without any trace of grinding or binding during engagement and release.

It may be necessary to repeat the striker adjustment several times (and possibly re-adjust the hinges) before the correct door to body match is produced.

Hood

REMOVAL & INSTALLATION

▸ See Figure 2

➡You'll need an assistant for this job.

1. Open the hood.
2. Matchmark the hood-to-hinge position.
3. Disconnect the washer hoses.
4. With an assistant supporting the hood, remove the hood-to-hinge bolts and lift off the hood.

To install:

5. With a helper, place the hood into position, aligning the matchmarks.
6. Tighten the hinge bolts to the body of the vehicle.
7. Connect the washer hoses.
8. Adjust if necessary.

ADJUSTMENT

▸ See Figures 3, 4, and 5

➡A tapered, self-centering bolt is used as the hood hinge set bolt. The hood cannot be adjusted with this bolt in place. Remove it and substitute a bolt and washer which will allow adjustment.

1. Loosen the hood to hinge bolts slightly. Adjust the hood fore-and-aft and left-and-right directions. Tighten the bolts to 10–15 ft. lbs. (13–20 Nm).
2. Adjust the front edge of the hood by turning the two cushions higher or lower. The hood should align with the fender edges.
3. Except on the Land Cruiser, remove the wiper arms, then remove the cowl cover below the windshield. Inside the cowl plenum, adjust the hinge-to-body bolts to control the height of the rear of the hood. Reinstall the cowl panel and wipers.
4. On the Land Cruiser, the rear hood height is adjusted by loosening the four mounting screws holding the hinge to the firewall.
5. Loosen the hood latch retaining bolts and adjust the latch by moving it up-down or left-right.
6. Close the hood and check the tension needed to release the hood. If the release requires excessive force, the latch is under tension and must be adjusted.

➡Be sure to tighten all fasteners after the adjustments are complete.

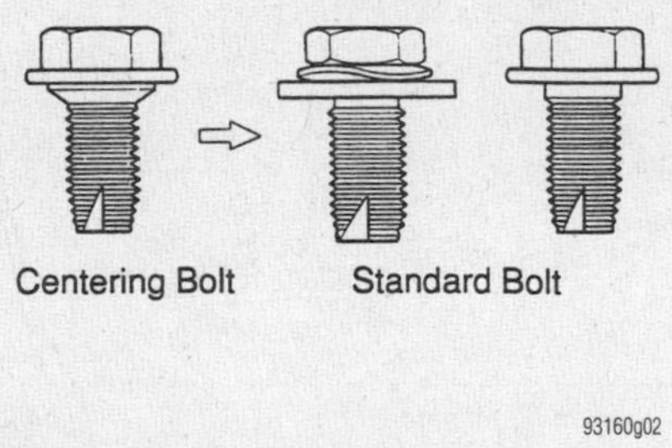

Fig. 2 View of the different types of hood mounting bolts

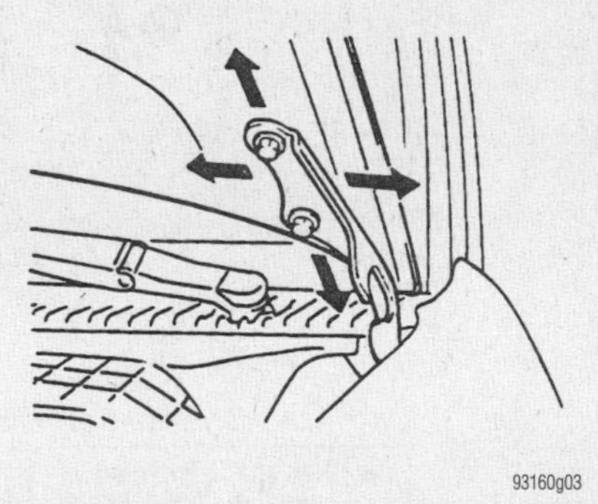

Fig. 3 The hood hinges are slotted so that the hood can move in several directions to aid adjustment

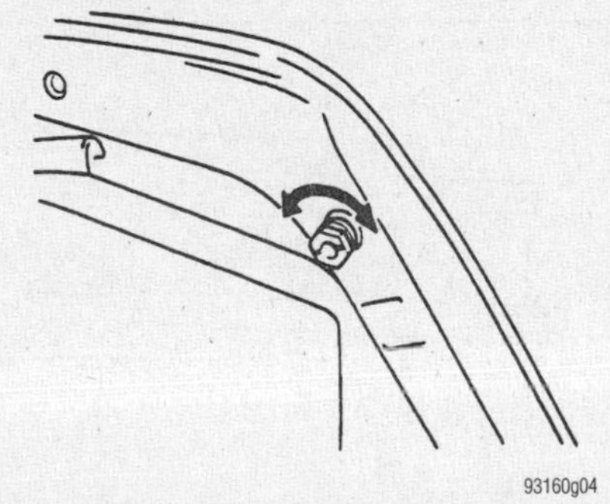

Fig. 4 Adjust the cushions by turning them left or right

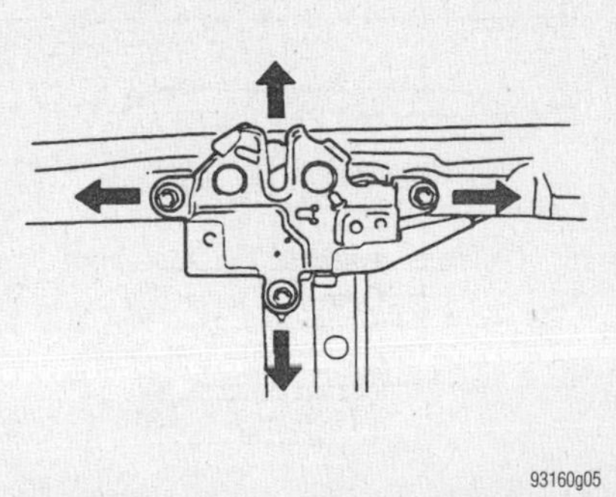

Fig. 5 The hood locking mechanism can also be moved to ensure proper adjustment

Tailgate

REMOVAL & INSTALLATION

◆ **See Figures 6 thru 12**

1. Remove the service hole cover.
2. Disconnect the tail gate link from the lock control.

➡**If needed, remove the outer gate handle.**

3. Remove the tailgate stay from the gate.
4. Unbolt the tailgate hinges.
5. Remove the tailgate and torsion bar.
6. Installation is the reverse of removal.

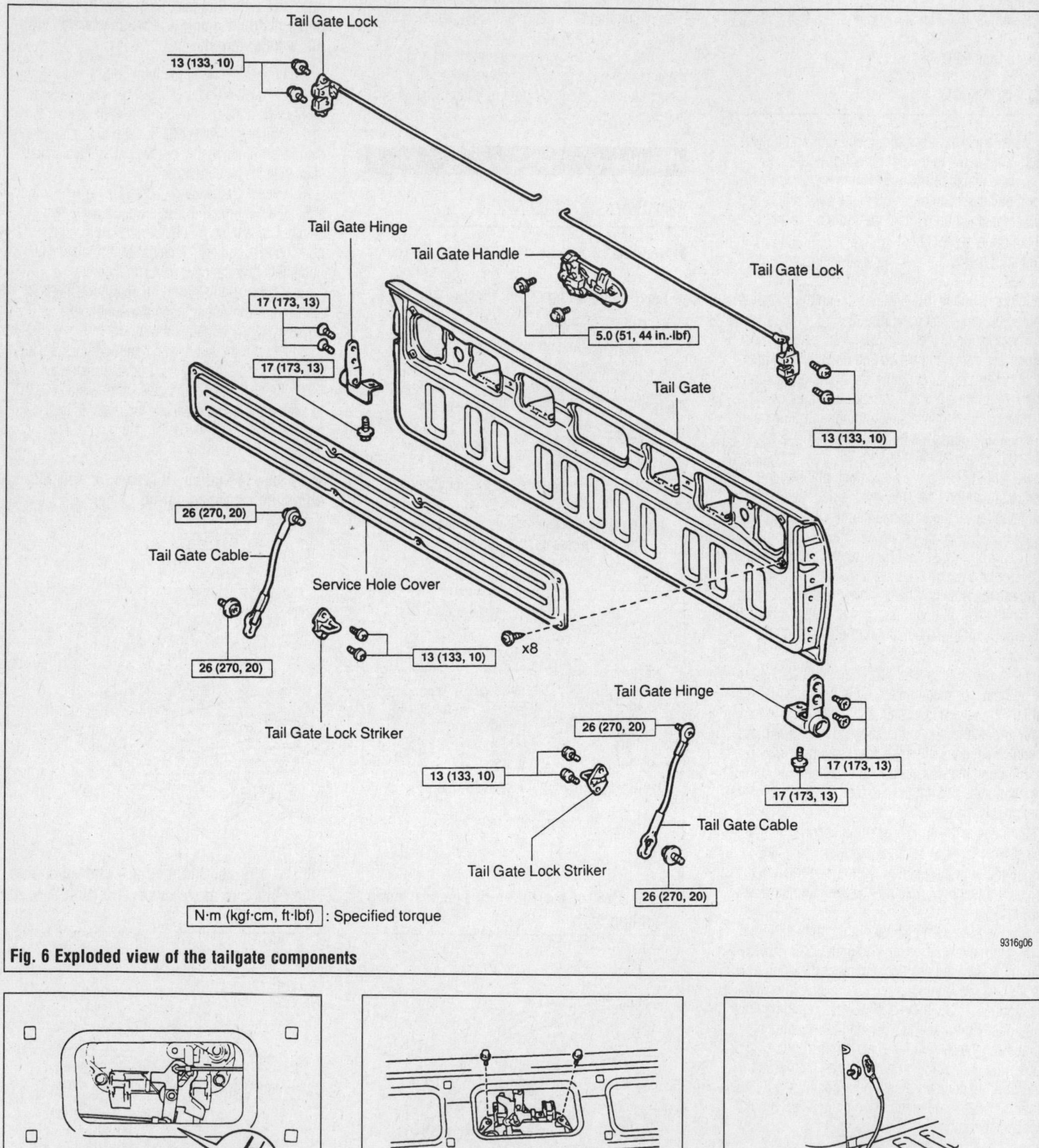

Fig. 6 Exploded view of the tailgate components

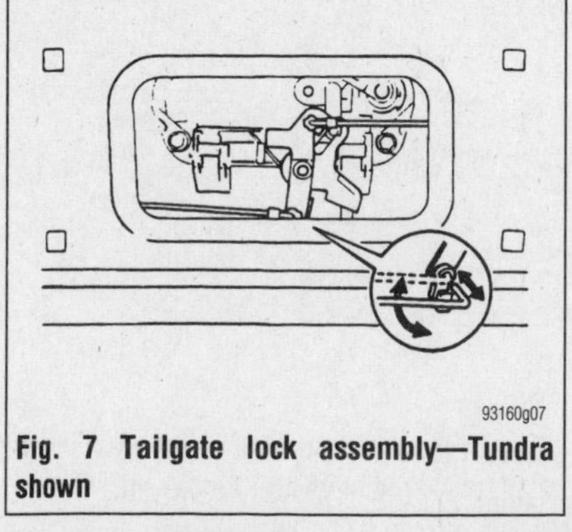

Fig. 7 Tailgate lock assembly—Tundra shown

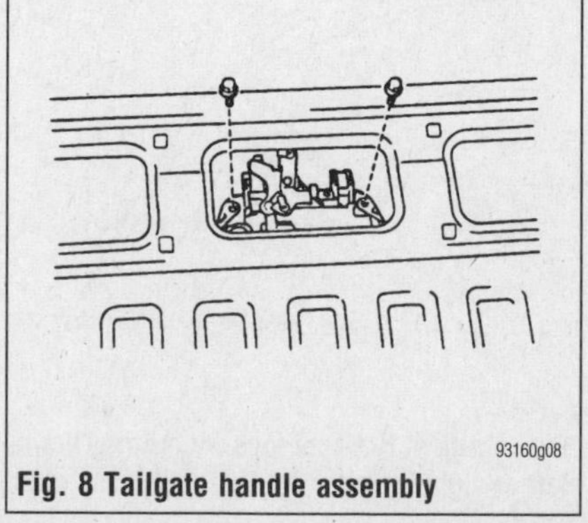

Fig. 8 Tailgate handle assembly

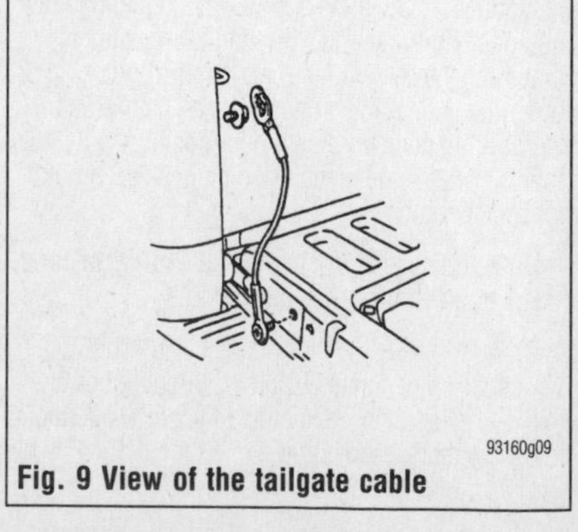

Fig. 9 View of the tailgate cable

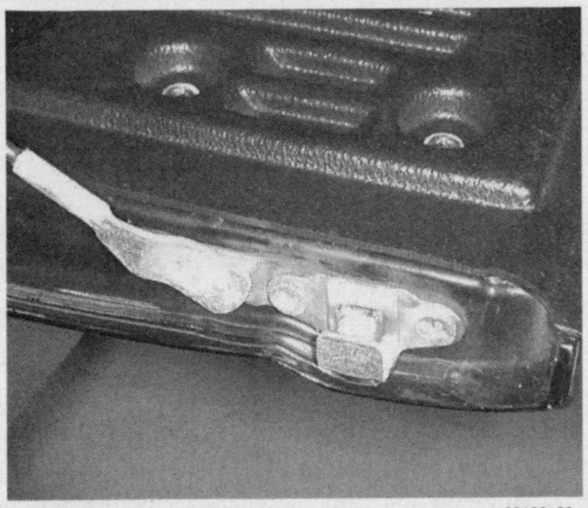

Fig. 10 Tailgate cable and lock assembly—Tacoma shown

Fig. 11 View of the tailgate cable as it attaches to the bed of the truck—Tacoma shown

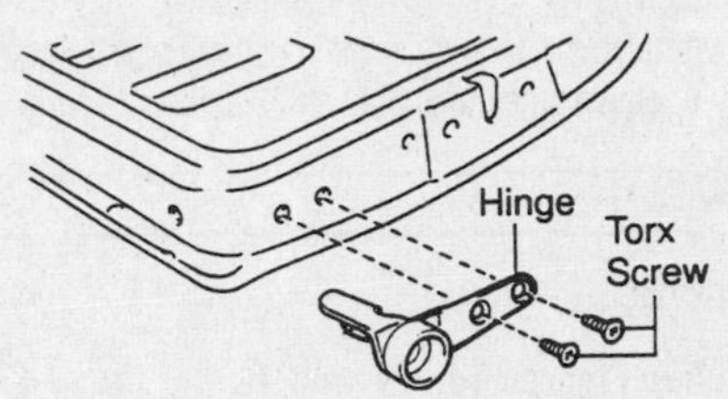

Fig. 12 Tailgate hinge and bolts

Rear Door

REMOVAL & INSTALLATION

➧ See Figure 13

➡**An assistant is required for this procedure.**

1. On Land Cruiser models, remove the inner door panel trim. Unplug any wiring connectors for harnesses running between the door and body.
2. Lower the door glass into the door all the way.
3. On Land Cruiser models, remove the bolts holding the door supports to the door.
4. Remove the bolts and clamps holding the torsion bar to the door. Remove the clip.
5. Disconnect the torsion bar and bolts from the door.

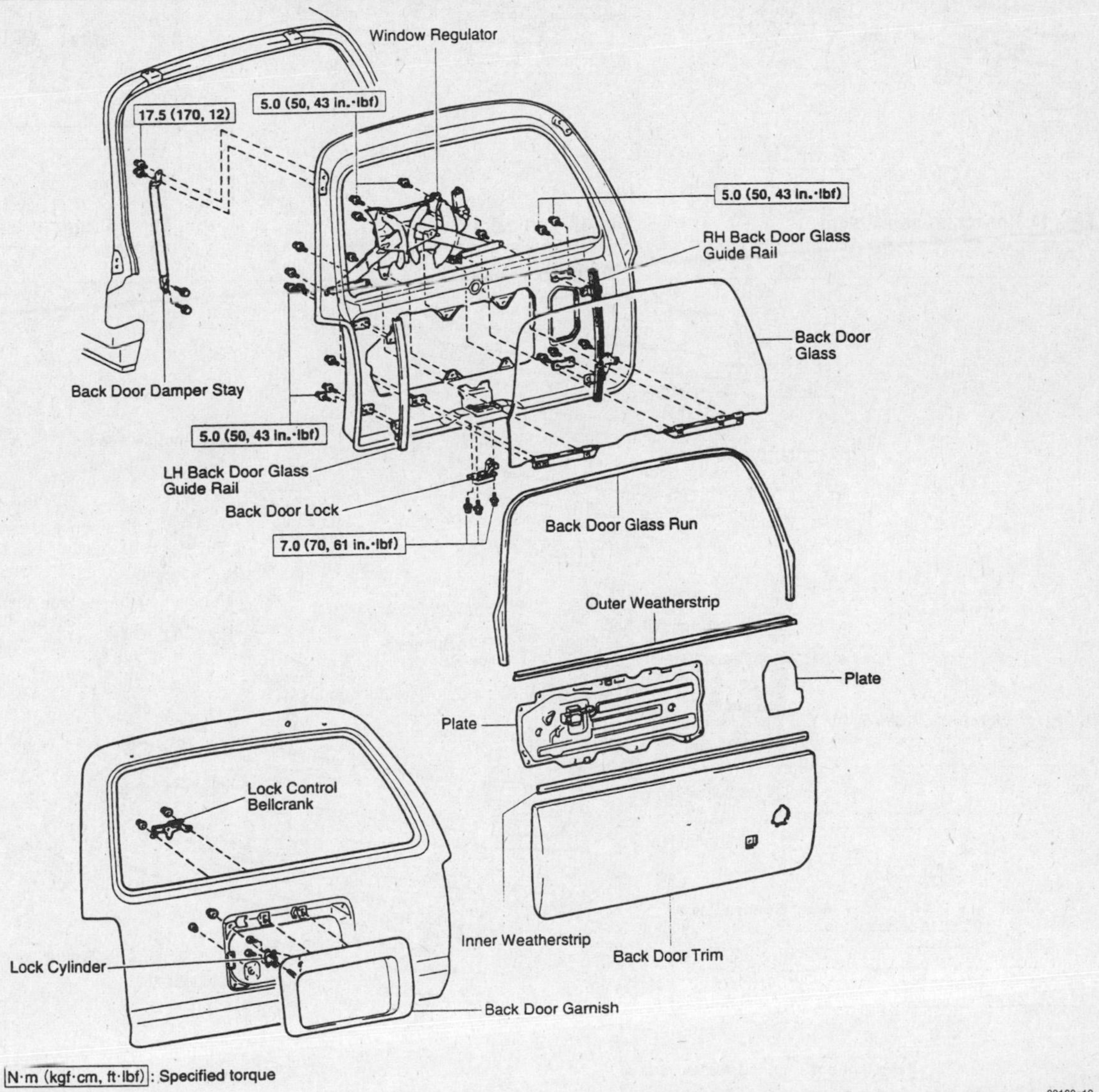

Fig. 13 Rear door components

6. Detach the torsion bar guide.
7. Remove the two bolts and the door stay.
8. Support the door, then remove the hinge bolts and the door.
9. Installation is the reverse of the removal procedure. Tighten the hinge bolts to 22 ft. lbs. (29 Nm).

ADJUSTMENT

4Runner

➧ **See Figures 14, 15, and 16**

1. To adjust the door fore-and-aft, as well as left-to-right, loosen the body side hinge nuts. When adjusted, retighten to 25 ft. lbs. (33 Nm).
2. To adjust the door vertically, as well as left-to-right, loosen the door side hinge bolts. When adjusted, retighten to 17 ft. lbs. (23 Nm).
3. Adjust the door striker as follows:
   a. Loosen the striker mounting screws to adjust.
   b. Using a plastic hammer, tap the striker to adjust.

Land Cruiser

1. Adjust the upper and lower rear doors fore-and-aft and left-to-right as follows:
   a. Adjust the door by loosening the door side hinge bolts.
   b. Move the hinge into the appropriate direction with your hand or a plastic hammer.
2. To adjust the upper and lower doors in the left-to-right and vertical directions, loosen the body side hinge bolts.
3. Adjust the door striker as follows:
   a. Check that the door fit and door lock linkage are adjusted correctly.
   b. Adjust the striker position by slightly loosening the striker mounting screws, then hitting the striker with a plastic headed hammer. Tighten the mounting screw when the adjustment is appropriate.

Bumpers

REMOVAL & INSTALLATION

➧ **See Figures 17 and 18**

1. Support the bumper.
2. Remove any trim pieces, corner moldings, etc. on the bumper.
3. Remove the nuts and bolts attaching the bumper to the frame.
4. Installation is the reverse of removal.

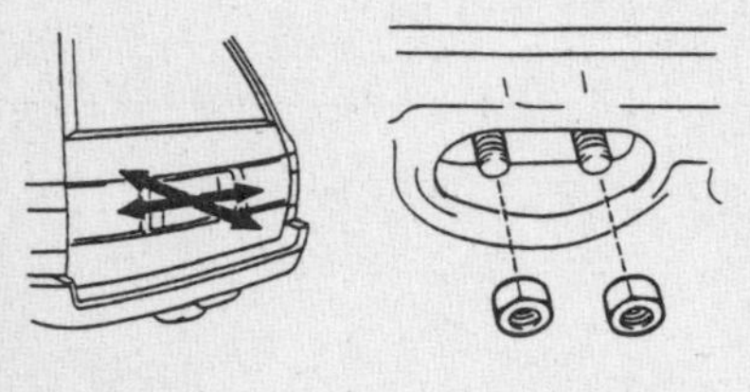

93160g13

Fig. 14 Horizontal adjustment

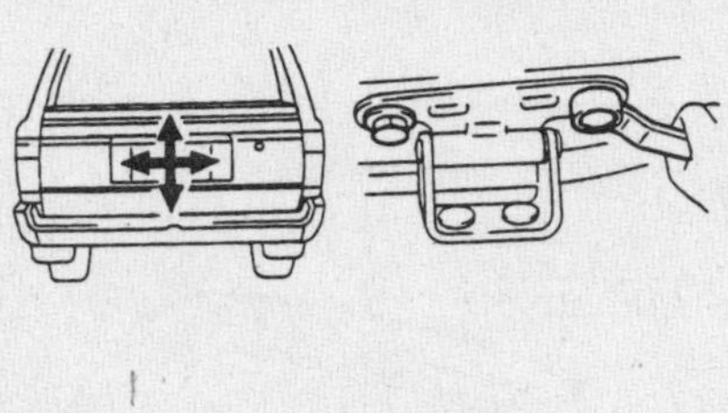

93160g14

Fig. 15 Vertical adjustment

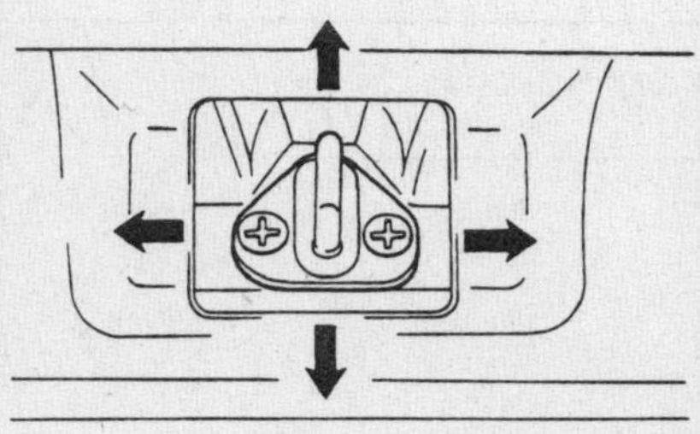

93160g15

Fig. 16 Door lock striker adjustment

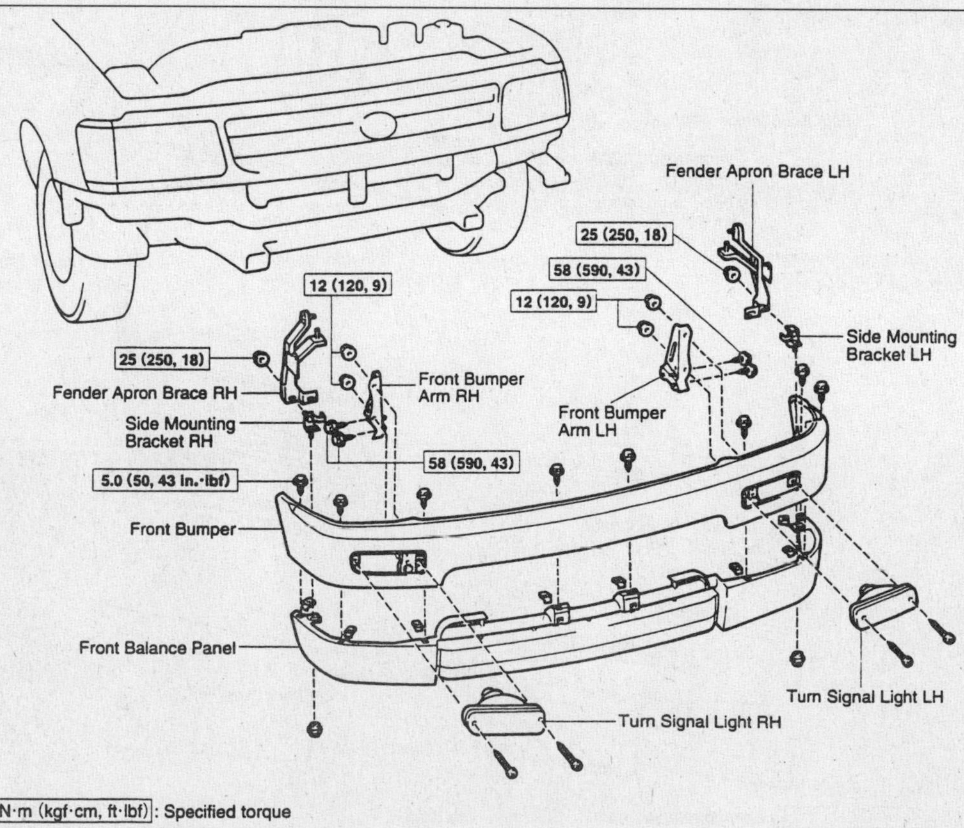

93160g11

Fig. 17 Exploded view of the front bumper—4Runner shown, other models similar

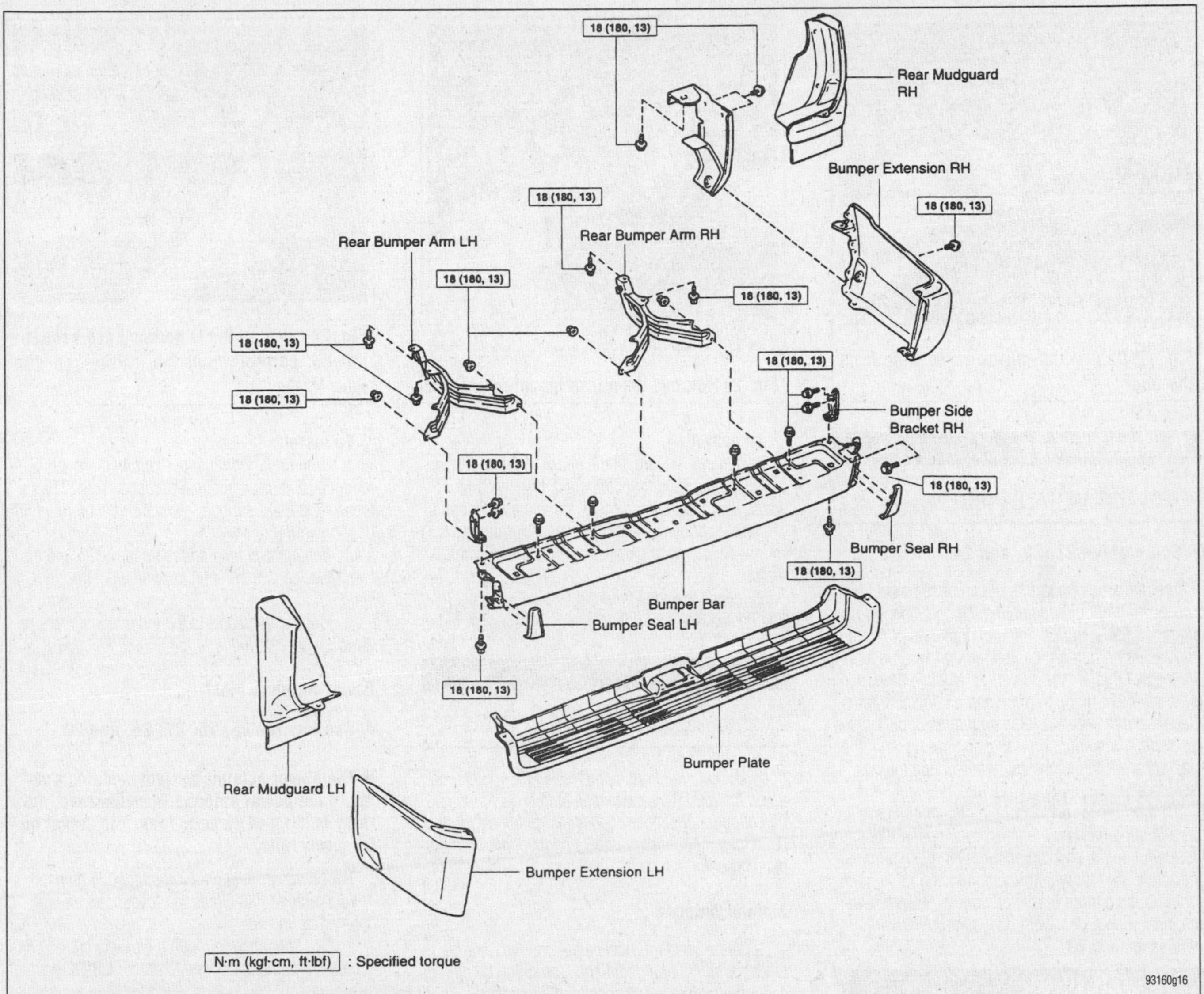

Fig. 18 Exploded view of the rear bumper mounting—4Runner shown, other models similar

Grille

REMOVAL & INSTALLATION

➧ **See Figures 19, 20, and 21**

1. Open and support the hood.
2. Remove the turn signal and parking lamps, as necessary.
3. Either unscrew the grille assembly or remove the retaining clips and remove the grille from the vehicle.
4. Installation is the reverse of removal.

Fig. 19 Removing the grille from the front of the vehicle

Fig. 20 Close up of a typical grille clip

Fig. 21 When re-installing the grille, make sure all of the mounting clips are properly aligned

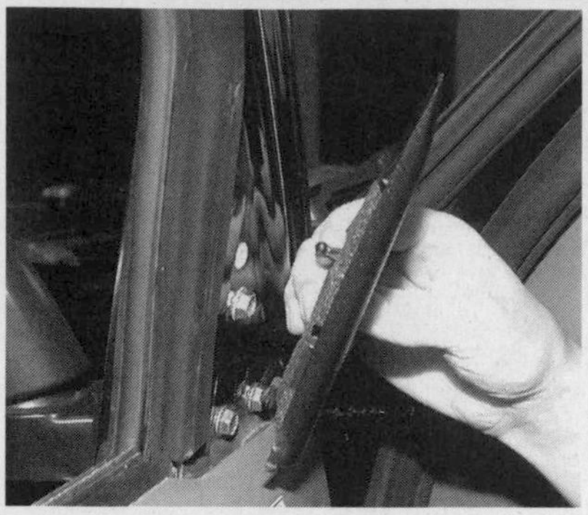
93160p08
Fig. 22 Detach the mirror cover plate from the door

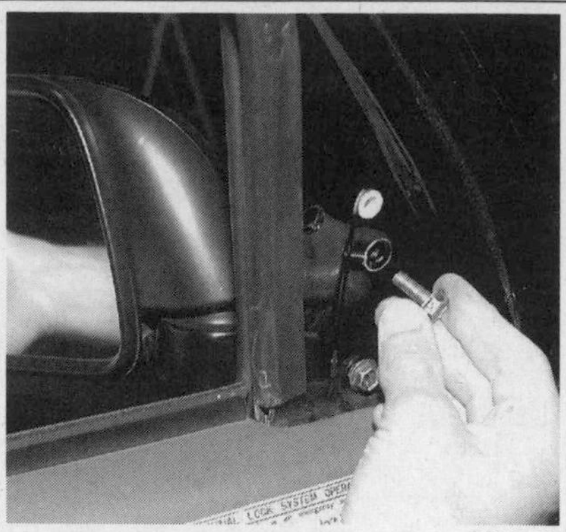
93160p36
Fig. 23 Remove the mirror mounting screws

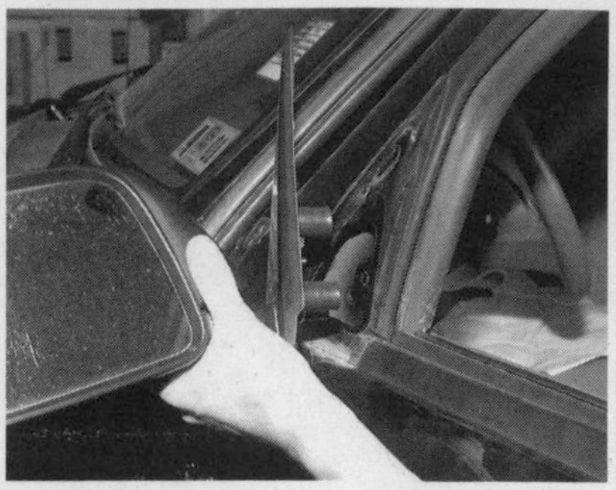
93160p35
Fig. 24 Once all the fasteners have been removed, carefully pull the mirror from the door frame

Outside Mirrors

REMOVAL & INSTALLATION

➧ **See Figures 22, 23, and 24**

The mirrors (in most cases) can be removed from the door without disassembling the door liner or other components. Both left and right outside mirrors may be either manual, manual remote (small lever on the inside to adjust the mirror) or, in some cases, electric remote. If the mirror glass is damaged, replacements may be available through your dealer or a reputable glass shop. If the plastic housing is cracked or damaged, the entire mirror unit must be replaced.

1. If the mirror is manual remote, check to see if the adjusting handle is retained by a hidden screw, usually under an end cap on the lever. If so, remove the screw and remove the adjusting knob.
2. Using a blunt plastic or wooden tool, remove the inner triangular cover from where the mirror mounts to the door.

⁂ WARNING

Don't use a screwdriver; the plastic will be marred.

3. Depending on the model and style of mirror, there may be concealment plugs or other minor parts under the cover. Remove them. If electric connectors are present, unplug them.
4. Support the mirror housing from the outside and remove the three bolts or nuts holding the mirror to the door.
5. Remove the mirror.

To install:

6. When installing, fit the mirror to the door, then install the nuts and bolts to hold it. Connect any wiring. Pay particular attention to the placement and alignment of any gaskets or weatherstrips around the mirror; serious wind noises may result from careless work.
7. Install the cover, pressing it firmly into position. Install the control lever knob if it was removed.

Antenna

REMOVAL & INSTALLATION

If your antenna mast is the type where you can unscrew the mast from the fender, simply do so with a pair of pliers. Most damaged antennas are simply the result of a truck wash or similar mishap, in which the mast is bent.

Manual Antenna

1. Disconnect the antenna cable at the radio by pulling it straight out of the set. Depending on access, this may require loosening the radio and pulling it out of the dash.
2. Working under the instrument panel, disengage the cable from its retainers.

➡On some models, it may be necessary to remove the instrument panel pad to get at the cable.

3. Outside, unsnap the cap from the antenna base.
4. Remove the screw(s) and lift off the antenna, pulling the cable with it, carefully.

To install:

5. When reinstalling, make certain the antenna mount area is clean and free of rust and dirt. The antenna must make a proper ground contact through its base to work properly.
6. Install the screws and route the cable into the cab. Make certain the cable is retained in the clips, etc.
7. Connect the cable to the radio; reinstall the radio if it was removed.

Power Antenna Mast

➧ **See Figures 25, 26, 27, 28, and 29**

➡The power antenna system contains a relay. If the power antenna is inoperative, the relay is the first place to look. The actual motor rarely fails.

The power antenna mast is replaceable on most Toyota vehicles. If the mast is damaged or broken, proceed as follows:

1. Perform this repair with the battery cables connected. Turn the ignition switch to the **LOCK** position.
2. Remove the antenna nut.
3. If equipped with a CD player, press the AM and FM buttons on the receiver and simultaneously turn the ignition switch to **ACC**.
4. For non-CD player units, press the AM button and simultaneously turn the ignition switch to **ACC**.
5. The antenna motor will run, unwinding the mast from the spool. have an assistant guide the mast so it doesn't fall and damage the bodywork. When fully extended, the mast will be released. Remove it, and leave the ignition in the **ACC** position.

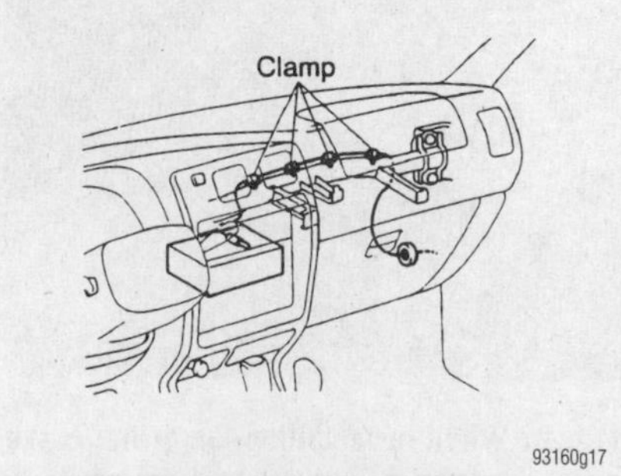

93160g17
Fig. 25 In most cases, you must remove the radio to detach the antenna cable

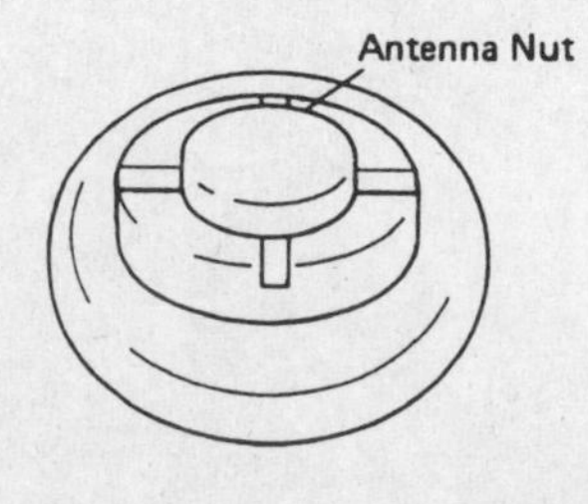

93160g18
Fig. 26 Remove the antenna nut

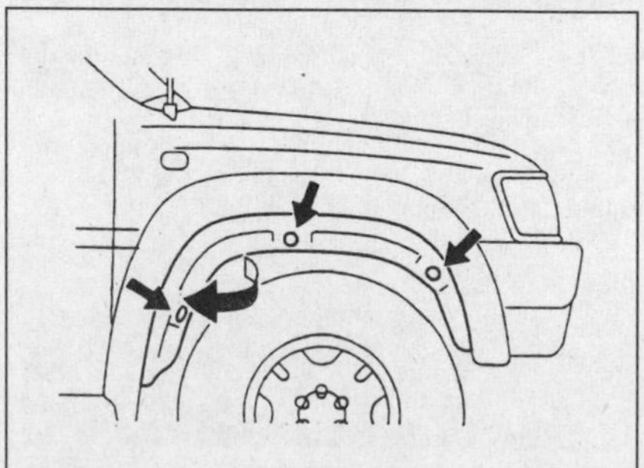
93160g19
Fig. 27 Detach the wheel well clips and remove the liner

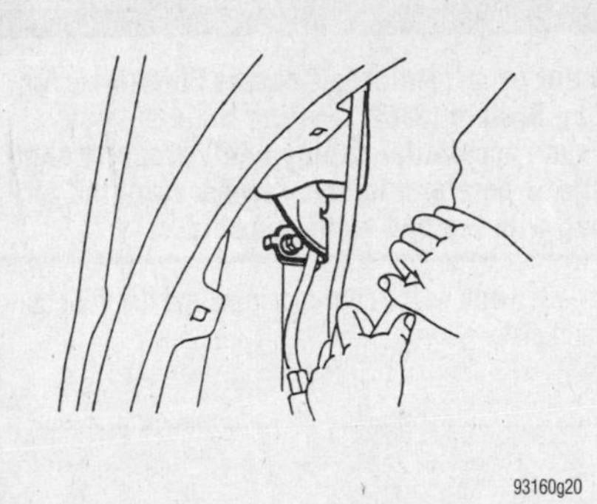

Fig. 28 Location of the antenna assembly retaining bolt

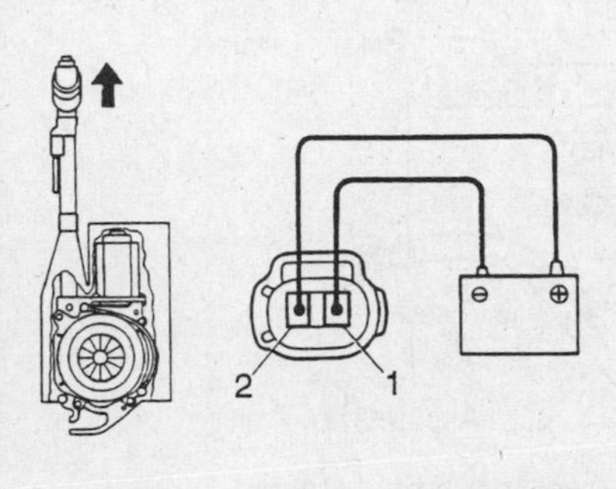

Fig. 29 Antenna motor and connector polarity

To install:

6. Insert the new cable so that the teeth face the rear of the vehicle. Feed the cable into the motor until the cable reaches the bottom, about 12 in. (30cm).
7. Have an assistant ready and prepared to guide the cable. Turn the ignition switch to **LOCK**. The motor will run, winding the cable onto the spool and drawing the antenna down into the mount.
8. If the cable does not wind, twist the cable at the top of the housing; the part at the bottom may have turned while being pushed down the hole.
9. Once wound onto the spool, install the antenna nut even if the antenna is not fully retracted. Test the antenna elevation and retraction; the mast will eventually retract fully.

Fenders

REMOVAL & INSTALLATION

1. Support the hood with a prop rod.
2. Clean all fenders and liberally apply penetrating oil.
3. Remove the fender support screws.
4. Detach the inner fender liner.
5. Remove the screws that attach the fender to the corner of the cab.
6. Detach all wiring harnesses that may be fastened to the fender.
7. Remove the running board if equipped.
8. Remove the upper fender retaining bolts.
9. Once all fasteners have been removed, lift the fender from the body.
10. The installation is the reverse of removal

Power Sunroof

REMOVAL & INSTALLATION

➡When removing any interior garnish pieces, always have a small supply of extra clips on hand. You will very likely break a few upon removal.

4Runner

➧ See Figure 30

1. Remove or disconnect the following components:
   - Rear room light
   - Back door scuff plate
   - Rear header trim
   - Back and rear doors scuff plates
   - Rear seat side garnish
   - Deck side trim
   - Front door scuff plate
   - Center pillar lower garnish
2. Unbolt the front seat belt shoulder anchor.
3. Using a taped flat-bladed tool, remove the center pillar upper garnish.
4. Remove the following parts:
   - Assist grips
   - Front pillar garnish
   - Control switch
   - Inner rear view mirror
   - Front room lamp
   - Sunvisors and holders
5. Remove the clips securing the headliner. Lower the headliner.
6. Unplug the drain hoses and connectors. Remove the nuts and bolts and roof housing assembly.
7. Reinstall in reverse order. Tighten the housing assembly bolts to 65 inch lbs. (7 Nm) and the seat belt shoulder anchor to 31 ft. lbs. (42 Nm).

Land Cruiser

1. Remove the following parts:
   - Back door scuff plate
   - Rear seat
   - Right and left quarter side trims
   - Rear seat side garnish
   - Rear door scuff plate
   - Cowl side trim
   - Front and rear door opening trims
   - Center pillar lower garnish
   - Front seat outer belt shoulder anchor
   - Center pillar upper garnish
   - Front seat outer belt shoulder anchor adjuster
   - Both rear seat outer belt shoulder anchors
   - Quarter pillar garnish
   - Rear pillar garnish
   - Assist grips
   - Front pillar garnish and sunvisors with holders
   - Inner rear view mirror
   - Front and rear room lamps
   - Back door opening trim
   - Sliding roof opening molding
2. Remove the control switch by unscrewing the cover. Separate the cover from the body, then unscrew the switch body. Unplug the connector. Remove the body with bracket.
3. Remove the clips retaining the headliner.
4. Unbolt the drive gear control relay, then unplug the connector.
5. Remove the gear mounting bolts and bracket. Separate the drive gear from the unit then unplug the connector.
6. Remove the sliding roof garnishes. Pry loose the inner side garnish clips.
7. Remove the sliding roof glass. Remove the nuts and shims. Be sure your have all six of the shims. Pull the glass upwards to remove it from the vehicle.
8. Remove the drip channel.
9. Remove the wind deflector.
10. Disconnect the drain hose, then remove the roof housing.
11. Adjust the drive rail to a closed and tilted down position. Using a flat-bladed tool, slide the link forward or backward to align the 2 marks shown in the illustration.

To install:

12. Adjust and install the drive gear assembly as follows:
    a. Remove the screw and cam plate cover.
    b. Remove the large screw, washers and shim.
    c. Turn the driveshaft with a screwdriver to align the housing and gear point mark.
    d. Install the cam plate cover with the screw.
    e. Install the drive gear assembly with the four mounting bolts.
    f. Plug in the connector.
13. Install the drive gear control relay and bracket, then attach the connector.
14. Install the remaining parts in the reverse order of removal.

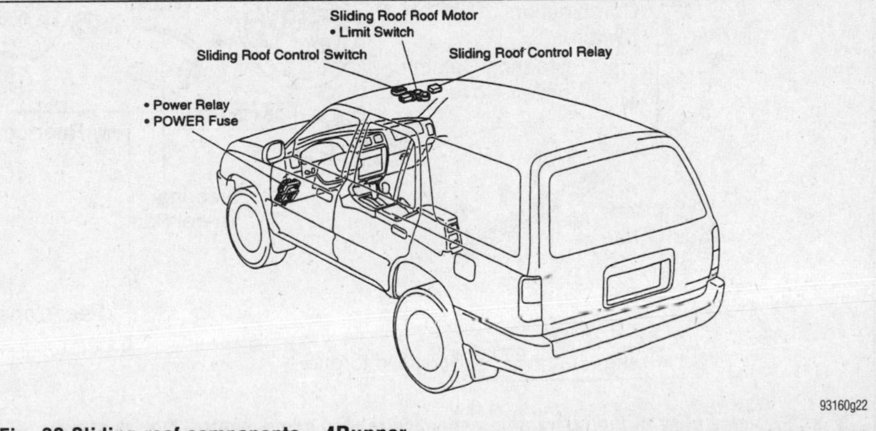

Fig. 30 Sliding roof components—4Runner

INTERIOR

Instrument Panel

REMOVAL & INSTALLATION

4Runner and Tundra

See Figures 31 and 32

1. Disconnect the negative battery cable.
2. Remove the steering wheel. For additional information, please refer to the following topic(s): Suspension and Steering, Steering Wheel.

CAUTION

The air bag system (SRS) must be disarmed before removing the steering wheel or instrument panel. Refer to Chassis Electrical, Air Bag System (SRS). Failure to do so may cause accidental deployment, property damage or personal injury. Always store the air bag with the pad facing upward.

3. Remove the cowl side trim and the front door scuff plate.

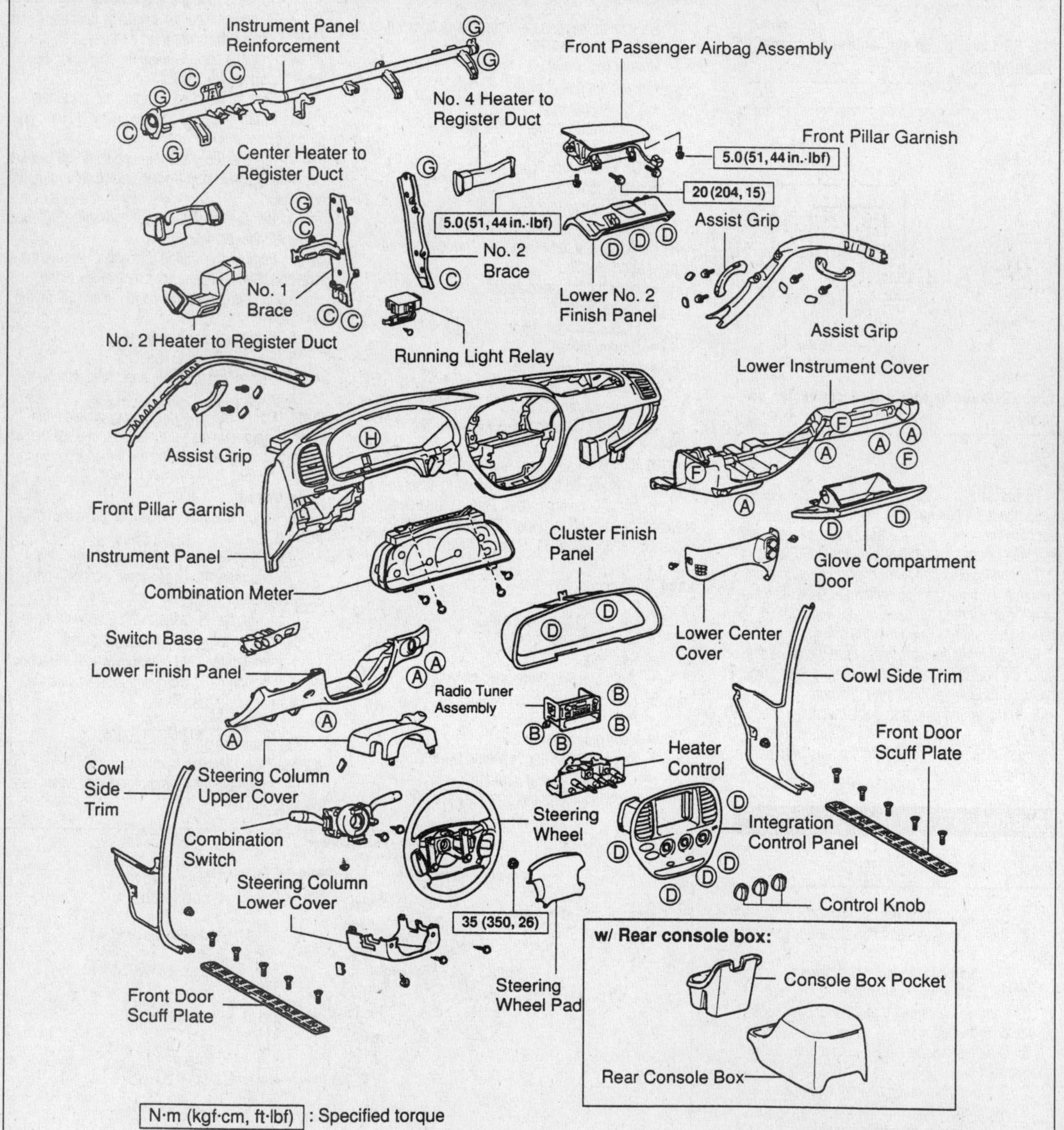

Fig. 31 Exploded view of the instrument panel and related components—Tundra shown

4. Unbolt the lower finish panel, then remove the hood and fuel tank release lever screws.
5. Remove the starter switch bezel.
6. Detach the No. 2 and No. 1 heater-to-register duct.
7. Unscrew the cluster finish panel, then remove.
8. Disconnect the harness for the combination meter, then unscrew and remove.
9. Remove the A/C switch, heater control knob and heater control panel.
10. Remove the 2 mounting screws. Using a flat-bladed tool, remove the panel.
11. Unplug the connectors. Separate the A/C control cable from the unit.
12. Remove the glove compartment door.
13. Remove the glove box lamp. Remove the bolts and the panel.
14. Remove the glove compartment door reinforcement.
15. Unhook the heater register duct. Remove the radio and side bracket.
16. Disconnect the air bag harness.
17. Remove the bolts in the upper portion of the glove box.
18. Remove the defroster nozzle.
19. Remove the instrument panel reinforcement.

To install:

20. Attach the instrument panel reinforcement.
21. Install the defroster nozzle.
22. Bolt in the upper portion of the glove box.
23. Plug in the air bag harness.

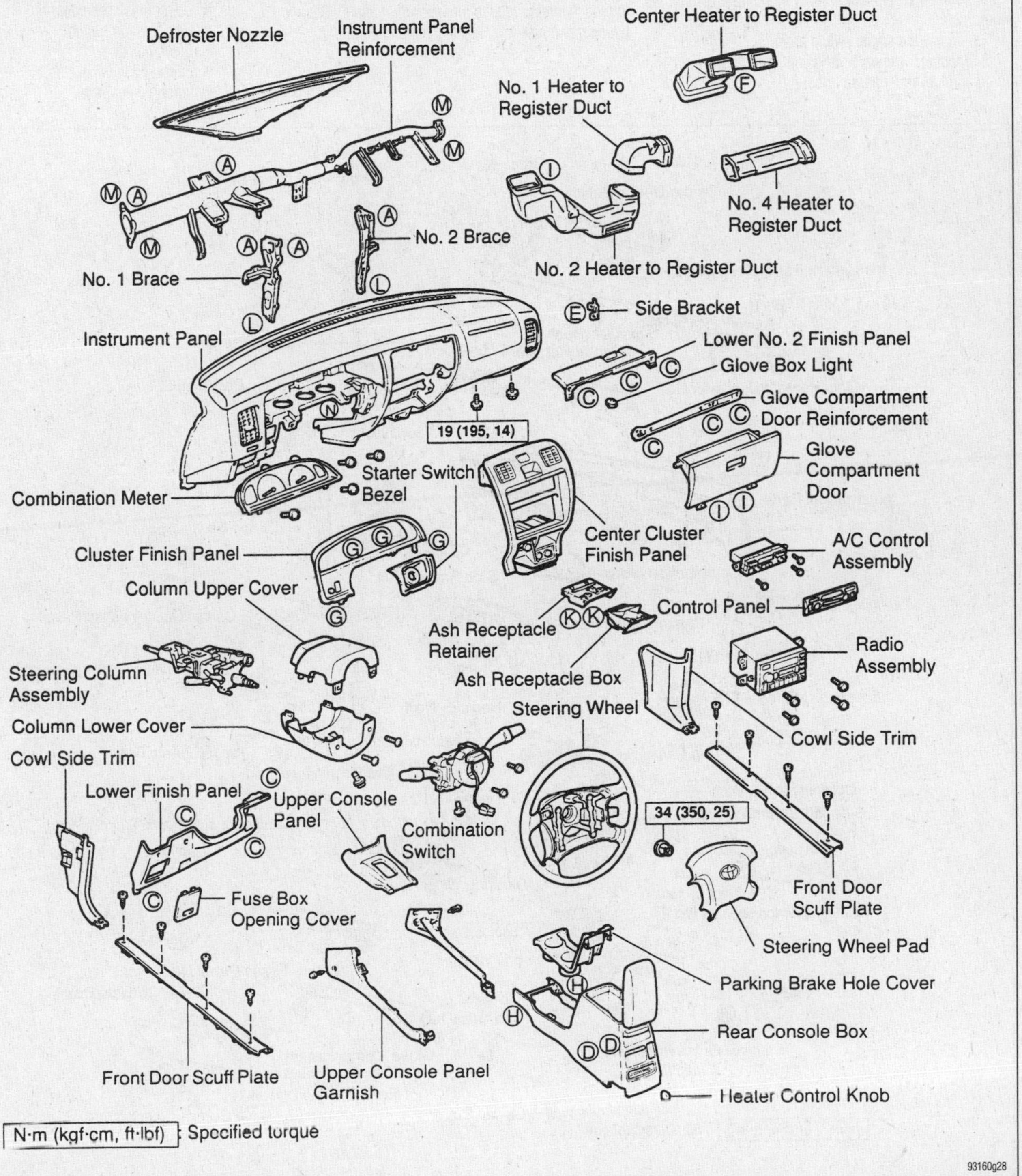

Fig. 32 Exploded view of the instrument panel—4Runner shown

24. Install the radio and hook-up the heater register duct.
25. Install the glove compartment door reinforcement.
26. Install the glove box lamp. Attach the bolts for the panel.
27. Install the glove box door.
28. Attach the A/C control cable. Plug the connectors.
29. Install the center cluster finish panel.
30. Attach the harness to the combination meter, then attach to the vehicle.
31. Tighten the cluster finish panel.
32. Attach the No. 2 and No. 1 heater-to-register duct.
33. Install the starter switch bezel.
34. Install the lower finish panel, then attach the hood and fuel tank release lever.
35. Install the cowl side trim and the front door scuff plate.
36. Install the steering wheel.
37. Connect the negative battery cable.

T100

See Figure 33

1. Disconnect the negative battery cable.
2. Remove the front pillar garnish.
3. Unscrew the front door scuff plate and the cowl side trims.
4. Remove the steering wheel. For additional information, please refer to the following topic(s): Suspension and Steering, Steering Wheel.

CAUTION

The air bag system (SRS) must be disarmed before removing the steering wheel or instrument panel. Refer to Chassis Electrical, Air Bag System (SRS). Failure to do so may cause accidental deployment, property damage or personal injury. Always store the air bag with the pad facing upward.

5. Remove the following:
   - Steering column cover
   - Hood lock release lever
   - Lower finish panel No. 1
   - Combination switch
   - Glove box door
   - Lower finish panel No. 2
   - Lower center panel

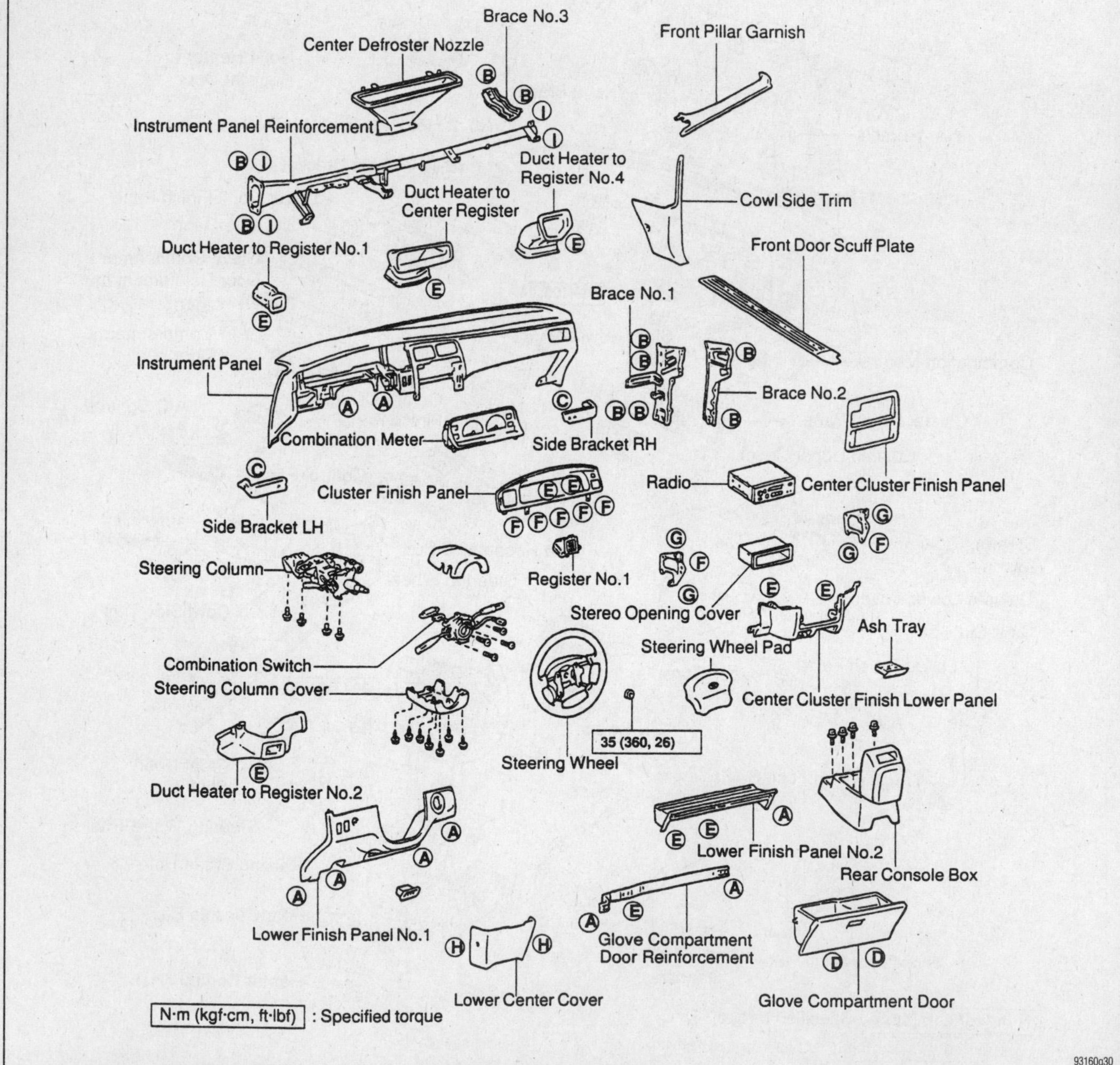

Fig. 33 Exploded view of the instrument panel and related components—T100 shown

6. Remove the screws retaining the center cluster finish panel, then detach the harness from the unit.
7. Remove the stereo opening cover.
8. Unscrew the combination meter from the dash.
9. Remove the following:
- No. 1 register
- Duct heater-to-register No. 1
- Duct heater-to-register No. 2
- Glove compartment door reinforcement
- Brace for the No. 1 and No. 2 registers
10. Detach the harness connections for the instrument panel, then remove the 2 bolts from the panel.
11. Unbolt the No. 3 brace, then remove the reinforcement.

To install:

12. Attach the reinforcement, then the No. 3 brace.
13. Attach the harness connections for the instrument panel, then tighten the 2 bolts for the panel.
14. Install the following:
- Brace for the No. 1 and No. 2 registers
- Glove compartment door reinforcement
- Duct heater-to-register No. 2
- Duct heater-to-register No. 1
- No. 1 register
15. Tighten the combination meter into place.
16. Attach the stereo opening cover.
17. Attach the cluster harness, then install and tighten the screws that retain the center cluster finish panel.
18. Install the following:
- Lower center panel
- Lower finish panel No. 2.
- Glove box door
- Combination switch
- Lower finish panel No. 1
- Hood lock release lever
- Steering column cover
19. Install the steering wheel.
20. Attach, then tighten the front door scuff plate and the cowl side trims.
21. Place the front pillar garnish into position and tighten.
22. Connect the negative battery cable.

Tacoma

➧ **See Figure 34**

1. Disconnect the negative battery cable.

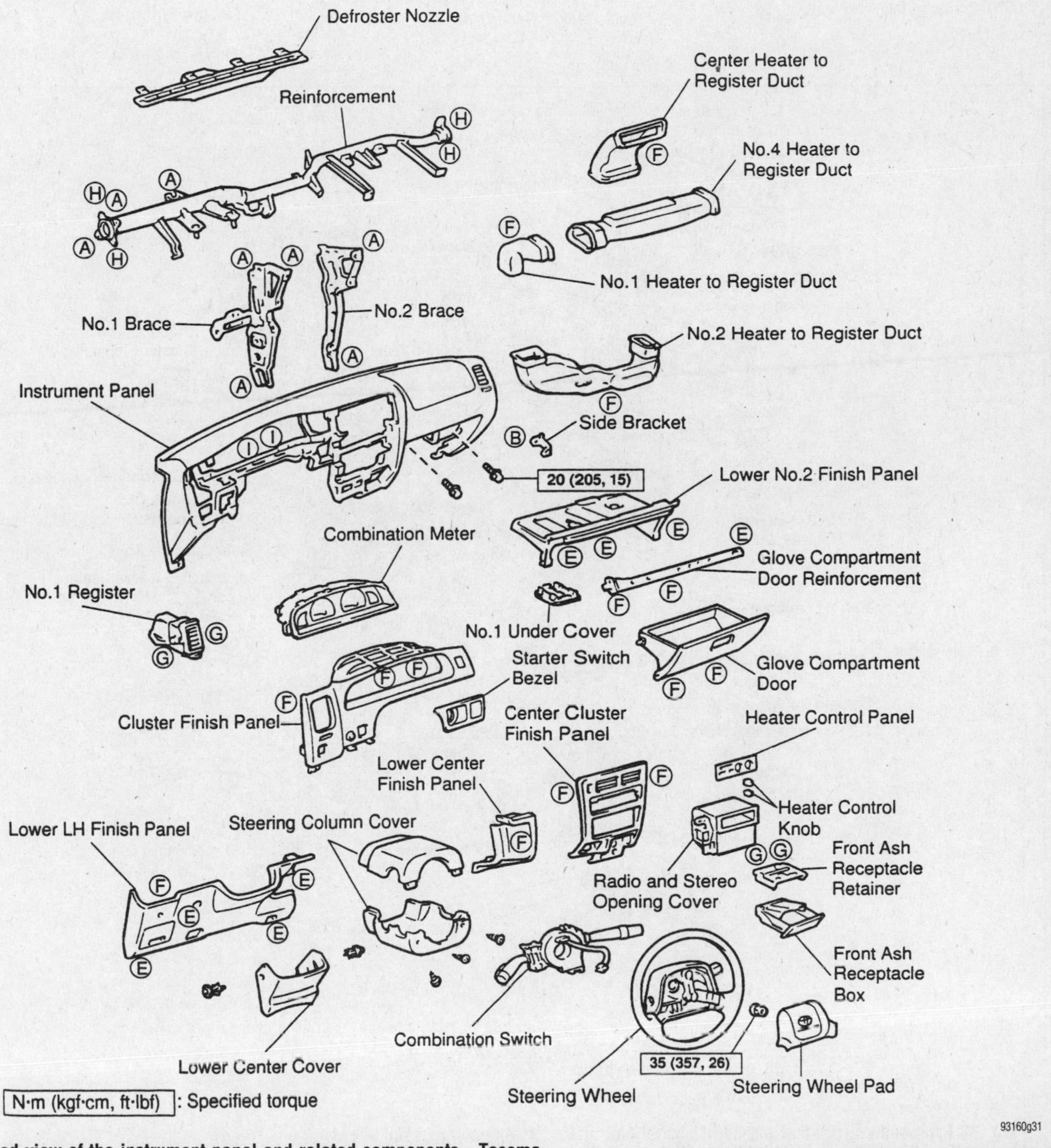

Fig. 34 Exploded view of the instrument panel and related components—Tacoma

2. Remove the steering wheel. For additional information, please refer to the following topic(s): Suspension and Steering, Steering Wheel.

CAUTION

The air bag system (SRS) must be disarmed before removing the steering wheel or instrument panel. Refer to Chassis Electrical, Air Bag System (SRS). Failure to do so may cause accidental deployment, property damage or personal injury. Always store the air bag with the pad facing upward.

3. Remove the following:
   - Steering column cover
   - Hood lock release lever
   - Combination switch
   - Fuse box cover
4. Remove the lower left hand finish panel.
5. Remove the following parts:
   - Starter switch bezel
   - No. 2 heater-to-register
   - Steering column
   - Clock
6. Remove the cup holder and the heater control knobs.
7. With the aide of a flat-bladed tool, remove the heater control panel.
8. Disconnect the hazard harness.
9. Remove the mounting screws for the center cluster finish panel.
10. Remove the heater control assembly.
11. Remove the radio.
12. Remove the screws mounting the cluster finish panel, then lower the panel.
13. Remove the combination meter screws, the speedometer cable. Disconnect the harness.
14. Remove the No. 1 register and the No. 1 heater-to-register duct.
15. Unscrew the glove compartment door and the reinforcement, then remove.
16. Unbolt the lower center instrument cover and remove the cover.
17. Separate the lower No. 2 finish panel from the dash.
18. Lift out the ashtray box and receptacle retainer.
19. Remove the stereo opening cover and the cigarette lighter harness.
20. Unbolt the side bracket for the instrument panel, then remove the instrument panel.
21. Unbolt the No. 1 and No. 2 brace for the instrument reinforcement. Remove the center heater-to-register duct.
22. Pull out the defroster nozzle.
23. Separate the reinforcement from the dash.
24. To install, reverse the removal procedure.
25. Connect the negative battery cable.

Land Cruiser

➧ **See Figure 35**

1. Disconnect the negative battery cable.

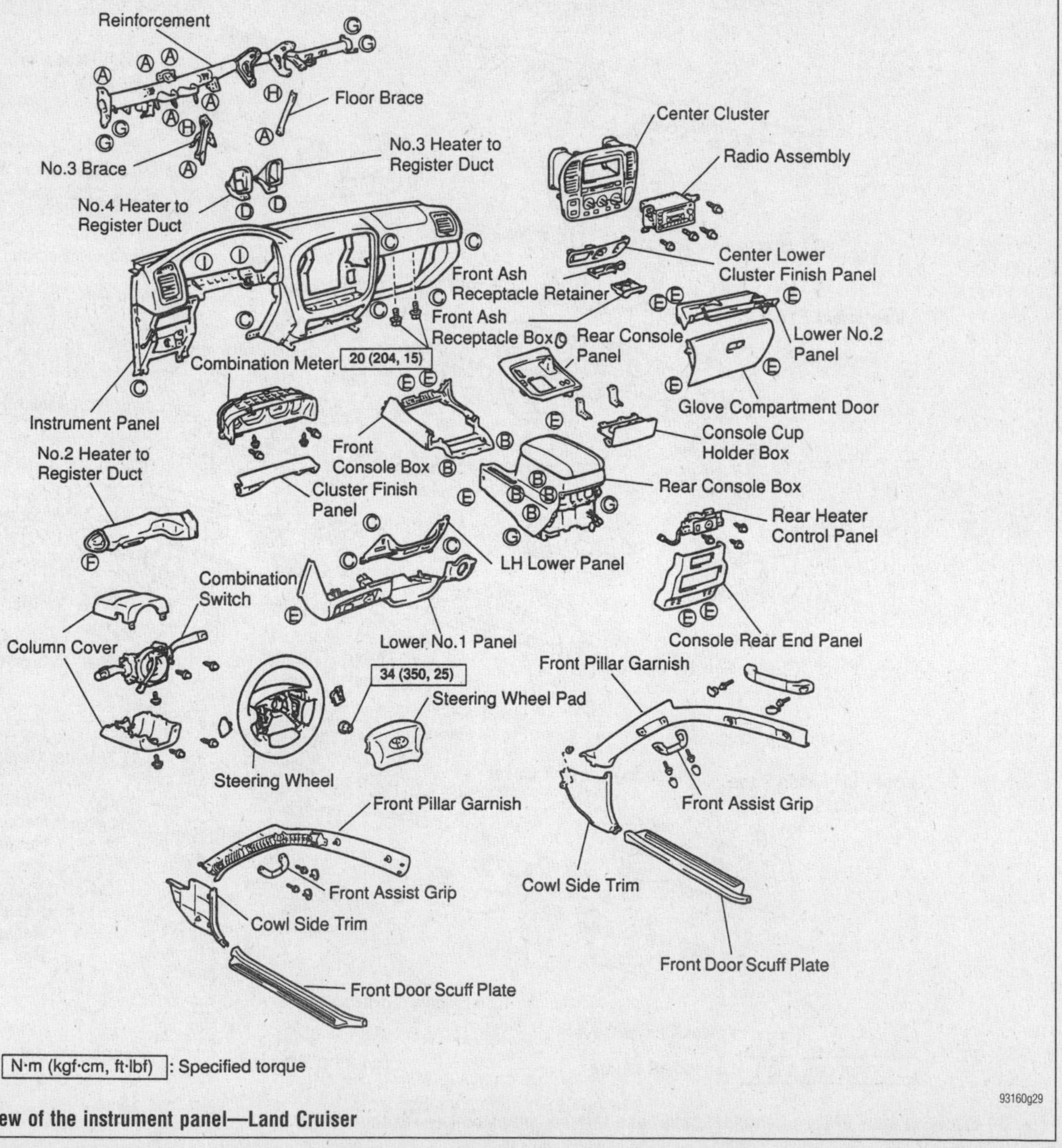

Fig. 35 Exploded view of the instrument panel—Land Cruiser

2. Remove the steering wheel. For additional information, please refer to the following topic(s): Suspension and Steering, Steering Wheel.

⁂ CAUTION

The air bag system (SRS) must be disarmed before removing the steering wheel or instrument panel. Refer to Chassis Electrical, Air Bag System (SRS). Failure to do so may cause accidental deployment, property damage or personal injury. Always store the air bag with the pad facing upward.

3. Apply strips of protective tape on the inside of each windshield pillar. This will protect the trim during removal.
4. Remove the upper and lower steering column covers.
5. Remove the hood release and fuel door release levers.
6. Remove the fuse box opening cover.
7. Unscrew the lower trim panel below the steering column.
8. Remove the lower instrument panel.
9. Disconnect the No. 2 heater-to-register duct.
10. Loosen the DLC3 and the fuse block.
11. Detach the No. 2 center cluster finish panel.
12. Remove the steering column.
13. Unbolt the cluster finish panel, then the combination meter.
14. Remove the center cluster finish panel assembly with the clock attached.
15. With the aid of a taped prytool, take off the 2 claws, then remove the cup holder hole cover.
16. Remove the ashtray.
17. Unscrew the center cluster finish panel with the heater control assembly, then disconnect the harness.
18. Remove the screws retaining the heater control assembly from the center cluster finish panel.
19. Remove the following:
    - Radio
    - Glove compartment door
    - Speaker panel
    - Speaker
    - Front console box
    - Rear console box
20. Loosen and remove the 5 screws and 9 bolts holding the instrument panel.
21. Remove the lower instrument panel reinforcement, then the No. 1 brace and the instrument panel.

To install:

22. Attach the No. 1 brace and lower instrument panel, then the instrument panel reinforcement.
23. Tighten the 5 screws and 9 bolts holding the instrument panel.
24. Install the following:
    - Radio
    - Glove compartment door
    - Speaker panel
    - Speaker
    - Front console box
    - Rear console box
25. Tighten the screws retaining the heater control assembly to the center cluster finish panel.
26. Connect the harness to the heater control, then attach the center cluster finish panel with the heater control assembly.
27. Reinstall the ashtray.
28. Place the cup holder hole cover into position.
29. Install the center cluster finish panel assembly with the clock attached.
30. Install the combination meter.
31. Attach the cluster finish panel.
32. Install the steering column.
33. Attach the No. 2 center cluster finish panel.
34. Install the DLC3 and the fuse block.
35. Insert and attach the No. 2 heater-to-register duct.
36. Install and tighten down the lower instrument panel.
37. Place the lower trim panel below the steering column, then tighten.
38. Attach the fuse box opening cover.
39. Place into position, then tighten down the hood release and fuel door release levers.
40. Attach the upper and lower steering column covers.
41. Install the steering wheel.
42. Connect the negative battery cable.

Door Panels

REMOVAL & INSTALLATION

➧ **See Figures 36 thru 50**

1. Remove the inner mirror control knob (if manual remote) and remove the inner triangular cover from the mirror mount.

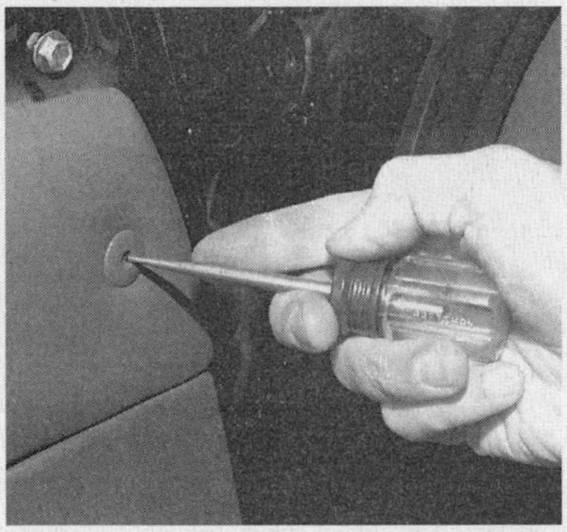

93160p01

Fig. 36 Use a scratch awl to depress the center of the upper door retaining clip pin

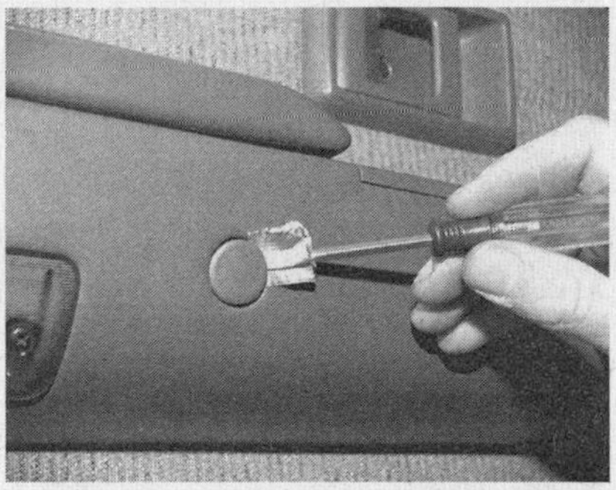

93160p02

Fig. 37 Use a small prytool, covered with tape to protect the interior panels from scratches, to remove any decorative cover plates

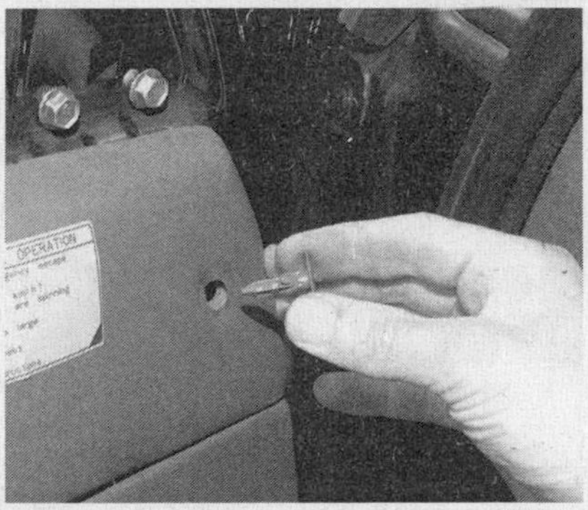

93160p15

Fig. 38 View of the trim panel screw being removed from the front driver's door—Tacoma

93160p03

Fig. 39 If possible, always use your hands to remove trim pieces. This will protect the interior from scratches

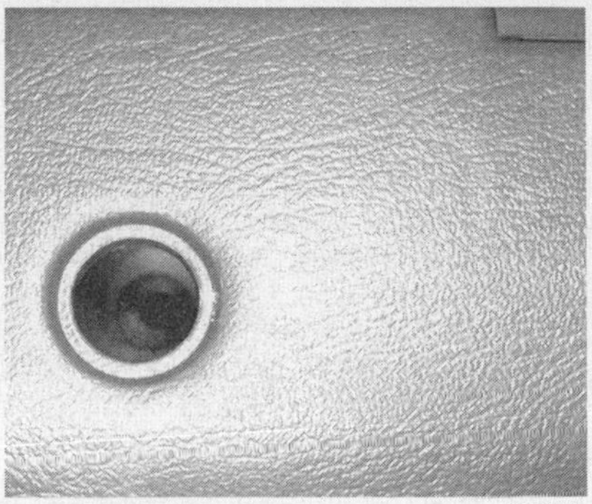

93160p04

Fig. 40 When removing interior panels, always look for hidden screws . . .

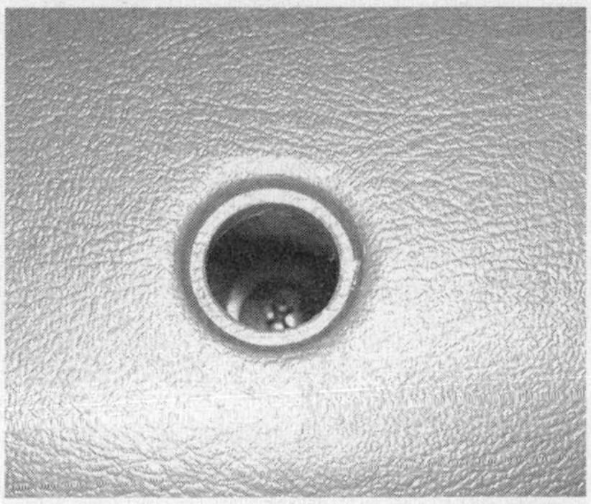

93160p14

Fig. 41 . . . for they are not always visible at first glance

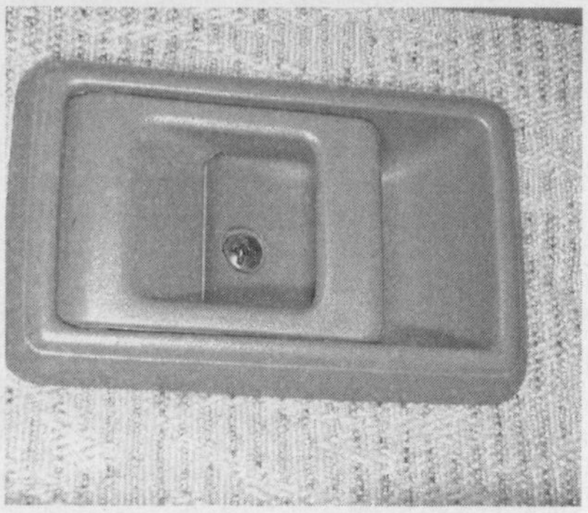

93160p10

Fig. 42 On Tacoma models, the interior door release handle must be removed

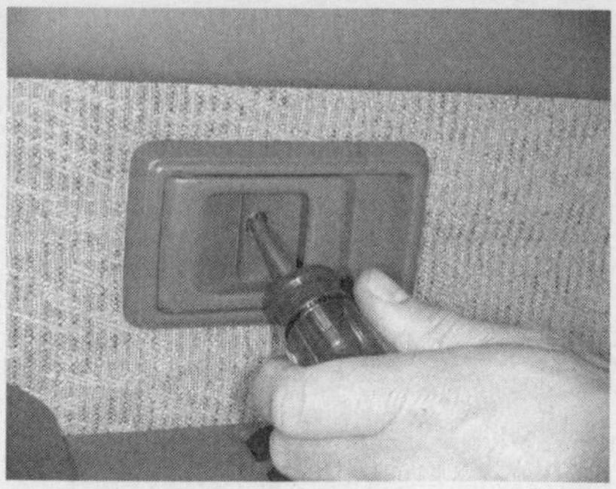

93160p05

Fig. 43 A Phillips screwdriver is all that is needed to loosen the interior door handle retaining screw . . .

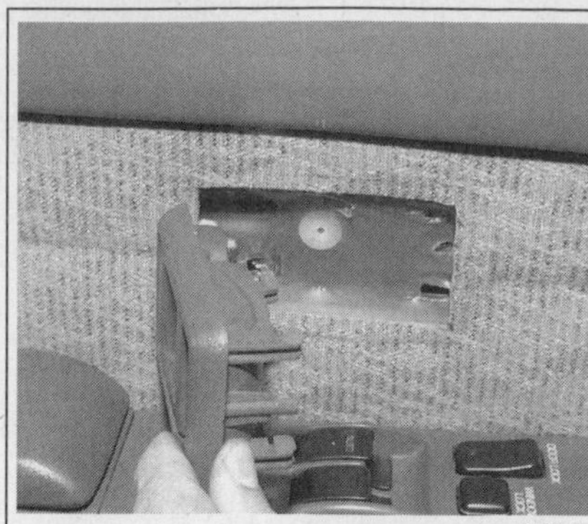

93160p16

Fig. 44 . . . then pry the handle away from the door with your fingers

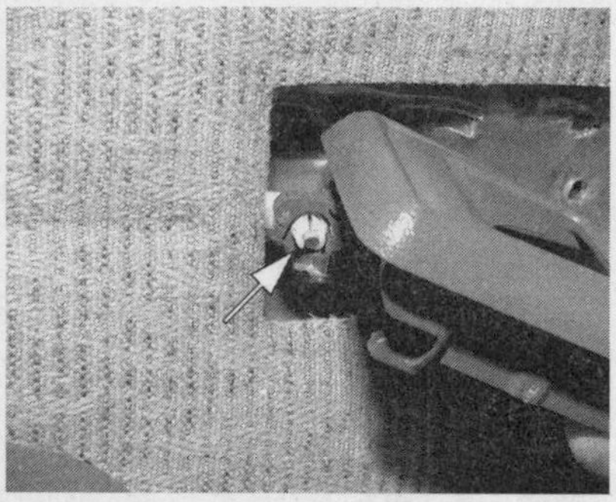

93160p17

Fig. 45 The actuator rod must be detached from the door handle before it can be removed from the vehicle

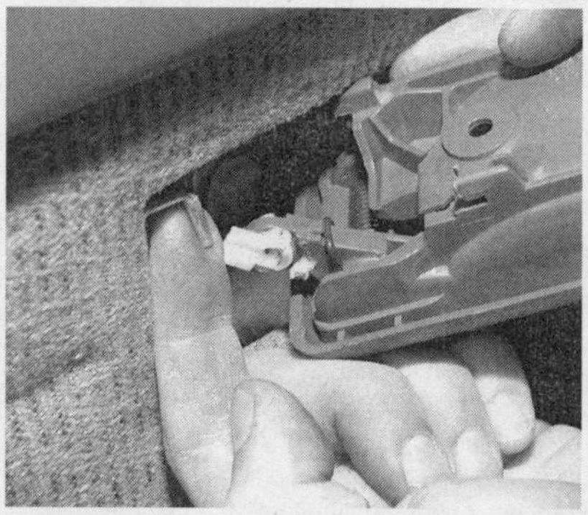

93160p18

Fig. 46 Do not let the rod disappear into the door

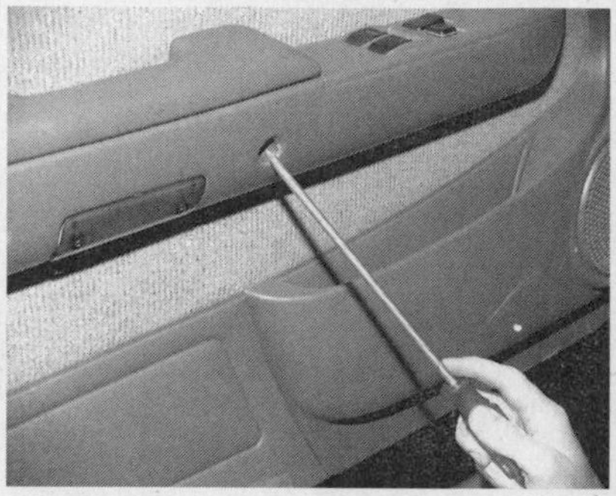

93160p07

Fig. 47 Long handle tools are a must. You will encounter numerous countersunk fasteners

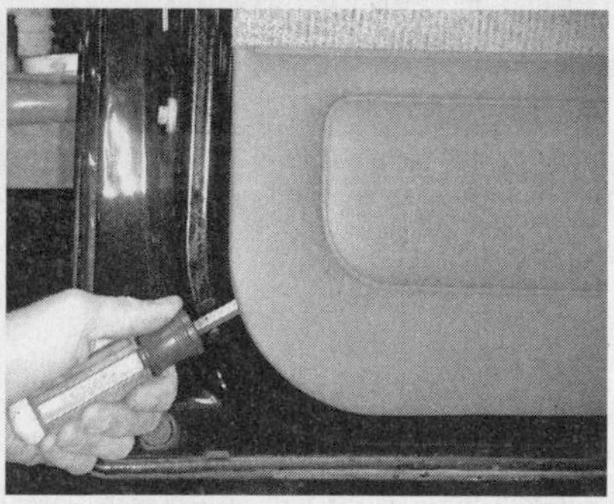

93160p06

Fig. 48 Although not used here, there are door panel clip removal tools, available at most local auto parts suppliers, which make removing the plastic clips much easier

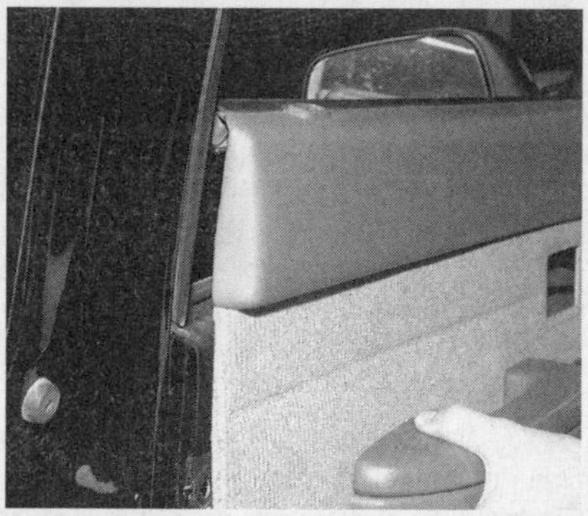

93160p19

Fig. 49 Once all retainers are removed, lift the door panel up and off the inner lip of the door frame . . .

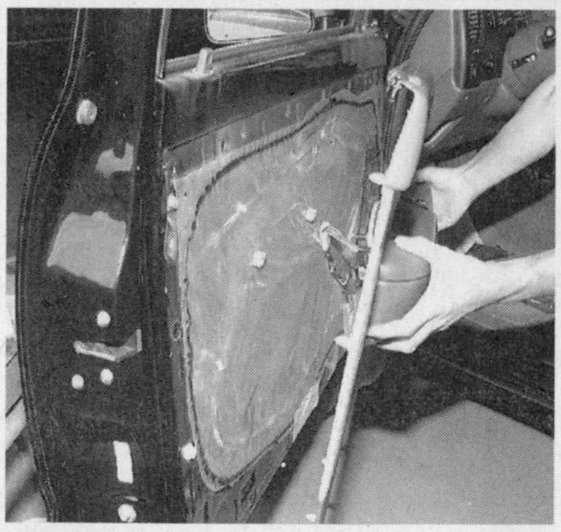

93160p20

Fig. 50 . . . then carefully remove the door panel from the vehicle

2. Remove the screws holding the armrest and remove the armrest. The armrest screws may be concealed behind plastic caps which may be popped out with a non-marring tool.

3. Remove the surround or cover for the inside door handle. Again, seek the hidden screw; remove it and slide the cover off over the handle.

4. If not equipped with electric windows, remove the window crank handle. This can be tricky, but not difficult. Install a piece of tape on the door pad to show the position of the handle before removal. The handle is held onto the crank axle by a spring clip shaped like the Greek letter omega;. The clip is located between the back of the crank handle and the door pad. It is correctly installed with the legs pointing along the length of the crank handle. There are three common ways of removing the clip:

a. Use a door handle removal tool. This inexpensive slotted and toothed tool can be fitted between the crank and the panel and used to push the spring clip free.

b. Use a rag or piece of cloth and work it back and forth between the crank and door panel. If constant upward tension is kept, the clip will be forced free. Keep watch on the clip as it pops out; it may get lost.

c. Straighten a common paper clip and bend a very small J-hook at the end of it. Work the hook down from the top of the crank and engage the loop of the spring clip. As you pull the clip free, keep your other hand over the area. If this is not done, the clip may vanish to an undisclosed location, never to be seen again.

5. In general, power door lock and window switches mounted on the door pad (not the armrest) may remain in place until the pad is removed. Some cannot be removed until the doorpad is off the door.

6. If the truck has manual vertical door locks, remove the lock knob by unscrewing it. If this is impossible (because they're in square housings), wait until the pad is lifted free.

7. Using a broad, flat-bladed tool, (not a screwdriver) begin to gently pry the door pad away from the door. You are releasing plastic inserts from plas-

tic seats. There will be 6–12 of them around the door. With care, the plastic inserts can be reused several times.

8. When all the clips are loose, lift up on the panel to release the lip at the top of the door. This may require a bit of jiggling to loosen the panel; do so gently and don't damage the panel. The upper edge (at the window sill) is attached by a series of retaining clips.

9. Once the panel is free, keep it close to the door and check behind it. Disconnect any wiring for switches, lights or speakers which may be attached.

➡Behind the panel is a plastic or paper sheet taped or glued to the door. This is a watershield and must be intact to prevent water entry into the car. It must be securely attached at its edges and not be ripped or damaged. Small holes or tears can be patched with waterproof tape applied to both sides of the liner.

To install:

10. When reinstalling, connect any wiring harnesses and align the upper edge of the panel along the top of the door first. Make sure the left-right alignment is correct; tap the top of the panel into place with the heel of your hand.

11. Make sure the plastic clips align with their holes; pop each retainer into place with gentle pressure.

12. Install the armrest and door handle bezel, remembering to install any caps or covers over the screws.

13. Install the window crank handle on vehicles with manual windows. Place the spring clip into the slot on the handle, remembering that the legs should point along the long dimension of the handle. Align the handle with the tape mark made earlier and put the crank over the end of the axle. Use the heel of your hand to give the center of the crank a short, sharp blow. This will cause the crank to move inward and the spring will engage its locking groove. The secret to this trick is to push the crank straight on; if it's crooked, it won't engage and you may end up looking for the spring clip.

14. Install any remaining parts or trim pieces which may have been removed earlier. (Map pockets, speaker grilles, etc.)

15. Install the triangle cover and the remote mirror handle if they were removed.

Door Locks

REMOVAL & INSTALLATION

➧ See Figure 51

1. Remove the door trim panel and the inner watershield.

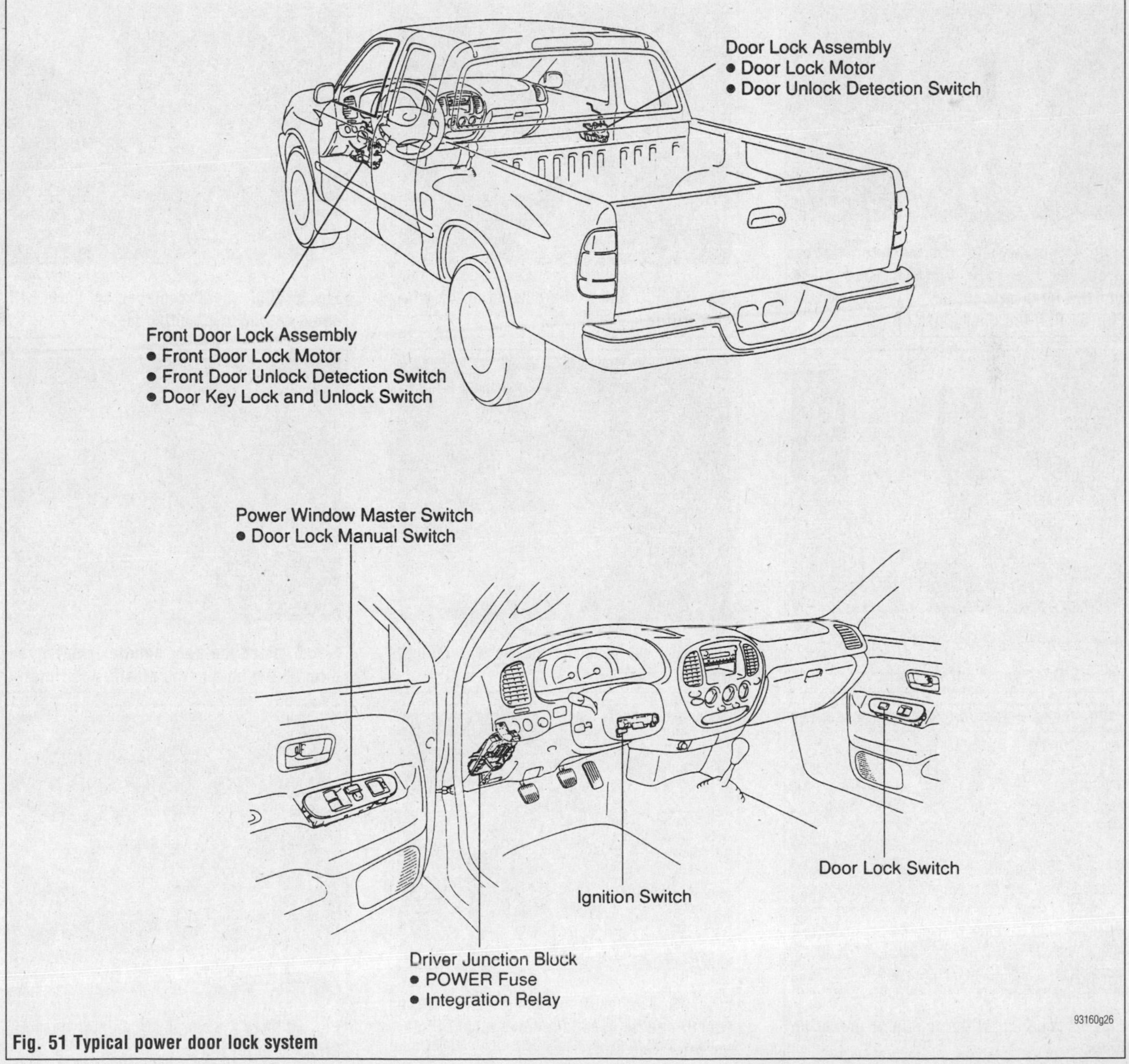

Fig. 51 Typical power door lock system

2. Disconnect the following:
  - Inside locking control link
  - Outside opening control link
  - Outside locking control link

3. Remove the door lock cylinder with a pair of pliers.

To install:

4. Install the lock cylinder and connect the links.
5. Loosen the mounting screws for the inside door handle and push it forward until resistance is felt. Move it backwards slightly and tighten the mounting screws.
6. Disconnect the control link form the outside door handle about 0.004 in. (1mm) from rest. Turn the adjuster on the link until it will fit into the mounting hole of the raised handle.

Door Glass and Regulator

REMOVAL & INSTALLATION

Door Glass

See Figures 52, 53, and 54

1. Lower the window.
2. If your vehicle has power windows, disconnect the negative battery cable.
3. Remove the door trim panel and the watershield.
4. Unscrew the armrest base and the inside door handle, then remove.
5. Remove the inner and outer weatherstrips.
6. Remove the 2 door glass channel mounting bolts and pull the window up and out of the door. Carefully pry the glass channel from the bottom of the window.

To install:

7. Coat the inside of the weatherstrip with soapy water and tap (with a plastic hammer) the glass channel onto the bottom of the window.
8. Slide the window into the door until the 2 glass channel mounting bolts can be fitted. Tighten the bolts.
9. Install the weatherstrips. Install the armrest base and inside door handle.
10. Install the watershield and the door trim panel.
11. If necessary, connect the negative battery cable.

Regulator

See Figures 55 thru 63

1. If your vehicle has power windows, disconnect the negative battery cable.

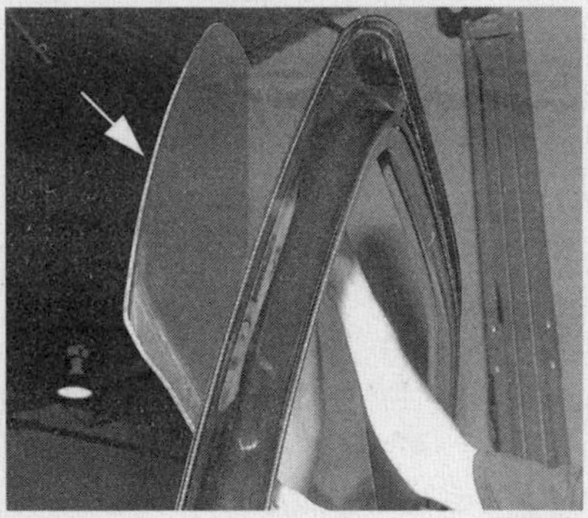
93160p32
Fig. 52 Pull the door glass up . . .

93160p33
Fig. 53 . . . and to the outside of the window frame

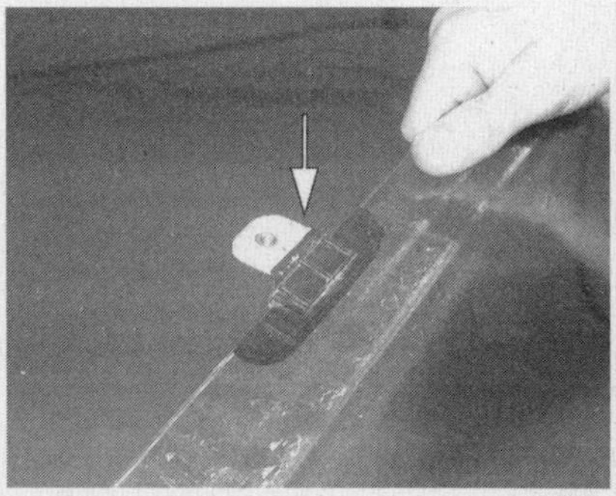
93160p34
Fig. 54 High quality replacement glass will come with new mounting tabs

93160p21
Fig. 55 Door panel wiring harness

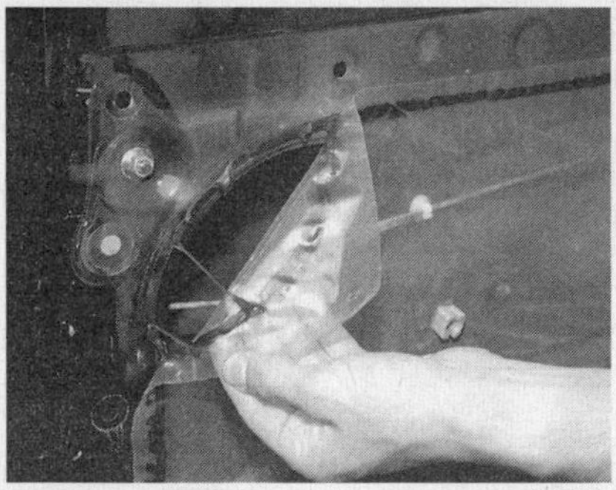
93160p22
Fig. 56 Peel back the plastic watershield from the door

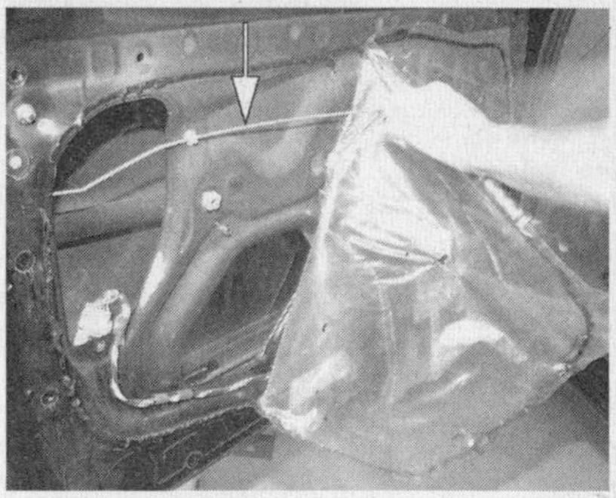
93160p23
Fig. 57 Feed the door handle actuator rod through the hole in the plastic door liner

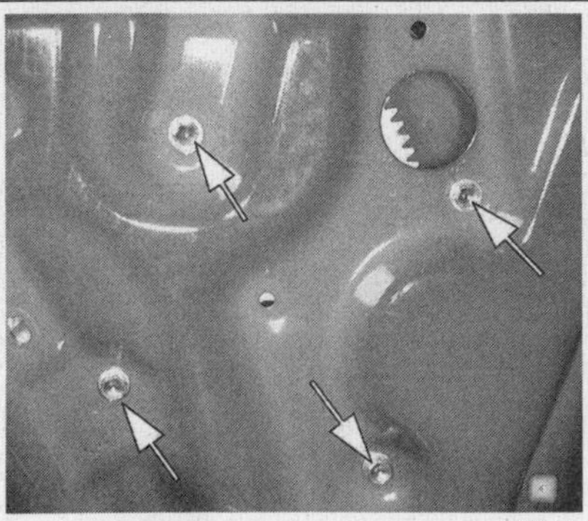
93160p25
Fig. 58 Location of the regulator mounting bolts

93160p27
Fig. 59 A ratchet, extension and 12mm socket can be used to remove most regulator mounting bolts

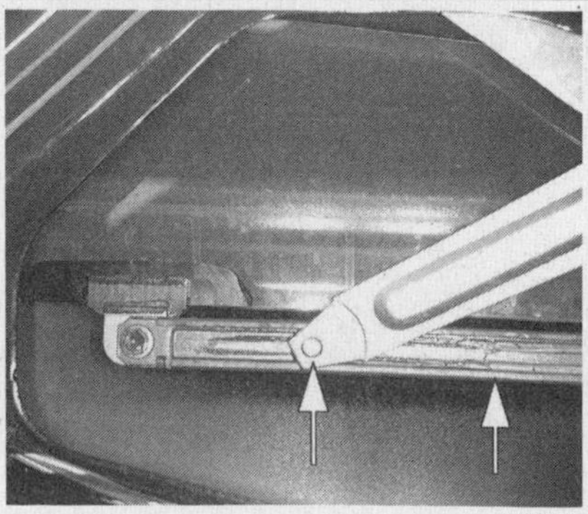
93160p29
Fig. 60 Keep the window regulator track lubricated at all times

Fig. 61 This junction must also be properly lubricated to prevent binding

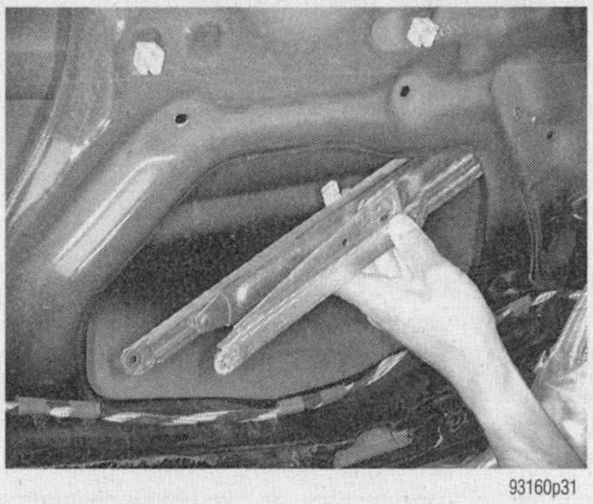

Fig. 62 Slide the door window regulator through the oval cutout in the door

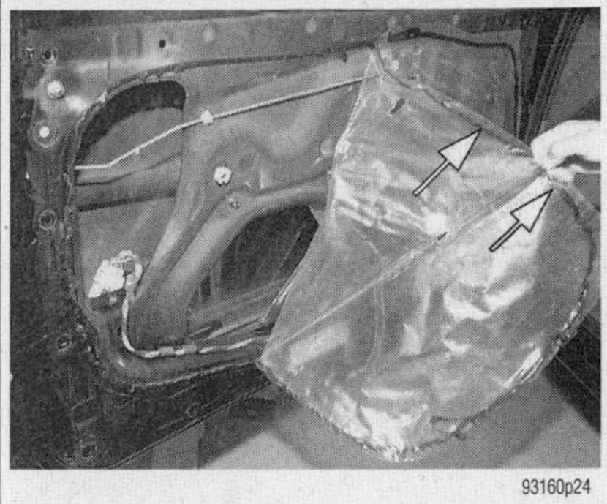

Fig. 63 Apply adhesive to the plastic liner upon installation

2. Remove the door trim panel.
3. Remove the watershield.
4. Remove the window.
5. If the truck has power windows, disconnect the electrical lead from the motor.
6. Remove the regulator mounting bolts, then lift the regulator out through the service hole. On models without a vent window, remove the 2 equalizer arm bracket mounting bolts.

To install:

7. Install the regulator and tighten the mounting bolts to 43 inch lbs. (5 Nm). On models with a vent window, install the 2 equalizer arm bracket mounting bolts.
8. Connect the lead to the power window motor if equipped.
9. Install the window, watershield and door trim panel.

Electric Window Motor

REMOVAL & INSTALLATION

See Figure 64

1. Disconnect the negative battery cable.
2. Remove the door panel.
3. Peel back the plastic door cover (watershield).
4. Remove the window regulator and motor assembly.
5. Detach the electrical wiring.
6. Remove the motor mounting bolts.
7. Pull the motor out of the hole cut into the lower portion of the door.
8. Installation is the reverse of removal.

Tailgate Window and Regulator

REMOVAL & INSTALLATION

1. Remove the inner tailgate trim.
2. Remove the tailgate plate and the watershield.
3. Disconnect the control link for the inside handle at the regulator, remove the 2 mounting screws and lift out the door handle.
4. Disconnect the inside lock knob link at the regulator and remove the knob and link.
5. Remove the upper door trim and the weather-stripping.
6. Move the locking assembly into the locked position and then raise the rear window until the regulator arms are in a straight line.
7. Disconnect the electrical lead at the regulator.
8. Detach the leads for the rear defogger at the window.
9. Disconnect the door lock control cables at the regulator side.
10. Detach the 2 remaining leads and the ground cable at the regulator.
11. Remove the regulator mounting bolts and then shimmy it side-to-side until the arms pull away from the glass.
12. Pull out the rear window and remove the regulator.

To install:

13. Slide the window into the tailgate.
14. Shimmy the regulator side-to-side until the arms position themselves in the glass channel and then install the regulator mounting bolts.
15. Connect the rear defogger leads to the window. Connect the 2 leads and the ground cable at the regulator.
16. Use the original clamps and connect the door lock control cables to the regulator.
17. Connect the power lead to the regulator.
18. Install the upper tailgate trim and weather-stripping.
19. Install the inside lock knob and link.
20. Install the inside handle and connect the control link to the regulator.
21. Seal the watershield with butyl tape 0.2 in. (6mm) in width. Insert the lower edge into the panel slit and then seal the slit with cotton tape, being careful not to block the trim clip seats.
22. Install the plate and lower tailgate trim.

Inside Rear View Mirror

REPLACEMENT

Twist-Off Style (Glass Mount)

1. Remove the negative battery cable on models equipped with a map light in the mirror assembly.
2. Detach any wiring from the mirror assembly.
3. Firmly grasp the base of the rear view mirror and twist it counterclockwise about $^1/_4$–$^1/_2$ turn.
4. Remove the mirror assembly from the window.
5. Installation is the reverse of removal.

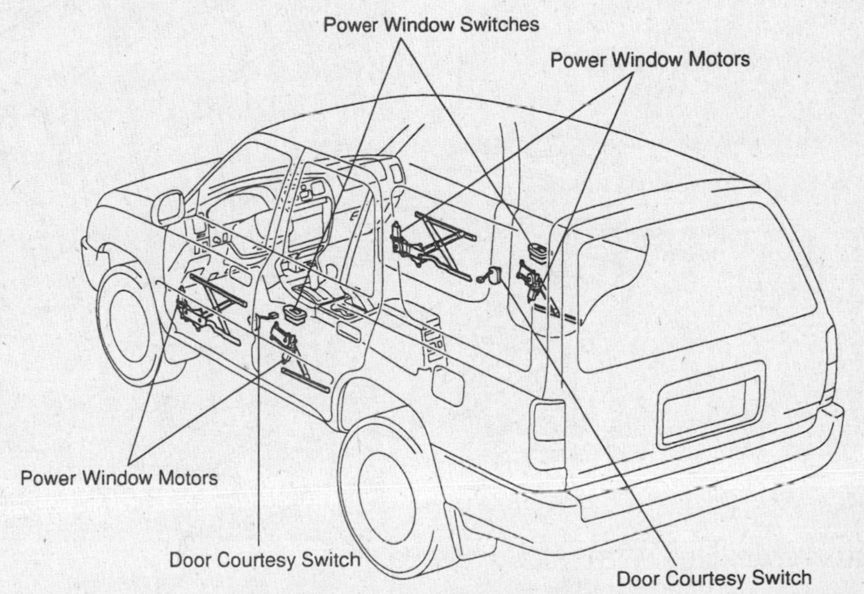

Fig. 64 Location of the power window motor and related components

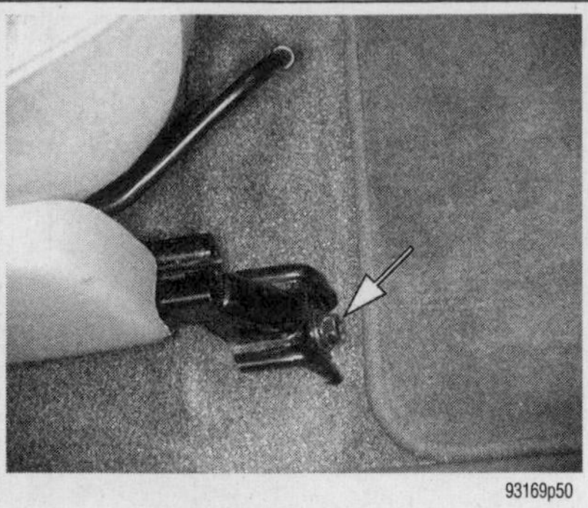

Fig. 65 Location of the front seat mounting bolt

Machine Screw Type

1. Carefully pry the cover (not all models have a cover plate) off using a suitable flat blade prytool.
2. Remove the rubber damper from the mirror stalk.
3. Remove the machine screw from the base.
4. Remove the mirror assembly.
5. Installation is in reverse order of removal.

Seats

REMOVAL & INSTALLATION

Front

➧ **See Figure 65**

1. Lift the carpet in any areas covering the seat track areas.
2. Remove the seat track-to-floor pan bolts and lift out the seat.

To install:

3. Apply sealer to the hole areas and install the seat.
4. Tighten the bolts to 25–33 ft. lbs. (34–45 Nm).
5. Place any carpeting back into position.

Rear

➧ **See Figure 66**

1. Release the seat back locks on each side of the seat.
2. Remove the covers and remove the bolts holding the front of the seat bottom to the floor pan. On

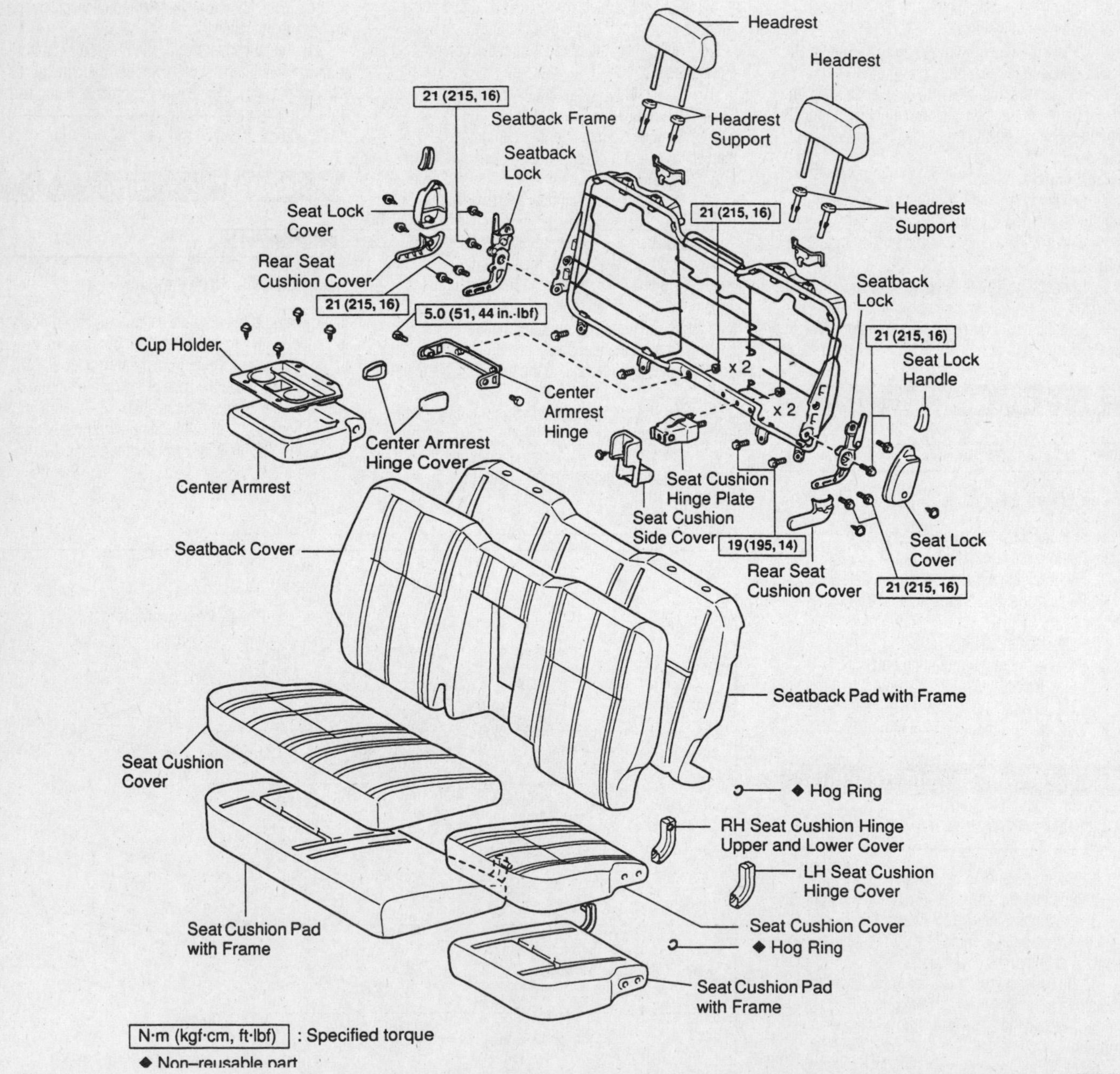

Fig. 66 Exploded view of the rear seat components—Tundra shown

4Runner, doing this removes only the seat bottom. Remove the seat back by removing the center hinge bolts and the pivot bolts at either side. Remove the seat and seat back.

To install:

3. Apply sealer to the hole areas and install the seat and back. Tighten the bolts. Tighten the bolts holding the seat to the floor to 13–29 ft. lbs. (18–39 Nm).

Power Seat Motor

REMOVAL & INSTALLATION

See Figure 67

1. Remove the negative battery cable.
2. Remove the seat.
3. Detach the connector from the power seat motor.
4. Unscrew the bolts that secure the power seat motor to the seat frame.
5. Remove the seat motor.
6. Installation is the reverse of the removal procedure.

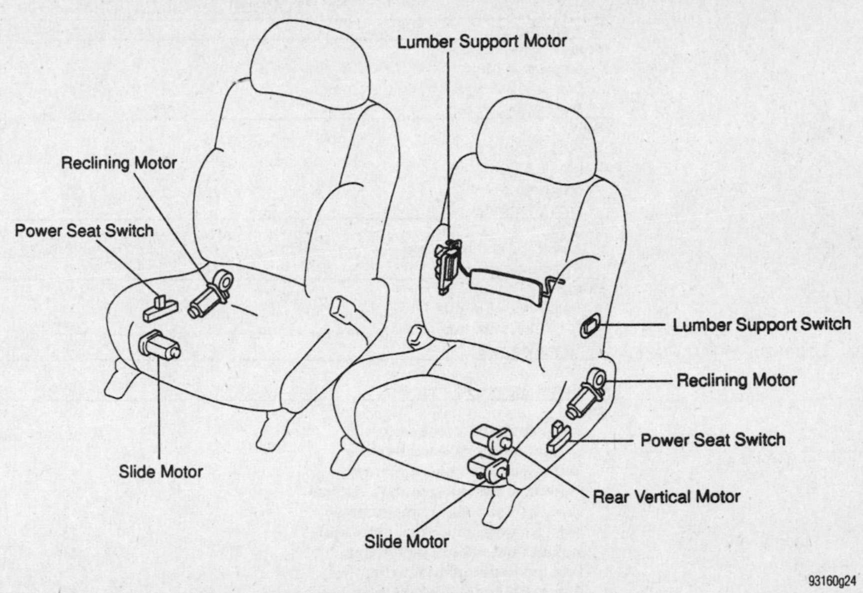

Fig. 67 Power seat motor and related component locations—4Runner

TORQUE SPECIFICATIONS — LAND CRUISER AND TUNDRA

Components	English Specifications (ft. lbs.)	Metric Specifications (Nm)
Front Bumper		
Front bumper arm-to-body	43	58
Front bumper cover side mounting bracket-to-arm	9	12
Front bumper cover-to-front balance panel	43 inch lbs.	4.9
Front bumper reinforcement-to-Body	37	50
Front bumper-to-front bumper side mounting bracket	43 inch lbs.	4.9
Rear Bumper		
Rear bumper arm-to-body	59	79
Rear bumper bar-to-rear bumper No. 2 reinforcement	33	45
Rear bumper bar-to-rear bumper reinforcement	22	29
Rear bumper No. 2 reinforcement-to-rear bumper arm	59	79
Hood		
Hood hinge-to-hood	10	13
Hood lock-to-body	69 inch lbs.	7.8
Hood support-to-body	16	22
Hood support-to-hood	16	22
Front Door		
Door check-to-body	20	27
Door check-to-door panel	44 inch lbs.	5.0
Door glass-to-window regulator	44 inch lbs.	5.0
Door hinge-to-body	17	23
Door hinge-to-door panel	17	23
Door lock-to-door panel Torx screw	44 inch lbs.	5.0
Door striker-to-body	17	23
Nut	44 inch lbs.	5.0
Outside handle-to-door panel	49 inch lbs.	5.5
Window regulator-to-door panel Bolt	44 inch lbs.	5.0
Instrument Panel		
passenger airbag assembly-to-Instrument panel	43 inch lbs.	5.0
ppassenger airbag-to-Instrument panel reinforcement M8	15	20
Tailgate		
Tailgate cable-to-body	20	26
Tailgate handle-to-tail gate	44 inch lbs.	5.0
Tailgate hinge-to-tail gate	13	17
Tailgate lock striker-to-body	10	13
Tailgate lock-to-tail gate	10	13
Tailgate shaft-to-tail gate	20	26
Tailgate-to-body	13	17
Front Seat		
Armrest-to-seatback assembly	27	37
Front seat-to-body	27	37
Seat cushion assembly-to-seat adjuster	14	19
Seatback assembly-to-seat adjuster	32	43
Rear Seat		
Center armrest hinge-to-center armrest	44 inch lbs.	5.0
Center armrest-to-seatback assembly	16	21
Seatback assembly-to-seatback lock	16	21

93160c01

TORQUE SPECIFICATIONS — T100

Components	English Specifications (ft. lbs.)	Metric Specifications (Nm)
Door		
Door hinge-to-body	19	25
Door hinge-to-door panel	19	25
Door lock-to-door panel	52 inch lbs.	5.9
Hood		
Hood hinge-to-hood	10	14
Hood lock-to-body	14	19
Hood hinge-to-hood	10	14
Hood lock-to-body	14	19
Bumpers	7	9.8
Bumper side support-to-bumper arm	9	13
Front bumper arm-to-body	45	61
Tailgate		
Tailgate hinge-to-tail gate	13	18
Tailgate lock striker-to-body	9	12
Tailgate lock-to-tail gate	9	12
Window		
Window regulator-to-door panel	48 inch lbs.	5.4
Seat		
Back panel trim-to-body (rear seat)	7	9.8
Front seat belt adjustable anchor-to-body	32	43
Inner track-to-seat back frame (sport type)	9.5	12.5
Inner track-to-seat back frame (split bench type)	9.5	12.5
Inner track-to-seat cushion frame (sport type)	13	18
Inner track-to-seat cushion frame (bench type)	13	18
Inner track-to-seat cushion frame (split bench type)	13	18
Outer track-to-seat cushion frame (sport type)	13	18
Outer track-to-seat cushion frame (bench type)	13	18
Outer track-to-seat cushion frame (split bench type)	13	18
Seat adjuster-to-seat cushion frame (sport type)	13	18
Seat adjuster-to-seat cushion frame (split bench type)	13	18
Seat adjuster-to-seatback (sport type)	32	43
Seat adjuster-to-seatback (split bench type)	13	18
Seat cushion-to-body (rear seat)	7	9.8
Seat track-to-body (sport type)	27	37
Seat track-to-body (bench type)	27	37
Seat track-to-body (split bench type)	27	37
Seat track-to-seatback (bench type)	13	18

93160c02

TORQUE SPECIFICATIONS — 4RUNNER AND TACOMA

Components	English Specifications (ft. lbs.)	Metric Specifications (Nm)
Front bumper		
Front bumper arm-to-body	43	58
Front bumper arm-to-front valance panel	43 inch lbs.	4.9
Upper retainer-to-front valance panel	43 inch lbs.	4.9
Hood		
Hood hinge-to-body	13	18
Hood hinge-to-hood	10	13
Hood lock-to-body	71 inch lbs.	8
Front door		
Door lock striker-to-body	9	12
Hinge set bolt	17	23
Outside handle-to-front door	43 inch lbs.	4.9
Window regulator-to-body	43 inch lbs.	4.9
Removable roof		
Removable roof handle-to-removable roof	26 inch lbs.	2.9
Removable roof hinge case-to-body	30 inch lbs.	3.4
Removable roof lock base-to-body	52 inch lbs.	5.9
Instrument panel		
Front passenger airbag assembly-to-instrument panel	42 inch lbs.	5.0
Front passenger airbag assembly-to-reinforcement	15	20
Steering wheel set nut	26	35
Tailgate		
B bolt:	17	24
C bolt:	19	28
Tailgate cable-to-tailgate	10	14
Tailgate hinge-to-body A bolt:	22	30
Tailgate lock striker-to-body	9	12
Seat		
Back panel trim-to-body	7	9.8
Seat adjuster-to-body	27	37
Seat cushion-to-body	7	9.8

93160c03

UNDERHOOD CHECKS

Overall condition and cleanliness

Drivebelts
☐ Good ☐ Fair ☐ Poor

Vacuum lines and fittings
☐ Good ☐ Fair ☐ Poor

Electrical wiring
☐ Good ☐ Fair ☐ Poor

Battery
☐ Good ☐ Fair ☐ Poor

Battery box
☐ Good ☐ Fair ☐ Poor

Battery hold-downs
☐ Good ☐ Fair ☐ Poor

Distributor cap
☐ Good ☐ Fair ☐ Poor

Spark plug wires
☐ Good ☐ Fair ☐ Poor

Air filter
☐ Good ☐ Fair ☐ Poor

Electrical relay boxes
☐ Good ☐ Fair ☐ Poor

Windshield washer reservoir
☐ Good ☐ Fair ☐ Poor

PCV valve
☐ Good ☐ Fair ☐ Poor

Fluid level and quality checks:

Oil
☐ Good ☐ Fair ☐ Poor

Brake master cylinder fluid
☐ Good ☐ Fair ☐ Poor

Clutch master cylinder fluid
☐ Good ☐ Fair ☐ Poor

Power steering fluid
☐ Good ☐ Fair ☐ Poor

Transmission fluid
☐ Good ☐ Fair ☐ Poor

Coolant
☐ Good ☐ Fair ☐ Poor

Fluid leaks

General

Power steering

☐ Good ☐ Fair ☐ Poor

Oil

☐ Good ☐ Fair ☐ Poor

Transmission fluid

☐ Good ☐ Fair ☐ Poor

Brake fluid

☐ Good ☐ Fair ☐ Poor

tch master cylinder

☐ Good ☐ Fair ☐ Poor

Cooling system

Radiator

☐ Good ☐ Fair ☐ Poor

ator hoses

☐ Good ☐ Fair ☐ Poor

oses

Good ☐ Fair ☐ Poor

Good ☐ Fair ☐ Poor

Receiver-drier

☐ Good ☐ Fair ☐ Poor

Fuel

Fuel lines

☐ Good ☐ Fair ☐ Poor

Carburetor

☐ Good ☐ Fair ☐ Poor

Fuel injectors

☐ Good ☐ Fair ☐ Poor

Fuel filter

☐ Good ☐ Fair ☐ Poor

Fuel pump

☐ Good ☐ Fair ☐ Poor

INTERIOR CHECKS

Instrument operation

☐ Good ☐ Fair ☐ Poor

Air-conditioning operation

☐ Good ☐ Fair ☐ Poor

Blower switch operates at all speeds

☐ Good ☐ Fair ☐ Poor

Cigarette lighter

☐ Good ☐ Fair ☐ Poor

Clock

☐ Good ☐ Fair ☐ Poor

Map light, dome light

☐ Good ☐ Fair ☐ Poor

Alarm system

☐ Good ☐ Fair ☐ Poor

Door locks, power or manual

☐ Good ☐ Fair ☐ Poor

Remote operation of locks

☐ Good ☐ Fair ☐ Poor

Window tint film

☐ Good ☐ Fair ☐ Poor

Power mirrors

☐ Good ☐ Fair ☐ Poor

Rear window wiper

☐ Good ☐ Fair ☐ Poor

Rear window defroster

☐ Good ☐ Fair ☐ Poor

Convertible top operation

☐ Good ☐ Fair ☐ Poor

Condition of plastic rear window (convertible)

☐ Good ☐ Fair ☐ Poor

Sunroof or T-top

☐ Good ☐ Fair ☐ Poor

Seat adjustments

☐ Good ☐ Fair ☐ Poor

Power seat operation

☐ Good ☐ Fair ☐ Poor

Console

☐ Good ☐ Fair ☐ Poor

Glove box

☐ Good ☐ Fair ☐ Poor

Emergency brake

☐ Good ☐ Fair ☐ Poor

Maintenance/service stickers

☐ Good ☐ Fair ☐ Poor

Interior fuel-filler door release

☐ Good ☐ Fair ☐ Poor

TRUNK INSPECTION

Proper key, key operation

☐ Good ☐ Fair ☐ Poor

Decklid/hatch fit

☐ Good ☐ Fair ☐ Poor

Weatherstripping

☐ Good ☐ Fair ☐ Poor

Interior trunk release

☐ Good ☐ Fair ☐ Poor

Gas-assisted trunk/hatch struts

☐ Good ☐ Fair ☐ Poor

Paint match

☐ Good ☐ Fair ☐ Poor

Floormats

☐ Good ☐ Fair ☐ Poor

Spare tire

☐ Good ☐ Fair ☐ Poor

Factory jack and tire-changing tools

☐ Good ☐ Fair ☐ Poor

Rust under floormat

☐ Good ☐ Fair ☐ Poor

Collision damage

☐ Good ☐ Fair ☐ Poor

Trailer wiring

☐ Good ☐ Fair ☐ Poor

Speaker wiring

☐ Good ☐ Fair ☐ Poor

Trunk courtesy light

☐ Good ☐ Fair ☐ Poor

TRUNK OPEN light on dash

☐ Good ☐ Fair ☐ Poor

USED CAR BUYING INSPECTION LIST

UNDERCAR CHECKS

CV joint boots
☐ Good ☐ Fair ☐ Poor

Exhaust system leaks
☐ Good ☐ Fair ☐ Poor

Exhaust system hangers
☐ Good ☐ Fair ☐ Poor

Non-stock exhaust components
☐ Good ☐ Fair ☐ Poor

Chassis (frame or unibody) condition
☐ Good ☐ Fair ☐ Poor

Driveshaft
☐ Good ☐ Fair ☐ Poor

Tires, from backside
☐ Good ☐ Fair ☐ Poor

Fluid leaks:

Fuel
☐ Good ☐ Fair ☐ Poor

Oil
☐ Good ☐ Fair ☐ Poor

Coolant
☐ Good ☐ Fair ☐ Poor

Power steering fluid
☐ Good ☐ Fair ☐ Poor

Transmission fluid
☐ Good ☐ Fair ☐ Poor

Rear transmission seal
☐ Good ☐ Fair ☐ Poor

Rear axle pinion seal
☐ Good ☐ Fair ☐ Poor

Brake lines:

Leaks
☐ Good ☐ Fair ☐ Poor

Crushed spots
☐ Good ☐ Fair ☐ Poor

Rust
☐ Good ☐ Fair ☐ Poor

Front suspension checks:

Shocks
☐ Good ☐ Fair ☐ Poor

Springs
☐ Good ☐ Fair ☐ Poor

Ball joints
☐ Good ☐ Fair ☐ Poor

Tie rod ends
☐ Good ☐ Fair ☐ Poor

Steering gear
☐ Good ☐ Fair ☐ Poor

Brakes
☐ Good ☐ Fair ☐ Poor

Bushings
☐ Good ☐ Fair ☐ Poor

Rear Suspension checks:

Shocks
☐ Good ☐ Fair ☐ Poor

Springs
☐ Good ☐ Fair ☐ Poor

Brakes
☐ Good ☐ Fair ☐ Poor

Rear axle pinion seal
☐ Good ☐ Fair ☐ Poor

Bushings
☐ Good ☐ Fair ☐ Poor

GLOSSARY

AIR/FUEL RATIO: The ratio of air-to-gasoline by weight in the fuel mixture drawn into the engine.

AIR INJECTION: One method of reducing harmful exhaust emissions by injecting air into each of the exhaust ports of an engine. The fresh air entering the hot exhaust manifold causes any remaining fuel to be burned before it can exit the tailpipe.

ALTERNATOR: A device used for converting mechanical energy into electrical energy.

AMMETER: An instrument, calibrated in amperes, used to measure the flow of an electrical current in a circuit. Ammeters are always connected in series with the circuit being tested.

AMPERE: The rate of flow of electrical current present when one volt of electrical pressure is applied against one ohm of electrical resistance.

ANALOG COMPUTER: Any microprocessor that uses similar (analogous) electrical signals to make its calculations.

ARMATURE: A laminated, soft iron core wrapped by a wire that converts electrical energy to mechanical energy as in a motor or relay. When rotated in a magnetic field, it changes mechanical energy into electrical energy as in a generator.

ATMOSPHERIC PRESSURE: The pressure on the Earth's surface caused by the weight of the air in the atmosphere. At sea level, this pressure is 14.7 psi at 32°F (101 kPa at 0°C).

ATOMIZATION: The breaking down of a liquid into a fine mist that can be suspended in air.

AXIAL PLAY: Movement parallel to a shaft or bearing bore.

BACKFIRE: The sudden combustion of gases in the intake or exhaust system that results in a loud explosion.

BACKLASH: The clearance or play between two parts, such as meshed gears.

BACKPRESSURE: Restrictions in the exhaust system that slow the exit of exhaust gases from the combustion chamber.

BAKELITE: A heat resistant, plastic insulator material commonly used in printed circuit boards and transistorized components.

BALL BEARING: A bearing made up of hardened inner and outer races between which hardened steel balls roll.

BALLAST RESISTOR: A resistor in the primary ignition circuit that lowers voltage after the engine is started to reduce wear on ignition components.

BEARING: A friction reducing, supportive device usually located between a stationary part and a moving part.

BIMETAL TEMPERATURE SENSOR: Any sensor or switch made of two dissimilar types of metal that bend when heated or cooled due to the different expansion rates of the alloys. These types of sensors usually function as an on/off switch.

BLOWBY: Combustion gases, composed of water vapor and unburned fuel, that leak past the piston rings into the crankcase during normal engine operation. These gases are removed by the PCV system to prevent the buildup of harmful acids in the crankcase.

BRAKE PAD: A brake shoe and lining assembly used with disc brakes.

BRAKE SHOE: The backing for the brake lining. The term is, however, usually applied to the assembly of the brake backing and lining.

BUSHING: A liner, usually removable, for a bearing; an anti-friction liner used in place of a bearing.

CALIPER: A hydraulically activated device in a disc brake system, which is mounted straddling the brake rotor (disc). The caliper contains at least one piston and two brake pads. Hydraulic pressure on the piston(s) forces the pads against the rotor.

CAMSHAFT: A shaft in the engine on which are the lobes (cams) which operate the valves. The camshaft is driven by the crankshaft, via a belt, chain or gears, at one half the crankshaft speed.

CAPACITOR: A device which stores an electrical charge.

CARBON MONOXIDE (CO): A colorless, odorless gas given off as a normal byproduct of combustion. It is poisonous and extremely dangerous in confined areas, building up slowly to toxic levels without warning if adequate ventilation is not available.

CARBURETOR: A device, usually mounted on the intake manifold of an engine, which mixes the air and fuel in the proper proportion to allow even combustion.

CATALYTIC CONVERTER: A device installed in the exhaust system, like a muffler, that converts harmful byproducts of combustion into carbon dioxide and water vapor by means of a heat-producing chemical reaction.

CENTRIFUGAL ADVANCE: A mechanical method of advancing the spark timing by using flyweights in the distributor that react to centrifugal force generated by the distributor shaft rotation.

CHECK VALVE: Any one-way valve installed to permit the flow of air, fuel or vacuum in one direction only.

CHOKE: A device, usually a moveable valve, placed in the intake path of a carburetor to restrict the flow of air.

CIRCUIT: Any unbroken path through which an electrical current can flow. Also used to describe fuel flow in some instances.

CIRCUIT BREAKER: A switch which protects an electrical circuit from overload by opening the circuit when the current flow exceeds a predetermined level. Some circuit breakers must be reset manually, while most reset automatically.

COIL (IGNITION): A transformer in the ignition circuit which steps up the voltage provided to the spark plugs.

COMBINATION MANIFOLD: An assembly which includes both the intake and exhaust manifolds in one casting.

COMBINATION VALVE: A device used in some fuel systems that routes fuel vapors to a charcoal storage canister instead of venting them into the atmosphere. The valve relieves fuel tank pressure and allows fresh air into the tank as the fuel level drops to prevent a vapor lock situation.

COMPRESSION RATIO: The comparison of the total volume of the cylinder and combustion chamber with the piston at BDC and the piston at TDC.

CONDENSER: 1. An electrical device which acts to store an electrical charge, preventing voltage surges. 2. A radiator-like device in the air conditioning system in which refrigerant gas condenses into a liquid, giving off heat.

CONDUCTOR: Any material through which an electrical current can be transmitted easily.

CONTINUITY: Continuous or complete circuit. Can be checked with an ohmmeter.

COUNTERSHAFT: An intermediate shaft which is rotated by a mainshaft and transmits, in turn, that rotation to a working part.

CRANKCASE: The lower part of an engine in which the crankshaft and related parts operate.

CRANKSHAFT: The main driving shaft of an engine which receives reciprocating motion from the pistons and converts it to rotary motion.

CYLINDER: In an engine, the round hole in the engine block in which the piston(s) ride.

CYLINDER BLOCK: The main structural member of an engine in which is found the cylinders, crankshaft and other principal parts.

CYLINDER HEAD: The detachable portion of the engine, usually fastened to the top of the cylinder block and containing all or most of the combustion chambers. On overhead valve engines, it contains the valves and their operating parts. On overhead cam engines, it contains the camshaft as well.

DEAD CENTER: The extreme top or bottom of the piston stroke.

DETONATION: An unwanted explosion of the air/fuel mixture in the combustion chamber caused by excess heat and compression, advanced timing, or an overly lean mixture. Also referred to as "ping".

DIAPHRAGM: A thin, flexible wall separating two cavities, such as in a vacuum advance unit.

DIESELING: A condition in which hot spots in the combustion chamber cause the engine to run on after the key is turned off.

DIFFERENTIAL: A geared assembly which allows the transmission of motion between drive axles, giving one axle the ability to turn faster than the other.

DIODE: An electrical device that will allow current to flow in one direction only.

DISC BRAKE: A hydraulic braking assembly consisting of a brake disc, or rotor, mounted on an axle, and a caliper assembly containing, usually two brake pads which are activated by hydraulic pressure. The pads are forced against the sides of the disc, creating friction which slows the vehicle.

DISTRIBUTOR: A mechanically driven device on an engine which is responsible for electrically firing the spark plug at a predetermined point of the piston stroke.

DOWEL PIN: A pin, inserted in mating holes in two different parts allowing those parts to maintain a fixed relationship.

DRUM BRAKE: A braking system which consists of two brake shoes and one or two wheel cylinders, mounted on a fixed backing plate, and a brake drum, mounted on an axle, which revolves around the assembly.

DWELL: The rate, measured in degrees of shaft rotation, at which an electrical circuit cycles on and off.

ELECTRONIC CONTROL UNIT (ECU): Ignition module, module, amplifier or igniter. See Module for definition.

ELECTRONIC IGNITION: A system in which the timing and firing of the spark plugs is controlled by an electronic control unit, usually called a module. These systems have no points or condenser.

END-PLAY: The measured amount of axial movement in a shaft.

ENGINE: A device that converts heat into mechanical energy.

EXHAUST MANIFOLD: A set of cast passages or pipes which conduct exhaust gases from the engine.

FEELER GAUGE: A blade, usually metal, or precisely predetermined thickness, used to measure the clearance between two parts.

FIRING ORDER: The order in which combustion occurs in the cylinders of an engine. Also the order in which spark is distributed to the plugs by the distributor.

FLOODING: The presence of too much fuel in the intake manifold and combustion chamber which prevents the air/fuel mixture from firing, thereby causing a no-start situation.

FLYWHEEL: A disc shaped part bolted to the rear end of the crankshaft. Around the outer perimeter is affixed the ring gear. The starter drive engages the ring gear, turning the flywheel, which rotates the crankshaft, imparting the initial starting motion to the engine.

FOOT POUND (ft. lbs. or sometimes, ft.lb.): The amount of energy or work needed to raise an item weighing one pound, a distance of one foot.

FUSE: A protective device in a circuit which prevents circuit overload by breaking the circuit when a specific amperage is present. The device is constructed around a strip or wire of a lower amperage rating than the circuit it is designed to protect. When an amperage higher than that stamped on the fuse is present in the circuit, the strip or wire melts, opening the circuit.

GEAR RATIO: The ratio between the number of teeth on meshing gears.

GENERATOR: A device which converts mechanical energy into electrical energy.

HEAT RANGE: The measure of a spark plug's ability to dissipate heat from its firing end. The higher the heat range, the hotter the plug fires.

HUB: The center part of a wheel or gear.

HYDROCARBON (HC): Any chemical compound made up of hydrogen and carbon. A major pollutant formed by the engine as a byproduct of combustion.

HYDROMETER: An instrument used to measure the specific gravity of a solution.

INCH POUND (inch lbs.; sometimes in.lb. or in. lbs.): One twelfth of a foot pound.

INDUCTION: A means of transferring electrical energy in the form of a magnetic field. Principle used in the ignition coil to increase voltage.

INJECTOR: A device which receives metered fuel under relatively low pressure and is activated to inject the fuel into the engine under relatively high pressure at a predetermined time.

INPUT SHAFT: The shaft to which torque is applied, usually carrying the driving gear or gears.

INTAKE MANIFOLD: A casting of passages or pipes used to conduct air or a fuel/air mixture to the cylinders.

JOURNAL: The bearing surface within which a shaft operates.

KEY: A small block usually fitted in a notch between a shaft and a hub to prevent slippage of the two parts.

MANIFOLD: A casting of passages or set of pipes which connect the cylinders to an inlet or outlet source.

MANIFOLD VACUUM: Low pressure in an engine intake manifold formed just below the throttle plates. Manifold vacuum is highest at idle and drops under acceleration.

MASTER CYLINDER: The primary fluid pressurizing device in a hydraulic system. In automotive use, it is found in brake and hydraulic clutch systems and is pedal activated, either directly or, in a power brake system, through the power booster.

MODULE: Electronic control unit, amplifier or igniter of solid state or integrated design which controls the current flow in the ignition primary circuit based on input from the pick-up coil. When the module opens the primary circuit, high secondary voltage is induced in the coil.

NEEDLE BEARING: A bearing which consists of a number (usually a large number) of long, thin rollers.

OHM: (Ω) The unit used to measure the resistance of conductor-to-electrical flow. One ohm is the amount of resistance that limits current flow to one ampere in a circuit with one volt of pressure.

OHMMETER: An instrument used for measuring the resistance, in ohms, in an electrical circuit.

OUTPUT SHAFT: The shaft which transmits torque from a device, such as a transmission.

OVERDRIVE: A gear assembly which produces more shaft revolutions than that transmitted to it.

OVERHEAD CAMSHAFT (OHC): An engine configuration in which the camshaft is mounted on top of the cylinder head and operates the valve either directly or by means of rocker arms.

OVERHEAD VALVE (OHV): An engine configuration in which all of the valves are located in the cylinder head and the camshaft is located in the cylinder block. The camshaft operates the valves via lifters and pushrods.

OXIDES OF NITROGEN (NOx): Chemical compounds of nitrogen produced as a byproduct of combustion. They combine with hydrocarbons to produce smog.

OXYGEN SENSOR: Use with the feedback system to sense the presence of oxygen in the exhaust gas and signal the computer which can reference the voltage signal to an air/fuel ratio.

PINION: The smaller of two meshing gears.

PISTON RING: An open-ended ring with fits into a groove on the outer diameter of the piston. Its chief function is to form a seal between the piston and cylinder wall. Most automotive pistons have three rings: two for compression sealing; one for oil sealing.

PRELOAD: A predetermined load placed on a bearing during assembly or by adjustment.

PRIMARY CIRCUIT: the low voltage side of the ignition system which consists of the ignition switch, ballast resistor or resistance wire, bypass, coil, electronic control unit and pick-up coil as well as the connecting wires and harnesses.

PRESS FIT: The mating of two parts under pressure, due to the inner diameter of one being smaller than the outer diameter of the other, or vice versa; an interference fit.

RACE: The surface on the inner or outer ring of a bearing on which the balls, needles or rollers move.

REGULATOR: A device which maintains the amperage and/or voltage levels of a circuit at predetermined values.

RELAY: A switch which automatically opens and/or closes a circuit.

RESISTANCE: The opposition to the flow of current through a circuit or electrical device, and is measured in ohms. Resistance is equal to the voltage divided by the amperage.

RESISTOR: A device, usually made of wire, which offers a preset amount of resistance in an electrical circuit.

RING GEAR: The name given to a ring-shaped gear attached to a differential case, or affixed to a flywheel or as part of a planetary gear set.

ROLLER BEARING: A bearing made up of hardened inner and outer races between which hardened steel rollers move.

ROTOR: 1. The disc-shaped part of a disc brake assembly, upon which the brake pads bear; also called, brake disc. 2. The device mounted atop the distributor shaft, which passes current to the distributor cap tower contacts.

SECONDARY CIRCUIT: The high voltage side of the ignition system, usually above 20,000 volts. The secondary includes the ignition coil, coil wire, distributor cap and rotor, spark plug wires and spark plugs.

SENDING UNIT: A mechanical, electrical, hydraulic or electromagnetic device which transmits information to a gauge.

SENSOR: Any device designed to measure engine operating conditions or ambient pressures and temperatures. Usually electronic in nature and designed to send a voltage signal to an on-board computer, some sensors may operate as a simple on/off switch or they may provide a variable voltage signal (like a potentiometer) as conditions or measured parameters change.

SHIM: Spacers of precise, predetermined thickness used between parts to establish a proper working relationship.

SLAVE CYLINDER: In automotive use, a device in the hydraulic clutch system which is activated by hydraulic force, disengaging the clutch.

SOLENOID: A coil used to produce a magnetic field, the effect of which is to produce work.

SPARK PLUG: A device screwed into the combustion chamber of a spark ignition engine. The basic construction is a conductive core inside of a ceramic insulator, mounted in an outer conductive base. An electrical charge from the spark plug wire travels along the conductive core and jumps a preset air gap to a grounding point or points at the end of the conductive base. The resultant spark ignites the fuel/air mixture in the combustion chamber.

SPLINES: Ridges machined or cast onto the outer diameter of a shaft or inner diameter of a bore to enable parts to mate without rotation.

TACHOMETER: A device used to measure the rotary speed of an engine, shaft, gear, etc., usually in rotations per minute.

THERMOSTAT: A valve, located in the cooling system of an engine, which is closed when cold and opens gradually in response to engine heating, controlling the temperature of the coolant and rate of coolant flow.

TOP DEAD CENTER (TDC): The point at which the piston reaches the top of its travel on the compression stroke.

TORQUE: The twisting force applied to an object.

TORQUE CONVERTER: A turbine used to transmit power from a driving member to a driven member via hydraulic action, providing changes in drive ratio and torque. In automotive use, it links the driveplate at the rear of the engine to the automatic transmission.

TRANSDUCER: A device used to change a force into an electrical signal.

TRANSISTOR: A semi-conductor component which can be actuated by a small voltage to perform an electrical switching function.

TUNE-UP: A regular maintenance function, usually associated with the replacement and adjustment of parts and components in the electrical and fuel systems of a vehicle for the purpose of attaining optimum performance.

TURBOCHARGER: An exhaust driven pump which compresses intake air and forces it into the combustion chambers at higher than atmospheric pressures. The increased air pressure allows more fuel to be burned and results in increased horsepower being produced.

VACUUM ADVANCE: A device which advances the ignition timing in response to increased engine vacuum.

VACUUM GAUGE: An instrument used to measure the presence of vacuum in a chamber.

VALVE: A device which control the pressure, direction of flow or rate of flow of a liquid or gas.

VALVE CLEARANCE: The measured gap between the end of the valve stem and the rocker arm, cam lobe or follower that activates the valve.

VISCOSITY: The rating of a liquid's internal resistance to flow.

VOLTMETER: An instrument used for measuring electrical force in units called volts. Voltmeters are always connected parallel with the circuit being tested.

WHEEL CYLINDER: Found in the automotive drum brake assembly, it is a device, actuated by hydraulic pressure, which, through internal pistons, pushes the brake shoes outward against the drums.

NOTES

MASTER INDEX